MW00355281

EVANGELIZOLOGY

Standard Topics in The Study of Evangelizing

Volume One: Introduction and Definition

By Thomas P. Johnston

Forewords by Darrell W. Robinson and Robert E. Coleman

Evangelism Unlimited, Inc.
P.O. Box 1152, Liberty, MO 64069-1152, U.S.A.
Webpage: www.evangelizology.org;
Email: 4thomasjohnston@gmail.com

2019 Edition

Unless otherwise noted, Scripture is quoted from the New American Standard Bible or the New American Standard Updated edition, © Copyright the Lockman Foundation 1960,1962, 1963, 1968, 1971, 1972, 1973, 1975, 1977, 1988, 1995. Used by permission.

Other Scripture cited are taken from BibleWorks 7, 8, 9, or 10 (BibleWorks, P.O. Box 6158, Norfolk, VA 23508, service@bibleworks.com), with the exception of some 14th-17th Century French and English versions; the Contemporary English Version, © American Bible Society 1991, imprimatur 22 Mar 1991; and the Good News Translation or Today's English Version, second edition, © American Bible Society 1978, 1992, imprimatur 10 Mar 1993.

Greek text is from the Nestle-Aland 27th edition (from BibleWorks 7, 8, or 9), unless otherwise noted. Hebrew citations from the Biblia Hebraica Stuttgartensia, unless otherwise noted. Likewise citations from Barclay-Newman (Barclay M. Newman, Jr., *A Concise Greek-English Dictionary of the New Testament* [1971, 1993),Friberg Lexicon (Timothy and Barbara Friberg, *Analytical Lexicon to the Greek New Testament* [1994, 2000]); Gingrich Lexicon (*Greek-English Lexicon of the New Testament and Other Early Christian Literature,* 3rd ed [2000]); Liddell-Scott Lexicon (*The Abridged Liddell-Scott Greek-English Lexicon*); Louw-Nida (*Louw-Nida Greek-English Lexicon of the New Testament Based on Semantic Domains* [1988]); Lust-Eynikel-Hauspie (*A Greek-English Lexicon of the Septuagint* [1992, 1996]); Thayer's (C. L. W. Wilke, C. G. Grimm and Joseph Henry Thayer, *A Greek-English Lexicon of the New Testament* (1851, 1861-1868,1879, 1889]); and Tischendorf (*The Constantinus Tischendorf Apparatus* [1869, 1872, 1984, 2003]).

Cover design by Cory Thomason. Some inside artwork by Mike Longinow (The Spiritual Battle, 174; Electric Bible, 539).

Dedication

I dedicate this work to my beloved wife of almost 35 years, Raschelle. I began these notes during the first year of our marriage, and have continued to work on them ever since. Without Raschelle's love, understanding, commitment, and sacrifice, this study would never have been possible.

Abbreviations

The following abbreviations are used (includes most versions of the Bible used):
    BBE=Bible in Basic English (Cambridge, 1949/1964);*
    BYZ=Byzantine Textform (Chilton, 2005; Bibleworks);*
    CEV=Contemporary English Version (1991);*
    CJB=Complete Jewish Bible (1998);*
    CSB=Holman Christian Standard (Nashville: Lifeway, 1999, 2000, 2002, 2003, 2009);*
    CSB17=Christian Standard Version (2017);*
    CSBO=CSB versions prior to the 2009 edition;*
    DRA=Douais-Rheims (1899);*
    DS=Denzinger, Heinrich, et al. *Symbols et Definitions de la Foi Catholique: Enchiridion Symbolorum* (Paris: Cerf, 2005).
    ESV=English Standard Version (2001, 2007, 2011);*
    FGN [or GEN]=French Geneva (1560; http://biblegeneve.com/nt1669, 1669);
    FJB [or FBJ]=French Jerusalem Bible (1973);*
    GNV [or EGN]=English Geneva Bible (1560; Hendricksen, 2007; Bibleworks, 1599);*
    GOT=Greek Orthodox Text (Athenian Bible Society, 1928, 2004; also Bibleworks)*
    FLF=French Lefevre Bible NT (bibliotheque national de France [online], 1530);
    FLV=French Louvain Bible (bibliotheque nationale de France [online], 1550);
    GNT=Good News Translation (American Bible Society, 1993);
    GWN=God's Word to the Nations (1995);*
    KJV=King James Version (1611/1769);*
    LXE=Brenton' English Translation of the Septuagint (1844; 1851);
    MIT=MacDonald Idiomatic Translation of the NT (2006);*
    MRT=French Martin (http://www.biblemartin.com/bible/bible_frm.htm, 1744);
    NA27=Nestle-Aland 27th (1993);*
    NAB=New American Bible (1900, 1970, 1986, 1991);*
    NAS [or NASB]=New American Standard (1976);*
    NAU=New American Standard Updated (1995);*
    NET=New English Translation (1996-2006);*
    NETS=New English Translation of the Septuagint (2007);*
    NIV=New International Version (1984, 2011);*
    NJB=[English] New Jerusalem Bible (1985);*
    NKJ [or NKJV]=New King James (1982);*
    NLT=New Living Translation (2004);*
    RPTE=Revised Patriarchal Greek Orthodox New Testament (1904, from 350 Gothic Text)
    RSV=Revised Standard Version (1952);*
    SEM=French Le Semeur (International Bible Society, 1992, 1999);
    TOB=French Traduction Oecumenique de la Bible (1988);*
    VUL=Latin Vulgate (435, 1969, 1975, 1983).*

Other Bible versions cited include: French Darby (1859/1884);* English Darby (1884/1890);* James Murdock NT (1851);* French Ostervald (http://lirelabible.com/bibles-php/index.php?version=ostervald-NT, 1744); French Segond (1910);* Wycliffe 1st ed (1382; Oxford, 1850); Wycliffe 2nd ed (1388);* Young's Literal (1862/1898);* as well as five German, three Italian, five Portuguese, and one Spanish translation.*

*Versions used from BibleWorks 8.0, BibleWorks 9.0, BibleWorks 10.0, and/or add-ons.

Forewords

What a TREASURE our Sovereign God has given to His church through Dr. Tom Johnston's *Understanding Evangelizology.* This book provides a wealth of comprehensive Biblical, historical, and statistical resource material on Evangelism.

Every theology professor, Bible teacher, student of theology, pastor, and leader will greatly profit by having Dr. Johnston's book of research on Evangelism in their basic "tool kit" for balanced Biblical studies. He provides an extensive bibliography on Personal Evangelism dated from the 1700's to 2005. The Biblical terms used in both the Old and New Testaments that form a foundation for Evangelism are set forth along with all the Greek words and Scripture references to Evangelism.

Dr. Johnston's book covers every conceivable subject that I could imagine on Evangelism. He gives excellent charts and illustrations as he outlines such subjects as the Biblical Theology of Evangelism; the Practical Theology of Evangelism; A Biblical Theology of Follow-up; and the Local Church Evangelism Strategy.

Dr. Tom Johnston is truly "scholarship on fire!" He is an outstanding theologian, professor, pastor, preacher, and he practices what he writes, teaches and preaches in his life of personal witness for Christ to those who need to know Him.

My only regret is that I did not have this book from the beginning of the pastoral and evangelistic ministry to which God called me.

Dr. Darrell W. Robinson
The Woodlands, Texas, 2006.

Evangelism begins before the foundation of the world when the Lamb is slain in the heart of God. That amazing act of redemptive love which came into focus at Calvary brings creatures of time to measure life now by the values of eternity. In so doing, we are made to face the cross on which the Prince of Glory died, and broken and contrite in spirit, offer ourselves to Him who poured out His blood for us.

That commitment to Christ, through the power of His Spirit, transforms us into an emissary of the Gospel as the love of God is shed abroad in our heart. The priorities of our Lord reorder our agenda of concern, and we begin to think in terms of His kingdom, which might be called a "mindset of eternity."

That is why these notes compiled by Tom Johnston are so helpful. They lift up evangelism from the biblical perspective, coming to groups with both theory and practical ministry of the Word.

What gives this kind of study authenticity is the author's own personal life-style. I have known Tom for a number of years, and can say that he sincerely seeks to practice what he teaches. He is a fearless witness, yet always compassionate, and ever seeking more understanding. I appreciate such a man, and it is a pleasure to commend his thoughts to you.

Dr. Robert E. Coleman
Deerfield, Illinois, 1992

Contents

Preface ix

Volume One: Introduction and Definition

1. The Work of the Gospel 1

   Outline:
   The Roman Road.. 1
   Submitting to God's Manner or Method of Salvation 2
   Undermining God's Manner or Method of Salvation 5
   Tools of the Trade 8
      Gospel Tracts 8
      Gospel Plans for Memorizing 14
      Gospel Plans from One Test of Scripture 19
      Memorizing Scripture Verses 22
      The Use of Quetionnaires or Surveys 23

   Appendixes:
   Chronological Bibliography.. 26
   Other Evangelism Resources 45
   Guillaume Husson's Tract Ministry in 1544.. 47
   On the Necessity of Regular Verbal Confession of Christ 48
   How Evangelizing May Be a Spiritual Benefit.. 51
   How a Lack of Initiative Evangelism Is Detrimental... 54
   Pillars of Evangelizology 55
   Toward a New Testament Theology of Personal Evangelism 56
   Considering Theological and Methodological Drift 57
   Considering Tests for Theologies 58

2. The Christian's Calling to Evangelism, and Metaphors Related to Evangelism...................... 63

   Outline:
   The Christian's Calling to Evangelism 66
   Metaphors Related to Evangelism 75

   Appendixes:
   Hearing to Believe—The Hearing of Faith.. 84
   Aggressive Evangelism's Point of No Return 101
   The Difficulty of Personal Soul-Winning from Trumbull 102
   Claude Monier's Self-Sacrificing Ministry in 1551 104
   The Evangelism Ministry of Two Teenage Girls, Isabeau and Pintarde, around 1689 105

3. The Role of the Evangelist 107

   Outline:
   Introduction 107
   Noticing the Obvious—On the Omission of Evangelists 113
   Is There a Gift of Evangelism, or Is It Rather the Gift of the Evangelist?........................ 123
   The Function of the Evangelist 127
   The Evangelist in the Bible 132
   Definition of an Evangelist 135
   Diversity in the Gift of the Evangelist 136
   Some Examples of Evangelists in the History of the Churches.. 137
   The Evangelist and Revival Ministry.. 143
   Some Common Reproaches Against Evangelists 150

   Appendixes:
   Comparing the Preaching of a Pastor, Revivalist, and Evangelist.................................... 154
   Comparing Special Events and Revivals 155

4. The Spiritual Passions and the Spiritual Battle 157

   Outline:
   Historic and Modern Statements on Initiative Evangelism... 157
   The Spiritual Passions 164
   The Spiritual Battle 168

Appendixes:
Thoughts on the Study of Evangelism 175
The Interrelationship of Message, Reception, and Propagation 184
Understanding the Importance of Evangelism Methodology 186
A Graphic Portrayal of Methodological Drift 187
Thoughts on Church Leadership and Theological Education Based on Ephesians 4:11 188
Understanding Classical Theological Education's Systemic Antipathy for Evangelism 190
Centrality of Evangelism for Theological Education 192
Evangelistic Theological Education and Schools of Thought 193
Keys to an Evangelistic Curriculum 207
    Select Reverse Chronological Historical-Theological Barriers and Disconnects 215
    Reverse Chronological Historical-Theological Tracts 217
    Second Council of Orange (A.D. 529), On Infant Baptism and Salvation 218
    Reversing the Chronological Historical-Theological Tracks 221
Considering the Ranges of Training Needed by Different Levels and Types of Leaders 222
Considering Approaches to Evangelism in Academic Settings 223

5. Steadfast Truths in Evangelism 225

Outline:
Timeless Realities of Evangelism 225
    Fear Is Inevitable 227
    Difficulties Are Inevitable 228
    Antagonism Is Inevitable 229
    Persecution Is Inevitable 231
Tremendous Truths in Evangelism 233
    God Deisres the Salvation of All Men 233
    God Is Always Present 234
    God's Word Is Always Effective 234
    The Harvest Is Always Ripe 234
    There Is Always a Need for Workers 235
    Sharing the Gospel Is Always Appropriate 236
    Sharing the Gospel Always Has a Positive Impact 236
    Victory Is Sure 236

Appendix:
Undermining the Primacy of Evangelism 239

6. Motivations and Urgency of Evangelism 241

Outline:
Motivations for Evangelism 241
    "For This Purpose I Labor" 241
    "The Love of Christ Compels Us" 243
    Other Motivations 244
The Urgency of Evangelism 246
    Jesus Is Coming Back Quickly 247
    The Lost Are Really Lost 250
    The Christian Is Accountable for the Lost Whom He Should Reach 257
    Time Is Short and the Harvest Is Ripe 261

Appendixes:
The Gospel of Christ or the Glory of God as Central Interpretive Motif? 264
Evangelism and Predestination 279
Thoughts on the Extent of the Atonement 281
Evangelism in the Pentateuch 285

7. Defining Evangelizing 289

Outline:
Select Historic Definitions of Evangelism 294
A Long Historic Look at Terms for Evangelism 298
Towards Translating Proclamational Words in the Old Testament 345
A Survey of the Translation of εὐαγγελίζω in the English New Testament 356
"Evangelize" in Several Translation Histories 364
On the Translation of Proclamational Terms in English Bibles 376
Turning the Tide—Unleashing the Word Evangelize! 385
Arguments Against and For Translating εὐαγγελίζω as "Evangelize" 389
    Arguments Against Translating εὐαγγελίζω as "Evangelize" 389

Reasons For Translating εὐαγγελίζω as "Evangelize"..393
Five Categories of New Testament Terms for Evangelizing:...401
   Person..402
   Method 417
      Verbs Used For Evangelism...417
      Categories of Communicatory Verbs Not Used For Evangelism 505
   Movement and/or Location 524
   Spiritual Dynamic 529
   Result of Evangelism Ministry...536
   Toward a Working Definition..557

Appendixes:
   Considering the Meaning of "Taking Oaths in the Name of the Lord" in Deut 6 and 10 563
   Considering the Meaning of "Lifting Up the Name of the Lord in Vain" in Exod 20 and Deut 5...........566
   Words Lightly Used in English Bible Translations?...567

Volume Two: Doctrine and Practice of Evangelism

8. The Doctrine of the Bible in Evangelism

9. The Doctrine of Conversion

10. The Church Doctrine of the Great Commission

11. God, Prayer, and Fasting in Evangelism

12. Spiritual Elements to Evangelism

13. Before Sharing the Gospel

14. Beginning a Spiritual Conversation

15. Getting into Spiritual Things

16. The Personal Testimony and Power of Story

17. What Is the Gospel?

18. Levels of Openness

19. Smokescreens and Objections (Street Apologetics)

20. Results, Reactions, and Responses

21. Commitment and the Prayer of the Sinner

22. Is an Invitation Necessary for Effective Evangelistic Preaching?

Volume Three: Follow-up, Discipleship, and the Local Church

23. Immediate Follow-Up and Evaluation

24. Baptism After Evangelism

25. The Parable of the Sower

26. Follow-Up Is Important

27. God and the Bible in Follow-Up

28. A Graphic Look at Biblical Follow-Up

29. Visitation Initiative—Toward a Local Church Evangelism Strategy

30. Four Categories of Evangelism Programs

31. Evangelism and Systematic Theology Revisited

   Alphabetical Bibliography of Evangelism
   Studies of Hebrew Terms
   Studies of Greek Terms
   Scripture Studies
   General Index

Preface

Walter Rauschenbusch began his *A Theology for the Social Gospel* with the following two sentences: "We have a Social Gospel. We need a systematic theology large enough to match it and vital enough to back it." I would like to change his logical progression a bit, and say: "We have a Great Commission. We need a theology of evangelism large enough to match it and vital enough to back it."

While God's Word was, is, and will always be very much sufficient to back up the Great Commission, these notes seek to look at evangelism from the Bible first, from the history of the churches and systematic theology second, and lastly from culture. This order is usually reversed in most works on evangelism. Even critical hermeneutics cannot look at the words of the Bible without first analyzing the recent historical approaches to words, phrases, arguments, and genres. In this process the priority of the message of the Bible can sometimes be lost due to linguistic arguments of some type or other.

I recently read in the preface of the 2nd volume of Matthew Henry's Bible Commentary the following, "*Brevis esse laboro, obscurus fio*—labouring to be concise I become obscure." It occurred to me that these words may relate to this present volume. Several years ago I determined that, due to the apparent lack of a comprehensive biblical overview of evangelism, brevity would not befit the subject at hand.

My late father, Arthur P. Johnston, conceived of a theology of missions and evangelism as an iceberg. 90% of the iceberg is under the waterline. Likewise, he taught that the 10% of missions and evangelism above the waterline corresponds to the principles and practice of the same. Meanwhile, the 90% below the waterline represent the theological foundations that buttress missions and evangelism. It would be foolish and self-defeating to teach the principles and practice of New Testament evangelism, without at the same time devoting some space to the 90% of biblical-historical-theological material that undergirds the same.

Therefore, my goal in making these class notes available is not to render obscure the work of the Gospel, nor to make evangelizing overly complex, but rather to highlight the teachings of the Bible, and to simultaneously examine avenues by which deviations from the Bible's teaching are constantly being made. Each chapter has biblical meat which drives an urgent evangelism, and likewise includes various theological or practical points which may undermine the very subject at hand. My desire is to show the breadth of issues related to the study of evangelism, hence evangelizology. Indeed, the Christian faith is like a well ordered row of dominos. When one domino moves, the remaining dominos likewise move. Hence, "A little leaven leavens the whole lump." Methodology of evangelism is often one of the first dominos moved, which ends up altering all of Christian doctrine itself. Therefore, while not discussing every point in any class, nor looking up every verse with my students, main points are highlighted during class, with the remaining material as a type of encyclopedic resource for further study and inquiry into evangelizology.

As far as evangelizology as a "Classical Theological" discipline. Since the writings of Augustine, particularly those compiled as *Contra Donatisten* (Against the Donatists), and since the so-called Soteriological Controversy which led to the Second Council of Orange (529 A.D.), Sacramental writings have framed the question of "Classical Theology." The Medieval authors, such as Master Peter "the Lombard" and Thomas Aquinas, only furthered the Sacramental cause. Schleiermacher and Schaff, in their writings on the "Study of Theology" did not very much alter the course set before them. The Evangelical Gospel and its corresponding evangelizing have had a tough go of it in historical writings. B. H. Carroll, fouding president of Southwestern Baptist Theological Seminary was correct in his assessment of this struggle. He spoke in 1906 to the Southern Baptist Convention on the creation of a "Department of Evangelism":

> "Let us give the report a rousing, unanimous endorsement.
> "The bedrock of Scripture underlies it. Experience demonstrates its wisdom and feasibility. If the Home Board may employ any man, it may employ evangelists. Altogether, then, with a ring, let us support this measure. If I were the secretary of this board I would come before this body in humility and tears and say: 'Brethren, give me evangelists. Deny not fins to things that must swim against the tide, nor wings to things that must fly against the wind.'" (Charles S. Kelley, *How Did They Do It?* [Insight, 1993], 14).

Alas, there will always be a battle involved for both the work of the evangelist and for New Testament evangelism! But we must not lose heart.

The question for contemporary Baptist and Conservative Evangelical academia comes by way of a plea off the pen of the Apostle Paul: "Therefore do not be ashamed of the testimony of our Lord, or of me His prisoner; but join with *me* in suffering for the gospel according to the power of God" (2 Tim 1:8). There is a shame involved in participation in Pauline or New Testament evangelism. Later Paul wrote, "At my first defense no one supported me, but all deserted me; may it not be counted against them" (2 Tim 4:16). Could the Apostles of the Lord in Jerusalem be counted among these "all"? Or is Paul speaking of his missionary team? Either interpretation is sorrowful. My request to the reader is to consider Paul's plea in 2 Timothy 1:8, while reading these note that are doubtless flawed and feeble. Please consider that any areas of disagreement or any errors you may find originate in a sincere desire to plumb the depths of Scripture in the area of biblical evangelizology.

As the Book of Proverbs says, "He who has knowledge spares his words, *And* a man of understanding is of a calm spirit. Even a fool is counted wise when he holds his peace; *When* he shuts his lips, *he is considered* perceptive" (Prov 17:27-28). Then two verses later we read, "A fool has no delight in understanding, But in expressing his own heart" (Prov 18:2). In this light, perhaps no one ought ever to write a book. And if someone did write down his thoughts, he ought to follow Proverbs 18:1, "A man who isolates himself seeks his own desire; He rages against all wise judgment." There is always a danger of isolating oneself by finding fault with everyone else. Knowledge can always be dangerous and lead to pride (1 Cor 8:1). May the reader be assured that this author recognizes that he also is in the midst of a journey to understand the depths of the teachings of the Word of God.

It is my prayer that these efforts will encourage new avenues of study into biblical evangelizing, allowing the very words of God's Word to motivate His children to evangelize in concert with what He has revealed in His Scriptures. This work is therefore offered to that end, that, according to God's will, He would usher in a needed awakening of New Testament evangelism among His people.

Thomas P. Johnston
Liberty, Missouri, U.S.A.
December, 2019.

CHAPTER 1

Introducing the Work of the Gospel

The Roman Road

The Urgency:

"Evangelism, in the New Testament sense of the word, is indispensable to Southern Baptist churches. Without it they will dwindle away and die. To a people who avoid catechisms and other similar methods of reaching 'unchurched' people, the choice is between a vital effort in evangelism and ceasing to exist altogether. What is more important, it is the choice between leading persons to him who is 'the way, the truth, and the life,' and of permitting them to go unchallenged into eternity, destined only for being everlastingly lost, which is the 'second death' (Rev 14:20)."[1]

Preliminary Questions:

Do you know Jesus as your Savior and Lord?
Before embarking on the journey of soul-winning, you need to be sure that you are saved...[2]
Here is a simple Gospel plan that we will use for this class. It is called the "Roman Road"

The Roman Road:[3]
1. God says that all are sinners, Rom3:10, 23[4]
2. God tells us the reason all are sinners, Rom 5:12
3. God tells us the result of sin, Rom 6:23
4. God tells us of His concern for sinners, Rom 5:8-9
5. God's way of salvation is made plain, Rom 10:9-10, 13
6. God tells us the results of salvation, Rom 5:1, 8:1
7. God gives the saved sinner assurance, Rom 8:16

Questions:

Have you confessed your sinful state to Christ?
Have you believed that Jesus Christ paid the full and complete penalty for your sins on the cross?
Have you asked God to forgive you of your sins by the blood of Jesus?
If you have not, please take a moment and do business with God...
Evangelism, or the work of the Gospel, will be irrelevant if you are not a born-again Christian. In fact,
   you will probably be antagonistic to this class if you are not truly saved!

GOSPEL SHARING PRACTICUM

Let's take a few minutes and share the Gospel with one another
Please use the Gospel tract provided and share it with your neighbor

---

[1]"Introduction," in Herschel H. Hobbs, *New Testament Evangelism: The Eternal Purpose* (Nashville: Convention Press, 1960), xi.

[2]"The first condition of success in personal work, and in all soul-saving work, is a personal experimental knowledge of Jesus Christ as Savior. It was because the Apostle Paul could say: 'This is a faithful saying, and worthy of all acceptation, that Christ Jesus came into the world to save sinners; OF WHOM I AM CHIEF' (1 Tim 1:15) that he had power in bringing other men to that Savior. It is the man who knows Jesus as his own Savior, who will have a longing to bring others to this wonderful Savior whom he has himself found; and it is the man who knows Jesus as his Savior who will understand how to bring others to the Savior whom he has found. There are many today who are trying to save others, who are not saved themselves" (R. A. Torrey, "Personal Work," Book One: *How To Work for Christ: A Compendium of Effective Methods* [New York: Revell, 1901], 15).

[3]It must be acknowledged that there are differing versions of the Roman Road, some perhaps having different theological or pragmatic purposes. For example, one version of the Roman Road began with Rom 1:20-21, emphasizing the general revelation of God, man's prior knowledge of God, and his subsequent suppression of that knowledge.

[4]See my chart on translations of Rom 3:23 in Chapter 17, "What Is the Gospel?"

Submission to God's Manner or Method of Salvation

Perhaps the most important issue in evangelism is a willingness or lack of willingness to submit to God's revealed method or manner of salvation! Consider that this was an issue that sparked much debate!

TEXT:

Acts 15:7-11, [7]And after there had been much debate, Peter stood up and said to them, "Brethren, you know that in the early days God made a choice among you, that by my mouth the Gentiles should hear the word of the gospel and believe. And God, who knows the heart, bore witness to them, giving them the Holy Spirit, just as He also did to us; and He made no distinction between us and them, cleansing their hearts by faith. Now therefore why do you put God to the test by placing upon the neck of the disciples a yoke which neither our fathers nor we have been able to bear? But we believe that we are saved through the grace of the Lord Jesus, in the same way as they also are."

Translations of the last phrase in Acts 15:11 [καθ᾽ ὃν τρόπον κἀκεῖνοι][5]

Byzan-tine	Vulgate	Tyn-dale (1534)	English Geneva (1560)	King James (1611, 1769)	English Darby (1884, 1890)	English Revised (1885)	ASV (1901)	NAS (1977)	NKJ (1982)	RSV (1952); NRS; ESV	NIV (1984)	CEV✠ (1995)	NLB (2004)	NET (2005)
καθ᾽ ὃν τρόπον κἀκεῖ-νοι	quemad-modum et illi	as they doo.	euen as they *do*	even as they	the same manner as they also[a]	in like manner as they	in like manner as they.[b]	in the same way as they also are	in the same manner as they	just as they will	just as they are	just as the Gentiles are	the same way…	in the same way as they are

[a]The French Darby, preceding the English Darby by 26 years, translated similarly, "de la même manière qu'eux aussi" (1858, 1885).
[b]The French Louis Segond (1910), New French Geneva (1977), and *Le Semeur* (1992, 1999), are similar to the ASV, "de la même manière qu'eux."
✠Indicates a Roman Catholic Bible translation.[6]
By the way, the 1545 Luther Bible translated this phrase as, "gleicherweise wie auch sie"

The Greek word τρόπον carries with it a strong degree of similitude. The OT LXX provides parallel examples, two using τρόπον and one not, both verses using the Hebrew *asher*:

Deut 23:23[24], "You shall be careful to perform what goes out from your lips, **just as** [*c-asher*] you have voluntarily vowed to the LORD your God, **what** [*asher*] you have promised"

   This verse includes parallelism which is somewhat lost in the NAS translation; the last phrase includes the word "mouth"; hence KJV, "which thou hast promised with thy mouth"; thus:
      Goes forth from your lips > willingly spoken with your mouth.
However of importance in this case is the dual use of the word *asher* in the Hebrew, which is once translated τρόπον in the Greek (English, "just as"), and ὅ in Greek (English, "what").

Deut 24:8, "**Be careful** against an infection of leprosy, that you **diligently observe and do** according to all that the Levitical priests shall teach you; **as** [*c-asher*] I have commanded them, so you shall **be careful to do**."

---

[5]The Greek word κἀκεῖνος used 21 times in the NT. Friberg, Thayer, and Gingrich lexicons all have an entry for the word κἀκεῖνος, e.g.:
   "2688 κἀκεῖνος (Griesbach κἀκεῖνος; see κἀγω, and references), κακεινη, κακεινο (by crasis from καί and ἐκεῖνος (cf. Winer's Grammar, sec. 5, 3; especially Tdf. Proleg., p. 97)); 1. ἐκεῖνος referring to the more remote subject; a. *and he* (Latin *et ille*): Luke 11:7; 22:12; Acts 18:19; ταῦτα κἀκεῖνα (A. V. *the other*), Matt. 23:23; Luke 11:42. b. *he also*: Acts 15:11; Rom. 11:23 (Rec. st καί ἐκεῖνος); 1 Cor. 10:6. 2. ἐκεῖνος referring to the nearer subject (cf. ἐκεῖνος, 1 c.); a. *and he* (Latin *et is*, German *und selbiger*): Matt. 15:18; John 7:29; 19:35 (L Tr WH καί ἐκεῖνος)" (Thayer, BibleWorks, 9.0).
   Louw-Nida, however, follows the "Scott" lexicon, which entry for κἀκεῖνος simply reads, "κἀκεῖνος, by crasis for καί ἐκεῖνος" ("κἀκεῖνος"; in Henry George Liddell and Robert Scott, *A Greek-English Lexicon Based on the German Work of Francis Passow*, with corrections by Henry Drissler [New York: Harper & Brothers, 1875]).
   [6]"Some committees have considered the possibility of explaining different Roman Catholic and Protestant beliefs by noting that one interpretation is held by Roman Catholics and another by Protestants. Such a procedure does not seem wise, for it tends to accentuate differences; nor is it necessary, since most diversities of interpretation can be covered more objectively by marginal annotations on alternative renderings, if the issue in question is important. Where the matter is not of great consequence, it is better simply to omit reference in the interest of joint undertakings" ("Guiding Principles for Interconfessional Cooperation in Translating the Bible," in Thomas F. Stransky, C.S.P., and John B. Sheerin, C.S.B., eds. *Doing the Truth in Charity: Statements of Pope Paul VI, Popes John Paul I, John Paul II, and the Secretariat for Promoting Christian Unity 1964-1980* [New York: Paulist, 1982], 159-69).

What is interesting in this verse is thrice use of "be careful unto thyself" [πρόσεχε σεαυτῷ], "keep to do exceedingly" [φυλάξῃ σφόδρα ποιεῖν], and "keep to do" [φυλάξασθε ποιεῖν]; in addition to the "just as I have commanded them" [ὃν τρόπον ἐνετειλάμην ὑμῖν].

The Migne Vulgate renders the Hebrew *c-asher* with the emphatic, *iuxta id quod praecepi eis*, or: "**according to what** I have commanded them" (DRA).

Deut 22:26, "But you shall do nothing to the girl; there is no sin in the girl worthy of death, **for just as** [*cy c-asher*] a man rises against his neighbor and murders him, so is this case"

Wherein the young girl raped in the field is not held guilty, because it is "just like" (Hebrew, *cy c-asher*; Greek ὅτι ὡς εἴ [lit. that as if when]) the man pounces on his neighbor putting him to death. Notice also the interesting emphasis in the last phrase in Deut 22:26, "even so *is* this matter" [Heb. *cen hadabar hatseh*; Gk. οὕτως τὸ πρᾶγμα τοῦτο], which is reminiscent of the emphasis of the last phrase in Acts 15:11.

Considering the method, Acts 15:7-11

Verse	Man	Hearing	Believing	God's place
v. 7		"…that by my mouth the Gentiles should hear the word of the gospel…"	…and believe"	"Brethren, you know that in the early days God made a choice among you…"
v. 8				"And God, who knows the heart, bore witness to them, giving them the Holy Spirit, just as He also did to us;"
v. 9			[…by faith]	"and He made no distinction between us and them, cleansing their hearts… []"
v. 10	"Now therefore why do you put God to the test by placing upon the neck of the disciples a yoke which neither our fathers nor we have been able to bear?"			
v. 11	"But we believe that we are saved…, in the same way as they also are"			"… through the grace of the Lord Jesus…"
Luther's Three*		Scriptures Alone Or: Sola Scriptura, "on the word alone"[7]	Faith Alone Or: Sola Fide, "through faith alone"	Grace Alone Sola Gratia

*These same three are also clearly taught in Rom 3:21-26 and 1 Cor 15:1-11 (e.g. Acts 16:30-31; cf. Rom 5:1-2; 15:25-27; Gal 3:26).

Some thoughts:

1. Notice that there are not multiple means of salvation, but just one, hearing and believing; the noun τρόπον is the masculine singular accusative of ὁ τρόπος, that there is one means of salvation:
   a. in this regard, consider the translation "by all means" in 1 Cor 9:22, which is derived from the use of the word "all"—the word "means" being supplied by the translators
   b. See the chart and discussion of Grudem's 11 "means of grace" at the opening of Chapter 13.

2. Likewise, consider that the noun ὁ τρόπος is not a hapax legomena, it is used 13 times in the New Testament, and 180 times in the LXX:
   a. For example in the OT, the noun is used to translate the compound Hebrew word *ka-asher*: the Israelites should take the land "in like manner as" to how God had told them, Deut 1:21; "in like manner as" they heard God's voice, Deut 4:33; "in like manner as" commanded by the Lord, Deut 5:16; etc.
   b. In the NT:
      1) Nominative use (1 NT use): "Manner" is used as the subject of the verb in Heb 13:5:
         BYZ, Ἀφιλάργυρος ὁ τρόπος, ἀρκούμενοι τοῖς παροῦσιν· αὐτὸς γὰρ εἴρηκεν, Οὐ μή σε ἀνῶ, οὐδ᾽ οὐ μή σε ἐγκαταλείπω.

---

[7]Philip Schaff, "The Evangelical Church Diet of Germany," *The Mercerberg Review*, vol 9 (1857), 5.

KJV, "*Let your* **conversation** *be* without covetousness; *and be* content with such things as ye have: for he hath said, I will never leave thee, nor forsake thee"

NAS, "Let **your character** be free from the love of money, being content with what you have; for He Himself has said, 'I will never desert you, nor will I ever forsake you,'"

2) Dative uses (2 NT use):

Phil 1:18:

BYZ, Τί γάρ; Πλὴν παντὶ τρόπῳ, εἴτε προφάσει εἴτε ἀληθείᾳ, χριστὸς καταγγέλλεται· καὶ ἐν τούτῳ χαίρω, ἀλλὰ καὶ χαρήσομαι.

KJV, What then? notwithstanding, every **way**, whether in pretence, or in truth, Christ is preached; and I therein do rejoice, yea, and will rejoice.

NAS, What then? Only that in every **way**, whether in pretence or in truth, Christ is proclaimed; and in this I rejoice, yes, and I will rejoice.

ESV, What then? Only that in every **way**, whether in pretence or in truth, Christ is proclaimed, and in that I rejoice. Yes, and I will rejoice,

2 Thess 3:16:

BYZ, Αὐτὸς δὲ ὁ κύριος τῆς εἰρήνης δῴη ὑμῖν τὴν εἰρήνην διὰ παντὸς ἐν παντὶ τρόπῳ. Ὁ κύριος μετὰ πάντων ὑμῶν.

KJV, "Now the Lord of peace himself give you peace always by all **means**. The Lord *be* with you all."

ASV, "Now the Lord of peace himself give you peace at all times in all **ways**. The Lord be with you all."

NAS, "Now may the Lord of peace Himself continually grant you peace in every **circumstance**. The Lord be with you all!"

ESV, "Now may the Lord of peace himself give you peace at all times in every **way**. The Lord be with you all."

3) Accusative uses (10 NT uses):

Acts 1:11, Christ is going to return "in like manner" [ὃν τρόπον] as He left,

Acts 7:28, The Hebrew slave asked Moses, Are you going to kill me "in like manner" as you killed the Egyptian yesterday?

2 Tim 3:8, False teachers act "in like manner" to those during the time of Moses

3. Likewise the girl with a spirit of divination was ridiculing Paul and Silas for preaching a singular "**way of salvation** [ὁδὸν σωτηρίας]." What a joke to pluralistic Greek society of that time!

    Acts 16:17, "Following after Paul and us, she kept crying out, saying, 'These men are bond-servants of the Most High God, who are proclaiming to you **the way of salvation.**'"

4. While Luther was correct in abolishing the Mass as a "**manner of receiving salvation**" or "**means of grace**," and replacing it with Scriptures alone, faith alone, and grace alone, he seemed unwilling to remove the sacramental grace associated with infant baptism. This left Anabaptists persecuted from both sides, the Church of Rome and even Magisterial Protestant churches.

5. As noted in the chart above, it was John Darby, in his 1884 translation of Acts 15:11, who gave us the translation of ὁ τρόπος as "manner", which led to a flurry of translations following suit (much like Darby's "make disciples" in Matt 28:19 took hold). However, it seems like this translation tendency ended with the RSV (1952) and the NIV (1984).

6. What is at stake is the vehemently argued **manner of salvation** (Acts 15:7), and hence of instantaneous **conversion** in space and time (Acts 15:11);[8] likewise at stake is the vehemently argued method of evangelizing (Gal 1:8-10).

7. Note the distinction when translating Acts 15:11:

    a. Wycliffe's (1388) translation of the Latin Vulgate: "But bi the grace of oure Lord Jhesu Crist we bileuen to be saued, as also thei"

    b. Johnston (2008): "But that through the grace of the Lord Jesus we believe unto salvation, in the same manner as they also."

8. Therefore, there is a manner or method of salvation, just as was acknowledged by August Hermann Francke (1663-1727):

    "As far as I am concerned, I must preach that should someone hear me only once before he dies, he will have heard not just a part, but the entire way of salvation and in the proper way for it to take root in his heart."[9]

---

[8]For differing views of conversion, and antagonism to instantaneous conversion, see Chapter 8.

9. A corollary to this "way of salvation" is "the words of eternal life", John 6:68

> John 6:68, "Simon Peter answered Him, 'Lord, to whom shall we go? You have words of eternal life. And we have believed and have come to know that You are the Holy One of God.'"

On Undermining God's Manner or Method of Salvation

1. Elymas the Magician provides an example of one who sought to make crooked the straight "ways of the Lord"—referring contextually to the way of salvation:

> Acts 13:6-12, "And when they had gone through the whole island as far as Paphos, they found a certain magician, a Jewish false prophet whose name was Bar-Jesus, [7] who was with the proconsul, Sergius Paulus, a man of intelligence. This man summoned Barnabas and Saul and sought to hear the word of God. [8] But Elymas the magician (for thus his name is translated) was opposing them, seeking to turn the proconsul away from the faith. [9] But Saul, who was also *known as* Paul, filled with the Holy Spirit, fixed his gaze upon him, [10] and said, 'You who are full of all deceit and fraud, you son of the devil, you enemy of all righteousness, will you not cease to make crooked the straight ways of the Lord? [11] 'And now, behold, the hand of the Lord is upon you, and you will be blind and not see the sun for a time.' And immediately a mist and a darkness fell upon him, and he went about seeking those who would lead him by the hand. [12] Then the proconsul believed when he saw what had happened, being amazed at the teaching of the Lord.

   a. Notice the terminology used for the teaching regarding the way of salvation:
      1) "Word of the Lord," Acts 13:7
      2) "The faith," Acts 13:8
      3) "The straight ways of the Lord," Acts 13:10
      4) "Teaching of the Lord," Acts 13:12

   b. Notice also the response: "the proconsul believed," Acts 13:12

   c. And notice the attack of Elymas the Magician, Acts 13:10-11:

      1) His attack against the Gospel was a result of all deceit and fraud

      2) His attack made him an enemy of all unrighteousness
         Long has the concept of "justification by faith alone" been the basis for attack and cruelty against the true church of God.[10]

      3) His attacks were relentless, "will you not cease"

      4) His attacks sought to "make crooked the straight ways of the Lord"
         Historically there have been reepeated attempts to make crooked the straight ways of the Lord, cf. Matt 24:26

2. Some thoughts:

   a. It behooves the Christian to know the way of salvation

   b. It behooves the Christian to know the attacks of the evil one on the straight ways of the Lord

   c. These notes, therefore, seek to look at both sides of the equation:
      1) What is the way of salvation, and how can a person communicate it clearly?
      2) What are some common deviations from the way of salvation, and how can they be detected and avoided?

---

[9]Paulus Scharpff, *History of Evangelism: Three Hundred Years of Evangelism in Germany, Great Britain, and the Unites States of America.* Helga Bender Henry, trans. (Grand Rapids: Eerdmans, 1964, 1966), 46.

[10]Notice the Roman Catholic "Council of Trent" (1545-1563), Canon 9 on Justification: "Canon 9. If anyone says that the sinner is justified by faith alone, meaning that nothing else is required to cooperate in order to obtain the grace of justification, and that it is not in any way necessary that he be prepared and disposed by the action of his own will [necessitating baptism in Rome's mind], let him be anathema" ("Council of Trent: 19th Ecumenical Council; from: http://www.forerunner.com/chalcedon/X0020_15._Council_of_Trent.html; accessed 8 Jan 2005; Internet).

The Need for Submission to the Confession of the Gospel of Christ:

This course is academics put into practice; it is submission to the confession of the Gospel of Christ!

2 Cor 9:13 (CSB), "Through the proof of this service, they will glorify God for **your obedience to the confession of the gospel of Christ**, and for your generosity in sharing with them and with others"

Like Naaman in 1 Kings 5, who had to submit to dunking himself in the Jordan 7 times, submission is always difficult;
While submitting to the Great Commission ought not be difficult, it is!
It is my prayer that we will constantly be teachable in the area of the confession of the Gospel of Christ!

Variations in Translating ἡ ὁμολογία in 2 Cor 9:13

Byzan-tine Text-form*	Holman Christian Standard (2004)	J. N. Darby Bible (1884/1890)	New Interna-tional Version (1984)	New American Standard (1977)	God's Word for the Nations (1995)	Revised Standard Version (1952)	English Geneva (1560)	King James (1611/1769)	French Le Semeur⸶ (IBS, 1992, 1999)**	New Jeru-salem⸶ (1985)	CEV⸶ (ABS, 1991)***	Bible in Basic English (1949/1962)
Most Evangelistic Translations										Least Evangelistic Translations		
τῇ ὑποταγῇ τῆς ὁμολο-γίας ὑμῶν εἰς τὸ εὐαγγέ-λιον τοῦ χριστοῦ	your obedience to the confession of the gospel of Christ	by reason of your subject-tion, by profess-sion, to the glad tidings of the Christ	The obedience that accom-panies your confes-sion of the gospel of Christ	for the obedience of your confes-sion unto the gospel of Christ	because of your commit-ment to spread the Good News of Christ	your obedience in acknow-ledging the gospel of Christ	for your voluntarie submis-sion to the Gospel of Christ	Your professed subjection unto the gospel of Christ	the obedience by which is expres-sed your faith in the Good News of Christ	for the obedience which you show in profes-sing the gospel of Christ	You believed the message about Christ, and you obeyed it by sharing gene-rously...	for the way in which you have given your-selves to the good news of Christ

⸶Indicates Bible versions affirmed as Roman Catholic by an imprimatur.

*Also known as the Robinson-Pierpont text of 2004/2005, this Greek text follows the priority of the Byzantine and Majority Text. It is used within the charts in addition to the Critical Greek Text in the tradition of Westcott-Hort-Tischendorf-Nestle-Aland-Metzger-Martini-Karavidopoulos. There are no variants in this text which differentiate the Nestle-Aland, 27th ed. from the Byzantine Textform. Hence all these translations are made from the same Greek original text.

**Actual French, "l'obéissance par laquelle s'exprime votre foi en la Bonne Nouvelle du Christ"; These notes refer to the 1999 French Le Semeur quite regularly, as it usually provides an example of the most non-proclamational and non-Evangelical reading of all the modern translations that I have studied (e.g. downplaying total depravity, justification by faith alone, and proclamation). The translation was made by the United Bible Society, printed by the International Bible Society, and marketed in the U.S. by the American Bible Society. It represents the impact of the "Guiding Principles for Interconfessional Cooperation in Translating the Bible" of the United Bible Society and the Roman Catholic Secretariat for the Promotion of Christian Union on June 2, 1968, revised on 16 November 1987 as "Guidelines for Interconfessional Cooperation in Translating the Bible: the New Revised Edition Rome." More details regarding this landmark document are found in my unpublished 2008 ETS paper, "Worldwide Bible Translation and Original Language Texts: An Analysis of the Impact of the 1968 and 1987 UBS and SPCU 'Guidelines for Interconfessional Cooperation in Translating the Bible'" (available at: http://www.evangelismunlimited.com/ubs-spcu_text20090116b.pdf (online); accessed 14 July 2012; Internet).

***The 1991 Contemporary English Version, marketed in the U.S. by the American Bible Society (copyright holder), available with apocryphal books and imprimatur by the Church of Rome, was made under the same 1987 "Guidelines" as the French Le Semeur described above.

You may be taking this course voluntarily, or involuntarily:

1 Cor 9:16-17, "For if I preach the gospel [lit. "evangelize"], I have nothing to boast of, for I am under compulsion; for woe is me if I do not preach the gospel [lit. "evangelize"]. For if I do this voluntarily, I have a reward; but if against my will, I have a stewardship entrusted to me."

Voluntary? [gladly; with a glad-heart]
Or, against your will? [grudgingly; Fr. contre-coeur[11]]

Either way, it is my prayer that this class will give you a reward!

---

[11]From the French Geneva translation published by Matthieu Berjon (Geneva, 1605).

Is this not merely submitting to God Himself?

> Heb 12:9, "Furthermore, we had earthly fathers to discipline us, and we respected them; shall we not much rather be subject to the Father of spirits, and live?"

Remember the reward for bold speech:

> Heb 10:35 (ASV), "Cast not away therefore your boldness, which hath great recompense of reward"

Translations of ἡ παρρησία in Heb 10:35

Passive [self-centered]	Passive [God-centered]						Active [God-centered and Verbally-centered]
Sure of yourselves	Being brave	Courage	Fearlessness	Hope	trist [trust]	Confidence	Boldness
Message (1993)	CEV (1991)✠	GNT (1993)✠	NJB (1985)✠	BBE (1949)	Wycliffe (2nd ed)	Tyndale (1534); Geneva; Bishops; KJV; RSV; NAS; NKJ; NIV; CSB; NET; ESV	Young's (1862); ERV; ASV
So don't throw it all away now. You were sure of yourselves then. It's *still* a sure thing!	Keep on being brave! It will bring you great rewards.	Do not lose your courage, then, because it brings with it a great reward	Do not lose your fearlessness now, then, since the reward is so great	So do not give up your hope which will be greatly rewarded	Therfor nyle ye leese youre trist, which hath greet rewarding	Cast not awaye therfore youre confidence which hath great rewarde to recompence	Ye may not cast away, then, your boldness, which hath great recompense of reward

- It appears that the progression goes from "keep a stiff upper lip" to "do not be afraid to speak out boldly for the Lord."
- Note that the Catholic translations appear to avoid using the term "cast away." Perhaps this is related to the Vulgate's use of the verb *amittere*; note also that the same Greek verb is used in Rev 3:2 in the Byzantine text.

Remember the blessing:

> Rev 12:11, "And they overcame him because of the blood of the Lamb and because of the word of their testimony, and they did not love their life even to death."

> Rev 20:4, "And I saw thrones, and they sat upon them, and judgment was given to them. And I *saw* the souls of those who had been beheaded because of the testimony of Jesus and because of the word of God, and those who had not worshiped the beast or his image, and had not received the mark upon their forehead and upon their hand; and they came to life and reigned with Christ for a thousand years."

Tools of the Trade:
Memorized and Printed

Introduction:

The following notes provide an overview of Gospel tracts, Gospel presentations, and Gospel literature used in contemporary evangelism. A discussion of the content of the Gospel takes place below in Chap 17.

Different Types of Printed Literature Used in Evangelism:[12]
   a.   Bible distribution (including New Testaments and Bible portions).
   b.   Books, such as *Left Behind* series by Tim Lahaye; *Jesus Freak* by D.C. Talk; C.S. Lewis, *Mere Christianity;* John R.W. Stott, *Basic Christianity,* etc.
   c.   Newspapers or Magazines (e.g. *Decision Magazine*).
   d.   Tracts or pamphlets...

A. Gospel Tracts:

Introduction:

"Pamphlet wars" occurred after Pope Boniface VIIIth published his *Unum Sanctum* (1302).[13]

Taborite manifestos [tracts] were distributed throughout Germany, Poland, Picardy, Venice, Oxford, Barcelona, and Dauphiné, affirming the "Four Articles of Prague," formulated in 1419-1420—even before the invention of the printing press in 1455!

   (1)   To give freedom for the preaching of the Word in the mother-tongue;
   (2)   To administer Communion in both kinds;
   (3)   To dispossess the Church of its earthly wealth; and
   (4)   To organize political life according to God's law, a public sin to receive a public punishment.[14]

William Caxton famously brought the printing press to the British Isles, setting up a press in Westminster in 1476,[15] and printing the first "handbill" or advertisement that same year.[16]

Later, Marguerite de Valois, sister of King of France, Francis I, was converted after reading Gospel tracts (in 1522)!

"But there was especially one soul, in the court of Francis I, who seemed prepared for the evangelical influence of the doctor from Étaples and the Bishop of Meaux. Marguerite, uncertain and unsure, in the midst of the corrupt society that surrounded her, sought something firm, and she found it in the Gospel. She turned herself to this new wind that was reinvigorating the world, and she inhaled with delight the emanations from heaven. She learned from several of the ladies in her court what was being taught by the new doctors; their writings were communicated to her, their small books, called in the language of the times 'tracts'; they spoke to her of 'the primitive church, the pure Word of God, worship in spirit and in truth, Christian liberty that removes the yoke of the superstitions and traditions of men to attach itself uniquely to God.' Soon this princess met Lefèvre, Farel, and Roussel; their zeal, their piety, their beliefs,

---

[12]For further information, see: Mark Ward, Sr., *The Word Works: 151 Amazing Stories of Men and Women Saved through Gospel Literature* (Greenville, SC: Ambassador Emerald Int'l, 2002); George Verwer, *Literature Evangelism* (Chicago; Moody, 1963); and Arthur M. Chirgwin, *The Bible in World Evangelism* (New York; Friendship, 1954).

[13]"Clement V"; available at: http://en.wikipedia.org/wiki/Clement_V (online); accessed: 5 Jan 2013 (Internet).

[14]Amedeo Molnar, "Czech Reformation and Mission," in *History's Lessons for Tomorrow's Mission: Milestones in the History of Missionary Thinking* (Geneva: World Student Christian Federation, 1960), 130.

[15]"William Caxton"; available at: http://en.wikipedia.org/wiki/William_Caxton (online); accessed: 5 May 2015; Internet.

[16]"'If it please any man, spiritual or temporal, to buy any Pyes of two and three commemorations of Salisbury Use, emprynted after the forme of the present letter, which ben well and truly correct, let hym come to Westminstre in to the Almonrye at the Red Pale and he shall have them good and chepe. *Supplico stet cedula.*' No advertisement of modern times, however ingeniously constructed, could have more points of interest that this fifteenth-century handbill" (Susan Cunnington, *The Story of William Caxton* [London: Harrap, 1917], 75).

everything in them struck her; but it was especially the Bishop of Meaux [Briçonnet], long acquaintance of hers, who became her guide in the path of faith."[17]

In February 1523, Francois Lambert d'Avignon (a.k.a. Johannes Serranus) first wrote a French tract from Wittenberg (where there was freedom of the press). It was "Reasons on account of which I rejected the life and habit of the Minorites [Minor Brothers, or Franciscans]." Then in March, Lambert wrote "Evangelical Commentary on the Rule of the Minorites."[18] Later in the summer, Lambert prepared other evangelical works. He wrote to Spalatin, "I have begun to prepare some things in French because messengers from Hamburg have come to me, asking for tracts in the French language."[19]

Throughout the history of the churches, churches and governments have issued decrees against Gospel literature, which has resulted in persecution:

1) Church of Rome's 19th Ecumenical Council, the Council of Trent, wrote "A Decree Concerning the Edition and Use of the Sacred Books" (April 1546), in which was limited freedom of the press to only those items with the approbation of a Roman Catholic Bishop, imposing the death penalty and confiscation of property on perpetrators (Article 3 of the Fourth Lateran Council).[20]

2) King Charles II's 1662 Seditious Printing Act, titled, "An Act for preventing the frequent Abuses in printing seditious treasonable and unlicensed Bookes and Pamphlets and for regulating of Printing and Printing Presses."[21]

---

[17]J.-H. Merle d'Aubigny, *Histoire de la Réformation du Seizième Siècle* (Paris: Firmin Didot Frères, 1867), 3:508-09. Translation mine.

[18]Roy Lutz Winters, *Francis Lambert of Avignon (1487-1530): A Study in Reformation Origins* (Philadelphia: United Lutheran Publication House, 1938), 45.

[19]Ibid., 49.

[20]"Furthermore, to check unbridled spirits, it decrees that no one relying on his own judgment shall, in matters of faith and morals pertaining to the edification of Christian doctrine, distorting the Holy Scriptures in accordance with his own conceptions,[5] presume to interpret them contrary to that sense which holy mother Church, to whom it belongs to judge of their true sense and interpretation,[6] has held and holds, or even contrary to the unanimous teaching of the Fathers, even though such interpretations should never at any time be published. Those who act contrary to this shall be made known by the ordinaries and punished in accordance with the penalties prescribed by the law.

"And wishing, as is proper, to impose a restraint in this matter on printers also, who, now without restraint, thinking what pleases them is permitted them, print without the permission of ecclesiastical superiors the books of the Holy Scriptures and the notes and commentaries thereon of all persons indiscriminately, often with the name of the press omitted, often also under a fictitious press-name, and what is worse, without the name of the author, and also indiscreetly have for sale such books printed elsewhere, [this council] decrees and ordains that in the future the Holy Scriptures, especially the old Vulgate Edition, be printed in the most correct manner possible, and that it shall not be lawful for anyone to print or to have printed any books whatsoever dealing with sacred doctrinal mattes without the name of the author, or in the future to sell them, or even to have them in possession, unless they have first been examined and approved by the ordinary, under penalty of anathema and fine prescribed by the last Council of the Lateran.[7]

"If they be regulars they must in addition to this examination and approval obtain permission also from their own superiors after these have examined the books in accordance with their own statutes. Those who lend or circulate them in manuscript before they have been examined and approved, shall be subject to the same penalties as the printers, and those who have them in their possession or read them, shall, unless they make known the authors, be themselves regarded as the authors. The approbation of such books, however, shall be given in writing and shall appear authentically at the beginning of the book, whether it be written or printed, and all this, that is, both the examination and the approbation, shall be done gratuitously, so that what ought to be approved may be approved and what ought to be condemned may be condemned.

"Furthermore, wishing to repress that boldness whereby the words and sentences of the Holy Scriptures are turned and twisted to all kinds of profane usages, namely, to things scurrilous, fabulous, vain, to flatteries, detractions, superstitions, godless and diabolical incantations, divinations, the casting of lots and defamatory libels, to put an end to such irreverence and contempt, and that no one may in the future dare use in any manner the words of Holy Scripture for these and similar purposes, it is commanded and enjoined that all people of this kind be restrained by the bishops as violators and profaners of the word of God, with the penalties of the law and other penalties that they may deem fit to impose" ("Council of Trent"; from: http://www.forerunner.com/chalcedon/X0020_15._Council_of_Trent.html; accessed: 8 Jan 2005; Internet).

[21]The first paragraph read as follows: "Whereas the well-government and regulating of Printers and Printing Presses is matter of Publique care and of great concernment especially considering that by the general licentiousnes of

Of there content:

In the 16th-18th Century tracts generally contained entire or partial messages of preachers (Martin Luther, Balthasar Hubmaier, John Calvin, and Auguste H. Francke). Francke, for example, purchased Bibles for the poor and gave them lessons in the Bible.[22] The movement he founded led to an awakening in Germany in 1689.[23] Also published at that time were the numbered articles for disputations, and other Gospel summaries.

In 1799 a new department of the "Book Society for promoting Religious Knowledge among the Poor" (c. 1750) was formed in London, it was called the "Religious Tract Society." Its original object was: "to form a society for the purpose of printing and distributing religious tracts."[24] They recognized two principles from the first:

a) "That there is a common Christian faith, in the expression and enforcement of which all evangelical believers may unite, irrespective of ecclesiastical or doctrinal distinctions; and

b) "That this faith may be set forth in so brief a compass and so simple a way, that even the smallest tract may contain the essentials of saving truth.

"…It was in the committee room of the Religious Tract Society , at the close of the year 1802, that the BRITISH AND FOREIGN BIBLE SOCIETY was originated, and on Tuesday, Feb. 1, 1803, that its rules were finally adopted; the diffusion of the streams thus naturally leading to the fountain-head. From the first, the two societies have labored together in brotherly union for the evangelization of the world.

"…Of the tracts produced under these conditions, there are now about 3,200 on the society's catalogue, from the single-page handbill to the important series of *Present-day Tracts*, in which some of the foremost scholars and thinkers of the day have employed their pens for the defence of the Christian faith. The tracts circulated in the year 1882-83, in the English language alone, amounted to 33,249,800."[25]

There appears to have been a shift in the mid-19th Century, when tracts were printed on one folded sheet of paper, called a billet or leaflet (e.g. Spurgeon's "Ark of Safety" tract), also being picked up in the English Roman Catholic "tractarian movement" (cf. John Henry Newman). Listen to Spurgeon, as he lectured on evangelism:

---

the late times many evil disposed persons have been encouraged to print and sell heretical schismatical blasphemous seditious and treasonable Bookes Pamphlets and Papers and still doe continue such theire unlawfull and exorbitant practice to the high dishonour of Almighty God the endangering the peace of these Kingdomes and raising a disaffection to His most Excellent Majesty and His Government For prevention whereof no surer meanes can be advised then by reducing and limiting the number of Printing Presses and by ordering and setling the said Art or Mystery of Printing by Act of Parliament in manner as herein after is expressed. The Kings most Excellent Majesty by and with the Consent and Advise of the Lords Spiritual and Temporal & Commons in this present Parliament assembled doth therefore ordaine and enact And be it ordained and enacted by the Authority aforesaid That no person or persons whatsoever shall presume to print or cause to be printed either within this Realm of England or any other His Majesties Dominions or in the parts beyond the Seas any heretical seditious schismatical or offensive Bookes or Pamphlets wherein any Doctrine or Opinion shall be asserted or maintained which is contrary to [the] Christian Faith or the Doctrine or Discipline of the Church of England or which shall or may tend or be to the scandall of Religion or the Church or the Government or Governors of the Church State or Common wealth or of any Corporation or particular person or persons whatsoever nor shall import publish sell or [dispose (or disperse)] any such Booke or Books or Pamphlets nor shall cause or procure any such to be published or put to sale or to be bound stitched or sowed togeather" ("An Act for preventing the frequent Abuses in printing seditious treasonable and unlicensed Bookes…"; from: http://www.british-history.ac.uk/report.aspx?compid=47336; accessed: 17 Sept 2008; Internet).

[22]"Francke was highly influenced by the considerations and writings of Spener. Himself influenced by the writings of Arndt, Spener had promoted a theology of preaching that perceived a primary need of the poor to have access to the Word of God" (Steliopoulos, "At Home with the Word of God: Pietism As Seen Through the Lens of August Hermann Francke"; available at: https://speliopoulos.wordpress.com/tag/august-hermann-francke/ [online]; accessed: 20 Dec 2015; Internet).

[23]"The enthusiasm of the students spilled over into the town, so that an *Erweckungsbewegung* originated. The German word *Erweckung* has no really adequate equivalent in English; perhaps 'quickening' or 'wakening' come closest. Students, aroused by Francke and his colleagues, founded circles for Bible reading, in which all kinds of citizens took part, wealthy merchants, but also artisans, and even women" ("Pietism, 4: The Second Generation of Pietists: August Hermann Francke"; available at: http://home.online.nl/piet.fontaine/volumes/vol26/index1.htm? vol26_ch1_part4.htm [online]; accessed: 20 Dec 2015; Internet).

[24]"Tract Societies, Religious" *Schaff-Herzog*, 4:2374.

[25]Ibid.

"When preaching and private talk are not available, you need to have a tract ready. This is often an effective method. Some tracts would not save a beetle; there is not enough in them to interest a fly. Get good, striking tracts, or none at all. But a touching gospel tract may be the seed of eternal life. Therefore, do not go without your tracts."[26]

In American Evangelicalism, Bill Bright's *Four Spiritual Laws,* published in the mid-1960s as a small multiple-page booklet, shifted the emphasis from a leaflet-type tract (format still used by the American Tract Society) to a booklet-style tract with multiple sheets, a staple, and graphics.

The content of todays Gospel tracts normally include:
a) Some type of introductory "hook"
b) The fact and price of sin
c) The death of Christ for sin
d) The need for commitment or to receive Jesus Christ as Savior and Lord.

Deviations from this rough outline provide uniqueness to each tract.

Further, Gospel tracts also represent different theologies of salvation and/or philosophies of evangelism:

A comparison of several "families" of Gospel tracts may prove beneficial. In my *Charts for a Theology of Evangelism* I have included several related charts that seek to identify theological tendencies and trends among Gospel tracts:
a) Chart 20, "Comparing Bridge Illustrations"
b) Chart 30, "Comparing Gospel Presentations" and
c) Charts 76-77, "Four Directions of Theological and Methodological Downgrade."

1) Theologically-driven tracts: e.g. *Eternal Life* and *GRACE*

2) The *Four Spiritual Laws*, *Bridge to Life*, and *Steps to Peace with God* "family" of tracts

3) The *Evangelism Explosion* approach (this is a memorized outline)

4) Matthias Media's [postmodern-oriented] *2 Ways to Live*

5) Humorous and pop culturally-relevant tracks (Jews for Jesus and Living Waters)

R. A. Torrey's Outline on "The Use of [Gospel] Tracts":[27]

a. Importance and Advantages:
1) Any person can do it
2) A tract always sticks to the point
3) A tract never loses its temper
4) Oftentimes people who are too proud to be talked, will read a tract when no one is looking
5) A tract stays by one
6) Tracts lead many to accept Christ.

b. Purposes for Which to Use a Tract:
1) For the conversion of the unsaved
2) To lead Christians into a deeper and more earnest Christian life
3) To correct error
4) To set Christians to work

c. Who Should Use Tracts:
1) Ministers of the Gospel should use them
2) Sunday School teachers
3) Traveling men
4) Business men
5) School teachers
6) Housekeepers

---

[26]Spurgeon, *The Soul Winner* (New Kensington, PA: Whitaker House, 1995), 160.

[27]R. A. Torrey, "The Use of Tracts"; available at: WholesomeWords.org; from R. A. Torrey, *How to Work for Christ: A Compendium of Effective Methods* (New York: Revell, 1901).

  d. How to Use Tracts:
      1) To begin a conversation
      2) Use a tract to close a conversation
      3) Use tracts where a conversation is impossible
      4) Use tracts to send to people at a distance

  e. Suggestions as to the Use of Tracts:
      1) Always read the tracts yourself before giving them to others
      2) Suit your tract to the person to whom you give it
      3) Carry a selection of tracts with you
      4) Seek the guidance of God
      5) Seek God's blessing upon the tract after you have given it out
      6) Oftentimes give a man a tract with words and sentences underscored
      7) Never be ashamed of distributing tracts.

General Outlines of Gospel Tracts:[28]

  a. **A.B.C.'s for a Better Life**:[29]
      Introduction: John 10:10
      1) A—Admit that you are a sinner, Rom 3:23
          Some others use different terminology here:
              (1) A—Acknowledge that you have sinned
              (2) A—Admit that you need Jesus
      2) B—Believe on Christ, Acts 16:31
      3) C—Confess your faith, Rom 10:9
          Some others use different terminology here:
              (1) C—Confess Jesus as Lord

  b. **"Bridge to Life"** of the Navigators:[30]
      1) The Bible teaches that God loves all men and wants them to know him. But man is separated
          from God and His love, 1 Tim 2:5.
      2) Because He has sinned against God, Isa 59:2, Rom 3:23.
      3) This separation leads only to death and certain judgment, Heb 9:27, 2 Thess 1:8-9.
      4) Jesus Christ, who died on the cross for our sins, is the way to God, 1 Tim 2:5-6, 1 Pet 3:18
      5) Yes. But only those who personally receive Jesus Christ into their lives, trusting Him to
          forgive their sins, can cross this bridge, John 1:12
      6) Everyone must decide individually whether to receive Christ, Rev 3:20, John 14:14

  c. *Eternal Life* tract (North American Mission Board):[31]
      Introduction: Cover: "Do you know for certain that you have eternal life and that you will go to
          heaven when you die?"
      Inside cover: "God wants you to know for sure"
      1) God's purpose is that we have eternal life, Rom 6:23; John 10:10; John 14:3
      2) Our need is to understand our problem, Rom 3:23; Eph 2:9; Rom 6:23; John 14:6
      3) God's provision is Jesus Christ, John 1:1, 14; 1 Pet 3:18; Rom 4:25; John 1:12
      4) Our response is to receive Jesus:
          a) We must repent of our sin, Acts 3:19; Acts 26:20
          b) We must place our faith in Jesus, Eph 2:8; James 2:19

---

[28]There are many examples of Gospel tracts. The following is a variety of popular tracts. Note all the tract
producing organizations in the bibliography at the end of this chapter, "III. Some Tract Publishers and Some Tracts,"
some publiahing houses print up to 300 different tracts. This listing of organizations is only a sampling which represents
many Protestant theological persuasions.

[29]Developed from "ABC's for a Better Life" (Chicago: Pacific Garden Mission, n.d.). See Chart 21 in my
Charts for a Theology of Evangelism for different listings of A.B.C.s.

It appears that quiet Italian Reformer Juan Valdes may have developed a plan similar to the ABC's in 1546,
titled *The Christian Alphabet* (Venice, 1546); (described in Leopold Witte, *A Glance at the Italian Inquisition: A Sketch
of Pietro Carnesecchi: His Trial ... and His Martyrdom in 1566*; translated from the German by John T. Betts [London:
The Religious Tract Society, 1885], 31).

[30]This is a conversational rendering of the "Bridge to Life" Gospel plan found in the next section on
memorization (*Bridge to Life* [Colorado Springs, CO: NavPress, 1969], 2-16).

[31]"Eternal Life" tract, revised 9/00 (Alpharetta, GA: North American Mission Board, 2000).

Three Important Questions:
- a) Does what you have been reading make sense to you?
- b) Is there any reason you would not be willing to receive God's gift of eternal life?
- c) Are you willing to place your faith in Jesus right now and turn from your sin?

You need to ask Jesus to save you, Rom 10:13

Follow-up information.

- d. **"Four Spiritual Laws"** of Campus Crusade for Christ:[32]
  1) God **Loves** You, and Offers a Wonderful **Plan** for Your Life, John 3:16, John 10:10.
  2) Man is **Sinful** and **Separated** from God. Therefore, He Cannot Know and Experience God's Love and Plan for His Life, Rom 3:23, 6:23.
  3) Jesus Christ is God's **Only** Provision for Man's Sin. Through Him You Can Know and Experience God's Love and Plan for Your Life, Rom 5:8, 1 Cor 15:3-6, John 14:6.
  4) We Must Individually **Receive** Jesus Christ as Savior and Lord; Then We Can Know and Experience God's Love and Plan for Our Lives:
     - a) We must receive Christ, John 1:12
     - b) We receive Christ through faith, Eph 2:8-9
     - c) We receive Christ by personal invitation, Rev 3:20
     - d) You can receive Christ right now through prayer
     - e) Do not depend on feelings: Fact—Faith—Feelings

- e. **"GRACE"** of the Billy Graham School of the Southern Baptist Theological Seminary:[33]
  1) G—"G" stands for God: Gen 1:1; Psa 19:1; Rev 4:11
  2) R—"R" stands for Rebellion: Lev 19:2; Rom 3:23; 5:12; 1 John 1:8; Isa 59:2; Rom 6:23; Heb 9:27; Matt 25:31, 46
  3) A—"A" stands for Atonement: John 3:16; Rom 5:1; John 1:14; Heb 4:15; Rom 5:8; 1 Pet 2:24; 3:18; 2 Cor 5:21; Acts 17:31
  4) C—"C" stands for Conversion: John 14:6; Acts 4:12; 17:30; Luke 3:3; Rom 6:23; Eph 2:8-9; John 1:12; Rom 10:9, 13; Acts 16:31; Rom 1:16
  5) E—"E" stands for Eternal Life: John 4:24; 1 John 5:12; 2 Cor 5:17; John 10:10; 14:27; 16:33; Rom 8:35, 37-38; 1 Thess 4:16-17
  6) The most important question: "Where do I stand in the sight of God?" 1 Thess 1:7-9; John 3:36; Matt 12:30; 1 Pet 1:3-5, 8-9
  7) Are you ready? 1 John 5:12-13
  8) Living daily in God's grace: 2 Cor 5:15

- f. **"Steps to Peace with God,"** by Billy Graham:[34]
  1) God's Plan: Peace and Life, Rom 5:1, John 3:16, John 10:10
  2) Man's Problem: Separation, Rom 3:23, 6:23
  3) God's Remedy: The Cross, 1 Tim 2:5, Rom 5:8, John 14:6, Eph 2:8-9.
  4) Man's Response: Receive Christ, Rev 3:20, John 1:12, Rom 10:9

- g. Unknown Source:
  "IF YOU DIE and Go To Hell … WHO CARES?"
  Answer:
  - No. 1 - John 3:16, God cares!
  - No. 2 - Matt 18:11, Jesus Cares!
  - No. 3 - Luke 15:7, All People In Heaven Care!
  - No. 4 - Rev 22:17, All saved People Care!
  - No. 5 - Luke 16:19-31, All People In Hell Care!
  - No. 6 - Rom 1:16, I Care!

  Now, Friend, The most important question is: DO YOU CARE?

---

[32]Bill Bright, *The Four Spiritual Laws* (San Bernardino, CA: Campus Crusade for Christ, 1965).

[33]© 2003 The Billy Graham School of Missions, Evangelism and Church Growth, 2825 Lexington Road, Louisville, KY 40280. Telephone: (502) 897-4108; Email: bgschool@sbts.edu.

[34]Billy Graham, "Steps to Peace with God" (Minneapolis: Billy Graham Evangelistic Association, n.d.).

h. Other tracts:
Many other tracts are available. For sample tracts and tract publishers, please see the section after the chronological bibliography at the end of this chapter.

B. Gospel Plans for Memorizing:

Introduction:

Repetitio mater est studiorum (repetition is the mother of learning)!

It is a very helpful to have a Gospel plan memorized for spontaneous sharing situations (1 Pet 3:15). When a Gospel plan is memorized, a good clear Gospel presentation can be made to the unsaved person. There are many Gospel plans for memorization available.[35]

Two comments may be made about memorized Gospel presentations. Firstly, there is a need for input from the person being witnessed to. An effort must be made to assure that they are following the presentation. Secondly, it is important to memorize the verses and their references corresponding with the Gospel presentation. This gives the power in the witness.

There are many different Gospel presentations that can be memorized. All those mentioned above can be used for memorization. Included are several of the most Gospel presentations meant specifically to be memorized:

1. **3 Circles: Life Conversation Guide**: see http://lifeonmissionbook.com/conversation-guide.

2. **The Bridge Illustration**:[36]
   a. God's Purpose:
      1) Abundant Life, John 10:10
      2) Eternal Life, John 3:16
   b. Our Problem:
      1) All Have Sinned, Rom 3:23 (Isa 53:6)
      2) Sin's Penalty, Rom 6:23; Heb 9:27
   c. God's Remedy:
      1) Christ Paid the Penalty, Rom 5:8, 1 Pet 3:18
      2) Salvation Not by Works, Eph 2:8-9 (Titus 3:5)
   d. Our Response:
      1) Must Receive Christ, John 1:12, Rom 10:9-10
      2) Assurance of Salvation, John 5:24 (1 John 5:13)

3. Dare 2 Share's "**Gospel Journey**":
   G—**G**od created us to be with Him (Genesis 1-2)
   O—**O**ur sins separate us from God (Genesis 3)
   S—**S**ins cannot be removed by good deeds (Genesis 4 – Malachi 4)
   P—**P**aying the price for sin, Jesus died and rose again (Matthew – Luke)
   E—**E**veryone who trust in Him alone has eternal life (John)
   L—**L**ife with Jesus starts now and lasts forever (Acts – Revelation).[37]

4. **Evangelism Explosion**'s Gospel Presentation:[38]
   a. The introduction (including the assurance questions, see *Evangelizology,* Chap 15)
   b. The Gospel:
      1) **Grace**:
         a) Heaven is a free gift

---

[35]Ronald Rand, *Won by One* (Ventura, CA; Regal, 1988) has many good examples of how to share one's faith from memorization, including, "Let's Be Friends" and "The ABCs of Christianity."

[36]*The 2:7 Series: Leadership Training Clinic Part I,* (Colorado Springs, Co: Navigators, 1988), 34.

[37]"Gospel Journey" is trademarked by Dare 2 Share; available at: http://www.dare2share.org/wp-content/uploads/2013/11/gospel-journey-4-up.pdf (online); accessed: 17 Oct 2015; Internet. I'm grateful to several students who have found this method helpful in their witness and training.

[38]For more details about Evangelism Explosion's "Gospel Presentation" please see Kennedy, D. James, *Evangelism Explosion,* Revised edition (Wheaton IL: Tyndale House, 1977), 16-44 or write Evangelism Explosion III, International, P.O. Box 23820, Fort Lauderdale, FL 33308 U.S.A. It must be noted that it contains excellent information concerning the personal presentation of the Gospel, including subjects of conversation and pertinent illustrations.

        b) It is not earned or deserved, Rom 6:23
    2) **Man**:
        a) Is a sinner, Matt 5:48, Rom 3:23
        b) Cannot save himself, Eph 2:8-9
    3) **God**:
        a) Is merciful—therefore doesn't want to punish.
        b) Is just—therefore must punish sin.
    4) **Jesus Christ**:
        a) Who He is—the infinite God-man, John 1:1, 14.
        b) What He did—He paid for our sins and purchased a place in heaven for us which He offers as a gift, Isa 53:6, 10, 4, (John 14:2), Rom 6:23.
    5) **Faith**:
        a) What it is not—mere intellectual assent nor temporal faith, Eph 2:8
        b) What it is—"trusting in Jesus Christ alone for our salvation"
  c. The Commitment
  d. The Immediate Follow-Up

5. **FAITH Visit Outline**:[39]
Introduction: Interests; Involvement; Inquiry.
F F is for FORGIVENESS, Eph 1:7a
A A is for AVAILABLE, John 3:16; Matt 7:21a
I I is for IMPOSSIBLE, John 3:16; James 2:13a; Rom 3:23
T T is for TURN, Luke 13:3b; 1 Cor 15:3b-4; Rom 10:9
H H is for HEAVEN, John 10:10; 14:3; Rom 10:9
Invitation: Inquire; Invite; Insure.

6. The Navigators' **Gospel Presentation** (from the *Topical Memory System*):[40]
  a. The fact of sin, Rom 3:23, 3:11, 12
  b. The price of sin, Rom 6:23, Rom 5:12, Gal 3:10
  c. The price must be paid, Heb 9:27, Rom 2:12, Heb 2:2-3
  d. The price has been paid by Christ, Rom 5:8, 1 Pet 3:18, Gal 3:13
  e. Salvation is a free gift, Eph 2:8-9, Rom 3:24, Titus 3:5
  f. Salvation must be received, John 1:12, Rev 3:20, Rom 10:9-10

7. **Plan of Salvation** (from B. Gray Allison, founding president of Mid-America Baptist Theological Seminary, Memphis, TN):[41]
  a. Salvation needed:
    1) Fact of sin: Rom 3:10; 23
    2) Consequences of sin: Isa 59:2; Rom 6:23
  b. Salvation provided—John 3:16
  c. Salvation accepted:
    1) Repentance required: Acts 20:20-21
    2) Faith is necessary: Acts 20:20-21
  d. Closing verses: Rev 3:20; Rom 10:9-13; Rom 6:23; John 1:12
    1) Confession: Matt 10:32-33
    2) Baptism: Matt 28:18-20
    3) Church membership: Matt 28:18-20; Acts 2:41, 47

8. **Roman Road**:[42]
  a. **Need** (Why?)
    1) God says that all are sinners, Rom 3:10, 23
    2) God tells us the reason all are sinners, Rom 5:12
  b. **Consequence** (What?) God tells us the result of sin, Rom 6:23
  c. **Remedy** (How?) God tells us of His concern for sinners, Rom 5:8-9

---

[39]"FAITH Visit Outline"; available at: http://www.lifeway.com/ev/files/evF_min_FAITH_VisitOutline.pdf; accessed 1 Nov 2013; Internet.

[40]*Topical Memory System,* Guidebook 1 (Colorado Springs: NavPress, 1969), 19.

[41]B. Gray Allison, "Plan of Salvation," leaflet, n.p., n.d.

[42]"Roman Road," (Chicago: Pacific Garden Mission, n.d.).

    d.   **Condition** (Who?) God's way of salvation is made plain, Rom 10:9-10, 13

    e.   **Results**: God tells us the results of salvation, Rom 5:1, 8:1

    f.   **Assurance**: God gives the saved sinner assurance, Rom 8:16

9.   ***Share Jesus Without Fear*** methodology by William Fay:[43]

    a.   The Five Questions:

        1) Do you have any kind of spiritual beliefs?

        2) To you, who is Jesus Christ?

        3) Do you think there is a heaven and hell?

        4) If you died, where would you go? If heaven, why?

        5) If what you are believing is not true, would you want to know?

    b.   Share Scriptures:

        1) Rom 3:23

        2) Rom 6:23

        3) John 3:3

        4) John 14:6

        5) Rom 10:9-10

        6) 2 Cor 5:15

        7) Rev 3:20

    c.   Bring to Decision:

        1) Are you a sinner?

        2) Do you want forgiveness of sins?

        3) Do you believe Jesus died on the cross and rose again?

        4) Are you willing to surrender your life to Jesus Christ?

        5) Are you ready to invite Jesus into your life and into your heart?

Introductory Discussion: Notice several presuppositions in many of the Gospel presentations above:

    a.   Belief in a way of salvation

    b.   Belief in a specific message of salvation

    c.   Belief in prayer as the means by which salvation is acquired

    d.   Belief in assurance of salvation[44]

---

[43]William Fay, *Share Jesus Without Fear* (Nashville: Broadman, 1999).

[44]It may be helpful to realize that Thomas Aquinas likened assurance of salvation to vainglory (Thomas Aquinas, *Summa Theologica*, SS, Q[132], "Of Vainglory"; available at: http://www.ccel.org/ccel/aquinas/summa.html; accessed: 19 June 2008; Internet). Likewise, the Council of Trent anathematized it.

See for example, Aquinas, SS, Q[132], A[1], "Since, however, that which is clear simply can be seen by many, and by those who are far away, it follows that the word glory properly denotes that somebody's good is known and approved by many, according to the saying of Sallust (Catilin.) [*The quotation is from Livy: Hist., Lib. XXII C, 39]: 'I must not boast while I am addressing one man.' ... Yet he is not truly virtuous who does virtuous deeds for the sake of human glory, as Augustine proves (De Civ. Dei v). ... It is requisite for man's perfection that he should know himself; but not that he should be known by others, wherefore it is not to be desired in itself. It may, however, be desired as being useful for something, either in order that God may be glorified by men, or that men may become better by reason of the good they know to be in another man, or in order that man, knowing by the testimony of others' praise the good which is in him, may himself strive to persevere therein and to become better. In this sense it is praiseworthy that a man should 'take care of his good name,' and that he should 'provide good things in the sight of God and men': but not that he should take an empty pleasure in human praise" (ibid.).

Aquinas, SS, Q[132], A[2], "Wherefore inordinate desire of glory is directly opposed to magnanimity. ... He that is desirous of vainglory does in truth fall short of being magnanimous, because he glories in what the magnanimous man thinks little of, as stated in the preceding Reply. But if we consider his estimate, he is opposed to the magnanimous man by way of excess, because the glory which he seeks is something great in his estimation, and he tends thereto in excess of his deserts" (ibid.).

Aquinas, SS, Q[132], A[4], "Gregory (Moral. xxxi) numbers vainglory among the seven capital vices. ... The capital vices are enumerated in two ways. For some reckon pride as one of their number: and these do not place vainglory among the capital vices. Gregory, however (Moral. xxxi), reckons pride to be the queen of all the vices, and vainglory, which is the immediate offspring of pride, he reckons to be a capital vice: and not without reason. For pride, as we shall state farther on (Q[152], AA[1],2), denotes inordinate desire of excellence. ... And since many vices arise from the inordinate desire thereof, it follows that vainglory is a capital vice. ... It is not impossible for a capital vice to arise from pride, since as stated above (in the body of the Article and FS, Q[84], A[2]) pride is the queen and mother of all the vices. ... For the reason why a man loves to be honored and praised is that he thinks thereby to acquire a certain renown in the knowledge of others" (ibid.).

1) Note that Paul stated that assurance in the living God was the reason for his persecutions, 1 Tim 4:10 [see Byzantine Textform, cf. English Darby], "for, for this we labour and suffer reproach, because we hope in a living God, who is preserver of all men, specially of those that believe"

2) Consider, for example, the textual variants and some translations of 1 John 5:13, one of the important verses which teaches assurance of salvation:

   1 John 5:13 (NAS), "These things I have written to you who believe in the name of the Son of God, in order that you may know that you have eternal life."

   1 John 5:13 (NKJ), "These things I have written to you who believe in the name of the Son of God, that you may know that you have eternal life, and that you may *continue to* believe in the name of the Son of God."

Aquinas then quite naturally continued in SS, Q[132], A[5], "Whether the daughters of vainglory are suitably reckoned to be disobedience, boastfulness, hypocrisy, contention, obstinacy, discord, and love of novelties?" These nouns explain regular accusations against Baptists, Evangelicals, and Protestants.

Consider also, Council of Trent, "Decrees Concerning Justification" (13 Jan 1547), Chapter IX, "Against the Vain Confidence of the Heretics": "But though it is necessary to believe that sins neither are remitted nor ever have been remitted except gratuitously by divine mercy for Christ's sake, yet it must not be said that sins are forgiven or have been forgiven to anyone who boasts of his confidence and certainty of the remission of his sins,[47] resting on that alone, though among heretics and schismatics this vain and ungodly confidence may be and in our troubled times indeed is found and preached with untiring fury against the Catholic Church. Moreover, it must not be maintained, that they who are truly justified must needs, without any doubt whatever, convince themselves that they are justified, and that no one is absolved from sins and justified except he that believes with certainty that he is absolved and justified,[48] and that absolution and justification are effected by this faith alone, as if he who does not believe this, doubts the promises of God and the efficacy of the death and resurrection of Christ. For as no pious person ought to doubt the mercy of God, the merit of Christ and the virtue and efficacy of the sacraments, so each one, when he considers himself and his own weakness and indisposition, may have fear and apprehension concerning his own grace, since no one can know with the certainty of faith, which cannot be subject to error, that he has obtained the grace of God" ("Council of Trent"; available at: http://www.forerunner.com/chalcedon/X0020_15._Council_of_Trent.html; accessed: 8 Jan 2005; Internet).

Original Language Texts and Translations of 1 John 5:13

NKJ: TNT; GNV; BSP; KJV; WEB; YLT; RWB	GOC	BYZ	NAS Syriac: MGI; BBE; RSV; NIV; NJB⚜; NLT; CSB; NET; MGI; ESV	NA27 =Nestle 19 (1949)	Latin Vulgate⚜ (Migne)	Nova Vulgata⚜	NAB⚜: WYC; DBY; ERV; ASV	From the Syriac: ETH: NOR; MRD
These things I have written to you	Ταῦτα ἔγραψα ὑμῖν	Ταῦτα ἔγραψα ὑμῖν	These things I have written to you	Ταῦτα ἔγραψα ὑμῖν,	Haec scribo vobis	Haec scripsi vobis,	I write these things to you	These I have written to you,
				ἵνα εἰδῆτε ὅτι ζωὴν ἔχετε αἰώνιον,	ut sciatis quoniam vitam habetis aeternam,	ut sciatis quoniam vitam habetis aeternam,	so that you may know that you have eternal life,	that you may know that you have the life which is eternal,
who believe in the name of the Son of God,	τοῖς πιστεύουσιν εἰς τὸ ὄνομα τοῦ υἱοῦ τοῦ θεοῦ,	τοῖς πιστεύουσιν εἰς τὸ ὄνομα τοῦ υἱοῦ τοῦ θεοῦ,	who believe in the name of the Son of God,	τοῖς πιστεύουσιν εἰς τὸ ὄνομα τοῦ υἱοῦ τοῦ θεοῦ.	qui creditis in nomine Filii Dei.	qui creditis in nomen Filii Dei.	you who believe in the name of the Son of God	who believe in the name of the Son of Aloha.
that you may know that you have eternal life,	ἵνα εἰδῆτε ὅτι ζωὴν αἰώνιον ἔχετε,	ἵνα εἰδῆτε ὅτι ζωὴν αἰώνιον ἔχετε,	in order that you may know that you have eternal life					
and that you may *continue to* believe in the name of the Son of God	καὶ ἵνα πιστεύητε εἰς τὸ ὄνομα τοῦ υἱοῦ τοῦ θεοῦ.	καὶ ἵνα πιστεύητε εἰς τὸ ὄνομα τοῦ υἱοῦ τοῦ θεοῦ.						

A Comparison of Some English Translations of 1 John 5:13

Particularistic				Universalistic
NAS (1977)	GWN (1995)	GNT⚜ (1993)	BBE (1949)	CEV⚜ (1991)
These things I have written to you who believe in the name of the Son of God, in order that you may know that you have eternal life	I've written this to those who believe in the Son of God so that they will know that they have eternal life.	I am writing this to you so that you may know that you have eternal life—you that believe in the Son of God	I have put these things in writing for you who have faith in the name of the Son of God, so that you may be certain that you have eternal life	All of you have faith in the Son of God, and I have written to let you know that you have eternal life.

C. Gospel Plans from One Text of Scripture:

Introduction:

There are times when the evangelist has a Bible and nothing else with which to share the Gospel. How does he make use of this most powerful weapon, without flipping from page to page in the Bible, and possibly confusing the open contact in the process? The following are some sample Gospel plans which may be helpful in sharing the Gospel from one Scripture passage.

1. **1 John 1:7-2:2**:

A very effective passage for those from a Roman Catholic background.

The following provides a sample dialogue:

Evangelist: "Hi, my name is _____ and this is _____, and we are with _____ church, and we are out telling people about Jesus. Have you ever heard of Jesus?"
Contact: "Oh yes, I've heard of Him all my life. I'm Catholic and I go to St. Joseph."
Evangelist: "Great. I hope you haven't heard too much about Him."

[Gauge their response to a somewhat humorous but poignant question]

Contact: "No, I haven't heard too much about Him!"

[Often this is the point where a person will show genuine interest, or their eyes will harden and they will close the door]

Evangelist: "Then, do you mind if I ask you a question?"
Contact: "Sure."
Evangelist: "If you died tonight, are you absolutely certain that you would go to heaven?"
Contact: "Yes, I'm pretty sure."
Evangelist: "And why is that?"
Contact: "Because I'm a good person."

[By this statement, you know that the contact is relying on his own righteousness to get to heaven, something that Rom 10:1-4 tells us is not enough]

[Here a lot of varying responses may be made, I will continue with a sample dialogue based on the use of 1 John 1:7-2:2; be open that God may place numerous other Scripture passages in your heart and on your mind at this point]

Evangelist: "That's very commendable, but one little problem, do you know what that problem is? It is sin. Can I show you a Scripture passage in the Bible?"
Contact: "Sure."
Evangelist: [read 1 John 1:7-10] "That's pretty strong isn't it?"
Contact: "Yes."
Evangelist: "Do you think that you've ever sinned? I know I have!"
Contact: "Yes, I have sinned."

[The contact may begin to look quietly at you as conviction from the Holy Spirit sets in. It is helpful to gauge the level of conviction of sin as you speak]

Evangelist: "Who should we confess to? Who is our confessor? This passage tells us [read 1 John 2:1-2]. By the way, propitiation means atoning sacrifice. Did you ever see the movie 'The Passion of Christ'?"
Contact: "Yes."
Evangelist: "When Jesus was hanging on the cross, God placed all the sins of the whole world on him at that time. Amazing!"

[Perhaps there will be no response as he is thinking about the atonement]

Evangelist: "So who is our only Confessor? Only Jesus is worthy to be our Confessor, our Advocate, and our Mediator, because only Jesus died on the cross for the sins of the world. Have you ever confessed your sins to Jesus before?"
Contact: "Yes. I do that every night."
Evangelist: "Amen! And you can be sure that He hears you. But I have a further question: have you ever asked Jesus to be your only Advocate or Lawyer before God?"
Contact: "No I don't think that I have?"

Evangelist: "At the end of this book of 1 John, the Apostle John explains what it means to receive Jesus Christ by faith.

[read 1 John 5:11-13]

[Amazingly, one young man who was under conviction exclaimed, "It's guaranteed!" as I read 1 John 5:13]

Evangelist: "If you would like to, you can ask Jesus to be your Lawyer before God the Father, and not only that! Would you like to receive the gift of forgiveness of sins and eternal life offered to you by the blood of Jesus?"
Contact: "Yes, I would."
Evangelist: "Here is a suggested prayer that you can pray to give your heart to Jesus. Why don't you read this prayer and tell me what you think of it."

[Reads the prayer quietly to himself]

Evangelist: "Do you mind reading it out loud?"
Contact: "Sure."

[reads sinner's prayer outloud]

Evangelist: "Now what did you think of that prayer? Do you agree with it?"
Contact: "Yes."
Evangelist: "Would you like to read it again out loud as a prayer to God, and ask Him to forgive you of your sins and invite Him to be your Savior?"
Contact: "Yes, I would."
Evangelist: "Then read it aloud right now, and I will pray along with you."
Contact: [reads sinner's prayer a second or third time]
Evangelist: "Praise the Lord. May I pray for you?" [praise the Lord for the contact's openness to the Gospel, for the contact's walk with the Lord, and for his spiritual growth]

[See Chapter 23 for ideas for immediate follow-up, and Chapter 26 for long-term follow-up ideas]

Here is an example of leading someone to Christ using 1 John 1:7-2:2. Oh the amazement of seeing God place conviction in the heart of someone as they listen to the Gospel proclaimed!

2. **John 3**:

Darrell Robinson introduced his readers to using this powerful portion of Scripture in evangelism.[45]

Likewise, I recommend the following as a possible opener:
Evangelist: "Have you found a good church since you have moved to _____?"
Contact: "Yes, I attend _____ [which in the mind of the evangelist is likely a non-conversionist church]
Evangelist: "Great, I'm glad you found a church home. Can you tell me, does your pastor [priest, etc.] ever speak about being born again?"
Contact: "No, I don't think so."
Evangelist: "Can I show you in the Bible where Jesus commands us to be born again?"
Contact: "Sure."

[Then the evangelist begins presenting the Gospel plan from John 3]

Evangelist: "Jesus told a very religious man in John 3 [read verse 3]. You see, Nicodemus was one of the rulers [read verses 1-2]. What do you think it means to be born again?"
Contact: "I'm not really sure"
Evangelist: "Jesus relates being born again to believing in verses 14-16. In the Old Testament, when the people of Israel were bit by poisonous snakes, all they had to do to survive was to look to the serpent. So now, all we need to do is look to Jesus to be saved from sin. What do you think it means to look to Jesus alone for your salvation?"
Contact: "I've never really thought about that before."

---

[45]Darrell Robinson, *Synergistic Evangelism* (Bloomington, IN: CrossBooks, 2009), 121-27.

Evangelist: "Well, looking to Jesus alone for your salvation means that you place your faith that when Jesus died on the cross for your sins, He did it all. He bought your salvation full and free. You cannot add a thing to what Jesus did for you. That's pretty amazing isn't it?"

Contact: "Yes, it is."

Evangelist: "Do you know how to receive this salvation full and free?"

Contact: "I'm not sure."

Evangelist: "You do this through believing in Jesus for your salvation. Can I read you several verses?

Contact: "Sure."

Evangelist: [read John 3:16-19]. "Do you see the importance of believing in Jesus as your Savior and Lord?"

Contact: "Yes, I think I do."

Evangelist: "Would you like to believe in Jesus as you Savior and receive Him as your Lord right now?

Contact: "Yes, I would like to."

Evangelist: "You can pray to God right now and ask Jesus Christ to be your Savior. Would you like to pray right now?"

Contact: "I don't know how to pray."

Evangelist: "Praying is just talking to God. He knows your heart, and He made your tongue. Just say, 'Oh God, I acknowledge that I am a sinner."

Contact: "Oh God, I acknowledge that I am a sinner."

Evangelist: "Please forgive me of my sins."

Contact: "Please forgive me of my sins."

Evangelist: "Thank you for sending Jesus to die on the cross for my sins."

Contact: "Thank you for sending Jesus to die on the cross for my sins."

Evangelist: "Please be my Savior and my Lord."

Contact: "Please be my Savior and my Lord."

Evangelist: "In Jesus' name, Amen."

Contact: "In Jesus' name, Amen."

[For further ideas, see Chapter 23 on "Immediate Follow-up"]

3. **Romans 3:19-26**:

This portion can be used for those who are assured of their own righteousness. It contains the essentials:
Sin, vv. 19-20
Righteousness apart from the law, vv. 21-23
Free justification by believing in Jesus, vv. 24-26

The evangelist may also want to highlight Rom 10:1-4 which discusses the same issues in different words.

4. **Isaiah 53**:

Consider sharing the Gospel using these verses (as did Philip in Acts 8). It may be especially important to people from a Jewish heritage. Again, the substitutionary atonement is clearly communicated in these verses.

5. **Ezek 36:25-27**:

These verses communicate the essence of God's part in the subsitutionary atonement. They can be used to encourage people who have no hope or do not understand that salvation is completely wrought in and through God's redeeming work in and through the cross of Christ alone.

D. Memorizing Scripture Verses:

Introduction:

The memorizing of Scripture is important for many reasons. It allows the Christian to meditate on the Word day and night as he is encouraged to do (e.g. Psa 1:2). Memorization also helps in sharing situations when a verse can be injected into the conversation without having to reach for a Bible and without breaking the rhythm of the conversation (although it is sometimes good to look directly to the Bible).

The apostles and other preachers in the Acts must have thought highly of memorization as many verses from the Old Testament were cited in their preaching. Here are some helpful hints in memorization especially as a witnessing tool:[46]

1. Some tips for memorizing:

    a. Decide on a salvation plan. All of the salvation plans mentioned above are effective in sharing the Gospel message. Choose one of these.

    b. Begin by memorizing the outline with the verses that follow each point:
        1) It is best to memorize one item at a time and then to move on to the next.
        2) The motto which Dawson Trotman used in memorizing Scripture was, "Memorize the reference 'for and aft.'" Memorizing the reference before and after each verse will help you know where the verse is found—which is very important in sharing situations.
        3) It is best to memorize one phrase at a time, without adding a new phrase until the earlier phrases are solidly memorized. Memorizing becomes like adding links to a memory chain.
        4) Writing the verses on a card is an effective way to have the verses available for memorization and meditation during free times during the day.
        5) Copying the verses in writing repeated times can also help to memorize the verses more exactly.

    c. You can test yourself by writing down the verses that you have memorized without looking at the Bible. Then check to see how well you have done. You can do this until you have each verse solidly memorized.

    d. Use the verses you have memorized in sharing situations. This will encourage you to continue memorizing, and it will show you what verses you need to memorize.

    e. "Review! Review! Review!" If repetition is the mother of learning, review is its father. Reviewing the verses on a regular basis allows them to be impressed upon our hearts.[47]

---

[46]*Topical Memory System* by NavPress is highly recommended as good source of helpful material to begin memorizing Scripture.

[47]Deuteronomy 6:6-7 speaks of having God's Word "on your heart" and the word for "teach diligently" in verse 7, *shanan,* is translated more accurately in the French *Nouvelle Édition de Génève: "Tu les inculqueras à tes enfants."* Webster's defines the meaning of inculcate as "to impress upon the mind by frequent repetition or persistent urging."

E. The Use of Questionnaires or Surveys:

Introduction:

    a. A questionnaire is a series of questions which are asked to another individual. In a survey the questions are compiled and statistics can be developed. Questionnaires can be effective in leading into the sharing of the Gospel. The person asking the questions may feel uncomfortable beginning a conversation about the Gospel. This is a case where a questionnaire can help bridge that fear.

    b. A target group needs to be selected in the development of a questionnaire. This can then allow the questionnaire to effectively reach the desired group. The target groups can be varied, from middle-aged Americans to Quebec's college students to American High school students. People in rural communities may have different interests than those in urban communities. These must all be weighed in forming a questionnaire.

1. Sample questionnaires:

    a. Spiritual Interest Questionnaire:[48]
      1) On a scale of 0-10, where do you rate your desire to be spiritual?
      2) What 3 words would you use to describe spirituality, and why?
      3) What 3 words would you use to describe Jesus? Why?
      4) On a scale of 0-10, where do you rate your desire to know Jesus? (If a positive response is given, ask if you can share what the Bible says about how to know God).

    b. Questionnaire developed for use in Quebec-city, Quebec, Canada (translated from French):
      1) According to you what does the world need most?
      2) What is the most important thing in your life?
      3) Where or to whom would you go if you had spiritual questions?
      4) What do you think of Jesus Christ?
      5) Do you think that it is possible to know God personally?
      6) If you were to die tonight, where would you go?
      7) If you stood before God and He asked you why should I let you into My heaven, what would you say?
      8) May I share how I came to know that I have eternal life?

    c. Religious Survey—developed for use in an "Evangelism in Contemporary Society" class:
      1) Are you the member of any religious group?
      2) What religious group is this? If not, were you brought up in the beliefs of a religious group?
      3) Were you brought up in this religion? If not, skip.
      4) At what period of your life did you become interested in this religion? If not, at what period did you become disinterested?
      5) Do you ever participate in religious services?
      6) How often do you participate in religious services?
      7) How far do you travel to these religious services?
      8) If you had children, would you rear them in this religion?
      9) To what religious writings do you adhere, if any?
      10) How often do you refer to this religious book?
      11) How do your religious beliefs influence the way you live?
      12) Do you seek to tell your acquaintances about your religious beliefs?
      13) Do you feel that your religion is the only true religion?
      14) Are you certain that if you died tonight you would achieve "salvation" in your religion?
      15) If you stood before the Supreme Being and He asked you, "Why should I let you into my heaven?" what would you answer?
      16) Can I show you a pamphlet which may assist you in your religious journey?

---

[48]This questionnaire was developed by David Elliott as he was Associate Pastor of Evangelism at Roanoke Baptist church in a New Age area of the older part of Kansas City, Missouri. We found it very effective for starting spiritual conversations.

  d. Neighborhood Questionnaire for Pastors:[49]
      1) According to you, what is the greatest need in _____ (city)?
      2) What advice do you have to a pastor of a church here in _____ (city)?
      3) How can we as a local church help you?

  e. Evangelism Unlimited's *Neighborhood Questionnaire III*:[50]
      1) According to you, what is the greatest need in this community?
      2) What advice do you have for a church here in this community?
      3) Are you actively involved in a church here in the area?
      4) If you were to attend a church, what would you look for?
      5) Have you come to the place in your spiritual life where you are certain that if you died tonight you would go to heaven?
      6) If you stood before God and He asked you, "Why should I let you into my heaven?" what would you answer?
      Immediate Evaluation (check off as appropriate):
          Needs expressed: ❑ Spiritual; ❑ Material; ❑ Psychological; ❑ Other? _____
          Did you speak about: ❑ God? ❑ Gospel? ❑ Bible study? ❑ Other? _____
          Spiritual Response: ❑ Open; ❑ Closed; ❑ Other _____
          Would another contact be worthwhile? ❑ Yes; ❑ No; ❑ Other _____.

  f. National Religious Survey:[51]
      1) Sex
      2) What is your profession?
      3) Do you practice a religion?
      4) What is it?
      5) At this time, with what frequency do you attend religious services?
      6) Are you married?
          a) How many children do you have?
          b) Do your children have religious instruction?
      7) A religion should be practiced:
          a) Because it is the parents' religion?
          b) Because it is your own conviction?
          c) Because the majority follows it?
      8) Which of the founders of world religions do you know the most about?
          Mohammed, Buddha, Jesus Christ, other_____
      9) To your understanding, who is Jesus Christ?
      10) In your opinion, how can a person become a Christian?
      11) In previous surveys it was verified that people sense a necessity to know God better. In your opinion, why?
      12) Do you yourself sense a need to know God better?

  g. Evangelism Explosion's "Assurance Questionnaire":[52]
      Introduction: I am _____ of _____. We're trying to determine people's religious thinking and assist anyone looking for a faith,
      1) Will you help us by giving your thoughts in response to five brief questions?
          (1) yes (2) no
      2) Of what religious group or church are you a member?
          (1) Baptist, (2) Catholic, (3) Christian Church, (4) Christian Science, (5) Congregational, (6) Episcopal, (7) Jewish, (8) Lutheran, (9) Mormon, (10) Methodist, (11) Presbyterian, (12) None, (13) Other

---

[49]This survey was one used with good results by Rob Stewart, the pastor of the Delta Evangelical Free Church, Vancouver, British Columbia.

[50]Available at www.evangelismunlimited.org.

[51]This survey comes from Campus Crusade's "Christ for the World" campaign (in the 1980s). This version was likely translated several times, as it came via Portugal and Holland.

[52]For more details about Evangelism Explosion's "Assurance Questionnaire," please see D. James Kennedy, *Evangelism Explosion* (Wheaton, IL: Tyndale House, 1977), 235 or write Evangelism Explosion III, International, P.O. Box 23820, Fort Lauderdale, FL 33308 U.S.A.

3) What local church do you attend?
   (1) _____, (2) None.
4) How often do you attend?
   (1) Weekly, (2) Often, (3) Seldom, (4) Never.
5) Have you come to the place in your spiritual life where you know that you have eternal life—that is, do you know for certain that if you died today you would go to heaven?
   (1) Yes, (2) Hope so, (3) No.
6) If you were to die today and stand before God and he said to you, "Why should I let you into my heaven?" what would you say?
   (1) Faith, (2) Works, (3) Unclear, (4) No answer.

Closing: This completes the questionnaire. You answers are interesting. Thank you for your help.

May I have a few more minutes of your time to share with you how I came to know I have eternal life and how you can know it too?

h. Conclusions:
   1) Questionnaire "b" gradually brings the focus into spiritual things, with some deep questions. The final question gives the surveyor the opportunity to share his/her faith in Jesus Christ.
   2) The National Religious Survey is, as its name suggests, a survey. It allows for the compiling of information in order to discern where an area is spiritually.
   3) The "Assurance Questionnaire" is a good general questionnaire for an area where people have a certain church affiliation. It allows the surveyor to share his/her faith if the person is open to it.

Conclusion:

Many weapons are available to the evangelist to allow him to share the Gospel. Most importantly is the word of God that provides the eternal seed of the Holy Spirit to transform the heart (cf. Deut 32:1-2; Isa 55:10-11; Luke 8:11; also see Chapter 6 for more on the power and necessity of the Word of God):

Chapter 1 Appendixes

Chronological Bibliography

I. Sample Books on Personal Evangelism—Arranged Chronologically:

The following books on evangelism are arranged chronologically. Generally not included are books on world missions, church planting, church growth, personal follow-up, discipleship, and a theology of evangelism. It may be noted, however, that there is a significant overlap of topics. An effort has been made to include books of all stripes, everywhere from a 1975 Papal Encyclical to W. B. Riley's 1904 *The Perennial Revival*. Inclusion in this list does not constitute an endorsement, but is meant to show the breadth of books on evangelism in the past century. These books may show that "There is nothing new under the sun," even in the area of evangelism. A similar bibliography is arranged alphabetically at the end of these notes.

2019 Denton, Ryan and Scott Smith, *A Certain Sound: A Primer on Open Air Preaching*. Grand Rapids: Reformation Heritage, 2019.

2018 Chan, Sam. *Evangelism in a Skeptical World: How to Make the Unbelievable News about Jesus More Believable*. Grand Rapids: Zondervan, 2018.

Kelley, Charles S., Jr. *Fuel the Fire: Lessons from the History of Southern Baptist Evangelism*. Nashville: Broadman, 2018.

Queen, Matt. *110 Evangelism Stories*. Fort Worth: Seminary Hill, 2018.

Queen, Matt. *Mobilize to Evangelize: The Pastor and Congregational Evangelism*. Fort Worth: Seminary Hill 2018.

Stone, Bryan. *Evangelism after Pluralism: The Ethics of Christian Witness*. Grand Rapids: Baker, 2018.

Wax, Trevin. *Eschatological Discipleship: Leading Christians to Understand Their Historical and Cultural Context*. Nashville: Broadman, 2018.

2017 Boland, Peter. *Open Air Preaching to the Glory of God: The Forgotten Power and Lost Art of Open Air Expository Exultation*. Published by author, 2017.

Cook, Brady. *Toolbox for Evangelism: Basic Christian Principles to Help You Share Your Faith*. Amazon, 2017.

Harrington, Bobby and Josh Patrick, *The Disciple Maker's Handbook: Seven Elements of a Discipleship Lifestyle*. Grand Rapids: Zondervan, 2017.

Heath, Elaine A. *The Mystic Way of Evangelism: A Contemplative Vision for Christian Outreach*, 2nd edition. Grand Rapids: Baker, 2008, 2017.

Johnston, Thomas P. *Consumed! A Passion for the Great Commission*. Liberty, MO: Evangelism Unlimited, 2017.

Jones, Peyton. *Reaching the Unreached: Becoming Raiders of the Lost Art*. Grand Rapids: Zondervan, 2017.

Newman, Randy. *Questioning Evangelism: Engaging People's Hearts the Way Jesus Did*. 2nd ed. Grand Rapids: Kregel, 2004, 2017.

O Deel, Ruth. *Evangelism from the Heart*. Christian Faith, 2017.

Reid, Alvin. *Sharing Jesus Without Freaking Out: Evangelism the Way You Were Born to Do It*. Broadman, 2017.

2016 Dever, Mark. *Understanding the Great Commission*. Church Basics Series. Nashville: Broadman, 2016.

Gaines, Steve and Ken Hemphill. *Share Jesus Like It Matters*. CreateSpace, 2016.

Gress, Carrie. DPhil. *Nudging Conversions: A Practical Guide to Brining Those You Love Back to the Church*. Beacon, 2016.

Hull, Bill. *Conversion and Discipleship: You Can't Have One Without the Other*. Grand Rapids: Zondervan, 2016.

Krahn, John H. *From Surviving to Thriving: A Practical Guide to Revitalize Your Church*. CSS, 2016.

Leeman, Jonathan, Gen. Ed. *Unashamed of the Gospel*. Nashville: Broadman, 2016.

Logan, Doug. *On the Block: Developing a Biblical Picture for Missional Engagement*. Chicgao: Moody, 2016.

Malone, Kelly and Kendi Howells Douglas. *City Church: Working Together to Transform Cities*, vol 5. Urban Ministry in the 21st Century, 2016.

Reid, Alvin and George Robinson. *WITH: Informal Mentoring and Intentional Disciple Making*. Rainer, 2016.

Scroggins, Jimmy and Steve Wright, *Turning Everyday Conversations Into Gospel Conversations*. Nashville: Broadman, 2016.

Teasdale, Mark R. *Evangelism for Non-Evangelists: Sharing the Gospel Authentically*. InterVarsity, 2016.

Washer, Paul. *Discovering the Glorious Gospel* (Biblical Foundations for the Faith, Book 2). Media Gratiae, 2016.

Washer, Paul. *The Gospel of Jesus Christ*. Grand Rapids: Reformation Heritage, 2016.

Wheeler, David and Alvin Reid. *Stop That, Start This: Get a Heart for Great Commission Discipleship*. Thomas Nelson, 2016.

2015 Addison, Steve. *Pioneering Movements: Leadership That Multiplies Disciples and Churches*. Downers Grove, IL: InterVarsity, 2015.

Avant, John, Roy Fish, Alvin Reid, et al. *Revival Revived: The 1995 Revival in Brownwood, Texas, and Its Impact for Revival Today* [Gospel Advance Books, Vol 5]. Gospel Advance, 2015.

Ballor, Jordan J. and Robert Joustra, *The Church's Social Responsibility: Reflections on Evangelism and Social Justice*. Christians' Library Press, 2015.

Booth, Susan. *The Tabernacling Presence of God: Mission and Gospel Witness*. Eugene, OR: Wipf and Stock, 2015.

Bredenhof, Wes. *To Win Our Neighbors for Christ: The Missiology of the Three Forms of Unity*. Grand Rapids: Reformation

Heritage, 2015.

Chafer, Lewis Sperry. *True Evangelism or Winning Souls by Prayer*. 1st ed. Philadelphia: Sunday School Times, 1911; 2nd ed., Philadelphia: Sunday School Times, 1919; Wheaton, IL: Van Kampen; Grand Rapids: Zondervan, 1967, 16th printing, 1981; Grand Rapids: Kregel, 1993; CreateSpace, 2015.Harvey, Michael. *Creating a Culture of Invitation in Your Church*. Monarch, 2015.

Frost, Michael. *Surprise the World: The Five Habits of Highly Missional People*. Downers Grove, IL: InterVarsity, 2015.

Henard, Bill. *Can These Bones Live: A Practical Guide to Church Revitalization*. Broadman, 2015.

Kellemen, Robert W. and Brian Croft. *Gospel Conversations: How to Care Like Christ*. Grand Rapids: Zondervan, 2015.

Payne, J.D. *Apostolic Church Planting: Birthing New Churches from New Believers*. InterVarsity, 2015.

Raymond, Erik. *Gospel Shaped Outreach* (with DVD's, Handbook, and Leader's Guide). Good Book, 2015.

Reid, Alvin. *GET OUT: Student Ministry in the Real World*. Rainer, 2015.

Sherrard, Michael. *Relational Apologetics: Defending the Christian Faith with Holiness, Respect, and Truth*. Grand Rapids: Kregel, 2015.

Tice, Rico and Carl Laferton. *Honest Evangelism: How to Talk about Jesus even when It's Tough*. Foreword by D.A. Carson. Good Book, 2015.

2014 Collier, Jarvis L. *Whatever Happened to Christian Evangelism?* Nashville, TN: Sunday School Publishing Board, 2014.

Dodson, Jonathan K. *The Unbelievable Gospel: Say Something Worth Believing*. Grand Rapids: Zondervan, 2014.

Geisler, David and Norman Geisler. *Conversational Evangelism: Connecting with People to Share Jesus*. Reprint of 2009 edition. Harvest House, 2014.

Harrington, Bobby and Bill Hull, *Evangelism or Discipleship: Can They Effectively Work Together?* [Kindle Edition]. Exponential, 2014.

Iorg, Jeff. *Unscripted: Sharing the Gospel as Life Happens*. New Hope, 2014.

Klumpenhower, Jack. *Show Them Jesus: Teaching the Gospel to Kids*. New Growth Press, 2014.

Lancaster, Daniel B. and David Garrison. *Making Radical Disciples: Multiply Disciples in a Discipleship Movement Using 10 Proven Reproducible Bible Studies (Follow Jesus Training)*. Amazon, 2014.

Lawless, Chuck. *Nobodies for Jesus: 14 Days Toward a Great Commission Lifestyle*. Rainer, 2014.

Lorick, Nathan and Ed Stetzer, *Dying to Grow: Reclaiming the Heart of Evangelism in the Church*. Kindle, 2014.

McKnight, Scot, *Kingdom Conspiracy: Returning to the Radical Mission of the Local Church*. Grand Rapids: Brazos, 2014.

Parr, Steve. *The Coffee Shop that Changed the World: Discovering the Net Effect*. Sisters, OR: Deep River Books, 2014.

Payne, Matthew Robert. *Prophetic Evangelism Made Simple: Prophetic Seed Sowing*. CreateSpace, 2014.

Schneider, Floyd. *Evangelism for the Fainthearted*, 3rd ed. Keybobby Books, 2014.

Shook, Kerry and Kris. *Be the Message: Taking Your Faith Beyond Words to a Life of Action*. Waterbrook, 2014.

Stiles, J. Mack. *Evangelism: How the Whole Church Speaks of Jesus*. Wheaton, IL: Crossway [9Marks], 2014.

Kim, Van Nam. *Multicultural Theology and New Evangelization*. University Press of America, 2014.

Washer, Paul. *Gospel Assurance and Warnings (Recovering the Gospel)*. Grand Rapids: Reformation Heritage, 2014.

Willard, Dallas. *The Great Omission*. Reprint edition. HarperOne, 2014.

Willis, Dustin and Aaron Coe, *Life on Mission: A Simple Way to Share the Gospel*. Nashville: Lifeway, 2014.

Wilson, Mark O. *Purple Fish: A Heart for Sharing Jesus*. Indianapolis, IN: Wesleyan Publishing, 2014.

2013 Batchelor, Julian. Evangelism: *How to do it and how to do it well* [Kindle edition]. Amazon, 2013.

Beeke, Joel R. and Paul M. Smalley, *Prepared by Grace, for Grace: The Puritans on God's Ordinary Way of Leading Sinners to Christ*. Grand Rapids: Reformation Heritage, 2013.

Benavides, Victor. *The Prepared Witness: A 30 Day Devotional*. Acworth, GA: M28 Evangelism, 2013.

Duckworth, Jessicah Krey. *Wide Welcome: How the Unsettling Presence of Newcomers Ca Save the Church*. Minneapolis: Fortress, 2013.

Flemming, Dean. *Recovering the Full Mission of God: A Biblical Perspective on Being, Doing and Telling*. Downers Grove, IL: InterVarsity, 2013.

Fordham, Keith and Tom Johnston. *The Worth and Work of the Evangelist—for Christ's Great Commission Church*. Liberty, MO: Evangelism Unlimited, 2013.

Greear, J. D. Stop Asking Jesus Into Your Heart: How to Know for Sure You Are Saved. Foreword by Paige Patterson. B&H Books, 2013.

McDonald, Larry S., Sharayah Colter, Matt Queen, and Daniel Akin, eds. *A Passion for the Great Commission: Essays in Honor of Alvin Reid*. Crossbooks, 2013; Towering Oaks, 2014.

Platt, David. *Follow Me: A Call to Die. A Call to Live*. Wheaton, IL: Tyndale, 2013.

Reid, Alvin. *AS YOU GO: Creating a Missional Culture of Gospel-Centered Students*. NavPress, 2013.

Reid, Alvin. *REVITALIZE Your Church Through Gospel Recovery* [Gospel Advance Books, Vol 1]. Reid, 2013.

Reid, Alvin and George Robinson, eds. *Story ESV Outreach Bible*. Crossway, 2013.

Reid, Alvin and David Wheeler. *Servant Evangelism* [Gospel Advance Books, Vol 3]. Gospel Advance, 2013.

Servant, David A. *The Disciple-Making Minister* [Kindle Edition]. Ethnos Press, 2013.

Servant, David A. *Forgive Me for Waiting So Long to Tell You This* [Kindle Edition]. Ethnos Press, 2013.

Threads, *Engage: A Practical Guide to Evangelism (Member Book)*. Nashville: Lifeway, 2013.

Washer, Paul. *The Gospel Call and True Conversion (Recovering the Gospel)*. Grand Rapids: Reformation Heritage, 2013.

Wheeler, David and Vernon M. Whaley. *Worship and Witness: Becoming a Great Commission Worshiper*. LifeWay, 2013.

2012 9Marks, *Reaching the Lost: Evangelism*, from "Healthy Church Study Guides." Wheaton, IL: Crossway, 2012.

Beeke, Joel R. *Puritan Evangelism: A Biblical Approach*, 2nd ed. Grand Rapids: Reformation Heritage, 2012.

Bolger, Ryan K., ed. *The Gospel after Christendom: New Voices, New Cultures, New Expressions*. Grand Rapids: Baker, 2012.

Cameron, Julia E. M. *Christ Our Reconciler: Presentations from the Third Lausanne Congress in Capetown, South Africa*. Downer's Grove: InterVarsity, 2012.

Chan, Francis and Mark Beuving, *Multiply*. Colorado Springs: David C. Cook, 2012.

Chandler, Matt, with Jared Wilson, *The Explicit Gospel*. Wheaton, IL: Crossway, 2012.

Chandler, Matt, Eric Geiger, and Josh Patterson, *Creature of the Word: The Jesus Centered Church*. Broadman-Holman, 2012.

Johnston, E. A. *Asahel Nettleton: Revival Preacher*. Asheville, NC: Revival Literature, 2012.

Kannel, Don. *Saved?* www.xulonpress.com, 2012.

McGrath, Alister E. *Mere Apologetics: How to Help Seekers and Skeptics Find Faith*. Grand Rapids: Baker, 2012.

McManis, Clifford B. *Biblical Apologetics: Advancing and Defending the Gospel of Christ*. Xlibris, 2012.

Moyer, Larry. *Show Me How to Illustrate Evangelistic Sermons: A Guide for Pastors and Speakers* (Show Me How Series). Grand Rapids: Kregel, 2012.

Moyer, Larry. *Show Me How to Preach Evangelistic Sermons* (Show Me How Series). Grand Rapids: Kregel, 2012.

Moyer, Larry. *Show Me How to Share Christ in the Workplace* (Show Me How Series). Grand Rapids: Kregel, 2012.

Packer, J. I. and Mark Dever, *Evangelism and the Sovereignty of God*. Downers Grove, IL: InterVarsity Press, 1961, 2012.

Parr, Steve R. and Thomas Crites. *Evangelistic Effectiveness: Difference Makers in Mindsets and Methods*. Duluth, GA: Georgia Baptist Convention, 2012.

Pathak, Joy and Dave Runyon. *The Art of Neighboring: Building Genuine Relationships Right Outside Your Door*. Grand Rapids: Baker, 2012.

Payne, J. D. *Kingdom Expressions: Trends Influencing the Advancement of the Gospel*. Thomas Nelson, 2012.

Piper, John, ed. *Finish the Mission: Bringing the Gospel to the Unreached and Unengaged*. Crossway, 2012.

Plummer Robert L. and John Mark Terry, eds. *Paul's Missionary Method: His Time and Ours*. Downers Grove, IL: IVP Academic, 2012.

Shivers, Frank. *How to Preach without Evangelistic Results*. Columbia, SC: Frank Shivers Evangelistic Association, 2012.

Shivers, Frank. *Spurs to Soul Winning: 531 Motivations for Winning Souls*. La Vergne, TN: Lightning Source, 2012.

Walker, Jeremy. *The Brokenhearted Evangelist*. Grand Rapids: Reformation Heritage, 2012.

Washer, Paul. *Ten Indictments against the Modern Church*. Digital: Chapel Library, 2012.

Washer, Paul. The Gospel's Power and Message (Recovering the Gospel). Grand Rapids: Reformation Heritage, 2012.

2011 Arnold, Terry. Foundations for Evangelism. Sydney, Australia: Ark House, 2011.

Benavides, Victor. *Breaking the Evangelism Code: Evangelism Today*. Bloomington, IN: CrossBooks, 2011.

Bonnke, Reinhard. *Evangelism by Fire: Keys for Effectively Reaching Others With the Gospel*. Charisma House, 2011.

Coleman, Robert E. *The Heart of the Gospel: The Theology Behind the Master Plan of Evangelism*. Grand Rapids: Baker, 2011.

DeYoung, Kevin and Greg Gilbert, *What Is the Mission of the Church? Making Sense of Social Justice, Shalom, and the Great Commission*. Crossway, 2011.

Goheen, Michael W. *A Light to the Nations: The Missional Church and the Biblical Story*. Grand Rapids: Baker, 2011.

Horton, Michael. *The Gospel Commission: Recovering God's Strategy for Making Disciples*. Grand Rapids: Baker, 2011.

Johnston, Thomas P., ed. *Mobilizing a Great Commission Church for Outreach*. Eugene, OR: Wipf and Stock, 2011.

MacArthur, John, ed. *Evangelism: How to Share the Gospel Faithfully*. Nashville: Nelson, 2011.

Medearis, Carl. *Speaking of Jesus: The Art of Not-Evangelism*. David C. Cook, 2011.

Payne, J. D. *Evangelism: A Biblical Response to Today's Questions*. Foreword by J. I. Packer. Colorado Springs: Biblica, 2011.

Root, Jerry and Stan Guthrie, *The Sacrament of Evangelism*. Chicago: Moody, 2011.

Steve Smith and Ying Kai, *T4T: A Discipleship Re-Revolution: The Story Behind the World's Fastest Growing Church Planting Movement and How it Can Happen in Your Community!* WIGTake Resources, 2011.

Thiessen, Elmer John, *The Ethics of Evangelism: A Philosophical Defense of Proselytizing and Persuasion*. Downers Grove, IL: InterVarsity, 2011.

Thompson, John L. *Urban Impact: Reaching the World through Effective Urban Ministry*. Eugene, OR: Wipf and Stock, 2011.

Van Gelder, Craig and Dwight J. Zscheile. *The Missional Church in Perspective: Mapping Trends and Shaping the Conversation*. Grand Rapids: Baker, 2011.

Wee, Yan T. *The Soul-Winner's Handy Guide*, 3rd ed. Singapore: Y. T. Wee, 2011.

Wheeler, David and Vernon Whaley. *Biblical Principles for Worship Based Evangelism* Broadman, 2011.

2010 Adeney, Frances S. *Graceful Evangelism: Christian Witness in a Complex World*. Grand Rapids: Baker, 2010, 2011.

Earley, David and David Wheeler, *Evangelism Is . . .: How to Share Jesus with Passion and Confidence*. Nashville: Broadman-Holman, 2010.

Geisler, Norman and Patrick Zukeran. *The Apologetics of Jesus: A Caring Approach to Dealing with Doubters*. Grand Rapids: Baker, 2010.

Greenway, Adam and Chuck Lawless. *The Great Commission Resurgence: Fulfilling God's Mandate in Our Time*. Nashville:

Broadman, 2010.

Hunter, George G. III. *The Celtic Way of Evangelism: How Christianity Can Reach the West… Again.* 10th anniversary edition. Abingdon, 2010.

Koo, Hongnak. *The Impact of Luis Palau on Global Evangelism.* Grand Rapids: Credo, 2010.

Leith, John H. *Reformed Theology and the Style of Evangelism.* Edited by James C. Goodloe IV. Lousville, KY: Geneva Press, 1973; Eugene, OR: Wipf & Stock, 2010.

Malone, Kelly. *The Sword of the Spirit.* Missional, 2010.

Platt, David. *Radical: Taking Back Your Faith from the American Dream.* Multnomah, 2010.

Putnam, Jim. *Real Life Discipleship: Building Churches that Make Disciples.* NavPress, 2010.

Roudkovski, Jake. *Personal Evangelism for Pastors: Investigation of a Relationship Between Pastoral Personal Evangelism and Baptisms in Selected Southern Baptist Churches.* Lambert Academic, 2010.

Shivers, Frank. *Evangelistic Preaching 101: Voices from the Past and Present on Effective Preaching.* La Vergne, TN: Lightning Source, 2010.

Sills, David. *Reaching and Teaching: A Call to Great Commission Obedience.* Moody, 2010.

Smith, Gordon T. *Transforming Conversion: Rethinking the Language and Contours of Christian Initiation.* Grand Rapids: Baker, 2010.

Tovey, Phillip. *Inculturation: The Eucharist in Africa.* Kiraz Liturgical Series 11. Piscataway Township, NJ: Gorgias, 2010.

2009 Azurdia, Arturo, *Connected Christianity: Engaging Culture Without Compromise.* Fearn, Ross-shire, Great Britain: Christian Focus, 2009.

Barrs, Jerram. *Learning Evangelism from Jesus.* Wheaton, IL: Crossway, 2009.

Dawson, Scott and Scott Lenning, *Effectively Sharing the Gospel in a Rapidly Changing World.* Grand Rapids: Baker, 2009.

Elliff, Tom. *What Should I Say to My Friend?* Richmond, VA: International Mission Board, 2009.

Geisler, Norman and David. *Conversational Evangelism.* Harvest House 2009.

Greenway, Adam and Bill Henard, eds. *Evangelicals Engage Emergent.* Broadman Academic, 2009.

Harney, Kevin G. *Organic Outreach for Ordinary People: Sharing Good News Naturally.* Grand Rapids: Zondervan, 2009.

Hemphill, Ken. *You Are Gifted: Your Spiritual Gifts and the Kingdom of God.* Broadman, 2009.

Hirsch, Alan. *The Forgotten Ways: Reactivating the Missional Church.* Foreword by Leonard Sweet. Grand Rapids: Brazos, 2009.

Johnson, Jeffrey A. *Got Style?—A Personality Based Evangelism.* Judson, 2009.

Johnston, Thomas, *Understanding Evangelizology.* Liberty, MO: Evangelism Unlimited, 2009. A revision of *Toward a Biblical-Historical Theology of Evangelizology,* 2006, 2007.

Koukl, Gregory. *Tactics: A Game Plan for Discussing Your Christian Convictions.* Grand Rapids: Zondervan, 2009.

Liederbach, Mark and Alvin Reid, *The Convergent Church: Missional Worshipers in an Emerging Culture.* Kregel, 2009.

McDowell, Sean. *Apologetics for a New Generation: A Biblical and Culturally Relevant Approach to Talking about God.* Harvest House, 2009.

Moyer, Larry. *Free and Clear: Understanding and Communicating God's Offer of Eternal Life.* Grand Rapids: Kregel, 1997, 2009.

Moyer, Larry. *Show Me How to Answer Tough Questions* (Show Me How Series). Grand Rapids: Kregel, 2009.

Moyer, Larry. *Show Me How to Share the Gospel* (Show Me How Series). Grand Rapids: Kregel, 2009.

Payne, Tony. *Six Steps to Talking about Jesus: Practical Training for Small Groups.* Kingsford, NSW, Australia: Matthias Media, 2009.

Reid, Alvin. *Evangelism Handbook: Biblical, Spiritual, Intentional, Missional.* Nashville: Broadman, 2009.

Robinson, Darrell. *Synergistic Evangelism.* Nashville: CrossBooks, 2009.

Shivers, Frank. *Christian Basics 101: A Handbook on Christian Growth.* Xulon Press, 2009.

Smith, Warren Cole. *A Lover's Quarrel with the Evangelical Church.* Authentic, 2009.

Solc, Josef. *Communicating on the Playing Field.* Xulon, 2009.

Speed, Jon. *Evangelism in the New Testament.* Lockman Foundation, 2009.

Strobel, Lee and Mark Mittelberg, *The Unexpected Adventure: Taking Everyday Risks to Talk with People about Jesus.* Grand Rapids: Zondervan, 2009.

Wheeler, David. *Servanthood Evangelism.* Alpharetta, GA: North American Mission Board of the SBC, 2009. A revision of Alvin Reid and David Wheeler, "Servanthood Evangelism," 1997.

Wimber, John. *Power Evangelism.* San Francisco: Harper and Row, 1986; North Pomfret, VT: Trafalgar Square, 2000; **2nd** revised and enlarged: Regal, 2009.

2008 Baucum, Tory K., *Evangelical Hospitality: Catechetical Evangelism in the Early Church and its Recovery for Today.* Pietist and Wesleyan Studies (Book 25). Scarecrow, 2008.

Beougher, Timothy K. *Richard Baxter And Conversion: A Study of Puritan Concept of Becoming Christian.* Mentor, 2008.

Bock, Darrell L. and Mitch Glaser, *To the Jew First: The Case for Jewish Evangelism in Scripture and History.* Grand Rapids: Kregel, 2008.

Boyd, David, *You Don't Have to Cross an Ocean to Reach the World.* Grand Rapids: Chosen, 2008.

Chilcote, Paul W. and Laceye C. Warner, eds., *The Study of Evangelism: Exploring a Missional Practice of the Church.* Grand Rapids: Eerdmans, 2008.

Dawson, Scott and Luis Palau, *The Complete Evangelism Guidebook: Expert Advice on Reaching Others for Christ.* Grand

Rapids: Baker, 2008.

Heath, Elaine A. *The Mystic Way of Evangelism: A Contemplative Vision for Christian Outreach*. Grand Rapids: Baker, 2008.

Johnston, Thomas P. *Inquisition and Martyrdom (1002-1572): Being a Historical Study of Evangelism and Its Repression*. Liberty, MO: Evangelism Unlimited, 2008, 2009.

Lindsley, Art. *Love, the Ultimate Apologetic: The Heart of Christian Witness*. Downers Grove, IL: InterVarsity, 2008.

Morgan, Christopher W. and Robert A. Peterson, *Faith Comes by Hearing: A Response to Inclusivism*. Downers Grove, IL: InterVarsity, 2008.

Payne, J. D. *Missional House Churches: Reaching Our Communities with the Gospel*. Paternoster, 2008.

Richardson, Rick, Terry Erickson, and Judy Johnson. *Reimaging Evangelism: Inviting Friends on a Spiritual Journey*, Participant's Guide. Downers Grove, IL: IVP Connect, 2008.

Robinson, George. *Striking the Match: How God Is Using Ordinary People to Change the World through Short-term Missions*. e3 Resources, 2008.

Shivers, Frank. *Revivals 101: A Concise 'How To' Manual on Revivals*. Sumter, SC: Victory Hill Publishing, 2008.

Waggoner, Brad J. *The Shape of Faith to Come: Spiritual Formation and the Future of Discipleship*. Nashville: Broadman, 2008.

2007 Everist, Norma Cook, ed. *Christian Education as Evangelism*. Minneapolis: Fortress, 2007.

Davis, D. Mark. *Talking about Evangelism: A Congregational Resource*. Cleveland: Pilgrim, 2007.

Davis, Freddy, *Worldview Witnessing: How to Confidently Share Christ with Anyone*. Otsego, MI: PageFree, 2007.

Dever, Mark. *The Gospel and Personal Evangelism*. Wheaton, IL: Crossway, 2007.

Hemphill, Ken and Paula Hemphill. *SPLASH: Show People Love and Share Him*. Auxano, 2007.

Henderson, Jim. *Evangelism Without Additives: What If Sharing Your Faith Meant Just Being Yourself?* WaterBrook, 2007.

Johnston, Thomas P. *Charts for a Theology of Evangelism*. Nashville: Broadman, 2007.

LeFlore, David. *Fast Food Evangelism: A Drive-Through Approach to Sharing the Gospel*. Orlando, FL: Bridge-Logos, 2007.

Phillips, Richard D. *Jesus the Evangelist: Learning to Share the Gospel from the Book of John*. Reformation Trust, 2007.

Pilavachi, Mike and Liza Hoeksma. *When Necessary Use Words: Changing Lives Through Worship, Justice and Evangelism*. Ventura: Regal, 2007.

Rainer, Thom. *Simple Church*. Nashville: Broadman, 2007.

Shore, John. *I'm OK—You're Not: The Message We're Sending to Unbelievers and Why We Should Stop*. Colorado Springs: NavPress, 2007.

Speidel, Royal. *Evangelism in a Small Membership Church*. Abingdon, 2007.

Stone, Bryan P. *Evangelism after Christendom: The Theology and Practice of Christian Witness*. Grand Rapids: Brazos, 2007.

Van Gelder, Craig. *The Ministry of the Missional Church: A Community Led by the Spirit*. Grand Rapids: Baker, 2007.

Welch, Bobby and Doug Williams with David Apple, *Faith Evangelism: Discipling for Evangelism and Ministry*, Journal 1. Nashville: Lifeway, 2007.

2006 Bechtle, Mike. *Evangelism for the Rest of Us: Sharing Christ within Your Personality Style*. Grand Rapids: Baker, 2006.

Cassidy, Michael. *A Passion for Preaching*. Pietermaritzburg, South Africa: African Enterprise, 1986, 2006.

Comfort, Ray and Kirk Cameron. *Way of the Master*. Gainesville: Bridge-Logos, 2006.

Dawson, Scott, ed. *The Complete Evangelism Handbook: Expert Advice on Reaching Others for Christ*. Grand Rapids: Baker, 2006.

Hybels, Bill. *Just a Walk Across the Room: Simple Steps Pointing People to Faith*. Grand Rapids: Zondervan, 2006.

Johnston, Thomas P. *Toward a Biblical-Historical Theology of Evangelizology*. Liberty, MO: Evangelism Unlimited, 2006, 2007.

Martin, Ralph and Peter Williamson, eds. *John Paul II and the New Evangelization: How You Can Bring the Good News to Others*. Ann Arbor: Servant, 2006.

Newman, Randy. *Corner Conversations: Engaging Dialogues About God and Life*. Grand Rapids: Kregel, 2006.

Palau, Luis and Timothy Robnett, *Telling the Story: Evangelism for the Next Generation*. Ventura, CA: Gospel Light, 2006

Peace, Richard, *Holy Conversation: Talking About God in Everyday Life*. Downer's Grove, IL: InterVarsity, 2006.

Pierson, Robert D. *Needs-Based Evangelism*. Nashville, TN: Abingdon, 2006.

Rahn, David and Youth for Christ. *3Story: Preparing for a Lifestyle of Evangelism: Participant's Guide*. Grand Rapids: Zondervan-Youth Specialties, 2006.

Reese, Martha Grace, *Unbinding the Gospel: Real Life Evangelism*. Afterword by Brian McLaren. St. Louis: Chalice, 2006.

Richardson, Rick. *Reimagining Evangelism: Inviting Friends on a Spiritual Journey*. Downers Grove, IL: InterVarsity, 2006.

Shivers, Frank. *Soul Winning [101] with Illustrations and Sermons: 275 Helps for Winning the Lost*. Sumter, SC: Hill Publishing, 2006.

Singlehurst, Laurence. *Sowing, Reaping, Keeping: People-Sensitive Evangelism*. Nottingham: InterVarsity Press, 2006.

Sire, James W. *Why Good Arguments often Fail: Making a More Persuasive Case for Christ*. Downers Grove, IL: InterVarsity, 2006.

Sprenger, Mike. *Blowing Your Cover: Workbook*. London: Monarch, 2006.

2005 Claydon, David, ed. *A New Vision, A New Heart, A Renewed Call*. Volumes One, Two, Three. Lausanne Occasional Papers from the 2004 Forum for World Evangelization Pasadena, CA: William Carey Library, 2005.

George, Timothy and John Woodbridge. *The Mark of Jesus: Loving in a Way the World Can See*. Chicago: Moody, 2005.

Henderson, Jim. *a.k.a. Lost: Discovering Ways to Connect with the People Jesus Misses Most*. WaterBrook, 2005.

Lawless, Chuck and Thom S. Rainer, eds. *The Challenge of the Great Commission: Essays on God's Mandate for the Local Church*. Pinnacle, 2005.

Smith, Sean. *Prophetic Evangelism: Empowering a Generation to Seize Their Day*. Shippensburg, PA: Destiny Image, 2005.

Stetzer, Ed and Eric Ramsey, *Strategic Outreach: A How-to Marketing Manual for Pastors and Church Leaders*. Vista, CA: Outreach, 2005.

Wilkins, Scott G. *REACH: A Team Approach to Evangelism and Assimilation*. Grand Rapids: Baker, 2005.

2004 Allison, Lon and Mark Anderson. *Going Public with the Gospel: Reviving Evangelistic Proclamation*. Downers Grove, IL: InterVarsity, 2004.

Beougher, Timothy and Alvin L. Reid. *Evangelism for a Changing World*. Wipf & Stock, 2004.

Cameron, Kirk and Ray Comfort. *The School of Biblical Evangelism: 101 Lessons*. Gainesville: Bridge-Logos, 2004.

Hunt, Stephen. *The Alpha Enterprise: Evangelism in a Post-Christian Era*. Aldershot, Hants, England: Ashgate, 2004.

Long, Jimmy. *Emerging Hope* (revision and expansion of *Generating Hope* [1997]). Downers Grove, IL: InterVarsity, 2004.

Moyer, R. Larry. *21 Things God Never Said: Correcting Our Misconceptions about Evangelism*. Grand Rapids: Kregel, 2004.

Newman, Randy. *Questioning Evangelism: Engaging People's Hearts the Way Jesus Did*. Grand Rapids: Kregel, 2004.

Piper, John. *Don't Waste Your Life*. Crossway, 2004.

Rausch, Thomas P., S.J., ed. *Evangelizing America*. Mahwah, NJ: Paulist, 2004.

Shivers, Frank. *The Evangelistic Invitation 101: 150 Helps in Giving the Evangelistic Invitation*. Sumter, SC: Hill Publishing, 2004.

Simpson, Michael L. *Permission Evangelism—When to Talk, When to Walk*. Colorado Springs: NexGen, Cook, 2004.

Sjogren, Steve, Dave Ping, and Doug Pollock. *Irresistible Evangelism: Natural Ways to Open Others to Jesus*. Loveland, CO: Group, 2004.

Tabb, Mark. *Mission to Oz: Reaching Postmoderns without Losing Your Way*. Chicago: Moody, 2004.

2003 Catholic Church. *Ministry through the Lens of Evangelization*. Washington: USCCB (United States Conference of Catholic Bishops), 2003.

Corbitt, J. Nathan and Vivian Nix-Early. *Taking It to the Streets: Using the Arts to Transform Your Community*. Grand Rapids: Baker, 2003.

Frost, Toby, Bill Sims, and Monty McWhorter. *The Evangelistic Block Party Manual*. Atlanta: NAMB, 2003.

Johnston, Thomas P. *Examining Billy Graham's Theology of Evangelism*. Eugene, OR: Wipf and Stock, 2003.

McRaney, Will. *The Art of Personal Evangelism*. Nashville: Broadman, 2003.

Myers, Joseph R. *The Search to Belong: Rethinking Intimacy, Community, and Small Groups*. Grand Rapids: Zondervan, 2003.

Rainer, Thom. *The Unchurched Next Door: Understanding Faith Stages as Keys to Sharing Your Faith*. Grand Rapids: Zondervan, 2003.

Shadrach, Steve, *The Fuel and the Flame: 10 Keys to Ignite Your College Campus for Jesus Christ*. Conway, AR: The Bodybuilders, 2003.

Van Engen, Charles E., Dean S. Gilliland, Arthur S. Glasser, and Shawn B. Redford. *Announcing the Kingdom: The Story of God's Mission in the Bible*. Grand Rapids: Baker Academic, 2003.

Webber, Robert. *Ancient Future Evangelism: Making Your Church a Faith Forming Community*. Grand Rapids: Baker, 2003.

2002 Bowen, John P. *Evangelism for Normal People*. Minneapolis, MN: Augsburg Fortress, 2002.

Cahill, Mark. *One Thing You Can't Do in Heaven*. Genesis Publishing; Rockwall, TX: Biblical Discipleship, 2002, 2003, 2004, 2005.

Carswell, Roger. *And Some as Evangelists: Growing Your Church through Discovering and Developing Evangelists*. Fearn, Ross-shire, Great Britain: Christian Focus, 2002, 2005.

Kallenberg, Brad. *Live to Tell: Evangelism in a Postmodern World*. Grand Rapids: Baker, 2002.

Legg. Steve. *A-Z of Evangelism: The Ultimate Guide to Evangelism*. London: Hodder and Stoughton, 2002.

McLaren, Brian D. *More Ready Than you Realize: Evangelism as Dance in the Postmodern Matrix*. Grand Rapids: Zondervan, 2002.

Reid, Alvin. *Radically Unchurched: Who They Are and How to Reach Them*. Grand Rapids: Kregel, 2002.

Reid, Alvin and Malcolm McDow, *Firefall*. Pleasant Word, 2002.

Robinson, Darrell. *Incredibly Gifted*. Hannibal Press: Garland, TX, 2002.

Stier, Greg. *Outbreak! Creating a Contagious Youth Ministry through Viral Evangelism*. Chicago: Moody, 2002.

Ward, Mark Sr., *The Word Works: 151 Amazing Stories of Men and Women Saved through Gospel Literature*. Greenville, SC: Ambassador Emerald Int'l, 2002.

2001 Barrs, Jerram. *The Heart of Evangelism*. Wheaton, IL: Crossway, 2001, 2005.

Conard, William W., ed. *Amsterdam 2000: The Mission of an Evangelist*. Minneapolis: World Wide Publications, 2001.

Rainer, Thom. *Surprising Insights from the Unchurched and Proven Ways to Reach Them*. Grand Rapids: Zondervan, 2001.

Sjogren, Steve. *101 Ways to Reach Your Community*. Colorado Springs: NavPress, 2001.

2000 Achtemeier, Mark and Andrew Purves, eds., *A Passion for the Gospel: Confessing Jesus Christ for the 21st Century*. Louisville: Geneva, 2000.

Baugh, Ken. *Getting Real: An Interactive Guide to Relational Ministry*. Colorado Springs: NavPress, 2000.

Carson, Donald A., ed. *Telling the Truth: Evangelizing Postmoderns*. Grand Rapids: Zondervan, 2000.

Chang, Curtis. *Engaging Unbelief: A Captivating Strategy from Augustine and Aquinas.* Downers Grove, IL: InterVarsity, 2000.

Hunter, George G., III. *The Celtic Way of Evangelism.* Nashville, TN: Abingdon, 2000.

Mittelberg, Mark with Bill Hybels, *Building a Contagious Church: Revolutionizing the Way We View and Do Evangelism.* Grand Rapids: Zondervan, 2000.

Pippert, Rebecca Manley and Ruth Siemens, *Evangelism: A Way of Life,* A Lifeguide Bible Study. Downers Grove, IL: InterVarsity, 2000.

Richardson, Rick. *Evangelism Outside the Box: New Ways to Help People Experience the Good News.* Downers Grove, IL: InterVarsity, 2000.

Schneider, Floyd. *Evangelism for the Fainthearted.* Grand Rapids, MI: Kregel, 2000.

Shepherd, Norman. *The Call of Grace: How the Covenant Illuminates Salvation and Evangelism.* Phillipsburg, NJ: P&R, 2000.

Silvoso, Ed. *Prayer Evangelism.* Ventura: Regal, 2000.

Strobel, Lee. *The Case for Faith.* Grand Rapids: Zondervan, 2000.

Wright, Linda Raney. *Christianity's Crisis in Evangelism: Going Where the People Are.* Portland: Multnomah, 2000.

1999 Careaga, Andrew. *E-vangelism: Sharing the Gospel in Cyberspace.* Lafayette, LA: Vital Issues, 1999.

Chapman, John C. *Setting Hearts on Fire: A Guide to Giving Evangelistic Talks.* Australia: St. Matthias, 1999.

Évangile et Évangélisme: XIIe-XIIIe Siècle. Cahiers de Fanjeaux 34. Toulouse, France: Éditions Privat, 1999.

Fay, William. *Share Jesus Without Fear.* Nashville: Broadman, 1999.

Laurie, Greg. *How To Share Your Faith.* Wheaton, IL: Tyndale, 1999.

MacArthur, John. *Nothing But the Truth: Upholding the Gospel in a Doubting Age.* Wheaton, IL: Crossway, 1999; Amazon: Kindle, n.d.

Morgenthaler, Susan. *Worship Evangelism.* Grand Rapids: Zondervan, 1999.

Water, Mark. *Sharing Your Faith Made Easy: An Easy-to-Understand Pocket Reference Guide.* Hendricksen, 1999.

1998 Jensen, Phillip and Phil Campbell. *Two Ways to Live: A Bible Study Explaining Christianity.* Kingsford, NSW, Australia: Matthias Media, 1998.

Moyer, R. Larry. *Larry Moyer's how-To Book on Personal Evangelism.* Grand Rapids: Kregel, 1998.

Reid, Alvin. *Introduction to Evangelism.* Nashville: Broadman, 1998.

Williams, Doug and Bobby H. Welch. *A Journey in Faith: Facilitator Guide.* Sunday School Board of the SBC, 1998.

1997 Coleman, Robert E. *The Master's Way of Personal Evangelism.* Wheaton: Crossway, 1997.

Long, Jimmy. *Generating Hope: A Strategy for Reaching the Postmodern Generation.* Downers Grove, IL: InterVarsity, 1997.

Miller, John C. *Powerful Evangelism for the Powerless* (revision of *Evangelism and Your Church* [1980]) Phillipsburg, NJ: Presbyterian and Reformed, 1997.

Moyer, R. Larry. *Free and Clear: Understanding and Communicating God's Offer of Eternal Life.* Grand Rapids: Kregel, 1997.

Pollard, Nicky. *Evangelism Made Slightly Less Difficult: How to Interest People Who Aren't Interested.* Downers Grove, IL: InterVarsity, 1997.

Reid, Alvin and David Wheeler. "Servanthood Evangelism." n.p., n.d. [1997].

Robinson, Darrell. *Total Church Life.* Nashville: Broadman, 1997.

Tidwell, Jerry N. *Outreach Teams that Win.* Nashville, TN: Lifeway, 1997.

Welch, Bobby. *Evangelism Through Sunday School: A Journey of Faith.* Nashville: Lifeway, 1997.

1996 Bahnsen, Greg L. Ed. by Robert R. Booth. Always Ready: Directions for Defending the Faith. Covenant Media, 1996.

Hawthorne, Steve and Graham Kendrick, *Prayer Walking: Praying On Site with Insight.* Charisma House, 1996.

Kennedy, D. James. *Evangelism Explosion, 4th Edition.* Wheaton, IL: Tyndale House, 1994, 1996.

Pickard, Nellie. *52 True Stories About Successful Witnessing.* Grand Rapids: Baker, 1996.

Rainer, Thom. *Effective Evangelistic Churches: Successful Churches Reveal What Works and What Doesn't.* Nashville: Broadman, 1996.

Setzler, Monitia, Barbara Oden, Gary Bulley, and David Strawn. *TouchPOINTS—Sowing Seeds, Volume One.* Nashville: On Target, 1996.

Sjogren, Steve. *Servant Warfare: How Kindness Conquers Spiritual Darkness.* Ann Arbor: Servant, 1996.

Stott, John, ed. *Making Christ Known: Historic Mission Documents from the Lausanne Movement 1974-1989.* Great Britain: Paternoster, 1996.

1995 Atkinson, Donald A. and Charles L. Roesel, *Meeting Needs/Sharing Christ: Ministry Evangelism in Today's New Testament Church.* Nashville: Lifeway, 1995.

Beougher, Timothy and Alvin Reid, eds., *Evangelism for a Changing World: Essays in Honor of Roy Fish.* Wheaton, IL: Harold Shaw, 1995.

Barna, George. *Evangelism that Works: How to Reach Changing Generations with the Unchanging Gospel.* Ventura: Regal, 1995.

Ford, Kevin. *Jesus for a New Generation.* Downers Grove: InterVarsity, 1995.

Green, Michael. *One to One: How to Share Your Faith with a Friend.* Nashville: Moorings, 1995.

John, J. *God's Top Ten: Rediscovering the Basic Building Blocks for Life.* Eastbourne, Great Britain: Kingsway, 1995.

Kramp, John. *Out of Their Faces and Into Their Shoes: How to Understand Spiritually Lost People and Give Them Directions to Find God.* Nashville: Broadman and Holman, 1995.

Penn-Lewis, Jessie. *Prayer and Evangelism*. Fort Washington, PA: Christian Literature Crusade, 1995.

Robinson, Darrell, *People Sharing Jesus*. Nashville: Nelson, 1995.

1994 Brennan, Patrick. *Re-Imagining Evangelization: Vision, Conversion, and Contagion*. Crossroad, 1994.

Callahan, Kennon L. *Visiting in an Age of Mission: A Handbook for Person-to-Person Ministry*. San Francisco: HarperSanFrancisco, 1994.

Drane, John. *Evangelism for a New Age*. Hammersmith, London: Marshall Pickering, 1994.

Ford, Leighton. *The Power of Story: Recovering the Oldest, Most Natural Way to Reach People for Christ*. Colorado Springs: NavPress, 1994.

Gumbel, Nicky. *Telling Others: The Alpha Initiative*. Eastbourne, Great Britain: Kingsway, 1994.

Hybels, Bill and Mark Mittelberg. *Becoming a Contagious Christian*. Grand Rapids: Zondervan, 1994.

Johnston, Thomas P. *The Mindset of Eternity*. Deerfield, IL: Evangelism Unlimited, 1994.

Joslin, Roy. Urban Harvest: Biblical Perspectives on Christian Mission in the Inner Cities. Evangelical Press, 1994.

Levicoff, Steve. *Street Smarts: A Survival Guide to Personal Evangelism and the Law*. Grand Rapids: Baker, 1994.

Mims, Gene. *Kingdom Principles for Church Growth*. Nashville: Broadman, 1994, 2001.

Murphee, Jon Tal. *Responsible Evangelism: Relating Theory to Practice*. Toccoa Falls, GA: Toccoa Falls College, 1994.

Ray, Michael D. *Soul Winning—The Heart Of God*. Hopewell Ministries, 1994.

Terry, John Mark. *Evangelism: A Concise History*. Nashville: Broadman and Holman, 1994.

1993 *Beginning Steps: A Growth Guide for New Believers* [NIV]. Atlanta: North American Mission Board, 1993.

Beougher, Timothy. *Overcoming Walls to Witnessing*. Minneapolis: Billy Graham Evangelistic Association, 1993.

Briner, Bob. *Roaring Lambs*. Grand Rapids: Zondervan, 1993.

Brueggemann. *Biblical Perspectives on Evangelism: Living in a Three-Storied Universe*. Nashville: Abingdon, 1993.

Kelley, Charles. *How Did They Do It? The Story of Southern Baptist Evangelism*. New Orleans: Insight, 1993.

Piper, John. *Let the Nations Be Glad: The Supremacy of God in Missions*. Grand Rapids: Baker, 1993.

Sjogren, Steve. *Conspiracy of Kindness*. Ann Arbor: Servant, 1993.

1992 Bierle, Donald A. *Surprised by Faith*. Excelsior, MN: H.I.S. Ministries, 1992.

Bolt, Peter. *Mission Minded*. London: St. Matthias Press, 1992.

Drummond, Lewis A. *The Word of the Cross: A Contemporary Theology of Evangelism*. Nashville: Broadman, 1992.

Faircloth, Samuel. *Church Planting for Reproduction*. Grand Rapids: Baker, 1992.

Larsen, David L. *The Evangelism Mandate: Recovering the Centrality of Gospel Preaching*. Wheaton: Crossway, 1992.

McIntosh, Gary and Glen Martin. *Finding Them, Keeping Them: Effective Strategies for Evangelism and Assimilation in the Local Church*. Nashville: Broadman, 1992.

Pannell, William. *Evangelism from the Bottom Up*. Grand Rapids: Zondervan, 1992.

Porter, Douglas. *How to Develop and Use the Gift of Evangelism*. Lynchburg, VA: Church Growth, 1992.

Wiles, Jerry. *How to Win Others to Christ: Your Personal, Practical Guide to Evangelism*. Nashville: Nelson, 1992.

1991 Banks, William L. *In Search of the Great Commission: What Did Jesus Really Say?* Chicago: Moody, 1991.

Beasley, Gary M. and Francis Anfuso. *Complete Evangelism: Fitting the Pieces Together*. South Lake Tahoe, CA: Christian Equippers, 1991.

Gilbert, Larry. *Team Evangelism—Giving New Meaning to Lay Evangelism*. Lynchburg: Church Growth, 1991.

Heck, Joel D. *The Art of Sharing Your faith*. Old Tappan, NJ: Revell, 1991.

Johnson, Ben Campbell. *Speaking of God: Evangelism as Initial Spiritual Guidance*. Atlanta: Westminster John Knox, 1991.

Stebbins, Tom. *Evangelism by the Book*. Camp Hill, PA: Christian, 1991.

Whitney, Donald S. *Spiritual Disciplines for the Christian Life*. Colorado Springs: NavPress, 1991.

1990 Bleecker, Walter S. *The Non-Confronter's Guide to Leading a Person to Christ*. San Bernardino, CA: Here's Life, 1990.

Brock, Charles. *Let This Mind Be in You*. Kansas City, MO: Church Growth, 1990.

Coleman, Robert E. *"Nothing To Do But To Save Souls."* Wilmore, KY: Wesley Heritage, 1990.

Lukasse, Johan. *Churches with Roots: Planting Churches in Post-Christian Europe*. Bromley: STL, 1990.

Neighbour, Ralph W. Jr. *Knocking on Doors—Opening Hearts*. Houston: Touch, 1990.

Neighbour, Ralph W. Jr. *Where Do We Go from Here? A Guidebook for the Cell Group Church*. Houston: Touch, 1990.

Ratz, Calvin, Frank Tillapaugh, and Myron Augsburger. *Mastering Outreach And Evangelism*. Portland, OR: Multnomah (with Christianity Today), 1990.

1989 Abraham, William J. *Logic of Evangelism*. Grand Rapids: Eerdmans, 1989.

Comfort, Ray. *Hell's Best Kept Secret*. Bellflower, CA: self-published, 1989; Springdale, PA: Whitaker House, 1989; New Kensington, PA: Whitaker House, 2002; revised with study guide, Kensington, PA: Whitaker House, 2004.

Petersen, Jim. *Living Proof*. Colorado Springs: NavPress, 1989.

Posterski, Donald C. *Reinventing Evangelism: New Strategies for Presenting Christ in Today's World*. Downer's Grove, IL: InterVarsity, 1989.

Walker, Louise Jeter. *Evangelism Today: An Independent Study Textbook*, 2nd ed. International Correspondence Institute, 1989.

1988 Aldrich, Joseph C. *Gentle Persuasion*. Portland, OR: Multnomah, 1988.

Fordham, Keith. *"The Evangelist"—The Heart of God*. Del City, OK: Spirit, 1988, 1991, 2002.

Pickard, Nellie. *What to Say When—: An Inspirational Guide to Witnessing*. Grand Rapids: Baker, 1988.

Rand, Ronald. *Won By One*. Ventura: Regal, 1988.

Scott, Bruce. *Gleanings for the Remnant*. Lynwood, IL: American Messianic Fellowship, 1988.

1987 Barrett, David B. *Evangelize! A Survey of the Concept*. Birmingham, AL: New Hope, 1987.

Bartlett, David L. and Ruth Fowler. *Moments of Commitment: Years of Growth: Evangelism and Christian Education*. St. Louis, MO: Christian Board of Publications, 1987.

Bright, Bill. *Witnessing Without Fear*. San Bernardino, CA: Here's Life, 1987.

Douglas, J. D., ed. *The Calling of an Evangelist: The Second International Congress for Itinerant Evangelists, Amsterdam, The Netherlands*. Minneapolis: World Wide, 1987.

Hinson, William H. *A Place to Dig in: Doing Evangelism in the Local Church*. Nashville: Abingdon, 1987.

Crossley, G. *Everyday Evangelism*. Evangelical Press, 1987.

Randall, Rob, *Witnessing: A Way Of Life*. Criteron Publications, 1987.

Reid, Gavin. *To Reach a Nation: The Challenge of Evangelism in a Mass-Media Age*. London: Hodder and Stoughton, 1987.

Wells, David F. *God the Evangelist: How the Holy Spirit Works to Bring Men to Christ*. Grand Rapids: Eerdmans, 1987; Exeter, United Kingdom: Paternoster Press, 1987.

Yamamori, Tetsuanao. *God's New Envoys: A Bold Strategy for Penetrating "Closed Countries."* Portland, OR: Multnomah, 1987.

1986 Cairns, Earle Edwin. *An Endless Line of Splendor: Revivals and Their Leaders from the Great Awakening to the Present*. Wheaton, IL: Tyndale House, 1986.

Cassidy, Michael. *A Passion for Preaching*. Pietermaritzburg, South Africa: African Enterprise, 1986, 2006.

Dale, Robert D. *Evangelizing the Hard-to-Reach*. Nashville: Broadman, 1986.

Hanks, Billie, Jr. *Everyday Evangelism: Evangelism as a Way of Life*. Nashville: Word, 1986.

Hulse, Erroll. *The Great Invitation*. Welwyn: Evangelical, 1986.

Jacks, Bob and Betty. *Your Home a Lighthouse*. Colorado Springs: NavPress, 1986, 1987.

McCloskey, Mark. *Tell It Often—Tell It Well*. San Bernardino, CA: Here's Life, 1986.

Miles, Delos, *Evangelism and Social Involvement*. Nashville: Broadman, 1986.

Wimber, John. *Power Evangelism*. San Francisco: Harper and Row, 1986; North Pomfret, VT: Trafalgar Square, 2000; revised and enlarged: Regal, 2009.

1985 Petersen, Jim. *Evangelism for Our Generation*. Colorado Springs, CO: NavPress, 1985.

Smith, Glenn C., ed. *Evangelizing Adults*. Washington, DC: Paulist National Catholic Evangelization Association; Wheaton, IL: Tyndale House, 1985.

1984 Armstrong, Richard Stoll. *The Pastor as Evangelist*. Philadelphia: Westminster, 1984.

Cocoris, Michael G. *Evangelism: A Biblical Approach*. Chicago: Moody, 1984.

Douglas, J. D., ed. *The Work of an Evangelist: International Congress for Itinerant Evangelists, Amsterdam, The Netherlands, 1983*. Minneapolis: World Wide Publishing, 1984.

Graham, Billy. *A Biblical Standard for Evangelists*. Minneapolis: World Wide, 1984.

Neighbour, Ralph Jr. *The Journey into Discipleship: The Journey into Lifestyle Evangelism and Ministry*. Memphis: Brotherhood Commission of the SBC, 1984, 1987.

Rockwell, Margaret. *Stepping Out: Sharing Christ in Everyday Circumstances*. Arrowhead Springs, CA: Here's Life, 1984.

Streett, R. Alan. *The Effective Invitation*. Old Tappan, NJ: Revell, 1984.

Trotman, Dawson. *Born to Reproduce*. Colorado Springs: NavPress, 1984.

Williams, Derek. *One in a Million*. Berkhamsted. UK: Word Books, 1984.

1983 Augsburger, Myron. *Evangelism as Discipling*. Scottsdale, PA: Herald, 1983.

Dayton, Edward R. *That Everyone May Hear: Reaching the Unreached*, 3rd ed. MARC—Mission Advanced Research and Communication Center, 1983.

Graham, Franklin with Jeanette Lockerbie. *Bob Pierce: This One Thing I Do*. Waco: Word, 1983.

Hanks, Billie, Jr. *Everyday Evangelism: How to Do It and How to Teach It*. Grand Rapids: Zondervan, 1983

Innes, Dick. *I Hate Witnessing! A Handbook for Effective Christian Communication*. Ventura, CA: Vision House, 1983.

Johnson, Ben. *An Evangelism Primer: Practical Principles for Congregations*. Atlanta: John Knox, 1983.

Kraft, Charles. *Communication Theory for Christian Witness*. Nashville: Abingdon, 1983.

Miles, Delos. *Introduction to Evangelism*. Nashville: Broadman, 1983.

Miller, Herb. *Fishing on the Asphalt: Effective Evangelism in Mainline Denominations*. St. Louis: Bethany, 1983.

Rueter, Alvin C. *Organizing for Evangelism: Planning an Effective Program for Witnessing*. Minneapolis: Augsburg, 1983.

Tuttle, Robert, Jr. *Someone Out There Needs Me: A Practical Guide to Relational Evangelism*. Grand Rapids: Zondervan, 1983.

Walker, Mickey. *Doulos: Personal Evangelism Notebook*. Bilbao, Spain: Operation Mobilization, 1983.

1982 Callender, Willard D. *How to Make a Friendly Call*. Valley Forge, PA: Judson, 1982.

Clapp, Steve. *Christian Education as Evangelism*. Champaign, IL: Crouse Printing, 1982.

Conn, Harvey. *Evangelism: Doing Justice and Preaching Grace*. Grand Rapids: Zondervan, 1982.

Eakin, Mary Mulford. *Scruffy Sandals: A Guide for Church Visitation in the Community*. New York: Pilgrim, 1982.

Krass, Alfred C. *Evangelizing Neopagan North America*. Scottsdale, PA: Herald, 1982.

Miles, Delos. *Master Principles of Evangelism: Examples from Jesus' Personal Witnessing*. Nashville: Broadman, 1982.

Reisinger, Ernest C. *Today's Evangelism*. Phillipsburg, NJ: P & R, 1982.

Roberts, Richard Owen. *Revival: What Is Revival? When Is Revival Needed? When Can Revival Be Expected? When Is*

Revival Dangerous? Will the Revival Last? Wheaton, IL: Tyndale House, 1982.

Sanders, Oswald J. *Effective Evangelism.* Kent, England: STL Books, 1982.

Savelle, Jerry. *Sharing Jesus Effectively: A Handbook on Successful Soul-Winning.* Tulsa, OK: Harrison House, 1982.

Walsh, John. *Evangelization and Justice: New Insight for Christian Ministry.* Maryknoll, NY: Orbis, 1982.

1981   Aldrich, Joseph C. *Life-Style Evangelism: Crossing Traditional Boundaries to Reach the Unbelieving World.* Portland, OR: Multnomah, 1981.

Bassett, Paul, *God's Way.* Ambassador, 1981.

Chapman, John C. *Know and Tell the Gospel: The Why and How of Evangelism.* London: Hodder and Stoughton, 1981; Colorado Springs, CO: NavPress, 1985.

Metzger, Will. *Tell the Truth: The Whole Message to the Whole Person by the Whole People.* Downers Grove, IL: InterVarsity, 1981, 1984.

Neville, Joyce. *How to Share Your Faith Without Being Offensive.* New York: Seabury, 1981.

Prince, Matthew. *Winning Through Caring: Handbook on Friendship Evangelism.* Grand Rapids: Baker, 1981.

Samuel, Leith. *Share Your Faith.* Grand Rapids: Baker, 1981.

Thompson, W. Oscar, Jr. *Concentric Circles of Concern.* Nashville: Broadman, 1981.

1980   Amberson, Talmadge R. *Reaching Out to People.* Nashville: Broadman, 1980.

Calver, Clive. *Sold Out: Taking the Lid Off Evangelism.* London: Lakeland, Marshall, Morgan and Scott, 1980.

Deville, Jard. *The Psychology of Witnessing.* Waco: Word, 1980.

Henderson, Robert T. *Joy to the World: An Introduction to Kingdom Evangelism.* Atlanta: John Knox, 1980.

Korthals, Richard G. *Agape Evangelism: Roots that Reach Out.* Wheaton, IL: Tyndale House, 1980.

Lessons in Assurance. Colorado Springs: NavPress, 1980.

Miller, John C. *Evangelism and Your Church.* Phillipsburg, NJ: Presbyterian and Reformed, 1980.

Peale, Norman Vincent. *The Positive Power of Jesus Christ: Life-Changing Adventures in Faith.* Wheaton, IL: Tyndale House, 1980.

Petersen, Jim. *Evangelism as a Lifestyle.* Colorado Springs, CO: NavPress, 1980.

Turnbull, Michael. *Parish Evangelism: A Practical Resource Book for the Local Church.* London: Mowbrays, 1980.

1979   Armstrong, Richard S. *Service Evangelism.* Philadelphia: Westminster, 1979.

Green, Michael. *Evangelism Now and Then: How Can What Happened in the Early Church Happen Now?* Downers Grove, IL: InterVarsity, 1979; Rev. Ed. Grand Rapids: Eerdmans, 2004.

Kraft, Charles H. *Communicating the Gospel God's Way.* Pasadena: William Carey, 1979.

McDill, Wayne. *Making Friends for Christ—A Practical Approach to Relational Evangelism.* Nashville: Broadman, 1979.

McPhee, Arthur. *Friendship Evangelism: The Caring Way to Share Your Faith.* Grand Rapids: Zondervan, 1979.

Misselbrook, Lewis. *Sharing the Faith with Others: A Program for Training in Evangelism.* Valley Forge, PA: American Baptist, 1979.

Pippert, Rebecca Manley. *Out of the Saltshaker and into the World: Evangelism as a Way of Life.* Downers Grove, IL: InterVarsity, 1979.

Routh, Porter. *Witness To The World.* Convention Press, 1979.

Sisson, Richard. *Training for Evangelism.* Chicago: Moody, 1979.

1978   Caldwell, Max L., ed., *Witness to Win: Positive Evangelism through the Sunday School.* Nashville: Convention, 1978.

Engel, James F. *Contemporary Christian Communications: Its Theory and Practice.* Nashville: Nelson, 1978, 1979.

Jauncey, James H. *One-on-One Evangelism.* Chicago: Moody, 1978.

Lavin, Ronald J., ed., *The Human Chain for Divine Grace: Lutheran Sermons for Evangelical Outreach.* Philadelphia: Fortress, 1978.

Menninger, Karl. *Whatever Became of Sin?* New York: Bantam, 1978.

Miller, Calvin. *A View from the Fields.* Nashville: Broadman, 1978.

Read, David Haxton Carswell. *Go and Make Disciples.* Nashville: Abingdon, 1978.

Smith, Bailey E. *Real Evangelism: Exposing the Subtle Substitutes for That Evangelism.* Nashville: Broadman, 1978; Nashville: World, 1999.

Sweazey, George E. *The Church as Evangelist.* San Francisco: Harper and Row, 1978.

1977   Dalaba, Oliver V. *That None Be Lost.* Springfield, MO: Gospel Publishing, 1977.

Ford, Leighton. *Good News Is for Sharing: A Guide to Making Friends for Christ.* Elgin, IL: David C. Cook, 1977.

Hendrick, John R. *Opening the Door of Faith: The Why, When, and Where of Evangelism.* Atlanta: John Knox, 1977.

Hogue, C. B. *I Want My Church to Grow.* Nashville: Broadman, 1977.

Kennedy, D. James. *Evangelism Explosion,* Revised Edition. 1970; Wheaton, IL: Tyndale House, 1977.

Little, Paul E., ed. *His Guide to Evangelism.* Downers Grove, IL: InterVarsity, 1977, 1979.

Miller, Herb. *Evangelism's Open Secrets.* St. Louis: Bethany, 1977.

1976   Borchert, Gerald L. *Dynamics of Evangelism.* Waco, TX: Word, 1976.

Colle, Beau. *CB for Christians.* Nashville: Broadman, 1976.

Dobbins, Gaines S. *Good News to Change Lives: Evangelism for an Age of Uncertainty.* Nashville: Broadman, 1976.

Gentry, Gardiner. *Bus Them in.* Grand Rapids: Baker, 1976.

Haney, David P. *The Ministry Evangelism Weekend: Preparation Manual.* Atlanta: Renewal Evangelism, 1976.

Havlik, John F. *The Evangelistic Church.* Nashville: Convention, 1976.

High School Evangelism. San Bernardino, CA: Campus Crusade for Christ, 1976.

Hogue, C. B. *Love Leaves No Choice: Life-style Evangelism.* Waco: Word, 1976.

Howard, David M. *The Great Commission Today.* Downers Grove, IL: InterVarsity, 1976.

Kuhne, Gary. *The Dynamics of Personal Follow-Up.* Grand Rapids: Zondervan, 1976.

Martin, Roger. *R. A. Torrey: Apostle of Certainty.* Murfreesboro, TN: Sword of the Lord, 1976.

McDill, Wayne *Evangelism in a Tangled World.* Nashville: Broadman, 1976.

Morgan, G. Campbell, *Evangelism.* Grand Rapids: Baker, 1976.

Northey, James. *Outreach: Toward Effective Open-Air Evangelism.* London: Salvationist, 1976.

Towns, Elmer. *Evangelize Thru Christian Education.* Wheaton, IL: Evangelical Teacher Training Association, 1976.

Warren, Max. *I Believe in the Great Commission.* Grand Rapids: Eerdmans, 1976.

Watson, David. *I Believe in Evangelism.* Grand Rapids: Eerdmans, 1976; London: Hodder and Stoughton, 1976.

1975 Dhavamony, Mariasusia, S.J. *Evangelisation.* Rome: Università Gregoriana, 1975.

Drummond, Lewis. *Leading Your Church in Evangelism.* Nashville: Broadman, 1975.

Eims, Leroy. *Winning Ways: The Adventure of Sharing Christ.* Wheaton, IL: Victor, 1975.

Engel, James F. and Wilbert Norton, *What's Gone Wrong with the Harvest? A Communication Strategy for the Church and World Evangelism.* Grand Rapids: Zondervan, 1975.

Fackre, Gabriel. *Word in Deed: Theological Themes in Evangelism.* Grand Rapids: Eerdmans, 1975.

Green, Hollis Lynn. *Why Wait Till Sunday? An Action approach to Local Evangelism.* Minneapolis: Bethany Fellowship, 1975.

Laney, James T. *Evangelism: Mandates for Action.* New York: Hawthorn, 1975.

Prior, Kenneth Francis William. *The Gospel in a Pagan Society: A Book for Modern Evangelists.* Downers Grove, IL: InterVarsity, 1975.

Neighbour, Ralph W. Jr., *Target-Group Evangelism.* Nashville: Broadman, 1975.

Paul VI. *Evangelii Nuntiandi.* Rome: Vatican, 8 Dec 1975.

Quere, Ralph W. *Evangelical Witness: The Message, Medium, Mission, and Method of Evangelism.* Minneapolis: Augsburg, 1975.

Smith, Morton, Reformed Evangelism. Multi-Communication, 1975.

Walker, Alan. *The New Evangelism.* Nashville: Abingdon, 1975.

Weber, Jaroy. *Winning America to Christ.* Nashville: Broadman, 1975.

Wiggins, Kembleton S. *Soul Winning Made Easier: The Psychology of Getting More Decisions.* Mountain View, CA: Pacific, 1975.

1974 Chafin, Kenneth L. *The Reluctant Witness.* Nashville: Broadman, 1974.

Fish, Roy. *Giving a Good Invitation.* Nashville: Broadman, 1974.

Mayfield, William H. *Restoring First Century Evangelism: for an Effective Program in Soul-Winning through the Rediscovery of the Witnessing Power of the Early Church: Evangelism Text Book and Training Manual.* Cincinnati: New Life, 1974.

Henrichsen, Walter A. *Disciples Are Made-not Born.* Wheaton, IL: Victor, 1974.

Johnson, Daniel E. *Building with Buses.* Grand Rapids: Baker, 1974.

Koyama, Kosuke. *Waterbuffalo Theology.* Maryknoll, NY: Orbis, 1974, 1999.

Pickering, Ernest D. *The Theology of Evangelism.* Clarks Summit, PA: Baptist Bible College, 1974.

Rand, Ronald R. *The Evangelism Helper.* Cincinnati, OH: The Vine, 1974.

Sherrod, Paul. *Successful Soul Winning: Proven Ideas to Challenge Every Christian to Be a Personal Worker.* Lubbock, TX: P. Sherrod, 1974.

Shoemaker, Helen S. *Prayer and Evangelism.* Waco, TX: Word, 1974.

Washburn, Alphonso V. *Reach Out to People: A People-to-People Emphasis.* Nashville: Convention, 1974.

1973 Coleman, Robert E. *They Meet the Master: A Study Manual on the Personal Evangelism of Jesus.* Old Tappan, NJ: Revell, 1973.

Fackre, Gabriel. *Do and Tell: Engagement Evangelism in the '70s.* Grand Rapids: Eerdmans, 1973.

Foust, Paul J. *Reborn to Multiply: Tested Techniques for Personal Evangelism.* St. Louis: Concordia, 1973.

Godfrey, George. *How to Win Souls and Influence People for Heaven.* Grand Rapids: Baker, 1973.

Hinkle, J. Herbert. *Soul Winning in Black Churches.* Grand Rapids: Baker, 1973.

Hogue, C.B. *Lifestyle Evangelism.* Atlanta, GA: Home Mission Board of the SBC, 1973.

Martin, O. Dean. *Invite: What Do You Do after the Sermon?* Nashville: Tidings, 1973.

1972 Anderson, Ken. *A Coward's Guide to Witnessing.* Carol Stream, IL: Creation House, 1972.

Brooks, W. Hal. *Follow Up Evangelism.* Nashville: Broadman, 1972.

Drummond, Lewis A. *Evangelism—The Counter Revolution.* London: Marshall, Morgan and Scott, 1972.

Feather, R. Othal. *Outreach Evangelism through the Sunday School.* Nashville: Convention, 1972.

Green, Hollis L. *Why Churches Die: A Guide to Basic Evangelism and Church Growth.* Minneapolis: Bethany Fellowship, 1972.

Hendricks, Howard G. *Say It with Love: The Art and Joy of Telling the Good News.* Foreword by Billy Graham. Wheaton, IL: Victor, 1972, 1973.

Jauncey, James H. *Psychology for Successful Evangelism.* Foreword by Leighton Ford. Chicago: Moody, 1972.

Neighbour, Ralph W., Jr., *The Touch of the Spirit.* Nashville: Broadman, 1972.

Poulton, John. *A Today Sort of Evangelism.* London: Lutterworth, 1972.

Turnbull, Ralph G., ed. *Evangelism Now.* Grand Rapids: Baker, 1972.

1971   Bisagno, John R. *How to Have an Evangelistic Church.* Nashville: Broadman, 1971.

Coggin, James E. *You Can Reach People Now.* Nashville: Broadman, 1971.

Grubb, Norman P. *Continuous Revival.* Fort Washington, PA: Christian Literature Crusade, 1971.

Lum, Ada. *How to Begin an Evangelistic Bible Study.* Downers Grove, IL: InterVarsity, 1971.

Mallough, Don. *Grassroots Evangelism.* Grand Rapids: Baker, 1971.

Starkes, M. Thomas. *Interfaith Witness.* Memphis: Brotherhood Commission, SBC, 1971.

White, Robert A. *How to Win a Soul.* Nashville: Southern Publication Association, 1971.

1970   Brown, Fred. *Secular Evangelism.* London: SCM, 1970.

Chantry, Walter J. Today's Gospel: Authentic or Synthetic. Banner of Truth, 1970.

Child, Kenneth. *In His Own Parish: Pastoral Care through Parochial Visiting.* London: SPCK, 1970.

Exum, Jack. *How to Win Souls Today.* Shreveport, LA: Lambert, 1970.

Havlik, John F. *People-Centered Evangelism.* Nashville: Broadman, 1970, 1971.

Green, Michael. *Evangelism in the Early Church.* Grand Rapids: Eerdmans, 1970.

Kennedy, Dennis James. *Evangelism Explosion.* Wheaton, IL: Tyndale House, 1970; rev ed., 1977; 3rd ed.; 4th ed., 1994, 1996.

Peters, George W. *Saturation Evangelism.* Grand Rapids: Zondervan, 1970.

Target, George W. *Tell It the Way It Is: A Primer for Christian Communicators.* London: Lutterworth, 1970.

1969   Bretscher, Paul G. *The Holy Infection: The Mission of the Church in Parish and Community.* In "The Witnessing Church Series." Saint Louis: Concordia, 1969.

Martin, Gerald E. *The Future of Evangelism.* Grand Rapids: Zondervan, 1969.

Mumma, Howard. E. *Take It to the People: New Ways in Soul Winning—Unconventional Evangelism* New York: World, 1969.

Murphey, Buddy. *Drawing the Net: The Soul Winners Workbook.* Corpus Christi, TX: Buddy Murphey, 1969.

Wilder, Jack B. *Biblical Blueprints for Building Witnessing Churches.* Tigerville, SC: Jewel, 1969.

1967   Henry, Carl F. H. and W. Stanley Mooneyham, eds. *One Race, One Gospel, One Task: World Congress on Evangelism, Berlin, 1966.* 2 vols. Minneapolis: World Wide Publications, 1967.

Metcalf, Harold E. *The Magic of Telephone Evangelism.* Atlanta: Southern Union Conference [of Seventh-Day Adventists], 1967.

Stott, John R. W. *Our Guilty Silence: The Church, The Gospel, The World.* Grand Rapids: Eerdmans, 1967, 1976.

1966   Ford, Leighton. *The Christian Persuader: A New Look at Evangelism Today.* New York: Harper and Row, 1966.

Krupp, Nate. *A World to Win: Secrets of New Testament Evangelism.* Minneapolis: Bethany Fellowship, 1966.

Little, Paul E. *How to Give Away Your Faith.* Downers Grove, IL: InterVarsity, 1966.

Rader, Lyell. *Re-discovering the Open Air Meeting; A Manual for Salvationist Soul-Winning.* Wilmore, KY: Asbury Theological Seminary, Evangelism Dept., 1966.

Scharpff, Paulus. *History of Evangelism: Three Hundred Years of Evangelism in Germany, Great Britain, and the United States of America,* trans. Helga Bender Henry. Grand Rapids: Eerdmans, 1966; trans *Geschichte der Evangelisation: Dreihundert Jahre Evangelisation in Deutschland, Großbritannien und USA.* Giessen, West Germany: Brunnen Verlag, 1964.

1965   Bender, Urie A. *The Witness.* Scottdale, PA: Herald Press, 1965.

Cullom, Peter E. *Visitation Evangelism Everywhere, as Did the Lord Jesus and Early Christians.* Washington, D.C.: Fishers of Men, 1965.

Graf, Arthur E. *The Church in a Community: An Effective Evangelism Program for the Christian Congregation.* Grand Rapids: Eerdmans, 1965.

McLarry, Newman R., ed., *Handbook on Evangelism: A Program of Evangelism for Southern Baptists.* Nashville: Convention, 1965.

Moseley, J. Edward, ed., *Evangelism—Commitment and Involvement.* St. Louis: Bethany, 1965.

Mueller, Charles S. *The Strategy of Evangelism: A Primer for Congregational Evangelism Committees.* Saint Louis: Concordia, 1965.

Riggs, Ralph, et al. *So Send I You—A Study In Personal Soul Winning.* Gospel Publishing, 1965.

Swearingen, Thomas E. and Mary G. *Heeding the Spirit in Evangelism.* Birmingham: Keystone, 1965.

1964   Augsburger, Myron. *Invitation to Discipleship: The Message of Evangelism.* Scottsdale, PN: Herald, 1964.

Leavell, Roland Q. *The Christian's Business: Being a Witness.* Nashville: Broadman, 1964.

Lovett, Cummings Samuel. *Witnessing Made Easy.* Baldwin Park, CA: Personal Christianity, 1964, 1971.

Wilson, Jim. *Principles of War: A Handbook on Strategic Evangelism.* Moscow, ID: Community Christian Ministries, 1964, 1983, 1991; under the title, *Against the Powers,* 1980.

Wood, Eernest J. *A Church Fulfilling Its Mission through Proclamation and Witness.* Nashville: SBC, 1964.

1963   Brown, Stanley C. *Evangelism in the Early Church: A Study in the Book of the Acts of the Apostles.* Grand Rapids: Eerdmans, 1963.

Coleman, Robert E. *The Master Plan of Evangelism.* Old Tappan, NJ: Revell, 1963.

Conant, J. E. *Soul-Winning Evangelism: The Good News in Action.* Grand Rapids, 1963.

Douglas, Mack R. *How to Build an Evangelistic Church.* Grand Rapids: Zondervan, 1963.

Olford, Stephen F. *The Secret of Soul-Winning.* Chicago: Moody, 1963, 1981.

1962 Davenport, Ray W. *A Syllabus for Classes in Personal Evangelism,* 6th Ed. Whittier, CA: Ray W. Davenport, 1962.

de Jong, Pieter. *Evangelism and Contemporary Theology: A Study of the Implications for Evangelism in the Thoughts of Six Modern Theologians.* Nashville: Tidings, 1962.

Edwards, Gene. *How to Have a Soul Winning Church.* Springfield, MO: Gospel Publishing, 1962.

Fletcher, Joseph. *Mission to Main Street: Five Study Units on the Work of the Church, the Function of the Lay Members, and the Place Where Witness Is Made.* Greenwich, CT: Seabury, 1962.

Hyles, Jack. *Let's Go Soul Winning: A Step by Step Guide in How to Lead a Soul to Christ.* Murfreesboro, TN: Sword of the Lord, 1962.

Rinker, Rosalind. *You Can Witness with Confidence.* Grand Rapids: Zondervan, 1962.

Southard, Samuel. *Pastoral Evangelism.* Nashville, Broadman, 1962; Atlanta: John Knox, 1981.

1961 Alabama Baptist State Convention, Department of Evangelism. *Evangelize or Die!* Montgomery: The Convention, 1961.

Autrey, C. E. *You Can Win Souls.* Nashville: Broadman, 1961.

Boer, Harry R. *Pentecost and Missions.* Lutterworth, 1961; Grand Rapids: Eerdmans, 1961, 1964.

Kuiper, Rienk Bouke *God Centered Evangelism.* Grand Rapids: Baker, 1961, 1975; Carlisle, PA: Banner of Truth, 1966, 1978.

Marty, Martin E. *The Improper Opinion: Mass Media and the Christian Faith.* Philadelphia: Westminster, 1961.

Messages on Evangelism: Delivered at Florida Baptist Evangelistic Conference, 1961. Orlando: Golden Rule, 1961.

Packer, J. I. *Evangelism and the Sovereignty of God.* Downers Grove, IL: InterVarsity, 1961.

Rice, John R. *The Golden Path to Successful Soul Winning.* Wheaton, IL: Sword of the Lord, 1961.

Sellers, James Earl. *The Outsider and the Word of God: A Study in Christian Communication.* New York: Abingdon, 1961.

Webster, Douglas. *What Is Evangelism?* London: Highway Press, 1961.

1960 Bayly, Joseph. *The Gospel Blimp.* Grand Rapids: Zondervan, 1960.

Cox, Harvey. *Manual for Church in World Witness: with Procedures for Church in World Conferences and Study Groups.* New York : Division of Evangelism, American Baptist Home Mission Societies, 1960.

Hobbs, Herschel H., *New Testament Evangelism: The Eternal Purpose.* Nashville, Convention, 1960.

Shoemaker, Samuel M. *With the Holy Spirit and with Fire.* New York: Harper and Brothers, 1960.

Stewart, James A. *Evangelism Without Apology: the Bob Jones University Lectures on Evangelism for 1959.* Grand Rapids: Kregel, 1960.

Tull, Nelson F. *Effective Christian Witnessing.* Memphis: Brotherhood Commission, SBC, 1960, 1971.

Washburn, Alphonso V. *Outreach for the Unreached.* Nashville: Convention, 1960.

1959 Autrey, C. E. *Basic Evangelism.* Grand Rapids: Zondervan, 1959; Memphis: Brotherhood Commission, SBC, 1960.

Feather, R. Othal. *A Manual for Promoting Personal Evangelism through the Sunday School.* Nashville: Convention Press, 1959.

Lovett, Cummings Samuel. *Soul-Winning Made Easy.* Baldwin Park, CA: Personal Christianity, 1959, 1978.

Lovett, Cummings Samuel. *Visitation Made Easy.* Baldwin Park, CA: Personal Christianity, 1959.

Sanderson, Leonard, ed. *Revival Plan Book.* Dallas: Division of Evangelism, Home Mission Board, Southern Baptist Convention, 1959-1960.

1958 Ellis, Howard W. *Evangelism for Teen-Agers.* New York: Abingdon, 1958.

Malone, Tom. *Essentials of Evangelism: Bob Jones University Lectures on Evangelism for 1958.* Murfreesboro, TN: Sword of the Lord, 1958.

McDormand, Thomas Bruce. *Evangelism and a Saving Faith for Modern Man.* 1958.

Powell, Sidney W. *Where Are the Converts?* Nashville: Broadman, 1958.

Sanderson, Leonard. *Personal Soul-Winning.* Nashville: Convention, 1958.

Sanderson, Leonard. *The Association in Evangelism.* Atlanta: Home Mission Board, SBC, 1958.

Sanderson, Leonard. *Using the Sunday School in Evangelism* Nashville: Convention, 1958.

1957 Colquhoun, Frank. *The Fellowship of the Gospel: A New Testament Study in the Principles of Christian Cooperation.* Grand Rapids: Zondervan, 1957.

Daniels, Elam Jackson. *Techniques of Torchbearing.* Grand Rapids: Zondervan, 1957.

Dean, Horace F. *Operation Evangelism: The Bob Jones University Lectures on Evangelism for 1957.* Grand Rapids: Zondervan, 1957.

Dean, Horace F. *Visitation Evangelism Made Practical: Reaching Your Community for Christ and the Church.* Grand Rapids: Zondervan, 1957.

Downey, Murray. *The Art of Soul-Winning.* Grand Rapids: Baker, 1957, 1983.

Freeman, Clifford Wade, ed. *The Doctrine of Evangelism [nineteen sermons].* Nashville: Baptist General Conference of Texas, 1957.

Grindstaff, Wilmer E. *Ways to Win: Methods of Evangelism for the Local Church.* Nashville: Broadman, 1957.

Misselbrook, Lawrence Richard. *Winning the People for Christ: An Experiment in Evangelism.* London: Carey Kingsgate, 1957..

Robinson, Godfrey C. and Stephen F. Winward. *The King's Business: A Handbook for Christian Workers.* England: Children's Special Service Mission, 1957, 1958; U.S. Edition, 1960.

Sanny, Lorne. *The Art of Personal Witnessing.* Chicago: Moody, 1957.

Shoemaker, Samuel M. *The Experiment of Faith: A Handbook for Beginners.* New York: Harper, 1957.

Templeton, Charles B. *Evangelism for Tomorrow.* New York: Harper, 1957.

1956 Gager, Leroy. *Handbook for Soul Winners.* Grand Rapids: Zondervan, 1956.

Gesswein, Armin Richard. *Is Revival the Normal?* Intro. by Billy Graham. Elizabethtown, PA: McBeth, 1956.

MacAulay, J. C. and Robert H. Belton. *Personal Evangelism.* Chicago: Moody, 1956.

McKay, Charles L. *The Call of the Harvest.* Nashville: Convention Press, 1956, 1976.

Short, Roy Hunter. *Evangelism through the Local Church* (New York: Abingdon, 1956.

1955 Adeney, David H. *The Unchanging Commission.* Chicago: Moody, 1955.

Hartt, Julian N. *Toward a Theology of Evangelism.* New York: Abingdon, 1955

Jones, Bob, Sr., *Evangelism Today: Where Is It Headed?* Greenville, SC: Bob Jones University, 1955.

Lee, Robert G. *How to Lead a Soul to Christ.* Grand Rapids: Zondervan, 1955.

O'Brien, John A. *Bringing Souls to Christ: Methods of Sharing the Faith with Others.* Introduction by Francis Cardinal Spellman. Garden City, NY: Hanover House, 1955.

Overholtzer, J. Irvin. *Handbook on Child Evangelism.* Grand Rapids: Child Evangelism Fellowship, 1955.

Sweeting, George. *The Evangelistic Campaign: A Book of Helps for Pastor and Evangelist.* Chicago: Moody, 1955.

1954 Chirgwin, Arthur Mitchell. *A Book in his Hand: A Manual of Colportage.* London: United Bible Societies, 1954.

Kantonen, Talto A. *The Theology of Evangelism.* Philadelphia: Muhlenberg, 1954.

Lawrence, J. B. *The Holy Spirit in Evangelism.* Grand Rapids: Zondervan, 1954.

1953 Sweazey, George E. *Effective Evangelism: The Greatest Work in the World.* New York: Harper and Row, 1953, 1976.

1952 Bryan, Dawson Charles. *Building Church Membership through Evangelism.* New York: Abingdon-Cokesbury, 1952.

Harrison, Eugene Myers. *How to Win Souls: A Manual of Personal Evangelism.* Wheaton, IL: Van Kampen, 1952; Wheaton, IL: Scripture Press, 1952.

Lewis, Edwin. *Theology and Evangelism.* Nashville: Tidings, 1952.

1951 Cook, Henry. *The Theology of Evangelism: The Gospel in the World of To-Day.* London: Carey Kingsgate, 1951.

Green, Bryan S. W. *The Practice of Evangelism.* London: Hodder and Stoughton, 1951, 1952; New York: Scribner, 1951.

Leavell, Roland Q. *Evangelism: Christ's Imperative Command.* Nashville: Broadman, 1951.

Munro, Harry C. *Fellowship Evangelism through Church Groups.* St. Louis: Cooperative Association, Bethany, 1951.

1950 Barnett, Minyard Merrill. *The Greatest of All Journeys: Soul Winner's Chart.* Fresno: CBF Press, 1950.

Ham, Edward E. *Fifty Years on the Battle Front with Christ: A Biography of Mordecai F. Ham.* Shelbyville, TN: Bible and Literature Missionary Foundation, 1950.

Head, Eldred Douglas. *Evangelism in Acts.* Fort Worth, TX: Southwestern Baptist Theological Seminary, 1950.

Rice, John R. *We Can Have Revival Now.* Wheaton, IL: Sword of the Lord, 1950.

Smith, Oswald J. *The Passion for Souls.* London: Marshall, Morgan and Scott, 1950, 1965.

1949 Dobbins, Gaines S. *Evangelism According to Christ.* Nashville: Broadman, 1949.

Matthews, C. E. *The Southern Baptist Program of Evangelism.* Atlanta: Home Mission Board, SBC, 1949.

Powell, Sidney Waterbury. *Toward the Great Awakening.* New York: Abingdon-Cokesbury, 1949.

Wells, Robert J. and John R. Rice, eds. *How to Have a Revival.* Wheaton, IL: Sword of the Lord, 1949.

Whitesell, Faris D. *Basic New Testament Evangelism.* Grand Rapids: Zondervan, 1949.

1948 Bryan, Dawson Charles. *Handbook on Evangelism for Laymen.* New York: Abingdon-Cokesbury, 1948.

O'Brien, John A. *Winning Converts: A Symposium on Methods of Convert Making for Priests and Lay People.* New York: P. J. Kennedy, 1948.

1947 Henry, Carl F. H. *The Uneasy Conscience of Modern Fundamentalism.* Grand Rapids: Eerdmans, 1947.

Kemp, Charles F. *Physicians of the Soul.* New York: Macmillan, 1947).

1946 Archibald, Arthur C. *New Testament Evangelism: How It Works.* Philadelphia: Judson, 1946, 1947.

Benson, Clarence H. *Techniques of a Working Church.* Chicago: Moody, 1946.

Cushman, Ralph Spalding. *The Essentials of Evangelism.* Nashville: Tidings, General Board of Evangelism, The Methodist Church, 1946.

Matthews, C. E. *The Department of Evangelism and the Simultaneous Revival Program.* Dallas: Baptist General Convention of Texas, 1946.

McCullough, William James. *Home Visitation Evangelism for Laymen: A Manual.* New York: American Baptist Home Mission Society, 1946.

Muncy, William L., Jr. *New Testament Evangelism for Today.* Kansas City, KS: Central Seminary, 1946.

Stone, John Timothy. *Winning Men; Studies in Soul-Winning.* New York: Revell, 1946.

White, Ellen G. *Evangelism.* Review and Herald, 1946.

Wood, Verda. *Ringing Door Bells : the Art of Visiting.* Nashville: Baptist Sunday School Board, 1946.

1945 Barton, Levi Elder. *Helps for Soul Winners.* Montgomery: Paragon, 1945.

Muncy, William L., Jr. *A History of Evangelism in the United States.* Kansas City, KS: Central Seminary, 1945.

Whitesell, Faris D. *Sixty-Five Ways to Give Evangelistic Invitations.* Grand Rapids: Zondervan, 1945.

1944 Berge, Selmer Alonzo. *Evangelism in the Congregation.* Minneapolis: Faith Action Movement, 1944.

1943 Beardsley, Frank G. *Religious Progress Through Revivals.* New York: American Tract Society, 1943.

Homrighausen, Elmer G. *Choose Ye This Day: A Study of Decision and Commitment in Christian Personality.* Philadelphia: Westminster, 1943.

1942 Appelman, Hyman. *The Call to Conversion: Have You Been Born Again?* Philadelphia: Blakiston; New York: Revell, 1942.

Blackwood, Andrew Watterson. *Evangelism in the Home Church.* New York: Abingdon-Cokesbury, 1942.

Leavell, Frank H. *Christian Witnessing.* Nashville: Broadman Press, 1942.

Leavell, Roland Q. *The Romance of Evangelism.* New York: Revell, 1942.

1941 Bothwell, Robert H. "New Testament Principles of Personal Evangelism." B.D. Thesis, Northern Baptist Theological Seminary, 1941.

Conant, J. E. *No Salvation without Substitution.* Grand Rapids: Eerdmans, 1941.

Ellis, Howard W. *Fishing for Men: Including a Suggested Scheme of Organization for Bands of "Fishermen" Together with a Plan and Program for Winning Those Who Are Lost and for Enlisting the Unenlisted Saved in the Service of Christ.* Grand Rapids: Zondervan, 1941.

Ownbey, Richard L. *Evangelism in Christian Education.* Nashville: Abingdon, 1941.

Rice, John R. *The Soul-Winner's Fire.* Wheaton, IL: Sword of the Lord, 1941.

1940 Murray, Arthur L. *Reaching the Unchurched.* New York: Round Table, 1940.

1939 Campbell, Robert C. *The Coming Revival.* Nashville: Broadman, 1939.

Leavell, Roland Q. *Helping Others to Become Christians.* Atlanta: Home Mission Board, SBC, 1939.

McFatridge, F. V. *The Personal Evangelism of Jesus* (Grand Rapids: Zondervan, 1939).

Scarborough, L. R. *Gay Lectures on Evangelism 1939.* 1939.

Trimble, Henry Burton. *To Every Creature.* Nashville: Cokesbury, 1939.

White, F. C. *Evangelism Today.* London: Marshall, Morgan, and Scott, 1939.

1938 Chambers, Oswald. *Workmen of God.* New York: Grosset and Dunlap, 1938.

Hamilton, William Wistar. *Highways and edges.* Nashville: Broadman, 1938.

Hedstrom, C. B. *"Pay Day—Some day": with Other Sketches from Life and Messages from the Word.* Grand Rapids: Zondervan, 1938.

1937 Bader, Jesse M., ed. *The New Message and Method of the New Evangelism: A Joint Statement of the Evangelistic Mission of the Church.* New York: Round Table, 1937.

Haynes, Carlyle B. *Living Evangelism.* Tacoma Park, WA: Review and Herald, 1937.

Morgan, G. Campbell, *The Great Physician* (New York: Revell, 1937).

Muncy, William L., Jr. *New Testament Evangelism.* Kansas City: Central Seminary Press, 1937.

Phillips, William A. *The Follow-Up in Evangelism.* Philadelphia: The John Mason Jackson Fund of the American Baptist Publication Society, 1937.

Spurr, Frederic C. *The Evangelism for OUR Time.* London: Epworth, 1937.

1936 Bailey, Ambrose M. *Evangelism in a Changing World.* New York: Round Table Press, 1936.

Clark, Elmer T., ed., *Methodism Vitalized,* Studies in Evangelism by Bishops John M. Moore, A. Frank Smith, W. N. Ainsworth, and Paul B. Kern. Nashville: Board of Missions, Methodist Episcopal Church, South, 1936.

Dodd, C. H. *Apostolic Preaching and Its Development.* London: Hodder and Stoughton, 1936.

Hough, Lynn Harold. *The Great Evangel.* Nashville: Cokesbury, 1936.

Houghton, Will H. *Lessons in Soul-Winning.* Chicago: Moody Bible Institute of Chicago, 1936.

Leavell, Roland Q. *Winning Others to Christ.* Nashville: Sunday School Board of the SBC, 1936; Nashville: Convention, 1936.

MacDonald, William C. *Modern Evangelism.* London: James Clarke, 1936, 1937.

Orr, J. Edwin. *This Is the Victory: 10,000 Miles of Miracle in America.* London: Marshall, Morgan and Scott, 1936; Grand Rapids: Zondervan, 1936.

Sunday School Board, *Ringing Door Bells: the Art of Visiting.* Nashville: Department of Young People's and Adult Sunday School Work, Sunday School Board, Southern Baptist Convention, 1936.

Warren, Max. *Interpreters: A Study in Contemporary Evangelism.* London: Highway Press, 1936.

Wilson, Walter Lewis. *Let's Go Fishing with the Doctor.* Findlay, OH: Fundamental Truth, 1936; Grand Rapids: Dunham, 1964.

1935 Crawford, Percy B. *The Art of Fishing for Men.* Philadelphia: The Mutual, 1935.

Hamilton, William Wistar. *The Fine Art of Soul-Winning.* Nashville: Sunday School Board of the SBC, 1935.

Mott, John R. *Cooperation and the World Mission.* New York: International Missionary Council, 1935.

Orr, J. Edwin. *The Promise Is to You: 10,000 Miles of Miracle—to Palestine.* London: Marshall, Morgan and Scott, 1935.

1934 Burroughs, Prince Emanuel. *How to Win to Christ.* Nashville: Sunday School Board of the SBC, 1934; Nashville: Convention, 1934.

Cartwright, Lin D. *Evangelism for Today.* St. Louis: Bethany, 1934, 1943.

Flake, Arthur. *Building a Standard Sunday School.* Nashville: Sunday School Board of the Southern Baptist Convention, 1934.

Lowry, Oscar. *Scripture Memory for Successful Soul-Winning.* New York: Revell, 1934.

Orr, J. Edwin. *God Can——? "10,000 Miles of Miracles in Britain."* London: Marshall, Morgan and Scott, 1934; Grand Rapids: Zondervan, 1934.

Wood, Frederick P. *Studies in Soul-Winning.* London: Marshall Brothers, National Young Life Campaign, 1934; Rev. Ed. London: Marshall, Morgan and Scott, 1934.

1933 De Blois, Austen Kennedy. *Evangelism in the New Age.* Philadelphia: Judson, 1933.

Smith, J. Oswald. *The Revival We Need.* Foreword by Jonathan Goforth. London: Marshall, Morgan and Scott, 1933; 1940.

1932 [Hocking Report]. *Rethinking Missions: A Laymen's Inquiry after One Hundred Years.* New York: Harper and Brothers, 1932.

Shoemaker, Samuel M. *The Conversion of the Church.* New York: Revell, 1932.

1930 Dodd, M. E. *Missions Our Mission.* Nashville: Sunday School Board of the SBC, 1930.

Massee, Jasper C. *The Pentecostal Fire: Rekindling the Flame.* Philadelphia: Judson, 1930

Massee, Jasper C. *Rekindling the Pentecostal Fire.* Butler, IN: Higley, 1930.

Reisner, Christian F. *Disciple Winners.* New York: Abingdon, 1930.

1929 Cooper, Raymond W. *Modern Evangelism: A Practical Course in Effective Evangelistic Methods.* New York: Revell, 1929.

Hamilton, William Wistar. *Wisdom in soul winning.* Nashville: Sunday School Board of the SBC, 1929.

Herrick, Carl E. *Modern Evangelism: A Practical Course in Effective Evangelistic Methods.* New York: Revell, 1929.

Kernahan, A. Earl. *Christian Citizenship and Visitation Evangelism.* New York: Revell, 1929.

Neil, Samuel Graham. *A Great Evangelism.* Philadelphia: Judson, 1929.

1928 Clark, Glenn, *Fishers of Men.* Boston: Little, Brown, 1928.

Cowan, John F. *New Youth Evangelism: for Workers Among Young People of To-day.* New York: Revell, 1928.

Lewis, Sinclair. *Elmer Gantry.* Berlin: E. Rowolht, 1928; New York: Harcourt, Brace, 1929.

Loud, Grover Cleveland. *Evangelized America.* New York, L. MacVeagh, the Dial Press, 1928; Toronto, Longmans, Green, 1928; Freeport, NY: Books for Libraries Press, 1971.

McDowell, William Fraser. *That I May Save Some.* New York: Abingdon, 1928.

Visser 't Hooft, W. A. *The Background of the Social Gospel in America.* Haarlem: H. D. Tjeenk Willink and Zoon, 1928; St. Louis, MO: Bethany Press, 1963, 1968.

1927 Taylor, Frederick Eugene. *The Evangelistic Church.* Philadelphia: Judson, 1927.

Zahniser, Charles Reed. *Case Work Evangelism: Studies in the Art of Christian Personal Work.* New York: Revell, 1927.

1926 Goodell, Charles L. *Motives and Methods in Modern Evangelism.* New York: Revell, 1926.

Scarborough, L. R. *How Jesus Won Men.* Nashville: Tennessee Sunday School Board, 1926.

Speer, Robert E. *The Church and Missions.* London: James Clarke, n.d.; New York, George H. Doran, 1926.

1925 Chappell, E. B. *Evangelism in the Sunday School.* Nashville: Methodist Episcopal Church, South, 1925.

Crume, Thomas Clinton. *Evangelism in Action.* Louisville: Pentecostal, 1925.

Kernahan, A. Earl. *Visitation Evangelism: Its Methods and Results.* New York: Revell, 1925, 1935.

Scarborough, L. R. *A Search for Souls: A Study in the Finest of the Arts—Winning the Lost to Christ.* Nashville: Tennessee Sunday School Board, 1925.

Stilwell, H. F. *The Stewardship of Evangelism.* New York: Board of Missionary Cooperation of the NBC, 1925.

1924 Rockey, Carroll J. *Fishing for Fishers of Men.* Philadelphia: United Lutheran, 1924.

1923 Fletcher, Lionel B. *The Effective Evangelist.* New York: George H. Doran, 1923; London: Hodder and Stoughton, 1923.

Sellers, Ernest O. *Personal Evangelism: Studies in Individual Efforts to Lead Souls into Right Relations to Christ.* Nashville: Sunday School Board of the SBC, 1923; New York: Doran, 1923.

1922 Conant, J. E. *Every Member Evangelism.* New York: Harper and Brothers, 1922; revised by Roy Fish, 1976.

Gage, Albert H. *Evangelism of Youth.* Philadelphia: Judson, 1922.

Hicks, Joseph P. *Ten Lessons in Personal Evangelism.* New York: Doran, 1922.

Scarborough, L. R. *Endued to Win.* Nashville: Sunday School Board of the SBC, 1922.

1921 Biederwolf, William E. *Evangelism: Its Justification, Its Operation and Its Value.* New York: Revell, 1921.

Hannan, F. Watson. *Evangelism.* New York: Methodist Book Concern, 1921.

1920 Bryan, O. E. *The Ethics of Evangelism.* Louisville: The Southern Baptist Theological Seminary, 1920.

Stewart, George, Jr. and Henry B. Wright, *Personal Evangelism among Students: Studies in the Practice of Friendship in School and College.* New York: Association, 1920.

1919 Johnston, Howard A. *Enlisting for Christ and the Church.* New York: Association, 1919.

Morgan, G. Campbell. *The Ministry of the Word.* New York: Revell, 1919.

Pell, Edward Leigh. *How Can I Lead my Pupils to Christ?* New York: Revell, 1919.

Scarborough, L. R. *With Christ After the Lost.* Nashville: Tennessee Sunday School Board, 1919; New York: George H. Doran, 1919; Nashville: Broadman, 1919, 1952, 1953.

1918 Stewart, George. *The Practice of Friendship: Studies in Personal Evangelism with Men of the United States Army and Navy in American Training Camps.* New York: Association, 1918.

Trumbull, Charles G. *What Is the Gospel? Straightforward Talks on Evangelism.* Philadelphia: Sunday School Times, 1918; New York: Harper and Brothers, 1918; Minneapolis: The Harrison Service, 1944.

1917 Condé, Bertha. *The Human Element in the Making of a Christian: Studies in Personal Evangelism.* New York: Scribner's, 1917.

Rauschenbusch, Walter. *A Theology for the Social Gospel.* New York: Macmillan, 1917; Nashville: Abingdon, 1978.

Torrey, Reuben A. *Individual Soulwinning.* Los Angeles: Biola, 1917.

Truett, George W. *A Quest for Souls.* New York: Doran, 1917; Nashville: Broadman, 1917.

1916 Faris, John T. *The Book of Personal Work.* New York: Doran, 1916.

1915 Ward, Harry Frederick. *Social Evangelism.* New York: Missionary Education Movement of the U.S. and Canada, 1915.

Weatherford, W. D. *Introducing Men to Christ: Fundamental Studies.* New York: Association Press, 1915.

1914 Burroughs, Prince Emanuel. *Winning to Christ.* Nashville: Tennessee Sunday School Board, 1914, 1923.

Riley, W. B. *The Crisis of the Church.* New York: Cook, 1914.

Scarborough, L. R. *Recruits for World Conquest.* New York: Revell, 1914.

1913 Dean, John Marvin. *Evangelism and Social Service.* Philadelphia: Griffith & Rowland, 1913.

1911 Kilpatrick, Thomas B. *New Testament Evangelism.* 1911.

Chafer, Lewis Sperry. *True Evangelism or Winning Souls by Prayer.* 1st ed. Philadelphia: Sunday School Times, 1911; 2nd ed., Philadelphia: Sunday School Times, 1919; Wheaton, IL: Van Kampen; Grand Rapids: Zondervan, 1967, 16th printing, 1981; Grand Rapids: Kregel, 1993, 2015.

1910 Evans, William. *Personal Soul-Winning.* Chicago: Moody, 1910.

Green, Oscar Olin. *Normal Evangelism.* New York: Revell, 1910.

Stone, John Timothy. *Recruiting for Christ: Hand to Hand Methods with Men.* New York: Revell, 1910.

1909 Hamilton, William Wistar. *Sane Evangelism.* Philadelphia: American Baptist, 1909. Contents: Introduction.

—Denominational evangelism, by G. W. Truett.

—Sane aggressive evangelism, by W. W. Hamilton.

—The primary mission of the churches of Jesus Christ, by L. R. Scarborough.

—Fundamentals of evangelism, by L. O. Dawson.

—New Testament evangelism, by B. H. Carroll.

—How the average pastor may make the regular service an evangelistic force, by E. C. Dargan.

—Personal evangelism, by H. A. Porter.

—The power of Pentecost, by L. G. Broughton.

—Methods in evangelism. by W. W. Hamilton.

—Caring for young converts, by W. W. Hamilton.

1908 Gordon, S. D. *Quiet Talks with World Winners.* New York: A. C. Armstrong, 1908.

Sheridan, Wilbur Fletcher. *The Sunday-Night Service: A Study in Continuous Evangelism.* Cincinnati: Jennings and Graham; New York: Eaton and Mains, 1908.

1907 Goodell, Charles L. *Pastoral and Personal Evangelism.* New York: Revell, 1907.

Harnack, Adolf and Wilhelm Hermann. *Essays on the Social Gospel.* London: Williams and Norgate, 1907.

MacLean, John Kennedy. *Triumphant Evangelism: The Three Years Mission of Dr. Torrey and Mr. Alexander in Great Britain and Ireland.* London: Marshall, 1907.

Peile, James H. F. *The Reproach of the Gospel: An Inquiry into the Apparent Failure of Christianity as a General Rule of Life and Conduct, with a Special Reference to the Present Time.* London: Longmans, Green, 1907.

Trumbull, Charles Gallaudet. *Taking Men Alive: Studies in the Principles and Practise of Individual Soul-Winning.* New York: The International Committee of the YMCA, 1907; 1915; New York: Revell, 1938.

1906 Mabie, Henry C. *Method in Soul-Winning: on Home and Foreign Fields.* New York: Revell, 1906.

1905 Davenport, Frederick Morgan, *Primitive Traits in Religious Revivals: A Study in Mental and Social Evolution.* New York: Macmillan, 1905.

Jowett, John Henry. *The Passion for Souls.* Chicago: Revell, 1905.

1904 Riley, W. B. *The Perennial Revival: A Plea for Evangelism.* Chicago: The Winona Publishing Company, 1904; Philadelphia: American Baptist Publication Society, 1916.

1903 Chapman, J. Wilbur. *Present Day Evangelism.* New York: Revell, 1903, 1913.

1902 Banks, Louis Albert. *Soul Winning Stories.* New York: American Tract, 1902; New York: George H. Doran, 1902.

1901 Mallalieu, W. F. *The Why, When and How of Revivals.* New York: Eaton and Mains; Cincinnati: Jennings and Pye, 1901.

Torrey, Reuben A. *How to Work for Christ: A Compendium of Effective Methods.* New York: Revell, 1901; Los Angeles: Revell, 1920 [includes Book One, "Personal Work;" Book Two, "Methods of Christian Work;" and Book Three, "Preaching and Teaching the Word of God"]. 518 pages.

Torrey, Reuben A. *Personal Work* [part one of *How to Work for Christ*]. New York: Revell, 1901.

Torrey, Reuben A., ed. *How to Promote and Conduct a Successful Revival.* Chicago: Revell, 1901.

Trumbull, Henry Clay. *Individual Work for Individuals: A Record of Personal Experiences and Convictions.* New York: The International Committee of the Young Men's Christian Associations, 1901.

1900 Johnston, James, ed. *Ecumenical Missionary Conference, New York, 1900: Report of the Ecumenical Conference on Foreign Missions, Held in Carnegie Hall and Neighboring Churches, April 21 to May 1.* New York: American Tract Society, 1900.

Torrey, Reuben A. *The Missionary's Message—The Full Gospel.* Los Angeles: Biola, n.d.

Torrey, Reuben A. *The Wondrous Joy of Soul Winning.* London: The "One by One" Working Band; Los Angeles: Biola, n.d.

1898 Gladden, Washington. *The Christian Pastor and the Working Church.* New York: Scribner's, 1898.

1897 Brealey, W. J. H. *Always Abounding: or, Recollections of the Life and Labours of the Late George Brealey, the Evangelist of the Blackdown Hills.* Kilmarnock, Scotland: John Ritchie, 1897; London: W. G. Wheeler, 1897; London: John F. Shaw, 1897; Glasgow: Pickering & Inglis, 1897; London: S. Bagster & Sons, 1897; New York: Gospel Pub. House, 1897.

1895 Doe, Walter P., ed. *Revivals. How to Promote Them. As Taught and Exemplified by...* New and enlarged edition. New York: E. B. Treat, 1884, 1895.

1894 Peck, Jonas O. *The Revival and the Pastor.* New York: Eaton and Mains; Cincinnati: Curts and Jennings, 1894.

1893 Torrey, Reuben A. *How to Bring Men to Christ.* New York: Revell, 1893; Chicago: Moody, 1910; Minneapolis: Bethany, 1977.

1892 Banks, Louis Albert. *The Revival Quiver.* Boston: Lee and Shepard, 1892.

Pierson, A. T. *From the Pulpit to the Palm-Branch: A Tribute to Charles Haddon Spurgeon.* New York, A.C. Armstrong, 1892.

Shindler, Robert Doy. *From the Usher's Desk to the Tabernacle Pulpit: The Life and Labors of Charles Haddon Spurgeon.* New York: American Tract Society, 1892; New York: A. C. Armstrong, 1892; London: Passmore and Alabaster, 1892.

1890 Knapp, Martin Wells. *Revival Kindlings.* Cincinnati: God's Revivalist Office, 1890.

1888 Gall, James. *The Evangelistic Baptism Indispensable to the Church for the Conversion of the World.* "Science of Mission." Edinburgh: Gall and Inglis, 1888.

Johnston, James, ed. *Report of the Centenary Conference on the Protestant Missions of the World Held in Exeter Hall (June 9th-19th), London, 1888.* New York: Revell, 1888.

Thwing, Charles Franklin. *The Working Church,* New York: Baker and Taylor, 1888; rev. ed. 1889; New York: Revell, 1913.

1887 Pierson, A. T. *Evangelistic Work in Principles and Practice.* New York: Baker and Taylor, 1887; London: Dickinson, 1888; rev. ed., London: Passmore and Alabaster, 1892.

1884 Hervey, George Winfred. *Manual of Revivals: Practical Hints and Suggestions from Histories of Revivals and Biographies of Revivalists, with Themes for the Use of Pastors and Missionaries Before, During, and After Special Services, Including the Texts, Subjects, and Outlines of the Sermons of Many Distinguished Evangelists.* New York: Funk and Wagnall's, 1884.

1876 Spurgeon, Charles Haddon. *Lectures to My Students: A Slection of Addresses Delivered to the Students of thte Pastors' College, Metropolitain Tabernacle.* London: Passmore and Alabaster, 1876, 1887, 1894, 1900.

1874 Fish, Henry Clay. *Handbook of Revivals: For the Use of Winners of Souls.* Boston: J. H. Earle, 1874.

1870 Bonar, Horatius. *Words to Winners of Souls.* Boston: American Tract Society, 1870.

1868 Earle, Absalom B. [and J. C. Buttre]. *Bringing in the Sheaves.* Boston: James H. Earle, 1868, 1869, 1872.

1859 Humphrey, Heman. *Revival Sketches and Manual: in Two Parts.* New York: American Tract Society, 1859.

1856 Taylor, William. *Seven Years Street Preaching in San Francisco: Embracing Incidents, Triumphant Death Scenes, Etc.* New York: Carlton and Porter, 1856, 1857, 1858.

1853 Spencer, Ichabod [pastor, 2nd Presbyterian, Brooklyn, NY; founder of Union Theological Seminary]. *Conversations with Anxious Souls Concerning the Way of Salvation.* New York: M. W. Dodd, 1853; Solid Ground, 2006.

Spurgeon, Charles H. *The Soul Winner; Or, How to Lead Sinners to the Saviour.* New York: Revell, 1853, 1895; London: Marshall, 1893; London: Passmore and Alabaster, 1895, 1897; Baltimore: Wharton, 1886; Grand Rapids: Zondervan, 1947, 1948; Grand Rapids: Eerdmans, 1963, 1964, 1995.

Stone, Barton Warren. *The Biography of Eld. Barton Warren Stone, Written by Himself: with Additions and Reflections by Elder John Rogers.* Cincinnati , OH: American Christian Publication Society, 1853; Forgotten Books, 2012.

1844 Andrew A. Bonar, *Memoir and Remains of Rev. Robert Murray McCheyne, Minister of St. Peter's, Dundee.* Philadelphia: Presbyterian Board, 1844; New York: Carter, 1849, 1860; Abridged version, Chicago: Moody, 1947; London: Banner of Truth, 1962, 1972, 1990; *Robert Murray McCheyne: A Biography.* Grand Rapids: Zondervan, 1983.

1832 Sprague, William B. *Lectures on the Revival of Religion.* 1832; London: Banner of Truth Trust, 1959.

1825 A chronology of select editions of Finney *On Revival* (oldest to newest):[53]

1825 (396 pages): Finney, Charles G. *Lectures on the Revivals of Religion: From Notes by the Editor of "New York Evangelist," Revised by the Author [1825].* From 6th American Edition, 2nd British Edition [hence 8th Edition]. London: Milner [Paternoster Row], 1838. 396 pages.

1835 (438 pages, 20cm): Finney, Charles G. *Lectures on the Revivals of Religion.* New York: Leavitt, Lord; Boston: Crocker and Brewster; London: Milner and Sowerby, 1835.

1839 (396 pages): Finney, Charles G. *Lectures on the Revivals of Religion.* 9th Edition. London: Thomas Tegg, 1839. 396 pages.

1868 (445 pages): Finney, Charles G. *Lectures on the Revivals of Religion: A New Edition.* Revised and enlarged. Oberlin, OH: E. J. Goodrich, 1868. 445 pages.

Arranged: Finney, Charles G. *Finney on Revival,* **arranged** by E. E. Shelhamer. **1834**, 1839, 1850, 1868; Minneapolis: Bethany House, 1988; 120 pages.

Modified: Finney, Charles G. *Lectures on Revival,* Kevin Walter Johnson, ed., a **modified** edition of *Lectures on Revivals of Religion,* **1835**; Minneapolis: Bethany House, 1988; 288 pages.

Finney, Charles G. *True and False Repentance: Evangelistic Sermons.* Grand Rapids: Kregel, 1966.

1792 Carey, William. "An Enquiry whether the Commission given by our Lord to His Disciples be not still Binding on Us," in *An Enquiry into the Obligations of Christians to use Means for the Conversion of the Heathen.* 1792.

1784 Fuller, Andrew. *The Gospel Worthy of All Acceptation.* 1784.

1769 Gill, John. *Body of Divinity.* London: George Keith, 1769; Tegg, 1839; Grand Rapids: Baker, 1978.

1749 Edwards, Jonathan. *An Account of the Life of the Late Reverent Mr. David Brainerd [1718-1747], Minister of the Gospel, Missionary to the Indians, from the Honourable Society in Scottland for the Propagation of Christian Knowledge…* Boston: Henchman, 1749 [334 pp.]; New York: American Tract Society, 1820 [360 pp.].

1736 Edwards, Jonathan. *Jonathan Edwards on Revival: A Narrative of Surprising Conversions* [1736], *The Distinguishing Marks of a Work of the Holy Spirit* [1941]; *An Account of the Revival of Religion in Northampton* [1740-1742]. Edinburgh: Banner of Truth, 1965.

1735 Gill, John. *The Cause of God and Truth.* London: Aaron Ward, 1735.

---

[53]There appears to be an interesting theological shift in Finney's approach to evangelism in approximately 1835. Note the comments in *Evangelizology,* Chapter 7, B. Some Historic Looks at and Terms for Evangelism; 7. Sample Terminology in the 19th and 20th Centuries; b. Charles Grandison Finney, *Lectures on Revival.*

1707	Hussey, Joseph. *The Glory of Christ Vindicated, ...* London: William and Joseph Marshall, 1707; Philadelphia: printed by Joseph Crukshank for John M'Gibbons, 1771.

1678	John Bunyan, *Pilgrim's Progress.* London: Nathaniel Ponder, 1678 [hundreds of editions following this one].

1660	van Braght, Thieleman J. *The Bloody Theater or Martyrs Mirror of the Defenseless Christians Who Baptized Only Upon Profession of Faith...,* trans. by Joseph F. Sohm (1660; 1748; 1837; 1853; Scottdale, PA: Herald Press, 2007).

1658	Baxter, Richard. *Call to the Unconverted to Turn and Live, and to Accept the Mercy While Mercy may Be Had, as Ever, They Would Find Mercy in the Day of their Extermity.* London: R.W., 1658.

1647	Owen, John (1616-1683). *Death of Death in the Death of Christ.* 1647; Edinburgh: Banner of Truth, 1959.

1564	Coverdale, Miles. *Certain most godly, fruitful, and comfortable letters of such true saintes and holy martyrs as in the late bloodye persecution gave their lyves.* London: J. Day, 1564.

1563	Foxe, John. *Acts and Monuments of these latter and perillous dayes....* London: J. Day, 1563, 1583.

1559	van Haemstede, Adrian-Cornelis. *De Geschiedenisse....* Dordrecht: Emden, 1559.

1556	Illyricus, Matthias Flavius. *Catalogus testium Veritatis qui ante nostram aetatem reclamarunt pape.* Basel: J. Oporinus, 1556.

1555	Rabus, Ludwig. *Historien der heyligen ausserwölten Gottes Zeügen, Bekennern und martyrern. Der dritte Theyl.* Strasbourg, 1555. [German martyrology]

	Sleidan, Johannes. *De statu religionis et republicae, Carolo Quinto Caesare Commentarii.* Strasbourg, 1555. [Latin church history]

1554	Crespin, Jean. *Histoire des vrays Tesmoins de la verite de l'evangile, qui de leur sang l'ont signée, depuis Jean Hus iusques autemps present* [*History of the True Witnesses to the Truth of the Gospel, Who with Their Blood Signed, from John Hus to the Present*]. Geneva, 1554, 1555, 1556, 1561, 1564, 1570; reproduction, Liège, 1964. [Most Protestant Martyrologies taught how to share the Gospel and take a stand for Jesus]

	Foxe, John. *Commentarii Rerum in Ecclesia Gestarum. Liber primus.* Strasbourg: W. Rihel, 1554, 1559.

1546	Askewe, Anne. *The first examinacyon Anne Askew, Lately martyred in Smythfelde.* London: J. Bale; Wessel: Dirk van der Straten, 1546.

1540	Calvin, John. "A Letter to Some Friends" (1540), "A Short Treatise" (1543), "Answer of John Calvin to the Nicodemite Gentlemen Concerning Their Complaint That He Is Too Severe" (1544), "Four Sermons" (1552), "A Response to a Certain Dutchman" (1562), in *Come Out From Among Them: 'Anti-Nicodemite' Writings of John Calvin.* Trans. By Seth Solnitsky. Dallas: Protestant Heritage, 2001.

1525	Francois Lambert d'Avignon. *Le Martyre de Jehan Chastellain.* Strasbourg, 1525.

1524	Hubmaier, Balthasar. *Von Ketzern and ihren Verbrennern* [*On Heretics and Those Who Burn Them*]. written in Schaffhausen, 1524.

1523	Luther, Martin. *Der Actus und hendlung der Degradation und verprennung der Christliche dreien Ritter und merterer Augustiner ordens geschehen zu Brussel.* Wittenberg, 1523; Lutehr also wrote his first hymn about these martyrs: "Eyn new lied von den zween Merterern Christi, zu Brussel von den Sophisten zu Löwen verbrant ("A new song of the two martyrs of Christ burned in Brussels by the Sophists of Louvain").[54]

---

[54]Akerboom, T.H.M. (University of Tilburg), "'A new song we raise'. On the First Martyrs of the Reformation and the Origin of Martin Luther's First Hymn"; *Perichoresis* 4/1 (2006), 53-77; from: http://www.emanuel.ro/wp-content/uploads/2014/06/P-4.1-2006-T.-H.-M.-Akerboom-A-New-Song-We-Raise.pdf (Online); accessed: 1 Nov 2017; Internet.

II. Other Evangelism Resources:

Sample Internet Evangelism Helps (alphabetical order; inclusion on this list is not meant to be an endorsement; all accessed 14 June 2012):

Tracts:
2 Ways to Live; available at: http://www.matthiasmedia.com.au/2wtl.
Bridge to Life: available at: http://www.lifebpc.com/resources/bridgelife.htm.
Chick Publications: available at: http://www.chick.com/catalog/tractlist.asp.
DigiTracts: The Roman Road: available at: http://www.fishthe.net/digitracts/roman.htm.
Four Spiritual Laws: available at: http://www.godlovestheworld.com.
The Good News: available at: http://www.thegoodnews.org.
Peace with God: available at: peacewithgod.net.
Salvation: available at: http://www.saved.com/index.htm.
The Story: available at: http://viewthestory.com/; also: http://vimeo.com/thestory.
There Is Hope: available at: http://www.evangelismunlimited.org/ThereIsHope_LegalSize.pdf.

Tract Publishers:
[In alphabetical order; inclusion on this list does not indicate an endorsement]
Agape Force Central, P.O. 386, Lindale, TX 75771: "These Are the Facts."
American Messianic Fellowship, Lynwood, IL 60411: "L'Chaïm," "A Fisherman's Life;" available at: www.amfi.org
American Tract Society, P.O. Box 462008, Garland, TX 75046-2008; available at: www.atstracts.org
As Chosen To Serve Ministries, 1123 W. Acacia Ave, Hemet, CA 92543; available at: www.actstracts.com
Bible tracts, P.O Box 188, Bloomington, IL 61702-0188.
Billy Graham Evangelistic Association, Charlotte, NC 28201: "Steps to Peace with God"; available at: www.billygraham.org
Cambridge Gospel Literature, P.O. Box 138, Cambridge, IA 50046.
Campus Crusade for Christ Int'l, San Bernardino, CA 92414: "Four Spiritual Laws," "The Spirit-Filled Life," "Your Most Important Relationship;" available at: www.ccci.org
Four Spiritual Laws: available at: http://www.godlovestheworld.com
Chick Publications, P.O. Box 662, Chino, CA 91710: "This Was Your Life," "Big Daddy," "Hi There!" available at: http://www.chick.com/catalog/tractlist.asp
Child Evangelism Fellowship Inc., P.O. Box 348, Warrenton, MO 63383: "Wordless Book"; available at: www.cefonline.com
Christian Equippers International, 2100 Eloise Ave., South Lake Tahoe, CA 96150, "Two Question Test"; available at: www.equipper.com
Collegiate Crusade for Christ, Inc., P.O. Box 6131, Norfolk, VA 23508.
Continuous Witness Training: Apprentice Manual. Alpharetta, GA: North American Mission Board, 1982, 1995.
Cross Evangelism Training: available at: http://www.shareasyougo.com/cross-evangelism
David Edwards Productions, Oklahoma City, OK 73156: "How to Make Life All Good;" available at: www.davetown.com
DigiTracts: The Roman Road: available at: http://www.fishthe.net/digitracts/roman.htm
EvangeCube; available at: available at: http://www.e3resources.org
Evangelism Explosion Int'l, P.O. Box 23820, Ft. Lauderdale, FL 33307, "Do You Know?" available at: www.eeinternational.org
Evangelism Tackle Box: available at: http://www.fishthe.net
Evangelism Unlimited, "There Is Hope" available at: http://www.evangelismunlimited.com/gospel-tracts.php
Every Believer a Witness, by Dennis Nunn; Dallas, GA: Living the New Life Ministries; available at: http://www.everybelieverawitness.org/about-us
Faith, Prayer & Tract League, Grand Rapids, MI 49504-1390.
Fellowship Tract League, P.O. Box 164, Lebanon, OH 45036; available at: www.fellowshiptractleague.org
Fishing for Souls.com: available at: http://www.fishingforsouls.com/home.html
Good News Publishers, 9825 W. Roosevelt Rd., Westchester, IL 60153; available at: www.gnpcb.org/home/tracts
The Good News: available at: http://www.thegoodnews.org
Gospel Journey: available at: http://www.dare2share.org/gospeljourney
Gospel Tract and Bible Society, Moundridge, KS 67107.
Gospel Tract Society, Inc., P.O. Box 1118, Independence, MO 64051.
Grace & Truth, 215 Oak Hillery, Danville, IL 61832.
Happy Heralds, Inc.; available at: www.happyheralds.org
Harvest Ministries (Greg Laurie). "Why Believe?"; available at: www.harvest.org
I Am Second: available at: http://www.iamsecond.com
International Tract Ministry.
International Bible Society, P.O. Box 35700, Colorado Springs, CO 80395; available at: www.IBSdirect.com
Jesus Name Project, Inc., P.O. Box 100, Chesterfield, MO 63006; "Jesus"; available at: jesusnameproject.org/home.html

Jews for Jesus, 60 Haight Street, San Francisco, CA 94102; available at: www.jewsforjesus.org
Know God: available at: http://www.harvest.org/knowgod
Literature Ministries International, PO Box 9028 Greenville Texas 75404. "What Every Catholic Should Know;" available at: www.litmin.com
Living Waters Ministries (Ray Comfort and Kirk Cameron); available at: www.livingwaters.com;
Way of the Master; available at: www.wayofthemaster.com
Matthias Media (Anglican Information Office, Sydney Square, Australia), *2 Ways to Live*; available at: http://www.matthiasmedia.com.au/2wtl
The Most Important Thing: available at: http://www.mostimportantthing.com
NavPress, Colorado Springs, CO 80993: "Bridge to Life"; for example, *Bridge to Life*: one version is available at: http://www.lifebpc.com/resources/bridgelife.htm
Need Him: available at: http://www.needhim.org
North American Mission Board, SBC, Alpharetta, GA 30202-4174: "Eternal Life", "Split-Time," "Your Life: A New Beginning"; available at: www.namb.net
Old Paths Tract Society, Shoals, IN 47581.
Osterhus Publishing House, 4500 W. Broadway, Minneapolis, MN 55422.
Pilgrim Tract Society, Inc., Randleman, NC 27317.
Pocket Testament League; available at: www.pocketpower.org.
Reasons to Believe: available at: http://www.reasons.org
Salvation: available at: http://www.saved.com/index.htm
Sonlife Ministries, Moody Bible Institute, 820 N. LaSalle Dr., Chicago, IL 60610: "Knowing God Personally"; available at: www.sonlife.com
The Story: available at: http://viewthestory.com/; see also: http://vimeo.com/thestory
Towne Press, 5301 Dewey Dr., Fair Oaks, CA 95628.
Western Tract Mission, 401 - 33rd St. West, Saskatoon, SK S7L 0V5.
World Home Bible League, 16801 Van Dam Road, South Holland, IL 60473: "Sun/Son Shine."
World Missionary Press, Inc., Box 120, New Paris, IN 46553; available at: www.wmpress.org.

Other Evangelism Resources:

EvangeCube: available at: http://www.e3resources.org.
Evangelism Tackle Box: available at: http://www.fishthe.net.
Fishing for Souls.com: available at: http://www.fishingforsouls.com/home.html.
Gospel Journey: available at: http://www.dare2share.org/gospeljourney.
I Am Second: available at: http://www.iamsecond.com.
Know God: available at: http://www.harvest.org/knowgod.
The Most Important Thing: available at: http://www.mostimportantthing.com.
Need Him: available at: http://www.needhim.org.
Reasons to Believe: available at: http://www.reasons.org.

Age Group and Sports Resources:

Max7: child evangelism website: www.max7.org.
Billy Graham Evangelistic Association sponsored to teach tweens to share their faith: available at: www.daretobeadaniel.com.
South African Sports Coalition: whole life coaching for soccer: available at: www.ubabalo2010.com.

Evangelism Training:

Billy Graham evangelism material: available at: www.jesus.net.
Cross Evangelism Training: available at: http://www.shareasyougo.com/cross-evangelism.
Way of the Master; available at: http://www.livingwaters.com.
Worcester, David. "How to Share Jesus Using Gospel Appointments." Collegiate Collective (September 22, 2014). Accessed October 2015. http://collegiatecollective.com gospel-4appointments-part-1/#.Vh-dlda-Qxc.

Other Resource:

Worcester, David. "How to Share Jesus Using Gospel Appointments." Collegiate Collective (September 22, 2014). Accessed October 2015. http://collegiatecollective.com/gospel-4appointments-part-1/#.Vh-dlda-Qxc

Guillaume Husson's Tract Ministry in 1544

"Guillaume Husson, Frenchman"

"During these approximate times of the year 1544, Guillaume Husson pharmacist, fugitive of Blois for the word of God, arrived in Rouen, and found lodging near the gate Martin-ville, with a widow: of whom among other things he inquired the hour that the Court of the Parliament was dismissed. Having heard from her that it was at ten o'clock, he went to the palace, and sowed several little booklets containing the doctrine of the Christian religion, and the abuses of human traditions: of which the Court became so shaken, that incontinent they shut the doors of the city, and made inquiries of all the hotel keepers to know what people they had in their [hotels]. The prior mentioned widow told them that a man had come in the morning to lodge at her home, that he had asked the time of the dismissal of the Court, and having stayed several two hours in the town, returned for lunch, and this done mounted a horse, and left. Having heard this they hurried off couriers to go after him: of which those who took the way to Dieppe, retained him midway, and brought him back to Rouen: where they inquired incontinent of his faith, of which he confessed without constraint: and that he came solely for the purpose of sowing the said booklets, and that he was heading for Dieppe to do the same.

"The next week he was condemned to be burned alive, and being that he was a man of some learning, they brought him a Doctor of the Sorbonne named De-landa, the Provincial Head of the Carmelite Order, in order to convert him to the faith that they call Catholic. After his sentence was pronounced against him, he was brought from the prison in a chariot before the Cathedral church, accompanied by this doctor: who had secured a torch to the fist of the patient, wanting to persuade him to make honorable amendment to the image that they call Our-Lady: but Husson not listening to him, on purpose allowed the torch to fall. For this reason his tongue was cut out, and thereafter he was brought to the veal market, where the said doctor gave a sermon that lasted for a long time. When this sluggard [*caphar*] said something of the grace of God, the patient gave him audience. But when he returned to the merits of the saints and similar dreams, he turned his head back. The venerable doctor seeing the countenance of Husson, lifted up his arms and with great exclamation said to the people that this man was damned, and from this moment on possessed of the devil.

"Hence after all the joking of the Monk was achieved, Husson was attached and hung in the air by a large pulley, his hands and feet tied behind his back. When the fire was lit, he stayed over the flame for a period of time without moving, if not to render his spirit he was seen to move by dropping his head. Upon leaving this spectacle was heard diverse comments and opinions of the people. Some said that he had a devil in his body: others maintained the contrary, alleging that if such was the case, he would have been in despair, being that the end which comes from the devil is despair. This holy Martyr in the midst of the flame, brought astonishment to a number of people: for some they remained foolish, the others were incited to know more clearly the true God of Israel, who in the midst of the blazing furnace can save those who invoke the name of his Son, only protector and liberator of his own."[55]

---

[55]Jean Crespin, *Histoire des vrays Tesmoins de la verite de l'evangile, qui de leur sang l'ont signée, depuis Jean Hus iusques autemps present* [*History of the True Witnesses to the Truth of the Gospel, Who with Their Blood Signed, from John Hus to the Present*] (Geneva: Crespin, 1570; Liège: Centre nationale de recherches d'histoire religieuse, 1964), 131-131v. Translation mine.

On the Necessity of Regular Verbal Confession of Christ

Question: Is it absolutely necessary for someone who believes in Jesus Christ as their Savior to regularly and verbally confess Him before unbelieving men to be saved?

To focus our attention on this question, let us begin by examining John 12:42-43:

> "Nevertheless even among the rulers many believed in Him, but because of the Pharisees they did not confess *Him*, lest they should be put out of the synagogue; for they loved the praise of men more than the praise of God."

The original question, when considered in light of these verses, expands to the following questions:

- Is faith alone necessary to salvation?
- And if so, does faith alone exclude the need for verbal confession, or is regular verbal confession a fruit of faith alone?
- Furthermore, is outward verbal confession unto salvation a one-time event, or does it entail regular verbal confession before both saved and unsaved men?
- How does seeking the praise of God and the praise of men, or pleasing God and pleasing man, fit into the regular verbal confession of Christ?

Let's begin with the last question and work our way to the first.

The Apostle Paul mentions the concept of pleasing God and pleasing man several times in his epistles, in the context of evangelistic activity:

> "For do I now persuade men, or God? Or do I seek to please men? For if I still pleased men, I would not be a bondservant of Christ" (Gal 1:10 NKJ)

> "For our exhortation *did* not *come* from error or uncleanness, nor *was it* in deceit. But as we have been approved by God to be entrusted with the gospel, even so we speak, not as pleasing men, but God who tests our hearts" (1 Thess 2:3 NKJ)

Therefore, it is clear from these verses, that obeying God is a much higher priority than is pleasing men. Likewise, it seems like the area of evangelism provides a touchstone for love and obedience of God first and foremost to be lived out in the life of the New Testament Christian.

For the next question: is verbal confession a one-time event, or does it necessitate repeated action?

The answer to this question seems to be lodged in the context and tense of the verses which require a verbal confession of Christ, as well as those that apply to its contrary, denial of Christ:

> "Therefore whoever confesses Me before men, him I will also confess before My Father who is in heaven. But whoever denies Me before men, him I will also deny before My Father who is in heaven" (Matt 10:32 NKJ)

> "Also I say to you, whoever confesses Me before men, him the Son of Man also will confess before the angels of God. But he who denies Me before men will be denied before the angels of God" (Luke 12:8 NKJ)

The context is one of evangelistic missionary work (Matthew 10) and of the other the fear of men (Luke 12). The verb form of the "confess" in Matthew is in the future active tense and in Luke is in the subjunctive aorist active tense. As far as the denying side, Matthew is a subjunctive aorist middle and Luke is a participle aorist middle, "he who is denying me."

Equally important in this discussion are some New Testament verses on shame:

> "For whoever is ashamed of Me and My words in this adulterous and sinful generation, of him the Son of Man also will be ashamed when He comes in the glory of His Father with the holy angels" (Mark 8:38 NKJ)

> "For whoever is ashamed of Me and My words, of him the Son of Man will be ashamed when He comes in His *own* glory, and *in His* Father's, and of the holy angels" (Luke 9:26 NKJ)

These verses make it clear that the necessary confession involves confession before those who could bring a feeling of shame to the one who is confessing Christ:

> Foremost, this shame refers to the fear of confession before a lost or unsaved audience, as in the case of Peter prior to the crucifixion. Peter feared confessing his knowledge of Christ three times when

specifically asked of such. His was a three-fold denial before various servants and sundry people the morning of the crucifixion of Christ.

Likewise, even before a saved audience the pastor and/or Christian may sometimes feel shame about discussing certain less accepted teachings of Scripture, such as total depravity and hell. Which shame is often concealed by equivocation and subtle double-speak.

It would seem that the latter fear is merely an extension of the former fear. Both amount to fearing man more than God. Both are reprimanded in the Bible.

The necessity of verbal confession, being more than a mere regular habit in the life of a Christian, comes from the five Great Commission passage and their many parallels:

The Great Commission raises the verbal proclamation of the Gospel to the place of being the prime motive in the life of the believer, everything in life is guided by its principle (see my notes on the Great Commission here)!

Likewise, this same emphasis was the obvious example of the Apostle Paul (1 Cor 9:22-23), whose example all Christians are called to follow (1 Cor 11:1):

"To the weak I became as weak, that I might win the weak. I have become all things to all *men*, that I might by all means save some. Now this I do for the gospel's sake, that I may be partaker of it with *you*" (1Cor 9:22 NKJ).

"Give no offense, either to the Jews or to the Greeks or to the church of God, just as I also please all *men* in all *things*, not seeking my own profit, but the *profit* of many, that they may be saved. Imitate me, just as I also *imitate* Christ" (1Cor 10:32-11:1 NKJ).

So, does faith alone snuff out the necessity for evangelizing to be the *a priori* in the life of the believer? No. It merely complements faith alone as the message unto which the Christian is called to share:

"But you *are* a chosen generation, a royal priesthood, a holy nation, His own special people, that you may proclaim the praises of Him who called you out of darkness into His marvelous light; who once *were* not a people but *are* now the people of God, who had not obtained mercy but now have obtained mercy." (1 Pet 2:9-10 NKJ)

Is this argumentation by sophistry or bending texts beyond their clear meaning? Not at all.

This clear teaching from the Bible may be snuffed out by focusing on speculative theological questions, as took place within the Church of Rome from Augustine to Aquinas and to the present day. However, it is only the regular verbal confession of Christ which makes sense of the teaching in Matthew 10. Anything less turns the missionary teaching of Jesus into paradox.

Is teaching the necessity of regular verbal confession of Christ before all men "over-emphasizing certain aspects of the Christian life," or, as the 2006 Vatican-World Council of Churches Inter-religious Consultation on Conversion stated, an **"obsession of converting others"**? Not at all. It is merely obeying what the Bible says over and over in numerous ways, both by teaching and by example.

So, is verbal confession of Christ necessary unto salvation by faith alone. The answer is found in Paul epistle to the Romans:

Paul's purpose is to explain salvation "from faith to faith" (Rom 1:14-17)

As part of this salvation "from faith to faith" the only necessity unto salvation is the verbal confession "with your mouth" that Jesus is Lord, accompanied by belief in the heart that God raised Him from the dead (Rom 10:9). The result being "you will be saved."

For, says the Apostle, "For with the heart one believes unto righteousness, and with the mouth confession is made unto salvation" (Rom 10:10).

Both verses 9 and 10 reiterate that Paul is speaking of salvation, having thus explained how the Gospel is "the power of God unto salvation for everyone who believes" (Rom 1:16) and how "the righteous shall live by faith" (Rom 1:17).

Thus saving faith begins with the verbal confession of the Lord Jesus. And saving faith is confirmed through the regular verbal confession of the Lord Jesus, and his word, yes even before an adulterous and sinful generation:

"For whoever is ashamed of Me and My words in this adulterous and sinful generation, of him the Son of Man also will be ashamed when He comes in the glory of His Father with the holy angels" (Mark 8:38 NKJ)

Could not the original question be restated in several other ways?

What of someone who claims to be a believer in Christ, but refuses to regularly and verbally confess Him before unbelieving men? Is that person truly saved, or not?

What of a professor who requires his students to regularly and verbally confess Christ as part of their grade, is this legalism or unwarranted?

What if some of his students are not saved, even if they are required to be so as an entrance requirement to the school?

How Evangelizing May Be a Spiritual Benefit

I invite you to the practice of personal and public evangelism for a lifetime…

A. In so doing, God promises you:
    1. Struggles and hardships;
    2. Tremendous joy and purpose;
    3. Inward and outward battles;
    4. Unexplainable peace!

B. The regular practice of personal evangelism, which is merely obedience of several of the key commands of Christ in Scripture (e.g. the Great Commission and the condition of confessing Christ before men):
    1. Gives focus, direction, and purpose to life
    2. Allows the evangelist to "preach the gospel to himself"—constantly applying lessons from the Bible and his evangelism ministry to his own life[56]
    3. Uncovers what are the most important theological, hermeneutical, and evangelistic issues in Scripture and in life
    4. Provides a coherent hermeneutic of the Scripture, as well as a Central Interpretive Motif for theology
    5. Guides and focuses all other ancillary theological or ministry studies
    6. Helps one understand persecution and suffering for the Gospel, both in the Bible, in the history of the Church, and in contemporary life
    7. Helps one understand the history of the churches and place of evangelism as a part of that history
    8. Allows the Christian to understand to a very small degree the spiritual hatred and blindness that Jesus experienced
    9. Shows the evangelist time and again the power of the Word of God both to blind or to break and open hearts to the Gospel

Perhaps most importantly of these is to learn to "make a distinction." The personal evangelist, in every conversation is seeking to essay the heart of the person with whom he is speaking. He is practically "making a distinction" on many levels:
    a. Is this person saved or lost?
    b. If he says that he are a Christian, how does this person view salvation? To what church do they belong, or to what church did they belong?
    c. If this person is not a Christian, what is their religious belief? From what religious background did they come?

All of these, and many more questions, come to the mind of the personal evangelist—he must be a master essayer, and in so doing he is learning to "make a distinction":

> Lev 10:10-11, "Then the LORD spoke to Aaron, saying: Do not drink wine or intoxicating drink, you, nor your sons with you, when you go into the tabernacle of meeting, lest you die. *It shall be* a statute forever throughout your generations, that you may distinguish between holy and unholy, and between unclean and clean, "and that you may teach the children of Israel all the statutes which the LORD has spoken to them by the hand of Moses."

So also, because of the practice of personal evangelism, the evangelist encounters numerous types of people with many variations of belief and commitment level:
One week of personal evangelism can sometimes provide more interaction with peoples of other religious systems that one semester of worldviews or world religions
    a. Further, from these encounters, because of his desire to bring Jesus to those individuals, the evangelist builds a database of convictions based on actual conversations with people who hold to various forms of belief
    b. From these conversations the evangelist learns approaches to share the gospel with people from these various belief systems
    c. At time during these conversations, the Holy Spirit teaches the evangelist "on the spot" powerful things to say to certain people that become life-long milestones of truth for that evangelist.

---

[56]A special thanks to Darin Smith for the thought to include the lesson of the evangelist "Preaching the gospel to himself"!

C. Or, if not, how can we know that we will…?

  1. Understand and utilize the teachings of the secular world, such as Plato, Aristotle, or Socrates, or insight from anthropology, psychology, and sociology, in a more effective or efficient way than those that have gone before us? What will be our ultimate source of authority?

  2. Correctly exegete culture, its fads and needs?

  3. Properly study and interpret the Bible, theology, or the history of the churches from the correct point-of-view (worldview), being there are so many points of view out there, and everyone promotes their own view as being correct and/or proper?

  4. There is only one way to know that what you are reading and learning from the Bible is truly from God—does it line up with God's Word as understood from being a careful doer of the Word?

  5. For all these to take place, evangelism must needs take a front seat!

D. Some characteristics of the Christian who has been active and urgent in sincere evangelism (remembering that even Judas Iscariot was sent out to evangelize in Matt 10:4):

  1. A resolute quality about a person who believes in God's ways enough to make it known and to stand against the tide and preach about it:
     a. Hence, Noah was called a "preacher of righteousness" (2 Pet 2:5), not merely a "righteous man"
     b. Was this not what also distinguished "righteous Lot" from the men of Sodom (2 Pet 2:7), Gen 19:7-9?

  2. A certain impatience, and even an intolerance, with other Christians' lack of action in evangelism and/or their lack of vital spiritual inertia, Gal 3:1-5; Phil 2:12-13:
     a. Some would perhaps negatively refer to this inner urging as "activism"
     b. Rather, it seems that this conviction must be included in the gift of the revival preacher, cf. Jer 5:30-31; 23:9-11

  3. A winsome desire to persuade others unto salvation, 2 Cor 5:10, accompanied by a general positive spirit, 2 Cor 6:10:
     a. Persuasion clearly accompanied Paul's ministry throughout his days, Acts 9:20-22; 17:2-4; 18:4; 19:8; 26:25-29; 28:23-24
     b. God's people are called to "win disciples" of all nations (Matt 28:19), which includes a need for godly persuasion

  4. A certain protectionism, possibly considered sectarianism, a spiritual caution, and a skeptical guardedness toward those who do not agree with their view of the Gospel or evangelism, Gal 1:6-10
     a. Sometimes this guardedness can be accompanied by a lack of openness to other approaches to evangelism and even a distrust of others
     b. Persecution because of the Gospel can also lead to a type of paranoya regarding enemies all around

  5. An unashamed singleness of focus, 1 Cor 2:2; 9:22-23; Col 1:28-29

  6. A holy boldness and spiritual sinew drawn from activity in spiritual warfare, Ezek 3:8-9; Acts 13:9-11; Gal 5:11

  7. An initiating spirit, a self-starter attitude:
     a. The self-starter attitude:
        1) Perhaps this attitude can best be explained by an "If I don't do it, who will?" attitude, leading to a very strong sense of personal responsibility.
        2) Perhaps it is the fact that God is calling individuals to do His will, as in Isaiah 6:8, "Whom shall I send, and who will go for Us?"
        3) Perhaps it is the individualistic, "Here am I send me" attitude, as exemplified by the prophet Isaiah in the same verse!
        4) Rather than denigrate this sense of personal responsibility as Type-A, Anal Retentive, or Obsessive-Compulsive, let's be grateful that God gives His people motivation!
     b. This self-starter and initiatory attitude has often pulled evangelists to:
        1) Perfect their own Gospel plan, Gospel tract, or evangelism program
        2) Develop their own revival plan
        3) Develop their own follow-up materials

    c.   This self-starter and initiatory attitude has often allowed evangelists to be at the vanguard of movements, awakenings, and spiritual institutions, such as:

        1) Planting new churches, lead others to plant churches, and sometimes even initiate what becomes over time new denominational groupings:

            a) Reformation groups, Wesley and the Methodists, etc.

            b) It must be remembered that John Calvin considered that God raised up Evangelists during the Reformation period[57]

        2) Founding evangelistic associations, colleges, orphanages or children's homes, hospitals, and other societies to further the cause of the Gospel among a people:

            a) Francke in Germany

            b) William Booth with the Salvation Army in England

            c) Presbyterian missionaries in Korea whom God used to transform that culture

        3) Translating the Bible into the language of a certain people for the purposes of better communicating the Gospel to them:

            a) Olivetan's French translation which became the French Geneva

        4) In fact, many hymn books in the past have come off the hands of bold evangelists:

            a) A. H. Francke in Germany

            b) D. L. Moody for the English

            c) R. Saillens in France

        5) The singleness of focus of the evangelists kept the societies they founded grounded in the evangelizing; it was not until either they had died or shifted away from evangelizing that the movements they founded dissipated into mere social service activities

    d.   Oh, the spiritual benefit of evangelists and their bold evangelism to any culture! Who can explain it?

        1) Consider what the Gospel accomplished in Reformation Germany and Switzerland

        2) Or consider the impact of House of Orange in the Netherlands and England

        3) Or consider the power of the Gospel at work in various eras of U.S. Church history.

---

[57]"Those three functions [apostles, prophets, and evangelists] were not instituted in the church to be perpetual… although I deny not, that afterward God occasionally raised up Apostles, or at least Evangelists, in their stead, as has been done in our time. For such were needed to bring back the Church from the revolt of Antichrist" (John Calvin, *Institutes of the Christian Religion;* trans by Henry Beveridge [London: Clarke, 1957] 2:319).

How a Lack of Initiative Evangelism Is Detrimental

There are many traps and dangers with a lack of regular initiative evangelism. These notes will seek to enumerate a few of these pitfalls.

A. Actively choosing to ignore the proclamational commands of the Great Commission:
    1. A lack of regular involvement in initiative evangelism leads to a callousness towards the proclamational elements of Christ's Great Commission;
    2. A lack of regular involvement in initiative evangelism leads to a callousness towards those who are regularly involved in the same, and animosity towards their encouragement to be involved in the same.

B. Actively choosing to reinterpret the Great Commission:
    1. The regular dousing of the Holy Spirit's call to share the Gospel leads to a quenching of His work through the Word of God;
    2. The regular dousing of the Holy Spirit's call to share the Gospel leads to interpreting away His calls to evangelism, and to reinterpretating them into calls for something other than initiative evangelism;
    3. The regular dousing of the Holy Spirit's call to share the Gospel leads to actively developing theological systems that are non-proclamational at their base and in their theology of conversion (enter Augustine, Lombard, and Aquinas);
    3. The regular dousing of the Holy Spirit's call to share the Gospel leads to active antagonism to those who are doing initiative evangelism, including actively mocking their evangelism efforts and actively opposing them (their jobs, their worth, etc.);
    4. The regular dousing of the Holy Spirit's call to share the Gospel leads to active persecution and annihilation of evangelists and any who heed their calls to conversion and salvation (enter the persecution of the 9th-10th Century Paulicians, the 11th-13th Century Cathars, the 14th-15th Century Lollards and Hussites, and the 16th-18th Century Baptists and Protestants).

C. Actively choosing to oppose the Great Commission:
    1. Active antagonism to Scripture teaching initiative evangelism and to people who actively evangelize leads to working against Christ and His eternal Word;
    2. Active antagonism to Scripture teaching initiative evangelism and people who actively evangelize leads to being ashamed of Christ before men (Mark 8:38), and therefore not confessing Christ before men (Luke 12:8-9);
    3. Active antagonism to Scripture teaching initiative evangelism and to people who actively evangelize leads to the loss of one's soul (Matt 10:32-33).

Pillars of Evangelizology

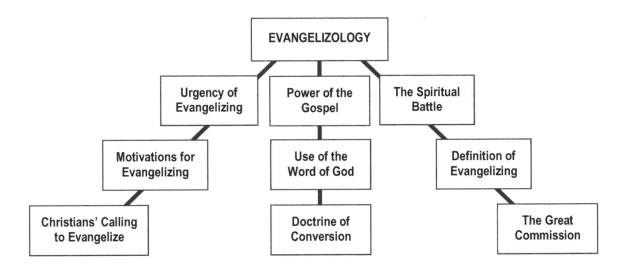

These pillars, among others, support or undergird New Testament evangelizing. Any movement away from the New Testament in any of these pillars will be a strong detriment to evangelizology, and ultimately do great harm to the local church, its evangelism, its growth, its preaching, its teaching, its health, and its overall ministry.

It is for this reason that the first 10 chapters of this book address these issues, seeking to provide a solid foundation for the practice of New Testament evangelizing.

By the way, it may be interesting to note how few of these pillars are specifically taught in the normal regiment of the "Classical Theological Disciplines"!

Toward a New Testament Theology of Personal Evangelism

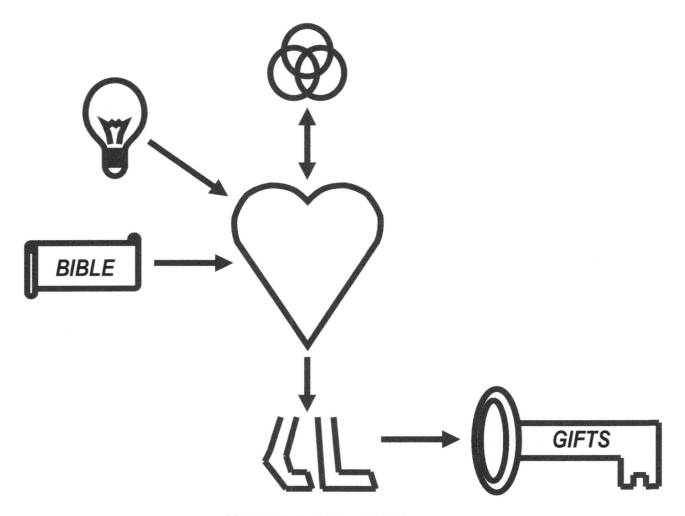

Matt 4:19 And He said to them,
"Follow Me, and **I will make you** fishers of men."

Mark 1:17 And Jesus said to them,
"Follow Me, and I will make you **become** fishers of men."

Luke 5:10, And Jesus said to Simon,
"Do not fear, from now on **you will be taking men alive**"
[my translation]

John 4:38, "**I sent you to reap** that for which you have not labored;
others have labored, and you have entered into their labor."

Considering Theological and Methodological Shift[58]

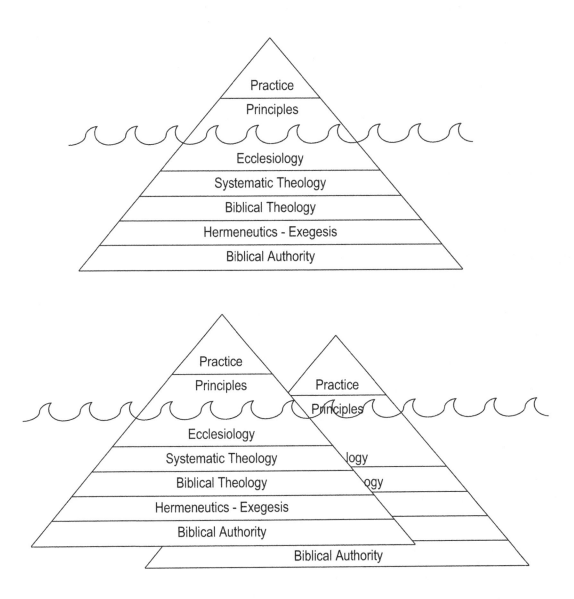

As with the iceberg, the theological foundations of many books on the principles and practice of evangelism are hidden under the surface. While the "new" ideas for the principles and practice of evangelism may be appealing, they may in fact be nothing more than the result of a shift in theology. The careful reader will be aware of the implications of varying views of man's sin and the atonement when he reads about "new" methodologies of evangelism.

The "Pillars of Evangelizology" on the previous page list central elements to New Testament theology. The very foundations of evangelizing can be removed from it, even sometimes while maintaining a veneer of evangelism. The need for theological discernment intensifies when seeking to maintain New Testament evangelizing!

---

[58]Charts taken from class notes by Arthur P. Johnston, "Theology of Missions and Evangelism" (Deerfield, IL: Trinity Evangelical Divinity School, 1986).

Considering Tests for Theologies

An Introduction to Critical Thinking

Postulate 1.1, No one will ever know everything:
>   To think that one can know everything is either arrogant or foolish, or both
>   Likewise, fullness of knowledge in any given area is impossible
>   Therefore, critical thinking is a matter of gradations of knowledge, from little to more
>   Therefore, critical thinking is a matter of understanding knowledge, not of full knowledge of everything
>   Therefore, rather than knowing everything, critical thinking is a matter of framing the question or worldview

Postulate 1.2, As born-again Christians, there are some things of which we have become convinced, not the least of which is obedience to the command of Christ, "You must be born again!":
>   2 Tim 3:14, "You, however, continue in the things you have learned and become convinced of, knowing from whom you have learned *them*."
>   John 14:6, "Jesus said to him, 'I am the way, and the truth, and the life; no one comes to the Father, but through Me'"

Conclusion 1, We must develop criteria by which knowledge can be critically judged, which is based upon that of which we have become convinced:
>   Therefore, the foundation of critical thinking is NOT knowing everything there is to know, an impossible task
>   The foundation is properly interpreting what we do know, by a proper set of criteria
>   Based on 1 Peter 1:17-25, the following is recommended as a foundational criteria:

> **Conversion by faith in the blood of Christ alone as communicated through the fully trustworthy words of the Bible**

> Further, for theological purposes, the following criteria are also recommended:

>> That elaborated from Acts 15:7-11; Rom 3:21-26:
>>   (1) Scriptures alone
>>   (2) Faith alone
>>   (3) Grace alone

>> As well as the theological principles elaborated during the 1895 Bible Conference in Niagara-on-the-Lake, Ontario, which have proved helpful to this end:
>>   (1) Inerrancy of Scriptures
>>   (2) Deity of Christ
>>   (3) Virgin birth of Christ (and likewise all of the Bible's miracles)
>>   (4) Substitutionary atonement
>>   (5) Bodily resurrection (after death to a literal heaven and hell)

Some related thoughts:

>   It is possible to continually learn and never to come to a knowledge of the truth?
>>   Yes, "always learning and never able to come to the knowledge of the truth" (2 Tim 3:7)
>>   Therefore showing the need to properly frame the question and understand the issues

>   Thus there is still the need for continuous study: "Be diligent to present yourself approved to God as a workman who does not need to be ashamed, handling accurately the word of truth" (2 Tim 2:15)

Postulate 2.1, The Bible provides an inerrant source of truth:
>   Psa 119:137-138, "Righteous art Thou, O LORD, And upright are Thy judgments. Thou hast commanded Thy testimonies in righteousness And exceeding faithfulness."
>   Psa 119:142, "Thy righteousness is an everlasting righteousness, And Thy law is truth."
>   Psa 119:160, "The sum of Thy word is truth, And every one of Thy righteous ordinances is everlasting."
>   John 17:17, "Sanctify them in the truth; Thy word is truth."

Postulate 2.2, The Bible frames truth and reality in certain ways

Conclusion 2.1, It is always preferable to allow the Bible to frame the question:

Isa 55:9, "For *as* the heavens are higher than the earth, So are My ways higher than your ways, And My thoughts than your thoughts."

Job 36:22-23, "Behold, God is exalted in His power; Who is a teacher like Him? Who has appointed Him His way, And who has said, 'Thou hast done wrong '?"

Psa 19:11-13, "Moreover, by them Thy servant is warned; In keeping them there is great reward. Who can discern *his* errors? Acquit me of hidden *faults*. Also keep back Thy servant from presumptuous *sins*; Let them not rule over me; Then I shall be blameless, And I shall be acquitted of great transgression."

Conclusion 2.2, Therefore, any other source of truth:

(1) Must be judged by the Bible,

(2) Must be considered suspect until it has been found to be faithful to the Bible, and

(3) Can only be trusted insofar as it is faithful to the Bible.

Conclusion 2.3, the truism, "All truth is God's truth," is fallacious in light of equating empirically derived "truth" with that "Truth" which is revealed in the Word of God!

Is not this dictum philosophically-posited based on its antithetical: "all falsehood is Satan's falsehood!" (cf. John 8:44)?

Does this dictum not imply that God's truth rightly understood will eventually merge with or coalesce with or melt into man's truth, as rightly understood?

In that case, what of Isa 55:9 (above)? Or 1 Cor 1:18-25?

> "For the message of the cross is foolishness to those who are perishing, but to us who are being saved it is the power of God. For it is written: 'I will destroy the wisdom of the wise, And bring to nothing the understanding of the prudent.' Where *is* the wise? Where *is* the scribe? Where *is* the disputer of this age? Has not God made foolish the wisdom of this world? For since, in the wisdom of God, the world through wisdom did not know God, it pleased God through the foolishness of the message preached to save those who believe. For Jews request a sign, and Greeks seek after wisdom; but we preach Christ crucified, to the Jews a stumbling block and to the Greeks foolishness, but to those who are called, both Jews and Greeks, Christ the power of God and the wisdom of God. Because the foolishness of God is wiser than men, and the weakness of God is stronger than men" (1 Cor 1:18-25).

Does not the above truism place man's truth at the same level as God's truth?

Or if not, does it not place stress on the interpreter of the Bible to find points of agreement between man's truth and God's truth?

And, therefore, does it not drastically alter one's emphasis and direction in the interpretation of Scripture?

And, therefore, does it not hinder the free interpretation of Scripture with itself, unhindered from any predetermined hermeneutical grids

And, was this not the problem of the Medieval Catholic interpreters, even to the time of Erasmus,[59] who left the so-called "literal sense" (the "unlearned" reading), and sought out Aritotle and Socrates wherever and whenever they could find them in Scripture, thereby bypassing the plain reading of text for the "greater good" of a learned reading?

William D. Dennison explained the all-encompassing use of the dictum "all truth is God's truth" in his essay on U.S. higher education[60]

Charles Finney, in his later life while presiding over a liberal arts college, seemed to forget the Isaiah 55:9 distinction between empirical truth and God's truth[61]

---

[59]"However, just as divine Scripture bears no great fruit if you persist in clinging only to the literal sense, so the great poetry of Homer and Vergil is of no small benefit if you remember that this is all allegorical, a fact that no one who has but touched his lips with the wisdom of the ancients will deny. . . . I would prefer, too, that you follow the Platonists among the philosophers, because in most of their ideas and in their very manner of speaking they come nearest to the beauty of the prophets and the gospels" (Raymond Himelick, *The Enchiridion of Erasmus* [Gloucester, MA: Peter Smith, 1970], 51).

[60]"Hence, it is not uncommon to find Christian academicians who employ the pious-clad phrase, 'all truth is God's truth,' to justify a methodology that utilizes the fundamental precepts of rationalism, empiricism, realism, idealism, romanticism, naturalism, materialism, existentialism, structuralism, or poststructuralism, without any critique of the foundational premises of those methodologies" (William D. Dennison, "Antithesis, Common Grace, and Plato's View of the Soul" *JETS* 54:1 [March 2011]: 112-13).

[61]"I have not yet been able to stereotype my theological views, and have ceased to expect ever to do so. The idea is preposterous. None put an omniscient mind can continue to maintain a precise identity of views and opinions. Finite minds, unless they are asleep or stultified by prejudice, must advance in knowledge. The discovery of new truth

Postulate 3.1, However, attacks on the Bible and its message are numerous; they come from such areas of study as:

Translation theories and translation from original language issues

Textual critical issues

Various methods and schools of interpretation (hermeneutics)

Theological schools of though

Ecclesiastical emphases

Various approaches to culture, the mission of the church, and evangelism

[Neither can any or all of these areas be fully known and understood by any one author or scholar]

Postulate 3.2, All Scripture is exhaled by God (2 Tim 3:16), whereby the one God speaks with one voice:

In other words, the Bible is not pluriform, pluralistic, nor subject to contradictions or multiple interpretations

Conclusion 3, One must concern oneself with developing proper criteria, based on that of which one is convinced, by which to judge the biblical-theological sciences:

Such as, conversion by the blood of Christ alone as communicated through the fully trustworthy words of the Bible.

Be ready because:

Developing any objective criteria will be attacked by broad-minded Christians and theologians, especially when those criteria are not in line with their predetermined conclusions about Scriptures and theology

With this in mind, several "tests for theologies" are proposed…

Proposed Basic Tests for Theologies

1. **The Biblical Authority Tests:**

    a.   What or whom is the stated authority upon which this theology is based (Matt 7:24-27; 1 Cor 3:11)?

    b.   What or whom is the actual basis for this theology (Acts 20:29-32)?

2. **The Gospel Tests:**

    a.   What does this theology do to the need for the death of Jesus Christ on the cross (Gal 2:21)?

---

will mollify old views and opinions, and there is perhaps no end to this process in finite minds in any world. True Christian consistency does not consist in stereotyping our opinions and views, and in refusing to make any improvement lest we should be guilty of change, but it consists in holding our minds open to receive rays of truth from every quarter and in changing our views and language and practice as often and as fast, as we obtain further information. I call this Christian consistency, because this course alone accords with a Christian profession. A Christian profession implies the profession of candor and of a disposition to know and obey all truth. It must follow, that Christian consistency implies continued investigation and change of views and practice corresponding with increasing knowledge. No Christian, therefore, and no theologian should be afraid to change his views, his language, or his practices in conformity with increasing light. The prevalence of such a fear would keep the world, at best, at a perpetual stand-still, on all subjects of science, and consequently all improvements would be precluded.

"Every uninspired attempt to frame for the church an authoritative standard of opinion which shall be regarded as an unquestionable exposition of the word of God, is not only impious in itself, but it is also a tacit assumption of the fundamental dogma of Papacy. The Assembly of [Westminster] Divines did more than to assume the necessity of a Pope to give law to the opinions of men; they assumed to create an immortal one, or rather to embalm their own creed, and preserve it as the Pope of all generations; or it is more just to say, that those who have adopted that confession of faith and catechism as an authoritative standard of doctrine, have absurdly adopted the most obnoxious principle of Popery, and elevated their confession and catechism to the Papal throne and into the place of the Holy Ghost. That the instrument framed by that assembly should in the nineteenth century be recognized as a standard of the church, or of an intelligent branch of it, is not only amazing, but I must say that it is highly ridiculous. It is as absurd in theology as it would be in any other branch of science, and as injurious and stultifying as it is absurd and ridiculous. It is better to have a living that a dead Pope. If we must have an authoritative expounder of the word of God, let us have a living one, so as not to preclude the hope of improvement. 'A living dog is better than a dead lion;' so a living Pope is better than a dead and stereotyped confession of faith, that holds all men bound to subscribe to its unalterable dogmas and unvarying terminology" (Charles G. Finney, "Preface," *Systematic Theology*, ed. by J. H. Fairchild [E. J. Goodrich, 1878; South Gate, CA: Porter Kemp, 1944], xi-xii).

b. How does it impact the Gospel message (1 Cor 15:2; 2 Cor 11:4; Gal 1:6-8; 2 Pet 2:1; Jude 4)?

c. Does it still require?
   1) The substitutionary atonement (2 Cor 5:21; 1 Pet 2:24; 3:18)?
   2) Conversion (John 3:3, 7; Acts 2:38)?
   3) Does it add anything to grace alone and faith alone (Eph 2:8-9)?

3. The Evangelistic Tests:

a. Does the theology compliment of alter the Great Commission mandate that Christ gave to His church (Matt 28:19-20; Mark 16:15; Luke 24:44-49; John 20:21; Acts 1:8)?

   1) Does this theology, especially in the pre-First Great Awakening history of the churches, hold true to a Great Commission hermeneutic[62] (Matt 24:14; 28:19-20)?

b. What does this theology do to the urgency of sharing the Gospel message (Matt 9:37-38; John 4:35; Acts 4:19-20; 5:29; 2 Cor 5:11)?

c. Does it undercut the need to be boldly preaching the Gospel (Acts 4:31; Eph 6:19-20)?

4. The Martyrs Test:

a. Can this theology be "tested by fire," in other words, was the blood of past Christian martyrs spent as a confirmation to their faith in this theology?

   While Augustine was partially right, *Martyrem non facit poena, sed causa* ["Punishment does not make the martyr, but the cause"],[63] as people are martyred for false theologies and lies, there is also an element wherein a commitment to the Christ is a commitment to die for Him and His Gospel (Matt 10:28, 39).

   Some theologies promise blessing in this life, without mentioning suffering for the Gospel now, nor emphasizing eternal life as the blessed hope.

   A commitment to suffer and die for the Gospel is the martyr's test, the test by fire, as described in 1 Peter 1:7:

   "In this you greatly rejoice, even though now for a little while, if necessary, you have been distressed by various trials, that the proof of your faith, *being* more precious than gold which is perishable, even though tested by fire, may be found to result in praise and glory and honor at the revelation of Jesus Christ; and though you have not seen Him, you love Him, and though you do not see Him now, but believe in Him, you greatly rejoice with joy inexpressible and full of glory, obtaining as the outcome of your faith the salvation of your souls" (1 Peter 1:6-9).

---

[62]See Chuck Kelley, *How Did They Do It? The Story of Southern Baptist Evangelism* (New Orleans: Insight, 1993), 119-31.

[63]Léon-E Halkin, "Hagiographie Protestante," in *Mélanges Paul Peeters II*, Analecta Bollandiana 68 (Bruxelles: Société des Bollandistes, 1950), 456; Jean-François Gilmont, "Les centres d'intérêt du martyrologe de Jean Crespin (1554-1570) révélés par la cartographie et les statistiques," *Miscellanea historiae ecclesiasticae,* Vol 5, Issue 61, 361.

CHAPTER 2
The Christian's Calling in Evangelism, and Metaphors Related to Evangelism

Introduction 1: Of the human element in evangelism:

The famous allocution of Augustine of Hippo, "Pick up and read!" (*Tolle lege*) begs a very interesting evangelistic-practical-historical question:

Is there the need for a human element in conversion?
>If so, what is that need?
>If not, what of the Great Commission, examples of evangelism, and the ministry of the evangelist in the NT?

Did Augustine not have a human element in his conversion when he picked up and read, as if it were completely by chance or by miraculous providential intervention when he heard a young girl singing in a neighboring yard, "Pick up and read" (~A.D. 387)?

>Could it be that Augustine's experience of hearing the little girl:
>>Provided this rhetorical giant the ammunition he needed to shake off his Manichean (Evangelical) past, and
>>Provided him the rhetorical bridge by which he could give a nod toward biblical evangelism—by somehow relating his "conversion" to his reading of the Bible (or: Scriptures alone), while, all the while, fully espousing a Sacramental view of conversion and salvation?

>If that was truly a divinely miraculous moment in his life, then when was his conversion? Or was it part of a complex conversion a process beginning in predestination, the prayers of a godly mother, his lurid past, hearing the voice, deciding to exert his strength to "put on Christ," culminating in his baptism by Ambrose?

>Is it legitimate to speak of the moment of conversion in light of predestination and election?

>If so, then what about the general election presupposition of a State-Church or Sacramental-system Church?

>If so, then what about the Sacrament of Baptism?

>According to Augustine, is not conversion vested in all the signs and symbols, Scriptures used, the very words uttered, and prayers raised to God in [Holy] Baptism?

What of the human element involved when Ambrose baptized him, was that a more legitimate human role than that of sharing the gospel?
And what role did baptism have in the timing of Augustine's "conversion" experience?

And what of that ritual of baptism, did it not have a human element (Ambrose), and did it not also have a physical element, a necessary physical sign or symbol ([Holy] Water), for which and of which Augustine so powerfully argued?

By the way, what did Augustine pick up and read? It is reported that after having heard of *St. Anthony's Life in the Desert,* he heard a childlike voice prompting him to "pick up and read," the 31 year-old rhetorician then picked up the Bible and read Rom 13:13-14:[64]

>Rom 13:13-14, "Let us behave properly as in the day, not in carousing and drunkenness, not in sexual promiscuity and sensuality, not in strife and jealousy. But put on the Lord Jesus Christ, and make no provision for the flesh in regard to *its* lusts."

---

[64]"Augustine of Hippo"; available at: http://en.wikipedia.org/wiki/Augustine_of_hippo; accessed: 29 May 2014; Internet.

So, Augustine's conversion seems to have approximated more a vow to monastic asceticism than it does repentance from sin and turning one's live over by faith, trusting in Christ's redemptive work alone for salvation (His blood) and the reception of His righteousness—a righteousness actually alien to sinful human nature (infant baptized or not):

And yet, Augustine's gift of rhetoric, being what it was and being so mighty, was such that his writings continue to be used by both adherents of a sacramental-works-oriented salvation, as well as by those who adhere to the three Protestant pillars of Scriptures alone, faith alone, grace alone.

Amazing!

So, what of the human element in evangelism? Is it necessary or not?

Perhaps from the comments above, it can be noted that there huge varieties of interpretation and application of segments of the Bible in Christian history, some of which have not been very keen to the human element in evangelism and conversion!

But what does the Bible have to say?

Introduction 2: *This [One] Thing I Do*!

In an interesting book by this title, Franklin Graham explained the ministry of Bob Pierce, founder of World Vision and grandfather of AERDO (Association of Evangelical Relief and Development Organizations), a book which explained the two things he did.[65] Interestingly, the title of this book was drawn from a pre-critical edition reading of 1 Cor 9:23:

1 Cor 9:23 (KJV), "And this I do for the gospel's sake, that I might be partaker thereof with *you*."

In context, the demonstrative "this" refers to "that I might save some" in v. 22 and "that I might win…" 6x in vv. 19-22. Or also to the preeminence of "evangelizing" for Paul in 1 Cor 9:16.

Translations of 1 Cor 9:23

Pre-Critical Greek		Combination						Critical Edition Greek*	
Byzantine Textform	Tyndale's NT (1534)	NIVO 1984	NIRV 1995	CSBO 1999	NET 2004	NLT 2007	ESV 2011	Wycliffe 2nd Edition (1388)	NA27
Τοῦτο δὲ ποιῶ διὰ τὸ εὐαγγέλιον,	"And this I do for the gospels sake"	"I do all this for the sake of the gospel"	"I do all of that because of the good news"	"Now I do all this because of the gospel"	"I do all these things because of the gospel"	"I do everything to spread the Good News"	"I do it all for the sake of the gospel"	"But Y do alle thingis for the gospel"	πάντα δὲ ποιῶ διὰ τὸ εὐαγγέλιον,
Other versions with similar translations	Bishops', English Geneva, KJV, Webster's, Young's, NKJ	NJB✳, NABO✳, TNIV, NAB✳, NIV		CSB				Rotherham, Noyes, Darby, ERV, ASV, RSV, NASB, NRS	

*The Critical Edition Greek merely follows the Latin Vulgate's *omnia autem facio propter evangelium*. That this Latin reading existed early in the Reformation is evident through Jacques LeFebvre d'Étaple's 1522 French translation: "Mais ie fais toutes choses po' levangile" [But I do all things for the gospel]. Note also that the Critical edition translations merely return to Wycliffe's translation of the Latin into English in this verse.

---

[65] "Pierce explained his change of heart resulting from an experience on a trip he took to China. He shared the event with Franklin Graham when, early in his ministry, Pierce's view of the mission of the church changed—it was a paradigm shift etched in his mind. Bob Pierce's encounter with the persecution of a young protégé of Dutch missionary Tena Hoelkeboer resulted in a major paradigm shift in his view of evangelism, similar to the impact of Bishop Thoburn's sermon on John R. Mott fifty years earlier.

"It is interesting that both Pierce and Mott had clearly etched in their memory the exact time when they changed from an exclusively soul-oriented evangelism to a combination of evangelism and social ministry. It would seem in their minds that these events represented a major paradigm shift for them. And so it was—it was a shift from a universal affirmative—the gospel, to a particular affirmative—the gospel and social concern or social ministry" (Thomas P. Johnston, *Examining Billy Graham's Theology of Evangelism* [Eugene, OR: Wipf & Stock, 2003], 91-93; citing Franklin Graham and Jeannette Lockerbie, *Bob Pierce: This One Thing I Do* [Dallas: Word, 1983]).

And yet, note the power of this one phrase, "And this I do":

> "This" [Τοῦτο] referring to the soul-winning discussed in vv. 19-22.
>
> "This" referring to the "evangelizing" mentioned in vv. 16-17.
>
> "This" referring to the "threshing" and "plowing" in v. 10 and the "sowing" and "reaping" in v. 11.

> "I do" [ποιῶ] describes an action in which Paul had become adept, "evangelizing."
>
> "I do" teaches that "evangelizing" is something to be done, following the example of Paul,
>   1 Cor 11:1.

Not, I would recommend, "All things"—as in the "wordless witness" of a Christian lifestyle.[66]

Introduction 3: So, what then is the chief end of the redeemed? Is it not "To sound His praise abroad"?—"To Proclaim His Excellencies"?

Anything less than evangelism at the heart of faith in Christ is Pharisaical belief—believing without verbal confessing for fear of man:

> John 12:42-43, "Nevertheless many even of the rulers **believed in Him**, but because of the Pharisees **they were not confessing** *Him*, lest they should be put out of the synagogue; for they loved the approval of men rather than the approval of God."

And if a verbal confession before men is important, should it even be done before antagonistic people? Absolutely!

> Mark 8:38, "For whoever is ashamed of Me and My words in this adulterous and sinful generation, the Son of Man will also be ashamed of him when He comes in the glory of His Father with the holy angels."

Is verbal confession so important that it becomes the foundational cornerstone for Evangelical theology and practice? Absolutely!

Yet, why is the command to evangelize sometimes considered the only command of Jesus to be obeyed conditionally?

---

[66]"21. Above all the Gospel must be proclaimed by witness. Take a Christian or a handful of Christians who, in the midst of their own community, show their capacity for understanding and acceptance, their sharing of life and destiny with other people, their solidarity with the efforts of all for whatever is noble and good. Let us suppose that, in addition, they radiate in an altogether simple and unaffected way their faith in values that go beyond current values, and their hope in something that is not seen and that one would not dare to imagine. Through this wordless witness these Christians stir up irresistible questions in the hearts of those who see how they live: Why are they like this? Why do they live in this way? What or who is it that inspires them? Why are they in our midst? Such a witness is already a silent proclamation of the Good News and a very powerful and effective one. Here we have an initial act of evangelization. The above questions will ask, whether they are people to whom Christ has never been proclaimed, or baptized people who do not practice, or people who live as nominal Christians but according to principles that are in no way Christian, or people who are seeking, and not without suffering, something or someone whom they sense but cannot name. Other questions will arise, deeper and more demanding ones, questions evoked by this witness which involves presence, sharing, solidarity, and which is an essential element, and generally the first one, in evangelization."[51]
"All Christians are called to this witness, and in this way they can be real evangelizers. We are thinking especially of the responsibility incumbent on immigrants in the country that receives them. …
"41. Without repeating everything that we have already mentioned, it is appropriate first of all to emphasize the following point: for the Church, the first means of evangelization is the witness of an authentically Christian life, given over to God in a communion that nothing should destroy and at the same time given to one's neighbor with limitless zeal.
"69. Religious, for their part, find in their consecrated life a privileged means of effective evangelization. At the deepest level of their being they are caught up in the dynamism of the Church's life, which is thirsty for the divine Absolute and called to holiness. It is to this holiness that they bear witness. They embody the Church in her desire to give herself completely to the radical demands of the beatitudes. By their lives they are a sign of total availability to God, the Church and the brethren.
"As such they have a special importance in the context of the witness which, as we have said, is of prime importance in evangelization. At the same time as being a challenge to the world and to the Church herself, this silent witness of poverty and abnegation, of purity and sincerity, of self-sacrifice in obedience, can become an eloquent witness capable of touching also non-Christians who have good will and are sensitive to certain values.
"In this perspective one perceives the role played in evangelization by religious men and women consecrated to prayer, silence, penance and sacrifice" (Paul VI, *Evangelii Nuntiandi* [8 December 1975], §21, 41, 69; emphasis mine; available at: http://listserv.american.edu/catholic/church/papal/paul.vi/p6evang.txt [online]; accessed: 8 Sept 2004; Internet).

The Christian's Calling to Evangelism

A. A Look at 1 Peter 2:9-10 (cf. Isa 43:21):

1. 1 Peter 2:9-10

Byzantine Textform (2004):

⁹ Ὑμεῖς δὲ γένος ἐκλεκτόν, βασίλειον ἱεράτευμα, ἔθνος ἅγιον, λαὸς εἰς περιποίησιν, ὅπως τὰς ἀρετὰς ἐξαγγείλητε τοῦ ἐκ σκότους ὑμᾶς καλέσαντος εἰς τὸ θαυμαστὸν αὐτοῦ φῶς· ¹⁰ οἱ ποτὲ οὐ λαός, νῦν δὲ λαὸς θεοῦ· οἱ οὐκ ἠλεημένοι, νῦν δὲ ἐλεηθέντες.

ASV (1901)

⁹But ye are an elect race, a royal priesthood, a holy nation, a people for *God's* own possession, that ye may show forth [follows KJV] the excellencies of him who called you out of darkness into his marvellous light: ¹⁰who in time past were no people, but now are the people of God: who had not obtained mercy, but now have obtained mercy.[67]

NASB (1995)

⁹But you are A CHOSEN RACE, A royal PRIESTHOOD, A HOLY NATION, A PEOPLE FOR *God's* OWN POSSESSION, so THAT YOU MAY PROCLAIM THE EXCELLENCIES[68] of Him who has called you out of darkness into His marvelous light; ¹⁰for you once were NOT A PEOPLE, but now you are THE PEOPLE OF GOD; you had NOT RECEIVED MERCY, but now you have RECEIVED MERCY.[69]

2. 1 Peter 2:9's Key Verb: ἐξαγγέλλω—to "sound forth," "publish," or "broadcast":

From Isaiah 43:20-21?

ASV (1901)

²⁰The beasts of the field shall honor me, the jackals and the ostriches; because I give waters in the wilderness, and rivers in the desert, to give drink to my people, my chosen, ²¹the people which I formed for myself, that they might set forth my praise.

NASB (1995)

²⁰"The beasts of the field will glorify Me,
The jackals and the ostriches,
Because I have given waters in the wilderness
And rivers in the desert,
To give drink to My chosen people.
²¹"The people whom I formed for Myself
Will declare My praise [Heb לִּי תְּהִלָּתִי יְסַפֵּרוּ; Gk τὰς ἀρετάς μου διηγεῖσθαι]."

> Note that the LXX in this case used διηγέομαι to translate *saphar*, and not ἐξαγγέλλω, as did Peter in 1 Pet 2:9:
> > Could it very well be that he may have translated the phrase from the Hebrew himself?
> > Or perhaps could it not be that he heard Jesus translate it that way in His itinerant teaching?
> Note also that in the LXX, the Hebrew verb *saphar* is translated using at least 6 different Greek verbs:[70]
> > 3 examples of ἀναγγέλλω, 2 examples of ἀπαγγέλλω, 2 examples of διαγγέλλω 6 examples of ἐξαγγέλλω, 10 examples of διηγέομαι, and 2 examples of ἐκδιηγέομαι.

Or from Isaiah 42:12?

ASV (1901)

"Let them give glory unto Jehovah, and declare his praise in the islands."

NASB (1995)

"Let them give glory to the LORD, And declare His praise in the coastlands."

> Hebrew: וּתְהִלָּתוֹ בָּאִיִּים יַגִּידוּ; Greek LXX: τὰς ἀρετὰς αὐτοῦ ἐν ταῖς νήσοις ἀναγγελοῦσιν
> Notice that instead of using the Heb verb *saphar*, Isaiah in this text used the Hebrew verb *nagad*;
> Notice on the same chart in Chapter 7 that the verb *nagad* is translated by two of the verbs mentioned above 23 examples of ἀναγγέλλω, 5 examples of ἀπαγγέλλω, and 1 use of ἀγαλλιάω;
> Note also that in this case, the LXX used ἀναγγέλλω to translate the Hebrew *nagad*, and not ἐξαγγέλλω as in 1 Pet 2:9 (Again, Peter may have translated the phrase from the Hebrew himself).

---

[67]*1901 American Standard Version* (Oak Harbor, WA: Logos Research Systems) 1994.

[68]In this phrase the caps are mine.

[69]*The New American Standard Bible, 1995 Update* (La Habra, California: Lockman) 1996.

[70]Chapter 7, "A Proclaimed or Spoken Witness in the Old Testament."

3. **1 Peter Lists of Descriptors for the Christian:**

   a. **Who we are?**
      1) A CHOSEN RACE (Isa 43:20; cf. Deut 7:6; 10:15)
      2) A royal PRIESTHOOD (Exod 19:6 [23:22 LXX], Isa 61:6 [1 Pet 2:5; Rev 1:6; 5:10; 20:6])
      3) A HOLY NATION (Exod 19:6 [23:22 LXX]; cf. Deut 26:19, "a holy people"; 1 Cor 1:2; 1 Pet 1:15-16)
      4) A PEOPLE FOR *God's* OWN POSSESSION (Isa 43:21; Exod 19:5 [23:22 LXX]; Deut 4:20; 7:6; 14:2; 26:18 [Titus 2:14])

   By the way, particularity emanates from each of these descriptors:

   The fourth descriptor is rendered in the KJV, "A peculiar people"

   Could it be rendered "a particular people"—as in "set aside" for purchasing?

   Interestingly, the word "particular" is found only 2 times in the entire NKJ (Zach 11:7; Eph 5:33)

   Likewise, the word "particular" is found once in the NAS (Dan 8:13)

   There seems to be a level of antagonism to the particular elements of redemption that may be transposed into certain Bible translations

   Notice, for example, the difference between Norton's translation of the Syriac and the three other translations: "multitude" versus "congregation" or "assembly"; there appears to be an clear ecclesiastical presupposition in these renderings

Translations of "A Peculiar People" in 1 Pet 2:9 (from the Greek)

Byzantine Text-form	Tyndale (1534); Geneva; Bishops; KJV; Webster's	Young's (1862...)	Darby (1884)	ERV (1885); ASV; NAS	Bible in Basic English (1949)	RSV (1952); GNT*	NKJ (1982)	NIV (1984)	TNIV (2001, 2005)	NLT (2004)	CSB (2005)	ESV (2007)
Original Greek	From the Greek	From the Greek	From the Greek	From the Greek	From the Greek	From the Greek	From the Greek	From the Greek	From the Greek	From the Greek	From the Greek	From the Greek
λαὸς εἰς περιποίησιν	a peculiar people	a people acquired	a people for a possession	a people for *God's* own possession	a people given up completely to God	God's own people	His own special people	a people belonging to God	God's special possession	God's very own possession	a people for His possession	a people for His own possession

Translations of "A Peculiar People" in 1 Pet 2:9 (from the Latin and the Syriac)

Latin Vulgate I✠	Latin Vulgate II✠	Wycliffe (1388)	Douay-Rheims✠ (1899)	NJB✠ (1985)	NAB✠ (1991); NET	CEV✠ (1991)	Etheridge (1849)[71]	Norton (1881)[72]	Murdock (1851)[73]	Magiera (2006)
1880 Migne edition	1979 Nova Vulgata	From the Latin	From the Latin	From the Latin	From the Latin (and Greek)	From the Greek and Latin	From the Syriac	From the Syriac	From the Syriac	From the Syriac
populus acquisitionis	populus in acquisitionem	a puple of purchasing	a purchased people	a people to be a personal possession	a people of His own	and special people	a congregation redeemed	a multitude delivered	a redeemed congregation	a redeemed assembly

b. What we do?

1) So that you may proclaim[74] the excellencies (Isa 43:21 [42:12]), cf. Ps 145:4 et al

a) By the way, the proclamational verbs in the phrase in the LXX translations of Isaiah 42 and 43 are both different than what is found in 1 Pet 2:9:

(1) Isa 42:12, "And declare His praise in the coastlands" = LXX: τὰς ἀρετὰς αὐτοῦ ἐν ταῖς νήσοις ἀναγγελοῦσιν [verb: ἀναγγέλλω]

(2) Isa 43:21, "Will declare My praise" = LXX: τὰς ἀρετάς μου διηγεῖσθαι [verb: διηγέομαι]

(3) 1 Pet 2:9, "that you may proclaim the excellencies" = Byz: ὅπως τὰς ἀρετὰς ἐξαγγείλητε [verb: ἐξαγγέλλω]

---

[71]"John Wesley Etheridge was an English nonconformist clergyman who was born near Newport, Isle of Wight, on 24th of February, 1804. He died in Camborne on 24th of May, 1866. Etheridge was educated by his father and later acquired a thorough knowledge of Hebrew, Greek, Latin, Syriac, German and French. In 1826 he attempted to enter the ministry and after a period of probation was received in full connection at the conference of 1831. Thereafter he spent two years at Brighton, when he removed to Cornwall. In 1838 his health began to fail and he was pensioned and went to live at Caen and Paris. His health improving, he accepted the pastorship of a Methodist church at Boulogne in 1842. Four years later he returned to his native land and was successively on the circuits of Islington, Bristol, Leeds, Penzance, Penryn, Truro and Saint Austell in Cornwall. Heidelberg conferred on him the degree of Ph.D. He published (The Apostolic Ministry and the Question of Its Restoration Considered) (1836) ; (Misericordia, or Contemplations of the Mercy of God) (1842): (Horae Aramaicae) (1843); (The Syrian Churches: Their Early History, Liturgies and Literature) (1846) (The Apostolical Acts and Epistles from the Peschitto, or Ancient Syriac, to which are Added the Remaining Epistles and Book of Revelation from a later Syriac Text) (1849); (The Targums of Onkelos and Jonathan ben Uzziel on the Pentateuch, with the Fragments of the Jerusalem Targum) (2 vols., 1863); (Life of Rev. Adam Clarke) (1858). Consult memoir by T. Smith (London 1871)" (from: http://aramaicnewtestament.org/peshitta/etheridge/; accessed: 19 Jan 2014).

[72]"William Norton of North Devon (England) was both an Aramaic and Greek Scholar who revealed the originality of Aramaic Peshitta NT (also known as Peshito-Syriac in 1800s) through his two books. His first book is 'A Translation, in English Daily Used, of the Peshito-Syriac Text, and of the Received Greek Text, of Hebrews, James, 1 Peter, and 1 John: With An Introduction On the Peshito-Syriac Text, and the Received Greek Text of 1881' (1889). His second book is 'A Translation in English Daily Used: of the Seventeen Letters Forming Part of the Peshito-Syriac Books' (1890)" ("William Norton"; available at: http://en.metapedia.org/wiki/William_Norton [online]; accessed: 14 Dec 2014; Internet).

[73]"James Murdock was born in Westbrook, Connecticut on 16 February, 1776 and died in Columbus, MS on 10 August, 1856. He graduated at Yale in 1797, and became successively preceptor of Hopkins grammar-school at New Haven, and of Oneida academy (now Hamilton college), NY. He studied theology under Timothy Dwight, and was licensed to preach as a Congregational minister in January, 1801, and settled as pastor of the church at Princeton, MA, in June, 1802, where he remained for thirteen years. In 1815 he became professor of ancient languages in the University of Vermont, and from 1819 till 1828 he was professor of sacred rhetoric and ecclesiastical history in Andover theological seminary. In 1829 he moved to New Haven and devoted the rest of his life to study, principally that of ecclesiastical history, the oriental languages, and philosophy. He was president of the Connecticut academy of arts and sciences, vice-president of the philological society of Connecticut, and one of the founders of the American oriental society. He received the degree of D. D. from Harvard in 1819" (from: http://aramaicnewtestament.org/peshitta/murdock/; accessed: 19 Jan 2014).

[74]The subjunctive mood of the verb ἐξαγγέλλω is used as a purpose clause, as explained in J. W. Wenham's *The Elements of New Testament Greek* (Cambridge: University Press, 1965), 161-62: "The Use of the Subjunctive… (2) **Purpose** (or **final**) **clauses**. Purpose clauses are introduced by ἵνα or ὅπως, both of which mean 'in order that' or 'that'."

b) Could it be that Peter translated from the Hebrew himself, as he was recalling lessons from the Hebrew with Jesus?
(1) Did Jesus teach His disciples in Greek or in Aramaic?
(2) Did Jesus quote from the OT to His disciples in Hebrew?

c) Notice the wide range of translations of the proclamational verb in modern English language translations…

Translations of τὰς ἀρετὰς ἐξαγγείλητε in 1 Peter 2:9

1	2	3	4	5	6	7	8	9	10	11	12	13
New Jerusalem Bible⌖ (1985)*	French Le Semeur** (1992, 1999)	New Living Translation (2004)	Tyndale Version (1534)	KJV75 (1611/ 1769)	American Standard Version (1901)	English Geneva (1560)	CEV⌖ (1995)***	Good News Trans⌖ (1992)°	New American Bible⌖ (1991)°°	NIV (1984)	NKJ (1982)	NAS (1977); CSB (2004); ESV (2007)
to sing the praises	so that you may celebrate very highly the marvelous works	as a result, you can show others the goodness of God	that ye shuld shewe the vertues	that ye should shew forth the praises	that ye may show forth the excellencies	that ye shulde shewe forthe the vertues	Now you must tell all the wonderful things that he has done.	chosen to proclaim the wonderful acts of God	so that you may announce the praises	that you may declare the praises	that you may proclaim the praises	that you may proclaim the excellencies
Worship-oriented	**Lifestyle-oriented**						**Proclamation-oriented; muted purpose clause**		**Proclamational-oriented; as purpose clause (apodosis)**			

*The New Jerusalem (1885) is a Roman Catholic translation, whose 1973 French older cousin (*Bible de Jérusalem*) seems to be the pattern for the French *Le Semeur*. Interestingly enough, the French *Jérusalem* followed pattern #9, 12, or 13, using "proclaim."

**Translation mine.

***American Bible Society's (ABS) *Contemporary English Version* (imprimatur: Most Reverend Daniel E. Pilarczyk, President, National Conference of Catholic Bishops [1991]), reorganized the descriptors: "But you are God's chosen and special people. You are a group of royal priests and a holy nation. God has brought you out of darkness into his marvelous light. Now you must tell all the wonderful things that he has done."

°Imprimatur: Most Reverend William H. Keeler, President, National Conference of Catholic Bishops (1993); also published by the ABS.

°°The 1991 American Bible is copyrighted by the Confraternity of Christian Doctrine (Washington, D.C.). Some of the oldest French Bibles also use announce (Fr. *Announcer*; cf. 1530 Lefèvre; 1534 Olivétan; 1550 Louvain).

c. The reason for our message? Our salvation!
1) For you once were NOT A PEOPLE, but now you are THE PEOPLE OF GOD (Hos 2:23 [1:9; 2:1]);
2) You had NOT RECEIVED MERCY, but now you have RECEIVED MERCY (Hos 2:23 [1:6; 2:1]).

B. Other OT Passages with This Same Emphasis:[76]
Introduction:
Examples of message are limited to the glory of God—there is an obvious shift in the NT to the salvation wrought in Christ
See emphasis on recipients of the message in bold, and salvation highlighted;
By the way, the word "salvation" is found 61 times in the NAS translation of the book of Psalms (e.g. Psa 24:5; 40:16; 51:12, 14; 65:5…), the word "glory" is found 55 times, and the phrase "glory of God" one time (Psa 19:1).
Exod 9:16, "But, indeed, for this cause I have allowed you [Moses] to remain, in order to show you My power, and in order to proclaim My name **through all the earth**"

---

[75]The word "shew" or "shew forth" was a favorite translation for the KJV for numerous proclamational terms, in addition to its visual meaning ("to cause to see," cf. 39:4; or "show," Luke 4:5; 17:14; 20:24, 47; 22:12; 24:40), or its abstract cognitive meaning ("to cause to know"; cf. Isa 40:14; Luke 20:37). The KJV used "shew" as a translation for *basar* (evangelize, bear tidings), *saphar* (count, recount, relate), for *nagad* (proclaim, be conspicuous), and for *shama* (make known, [cause] to hear). In the NT the KJV translated the following as "shew": ἀναγγέλλω, ἀπαγγέλλω, εὐαγγελίζω, διηγέομαι, προκαταγγέλλω, etc. For a complete analysis, see Chapter 7, "Defining Evangelizing."

[76]For a more complete look at OT proclamational verbs, see Chapter 7, "Defining Evangelizing"; F. "Toward Translating Proclamational Words in the Old Testament."

1 Chr 16:8-9, "Oh give thanks to the LORD, call upon His name; Make known His deeds **among the peoples**. Sing to Him, sing praises to Him; Speak of all His wonders"

1 Chr 16:23-24, "Sing to the LORD, all the earth; Proclaim good tidings of His salvation from day to day. Tell of His glory among the nations, His wonderful deeds **among all the peoples**"

Psa 9:11, "Sing praises to the LORD, who dwells in Zion; Declare **among the peoples** His deeds"

Psa 9:14, "That I may tell of all Your praises, That in the gates of the daughter of Zion I may rejoice in Your salvation"

Psa 22:31-32, "Posterity will serve Him; It will be told of the Lord **to the *coming* generation**. They will come and will declare His righteousness **To a people who will be born**, that He has performed *it*."

Psa 26:6-7, "I shall wash my hands in innocence, And I will go about Your altar, O LORD, That I may proclaim with the voice of thanksgiving And declare all Your wonders"

Psa 35:28, "And my tongue shall declare Your righteousness *And* Your praise all day long"

Psa 40:5, "Many, O LORD my God, are the wonders which You have done, And Your thoughts toward us; There is none to compare with You. If I would declare and speak of them, They would be too numerous to count"

Psa 40:9-10, "I have proclaimed glad tidings of righteousness **in the great congregation**; Behold, I will not restrain my lips, O LORD, You know. I have not hidden Your righteousness within my heart; I have spoken of Your faithfulness and Your salvation; I have not concealed Your lovingkindness and Your truth **from the great congregation**"

Psa 51:12-15, "Restore to me the joy of Your salvation And sustain me with a willing spirit. *Then* I will teach transgressors Your ways, And sinners will be converted to You. Deliver me from bloodguiltiness, O God, the God of my salvation; *Then* my tongue will joyfully sing of Your righteousness. O Lord, open my lips, That my mouth may declare Your praise."

Psa 64:9, "Then all men will fear, And they will declare the work of God, And will consider what He has done"

Psa 71:8, "My mouth is filled with Your praise And with Your glory all day long"

Psa 71:15-17, "My mouth shall tell of Your righteousness *And* of Your salvation all day long; For I do not know the sum *of them*. I will come with the mighty deeds of the Lord GOD; I will make mention of Your righteousness, Yours alone. O God, You have taught me from my youth, And I still declare Your wondrous deeds"

Psa 71:24, "My tongue also will utter Your righteousness all day long; For they are ashamed, for they are humiliated who seek my hurt"

Psa 73:28, "But as for me, the nearness of God is my good; I have made the Lord GOD my refuge, That I may tell of all Your works"

Psa 75:1, "Men declare Thy wondrous works" [διηγήσομαι πάντα τὰ θαυμάσιά σου]

Psa 75:9, "But as for me, I will declare *it* forever; I will sing praises to the God of Jacob"

Psa 78:4, "We will not conceal them **from their children**, But tell **to the generation to come** the praises of the LORD, And His strength and His wondrous works that He has done"

Psa 79:13, "So we Your people and the sheep of Your pasture Will give thanks to You forever; To all generations we will tell of Your praise"

Psa 89:1, "I will sing of the lovingkindness of the LORD forever; To all generations I will make known Your faithfulness with my mouth."

Psa 92:1-3, "It is good to give thanks to the LORD And to sing praises to Your name, O Most High; To declare Your lovingkindness in the morning And Your faithfulness by night, With the ten-stringed lute and with the harp, With resounding music upon the lyre"

Psa 92:14-15, "They will still yield fruit in old age; They shall be full of sap and very green, To declare that the LORD is upright; *He is* my rock, and there is no unrighteousness in Him"

Psa 96:2-3, "Sing to the LORD, bless His name; Proclaim good tidings of His salvation from day to day. Tell of His glory **among the nations**, His wonderful deeds **among all the peoples**."

Psa 102:21, "That *men* may tell of the name of the LORD in Zion And His praise in Jerusalem"

Psa 105:1-2, "Oh give thanks to the LORD, call upon His name; Make known His deeds among the peoples. Sing to Him, sing praises to Him; Speak of all His wonders"

Psa 106:2, "Who can speak of the mighty deeds of the LORD, Or can show forth all His praise?" (LXX. ἀκουστὰς ποιήσει πάσας τὰς αἰνέσεις αὐτοῦ; Fr. Qui publiera toute sa louange?)

Psa 107:22, "Let them also offer sacrifices of thanksgiving, And tell of His works with joyful singing"

Psa 118:17, "I will not die, but live, And tell of the works of the LORD"

Psa 145:4, "One generation shall praise Your works **to another**, And shall declare Your mighty acts"[77]

Psa 145:6-7, "Men shall speak of the power of Your awesome acts, And I will tell of Your greatness. They shall eagerly utter the memory of Your abundant goodness And will shout joyfully of Your righteousness"

Psa 145:11-12, "They shall speak of the glory of Your kingdom And talk of Your power; To make known to the sons of men Your mighty acts And the glory of the majesty of Your kingdom"

---

[77]Notice what the Babylonian Talmud said about Psa 145: "Said R. Eleazar bar Abina, 'Whoever says the Psalm, "Praise of David" (Psa 145) three times a day may be assured that he belongs to the world to come'" ("Bavli Berakhot," Chapter One, Folio 2A, M. III.3.,A. in Jacob Neusner, *The Babylonian Talmud: A Translation and Commentary* [Peabody, MA: Hendricksen, 2005, 2011] 1:18).

Psa 145:21, "My mouth will speak the praise of the LORD, And all flesh will bless His holy name forever and ever"

Psa 149:6, "*Let* the high praises of God *be* in their mouth"

Isa 12:4-5, "And in that day you will say, 'Give thanks to the LORD, call on His name. Make known His deeds **among the peoples**; Make *them* remember that His name is exalted.' Praise the LORD in song, for He has done excellent things; Let this be known throughout the earth"

Isa 38:19, "It is the living who give thanks to You, as I do today; A father **tells his sons** about Your faithfulness"

Isa 40:9, "Get yourself up on a high mountain, O Zion, bearer of good news (Gk. ὁ εὐαγγελιζόμενος; Lat. *evangelizas*), Lift up your voice mightily, O Jerusalem, bearer of good news; Lift *it* up, do not fear. Say to the cities of Judah, 'Here is your God!'"

Isa 42:12, "Let them give glory to the LORD And declare His praise in the coastlands."

Isa 43:21, "The people whom I formed for Myself Will declare My praise"

Isa 48:20, "Go forth from Babylon! Flee from the Chaldeans! Declare (Gk. ἀναγγείλατε) with the sound of joyful shouting (Gk. φωνὴν εὐφροσύνης), proclaim (Gk. ἀκουστὸν) this, Send it out (Gk. ἀπαγγείλατε) to the end of the earth (cf. Acts 1:8); Say, 'The LORD has redeemed His servant Jacob'"

Isa 52:7, "How lovely on the mountains Are the feet of him who brings good news, Who announces peace And brings good news of happiness, Who announces salvation, *And* says to Zion, 'Your God reigns!'"

Isa 60:6, "…And will bear good news of the praises of the LORD" (καὶ τὸ σωτήριον κυρίου εὐαγγελιοῦνται)

Isa 66:19, "I will set a sign among them and will send survivors from them to the nations: Tarshish, Put, Lud, Meshech, Rosh, Tubal and Javan, to the distant coastlands that have neither heard My fame nor seen My glory. And they will declare My glory among the nations" (καὶ ἀναγγελοῦσίν μου τὴν δόξαν ἐν τοῖς ἔθνεσιν).

C. Other OT Passages:

Speak of singing the high praises of God, Psa 18:49; 40:3; 92:4; 108:3; 109:30; 117:1; 119:171; 148:13

In first person, Isa 45:22

In second person, Psa 16:2; 96:10

In passive mood, Psa 66:8; 67:1-3

Speak of no one declaring in the grave, Psa 30:9; 88:11-12

Speak of the heavens declaring, Psa 19:1; 50:6; 89:5; 97:6

Further OT passages emphasize the message to be shared:

Isa 45:24-25, "They will say of Me, '**Only in the LORD are righteousness and strength**.' Men will come to Him, And all who were angry at Him will be put to shame. In the LORD all the offspring of Israel Will be justified and will glory."

Isa 49:6 (cf. Acts 13:47), "He says, 'It is too small a thing that You should be My Servant To raise up the tribes of Jacob and to restore the preserved ones of Israel; I will also make You a light of the nations So that My salvation may reach to the end of the earth.'"

Isa 52:10, "The LORD has bared His holy arm In the sight of all the nations, That all the ends of the earth may see The salvation of our God."

D. Some NT passages with this same emphasis (an extensive study of NT verbs for proclamation is found in Chapter 7 and a study of NT nouns for the message is found in Chapter 17):

Acts 2:11, "we hear them in our *own* tongues speaking of the mighty deeds of God" (as a fulfillment of the above admonitions!)

Eph 1:6, "to the praise of the glory of His grace" (Gk, εἰς ἔπαινον δόξης τῆς χάριτος αὐτοῦ; Fr NEG, "pour célébrer la gloire de sa grâce").

Eph 3:8, "unto the Gentiles to evangelize the unfathomable riches of Christ" (Gk, εὐαγγελίσασθαι τὸν ἀνεξιχνίαστον πλοῦτον τοῦ Χριστοῦ).

E. Some Verses on Believing without Evangelizing:

1. Knowing Christ without evangelizing = believing in vain:

   2 Cor 6:1-2, "And working together *with Him*, we also urge you not to receive the grace of God in vain—for He says, 'At the acceptable time I listened to you, And on the day of salvation I helped you'; behold, now is 'the acceptable time,' behold, now is 'the day of salvation'—

2. Believing the Gospel without evangelizing = shame for the Gospel:

   Rom 1:14-17, "I am under obligation both to Greeks and to barbarians, both to the wise and to the foolish. Thus, for my part, I am eager to [evangelize among] preach the gospel to you also who are in Rome. For I am not ashamed of the gospel, for it is the power of God for salvation to everyone who believes, to the Jew first and also to the Greek. For in it *the* righteousness of God is revealed from faith to faith; as it is written, 'But the righteous *man* shall live by faith.'"

   2 Timothy 1:8-11, "Therefore **do not be ashamed** of the testimony of our Lord, or of me His prisoner; but join with *me* in suffering for the gospel according to the power of God, who has saved us, and called us with a holy calling, not according to our works, but according to His own purpose and grace which was granted us in Christ Jesus from all eternity, but now has been revealed by the appearing of our Savior Christ Jesus,

who abolished death, and brought life and immortality to light through the gospel, for which I was appointed a preacher and an apostle and a teacher."

Mark 8:38, "For whoever is ashamed of Me and My words in this adulterous and sinful generation, the Son of Man will also be ashamed of him when He comes in the glory of His Father with the holy angels."

3. Believing without evangelizing = a spirit of timidity or the fear of men:

2 Tim 1:7, "For God has not given us a spirit of timidity, but of power and love and discipline."

John 12:42-43, "Nevertheless many even of the rulers believed in Him, but because of the Pharisees they were not confessing *Him*, lest they should be put out of the synagogue; for they loved the approval of men rather than the approval of God."

F. Conclusion:

Historically, the Baptist Doctor of Theology, Balthasar Hubmaier, therefore followed the clear testimony of Scripture in 1524 by placing the spoken Gospel at the beginning of his "26 Conclusions":

I.   Every Christian is obliged to give an account of his hope, and therefore his belief, if anyone asks about it. (First Peter 3)

II. If anyone confessed Christ before men, not fearing them, though they rage as lions, Christ will confess him, in the presence of the Father, (Matt. 10 Mark 8)

III. With the heart one believes unto righteousness, and with the mouth confession is made unto eternal salvation. (Romans 10)

IV. It may be that you will believe, but will not understand. (Isaiah 6) I have believed, therefore I have spoken (Psalm 115). How shall they believe on him of whom they have not heard? (Romans 10)[78]

G. Comparing this truth with some other concepts...

Select Comparative Purposes for Man's Life

#	Person	Purpose
1	Darwin	Survival of the fittest; Be the fittest and survive!
2	Greek Golden Mean	Moderation in all things: Find out what's good for you, and live a balanced life!
3	Highest Virtue of Greek Philosophy / Opposite of which is the First Cardinal Sin of Church of Rome	Humility—Be Humble! / Pride—Don't Be Proud![79]
4	Plato	Know yourself; To yourself be true!
5	Gandhi	Make Christians better Christians, Moslems better Moslems, and Hindus better Hindus
6	Rick Warren	Know your purpose; Live the five purposes for which God made you!
7	Westminster Confession	Glorify God!
8	1 Peter 2:9	Declare the excellencies of God and of His salvation!

---

[78]Balthasar Hubmaier, "Conclusions of Balthasar Friedberg, Pastor at Waldshut and a Spiritual Brother of Ulrich Zwingli. They are Addressed to John Eck at Ingolstadt, But He Forbade Them to Be Examined," from "The Writings of Balthasar Hubmaier," collected and photographed by W. O. Lewis, translated by G. D. Davidson (Liberty, MO: Archives, William Jewell College Library), 1:38.

[79]The "vainglory of the heretics" for Thomas Aquinas appeared to be assurance of sins forgiven and assurance of salvation.

Metaphors Related to Evangelism

A. The Christian as a Light in the World:

1   Jesus is the source of light, Luke 2:32, John 1:4-9, 8:12, 9:5, 12:35, 46, Acts 13:47, 1 Pet 2:9 (cf. Psa 132:17; Isaiah 42:6)
   a.   This source of light comes from God: 1 John 1:5, 2:8.
   b.   The Gospel of Jesus Christ radiates this light, 2 Cor 4:4
   c.   This is the light of the knowledge of the glory of God in the face of Christ, 2 Cor 4:6 (cf. Heb 1:3).

2.   The Bible is the instrument by which mankind can come to know and understand this light, Psa 119:105, 130.

3.   The followers of Jesus as light, Matt 5:14, 12:36, Eph 5:8, Philippians 2:15, 1 Thess 5:5

4.   Exhortations concerning the Christian and light:

   a.   Old Testament teaching:
      1)   Judges 5:31, "Thus let all Thine enemies perish, O Lord; But let those who love Him be like the rising sun in its might."
      2)   Psa 37:6, "And He will bring forth your righteousness as the light, and your judgment as the noonday."
      3)   Psa 97:11 (NIV), "Light is shed upon the righteous and joy on the upright in heart."
      4)   Proverbs 4:18, "The path of the righteous is like the light of dawn, That shines brighter and brighter until the full day."
      5)   Proverbs 13:9 (NIV), "The light of the righteous shines brightly, but the lamp of the wicked is snuffed out."
      6)   Isaiah 42:6 and 49:6 seemed to be combined by Paul in Acts 13:47; clearly Isa 42:6 refers to the covenant people of God and 49:6 refers to the Messiah; interesting in this context, through Paul's use of Isa 49:6, is the idea that Paul was fulfilling the work of messianic prophecy by his own evangelism efforts (cf. Col 1:24-26):
         a)   Isa 42:6, "I am the LORD, I have called you in righteousness, I will also hold you by the hand and watch over you, And I will appoint you as a covenant to the people, As a light to the nations, To open blind eyes, To bring out prisoners from the dungeon, And those who dwell in darkness from the prison"
         b)   Isa 49:6, "I will make you a light of the nations So that My salvation may reach to the ends of the earth"
      7)   Daniel 12:3, "And those who have insight will shine brightly like the brightness of the expanse of heaven, and those who lead the many to righteousness, like the stars forever and ever."

   b.   The Christian has been called into fellowship with God through the light of the Gospel:
      1)   "The light of the Gospel," 2 Cor 4:4
      2)   "The light of the glory of God in the face of Christ," 2 Cor 4:6
      3)   "Called into His marvelous light," 1 Pet 2:9

   c.   The Christian is to live consistent with his calling into the light:
      1)   "Walk in the light," John 12:35-36, Eph 5:8
      2)   "Do not walk in darkness," 1 John 1:5-7
      3)   "For you are all sons of light and sons of day. We are not of the night nor of the darkness; so then let us not sleep as others do, but let us be alert and sober." 1 Thess 5:5-6 (cf. v. 8, Eph 5:14)
      4)   "The one who says he is in the light and yet hates his brother is in darkness until now," 1 John 2:9

   d.   The Christian is to shine forth this light for others to see:
      1)   Not to hide the light, Matt 5:14-16
      2)   "For thus the Lord commanded us, 'I have placed You as a light for the Gentiles, that You should bring salvation to the end of the earth.'" Acts 13:47
      3)   "...Children of God in the midst of a crooked and perverse generation among whom you appear as lights in the world, holding fast the word of life" Phil 2:15-16
      4)   "To bring to light" the Gospel truth, Eph 3:8-10
      5)   "And fixing their gaze on him, all who were sitting in the Council saw his face like the face of an angel." Acts 6:15 (cf. Exod 34:30)

   e.   A warning concerning the light: the removal of the lampstand, Rev 2:5.

5. A Christian as light and evangelism: The only way other people will know to glorify God when they see us walking in the light is if they have heard the motivation behind such a life, the Gospel of Jesus Christ—otherwise a humanistic works salvation is communicated. The Christian is a light to the world by walking in fellowship with the Lord and verbally communicating the Gospel to others.

B. The Christian as Salt:

1. Five possible understandings of the metaphor "salt":[80]

    Introduction: the real issue in understanding why there are differing interpretations of "salt" seems to be the predetermined view of Christ and Culture.[81] The question revolves around a natural or supernatural interpretation of the metaphor, i.e. is the "salt value" added to a person, people, or culture because of the Holy Spirit residing in individual hearts leading to divinely wrought works (Eph 2:10), or is it something unrelated or tangential to individual salvation? Rather, is the "salt value" something which Christians need to work, through involvement in politics, social action, economic revitalization, etc.?

    1) "That which is born of the flesh is flesh, and that which is born of the Spirit is spirit," John 3:6
    2) It is the Spirit who gives life; the flesh profits nothing; the words that I have spoken to you are spirit and are life," John 6:63
    3) "But a natural man does not accept the things of the Spirit of God, for they are foolishness to him; and he cannot understand them, because they are spiritually appraised," 1 Cor 2:24

    Robert Speer spoke to this constant battle within Christendom at the 1900 New York Ecumenical Missionary Conference:

    > "It is the aim of foreign missions that is to be defined, and not the aim of the Christian Church in the world, or of the Christian nations of the world. There are many good and Christian things which it is not the duty of the foreign missionary enterprise to do. Some things are to be laid, from the beginning, upon the shoulders of the new Christians; some are to be left to be discharged in due time by the native Christian churches that shall arise, and there are many blessings, political, commercial, and philanthropic, which the Christian nations owe to the heathen world, which are not to be paid through the enterprise of foreign missions. It is the aim of a distinctive, specific movement that we are to consider.
    > "It will help us in defining it to remind ourselves, for one thing, that we must not confuse the aim of foreign missions with the results of foreign missions. There is no force in the world so powerful to accomplish accessory results as the work of missions. Wherever it goes it plants in the hearts of men forces that produce new lives; it plants among communities of men forces that create new social combinations. It is impossible that any human tyranny should live where Jesus Christ is King. All these things the foreign mission movement accomplishes; it does not aim to accomplish them. I read in a missionary paper a little while ago that the foreign mission that was to accomplish results of permanent value must aim at the total reorganization of the whole social fabric. *This is a mischievous doctrine.* We learn nothing from human history, from the experience of the Christian Church, from the example of our Lord and His apostles to justify it. They did not aim directly at such an end. They were content to aim at implanting the life of Christ *in* the hearts of men, and were willing to leave the consequences to the care of God. It is a dangerous thing to charge ourselves openly before the world with the aim of reorganizing States and reconstructing society. How long could the missions live, in the Turkish Empire or the Native States of India, that openly proclaimed their aim to be the political reformation of the lands to which they went? It is misleading, also, as Dr. Behrends once declared, to confuse the ultimate issues with the immediate aims; and *it is not only misleading, it is fatal.* Some things can only be secured by those who do not seek them. Missions are powerful to transform the face of society, because they ignore the face of society and deal with it at its heart. They yield such powerful political and social results because they do not concern themselves with them"[82]

    Note the poignant words of Mordecai Ham on a similar topic (as an appendix to Chapter 10).

---

[80]Thomas P. Johnston, *Charts for a Theology of Evangelism*, Chart 60, "Five Interpretations of Salt in Matthew 5:13," 97.

[81]H. Richard Niebuhr, *Christ and Culture* (New York: Harper and Row, 1951).

[82]Robert E. Speer, "The Supreme and Determining Aim," in *Ecumenical Missionary Conference: New York, 1900* (New York: American Tract Society, 1900), 74-75; emphasis mine.

   a. A blessing to culture (Gen 12:1-3)—meaning God blessing others spiritually:

      1) As the blessing is passed on through making God's salvation known through all the earth, Psa 67:1-2

      2) Is this not having our speech be seasoned with salt, to know how to respond that we may give grace to those who hear (Eph 4:29; Col 4:6; 1 Pet 3:15)?

      3) God gives rejoicing and righteousness as people repent and get right with God, 2 Chr 30:23; 31:1; Acts 8:8

   b. A seasoning to culture—meaning God's physical blessing of a culture, resulting from His supernatural blessing, and due to His favor on His own, Acts 27:42-43; 1 Cor 7:14

   c. Supernatural antiseptic—meaning, Word of God, accepted or rejected, brings about a fear of God, an antiseptic against sin, wickedness, and evil

   d. Sign to solemnize a contract—as the sign of a covenant (cf. new Covenant), Lev 2:13; Num 18:19.

   e. A preservative of culture[83]—meaning, expanding on this idea, redeeming culture (through natural means)[84]

      1) This analogy is typically combined with light to produce the "two commands—one spiritual (supernatural) = light; and one physical (natural) = salt[85]

      2) A question can follow: what is there worth preserving in human culture (1 Pet 1:18)?

Five Interpretations of "Salt" in Matthew 5:13[86]

Supernatural Interpretations				Naturalistic
A Blessing to Culture	**Seasoning within Culture**	**Antiseptic to Culture**	**Contractual Arrangement**	**Preservative of Culture**
"And in you all the families of the earth will be blessed," Gen 12:3	"They are the majestic ones," Ps 16:3; Job 6:6; Col 4:6	The cleansing through the word of Christ, John 15:3	"Salt of the covenant of your God," Lev 2:13; Num 18:19; 2 Chr 13:5	Turn blessings into commands; "Be the salt of the earth"

  2. In contemporary American culture, the preservative interpretation has taken the field. For example from an email from a Christian college chaplain stated (in 2002):

> SALTY!!!! No preaching, no hard core evangelism but I don't think ANYBODY walked away not having tasted, smelled, seen, and heard the love of Jesus from _____ [the college] this weekend. People were OVERWHELMED at the generosity of _____ [the college] students. This is true for each of these events and I'm guessing for other times as well (softball teams, baseball teams and more).

  3. Unfortunately for the "redeeming culture" interpretation of salt is this statement from Charles Colson:

> When we turn to the New Testament, admittedly we do not find verses specifically commanding believers to be engaged in politics or the law or education or the arts. But we don't need to, because the cultural mandate given to Adam till applies.[87]

Therefore, according to Colson, the co-commission of socio-political-economic transformation is *not* found in the New Testament. This lack of New Testament verses is perhaps why the metaphor of

---

[83]"Conversely, it is the churches which visibly demonstrate the righteousness and peace of the kingdom which will make the greatest evangelistic and social impact on the world. The salt must retain its saltiness, Jesus said; otherwise it is good for nothing (Matt 5:13)" (John R. W. Stott, "Evangelism and Social Responsibility," in John R. W. Stott, ed., *Making Christ Known: Historic Mission Documents from the Lausanne Movement, 1974-1989* [Grand Rapids: Eerdmans, 1996], 198).

[84]Charles Colson and Nancy Pearcey, *How Now Shall We Live?* (Wheaton, IL: Tyndale House, 1999), x, 295-96.

[85]See many of John R. W. Stott's writings on the Great Commission, the Sermon on the Mount, *Balanced Christianity*, etc.

[86]Note also Chart 60, "Five Interpretations of 'Salt' in Matthew 5:13," *Charts for a Theology of Evangelism* (Nashville, Broadman, 2007), 97.

[87]Charles Colson and Nancy Pearcey, *How Now Shall We Live?* 296.

"salt" in Matthew 5:13 (with its multitudinous possible meanings) is so strongly argued as a prooftext for socio-political involvement.

4. Similarly, note the ironic words of Wolfhart Pannenberg that conversionist churches are "most relevant" to society, even though they supposedly have lost "openness to the human situation":

> It has frequently been noted that the mainline and accommodating churches are in decline, while conservative churches continue to grow. Evangelicals and fundamentalists are not embarrassed to challenge the prevailing patterns of thought and behavior associated with secularity. This growth, however, does not come without paying a price. That price includes a loss of openness to the human situation in all of its maddening variety, and a quenching of the unprejudiced search for truth. *That said, the irony is that those churches that are dismissed as irrelevant by more "sophisticated" Christians often turn out to be most relevant to our secular societies.*[88]

Concluding Thoughts:

Perhaps the most disheartening part of the "naturalistic" view is that it undermines the importance of being "born again" or "born from above" along with its corollary, the promised presence of the Holy Spirit (John 3:5-8; 6:63; 7:39; 14:17, 26; 15:26; 16:13; 20:22; Acts 1:5…). It appears to be like a slap in the face to God, saying that the presence of His Spirit (Jesus who baptizes in the Spirit, Matt 3:11; Mark 1:8; Luke 3:16; in the Spirit giving words, Matt 10:20; Mark 13:11; Luke 12:12) in the life of the believer is of little value or of no account (James 4:5 [Num 23:9]; Luke 11:13). Could this lack of consideration of the impact of the Holy Spirit not be blasphemy against the Holy Spirit (Matt 12:31-32; Mark 3:29; Luke 12:10)?

With its rationalism and sophistication, the "naturalistic" view of conversion, evangelism, and cultural impact cannot give an adequate answer to the issues of the Holy Spirit. They have de-spiritized Christianity and framed the Holy Spirit out of the question. Romanism has not fared any better, selling the Holy Spirit for a price (for Baptism, absolution, or Masses to be said for the dead). Perhaps this is why R. A. Torrey, superintendent of Moody Bible Institute, who from an intellectual standpoint was combating German rationalism, as well as perhaps the constant Evangelical drift into Unitarianism and the errors of Roman Catholicism, wrote several books on the subject of The Holy Spirit.[89]

C. Other Biblical Metaphors Relating the Christian and Evangelism:

Introduction: Billy Graham in his 1947 sermon "Retreat! Advance! Stand!" spoke of some of the following metaphors (this type of listing seemed to be part of Graham's regular preaching early on):

> We young Christians have the Word of God. Our Great Commander has said, "Go and take this message to a dying world." …
> Let us remember that the Apostle Paul exhorted the Christians centuries ago to preach only the Word. Remember, we are sowing seed....
> We are holding light....
> We are blowing a trumpet....
> We are kindling a fire ....
> We are striking with a hammer....
> We are using a sword....
> We have bread for a hungry world....
> We have water for a famishing people.... We must never give up. Keep using the Word.[90]

1. Old Testament Metaphors:[91]

a.   The Christian as a **winner of souls**, Prov 11:30, "And he who wins souls is wise."
     Literally, "he who snatches souls is wise" (cf. Jude 23)

---

[88]Wolfhart Pannenberg, "The Present and Future Church," *First Things,* November 1991, 48-51 (emphasis mine). Pannenberg was Professor of Systematic Theology on the Protestant Theological Faculty at the University of Munich, Germany.

[89]Sample R. A. Torrey books on the Holy Spirit: *Baptism with the Holy Spirit* (1895); *The Holy Spirit* (1900); *The Person and Work of the Holy Spirit* (1910).

[90]Billy Graham, *Calling Youth to Christ* (Grand Rapids: Zondervan, 1947), 44-45. These were repeated almost verbatim in Billy Graham, *Peace with God* (Garden City, NY: Doubleday, 1953), 167-68.

[91]See also Chapter 7, I. Five Categories of New Testament Terms for Evangelism, 1. Person, d. Some Old Testament Precedents.

NT parallel—"winning disciples," Matt 28:19; Acts 14:21 (NIV); cf. 1 Cor 9:19-23
NT parallel—"fishing for men," Matt 4:19; Mark 1:17; "taking/capturing men alive," Luke 5:10

Various English Translations of "Winning Souls" (*laqach nephesh*) in Prov 11:30

From Hebrew												From Latin		From Greek LXX
Geneva (1560); Bishops; KJV; Darby; ERV; ASV; NAS; NKJ; NIV; Stern; NET	Isaac Leeser (1853)	Young's (1862, 1887, 1898)	Rotherham (1868)	Cambridge (1949, 1962)	RSV (1952)	NJB‡ (1985)	NAB‡ (1991)	NLT (2007)	ESV (2011)	CSB (2005)		Wycliffe, 2nd Ed (1388)	Douai-Rheims‡ (1899)	Brenton (1851)
winneth soules	draweth souls	is taking souls	rescueth souls	takes away souls	takes away lives	capti-vates souls	takes lives away	wins friends	captures souls	takes lives		he that takith soulis	gaineth souls	cut off before their time
The fruite of the righteous is as a tree of life, and he that winneth soules, is wise.	The fruit of the righteous is of the tree of life, and the wise draweth souls to himself.	The fruit of the righteous *is* a tree of life, And whoso is taking souls *is* wise.	The fruit of the righteous, is a tree of life, and, he that rescueth souls, is wise	The fruit of righteous ness is a tree of life, but violent behaviour takes away souls.	The fruit of the righteous is a tree of life, but lawlessne ss takes away lives.	The fruit of the upright is a tree of life: the sage captivates souls.	The fruit of virtue is a tree of life, but violence takes lives away.	The seeds of good deeds become a tree of life; a wise person wins friends.	The fruit of the righteous is a tree of life, and whoever captures souls is wise.	The fruit of the righteous is a tree of life, but violence takes lives.		The fruyt of a riytful man is the tre of lijf; and he that takith soulis, is a wijs man.	The fruit of the just man is a tree of life: and he that gaineth souls, is wise.	Out of the fruit of righteous ness grows a tree of life; but the souls of transgres sors are cut off before their time.

b. The Christian as a **courier** [**postman**] of God's decrees, 2 Chr 30:6-12 (Gk. οἱ τρέχοντες, i.e. runners, from τρέχω, to run; cf. Rom 9:16; 1 Cor 9:24; Gal 5:7; note also in 1 Cor 15:3, hand delivered [Gk. παραδίδωμι], Fr. Geneva *je vous ai baillé*, "which I packaged to you"):

1) Went forth
2) Had a message of repentance, 2 Chr 30:6-9:

> "O sons of Israel, return to the LORD God of Abraham, Isaac and Israel, that He may return to those of you who escaped *and* are left from the hand of the kings of Assyria. Do not be like your fathers and your brothers, who were unfaithful to the LORD God of their fathers, so that He made them a horror, as you see. Now do not stiffen your neck like your fathers, but yield to the LORD and enter His sanctuary which He has consecrated forever, and serve the LORD your God, that His burning anger may turn away from you. For if you return to the LORD, your brothers and your sons *will find* compassion before those who led them captive and will return to this land. For the LORD your God is gracious and compassionate, and will not turn *His* face away from you if you return to Him."

3) "But they laughed them to scorn and mocked them," 2 Chr 30:10
4) "Nevertheless some men of Asher, Manasseh and Zebulun humbled themselves," 2 Chr 30:11

c. The Christian as a **one who makes known to those that do not know**, Ezra 7:25, "And you, Ezra, according to the wisdom of your God which is in your hand, appoint magistrates and judges that they may judge all the people who are in *the province* beyond the River, *even* all those who know the laws of your God; and you may teach anyone who is ignorant *of them*."

1) Last line reads literally, "and those who [do] not know, [let them] know."
2) Heb. וְדִי לָא יָדַע תְּהוֹדְעוּן; Gk. καὶ τῷ μὴ εἰδότι γνωριεῖτε;
3) Notice that this was a commission from King Artaxerxes!

d. The Christian as a **beggar telling another beggar where to find bread**, 2 Kings 7:1-9, esp. v 9, "Then they said to one another, 'We are not doing right. This day is a day of good news, but we are keeping silent; if we wait until morning light, punishment will overtake us. Now therefore come, let us go and tell the king's household.'"

1) "This is a day of good new, but if we are keeping silent'; cf. Acts 18:9-10;
2) Gk. ἡμεῖς ποιοῦμεν ἡ ἡμέρα αὕτη ἡμέρα εὐαγγελίας ἐστίν καὶ ἡμεῖς σιωπῶμεν

e. Christians as **itinerating teams of officials sent out to teach** the Word of God, 2 Chr 17:7-9 (e.g. Luke 10:1; cf. Matt 10:23)

f. The Christian as a **bearer of Good News** (an evangelist!), Isa 40:9, 52:7

g. The Christian as a **sower of seed**, Psa 126:5-6 (cf. Eccl 11:6; Isa 32:20; Amos 9:13), cf. "bringing in the sheaves"

h. The Christian as a **spiritual watchman** (ὁ σκοπὸς), Ezek 3:16-21 (cf. Jer 6:17)

i. The Christian as a **watchman who sounds the trumpet**, Ezek 33:2-7; Joel 2:1 (cf. Isa 58:1)

j. The Christian as **one who stands in the gap**, Ezek 22:30 (cf. Psa 106:23)

k. The Christian as one who **leading others to righteousness**, Dan 12:3

l. The Christian as a **messenger**:
1) Mal 2:7, "For the lips of a priest should preserve knowledge, and men should seek instruction from his mouth; for he is the messenger [Heb *mal'ak*; Gk ὁ ἄγγελος] of the LORD of hosts"
2) 2 Chr 36:15-16, "The LORD, the God of their fathers, sent *word* to them again and again by His messengers [Heb *mal'ak*; Gk ὁ προφήτης], because He had compassion on His people and on His dwelling place; but they *continually* mocked the messengers [Heb *mal'ak*; Gk ὁ ἄγγελος] of God, despised His words and scoffed at His prophets [Heb *nabyi'*; Gk ὁ προφήτης], until the wrath of the LORD arose against His people, until there was no remedy.

m. The Christian as a **shepherd finding lost sheep**, Ezek 34:4

n. The Christian as **one with insight** giving understanding to others, Dan 11:33, "And those who have insight among the people will give understanding to the many…"

o. The Christian as **one converting sinners**, Psa 51:13

p. The Christian as **turning many back from iniquity**, Mal 2:6

2. The Christian as a co-laborer with God in sharing the Gospel:

a. A fellow worker (ὁ συνεργός) with God, 1 Cor 3:9 (cf. Isa 52:6; Deut 31:7)

b. As servants of God (ὡς Θεοῦ διάκονοι), 2 Cor 6:4

3. The Christian as one working together with Christ (cf. Rom 15:8):

a. Gathering with Christ, Matt 12:30; cf. Jer 23:1-2; Zech 11:16

b. The Lord worked with them, Mark 16:20, or Christ worked through him, Rom 15:18

c. A branch in the vine of Christ, bearing much fruit, John 15:5

d. Sent by Christ, John 13:20, 17:18, 20:21 (the apostles were referred to as "servants of the Word," Luke 1:2)

e. Working together with Christ, 2 Cor 6:1-2

f. "Doing the Lord's work," 1 Cor 16:10; Phil 2:30

g. The Christian as an ambassador of reconciliation in Christ, 2 Cor 5:18-20
1) The call of the ambassador, 5:18-19
2) The role of the ambassador, 5:19-20
3) The message of the ambassador, 5:19-21

h. Evangelism as extending the work of Christ, Acts 13:47, Eph 2:17
1) "Manifesting the life of Jesus," 2 Cor 4:11
2) "Filling up that which is lacking in Christ's afflictions," Col 1:24

   i.   The Christian as giving off the scent of Christ, 2 Cor 2:14-17:
       1) The scent being the knowledge of Christ, 2:14
       2) Giving an odor of death to those who are perishing, 2:15-16
       3) Giving an odor of life to those who are being saved, 2:15-16

   j.   Titles indicating co-laboring with Christ:
       1) Apostle of Jesus Christ, 1 Cor 1:1, 2 Cor 1:1, Eph 1:1, Col 1:1, 1 Tim 1:1, 2 Tim 1:1
       2) Minister of Jesus Christ (λειτουργὸν Ἰησοῦ χριστοῦ), Rom 15:16
       3) Prisoner of Christ Jesus, Philm 1:1
       4) Bond-servant of Jesus Christ (δοῦλος Ἰησοῦ Χριστοῦ), Rom 1:1, Phil 1:1, Titus 1:1
       5) The called of Jesus Christ, Rom 1:6

4. The Christian as a fellow-worker with the Gospel:
   a. Priest of the Gospel of God, Rom 15:16 (ἱερουργοῦντα τὸ εὐαγγέλιον τοῦ Θεοῦ)
   b. Servant/minister of the Gospel, Eph 3:7, Col 1:23 (ὁ διάκονος)
   c. A fellow-partaker with the Gospel, 1 Cor 9:23 (ὁ συγκοινωνός)
   d. A participant with the Gospel, Phil 1:5 (τῇ κοινωνίᾳ ὑμῶν εἰς τὸ εὐαγγέλιον)
   e. The Christian as a sower sowing the seed of the Gospel, Matt 13:3, 19ff., Mark 4:3, 14ff.,
       Luke 8:5, 11ff.
   f. Entrusted with the Gospel, 1 Thess 2:4
   g. Clay pots with the Gospel treasure, 2 Cor 4:7
   h. Parallel designations:
       1) Servants of the new covenant, 2 Cor 3:6
       2) An agent of God's forgiveness, Matt 18:18, John 20:23

5. The Christian as a Worker in the Harvest:
   a. The call for workers, Matt 9:37-38; Luke 10:2
   b. The support of workers in the harvest, Matt 10:10; 1 Cor 9:14

6. Other New Testament Metaphors:
   a. The Christian as **fisher of men**, Matt 4:19, Mark 1:17

       1) The progression:
           Matt 4:19 (NAS), "And He said to them, 'Follow Me, and I will make you fishers of men.'"
               Byz, Δεῦτε ὀπίσω μου, καὶ ποιήσω ὑμᾶς ἁλιεῖς ἀνθρώπων.
           Mark 1:17 (NAS), "And Jesus said to them, 'Follow Me, and I will make you **become** fishers of
               men.'"
               Byz, Δεῦτε ὀπίσω μου, καὶ ποιήσω ὑμᾶς γενέσθαι ἁλιεῖς ἀνθρώπων.

       2) By the way, Jesus did not say:
           "Follow Me, and I will help you connect with God"
           "Follow Me, and I will make you worshippers of My Father"
           "Follow Me, and I will make you worshippers of Me"
           "Follow Me, and I will make you into completed men/completed people"
           "Follow Me, and I will teach you to love your neighbor as yourself"
           "Follow Me, and I will teach you to love one another"

       3) Rather He gave them a mission, even as He called them!

   b. The Christian as a **catcher of men**, Luke 5:10, "capturing men alive" [ζωγρέω]:

       "But let us remember, every man in the world is going to be 'taken alive'—by some one. The Greek
       zogreo, meaning 'to take alive,' is found only twice in the entire New Testament: in Luke 5:10 and
       2 Timothy 2:26. In one case Jesus promises to enable his disciples to take men alive for the Kingdom. In
       the other case, Paul speaks of those who have been taken alive by the Devil. It is the same outcome in both
       cases, but with a very different outcome! By one or the other fisher of men every soul will eventually be
       taken,—taken alive unto death, or taken alive unto eternal life."[92]

---

[92]C. G. Trumbull, *Taking Men Alive: Studies in the Principles and Practise of Individual Soul-Winning* (New
York: The International Committee of the YMCA, 1907; 1915; New York: Revell, 1938), 30.

c. **Sent to reap**:

"I sent you to reap [Ἐγὼ ἀπέστειλα ὑμᾶς θερίζειν] that for which you have not labored; others have labored, and you have entered into their labor." John 4:38.

d. The Christian as **calling** men to repentance, Matt 22:3 (cf. Matt 9:13; Luke 5:32)

e. The Christian as a **delivery person**, 1 Cor 15:3[93]

f. The Christian as **bearing fruit** that remains, John 4:36; 5:8, 16 (cf. Rom 1:13):

Four NT Aspects of Bearing Fruit

Fruit = Souls (e.g. fishing for men)	Fruit = Behaviors (e.g. justice versus bloodshed)	Fruit = Inner Virtues (e.g. "Fruit of the Spirit")	Fruit = Actions and Impact of False Teachers
John 4:35-38; 15:8	**Isaiah 5:1-7**	**Gal 5:22-23**	**Matt 7:15-20**

g. The Christian as **fighting the good fight** and **running a race**:

1) 1 Cor 9:24-27 (not the context of 1 Cor 9:16-23)

2) 2 Tim 4:7, "I have fought the good fight, I have finished the course, I have kept [guarded] the faith":
   a) Paul could say that he fought the good fight
   b) He had finished the course
   c) He had preserved the faith, by maintaining its purity and passing it on to others, both through evangelism and through his teaching and writings! This was written in a book with a litany of people who had not persevered in the Gospel (2 Tim 1:15; 2:16-18; 3:5, 8-9; 4:3-4, 10, 16)

h. Evangelism is **the direction in the Christian's armor**, Eph 6:15:

The Christian life is meant to be one of "going"—with the gospel's call as the direction for that going.

1) "Having shod your feet with the preparation of [zeal for] the Gospel of peace." (cf. Luke 1:2)
   a) καὶ ὑποδησάμενοι τοὺς πόδας ἐν ἑτοιμασίᾳ τοῦ εὐαγγελίου τῆς εἰρήνης·
   b) Charles Hodge (in his commentary on this verse) recommended the translation of ἡ ἑτοιμασία as "alacrity"
   c) Preparation is not only having the right weapons, but rather having the weapons aimed and ready to fire: consider, for example, the image of an archer with bow stretched, aimed, and ready to shoot:
   Psa 11:2, "For, behold, the wicked bend the bow, They make ready their arrow upon the string [ἡτοίμασαν βέλη εἰς φαρέτραν], To shoot in darkness at the upright in heart."

2) French Segond revisée Genève: *"Mettez pour chaussures à vos pieds le zèle que donne l'Évangile de paix"*

3) Consider different ways of translating the word ἡ ἑτοιμασία, from passive (preparation) to positive (eagerness), and to active (zeal)…

---

[93]Chapter 7, I., "Five Categories of New Testament Terms for Evangelism," includes a chart on the use of this verb in 1 Cor 15:3.

Translations of the phrase ἐν ἑτοιμασίᾳ in Ephesians 6:15
From "Equipment" to "Zeal"

Translations	"Equipment of"	"Preparation of"	"Availability to serve"*	"Readiness given by"	"Prepared by"	"Momentum to announce"	"Desire to tell"	"Eagerness to spread"	"Zeal which comes from"
FROM PASSIVE PREPARATION?			→	OR		→			TO ACTIVE INVOLVEMENT?
Byzantine Textform	RSV (1952)	[Jerome, 435]; English Geneva (GNV) (1560); KJV (1622/1769); ASV (1901); NAS (1977); NKJ (1982)	IBS's French *Le Semeur* (1992, 1999)	NIV (1984); ESV (2001); CSB (2003)	Tyndale (1534)	French *Traduction Oecumenique de la Bible* (TOB) (1988)	CEV⌧ (1991)	New Jerusalem Bible⌧ (1985)	French Louis Segond (1910); French Jerusalem⌧ (1973); French New Geneva (1975); Bible *Français Courant* (1997)
καὶ ὑποδησάμενοι τοὺς πόδας ἐν ἑτοιμασίᾳ τοῦ εὐαγγελίου τῆς εἰρήνης	and having shod your feet with **the equipment of** the gospel of peace	And your fete shod with **the preparation of** the gospel of peace	Having for shoes on your feet **the availability to serve** the Good News of peace**	And, as shoes for your feet, having put on **the readiness given by** the gospel of peace	and shood with showes **prepared by** the gospell of peace	And, as shoes on [your] feet, **the momentum to announce** the gospel of peace***	Your **desire to tell** the good news about peace should be like shoes on your feet	Wearing for shoes on your feet **the eagerness to spread** the gospel of peace	Place as shoes on your feet **the zeal which comes from** the Gospel of peace****

*Notice how the International Bible Society's French *Le Semeur* is the least Evangelical French translation, changing the proclamation of the Gospel into service. This emphasis seems to be no coincidence. In these notes we shall see translation after translation which follows this non-proclamational or even anti-proclamational pattern.

**French: "*Ayez pour chaussures à vos pieds la disponibilité à servir la Bonne Nouvelle de la paix.*" Translation mine.

***French: "*et, comme chaussures aux pieds, l'élan pour annoncer l'Évangile de la paix.*" Translation mine.

****French: "*Mettez pour chaussure à vos pieds le zèle que donne l'Évangile de paix.*" Translation mine.

    i. The Christian as a **sent one**, as the name apostle signifies, "whom He also named as apostles," Luke 6:13
        1) Mark 3:14, "And He appointed twelve, so that they would be with Him and that He *could* send them out to preach [καὶ ἵνα ἀποστέλλῃ αὐτοὺς κηρύσσειν]"
        2) Mark 6:7, "And He summoned the twelve and began to send them out in pairs [καὶ ἤρξατο αὐτοὺς ἀποστέλλειν δύο δύο], and gave them authority over the unclean spirits"
        3) Luke 9:2, "And He sent them out to proclaim [Καὶ ἀπέστειλεν αὐτοὺς κηρύσσειν] the kingdom of God and to perform healing"
        4) Luke 10:1, "Now after this the Lord appointed seventy others, and sent them in pairs [καὶ ἀπέστειλεν αὐτοὺς ἀνὰ δύο] ahead of Him to every city and place where He Himself was going to come"
        5) Luke 10:3, "Go; behold, I send you [Byz. ἐγὼ ἀποστέλλω ὑμᾶς] out as lambs in the midst of wolves"

D. Some Verses on Self-Sacrifice:

    1. Matt 10:39, "He who has found his life shall lose it, and he who has lost his life for My sake shall find it." There are a number of parallels to this verse in the Gospels:

    Using the phrase "wishes to save his life" (three uses):
        Matt 16:25, "For whoever wishes to save his life shall lose it; but whoever loses his life for My sake shall find it"
        Mark 8:35, "For whoever wishes to save his life shall lose it; but whoever loses his life for My sake and the gospel's shall save it"
        Luke 9:24, "For whoever wishes to save his life shall lose it, but whoever loses his life for My sake, he is the one who will save it"

    Using the phrase "found his life":
        Matt 10:39

Using the phrase "seeks to keep":

> Luke 17:33, "Whoever seeks to keep his life shall lose it, and whoever loses *his life* shall preserve it"

> > "Keep" in the NASB is from a variant reading [περιποιέω]; the Byzantine Textform uses the word "save" [σώζω]

> > "Shall preserve" in the NASB is from the Greek ζῳογονέω, meaning to "give life to" [1 Tim 6:13], or "keep alive, preserve alive" [Luke 17:33; Acts 7:19]:

> > > Notice another variant in this word group, as the Byzantine Textform does not use ζῳογονέω in 1 Tim 6:13, but rather ζῳοποιέω, meaning "to make alive" (12 NT uses, including 2 in John 5:21)

> > > Use of ζῳογονέω in 1 Tim 6:13 may be wrongly taken to imply a universal salvation

> > > Not to be confounded with ζωγρέω as in Luke 5:10.

Using the phrase "loves his life":

> John 12:25, "He who loves his life loses it; and he who hates his life in this world shall keep it to life eternal"

On Finding and Losing One's Life

Verse	Protasis		Apodosis	
	Condition	Result	Condition	Result
Matt 10:39	He who has found his life	Shall lose it	And he who has lost his life for My sake	Shall find it
Matt 16:25	For whoever wishes to save his life	Shall lose it	But whoever loses his life for My sake	Shall find it
Mark 8:35	For whoever wishes to save his life	Shall lose it	But whoever loses his life for My sake and the gospel's	Shall save it
Luke 9:24	For whoever wishes to save his life	Shall lose it	But whoever loses his life for My sake	He is the one who will save it
Luke 17:33	Whoever seeks to keep [save] his life	Shall lose it	And whoever loses *his life*	Shall preserve it
John 12:25	He who loves his life	Loses it	And he who hates his life in this world	Shall keep it to life eternal

2. 1 Cor 9:19, "For though I am free from all *men*, I have made myself a slave to all, that I might win the more"

    Notice the 1560 English Geneva Bible here: "For thogh I be fre from all men, yet haue I made my self seruant vnto all men, that I might winne the mo."

    The Nestle-Aland, 27th ed. reads: Ἐλεύθερος γὰρ ὢν ἐκ πάντων πᾶσιν ἐμαυτὸν ἐδούλωσα, ἵνα τοὺς πλείονας κερδήσω·

    If the verb δουλόω (8 NT uses; e.g. Titus 2:3; 2 Pet 2:19) is translated as a verb in the English, we get: "For though I am free from all *men*, I have enslaved myself to all, that I might win the more"

3. 2 Cor 12:15, "And I will most gladly spend and be expended for your souls. If I love you the more, am I to be loved the less?"

    Note the use of the verb δαπανάω (spend) and its cognate ἐκδαπανάω (expend, used in the future passive, be expended)

    Notice the 1530 Lefèvre on the first phrase: *"Et moy tres volontier me donneray / & encore plus feray / moy mesme habandonner pour vos ames"*

    > My translation of Lefèvre, "And me very voluntarily would give myself / and even more would make / myself abandoned for your souls"

    > Does this not sound like Rom 9:3 (see below)?

    The 1550 Louvain tweaked this verse: *"Et moy tresvolontier donneray, & feray mesme aussi donné pour voz ames"*

    > My translation of the Louvain: "And me very voluntarily would give, and would even also [cause to] give for your souls

3. Rom 9:3, "For I could wish that I myself were accursed, *separated* from Christ for the sake of my brethren, my kinsmen according to the flesh"

    The Greek εὔχομαι (pray) is in the imperfect middle 1st person singular, "I pray myself"
    > Notice the Douay-Rheims use of the past tense, which changes the meaning: "For I **wished** myself to be an anathema from Christ, for my brethren, who are my kinsmen according to the flesh"

    The ASV uses the transliterated anathema: "For I could wish that I myself were anathema from Christ for my brethren's sake, my kinsmen according to the flesh"

    One is reminded of 1 Cor 9:16, "for woe is me if I do not preach the gospel"

4. 1 Cor 9:16-17 [my translation of εὐαγγελίζω]: "For if I evangelize, I have nothing to boast of, for I am under compulsion; for woe is me if I do not evangelize. For if I do this voluntarily, I have a reward; but if against my will, I have a stewardship entrusted to me"

5. 2 Tim 4:6, "For I am already **being poured out as a drink offering** [Ἐγὼ γὰρ ἤδη σπένδομαι], and the time of my departure has come."

Chapter 2 Appendixes

Hearing to Believe—The Hearing of Faith

Introduction:

Without first hearing the Gospel, there is no salvation. It is no surprise, therefore, that hearing to believe is the essence of evangelical soteriology and methodology!

There is an **absolute necessity** for a verbal witness for the salvation message to be communicated for salvation (note in my Book of Charts, "A Verbal Order of Salvation")

The Two Sides of a Theology of Salvation

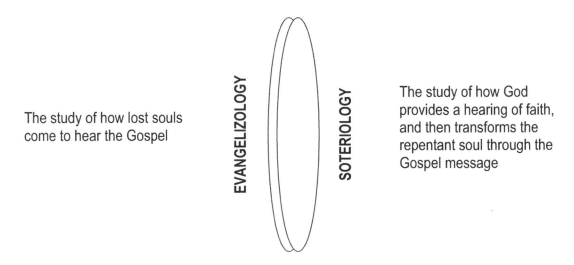

The study of how lost souls come to hear the Gospel

EVANGELIZOLOGY

SOTERIOLOGY

The study of how God provides a hearing of faith, and then transforms the repentant soul through the Gospel message

Often the evangelizing side of this theological equation is either:
  (1) Ridiculed as base and unlearned,[94]
  (2) Buried in [infant] Baptism, leading to an antagonism to evangelists and evangelizing,[95] or
  (3) Ignored or assumed (as in the Westminster Shorter Catechism[96] and the Westminster Confession[97]) based on 1,000+ years of theological precedent.

---

[94]"In his well known *Faṣl al-maqāl* — oftentimes referred to as his *Decisive Treatise*, though the more literal rendering of the title is 'Book of the Distinction of Discourse and the Establishment of the Relation of Religious Law and Philosophy'—Averroes reasons to the priority of philosophical demonstration in the attainment of truth and the interpretation of scripture over religious literalism. While clearly setting aside the possibility of a double truth, Averroes nevertheless maintains a distinction of discourse based on a human educational psychology in which people are seen generally to fall under three classifications. Some are in fact intellectually weak in argumentative skills and easily swayed to assent by emotions under the influence of rhetoric; some see reality through foundational assumptions and build their thinking and reasoning on those, being persuaded to give assent by dialectical engagement; and some are skilled in philosophical logic and reasoning through the method of demonstration and so give assent to truth per se and with necessity because such is the nature of the product of demonstration. There he goes on to explain that those skilled in philosophical demonstration should not be so incautious or even destructive as to reveal truths and interpretations of scripture obtained by demonstration to those unable to understand" (Richard Taylor, "Averroes on Creation" [unpublished paper, beta copy], given at "Aquinas and the 'Arabs'" (Sorbonne, Paris) 31 May 2012; available at: http://academic.mu.edu/taylorr/AAP_Papers/ Taylor_Paris_31_May_2012.html (online); accessed 6 June 2012; Internet).

[95]Please see the Appendix following Chapter 10, on the Second Council of Orange of 529 A.D.

[96]"29. How are we made partakers of the redemption purchased by Christ? A. We are made partakers of the redemption purchased by Christ, by the effectual application of it to us by his Holy Spirit.

"30. How doth the Spirit apply to us the redemption purchased by Christ? A. The Spirit applieth to us the redemption purchased by Christ, by working faith in us, and thereby uniting us to Christ in our effectual calling.

Yet it is commanded in the Bible, it is exemplified in the Bible, its necessity is taught in the Bible. It cannot and must not be ignored!

Further, it is at the point of a "hearing of faith" where the divine miracle of salvation is first initiated: Those who ears are closed and unable to hear are given the gift of hearing the Gospel by the power of the Holy Spirit. Praise the Lord!

A. OT Antecedents:

1. From a dispensational distinction:
   a. OT focus on the hearing of the words of the curse and not repenting:

   Deut 29:18-20 (NKJ), "so that there may not be among you man or woman or family or tribe, whose heart turns away today from the LORD our God, to go *and* serve the gods of these nations, and that there may not be among you a root bearing bitterness or wormwood; and so it may not happen, when he hears the words of this curse, that he blesses himself in his heart, saying,`I shall have peace, even though I follow the dictates of my heart'-- as though the drunkard could be included with the sober. The LORD would not spare him; for then the anger of the LORD and His jealousy would burn against that man, and every curse that is written in this book would settle on him, and the LORD would blot out his name from under heaven."

   b. A NT focus on hearing the curses and repenting, then promises and believing:

   Gal 3:22 (NKJ), "But the Scripture has confined all under sin, that the promise by faith in Jesus Christ might be given to those who believe."

2. OT reading the Law of God so that the people actually hear it with their own ears, e.g.:

   Deut 31:11, "when all Israel comes to appear before the LORD your God in the place which He chooses, you shall read this law before all Israel in their hearing."

   Deut 31:28, "Assemble to me all the elders of your tribes and your officers, that I may speak these words in their hearing and call the heavens and the earth to witness against them."

3. OT calling the people to "hear the word of the Lord," e.g.:

   Josh 3:9, "So Joshua said to the children of Israel, 'Come here, and hear the words of the LORD your God.'"

   This phrase from Josh 3 is oft repeated in the OT, e.g. Josh 24:27; 1 Kgs 22:19; 2 Kgs 7:1; 20:19;
   2 Chron 18:18; Isa 1:10; 28:14; 39:5; 66:5; Jer 2:4; 9:20; 10:1; 17:20; 19:3; 21:11; 22:2, 29; 29:20; 31:10; 34:4; 42:15; 44:26; Eek 6:3; 13:2; 16:35; 20:47; 25:3; 34:9; 36:1, 4; 37:4; Hos 4:1; Amos 3:1; 7:16.

   Relation to evangelism:

   Acts 19:10, "And this continued for two years, so that all who dwelt in Asia **heard the word of the Lord Jesus**, both Jews and Greeks."

"31. What is effectual calling? A. Effectual calling is the work of God's Spirit, whereby, convincing us of our sin and misery, enlightening our minds in the knowledge of Christ, and renewing our wills, he doth persuade and enable us to embrace Jesus Christ, freely offered to us in the gospel" ("Westminster Shorter Catechism"; available at: http://www.shortercatechism.com/resources/wscformats/BPC_wsc.doc [online]; accessed: 1 Dec 2005; Internet).

[97]"CHAPTER XXVIII. *Of Baptism.* I. Baptism is a sacrament of the New Testament, ordained by Jesus Christ, not only for the solemn admission of the party baptized into the visible Church, but also to be unto him a sign and seal of the covenant of grace, of his ingrafting into Christ, of regeneration, of remission of sins, and of his giving up unto God, through Jesus Christ, to walk in newness of life: which sacrament is, by Christ's own appointment, to be continued in his Church until the end of the world.

"VI. The efficacy of baptism is not tied to that moment of time wherein it is administered; yet, notwithstanding, by the right use of this ordinance, the grace promised is not only offered, but really exhibited and conferred by the Holy Ghost, to such (whether of age or infants) as that grace belongeth unto, according to the counsel of God's own will, in his appointed time" (Westminster Confession; available at: http://www.reformed.org/documents/ westminster_conf_of_faith.html (online); accessed: 18 Sept 2012; Internet).

A. Ears to Hear:

1. The need for ears to hear:
   a. Jesus said repeatedly (NKJ): "He who has ears to hear, let him hear!" Ὁ ἔχων ὦτα ἀκούειν ἀκουέτω), Matt 11:15; 13:9, 43; Mark 4:9, 23; 7:16; Luke 8:8; 14:35
      1) Which makes this statement the most repeated statement of Jesus, "love one another" being found 5 times in John 13:34-35; 15:12, 17!
   b. Listen to this rebuke of Jesus:

      Mark 8:17-21, "And Jesus, aware of this, said to them, 'Why do you discuss *the fact* that you have no bread? Do you not yet see or understand? Do you have a hardened heart? Having eyes, do you not see? And having ears, do you not hear? And do you not remember, when I broke the five loaves for the five thousand, how many baskets full of broken pieces you picked up?' They said to Him, 'Twelve.' 'And when *I broke* the seven for the four thousand, how many large baskets full of broken pieces did you pick up?' And they said to Him, 'Seven.' And He was saying to them, 'Do you not yet understand?'"

2. On God giving ears to hear:
   Psa 40:6, "Sacrifice and meal offering Thou hast not desired; My ears Thou hast opened; Burnt offering and sin offering Thou hast not required."
   Isa 32:3, "Then the eyes of those who see will not be blinded, And the ears of those who hear will listen."
   Matt 13:16-17, "But blessed are your eyes, because they see; and your ears, because they hear. For truly I say to you, that many prophets and righteous men desired to see what you see, and did not see *it*; and to hear what you hear, and did not hear *it*"
   Rom 4:17, "(as it is written, 'A father of many nations have I made you') in the sight of Him whom he believed, *even* God, who gives life to the dead and calls into being that which does not exist"
   2 Cor 4:4, "in whose case the god of this world has blinded the minds of the unbelieving, that they might not see the light of the gospel of the glory of Christ, who is the image of God"[98]

      Wycliffe's translation of this verse is particularly striking:
      2 Cor 4:3-4 For if also oure gospel is kyuerid, in these that perischen it is kyuerid; ⁴ in which God hath blent the soulis of vnfeithful men of this world, that the liytnyng of the gospel of the glorie of Crist, which is the ymage of God, schyne not."

3. Christ giving understanding:
   Matt 15:10, "When He had called the multitude to *Himself*, He said to them, 'Hear and understand'"
   Acts 16:14, "And a certain woman named Lydia, from the city of Thyatira, a seller of purple fabrics, a worshiper of God, was listening; and the Lord opened her heart to respond to the things spoken by Paul"

B. Hearing to know God's Word:
   Deut 4:6, "the peoples who hear all these statutes will say 'surely this great nation is a wise and understanding people.'"
   Psa 78:1, "Listen, O my people, to my instruction; Incline your ears to the words of My mouth."
   Prov 2:2, "Make your ear attentive to wisdom, Incline your heart to understanding." (cf. Pr. 4:1, 10, 20, 5:1, 7)
   Isa 1:2, "Listen, O heavens, and hear, O earth; For the Lord speaks."
   Luke 16:31, "But He said to him, 'If they will not listen to Moses and the Prophets, neither will they be persuaded if someone rises from the dead.'"

C. Hearing to Fear the Lord:
1. Deut 5:28-29
2. 1 Kgs 8:41-43 (cf. vs. 59-60)

D. Hearing to Make the Gospel Known (cf. Matt 13:29):

1. Some OT prophecies and examples:
   Jer 6:10, "To whom shall I speak and give warning, That they may hear? Behold, their ears are closed, And they cannot listen. Behold, the word of the LORD has become a reproach to them; They have no delight in it."

---

[98]"And there is another method of preaching the gospel; *believing it to be the power of God unto salvation;* preaching it in the *expectation* that He who first brought light out of darkness can and will at once and instantaneously take the darkest heathen heart and create light within" (J. Hudson Taylor, "The Source of Power," *Ecumenical Missionary Conference, New York, 1900* [New York, American Tract Society, 1900]: 1:91; emphasis mine).

Ezek 40:4, "And the man said to me, 'Son of man, see with your eyes, hear with your ears, and give attention to all that I am going to show you; for you have been brought here in order to show *it* to you. Declare to the house of Israel all that you see.'"

Ezek 44:5-8, "And the LORD said to me, 'Son of man, mark well, see with your eyes, and hear with your ears all that I say to you concerning all the statutes of the house of the LORD and concerning all its laws; and mark well the entrance of the house, with all exits of the sanctuary. And you shall say to the rebellious ones, to the house of Israel, "Thus says the Lord God, 'Enough of all your abominations, O house of Israel, when you brought in foreigners, uncircumcised in heart and uncircumcised in flesh, to be in My sanctuary to profane it, *even* My house, when you offered My food, the fat and the blood; for they made My covenant void-- *this* in addition to all your abominations. And you have not kept charge of My holy things yourselves, but you have set *foreigners* to keep charge of My sanctuary.'"'"

2. The Gospel was first proclaimed by Jesus Christ:
    1 John 1:5, "And this is the message we heard from Him and announce to you, that God is light, and in Him is no darkness at all."

3. NT examples of hearing to make known:
    Acts 18:9-10, "And the Lord said to Paul in the night by a vision, 'Do not be afraid any longer, but go on speaking and do not be silent; for I am with you, and no man will harm you, for I have many people in this city.'"
    1 Thess 1:5, "For our Gospel did not come to you in word only [but that was part of it], but also in power and in the Holy Spirit and with full conviction."
    Col 1:5-7 (NKJ), "because of the hope which is laid up for you in heaven, of which you heard before in the word of the truth of the gospel, which has come to you, as *it has* also in all the world, and is bringing forth fruit, as *it is* also among you since the day you heard and knew the grace of God in truth; as you also learned from Epaphras, our dear fellow servant, who is a faithful minister of Christ on your behalf"
    Heb 4:2, "For indeed we have had the good news preached to us, just as they also; but the word they heard did not profit them, because it was not united by faith in those who heard."

E. Hearing to Be Able to Obey:
Deut 15:5, "if only you listen obediently [Gk. ἀκοῇ εἰσακούσητε] to the voice of the LORD your God, to observe carefully all this commandment which I am commanding you today"
Psa 18:44, "As soon as they **hear**, they obey me; foreigners submit to me."
Psa 119:4, 11, "**Thou hast ordained Thy precepts**, That we should keep them diligently. **Thy word** I have treasured in my heart, That I may not sin against Thee."
John 10:16, "And I have other sheep, which are not of this fold, I must bring them also, and they shall **hear** my voice; and they shall become one flock with one shepherd."
John 17:6, "I manifested Thy name to the men whom Thou gavest Me out of the world; Thine they were, and Thou gavest them to Me, and they have kept **Thy word**."
Eph 4:20-24, "But you did not learn Christ in this way, **if indeed you have heard Him** and have been taught in Him, just as truth is in Jesus, that, in reference to your former manner of life, you lay aside the old self, which is being corrupted in accordance with the lusts of deceit, and that you be renewed in the spirit of your mind, and put on the new self, which in *the likeness of* God has been created in righteousness and holiness of the truth."

F. The Christian Speaking so that People Hear to Give an Opportunity to Believe:
Gen 15:4, 6, "Then behold, the word of the LORD came to him, saying … Then he believed in the LORD; and He reckoned it to him as righteousness."
Luke 1:45, "And blessed *is* she who believed that there would be a fulfillment of what had been spoken to her by the Lord."
John 4:41, "And many more believed because of his word."
John 4:42, "And they were saying to the woman, 'It is no longer because of what you said that we believe, for we have heard for ourselves and know that this One is indeed the Savior of the world.'"
John 4:50, "The man believed the word that Jesus spoke to him, and he started off."
John 17:8, "for the words which Thou gavest Me I have given to them; and they received them, and truly understood that I came forth from Thee, and they believed that Thou didst send Me."
John 17:20, "I do not ask in behalf of these alone, but for those also who believe in Me through their word."
Acts 14:1, " and [they] spoke in such a manner that a great multitude believed, both Jews and Greeks."
Acts 18:8, "And Crispus, the leader of the synagogue, believed in the Lord with all his household, and many of the Corinthians **when they heard were believing** and being baptized"
Acts 18:9-10, "but go on speaking and do not be silent for I have many people in this city."
Rom 10:14, "And how are they to believe in Him whom they have not **heard**? And how shall they **hear** without a **preacher**?"
Rom 10:17, "Faith comes from **hearing** and **hearing** from the word of Christ."

1 Cor 15:11, "Whether then *it was* I or they, so **we preach** and so **you believed**"

Eph 1:13 (ASV), "in whom ye also, **having heard** the word of the truth, the gospel of your salvation, -- in whom, **having also believed**, ye were sealed with the Holy Spirit of promise"

1 Pet 1:23-25, "For you have been born again ... through the living and abiding word of God. ... And this is the word which was preached to you."

Translations of Hearing and Believing in Eph 1:13

Greek Orthodox Text*	Bishops Bible (1595)	Bible in Basic English (Cambridge, 1949)	NASB (1977)	NIV (1984)	New Jerusalem Bible⌧	Cont. English Version (1991)⌧
ἐν ᾧ καὶ ὑμεῖς ἀκούσαντες τὸν λόγον τῆς ἀληθείας, τὸ εὐαγγέλιον τῆς σωτηρίας ὑμῶν, ἐν ᾧ καὶ πιστεύσαντες ἐσφραγίσθητε τῷ Πνεύματι τῆς ἐπαγγελίας τῷ Ἁγίῳ,	In whom also ye, after that ye heard the worde of trueth, the Gospell of your saluation, wherin also after that ye beleued, were sealed with the holy spirite of promise	In whom you, having been given the true word, the good news of your salvation, and through your faith in him, were given the sign of the Holy Spirit of hope	In Him, you also, after listening to the message of truth, the gospel of your salvation-- having also believed, you were sealed in Him with the Holy Spirit of promise	And you also were included in Christ when you heard the word of truth, the gospel of your salvation. Having believed, you were marked in him with a seal, the promised Holy Spirit,	Now you too, in him, have heard the message of the truth and the gospel of your salvation, and having put your trust in it you have been stamped with the seal of the Holy Spirit of the Promise,	Christ also brought you the truth, which is the good news about how you can be saved. You put your faith in Christ and were given the promised Holy Spirit to show that you belong to God.
	The verb "hear" is used in the: Wycliffe, Tyndale, Coverdale, Geneva, KJV, ERV, ASV, RSV, NKJ, NLT, CSB, NET, and ESV	Changed "hearing" to "having been given"; barely related to the Greek ἀκούω	Changed "hearing" to "listening"; thereby moving from proclamation to reception	Made two sentences out of the verse, thereby separating hearing from believing; other translations using two sentences: CET**, GNT**, and NLT	Note antagonism to the verb "believe", using rather "put your faith"	Complete removal of "hearing"; replacing the evangelist with Christ; divide "hearing" and "believing" into two sentences; also antagonism to verb "believe" as NJB

*No distinction between the Greek Critical edition text and the Greek Byzantine Textform. The Greek Orthodox Text was chosen due to capitalization of the words Holy Spirit.

Translating ὅτι ἔσται in Luke 1:45
A Case Study on Hearing and Believing: Mary's Faith

Byzantine Text	Douais-Rheims⌧ (1899)	KJV	CSB	Tyndale (1534); Geneva; Bishops	NIV	NAS
Basis of Faith	She believed because she is by nature blessed					She is blessed because she believed
Focus of Faith	Based on her nature					Based on God who fulfills His Word
Result of Faith	Fulfillment based on her faith					Fulfillment based on God's character
Καὶ μακαρία ἡ πιστεύσασα, ὅτι ἔσται τελείωσις τοῖς λελαλημένοις αὐτῇ παρὰ κυρίου.	And blessed art thou that hast believed, because those things shall be accomplished that were spoken to thee by the Lord	And blessed *is* she that believed: for there shall be a performance of those things which were told her from the Lord.	She who has believed is blessed because what was spoken to her by the Lord will be fulfilled!	And blessed arte thou that belevedst: for thoose thinges shalbe performed wich were tolde the from the lorde	Blessed is she who has believed that the Lord would fulfill his promises to her!	And blessed *is* she who believed that there would be a fulfillment of what had been spoken to her by the Lord

G. Hearing to Give Grace—A Study of Ephesians 4:29:

Introduction:

    a. The reception of grace is no small matter, and no laughing matter; many in the history of the churches have been burned alive for this one matter: how is grace conferred? Is it through the spoken word or through the physical symbol of a sacrament?

    b. The issue of how grace is received goes back to Augustine in 412 A.D., who argued for a sacramental position; i.e. that grace was communicated through the physical species of the symbol [in the sacrament] by virtue of what it represented ("What you loose on earth shall be loosed in heaven," Matt 16:19; 18:18)

    c. This makes the matter of binding and loosing more prominent in sacramental churches than the content of what is spoken and understood, except for the use of the necessary words for the proper enactment of the Sacrament by the person who has received the proper Sacrament to say those words in the proper way!

Understanding Views of the Disbursement of Grace

Category	Sacramental	Median Position	Evangelical
Grace is conferred via:	The Signs and Symbols of the Sacraments (water, a Host, Oil, etc)	Good works; or even perhaps, Good thinking ("the divinely inspired Plato")	Words, especially the words of the Bible, and especially those words related to the Gospel of Jesus Christ
Grace is normally conferred by:	The priest who has received the Sacrament of Holy Orders from a Bishop who is in right relationship with the properly elected figurehead (Patriarch of Constantinople, Vicar of Christ [in Rome], Archbishop of Canterbury, etc.)	Anyone who does good works	By one who, believing in the personal Gospel, is evangelizing
Some exceptions	Heretics can baptize into the Church of Rome, by use of the Trinitarian formula, even though it is likely that they are unaware that they are so doing (this allows Rome to apply its version of "church discipline" to heretics and schismatic's)	God can even use the good works of those in other religious groups to communicate His grace to mankind!	In order to communicate His word, God has used a donkey; To communicate in preparation for the Gospel, God has used visions (Acts 9; 10) And to prepare for the coming of Jesus, God used angels (Luke 2)
The work of the Holy Spirit	The Holy Spirit works *ex opere operato* through the Sacraments[99]	The Holy Spirit works through our lives and lifestyle	The Holy Spirit works through the Word of God, which is the Sword of the Spirit (Eph 6:17)

---

[99]"Canon 8. If anyone says that by the sacraments of the New Law grace is not conferred ex opere operato, but that faith alone in the divine promise is sufficient to obtain grace, let him be anathema" (*Council of Trent* [1545-1564], "Canons on Sacraments in General" [3 Mar 1547]; available at: http://www.forerunner.com/chalcedon/X0020_15._ Council_of_Trent.html; accessed: 8 Jan 2005; Internet).

1.   While there are a number of verses on this subject, Ephesians 4:29 is important:
     Eph 4:29 (NAS), "Let no unwholesome word proceed from your mouth, but only such *a word* as is good for edification according to the need *of the moment*, that it may give grace to those who hear."

Variations in Translating Ephesians 4:29
Variations on Ministering Grace

Byzantine Greek	French Geneva (1560-1669)[100]	English Geneva (1560)	KJV (1611/1769)	NAS (1977)	NIV (1984)	ABS' GNT* (1993)	ABS' CEV* (1991)
Ministry Emphasis	"Give grace"	"Minister grace"	"Minister grace"	"Give grace"	"Benefit [others]"	"Do good"	"Help others"
Πᾶς λόγος σαπρὸς ἐκ τοῦ στόματος ὑμῶν μὴ ἐκπορευέσθω,	Let nary an infected proposal escape from your mouth:	Let no corrupt comunication proceed out of your mouths:	Let no corrupt communication proceed out of your mouth,	Let no unwholesome word proceed from your mouth,	Do not let any unwholesome talk come out of your mouths,	Do not use harmful words,	Stop all your dirty talk.
ἀλλ᾽ εἴ τις ἀγαθὸς πρὸς οἰκοδομὴν τῆς χρείας,	but that which is good unto usefulness for edifying,	but that which is good, to ye vse of edifying,	but that which is good to the use of edifying,	but only such *a word* as is good for edification according to the need *of the moment*,	but only what is helpful for building others up according to their needs,	but only helpful words, the kind that build up and provide what is needed,	Say the right thing at the right time
ἵνα δῷ χάριν τοῖς ἀκούουσιν.	in order that it give grace to those who hear it.	that it may minister grace vnto the hearers.	that it may minister grace unto the hearers.	that it may give grace to those who hear.	that it may benefit those who listen.	so that what you say will do good to those who hear you.	And help others by what you say.
Analysis by Phrase	1) Emphatic negative; 2) Emphasis on verb "usefulness"; 3) Use of word "grace"	1) Removal of emphatic negative, use of corrupt; 2) Softening of "usefulness," no use of "need" 3) "give" changed to "minister"; "hear" as participle changed to noun, "hearers"	[See comments with English Geneva]	1) "Corrupt" softened to "unwholesome" 2) Additions of words from apodosis provide helpful guides, including use of the word "need" 3) Return to verbal use of "hear"	1) Follow NAS precedent, while removing word "word"; 2) Change "good" to "helpful"; 3) Combine two words "give grace" into an abstract verb, "benefit"; "listen" seems to place the responsibility on the hearer rather than the speaker!	1) Serious downgrade of "corrupt" and change from singular to plural "word" 2) Follow NIV precedent, using "helpful" rather than "good" 3) Replace "minister grace" with "do good"!*	1) Limit "corrupt word" to "dirty talk"; remove the emphasis on the mouth; 2) Remove "needful edification," replacing it with "right timing" (kairos); 3) "Give grace" reduced to "help others"**

*A clear view of ministry in changing "giving grace" or "ministering grace" with "doing good" or "helping others"!

2.   Unpacking the three phrases in Ephesians 4:29:

   a.   The plural command, as protasis:

      1)   Let not proceed forth from your mouth:
           Obviously dealing with the word which goes forth from the mouth—including evangelizing!

      2)   Any [or all] infected—unwholesome—corrupting word (σαπρός, meaning: rotten, decayed; hence corrupt):
           a)   The translator's view of man's sinfulness is wrapped up in the translation of this word
           b)   A more moderating translation is "worthless"

100"Que nul propos infect ne sorte de vostre bouche: mais celui qui est bon à l'usage d'edification, afin qu'il donne grace à ceux qui l'oyent" (Eph 4:29; 1669 *Bible de Genève*; from: http://biblegeneve.com/bibles-php/index.php?version=nt1669-cm; accessed: 29 June 2006; Internet).

        c) For example, the NAS includes 10 uses of the English "corrupt" or some form of it in the translation of:

            διαφθείρω (verb) in Rev 19:2; word otherwise translated as:

                "Decayed" in 2 Cor 4:16

                "Depraved" in 1 Tim 6:5

                "Destroyed" in Luke 12:33; Rev 8:9; 11:18 (twice)

            μιασμός (noun) in 2 Pet 2:10

            φθαρτός (adjective) in Rom 1:23

            φθορά (noun) in Rom 8:21; Gal 6:8; 2 Pet 1:4; 2:19

            φθείρω (verb) in 1 Cor 15:33; 2 Cor 7:2; Eph 4:22

      3) Issue: what proceeds forth from your mouth is important, and it ought not be a corrupt

    b. Apodosis:

      1) But that which is good…

      2) Needful for edification

    c. Resulting clause:

      1) That it may give grace:

        a) Here God's Word specifically states that words give grace!

        b) By virtue of silence, it is clear that a physical symbol [or Sacrament] does not need to be added to the words so that those words truly give grace!

      2) To those who listen [or hear]

        a) "So then faith comes by hearing, and hearing by the word of God," Rom 10:17

Conclusion:

Spoken words do give grace!

Our words ought to give grace to those who hear!

H. "Through the Foolishness of Preaching"—A Study of 1 Cor 1:17-21:

1. God's call to evangelize as a priority:

    1 Cor 1:17 (HCSB), "For Christ did not send me to baptize, but to evangelize-- not with clever words, so that the cross of Christ will not be emptied of its effect."

    1 Cor 1:17 (NAS), "For Christ did not send me to baptize, but to preach the gospel, not in cleverness of speech, that the cross of Christ should not be made void."

2. The unique power of the "word of the cross" unto salvation:

    1 Cor 1:18 (NKJ), "For the message of the cross is foolishness to those who are perishing, but to us who are being saved it is the power of God."

3. God saving "them that believe" "through the foolishness of preaching":

    1 Cor 1:21 (KJV), "For after that in the wisdom of God the world by wisdom knew not God, it pleased God by the foolishness of preaching to save them that believe."

On the Addition of the Concept of Message to Preaching in 1 Cor 1:21
Marking a Shift from Method to Message?[101]

Issue	Versions without the Addition of the Concept of "Message"	First Apparent Addition of Concept of the "Message"	Continued Translation without Addition of the Concept of "Message"	Two Transitory Translations*	Groundswell of the Addition of "Message"	Do not Add "Message"
Sample Verse	Tyndale (1534), "For when the worlde thorow wysdome knew not God in the wysdome of God: it pleased God thorow folisshnes of preachinge to save them that believe"	Rotherham (1868-1902), "For, seeing that, in the wisdom of God, the world, through its wisdom, did not get to knew God, God was well-pleased—through the foolishness of the thing proclaimed, to save them that believe"	Noyes (1869), "For since, in the wisdom of God, the world by its wisdom knew not God, it pleased God by the foolishness of preaching to save those who believe"	BBE (Cambridge, 1949), "For because, by the purpose of God, the world, with all its wisdom, had not the knowledge of God, it was God's pleasure, by so foolish a thing as preaching, to give salvation to those who had faith in him" RSV (1952), "For since, in the wisdom of God, the world did not know God through wisdom, it pleased God through the folly of what we preach to save those who believe"	NASB (1977), "For since in the wisdom of God the world through its wisdom did not *come to* know God, God was well-pleased through the foolishness of the message preached to save those who believe"	NET (2006), "For since in the wisdom of God the world by its wisdom did not know God, God was pleased to save those who believe by the foolishness of preaching"
Other Versions	Bishops, Geneva, KJV, Webster's, Young's		Darby, ERV, ASV		NKJ, NIV, NIRV, TNIV, HCSB, ESV	NLT

*It is interesting to consider that these translations, along with the NIV, were commissioned during Eugene Nida's role as "Executive Secretary of Translations" for the American Bible Society from 1946-1981.

---

[101]This is quite similar and parallel to the addition of the word "gospel" to the translation of the verb "evangelize," which was in the translated as "preach" or "proclaim " from the 16th Century on until John Darby translated that verb as "preach glad tidings" in his 1884 English translation. The addition of the predicate noun stuck after that time (see Chart, "A Translation History of Translating Evangelize as Evangelize" in Chapter 17).

Shifts from Method to Message in Gal 1:8-9

Passage	Method and Message	Word-for-Word	Transition, Phase 1	Transition, Phase 2	Transition, Phase 3	Transition, Phase 4	Transition, Phase 5	Emphatic on Message	Emphasis on the Preacher
Gal 1:8	Tyndale (1534), "Neverthelesse though we oure selves or an angell from heven preache eny other gospell vnto you the that which we have preached vnto you holde him as a cursed"	Geneva (1560), "But though that we, or an Angel from heauen preach vnto you otherwise, then that which we haue preached vnto you, let him be accursed"	Young's (1862), "but even if we or a messenger out of heaven may proclaim good news to you different from what we did proclaim to you—anathema let him be!"	Rotherham (1868-1902), "But, even if, we, or, a messenger out of heaven, announce a glad-message [[unto you]] aside from that which we announced unto you, accursed, let him be!"	Noyes (1869), "But even if we or an angel from heaven should preach a gospel to you contrary to that which we preached to you, let him be accursed!"	ERV (1885), "But though we, or an angel from heaven, should preach unto you any gospel other than that which we preached unto you, let him be anathema"	NIV (1984), "But even if we or an angel from heaven should preach a gospel other than the one we preached to you, let him be eternally condemned!"	NIRV (1998), "But suppose even we should preach a different 'good news.' Suppose even an angel from heaven should preach it. I'm talking about a different one than the good news we gave you. Let anyone who does that be judged by God forever"	BBE (Cambridge, 1949), "But even if we, or an angel from heaven, were to be a preacher to you of good news other than that which we have given you, let there be a curse on him"
Gal 1:9	Tyndale (1534), "As I sayde before so saye I now agayne yf eny man preache eny other thinge vnto you then that ye have receaved holde him accursed"	Geneva (1560), "As we sayd before, so say I now againe, If any man preach vnto you otherwise, then that ye haue receiued, let him be accursed"	Young's (1862), "as we have said before, and now say again, If any one to you may proclaim good news different from what ye did receive—anathema let him be!"	Rotherham (1868-1902), "As we have said before, even now, again, I say: If anyone is announcing unto you a glad-message aside from that which ye accepted, accursed, let him be!"	Noyes (1869), "As we have said before, so I now say again, If any one preach a gospel to you contrary to that which ye received, let him be accursed!"	ERV (1885), "As we have said before, so say I now again, If any man preacheth unto you any gospel other than that which ye received, let him be anathema"	NIV (1984), "As we have already said, so now I say again: If anybody is preaching to you a gospel other than what you accepted, let him be eternally condemned!"	NIRV (1998), "I have already said it. Now I will say it again. Anyone who preaches a 'good news' that is different from the one you accepted should be judged by God forever"	BBE (Cambridge, 1949), "As we have said before, so say I now again, If any man is a preacher to you of any good news other than that which has been given to you, let there be a curse on him"
Other Similar Versions	Bishops, KJV, Webster's, NKJ	Etheridge, Murdock			RSV, NASB, NET, ESV	ASV, NIV, TNIV, HCSB	NJB✸, NAB✸	NLT	

Or Consider the Addition of "Message" into οὐδὲν προσανέθεντο in Gal 2:6

Description	Straight negation	Addition of Explanatory Clause	Different Verb and Adjective	Different Verb	Different Verb	Addition of Adjective	Addition of "Message"
Phrase in Question	"Added nothing to me"	"Above that I had"	"Communicated nothing new"	"Imparted nothing to me"	"Contributed nothing to me"	"Added nothing new to me"	"Added nothing to my message
Sample Translation	Tyndale, "Of the which seme to be great (what they were in tyme passed it maketh no matter to me: God loketh on no mans person) neverthelesse they which seme great added nothynge to me"	Geneva (1560), "But by them which seemed to be great, I was not taught (whatsoeuer they were in time passed, I am nothing the better: God accepteth no mans person) for they that are the chiefe, did adde nothing to me aboue that I had"	Noyes (1869), "But from those who were reputed to be somewhat— whatever they were, it matters not to me, (God accepteth no man's person,) for to me those in reputation communicated nothing new"	ERV (1885), "But from those who were reputed to be somewhat (whatsoever they were, it maketh no matter to me: God accepteth not man's person)—they, I say, who were of repute imparted nothing to me"	NAS (1977), "But from those who were of high reputation (what they were makes no difference to me; God shows no partiality)-- well, those who were of reputation contributed nothing to me"	RSV, "But from those who were reputed to be somewhat (whatsoever they were, it maketh no matter to me: God accepteth not man's person)--they, I say, who were of repute imparted nothing to me"	NIV (1984), "As for those who seemed to be important-- whatever they were makes no difference to me; God does not judge by external appearance-- those men added nothing to my message"
Other Similar Translations	Bishops, KJV, NKJ, NAB✳, HCSB, ESV		Darby	ASV			NJB✳, NIRV, TNIV, NET

I. The Christian Speaking, so that People Hear to Be Saved:

Acts 11:14, "and he shall speak words to you by which you will be saved, you and your household."
1 Thess 2:16, "keeping us from speaking to the Gentiles that they might be saved."
[κωλυόντων ἡμᾶς τοῖς ἔθνεσι λαλῆσαι ἵνα σωθῶσιν]

J. The Parallel Concept of God Speaking:

John 6:45, "It is written in the prophets, 'And they shall all be taught of God.' Everyone who has **heard** and **learned** from the Father, **comes** to Me."
Eph 2:17-18, "And **He came and preached** [evangelized] peace to you who were far away, and peace to those who were near; for through Him we both have our access in one Spirit to the Father."
Eph 4:20-21, "But you did not learn Christ in this way, **if indeed you have heard Him** and have been taught in Him, just as truth is in Jesus"

Synthesizing Some of Verses on Hearing and Believing

	Matthew 13:23	John 6:45	Acts 15:7	Galatians 3:2	Ephesians 1:13 (ESV)
Introduction	"And the one on whom seed was sown on the good soil,	"It is written in the prophets, 'And they shall all be taught of God.'	"Brethren, you know that in the early days God made a choice among you,	"This is the only thing I want to find out from you:	"In him you also,
Hearing (Man)	this is the man who hears the word	Everyone who has heard	that the Gentiles by my mouth should hear the word of the gospel	by the works of the Law, or by hearing	when you heard the word of truth, the gospel of your salvation,
Understanding (God)	and understands it;	and learned from the Father,			
Response		comes to Me."	and believe."	with faith?"	and believed in him,
Result	who indeed bears fruit, and brings forth, some a hundredfold, some sixty, and some thirty."			did you receive the Spirit	were sealed with the promised Holy Spirit"

K. Preparation for a Hearing of Faith

On the removal of the veil:
>   Hypothetical or actual?

2 Cor 3:16-17 on Conversion: From Actual to Hypothetical

NKJ	BYZ	BGT	NAS
15 But even to this day, when Moses is read, a veil lies on their heart. 16 Nevertheless when one turns to the Lord, the veil is taken away.	15 Ἀλλ' ἕως σήμερον, ἡνίκα ἀναγινώσκεται Μωϋσῆς, κάλυμμα ἐπὶ τὴν καρδίαν αὐτῶν κεῖται. 16 Ἡνίκα δ' ἂν ἐπιστρέψῃ πρὸς κύριον, περιαιρεῖται τὸ κάλυμμα.	15 ἀλλ' ἕως σήμερον ἡνίκα ἂν ἀναγινώσκηται Μωϋσῆς, κάλυμμα ἐπὶ τὴν καρδίαν αὐτῶν κεῖται· 16 ἡνίκα δὲ ἐὰν ἐπιστρέψῃ πρὸς κύριον, περιαιρεῖται τὸ κάλυμμα.	15 But to this day whenever Moses is read, a veil lies over their heart; 16 but whenever a man turns to the Lord, the veil is taken away.

The difference between the hypothetical and the actual is found in the verb forms—subjunctive or indicative:
>   "Is read" (in BYZ) is indicative: ἀναγινώσκεται;
>   "Is read" (in BYZ) is subjunctive: ἀναγινώσκηται.

Conversion (ἐπιστρέφω, also: repentance or heart-change) is not merely theoretical vaguely applied to actual events, but visa-versa, it is actual fact, which then receives a theoretical explanation.

Consider for example:
>   Nicodemus and his heart-change, occasioned by a change in "hearing" with spiritual understanding;
>   The Woman at the Well and her heart-change, exemplified by "hearing" with spiritual understanding.

L. The Hearing of Faith:

Introduction:
>   Aka. in Latin, *ex auditu fidei*; in Greek: ἐξ ἀκοῆς πίστεως
>   In this study the word faith remains constant (as ἡ πίστις or *pistis*), but the words used for the act of "hearing" varies:

1) With the verb ὑπακούω, meaning "to hear, hearken, [by implication] obey":

>   Acts 6:7 (ASV), "And the word of God increased; and the number of the disciples multiplied in Jerusalem exceedingly; and a great company of the priests **were obedient to the faith**"
>   BYZ: Καὶ ὁ λόγος τοῦ θεοῦ ηὔξανεν, καὶ ἐπληθύνετο ὁ ἀριθμὸς τῶν μαθητῶν ἐν Ἰερουσαλὴμ σφόδρα, πολύς τε ὄχλος τῶν ἱερέων ὑπήκουον τῇ πίστει.
>   My translation: "And the word of God was growing, and the number of disciples was multiplying exceedingly in Jerusalem, even a great company of the priests **were hearing with faith**"

>   Rom 10:16 (ASV), "But they did not all hearken to the glad tidings. For Isaiah saith, Lord, who hath believed our report?"
>   BYZ: Ἀλλ' οὐ πάντες ὑπήκουσαν τῷ εὐαγγελίῳ. Ἡσαΐας γὰρ λέγει, Κύριε, τίς ἐπίστευσεν τῇ ἀκοῇ ἡμῶν;
>   My translation: "But they did not all hearken to the gospel. For Isaiah said, Lord, which person has believed what we have caused them to hear?"
>   Some thoughts:
>   >   The hearing is found twice in this verse, once as the active verb in the first clause; and then as the noun upon which the verb "having faith" or "believing" is acting
>   >   Paul, taking the noun *shemuw'ah* (that which is reported) in Isa 53:1, turns it into the verb harken in the first clause of Rom 10:16
>   >   Further, Paul did not quote the second part of Isa 53:1—on the divine side of evangelizing, "To whom has the arm of the Lord been revealed?" Although these verses are in actuality answering that very question!

2) With the noun ἡ ἀκοή, meaning to hear, cause to hear:

>   Rom 10:17 (NKJ), "So then faith *comes* by hearing, and hearing by the word of God"
>   BYZ: Ἄρα ἡ πίστις ἐξ ἀκοῆς, ἡ δὲ ἀκοὴ διὰ ῥήματος θεοῦ.
>   My translation: "Thus, faith from hearing, but hearing through the word of God."
>   Thoughts:
>   >   Therefore, is not Paul answering the question of Isa 53:1b, "To whom has the arm of the Lord been revealed?"?

Yes, the issue is "calling on the name of the Lord to be saved," Rom 10:13
But even before that, the issue is a hearing of faith!
It appears that this verse is the climax of Paul's explanation of his evangelizing, as expressed in
    Rom 10:15

Gal 3:2, "This is the only thing I want to find out from you: did you receive the Spirit by the works of the Law, or by hearing with faith?" (e.g. Acts 10:44)
    BYZ: Τοῦτο μόνον θέλω μαθεῖν ἀφ᾽ ὑμῶν, ἐξ ἔργων νόμου τὸ πνεῦμα ἐλάβετε, ἢ ἐξ ἀκοῆς πίστεως;

Translations of the "Hearing of Faith [ἐξ ἀκοῆς πίστεως] in Galatians 3:2

Vulgate⚹	Fr Geneva, Segond, NEG	English Geneva	KJV, DRA⚹, ASV, NKJ	NAS, ESV, CSB	NAB⚹	NIV, NET	NJB⚹	Le Semeur (trans mine)*	CEV⚹
ex auditu fidei	by the preaching of the faith [Par la predication de la foi]	by the hearing of faith *preached*	by the hearing of faith	by hearing with faith	from faith in what you heard	by believing what you heard	by believing in the message you heard	because you welcomed with faith the Good News that you heard	by hearing about Christ and having faith in him
Word for word translation of the Greek; order unchanged	The noun ἀκοή is rendered "preaching"	The noun ἀκοή is rendered the participle, "hearing" with the addition of verb "preached"	The verb "preached" is eliminated	Removal of definite article "the"	The words hear and faith are reversed	Faith is turned into the verb believing	Add the words "the message" emphasi-zing the supplied message rather than the verbal communica-tion of the message (cf. Gal 1:8-9)	Rearrange as NAB, NIV, NET, and NJB; add main verb "welcome" or "receive" to "with faith"; faith becomes secondary; add "the Good News"	Add the words "about Christ and having" which further dividing "hearing of faith"; concept of "hearing of faith" is completely lost

*French original: "parce que vous avez accueilli avec foi la Bonne Nouvelle que vous avez entendue"

Gal 3:5, "Does He then, who provides you with the Spirit and works miracles among you, do it by the works of the Law, or by hearing with faith?"

Heb 4:2 (mine), "For indeed we were evangelized, just as they also; but the word they heard did not profit them, because it was not united by faith in those who heard."
    BYZ: Καὶ γάρ ἐσμεν εὐηγγελισμένοι, καθάπερ κἀκεῖνοι· ἀλλ᾽ οὐκ ὠφέλησεν ὁ λόγος τῆς ἀκοῆς ἐκείνους, μὴ συγκεκραμένους τῇ πίστει τοῖς ἀκούσασιν.

3) Consider the "hearing with gladness" of Herod:

Of Herod:
    Mark 6:19-20 (NKJ), "Therefore Herodias held it against him and wanted to kill him, but she could not; for Herod feared John, knowing that he *was* a just and holy man, and he protected him. And **when he heard** him, he did many things, and **heard him gladly**."
    BYZ: καὶ ἀκούσας αὐτοῦ, πολλὰ ἐποίει, καὶ ἡδέως αὐτοῦ ἤκουεν.

Of the Common People:
    Mark 12:37 (NKJ), "Therefore David himself calls Him 'Lord'; how is He *then* his Son?" And the common people **heard Him gladly**."
    BYZ: καὶ ὁ πολὺς ὄχλος ἤκουεν αὐτοῦ ἡδέως.

The adverb "gladly" describes how Herod heard John the Baptist, or how the people listened to Jesus:
    ἡδέως: Liddell-Scott: "Adv. ἡδέως, *sweetly, pleasantly, with pleasure,* Soph., Eur., etc.; ἡδέως ἂν ἐροίμην I would *gladly* ask, should like to ask, Dem.;- ἡδ. ἔχειν τι to be *pleased* or *content* with, Eur.; ἡδ. ἔχειν πρός τινα or τινί to be *kind, well-disposed* to one, Dem.:-Comp. ἥδιον Plat., etc.:-Sup., ἥδιστα Id."
    (Liddell-Scott, BibleWorks 10.0);
    ἡδέως: Gingrich: "ἡδέως adv. *gladly* 2 Cor 11:19. ἡ. ἀκούειν *like to hear* Mk 6:20; 12:37. Superlative ἥδιστα *very gladly* 2 Cor 12:9, 15.*"

Comparative translations of ἤκουεν αὐτοῦ ἡδέως in Mark 12:37

Heard him gladly	Were hearing him gladly	Was hearing him gladly	Gave ear to him gladly	Heard him with pleasure	Heard this with delight	Listened to him with delight	was listening to Him with delight	Enjoyed listening to Him
Tyndale (1534); Geneva (1560 and here); Bishops; KJV; DRA✲; Darby; ERV; ASV; RSV; NKJV; ESV	Young's (1862f.)	Rotherham (1868f.)	BBE (1949f.)	Murdock (1851)	NAB✲ (1991, 2010)	NIV (1984, 2011); NJB✲	NET (1996f.); HCSB;	NASB (1977)

M. Other than a Hearing of Faith:

1. Stopped up their ears, Psa 58:3-5

2. Have ears but cannot hear:
    Psa 115:6, 8, "They have ears, but they cannot hear; … Those who make them will become like them, Everyone who trusts in them."
    Psalm 135:17-18, "They have ears, but they do not hear; Nor is there any breath at all in their mouths. Those who make them will be like them, *Yes*, everyone who trusts in them."
    Ezek 12:2, "Son of man, you live in the midst of the rebellious house, who have eyes to see but do not see, ears to hear but do not hear; for they are a rebellious house."

3. Being deaf, Isa 43:8

4. Dull of hearing, Isa 6:10:
    Matt 13:15, "For the heart of this people has become dull, And with their ears they scarcely hear, And they have closed their eyes Lest they should see with their eyes, And hear with their ears, And understand with their heart and return, And I should heal them"
    Eph 4:18 (French 1669 Geneva), "Ayans leur entendement obscurci de tenebres [Having their hearing obscured by darkness]"
    Acts 28:27, "with their ears they scarcely hear"
    Rom 1:31 (NKJ), "undiscerning"; (NAS), "without understanding"

Sample Translations of ἀσύνετος in Rom 1:[30]31

Lacking discernment*	Lacking Understanding			Lacking wisdom	Lacking intelligence					Lacking conscience	Lacking feeling
NKJ, CSB	Geneva, KJV, NAS	NIV (2011)	NLT	Wycliffe	Young's	NEG	RSV, ESV	NJB✲	CEV✲	GNT✲	Noyes, NIV (1984), NAB✲
undiscerning	without understanding	have no understanding	refuse to understand	vnwise	unintelligent	devoid of intelligence	foolish	without brains	stupid	have no conscience	senseless

*The 1669 French Geneva has for this word, "without hearing" [sans entendement]

5. A corrupt (federal) or corrupted (natural) hearing, 2 Tim 3:8:

    Context: 2 Tim 3:8, "And just as Jannes and Jambres opposed Moses, so these *men* also oppose the truth, **men of depraved** [καταφθείρω] **mind**, rejected as regards the faith."

    Importance: Does this relate to the opposite of a hearing of faith (Gal 3:2, 5; Heb 4:2): i.e. a corrupt hearing?

    An overview of several lexicons:
    Barclay-Newman (1971, 1993): 3354 καταφθείρω (pf. pass. κατέφθαρμαι) corrupt, deprave, ruin

Friberg (1999, 2000): 15397 καταφθείρω pf. pass. ptc. κατεφθαρμένος; literally *destroy* (2P 2.12); figuratively, of the mind *corrupt, deprave, ruin* (2T 3.8)

Liddell-Scott (public domain): 22685 καταφθείρω: κατα-φθείρω, f. -φθερῶ, *to destroy* or *spoil utterly, bring to naught*, Aesch., Soph., etc

Louw-Nida (1988): 88.266 φθείρω ; διαφθείρω ; καταφθείρω: to cause someone to become perverse or depraved, as a type of moral destruction–'to deprave, to pervert, to ruin, to cause the moral ruin of.' φθείρω: ἔκρινεν τὴν πόρνην τὴν μεγάλην ἥτις ἔφθειρεν τὴν γῆν ἐν τῇ πορνείᾳ αὐτῆς 'he condemned the great harlot who was leading the world into moral ruin with her immorality' Re 19.2. διαφθείρω: διαφθεῖραι τοὺς διαφθείροντας τὴν γῆν 'to destroy those who ruin the earth' or '... cause the earth to be depraved' Re 11.18; διαπαρατριβαὶ διεφθαρμένων ἀνθρώπων τὸν νοῦν 'constant arguments from those whose minds are depraved' 1 Tm 6.5. καταφθείρω: ἄνθρωποι κατεφθαρμένοι τὸν νοῦν 'people with depraved minds' 2 Tim 3:8.

Thayer's (1889): 857 καταφθείρω καταφθείρω: perfect passive participle κατεφθαρμένος; 2 future passive κατεφθαρήσομαι; (see κατά, III. 4.) **1.** *to corrupt, deprave*; κατεφθαρμένοι τὸν νοῦν, corrupted in mind, 2 Tim. 3:8. **2.** *to destroy*; passive *to be destroyed, to perish*: followed by ἐν with the dative indicating the state, 2 Pet. 2:12 R G. (From Aeschylus down.)*

English Translation History of 2 Timothy 3:8

Greek Byzantine	Latin Vulgate	Wycliffe (1388)	Tyndale (1534)	English Geneva (1560)	Bishops (1595)	KJV (1611, 1769); Websters; NKJ	Murdock (1852)	Youngs (1862); Darby; ERV; DRA; ASV; ESV	Bible in Basic English (1949)	RSV (1952)	NAS (1977); NIV	NJB (1985)	CEV (1991)	GNB (1993)	NET (2004)
ἄνθρωποι κατεφθαρμένοι τὸν νοῦν	homines corruptimente	men corrupt in vndirstonding	men they are of corrupt myndes	men of corrupte mindes	Men of corrupt myndes	men of corrupt minds	men whose mind is corrupted	men corrupted in mind	men of evil minds	men of corrupt mind	men of depraved mind	so these men defy the truth, their minds corrupt	Their minds are sick	people whose minds do not function	so these people–who have warped minds

French Translation History of 2 Timothy 3:8

Greek Byzantine	Latin Vulgate	Wycliffe (1388)	French Lefèvre (1522)	French Louvain (1550)	French Geneva (1560)	French Segond (1910); NEG	New Geneva (1977)	French Martin (1707)	French Ostervald (1744)	Bible de Jerusalem (1973)	French Le Semeur (1992, 1999)
		Corrupt understanding	Corrupt of hearing					Corrupted spirit			Distorted intelligence
ἄνθρωποι κατεφθαρμένοι τὸν νοῦν	homines corruptimente	men corrupt in vndirstonding	They are men corrupt of hearing	Men corrupt of hearing	people all corrupt of hearing	Being corrupt of hearing	being corrupt of hearing	[being] people who have a corrupted spirit	people of corrupted spirit	men with a corrupted spirit	Their intelligence is distorted
			Ilz sont hommes corcumpus dentendement	hommes corrompu d'entendement	gens du tout corrompus d'entendement	Étant corrompus d'entendement	étant corrompus d'entendement	[étant des] gens qui ont l'esprit corrompu	gens d'un esprit corrompu	hommes à l'esprit corrompu	Ils ont l'intelligence faussée

Does this verse refer to deafness (i.e. no hearing), Psa 58:4-5; Isa 43:8; dull hearing, Isa 6:10; or a corrupt hearing, 2 Tim 3:8?

Notice some further Scriptures:

Heb 4:2, hearing not profitable, because it was not united with faith

Heb 4:6, those hearing failed to enter, because of disobedience

1 Pet 2:8, those who stumbled, stumbled because they were disobedient to the word, and to this doom they were also appointed.

6.   The Gospel veiled, 2 Cor 4:3-4

7.   The snatching of the seed:

   a.   "And they do not understand," Matt 13:19; cf. Mark 4:15
      1)   "Lest they should see with their eyes, And hear with their ears, And understand with their heart and return, And I should heal them," Matt 13:15
      2)   "And while hearing, they may hear and not understand lest they return and be forgiven," Mark 4:12

   b.   "So that they may not believe and be saved," Luke 8:12

N.   Hearing, Receiving, But Not Persevering:

Introduction: A disconcerting set of verses for evangelism, but especially for theological reflection, are those in which some seem to hear and believe, but do not persevere for certain reasons:

1.   The seed sown in the rocky soil:

Matt 13:20-21, "And the one on whom seed was sown on the rocky places, this is the man who hears the word, and immediately receives it with joy; yet he has no *firm* root in himself, but is *only* temporary, and when affliction or persecution arises because of the word, immediately he falls away"

Mark 4:16-17, "And in a similar way these are the ones on whom seed was sown on the rocky *places*, who, when they hear the word, immediately receive it with joy; and they have no *firm* root in themselves, but are *only* temporary; then, when affliction or persecution arises because of the word, immediately they fall away."

Luke 8:13, "And those on the rocky *soil are* those who, when they hear, receive the word with joy; and these have no *firm* root; they believe for a while, and in time of temptation fall away"

In all three Gospels, the hearer hears, receive it with joy, and yet fall away [scandalize; Gk. in Matt and Mark σκανδαλίζω; Luke: ἀφίστημι]

The seed sown among the thorns, which is also a part of the regular ministry of evangelism and discipleship, provides yet another complication to neat theological categories (See a discussion of levels of openness and responses to the Gospel in Chapters 18, 20)

2.   Simon the Sorcerer:

Acts 8:13, "And even Simon himself believed; and after being baptized, he continued on with Philip; and as he observed signs and great miracles taking place, he was constantly amazed"

Acts 8:21, "You have no part or portion in this matter, for your heart is not right before God."

It is clear that Simon, the archetypal false-teacher in the Book of Acts (from which we get the oft-used term "Simony"), heard, believed, and was baptized; yet Peter stated, "You have no part or portion in this matter"!

3.   It ought not be a surprise that these people truly exist in churches today:

   a.   Paul said "from among your own selves men will arise" (Acts 20:30), and likewise he had trouble with false brethren (2 Cor 11:26), many peddlers of the word (2 Cor 2:17), and even super-apostles (2 Cor 11:5) and false apostles (2 Cor 11:13)

   b.   Ananias and Sapphira were members of the church (Acts 5), as was Diotrephes (3 John)!

O.   The Result of a Hearing of Faith:

1.   The question: "To whom has the arm of the Lord been revealed?"

"But though He had performed so many signs before them, *yet* they were not believing in Him; that the word of Isaiah the prophet might be fulfilled, which he spoke, 'LORD, who has believed our report? And to whom has the arm of the Lord been revealed?' For this cause they could not believe, for Isaiah said again, 'He has blinded their eyes, and He hardened their heart; lest they see with their eyes, and perceive with their heart, and be converted, and I heal them'" (John 12:37-40)

However, they did not all heed the glad tidings; for Isaiah says, 'LORD, who has believed our report?' [17] So faith *comes* from hearing, and hearing by the word of Christ" (Rom 10:16-17)

Therefore, is not the particularity of salvation at the point of the self-revelation of God?

(cf. John 8:43-47)

2. Receiving a love for the truth:

    2 Thess 2:10, "and with all unrighteous deception among those who perish, because they did not receive the love of the truth, that they might be saved"

Translations of the Word "Receive" in 2 Thess 2:10

Tyndale (1534), Geneva, Bishops, KJV, ERV, DRA✲, ASV	NAS (1977), NKJ	Darby (1884)	HSCB (2003)	NJB✲ (1985)	RSV (1952), NIV, NLT, ESV	GWN (1995)	NET (2005)	Bible in Basic English (1949)
Because they received not the	Because they did not receive the	Because they have not received the	Because they did not accept the	Because they would not accept the	Because they refused to	Those who refused to	Because they found no place [in their hearts for]	Because they were quite without that

3. The individual manifestation (revelation) of God:

    "But when the kindness of God our Savior and *His* love for mankind appeared, [5] He saved us…" (Titus 3:4-5)

    a. The when [ὅτε] of the individual revelation, Tit 3:4
    b. The what of the individual revelation of God:
        1) The kindness [ἡ χρηστότης] of God, Tit 3:4
            a) As opposed to diobedience, deception, and slavery, Tit 3:3
        2) The love [ἡ φιλανθρωπία] of God, Tit 3:4
            b) As opposed to deserving hate and hating one another, Tit 3:3
        3) The grace [ἡ χάρις] of God, Tit 2:11
    c) The result of individual revelation:
        1) Bringing salvation to all to whom it is revealed, Tit 3:5

Concluding Thoughts:

1. Now comes the question: when and where does this hearing take place?
    a. In the church only?
    b. Outside the church?

2. And another question: by whom does this hearing take place?
    a. To acquaintances only?
    b. To strangers also?

3. And a third question: ought the Christian go out of his way to share the Gospel?
    a. Ought he go or merely stay?
    b. Should he make an effort, or let the person come to him?

4. And a last question: if some are not open to hear, what does this imply?
    a. That the method of evangelism was wrong?
    b. That the Gospel presentation was wrong?
    c. That their heart was not receptive?

5. And yet even among "receptive" persons, there will still be those who are pseudo-Christians!

Aggressive Evangelism's Point of No Return?

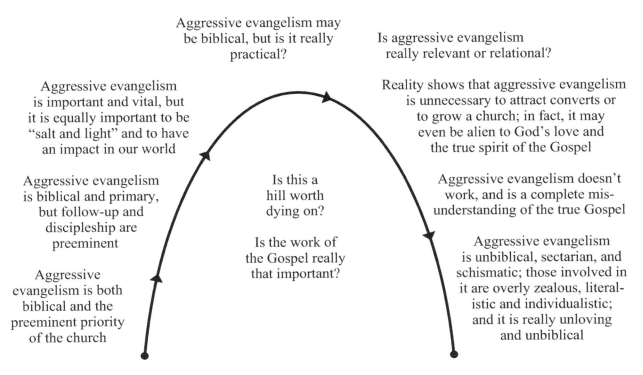

Aggressive evangelism may
be biblical, but is it really
practical?

Is aggressive evangelism
really relevant or relational?

Aggressive evangelism
is important and vital, but
it is equally important to be
"salt and light" and to have
an impact in our world

Reality shows that aggressive evangelism
is unnecessary to attract converts or
to grow a church; in fact, it may
even be alien to God's love and
the true spirit of the Gospel

Aggressive evangelism
is biblical and primary,
but follow-up and
discipleship are
preeminent

Is this a
hill worth
dying on?

Aggressive evangelism doesn't
work, and is a complete misunderstanding of the true Gospel

Is the work of
the Gospel really
that important?

Aggressive
evangelism is both
biblical and the
preeminent priority
of the church

Aggressive evangelism
is unbiblical, sectarian, and
schismatic; those involved in
it are overly zealous, literalistic and individualistic;
and it is really unloving
and unbiblical

Food for Thought:

Notice that this cycle resembles a bell curve. At least on the aggressive evangelism side, it seems like the number of Christians increase as zeal for evangelism decreases.

Can you relate to this cycle? Have you experienced this cycle?

How long does it take for a person, church, denomination, or movement to move through this cycle?

Where on the cycle does a person become resentful of someone who is aggressively evangelistic?

How long can a person keep up a façade of being evangelistic when they cease believing in its necessity?[102]

Where are you on this cycle?

Note, for example, the following quote from Mark Mittelberg. Is it possible to place him on this cycle based on this quote?

"Inherent in all this is the fact that for most people today the movement toward Christ will be a *process*. Contrast this to what I said previously about earlier forms of evangelim, which were largely designed to be an *event* that reminded semireligious people of what they already knew and then challenged them to commit to it right there on the spot. Rather, the process approach deepens the trust of secular people over time, along the way, urges tyhem to put their faith in Christ."[103]

---

[102]For example, note Chuck Templeton who continued to be involved in crusade evangelism even after he no longer believed in salvation by grace alone, through the Scriptures alone, by hearing and believing alone: "How does a man who, each night, tells ten to twenty thousand people how to find faith confess that he is struggling with his own?" (Templeton, *Farewell to God: My Reasons for Rejecting the Christian Faith* [Toronto: McClelland and Stewart, 1996], 11).

[103]Mark Mittelberg, *Building a Contagious Church* (Grand Rapids: Zondervan, 2000), 60.

The Difficulty of Personal Soul-Winning from Trumbull

Individual Work the Hardest Work

Individual soul-winning is not easy work. It is hard. It is the hardest work that God asks us to do for him. Before trying to reason out why, or to argue that the simple extending to a fellow-man of an invitation to share with us the richest joy of our life *ought* to be an easy thing to do, let us frankly admit that it is hard, and face that fact to begin with.

For any one who has ever tried the work knows this. Even those whose professional and only life-business is soul-saving find it difficult. Ask any minister-friend which is easier for him to do: to preach a sermon, or to seek an opportunity to talk alone with an individual about that one's spiritual welfare.

Many a man who is eloquent before a large congregation is dumb before a single individual. Such a man often confesses that he is not an effective worker in an "inquiry meeting." Even in a season of special religious interest he wants to turn the work of conversing with individuals over to somebody else.

Bossuet, the great French preacher, said frankly as to this very matter: "It requires more faith and courage to say two words face to face with one single sinner, than from the pulpit to rebuke two or three thousand persons, ready to listen to everything, on condition of forgetting all."

Men who have a national and an international fame as preachers to a multitude actually say-not only think, but say-that they cannot speak to an individual soul for Christ. In some instances these preachers speak of it as if they counted a sinner's personality too sacred to speak a word to, even to save his soul or to honor Christ. In other cases, they speak of their inability as an amiable weakness, instead of as a pitiable moral and spiritual defect, which proves them incompetent for their position and profession.[104]

Will It Grow Easy?

If it is so hard even for the trained minister, it is not to be expected that laymen will do it more easily. But if it is our greatest work, and if it is Christ's preferred method because it is the most effective method, have we the satisfaction and encouragement of knowing that this work will grow easy as we go on in its accomplishment? Will long-continued practice bring ease and facility?

It is to be hoped not. And judging from the experience of others we are not likely to be in danger, in this field, from the peril of easy accomplishment, which usually means loss of effectiveness.

If it "takes it out" of a man to sell goods, or write life insurance, or solicit advertising, or do anything else that means bringing another across from his position to ours, is there anything we ought to be more sharply watchful against in ourselves than slipping into a superficial "facility" in soul-winning? We not only must not expect the work to grow easy, but we must realize that if it does so, something is wrong. Anything but the "facile" man here!

Dr. Trumbull was often spoken of as being a man of exceptional "tact." He practiced pretty constantly at individual soul-winning from the time when he first found his Saviour, at twenty-one, until his death more than fifty years later. People who knew him and his ways, and his life-long habit, have said of him, "Oh, it was 'second nature' to Dr. Trumbull to speak to a man about his soul. He fairly couldn't help doing it, it was so easy for him. I never could get his ease in the work." And in so saying they showed how little they knew of him or of the demands of this work upon every man.

The book on "Individual Work" was written after its author was seventy years of age. Hear what he had to say as to the "ease" which his long practice had brought him:

From nearly half a century of such practice, as I have had opportunity day by day, I can say that I have spoken with thousands upon thousands on the subject of their spiritual welfare. Yet, so far from my becoming accustomed to this matter, so that I can take hold of it as a matter of course, I find it as difficult to speak about it at the end of these years as at the beginning. Never to the present day can I speak to a single soul for Christ without being reminded by Satan that I am in danger of harming the cause by introducing it just now. If there is one thing that Satan is sensitive about, it is the danger of a

---

[104]Here the author quotes from his father's book: H. Clay Trumbull, *Individual Work for Individuals: A Record of Personal Experiences and Convictions* (New York: The International Committee of the Young Men's Christian Association, 1901), 8, 9-10, 169-70.

Christian's harming the cause he loves by speaking of Christ to a needy soul. He [Satan] has more than once, or twice, or thrice, kept me from speaking on the subject by his sensitive pious caution, and he has tried a thousand times to do so. Therefore my experience leads me to suppose that he is urging other persons to try any method for souls except the best one.

Have we not the answer here to the question which was passed over a moment ago, as to why this work is the hardest work in the world? Just because it is the most effective work for Christ, the Devil opposes it most bitterly, and always will while he is permitted to oppose anything good. The Devil strikes hardest and most persistently at the forces which will, if effective, hurt his cause most. He devotes his chief energies to those from whom he has most to fear; their sides he never leaves. Therefore the worker who seeks to win individuals to Christ may rest assured that he has, by entering upon that work, served notice upon the Devil for a life-and-death conflict; and that notice will be accepted by the Devil as an obligation to swerve the worker from his purpose whenever, by any subtle means in the Devil's power, this can be done. Let us write down large in our mental or real note-books the Devil's favorite argument:

His favorite argument with a believer is that just now is not a good time to speak on the subject. The lover of Christ and of souls is told that he will harm the cause he loves by introducing the theme of themes just now.

This, then, is what we face when we enter upon this work. The greatest and hardest work in the world, it will never grow easy, but it will never grow small. If it always remains the hardest, it always remains also the greatest. There is a character-challenge in continued difficulties that assures this work a quality of success to which easy work could never attain.

One who was making a study of the incidents in Dr. Trumbull's book started to group together first those cases that seemed to be complicated by some special difficulty, some factor that offered a noticeable obstacle to doing individual work in that case. He put down one incident, and another, and another, and another. And then he gave up that plan of classifying, for he found that he would have to put into that first group practically every case in the book! In the record of fifty years' work by one to whom this work was said to be "easy" because it had become "second-nature," there was scarcely a single instance that had not its own peculiar obstacle or reason for holding off!

Shall we not take encouragement by remembering this the next time we are tempted to discouragement by the peculiar difficulties that beset our path? As it was in that volume, so it will be in life. There will seldom be an opportunity free from some strong reason why we had better "do it later." But the Devil is back of the reason.[105]

---

[105]Charles G. Trumbull, *Taking Men Alive: Studies in the Principles and Practise of Individual Soul-Winning* (New York: The International Committee of the Young Men's Christian Association, 1907; 1915; New York: Revell, 1938), 42-46.

Claude Monier's Self-Sacrificing Ministry in 1551

M. Claude Monier, from Auvergne [a region in south central France]

Claude Monier, an educated man, native of St. Amand of Talande, also of La Chaire, three leagues from Issoère in Auvergne [county]: after having been instructed for some time in the public schools of this town, and in Clermont, capital city of Auvergne, having been taught from his youth a special fear of God and the knowledge of His Holy Word, became hated and suspect by the haters of the same, so much so that he lost his charge as a teacher. So he left in the direction of Auvergne and other villages around the same, publicly preaching the Word of God, up until the time that he was persecuted, and constrained to retire to the land of the Gospel [Switzerland], and the Reformed Church by the Word of God. After which he retired to Lausanne, city in the jurisdiction of the Lords of Bern, and studied there for some time. Since finding himself in Lyon, he had the charge of several children, who he instructed in the Holy Letters: so much so that in a little time he became known of several faithful, who rejoiced in his holy conversation: for he was gifted with a tender spirit, peaceable and meek, according to the testimony given him by several faithful witnesses, who were familiar with his good life, and the pure doctrine that he announced to each one who he was able to encounter there: as is also manifestly noted by the fruit of his life and [as] the true mark that follows the said doctrine. For it soon came about, on a Sunday the fifth of July 1551, having been in the home of his friend to give him advice to hold himself away from the Provost [of the town] who had come to take him: after having guided the friend and done the action of a true Christian: returning from his trip, there came upon him the Provost suspicious to take Monier, and brought him as a prisoner to the *Official* [prison], after which he was questioned on several things. Thus it would be that God would give him the grace that while being a prisoner he wrote part of the judicial acts and interrogations held against him, we have here his letter containing his entire confession, in the strength to which it was put into writing for the faithful, as follows…[106]

[He was slowly burned while hanging over a fire in Lyon, France, on the 20th of October 1551—97 days after his arrest].

---

[106]Jean Crespin, *Histoire des vrays Tesmoins de la verite de l'evangile, qui de leur sang l'ont signée, depuis Jean Hus iusques autemps present* [*History of the True Witnesses to the Truth of the Gospel, Who with Their Blood Signed, from John Hus to the Present*] (Geneva, 1570; reproduction, Liège, 1964), 182. Translation mine.

The Evangelism Ministry of Two Teenage Girls, Isabeau and Pintarde, around 1689

"Two young women that God had raised up in the Cévennes region [of France] for the consolation of His people provided much edification to Mr. Brousson [desert church evangelist/preacher, martyred in 1698]. He spoke of them with great delight. One was named Isabeau Redosteire. She was approximately 18 years old. She was the daughter of a little peasant from a little village called Milieyrines. The other was named Pintarde. This one was approximately 16 or 17 years old and was the daughter of a peasant from the region of Gros, near St.-Hippolyte. One and the other traveled separately, from place to place and from desert to desert, gathering people wherever they went where they exhorted the people by the Word of God to be converted, to be sanctified, to take hold of zeal, to come out of the impurities of Babylon, to give glory to God, to serve Him with purity, and to be faithful to Him unto death. They joined this exhortation with ardent and admirable prayers that they took from the Book of Psalms and the ancient prophets, which were perfectly appropriate to the state of the Church in France, and which they expressed with inconceivable power. They were of such a modest character, so humble, so simple, and so full of piety, that Mr. Brousson was greatly delighted in admiration of them. After they had worked one and the other for about two years unto the salvation and consolation of the faithful, they were arrested and brought before Mr. de Bâville who said to them:

"'So! You are then these girls who are getting mixed up with preaching?'

"'We have done,' said they, 'several exhortations to our brothers, and we have prayed with them when the occasion presented itself. If you call that preaching, then we have preached.'

"'Do you not know,' said the commissary, 'that the king prohibits that?'

"'We are well aware of that,' said they, 'but the King of kings, the God of the heavens commands it, and we are obligated to obey God rather than men.'

"So the commissary told them that they had merited death and that they could not expect any treatment less rigorous than that which was realized and experienced by those who, like them, had preached [the Gospel] against the prohibition of the king.

"'Your threats are incapable of astonishing us,' said they [the girls], 'and we are completely disposed to suffer death for the glory of God for the service to which we are committed.'

"Such a zealous and Christian answer astonished the commissary. He feared that the girls, who were so young, and so prepared for martyrdom, would make an impression on the spirits [of the people] if he condemned them to death and had them executed in public. So he contented himself to condemn them to perpetual life in prison. One was brought to the Tower of Constance, in [the town] Aigue-Mortes, where, after having suffered many terrible treatments, she died in complete resignation to God's divine will and in the perseverance that nothing can weaken nor shake. The other was closed up in the Chateau of Sommières, where she also suffered much, but with an unshakable constancy and perseverance."[107]

---

[107]Antoine Court [d. 1760], *Claude Brousson* (Paris: Librairie Protestante, 1961), 54-56.

CHAPTER 3

The Role of the Evangelist

Introduction:

B. H. Carroll, founder of Southwestern Baptist Theological Seminary, pled with delegates to the Southern Baptist Convention Meeting in Chatanooga, TN, 14 May 1906, "Brethren, give me evangelists"? Here is the context of these potent words:

> "The bedrock of Scripture underlies it. Experience demonstrates its wisdom and feasibility. If the Home Mission Board may employ any man, it may employ evangelists. Altogether, then, with a ring, let us support this measure. If I were the secretary of the board I would come before this body in humility and tears and say: 'Brethren, give me evangelists. Deny not fins to things that must swim against the tide, nor wings to things that must fly against the wind.'"[108]

Today, if you ask any pastor, "Do you want your church to grow?" The obvious answer is, "Yes!"
Then who should he contact? Today, there are two main choices, the Church Growth consultant or the God-called evangelist.
The following chart uses exaggeration to compare and contrast these approaches and their potential results…

Comparing the Ministry of the Church Sociologist with that of the God-Called Evangelist*

	Church Sociologist*	**God-Called Evangelist***
Contemporary View	In vogue, relevant	Old-fashioned, irrelevant
Qualifications	Man trained, man taught, and man equipped; Man sent (Jer 23:21)	God called, God gifted, God equipped; Sent out by God
Source of calling	Based on adequate training and experience in an empirical science founded by men (1 Chron 12:32)	Office established by God in His eternal Word, Eph 4:11 (cf. Acts 21:8)
Student of…	Student of culture, whether contemporary church culture or the culture at large, drawing conclusions from studies of these cultures	Student of the Word of God, framing the issues, questions, answers, and preaching by the eyeglasses of the Word of God, Deut 6:8
Method	Assess and recommend changes in: worship styles, preaching, dress, hairstyles, nomenclature, architecture, staffing, organizational structure, fellowship, small groups, outreach, etc. (e.g. Christian Schwarz, *Natural Church Development*; et al.)	Preach, teach, and lead evangelism by revivals and personal soul winning
Basis	Contemporary church growth literature, business models, church sociology Consider however: Prov 14:12 (16:25), "There is a way *which seems* right to a man, But its end is the way of death" 1 Cor 2:14, "But a natural man does not accept the things of the Spirit of God; for they are foolishness to him, and he cannot understand them, because they are spiritually appraised" Isa 55:8-9; Prov 3:5-6	Message and methods of evangelism in the Bible: 1 Pet 1:23-25, "for you have been born again not of seed which is perishable but imperishable, *that is*, through the living and abiding word of God. For, 'All flesh is like grass, 'And all its glory like the flower of grass. 'The grass withers, 'And the flower falls off, 'But the word of the Lord abides forever.' "And this is the word by which you were evangelized."

---

[108]B. H. Carroll, "Shall the Atlanta Board Be Instructed to Employ Evangelists and to Call for an Extra $25,000 for Their Support?" *Baptist Standard* (31 May 1906) 14:1-2; cited in Charles S. Kelley, Jr., *How Did They Do It? The Story of Southern Baptist Evangelism* (New Orleans: Insight, 1993), 14.

	Church Sociologist*	God-Called Evangelist*
Substance	Seeking to principalize, standardize, and package the love of God giving genuine care (such as the "seven touches of the Gospel"?) and combining these principles with the latest marketing techniques of "Madison Avenue" and the latest business models from the *Harvard Business Review* or *Fortune 500 Magazine*	The love of God being shed abroad in the believer's heart allows that believer to be: 1) Genuine 2) Biblical 3) Use truly indigenous methods 4) Remain focused on evangelism and the Gospel message
Is it biblical?	The usefulness of the study depends upon the doctrinal presuppositions of the researcher; which are often nuanced and very difficult to ascertain	Imminently biblical, necessitates biblical methods and message; discernment also needed here
Agent of change	Administrative prowess: transformational leadership models and change agent training	The Holy Spirit working through the Word of God; the foolishness of the Word preached (1 Cor 1:18)
Results of change	Outward form is changed (2 Tim 3:5): names, administration, appearances, sometimes message is diluted to adapt to cultural norms	Inner hearts are transformed
Ultimate focus	Numbers of people in church	Number of souls truly saved
Impact of change	Temporary influx of people	An eternal Gospel (Rev 14:6) with lasting impact (Eph 2:5)
Depth of change	Shallow	To the inner heart (Heb 4:12-13)
Biblical analysis?	Wood, hay, and stubble	Gold, silver, and precious stones

*Disclaimer: This chart is not meant to discount all church sociologists, nor the usefulness of their findings. Rather it is meant to clarify extremes by way of comparison to portray sometimes overlooked points. Some church sociologists truly love the Bible, the Gospel, and evangelism. Others, however, approach the sociology of the church as a mere socio-cognitive-scientific study, sometimes either avoiding or equivocating away the supernatural elements of true church growth, such as the preaching of the Gospel and the need for conversion.[109] Likewise, not all those who call themselves "evangelists" follow the biblical patterns and norms for their evangelistic ministry. Discernment is needed on both sides!

There is a remarkable difference in the approach and results of these two extremes. Perhaps this was why God differentiated between Philip and Simon the Sorcerer in Acts 8?

Biblical Food for Thought:

When does a pollster become a soothsayer (for the Hebrew 'anan)?

Deut 8:14 (KJV), "For these nations, which thou shalt possess, hearkened unto observers of times, and unto diviners: but as for thee, the LORD thy God hath not suffered thee so *to do*"

Various Translations of the Hebrew 'anan in Deut 18:14

Bishop's	KJV	Young's	BBE	NET	DRA, RSV, NKJ, NJB	NLT	GWN; ESV; CSB	Wycliffe	Darby	ERV, ASV	NIV	NASB
regarders of tymes	observers of times	observers of clouds	readers of signs	omen readers	soothsayers	sorcerers	fortune-tellers	that worchen bi chiteryng of briddis	those that use auguries	Those who practice augury	Those who practice sorcery	Those who practice witchcraft

---

[109]In this light, consider, for example, Christian Schwarz' *ABC's of Natural Church Development* (Carol Stream, IL: ChurchSmart, n.d.) and his *Natural Church Development: A Guide to Eight Essential Qualities of Healthy Churches* (Carol Stream, IL: ChurchSmart Resources, 1998). Schwarz made use of the complexities of Christological language to explain his naturalistically-oriented approach, leading him to posit "Functionality as a Theological Criterion" in his *Paradigm Shift in the Church: How Natural Church Development Can Transform Theological Thinking* (1999).

Being an "observer of the times" appears to stand in juxtaposition to "understanding the times" in 1 Chronicles 12:32, a common verse used by those who peddle in parsing contemporary culture:

> 1 Chron 12:32, "And of the sons of Issachar, men who understood the times, with knowledge of what Israel should do, their chiefs were two hundred; and all their kinsmen were at their command"

Some have inverted the old adage as follows, "He is so earthly minded, that he is no heavenly good!"

Historical Food for Thought:

Ever since "church growth" became a marketed term among U. S. Evangelicals (circa. McGavran's *Understanding Church Growth*, 1970), Evangelical churches in the U.S. have for the most part been in decline.

Furthermore, "church growth" was not only popularized by McGavran. Methodist missionary to India and Bishop Jarrell Waskom Pickett's "mass movements" methodology was front and center as "The Most Natural Way of Approach to Christ" in the Madras [India] 1938 International Missionary Council's (IMC) evangelism papers:[110]

According to Arthur McPhee, who wrote his Ph.D. dissertation on Pickett,[111] Pickett was very influencial in modern India:

> "Following [India's] independence, in 1947, no expatriate surpassed Pickett in political influence. He had unusual access to Prime Minister Nehru, knew all the members of his cabinet well, and was a close friend of B. R. Ambedkar, Nehru's Law Minister and Rajkumari Amrit Kaur, his Health Minister."[112]

Pickett also seems to have become the *de facto* grandfather of the modern AERDO—American Evangelical Relief and Development Organizations:

> "Donald Elbright, one time Director of Famine Relief for the National Christian Council of India, wrote, during the communal riots following Independence and Partition, 'Bishop J. W. Pickett … did more than any one non-government person to organize voluntary relief in Delhi.'"[113]

Several points of caution:

1) One origin of an Evangelical emphasis on socio-political action was Pickett's influence on Madras and McGavran:

> "In 1933, Pickett published *Christian Mass Movements in India*. After reading this book, McGavran became a disciple of Pickett. Herbert Works writes, 'It is no surprise, therefore, that the inscription he wrote inside the cover of his book *How Churches Grow*, nearly thirty years after this India experience, says, "To J. Waskom Pickett, at whose fire I lit my candle."'[114] McGavran researched with Pickett and co-authored *Church Growth and Group Conversion* in 1936."[115]

2) A shift to the center on socio-policial action necessitates a rearrangement of one's view of the Great Commission

3) The change in the Great Commission, adhered to in Pickett's mass movement methodology, seemed to appease both moderate and remaining conservative factions of the IMC movement. It must be noted that some Evangelical mission organizations began to pull out of the IMC in 1917, when they formed the IFMA—Independent Foreign Missions Association of North America

---

[110]*Evangelism*, "The Madras Series," Vol 3 (New York: International Missionary Council, 1939), 3, 4, 5, 10, 14, 24, 42, 58-79, 85, 88-89, 95, 105, 121, 201-02, 279, 363-76. Donald McGavran is mentioned by name in this conference resource in connection to Pickett's "mass movements" on page 76.

[111]Arthur Gene McPhee, "Pickett's Fire: The Life, Contribution, Thought, and Legacy of J. Waskom Pickett, Methodist Missionary to India." Ph.D. Dissertation, Asbury Theological Seminary, Wilmore, KY, 2001.

[112]Art McPhee, "Bishop J. Waskom Pickett's Rethinking on 1930s Missions in India," *International Journal of Frontier Missions*, 19:3 (Fall 2002), 31.

[113]Ibid.

[114] Herbert M. Works, Jr., "Donald A. McGavran: The Development of a Legacy," *Global Church Growth*, Vol. XXVII, No. 3 (July-August-September, 1990), 8.

[115]Thomas P. Johnston, "A Historical and Theological Evaluation of Christian Schwarz's 'Natural Church Development'"; unpublished paper, 2000.

4) Twelve years after Madras, the International Missionary Council movement merged into the World Council of Churches, in Amsterdam (1948).

Biblical Food for Thought:

Some thoughts about the Priest of Zeus, Acts 14:12-19:

He had chosen to represent the most powerful deity in the Greek Pantheon—Zeus, Acts 14:13

His was either a religious newcomer or had a very prestigious position in that city, "whose *temple* was just outside the city," Acts 14:13

He had no problem syncretizing his religion with another one—"wanted to offer sacrifice," Acts 14:13

He had no problem worshipping the creature rather than the creator—"wanted to offer sacrifice," Acts 14:13

He was catching the religious wave of public opinion—"wanted to offer sacrifice with the crowds," Acts 14:13

He used a genuine Spirit-given miracle to further his own selfish ends, Acts 14:13

He did not want to be outdone by Paul

His goal was seemingly to use the miracle to get the attention back on him

Is this not sin against the Holy Spirit, similar to Nadab and Abihu, Lev 9:23-10:3?

His town led to the most violent opposition that Paul ever faced in his ministry—"they stoned Paul and dragged him out of the city, supposing him to be dead" Acts 14:19

What does God bless, sociological research or His Word?

"For you have been born again not of seed which is perishable but imperishable, *that is*, through the living and abiding word of God. For,

'All flesh is like grass,

'And all its glory like the flower of grass.

'The grass withers,

'And the flower falls off,

'But the word of the Lord abides forever.'

"And this is the word by which you were evangelized" (1 Pet 1:23-25, NAS with my revision of v. 25).

God has chosen to bless His Word, proclaimed by His servants in His way![116] Aren't God's ways always superior (Isa 55:8-9)? Notice the context of these verses quoted by Peter:

[6] Seek the LORD while He may be found; Call upon Him while He is near.

[7] Let the wicked forsake his way, And the unrighteous man his thoughts;

And let him return to the LORD, And He will have compassion on him; And to our God,

For He will abundantly pardon.

[8] "For My thoughts are not your thoughts, Neither are your ways My ways," declares the LORD.

[9] "For *as* the heavens are higher than the earth, So are My ways higher than your ways, And My thoughts than your thoughts.

[10] "For as the rain and the snow come down from heaven, And do not return there without watering the earth, And making it bear and sprout, And furnishing seed to the sower and bread to the eater;

[11] So shall My word be which goes forth from My mouth; It shall not return to Me empty, Without accomplishing what I desire, And without succeeding *in the matter* for which I sent it. (Isa 55:6-11)

Also note this statement by English evangelist Roger Carswell in his book, *And Some as Evangelists: Growing your Church through Discovering and Developing Evangelists*:

"My plea is for the setting aside of gifted believers to be devoted to the full-time work of evangelism, in the same way that pastors and missionaries are appointed for their task. They will spearhead evangelistic endeavour in their locality and beyond. Their emphasis will be the proclaiming of the gospel. Christ crucified will be their abiding theme."[117]

Does not the plea of Carswell sound similar to the plea of B. H. Carroll as listed above?

---

[116]"Do not believe, dear friends, that when you go into revival meetings or special evangelistic services, you are to leave out the doctrines of the Gospel, for then you ought to proclaim the doctrines of grace more, rather than less" (Charles H. Spurgeon, *The Soul Winner* [New Kensington, PA: Whitaker House, 1995], 14).

[117]Roger Carswell, *And Some as Evangelists: Growing Your Church through Discovering and Developing Evangelists* (Fearn, Ross-shire, Great Britain: Christian Focus, 2002, 2005), 91.

Rather than come up with a new program, new terminology, a new methodology, or a new organizational structure, God calls His servants to "rekindle the gift of God."

2 Tim 1:6 (RSV), "Hence I remind you to rekindle the gift of God that is within you through the laying on of my hands"

Comparative Translations of 2 Tim 1:6

[ordered chronologically by first known usage for the translation of ἀναζωπυρεῖν]

Byzantine Textform	Latin Vulgate	Wycliffe 2nd edition	Tyndale (Bishop's; Geneva; KJV; Webster's; Young's; English Revised; Douay-Rheims✳; ASV; NKJ)	Murdock	Darby (RSV; NET)	New American Bible✳	Bible in Basic English	NASB	NIV (NJB✳; NLT; ESV)	HCBS	Good News Trans✳	Cont English Version✳
Ἀναζω-πυρεῖν	Resus-cites	Reise ayen	Stere up (stir up)	Excite	Rekindle	Stir into flame	Let … have living power	Kindle afresh	Fan into flame[s]	Keep ablaze	Keep alive	Make full use of
Δι᾽ ἣν αἰτίαν ἀναμιμνήσκω σε ἀναζω-πυρεῖν τὸ χάρισμα τοῦ θεοῦ, ὅ ἐστιν ἐν σοὶ διὰ τῆς ἐπιθέσεως τῶν χειρῶν μου.	ropter quam causam admoneo te ut resuscites gratiam Dei quae est in te per inposi-tionem manuum mearum	For which cause Y moneste thee, that thou reise ayen the grace of God, that is in thee bi the settyng on of myn hondis.	Wherfore I warne the that thou stere vp the gyfte of god which is in the by the puttynge on of my hondes.	Wherefore I remind thee, that thou excite the gift of God, that is in thee by the imposition of my hands.	For which cause I put thee in mind to rekindle the gift of God which is in thee by the putting on of my hands.	For this reason, I remind you to stir into flame the gift of God that you have through the imposition of my hands.	For this reason I say to you, Let that grace of God which is in you, given to you by my hands, have living power.	And for this reason I remind you to kindle afresh the gift of God which is in you through the laying on of my hands.	For this reason I remind you to fan into flame the gift of God, which is in you through the laying on of my hands.	Therefore, I remind you to keep ablaze the gift of God that is in you through the laying on of hands.	For this reason, I remind you to keep alive the gift that God gave you when I laid my hands on you.	So I ask you to make full use of the gift that God gave you when I placed my hands on you.

Thoughts on Calling the Biographers of Jesus "Evangelists":

Introduction: Historically, the biographers of Jesus have been titled "Evangelists"—What are the possible ramifications of calling them by such a title?

This section will address this issue and explore some of its ramifications

Possible Reasons for Calling the Authors of the Four "Gospels" Evangelists:

Because Mark begins his biography of Jesus with the words "The beginning of the gospel of Jesus Christ" [Ἀρχὴ τοῦ εὐαγγελίου Ἰησοῦ χριστοῦ];

Because John explained that the purpose of his biography of Jesus was evangelistic:

"And truly Jesus did many other signs in the presence of His disciples, which are not written in this book; but these are written that you may believe that Jesus is the Christ, the Son of God, and that believing you may have life in His name." John 20:30-31 (NKJ).

To confuse the meaning of the word "Evangelist" and its role in the local church"

"And He Himself gave some *to be* apostles, some prophets, some evangelists, and some pastors and teachers, for the equipping of the saints for the work of ministry, for the edifying of the body of Christ." Eph. 4:11-12 (NKJ)

Reasons for Not Calling the Authors of the Four "Gospels" Evangelists:

Because Philip was the only person named an "Evangelist" in the New Testament:

> "On the next *day* we who were Paul's companions departed and came to Caesarea, and entered the house of Philip the evangelist, who was *one* of the seven, and stayed with him." Acts 21:8 (NKJ)

Therefore, it is more exegetically consistent to allow the Bible to supply the meaning of the term "Evangelist"—by examining the ministry of Philip.

And since Philip did not write a "Gospel"—therefore, writing a gospel did not constitute why only he was called an "Evangelist" by Luke.

Because calling the authors of the Gospels "Evangelists" confuses how the Bible uses the term

Because also, we never read in the Book of Acts of Mark or Luke "evangelizing" [εὐαγγελίζω]:

We find Matthew and John evangelizing as part of the twelve in Luke 9:6; Acts 5:42;

Jesus evangelized in Matt 11:5; Luke 4:18, 43; 7:22; 8:1; 20:1;

Philip "evangelized" as noted in Acts 8:4, 12, 35, 40;

Peter and John "evangelized" in Acts 8:25; Peter evangelized in Acts 10:36

And likewise, although never titlted with the title "Evangelist," Paul evangelized in Acts 13:32; 14:7, 15, 21; 15:35; 16:10; 17:18; Rom 1:15; 15:20; 1 Cor 1:17; 9:16, 18; 15:1-2; 2 Cor 10:16; 11:7; Gal 1:8-9. 11, 16, 23; 4:13; Eph 3:8.

Corrollary Issue:

Possible reasons for Calling the Biographies of Jesus "Gospels":

Possible reasons for Not Calling the Biographies of Jesus "Gospels":

Has Calling the Biographies of Jesus "Gospels" confused the use of the word gospel by Jesus in the "Gospels" or by Paul in the Pauline corpus?

E.g. see the impact of adding adjectives to the word "gospel" in the introduction of Chap 17.

Conclusions:

The use of "Gospels" for the biographies of Jesus renders confusion as to what is the "Gospel"

The use of "Evangelists" for the authors of the "Gospels" confuses what the function and role of the "Evangelist" really is—advancing the cessationist notion that it is a closed office.

A. Noticing the Obvious—On the Omission of Evangelists:

Introduction: But something is drastically wrong in the church today; we seem to have forgotten the evangelist! (Eph 4:11—"and some as evangelists")

> "Where are they? Where have they gone? It's almost like an endless search for Bigfoot. They have become a myth and legend of yesterday's phenomena. Do I dare say the name? Be prepared if you say it, you will in doubt catch the glaring eye of today's Evangelical world with their endless excuses of an outdated mode and out-of-style. I believe much of what we see today with the up-rise of wickedness and evil is grounded in the willful neglect of the office of an Evangelist within the Local Church"[118]

1. **Not surprisingly, the evangelist is usually ignored in the development of curricula for teaching theology, and even for theological education. For example:**

   a. The Puritan William Ames (1629);[119]

   b. The Lutheran Freidrich Schleiermacher (1830);[120] and

   c. The Northern Baptist University of Chicago's Philip Schaff (1902).[121]

   RESULT 1: Evangelists (and their corrolary activity "evangelism") are considered irrelevant or unnecessary in mainstream theological education.

---

[118]Jeff Rose, "The Forgotten Evangelist: An Indictment Against Contemporary American Evangelicalism"; available at: http://us9.campaign-archive1.com/?u=e8556cd67e3728a96332fb7d6&id=2980653ec6&e=055e660084 (online); accessed 23 Feb 2015; Internet.

[119]Puritan divine William Ames, in his *The Marrow of Theology,* trans. John D. Eusden (1629; Grand Rapids: Eerdmans, 1997), apparently had nothing to say of the responsibility of the Christian in evangelism, much less of the work of evangelism. This was an unusual omission in light of the fact that his second book dealt with the Christian life. He divided this book into two sections, "religion" and "justice." Interestingly for the history of evangelism among congregationalists and in theological studies in the United States, "Both Thomas Hooker and Increase Mather recommended the *Marrow of Theology* as the only book beyond the Bible needed to make a student into a sound theologian" (ibid., back cover).

[120]Schleiermacher made "how to deal with converts" a subject for Christian education, never mentioning how people would become converts, nor the work of evangelism. This is an incredible omission given how much of the book of Acts is devoted to evangelization, and also given that his "Brief Outline on the Study of Theology" has been very influential on determining what courses need to be taught in seminaries—if you follow his outline, you will never have a course in personal evangelism (that figures, most seminaries don't anyway):

"§296. On similar grounds, those who live within the neighborhood or vicinity of the congregation—as religious strangers, as it were—may also become subjects of similar activity [catechetics]. This requires a theory of how to deal with converts. For the more definitely the principles of catechetics are set forth the easier it will be to derive this theory from them.

"§297. However, since this activity is not so naturally grounded certain indications should be drawn up for recognizing whether it is properly motivated. For it is possible to err in both directions here: in hasty self-confidence and in anxious hesitation.

"§298. Conditionally, the theory of missions might also be attached here, one which is as good as completely lacking at the present time. It could most easily be attached if it were possible to assume that all efforts of this kind are successful only where a Christian congregation is in existence" (Friedrich Schleiermacher, *Brief Outline on the Study of Theology,* 2nd ed., trans. Terrence N. Tice [1830; Richmond, VA: John Knox, 1966], 102).

Schleiermacher's view of conversion as "quiescent self-consciousness" shaped his view of the work of conversion as a process of informing the self (see Friedrich Schleiermacher, *The Christian Faith,* 2nd ed. [Edinburgh: Clark, 1960], 478-479). In fact, he opposed instantaneous conversion: "The idea that every Christian must be able to point to the very time and place of his conversion is accordingly an arbitrary and presumptuous restriction of divine grace, and can only cause confusion" (ibid., 487).

[121]The thirty-second chapter of thirty-four in practical theology is titled "Evangelistic." In two pages Schaff described "The new branch of theological learning, demanded by the growing zeal in missions" (Philip Schaff, *Theological Propædeutic: A General Introduction to the Study of Theology,* 5th ed. [New York: Scribner, 1902], 517). Perhaps Schaff was perhaps referring to the work of Gustav Warneck, who wrote *An Outline of a History of Protestant Missions from the Reformation to the Present Time,* ed. by George Robson, translated from the 7th German ed. (New York: Revell, 1901), which became foundational in the study of the Protestant mission movement. Schaff then went on to include two other sections on missions: "Epochs of Missions" and "Missionary Literature." While quoting the Great Commission in his section titled "Evangelistic," Schaff never addressed conversion, but rather dealt with missions from a historical and ecclesial point of view, culminating in a post-millenial triumphalism: "The extraordinary progress of missionary zeal and enterprise is phenomenal, and one of the greatest evidences for the vitality of Christianity, and an assurance of its ultimate triumph to the ends of the earth..." (Schaff, *Theological Propædeutic,* 522).

2. **Similarly, the evangelist is often forgotten, overlooked, or explained away in Protestant textbooks on systematic theology:**

     a. John Calvin's *Institutes of the Christian Religion* (~1545 A.D.):

     "By *Evangelists,* I mean those who, while inferior to the rank of the apostles, were next them in office, and even acts as their substitutes. Such were Luke, Timothy, Titus, and the like; perhaps, also, the seventy disciples whom our Saviour appointed in the second place to the apostles (Luke x. 1). According to this interpretation, which appears to me to be consonant both to the words and the meaning of Paul, those three functions [apostles, prophets, and evangelists] were not instituted in the church to be perpetual, but only to endure so long as churches were to be formed where none had previously existed, or at least where churches were to be transferred from Moses to Christ; although I deny not, that afterward God occasionally raised up Apostles, or at least Evangelists, in their stead, as has been done in our time. For such were needed to bring back the Church from the revolt of Antichrist."[122]

     [Notice that in this definition, although he does state that the Evangelist is not a perpetual office (as is taught in Roman Catholicism), Calvin states that the Reformers were "Evangelists." Viewing the Reformers in this light is a refreshing statement from one who lived during that time period and experienced first-hand the fiery evangelism of Guillaume Farel (who urged Calvin to stay in Geneva) and of others, such as Robert Olivétan, by whom Calvin himself was led to Christ.]

     1) Gustav Warneck (1903): Although not a systematic theologian, Warneck, the "father" of modern Protestant missiology, also affirmed a similarly limited view of evangelism after a church was planted in a culture.[123] Therefore Warneck logically placed the planting of a church as logically above or higher than that of saving souls.

     b. However, B. H. Carroll, founding president of Southwestern Baptist Theological Seminary, when arguing for the hiring of evangelists as part of the Home Mission Board of the Southern Baptist Convention in 1906, stated:

     "Five distinct gifts are here mentioned, namely, apostles, prophets, evangelists, pastors and teachers. And if the first two, whose credentials and powers were extraordinary, must cease with the completion of the canon of Scriptures, and with the accrediting of the church and the laying of the foundations once for all (see I Cor. 12th, 13th, and 14th chapters and Eph. 2:20), certainly the other three must abide till the Master comes."[124]

     c. Millard Erickson (1985);[125]

     d. Wayne Grudem (1994);[126]

---

[122]John Calvin, *Institutes of the Christian Religion;* trans by Henry Beveridge (London: Clarke, 1957) 2:319.

[123]"This last task is the task of missions [the solid founding of the Christian church]; the limitation of this task to mere evangelisation confounds means and goal. Mere preaching does not suffice; it is to be the means of laying the foundation of the Church. ...mere announcement of the Gospel is not sufficient for this" (Gustav Warneck, *Outline of the History of Protestant Missions,* 3rd English edition [translated from 8th German edition of 1904] [New York: Revell, 1906], 406-07).

[124]B. H. Carroll, "Shall the Atalanta Board Be Instructed to Employ Evangelists and to Call for an Extra $25,000 for Their Support?" *Baptist Standard* (31 May 1906) 14:1-2; cited in Charles S. Kelley, Jr., *How Did They Do It? The Story of Southern Baptist Evangelism,* 197.

[125]Millard Erickson explains the Great Commission in Matthew (see Erickson, *Christian Theology* [Baker, 1985], 131), and he spends 3 pages describing evangelism as a "Function of the Church" (*ibid.,* 1052-54). He discusses the Great Commission, but he *never once* speaks about the evangelist or the role of the evangelist as a leader in the church.

[126]Wayne Grudem gave two sentences on evangelism as the mandate of the church (Wayne Grudem, *Systematic Theology* [Grand Rapids: Zondervan, 1994], 868), stating, "This evangelistic work of declaring the Gospel is the primary ministry that the church has toward the world." He then changed the focus to "a ministry of mercy," going on to discuss deeds of mercy that adorn "the gospel that it professes." He chastises those who would overemphasize one of the three (worship, evangelism, or edification; *ibid.,* 869), and yet he felt it is necessary to devote an entire chapter to worship (*ibid.,* 1003-15), while only discussing evangelism in several limited sentences here and there, such as in two pages on the "Gospel Call" (*ibid.,* 694-95). In his chapter on church leadership, "Church Government" (*ibid.,* 904-49), he never once discussed the evangelist as a leader in the church! Interestingly from a theological perspective, evangelism was considered 10 of 12 "means of grace" within the church (*ibid.,* 958-59). This being said, Grudem has far more on evangelism than any theology that I have seen.

e. Historically, Rome framed the "Evangelist" out of its theology very early (at least as far as extant authors), due to its fascination with sacramentalism, rather than salvation by grace through faith through the instrumentality of the Word of God preached:

1) Augustine's theology had no use for the preaching of the Evangelist unto salvation;

2) Peter Lombard framed the Evangelical view of conversion out of his *Sentences*;

3) Thomas Aquinas, in his animos against the Albigenses and Waldenses, organized his *Summa* much like the questions in an Inquisition chamber, also removing the concept of hearing unto salvation out of His theology;

4) With these men as the framers of the "classical approach to theology" it is no wonder that most theologies do not address the issues of evangelism nor the Evangelist.

f. Likewise with contemporary Rome: the *Catechism of the Catholic Church* (1993) does not contain the words Evangelism or Evangelist in its index, although the word "Evangelist" was used [in a different manner] at the "21st Ecumenical Council"—Vatican II.

The encyclical, *Evangelii Nuntiandi* of Paul VI (8 December 1975) used the word evangelist twice. Early in the encyclical he spoke of "John the Evangelist," Then later Paul VI discussed the role of the evangelist as follows:

> The world which, paradoxically, despite innumerable signs of the denial of God, is nevertheless searching for Him in unexpected ways and painfully experiencing the need of Him--the world is calling for evangelizers to speak to it of a God whom the evangelists themselves should know and be familiar with as if they could see the invisible [Bull *Apostolorum Limina* (23 May 1974), VII: AAS 66. 90-91]. The world calls for and expects from us simplicity of life, the spirit of prayer, charity towards all, especially towards the lowly and the poor, obedience and humility, detachment and self-sacrifice. Without this mark of holiness, our word will have difficulty in touching the heart of modern man. It risks being vain and sterile.[127]

[My notes in Chapter 7, provide statistical information on Rome's use of words beginning with "evangel" and "Gospel"]

g. Conclusion: The evangelist is absent from virtually all systematic theologies! What is the definitional construct that has led to this exclusion of a concept and office that are obviously in the Bible?

RESULT 2: Most books on theology do not deal with man's side of conversion, hearing and receiving; therefore they cannot be said to be fully biblical, nor balanced as they consider a theology of conversion.[128]

---

[127]Paul VI, *Evangelii Nuntiandi* (Rome: 8 Dec 1975), §76.

[128]The evangelist, evangelism, and man's side of conversion (speaking, hearing, and believing) are not the only omissions of clearly biblical teaching in textbooks of theology, which then frame the question for classes in "theology." Neither do any theology textbooks, of which I am aware, have chapters on false teachers and their false teaching (which would be helpful introduction to a course in theology), nor on persecution in the Bible, another well-attested topic in the NT.

3. **Likewise, the evangelist is framed out of in most courses on ecclesiology—or: how the local church ought to operate:**[129]

   a. Comparing NT terms for church leaders:
     1) The English word "pastor" is found only once in the NT (Eph 4:11, as the translation for poimh,n [shepherd]):
       a) The word ὁ ποιμήν (shepherd) is found 18 times in the NT
       b) Te verbal form ποιμαίνω [to shepherd] is found 11 times
       c) For a total of 29 uses
     2) The word "evangelist" is found three times in the NT (from ὁ εὐαγγελιστής in Acts 21:8; Eph 4:11; 2 Tim 4:5
       a) And the verb εὐαγγελίζω found 54/55 times
       b) The noun εὐαγγέλιον is found 77 times in the NT
       c) For a total of 134/135 uses

   b. Therefore, those who write or teach about the pastor in ecclesiology (and rightfully they should), and yet ignore the person and ministry of the evangelist are perhaps **not** teaching the whole counsel of NT ecclesiology!

RESULT 3: The evangelist is not considered a part of regular church life in the New Testament church; his role and place is either ignored or shunned.

4. **The evangelist and evangelism are nearly forgotten in the history of the churches:**[130]

   a. How often is the evangelistic ministry of Henry of Lausanne, who evangelized Southern France, characterized as heretical?[131] How much time is spent discussing the evangelistic methodologies of the so-called "Albigenses"?

   b. How much time is spent discussing the evangelistic methodologies of Peter Valdo and the Waldenses? Meanwhile they were being persecuted by the Dominicans and Franciscans who

---

[129]Also, a typical Evangelical course in ecclesiology was organized as follows, briefly discussing evangelism in general as a function of the church, but never expounding on the centrality of evangelism or the Great Commission, and never discussing the evangelist as a leader in the church (for example, note what is included in the actual course outline from the conservative Paul Feinberg, Trinity Evangelical Divinity School, 1985):
A. The Church as an organization—visible church (local church)
  1. Mission or function of the church
  2. Organization of the church, i.e. government
  3. Officers of the church
    a. Elder (deacons) and divorce issue
    b. Male and female officers in the church
  4. Ordinances in the church
    a. Sacraments vs. sacraments
    b. Three ordinances viewpoint
    c. Lord's supper views
    d. Baptismal views
B. The Church as an organism—invisible church (universal church)
  1. Relationship of Old Testament to New Testament
  2. Relationship of New Testament Church to Old Testament Covenants
  3. Relationship of New Testament Church to seed of Abraham
  4. Relationship of New Testament Church to Kingdom of God, Kingdom program.
Notice that there was nothing in this course on ecclesiology from a very conservative perspective on the evangelist or evangelism. Is that typical of what we read about the church in the Book of Acts?

[130]For example, Kenneth Scott Latourette, in his *Christianity Through the Ages* (New York: Harper and Row, 1965) doesn't mention Henry of Lausanne at all. Earle Cairns, in his *Christianity Through the Ages* (Grand Rapids: Zondervan, 1996) doesn't seem to mention Henry of Lausanne either. Cairns, however, does speak of Guillaume Farel, as "a red-headed, hot-tempered, strong-voiced, prophetic individual" (*ibid.,* 303). Farel was the evangelist used of God to help usher in the reformation into Neuchatel and Geneva. Robert Baker in several sentences treated the ministry of Henry of Lausanne, saying that he had "a long and active ministry" based on an "evangelical nature" (Robert Baker, *A Summary of Christian History* [Nashville: Broadman, 2002], 185). These are conservative books that barely touch on the vital ministry of the evangelist in the history of the churches.

[131]Harold O.J. Brown, *Heresies: Heresy and Orthodoxy in the History of the Church* (Peabody, MA: Hendrickson, 1984), 261

falsely took the name of "preaching orders", and Francis of Assisi who is lauded as a wonderful evangelist,[132] with whom Lewis Drummond even compared Billy Graham's "wholistic" ministry![133]

c. How often is the preparatory evangelistic ministry of the evangelist Guillaume Farel forgotten when discussing Neuchatel's severing itself from the domination of the Papacy, followed by Geneva, before he pled for Calvin to stay in Geneva? Or if he is mentioned, the characterizations used are often not very positive.

d. Many Reformation Church historians and historical theologians may suffer from a focus on differing views on Baptism and the Lord's Supper,[134] or who was the theological precedent for so-and-so,[135] but they often completely ignore the most important factor in history, the Word of God proclaimed (evangelism), the hearing of faith, and conversion—without which souls are NOT saved and the true church disappears. Usually before the Gospel was proclaimed in churches and cathedrals, it was first proclaimed on the "highways and hedges":

1) How often is it shared that Francois Lambert d'Avignon, who removed his strict Franciscan garb after Zwingli led him to Christ, taught for Luther in Marbourg, yet he did not agree with Luther on consubstantiation?

2) How often is Balthasar Hubmaier remembered? Who left his prominent position as founding chaplain of *zur schönen Maria* [Beauteous Mary] in Regensburg, to follow the Reformers of the German Swiss Reformation, one branch of which became Anabaptist. He led a revival in the town of Waldshut before Archduke Ferdinand framed it as a "peasant's revolt" (against

---

[132]"On the Continent was the gentlest and loveliest of medieval characters, *Francis of Assisi* (1182-1226)" (V. Raymond Edman, *Light in the Dark Ages* [Wheaton, IL: Van Kampen, 1949], 290-91).

[133]"In light of this truth [love for a brother], an evangelism that accepts the full revelation of God in Scripture must be holistic in nature. This means that human needs, whether they are spiritual, physical, cultural, or economic, must be addressed by God's people. ... Moreover, no one saw this truth more clearly than the renowned medieval man of God, St. Francis of Assisi" (Lewis A. Drummond, *The Canvas Cathedral: Billy Graham's Ministry Seen through the History of Evangelism* [Nashville: Thomas Nelson, 2003], 211). "As we looked into the life and service of St. Francis of Assisi, we learned that the man of God was a fervent evangelist. Like Graham, he too longed to see people come to faith in Jesus Christ. But history also attests to the fact that Francis felt a deep burden for the physical and social needs of his fellowman" (Ibid., 223).

[134]In focussing on the differences, church historians follow the precedent of Jacques Benigne Bossuet (1627-1704) used in his multiple-volumed *Histoire des variations des églises Protestantes* (Paris, 1688, 1740, 1760, 1821), which was a vehement attack on Protestantism. An argument that Bossuet brought forth, in order to refute the validity of Evangelicalism-Protestantism, was to highlight the differences between the Reformers. (1) Note how he began his book: "Two things mark the disorder in these heresies: one is pulled from the genius of the human spirit, that since it has quenched once of the taste of novelty, never ceases in seeking it with an unmitigated appetite for this tender deceptiveness: the other is pulled from the difference that God works through mankind's actions. The Catholic truth, having come from God, in the first place has its perfection: the heresy, feable production of the human spirit, cannot be made except by pieces that do not fit together. While one wants to reverse, against the precepts of the wise [note: Prov 22:28], *the ancient boundaries laid by our fathers,* and reform the doctrine once received by the faithful, one engages oneself without perceiving all the results of what one advances. It is a false brilliance begun by hazardous means, that causes the reformers to reform themselves every day: to such a degree that they can never say when they will be done with their innovations, nor ever please themselves by them.

"Such are the solid and unshakable principles by which I plan to prove that to the protestants the falsehood of their doctrine through its continual variations, and in the changing manner in which they have explained their dogmas; I am not speaking of a particular, but of the whole of the Church, in the books to which they refer as Symbols, that is to say, those which they have made to express the common consent of their Churches, in one word, in their own confessions of faith, written [*ârretées*], signed, published, in which they have given doctrine as if it were a doctrine that contained only the pure word of God, and which has however changed in so many ways in its principle articles" (*ibid.*, 1:8. Translation mine). (2) Also note the table reference to volume 2, page 305, "The diverse confessions of faith mark the disunity of the party" (Fr. *Les diverses Confessions marquent la désunion du parti"*] (*ibid.*, 2:342). In doing so, Bossuet ignored or discounted the *Gospel principles* which united them against the sacramental salvation of Roman Catholicism.

[135]There is a non-spiritual view among the Roman Catholic inquisitors of the time, that no one can learn from the Holy Spirit through the Bible, "Who taught you that?" They must learn their heretical views (like justification by faith alone or the ineffectiveness of absolution from a priest) from a specific person before them (therefore they must find human provenance for "heresy").

the Catholic church and the crown), and therefore attacked the city, killing many of its inhabitants. Hubmaier was burned at the stake in 1528.

3) Listen to the sentence against Quirinus Pieters of Groeningen, from the Archives of the Secretary of the City of Amsterdam, the Netherlands (1545):

> "Whereas Quirinus Pieters, a native of Groeningen, has embraced the unbelief and heresy of the Anabaptists, having been rebaptized about six years ago, by Menno Simons, a teacher of the aforesaid sect, and whereas he holds pernicious views concerning the sacraments of the holy church, and, moreover, has induced others, into such unbelief and errors, persuading them into it, directly contrary to the holy Christian faith, the ordinances of the holy church, and the decrees of his Imperial Majesty, our gracious lord; and whereas he obstinately continues in the aforesaid unbelief, therefore, my lords the judges, having heard the demand made by my lord the bailif concerning the aforesaid Quirinus Pieters, as also his answer and confession, and having fully considered the circumstances of said matter, sentence the aforesaid Quirinus Pieters to be burned by the executioner; and furthermore, declare his property confiscated for the benefit of the exchequer of his Imperial Majesty. Pronounced this sixteenth day of April, A.D. 1545, in the presence of the entire bench of judges, except Sir Henry Dirks, Burgomaster"[136]

4) Listen to a portion of the inquisition record of Anabaptist Dirk Pieters in Amsterdam, Holland (1546):

> "Q. The apostles certainly went forth to teach; where did they go teach?
> "A. Whithersoever they came, they went into the synagogues, and preached the Gospel of Christ."
> "Q. We have heard that you also teach wherever you go?
> "A. O Lord, what should I preach; we may read the Gospel together.
> "Q. Where did you read it together?
> "A. At the dyke.
> "Q. With whom did you read it?
> "A. This I do not know.
> "Q. How should you not know with whom you read it?
> "A. How should I know it, sometimes with this one, sometimes with another.
> "They therefore mentioned the names of a good many, and said: "Do you know this and that one?
> "A. Yes, I know them.
> "Q. Have you any books of Menno Simons and of David Joris?
> "A. No, I have no books in the house, except a Bible and a Testament, and a little book on the faith."[137]

e. May God forgive us these omissions of His work through His word, and allow this unfortunate misplaced emphasis to be remedied![138]

RESULT 4: Ignorance as to the soteriological (salvation) issues in the history of the churches, along with ignorance of the only way that souls were saved and added to God's true church in the history of the churches.

RESULT 5: The reframing of sources and topics in the history of the churches to accommodate the sacramental position of the Roman Catholic church, wherein not only was the evangelist not needed, but he was to be extirpated from the world by death; for example:

Why Protestants use Augustine?
    To affirm the antiquity of Reformation thought
    To affirm doctrines, such as predestination and biblical authority

But why do Roman Catholics use Augustine?
    To affirm the centrality of the Church of Rome, and her unique place in salvation

---

[136]Thieleman J. van Braght, *The Bloody Theater or Martyrs Mirror of the Defenseless Christians Who Baptized Only Upon the Confession of Faith, and Who Suffered and Died for the Testimony of Jesus, Their Savior, From the Time of Christ to the Year A.D. 1660*, trans from the Dutch by Joseph Sohm, 2nd English edition (1660; 1837; 1886; Scottdale, PA: Herald Press, 2007), 474-75.

[137]Ibid., 477.

[138]This author has used E. H. Broadbent's *The Pilgrim Church* (1931; Grand Rapids: Gospel Folio Press, 1999), in church history classes. Broadbent focused on the persecuted church, and did speak of evangelism at certain points. Most French Protestant church Reformation histories seem to emphasize evangelism far more than those in English (e.g. Franck Puaux and Merle d'Aubigny).

To affirm the centrality of the Eucharist for salvation, and the other sacraments of Rome

To disaffirm the "Free Church," "self-rule," or "local church autonomy" [likewise the "Freedom of Conscience"] of the Donatist churches of North Africa (cf. Augustine's *Contra Donatisten*)

To disaffirm the teaching of the "Manicheans" (which seems to be a code word for Evangelical thought; cf. Augustine's *Contra Manichean*)

May the able reader take note of how Augustine is quoted by both Peter the Lombard and Thomas Aquinas. The citations are often shocking and almost never evangelical in their orientation.

What remains in print related to knowledge of early church theology and practice (including information about evangelism and evangelists)?

Throughout the Middle Ages (800-1500), only those things from the history of the church which favored Rome were published in Latin-speaking Europe; all other writings disappeared or where destroyed.

The same is true, to a lesser degree, in the Eastern church, which has not had the monolithic hierarchy of Rome.

This is why the study of Patristics and Medieval theology is very lopsided, non-evangelistic, and non-Evangelical; the lines of demarcation are very clear:

Track with Rome's progress into philosophical and sacramental theology (from the earliest "fathers"), or

Track with the combed-through fragments about the persecuted Evangelical church through the ages

Perhaps it is for this reason that most studies of evangelism and evangelists begin in the post-Reformation era (e.g. early on I began my study of evangelists with the First Great Awakening in the U.S.)

By way of final analysis, it would seem that American Evangelical thought has capitulated to teaching the history of the churches using the worldview framing as described in Jacques Benigne Bossuet's derisive *Histoire des variations des eglises Prostantes* [History of the Variations of Protestant churches].[139]

5. The omission of "evangelize" and even "evangelist" in modern Bible translation:

a. The systemic removal of the verb "evangelize" by translators is especially clear in several instances (see charts in Chapter 7):

1) The change from the 36 uses of evangelize in the 1382 Wycliffe to 3 in the 1388.
2) The change from the 37 uses in the 1530 Catholic Lefevre to 4 uses in the 1550 Catholic Louvain Bible
3) On the removal of "evangelize" when translating from French into English:
    a) The 1560 French Geneva had 24 uses of the verb "evangelize":
        1) Its English counterpart, the English Geneva, 0 uses
    b) The 1859 John Darby French translation had 21 uses:
        1) His English translation had 0 uses
    c) Isn't that strange?

---

[139]The first paragraph should suffice to give the reader a feel for the emotional qualities of this four volume work: "If Protestants knew thoroughly how their religion was formed; with how many variations and with what inconstancy their confessions of faith were drawn up; how they first separated themselves from us, and afterwards from one another; by how many subtilties, evasions, and equivocations they laboured to repair their divisions, and to re-unite the scattered members of their disjointed reformation; this reformation of which they boast would afford them but little satisfaction, or rather, to speak my mind more freely, it would excite in them only feeling of contempt. It is the history of these variations, these subtilties, these equivocations, and these artifices, which I design to write; but in order to render this detail more useful to them, some principles must be laid down which they cannot contravene, and which the current of a narration would not permit me to deduce, when once engaged in it" (Jacques-Benigne Bossuet, *The History of the Variations of the Protestant Churches* [pub. in French: 1688, 1740, 1760, 1821; this Engl. trans., Dublin: Richard Coyne, 1829], 1).

Variant Translations of "Evangelist" in the New Testament

Text	Byzantine Textform	English Geneva (1560); cf. Tyndale; Bishop's; KJV; Webster's; Murdock; Darby; English Revised; DRA‡; ASV; RSV; NAS; NKJ; NIV; NRSV; ESV; CSB	Young's Literal (1862)	Bible in Basic English (1949)	New Jerusalem Bible‡ (1985)	ABS' Contemp English Version‡ (impr. 1991)	IBS' French Le Semeur (1992, 1999)*	ABS' Good News Trans‡ (impr. 1993)	God's Word to the Nations (1995)	New Living Translation (2004)
	τοῦ εὐαγγελισ-τοῦ	the Euangelist [or: evangelist]	the evangelist	the preacher	the evangelist	The preacher	the evangelist	the evangelist	a missionary	the Evangelist
Acts 21:8b	αἱ εἰσελθόντες εἰς τὸν οἶκον Φιλίππου τοῦ εὐαγγελισ-τοῦ, ὄντος ἐκ τῶν ἑπτά, ἐμείναμεν παρ' αὐτῷ.	and we entred into the house of Philippe the Euangelist, which was one of the seuen Deacons, and abode with him.	and having entered into the house of Philip the evangelist -- who is of the seven -- we remained with him,	where we were guests in the house of Philip, the preacher, who was one of the seven.	Here we called on Philip the evangelist, one of the Seven, and stayed with him.	and stayed with Philip, the preacher. He was one of the seven men who helped the apostles	We brought ourselves to the house of Philip, the evangelist— he was one of the seven men that was elected in Jerusalem—, and we stayed with him	There we stayed at the house of Philip the evangelist, one of the seven men who had been chosen as helpers in Jerusalem.	He was a missionary and one of the seven men who helped the apostles.	And stayed at the home of Philip the Evangelist, one of the seven men who had been chosen to distribute food.
	τοὺς δὲ εὐαγγελισ-τάς	And some Euangelists [or: evangelists]	some as proclaimers of good news	and some, preachers of the good news	to some, evangelists	mission-aries	others as evangelists	others to be evangelists	missiona-ries	the evangelists
Eph 4:11	Καὶ αὐτὸς ἔδωκεν τοὺς μὲν ἀποστόλους, τοὺς δὲ προφήτας, τοὺς δὲ εὐαγγελισ-τάς, τοὺς δὲ ποιμένας καὶ διδασκάλους,	He therefore gaue some to be Apostles, and some Prophets, & some Euangelists, and some Pastours, and Teachers,	and He gave some as apostles, and some as prophets, and some as proclaimers of good news, and some as shepherds and teachers,	And he gave some as Apostles, and some, prophets; and some, preachers of the good news; and some to give care and teaching	And to some, his 'gift' was that they should be apostles; to some prophets; to some, evangelists; to some, pastors and teachers;	Christ chose some of us to be apostles, prophets, mission-aries, pastors, and teachers.	It's him who gave some as apostles, others as prophets, others as evangelists, and others also as pastors and instructors	It was he "who gave gifts to the people"; he appointed some to be apostles, others to be prophets, others to be evangelists, others to be pastors and teachers.	He also gave apostles, prophets, missionaries, as well as pastors and teachers as gifts to his church.	Now these are the gifts Christ gave to the church: the apostles, the prophets, the evangelists, and the pastors and teachers.

	Byzantine Textform	Eng Geneva (1560); KJV; et al.	Young's Literal (1862)	BBE (1949)	NJB✴ (1985)	CEV✴ (impr. 1991)	IBS' Semeur (1992, '99)*	GNT✴ (impr. 1993)	GWN (1995)	NLT (2004)
	ἔργον ποίησον εὐαγγελισ-τοῦ	doe the worke of an Euangeliste	do the work of one proclaiming good news	go on preaching the good news	do the work of preaching the gospel	You must work hard to tell the good news*	Properly fulfill your role of preacher of the Gospel	do the work of a preacher of the Good News	Do the work of a missionary	Work at telling others the Good News
2 Tim 4:5	Σὺ δὲ νῆφε ἐν πᾶσιν, κακοπάθη-σον, ἔργον ποίησον εὐαγγελισ-τοῦ, τὴν διακονίαν σου πληροφό-ρησον.	But watch thou in all things: suffer aduersitie: doe the worke of an Euangeliste: make thy ministerie fully knowen.	And thou—watch in all things; suffer evil; do the work of one proclaiming good news; of thy ministration make full assurance,	But be self-controlled in all things, do without comfort, go on preaching the good news, completing the work which has been given you to do	But you must keep steady all the time; put up with suffering; do the work of preaching the gospel; fulfil the service asked of you.	But you must stay calm and be willing to suffer. You must work hard to tell the good news and to do your job well.	But you, keep, in all circum-stances, control of yourself. Put up with suffering. Properly fulfill your role of preacher of the Gospel.*** Fully acomplish your ministry.	But you must keep control of yourself in all circum-stances; endure suffering, do the work of a preacher of the Good News, and perform your whole duty as a servant of God.	But you must keep a clear head in everything. Endure suffering. Do the work of a missionary. Devote yourself completely to your work.	But you should keep a clear mind in every situation. Don't be afraid of suffering for the Lord. Work at telling others the Good News, and fully carry out the ministry God has given you.

*The ABS' Contemporary English Version has removed any noun to correspond with the word "evangelist" from this text of Scripture.

**French texts (translation mine): Acts 21:8, "Nous nous sommes rendus à la maison de Philippe, l'évangéliste—c'était l'un des sept hommes que l'on avait élus à Jérusalem—, et nous avons logé chez lui"; Eph 4:11, "C'est lui qui a fait don de certains comme apôtres, d'autres comme *prophètes, d'autres comme évangélistes, et d'autres encore comme pasteurs et enseignants."; 2 Tim 4:5, "Mais toi, garde, en toute circonstance, le contrôle de toi-même. Supporte les souffrances. Remplis bien ton rôle de prédicateur de l'Evangile [Autre traduction: *Fais le travail d'un évangéliste*.]. Accomplis pleinement ton ministère."

***Le Semeur contains a footnote: "Other translation: *Do the work of an evangelist.*"

RESULT 6: As the person of the evangelist disappears from the text of the Bible, so will the office and role of the evangelist disappear as God intended through His Word.

6. Conclusion: Further thoughts on omission of evangelists:

a. One answer to this omission prior to the Reformation may be the strict control of the Catholic church over books and publishing, as it suppressed, sought, and seeks to suppress "heresy":

> "Thematically the major omission from this study is a detailed consideration of the detection of heresy in texts, as opposed to people. Deciding whether certain written propositions represented error and heresy was of course closely allied to testing the suspicion of heresy that surrounded the author, writer, compiler, reader, or hearer of those words."[140]

That strict control continued throughout most of Europe prior to the Enlightenment. And as a result of this control, the Roman Catholic church defined parameters of what was appropriate and inappropriate, what was heretical and what was orthodox. Through Peter the Lombard and Thomas Aquinas, the Catholic church framed the theological debates which continue today. Evangelicals were framed out of the question in Catholic works, as they were defined as Manicheans. Likewise, evangelization was repressed as unorthodox, and finally led to bloodshed with the imprisonment and burnings of the Waldenses and Albigenses following the 3rd and 4th Lateran Councils (1179 and 1215 respectively).

b. A second answer to this question may lie in the fact that most scholarly books are written by scholars who are disinterested in or reproachful of evangelism. This may also be the case with publishing companies, as well as scholarly organizations and their journals.

---

[140]Ian Forrest, *The Detection of Heresy in Late Medieval England* (Oxford: Clarendon, 2005), 3.

c. A third answer, being theological in nature, is that most state-type churches do not adhere to conversionism. Since evangelism and evangelists require a conversionistic theology of salvation, they are shunned as heretical or fanatical, or ignored as schismatic

d. A fourth answer, dealt in chapter 7, is that the verb "evangelize" has not been used in our English translations since it was removed from the Wycliffe second edition of 1388. Therefore, it is only those who rightfully take the NT concept of "preach" out into the streets who acknowledge and practice evangelism.

e. A fifth concern is the contemporary effort to remove the word "evangelist" from 2 Tim 4:5 (using dynamic equivalence arguments), as noted above in Rome's 1985 *New Jerusalem Bible*, the 1999 International Bible Society's French *Le Semeur*, and the 1995 American Bible Society's *Contemporary English Version*!

f. Perhaps most common among Evangelicals is the view of John Calvin and Gustav Warneck,[141] that the evangelist was only a temporary need in the church. A similar view was held by Lewis Sperry Chafer, founder of what became Dallas Theological Seminary:

> The evangelist of the Scriptures is, without question, the messenger to the unevangelized, preparing the way for the pastor and teacher in his more constant ministry in the church. The evangelist, therefore, finds his fullest divine mission as a pioneer missionary to the hithertofore unevangelized. …
>
> The discussion of the fundamental error of the church, in unduly magnifying the work of the evangelist and neglecting her own God-appointed ministry in salvation [prayer], will be the theme of the succeeding chapters.[142]

---

[141]Gustav Warneck, *Outline of the History of Protestant Missions*, 3rd English edition; from 8th German edition of 1904 (New York: Revell, 1906), 406-07.

[142]Lewis Sperry Chafer, *True Evangelism or Winning Souls by Prayer* (1st ed. Philadelphia: Sunday School Times, 1911; 2nd ed., Philadelphia: Sunday School Times, 1919; Wheaton, IL: Van Kampen; Grand Rapids: Zondervan, 1967; Grand Rapids: Kregel, 1993), 15, 17.

B. Is There a Gift of Evangelism, or Is It Rather the Gift of the Evangelist?

Introduction to spiritual gifts: John 16:14—"He shall glorify Me":
   a. The Holy Spirit is to glorify Christ;
   b. It follows that all the spiritual gifts of the Holy Spirit glorify Christ;
   c. Evangelism focuses on sharing about the person and work of Christ, Acts 8:5; 1 Cor 15:1-5;
   d. Therefore, all the gifts of the Spirit must be evangelistic!
   e. Also, since the Holy Spirit gives gifts to each believer (1 Cor 12:7), every believer is gifted to evangelize!

1. Understanding the gifts and the offices:
   a. Four NT passages enumerate the spiritual gifts and offices: Rom 12:6; 1 Cor 12:7; Eph 4:7; 1 Pet 4:10

NT Enumeration of Spiritual Gifts and Offices*

Enumeration	Romans 12:6-8	1 Cor 12:8-11	1 Cor 12:28-30	Eph 4:11	1 Peter 4:10-11
1. Apostle			1. Apostle	1. Apostles	1. Speaks
2. Prophet/Prophecy	1. Prophecy	6. Prophecy	2. Prophets	2. Prophets	
3. Evangelist				3. Evangelists	
4. Pastor/Showing mercy	7. Showing mercy			4. Pastors	
5. Teacher/Teaching	3. Teaching		3. Teachers	5. Teachers	
6. Exhortation (revivalist)	4. Exhortation				
7. Word of wisdom		1. Word of wisdom			
8. Word of knowledge		2. Word of knowledge			
9. Service/Helps	2. Service		6. Helps		2. Serves
10. Giving	5. Giving				
11. Leading/Administration	6. Leading		7. Administration		
12. Faith		3. Faith			
13. Gifts of healing		4. Gifts of healing	5. Gifts of healing		
14. Worker of miracles		5. Effecting of miracles	4. [workers of] Miracles		
15. Distinguishing of spirits		7. Distinguishing of spirits			
16. Speaking in tongues		8. Various kinds of tongues	8. Various kinds of tongues		
17. Interpretation of tongues		9. Interpretation of tongues	9. Interpretation of tongues		

*Some consider other gifts as spiritual gifts: martyrdom (cf. 1 Cor 13:3); apostleship = church planter or cross-cultural missionary. The OT also contains additional gifts (craftmanship on the Temple, singing, or playing instruments).

   b. There are distinct gifts and offices, with some overlap:

   1) Two offices (in Eph 4:11) that have both a spiritual gift and an office are: prophet/prophecy, and teacher/teach

   2) Three other offices are: apostle, evangelist, and pastor/shepherd

   3) All other spiritual gifts are not directly linked to an specific office

   4) The gift of evangelism is **not** in the lists of the New Testament:
      a) It seems to be confusing to speak of a gift of evangelism, as the Great Commission mandates that all believers bear verbal witness to the Gospel
      b) It seems best to allow that all ought to share the Gospel, and that some are particularly gifted to lead the church in this area.

      "God uses not so much gifts for evangelism but the faithfulness of thousands and millions of

Christians who would never say evangelism is their gift" (Mark Dever)[143]

5) By the way, what was the office of Zenas in Titus 3:13?

Some questions:

Is ὁ νομικός a sixth office to those of Eph 4:11, or is it a parallel term for a teacher [ὁ διδάσκαλος] as found in Eph 4:11?

Also from the context of Titus 3:13, Zenas seemed to be a travelling teacher, as did Apollos (cf. Acts 18:24, 27; 19:1); these travelling teachers would parallel the teacher sent out by King Jehoshaphat in 2 Chron 17:7-9;

Paul called the ministry of Apollos a "watering" ministry (1 Cor 3:6), as opposed to his own "planting" ministry.

a) The word ὁ νομικός is found 9 times in the NT (once in Matthew [22:35]; 6 times in the Gospel of Luke [sometimes used in parallel with "scribe" in Matt and Mark]; and twice in Titus [3:9, 13])

b) Other words with similar meaning are:
(1) The word for "scribe": ὁ γραμματεύς (67 NT uses)
(2) The word translated "advocate" in John 2:2: ὁ παράκλητος (5 NT uses; 4 in John 14-16)

Sample Translations of ὁ νομικός in Titus 3:13

Latin Vulgate	Wycliffe's 2nd ed (1388)	Fr. LeFevre (1522); Fr. Geneva; Fr. Martin	Tyndale (1534); Bishops; KJV; Webster's; Young's; Darby; DRA✠; ASV; RSV; NAS; NKJ; CEV✠; GNT✠; ESV; NLT; NET	Fr. Louvain✠ (1550)	English Geneva (1560)	Fr. Ostervald (1744); Fr. Geneva Rev.	Murdock (1852)	Fr. Le Semeur (1992, 1999)
skilled [or experienced] in the law	a wise man of lawe	doctor in the law	the lawear [the lawyer]	wise in the law	the expounder of the Law	the doctor in the law	Scribe	the lawyer
legis peritum		docteur de la loi		sage en la loi		le docteur de la loi		le jurist

---

[143]Mark Dever, *The Gospel And Personal Evangelism* (Wheaton, IL: Good News, 2007).

2. The following diagram charts some issues in adhering to a gift of evangelism and the ministry of the evangelist:[144]

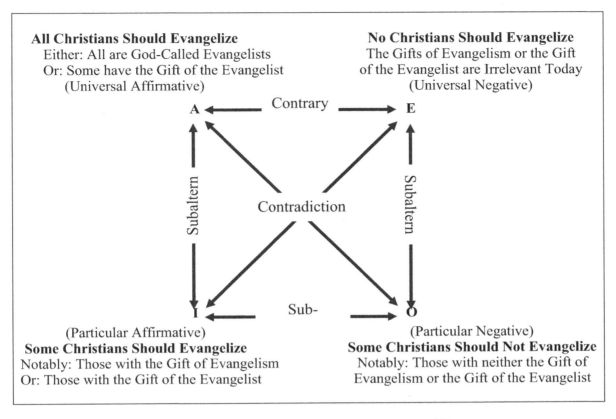

3. C. Peter Wagner's possible move around the square of opposition: [145]

a. "The gift of evangelist is the special ability that God gives to certain members of the Body of Christ to share the gospel with unbelievers in such a way that men and women become Jesus' disciples and responsible members of the Body of Christ" (157).

b. "For another thing, every true Christian is a witness for Jesus Christ whether or not they have the gift of evangelist. Furthermore, Christians need to be prepared to share their faith with unbelievers and lead them to Christ whenever the opportunity presents itself" (161).

c. His use of the equivocal "witness for Jesus Christ" aside, Wagner made three statements that seem to undermine the universal affirmative that he stated:
   1) Many Christian circles "tend to overemphasize it [evangelism]" (160).
   2) "The gift of the evangelist is probably the most frequently projected of all gifts" (163).
   3) He figured that "approximately 5 to 10 percent of its active adult membership have been given the gift of evangelist" (160).
      a) The 5 to 10 percent figure was presumably derived from personal observation of those members of D. James Kennedy's church involved in his Evangelism Explosion program. Wagner surmised that since this number were involved in his evangelism program, they must be the ones who had the gift of evangelism.[146]

---

[144]From Johnston, *Charts for a Theology of Evangelism*, Chart 18A, "Should All Christians Evangelize?", 38.

[145]C. Peter Wagner, *Your Spiritual Gifts Can Help Your Church Grow* (Ventura, CA: Regal, 1979, 1994), 157-63.

[146]Thom Rainer explained his interview of C. Peter Wagner in a spiritual gifts seminar (Southern Baptist Seminary, 1997), as he noted also in his *The Book of Church Growth: History, Theology, Principles* (Nashville: Broadman, 1993), 116 n6.

4. Relation of the Gift to the Command:

    a. The gift of the evangelist does not negate the command for other Christians who are not or may not want to be gifted as evangelists:
        1) The command and the metaphors for the follower of Jesus still apply to *all Christians*, who are to be verbal witnesses
        2) The work of evangelism needs to be accomplished through the obedience of every Christian if the task is to be accomplished:
            a) The preaching of the Gospel to the whole world, Matt 24:14, Mark 16:15
            b) That everyone may have a chance to hear the Gospel, Rom 10:13-15

    b. The gift of the evangelist intensifies and focuses the life of the evangelist in seeking to accomplish the task assigned to him:
        1) The evangelist must accomplish the work which is given to him:
            a) As for the case of Jesus, John 4:34, 17:4
            b) As for the apostle Paul, 1 Cor 9:16-17
            c) As for all Christians, Matt 25:44-51, 2 Tim 2:4
        2) The evangelist must not allow himself to get ensnared in the cares of the world, Matt 13:22, 1 Cor 9:26-27, 2 Tim 2:4, Heb 12:1

    c. Just as the gift of "giving" does not exclude other Christians from giving, just as the gift of "mercy" does not exclude other Christians from showing mercy, similarly, neither does the office of the evangelist, nor even the possibility of a gift of evangelism, exclude that all Christians ought to be about the business of proclaiming the Gospel.

    d. Lawrence O. Richards wrote:

        "The evangelist is that person specially, charismatically gifted by God to bring others to a knowledge of Jesus Christ and to lead others to do the same."[147]

5. Summary:

    The evangelist must be found doing what the Master has set out for him to do. If not he will be like the wicked slave who buried his talent (Matt 25:24-30), or like the unrighteous servant who was not doing his masters bidding (Matt 24:45-51). It is a serious charge with great eternal rewards for the obedient, or tremendous eternal regrets for the disobedient.

    "Blessed is that slave whom his master finds so doing when he comes," Matt 24:46.

    Let's listen in to the prayer of the evangelist of the Swiss Reformation, Guillaume Farel:

    "When will Christ be all in all? When will the only study, the only consolation, the only desire of all be to know the Gospel, to cause it to advance everywhere, and to be firmly persuaded, as our ancestors, of this primitive church, dyed by the blood of martyrs, who understood that knowing nothing, except the Gospel, is to know everything."[148]

---

[147]Lawrence O. Richards, *A Theology of Pastoral Ministry* (Grand Rapids: Zondervan, 1981), 212.

[148]Franck Puaux, *Histoire de la Réformation en France*, 1:60. Translation mine.

C. The Function of the Evangelist:

1. The Function of the Evangelist:

    a. The evangelist is a leader gifted and necessary for the building up of the church, Eph 4:11:

        1) A gift given to the church:

            a) Showing the priority of the church over the gift of evangelism—as it is a gift given *to* the church

            b) Indicating the evangelist has a ministry for the church.

            c) It is the only gift given with an emphasis outside the Church.

        2) Note the order in the listing: apostles, prophets, evangelists, pastors and teachers:

            a) Shows the importance of evangelists to the life of the church (noting that it is omitted in listings of spiritual gifts, e.g. 1 Cor 12:28)

            b) Shows the importance of the person as opposed to the gift, as in all the other offices mentioned.

        3) If it is accepted that the gift of apostleship has ceased, since no living person was alive at the baptism of Jesus on through His resurrection (cf. Acts 1:21-22), then the rest of the gifts appear to have a chronological component:

            a) Like John the Baptist (cf. Mal 4:5), the prophet is God's preparation for the Gospel; he preaches repentance for the forgiveness of sin

            b) Like Philip, the evangelist evangelizes and leads people to Christ

            c) The pastor nurtures the new believer in the local church

            d) The teacher teaches him to "obey all that I have commanded you" (cf. Matt 28:20).

        4) Understanding the gift of the evangelist:

            a) Some equate the gift of the evangelist only with a **gift of harvesting**:

                (1) Focusing only on the harvesting emphasis of the evangelist may discourage average Christians from evangelizing, since they will not have the success of the evangelist, presumably not being gifted that way;

                (2) Focusing only on harvesting may encourage a sense of pride in the evangelist being the "hired gun" to bring in a harvest;

                (3) Focusing only on harvesting may create an undue emphasis only on the invitation, rather than on need for the preaching of the entire message of the Gospel

                (4) Focusing only on harvesting can pressure the evangelist to log high numbers of responses, rather than on keeping the biblical message of the Gospel pure and strong

                (5) Focusing only on harvesting can lead to a segmented or rational approach to evangelism (go primarily to those we deem to be receptive) rather than to the "all nations," "all creation," and "highways and byways" approach of the New Testament

                (6) And yet, many a church is blessed by the supernatural harvesting ability of Christ's evangelists—as harvesting souls ought to be the evangelist's primary passion.

            b) Rather, the gift of the evangelist seems to be a **supernatural office focused only on the proclamation the Gospel**:

                (1) Are not all Christians to be proclaimers (Luke 4:46-47; Acts 8:4)? Yes.

                (2) Are not all pastors to proclaim the Word, 2 Tim 4:2? Yes.

                (3) However, in the wisdom of Christ, He has set aside certain leaders in his Church to focus only upon the proclamation of the Gospel

                (4) And in His wisdom, Christ listed the evangelist prior to the pastor in the list of offices given to His Church

            c) In addition, the gift of the evangelist (ὁ εὐαγγελιστής) is clearly **to proclaim the Gospel to the lost** (both within and outside of the church):

                (1) This seems to fit with the uses of εὐαγγελίζω in the NT (evangelizing rather than merely preaching/homiletics);

                (2) This provides a differentiation between the Gospel ministry of the pastor and the Gospel ministry of the evangelist;

(3) Another differentiation may be needed here between the revivalist (ministry primarily to the church) and the evangelist (ministry outside the church);

(4) One can see already that if the evangelists ministry is primarily outside the church, then it involves personal evangelism, street evangelism, and mass evangelism.

d) Whatever the case, if the evangelist's ministry ought to focus:

(1) **Outside the church** in evangelizing:
  (a) His visibility before the church who is or churches who are supporting him will be in his role outside the church (often unnoticed by church members)
  (b) Churches can function without an evangelist, but if so they are not NT churches

(2) **Inside the church** in evangelizing, training in evangelism, and providing a focus for the mission of the church:
  (a) Evangelizing the lost that inadvertantly are a part of the church
  (b) Training all Christians to be about the business of evangelizing
  (c) Strategic planning, allowing that evangelizing remains the main, onlym, and primary focus of every aspect of church life

e) By giving a leader in the church the unique focus of evangelizing, God has provided that evangelizing (and the Great Commission) are not ignored, overlooked, nor forgotten in the ministry of the local church:

(1) Whereas **in contemporary practice**, the order of the last three persons in Eph 4:11 may be "teachers, pastors, and evangelists (last)"
  (a) Teachers:
    [1] Train the seminary students for pastoral ministry
    [2] Develop the curricula
    [3] Write the books used in the classes
    [4] Teach the seminars, and
    [5] Provide consultation to local churches
  (b) Pastors lead the church and shepherd the flock of God (the word for pastor in Eph 4:11 is actually "shepherd"); his focus is the flock, not necessarily the lost outside the church
  (c) Evangelists struggle to maintain their financial support, keep their calendars full, sometimes ministering in declining churches that will invite them in, and seek to keep soul-winning a priority where they are allowed to minister

(2) However, God foreordained in His word that **the inspired order ought to be**: "evangelists, pastors and teachers":

  (a) Evangelists should:
    [1] Train seminary students for pastoral ministry:
      [a] Was this not what Moody, R.A. Torrey, and others did through Moody Bible Institute 100 years ago?
    [2] Develop the curricula:
      [a] The removal of NT evangelism from curriculum today is the most crucial missing element in much of seminary education today
      [b] The mantra of "shared governance" in higher education almost assures that evangelism cannot and will not remain the focus of higher education
    [3] Write the books used in the classes:
      [a] Evangelists rarely write books; and often if they do they will not be published by most publishing companies
    [4] Teach the seminars, and
      [a] The "seminars" taught by evangelists are called "revivals"
      [b] Their result is a focus on the gospel, the conversion of the lost, training and motivation in soul winning, and a perennial focus on evangelism
    [5] Provide consultation to local churches
      [a] Evangelists are not often considered as consultants to local churches
      [b] Churches rather look to "Church Growth Experts" trained in the empirical science of church sociology

         (b) Pastors should:
            [1] Shepherd the church of God (Acts 20:28)
            [2] While doing the work of an evangelist (2 Tim 4:5)

         (c) Teachers, in submission to evangelists and pastors, should:
            [1] Teach them to observe all that Jesus commanded (Matt 28:20)
            [2] Which includes the command to win disciples (Matt 28:19)

      (3) Note in this light three charts at the end of Chapter 3, "Thoughts on Church Leadership Theological Education Based on Ephesians 4:11," "Centrality of Evangelism for Theological Education," "Evangelistic Theological Education and Schools of Thought"

   f) The evangelist is given to the church to keep it on target:
     (1) The only purpose of the evangelist is to evangelize, which is preaching the Gospel and calling sinners to repentance
     (2) He is listed before the pastor, because his role is more important to the local church than that of the pastor, as he is called to keep the church on target
     (3) If a church under the leadership of the pastor forgets or ignores the preeminence of evangelism (which we have seen in detail in theological literature), it actually begins to work against the Great Commission
     (4) Revival is needed to keep the local church focused and targeted on soul-winning

  b. Jesus gave instructions to his apostles, sending them out as itinerant evangelists (organized from shortest to longest):

   1) Mark 6

   2) Luke 9

   3) Luke 10

   4) Matt 9:35-11:1

   5) Some conclusions about the ministry of the evangelist:

     a) Jesus sent out His disciples as wandering preachers:
       (1) Wandering preachers have no political clout, nor do they have earned respect in the community
       (2) Wandering preachers have no established long term relationships
       (3) Wandering preachers have:
         (a) No building to invite people to
         (b) No money to:
            [1] Help the poor or feed the hungry
            [2] Provide entertainment for the people (as Simon the Magician was fond to do, Acts 8)
       (4) Wandering preachers are strangers and aliens who speak with an accent—"You're not from these parts, are you?"
       (5) Wandering preachers do not have a ministry directed primarily to their own hometown, family, or friends

     b) It is clear to see from the list above, that the grocery list of contemporary evangelism methodologies do not coincide with the wandering methodology taught by Jesus

  c. The Evangelist, His Life and Witness:

   1) Accountability to the character traits of 1 Tim 3 and Titus 1:
     a) Sometimes men who are not qualified to be Pastors or Missionaries will seek to become Evangelists
     b) There is great danger to the church and to the harvest if Evangelists are not held to the same moral and ethical standards as pastors or missionaries; being called by God to the ministry of the Evangelist is an honor, not a calling of last resort if all else fails!

2) Accountability to the Local church:
    a) It is vital that an Evangelist submit to the authority of a local New Testament church
    b) Keith Fordham in his book, *The Evangelist—The Heart of God*, discussed three levels of relationship of an evangelist with a local church:
        (1) Staff evangelist: In this scenario, the evangelist is on the staff of the church, however, he is allowed 20-25 weeks out of the year to preach revivals outside of the church, reporting back to the church about those activities
        (2) "Our Evangelist": This is "staff evangelist" in name only, needing to raise his support from outside the church
        (3) Member in name only: The evangelist joins a church but has no assistance or support from the pastor or the church
    c) To Keith's three scenarios, I will add a fourth option:
        (4) Evangelist with no home church base: Sadly some evangelists have completely cut ties with the local church due to bad experiences on both sides. This lack of submission to a local church appears dangerous.

3) Conclusion:
    a) It would be good for churches, prior to using an evangelist, to get information on the church where the evangelist is a member and ask for a reference
    b) Submission to a local church and its pastor should be a must for every evangelist, as well as evidence of the character traits of 1 Tim 3 and Titus 1 in his life

d. Concluding comments:

1) Built into the term evangelist are the following:

a) It is a proclamational gift:
    (1) This proclamational orientation flies in the face of the numerous contemporary non-proclamational approaches to evangelism, as well as the many denominational groupings that are either non-proclamational or anti-proclamational in their theology

b) It is directed specifically and only to the proclamation of the Gospel:
    (1) It is not primarily a gift directed only to church growth (and once the church can support its ministries, the evangelist is no longer needed)
    (2) The evangelist is not primarily gifted to raise funds, for himself, for the church, or for some other institution

c) Athough the evangelist is a leader in the church, the gift is directed to preaching the Gospel to the lost outside the church:
    (1) Although church revivals have their place, the primary gift of the evangelist is to preach to the lost (Rom 15:20; 2 Cor 10:16)
        (a) There has to be a way to reorient the ministry of evangelists outside the church, like the ministries of Wesley and Whitefield, the circuit riders under Francis Asbury, or the camp meeting movement of the 19th Century
    (2) In this light, the evangelist, by his example and teaching, is gifted specifically to lead the church into the fulfillment of the Great Commission, which may otherwise be neglected by the pastor and teacher

d) The evangelist is given to the church to preach the Gospel to the lost and persuade them to come to Christ for salvation:
    (1) Again this emphasis flies in the face of people, denominations, and theologies that do not ascribe to evangelism, conversion, persuasion

2) It is a gift most often associated with itinerant ministry:

a) The ministry of the evangelist calls for travelling from one place to another (cf. the "Go" in Chapter 10 on the Great Commission)
    (1) In the OT it is associated with one who runs:
        (a) 2 Sam 18:19-31 used the verb "evangelize 5 times associated with one who runs to bring news
        (b) In 2 Chron 30:6 couriers were sent out with a message from King Hezekiah

(2) Paul seems to pick up on this running aspect of his message and ministry:
  (a) "Finally, brethren, pray for us, that the word of the Lord may run *swiftly* and be glorified, just as *it is* with you," 2 Thess 3:1 (NKJ)
  (b) "So that in the day of Christ I may have cause to glory because I did not run in vain nor toil in vain," Phil 2:16; cf. 1 Cor 9:24, 26; Gal 2:2; 5:7

b) There is an urgency in itinerant ministry:
  (1) An urgency built in to a travelling ministry, making the most of every opportunity
  (2) There is an urgency built into the shortness of time in any one area
  (3) There is an urgency in maintaining support as an itinerant evangelist

c) There is a breadth and depth of knowledge and experience from itinerating ministry

d) There is the opportunity to perfect the ministry due to the routine of repetition of sermons, sermon series, and other aspects of planning revival meetings

e) There is fatigue involved in revival meetings:
  (1) Fatigue for the church and plastor in hosting a revival meeting
  (2) Fatigue for the evangelist, because life on the road is hard on family, friends, etc.

f) Hosting an evangelist for special meetings provides times and seasons in churches:
  (1) Seasons for outreach and harvest
  (2) Seasons for the church to refocus on the importance of evangelism, the Gospel, and conversion
  (3) Even though hosting an evangelist can bring fatigue, it is only for a short time:
    (a) While the congregation can look forward to the beginning and end of the revival
    (b) The evangelist travels home (if he can) only to move on to the next revival

3) In this light, it would seem that the gift of the evangelist is not only a gift of harvesting, but rather a calling to evangelize or preach the Gospel, and to prompt and lead the church to do the same:

a) As far as evangelizing, the New Testament is balanced between personal evangelism and mass evangelism:
  (1) Such was the case with Jesus, who preached to the crowds, and dealt with individuals
  (2) Such was also the case with Philip, the only named evangelist, who was involved in both mass evangelism (in Samaria) and personal evangelism (with the Ethiopian Eunuch)

b) Thus there need be no competition between crusade/revival evangelism and personal evangelism, as has been regularly a problem in the church, for example:
  (1) C.G. Trumbull (1907)[149]
  (2) Jim Petersen (1980)[150], on "the limitation of proclamation"

c) In this light, see the addendum at the end of *UE,* Chapter 3 titled, "A Graphic Portrayal of Methodological Drift"

4) Since all Christians ought to evangelize (Luke 24:46-47), and since all pastors should do the work of an evangelist (2 Tim 4:5), it would seem then that God has endued evangelists to keep evangelism *the* priority in the church—as evangelism is his only calling!

5) It is no wonder that many churches are dying who no longer seek or use the evangelist whom Christ gifted for the upbuilding of His church!

---

[149]Charles G. Trumbull, *Taking Men Alive: Studies in the Principles and Practise of Individual Soul-Winning* (New York: The International Committee of the Young Men's Christian Association, 1907; 1915; New York: Revell, 1938), 42-46.
  [150]Jim Petersen, *Evangelism as a Lifestyle* (Colorado Springs: NavPress, 1980), 75.

D. The Evangelist in the Bible:

1. **Old Testament Prophecies** concerning the evangelist:

   a. Psa 68:11, "The Lord gives the command; The women who proclaim the *good* tidings (Gk εὐαγγελιζομένοις; Lat *evangelizantibus*) are a great host"

   b. Isa 41:27 (KJV), "The first *shall say* to Zion, Behold, behold them: and I will give to Jerusalem one that bringeth good tidings" (Gk παρακαλέσω; Lat *evangelistam*)

   c. Isa 52:7, "How lovely on the mountains Are the feet of him who brings good news (Gk εὐαγγελιζομένου ἀκοὴν εἰρήνης; Lat *adnuntiantis et praedicantis pacem*), Who announces peace And brings good news of happiness (Gk εὐαγγελιζόμενος ἀγαθά ὅτι ἀκουστὴν ποιήσω τὴν σωτηρίαν σου; Lat *adnuntiantis bonum praedicantis salutem*), Who announces salvation, *And* says to Zion, 'Your God reigns!'" (cf. Rom 10:15)

   d. Nahum 1:15, "Behold, on the mountains the feet of him who brings good news (Gk εὐαγγελιζομένου; Lat *evangelizantis*), Who announces peace! Celebrate your feasts, O Judah; Pay your vows. For never again will the wicked one pass through you; He is cut off completely"

2. **Old Testament Examples** of Itinerant Ministries:

   a. The itinerating "couriers" in 2 Chron 30:6-12

   b. The itinerating teams of teachers in 2 Chron 17:7-9

3. **Philip the evangelist**:

   a. The only named evangelist in the Bible, Acts 21:8

   b. An example of the ministry of Philip, Acts 8:5-40

   [the verb εὐαγγελίζω used five times in this chapter—almost 1/10th of all NT uses; interestingly, the only chapter that uses the verb more times is Galatians 1]

   1) Crusade ministry—Samaria:

      a) Consider the antithetic parallel provided by Luke of the naturally-based ministry of Simon the Sorcerer (also note the A-B-A-C pattern of the text):

Carnal and Spiritual Evangelists Compared

	Philip the Evangelist	Simon the Sorcerer	Similar/ Different
Summary	A Preacher ——— A Spiritual Ministry	An Entertainer ——— A Carnal Ministry	Different
Ministry	Evangelist, 21:8	Practicing magic, 8:9	Different
Method	Proclaiming, 8:5 Included verbal (hearing) and healings (saw signs), 8:6-7, 13 Preaching, 8:12	Practicing magic, 8:9 His magic arts, 8:11	Different
Length of ministry	[short time]	Long time, 8:11	Different
Message	Christ, 8:5 Kingdom of God and the name of Jesus Christ, 8:12	Claiming to be someone great, 8:9 "This man is the called the Great Power of God," 8:10	Different
Focus of Message	Christ	Simon himself	Different
Audience	The crowds with one accord, 8:6 City, 8:8 Men and women, 8:12	The people of Samaria, 8:9 Smallest to greatest, 8:10	Same
Appeal	Giving attention, 8:6	Giving attention, 8:10, 11	Same
Signs	Performed signs, 8:6; cast out unclean spirits, paralyzed and lame healed, 8:7; signs and great miracles, 8:13	Magic arts, 8:11	Different
Result of ministry	Rejoicing, 8:8	Astonishment, 8:9	Different

b) Note the apostolic (Peter's and John's) affirmation of Philip's ministry, and of their emulation, v. 25 (πολλάς τε κώμας τῶν Σαμαριτῶν εὐηγγελίζοντο); v. 40 (καὶ διερχόμενος εὐηγγελίζετο τὰς πόλεις πάσας ἕως τοῦ ἐλθεῖν αὐτὸν εἰς Καισάρειαν)

c) Note also:
  (1) God is well aware that bad evangelists will travel around, such as "savage wolves" (Acts 20:29), "peddlers of the word" (2 Cor 2:17), "false prophets" (2 Pet 2:1), and "certain persons" who have crept in unnoticed (Jude 3)
  (2) Yet it seems to be part of His economy for the church, "for there must also be factions among you, so that those who are approved may become evident" (1 Cor 11:19)
  (3) Therefore, God's word gives appropriate warnings and examples to the church

2) Personal evangelism ministry—Ethiopian Eunuch:
  a) Note that in this case, the evangelist's ministry ended with Baptism (as in Samaria, Acts 8:12)—even though there was no immediate local church to which the convert could go in Ethiopia!

4. John the Baptist:

a. John the Baptist came with a prophecied message: "Prepare ye the way of the LORD!" (Isa 40:3; cf. Mal 3:1)

1) This message described the role of John the Baptist—preparing the way for Christ
  a) Malachi 3 emphasized this preparatory role of John the Baptist: "Behold, I am going to send My messenger, and he will clear the way before Me"
  b) Notice that Christ in Isaiah 40:3 was called "the LORD" or YHWH!

2) This phrase describes the message of John the Baptist—that people ought to prepare themselves for the coming of the Lord:
    a) The verb "prepare" is in the plural, "Prepare ye"
        (1) In this statement, it is not so much that John was preparing the way,
        (2) Rather, he was exhorting the people to prepare the way; hence, prepare their hearts to give heed to the way
    b) Is this not a parallel to "the kingdom of heaven is near [at hand]," Matt 3:2?
    c) Notice also that John's ministry consisted uniquely preaching and baptizing:

> "And many came to Him and were saying, 'While John performed no sign, yet everything John said about this man was true,'" John 10:41

        (1) Therefore, one cannot argue that a necessary preparation for the Gospel consists of performing miracles (supernatural), nor feeding, healing, clothing (natural), apologetic arguments (natural), nor even longterm relationship (natural)

3) Any evangelist today is crying out "prepare ye the way of the LORD," to all who will listen:
    a) We are not the message, but bear witness to Him who is the message (1 Cor 15:1-5; Col 1:28-29)
    b) Not all receive the message, but only those whose hearts are ready, having "ears to hear"

b. The first part of the verse preceeds this message: "The voice of one calling in the desert"
   1) There is a way in which the evangelist always seems to be a voice calling in the desert place
    a) His role is not to be politically correct
    b) Perhaps this is why the evangelist has challenges in mainstreaming into academia
   2) It seems to this author, that there must come a resignation to being "a voice calling in the desert place"
    a) Lest the evangelist be sidetracked into secondary matters
    b) Or lest the evangelist mainstream his message to please culture
   3) It also seems that the evangelist must be ready to "Fight the good fight," 1 Tim 1:18; 6:12; cf. 2 Tim 4:7
    a) Remembering that "the battle is the Lord's," 1 Sam 17:47

5   Jesus:
a. The spiritual giftedness of Jesus: All the gifts of the Spirit were found in Jesus Christ, thus allowing Him to be a worthy example for all Christians, including the evangelist.
b. The ministry of Jesus with respect to evangelism, Mark 1:14-39; Luke 4:43-44, 8:1-3; John 3:34

6. The apostle Peter:
a. Peter's ministry as an evangelist, Acts 2:14-40, 3:1-26, 4:1-31, 10:1-48
b. Peter's calling seems to be particularly geared to Jews, Gal 2:7-8
c. Notice that Peter had to be prompted to share the Gospel when God led him to Cornelius and his household (being that he seemed more concerned with the prohibition of associating with Gentiles), Acts 10:28-29, 33

7. The apostle Paul:

a. The ministry of the apostle Paul:
   1) Paul's ministry in Acts exemplified the ministry of an itinerant evangelist
   2) Paul's ministry as an evangelist began from the time of his conversion, Acts 9:20
   3) The last words about Paul in the book of Acts show him preaching and teaching about Jesus Christ, Acts 28:31

b. The attitude of the apostle Paul with respect to ministry:
   1) Paul saw himself as a servant of the Gospel, Eph 3:6-7
   2) Paul had the attitude of complete self-sacrifice for the sake of the Gospel, 1 Cor 9:19, 22-23; 2 Cor 12:15
   3) Paul had an attitude of complete financial sacrifice for the sake of the Gospel, 2 Cor 12:15

c. Paul specifically felt that he was entrusted with the Gospel to the Gentiles, Gal 2:7-8
   1) Notice that he was entrusted with a message, not a response to the message
   2) Note that Paul still went "to the Jew first," Rom 1:16, which was also his example in Acts 13:46; 18:6; 19:9

8. **The interesting case of Timothy:**
    a. Timothy's reception of spiritual gifts, 1 Tim 4:14; 2 Tim 1:6
    b. The command given to Timothy: "Do the work of an evangelist!" 2 Tim 4:5
        1) Why is this command given to Timothy?
        2) To whom can this commandment be applied?
        3) What is the weight of the command being found in a second person voice?

9. **The Authors of the Gospels** (Matthew, Mark, Luke and John) are traditionally called "The Evangelists."

    a. They wrote, and thus verbally proclaimed, the Good News of Jesus Christ in telling of His life (e.g. Mark 1:1, "The beginning of the gospel of Jesus Christ, the son of God"—Ἀρχὴ τοῦ εὐαγγελίου Ἰησοῦ Χριστοῦ υἱοῦ τοῦ θεοῦ)
        1) Yet even a knowledge of the facts of the life of Christ is not enough to understand the impact of his life and death, Luke 24:25-26
        2) Jesus had "many more things to say" for which the disciples were not ready (John 16:12), showing the canonical necessity for the epistles of Paul (and the "Pauline Gospel") and the other epistles.

    b. Their accounts of the life of Jesus provide Christians their only inspired source of biographical material on the life and death of Jesus Christ, as well as God's provision for man's salvation, e.g. John 20:30-31 (also remembering that the whole Bible points to Jesus, Luke 24:44-45, John 5:39, 46).

    c. The Catholic church has emphasized the imitation of Christ since the Middle Ages, as opposed to the proclamation of the Gospel. For this reason they seem to emphasize the work of the Gospel writers as "the evangelists"
        1) This seems to be the example of cessationism in the role of the evangelist in the ministry of the church which Calvin also taught (see above).

Some concluding thoughts:

We may revere the Wesley, the Whitefield, the Moody, and the Sankey. We may look up to them and their ministries. And yet in the same breath some may say, "That's not for today!"

Why is it not for today? Because they ministered prior the industrial age, prior to the atomic age, Gen X, or postmoderns, prior to the age of telephone, television, and radio, or before the age of computers, DVDs, X-Box, and I-Pod.

Could it be that with a cultural slide of hand we invalidate a New Testament office and the method of our forebears of the Gospel?

E. Definition of an Evangelist:[151]

An evangelist is a Christian who has been gifted as an evangelist by the Holy Spirit (1 Cor 12:7), and who is actually actively using that gift in the way in which God has directed Him through the proclamation of the Gospel. The gift of the evangelist always revolves around the evangelizing the lost (by virtue of the word εὐαγγελιστής, Eph 4:11). Thus if an evangelist is exercising his spiritual gift it must relate to the proclamation of the Good News of Jesus Christ, His death and resurrection (Luke 24:46-47; 1 Cor 15:3-4).

The predominant New Testament method of evangelism revolves around itinerant street preaching and personal evangelism. Jesus was an itinerant evangelist (Mark 1:38; Luke 4:42-43; 8:1-3), He sent out His disciples as itinerant evangelists (Luke 9:6; 10:1), the apostles in the Book of Acts practiced itinerant evangelism (Acts 8:25), as did Philip (Acts 8:40) and the Apostle Paul.

The evangelist is given to the local church to keep the focus of the church on winning the lost to Christ. As churches so easily drift away from evangelism, they need evangelists to keep them focused on fulfilling the Great Commission, the proclamation of the Gospel, and soul-winning.

---

[151]See Keith Fordham, *"The Evangelist"—The Heart of God* (Del City, OK: Spirit, 1988) for an excellent book on the ministry of the evangelist.

The gift of the evangelist is given as a leadership gift to the church (Eph 4:11) and thus implies exemplary responsibility (1 Tim 3:1-13, Titus 1:5-9). As a result, the evangelist must submit to the requirements of church leadership, church membership, as well as church discipline.

All pastors are to exercise the ministry of an evangelist, "Do the work of an evangelist" (2 Tim 4:5), thus being "pastors-evangelists," as mentioned by W. A. Criswell.

F. Diversity in the Gift of the Evangelist:

Introduction: The Conference of Southern Baptist Evangelists includes evangelists with a number of different emphases:
Proclamational/harvest evangelists
Music evangelists
Children's evangelists
Etc.

1. A look at different aspects in the process of evangelism:
   a. There are some in the Bible who sow the seed, Psa 126:6, Matt 13:1-9, 18-23 (Mark 4, Luke 8), John 4:36-38
   b. The same person or another harvests, Psa 126:6, John 4:36-38
   c. The follow-up of the person may also be done by another person, 1 Cor 3:4-9.

2. Practical outworking of the diversity in the gift of the evangelist (this section assumes a gift of evangelism for the sake of illustration, whereas this is never mentioned as an actual gift):

   a. Because of the circumstances around the evangelism and the personality of the evangelist, some seem to be more gifted in one phase of evangelism more than in the others (1 Cor 3:5-8).

   b. Some evangelists may be more gifted in different areas of evangelism. There is no end to the aspects of evangelism, just as there is no end to the ministry of the evangelist—if it is accomplished biblically. Some clearly different aspects of the gift of evangelism are:
      1) The gift for personal evangelism:[152]
         Evangelism, Eph 4:11
      2) The gift for home evangelistic Bible studies:
         Evangelism, Eph 4:11 + hospitality, Rom 12:13, Heb 13:2, 1 Pet 4:7
      3) The gift for teaching evangelism:
         Evangelism, Eph 4:11 + teaching, Rom 12:7, 1 Cor 12:28, Eph 4:11
      4) The gift for organizing and leading evangelism:
         Evangelism, Eph 4:11 + administrative leadership, Rom 12:8
      5) The gift of evangelistic or revival preaching:
         Evangelism, Eph 4:11 + exhortation, Rom 12:8 + speaking, 1 Pet 4:11
      6) The gift of crusade evangelism:
         Evangelism, Eph 4:11 + administrative leadership, Rom 12:8 + exhortation, Rom 12:8 + speaking, 1 Pet 4:11
      7) Summary: The above are exemplary and not prescriptive. It would not be wise to limit the Holy Spirit in how He chooses to use His people in His work. However, this clearly portrays the breadth of possibilities within the scope of the gift of evangelism.

   c. The evangelist should seek to complete the evangelism process if possible, à la Matthew 28 (follow-up on the individual), without hindering the use of his gift, if others can help him in the follow-up. Remembering that the evangelist is responsible for those who come to Christ through his ministry. Thus, he must do the best he can do, and seek to ensure the best possible follow-up.[153]

---

[152]Although it may be that some have the gift of personal evangelism, this does not exonerate other Christians from taking part in the verbal proclamation of the Gospel to others.
[153]This will be discussed in detail later in the notes.

G. Some Examples of Evangelists in the History of the Churches:

(Roughly organized by their death)

Introduction: Developing this list of evangelists led me to research the martyrs of the Reformation period, which then led me into a study of the later Middle Ages. I have compiled the names and notes in Part One of a chronological chart titled, "Evangelism in the Western Church," available at www.evangelismunlimited.org.

The fact that few or no examples have made their way down to us through the pages of "church history" has been discussed in this chapter at the end of Section A. Also, the whole idea of burning alive, corresponded with Thomas Aquinas' view that obstinat (unrepentant) heretics ought to be excommunicated, or extirpated from the world through death. Burning of bodies and books, as well as the confiscation and/or destruction of property, assisted in erasing from "Medieval Church history" the memory of almost all its evangelists; by the way, the same would likely happen today, if the Catholic church had the political and intellectual power and wherewithall.

1. **Patrick** (389-447): Born into a Celtic Church [Evangelical] family in Britain, Patrick was sold as a slave by Irish marauders. He returned after being trained in the faith, to the country of those who had sold him into slavery, and is credited with evangelizing Ireland. His primary antagonists during his ministry appear to be Druid priests.[154]

2. **Columba** (b. 521): A Celtic missionary, Columba left Ireland in 563, establishing himself on the Island of Iona. From this island training institute, Columba sent missionaries out to preach the gospel, going out into the work of evangelism himself. He was credited with leading King Brude of the Picts to Christ.[155]

3. **Boniface [Winifrid]** (~680-755): Boniface's allegiance to Rome is much debated. Whatever the case, he is credited with evangelizing much of the Low Lands (West and East Frisians) and present day Germany (Thuringia and Bavaria). Boniface is remembered for having felled the sacred oak of Thundergod at Feismar, which had been a source of Druid worship.[156]

4. **Anskar of Corbey** (b. 801): Born in France, Anskar is considered the "Apostle to the North." He is credited for helping evangelize Denmark, Norway, and Sweden.

5. **Peter de Bruys** (of Cluny, d. 1126) who evangelized in Southeastern France (Dauphiné). Was burned alive in 1126 in St. Gilles, France.

6. **Henry of Lausanne** (d. 1148, after 14 years in prison) who also evangelized in Southern France in the early 12ᵗʰ Century establishing and encouraging the Cathar churches (described as 16 separate church bodies by the Inquisitor Reinerius Saccho), later to be called the Albigensian church. Henry's ministry was strongly opposed by the Roman Catholics leaders: **Peter the Venerable** of Cluny [who is still upheld as a "reformer" of his day], Cistercian **Bernard of Clairvaux**,[157] and **Pope Innocent II** (who had Henry imprisoned following the Council of Pisa in 1134). This same antagonism became deadly during and through the ministries of [St] Dominic and his Dominican inquisitors, as well as [St] Francis of the Fransiscans (whose antagonism to the Albigensian evangelism may have led him to say, "Preach the Gospel often, and if necessary use words").

7. **Peter Waldo** (also **Vaudez**, **Valdez**, or **Valdo**): began preaching against the sins of the Pope in Lyon France (1160); he was converted in 1170, and began to evangelize in the streets in 1173. Lyon Archbishop **Guichard de Pontigny** worked with **Waldo** and his followers who were called **Waldenses** (or **Vaudois**), beginning in 1173. In 1179, when a new archbishop was named, **Jean de Bellesmains**, **Waldo** was kicked out of Lyons and branded as a heretic; the Waldenses were

---

[154]Ruth A. Tucker, *From Jerusalem to Irian Jaya: A Biographical History of Christian Missions* (Grand Rapids: Zondervan,), 38-40.

[155]Ibid., 40-42.

[156]V. Raymond Edman, *Light in the Dark Ages* (Wheaton, IL: Van Kampen, 1949), 189-93.

[157]Dominique Iogna-Prat, "L'argumentation défensive: de la Polémique grégorienne au 'Contra Petrobrusianos' de Pierre le Vénérable," in *Inventer l'hérésie: Discours polémiques et pouvoirs avant l'inquisition*, Monique Zerner, ed., Collection du centre d'études médiévales de Nice, vol. 2 (Paris: C.I.D., 1998), 88.

excommunicated as heretics by Pope Lucius III in 1184—which meant that they were to be hunted down and extirpated from the world by death.[158]

8. **John Wycliffe** (1329-1384) and the **Lollards**: Wycliffe, apparently the first Englishman to use "evangelist" in his translation of the New Testament, appears to be a theologian with the heart of an evangelist. His teaching and translation of Scripture led to a formidable movement of English lay preachers called **Lollards**.

9. **Balthasar Hubmaier** (1484-1528), receiving his Doctor of Theology under Johann Eck (who disputed Luther at Leipzig in 1519) at Ingolstadt, Catholic priest of Beauteous Mary in Regensberg from 1519-1521, converted to evangelical principles of salvation in 1522-1523, began preaching salvation by faith alone and refuting the errors of the Catholic church. He was rebaptized by Wilhelm Reublin in 1525, and taught that all Christians must preach the Gospel in his *Summa of the Entire Christian Life* (1525). Led a revival at Waldshut, where thousands were baptized in one year. He was tortured on a rack by Zwingli in Zurich (1525-1526), and in 1528 in was turned over by Leonhard von Liechtenstein to the Roman Catholic Archduke Ferdinand. He was again tried on a rack to be forced to recant (February 1528), and was burned alive for heresy in Vienna (10 March 1528).[159]

10. **Francois Lambert d'Avignon** (1487-1530) was saved out of the life of a Observant [strict] Franciscan monastery by reading Luther on the Bible (1522). Escaped when traveling on official business for his order (1523), went to Switzerland, where he was converted under the ministry of **Ulrich Zwingli**, who told him during a sermon, "Brother, you're wrong." **Francois** then travelled into Germany, evangelizing. He ended up assisting **Martin Luther** by teaching theology in Marburg, and assisting in the Reformation of the Kingdom of Hesse.

11. **Alexandre Canus** (d. 1533), having left the order of the Dominicans in Normandy, France, went to Neuchatel, Switzerland, and was taught under French evangelist **Guillaume Farel**. He decided to return to France, and as he preached in Strasbourg, he was arrested and sent to Paris were he endured great torture. He was condemned to be burned alive, and in the process was able to give excellent witness of the Gospel and the grace of God before he died.[160]

12. **Pierre Robert Olivétan** (d. 1538) The cousin of John Calvin, who led him Calvin to Christ and was involved in regular evangelistic trips into the foothills of the Alps (travelling through the territory of the Duke of Savoy at night).[161] He also completed the translation of the Bible into French in 1534 (revised as the Geneva Bible in 1560). Olivétan died mysteriously on a trip to Rome in 1538 presumably to discuss issues of Hebrew translation.[162]

13. The 67+ **Bible colporteurs** who brought Bibles into France from Switzerland, evangelizing and selling their Bibles (which at that time were quite large). Many of them were burned at the stake, some of them with their Bibles hanging around their necks, and some of them had their tongue cut out so they could not preach as they were being burned.[163] For example:

    a. **Guillaume Husson** (d. 1544): He had a tract distribution methodology that got him arrested and martyred in Rouen, France (see in Appendixes of Chapter 1).

---

[158]Michel Rubellin, "Au temps où Valdès n'étais pas hérétique: hypothèses sure le rôle de Valdès à Lyon," in Monique Zerner, ed., *Inventer l'hérésie? Discours polémiques et pouvoirs avant l'inquisition* [Inventing heresy? Polemic discourses and powers before the inquisition], Collection du centre d'études médiévales de Nice, vol. 2 (Paris: C.I.D., 1998), 217.

[159]"Balthasar Hubmaier: Truth is unkillable!" Accessed 11 Aug 2006; available at http://www.cat.xula.edu/tpr/people/ h%FCbmaier/; Internet.

[160]Jean Crespin, *Histoire des vrays Tesmoins de la verite de l'evangile, qui de leur sang l'ont signée, depuis Jean Hus iusques autemps present* (Geneva, 1570; reproduction, Liège, 1964), 78a-b.

[161]"Mais cela ne l'empêchait pas d'inspirer à tous une vive sympathie. Andronicus, en effet, écrivait à Bucer, en 1533: Olivétan, qui n'est pas tant ton Olivétan que notre Olivétan à tous *(non tam tuus quant omnium)* a été envoyé au Piémont, dans une moisson du Seigneur, la plus dangereuse de toutes" (Lortsch, *Histoire de la Bible en France*; accessed: 5 March 2005; from: http://www.bibliquest.org/ Lortsch/ Lortsch-Histoire_Bible_France-1.htm; Internet, 2:4). "En octobre 1532, Gonin et Guido se remirent en route, emmenant avec eux Saunier et Olivétan. Ce dernier se rendait aux Vallées pour y annoncer l'Évangile. Mais ce voyage avait aussi pour but de recueillir auprès des Vaudois les dons nécessaires pour l'impression de la Bible" (ibid., 2:5).

[162]Ibid.

[163]Ibid., 1:30-33.

   b.   **Claude Monier** (d. 1551): evangelist and teacher, was arrested and burned alive in Lyon, France (see in Appendixes of Chapter 2).

   c.   **Philbert Hamelin** (d. 1557): He emphasized evangelism and church planting, and was martyred in Bordeaux, France (see in Appendixes of Chapter 15)

14. **Menno Simons** (1496-1561):

    "At the time [1539] the tyranny and persecution against the God-fearing Christians was very dreadful, so that envious papists, who hated the truth, caused likenesses of many of the principal teachers and overseers of the church of Jesus Christ to be made, and posted on doors, gates, and other public places, promising a large sum of money, to such as should deliver them into the hands of the officers and executioners. And since the God-fearing Menno Simons, who was zealous for God, was one of the principal teachers and elders in this bloody and perilous time, who, by his glorious admonitions, and writings from the Word of God, so flourished, that none of his adversaries dared come before him in an open and free scriptural disputation, though he at various times and very earnestly requested it; through which sound doctrine and Christian admonition, and the power of the Most High, said Menno Simons, drew, turned, and won to God a great number of men, from dark and erring popery; yea, from dumb idols, to the living God.

    "Therefore the servants of the antichrist were embittered the more against him, and, in order to quench and hinder this, caused, A. D. 1543, a dreadful decree to be proclaimed against him throughout all West Friesland [in the Netherlands]; in which all malefactors and murderers were offered remission of their crimes, the pardon of the Emperor, the freedom of the country, and one hundred Carl Guilders, if they could deliver Menno Simons into the hands of the torturers and executioners. But though these men thirsted with such exceeding tyranny and great bitterness for his blood, and sought and persecuted him unto death, yet the Almighty God preserved him, and almost miraculously protected him from the designs of all his enemies, so that they could not execute their tyrannical desires on him; for he died a natural death, as God had appointed it to him, at Wuestefeld, near Lubeck, on the 13th of January, in the year 1559, in his sixty-sixth year. Psa 31:15; Job 14:5; Psa 139:16."[164]

15. The antagonistic Cardinal of Tournon called the pastors and delegates of the Reformed church "**Evangelists**" before Charles IX, King of France, after Theodore Beza spoke in 1562.[165]

16. **Guillaume Farel** (1489-1565), the 16th Century evangelist who brought the Reformation to Neuchâtel, Switzerland and then to Geneva. The same urged Jean Cauvin (John Calvin) to remain in Geneva to teach the people the Word of God.[166] The French historian Franck Puaux wrote of Farel, "The place occupied by Farel in the history of the French Reformation is so great that its life [existence] can be completely attributed to him."[167]

17. **Jean de Labadie** (1610-1674), a post-Reformation, pre-Pietist preacher in Southern France, who preached 50 consecutive sermons on the text "Repent Ye", the last sermon being 2½ hours long.[168]

18. **Isabeau and Pintarde** (d. ~1689): two young peasant girls (17 and 18 years old) turned itinerant preachers, arrested and imprisoned for life in separate places (never to be heard from again; see their story in Appendixes of Chapter 2).

19. **Claude Brousson** (d. 1698), the underground itinerant preacher who restarted some of the scattered Reformed churches after the Revocation of the Edict of Nantes (1685) in the underground church movement called "Les églises du desert" (the desert churches). Preacher to the royal court in the Netherlands, Brousson died by strangulation and being stretched on the rack during his third missionary journey in France.[169]

20. **Philipp Jakob Spener** (1635-1705), who wrote *Pia Desideria* (Pious Desires) is considered the founder of German Pietism, a parallel movement to English Puritanism.

---

[164]Thieleman J. van Braght, *The Bloody Theater of Martyrs Mirror of the Defenseless Christians Who Baptized Only Upon Profession of Faith…*, trans by Joseph F. Sohm (1660; 1748; 1837; 1853; Scottdale, PA: Herald Press, 2007), 454-55.

[165]Jean Crespin, *Histoire des vrays tesmoins* (Geneva: Crespin, 1570), 584b.

[166]Puaux, *Histoire de la Réformation Française* (Paris: Michel Lévy Frères, 1859), 1:121-29, 137ff..

[167]*Ibid.,* 121; translation mine.

[168]Paulus Scharpff, *History of Evangelism: Three Hundred Years of Evangelism in Germany, Great Britain, and the Unites States of America.* Helga Bender Henry, trans. (Grand Rapids: Eerdmans, 1964, 1966), 25.

[169]From Matthieu Lelièvre, *Portraits et Récits Huguenots,* 274-82; translated and quoted by Rubens Saillens in his *The Soul of France* (London: Morgan and Scott, 1917), 85-87.

21. German Pietist evangelist **Ernst Christoph Hochmann von Hochenau** (1660-1721) was eventually kicked out of the Lutheran church and founded the Philadelphia churches in Germany and into Scandinavia.

22. **August Hermann Francke** (1663-1727) was an influential Pietist leader-evangelist. Over ½ million of his sermons were in print by his death, as were many editions of his hymnbook.[170] Francke once said:

> "As far as I am concerned, I must preach that should someone hear me only once before he dies, he will have heard not just a part, but the entire way of salvation and in the proper way for it to take root in his heart."[171]

> "His desire was 'a life changed, a church revived, a nation reformed, a world evangelized.'"[172]

Time of the First Great Awakening (circa 1740)
(evangelists roughly organized by the year of their birth)

It is often at this point at which most English histories of evangelism and discussion of evangelists in the history of the churches begin. Interestingly, it appears almost anathema to speak of evangelism or evangelists prior to the First Great Awakening in English Church Histories!

23. John Wesley (1703-1791), a founder of Methodism.
24. Jonathan Edwards (1703-1758), pastor, author of *A Faithful Narrative of the Surprising Work of God* (1738; which was like an evangelism primer), and president of the College of New Jersey (later called Princeton University) for one year prior to his death.
25. John Whitefield (1714-1770), evangelist.
26. Col. Samuel Harris (1724-1794), Apostle to Virginia.[173]
27. John Gano (1727-1804), personal evangelist, founding pastor of First Baptist Church, New York City, assisted in founding what became Brown University, Rhode Island, and was chaplain for George Washington (whom he allegedly Baptized).

> "Gano served as pastor of the New York Church until 1787, however, he made long itinerant trips evangelizing throughout the thirteen colonies, asserting, 'I... had a right to proclaim free grace wherever I went.' Gano travelled throughout the South, Middle Atlantic States, and New England, sometimes being away from home for as long as two years."[174]

28. Francis Asbury (1745-1816), American Methodist circuit-rider and leader.

---

[170]"A.H. Francke was a pioneer in this literary activity with his Canstein Bible, the first edition of which appeared in 1712. Francke's various writings, including his theological papers and above all his sermons, came out in quick succession in pamphlet form. Between 1717 and 1723 alone more than a half-million pieces of his materials, including about 350,000 sermons, were distributed in addition to the *Predigtbuch (Book of Sermons)* and the Halle songbooks" (Paulus Scharpff, *History of Evangelism*, 52).

[171]Ibid., 46. Consider also this excerpt from Francke: "It would further be useful, and it is highly necessary, that ministers should not only preach up the necessity of conversion, and instruct their hearers to depend on the grace of Christ for it, but also that they should, very frequently, in their sermons explain the nature and the whole progress of conversion, sometimes more largely and distinctly, and at other times more briefly, endeavoring thereby to lead their hearers into a true knowledge of the state of their souls; and showing them how they must repent of their sins, what they must do to be saved from their natural misery and ruin, and, in short, how they may obtain the full salvation of the gospel; that so every one may be able to give an answer to that most important question, 'What must I do that I may be a child of God and inherit eternal life?'" ("August Hermann Francke: Pioneer Philanthopist and Charity Leader"; available at: http://www.path2prayer.com/article/802/revival-and-holy-spirit/books-sermons/new-resources/famous-christians-books-and-sermons/august-hermann-francke-pioneer-philanthropist-and-charity-leader [online]; accessed: 20 Dec 2015; Internet).

[172]Dan Graves, "August Francke: Unto Us a Son Is Given"; available at: http://www.christianity.com/church/church-history/timeline/1601-1700/august-francke-unto-us-a-son-is-given-11630140.html (online); accessed 20 Dec 2015.

[173]I am grateful for the research of Jacob Willard into the history of English evangelists. He named four evangelists at the "Fellowship of Evangelists" gathering at Antioch Bible Baptist Church (Gladstone, MO) on May 30, 2015, three of whom I did not yet have on this brief listing of evangelists: Samuel Stearns Day, Samuel Harris, and Henry Morehouse. My understanding from Jacob is that he has developed a biographical database of English-speaking evangelist who ministered in the United States—which listing has grown to over 1,000 evangelists!

[174]"John Gano"; available at: http://en.wikipedia.org/wiki/John_Gano (Online); 9 Aug 2014; Internet.

29. Robert Haldane (1764-1842), Scotish churchman, who went from the Royal Navy, joined the "Society for the Propagation of the Gospel at Home," and moved to Geneva, helping usher in the French Protestant "Reveil"—or revival.
30. Charles Finney (1792-1875), author of *Lectures on Revival*.
31. Ichabod S. Spencer (1798-1854), author of *Conversations with Anxious Souls Concerning the Way of Salvation*, Pastor of Second Presbyterian Church, Brooklyn, NY, and founder of Union Theological Seminary.[175]
32. John Mason Peck (1789-1858), first Home Missionary [evangelist and church planter] with the Southern Baptist Convention, founder of Rock Springs Seminary [later Shurliff College, now University of Southern Illinois, Edwardsville Campus].
33. Samuel Stearns Day (1808-1871), Baptist evangelist and then missionary to India.
34. Jacob Knapp (1799-1874), 40 years as itinerant evangelist:

> "Jacob Knapp was used of God to win over 100,000 people to Jesus Christ, he preached over 16,000 sermons, he influenced hundreds of men to enter the ministry, and he brought into Baptist work the practice of holding 'protracted' revival campaigns. He ought to be one of the best-known and most-appreciated figures in Baptist history."[176]

35. Henry Morehouse (1840-1880), English evangelist.
36. Dwight L. Moody (1837-1899), cross-Atlantic evangelist and founder of Moody Bible Institute
37. R. A. Torrey (1856-1928), evangelist, president of Moody Bible Institute, and author of *How to Work for Christ*
38. J. Wilbur Chapman (1859-1918), initiator of simultaneous revivals
39. Billy Sunday (1862-1935), crusade evangelist
40. George Truett (1867-1944)
41. W. W. [William Wilstar] Hamilton (1869-), Director of Evangelism, Home Mission Board, SBC; author of 36 books.
42. Dr. Robert E. Neighbour (-1945), started the Baptist Bible Union (in Atlanta, GA), wrote 94 books, including 2 hymn books, and started 82 churches.
43. L. R. Scarborough (1870-1945)
44. W. B. Riley, pastor of First Baptist, Minneapolis, and founder of Northwestern Bible College and K.T.I.S. radio
45. Mordecai Ham (1878-1961)
46. E. Stanley Jones (1884-1972)
47. Bob Jones, Sr. (1883-1968)
48. Charles E. Fuller (1887-1968), founding director, the Old Fashioned Revival Hour[177]
49. Charles E. (C.E.) Matthews, director of evangelism for the Home Mission Board of the SBC
50. William "Billy" McCarrell, 1912 graduate of Moody Bible Institute, pastor of Cicero Bible Church, Chicago, IL; founder of Independent Fundamental Christians of America.
51. Dr. Walter R. MacDonald, aka. "Happy Mac"[178]
52. John R. Rice (1895-1980)
53. Hyman Appelman (1902-1983)
54. E. J. Daniels (1908-1987)
55. T. W. Wilson (1919-2001)
56. W. A. Criswell (1909-2002), pastor-evangelist of First Baptist Church, Dallas, TX
57. Bill Bright (1921-2003), founder of Campus Crusade for Christ
58. Adrian Rogers (1931-2005), pastor-evangelist of Bellevue Baptist church, Memphis, TN
59. D. James Kennedy (1930-2007), founder of Evangelism Explosion
60. Billy Graham (1918-2018)

---

[175]Ichabod Spencer, *Conversations with Anxious Souls Concerning the Way of Salvation* (New York: M. W. Dodd, 1853; Solid Ground, 2006).

[176]"Do You Know Jacob Knapp"; available at: http://ministry127.com/christian-living/do-you-know-jacob-knapp (online); accessed 5 Mar 2013; Internet.

[177]J. Elwin Wright, *The Old Fashioned Revival Hour and the Broadcasters* (Boston: Friendship, 1940).

[178]David Otis Fuller dedicates his edition of Charles H. Spurgeon's *The Soul Winner* to "Happy Mac" in this way, "Dedicated to 'Happy Mac' (Walter R. MacDonald) one of the greatest soul-winners and personal workers in Christian work today, to whom I owe much of what I have learned in winning souls to the Lord Jesus Christ" (Charles H. Spurgeon, *The Soul Winner,* condensed and edited by David Otis Fuller [Grand Rapids, MI: Zondervan, 1948]).

Current

61. Luis Palau (1934-)
62. Junior Hill (~1936-)
63. Bailey Smith (1939-), President of the SBC, 1981-1982
64. Jim Wilson
65. Keith Fordham, entered ministry in 1968, entered evangelism, 1974
66. Ray Comfort (1949-)
67. Franklin Graham (1952-)[179]
68. Johnny Hunt (1952-), Evangelist, Pastor of First Baptist Church Woodstock in Woodstock, Georgia, and Senior Vice President of Evangelism and Leadership, North American Mission Board, SBC.
69. Greg Laurie (1952-)[180]
70. Frank Shivers
71. Roger Carswell
72. Bill Britt
73. Brian Fossett
74. Eric Ramsey
75. Eric Fuller
76. Many more can be added to this list of God-called evangelists, including those from many countries around the world who are faithful to proclaim Christ in their language and culture. And God is still gifting and calling evangelists into the harvest today![181]

Conclusion: Evangelists in the history of the churches have:

a. Evangelized the Gospel, leading people to Christ
b. Planted and multiplied evangelistic churches
c. Started and multiplied spiritual movements and awakenings (incl. the Reformation)
d. Established new denominational groupings when expedient or necessary
e. Started most Bible schools, colleges, and seminaries
f. Promoted lively congregational singing and edited songbooks
g. Started tract societies, Bible societies, and publishing houses
h. Started Sunday School, orphanages, Christian camps, and other education programs for children
i. Started magazines, journals, newspapers, websites, blogs, and twitter feeds

This list, probably incomplete, is worthy of further study into this important office in Christ's church.

Truly, evangelists have been sparkplugs injecting life and vitality into Christ's church for millennia. Thank the Lord for His evangelists!

---

[179]Franklin Graham, *Rebel with a Cause* (Nashville: Nelson, 1995).

[180]Greg Laurie, *Lost Boy: My Story* (Ventura, CA: Regal, 2008).

[181]A list of current members of COSBE (the Conference of Southern Baptist Evangelists) is available at: http://www.sbcevangelist.org/~evangelists/evangelists.php?&set=1; accessed: 8 Dec 2013; Internet.

H. The Evangelist and Revival Ministry:

Introduction: Is there a similar but perhaps separate call between the ministry of an evangelist and the ministry of a revivalist? And if there is a separate call, what does the ministry of a revivalist entail?

1. **Two separate callings in the Bible?**
   a. Is "some as prophets" in Eph 4:11 speaking of Christ's gift of the revivalist?
   b. Can we make a distinction between the call to warn the wicked and the call to warn the righteous, Ezek 3:16-21?
   c. Peter was called to Jews and Paul was called to Gentiles, Gal 2:7-8; and yet Paul ministered to all men, Col 1:28-29, both Jews and Greeks, 1 Cor 9:18-22

2. **Biblical mandate for revival:**

   a. **Why revival?**

      1) God's people are bent on turning from God, Hosea 11;7
         a) This wandering is prophesied throughout the Bible, e.g. Deut 31:14-30 (cf. Psa 80)

      2) How quickly God's people in all ages forget, Psa 106:13-14

      3) The old levain needs to be regularly purges, 1 Cor 5:7-8

      4) Much of the OT and NT teaching about false prophets can be applied to the church, and indicates the continued need for revival within the church, cf. Matt 7:15-23; Acts 20:28-32
         a) These false prophets will be many, and they will deceive many, Matt 24:10-11 (et al)
         b) These false prophets will target the flock of God, the church, Acts 20:29-30 (et al)

   b. **Can [there be] revival? Deuteronomy 32:**

      1) Note that Jonathan Edwards' sermon "Sinners in the Hand of an Angry God" came from Deut 32:35, which is directed to God's people. Note the multiple time elements in this verse (reminiscent of "now" evangelism, 2 Cor 6:2; or of "today" evangelism, Heb 4:7):

Unpacking the Urgency in Deuteronomy 32:35

Time Elements		Subject	
		Vengeance is mine	לִי נָקָם; ἐκδικήσεως
		And retribution	וְשִׁלֵּם; ἀνταποδώσω
In due time	לְעֵת; ἐν καιρῷ	Their foot will slip	תָּמוּט רַגְלָם; ὅταν σφαλῇ ὁ ποὺς αὐτῶν
Near	קָרוֹב; ἐγγὺς	The day of their calamity	יוֹם אֵידָם; ἡμέρα ἀπωλείας
With haste*	וְחָשׁ; καὶ πάρεστιν	Impending things upon them*	עֲתִדֹת לָמוֹ; ἕτοιμα ὑμῖν

*The last line in the Greek appears to read, "is already present" or "has already arrived";[182] this line seems to answer the prophecied purpose for the Song of Moses, which was to wake the slumbering Israelites out of their sleep of apostasy (Deut 31:17, "so that they will say in that day, 'Is it not because our God is not among us that these evils have come upon us?'"), for their calamnity will literally be upon them "in that day"—and this fact will be combined with a hearing of faith, in that they are prophecied to believe the warnings of the Psalm of Moses.

   2) These time elements are found in numerous other OT Scripture:
      Lev 26:16, "I, in turn, will do this to you: I will appoint over you a sudden terror, consumption and fever that shall waste away the eyes and cause the soul to pine away; also, you shall sow your seed uselessly, for your enemies shall eat it up" (cf. Psa 78:33)
      Psa 73:18-19 (the Psalm seems to be an exposition of Deut 32:35):
      (1) "Surely Thou dost set them in slippery places;
      (2) "Thou dost cast them down to destruction.
      (3) "How they are destroyed in a moment! [πῶς ἐγένοντο εἰς ἐρήμωσιν ἐξάπινα]
      (4) "They are utterly swept away by sudden terrors! [ἐξέλιπον ἀπώλοντο διὰ τὴν ἀνομίαν αὐτῶν]"

---

[182]The Greek verb πάρειμι is defined in the Louw-Nida Lexicon in this way: "85.23 πάρειμι; παράκειμαι: to be present at a particular time and place – 'to be present, to be here, to be there, to be at hand.'" (BibleWorks 9).

Isa 13:6, "Wail, for the day of the LORD is near! It will come as destruction from the Almighty"

Isa 48:3 "I declared the former things long ago And they went forth from My mouth, and I proclaimed them. Suddenly I acted, and they came to pass"

Isa 55:6-7, "Seek the LORD **while He may be found**; Call upon Him **while He is near**. Let the wicked forsake his way, And the unrighteous man his thoughts; And let him return to the LORD, And He will have compassion on him; And to our God, For He will abundantly pardon.

Joel 1:15, "Alas for the day! For the day of the LORD is near, And it will come as destruction from the Almighty"

Joel 2:1-2, "Blow a trumpet in Zion, And sound an alarm on My holy mountain! Let all the inhabitants of the land tremble, For the day of the LORD is coming; Surely it is near, A day of darkness and gloom, A day of clouds and thick darkness. As the dawn is spread over the mountains, *So* there is a great and mighty people; There has never been *anything* like it, Nor will there be again after it To the years of many generations."

Obad 1:15, "For the day of the LORD draws near on all the nations. As you have done, it will be done to you. Your dealings will return on your own head."

Zeph 1:7, "Be silent before the Lord God! For the day of the LORD is near, For the LORD has prepared a sacrifice, He has consecrated His guests."

Zeph 1:14, "Near is the great day of the LORD, Near and coming very quickly; Listen, the day of the LORD! In it the warrior cries out bitterly."

3) None of the Acts sermons to Jews quote Deuteronomy 32, yet they quote other parallel passages—i.e. the message of revival is found repeated throughout the Old Testament many times and in many ways.

4) By the way, the "Song of Moses" in Deuteronomy 32 is provides us ***the hermeneutical grid*** to the entire Torah (cf. Deut 31:19-21). Therefore, it's message of the certainty of depravity and apostasy must not be ignored in scholars' quest for a secondary "Central Interpretive Motif" (i.e. which then becomes the central view of the atonement in the NT)—as is often done! The total depravity and sure apostasy, even of God's people, is prophecied! Hence is constantly needed a work of God, or revival!

Some hermeneutical and linguistic markers asking the reader of Deuteronomy to focus on the message of Deut 32:
The fact that Moses directly taught this text to the people, which is the only use of the verb "teach" directly related a portion and with the use of Moses' name in the entire Pentateuch, Deut 31:22; 32:44 (LXX)
The use of "until the end/until complete" in Deut 31:24, 30
The direct context of the "all the words of this song" (Deut 32:44), and the "all these words" (Deut 32:45), are immediately followed by "this word is not a futile thing" in Deut 32:47.

c. **Is there a specific formula for revival, such as 2 Chron 7:14 (à la [middle-to-later] Finney)?**

1) A+B+C+D=E+F+G

2) A (If My people)—the three protases, "if clauses," are in v. 13 (God's judgment)
    + B (humble themselves and pray)
        + C (and seek My face)
            + D (and if they turn from their wicked ways)
                = E (then I will hear from heaven)
                    + F (forgive their sin)
                        + G (heal their land)

3) A type of formula approach to revival has biblical legitimacy; yet it can be applied in a selfish way, as people want to have a healing of their land without first a turning from their wicked ways; therefore this promise needs to be compared with other plenary material (aka. *sensus plenior*) on the subject

4) Often this type of formula is used to emphasize the apodoses, blessings, and not the Protasis (in v. 13); the two examples of false repentance in Genesis, Cain and Esau, had concern for their punishment, without true contrition that they had sinned against the living God

5) This type of formula approach can also be applied, and is often applied, to verses on prayer ("Name it and claim it"), and especially to promises of divine healing ("Get your healing")!

3. **Biblical ministry tending toward a "revival" ministry**—calling to repentance:

Introduction:

> 1 Kings 18:17-18, "And it came about, when Ahab saw Elijah that Ahab said to him, 'Is this you, you troubler of Israel?' And he said, 'I have not troubled Israel, but you and your father's house *have*, because you have forsaken the commandments of the LORD, and you have followed the Baals'"

> 2 Chron 30:6-12

> Isa 58:1, "Cry loudly, do not hold back; Raise your voice like a trumpet, And declare to My people their transgression And to the house of Jacob their sins"

> Jer 35:14-15, "But I have spoken to you again and again; yet you have not listened to Me. Also I have sent to you all My servants the prophets, sending *them* again and again, saying: 'Turn now every man from his evil way and amend your deeds, and do not go after other gods to worship them. Then you will dwell in the land which I have given to you and to your forefathers; but you have not inclined your ear or listened to Me'"

> Ezek 3:18, "When I say to the wicked, 'You will surely die,' and you do not warn him or speak out to warn the wicked from his wicked way that he may live, that wicked man shall die in his iniquity, but his blood I will require at your hand"

> Ezek 33:8, "When I say to the wicked, 'O wicked man, you will surely die,' and you do not speak to warn the wicked from his way, that wicked man shall die in his iniquity, but his blood I will require from your hand."

> Luke 3:19-20, "But when Herod the tetrarch was reproved by him on account of Herodias, his brother's wife, and on account of all the wicked things which Herod had done, he added this also to them all, that he locked John up in prison."

> Acts 14:14-15, "But when the apostles, Barnabas and Paul, heard of it, they tore their robes and rushed out into the crowd, crying out and saying, 'Men, why are you doing these things? We are also men of the same nature as you, and preach the gospel to you in order that you should turn from these vain things to a living God, who made the heaven and the earth and the sea, and all that is in them.'"

   a. A call to repentance, Jer 4:3-4, 14-16, 5:1-10, 23, 13:9-10, Ezek 5:5-6; 18:30-32; 33:11

   b. A call to turn from sin, Jer 13:25-27, 18:11, 19:3-11, 25:5, Ezek 16:2, 43:10

   c. A call to turn from apostasy, Jer 8:1-5 (cf. Jer 14:7)

   d. A call back to a first love, Jer 2:2

   e. A warning of impending destruction, Jer 6:1-8, 9:11-16, 11:9-15, Ezek 9:4-8, 12:14-20, 11:5-12

   f. A cry of judgment of false prophets, Jer 5:31, 14:13-18, 23:9-32, 2:21-23, Ezek 13:1-24

4. **By the way, false prophets were anti-revival ministry:**

   a. **Their message did not include repentance:**

      1) "You shall say to them, 'Thus says the Lord, do men fall and not get up again? Does one turn away and not repent? Why then has this people, Jerusalem, turned away in continual apostasy? They hold fast to deceit, they refuse to return. I have listened and heard, they have not spoken what is right; no man has repented of his wickedness, saying 'What have I done?' Everyone has turned to his course, like a horse charging into battle," Jer 8:4-6

      2) "Also among the prophets of Jerusalem I have seen a horrible thing: The committing of adultery and walking in falsehood; And they strengthen the hand of evildoers, so that no one has turned back from his wickedness. All of them have become to Me like Sodom, and her inhabitants like Gomorrah," Jer 23:14

   b. **Rather their message was peace and love** (e.g. a "positive message"):

      1) "They have lied about the Lord and said, 'Not He; misfortune will not come upon us, and we will not see sword or famine,'" Jer 5:12

      2) "Saying, 'peace, peace,' but there is no peace," Jer 6:14

      3) "This is the Temple of the Lord, the temple of the Lord, the temple of the Lord," Jer 7:4

      4) "Saying, 'Peace, peace,' but there is no peace," Jer 8:11

      5) "You will not see the sword nor will you have famine, but I will give you lasting peace in this place," Jer 14:13

      [See my CTE, Chart 38, on the four quadrants of preaching][183]

      a) **This message is called preaching the apodosis without preaching the protasis (cf. Deut 28)**

      b) **Note the clear example of this misplaced emphasis in their murder plot against Jeremiah for his preaching, Jer 26:8-9; they ignored that he was sharing all that God had told him, Jer 26:2, "Do not omit a word!" (e.g. Psa 119:13; Acts 20:27)**

---

[183]Johnston, *Charts for a Theology of Evangelism*, Chart 38, "Preaching the Whole Counsel of God: Old Testament and New Testament," 70-71.

> They ignored that Jeremiah was primarily preaching the protasis, Jer 26:4-5, with 26:6 being the apodosis
>
> **c)** Note Jeremiah's clear example of preaching both protasis and apodosis regarding keeping the Sabbath, 17:21-27

6) "They keep saying to those who despise Me, 'The LORD has said, You will have peace,' and as for everyone who walks in the stubbornness of his own heart, They say, 'Calamity will not come upon you,'" Jer 23:17

7) "I had a dream, I had a dream," Jer 23:25
8) "You will not serve the king of Babylon," Jer 27:9
9) "You will not serve the king of Babylon," Jer 27:14
10) "Behold, the vessels of the Lord's house will now shortly be brought again from Babylon," Jer 27:16
11) "Thus says the Lord of hosts, the God of Israel, 'I have broken the yoke of the king of Babylon. Within two years I am going to bring back to this place all the vessels of the Lord's house, which king Nebuchadnezzar king of Babylon took away from this place and carried to Babylon. I am also going to bring back to this place Jeconiah the son of Jehoiakim, king of Judah, and all the exiles of Judah who went to Babylon,' declares the Lord, 'for I will break the yoke of the king of Babylon,'" Jer 28:2-4
12) "Thus says the Lord, 'Even so will I break within two full years the yoke of Nebuchadnezzar king of Babylon from the neck of all nations," Jer 28:11

c. False prophecy leads to a lack of repentance:
1) "So that no one has turned back from his wickedness, all of them have become to Me like Sodom, and her inhabitants like Gomorrah," Jer 23:14
2) "Therefore My people go into exile for their lack of knowledge; And their honorable men are famished, And their multitude is parched with thirst. Therefore Sheol has enlarged its throat and opened its mouth without measure; And Jerusalem's splendor, her multitude, her din *of revelry*, and the jubilant within her, descend *into it*." Isa 5:13-14

d. Some thoughts on how the message can change so subtly, quickly, and drastically:

1) It happens in little stages!
   a) It includes turning from and turning to, 2 Tim 4:4
   b) Turning from and too may include **allegorizing** the text, such as:
      (1) Expunging evangelism from Phil 1:12-18 (of which I was guilty at one time!)
      (2) Preaching 2 Cor 6:3-10 without ever mentioning evangelism!
   c) It includes adding and **subtracting** (Deut 4:2; 12:32; Prov 30:6; Rev 22:18), normally (seemingly) in the opposite order: subtracting then adding
      (1) Preaching 2 Tim 4:9-18 only from a relational point-of-view, without mentioning anything negative (e.g. vv. 14-16), but merely noting the positive relational elements of the passage
   d) "Adding and subtracting" is usually most noticeable in the **subtracting**, e.g. subtracting key doctrines such as total depravity, literal hell, the imminent return of Christ
   e) Then in order to support the omission of these doctrines, other doctrines and sources of authority (e.g. culture) need to replace them

2) There seem to be several "points-of-no-return":
   a) **Theologically**: conceding the depravity of man—whereby man is no longer considered too depraved to add to his salvation, Jude 11, "they have perished in the rebellion of Korah" (cf. Num 16:3, "You have gone far enough, for all the congregation are holy, every one of them, and the LORD is in their midst; so why do you exalt yourselves above the assembly of the LORD?")—did not Korah teach the basic moral goodness of all people?
   b) **Practically**: conceding the absolute need for instantaneous conversion—when it is no longer deemed absolutely necessary for a person to be born again to be a saved Christian (John 3:3, 7)

❖   ❖   ❖   ❖   ❖

5. **False Prophets (and Kings) Also Persecuted True Prophets:**
   a. Zedekiah son of Chenaanah (the false prophet who "spoke" in the name of the Lord) struck Micaiah (a true prophet) on the cheek, 1 Kings 22:24
   b. Pashhur son of Immer, a false prophet, had Jeremiah beaten and put in the stocks (near where he was street witnessing, Jer 7:2ff., cf. 11:6), Jer 20:1-6
   c. "When Jeremiah finished speaking all that the Lord had commanded him to speak to all the people, the priests and the prophets and all the people seized him, saying, 'You must die! Why have you prophesied in the name of the Lord saying, "This house will be like Shiloh and this city will be desolate, without inhabitant"?'" Jer 26:8-9
   d. "Then the priests and the prophets spoke to all the officials and to all the people, saying, 'A death sentence for this man [Jeremiah]! For he has prophesied against this city as you have heard in your hearing,'" Jer 26:11. "Then the officials and all the people said to the priests and the prophets, 'No death sentence for this man! For he has spoken to us in the name of the Lord our God,'" Jer 26:16
   e. "Indeed, there was also a man who prophesied in the name of the LORD, Uriah the son of Shemaiah from Kiriath-jearim; and he prophesied against this city and against this land words similar to all those of Jeremiah. When King Jehoiakim and all his mighty men and all the officials heard his words, then the king sought to put him to death; but Uriah heard *it*, and he was afraid and fled and went to Egypt. Then King Jehoiakim sent men to Egypt: Elnathan the son of Achbor and *certain* men with him *went* into Egypt. And they brought Uriah from Egypt and led him to King Jehoiakim, who slew him with a sword and cast his dead body into the burial place of the common people," Jer 26:20-23
   f. Hananiah son of Azzur contradicted the prophecy of Jeremiah and broke the yoke that he used in his prophecy, Jer 28:1-14
   g. "Now Shephatiah the son of Mattan, and Gedaliah the son of Pashhur, and Jucal the son of Shelemiah, and Pashhur the son of Malchijah heard the words that Jeremiah was speaking to all the people.... Then the officials said to the king, 'Now let this man be put to death....' So King Zedekiah said, 'Behold, he is in your hands; for the king can *do* nothing against you.' Then they took Jeremiah and cast him into the cistern *of* Malchijah the king's son, which was in the court of the guardhouse; and they let Jeremiah down with ropes. Now in the cistern there was no water but only mud, and Jeremiah sank into the mud," Jer 38:1-6

Similarly it seems that those who shift away from total depravity and the need to be born again (thereby conceding the need for NT evangelism), shun and then persecute those who do believe the same.

6. **Some ratios related to false and true prophets:**

   Introduction: One of the saddest truths about Gospel ministry relates to the many and the few (by no means exhaustive):
   1) "For **many** will come in My name, saying, 'I am the Christ,' and will mislead **many**," Matt 24:5
   2) "**Many** false prophets will arise and will mislead **many**," Matt 24:11
   3) "For we are not like **many**, peddling the word of God, but as from sincerity, but as from God, we speak in Christ in the sight of God," 2 Cor 2:17
   4) "And He was saying to them, 'The harvest is plentiful, but the laborers are **few**; therefore beseech the Lord of the harvest to send out laborers into His harvest,'" Luke 10:2
   5) "Children, it is the last hour; and just as you heard that antichrist is coming, even now **many** antichrists have arisen; from this we know that it is the last hour," 1 John 2:18
   6) "Beloved, do not believe every spirit, but test the spirits to see whether they are from God; because **many** false prophets have gone out into the world," 1 John 4:1
   7) "For **many** deceivers have gone out into the world, those who do not acknowledge Jesus Christ *as* coming in the flesh. This is the deceiver and the antichrist," 2 John 1:7

   a. Ratios of false prophets to true prophets:
      1) 850:1, 1 Kings 18:19
      2) 400:1, 1 Kings 22:6
      Someone once said, "One man and God is a majority!"

   b. Ratio of righteous men to a true prophet of God:
      1) 7,000:1, 1 Kings 19:18

   c. Ratio of angelic forces protecting versus enemies of God's prophet:
      1) "Do not fear, for those who are with us are more than those who are with them," 2 Kings 6:16

d.   Other interesting ratios:

1)   12:5,000, disciples who remained compared to those who ate and were filled, John 6:10, 66-67

2)   1:10, healed lepers exhibited faith, Luke 17:12-19

3)   1:12, one betrayer among the apostles, John 6:70-71

4)   11:11 of the remaining disciples fled when Jesus was arrested, Matt 26:31, 56

Some lessons from these numbers:

1)   We ought not get to enthralled with large numbers, but rather with faithfulness in Gospel proclamation

2)   We ought not consider that true Gospel ministry will gain or maintain a majority in a society, although the majority of populations that are saved have been the case in rare instances in the history of the churches

3)   We ought not make decisions based on desiring a majority:

a)   Of church participation: perhaps desiring a majority of churches was a pitfall that Billy Graham fell into?

b)   Of the goal of a converted society: perhaps this goal has led the Church Growth movement to study sociology rather than the Bible, as it has sought "people movements," leading to the notion of "disciple a nation" which seems to have drifted from NT evangelism

4)   We ought to content ourselves with being in the minority, rather than being "greater than our Master," John 15:20

5)   True evangelism is always an uphill battle, 1 Cor 16:8-9

7.   **Types and characteristics of revival:**

a.   In the Old Testament:

1)   Revival teams went thoughout the land, 2 Chron 17:7-9:

Then in the third year of his reign he sent his officials, Ben-hail, Obadiah, Zechariah, Nethanel and Micaiah, to teach in the cities of Judah; and with them the Levites, Shemaiah, Nethaniah, Zebadiah, Asahel, Shemiramoth, Jehonathan, Adonijah, Tobijah and Tobadonijah, the Levites; and with them Elishama and Jehoram, the priests. They taught in Judah, *having* the book of the law of the LORD with them; and they went throughout all the cities of Judah and taught among the people.

2)   King Jehoshaphat went throughout the land, 2 Chron 19:4:

So Jehoshaphat lived in Jerusalem and went out again among the people from Beersheba to the hill country of Ephraim and brought them back to the LORD, the God of their fathers.

3)   The couriers from Judah went throughout the land of Israel, 2 Chron 30:6-11:

The couriers went throughout all Israel and Judah with the letters from the hand of the king and his princes, even according to the command of the king, saying, "O sons of Israel, return to the LORD God of Abraham, Isaac and Israel, that He may return to those of you who escaped *and* are left from the hand of the kings of Assyria. Do not be like your fathers and your brothers, who were unfaithful to the LORD God of their fathers, so that He made them a horror, as you see. Now do not stiffen your neck like your fathers, but yield to the LORD and enter His sanctuary which He has consecrated forever, and serve the LORD your God, that His burning anger may turn away from you. For if you return to the LORD, your brothers and your sons *will find* compassion before those who led them captive and will return to this land. For the LORD your God is gracious and compassionate, and will not turn *His* face away from you if you return to Him." So the couriers passed from city to city through the country of Ephraim and Manasseh, and as far as Zebulun, but they laughed them to scorn and mocked them. Nevertheless some men of Asher, Manasseh and Zebulun humbled themselves and came to Jerusalem.

4)   A proclamation was circulated under the guidance of Ezra, Neh 8:14-15 (following Deut 31:10-13):

And they found written in the law how the LORD had commanded through Moses that the sons of Israel should live in booths during the feast of the seventh month. So they proclaimed and circulated a proclamation in all their cities and in Jerusalem, saying, "Go out to the hills, and bring olive branches, and wild olive branches, myrtle branches, palm branches, and branches of *other* leafy trees, to make booths, as it is written."

b. In the New Testament:

Introduction: Note in my CTE, Chart 82, on the "Reformation Pattern and New Testament Revival"

1) **Under John the Baptist** (the divine *preparatio evangelica*—preparation for the Gospel), Matt 3:1-12; Luke 3:1-10
    a) Included no miracles, John 10:41
    b) Included preaching repentance for the forgiveness of sins, Matt 3:2; Luke 3:3 (cf. Luke 24:47)
    c) Included baptism, Matt 3:6
    d) Included the public confession of sins, Matt 3:6
    e) Included individual spiritual advice to three types of inquirers, Luke 3:10-14—Is this were the inquiry room idea comes from? (cf. Acts 13:43)
    f) Included warning of judgment and against false assurance, Matt 3:7-10; Luke 3:7-9
    g) Included telling about Jesus' might, baptism, and judgment, Matt 3:11-12; Luke 3:15-17
    h) Included teaching how to pray, Luke 11:1

2) **Under Jesus in Galilee**, Luke 10-11 (some uses of ὄχλος, Luke 6:17-19; 7:11-12; 8:40; 9:37; 13:17; 22:47):
    a) The sign of revival, "As the crowds were increasing," Luke 11:29 (cf. Luke 12:1)
    b) As part of the revival, Jesus sent out his disciples evangelizing individually (Luke 9:1-6) and two-by-two (Luke 10:1), "to every city and place where He Himself was going to come."
    c) He preached judgment on the cities that had seen the most miracles, Luke 10:13-15
    d) The disciples experienced the miraculous, Luke 10:17-20
    e) Jesus faced opposition, Luke 10:25-29; 11:14-26, 53-54
    f) Jesus preached judgment on those who were following Him, Luke 11:29-32
    g) Preached judgment against false teachers (Pharisees), Luke 11:37-52

3) **Under Philip in Samaria**, Acts 8:5-25
    a) Began and ended in the midst of itinerant evangelism, Acts 8:4-5, 25, 40
    b) Included preaching Christ, Acts 8:5-6, 12, 14
    c) Included crowds of people, Acts 8:6
    d) Included miracles, Acts 8:6-7, 13
    e) Resulted in rejoicing, Acts 8:8
    f) Included antithetical example of a false preacher, Simon the Sorcerer, Acts 8:9-11, 13, 18-24
    g) Included baptism, Acts 8:13

4) **Under Paul in Ephesus**, Acts 19
    a) Began and ended with itinerant ministry, Acts 19:1, 21-22, 20:1
        (1) This ministry included a ministry team, Acts 19:22, 29
    b) Included dealing with false or partial teaching, Acts 19:1-7
    c) Was a long term ministry:
        (1) Three months of preaching in the synagogue, Acts 19:8
        (2) Two years of reasoning in the School of Tyrannus, Acts 19:9-10
        (3) A total of three years of ministry in Ephesus, Acts 20:31
    d) Included "extraordinary miracles," Acts 19:11-12
    e) Included imitators, Acts 19:13-16
    f) The method:
        (1) Found some disciples (εὑρίσκω), Acts 19:1
        (2) Bold speech (παρρησιάζομαι), reasoning (διαλέγομαι), and persuading (πείθω), Acts 19:8
        (3) Reasoning (διαλέγομαι), Acts 19:9
        (4) Declaring (ἀναγγέλλω) and teaching (διδάσκω), Acts 20:20
        (5) Publicly and house to house (δημοσίᾳ καὶ κατ' οἴκους), Acts 20:20
        (6) Solemnly testifying (διαμαρτύρομαι), Acts 20:21
        (7) Preaching (κηρύσσω), Acts 20:25
        (8) Declaring (ἀναγγέλλω), Acts 20:27
        (9) Not ceasing (οὐκ παύω) to admonish (νουθετέω), Act 20:31 (not ceasing to)

(10) Hands ministered (ὑπηρέτησαν αἱ χεῖρες αὗται) … working hard (κοπιάω),
Acts 20:34-35
    g) The message:
      (1) To believe in Jesus, Acts 19:4
      (2) The kingdom of God, Acts 19:8
      (3) Christ was magnified, Acts 19:17
      (4) The word of the Lord, Acts 19:20
      (5) Repentance toward God and faith in our Lord Jesus Christ, Acts 20:21
      (6) The gospel of the grace of God, Acts 20:24
      (7) The kingdom, Acts 20:25
      (8) The whole purpose of God, Acts 20:27
      (9) The words of the Lord Jesus, Acts 20:35
    h) Included baptism, Acts 19:5
    i) Included coming, confessing, and disclosing of practices, Acts 19:18, and the burning of books of magic (worth $5 million?!), Acts 19:19
      (1) Question: It seems that Paul's primary message was not to blaspheme the worship of Diana, Acts 19:37
      (2) The burning of the books seemed to mark that his ministry in Ephesus was finished, and that he should move on, Acts 19:21
    i) Included fierce opposition and a riot, Acts 19:23-41
    j) Including the founding of a church with elders (organized leadership), Acts 20:17
      (1) Paul may have made become friends with some political leaders, "Asiarchs," Acts 19:31

  c. Some current types of revival (some less valid than others):
    1) Evangelistic revival
    2) Healing services
    3) Consecration revival
    4) Prayer revival
    5) Teaching revival

I. Some Common Reproaches Against Evangelists:

Introduction: It seems like the more closely alligned our lives are to the Gospel, the more real are the biblically-taught reproaches against us:[184]
  a. The fact of dishonor and evil report, 2 Cor 6:8
  b. Being seen as impostors, 2 Cor 6:8 (RSV, NJB, SEM); cf. Matt 27:63; 1 Tim 4:1; 2 John 1:7
  c. Refusing to become overly boastful, but to boast in the Lord, 2 Cor 10:12-18; 11:30; 12:9-10:
    1) Notice that in his 2 Corinthians 11 curriculum vitae (compare with Philippians 3), Paul did not list his status as to the Law, nor his education, nor the revivals under his ministry (such as in Ephesus), nor the growing churches he founded, nor the evangelists, missionaries, and ministers that he trained (such as Timothy or Priscilla and Aquila)
    2) Notice in the grocery list of weaknesses, Paul did not mention that he was a persecutor of the church (in this context), nor any of his sins against the moral law of God
    3) Notice that "frequent journeys" were a burden to him, 2 Cor 11:26

1. Some reproaches against Jesus (not including the main accusations that led Him to the cross, as found repeated in the accusations against Stephen [Acts 6] and then Paul [Acts 21]):
  a. He's demon-possessed, John 8:48
  b. He had an illegitimate birth, John 8:41

2. Reproaches against Paul and his ministry in the Bible:[185]
  a. He's too single-minded for souls, 1 Cor 9:22-23
  b. He's in it for the money, 2 Cor 2:17 (cf. Jude 11)
  c. He's carnally minded, 2 Cor 10:2

---

[184]See also Chapter 11, God's Place in Evangelism," A. "Several Passages Exemplifying the Relationship of God and Man."

[185]See also Chapter 4, "Spiritual Passions and the Spiritual Battle," "The Spiritual Battle," IV., "Further Issues in the Spiritual Battle."

    d. He deceives people—about assurance of salvation?[186] 2 Cor 6:8

    e. He's too negative, 2 Cor 6:10

    f. He's so narrow minded, 2 Cor 6:11-12

    g. He lacks the proper appearance, 2 Cor 10:1, 7

    h. He's not that great a preacher, in fact, "his speech [is] contemptible" (ἐξουθενημένος, contemptible, having no value, worthless), 2 Cor 10:10

    i. He's untrained in matters of higher learning, 2 Cor 11:6 (NKJ), "Even though *I am* untrained in speech, yet *I am* not in knowledge"; NEG, "Si je suis un ignorant sous le rapport du langage, je ne le suis point sous celui de la connaissance"; [ἰδιώτης τῷ λόγῳ; "untrained in the letters"]

    j. He doesn't care about those he leads to Christ nor the churches he establishes, he just leaves them on their own and goes elsewhere, 2 Cor 11:28-29 (cf. Mark 1:35-39; Luke 4:42-43)

3. Medieval reproaches:

    a. Inquisitor of Carcassone, France, Jacques Fournier (1318-1325), later became Avignon Pope Benedict XII (1334-1342); his claim to fame was finding the woman who had slept with an Albigensian priest from the small town of Pamiers, whereupon he devasted that town to get every savory detail of all the immorality that he could find; he later made multiple copies of the chronicle of his inquisitions, thereby sealing his selectability for the job of Pope.[187]

    b. Likewise, Reinerius Saccho, former Waldensian become their inquisitor, wrote of the Waldenses:

> "Even though they praise continence, they satisfy nevertheless their carnal lusts by the most dirty means, explaining in this way the words of the Apostle: '*It is better to be married than to burn.* Better to satisfy one lust by a shameful act than to conserve temptation in one's heart.'"[188]

    c. Likewise, Luther, other Reformers, and Protestants (up to the present day), were called libertarians and antinomians, as they broke their vows of celibacy, in order to live according to Scriptures

    d. In the questioning of a 15 year old Anabaptist lad named Jacques Dosie, in Leeuwaerden, the Netherlands (1550), the woman who questioned him said, "I know that there are such sects, who are very wicked and kill people, and also have their goods and wives in common." Jacques replied, "Oh, no, my lady, we are quite unjustly charged with these wicked things, and occasion is thereby sought, to persecute us; but we must suffer all this with patience."[189]

---

[186]"The fundamentalist approach is dangerous, for it is attractive to people who look to the Bible for ready answers to the problems of life. It can deceive these people, offering them interpretations that are pious but illusory, instead of telling them that the Bible does not necessarily contain an immediate answer to each and every problem. Without saying as much in so many words, fundamentalism actually invites people to a kind of intellectual suicide. It injects into life a false certitude, for it unwittingly confuses the divine substance of the biblical message with what are in fact its human limitations" ("Pontifical Commission on Biblical Interpretation"; available at: http://www.ewtn.com/library/CURIA/PBCINTER.htm; accessed: 17 Oct 2009; Internet).

[187]Jean Duvernoy, *Le register d'inquisition de Jacques Fournier, éveque de Pamiers (1318-1325)* [in Latin] (Toulouse: Privat, 1965); French trans., Civilisation et société 43 (Paris: La Haye, 1978).

[188]"Témoignage rendu aux vaudois par un inquisiteur" (testimony given of the Waldenses by an inquisitor), in Franck Puaux, *Histoire de la Réformation Française* (Paris: Michel Lévy Frères, 1859), 1:425; taken from Bossuet, *Histoire des variations,* 11:55-54 (sic); translated into English by Thomas P. Johnston. Franck Puaux appended to this portion of the quote the following: "Reinerius slanders the Waldenses and seems too strong in his feelings. One passage in their apology relative to this accusation of being libertines, will suffice to refute him. It is this odious vice, say the Waldenses, that enticed David to kill his faithful servant, that pushed Amnon to corrupt his sister Tamar, and that consumed the inheritance of the prodigal son. Balaam chose it to make the children of Israel sin, which occasioned the death of twenty-four thousand persons. It is the same sin which occasioned the blinding of Samson and the fall of Solomon. The beauty of the woman have made a number perish. Fasting, prayer, and distance, such are the only remedy to oppose this evil. We can win over other vices by battling, but this one we can only surmount through fleeing… Joseph provides us an example."

[189]Thieleman J. van Bracht, *The Bloody Theater of Martyrs Mirror of the Defenseless Christians Who Baptized Only Upon Profession of Faith…*, trans by Joseph F. Sohm (1660; 1748; 1837; 1853; Scottdale, PA: Herald Press, 2007), 498.

4. Similar contemporary reproaches against evangelists:

   a. Evangelists focus all their time on fundraising (2 Cor 10:2):

      1) Why can't they get a real job? (1 Cor 9:11)
         a) Evangelism is work, 1 Cor 3:9; 6:1; 2 Tim 4:5
         b) Bible study is work, 2 Tim 2:15 (cf. Acts 6:4)

      2) Why can't they get a real life? (1 Cor 9:5)

      3) Evangelists should be funded for their spiritual work, 1 Cor 9:6-14
         a) "The worker is worthy of his support," Matt 10:10 (in the context of itinerant evangelism)
         b) Evangelists should also take care not to become "peddlers of the word," 2 Cor 2:17

   b. Some evangelists are crooks!

      Or… what about the possibility that there are bad evangelists who are fleecing the flock?

      1) Are there not also pastors who are fleecing the flock? Getting paid with no concern for evangelizing?
         a) Not doing the work of an evangelist, 2 Tim 4:5
         b) Nor working in the harvest, to be worthy of wages, Matt 10:10

      2) Note Phil 3:17-4:1:

         "Brethren, join in following my example, and observe those who walk according to the pattern you have in us. For many walk, of whom I often told you, and now tell you even weeping, *that they are* enemies of the cross of Christ, whose end is destruction, whose god is *their* appetite, and *whose* glory is in their shame, who set their minds on earthly things. For our citizenship is in heaven, from which also we eagerly wait for a Savior, the Lord Jesus Christ; who will transform the body of our humble state into conformity with the body of His glory, by the exertion of the power that He has even to subject all things to Himself. Therefore, my beloved brethren whom I long *to see*, my joy and crown, so stand firm in the Lord, my beloved."

         a) Paul sadly aknowledged that there were many false teachers and peddlers, who were leading Christians away

         b) Yet, Paul continued on in the ministry, and told Christians to take note of those who followed in the pattern of his life (cf. Acts 17:2-3)
            (1) So as you have us as an example/type/pattern [καθὼς ἔχετε τύπον ἡμᾶς], Phil 3:17; cf. 1 Thess 1:7; 2 Thess 3:9; 1 Tim 4:12; Tit 2:7
            (2) According to the custom of Paul [κατὰ δὲ τὸ εἰωθὸς τῷ Παύλῳ], Acts 17:2-3

   c. Evangelists travel too much, 2 Cor 11:26

   d. Evangelists don't care about follow-up (or discipleship), Phil 1:22-25:[190]
      1) Isn't the Great Commission to "make disciples" not just "make converts"?[191]
      2) There's a lot more to the Christian life than just winning souls!

   e. Evangelists do more harm than good for the church (cf. 2 Cor 6:3):
      1) He won't make a good appearance for our church, 2 Cor 10:1, 7
      2) He may ruin our image in the community:
         "We've worked real hard to get a good image in this community, we don't want it ruined by handing out tracts or bringing in an evangelist"

   f. Evangelists transfer their spiritual giftedness to all other Christians, expecting them to be soul winners like they are, and making them feel guilty if they are not[192]

---

[190]It is not interesting that "teachers" are not judged because they do not "do follow-up," nor in fact "pastors"! This omission is unusual: (1) being that I have met a number of "teachers" who lack depth of concern about their students, and likewise for "pastors"; and further (2) pastors and teachers have greater responsibility for involvement in follow-up because of the order of the leadership gifts in Eph 4:11.

[191]See Chapter 26, "Follow-up Is Important" (especially the chart on the translation of the verb μαθητεύω in Matt 28:19) and Chapter 10, "The Great Commission" (on the emphasis of the five Great Commission passages).

[192]See C. Peter Wagner quote above.

g. "Most evangelists are monarchianists":
    1) The accusation is that evangelists confuse the work of the three persons of the Trinity—perhaps this is a high church accusation against the power of the Holy Spirit in preaching and converting sinners, since high church Anglicans view that conversion takes place at infant baptism (see my analysis of the Second Council of Orange, Appendix of Chapter 10)
    2) Similarly, it also seems to assume that most evangelists are generally untrained (2 Cor 11:6), and therefore do not have "good theology" (e.g. Acts 4:13; cf. 2 Tim 2:15; 2 Pet 3:16)
    3) The backside of this type of thought is: If evangelists had better training and theology, then they would not be so evangelistically-oriented; they would rather be more tame and subdued, perhaps even sacramentally-oriented

h. Evangelists have codependency issues:[193]

    1) They are codependent on churches and make churches codependent on them:
        a) They make churches, pastors, and lay people codependent upon them to lead people to Christ
        b) They make churches, pastors, and lay people codependent on the need for regular revival services
        c) They make churches, pastors, and lay people codependent on them to reproduce the successes of past generations
        d) They make churches, pastors, and lay people codependent on them financially

    2) Yet, is it not the case that, much like Paul and his antagonists, the superapostles…
        a) The true evangelist is humbly seeking to obey the mandates of the Word of God?
        b) The true evangelist is humbly seeking to persuade lost souls to be saved?
        c) The true evangelist is willing to suffer privation and persecution to advance the gospel?

    3) The accusation of codependency is a mean-spirited attempt to discourage men who are with Christ after the lost!

h. Conclusion: While these reproaches are *not true* for many evangelists, they come with the territory. It is amazing that Paul experienced the same, and that the NT recorded it for us!

Conclusion: Billy Graham and his team prayed against the following four pitfalls by which other evangelists had fallen (for the most part, these fall into the category of ethical behavior):
a. Sexual immorality
b. Exaggeration of numbers
c. Speaking against the Lord's anointed
d. Financial indiscretion
    And God spared Graham and his team from these pitfalls in a ministry that lasted over 70 years—from 1937 to 2018!

Conclusion:

Roger Carswell made the following six recommendations to local churches as regards evangelists in his book, *And Some as Evangelists*:
a. Churches should pray for more evangelists
b. Churches should look for evangelists
c. Churches should train evangelists
d. Churches should use evangelists
e. Churches should pray for evangelists
f. Churches should support evangelists.[194]

---

[193]"Codependency is defined as a psychological condition or a relationship in which a person is controlled or manipulated by another who is affected with a pathological condition (typically narcissism or drug addiction); and in broader terms, it refers to the dependence on the needs of, or control of, another" ("Codependency"; available at: http://en.wikipedia.org/wiki/Codependency; accessed 8 June 2014; Internet).

[194]Roger Carswell, *And Some as Evangelists*, 92-106.

Appendixes for Chapter 3

Comparing the Preaching of a Pastor, Revivalist, and Evangelist

Introduction: There are some biblical and practical differences between the preaching of pastor and that of a travelling evangelist or revivalist (3 of the 5 offices listed in Eph 4:11, i.e. prophet, evangelist, pastor). I have sought to highlight a few of these for the sake of comparison. There seems to be two types or typologies of preaching into which pastors eventually drift, what I call doctrinal and relevant, with possibly a midpoint emphasizing the preaching of application only. These are also included for the sake of comparison.

Categories	Pastor	Revivalist	Evangelist
Itinerancy	Stationary	Travelling	Travelling
Primary Audience	To saved and baptized people (Matt 28:19), hence Matt 28:20 ministry	To saved and baptized people (Matt 28:19), hence Matt 28:20 ministry	Unsaved (and unbaptized) people, hence Matt 28:19 ministry
Primary Content of Sermons	"Teaching them to observe all that I have commanded you," Matt 28:20	Must preach repentance "so as to make ready a people prepared for the Lord" Luke 1:17	Duty-bound to preach repentance: "so as to make ready a people prepared for the Lord" Luke 1:17
	i.e. the whole council of God (Acts 20:27)	Consecration; commitment; and sanctification (cf. Acts 20 sermon)	The Gospel (1 Cor 15:1-8)
Secondary Content of Sermons	The Gospel (1 Cor 15:1-8)	The whole council of God (Acts 20:27)	The whole council of God (Acts 20:27)
Repitition of sermons	Preaches most sermons one time only	Repeats the same sermon multiple times	Repeats the same sermon multiple times
Repitition of illustrations	Can use a good illustration one time	Can repeat a good illustration many times	Can repeat a good illustration many times
Emphasis	Emphasizes exhortation and establishing (see verbs in *Evangelizology*, Chap. 26)	Emphasizes exhorting saved to commitment, holiness, and obedience	Emphasizes evangelizing lost and exhorting saved to evangelism (see verbs in *Evangelizology*, Chap. 7)
Primary sermon type	Often expository and/or doctrinal	Often expository or topical textual	Often topical or topical textual
Primary Response	Saved souls consecrate their lives more fully to Jesus	Saved souls convicted to immediate consecration their lives to Jesus	Lost souls convicted to immediate repentance, saved souls convicted to be involved in soul-winning
Secondary Response	Lost souls convicted to turn to Jesus; saved souls may commit to baptism, membership, a call to the ministry	Lost souls convicted to turn to Jesus; saved souls may commit to baptism, membership, a call to the ministry	Saved souls commit NT baptism, membership in a NT church, or a call to the ministry

Comparing Special Events and Revivals

Introduction: Today there are two tendencies, either comparing or excluding revivals as special events. While similar, this chart compares the similarities and differences, while adding a column for the combination of the two.

Categories	Special Events	Revivals	Revivals with Attractional Events
Emphasis	An attractional event	The preaching of the Gospel	The preaching of the Gospel
Focus	Getting people to come	Decisions for Christ	Decisions for Christ
Result	Public relations efforts for the existence of, location of, staff of, and size of the church	Souls saved and eternal decisions made	Numbers of people coming under the influence of the hearing of the Gospel
Consideration I	Those who appreciate special events (e.g. theatrical events or Block Parties), often decry revivals as irrelevant	Those who plan revivals often have used and do use Special Events to attract people to the revival (including Pizza Blast for youth, hot dog meals for children and families, and the first "Wild Game" suppers for men)	Those who plan revivals often have used and do use Special Events to attract people to the revival (including Pizza Blast for youth, hot dog meals for children and families, and the first "Wild Game" suppers for men)
Consideration II	Whereas special events can be and are planned and executed without any evangelism (such as in selling cars)	It is fairly difficult to conduct a revival without an emphasis on decisions (although some are preached as "Prayer Revivals," "Deeper Life" revivals, or "End Times" conferences)	Seeking to combine the two, revival and special events, necessitates a single-minded purpose for souls, if the events are to remain evangelistic, without morphing into non-evangelistic public relations

CHAPTER 4

Spiritual Passions, and
The Spiritual Battle

Historic and Modern Statements on Initiative Evangelism:

Have biblical Christians been characterized by aggressive evangelism in the past? Yes.

Balthasar Hubmaier (1524, 1525; Doctor of theology turned Reformation Anabaptist, burned alive in 1528):

> I. Every Christian is obliged to give an account of his hope, and therefore his belief, if anyone asks about it. (First Peter 3).
> II. If anyone confessed Christ before men, not fearing them, though they rage as lions, Christ will confess him, in the presence of the Father. (Matt. 10 Mark 8).
> III. With the heart one believes unto righteousness, and with the mouth confession is made unto eternal salvation. (Romans 10).[195]

> Man must, by word and deed, confess and magnify the name and praise of Christ, so that others through us may become holy and blessed. Just as we, through others who have preached Christ to us, have come to faith, and that the kingdom of Christ may be increased.[196]

William Farel (1529, French-Swiss Evangelist, the man who urged Calvin to remain in Geneva):

> The keys to the kingdom of heaven (Luke 11:52; Matt 23:13) are the knowledge of God, the Word of God, the sacred gospel (John 21:24), the shepherd of souls. Man is neither able to grant nor entrust these to another: but God alone gives His Holy Spirit, working the understanding of the Scriptures, sending him forth to preach the sacred gospel (Matt 28:18-20; Mark 16:15; John 20:30-31): to which the one who believes, heaven is opened to him. He is set free, his sins have been pardoned: for by faith his heart is cleansed (Acts 15:8-9), and he is saved. But to him who does not believe, heaven is closed to him (John 3:18), he is bound, his sins are retained: for he does not believe in the name of the Son of God: therefore his sin remains (Matt 23:13-36).[197]

John Calvin (1543, French-Swiss Reformer):

> First, let us be mindful that when we first enter his school, Jesus Christ gives us this lesson: if we are ashamed of him before men, he will likewise be ashamed of us when he appears in his majesty with the angels of God (Luke 9:26). So behold how our Lord is not satisfied if we recognize him in secret, and in our hearts. Rather, he strictly requires that we declare by an outward profession before men that we are his. He does not avow us as of his kingdom except upon this condition. And it is no wonder. For what St. Paul says cannot fail, that as one believeth with the heart unto righteousness, likewise one confesses with the mouth unto salvation (Rom. 10:10). By this he signifies that there can be no true faith before God unless it produces confession before men. In short, our Lord calls us all to confess his name. Whoever draws back from doing so must seek another master.[198]

---

[195]Balthasar Hubmaier, "Conclusions of Balthasar Friedberg, Pastor at Waldshut and a Spiritual Brother of Ulrich Zwingli. They Are Addressed to John Eck at Ingolstadt, but He Forbade Them to Be Examined," from "The Writings of Balthasar Hubmaier," W. O. Lewis, ed., trans by G. D. Davidson (1524; Liberty, MO: Archives, William Jewell College Library), 1:37.

[196]Balthasar Hubmaier, "Summary of the Entire Christian Life," from "The Writings of Balthasar Hubmaier," W. O. Lewis, ed., trans by G. D. Davidson (1525; Liberty, MO: Archives, William Jewell College Library), 1:39.

[197]William Farel, "William Farel's Summary" (trans. by James T. Dennison, Jr.), Chapter XVII, "Concerning the Keys of the Kingdom of Heaven," in James T. Dennison, Jr., ed., *Reformed Confessions of the 16th and 17th Centuries in English Translation*, volume 1: 1523-1552 (Grand Rapids: Reformation Heritage, 2008), 66-67.

[198]John Calvin, "A Shorter Treatise Setting forth what the Faithful Man Must Do when He Is among Papists and He Knows the Truth of the Gospel (1543)," in *Come Out From Among Them: Anti-Nicodemite Writings of John Calvin,* Seth Skolnitsky, trans. (Dallas: Protestant Heritage, 2001), 51-52.

Scriptural Instruction (Anabaptist "First Confession," Amsterdam, 1627):

Therefore the believer, according to the command of Christ, must confess openly before men, to the honor of his Creator and Redeemer, what he believes and experiences in his heart, no matter, what sufferings may result him on that account. He can not do otherwise, for he must hearken unto God more than unto men (Mark 16:16; John 3:11; Rom 10:10; 1:5, 16, 25; Acts 4:19, 20); for the Lord hath said: "Whosoever therefore shall confess me before men, him will I confess before my Father which is in heaven." Matt 10:32; Luke 9:26. John says: "Every spirit that confesseth that Jesus Christ is come in the flesh is of God" (1 John 4:2), and Paul explains: "We having the same spirit of faith, according as it is written, I believed, and therefore I have spoken; we also believe, and therefore we speak (2 Cor 4:13).

That, therefore, oral confession proceeding from sincere faith conduces to salvation, Paul testifies with these words: "If thou shalt confess with thy mouth the Lord Jesus, and shalt believe in thine heart that God raised him from the dead, thou shalt be saved. For with the heart man believeth unto righteousness; and with the mouth confession is made unto salvation" (Rom 10:9, 10).[199]

Richard Baxter (1656, English Puritan):

The work of conversion, of repentance from dead works, and faith in Christ, must be taught first and in a frequent and thorough manner. The stewards of God's household must give to each their portion in their season. We must never go beyond the capacities of our people, nor should we teach Christian maturity to those who have not yet learned the first lesson.[200]

Increase Mather (President, Harvard [1685-1701], stated in 1683):

"There is already a great death upon religion, little more left than a name to live.... Consider we then how much it is dying representing the [very] being of it, by the general failure of **the work of conversion**, whereby only it is that religion is propagated, continued and upheld in being, among any people. As converting doth cease, so does religion die away; though more insensibly, yet most irrecoverably.... How much it is dying, respecting the visible profession and practice of it, partly by the formality of churches, but more by the hypocrisy and apostasy of formal hypocritical professors."[201]

Ludwig von Zinzendorf (n.d., German Pietist and Moravian leader):

"I have but one passion - it is He, it is He alone. The world is the field and the field is the world; and henceforth that country shall be my home where I can be most used in winning souls for Christ."[202]

Gilbert Tennent (1740, son of William Tennent, founder of the Log Cabin School, now Princeton University):

What if some instances could be shown of unconverted ministers being instrumental in convincing persons of their lost state? The thing is very rare and extraordinary. And, for what I know, as many instances may be given of Satan's convincing persons by his temptations. Indeed, it's a kind of chance-medly, both in respect of the father and his children, when any such event happens. And isn't this the reason why a work of conviction and conversion has been so rarely heard of for a long time in the churches till of late, that the bulk of her spiritual guides were stone-blind and stone-dead?[203]

---

[199]Thieleman J. van Braght, *The Bloody Theater or Martyrs Mirror of the Defenseless Christians Who Baptized Only Upon the Confession of Faith, and Who Suffered and Died for the Testimony of Jesus, Their Savior, From the Time of Christ to the Year A.D. 1660*, trans from the Dutch by Joseph Sohm, 2nd English edition (1660; 1837; 1886; Scottdale, PA: Herald Press, 2007), 29.

[200]Richard Baxter, *The Reformed Pastor* (Portland, OR: Multnomah, 1982; based on William Orme's edition of 1920, first edition, 1656), 15. "The work of conversion is the first and most vital part of our ministry. For there are those who are Christian only in name, who have need to be truly 'born again.' ... The next part of the ministry is the upbuilding of those that are truly converted'" (ibid., 73). Baxter even extolled the benefits of personal ministry [evangelism], "Personal ministry is a vital advantage for the conversion of many souls" (ibid., 106), and encouraged church members in personal witness, "(2) Urge them to step out and visit their poor, ignorant neighbors. (3) Urge them to go often to the impenitent and scandalous sinners around them, to deal with them in all possible skill and earnestness" (ibid., 136).

[201]Increase Mather quoted in Isaac Backus, *A History of New England With Particular Reference to the Denomination of Christians Called Baptists,* vols. 1-3, 2nd ed. with notes (1777, 1784, 1796; Newton, MA: Backus Historical Society, 1871; New York: Arno Press and The New York Times, 1969), 1: 458-59.

[202]"Mission quotes," available at: http://www.thebiblechannel.org/Missions_Quotes/missions_quotes.html; accessed 25 Oct 2006.

[203]Gilbert Tennent, "The Danger of Unconverted Ministry"; accessed: 20 Oct 2008; from: http://www.sounddoctrine.net/Classic_Sermons/Gilbert%20Tennent/danger_of_unconverted.htm; Internet.

John Wesley (1740s, Anglican Evangelist, founder of what became the Methodist-Episcopal church):

> You have nothing to do but to save souls. Therefore spend and be spent in this work. And go always, not only to those that want you, but to those that want you most. Observe: It is not your business to preach so many times, and to take care of this or that society; but to save as many souls as you can; to bring as many sinners as you possibly can to repentance, and with all your power to build them up in that holiness without which they cannot see the Lord.[204]

Charles Grandison Finney (1834, from his early writings as an American revivalist):

> "It is the great business on earth of every Christian to save souls. … *Now if you are thus neglecting the MAIN BUSINESS of life, what are you living for?*"[205]

Charles Haddon Spurgeon (1879, English Baptist preacher and statesman):

> "Jesus Christ came not into the world for any of these things, but He came to seek and to save that which was lost; and on the same errand He sent His Church.... The business of the Church is salvation. The minister is to use all means to save some; he is no minister of Christ if this be not the one desire of his heart."[206]

> "They called Mr. Whitfield's chapel at Moorfields, 'The Soul-trap.' Whitefield was delighted, and said he hoped it would always be a soul-trap. Oh, that all our places of worship were soul-traps, and every Christian a fisher of men, each one doing his best, as the fisherman does, by every art and artifice, to catch those he fishes for! Well may we use all means to win so great a prize as a spirit destined for eternal weal or woe. The diver plunges deep to find pearls, and may we accept any labour or hazard to win a soul. Rouse yourselves, my brethren, for this is God-like work, and may the Lord bless you in it."[207]

William Booth (n.d., Founder, Salvation Army):

> "'Not called!' did you say? 'Not heard the call,' I think you should say. Put your ear down to the Bible, and hear him bid you go and pull sinners out of the fire of sin. Put your ear down to the burdened, agonized heart of humanity, and listen to its pitiful wail for help. Go stand by the gates of hell, and hear the damned entreat you to go to their father's house and bid their brothers and sisters, and servants and masters not to come there. And then look Christ in the face, whose mercy you have professed to obey, and tell him whether you will join heart and soul and body and circumstances in the march to publish his mercy to the world."[208]

A. B. Simpson (1880s, Founder, Christian and Missionary Alliance):

> "Let our churches exist for this; Let our ministers preach for this; Let our seminaries and colleges be on fire with this one theme; Let our laborers toil for this; Let our consecrated women sacrifice for this; Let our homes be furnished and our wardrobes be purchased with reference to this; And let the whole army of true hearts prove to the world around and the heavens above that they understand the meaning of the cross of Calvary, the cry of dying souls, and the glory of the Coming Kingdom."[209]

J. Hudson Taylor, speaking about China's unsaved millions (1890s, Founder, China Inland Mission):

> "Do you believe that each unit of these millions is a precious soul? And that 'there is none other name under heaven given amongst men whereby they must be saved' than the name *of Jesus*? Do you believe that He alone is 'the Door of the Sheepfold'; is 'the Way, the truth, and the Life'? that 'no man cometh unto the Father but by Him'? If so, think of the state of these unsaved ones; and solemnly examine yourself in the sight of God, to see whether you are doing *your utmost* to make him known to them."[210]

---

[204]John Wesley, "Charge to His Preachers," in Robert E. Coleman, *"Nothing to Do but to Save Souls"* (Grand Rapids: Zondervan, 1990), 1.

[205]Charles Grandison Finney, *Finney on Revival,* arranged by E. E. Shelhamer (1834, 1839, 1850, 1868; Minneapolis: Bethany House, 1988), 78.

[206]Charles H. Spurgeon, "Soul-Saving Our One Business," in *The Soul-Winner* (Grand Rapids: Eerdmans, 1963), 252-53.

[207]Ibid., 271.

[208]"Mission quotes," available at: http://www.thebiblechannel.org/Missions_Quotes/missions_quotes.html; accessed 25 Oct 2006.

[209]From a plaque on the wall of Crown College, St. Bonifacius, MN.

[210]"Mission quotes," available at: http://www.thebiblechannel.org/Missions_Quotes/missions_quotes.html; accessed 25 Oct 2006.

B. H. Carroll, Founder, Southwestern Baptist Theological Seminary, at the Southern Baptist Convention Meeting in Chatanooga, TN, "Brethren, give me evangelists" (14 May 1906):

"The bedrock of Scripture underlies it. Experience demonstrates its wisdom and feasibility. If the Home Mission Board may employ any man, it may employ evangelists. Altogether, then, with a ring, let us support this measure. If I were the secretary of the board I would come before this body in humility and tears and say: 'Brethren, give me evangelists. Deny not fins to things that must swim against the tide, nor wings to things that must fly against the wind.'"[211]

C. G. Trumbull (1907):

"The successful fisherman embodies the very characteristics which it is the duty for every soul-winner to have,—and that ought to mean every follower of Christ."[212]

L. R. Scarborough (1919 and 1914; Chair of Fire and President, Southwestern Baptist Theological Seminary):

"The divine obligation of soul-winning rests without exception upon every child of God."[213]

"The churches which do not constantly seek to win men to a saving knowledge of the truth and enlist them in Christ's service have missed the mark of the divine purpose and requirement. Soul-winning is the main task of every organization claiming to be the church of Christ."[214]

"It is not wise to say that *soul winning* is the main thing or that *soul building* is the main thing. They are Siamese twins of God's gospel, going hand in hand, and they ought to keep up with each other.... And this leads me to say that the main thing in the Kingdom of God is the evangelistic spirit, the martial note and conquest tread."[215]

W. B. Riley (1916 and 1914; Pastor, First Baptist Church, Minneapolis, and Founder of Northwestern Bible College):

"Other things are important; this thing is absolutely necessary.... But the indispensable thing is that the soul be saved."[216]

"Every true convert to Christ is a commissioned evangelist.... The method of the Wesleyans was in perfect accord with the prescription of the Word; and was equally adapted to the eighteenth, nineteenth, or twentieth century—'All at it: always at it'—every convert to Christ a commissioned Evangelist."[217]

George Truett (1917; Pastor, First Baptist church, Dallas, Texas):

"Oh, my fellow Christians, let us see to it that you and I, like Andrew, do our best to win people to Christ! What argument shall I marshal to get us to do that thing right now, and to do that thing as we never did it before, and to get us to do that thing these passing days, linking our lives with God with a devotion, and giving ourselves with a humility and personal appeal, such as we never knew before? What great arguments shall I marshal to get us to do that right now? Shall I talk about duty? Then this is our first duty. And what great word that word duty is! Robert E. Lee was right, that matchless man of the South, when he wrote to his son saying: 'Son, the great word is duty.' Shall I talk about duty? My fellow Christians, your duty and mine, primal, fundamental, preeminent, supreme, tremendously urgent, is that we shall tell these around us that we want them saved."[218]

---

[211]B. H. Carroll, "Shall the Atlanta Board Be Instructed to Employ Evangelists and to Call for an Extra $25,000 for Their Support?" *Baptist Standard* (31 May 1906) 14:1-2; cited in Charles S. Kelley, Jr., *How Did They Do It? The Story of Southern Baptist Evangelism* (New Orleans: Insight, 1993), 14.

[212]Charles G. Trumbull, *Taking Men Alive: Studies in the Principles and Practise of Individual Soul-Winning* (New York: The International Committee of the YMCA, 1907; 1915), 13.

[213]L. R. Scarborough, *With Christ After the Lost* (Nashville: Broadman, 1919, 1952), 2.

[214]Ibid., 62.

[215]L. R. Scarborough, *Recruits for World Conquest* (New York: Revell, 1914), 58.

[216]W. B. Riley, *The Perennial Revival* (Philadelphia: American Baptist, 1916), 35.

[217]W. B. Riley, *The Crisis of the Church* (New York: Charles C. Cook, 1914), 79, 80.

[218]George W. Truett, *Quest for Souls* (New York: Doran, 1917), 72.

J. E. Conant (1922):

"The main work of the whole Church in the whole world throughout the whole Age is witnessing to the salvation there is in Christ. Anything outside of this forfeits the promised presence and blessing of him who said, 'Lo, I am with you all the days, even unto the consummation of the Age.'"[219]

C. E. Matthews (1949; Secretary of Evangelism, HMB of the SBC):

"[Without mass or personal evangelism] The church quits majoring on the saving of souls and places chief emphasis on fellowship and social service, leaving the lost in the community to die in their sins."[220]

Roland Q. Leavell (1951; President, New Orleans Baptist Theological Seminary):

"The Great Commission is the *Magna Charta* of evangelism. It is the marching order of the supreme Commander. It is the proclamation of the King of kings to all his kingdom citizens. It is Christ's imperative for all who name his name."[221]

Malla Moe (n.d., missionary to South Africa with the Scandinavian Alliance Mission, renamed the Evangelical Alliance Mission [TEAM]):

"What are we here for, to have a good time with Christians or to save sinners?"[222]

Robert G. Lee (1960s; Pastor, Bellevue Baptist church, Memphis, TN, and President of the SBC):

"McCary: Dr. Lee, what in your opinion is the number one task of the church? Lee: I believe it is to win people to faith in the Lord Jesus Christ. Dr. Conwell of 'Acres of Diamonds' said that whenever a church calls a pastor who doesn't preach to save souls, or elects a deacon who doesn't work to save souls, or selects a teacher who doesn't teach to save souls, or admits to the choir anybody who sings without any desire to save souls—that church fails by that much to have the approval of God. In bringing men to Jesus we should be compassionate crusaders, not gay tourists. Fishing for men is the greatest business in the entire universe. We must look on the business of rescuing the unsaved as being as important as getting a doctor for a sick child when it is desperately ill; as serious a matter as getting out the fire department when the house is on fire; as imperatively necessary as administering the antidote when poison is in the stomach. We must believe that we are engaged in the greatest work that ever moved God's heart or any human heart in compassion. We must believe that it is the most important work that ever moved God's arm in power or sent a man's feet on Christian visitation—as well as the greatest work that ever laid claim upon the talents, education and abilities of Christians everywhere.

"Dr. Lyman Beecher once was asked what he considered the greatest thing a human being could do. He replied, 'The greatest thing a human being can do is to bring another human being to Jesus as Saviour. Saving souls was the life passion of Jesus. The redemption of poor sinners was more to Him than the glory He had with God before the world was. Soul saving was the only business big enough to bring Jesus out of the ivory palaces of heaven and into this world of woe and wickedness; to bring Him from the heights of deity to the depths of humanity. A winner of souls has the biggest job in the world.'"[223]

Billy Graham (1947, 1953, 1955, 1957, 1966, Southern Baptist Evangelist):

"God's purpose for you and me after we have been converted is that we be witnesses to his saving grace and power. Are you a daily and constant witness? Are you one of God's minutemen? Are you a commando for Christ? *He expects you to witness at every given opportunity.*"[224]

"*The church is for the spreading of the Gospel.* The church is commanded to "Go ye into all the world and preach the gospel" and to baptize those who believe. *The basic and primary mission of the church is to proclaim Christ to the lost.* The need of the world today is sending forth its S.O.S., asking the church to come to its help. The world is being overwhelmed by social, moral, and economic problems. Its people are going

---

[219]Conant, *Every-Member Evangelism*, 29.

[220]C. E. Matthews, *The Southern Baptist Program of Evangelism* (Atlanta: Home Mission Board of the Southern Baptist Convention, 1949), 9.

[221]Roland Q. Leavell, *Evangelism: Christ's Imperative Commission* (Nashville: Broadman, 1951), 3.

[222]"Mission quotes," available at: http://www.thebiblechannel.org/Missions_Quotes/missions_quotes.html; accessed 25 Oct 2006.

[223]"Interview with the Prince of Preachers, Dr. Robert G. Lee" (Studio Hall, CA: World Literature Crusade, n.d.), 6-7. Interviewed by its founder and president, Dr. Jack McAlister.

[224]Billy Graham, "Retreat! Stand! Advance!" *Calling Youth to Christ* (Grand Rapids: Zondervan, 1947), 44 (emphasis mine).

down, swept under the waves of crime and shame. The world needs Christ. The mission of the church is to throw the lifeline to the perishing sinners everywhere."[225]

"There are many others that are slothful about witnessing for Christ. How long has it been since you spoke to a soul about Christ? How long has it been since you won another person to a saving knowledge of Jesus Christ? There are scores of people that you contact every day that need the Saviour, and yet not one word has ever escaped your lips trying to win them to know Christ. You are guilty of the sin of slothfulness, and others will be lost because you are guilty of this sin."[226]

"I say this. I that if you are not witnessing for Christ and if you do not have a burning evangelistic fervor within your soul, it could be a sign that you have never repented of sin and have never been born again, because when you are born again of the Holy Spirit, Christ comes to live within you and when Christ lives within you there is that compassion and that fervency and that desire to win others to a knowledge of Jesus Christ."[227]

"This book will convince the reader that the primary responsibility of the Church in our time is that of evangelism, and that the related ministries of the Church, important as they are, are designed to support and advance the blessings and benefits of the Gospel of the risen Lord Jesus Christ."[228]

Bailey Smith (1978, Southern Baptist Evangelist and revivalist):

"It is sadly true that most Christians never win another soul to Christ. They are apparently not too impressed with the idea that the Gospel is good news for surely if they believed that they couldn't keep from telling it. No Christian, irrespective of his other gifts, is exempt from being a verbal witness for Christ."[229]

"J. T. Packard says, 'Every Christian, therefore, has a God-given obligation to make known the Gospel of Christ. And every Christian who declares the Gospel message to any fellow-man does so as Christ's ambassador and representative, according to the terms of the Great Commission.
"Let me repeat the too-often-forgotten truth. Witnessing is every Christian's responsibility. Escape cannot be found in some other achievement in Christian service. Oh, dear Christian, get hot on the trail for the souls of men."[230]

W. A. Criswell (1980, Pastor, First Baptist church, Dallas, TX, and Founder of Criswell College):

"The pastor is to win souls to Jesus. If the pastor is under authority to do the work of an evangelist, then he must do the same thing; namely, he must use his church organization to win the lost. To what better use could they be dedicated? And what a powerful instrument for witnessing the pastor has in the marching members of his many-faceted ministry through the church. The way the church is put together is inherently, intrinsically made for soul-winning, for reaching people." [231]

Roy Fish (2006, Professor of Evangelism, Southwestern Baptist Theological Seminary):

"Churches exist for evangelism like fire exists for burning."[232]

Luis Palau (2006, Evangelist):

"I believe evangelism is the main work of the Church of Jesus Christ. I've debated that point with many good friends, including one of my mentors, who believed that if you build up the local church and worship right on Sunday morning, emphasizing solid biblical exposition, the people will automatically give witness to their faith at work and around the community come Monday.
"At the World Congress on Evangelism in Berlin in 1966, one of evangelical Christianity's most respected statesmen said, 'Evangelism happens when the people walk with God.' But 30 years of experience tells me that it doesn't work that way. I know great worshipping people who just don't share their faith, and godly men and

---

[225]Billy Graham, *Peace with God* (Minneapolis: Grason, 1953, 1984), 185 (emphasis mine).

[226]Billy Graham, "Slothfulness," in *Freedom from the Seven Deadly Sins* (Grand Rapids: Zondervan, 1955), 94-95.

[227]Billy Graham, "The World Need and Evangelism," in C. Wade Freeman, *The Doctrine of Evangelism* (Nashville: Baptist General Convention of Texas, 1957), 29-30.

[228]Billy Graham, "Preface," in Paulus Scharpff, *History of Evangelism* (Grand Rapids: Eerdmans, 1966), vii.

[229]Bailey Smith, *Real Evangelism* (Nashville: Broadman, 1978), 161.

[230]Ibid., 162.

[231]W.A. Criswell, *Criswell's Guidebook for Pastors* (Nashville, TN; Broadman Press, 1980), 227, 233.

[232]Roy Fish, "What Has Happened to the Fire?" Sermon preached at Lifeway Ridgecrest Conference Center, Fire Mountain, NC, 31 July 2006.

women for whom evangelism never happens. If evangelism happened naturally, the Lord wouldn't have repeatedly commanded it. Evangelism must stay the priority for us to continue to work for Christ."[233]

Mark Cahill (2002, Evangelist):

"Oswald J. Smith said, 'Oh my friends, we are loaded down with countless church activities, while the real work of the church, that of evangelizing the world and winning the lost, is almost entirely neglected!' Don't neglect the call of the church to reach the lost. As one preacher put it, 'God's top priority is the salvation of every single soul.' We should desire to be used by God in what really matters to His heart."[234]

But I believe that one of the greatest sins believers can commit is not to tell the unsaved about the only thing that can save them. Jesus told the woman caught in adultery, 'Go, and sin no more' (John 8:11). As a believer, you know that God hates sin, so please, 'go, and sin no more' by making sure you tell everyone you encounter about Jesus."[235]

Are these views of the centrality of evangelism relics from the past, or do they flow supernaturally from the Word of God? Are these views the result of the culture of the author? In answer to these questions, I commend to you the Spiritual Passions and the Urgencies of Evangelism.

---

[233]Luis Palau, "Nothing Is More Important," in Luis Palau and Timothy Robnett, *Telling the Story: Evangelism for the Next Generation* (Ventura, CA: Gospel Light, 2006), 106-07.

[234]Mark Cahill, *One Thing You Can't Do in Heaven* (Rockwall, TX: Biblical Discipleship, 2002, 2005), 48.

[235]Ibid., 208-09.

The Spiritual Passions

A. A Passion for the Word of God:

1. Luther on the Bible—we will note the Bible on the Bible below!

    a. The Primacy of the Word of God as Absolute Authority, *Pagan Servitude of the Church* (1520):

    > "As we have said, God never has dealt, and never does deal, with mankind at any time otherwise than by the word of promise. Neither can we, on our part, ever have to do with God otherwise than through faith in his word and promise....
    >
    > "For anyone readily understands that these two, promise and faith, are necessarily yoked together."[236]

    b. The Hearing of Faith, *Commentary on Galatians* (Gal 3:1-5 [twice, ἐξ ἀκοῆς πίστεως];
        cf. Heb 2:1-3; 3:7-8, 14-17; 4:2-3, 7-13; Rom 1:5, "unto the obedience [which comes from
        hearing] of faith" [εἰς ὑπακοὴν πίστεως]):

    > "A man therefore is made a Christian, not by working, but by hearing: wherefore he that will exercise himself to righteousness, must first exercise himself in hearing the Gospel....
    >
    > "My adversaries think that faith, whereby we receive the Holy Ghost, is a light matter: but how high and hard a matter it is, I myself do find by experience, and so do all they which with me do earnestly embrace the same....
    >
    > "The faithful do find by their own experience, how gladly they would hold and embrace the Word when they hear it, with a full faith, and abandon the opinion of the law and of their own righteousness..."[237]

    c. "The Outward Word," *Smalcald Articles* and the *Larger Catechism:*

    > "And in those things which concern the spoken, outward Word, we must firmly hold that God grants His Spirit or grace to no one, except through or with the preceding outward Word, in order that we may [thus] be protected against the enthusiasts, i.e., spirits who boast that they have the Spirit without and before the Word, and accordingly judge Scripture or the spoken Word, and explain and stretch it at their pleasure, as Muenzer did, and many still do at the present day, who wish to be acute judges between the Spirit and the letter, and yet know not what they say or declare. For [indeed] the Papacy also is nothing but sheer enthusiasm, by which the Pope boasts that all rights exist in the shrine of his heart, and whatever he decides and commands with [in] his church is spirit and right, even though it is above and contrary to Scripture and the spoken Word.... Without the outward Word, however, they were not holy, much less would the Holy Ghost have moved them to speak when they still were unholy [or profane]; for they were holy, says he, since the Holy Ghost spake through them."[238]

    Also:

    > "For the Word of God is the sanctuary above all sanctuaries, yea, the only one which we Christians know and have. For though we had the bones of all the saints or all holy and consecrated garments upon a heap, still that would help us nothing; for all that is a dead thing which can sanctify nobody. But God's Word is the treasure which sanctifies everything, and by which even all the saints themselves were sanctified. At whatever hour then, God's Word is taught, preached, heard, read or meditated upon, there the person, day, and work are sanctified thereby, not because of the external work, but because of the Word which makes saints of us all. Therefore I constantly say that all our life and work must be ordered according to God's Word, if it is to be God-pleasing or holy. Where this is done, this commandment is in force and being fulfilled....
    >
    > "Now, they are so mad as to separate faith and that to which faith clings and is bound though it be something external. Yea, it shall and must be something external, that it may be apprehended by the

---

[236]Martin Luther, "Pagan Servitude of the Church," in John Dillenberger, *Martin Luther: Selections from His Writings Edited and with Introduction* (Garden City, NY: Doubleday, Anchor, 1961), 277.

[237]Martin Luther, *A Commentary on St. Paul's Epistle to the Galatians Based on Lectures Delivered at the University of Wittenberg in the Year 1531*. Based on the 'Middleton' edition of the English version of 1575 (Westwood, NJ: Revell, n.d.), 211.

[238]Martin Luther, "Of Confession," Smalcald Articles, Part 3, Section 8 [on-line], accessed 11 October 2001, available from http://www.frii.com/~gosplow/ smalcald.html#smc-03h; Internet.

senses, and understood and thereby be brought into the heart, as indeed the entire Gospel is an external, verbal preaching."[239]

Conclusion: Several Pertinent Questions about Luther:

    a. Was Luther' approach to the Bible on salvation biblical? Yes, as we shall show below.

    b. Do Luther's thoughts on this topic parallel those of Baptist Confessions? Yes.[240]

    c. How do Luther's emphases impact personal evangelism?
        1) The Primacy of the Word
        2) The Hearing of Faith
        3) The Outward Word as a hermeneutical principle.

2. Summary of Psalm 119 on Biblical Authority:

Introduction:

"In our German version it has an appropriate inscription, "The Christian's golden A B C of praise, love, power, and use of the word of God;" for here we have set forth in inexhaustible fullness what the word of God is to a man, and how a man is to behave in relation to it."[241]

    a. God's Word is eternal:
        a) Psa 119:89, 144, 152, 160
        b) Psa 119:160, "The sum of Thy word is truth, And every one of Thy righteous ordinances is everlasting."

    b. God's Word is righteous/right/upright:
        a) From *tsedeq*: Psa 119:62, 75, 106, 123, 138, 144, 160, 164
        b) From *yashar*: Psa 119:128, 137
        c) Psa 119:137-138, "Righteous art Thou, O Lord, And upright (*yashar*) are Thy judgments. Thou hast commanded Thy testimonies in righteousness (*tsedeq*) And exceeding faithfulness."

    c. God's Word is truth:
        a) Psa 119:43, 142, 151, 160
        b) Psa 119:160, "The sum of Thy word is truth, And every one of Thy righteous ordinances is everlasting."

    d. God's Word is faithful:
        a) Psa 119:86, "All Thy commandments are faithful; They have persecuted me with a lie."
        b) Psa 119:138, "Thou hast commanded Thy testimonies in righteousness And exceeding faithfulness."

---

[239]Martin Luther, "Larger Catechism," from: ttp://www.iclnet.org/pub/resources/text/wittenberg/ wittenberg-luther.html#sw-lc; accessed 19 October 2001; Internet.

[240]"Second London Confession (1677), Chap 20, Of the Gospel, and of the extent of the Grace thereof.

"I. THE Covenant of Works being broken by Sin, and made unprofitable unto Life; God was pleased to give forth the promise of *Christ,* the Seed of the Woman, as the means of calling the Elect, and begetting in them Faith and Repentance; in this Promise, the Gospel, as to the substance of it, was revealed, and therein Effectual, for the Conversion and Salvation of Sinners.

"2. This Promise of *Christ,* and Salvation by him, is revealed only by the Word of God; neither do the Works of Creation, or Providence, with the light of Nature, make discovery of *Christ,* or of *Grace* by him; so much as in a general, or obscure way; much less that men destitute of the Revelation of him by the Promise, or Gospel; should be enabled thereby, to attain saving Faith, or Repentance.

"3. The Revelation of the Gospel unto Sinners, made in divers times, and by sundry parts; with the addition of Promises, and Precepts for the Obedience required therein, as to the Nations, and Persons, to whom it is granted, is meerly of the Soveraign Will and good Pleasure of God; not being annexed by vertue of any Promise, to the due improvement of mens natural abilities, by vertue of Common light received without it; which none ever did make, or can so do: And therefore in all Ages the preaching of the Gospel bath been granted unto persons and Nations, as to the extent, or streightning of it, in great variety, according to the Councell of the Will of God.

"4. Although the Gospel be the only outward means, of revealing *Christ,* and saving Grace; and is, as such, abundantly sufficient thereunto; yet that men who are dead in Trespasses, may be born again, Quickened or Regenerated; there is morover necessary, an effectual, insuperable work of the Holy *Spirit,* upon the whole Soul, for the producing in them a new spiritual Life; without which no other means will effect their Conversion unto God." (William L. Lumpkin, *Baptist Confessions of Faith,* rev. ed. [Valley Forge: Judson, 1959, 1969]).

[241]C. F. Keil and Franz Delitzsch, *Commentary on the Psalms* (Grand Rapids: Eerdmans, 1986), 5:3:243.

B. The Spiritual Passions and Evangelism:

Introduction:

    a.   Jesus said that "we cannot serve two masters," Matt 6:24

    b.   Alexander I. Solzhenitsyn wrote, "There is no room in us for two passions."[242]

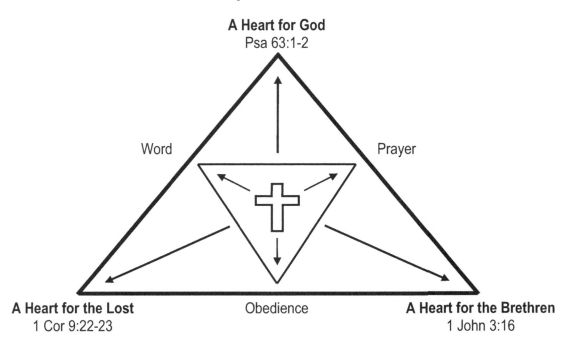

The Spiritual Passions

1.   Christ is the center:
    a. A passion to know Christ, Phil 3:8-10
    b. He is the focus, Rom 8:29, Heb 12:1-2
    c. We must abide in Him, John 15:1-8, 1 John 2:27-28

2.   Three central passions to Christian growth:

    a. A passion for the Word, 1 Pet 2:2
        1) An intense searching in the Word, Prov 2:1-9 (Psa 119:82)
        2) Developing a heart for the Word, Psa 119:71-72
        3) The goal: a passion for the Word, Psa 119:40, 97, 105, 131, 147-148

    b. A passion for Prayer, John 15:7
        1) Seeking the Lord in Prayer, Deut 4:29, Jer 29:12-13

    c. A Passion for Obedience, 1 John 2:3
        1) The importance of obedience in the Old Testament, Deut 4:1-2, 5, 14, 40, Jos. 1:8, Psa 103:18, 119:57, 60 (see Jos. 8:35, 11:15 for examples of obedience)
        2) The importance of obedience in the New Testament, John 3:36, 14:21, 1 John 2:3-6, 5:2, 2 John 6, Rev 2:5, 26, 3:10 (Christ as an example of obedience, Luke 2:51, Heb 5:7-10)

    d. Complimentary passions:
        1) A passion for salvation, Psa 119:81
        2) A passion for righteousness, Matt 5:6

---

[242]Alexander I. Solzhenitsyn, *The First Circle* (San Francisco: Harper and Row, 1966), 236.

3. Growing in these spiritual passions:

   a. A heart for God, Psa 63:1-2
     1) Drawing near to God, Jms 4:8
     2) Seeking God, I Chr 16:10-11, 2 Chr 7:14, Isa 55:6-7, Jer 29:12
     3) A thirsting for God, Psa 42:1-2, 63:1-2, 143:6, Isa 55:1-2, John 4:13-14
     4) Desiring nothing but God, Psa 73:25
     5) An intense love for God, Deut 6:5, Matt 22:36-37
     6) A fear of God, 2 Cor 5:11, 7:1, 1 Pet 2:17 (cf. Jer 2:19)

   b. A heart for the lost, 1 Cor 9:19-23 (cf. Phil 3:18-19):[243]
     1) Following God's example, John 3:16, Rom 5:8
     2) Obeying God, Mark 1:17, 16:15
     3) Following Paul's example (e.g. 1 Cor 11:1), 1 Cor 9:19-23, Col 1:28-29

   c. A heart for the brethren, 1 John 3:16[244]
     1) Learning to care for the brethren, 1 Thess 5:11
     2) "Through love serve one another," Gal 5:13
     3) Giving one's life for the brethren, John 15:12-13, 1 John 3:16
     4) Applying all one's efforts, Col 1:28-29

4. Evaluative Thoughts:
   a. Which passion coincides with the Great Commission mandate?
   b. Which passion coincides with the calling of the disciples to be (1) "fishers of men," Mat 4:19; Mark 1:17; or (2) "taking men alive," Luke 5:10?

---

[243]This attitude is often exemplified in vibrant growth periods in the history of the churches. John Knox said, "Give me Scotland or I die!" John Wesley said, "The world is my parish." William Booth said, "My ambition is the souls of men!" Jim Elliot wrote, "I want to be a fork in the road of every man for or against Christ" [my paraphrase].

[244]For greater depth in the Christian's attitudes toward his brothers, please see in T. Johnston, *Mindset*, Chap 11, II.D., "The Special Dimension of Christian Relationships."

The Spiritual Battle

Introduction—Reality Therapy:

A. Sharing Christ is stressful!

Consider that the Apostle Paul wrote of the stress he experienced related to the efforts he exerted in obeying Christ's Great Commission:
> "To this present hour we are both hungry and thirsty, and are poorly clothed, and are roughly treated, and are homeless." 1 Cor 4:11
> "Why are we also in danger every hour?" 1 Cor 15:30.

B. Sharing Christ is inconvenient!

C. Sharing Christ is time consuming!

D. Sharing Christ takes effort and is difficult!

> "Individual soul-winning is not easy work. It is hard. It is the hardest work that God asks us to do for Him. Before trying to reason out why, or to argue that the simple extending to a fellow-man of an invitation to share with us the richest joy in our life *ought* to be an easy thing to do, let us frankly admit that it is hard, and face the fact to begin with.
> "For any one who has ever tried the work knows this. Even those whose profession and only life-business is soul-saving find it difficult. Ask any minister-friend which is easier for him to do: to preach a sermon, or to seek an opportunity to talk alone with an individual about that one's spiritual welfare. …
> "Bossuet, the great French preacher, said frankly as to this very matter: "It requires more faith and courage to say two words face to face with one single sinner, than from the pulpit rebuke two or three thousand persons, ready to listen to everything, on the condition of forgetting it all."[245]

E. Sharing Christ brings persecution!

But Also...

F. Sharing Christ brings joy and peace in the Christian life!

G. Sharing Christ brings gratitude for what Christ has done for us (cf. Philemon 6, NIV)!

H. Sharing Christ gives the Christian purpose!

Luis Palau wrote…

> "After all, the number one responsibility of the Christian is not to retire young in order to spend endless hours chasing a little white golf ball. If only people would get as excited about building the kingdom of God as they do about their handicap on the golf course.
> "Yes, evangelism is spiritual warfare. In evangelism, we engage Satan nose to nose and try to steal his prey. So we should expect a few doors slammed in our face and more severe attacks on ourselves and our families.
> "But there's near ecstatic joy in obeying the Lord. A few inconveniences such as cynicism, rejection and, yes, even imprisonment only seemed to heighten the happiness of Jesus' first-century followers.
> "'As soon as ever you have won a soul, you won't care about any of the other things,' Moody said. There's no greater thrill than giving out the gospel and leading people into the eternal kingdom of God Almighty. So give evangelism all you've got. This life is your only chance."[246]

I. The Spiritual Battle and Proclamation:

Introduction: Knowledge that we are in a spiritual battle. When we are born into the world, we enter a spiritual battlefield. The Bible clearly describes the battle, as well as the weapons, the tactics and the casualties of war. This is the sobering arena into which evangelism comes to wage war against the Prince of the power of the air.

A. The spiritual battle explained:
1. Eph 6:10-20
2. 2 Cor 10:3-5

---

[245]Charles G. Trumbull, *Taking Souls Alive,* 42-43.
[246]Luis Palau, "Nothing Is More Important," 114.

B. Aspects of the spiritual battle:
1. The focus of the spiritual battle is the bold proclamation of the Gospel, Eph 6:19-20; Phil 1:14, 18
2. God even turns imprisonment into progress for the Gospel, Phil 1:12
3. The bold proclamation of the Gospel has opponents, Phil 1:28, (notice that opposition to the Gospel was why Paul was in prison)

C. Admonitions for spiritual battle:
1. Living worthy of the Gospel, Phil 1:27-28
2. Unity in the fight, Phil 1:27; 4:2-3
3. Don't be alarmed by opponents, Phil 1:28
4. Not fearing the edict of the king, Heb 11:23 (but rather fearing God, Luke 12:4-5)

II. The Spiritual Battle and Instantaneous Conversion:

A. The bold proclamation of the Gospel is inseparably linked with instantaneous conversion, Col 1:13-14; Eph 2:4-10

B. The kingdom of darkness explained, Eph 2:1-3

C. Transfer into the kingdom of light, Col 1:13-14

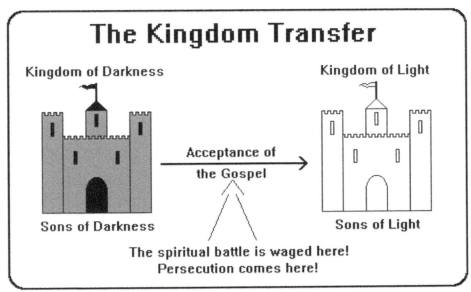

III. Nuts and Bolts of the Spiritual Battle:

A. The focus of the spiritual battle:
1. The Knowledge of God, 2 Cor 10:5
2. Submission to God, Psa 2:1-3, cf. pride, 1 John 2:15-17
3. Submission to the Word of God, 1 John 4:6

B. The relation of evangelism to the spiritual battle:
1. Evangelism brings knowledge of God, preaches submission to God and submission to the Word of God.
2. The Gospel, when accepted, causes the individual to be brought out of the kingdom of darkness into the kingdom of light, Col 1:13-14 (cf. Luke 10:18)
3. All heaven rejoices at the repentance of one man, Luke 15:7.

C. The kingdom transfer:
1. Satan, the enemy of our souls, dislikes this transfer more than anything, because it lessens his grip on the lives of people and allows the atonement of Christ to be effective in another life.
2. Satan, the adversary of the Christian (1 Pet 5:8-9), seeks to hinder the testimony of the Christian in any way he can, 2 Cor 10:4-5:
   a. Through sin—rendering the servant of God ineffective

b. Through false teaching—adding to or subtracting from the Gospel

c. Through discouragement and fear, Acts 18:9-10

IV. The Enemy's Playbook:

A. Notice some Satanic methods of stopping Christians from evangelizing:[247]

Introduction:
The general term, "plots of the Jews" [ταῖς ἐπιβουλαῖς τῶν Ἰουδαίων], Acts 20:19 (cf. Acts 9:24; 20:3; 23:30)
Leading to, "trials" [πειρασμῶν], Acts 20:19

1. Accusing of and arresting evangelists for disturbing the peace, Acts 4:2; 5:28; 16:20; 24:5 (cf. Luke 23:14, "as one who incites the people to rebellion"; Acts 16:36):[248]
Acts 24:5, "For we have found this man [Paul] a real pest and a fellow who stirs up dissension among all the Jews throughout the world, and a ringleader of the sect of the Nazarenes."
Pest = Gk. ὁ λοιμός; Lat. *pestiferum*
Stirs up (GK. κινέω; Lat. *concitantem*); dissension (Gk. ἡ στάσις; Lat. *seditiones*)
Ringleader = Gk. ὁ πρωτοστάτης; Lat. *auctorem seditionis*
Sect = Gk ai;resij; Lat. *sectae*

2. Accusing evangelist of perverting (διαστρέφω) the people with their teaching, Luke 23:2

3. Persecuting and forcing the evangelist to leave town, Acts 13:50; 14:5-6

4. Denying any miracles, Acts 4:16, or beginning to worship the person doing the miracle, Acts 14:11-12

5. Making evangelism illegal, Acts 4:17-18 (notice the use of the word "speak" [both λαλέω and φθέγγομαι in this passage]; cf. 1 Thess 2:14-16)

6. Sending impostors [literally, those "who feign themselves as righteous men", ὑποκρινομένους ἑαυτοὺς δικαίους εἶναι] to track the evangelist and betray him, Luke 20:20[249]

---

[247]See also Chapter 3, "The Gift of the Evangelist and Revival," Section F, "Some Common Reproaches against Evangelists."

[248]"Those among them that have not yet accepted the Christian religion do not restrain others from it or abuse the converts to it. While I was there, only one man among the Christians was punished. This newly baptized convert, in spite of all our advice, was preaching in public on the Christian worship more zealously than wisely. He grew so heated that he not only put our worship before all others, but condemned all other rites as profane and loudly denounced their celebrants as wicked and impious men fit for hell fire. After he had been preaching these things for a long time, they seized him. They convicted him not on a charge of disparaging their religion, but of arousing public disorder among the people, and sentenced him to exile" (Thomas More [Lord Chancellor of England, 1529-1532], *Utopia* [1516; Arlington Heights, IL: AHM Publishing, 1949], 71).

Almost 200 years later, Claude Brousson was condemned to be stretched on a wheel and put to death for disturbing the peace. His arrest warrant read as follows: "Being informed that the named Brousson continues to inspire a spirit of revolt among the people, and brings as many as possible to contradict the orders of the King [by converting them to the Reformed faith], which merits that he be punished as a disturber of the public peace [lit. *Perturbater du répos public*]" (From copy of official paper, in Walter C. Utt and Brian E. Strayer, *The Bellicose Dove: Claude Brousson and Protestant Resistance to Louis XIV, 1647-1698* [Brighton, Great Britain: University of Sussex, 2002], inside cover; translation mine).

[249]Consider the "councils of vigilance" promulgated by Pius X in his *Pascendi Dominici Gregis*: "We decree, therefore, that in every diocese a council of this kind, which We are pleased to name the 'Council of Vigilance,' be instituted without delay. The priests called to form part in it shall be chosen somewhat after the manner above prescribed for the censors, and they shall meet every two months on an appointed day in the presence of the Bishop.

7. Accusations of libel and intolerance due to evangelism, Acts 6:8-15

8. Accusing of and arresting evangelists for insubordination to government and insurrection, Acts 5:28; 16:20-21 (cf. Luke 23:2)

9. Mixing Christianity with other religions (syncretism), Acts 14:8-13

10. Creating riots due to spiritism, Acts 16:16-21

11. Instilling fear due to past persecution, Acts 18:9-10

12. Arresting indigenous people [men of peace] who take in the evangelists, Acts 17:6

13. Creating copycats who are in it for their own glory, Acts 19:13-16 (e.g. pseudo-Christian cults, such as the Mormons, Jehovah's Witnesses, Children of God, etc.)

14. Creating riot—due to economic loss and the possible discrediting of illicit business, Acts 19:23-27

15. Creating social unrest due to potential loss of a religious monopoly, majority, or superiority, Acts 17:27-28; 24:6

16. Seizing the property of Christians due to evangelism, Heb 10:32-34[250]

17. Forcing exile because of the Gospel, Rev 1:9; cf. Acts 18:2

18. Getting the evangelist sidetracked on vain and worldly discussions, requiring some special "knowledge," 1 Tim 6:20-21
     1 Tim 6:20-21, "O Timothy, guard what has been entrusted to you, avoiding worldly *and* empty chatter *and* the opposing arguments of what is falsely called 'knowledge'—which some have professed and thus gone astray from the faith. Grace be with you."

B. Further methods of Satan:
   1. Deceiving—He is the great deceiver, Rev 12:9; 13:14; cf. 2 Tim 2:13
   2. Lying—He is the father of lies, John 8:44

They shall be bound to secrecy as to their deliberations and decisions, and in their functions shall be included the following: they shall watch most carefully for every trace and sign of Modernism both in publications and in teaching, and to preserve the clergy and the young from it they shall take all prudent, prompt, and efficacious measures" (Pius X, *Pascendi Dominici Gregis*: Encyclical on the Doctrine of the Modernists, 8 Sept 1907; available at: http://www.newadvent.org/docs/pi10pd.htm (online); accessed 2 Dec 2002; Internet).

[250]"We excommunicate and anathematize every heresy raising itself up against this holy, orthodox and catholic faith which we have expounded above. We condemn all heretics, whatever names they may go under. They have different faces indeed but their tails are tied together inasmuch as they are alike in their pride. Let those condemned be handed over to the secular authorities present, or to their bailiffs, for due punishment. Clerics are first to be degraded from their orders. The goods of the condemned are to be confiscated, if they are lay persons, and if clerics they are to be applied to the churches from which they received their stipends. Those who are only found suspect of heresy are to be struck with the sword of anathema, unless they prove their innocence by an appropriate purgation, having regard to the reasons for suspicion and the character of the person. Let such persons be avoided by all until they have made adequate satisfaction. If they persist in the excommunication for a year, they are to be condemned as heretics. Let secular authorities, whatever offices they may be discharging, be advised and urged and if necessary be compelled by ecclesiastical censure, if they wish to be reputed and held to be faithful, to take publicly an oath for the defence of the faith to the effect that they will seek, in so far as they can, to expel from the lands subject to their jurisdiction all heretics designated by the church in good faith. Thus whenever anyone is promoted to spiritual or temporal authority, he shall be obliged to confirm this article with an oath. If however a temporal lord, required and instructed by the church, neglects to cleanse his territory of this heretical filth, he shall be bound with the bond of excommunication by the metropolitan and other bishops of the province. If he refuses to give satisfaction within a year, this shall be reported to the supreme pontiff so that he may then declare his vassals absolved from their fealty to him and make the land available for occupation by Catholics so that these may, after they have expelled the heretics, possess it unopposed and preserve it in the purity of the faith—saving the right of the suzerain provided that he makes no difficulty in the matter and puts no impediment in the way. The same law is to be observed no less as regards those who do not have a suzerain" ("Canon 3," Fourth Lateran Council [1215]; from: http://www.dailycatholic.org/history/12ecume1.htm; accessed 28 June 2003).

C. Remember the focus of the spiritual battle:
1. The message you share, Acts 4:1-3; 5:28; 2 Tim 4:14-15
    a. By the way, isn't a focus on the message the lion's share of Christian Doctrine I and II, or Theology I and II?
    b. This is one place where Satan has clearly attacked in the history of the Church!

2. The fact that you are sharing it, Acts 4:18-21
    a. Antagonism to evangelism is found throughout The history of the churches, just read the recent anti-proselytism writings of the World Council of Churches and the Roman Catholic Church.

3. Regardless, stay obedient to the voice of the Holy Spirit, Acts 5:17-21
    a. Remember the jealousy of the Chief Priests and Sadducees, Acts 5:17; 13:45; 17:5

4. This may lead to anger against you, Acts 5:33

D. Some Admonitions Related to the Spiritual Battle:
1. Don't be alarmed, Phil 1:28
2. Be strong, Eph 6:10
3. Do not fear, Deut 20:2-4…
4. Come what may, the victory is the Lord's, persevere for the Lord!

V. Areas of Spiritual Battle:

Areas of Spiritual Battle

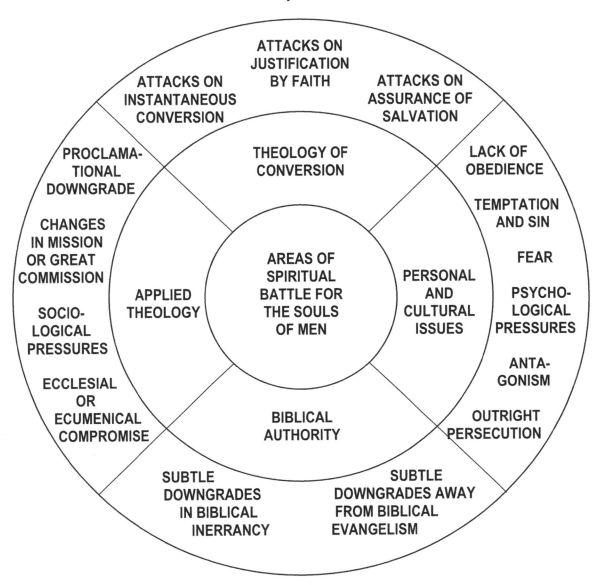

The areas of conflict in the spiritual battle are multi-varied and multi-facetted. As noted in the chart above, they cover most all areas of theological inquiry. The evangelistic student of the Bible should keep in mind the complexity of the battle in which he is engaged. Satan is a ruthless enemy, and will stop at nothing to undermine the proclamation of the Gospel by God's servants.

Conclusions:

A. As Christians, we ought to be aware of the spiritual battle for and against us.

B. In the Christian life and in evangelism, we need to be aware of the spiritual battle so that we can be as effective as possible for our Lord.

C. As pastors, theologians, and evangelists, we need to properly understand the centrality of evangelism both in theology and practice:
1. Evangelism unites message and method
2. We spend a lot of time seeking to understand the message from the Bible, how about the method?

3. The spiritual battle shows the link between the message and method—water down the method, and simultaneously the message has been watered down (no matter how one might deny this symbiotic relationship).

D. And yet, even with this battle going on, upon being let out of prison to defend himself before the large throng who were there in the auditorium with Agrippa, Bernice, and Festus, Paul still had the courage and expectation that King Agrippa may be saved:

> "'King Agrippa, do you believe the Prophets? I know that you do.
> "And Agrippa *replied* to Paul, 'In a short time you will persuade me to become a Christian.'
> "And Paul *said*, 'I would to God, that whether in a short or long time, not only you, but also all who hear me this day, might become such as I am, except for these chains'" (Acts 26:27-29).

Chapter 4 Appendixes

Thoughts on the Study of Evangelism

Introduction:

The study of evangelism is much like the study of Physical Chemistry. Physical Chemistry combines the study of calculus, physics, and chemistry. A thorough knowledge of each area is needed to properly study physical chemistry. Similarly, in evangelism, interpretation, theology, and practice are fully intertwined. They cannot be separated. The interpretation of the Bible, systematic theology, and the practice of evangelism go hand-in-hand. Each influences the other. This renders the study of evangelism particularly polemic, as it involves a practical clash of systems of theology.

Because of the divergence of theological views, as well as the cycles of revivalism within the history of the church, there are many approaches to the study of evangelism. The following notes seek to explain my approach as opposed to some others in the study of evangelism.

A. The Reality of the Difficulty in the Study of Evangelism:

1. There is a sense in which training in evangelism is impossible:
   a. For:
      1) It is impossible [for man] to teach wisdom
      2) It is impossible [for man] to teach a love for God or a love for man
      3) It is impossible [for man] to teach a burden for the lost
      4) These issues which are impossible for man are the responsibility and work of the Holy Spirit who transforms "from glory to glory," 2 Cor 3:18

   b. However, what can be done is to work with the Holy Spirit who Himself teaches a love for the lost and a burden for the lost:
      1) Provide an environment where in the teachings of the Scriptures are considered and memorized, allowing the Holy Spirit to do His work in hearts
      2) Provide multiple opportunities for students to converse with lost people so that they can experience first hand the lostness and ignorance of people, again allowing the Holy Spirit to develop a burden
      3) Provide tools to instill confidence in testifying
      4) Explain theological and practical pitfalls through which people in the past have lost their evangelistic zeal

2. There is also a sense in which training in evangelism is unnecessary:
   a. For:
      1) The former Demoniac from Gerasenes was given no evangelism training, Mark 5:19-20
      2) Jesus specifically told his disciples not to prepare a defense when they were arrested, as God would give them the words to speak, Luke 21:14-15
      3) Paul [Saul] immediately began to preach Jesus, without any [revealed] special post-conversion training, Acts 9:20
   b. However, there is another sense in which evangelism training is vitally necessary:
      1) Jesus called his disciples to follow him, so that he could make them become fishers of men, Mark 1:17, "And Jesus said to them, 'Follow Me, **and I will make you become** [καὶ ποιήσω ὑμᾶς γενέσθαι] fishers of men'" (cf. Matt 4:19; Luke 5:11)
      2) Moses was a man powerful in word and deed in part because of his education, Acts 7:22
      3) Paul taught the Corinthian church to be involved in evangelism, even as he was, 1 Cor 9:16-11:1
   c. Also, there are so many differing and conflicting views of evangelism, theology of evangelism, and systematic theology, that a well-reasoned approach is needed to remain true to New Testament Evangelism.
   d. These notes, therefore, are designed to provide a mastery of the subject of evangelism (knowing that evangelism is of will never completely mastered by anybody, other than the Apostle Paul, of whom God said, "Be imitators of me [Paul], just as I [Paul] also am of Christ," 1 Cor 11:1;

which quote raises the methodology of Paul as found on the pages of the Book of Acts as not only being worthy of imitation, but as being required for imitation by the imperative):

"Wherefore, if ye hear any man bringing you any other gospel than that ye heard of me [Paul], or bragging that he will deliver better things than ye received from me, let him and his disciples be accursed."[251]

"For the overthrowing of their wicked and blasphemous doctrine, thou hast here in plain text like a thunderbolt, wherein Paul subjecteth both himself and an angel from heaven, and doctors upon earth, and all other teachers and masters whatsoever, under the authority of Scripture. This queen ought to rule, and all ought to obey and be subject unto her."[252]

"Wherefore we must diligently weigh and consider the force of the argument, which is so often repeated in the Book of Acts."[253]

"Whereby they would bring us into bondage, and force us to say that we are justified, not by faith alone, but by faith formed and adorned with charity. But we set against them the Book of Acts."[254]

3. Lastly, there are people who will likely cringe at being required to take a class in personal evangelism:

  a. Those who are not genuinely saved:

  1 Cor 2:14, "But a natural man does not accept the things of the Spirit of God; for they are foolishness to him, and he cannot understand them, because they are spiritually appraised."

  b. Those who do not practice regular personal evangelism:

  Prov 26:16, "The sluggard is wiser in his own eyes Than seven men who can give a discreet answer."

  c. Those with fear:

  Acts 18:9-10, "And the Lord said to Paul in the night by a vision, 'Do not be afraid *any longer*, but go on speaking and do not be silent; for I am with you, and no man will attack you in order to harm you, for I have many people in this city.'"

B. Thoughts on Approaches to the Study of Evangelism:

1. Training in Evangelism may emphasize one of eleven contemporary methods (for more examples see the 122 methods in my *Book of Charts on a Theology of Evangelism*):
  a. Apologetic evangelism
  b. Block party evangelism
  c. Church evangelism/revivals/crusades
  d. Door-to-door evangelism
  e. Event evangelism
  f. Postmodern evangelism
  g. Prayer evangelism
  h. Relational evangelism (Living Proof/Contagious Christian/etc.)
  i. Servant evangelism
  j. Street evangelism
  k. Worship evangelism

  l. Food for thought:

  When do methods of sharing the Gospel become an attempt to make the folly of the message preached into the wisdom of the world? Was this one of the problems in Corinth?

  "For, I think, God has exhibited us apostles last of all, as men condemned to death; because we have become a spectacle to the world, both to angels and to men. We are fools for Christ's sake, but you are prudent in Christ; we are weak, but you are strong; you are distinguished, but we are without

---

[251]Martin Luther, *A Commentary on St. Paul's Epistle to the Galatians*, based on lectures delivered at the University of Wittenberg in 1531, translation based on the 'Middleton" edition of the English version of 1575, edited by Philip S. Watson (Westwood, NJ: Revell, n.d.), 69-70.
[252]Ibid., 70.
[253]Ibid., 201.
[254]Ibid., 205.

honor. To this present hour we are both hungry and thirsty, and are poorly clothed, and are roughly treated, and are homeless; and we toil, working with our own hands; when we are reviled, we bless; when we are persecuted, we endure; when we are slandered, we try to conciliate; we have become as the scum of the world, the dregs of all things, *even* until now," 1 Cor 4:9-10

Rather Paul wrote to the Corinthian church:

> "Let no man deceive himself. If any man among you thinks that he is wise in this age, let him become foolish that he may become wise. For the wisdom of this world is foolishness before God. For it is written, 'HE IS THE ONE WHO CATCHES THE WISE IN THEIR CRAFTINESS'; and again, 'THE LORD KNOWS THE REASONINGS OF THE WISE, THAT THEY ARE USELESS.' So then let no one boast in men," 1 Cor 3:18-21

It would seem that morphing into an apologetic evangelism can be using man's categories of reasoning, and likewise, other types of evangelism seem to follow sociological patterns of man's reasoning. In any case, it is dangerous to inject the "wisdom of the world" into evangelism, as it seems to be changing the foundation:

> "According to the grace of God which was given to me, as a wise master builder I laid a foundation, and another is building upon it. But let each man be careful how he builds upon it. For no man can lay a foundation other than the one which is laid, which is Jesus Christ," 1 Cor 3:10-11

2. Analyzing twelve "academic" approaches to evangelism:

Introduction:

1) There is a **crisis of methodology** which is attacking conservative churches today. For example, several years ago I attended a church planting retreat in which I heard an interesting statement:

   "People are not resistant to the Gospel; they are resistant to our methods"?!?

   What was this statement communicating? Was it saying that the Gospel is **not** the stumbling block, but rather the stumbling block is **"our methods"** [of evangelism]? Granted in church planting one needs to consider styles of music and ambience, but does this statement not imply that if couched in the proper methodology, the Gospel will be more likely to be received by people. This last is the exact point of Steve Sjogren et al, *Irresistible Evangelism*. However, it does not seem to correspond with the marks of New Testament evangelism.

2) Perhaps Schleiermacher in his antagonism to evangelism made a good point: "this activity [a theory of how to deal with converts] is not so naturally grounded."[255] No, it is not naturally grounded, it is supernaturally grounded!

   Therefore, from Schleiermacher (1830) to the current day, evangelism is not considered a part of the "Classical Disciplines" to be taught in a school of theology.

   In making this designation, the 19th Century Lutheran (and therefore Protestant) Schleiermacher merely followed Peter the Lombard's (anti-Evangelical) philosophical approach to conversion and theology, as expanded in Thomas Aquinas' anti-Albigensian *Summa Theologica*!

3) Lately, in tending toward the natural elements of evangelism and church growth, Donald McGavran emphasized the sociological study of people movements (or mass conversions), in a book he coauthored with J. Waskom Pickett in 1936, *Church Growth and Group Conversion*. This book built on the studies of Pickett published in his 1933, *Christian Mass Movements in India*. Similar to Schleiermacher's comment, the entire Church Growth movement, though it can be helpful, is built on a naturalistic premise of sociological analysis!

4) How can evangelism and conversion be studied scientifically, when it is a miracle of God? Note Mark 5:26-30:

   > "And He was saying, 'The kingdom of God is like a man who casts seed upon the soil; and he goes to bed at night and gets up by day, and the seed sprouts and grows—how, he himself does not

---

[255]Friedrich Schleiermacher, *Brief Outline on the Study of Theology*, 2nd ed., trans. Terrence N. Tice [1830; Richmond, VA: John Knox, 1966], 102.

know. The soil produces crops by itself; first the blade, then the head, then the mature grain in the head. But when the crop permits, he immediately puts in the sickle, because the harvest has come.'"

5) Here are several directions, natural and supernatural, in which a study of evangelism can proceed and has proceeded…

a. **Apologetics**—providing rational proofs for:
1) Rationality of Christianity
2) Truthfulness of the Bible
3) Proofs for the resurrection
4) Rational proofs for the existence of God, etc.

b. **Communications Theory**: methods of communicating in a given culture

c. **Church Growth Methodologies**:
1) Seeking to use techniques in evangelism consistent with producing "people movements"
2) Methodologies of planting churches, and the evangelistic techniques that flow from them

d. **Church Sociology**:
1) The study of the church as a social group, and the study of principles of assimilation of persons into a group setting
2) Some church sociologists have given their lives to study the sociology of the church. With findings generated from their surveys, they sometimes use their interpretation of public opinion to usurp the sole authority of the Word of God

e. **Cultural Anthropology/Cultural Exegesis**:
1) The study of language, culture, history, and/or religion in a certain people to determine the best way to reach them with the Gospel (e.g. "Postmodern Evangelism Strategies")
2) The watchword for this emphasis may be: "Engage Culture"

f. **Discipleship Evangelism**:
1) Placing discipleship as primary over evangelism, thus focusing on the personal life and habits of the evangelist which will enable him to live a more consistent lifestyle in order to reproduce disciples
2) Focusing on one-on-one mentoring
3) Focusing on "multiplication" rather than "addition"

g. **Sales and Marketing**: The use of business models of sales and marketing which lead to viewing evangelism:
1) As hot, lukewarm, or cold contacts
2) As marketing, such as Norm Whan's "Phones for You" telemarketing for the church
3) As developing prospect files, as a salesman develops his clients
4) As using commercials or billboards to advertise the church and its programs

h. **Public Relations**: similar to sales and marketing (*contra* Matt 10:22; 24:9; Mark 13:13; Luke 7:26; 21:17; John 15:18-21; 1 John 3:13)

i. **Persuasive Techniques**: teaching persuasive techniques in order to improve percentages of converts, such as:
1) The "A and B Close"
2) Psychology of mass movements/mass conversions
3) A Socratic series of questions

j. **Psychology and Conversion**:
1) Being "born again" as a "new start" in life, perhaps unrelated to repentance of sin and belief in the Gospel
2) The psychological need for people to make resolutions and commitments to which they hold, which is sometimes equated with encouraging a psychological "new birth"

k. **Individual Methodologies**: viewing evangelism as only one specific method:
1) Use of a certain tract, e.g. the *Four Spiritual Laws* or the *Two-Question Test* tract
2) Requiring some act of service as a preparation to the Gospel, e.g. Servant Evangelism (Francis of Assisi; etc.)

    l.   **New Testament Evangelism**: looking to the pages of the New Testament for both message and method of evangelism.

3.   Understanding the Issues:

    a.   There exists the desire to combine several of the above methodologies. The danger here is to mix revealed truth with empirical truth. Revealed truth is often over-ruled in this case (unfortunately when the two are mixed, "**culture** [unfortunately] **trumps theology**"; whereas the Bible is "living and active" in any culture [Heb 4:12], and it contains "no admixture" of error [Jer 23:28]; see in my *Charts for a Theology of Evangelism,* Chart 64, "The Missional Clash")

       Could Jude 10 fit here?

          Jude 10 (NKJ), "But these speak evil of whatever they do not know; and whatever they know naturally, like brute beasts, in these things they corrupt themselves"

    b.   Do any additions to NT evangelism not constitute what is sometimes called, "Evangelism outside the Box"?

       1)   These insertions are often what sell books, fill conferences, and unfortunately undermine theology. [256] In this case, Christians can become like the unsaved Athenians (Acts 17:21, "Now all the Athenians and the strangers visiting there used to spend their time in nothing other than telling or hearing something new")?

       2)   By the way, the phrase "Outside the Box," presupposes an "Inside the Box"—could "Outside the box" refer to going "**beyond**" [see KJV: Num 22:18; 24:13; cf. 1 Kgs 22:14; 2 Chr 18:13] "the things that are revealed" [Deut 29:29]?

       3)   Just as when Adam and Eve were tempted with the tree of knowledge, Satan continues to tempt the people of God with the world's "knowledge." Satan would have us think that there are much better truths and greater realities outside of the confines of the Word of God. It is an old trick, but there are many who follow the muse's voice in every generation. And they are usually rewarded with the things that Satan can give, fame and fortune.

    c.   These notes are based on the view that God has provided **sufficient revelation** (i.e. the sufficiency of Scriptures) of Himself and His purposes in His Word (and particularly as it relates to the New Testament) to provide not only for our salvation, "the Gospel." but also **to teach us how to propagate that salvation,** "the work of the Gospel."

    d.   Now, additions to the Scripture [in evangelism] are dangerous, as:

       1)   Additions are condemned in Scripture, cf. Deut 4:2; 12:32; Rev 22:18-19

       2)   Additions necessarily lead to subtractions from Scripture, e.g. note the order in Deut 4:2 and 12:32, cf. Jer 26:2

       3)   Additions inherently cause movement to the right or the left (cf. Deut 5:32; 17:11, 20; Jos 1:7; 23:6; Prov 4:25). By the way, their existence shows that movement away from the Scriptures has already taken place!

       4)   Additions cause the teacher to be teaching something the Lord has not commanded:

          "Now Nadab and Abihu, the sons of Aaron, took their respective firepans, and after putting fire in them, placed incense on it and offered strange fire before the LORD, **which He had not commanded them**" (Lev 10:1)

---

[256]"When I ask ministerial students whether the word *evangelism* carries positive or negative connnotations, the response is usually 85% negative. *Evangelism* and *evangelist* brings mental pictures of televised money grubbers, abrasive fundamentalists, manipulative proselityzing, or simple religious formulas. No wonder it seems so unappealing.

    "Isn't there a better way? …

    "ANOTHER KIND OF EVANGELISM

    "What if I told you that there is a different way to share the gospel? What if we discovered an authentic, relational, no-pressure approach that is engaging, adventurous, and really works? Would you be interested? *Purple Fish* provides that" (Wilson, Mark O. *Purple Fish: A Heart for Sharing Jesus.* Indianapolis, IN: Wesleyan Publishing, 2014.).

5) Additions cause the teacher to be teaching what is in his own heart:

"Then he went up to the altar which he had made in Bethel on the fifteenth day in the eighth month, even in the month **which he had devised in his own heart**; and he instituted a feast for the sons of Israel and went up to the altar to burn incense" (1 Kings 12:33)

"It shall be a tassel for you to look at and remember all the commandments of the LORD, so as to do them and **not follow after your own heart and your own eyes**, after which you played the harlot, so that you may remember to do all My commandments and be holy to your God" (Num 15:39-40; Prov 3:5)

6) Additions cause the teacher to apply the worthless reasonings of man to evangelism:

"For the word of the cross is foolishness to those who are perishing, but to us who are being saved it is the power of God. For it is written, 'I WILL DESTROY THE WISDOM OF THE WISE, AND THE CLEVERNESS OF THE CLEVER I WILL SET ASIDE' [Isa 29:14]. Where is the wise man? Where is the scribe? Where is the debater of this age? Has not God made foolish the wisdom of the world? **For since in the wisdom of God the world through its wisdom did not** *come to* **know God, God was well-pleased through the foolishness of the message preached to save those who believe.** For indeed Jews ask for signs and Greeks search for wisdom; but we preach Christ crucified, to Jews a stumbling block and to Gentiles foolishness, but to those who are the called, both Jews and Greeks, Christ the power of God and the wisdom of God. Because the foolishness of God is wiser than men, and the weakness of God is stronger than men" (1 Cor 1:18-25)

"Let no man deceive himself. If any man among you thinks that he is wise in this age, he must become foolish, so that he may become wise. For the wisdom of this world is foolishness before God. For it is written, '*He is* THE ONE WHO CATCHES THE WISE IN THEIR CRAFTINESS' [Job 5:13]; and again, '**THE LORD KNOWS THE REASONINGS of the wise, THAT THEY ARE USELESS.**' So then let no one boast in men [Psa 94:11]" (1 Cor 3:18-21)

7) Additions necessarily reframe the question

8) Additions reduce the power of Scripture (cf. Jer 23:28)

9) Additions hinder the proper proclamation of the Gospel

e. Scriptures encourage the study of the word of God, not the study of culture:

1) Verses and examples of those who were "mighty in the Scriptures" abound, e.g. Acts 6:2-4; 17:2, 11; 18:24, 28; etc…

2) Verses encouraging the study of culture are from inference and are very rare, e.g. 1 Chr 12:32; Luke 16:8; 1 Cor 9:18-22

3) There are verses even countering the wisdom of man, 1 Cor 1:18-25

4) Rather, it would seem that there are even biblical examples of "students of culture" who were on the other side:
   a) Simon the sorcerer, Acts 8 (antithetic to Philip the Evangelist)
   b) Elymas the magician, Acts 13 (antithetic to the Apostle Paul)
   c) The priest of Zeus, Acts 14 (antithetic to the Paul and Barnabas).

5) Consider again the ill advice of the brothers of Jesus as to how "to be known publicly," John 7:1-10—Jesus, however, was acting under a different set of presuppositions, John 2:23-25

6) Perhaps 1 John 2:15-17 speaks to the issue of culture:
   a) "Do not love the world, nor the things of the world":
      1) Clearly one needs to take care lest he grows in love with the world's mindset and the world's priorities
      2) Academia has tended to discount this possibility by labeling those concerned with a cognitive separation from worldliness (including the Apostle John in his writings) as Gnostic, Manichean, and Docetic
   b) "If anyone loves the world, the love of the Father is not in him":
      1) There comes a point in which a fascination with the world, its trends, its fads, and its movers and shakers turns into a love affair with the world
      2) The Christian's love affair or holy obsession should be with God's revelation of Himself and His salvation in the Bible, not with the constantly changing (and yet remaining the same in their essence) trends of the world

- c) "All that is in the world, the lust of the flesh":
  1) More than mere sexual immorality, there is a lust to please the fleshly or carnal nature, or carnal man
  2) Was this desire to please carnal man what led the opponents of Paul to preach circumcision along with the Gospel to avoid persecution, Gal 5:11?
  3) Was it not this same desire to please carnal man, his thinking and his thoughts, that led the apostles James and Peter to find fault with Paul's evangelism, because it was not oriented enough to social service for the poor, Gal 2:10?
- d) "The lust of the eye":
  1) Yes, outward visual sin is prominent, but so is inward visual sin
  2) There is a fascination these days with "worldview", notice the last word in this compound word, "view"—the way we cognitively see things
  3) While this fascination is not new (see Chapter 17 on *Weltanschauung*), John provides a cautionary note to falling in love with the world's worldview
- e) "And the [boastful] pride of life":
  1) Yes, there is a worship of the bios today, much as explained in Rom 1:22-23
  2) There is also a pride of knowing, as perhaps alluded to in Eph 2:3 as a "lust of the mind"
  3) In evangelism, there tends to be a pride in knowing beyond the clear teachings of the Scriptures, needing to go beyond Scripture to know:
     (a) Almost a type of evangelistic Gnosticism, which sometimes leads persons to become very zealous that they have found the panacea by which many will be saved, and that without persecution to the evangelist (Gal 6:12)!
     (b) Usually these zealous persons have found nothing more than a way to please either the lust of unsaved man's fleshly orientation, by adding "service to mankind" to the Gospel, or unsaved man's worldview by bringing in some new apologetic-orientation, based on how some unsaved thinker in the past framed the question
- f) "Is not from the Father but is from the world"
  1) From God's view of the academic-cognitive, the provenance of a thought is as important as the thought itself: does it come from Him or does it come from the world?
  2) Again, we are driven back to the Father in evangelism:
     (a) What has He taught in His word?
     (b) How has He framed the question?
     (c) What exact words has He chosen to use?
- g) "And the world is passing away, and also its lusts":
  1) John reminds his readers that man's thoughts, man's carnal methods, and man's worldview is passing away
- h) "But he who does the will of God abides forever":
  1) He who does God's will abides, leaving one to wonder about those who do it their own way
  2) We reproduce after our kind:
     (a) Those who "sow to the flesh, will from the flesh reap corruption, and those who sow to the Spirit will from the Spirit reap eternal life," Gal 5:8
     (b) "You will know them by their fruits. Grapes are not gathered from thorn *bushes*, nor figs from thistles, are they?" Matt 7:6
  3) Let's submit to God and His Word in evangelism!

f. Some thoughts on "dumbing-down evangelism":
  1) On the other hand, some may say, "why do you make it so complicated," or "why do you spend so much time on theology and definition"?
  2) Poorly equipped evangelists will fall prey to unbiblical or tangential theologies of evangelism, under the guise of KISS—Keep It Simple Sam.
  3) While the Gospel is simple, and it takes the faith of a child, evangelism is not simplistic. On the contrary, it is quite a complex field of study for which almost every Christian of all stripes have strong feelings.

4) The study of evangelism needs to match the intellectual rigor of any other field of theological endeavor. Anything less undermines the cross of Christ and the work of the Gospel.

C. The real question of these notes—Are you an Evangelical?

1. Do you believe that men are saved only through a Gospel proclaimed?

2. Is there any wiggle room? Can they be saved some other way (living a virtuous life, following the example of the lifestyle of Christ, going through one or more rituals in a church, etc.)? Is there any other way to be saved, other than hearing the Gospel and receiving it by faith? You need to be sure! These are non-negotiable questions!

3. Are you proclamational? Are you an Evangelical?

4. Do you believe that proclamation is reserved for those inside of the church only? Do you thus believe that those who do not enter the walls of your church are unworthy of being saved or perhaps they are not elect because they will not or have not enter the walls of your church? In this case, salvation is reserved only to those who will enter a select physical space (the church), and we know that many will never enter a Baptist church because they have some predisposed prejudice against it.

5. Is entering a church building therefore part of the order of salvation? If it is, then, is entering a church building a sure preparation for salvation, i.e. all who enter the building will be sure to be saved? Thus it is not hearing the Gospel with faith that saves; it is entering a building that saves. And if it is sure to all who enter, then all who enter the church, whether they hear the Gospel or not, and whether they respond by faith or not, will be saved. But this is absurd.

6. In this light, what of the 90-95% who will never enter your church? Are you committed to the Gospel to such a degree that you are willing to proclaim it outside the safety of your church? Are you willing to go to the highways and byways to reach the vast majority who will never step their foot into your church? Are you willing to obey the commission to "Go into all the world and preach the Gospel to all creation"?

7. Are you an Evangelical or not? You need to be sure!

8. Do you believe that God will save the elect outside the four walls of the church no matter what you do or don't do? Do you believe that requiring you to share the Gospel outside the walls of a church is adding a human work to the order of salvation? (it is actually subtracting a divine command) Then I pray answer, how will those outside the four walls of the church be saved? Is salvation only for us and for the members of our family within the safety of the church?

9. Are you an Evangelical?

10. If therefore the Gospel must needs be proclaimed outside the walls of your church to fulfill the Great Commission, how are you to accomplish this proclamation? Are you doing anything now? Are lost people hearing the Gospel proclaimed from your lips? If not, why not?

11. Perhaps the Great Commission is not the main command of Christ to His church? Can it be that past generations have gotten it all wrong? Perhaps they "overemphasized certain aspects of the Christian life"? Perhaps the fact that at the end of his life Jesus gave a clear command to His disciples, which was actually obeyed in the book of Acts, is not that big a deal? Perhaps the many other commands of Scripture actually snuff out the priority of the Great Commission for the church? Perhaps the Great Commission is not about evangelism? Perhaps evangelism is not that important after all? Maybe it is secondary or tertiary to the ministry of the local church?

12. Are you an Evangelical?

13. Perhaps you would prefer to be monastic and focus on your lifestyle and living your personal spiritual virtues? Perhaps you would prefer to call yourself a socialist and focus on human need wherever and whenever you find it?

14. Are you an Evangelical?

15. Then, is the Bible a reliable guide for evangelism or do we need to look elsewhere? Does the Bible lack sufficiency in this one area? You need to make up your mind!

16. If the Bible is not reliable for teaching us how to propagate the Gospel, then what is? Please tell me? What other subject is more reliable and inerrant than the Bible? Can we trust the winds and fads of culture as a more reliable source of authority for evangelism than the Bible?

17. Does "inerrant in matters of faith and practice" not include evangelism? Is evangelism not a part of practice in the Christian life?

18. Are you an Evangelical or not?

19. Jesus Christ died on the cross for you. He was abandoned, even by His disciples. Are you willing to abandon all to obey Christ in the area of evangelism? Friends, family, lose a job, leave a good paying job, leave your country of origin, learn a new language, or become an itinerant preacher without home? What sacrifice is Christ asking from you? Is any sacrifice too great in light of the cross?

20. Are you an Evangelical?

21. What about some of the **Baptist distinctives** for which our forefathers were martyred? Notice how closely related they are to evangelism: (1) **Freedom of Speech**—freedom to proclaim the Gospel; (2) **Priesthood of the believer**—freedom to individually receive salvation without a state church or other intermediary, other than the Word of God, the Holy Spirit, and Christ; (3) **Freedom of conscience**—freedom to individually believe according to conscience and freedom to assemble outside of a state regulated church; and (4) **Regenerate membership**—church membership only for the professing (those baptized as believers). Yes, these are distinctives for other Evangelical denominations as well, but they are special distinctives for Baptists.

22. Are these Baptist distinctives special to you? Are you grateful for them? Do you make full use of the freedoms we have in this country?

23. This school [where the author teaches] is both Baptist and Evangelical, and that's why students are required to take evangelism:

    "2. The need of the churches for trained ministers makes theological education necessary."

    ...

    "To the churches were given tasks of a practical nature, including evangelism, disciple-making, and disciple-teaching (Matt 28:18-20; Acts 1:8). They fail in their mission when they cease to fulfill their divinely appointed work. ... Thus, there is a need for the training of those whom God has called to lead churches that they may fully understand the gospel and become skillful in proclaiming it."[257]

    This course in evangelism is designed to flow from the Bible. *It seeks to frame the questions and answer the questions in, with, and by the Bible.* (**"The Bible asks the question, the Bible answers the question, and the Bible provides us the very terminology to properly answer the question"**) This course will not focus on one plan, one method, one time, one culture, or one worldview.

24. This course is only a beginning, the beginning of the mastery of the most important subject in Christianity, obedience to the Great Commission of our Lord and Savior, Jesus Christ. Evangelism is a subject that must be mastered, but is never mastered. It is continually learned, but never completely learned. The mandate for the work of the Gospel must be reawakened every day in every period of life. It cannot and it must not become passé. It cannot be relegated to the youth group, those with the gift of evangelism, or to the hired clergy. It is God's mandate for all of His obedient disciples—including you, if you are a born again Christian.

25. Are you a follower of Jesus? Then come on, let's follow Him, "diligently search the Scriptures" in one of the most important subjects there is—evangelism, and learn what it means to become fishers of men!

---

[257]"Appendix VIII: Southern Baptist Education Background and History," *Faculty Handbook* (Kansas City, MO: Midwestern Baptist Theological Seminary, 2003 update), 94; this document was adapted from *The Southern Baptist Organizational Manual*, A25-A30.

The Interrelationship of
Message, Reception, and Propagation[258]

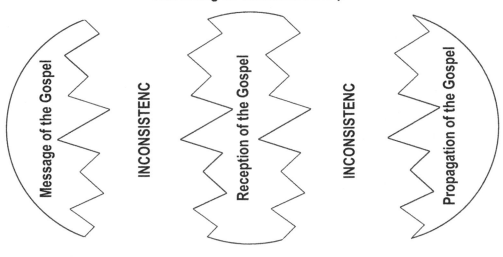

**Fragmented Approach
Assuming no interrelationship**

Message of the Gospel — INCONSISTENC — Reception of the Gospel — INCONSISTENC — Propagation of the Gospel

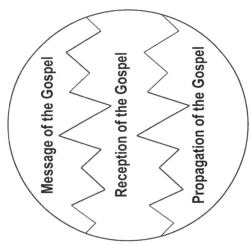

**Non-fragmented Approach
Acknowledging interrelationship**

Message of the Gospel — Reception of the Gospel — Propagation of the Gospel

It is often forgotten that message, reception, and propagation go hand-in-hand. If the message is changed (sometimes hard to detect), then the method of receiving the Gospel must accommodate that change. Then, as the method of receiving the Gospel changes, then the method of propagating the Gospel must change to accommodate the original change in the message. Of the three, perhaps the method of receiving the Gospel is easiest to discover. One will consider the difference of receiving "grace" by partaking in the Eucharist in Roman Catholicism versus repenting and believing in an Evangelical church.

My thesis is that the Bible not only gives us the words and parameters for the message of the Gospel, but it also gives us the words and parameters for the reception of the Gospel and for its propagation.

---

[258]Chapter 31 is devoted to this topic.

Some will dissociate message and method (propagation) by saying that the message comes from the Bible, but the method must be provided by culture. Herein lies a subtle way wherein "Baal" [culture] may enter the church!

Billy Graham, when asked the following question in 1967, "Do you still believe in the same fundamental doctrines that you did when you began preaching?" answered, "Yes, but methods change."[259] Fortunately for Graham, he used the same method all his life, with few exceptions, that is verbal proclamation. However, towards the end of his life, others working with him taught service and lifestyle as complementing methodologies. Graham's message and invitation did undergo change, as he broadened the scope of churches sponsoring his crusades. Likewise his definition of evangelism changed correspondingly.[260]

Indeed, there is an inter-relationship between message and method, between message, reception, and propagation.

---

[259]O. Charles Horton, "An Analysis of Selected Published Sermons of Billy Graham" (Th.M. thesis, New Orleans Baptist Theological Seminary, 1967), 96.

[260]Thomas P. Johnston, *Examining Billy Graham's Theology of Evangelism* (Eugene, OR: Wipf & Stock, 2003).

Understanding the Importance of Evangelism Methodology;
Or, the unforeseen impact of the move from revival to personal evangelism methodology

1. Historical:
   a. The revival strategy was held as the major evangelistic approach among American Evangelicals until the late-1950s
   b. When the primary emphasis of evangelism methodology shifted toward personal evangelism strategies in the late 1950s, simultaneously, the emphasis on harvest revivals began to wane (like the swing of a pendulum)
   c. In the North, the revival ministry became almost non-existent in the 1970s, whereas Evangelism Explosion and Continuous Witness Training gained in prominence in some evangelical denominations
   d. When personal evangelism strategies went out of vogue with the advent of relational and lifestyle evangelism in the late 1970s and early 1980s, especially in the North, there was very little to replace them, as revivals had already been rejected a generation before; it was at this point that special event evangelism and servant evangelism began to fill the void left by the rejection of initiative personal evangelism.

2. Unforeseen Methodological Byproducts:
   a. An emphasis on revival ministry almost always included a simultaneous emphasis on the use of personal evangelism.
   b. However, personal evangelism did not usually simultaneously encourage the use of revival ministry, as it often replaced it as being "more effective" in providing "lasting results."
   c. The rejection of revival evangelism as unacceptable had tragic repercussions, which eventually cause it to turn against the initiative personal evangelism that it was used to affirm, as well as to turn against the evangelism methodologies of the Bible as culturally irrelevant.
   d. Finally, in order to affirm non-biblical approaches to evangelism methodology, non-evangelical approaches to a theology of conversion were gradually adopted, resulting in the final phase of drift into liberalism.

3. Overview of Methodological and Theological Drift:
   a. As the use of revival methodology was waning, so the applicability of the Bible in the area of evangelism methodology waned.
   b. As the use of revivals waned, so the emphasis on conversion and the substitutionary atonement began to be replaced with a progressive enlightenment approach to conversion as evident in some discipleship emphases, in sectors of the spiritual disciplines movement, and in the emergent church movement.
   c. As the authority of the Bible waned in determining methodology, society and culture as a source of methodological authority began to replace the Bible.
   d. Then, as the prominence of cultural interpretations changed the methodology of evangelism, the methodology of conversion also had to adapt to non-evangelical methodologies learned from culture.

4. Conclusions:
   a. There is a need to revalidate the Bible as the authoritative source for evangelism methodology
   b. There is a need to revalidate revival as a biblical methodology of evangelism
   c. There is a need to move the pendulum back to the full affirmation of revival methodology as an important, relevant, and necessary methodology of evangelism
   d. Simultaneously, there is a need to reactivate emphases on:
      1) Street preaching, street evangelism, and tract distribution
      2) Tent revivals and open air services
      3) Camp meetings (the name is secondary to the method).

A Graphic Portrayal of Methodological Drift
Or, portraying the shift from revival, to personal evangelism, to relational evangelism

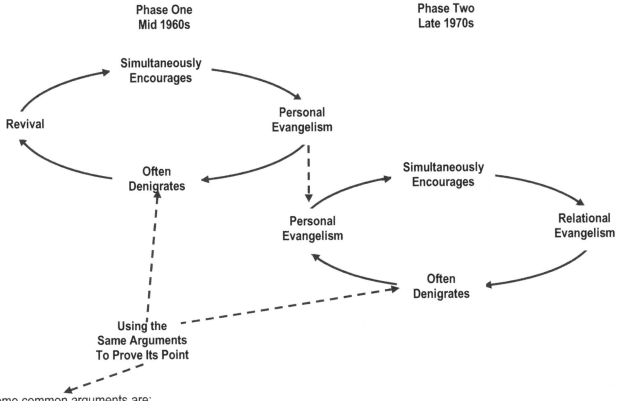

Some common arguments are:

- Evangelism methodology "X" does not work in our time, or in our culture;
- Likewise, evangelism methodology "X" is out of fashion, out-dated, and irrelevant;
- Man is now more relational than he used to be X, Y, or Z numbers of years ago, and it now takes longer to build relationships and earn a person's trust;
- "Postmodern Man" is less rationally-oriented, than was modern man X, Y, or Z numbers of years ago, therefore new (existential or postmodern) methods are needed to propagate the Gospel (lifestyle, community, non-propositional, story, etc.)

The only problem is that none of these arguments are rooted in the Bible nor in theology; meanwhile biblical anthropology does not change, nor did it change from Genesis to Revelation; man is the same sinner today as he was 2,000 years ago, and Satan is the same deceiver that he was 4,000 years ago. However, the result of accepting these arguments in practice of evangelism is an undermining of theology by culture. Hence the false-dichotomy, "I'm a practitioner, not a theologian."

The corollary argument becomes that the methods of evangelism don't need to be rooted in the Bible or theology, because the Bible either:

- Does not include teaching on method of evangelism, in which case we ought to take our lead from culture, in which case sociologists will fill in the details with their constant surveys and findings, some of which are helpful, and some of which contradict Scripture;
- Or if the Bible does teach specifically about methods of evangelism, it teaches all methods and approaches, which are proven by the proof texting of methods from non-evangelistic passages.

The problem with the cultural change argument is: "there is nothing new under the sun" (Eccl 1:3-11). Rather there seems to be the worship of the new (Acts 17:21), which is a major problem in academia. The impact of these shifts allows the insertion of methodological leaven into the theological lump of dough (Gal 5:7-9).

Some Thoughts on Church Leadership and Theological Education, Based on Ephesians 4:11

Introduction: Please note Chart 17 in my *Book of Charts for a Theology of Evangelism*.[261] In that chart, it can be noted that there are several approaches to understanding the contemporaneous nature of the five leadership gifts in Ephesians 4:11.

QUESTIONS	EVANGELISTS	PASTORS	TEACHERS
(1) Could there be a chronological emphasis in these leadership roles	Winning the lost	Shepherding those that are won	Teaching those that are won
(2) Likewise, may there be a relationship of the three gifts to the main verbs in Matthew's Great Commission?	"Go, win disciples of all nations"	"Baptizing them in the name of the Father, and of the Son, and of the Holy Spirit"	"Teaching them to observe all that I have commanded you"
(3) What may well be the primary target group of each leader?	Lost souls outside the church	Church members	Church members
(4) What may well be the primary ministry emphasis of each leader?	Evangelizing the lost	Helping the hurting, primarily within the congregation	Teaching the ignorant, and/or mentoring the weak
(5) In what way may this gift assist in the growth and development of the church?	Keeps the church focused outward in fulfilling the Great Commission; brings the saved into the church	Shepherds the hurting members of the church, and nurtures them to minister to one another	Gives both doctrinal and practical teaching to church members so that they can "obey all that I have commanded you"
(6) The gift of the evangelist notwithstanding, what type of evangelism may emerge from each gift developing its own style of evangelism?	Initiative or expectant evangelism; proclamational evangelism	Servant evangelism; relational evangelism; incarnational evangelism	Apologetic evangelism
(7) What Great Commission may each tend to emphasize?	Mark 16:15; Luke 24:46-47; Acts 1:8	John 20:21	Matt 28:19-20
(8) If each could envision their ideal church, what would it likely look like?	**A soul-winning church**, where people are being saved daily	**A loving church**, where members are loving and caring for one another	**A well-taught church**, where members are solidly rooted on the Word of God
(9) When each leader is visionary in his area, what would he likely envision?	New ideas for reaching the lost, and educating and equipping others to reach the lost	New ideas for small groups and fellowship, and other means of nurture	New ideas for educating church members: new classes, new curricula, and new teaching methods
(10) What kind of energy does each leader provide the church?	Enthusiasm; innovation; initiative	Care giving; humility; nurture	Structure; systems; administration and organization for learning
Proposal 1	**There seems to be a constant tug-of-war between these three visions for the church, which could easily cause division in the church, as each has biblical reasons why his vision for the local church is primary.**		

---

[261]Johnston, *Charts*, 37.

QUESTIONS	EVANGELISTS	PASTORS	TEACHERS
(11) What may be some verses to affirm each of the respective visions of each God-ordained leader?	Matthew's, Mark's, and Luke's Great Commissions, and the example of the Book of Acts	The Greatest Commandment, and other commandments to love, pastor, and shepherd	Matthew's Great Commission, and other admonitions related to teaching and learning
(12) What may be the result of ignoring each leader in the local church?	Little conversion growth; little evangelistic zeal; an inward focus	A cold church; an uncaring church; no fellowship	A superficial church; an ignorant church; an unfed or starving church
Proposal 2	**It is obvious that <u>each leader</u> is indispensable for the proper functioning and growth of the local church. Therefore, it is not a question of either/or, but rather of a question of emphasis**		
(13) With these differentiations in mind, who may each of these three leaders want to imitate, leading to dissension?	"I am of Paul," 1 Cor 1:12	"I am of Christ," 1 Cor 1:12	"I am of Apollos," 1 Cor 1:12
(14) However, which apostolic leader was meant to be imitated in the Bible? Why may that be so?	Paul's evangelism methodology, 1 Cor 11:1; Gal 1:8-9; Phil 4:9; 2 Tim 4:5; also as to hard work, Acts 20:34-35	Jesus said, "Follow Me, and I will make you become fishers of men," Mark 1:17; John 13:34-35	1 Pet 3:15; e.g. Acts 17:22-31
THE GIFTS IN THEOLOGICAL HIGHER EDUCATION			
(15) The writings of which leader are more likely to be found in the early history of the church?	Not the writings of the evangelist; they are virtually non-existent prior to the invention of the printing press	Some writings of the pastor, such as the *Didache* and other ecclesiastical codes (due to the state-church's interest in such)	The writings of some teachers have been passed on by the pen of monks of the "Dark Ages," Augustine, Peter the Lombard, Aquinas, etc.
(16) Which leaders' point-of-emphasis would most likely be in vogue in most theological schools of higher educational?	Not evangelism, as U.S. educational history confirms	Nor nurture, due to the competitive nature of gaining knowledge and grades	The teachers point-of-view, however, is primarily emphasized in theological schools of higher education, as U.S. history confirms
(17) What may be the ramifications of leadership gift of "the teacher" being overly-emphasized in theological schools of higher educational?	An inevitable shift away from evangelism, leading to an antagonism to evangelism, and its removal from the curriculum, as U.S. educational history confirms	A subtle move away from biblical nurture to secular philosophical and psychological models	Encouraging academic excellence (to the glory of God), while teaching the balance of all views (the Greek "Golden Mean"); in this context evangelism is often considered too single-minded, sectarian, and fanatical
(18) How can each of the three emphases be maintained in pastoral training and equipping?	(a) Must emphasize the priority of a converted student-body (otherwise evangelism can no longer be required, and it will soon disappear)	(a) Maintaining a converted student body provides the basis for expecting biblical holiness, discipline, and nurture	(a) Must maintain an evangelistic and biblically-founded faculty to avoid drifting toward persuasive words of wisdom, wisdom of the world, and sins of the mind
	(b) Must constantly encourage and promote an evangelistic spirit and practice on and off campus	(b) Must maintain godly fellowship and discipleship on campus	(b) To keep from drifting into secularism in every area of study, one must encourage the study of the Bible first and foremost in every academic discipline

Questions for further consideration:

A. What can we learn from the diversity of the leadership gifts in the leadership of the church?

B. What can we learn from the order of the three leadership gifts?

1. Could there be a prioritative pattern in the three (to maintain evangelism as a priority, it is placed first and not last)?

2. Consider revivalism in the history of the American churches, what have been the observable results of the emphases of each of these leadership gifts (evangelists, pastors, and teachers)?

3. In what order are the leadership gifts normally emphasized?

4. What may be the long-term results of a de-emphasis of each gift in the ministry of the local church?

Understanding Classical Theological Education's Systemic Antipathy for Evangelism

Richard L. Bushman, editor of *The Great Awakening*, shows great insight in explaining the antipathy of the Old Light establishment to the Great Awakening, and its impact on views of education. These antithetical views continue to be projected against conversionist schools of theological education to this very day, almost 300 years later!

The contemporary educator, therefore, must assess the original foundation of theological education and thelogical curriculum from this point of view. He must also consider that the natural drift of every school of theological education is away from conversionism and its close relative, revival.

Consider then the insightful comments of Bushman:

> "Well before the Awakening, Gibert Tennent and the other Log College graduates were discontented with the dominant faction in the Synod of Philadelphia. Looking to Scotland or Ulster for their models, most of these conservatives valued rigid orthodoxy and a traditional education over piety and spirited preaching. They disparaged the training William Tennent gave his students and resented their intensity and aggressiveness. In a move to exclude Log College men, the synod of 1738 required that all their candidates for a preaching license present a degree from Harvard, Yale, or a European university. To prevent Tennent's men from capturing vacant congregations or from evangelizing people without a church, the synod also forbade preaching before such groups without unanimous approval from the presbytery. Angered by the implicit rebukes, Gilbert Tennent and his friends contested the rules, but without success."[262]

The non-conversionistic, or may it be said, anti-conversionistic sentiment of the European Universities was foundational to the antagonism of the Old Side Presbyterians against the good attempt at a conversionistic education at William Tennent's Log Cabin School. This Old Side antagonism and the tax structures of that time led to the early growth of the Baptist denomination.

> "By the time Williams wrote, the revival ferment had already begun to split the churches. The most dramatic division occurred in the Presbyterian synod in 1741 when the tension between the Log College men and the European-oriented conservatives came to a head. When the synod met again, Robert Cross, one of the long time enemies of the Log College men, read a *Protestation* which culminated with the demand that the revivalists be excluded from the synod (No. 25). After a confused and heated clash, the signers of the protest were found to be in the majority, and the Log College men withdrew. For four years they subsited only as the 'Conjunct Presbyteries of New Brunswick and Londonberry," the areas in New Jersey and Southern Pennsylvania where most of the Log College men labored, and were popularly called New Side Presbyterians in contrast to the Old Side conservatives. In 1745 the Conjunct Presbyteries joined the New York Presbytery, which had long been restive in the Synod of Philadelphia, to form the Synod of New York. So long as rival animosities still rankled, New Side and Old Side were irreconcilable, but the disadvantages of a divided church became more obvious, proposals for reunification were made. Finally in 1758 the two synods made their peace. By then the dominance of the Awakening party within the Presbyterian Church was assured, and Gilbert Tennent moderated the first combined meeting.

> "In New England where there was no central ecclesiastical power to fight over, seperations occurred in individual congregations. Small groups, or even an individual like Nathan Cole, broke away to find more moving preaching or to sit under less constraining ecclesiastical rule. Some shortly returned to their old church. Others, like the group in Norwich, Connecticut, formed their own church and ordained a minister, usually a layman like themselves (No. 26). The established church attempted to discipline these schismatics to no effect. The Seperates believed the pastor and their former brethren to be without authority and scoffed at their censures and excommunication. The established church was no more successful in collecting ecclesiastical taxes. The Seperates refused to pay on grounds of conscience, contending that forced payment was an unwarranted invasion on their right to worship as they pleased. They went to prison rather than compromise. Relief came only gradually as individual town meetings found the tax laws impossible to enforce and as many Separates became Baptists, a denomination officially tolerated and exempt."[263]

It is interesting to note that Wycliffe in his day reportedly had a negative opinion of the Universities and Colleges run by the Catholic Church in his country. The Council of Constance rebuked the following Article of Wycliffe, provided here with a summary of their assessment by Jacques Lenfant:

---

[262]Richard L. Bushman, ed. *The Great Awakening: Documents on the Revival of Religion, 1740-1745* (Chapel Hill, NC: University Press for the Institute of Early American History and Culture, 1969), 85.
[263]Ibid., 86-87.

Art. XXIX. "Universities and Colleges, with the Degrees therein taken, where introduc'd by a Pagan Vanity, and are of no more Service to the Church than they are to the Devil."

This Article is declar'd false, injurious, contrary to good Manners, suspected of Unsoundness in Faith, and even Heretical according to the larger Censure. 1. Because the Church establish'd those Foundations, with a good Intention, for the publick Benefit. 2. Because the Universities have produc'd an abundance of Persons eminent for Learning and Piety, who have been very great Blessings to the Church, as the Bernards, Anselms, and Thomas Aquinas. 3. Because in the old and new Law, mention is made of Doctors, and it cannot be suppos'd, without Blasphemy, that they deriv'd their Authority and Origin from a Piece of Heathenish Vanity, as to which several Passages of Scripture are quoted, and particularly Acts xiii.1. and Ephes. Iv.11. 4. Because it ought not seem strange, that there are several Degrees in the Sciences, any more than several Degrees of Freedom in the Arts, and that this Vanity contributes extremely to the Maintenance of good Order, and the keeping up of Emulation. Lastly, They quote a Decretal of Pope Honorius III. for the Maintenance of Universities and Scholars.[264]

The suspicion of Wycliffe as to the purposes and methods of the Catholic Church in educating young minds can be inversed as it goes to those who do not appreciate an Evangelical education, as seen above. The education of students is a true battleground in the world of ideas!

---

[264]Jacques Lenfant, *Histoire du Concile de Constance*, new edition; translated by Stephen Whatley (Amsterdam: Pierre Humbert, 1727), 1:227.

Centrality of Evangelism for Evangelical Theological Education
(note the shift from supernatural to natural)

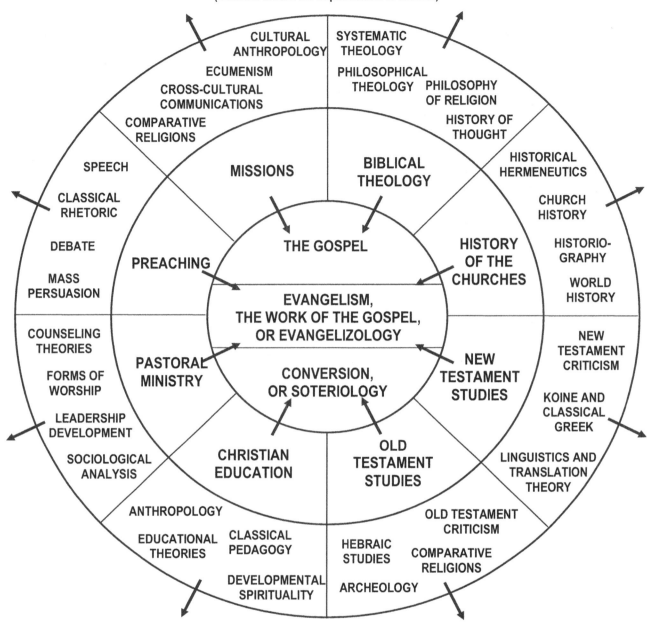

What makes an education distinctively Christian? It is the Gospel. An Evangelical Christian education begins with a focus on the Gospel, conversion, and the work of conversion (evangelism). Conversion was the starting point for conversionist American universities of higher education, those that followed in the footsteps of the First Great Awakening (e.g. Yale in the 18th Century; Princeton, Wheaton College, and William Jewell College in the 19th Century).

However, when the work of conversion, conversion itself, and then the personal Gospel were lost (seemingly in that very order) then those schools that succumbed to this drift gradually became secular universities, as their U.S. predecessor, Harvard University. Therefore, in the present, it is necessary for Christian schools of higher learning to maintain their conversionist distinctive by focusing on three things: the personal Gospel, conversion, and the work of the Gospel (evangelism). Otherwise their classes will drift away from the Bible and into a variety of secular fields, as noted in the above chart (2 Tim 4:4).

By the way, every field of study in the area of divinity has its secular counterpart, which can easily usurp the authority of Scripture in any of these fields.

Evangelistic Theological Education and Schools of Thought

Question 1: Is it possible to posit a thoroughly Evangelical or evangelistic curriculum for theological education? Several problems emerge.

Problem 1.1, no area of inquiry is devoid of theological nuance among the various theological conceptions.

Problem 1.2, each are of inquiry has (a) the possibility of and (b) the probability of pushing its own worldview on its students through use of the lens of its area of inquiry

Problem 1.2.1, part of the "worldview lens" of any area of inquiry includes a view of evangelism, either for it or against it, or some dialectic between these two extremes.

Problem 1.2.2, these views of evangelism, advanced through the classrooms of professors of various areas of theological inquiry simultaneously consist of:

Views of the authority (and application) of Scripture;

Views of the atonement (and the gospel); and

Views of evangelism (or: the propagation of the gospel).

TABLE 1

Areas of Theological Inquiry	Five Views of the Atonement	Textbooks for Classes (and School Curricula)
Old Testament	Substitutionary	Old Testament (Lexicons and Commentaries)
New Testament	Reconciliation	New Testament (Lexicons and Commentaries)
Systematic Theology	Christus Victor	Systematic Theology
The History of the Churches	Liberation Model	The History of the Churches
Missions and Evangelism	Moral Influence	Missions and Evangelism
Preaching and Pastoral		Preaching and Pastoral
Christian Education And Music		Christian Education and Music

Expansion 1.2, doctoral education:

1.2.1, Professors receive doctoral degrees from institutions that have the authority to grant doctoral degrees, the majority of which are clearly non-Evangelical and non-evangelistic;

1.2.2, Professors are strongly influenced, not only by the subjects they study, by perhaps more importantly, by the means in which their subject was framed in the schools where they did their theological studies;

1.2.3, Most professors have had their training in a non-evangelistic environment, and perhaps an anti-evangelistic environment;

1.2.4, For the professor to properly teach from within an evangelistic *a priori*, it is highly likely that he will need to reframe his thinking and the educational paradigms by which his approach to Scripture and to his area has been shaped.

Expansion 1.3, textbooks:

1.3.1, Authors from each area of theological inquiry write textbooks based upon their theological conceptions (as exemplified by the Five Views of the Atonement)

1.3.2, Therefore areas of inquiry in each field have and can be taught from the rainbow of theological persuasions

Problem 1.4. Each of the above approaches to the atonement proceed from or lead to a different view of the mission of the church

    1.4.1, Approximate (and ever changing) views of mission linked to each view of the atonement are:

        1.4.1.1, The Moral Influence theory tends toward a sacramental (or lifestyle) approach to the mission of the church, wherein those who are not a part of the church are guided into its fellowship through the sacraments or by adherence to a certain moral code

        1.4.1.2, The Liberation Model drives its members out into the world to alleviate political, economic, and social ills wherever and whenever they find them

        1.4.1.3, The Christus Victor Model seek intellectual, philosophical, and moral unity within and outside of the church, while moving from an individual to a societal approach to mission, trying to find Christ's saving activities incarnated in and through the unified church

        1.4.1.4, The Reconciliation Model of mission remains primarily individual, but emphasizes relationship over the simple Gospel; in this model "it's all about relationship": more man to man, than man to God

        1.4.1.5, The Substitutionary Model, sometimes viewed as forensic or objective or judicial, leads to an evangelistic view of the Great Commission

    1.4.2, Only belief in the substitutionary atonement truly safeguards the evangelistic spirit

Problem 1.5, In some areas of study it is more easy to hide, mask, or nuance one's theological views:

    1.5.1, Some approaches to theology, with accompanying views about evangelism and the Great Commission, seem to be *ex vocati* or *ex professo* (or by virtue of calling or subject area)

    1.5.2, For example, the Old Testament teaching about evangelism is somewhat obscure (although I devote a major sections of Chapters 7 and 10 to the subject), so an OT professor may or may not feel the need to express his views on evangelism forthrightly:

        1.5.2.1, The predominant OT view, outside of a Pauline interpretation, tends toward an "in this life" Lifestyle or Relational Evangelism, rather than to the NT intentional evangelism

        1.5.2.2, Jesus spoke of Pharisees and Saduccees during His time. Interesting is that these schools of thought still exist within Jewish life:

            1.5.2.2.1, Saduccees did not believe in the spiritual. Likewise there are non-spiritual approaches to OT interpretation today, along with Hebrew and Semitic programs that teach along those lines

            1.5.2.2.2, Pharisees did believe in the spiritual elements of interpretation. Paul was formerly a Pharisee. Likewise there are schools that teach Hebrew and Semitic throught from a spiritual *a priori.*

        1.5.2.3, The president and trustees of a school would be wise to discern which school of thought predominates in a professor they are about to hire:

            1.5.2.3.1, Among other possible points of interpretation, the relation of Isa 14 and Ezek 28 as speaking of Satan may provide a reference point for discernment here.

    1.5.3, For example, Pastoral counseling tends to emphasize views, some of which may be considered diametrically opposed to NT initiative evangelism:

        1.5.3.1, A life here-and-now emphasis, which was not the Pauline view as expressed in 1 Cor 15:19 (as an example)

        1.5.3.2, The nurturing of an introspective and individual focus, which is opposed to the others-oriented focus of the Gospel, "not seeking my own profit, but the profit of the many, so that they may be saved" (1 Cor 10:33)

        1.5.3.3, Additionally, Paul seemed obsessed with the Gospel and the salvation of others, "I have become all things to all men, that I may by all means save some. And I do all things for the sake of the gospel, that I may become a fellow partaker of it" (1 Cor 9:22-23)

Problem 1.6, differences of opinion on faculties in decision-making as regards programs, curricula, and the hiring of faculty often follow *ex vocati* or *ex professo* determinations:[265]

1.6.1, If there is a spiritual basis in decision-making in the first place, the decisions of faculty often follow the patterns of the *ex vocati* or *ex professo*

1.6.2, Hence, faculty members whose studies major in naturalistic conceptions of salvation or spiritual growth tend to pull together and vote against those who have greater supernatural conceptions of salvation

1.6.3, In addition, accrediting agencies, urging shared governance between faculty and administration, may further compound the problem

1.6.4, Often lines of demarcation within faculty fall on several continua:

1.6.4.1, There can be an Old Testament (Hebraic) worldview and a New Testament (Greek and/or Pauline) worldview clash

1.6.4.2, The soul-winning versus soul-building continuum, leading to a perceived or hidden evangelism versus discipleship clash

1.6.4.3, The old proclamation (Evangelical) versus lifestyle (Monastic) clash also exists in the developing of theological and ministry curricula

Problem 1.7, Additionally, no one professor is static in his views, but some changes do occur over time, in one direction or another.

Question 2: Is it possible to develop a thoroughly Evangelical or evangelistic curriculum for theological education, which highlights the Substitutionary Atonement?

Answer 2.1, It is very difficult for a number of reasons:

2.1.1, Schools of higher education tend to gravitate toward the new (e.g. Acts 17:21)

2.1.2, Publishing houses tend to publish and make money from what is new or novel, and these books become popular, are desired by students, influence trends, and are often made available as textbooks

2.1.3, Curricula are often developed from what is available as textbooks, and are therefore subject to market pressure, as well as by the fields in which degrees of higher learning are offered

2.1.4, Enrollment also puts pressure on schools:

2.1.4.1, A further pressure on the curricula is the interests of prospective students when they are considering a higher education

2.1.4.2, Therefore the student pool becomes a market pressure to drive schools to form classes and curricula to attract prospective students

2.1.4.3, The result is that schools tend to offer what is most attractive for the "yet-to-be-trained" student (on the master's level), whereas on the college level there may be greater parental input into the decision of a school

2.1.4.4, It goes without saying that the "yet-to-be-trained" student may not have the full benefit of theological depth necessary to understand what is important for his education, as he generally lacks both experience and education: that is why he is going to school for an education

2.1.4.4.1, the astute reader will see the circularity of the situation: yet-to-be-trained students influencing the forming of the curriculum for which they are yet-to-be-trained to understand why they need it

2.1.4.4.2, another circularity also exists, as it relates to ministry or occupation: yet-to-be-trained students, who have not yet experienced the ministry or occupation for which they are being trained, are shaping curriculum decisions to prepare them for the ministry or occupations which they have not yet experienced.

---

[265] As a professor of sociology, Neil Gross was debunking Senator Ted Cruz's characterization of radical liberal bias in higher education. In so doing, Gross made the following statement: "Radical academics, it turns out, are overrepresented not at elite research universities, like Harvard, but at small liberal-arts colleges. Most are concentrated in a handful of social sciences and humanities fields, like mine, sociology (in which radicals are nevertheless in the distinct minority), and in tiny interdisciplinary programs like women's studies and African-American studies" (Neil Gross, "The Actual Politics of Professors" [*The Chronicle of Higher Education* (online)]; available at: http://chronicle.com/blogs/conversation/2013/03/05/the-actual-politics-of-professors/; accessed: 12 Mar 2014; Internet).

2.1.5, Accrediting agencies guide schools to gravitate toward the status quo in theological education, both for accreditation, as well as in the credentialing of their faculty

    2.1.5.1, The downgrading of U.S. education into a caucophony of competing vanilla or "Brand X" schools with little or no denominational, theological, revivalist, or historical distinctives is one of the saddest developments in the last 100 years of U.S. higher education

        2.1.5.1.1, Christian liberal arts colleges, in this scenario, become little more than Christianized "finishing schools" for high school graduates,[266] whereas,

        2.1.5.1.2, Seminaries and schools of theology, in this same scenario, propagate a non-denominational pavlum of a-theological ideas

2.1.6, Societies, where papers must be read for a professor to further his rank as a professor, tend to drift toward non-Evangelical theology, subtly or not-so-subtly encouraging faculty to shed their distinctive denominational or Evangelical positions

    2.1.6.1, Perhaps the most potent trump card of these societies are the editorial boards of their journals, here is the reality:

        2.1.6.1.1, The Association of Theological Schools (also known as ATS) acts as the accrediting agency for most theological institutions in the U.S.

        2.1.6.1.2, ATS requirements for faculty to be promoted from Assistant Professor, to Associate Professor, and then to Full Professor, includes the publishing of at least 3 papers in scholarly journals

        2.1.6.1.3, The editorial boards of scholarly journals often publish material that is free from too much sectarian sentiment (à la Thomas Jefferson)

        2.1.6.1.4, It is not long for those few professors who actually (1) hold a Ph.D., (2) have a teaching position, (3) have some revivalistic views, and (4) actually take the time to write papers, to find that their views are not readily accepted by mainstream academia, as represented on the editorial boards

        2.1.6.1.5, These select professors, in order to remain credible in their field, and be promoted by their institution, must therefore make careful adjustments of their sectarian bias (e.g. interest in evangelizing others to their particular church) in order to move up the ranks: kind of an intellectual "Catch 22"

        2.1.6.1.6, Whereas those professors with a less sectarian focus have the road open to them to publish, receive promotions, and even possibly become administrators who decide what classes should and should not be taught, as well as who should or who should not teach them!

2.1.7, Often it is those with degrees in educational philosophy who administer theological schools of higher education, and not necessarily those with theological training or evangelistic hearts (the exception to this rule is current Southern Baptist seminaries), allowing schools to fall prey to the latest educational management techniques:

    2.1.7.1, An alarming trend of the last 50 years, in theological schools of higher learning, has been the trend toward minimalistic-original language and minimalistic-theologically-based degrees, which focus almost exclusively on secular educational models for the church (sociology and anthropology) or individuals (psychology or counseling)

    2.1.7.2, This trend has often allowed for: (1) less emphasis upon evangelism, (2) less emphasis upon denominational distinctives, then (3) less emphasis upon the Bible and original languages, and then (4) less emphasis upon historical theology

2.1.8, Therefore, there seems to be a self-perpetuating unseasoned blanding in schools of theology and areas of theological education, with the addition of the market pressure of the new.

---

[266]"I speak, I am sure, for the faculty of the liberal arts colleges and for the faculties of the specialized schools as well, when I say that a university has no real existence and no real purpose except as it succeeds in putting you in touch, both as specialists and as humans, with those human minds your human mind needs to include. The faculty, by its very existence, says implicitly: 'We have been aided by many people, and by many books, and by the arts, in our attempt to make ourselves some sort of storehouse of human experience. We are here to make available to you, as best we can, that experience'" (John Ciardi, "Another School Year: Why?" [Ruttger's *Alumni Monthly*, 1954]; available at: http://jonboeckenstedt.wordpress.com/2008/11/21/another-school-year-why-by-john-ciardi/; accessed: 6 Jan 2010).

Problem 2.2, Are the "classical areas of theology" doing any favors to an Evangelical education, or might they be changed? If so, when and how? Or, restated, is there a way off of the perpetual motion machine called "classical areas of theological education"?

Answer 2.2.1, by "classical areas of theological study" how far back is one required to go?

2.2.1.1, To Philip Schaff's *Theological Propædeutic* (5th ed., 1902), or

2.2.1.2, To Friedrich Schleiermacher's *Kurze Darstellung des theologischen Studiums zum Behuf einleitender Vorlesungen* (2nd ed., 1830), or

2.2.1.3, To Aquinas' *Summa* (A.D. 1275)—the summary of Aquinas' arguments derived from and gathered for the inquisition chambers, where inquisitors argued against the proclamational theology of the Albigenses and Waldenses, or

2.2.1.4, To Peter the Lombard's *Sentencia* (A.D. 1161)—incredibly philosophical, sacramental, and also non-proclamational organization of theology (whose organization of his four books of sentences shaped the Medieval scholastic approach to the organization of areas of theological inquiry)

2.2.1.5, Summary: in these examples, the farther back one goes into the "classical discipline of theology" the farther away one goes from an Evangelical theology. It seems like medieval scholasticism shaped contemporary the "classical disciplines of theology."

Answer 2.2.2, Therefore, it would seem that the normal approaches to the "classical areas of theological education" do no favors to:

2.2.2.1, The fulfillment of the Great Commission

2.2.2.2, The field of evangelism,

2.2.2.3, An evangelical theological education

2.2.2.4, Both evangelism and the Great Commission were either intentionally anathemized and perhaps later unintentionally omitted from most scholastic discussions

Question 2.2.3, Is it possible to find release from the question-framing of the "Classical" Conceptions of Theology?

2.2.3.1, The question framing at issue encompasses concepts and terms, both in the order they are discussed (thus their importance) and the relative weight assigned to them

2.2.3.2, Furthermore, there is significant pride associated with fluency in the "special knowledge" (gnosis if you will) that training in the "classical disciplines" provides, as well as association with schools of reknown that provide such training

2.2.3.3, However, it may be that falling prey to the question-framing of the so-called "Classical Disciplines" may be the first step to accepting the resulting theologies of the "classical" theologians, perhaps without even being aware of the same

2.2.3.4, The answer seems clearly to believe that the Bible (and all the words therein) is without error, and framing the question and teaching with that same zeal

2.2.3.5, It is therefore necessary, that the inerrantist constantly battle the tendency to drift into non-biblical modes of "framing the question" (which are most commonly used in the supermarket of ideas)—even if this means ridicule as an unsophisticated teacher

Question 2.3, How to formulate a thoroughly Evangelical or evangelistic ministry education, with its center and focus being the fulfillment of the Great Commission?

Answer 2.3.1, It seems that a thoroughly Evangelical or evangelistic theological education should be possible:

2.3.1.1, The history of education in the U.S. shows us that a thoroughly Evangelical theological education was taking place at:

2.3.1.1.1, the early Princeton Log Cabin schoolhouse of Gilbert Tennent, and

2.3.1.1.2, in the many of the early Bible School movement, such as Nyack Bible college and Moody Bible institute

2.3.1.2, This same has been true, in varying degrees, for many denominational schools founded in the U.S.

Problem 2.3.2, How can evangelistic spirit be safeguarded?

    2.3.2.1, Some have maintained that being non-accredited will keep the school from drifting:

        2.3.2.1.1, Such was the case for early years of Moody Bible Institute

            2.3.2.1.1.1, Seeking accreditation in the early Moody ethos was like selling out to the world

            2.3.2.1.1.2, There were many denominational schools in the early 20th Century that were examples to them to keep from drifting into becoming "mainstream" or culturally-acceptable

            2.3.2.1.1.3, Despite protests that accrediting agencies have no theological agenda, there are some areas wherein pressure is exerted:

                2.3.2.1.1.3.1, Shared governance shifts to power of governance from the President as the agent of the Board of Trustees to protect the constitution and doctrinal stance of the school, giving it to the administration + the faculty, often resulting in a drift from the doctrinal stance of the school

                2.3.2.1.1.3.2, Curricula decisions, by their very organization, frame the question and shape the education, including what courses are taught and what professors are needed (or not needed) in order to fulfill the requirements of a given degree

                2.3.2.1.1.3.3, Even agencies providing library books (the growth of which is strongly promoted by accreditors), as well as comparing libraries with comparable institutions, pushes an institution to become mainstream

        2.3.2.1.2, However, market pressure, time, and a change of vision and mission take their toll upon such institutions:

            2.3.2.1.2.1, Such is the case, for example, in considering the transfer of credits, seeking to align classes to promote the maximum transfer of credits to secular schools

            2.3.2.1.2.2, The need for new students can drive schools to fall prey to market pressures in the development of programs of study

            2.3.2.1.2.3, Funding is a major pressure, as competition against government-funded institutions has almost annihilated Christian higher education in the U.S. (considering that there was no public university prior to 1830, before 1830 all colleges were denominational at their origin)

    2.3.2.2, Some have maintained that remaining denominationally or privately funded will safeguard them from drift:

        2.3.2.2.1, Such schools have seen the historical drift of other schools due to their funding sources (such as the Duke Family, the Rockefeller Foundation, or the U.S. government)

        2.3.2.2.2, Some schools (such as Trinity Evangelical Divinity School) were forced to keep their endowment income low (e.g. below 25% of operating income), in order to force them to remain dependent upon churches and individual donors for their income

    2.3.2.3, Some have sought to avoid or slow drift through maintaining denominational control of schools, through board members and funding:

        2.3.2.3.1, Schools that have maintained a majority of Board members from a particular denomination (e.g. the SBC seminaries), have definitely slowed the drift:

            2.3.2.3.1.1, This requirement of SBC seminaries allowed for their recapture by conservatives in the convention in the middle 1990s—a positive historical anomaly in the history of U.S. churches!

        2.3.1.3.2, The changing of the constitution of the Board of Trustees away from denominational affiliation, for whatever reason (fund raising, student recruitment, faculty pressure, accreditation, or government pressure), has led to the theological demise of virtually every U.S. Evangelical institution founded prior to 1850, and many founded after that time

    2.3.2.4, Many Baptist institutions have required classes in Basic Evangelism and Church Evangelism:

        2.3.2.4.1, Requiring these classes is important and commendable

        2.3.2.4.2, However, one danger that has been evidenced is the gradual drift of all other classes in the institution so far from evangelism, so that the evangelism class and its professor become like a white elephant at the school; this dichotomy continues until the spiritual and psychological ethos allow the evangelism class to be changed to something else, such as discipleship, personal spiritual disciplines, the responsible self, or transformational leadership

2.3.2.4.3, A sure way to dissociate evangelism from the curriculum is to admit unsaved students (which is usually done [1] for the sake of enrollment, and also presumably [2] for the [likely or unlikely] evangelism of that unsaved student). Such a decision practically requires the elimination of evangelism as a requirement (as unsaved students cannot be led to do evangelism, nor does their acceptance into the school assure their predestination unto salvation); thus quickly accelerates the secularization of any school

2.3.2.5, Some have posited requiring involvement of all faculty and students in weekly evangelism:

2.3.2.5.1, such was/is currently the case for Criswell College and Mid-America Baptist Theological Seminary

2.3.2.5.2, requiring evangelism of all faculty and students does not insure against the insertion of a Judas into the school (notice that Judas also went out in evangelism, Matt 10:4), but it sure seems to help maintain a positive evangelistic focus in the school from the top down!

2.3.2.6, Some have required all graduates to plant a church as a graduation requirement (e.g. Jakarta Baptist Seminary, Jakarta, Indonesia)

2.3.2.6.1, While this is certainly practical and positive, some churches in the U.S. are planted without evangelism, and many church planting books are methodological with very little on doctrine or evangelism

2.3.2.7, In conclusion, two approaches emerge, required or voluntary evangelism?

2.3.2.7.1, the evangelistic spirit of Mid-America (requiring weekly evangelism by its administration, faculty, staff, and students) has been maintained on campus

2.3.2.7.2, whereas, a voluntary spirit of participation, as is practiced at the seminary where I teach, Midwestern Baptist Theological Seminary, has provided for a salting of the campus atmosphere due to regular encouragement from the administration

2.3.2.7.3, meanwhile, the curriculum and professors will always need separate attention

Answer 2.3.3, Keys to maintaining an evangelistically-focused curriculum

2.3.3.1, Assure that evangelism professors and evangelistic professors remain a significant percentage of the faculty:

2.3.3.1.1, This percentage will be necessary to maintain a majority when curriculum issues, including core courses, required courses, and programs of study are brought to committee and then voted upon by the faculty

2.3.3.1.1.1, The percentage of the faculty is directly tied to the required classes in the curriculum, the core courses being the most important ones

2.3.3.1.1.2, The perceptive reader may consider seminary programs in Christian Education and Counseling, for example, that include a wide diversity of classes which can only be taught from their own perspective and following their own agenda

2.3.3.1.1.3, Likewise, it may be that most of the seminary curriculum can be leveraged for Great Commission causes with some rearranging of class names and emphases, as will be noted below, without compromising outcomes, but actually enhancing them from a Great Commission point-of-view

2.3.3.1.2, Maintaining a significant percentage of evangelism professors will necessitate a significant number of required evangelism classes in the curriculum:

2.3.3.1.2.1, Understanding that each required class = a percentage of a full-time professor, depending on the size of the school; let's compare four hypothetical schools W, X, Y and Z, with four hypothetical curricula:

2.3.3.1.2.1.1, At school W, 2 required core M.Div. courses = one full-time faculty position to teach those classes

2.3.3.1.2.1.1.1, At school W, therefore, 4 required NT classes = 2 full-time NT faculty positions; these hypothetical classes include

(1) Introduction to NT One
(2) Introduction to NT Two
(3) Introduction to Greek One
(4) Introduction to Greek Two

2.3.3.1.2.1.1.2, At school W, let's assume a parallel scenario for OT as with NT = 2 full-time OT faculty positions

2.3.3.1.2.1.1.3, At school W, let's assume 2 required core M.Div. classes in theology = 1 full-time faculty position

2.3.3.1.2.1.1.4, At school W, there is one required core M.Div. class in ethics and philosophy of religion = ½ a full-time professor

2.3.3.1.2.1.1.5, At school W, there is one required core M.Div. class in missions = ½ a full-time professor

2.3.3.1.2.1.1.6, Therefore at hypothetical school W, out of 6 full-time faculty positions, there are 5½ non-evangelism faculty positions (according to normal job description), and ½ evangelism faculty positions by job description (or $0.5/6 = 8\%$)

2.3.3.1.2.1.2, At school X, 2 required core M.Div. courses = one full-time faculty position to teach those classes

2.3.3.1.2.1.2.1, At school X, therefore, 4 required NT classes = 2 full-time NT faculty positions; these hypothetical classes include

(1) Introduction to NT One
(2) Introduction to NT Two
(3) Introduction to Greek One
(4) Introduction to Greek Two

2.3.3.1.2.1.2.2, At school X, let's assume a parallel scenario for OT as with NT = 2 full-time OT faculty positions

2.3.3.1.2.1.2.3, At school X, let's assume 2 required core M.Div. classes in theology = 1 full-time faculty position

2.3.3.1.2.1.2.4, At school X, there is one required core M.Div. class in evangelism = ½ a full-time professor

Let's give the evangelism professor a core M.Div. course in missions to bring his load to 1 full-time professor (meaning either missions or evangelism is likely short-changed)

2.3.3.1.2.1.2.5, Therefore at hypothetical school X, out of 6 full-time faculty positions, there are 5 non-evangelism faculty positions (according to normal job description), and one evangelism faculty positions by job description (or $1/6 = 17\%$)

2.3.3.1.2.1.3, At school Y, 2 required core M.Div. courses = one full-time faculty position to teach those classes

2.3.3.1.2.1.3.1, At school Y, therefore, 3 required NT classes = 1½ full-time NT faculty positions; these hypothetical classes include:

(1) Introduction to NT
(2) Introduction to Greek One
(3) Introduction to Greek Two

2.3.3.1.2.1.3.2, At school Y, let's assume a identical scenario for OT as NT = 1½ full-time OT faculty positions

2.3.3.1.2.1.3.3, At school Y, let's assume 3 required core M.Div. classes in evangelism = 1½ full-time faculty positions, teaching:
(1) Introduction to Evangelism
(2) Church Evangelism
(3) History of Great Commission Activity

2.3.3.1.2.1.3.4, At school Y, let's assume 3 required core M.Div. classes in missions = 1½ full-time faculty positions, teaching:
(1) Introduction to Missions
(2) Interfaith Evangelism
(3) Cross-Cultural Church Planting

2.3.3.1.2.1.3.5, Therefore at hypothetical school Y, out of 6 full-time faculty positions, there are 3 non-evangelism faculty positions (according to normal job description), and 3 evangelism faculty positions by job description (or 1/2 = 50%)

2.3.3.1.2.1.4, At school Z, 2 required core M.Div. courses = one full-time faculty position to teach those classes

2.3.3.1.2.1.4.1, At school Z, therefore, 4 required Bible classes = 2 full-time NT faculty positions; these hypothetical classes include:
(1) Introduction to NT
(2) Introduction to OT
(3) Introduction to Greek One
(4) Introduction to Greek Two

2.3.3.1.2.1.4.2, At school Z, let's assume 4 required core M.Div. classes in evangelism = 2 full-time faculty positions, teaching:
(1) Introduction to Evangelism
(2) Exegetical Evangelism (emphasizing Applied Bible or Gospelology)
(3) Church Evangelism
(4) History of Great Commission Activity

2.3.3.1.2.1.4.3, At school Z, let's assume 4 required core M.Div. classes in missions = 1½ full-time faculty positions, teaching:
(1) Introduction to Missions
(2) Interfaith Evangelism
(3) Cross-Cultural Church Planting
(4) Ecumenics

2.3.3.1.2.1.4.4, Therefore at hypothetical school Z, out of 6 full-time faculty positions, there are 2 non-evangelism faculty positions (according to normal job description), and 4 evangelism faculty positions by job description (or 2/3 = 67%)

Quick Comparative of Hypothetical Schools W, X, Y, and Z

	School W		School X		School Y		School Z	
Number of Non-Evangelism Courses	11	92%	10	83%	6	50%	4	33%
Number of Evangelism Courses	1	8%	2	17%	6	50%	8	67%
Total Number of Required Courses	**12**		**12**		**12**		**12**	
Number of Non-Evangelism Faculty	5.5	92%	5	83%	3	50%	2	33%
Number of Evangelism Faculty	0.5	8%	1	17%	3	50%	4	67%
Total Number of Resulting Faculty	**6**		**6**		**6**		**6**	

Quick Comparative of Courses Offered in Hypothetical Schools W, X, Y, and Z

Area	Courses	School W	School X	School Y	School Z
NT	Introduction to NT One Introduction to NT Two Introduction to Greek One Introduction to Greek Two	4	4	3	3
OT	Introduction to OT One Introduction to OT Two Introduction to Hebrew One Introduction to Hebrew Two	4	4	3	1
Other	Theology One Theology Two Ethics and Philosophy of Religion	3	2	0	0
Number of Non-Evangelism Courses		**11**	**10**	**6**	**4**
Evangelism	Introduction to Evangelism Church Evangelism History of Great Commission Activity Exegetical Evangelism	1	1	3	4
Missions	Introduction to Missions Interfaith Evangelism Cross-cultural Church Planting Ecumenics	0	1	3	4
Number of Evangelism Courses		**1**	**2**	**6**	**8**
Total Number of Required Courses		**12**	**12**	**12**	**12**

2.3.3.1.2.1.4, The differences between hypothetical schools W, X, Y, and Z are quite stark:

2.3.3.1.2.1.4.1, While preaching, pastoral duties, and other course are not included in this comparative, the differences portray a completely different approach to educational emphasis

(1) School W represents the average M.Div. curriculum of many seminaries, with a very low percentage of evangelistic classes (8%); and often the class is not taught as evangelism, but rather as social transformation, spiritual disciplines, or discipleship

(2) School X would be a more "Evangelical" model of what is common today (17%); students have to be self-motivated to gain an evangelistic heart, as it does not likely come through in too many other classes (depending on the professor's heart)

(3) Schools Y and Z are hypothetical, but interesting from an evangelistic and missional point-of-view (50% or 67%)

2.3.3.1.2.1.4.2, Likewise, the make-up of the faculty would drastically alter the faculty committee membership (merely by virtue of what professors are called upon to teach), decisions brought by committees to the faculty, and decisions of the faculty as regards programs and courses of study

2.3.3.1.2.1.4.3, In the curricula delineated for schools W, X, Y, and Z:
(1) Does not each curriculum display or portray a view of what is important to the school, its administration, and/or supporting churches?
(2) Do they not each curricula actually show different views as to the importance of the Great Commission?
(3) Are these differences in emphasis not a part of the spiritual battle being waged in the world of ideas (Eph 6:10-20)?

2.3.3.1.2.1.4.4, As to individual course titles and content:
(1) Do not "Interfaith Evangelism" and "Exegetical Evangelism" cover essentially the same material as is normally taught in "Systematic Theology" classes, but from a very practical rather than theoretical-philosophical point-of view?
(2) Does not "History of Great Commission Activity" cover the most important elements of what is normally taught in a "Church History" class, but from a clearly evangelistic point-of-view not generally discussed in "Church History" classes?

2.3.3.1.2.1.4.4, Furthermore, it is not highly likely that the students who graduate from each hypothetical school would have very different ministries upon graduation!

2.3.3.1.2.2, Perhaps these stark differences in the emphasis of education portrays why the most heated arguments among the faculty in the seminary relate to changes in curriculum and required courses!

2.3.3.2, Likewise, one must assure that enough evangelism classes remain in the core of required courses, for example:

2.3.3.2.1, A personal evangelism class, along with a practicum element

2.3.3.2.2, A church evangelism class, to explain evangelistic programs from a local church point of view

2.3.3.2.3, An evangelistic preaching class, to focus on practical elements of evangelistic preaching

2.3.3.2.4, An inter-faith evangelism class, which teaches ways to reach people with the Gospel who come from differing religious backgrounds

2.3.3.2.5, An applied Bible in evangelism (a.k.a. "Gospelology"), deepening thoughts in exegetical evangelism:
2.3.3.2.5.1, It is anticipated that "applied Bible in evangelism" (or "Gospelology") would be a full year or two semester course

2.3.3.2.6, A history of evangelism course, taught in a reverse chronological way:
2.3.3.2.6.1, By "reverse chronological" is meant beginning with the present and working back century by century
2.3.3.2.6.2, This "reverse chronological" approach would avoid the disconnect that often occurs between various phases in the history of the churches, leading professors and students to study tangential histories, only to find that they have no relationship to the current times
2.3.3.2.6.3, It is anticipated that "history of evangelism" would be a full year or two semester course

2.3.3.2.7, A macro-ecclesiology class (ecumenics), to explain multi-church cooperative evangelism efforts, their strengths and weaknesses

2.3.3.3, Fight to maintain an evangelistic curriculum:

2.3.3.3.1, Curriculum yields the graduate, and the graduate yields the impact and public image of the school
2.3.3.3.1.1, This appears why Education and Counseling Programs seem to crowd the curriculum with their classes and very few electives, it appears that they want to frame as much of the question as possible for their graduates, and likewise leverage as many professors as possible for their majors

2.3.3.3.2, There is a strong and almost inevitable tendency that the curriculum drifts to the status quo of philosophical and speculative theology (as noted above)

2.3.3.3.3, Reasons for this drift are two-fold:
2.3.3.3.2.1, Most curricula drift in this direction, thus it is merely flowing downstream

2.3.3.3.2.2, As the number of professors increases in non-evangelistic areas, by and large, they eventually vote for their areas of expertise and against evangelism

2.3.3.3.3, Strong evangelistic leadership is needed from the administration, but also from a majority of the faculty, to maintain a strongly-focused evangelistic curriculum

Problem 2.4, False teaching creeps in from within and from without (Acts 20:29-30):

2.4.1, The reality of false teaching from within may creep into schools in several ways (Matt 18:7; Luke 17:1):

2.4.1.1, False teaching comes from within the schools themselves, through professors who drift from their theological positions, or never maintained them in the first place

2.4.1.2, False teaching creeps into schools because some students are constantly wanting to learn the new (Acts 17:21), or year-after-year wanting to learn "outside the box" of biblical revelation (Matt 7:24-27)

2.4.1.2.1, The *Add Novitam* fallacy (fallacy of the new) dominates academic publishing and may guide student enrollment, may also encourage professors toward "freethinking"

2.4.1.3, False teaching also creeps into schools via the drift of local churches and/or the denomination to which they are attached.

2.4.2, As touched on above, some areas of study invite non-Evangelical thought (as noted above):

2.4.2.1, Some areas of study find their very existence because of the human sciences, apart from the revealed truth in the Bible, such as philosophy, sociology, psychology, and communications theory

2.4.2.2, Other areas of study tend to emphasis the history of human thought, such as philosophy of religion and comparative religions

2.4.2.3, In Bible study, some Bible portions and books of the Bible are focal points for non-Evangelical theology, such as the Minor Prophets, the Synoptic Gospels, and James

2.4.2.4, Also in Bible study, some textbooks study the text type, the textual transmission, and other "scientific" approaches to the text, while virtually ignoring the message of the text, such are textual criticism and forms of so-called higher criticism (source, form, redaction, historical socio-anthropological, feminist, etc.)

2.4.3, For this reason, one can only be held liable for one's own generation, and for working to protect the next generation as much as possible:

2.4.3.1, Consider in this light the sin of Hezekiah, as explained in Isaiah 39, who had no regard for the next generation

Problem 2.5, Over time, evangelistic and then theological drift will occur (Book of Judges).

2.5.1, It would seem that from a biblical standpoint, the only way to deter inevitable drift is God-ordained revival led by God-called evangelists:

2.5.1.1, It is difficult, but necessary, to administer a revivalistic spirit in a school

2.5.1.2, He who would do so, would be flying against the wind and swimming against the current[267]

2.5.2, The hope of revival causes generation-after-generation of the disheartened students or faculty members to take hope in the Lord: He will keep His church; He will further His cause; He is the Lord of the harvest!

2.5.3, However, revivalism is impossible without a certain hermeneutic and set of doctrinal convictions:

2.5.3.1, Some schools have drifted so far from the doctrinal basis upon which a campus-wide revival is possible, so as to make campus-wide revival almost impossible

2.5.3.2, Furthermore, some administrators and faculty are so antagonistic to revival, that they would rather close the doors of their school than to experience a God-ordained revival!

2.5.4, Yet, may doctrinal convictions conducive to revival be discovered or recovered?

2.5.4.1, Nothing is impossible with God!

---

[267]B. H. Carroll, "Shall the Atlanta Board Be Instructed to Employ Evangelists and to Call for an Extra $25,000 for Their Support?" *Baptist Standard* (31 May 1906) 14:1-2; cited in Charles S. Kelley, Jr., *How Did They Do It? The Story of Southern Baptist Evangelism* (New Orleans: Insight, 1993), 14.

2.5.4.2, However, the status quo is "You can't go back 30-50 years" (choose the appropriate length of time depending on the institution)

2.5.4.3, How may doctrinal convictions conducive to a revivalistic spirit in a school be discovered? Often this calls for a return to doctrinal distinctives

Question 3: Is it possible to develop systems by which schools, theologians, and professors may be analyzed to determine their Evangelical or evangelistic credentials?

Answer 3.1, A number of theological determinations have been posited over time:

3.1.1, Adherence to the Apostles Creed, the Nicene Creed, the Creed of Chalcedon, the Creed of Athanasius, the "Three Symbols of the Catholic Church," all the decrees of Rome, etc.

3.1.1.1, While interesting and helpful from the standpoint of historical theology, these creeds have done very little to protect the church from false teaching in areas other than the Trinity and Christology (and have failed to keep churches from a Unitarian or Idolatrous drift)

3.1.1.2, In fact, when the history of all the churches is analyzed, these creeds have accelerated the Church toward philosophical and sacramental theology

3.1.2, Adherence to the five points of the Synod of Dort:

3.1.2.1, Hence a strict Calvinism as a deterrent to false teaching

3.1.2.2, Strict Calvinism has been helpful, as a literal interpretation of Scripture is needed for many of the conclusions of Dort

3.1.2.3, one danger lies in the philosophical derivation of the doctrine of Limited Atonement

3.1.2.4, another danger lies in the presupposed Covenant relationship, resulting in infant baptism being the sign of a child entering into the Covenant family

3.1.2.4.1, The rampant sexual immorality in Amsterdam, Holland, the Netherlands, and the closed doors of its downtown Oudekirk (Old Church), is an example of the need for each generation to humbly receive the faith of its parents, the waters of infant baptism failing to pass on that charism, even though Calvin taught that such was the case.

3.1.3, Adherence to the nine points of the British Evangelical Alliance (1846):

3.1.3.1, Hence Evangelicalism as a minimum point of agreement for comity agreements (cooperation) in missions, evangelism, and church planting

3.1.3.2, While very helpful in its time period right after the onslaught of Socinianism, the nine points were somewhat minimalistic (after Albrecht Ritschl's downgrade, belief in "Atonement" needed to be clarified to belief in the "Substitutionary Atonement")

3.1.4, Adherence to the proto-Fundamentals (the Portland Evangelical Test of the 1869 YMCA)

3.1.5, Adherence to the Five Fundamentals of the Niagara Bible Conference (1895):

3.1.5.1, Hence Fundamentalism as a minimum point of agreement for cooperation in evangelism, education, and publishing

3.1.5.2, These Five Fundamentals are: Biblical inerrancy, the deity of Christ, the Virgin Birth, Substitutionary Atonement, and Bodily Resurrection (to a literal heaven or hell)

3.1.5.3, Notice that the Five Fundamentals do not discuss (for example): water baptism, baptism in the Spirit, speaking in tongues, the extent of the atonement, or degrees of separation

3.1.6, Adherence to the various church Confessions published over time:

3.1.6.1, Hence the James P. Boyce's "Abstract of Principles" became the document to be signed by all SBTS professors

3.1.6.2, Hence the "Baptist Faith and Message 2000" is currently used as the document by which all SBC seminaries must comply to receive SBC Cooperative Program funding

3.1.7, Many of these theological dictates have served various generations in protecting the proclamation of the Gospel, the pressures of the reinterpretation of future generations and succumbing to market pressures have shown that each of these have had various gradations of success over time:

3.1.8, Even good guidelines, such as the 1963 Baptist Faith and Message, did not deter the Presidents of the SBC seminaries and their professors from drifting; it took the conservative resurgence to pressure the schools back to their roots theologically

Answer 3.2, To reduce the rate of the inevitable theological drift, two items have generally been helpful in curbing the speed of that drift in Christian schools of higher education:

  3.2.1, Keeping the school closely aligned to the teaching of the Bible, the Word of God:
    3.2.1.1, Constantly studying the text of the Bible in every class
    3.2.1.2, Truly keeping the Bible first and foremost in every area of study (which needs diligent accountability and constant reappraisal)

  3.2.2, Keeping a school closely aligned to the local church has proven helpful in curbing the theological drift, and maintaining a theologically-sound faculty:

    3.2.2.1, One way of keeping schools closely aligned to local churches is through hiring pastors to be the administrators of schools
      3.2.2.1.1, Pastors may have a higher likelihood of being closer to the grassroots than scholars and educators
      3.2.2.1.2, The problem is that pastors may not have the level of education to discern the nuanced positions of faculty members, who know the answers that the untrained want to hear, and are trained in hiding their false teaching (Deut 29:18-19)

    3.2.2.2, Some schools have actually been housed in local churches, being run as a ministry of a particular local church under the authority of the pastor
      3.2.2.2.1, These church-based schools tend to be the most conservative
      3.2.2.2.2, However, changing pastors, growth in student population, pressures to broaden the curriculum, and new administrators tend to draw the schools away from the funding base of the local church over time

Answer 3.3, The issue of theological drift over time needs constantly to be addressed:

  3.3.1, Hence comes the constant cry from each generation: "Will You not Yourself revive us again, / That Your people may rejoice in You?" (Psa 85:6).

Keys to an Evangelistic Curriculum

Ideally speaking, in order to assure an evangelistic curriculum…

A. General Considerations:

1. Hire only thoroughly evangelistic faculty
   a. Proven by the unprompted and voluntary regular practice of personal evangelism
   b. And using the Baptist Faith and Message 2000 (or similar basis) as a doctrinal foundation

2. Emphasize NT evangelism throughout the curriculum:

   a. Every class is to have an evident evangelistic component:
      1) Any class that does not or cannot have an evangelistic component, ought not be in the curriculum

   b. Every semester that a student is enrolled, they should take a class which they are learning and practicing direct evangelism

   c. Daily organized opportunities are provided for students to be involved in direct evangelistic ministry:
      1) Students not involved in the organized daily evangelistic ministries (for no valid reason) should be dropped from the program
      2) Faculty will also be required to be leaders of evangelistic activities

3. Emphasize preeminently the Bible and its teachings in every class

   a. Hence, every class is a Bible class
      1) Any class that cannot or does not have the Bible as its primary textbook ought not be in the curriculum

   b. The full curriculum should allow for three different passes over the content of the Bible:

      1) First, as a survey of the Bible's direct teaching (NT and OT)

         a) Undergirded by a thorough study of Bibliology (BI), which would include:

            (1) A study of the many roles of the Bible:
               (a) The role of the Bible in the conversion process;
               (b) The role of the Bible in spiritual growth;
               (c) The role and place of the Bible in evangelizing; and
               (d) The role of the Bible in worship

            (2) A history of how the Bible came down to the present time in its various emanations;

            (3) A study of versions of the Bible and original language sources:
               (a) English versions of the Bible, their uniquenesses and differences
               (b) Original language versions of the Bible, their characteristics and place
               (c) The importance of the original languages, and the place of original languages in understanding Scripture and interpreting Scripture

            (4) Bible translation:
               (a) The need for good original language sources
               (b) The place of theological presuppositions in Bible translation work
               (c) The ultimate goal of Bible translation work.

b) A survey of all OT books;

c) A survey of all NT books.

2) Second, as a particular application for or Gospelology (GO):

    a) The Early Church's move to philosophical and speculative theology (from the writings that remain) provides a poor framing of the question; for example:

        (1) Sometimes it appears that theology is taught as the science of poisonous questions:

            1 Tim 6:3-5 (ESV), "If anyone teaches a different doctrine and does not agree with the sound words of our Lord Jesus Christ and the teaching that accords with godliness, he is puffed up with conceit and understands nothing. He has an unhealthy craving for controversy and for quarrels about words, which produce envy, dissension, slander, evil suspicions, and constant friction among people who are depraved in mind and deprived of the truth, imagining that godliness is a means of gain."

        (2) Rather, one should leave unanswered questions with the mind of God, and rather consider those areas that are clearly taught in Scripture:

            Deut 29:29, "The secret things belong to the LORD our God, but the things revealed belong to us and to our sons forever, that we may observe all the words of this law."

    b) What of the primary issue of the wrath of God in both the OT and NT? Should this not be front and center in Gospelology?

    c) What of gospel proclamation, the hearing of faith, verbally receiving Christ, etc.?

    d) "Systematic theology" needs to be reframed as Gospelology, much as was done through the Bible School movement in the U.S., wherein the Book of Romans rightfully became the fountional document for so-called "theology"

3) Third, the use of the Bible in the History of the Churches (HC), including:
    a) Availability or lack of availability of Bibles to the laity in HC
    b) Applications of or misapplications of Scripture in GO in HC
    c) Emphases and uses of the Bible in preaching in HC
    d) NT evangelism in HC
    e) This last course of study (HC), would be taught in a "reverse chronological" order as described in the prior Appendix

4. Conscientiously avoid philosophical theology and speculative theology in every class area: NT and OT book studies, Gospelology (GO), and history of the churches (HC):

a. It must be understood that at least since Peter the Lombard (d. 1164), Christian religious studies have been captivated by sacramental speculative theology
    1) While the Bible was simultaneously forbidden to lay people, and to most monks and clergy (even in Latin), something other than the Bible (sacramental theology) had to be used as the foundation for monastic eduction and preparation
    2) This 800 years of influence upon all areas of biblical, historical, and theological studies cannot be overestimated

b. While the Reformation was a massive improvement over Medieval scholasticism, it only touched portions of the reclarifications needed in Christian religious studies, as can be noted by:
    1) Continued Protestant forcible use of infant baptism upon all members of their society, and that as a covenantal and salvific act
    2) Luther's use of Augustine's renumbering of the Ten Commandments (subsuming the 2nd as part of the 1st, and dividing the 10th into two)
    3) Calvin's use of Augustine's broad theological categories, in addition to his theological Central Interpretive Motif

c. Perhaps the following chart displays the historical development of the seminary body of education:

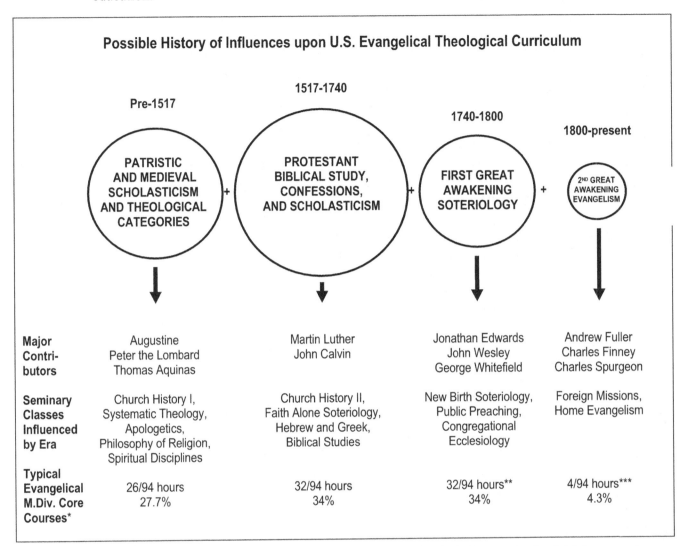

Possible History of Influences upon U.S. Evangelical Theological Curriculum

	Pre-1517	**1517-1740**	**1740-1800**	**1800-present**
	PATRISTIC AND MEDIEVAL SCHOLASTICISM AND THEOLOGICAL CATEGORIES	PROTESTANT BIBLICAL STUDY, CONFESSIONS, AND SCHOLASTICISM	FIRST GREAT AWAKENING SOTERIOLOGY	2ND GREAT AWAKENING EVANGELISM
Major Contributors	Augustine Peter the Lombard Thomas Aquinas	Martin Luther John Calvin	Jonathan Edwards John Wesley George Whitefield	Andrew Fuller Charles Finney Charles Spurgeon
Seminary Classes Influenced by Era	Church History I, Systematic Theology, Apologetics, Philosophy of Religion, Spiritual Disciplines	Church History II, Faith Alone Soteriology, Hebrew and Greek, Biblical Studies	New Birth Soteriology, Public Preaching, Congregational Ecclesiology	Foreign Missions, Home Evangelism
Typical Evangelical M.Div. Core Courses*	26/94 hours 27.7%	32/94 hours 34%	32/94 hours** 34%	4/94 hours*** 4.3%

*Based on the 2011 M.Div. of Trinity Evangelical Divinity School (from: http://www.teds.edu/academics/programs/master-of-divinity; accessed: 13 Dec 2011).

**The "Practical Ministries" courses that do not have a specifically spiritual bent have been combined under the "First Great Awakening." Historically, they probably represent a category not found in this chart, that of the Liberal Arts education, from the days of John Leverett, President of Harvard College (1708-1724); he was "Harvard's first secular president" (from: http://www.harvard.edu/history/presidents/leverett; accessed: 13 Dec 2011). Some courses in this category are "Anthropology for Ministry," "Cultural Hermeneutics," "Issues in Counseling Ministry," and "Educational Ministries in the Local Church."

***"Foundations of Christian Mission" and "Foundations of Evangelism" represent the only two courses specifically Great Commissional oriented in the typical Evangelical seminary core as viewed by their course description and purpose (on the numerous views of the Great Commission, see Chapter 10).

1) It must be understood that Patristic and Medieval theological categories formulate the Christian faith in a sacramental direction:
    a) Focusing on "Signs and Symbols"—sacramentalism (see Peter the Lombard)
    b) Focusing on speculation about Christological exactness, which was no less than a tangential way of addressing sacramentalism and of calling non-sacramental Christians heretics

2) Likewise, it must be understood that prior to the Second Great Awakening there was very little emphasis on teaching evangelism (or its more acceptable corollary, missions) as part of theological education in the U.S.

3) If this approximates the facts, then books and teaching evangelism methodologies must find their roots in Second Great Awakening methodologies

4) Therefore, it follows that all "classical forms of theology," prior to the Second Great Awakening, did not include evangelism in their curriculum, and some were perhaps quite antagonistic to including evangelistic ideas and concepts in their curricula

5) Thus, merely removing the Second Great Awakening emphasis of evangelism from the curriculum is quite a simple task, as it is not addressed historically in the "Classical Categories" of seminary education

6) For this reason, it is posited that question-framing in certain theological areas, especially those developed prior to the Reformation, would be a good idea, in order to re-frame those subjects in a way that is friendly to evangelism, rather than antagonistic or neutral to evangelism and the Great Commission

d. New nomenclature (titles):

1) Because organizational titles lead to question-framing:
   a) Renaming "Systematic Theology" to "Gospelology"
   b) Renaming "Church History" to "History of the Churches," and that perhaps being taught in a "reverse chronological" sense (see below)

2) Perhaps these new titles will assist students and professors in breaking historical ties with the "traditions of men" in these areas, a.k.a. "classical areas of theology"

5. Maintain a primary emphasis on Greek (NT and OT LXX) and a secondary emphasis on Hebrew (to deepen LXX studies):
   a. Focus on Classical Greek for NT and OT LXX studies
   b. Furthermore, OT studies often provide a seedbed for multiple views of the atonement and hence of multiple missions for the people of God, which are then imported into the NT church, NT Great Commission, and NT evangelism for pragmatic reasons

B. New Testament:

1. Survey all NT books with a view to explaining their plain teaching

2. Provide a clear study on the interrelationship of the OT and NT, which includes not only Rom 9-10, but also Galatians and Hebrews (esp. Heb 7-9)

C. Old Testament:

1. Emphasize Jesus and the Gospel in the OT, rather than source criticism and its many cousins

2. Emphasize the clear message of the Books of the OT, rather than prolonged explanations of genres, methods of composition, and varieties of interpretative schemes (*Geschichts*)

3. In Hebrew language classes, utilize Psa 119 and the Deuteronomy 1, 4-5 for preliminary studies, rather than the Book of Genesis 1-3 (as appears to be the norm)

D. Gospelology (or: Evangelology):

1. Emphasize the revealed biblical message of the Gospel first and foremost, e.g. the Book of Romans as the foundation for the NT Gospel; "The Gospel According to Paul"

2. Do not allow philosophical theology to frame the organization of any classes (thereby proactively avoiding the "traditions of men" in teaching theology: prolegomena, theism, etc.)
   a. If the Bible does not clearly address a question, then ought it be discussed in class or serve as a core course?
   b. Furthermore, if the Bible does not give a clear answer, clarity ought not be sought beyond the words of the Bible, nor should the tertiary topic become the Central Interpretive Motif interpreting thought and practice
   c. Rather, the centers of interpretation and application should be:
      1) God's wrath for sin
      2) The cross of Christ and the Gospel of Christ

3) The Great Commission
4) The Bible as the very words of God

3. Consciously and constantly seek biblical ways to organized and frame questions and issues, for example:
   a. Deut 5, 27-28 on God's priorities
   b. Deut 30 on God relationship to man
   c. Deut 31-32 on revival, as God's institution for keeping His people close to Him
   d. Judges for cycles in the history of the churches
   e. Dan 2, 7, 9 on the main structures of history[268]
   f. Matt 10 and Luke 10 on evangelism, as well as Matt 13, etc.
   g. John 3 and 4 on conversion
   h. John 14-16 on the Trinity
   i. Acts on pastoral ministry
   j. Acts 14 and 17 on cross-cultural missions (as well as Deut 4 and 12), 1 Cor 9, etc.
   k. Romans as the heart of the Gospel message
   l. 1 Tim and Titus on the functions of the local church
   m. Rev 20-21 on the eternal states

4. Perhaps this method of study provides for a healthy cross-polenization of areas of study (Bible, Gospelology, and biblical languages)

E. History of the Churches (HC):

1. Because a study of the HC, particularly in the first six centuries, frames the questions of theology and practice, it is necessary to consciously reframe the issues to redirect these classes to those matters that are of biblical importance, to avoid falling into speculative theology by default or in ignorance:

   a) Because there is often a disconnect between teaching speculative theology in HC and the current experience of the church...

   b) This author recommends that HC be taught in a reverse chronological fashion: beginning where we are today, and working our way back century by century

   c) In this way, students and professors will be able to discern lines of thought, including especially the Bible and evangelism, with greater clarity, as they work their way back

   d) It may be that students and professors will discern that some aspects of biblical Christianity drift into oblivion when crossing certain periods or phases in history, not because the Bible has changed, and not because faith in Christ has changed, but because the reporting on the church has changed, and the available documents providing information has diminished; phases in question include:
      1) Moving from the English and American First Great Awakening (1730-1740) back to the 17th Century Protestant scholastic period
      2) Moving from the Reformation era (1517-1572) into the pre-Reformation movements (Hus and Wycliffe)
      3) Moving from Hus (1415) and Wycliffe (1384) into the Roman Catholic scholastic and inquisition eras (11th-13th Centuries), with their almost unknown evangelists (Henry of Lausanne and Peter de Bruys) and churches (the 16 different denominations of the Cathars, acc. to Reinerius Saccho)[269]
      4) Moving from the Early Medieval formalization of sacraments and monasticism (7th-9th Centuries) into the Early Church period (2nd-5th Centuries)

---

[268]E.g. John [Johannes] Sleidan [1506-1556], *The Key of History or the Four Chief Monarchies*, two books in one binding (Strasbourg, 1556; London, 1627).

[269]Reinerius Saccho, *Summa de Catharis et Leonistis* (1250).

    e) When attempting to decipher the Middle Ages or the Early Church, it appears that a "reverse chronological" approach will assist in properly identifying the issues and connecting the dots historically-speaking from each era into the prior era:

        1) Many theologies (such as Philip Schaff's *Creeds of Christendom*) and histories jump from the iconoclastic [statues] controversy (9th Century) to the Reformation era (16th Century) with very few connecting thoughts

2. For example:
   a) Look for and emphasize evangelism, church planting, and true church growth in every century of HC
   b) Look for and emphasize the NT Gospel and movement away from it in every century of HC
   c) Availability or lack of availability of Bibles to the laity in HC
   d) Emphases and uses of the Bible in available sermons in HC
   e) The proper application of or misapplication of Scripture in AB in HC

3. It is clear that there are few materials that approach HC in the above prescribed fashion, necessitating research and curriculum development in this area, as mentioned below
   a) The need for updated materials would be enhanced by a new paradigm of "reverse chronological" teaching

4. HC students who have completed the "reverse chronological" methodology would now be prepared for advanced studies:
   a) They may want to consider and teach how early church theological categories have been used against Evangelical Christians and NT evangelism for almost 2 millennia (such as Marcionite, Manichean, Docetic, Modalistic, Pelagian, etc.)

Charting Some Ideas:

Comparing Classical Philosophical Theoretical Core Courses with the New Great Commission Paradigm

It appears that Evangelical seminary education in the U.S. has either begun or evolved into the following pattern:
1. A traditional classical philosophical-theoretical training curriculum with one or two Great Commission classes included to "salt" the curriculum
2. The traditional classical theoretical courses are taught mainly by Evangelicals, who seek to keep from drifting into non-Evangelical thought, although they use the philosophical-theoretical forms and questions (as they have received their higher education training in that paradigm)

In that light, it would appear that a curriculum needs to be developed from a Great Commission *a priori* instead…

Area	Required "Core" Courses (3 hours each)	Old Classical Philosophical-Theoretical	New Great Commission Paradigm
NT	Introduction to NT One and Two Introduction to Greek One and Two	12	9
OT	Introduction to OT One and OT Two Introduction to Hebrew One Introduction to Hebrew Two	12	3
Other Philosophical-Theoretical	Theology One and Two History of Christianity One and Two Ethics and Philosophy of Religion Introduction to Apologetics	18	0
Other Philosophical-Practical	Personal Spiritual Disciplines Pastoral Care and Counseling Principles of Preaching Christian Education Church Administration	15	3
Number of Non-Great Commission-Focused Courses		**57**	**15**
Evangelism	Introduction to Evangelism Church Evangelism (how to use CWT, EE, etc.) Evangelistic Preaching (including giving an invitation) History of Great Commission Activity (evangelism and church planting) Exegetical Evangelism (OT and NT evangelistic themes) The Work of an Evangelist (revival series, preparation, etc.) Practical Follow-up and Discipleship	3	21
Missions	Introduction to Missions Applied Bible in Missions Interfaith Evangelism Cross-Cultural Church Planting Ecumenics	3	15
Gospelology and History of the Churches	Applied Bible One (focusing on the Gospel) Applied Bible Two (focusing on conversion) History of the Great Commission One and Two	0	12
Number of Great Commission-Focused Courses		**6**	**48**
Total Number of Required "Core" Courses		**63**	**63**
Number of Concentration Hours and Elective Hours		**29**	**29**
Total M.Div. Hours		**92**	**92**

The weight and emphasis of each "core" curriculum is definitely quite different, with only 7 of the 21 courses overlapping, or 1/3rd of the current classical philosophical-theoretical courses; result:
From 9.5% to 66% Great Commission-focused faculty; from 90.5% theoretical faculty to 33% theoretical faculty
From 9.5% to 66% Great Commission-focused "core" courses; from 90.5% to 33% theoretical courses.

Concluding Comments:

1. Upon nascent investigation, it appears that the above curriculum corresponds with some of the logic behind:
   a. Bethlehem Chapel in Prague, Czechoslovakia, 1391, appeared to be training pastors and evangelists from a biblical perspective, with which John Hus was associated in 1402
   b. The early Reformation schools around the Luther in Wittenberg and later around Calvin in Geneva, who intentionally sought to avoid the pitfalls of Medieval scholasticism
   c. Evangelist Gilbert Tennent's "Log Cabin School," from which evolved Princeton University, appears to have been a home school with an evangelistic curriculum
   d. The early development of the U.S. Bible School movement in the late 19th and early 20th Centuries (such as Nyack Bible College and Moody Bible Institute), as many mainstream denominational schools were drifting from their biblical moorings
   e. Rather than "evangelism" being the one Great Awakening course thrust into an unwelcoming environment of classical philosophical-theology, evangelism, along with conversion, the Gospel, and the Great Commission would be front-and-center in the curriculum

2. Furthermore, it also appears that there are few if any textbooks suitable for this programs of study in the areas of Gospelology and History of the Churches:
   a. Because this paradigm of education appears new (in some ways), extensive bibliographic investigation will be necessary to ascertain if properly oriented books are available to fit the biblical paradigm, particularly in HC
   b. It appears that in both cases (GO and HC), it will be necessary to develop a new paradigm of curricula and new books to complement the new paradigm
   c. Further, there will need to be buy-in to the concepts and ideas of a completely Bible-based curriculum for higher education, so that trained evangelist-teachers can develop the necessary textbooks to be published and made available to students.

3. Finally there is the question of schools:
   a. Could existing accredited colleges and/or seminaries be retooled to accommodate a complete curriculum revision under the new paradigm?
   b. Would this paradigm necessitate a new movement of new schools being planted?
   c. Would there not be significant pressure from many sectors against this type of initiative?

Select Reverse Chronological
Historical-Theological Barriers and Disconnects

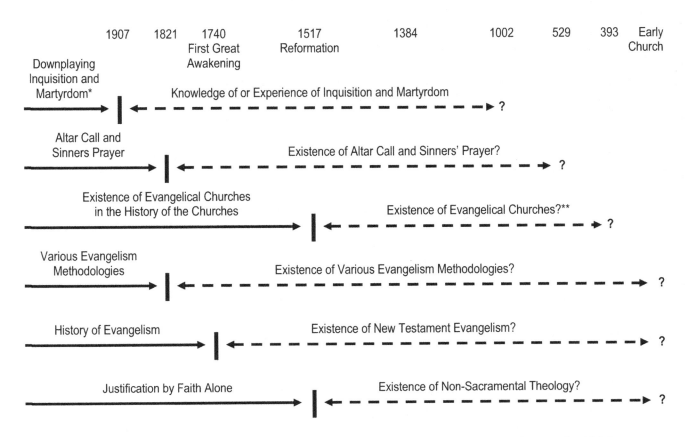

*Including also: the Evangelical teaching of Pre-Reformation Lights: Wycliffe and Hus; and the historical context in which the Franciscans and Dominicans were founded.

**Likewise existence of non-magisterial churches (i.e. non-state churches).

It is unknown to this author when it was forgotten that most or all of the Early Church Heresies (and Creeds) were at some point turned against the NT church, NT evangelism, and/or the Pauline Gospel (Adolf Harnack appears to have addressed this issue in his 1894 *History of Christian Dogma*). In this case, use of the Early Church Heresies is another change in the early 20th Century.

The obvious questions emanating from this study are: why, how, and what? Why is there a veil over these issues? How did it come to be that a veil was drawn over these issues? And what about the form of the Bible passed down from each of these time periods? Does it really matter, or is it merely meddling over trivialities of the past?

An explanation of the dates chosen:

> 1907, year of [Pope] Pius X's "*Pascendi Dominici Gregis:* On the Doctrine of the Modernists" in which "Counsels of Vigilance" commanded to be formed in every diocese, "with the task of noting the existence of errors and the devices by which new ones are introduced and propagated," and then "to extirpate the errors already propagated and to prevent their further diffusion, and to remove those teachers of impiety through whom the pernicious effects of such diffusion are being perpetuated" (Rome, 8 Sept 1907).

> 1821, when Charles Finney published his writings on revival in the *New York Evangelist*.

> 1740, date when the First Great Awakening began to spread.

> 1384, death of John Wycliffe

> 1002, "First executions of Cathars in France, at Orléans and Toulouse. Ten canons of the Collegiate Church of the Holy Cross sent to the stake" (Zoé Oldenbourg, "Chronological Table," in *The Massacre of Montségur*, Peter Green, trans [New York: Pantheon, 1962], 390-95; translation of *Le Bucher de Montségur* [Paris: Gallimard, 1959]).

> 529, year of the Second Council of Orange, for a reading of its canons and an analysis from an evangelistic point of view, please see the Appendix after Chapter 10.

393, year of Augustine's sermon, "On Faith and Creed," in which he differentiated between the Catholic faith and the faiths of the schismatics (e.g. Donatists) and heretics. He later urged the use of political pressure and extra taxation against Donatists to force them back into the Catholic church:

"Nor is this the actual question in dispute with them; but they carry on their unhappy strife solely on the question of communion, and in the perversity of their error maintain rebellious hostility against the unity of Christ" (Augustine, "A Treatise concerning the Correction of the Donatists" (417 A.D.) [Epistle CLXXXV], ch 1, §1).

"But God in His great mercy, knowing how necessary was the terror inspired by these laws, and a kind of medicinal inconvenience for the cold and wicked hearts of many men, and for that hardness of heart which cannot be softened by words, but yet admits of softening through the agency of some little severity of discipline, brought it about that our envoys could not obtain what they had undertaken to ask" (ibid., ch. 7, §26).

Chronological Historical-Theological Tracks:
A Graphic Portrayal of Disconnects in the Study of the History of the Churches;
Or: The Stairstep Approach to Teaching the History of the Churches

The Problem

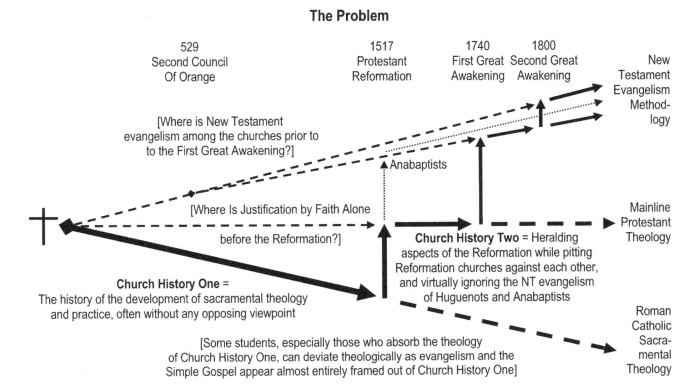

The solid black line attempts to portray the lines in which "Church History" is normally taught. Several questions emerge when the issues are considered:

Where are the New Testament churches prior to 1740, 1611, 1524, 1415, or 1380, or did they not exist? Likewise, was there New Testament evangelism prior to these dates?

Has not God reserved unto Himself, in the history of the churches, even the seven thousand that have not bowed the knee to Baal (cf. 1 Kings 19:18)?

Anabaptists, through whom a clear New Testament pattern emerged, have been marginalized, largely through the fallacy of composition, identifying Thomas Muntzer as the paragon of Anabaptists. These are denoted by a dotted line in the chart.

Likewise, the clear lines of cooperation and mutual support between the Alpine Waldenses and the Geneva Reformation are again blurred and ignored, forming a wall of separation between "Church History One" and "Church History Two" and muzzling the possibility of a pre-Reformation New Testament pattern.

This chart may also explain why it is difficult to maintain an Evangelical theological position if one studies deeply in the "Church History" prior to the Reformation. In fact, a "Church History One" class can be used to Romanize unsuspecting students, thereby turning them into janissaries. Consider:

Augustine (~A.D. 397-426): "All doctrine consists of things [objects] and signs" [*Omnis doctrina vel rerum est, vel signorum*], (*De doctrina Christiana*, bk. 1, c2, n2).

Peter the Lombard (~A.D. 1060): "All doctrine consists of things and signs" (*Four Books of Sentences*, bk 1, dist 1, c1, n1).

Thomas Aquinas: (~A.D. 1274):
"God is known by natural knowledge through the images of His effects" (*Summa*, FP, Q[12], A[12], Reply to Objection 2).
"But now we are speaking of sacraments in a special sense, as implying the habitude of sign: and in this way a sacrament is a kind of sign" (TP, Q[60], A[1], I Answer That).
"I answer that, Signs are given to men, to whom it is proper to discover the unknown by means of the known. Consequently a sacrament properly so called is that which is the sign of some sacred thing pertaining to man; so that properly speaking a sacrament, as considered by us now, is defined as being the 'sign of a holy thing so far as it makes men holy'" (TP, Q[60], A[2], I Answer That).

Second Council of Orange (A.D. 529), On Infant Baptism and Salvation:[270]

	About Infant Baptism	**About Believer's Baptizers**
Prior to Receiving Baptism	Outside the [holy] water of Baptism persons cannot understand the Gospel; Outside the [holy] water of Baptism persons cannot respond to the Gospel, even when and if it is effectively shared with them in the power of the Holy Spirit: Otherwise that is placing too much emphasis on their own rational humanity (hence, humanism or rationalism) Otherwise, that is not believing in the Council of Orange's definition of "total depravity" The operations of God's grace are all about the sign and symbol of the sacrament, which is in this case is dispensed through and only through the [Holy] Water of Holy Baptism[271]	Simply preaching the Gospel to lost persons is illegitimate, since only through the waters of Baptism can anyone be cleansed of original sin, and thereby understand the gospel and receive salvation Those who preach the Gospel indiscriminately expecting lost people to believe merely from hearing the Gospel with a hearing of faith: • Must not understand that the Holy Spirit must be dispensed with the sign of water • Must not understand that man in his own rational being cannot comprehend the things of God (hence Luther was accused of being a "humanist") Therefore, anyone who evangelizes indiscriminately must not believe in total depravity, making them "semi-Pelagian" (as it was described in those days), whereas through Infant Baptism they had already received Christ
What Baptism Does?	Second Council of Orange "According to the catholic faith we also believe that after grace has been received through [infant] baptism, all baptized persons have the ability and responsibility, if they desire to labor faithfully, to perform with the aid and cooperation of Christ what is of essential importance in regard to the salvation of their soul."	The Anabaptist Balthasar Hubmaier "Summary of the Entire Christian Life" (1525) "From all this it follows that the outward baptism unto Christ is nothing else than a public profession of the inward obligation. By it, man confesses publicly that he is a sinner, and admits his guilt. Yet he believes that Christ, through His death, has atoned for his sins, and by His resurrection has made him righteous in the sight of God,

---

[270]"CONCLUSION. And thus according to the passages of holy scripture quoted above or the interpretations of the ancient Fathers we must, under the blessing of God, preach and believe as follows. The sin of the first man has so impaired and weakened free will that no one thereafter can either love God as he ought or believe in God or do good for God's sake, unless the grace of divine mercy has preceded him. We therefore believe that the glorious faith which was given to Abel the righteous, and Noah, and Abraham, and Isaac, and Jacob, and to all the saints of old, and which the Apostle Paul <sic> commends in extolling them (Heb. 11), was not given through natural goodness as it was before to Adam, but was bestowed by the grace of God. And we know and also believe that even after the coming of our Lord this grace is not to be found in the free will of all who desire to be baptized, but is bestowed by the kindness of Christ, as has already been frequently stated and as the Apostle Paul declares, "For it has been granted to you that for the sake of Christ you should not only believe in him but also suffer for his sake" (Phil. 1:29). And again, "He who began a good work in you will bring it to completion at the day of Jesus Christ" (Phil. 1:6). And again, "For by grace you have been saved through faith; and it is not your own doing, it is the gift of God" (Eph. 2:8). And as the Apostle says of himself, "I have obtained mercy to be faithful" (1 Cor. 7:25, cf. 1 Tim. 1:13). He did not say, "because I was faithful," but "to be faithful." And again, "What have you that you did not receive?" (1 Cor. 4:7). And again, "Every good endowment and every perfect gift is from above, coming down from the Father of lights" (Jas. 1:17). And again, "No one can receive anything except what is given him from heaven" (John 3:27). There are innumerable passages of holy scripture which can be quoted to prove the case for grace, but they have been omitted for the sake of brevity, because further examples will not really be of use where few are deemed sufficient.

"According to the catholic faith we also believe that after grace has been received through baptism, all baptized persons have the ability and responsibility, if they desire to labor faithfully, to perform with the aid and cooperation of Christ what is of essential importance in regard to the salvation of their soul. We not only do not believe that any are foreordained to evil by the power of God, but even state with utter abhorrence that if there are those who want to believe so evil a thing, they are anathema. We also believe and confess to our benefit that in every good work it is not we who take the initiative and are then assisted through the mercy of God, but God himself first inspires in us both faith in him and love for him without any previous good works of our own that deserve reward, so that we may both faithfully seek the sacrament of baptism, and after baptism be able by his help to do what is pleasing to him. We must therefore most evidently believe that the praiseworthy faith of the thief whom the Lord called to his home in paradise, and of Cornelius the centurion, to whom the angel of the Lord was sent, and of Zacchaeus, who was worthy to receive the Lord himself, was not a natural endowment but a gift of God's kindness" (Second Council of Orange; available at: From: http://www.fordham.edu/halsall/basis/orange.txt [online]; accessed: 5 June 2009; Internet).

[271]"I answer that, God is said to be in a thing in two ways; in one way after the manner of an efficient cause; and thus He is in all things created by Him; in another way he is in things as the object of operation is in the operator; and this is proper to the operations of the soul, according as the thing known is in the one who knows; and the thing desired in the one desiring" (Thomas Aquinas, Summa, FP, Q[8], A[2], "Whether God is everywhere?"; available at: http://www.ccel.org/ccel/aquinas/summa.html [online]; accessed: 19 June 2008; Internet).

		our heavenly Father. Therefore he has determined to confess openly and publicly the faith and name of Jesus Christ."
After Receiving Baptism	They will not refuse the grace of God, although they will need to add works to the graces that they receive by the Holy Sacraments of the Holy Roman Church Likewise they do not need to hear the Gospel again, since they have already responded to the Gospel (through receiving baptism)	[Since Orange placed the focus on the holy waters of Baptism, everything is fine once persons have submitted to water Baptism] [Makes one wonder if this was why the so-called "Albigenses" or "Cathars" of the Middle Ages emphasized waterless Spirit-Baptism]
Therefore	Someone who tries to evangelize a baptized person is *ipso facto* a heretic Likewise, someone who tells an infant baptized person that he is not converted is a heretic: • Doubting the effectiveness of the Sacrament as taught by the Catholic Church, and • Causing the Baptized Catholic person to doubt their salvation!	
Interestingly	Those who vehemently oppose a so-called "sinner's prayer," seem to have no problem with the prayer of the priest or pastor over the "Holy Water" to infuse that water with the graces it signifies	Meanwhile, the prayer of a thinking child or adult, repenting and confessing sin and requesting from God to receive Jesus Christ as Savior, is made to be somehow inferior to the prayer over the water to be poured or sprinkled over the head of a baby who, very likely, does not even have their eyes open yet!

Council of Trent (A.D. 1547), Order of Salvation:[272]

Wording of Decree	Historical-Theological Analysis
"Now they [adults] are disposed to justice when,	Begins with individual personal disposition, i.e. non-Total Depravity
"Aroused and aided by divine grace,	Grace = infant baptism = plays a starting and assisting role, i.e. it is not "grace alone"
"Receiving faith by hearing,	Hearing what? Clearly not a "hearing of faith," nor hearing "Scriptures alone" Spiritual input thermostat #1? Unclear.
"They are moved freely toward God,	They exert their own will to move toward God, not undeserved favor
"Believing to be true what has been divinely revealed and promised,	I.e. "divine revelation" in Scripture, Tradition, and the Church Spiritual input thermostat #2? Unclear.
"Especially that the sinner is justified by God by his grace,	Is this teaching the substitutionary atonement? No, it's the grace of infant baptism + the other sacraments.
"Through the redemption that is in Christ Jesus;	What about the cross? What about the Gospel?
"And when, understanding themselves to be sinners	Does not seem that God shows them their sinfulness especially by the work of the Holy Spirit through the Word of God? E.g. John 16:8 Spiritual input thermostat #3? Unclear.
"They, by turning themselves from the fear of divine justice,	Not repenting of their sin? Notice again the emphasis on what man can do. Spiritual input thermostat #4? Unclear.

---

[272]"Now, they are disposed to that justice when, aroused and aided by divine grace, receiving faith by hearing, they are moved freely toward God, believing to be true what has been divinely revealed and promised, especially that the sinner is justified by God by his grace, through the redemption that is in Christ Jesus; and when, understanding themselves to be sinners, they, by turning themselves from the fear of divine justice, by which they are salutarily aroused, to consider the mercy of God, are raised to hope, trusting that God will be propitious to them for Christ's sake; and they begin to love Him as the fountain of all justice, and on that account are moved against sin by a certain hatred and detestation, that is, by that repentance that must be performed before baptism; finally, when they resolve to receive baptism, to begin a new life and to keep the commandments of God. Of this disposition it is written: He that cometh to God, must believe that he is, and is a rewarder to them that seek him; and, Be of good faith, son, thy sins are forgiven thee; and, The fear of the Lord driveth out sin; and, Do penance, and be baptized every one of you in the name of Jesus Christ, for the remission of your sins, and you shall receive the gift of the Holy Ghost; and, Going, therefore, teach ye all nations, baptizing them in the name of the Father, and of the Son, and of the Holy Ghost, teaching them to observe all things whatsoever I have commanded you; finally, Prepare your hearts unto the Lord" (Council of Trent, Decree Concerning Justification" [from 13 Jan 1547], Chap 6, "The Manner of Preparation"; available at: http://www.forerunner.com/chalcedon/X0020_15._Council_of_Trent.html ; accessed 8 Jan 2005; Internet).

"To which they are salutarily aroused,	Spiritual input thermostat #5? Unclear who arouses this knowledge in them.
"To consider the mercy of God,	Not receive the grace of God through faith, and a prayer to confess sins and confess Christ? Notice again the emphasis on man's ability to understand his own predicament Spiritual input thermostat #6? Unclear.
"Are raised to hope,	From whence does this hope come? Spiritual input thermostat #7? Unclear.
"Trusting that God will be propitious to them for Christ's sake;	Not to save them? God shows His grace "to them" by empowering the Sacraments of the Church with His Holy Spirit. Oh, also there's still purgatory which quenches the Blessed Hope!
"And they begin to love Him as the fountain of all justice,	Faith is transformed into some type of metaphysical love that man develops for God? Man's response of love included in the *ordo salutis*? Spiritual input thermostat #8? Unclear.
"And on that account are moved against sin by a certain hatred and detestation,	What about God's hatred of sin? Is this not salvation as a hatred of the vices and a love of the virtues? Spiritual input thermostat #9? Unclear.
"That is, by that repentance that is performed before baptism;	Is repentance an action to be performed? Makes repentance an act of man (e.g. penance) Spiritual input thermostat #10? Is repentance a performance of something?
"Finally, when they are resolved to receive baptism,	Herein is salvation for the Catholic church, the resolution to receive baptism; building upon the Second Council of Orange (529) Spiritual input thermostat #11? Another work of man.
"To begin a new life and to keep the commandments of God	Baptism is only the beginning of salvation, to which must be added all the commandments of Christ and the means of grace given to His Church (i.e. the Sacraments of the Catholic Church). Where's the finality of salvation here? It does not exist, which leads to chapter 9 "Against the Vain Confidence of the Heretics"!

Reversing the Chronological Historical-Theological Tracks

A Proposed Solution

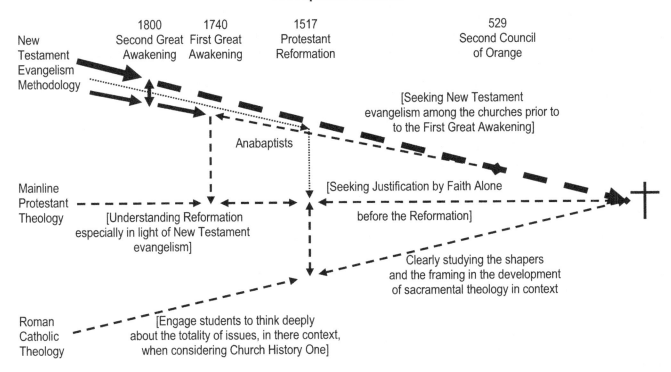

The proposed answer to this historiographic dilemma is to work back from the present, as delineated in the above chart. Avoiding false historical disjunctures and intense study of original texts may elicit some helpful material. It must be understood, however, that historical precedent never supercedes the biblical record as far as authority. Thus, the Bible stands head and shoulders above any interpretation of or findings in the history of the churches.

The additional complexity noted by the two heavy lines at the top of the chart represent the two supposed differences over which Baptists are splitting today: supposed First Great Awakening methodology (preaching without an invitation or sinner's prayer); and the supposed Second Great Awakening methodology (preaching with an invitation and a sinners prayer). The intensity of the debate over these issues and the shunning that id practiced as a result is almost comical were it not so serious in light of the other issues represented, which have much more stern consequences upon the eternal destiny of billions.

May God bless His people with unity around the biblical record!

Some histories that this author has found that seek to address the missing pieces in history are books such as:

(1) Various Protestant or Baptist Martyrologies, such as *Foxe's Book of Martyrs* (unabridged edition) or Thieleman J. van Braght, *The Bloody Theater or Martyrs Mirror* (1660; Scottdale, PA: Herald Press, 2007)

(2) Baptist histories, such as Henry Vedder's *A Short History of Baptists* (Philadelphia: Judson, 1907) and Thomas Armitage's *A History of Baptists* (New York: Taylor, 1886); and

(3) James A. Wylie's *The History of Protestantism* (London: Cassell, 1889); Wylie, by the way, authored *The Papacy: Its History, Dogmas, Genius and Prospects*, which was awarded a prize by the [British] Evangelical Alliance in 1851. He joined the Free Church of Scotland in 1852, received an Honorary Doctorate from Aberdeen University in 1856, and was lecturer on Popery at the Protestant Institute from 1860-1890 [possibly at St. Andrews University].

One the other hand, it appears that if a book is broad-based to cover the entire history of the church, one of the taboos is to speak negatively of the development of sacramental theology within the remaining records passed down of history from the monks of the Church of Rome.

Considering the Ranges of Training Needed
By Different Levels and Types of Leaders

Does one-size-fits-all Master of Divinity prepare church leaders for every level of pastoral leadership?

Does a Director of Mission encounter issues and difficulties different than the average pastor?

Does the State Executive or Seminary President encounter issues that differentiate his role and responsibilities from that of the DOM?

How can and should pastoral training be framed to meet the needs for men who change positions in level of leadership responsibility?

Is the average D.Min. or Ph.D. adequate for preparing the pastor to move from his local church responsibilities to other levels of responsibility, or is all he needs is advanced research in one the fields already covered in his M.Div.?

Are there some things that can only be learned by failure or on-the-job training?

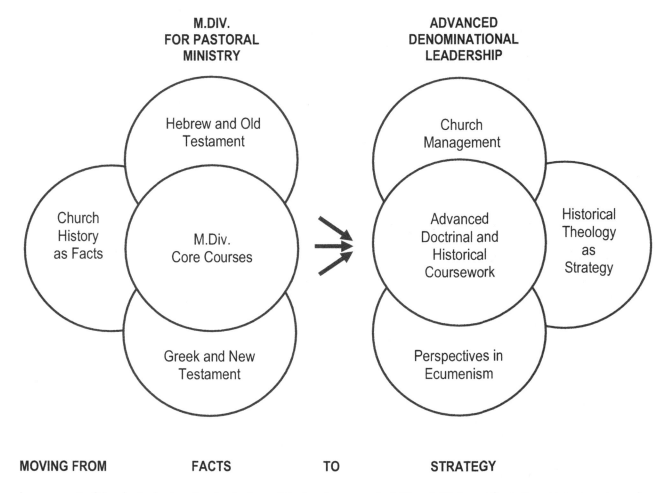

MOVING FROM   FACTS   TO   STRATEGY

In a way, all of theological education is strategy. It just so happens that Church History reflects the strategic nature of theological education more clearly than do other areas. Consider however:

- How does one teach theology or doctrine, and why?
- How does one teach evangelism, and why?
- How does one teach exegesis and why?

Each area reflects the strategic nature of the topic and how it can be leveraged either for the Gospel and the Great Commission or against it.

Considering Approaches to Evangelism in Academic Settings
With a Proposed Great Commission Grading Scale
Thomas P. Johnston, Ph.D.

N	M	L	K	J	I	H	G	F	E	D	C	B	A
0	0	1	2	3	3	4	5	6	7	8	9	9	10
Evangelism Prohibited		Evangelism Discouraged		Evangelism Tolerated		Evangelism Encouraged (at least by administration)							
Secular education, perhaps philosophical core or liberal arts core													
Open hostility to Evangelical Christianity on school property	Open antagonism to any vestige of Evangelical Christianity in the curriculum	Tight parameters placed upon any evangelistic student organizations on campus	Limited freedom to discuss evangelism or Evangelicalism in the classroom	Freedom allowed to student organizations who proselytize on campus property	Bible core, but no evangelism taught; Rather evangelism frowned upon as non-academic	Evangelism considered peripherally in some classes; But not taught as a separate class	Evangelism classes not required of any major; Taught as a free elective	Evangelism classes not required of all students; However, required for limited majors	Evangelism classes taught; One class required of all students; other evangelism classes taught for a specific major or as free electives	Two evangelism classes required of all students: Basic Evangelism and Church Evangelism	Evangelism major offered and promoted		Majors for evangelism and evangelists
Evangelism courses not in the curriculum (not deemed a necessary or integral part of a good education)						" All our classes are evangelism!"	Indirect evangelism taught (service, lifestyle, relationship)	Direct evangelism taught (initiative, expectant, New Testament)	Indirect evangelism taught (service, lifestyle, relationship)	Direct evangelism taught (initiative, expectant, New Testament)	Direct evangelism taught, as well as how to make it happen in the local church		
Students admitted regardless of their spiritual standing							Unsaved students not admitted						
State Schools				Christian Liberal Arts Schools			Christian Colleges, Seminaries, and Bible Colleges						
Do not allow Christian organizations to proselytize openly		Allow Christian organizations to proselytize in certain ways		Christian organizations usually do not have a place in these schools, as they are or were formerly denominationally-controlled			Evangelism is not officially organized			Evangelism is officially organized		Evangelism is expected DNA of entire community	

CHAPTER 5
Steadfast Truths in Evangelism

"When God permits pastors to die for the Gospel,
they preach more loudly and more effectively from the casket than they did during their lifetime."
Claude Brousson, *Lettres aux Pasteurs réfugiés*, 1683[273]

I. Timeless Realities of Evangelism:

Introduction:
> V. Raymond Edman gave this advice to Wheaton College students, "Never doubt in the dark what you saw in the light."[274]

In evangelism there are some realities that must be faced, in order to become effective in evangelism—note this possible progression in the life of the Apostle Paul…

"Reality Therapy" in the Life of the Apostle Paul

Nascent Optimism ➜	Alarm at Antagonism ➜	Humble Realism ➜	Divine Perspective ➜	Humble Submission ➜	Holy Motivation ➜	Holy Expectation
Note the Apostle Paul's early optimism as to the receptivity of religious leaders in Jerusalem, Acts 22:19-20	Paul warned the Philippian church not to be alarmed by opponents to the Gospel, Phil 1:28	Hard lessons learned through trial and persecution because of sharing the Gospel, Rom 5:3-5	Recognizing that the trials for the Gospel result in glory for those who receive it, Eph 3:13	Sacrificial submission to God's will and working in the midst of the trials that come from evangelism, Rom 9:1-3, 18	Desire to bear fruit; sense of divine obligation; eager evangelizing, Rom 1:13-15	Expecting the Gospel itself to be powerfully at work when evangelized, Rom 1:15-17

It was therefore important for the Apostle Paul to remind new believers that trials and afflictions were a part of their destiny as Christians:
> Acts 14:21-22, "And after they had preached the gospel to that city and had made many disciples, they returned to Lystra and to Iconium and to Antioch, strengthening the souls of the disciples, encouraging them to continue in the faith, and *saying*, '**Through many tribulations we must enter the kingdom of God.**'"
> Rom 8:17, "and if children, heirs also, heirs of God and fellow heirs with Christ, **if indeed we suffer** with *Him* in order that we may also be glorified with *Him*."
> 1 Thess 3:1-4, "Therefore when we could endure *it* no longer, we thought it best to be left behind at Athens alone; and we sent Timothy, our brother and God's fellow worker in the gospel of Christ, to strengthen and encourage you as to your faith, so that no man may be disturbed by these afflictions; **for you yourselves know that we have been destined for this**. For indeed when we were with you, we *kept* telling you in advance that **we were going to suffer affliction**; and so it came to pass, as you know."

And even in the midst of trial, Paul was content that his past and present sufferings were worth it, as long as those who had believed remained faithful:
> 1 Thess 3:6-8, "But now that Timothy has come to us from you, and has brought us good news of your faith and love, and that you always think kindly of us, longing to see us just as we also long to see you, for this reason, brethren, **in all our distress and affliction** we were comforted about you through your faith; for now we *really* live, if you stand firm in the Lord."

---

[273]Léopold Nègre, *Vie et Ministère de Claude Brousson, 1647-1698* (Paris: Sandoz et Fischbacher, 1878), front cover; translation mine.
[274]V. Raymond Edman, *The Disciplines of Life* (Minneapolis: World Wide, 1948), 33.

For example, "Suffer hardship with me" [συγκακοπάθησον] 2 Tim 1:8:

On the Translations of κακοπαθέω and συγκακοπαθέω in 2 Tim 1:8

Wycliffe*	DRA‡	NAB‡	NET	NJB‡	NKJ	NASB; NIV	RSV; CSB; ESV	ERV; ASV	Geneva; KJV	Tyndale; Bishops	Young's; Darby
Travel thou together in the gospel	Labor with the gospel	Bear your share of hardship for the gospel	Accept your share of suffering for the gospel	Share in my hardships for the sake for the gospel	Share with me in the sufferings for the gospel	Join with *me* in suffering for the gospel	Share in suffering for the gospel	Suffer hardship with the gospel	Be partaker of the afflictions of the Gospel	Suffer adversity with the gospel	Do thou suffer evil along with the good news
"Therfor nyl thou schame the witnessyng of oure Lord Jhesu Crist, nether me, his prisoner; but trauele thou togidere in the gospel bi the vertu of God"	Be not thou therefore ashamed of the testimony of our Lord, nor of me his prisoner: but labour with the gospel, according to the power of God	So do not be ashamed of your testimony to our Lord, nor of me, a prisoner for his sake; but bear your share of hardship for the gospel with the strength that comes from God	So do not be ashamed of the testimony about our Lord or of me, a prisoner for his sake, but by God's power accept your share of suffering for the gospel	So you are never to be ashamed of witnessing to our Lord, or ashamed of me for being his prisoner; but share in my hardships for the sake of the gospel, relying on the power of God	Therefore do not be ashamed of the testimony of our Lord, nor of me His prisoner, but share with me in the sufferings for the gospel according to the power of God	Therefore do not be ashamed of the testimony of our Lord, or of me His prisoner; but join with *me* in suffering for the gospel according to the power of God	Do not be ashamed then of testifying to our Lord, nor of me his prisoner, but share in suffering for the gospel in the power of God	"Be not ashamed therefore of the testimony of our Lord, nor of me his prisoner: but suffer hardship with the gospel according to the power of God"	"Be not therefore ashamed of the testimonie of our Lord, nether of me his prisoner: but be partaker of the afflictions of the Gospel, according to the power of God"	Be not a shamed to testyfye oure lorde nether be a shamed of me which am bounde for his sake: but suffre adversite with the gospell also thorow the power of god	"therefore thou mayest not be ashamed of the testimony of our Lord, nor of me his prisoner, but do thou suffer evil along with the good news according to the power of God"

*A translation of the Latin Vulgate.

On the Translations of κακοπαθέω and συγκακοπαθέω in 2 Tim 2:3

Latin (Migne): Labora		Greek (Critical edition): Συγκακοπάθησον						Greek (Byzantine textform): Σὺ οὖν κακοπάθησον				
Wycliffe	DRA‡	NJB‡	NAB‡	NIV	ERV; ASV; NASB	RSV; CSB; ESV	Darby; NET	NKJ	KJV	Tyndale; Geneva	Bishops	Young's
Trauele thou as a good knyyt of Crist Jhesu	Labour as a good soldier of Christ Jesus	Bear with your share of difficulties, like a good soldier of Christ Jesus	Bear your share of hardship along with me like a good soldier of Christ Jesus	Endure hardship with us like a good soldier of Christ Jesus	Suffer hardship with *me*, as a good soldier of Christ Jesus	Share in suffering as a good soldier of Christ Jesus	Take thy share in suffering as a good soldier of Jesus Christ	You therefore must endure hardship as a good soldier of Jesus Christ	Thou therefore endure hardness, as a good soldier of Jesus Christ	Thou therefore suffer affliction as a good souldier of Iesus Christ	Thou therfore suffer afflictions as a good souldier of Iesus Christe	thou, therefore, suffer evil as a good soldier of Jesus Christ

Therefore, our goal as Christians is **not** to avoid all trial and difficulty at all cost. Rather our goal is to be obedient to the One who called us:

2 Cor 11:7 (Rotherham), "Or, a sin, did I commit—abasing myself, that, ye might be exalted,—in that, free of charge, God's glad-message, I announced unto you?" [slight variation in punctuation]

A. Fear Is Inevitable:

Introduction:
- a. In a day when teens are competing in "Fear Factor," it is inconceivable that Christians are scared to tell of Christ… But that's the way it is!
- b. Listen to some of the closing words of Jean Bertrand to his judges and executioners:

> "Therefore noting that they would be able to get nothing more from him, the lawyer for the King told him, if he wanted to recant, Jesus Christ forgives, it would also be forgiven him, and that he would pray the lords for him. Bertrand responded that it is written, that in this one must not fear men, who only have power over the body, but that one must fear God, who has power over the body and the soul, and who is able to put all into the Gehenna of fire. He also promised that those who will confess Him before men, will be confessed similarly before God His Father; adding that he was not expecting to lose even one hair from his head, seeing as they were all counted."[275]

1. The principle of fear:
   - a. The positive **fear of God**, 2 Cor 5:11
   - b. The negative **fear of man**, Luke 12:4-5 (cf. Isa 51:7, e.g. I Sam. 15:24, Matt 14:5, 21:46), "Peer-pressure"
     1) The pressure to conform, Rom 12:1-2
     2) Loving the approval of man, John 12:42-43 (cf. Rom 2:29)
     3) Fear because of the risk of breaking a relationship, Matt 10:35-36
     4) "The fear of man brings a snare, But he who trusts in the Lord will be exalted," Prov 29:25
     5) "Cursed is the man who trusts in mankind and makes flesh his strength, and whose heart turns away from the Lord." Jer 17:5
   - c. Aspects of fear:
     1) Fear in evangelism, Phil 1:14 (cf. 2 Cor 7:5)
     2) Fear to acknowledge Christ, John 7:13 (cf. John 12:42-43)

2. Examples of fear in evangelism:
   - a. The apostle Paul, <u>Acts 18:9-10</u>, 1 Cor 2:3, 2 Cor 7:5
   - b. Those who were encouraged by the imprisonment of Paul, Phil 1:14
   - c. Consider the admonition of Paul to Timothy in 2 Tim 1:7:

Translating ἡ δειλία in 2 Tim 1:7

Introduction: Does it not seem like Paul is encouraging Timothy not to be a *femmelette* (effeminate) in 2 Tim 1:7?

Byzantine Greek	Wycliffe (1388)	Tyndale (1534); Geneva; KJV; DRA; NKJ; NET; ESV	Darby (1884); NAB	ERV (1885); ASV; CSB	RSV (1952); NAS; NIV; NJB	NLT (2004)
δειλία	Dread	Fear	Cowardice	Fearfulness	Timidity	Fear and timidity
Οὐ γὰρ ἔδωκεν ἡμῖν ὁ θεὸς πνεῦμα δειλίας	For whi God yaf not to vs the spirit of drede	For god hath not geven to vs the sprete of feare	For God has not given us a spirit of cowardice	For God gave us not a spirit of fearfulness	for God did not give us a spirit of timidity	For God has not given us a spirit of fear and timidity

All other OT LXX uses of ἡ δειλία:
- Lev 26:36, "As for those of you who may be left, I will also bring **weakness** into their hearts in the lands of their enemies…."
- Psa 55:4, "My heart is in anguish within me, And the **terrors** of death have fallen upon me."
- Psa 89:40 (Brenton), "Thou hast broken down all his hedges; thou hast made his strong holds a **terror**."
- Prov 19:15, "**Cowardice** [ἡ δειλία] possesses the effeminate *man* [ἀνδρογύναιος]; and the soul of the sluggard shall hunger."

---

[275]"Jean Bertrand [martyred in 1556]," Jean Crespin, ed. *Histoire des vrais tesmoins de la verite de l'evangile, qui de leur sang l'ont signée, depuis Jean Hus iusques autemps present* [*History of the True Witnesses to the Truth of the Gospel, Who with Their Blood Signed, from John Hus to the Present*] (Geneva, 1570; Liège, 1964), 433. Translation mine.

Notice also the reverse gender emphasis in Paul:
1 Cor 16:13 reads, "act like men" [the plural command ἀνδρίζεσθε is from ἀνδρίζομαι]

3. The results of fear:
   a. Positive: greater dependency on God, Jos. 1:9, Acts 18:9-10, Eph 6:19-20
   b. Negative:
      1) Denial of Christ, Matt 26:69-75
      2) Silence, Acts 18:9-10 (cf. 2 Kings 7:9)
      3) Inaction, laziness and compromise, Prov 22:13, 25:26
      4) Serving the creature rather than the Creator, Rom 1:25

4. God wants the Christian to overcome fear:
   a. The importance of prayer, Eph 6:19-20 (a continual need)
   b. Through putting one's confidence in God, Psa 27:1, 56:4-5, 12
   c. The command to be strong and courageous, Deut 31:6, 7, 23, Joshua 1:6, 9, 18, Prov 28:1
      1) The "be strong" verb [chazaq] is translated in the Greek LXX using ἀνδρίζομαι, "act like men," [ἀνδρίζου] which is picked up by Paul in 1 Cor 16:13, the only use of this verb in the NT
      2) The singular imperative in the OT is replaced by the plural imperative in 1 Cor 16:13, addressed to the entire church!
   d. The admonition to stand firm, 1 Cor 15:58, Heb 3:6
   e. God's encouragement, "Do not fear," Deut 31:6, 8, 23, Jos. 1:6, 9, Acts 18:9-10

5. God helps the Christian overcome fear:
   a. He forgives us for times that we have not told of Him, John 21:15-17
   b. The importance of a knowledge of God's presence, Deut 31:8, Jos. 1:5, 9, Matt 28:19-20, Acts 18:9-10
   c. The importance of faith in God, Psa 27:1, Prov 3:25-26
   d. God sees, knows and will judge everything, Gen 16:13, Psa 32:8, Isa 51:8
   e. God is salvation and defense for the Christian, Psa 27:1
   f. The importance of good examples to give courage, Phil 1:14
   g. It is possible to evangelize without fear, Phil 1:14

6. Summary: Fear Is Inevitable, but it can be overcome. Praise the Lord!

B. Difficulties Are Inevitable:

1. Difficulties in Evangelism:
   a. Evangelism is hard work, e.g. 2 Cor 1:8-9:
      1) "Sow with tears," Psa 126:5-6.
      2) "Others have labored," John 4:38.
      3) "Struggle in the cause of the Gospel," Phil 4:3, "Contended" (NIV)
   b. The Gospel lifestyle often brings rejection, 1 Cor 4:9-13 (e.g. Acts 17:5), 2 Cor 6:8-10 (cf. Jesus Himself was the stone rejected by the builders, Psa 118:22-23; Acts 4:11)
   c. There is suffering in evangelism, 2 Tim 1:8 (e.g. Acts 9:16)
      1) "Why are we also in danger every hour?" 1 Cor 15:30
   d. There are adversaries to the bold proclamation of the Word, 1 Cor 16:8-9, Phil 1:17:

      "But I shall remain in Ephesus until Pentecost; for a wide door for effective *service* has opened to me, and there are many adversaries" 1 Cor 16:8-9.

   e. Other Christians may desert the evangelist, 2 Tim 4:16-17 (cf. Matt 26:56)
   f. Jesus prophesied that though there are few workers (Matt 9:37; Luke 10:2), yet there are many false prophets and false teachers (Matt 24:11; Mark 13:6; Luke 21:8; cf. 1 John 4:1)

2. Difficulties in seeing responses to the Gospel:
   a. Some are blind to the Gospel message, Isa 6:9-10, Matt 13:4, 19, Acts 28:26-27, 2 Cor 3:15, 4:3-4
   b. Only a few will ever accept the Gospel, Matt 7:13-14, 1 Cor 7:16, 9:22 ("all" > "some").

3. Difficulties in seeing the continued impact of the Gospel in lives:
   a. Some who "accept" the Gospel fall away from the Lord, Matt 13:18-23
   b. Sorrow for some people's lack of spiritual growth, 2 Cor 2:1

    c. There is a burden for those who come to know the Lord, 2 Cor 11:28

4. Difficulties in life:
   a. Sleeplessness, 2 Cor 6:5, 11:27
   b. Hunger, 1 Cor 4:11, 2 Cor 6:5, 11:27, "often without food."
   c. Hardships in travel, 2 Cor 11:26 (e.g. Acts 27:9ff.)
   d. Living in need, Phil 4:11-12 (cf. 1 Cor 4:11)

5. Even difficulties from false brethren, 2 Cor 11:26 (e.g. 1 Cor 4:6-13):

6. Two results of difficulties (i.e. of Paul's imprisonment):
   a. Discouragement:
      Eph 3:13, "Therefore I ask you not to lose heart at my tribulations on your behalf, for they are your glory."
   b. Greater courage in evangelism:
      Phil 1:12-14, "Now I want you to know, brethren, that my circumstances have turned out for the greater progress of the gospel, so that my imprisonment in *the cause of* Christ has become well known throughout the whole praetorian guard and to everyone else, and that most of the brethren, trusting in the Lord because of my imprisonment, have far more courage to speak the word of God without fear."

7. Overcoming difficulties:
   a. Trusting in God's sovereignty over circumstances, 1 Cor 16:9
   b. Trusting in God's faithfulness, 1 Thess 5:24 (cf. Isa 49:14-15)
   c. Perseverance in God's will, Gal 6:9
   d. Rejoicing in the Lord, 1 Pet 4:12-16

8. Conclusion: Yes, difficulties in evangelism abound. Nevertheless, the Lord remains true to His promises! "For the Lord will not abandon His people, nor will He forsake His inheritance," Psa 94:14.

C. Antagonism Is Inevitable!

1. Seeking to live uprightly:
   a. Be blameless, Acts 24:16, Eph 1:4, Phil 2:15
   b. Give no offense, 1 Cor 10:32-33, 2 Cor 6:2

2. Reasons for antagonism:
   a. The world's hatred of Jesus and His followers, John 15:18-20 (cf. Psa 25:19)

On the Translation of ἀφιλάγαθος in 2 Tim 3:3
[Issue: Haters of those who do good? Or haters of good?]

Context: 2 Tim 3:1-5 (NKJ) "But know this, that in the last days perilous times will come: For men will be lovers of themselves, lovers of money, boasters, proud, blasphemers, disobedient to parents, unthankful, unholy, unloving, unforgiving, slanderers, without self-control, brutal, **despisers of good**, traitors, headstrong, haughty, lovers of pleasure rather than lovers of God, having a form of godliness but denying its power. And from such people turn away!"

Byzantine	Geneva (1560); Bishops (1595)	Geneva (1599)	KJV (1611, 1769); Webster's	Murdock (1852)	Young's (1862)	Tyndale (1534)	NIV (1984)	Darby (1884)	English Rev (1885); ASV	Douay-Rheims* (1899)	Bible in Basic Eng (1949)	RSV (1952); NASB	NKJ (1982)	CSB (2003)	NLT (2004)	NET (2005)
	Referring to individuals who do good					Open		Referring to the concept of good								
ἀφιλ-άγαθοι	despisers of them which are good	no louers at all of them which are good	despisers of those that are good	haters of the good	not lovers of those who are good	despisers of the [sic] which are good	not lovers of the good	having no love for what is good	no lovers of good	without kindness	hating all good	haters of good	despisers of good	without love for what is good	They will ... hate what is good	opposed to what is good

*Interestingly, while the 1522 French Lefèvre followed the Latin Vulgate: "without benificity" (as the Douay-Rheims above), the French Geneva (1616) translated this term as "haïssans les bons" (hating the good [people]); likewise, the French Martin (1707) and the French Geneva Revised (1977) added the word "gens" (people), translating ἀφιλάγαθος as referring to those who do good: "ennemis des gens de bien" (enemies of people of good). The French Darby and all the other translations changed the translation to refer to the concept of good, as exemplified above.

b. Professing Christians share in the sufferings of Christ, 2 Cor 1:5 (e.g. Acts 5:41)
c. The sinfulness of man, John 3:20
d. Jealousy, Acts 5:17-18, 13:45, 17:5
e. Evangelism draws opposition, Phil 1:27-28

3. Examples of antagonism:
   a. David was lonely and afflicted, Psa 25:16
   b. Jesus had pretenders following Him to catch Him in His words, Luke 20:20
   c. Throughout the Acts, antagonism to the Gospel was evident, Acts 4:1-2
   d. False brethren, 2 Cor 11:26
   e. Alexander the Coppersmith, 2 Tim 4:14-15

4. Describing this antagonism:
   a. A battle:
      2 Cor 10:3-5 (NKJ), "For though we walk in the flesh, we do not war according to the flesh. [4] For the weapons of our warfare *are* not carnal but mighty in God for pulling down strongholds, [5] casting down arguments and every high thing that exalts itself against the knowledge of God, bringing every thought into captivity to the obedience of Christ."
   b. Conflict:
      1 Thess 2:2, "but after we had already suffered and been mistreated in Philippi, as you know, we had the boldness in our God to speak to you the gospel of God **amid much opposition**"

Translating ἐν πολλῷ ἀγῶνι in 1 Thess 2:2

(Degree: from "Least struggle" at left to "Most struggle" at right)

Degree	Vulgate (435)	Wycliffe, 2nd ed. (1388)	Douay-Rheims* (1899)	Bible in Basic English (1945/1962)	Complete Jewish Bible (1998)	New American Bible* (1901)	English Geneva (1560)	King James Version (1611/1769)	Young's Literal (1962)	English Revised (1885)	American Standard (1901)	English Standard Version	New American Standard (1977)	NET Bible (2004, 2005)	God's Word for the Nations (1995)	Revised Standard Version (1952)	New Jerusalem Bible* (1985)	New Revised Standard (1989)	New Living Trans (2004)
Ἐν	in	in	in	though	even under	with	with	with	in	in	in	in the midst of	amid	in spite of	in spite of	in the face of	in spite of	in spite of	in spite of
πολλῷ	multa	myche	much	every-thing	great	much	muche	much	much	much	much	much	much	much	strong	great	great	great	great
ἀγῶνι	sollici-tudine*	bisy-nesse	careful-ness	was against us	pressure	struggle	striuing	conten-tion	conflict	conflict	conflict	conflict	opposi-tion	opposi-tion	opposi-tion	opposi-tion	opposition	opposition	opposition
Full transla-tion	in multa sollici-tudine	in myche bisy-nesse	in much careful-ness	though everything was against us	even under great pressure	with much struggle	with muche striuing	with much conten-tion	in much conflict	in much conflict	in much conflict	in the midst of much conflict	amid much opposi-tion	in spite of much opposi-tion	in spite of strong opposi-tion	in the face of great opposi-tion	in spite of great opposition	in spite of great opposition	in spite of great opposition

*meaning, "uneasiness of mind, care, disquiet, apprehension, anxiety, solicitude" (C. T. Lewis, *An Elementary Latin Dictionary* [1890]).

Translating ἐν πολλῷ ἀγῶνι in 1 Thess 2:2 in French

French Lefèvre✠ (1522/1530); Louvain✠ (1550)*	French Jerusalem Bible✠ (1973)*	Ecumenical Translation—TOB (1988)*	Bible en français courant (1997)	IBS' Le Semeur✠ (1992/1999)	French Geneva (1616)	French Darby (1859/1885)	Louis Segond (1910); New Geneva Revised (1976)	French Martin (1707); French Ostervald
with great care	in the midst of a difficult struggle	in the midst of many struggles	regardless of strong opposition	in the midst of a great opposition	with a great battle	with many battles	in the midst of many battles	in the midst of great battles
Care	**Struggle**	**Struggles**	**Opposition**		**Battle**	**Battles**		
en grands soing	au milieu d'une lutte pénible	à travers bien des lutes**	malgré une forte opposition.	au milieu d'une grande opposition	avec un grand combat	avec beaucoup de combats	au milieu de bien des combats	au milieu de grands combats

*It seems like the first three translations soften the level of conflict due to their reliance on the Latin Vulgate.
**"Lutes" could also be translated wrestlings, which may give the impression of inner conflict of soul.

5. Overcoming antagonism:
    a. Being aware of the antagonism, 2 Tim 4:15
    b. Boldness is key to overcoming opposition, 1 Thess 2:2
    c. Ministering regardless of the antagonism, <u>1 Cor 16:8-9</u>
    d. Warning the antagonistic, Acts 28:25-29

6. Conclusion: Antagonism is inevitable in evangelism!

D. Persecution Is Inevitable (2 Tim 3:12):

Introduction: Prior to being saved, the Apostle Paul was filled with a demonic spiritual rage against the people of God (Acts 26:11), something he regretted later (1 Tim 1:13); therefore:
    a. He understood that there were particular individuals who vehemently opposed the Gospel message, as he himself had, e.g. 2 Tim 4:14-15
    b. He knew that their only hope was that they be saved
    c. And he knew, not only that God was working out His perfect will in the midst of persecution
    d. But that persecution was essential to spiritual growth and vitality, Rom 5:3-5

1. The reality of persecution: It cannot be avoided!
    a. God's Word promises persecution, sorrow, and tribulation, Matt 10:17-18; Mark 13:9; John 16:20-22, 33, Acts 14:22, Phil 1:29-30, 1 Thess 3:3-4; etc.
    b. All faithful Christians will be persecuted, 2 Tim 3:12
    c. Persecution is happening to Christians all over the world, 1 Pet 5:8-9.
    d. "But an hour is coming for everyone who kills you to think that he is offering service to God." John 16:2

2. Reasons for the Persecution (most of these are in the context of evangelism):[276]
    a. **Spiritual Battle**, Eph 6:12
    b. Persecution because of **Jesus Christ**, John 15:18-20
    c. Persecution because **the cross** is an offense, 1 Cor 1:23
    d. Persecution for **the Gospel**, 2 Tim 1:8
    e. Persecution "because of their testimony of Jesus and because of the word of God," Rev 20:4
    f. Persecution for being a **Christian**, 2 Tim 3:12
    g. Interestingly, in and through their persecution, the ungodly receive an apologetic for their rage against God:

    Psa 22:7-8 (NKJ), "All those who see Me ridicule Me; They shoot out the lip, they shake the head, *saying*, 'He trusted in the LORD, let Him rescue Him; Let Him deliver Him, since He delights in Him!'"

---

[276]T. Johnston, *Mindset*, Chap 6, IV.B & D deal with persecution in greater detail, in the context of persecution as a result of a verbal witness of the Gospel and evangelism through persecution.

1) The ungodly are living by the age-old friends of Job dictum, "If they hadn't done something bad, bad things wouldn't be happening to them"—although they would likely deny it!
2) The ungodly are transferring their rage against the righteous demands of God waging war within their own souls, and taking it out on those who are living godly under those same righteous demands
   a) Thus eating the righteous as one eats bread (Psa 14:4; 53:4)
3) In their self-vindication via persecution, the ungodly reach the height of their arrogance; Yes, pride is is to them as a necklace! (Psa 73:6)

3. Evangelism through Persecution:

   a. Persecution should not be sought, but it will be there. Rather, the Christian should seek to live to be at peace with all men, Rom 12:18, 14:19, 2 Cor 13:11, 1 Thess 5:13, 1 Tim 2:1-2, Heb 12:14.

   b. Persecution should be seen from God's perspective:
      1) It is in God's will, Psa 105:25, Matt 5:10-11, John 16:33
      2) In how it helps advance the Gospel, Luke 21:12-13, Phil 1:12-14.
      3) From the perspective of eternity, 2 Cor 4:16-18
      4) God might be testing our faith in Him, Psa 105:18-19

   c. God's Help to Overcome Persecution:
      1) Introduction: Persecution can be overcome through, 2 Tim 1:8-12:
         a) Faith and trust in the God of the Gospel (cf. Prov 3:25-26)
         b) A decision of the will not to be ashamed, but to go forward:
            (1) "Be strong and courageous," Deut 31:6, 7, 23, Joshua 1:6, 9, 18, 23
            (2) Continuing with perseverance, Gal 6:9
         c) Looking to the promised victory, Deut 11:25
      2) God as a refuge and strength, Psa 46:1, 91:1-2
      3) He tells us not to fear: "Fear not!" Deut 31:8, Jos. 1:5, 9, Isa 41:10, 13, Matt 10:28-33, Luke 12:4-5, 8-9
      4) He is present with us: "I am with thee," Deut 31:6, 7, 23, Jo. 1:5, 9, Matt 28:20, Heb 13:5
      5) He encourages through times of fear, Acts 18:9-10
      6) He gives us the appropriate words at that time, Luke 21:14-15

4. Let's remember that Christ gave His life to make the Gospel available to us!

II. Tremendous Truths in Evangelism:

A. God Desires the Salvation of All Men!

1. Ezek 18:23, "'Do I have any pleasure in the death of the wicked,' declares the Lord God, 'rather than that he should turn from his wicked ways and live?'"

2. Ezek 18:32, "'For I have no pleasure in the death of anyone who dies,' declares the Lord God, 'Therefore, repent and live.'"

3. Ezek 33:11, "Say to them, 'As I live,' declares the Lord God, 'I take no pleasure in the death of the wicked, but rather that the wicked turn from his ways and live. Turn back, turn back from your evil ways! Why then do you die, O house of Israel?'"

4. 1 Tim 2:3-4, "This is good and acceptable in the sight of God our Savior, who desires all men to be saved and to come to the knowledge of the truth." (note v. 7)

5. 2 Pet 3:9, "The Lord is not slow about His promise, as some count slowness, but is patient toward you, not wishing any to perish but for all to come to repentance."

6. For example, note the words of the 17th Century Puritan, John Owen:

   "Sufficient we say, then, was the sacrifice of Christ for the redemption of the whole world, and for the expiation of all the sins of all and every man in the world.... This fullness and sufficiency of the merit of the death of Christ is a foundation unto two things:—First, The general publishing of the gospel unto 'all nation," with the right that it hath to be preach to 'every creature,' Matt xxviii.19; Mark xvi.15; because the way of salvation which it declares is wide enough for all to walk in.... Secondly, That preachers of the gospel ... may from hence justifiably call upon every man to believe, with assurance of salvation to every one in particular upon his so doing, and being fully persuaded of this, that there is enough in the death of Christ to save every one that shall so do; leaving the purpose and counsel of God ... to himself."[277]

7. Paul's desire was to have an impact on "every man" he encountered—note his repetition of these words:

   "And we proclaim Him [Christ], admonishing every man and teaching every man with all wisdom, that we may present every man complete in Christ. And for this purpose also I labor, striving according to His power, which mightily works within me" (Col 1:28-29, NAS)

Considering Translations of Col 1:28

Analysis	Greek Byzantine	Geneva (1560)	KJV (1611/1769)	Darby (1884)	Bible in Basic English (1949)	Holman (2003)	Cont English Version* (1991)
Paul's message	ὅν	Whome	Whom	Whom	Whom	... Him	...the message about Christ
Paul's methodology	ἡμεῖς καταγγέλλομεν (emphatic subject)	we preache	we preach	*we* proclaim	we are preaching	We proclaim	We announce
	νουθετοῦντες	admonishing	warning	Admonishing	Guiding	warning	Warn
	διδάσκοντες	teaching	teaching	Teaching	Teaching	teaching	Teach
Paul's audience	πάντα ἄνθρωπον (twice)	euerie man (twice)	Every man (twice)	every man (twice)	every man (once)	everyone (once)	everyone (once)
Paul's mindset	ἐν πάσῃ σοφίᾳ	in all wisdome	in all wisdom	in all wisdom	in all wisdom	with all wisdom	...and we use all our wisdom to...
Paul's goal	ἵνα παραστήσωμεν πάντα ἄνθρωπον τέλειον ἐν χριστῷ Ἰησοῦ·	that we may present euerie man perfect in Christ Iesus	that we may present every man perfect in Christ Jesus	to the end that we may present every man perfect in Christ	so that every man may be complete in Christ	so that we may present everyone mature in Christ	so that all Christ's followers will grow and become mature

---

[277] John Owen, *The Death of Death in the Death of Christ* (Edinburgh: Banner of Truth, 1959), 184-86.

B. God Is Always Present!

1. Deut 31:6, "Be strong and courageous, do not be afraid or tremble at them, for the Lord your God is the one who goes with you. He will not leave you or forsake you."
2. Jos. 1:5, "Just as I have been with Moses, I will be with you; I will not fail you nor forsake you."
3. Jos. 1:9, "Do not tremble or be dismayed for the Lord your God is with you wherever you go."
4. Psa 139:7-10, "Where can I go from Thy Spirit? Or where can I flee from Thy presence? If I ascend to heaven, Thou art there; If I make my bed in Sheol, behold Thou art there. If I take the wings of the dawn, If I dwell in the remotest part of the sea, Even there Thy hand will lead me, And Thy right hand will lay hold of me."
5. Matt 28:19-20, "Go therefore and make [win] disciples of all nations ... and lo, I am with you always, even to the end of the age."
6. Acts 18:9-10, "And the Lord said to Paul in the night by a vision, 'Do not be afraid *any longer*, but go on speaking and do not be silent; for I am with you, and no man will attack you in order to harm you, for I have many people in this city.'"

C. God's Word Is Always Effective!

1. Isa 55:11, "So shall My word be which goes forth from My mouth; it shall not return to Me empty, without *accomplishing* what I desire, And without *succeeding* in the matter for which I sent it."
   a. It will always accomplish God's desire (planting, watering, reaping or hardening - cf. 2 Cor 10:4-5, e.g. Jer 6:10, 36:24)!
   b. It will always have success in God's will!

2. Jer 1:9-10, "Then the Lord stretched out His hand and touched my mouth, and the Lord said, 'Behold, I have put My words in your mouth. See I have appointed you this day over the nations and over the kingdoms, To pluck up and to break down, To destroy and to overthrow, to build and to plant.'"
   a. The condemning aspect of God's Word (cf. Psa 149:6-9, Prov 10:29, 2 Cor 2:16)
   b. The edifying aspect of God's Word (cf. Prov 10:29, 2 Cor 2:16)

3. Rom 1:16, "For I am not ashamed of the Gospel, for it is the power (δύναμις) of God for salvation to everyone who believes, to the Jew first and also to the Greek."

4. Heb 4:12-13, "For the word of God is living (ζῶν) and active (ἐνεργὴς) and sharper than any two edged sword, and piercing as far as the division of soul and spirit, of both joints and marrow, and able to judge the thoughts and intentions of the heart."

5. Application: The important thing is to get the Word out, the response to the Word rests on those who heard. Ours is to get the Word out, Ezek 3:16-21.

D. The Harvest Is Always Ripe!

1. John 4:35-36 (NKJ), "Do you not say, 'There are still four months and *then* comes the harvest'? Behold, I say to you, lift up your eyes and look at the fields, for they are already white for harvest! And he who reaps receives wages, and gathers fruit for eternal life, that both he who sows and he who reaps may rejoice together."

   Leon Morris explained this text as follows:

   > "Thus four months elapsed between the end of seed-time and the beginning of harvest. This might well have given rise to the proverbial saying indicating that there is no hurry for a particular task. The seed may be planted, but there is no way of getting round the months of waiting. Growth is slow and cannot be hurried. But Jesus did not share this view when applied to spiritual things. He had an urgent sense of mission and these words convey something of it to the disciples. They must not lazily relax, comfortable in the thought that there is no need to bestir themselves. The fields are even now ready for harvest. There may even be the thought that in the kind of harvest in which they were engaged (unlike those in farms and the like) there is no necessary interval between sowing and reaping. The disciples must acquire a sense of urgency in their task."[278]

   We have here, in fact, a fulfillment of the prophecy of Amos:

   > Amos 9:13 (NKJ), "'Behold, the days are coming,' says the LORD, 'When the plowman shall overtake the reaper, And the treader of grapes him who sows seed; The mountains shall drip with sweet wine, And all the hills shall flow *with it.*'"

   It appears that the urgency communicated in this passage is so problematic that it is not without textual variants to change this meaning!

---

[278]Leon Morris, *The Gospel According to John* (Grand Rapids, MI: Eerdmans, 1971), 279-80.

The Punctuation of John 4:35-36

Byzantine Textform	New King James (1982)	Comments	New American Standard Bible (1977)	Critical Edition Text
35 Οὐχ ὑμεῖς λέγετε ὅτι Ἔτι τετράμηνός ἐστιν, καὶ ὁ θερισμὸς ἔρχεται; Ἰδοὺ, λέγω ὑμῖν, ἐπάρατε τοὺς ὀφθαλμοὺς ὑμῶν, καὶ θεάσασθε τὰς χώρας, ὅτι λευκαί εἰσιν πρὸς θερισμὸν ἤδη. 36 Καὶ ὁ θερίζων μισθὸν λαμβάνει, καὶ συνάγει καρπὸν εἰς ζωὴν αἰώνιον· ἵνα καὶ ὁ σπείρων ὁμοῦ χαίρῃ καὶ ὁ θερίζων.	"Do you not say, 'There are still four months and *then* comes the harvest'? Behold, I say to you, lift up your eyes and look at the fields, for they are already white for harvest! 36 "And he who reaps receives wages, and gathers fruit for eternal life, that both he who sows and he who reaps may rejoice together.	Because of the change in punctuation in the Greek behind these two translations, the readiness of the Gospel may be downplayed in the NASB, whereas it is more emphatic in the NKJ. Posited steps to market this change: Step 1: Out of the thousands of available manuscripts, find one or more that omit the "and" separating the "already" from the phrase that follows it; Step 2: Provide reasons why it is a better reading without the "and"; Step 3: Adapt the punctuation to move the adverb to modify the next phrase. Step 4: Provide reasons why that change renders a preferable reading.	"Do you not say, 'There are yet four months, and *then* comes the harvest '? Behold, I say to you, lift up your eyes, and look on the fields, that they are white for harvest. 36 "Already he who reaps is receiving wages, and is gathering fruit for life eternal; that he who sows and he who reaps may rejoice together.	35 οὐχ ὑμεῖς λέγετε ὅτι ἔτι τετράμηνός ἐστιν καὶ ὁ θερισμὸς ἔρχεται; ἰδοὺ λέγω ὑμῖν, ἐπάρατε τοὺς ὀφθαλμοὺς ὑμῶν καὶ θεάσασθε τὰς χώρας ὅτι λευκαί εἰσιν πρὸς θερισμόν. ἤδη 36 ὁ θερίζων μισθὸν λαμβάνει καὶ συνάγει καρπὸν εἰς ζωὴν αἰώνιον, ἵνα ὁ σπείρων ὁμοῦ χαίρῃ καὶ ὁ θερίζων.

*Was not a similar change in Punctuation was used in the Revised Standard Version (1952) perhaps removing an argument for the deity of Christ from Romans 9:5? Rom 9:5 (RSV), "to them belong the patriarchs, and of their race, according to the flesh, is the Christ. God who is over all be blessed for ever. Amen"; the RSV translation followed a variant in wording and punctuation recommended by the "critical edition" Greek text of that time (Nestle-Aland, 25th edition, 1949).

The John 4:35-36 change in punctuation was brought to my attention in 2006 by a former student, Nathan Dawson ☺ Thank you! It must be stated that the earliest manuscripts have no punctuation,[279] and also that the Byzantine Textform though from a different provenance follows the Greek Orthodox Text, as is generally the case.

By the way, the American Bible Society's *Contemporary English Translation* is replete with changes in punctuation in significant passages, including using paragraph breaks and section breaks to divorce ideas from each other (including a paragraph break between Rom 5:8 and 9). This method is also used in other language translations that seem to have Rome's fingerprints on them, including a number of UBS translations after the implementation of the 1968 and 1987 SPCU and UBS "Guidelines for Interconfessional Cooperation in Translating the Bible."[280]

2. Matt 9:37, "The harvest is *plentiful,* but the workers are few."
3. Luke 10:2, "The harvest is *plentiful,* but the laborers are few."
4. John 12:32, "And I, if I be lifted up from the earth, will draw all men to Myself."
5. Application: Prov 10:5.

E. There Is Always a Need for Workers!
1. Ezek 22:30, "And I searched for a man among them who should build up the wall and stand in the gap before Me for the land, that I should not destroy it; but I found no one."
2. Matt 9:37, "The harvest is plentiful, but the workers are few."
3. Luke 10:2, "The harvest is plentiful, but the laborers are few."
4. Rom 10:14-15, "How then shall they call upon Him in whom they have not believed? And how shall they believe in Him in whom they have not heard? And how shall they hear without a preacher? And how shall they preach unless they are sent? Just as it is written, "How beautiful are the feet of those who bring glad tidings of good things."
5. Application:
   a. One student said, "Need doesn't constitute a call." But it did for God who sent Jesus because of a needy world. It's the Great Commission that constitutes the call of God on our life!
   b. Prov 10:5. Now is the harvest time for the church!

---

[279] "There are, of course, few or no punctuation marks in the oldest MSS, and we are dependent on our sense of the fitness of things" (*ibid.*, 280, footnote 87).

[280] For a more complete explanation, please see my paper, "Worldwide Bible Translation and Original Language Texts: An Analysis of the Impact of the 1968 and UBS and SPCU 'Guidelines for Interconfessional Cooperation in Translating the Bible'"; available at: http://www.evangelismunlimited.com/ubs-spcu_text20090116b.pdf (Online); accessed: 1 Dec 2017; Internet.

F. Sharing the Gospel Is Always Appropriate!

Introduction: While it is important that it be done with appropriately, winsomely, and with humility!
1. Psa 71:15, "My mouth shall tell of Thy righteousness, And of Thy salvation all day long." (cf. Psa 34:1; 35:28; 40:16; 70:4; 71:8, 24; 75:9; Eccl. 11:6)
2. Prov 3:27, "Do not withhold good from those to whom it is due, When it is in your power to do it." (cf. Prov 24:11-12)
3. Ezek 2:7, "But you shall speak My words to them whether they listen or not, for they are rebellious." (cf. Ezek 3:11; 1 Cor 9:17)
4. John 9:4, "We must work the works of Him who sent Me, as long as it is day; night is coming, when no man can work." (cf. John 5:17)
5. 2 Cor 2:14, "But thanks be to God who always leads us in His triumph in Christ, and manifests through us the sweet aroma of the knowledge of Him in every place."
6. 2 Cor 6:2, "For He says, 'At the acceptable time I listened to you, And on the day of salvation I helped you'; behold, now is 'the acceptable time,' behold, now is 'the day of salvation.'" (cf. Eph 5:15-16)
7. Eph 5:15-16, "Therefore be careful how you walk, not as unwise men, but as wise, making the most of your time, because the days are evil."
8. Col 4:5-6, "Conduct yourself with wisdom toward outsiders, making the most of the opportunity. Let your speech always be with grace, seasoned, as it were, with salt, so that you may know how you should respond to each person." (cf. Eph 4:29, 5:15-16)
9. 2 Tim 4:2, "Preach the word; be ready in season (εὐκαίρως) and out of season (ἀκαίρως); reprove, rebuke, exhort, with great patience and instruction."
10. Application: We should never have to apologize for speaking about Jesus (cf. Mark 1:19-20, the example of Christ).

G. Sharing the Gospel Always Has an Impact!

Introduction: Many of the prior verses could be placed here, such as Isaiah 55:10-11; see point D. God's Word is Always Effective.
1. Psa 40:3, "And He put a new song in my mouth, a song of praise to my God; many will see and fear, and will trust in the Lord." (cf. Psa 67:7)
2. Psa 67:2, "That Thy way may be known in the earth, Thy salvation among all nations."
3. Isa 25:9, "And it will be said in that day, 'Behold this is our God for whom we have waited that He might save us, this is the Lord for whom we have waited; let us rejoice and be glad in His salvation."
4. Jer 6:10, "To who shall I speak and give warning, that they may hear? Behold, their ears are closed, and they cannot listen. Behold the Word of the Lord has become a reproach to them; they have no delight in it."
5. Ezek 2:4-5, 7, "And I am sending you to them who are stubborn and obstinate children; and you shall say to them, 'Thus says the Lord God.' As for them, whether they listen or not—for they are a rebellious house—they will know that a prophet has been among them. … But you shall speak My words to them whether they listen or not, for they are rebellious."

H. Victory Is Sure!

1. Deut 11:25, "There shall be no man able to stand before you; the Lord your God shall lay the dread of you and the fear of you on all the land on which you set foot, as He has spoken to you."
2. Joshua 1:8, "…Then you will make your way prosperous, and then you will have success."
3. 2 Cor 2:14, "But thanks be to God, who always leads us in His triumph in Christ, and manifests through us the sweet aroma of the knowledge of Him in every place."
4. 1 John 5:4, "For whatever is born of God overcomes the world; and this is the victory that overcomes the world—our faith."
5. Application: The example of the Apostle Paul, 2 Tim 4:7

III. Conclusion:

As a Christian, if you are not concerned primarily for the souls of men, your primary concern is secondary. Satan loves to lead Christians to major on the minors. If he can get us concerned about money, a church building, an excellent education, a positive image in the eyes of the world, or anything that at the heart does not have souls as a priority, he is content.

"But," you say, "very few Christians have souls as their priority. It must be those who are gifted in evangelism who need this passion." The fact that most of the prophets in the day of Elijah, Micaiah, or Jeremiah were false prophets did not make them right. The majority vote does not qualify when it comes to obeying God's commands. Concerning the fact that only those gifted in evangelism seem to have this heart for evangelism. This is an *ipso facto* argument. Since by definition anyone who has a heart for evangelism also has the "gift of evangelism," it follows that all those who have the "gift of evangelism" also possess the corresponding heart. Yet, it is my strong feeling due to the Great Commission and the many other comments of Scriptures that all Christians need to "fan the flames" of a heart for the lost.

Only with a heart for the lost will we be able to live as Christ would have us live: with eternity continually in focus. It is when I perceive the tremendous spiritual needs of the lost around me that I begin to perceive the immensity of my lost estate. When I understand my great needs, then I can have fellowship with other believers with a perspective to encourage them towards the Lord (Heb 10:24). As I see the needs around me and begin to see the depth of my need, then I am able to develop a thirst for the Lord which I ought to be developing (Psa 42:1-2). A heart for the lost allows me to develop a heart for God—what an amazingly simple, yet extremely difficult thing!

So my growth in the three primary relationships depends on my developing a heart for the lost:[281]

Where does Christ fit into all this? He is the center of our lives. He is the focus of our reason for being. All that really matters is Christ (Eph 1:10; Col 1:16-18). Nothing else in life matters more than Christ. What have you done with Christ? This is what really matters. It follows that what others have done with Christ is the only thing that really matters for them. Are they living for Him? Do they know Him? Have they heard of Him? Are they heeding His word?

It is with deep humility that the Christian who sees the lostness of souls around him, who sees his own need for the Master, and who understands some of the needs of Christians around him, can minister to others of similar lowly estate. The great theological denominator under which every human being can be identified is sin. And because of the universal problem of sin, the focus shifts to the universal remedy for sin: Jesus Christ. He has done it all. Praise His name!

Therein is the mindset of eternity. Seeing others and ourselves in an eternal context. A context that causes us to lament our sin and cry out for salvation which is found only in and by the blood of Jesus Christ. A mindset which sets the pace for all our relationships, the use of our time, the use of our money, our minds:

> "All for Jesus, All for Jesus!
> "All my being's ransomed pow'rs:
> "All my thots and words and doings,
> "All my days and all my hours.
>
> "All for Jesus! All for Jesus!
> "All my days and all my hours;
> "All for Jesus! All for Jesus!
> "All my days and all my hours."[282]

At the Christmas conference in 1784, John Wesley gave this injunction to the preachers:

> "You have nothing to do but save souls. Therefore spend and be spent in this work. And go always, not only to those who want you, but to those that want you most. Observe: It is not your business to preach so many times, and take care of this or that society; but to save as many souls as you can. to bring as many sinners

---

[281] An enlargement of this illustration is found in Chapter 27: A Graphic Look at Biblical Follow-Up, "Developing the Spiritual Passions."

[282] Words by Mary D. James, "All for Jesus" in *Church Hymnal* (Hillsboro, KS: Mennonite Brethren, 1953), 284.

as you possibly can to repentance, and with all your power to build them up in that holiness without which they cannot see the Lord."[283]

---

[283]Setting from Dawson C. Bryant, *Building Church Membership Through Evangelism* (Nashville: Abingdon-Cokesbury, 1952), 8, and quote from Robert E. Coleman, *"Nothing to Do But To Save Souls!"* (Grand Rapids: Francis Asbury Press of Zondervan, 1990), 1.

Chapter 5 Appendix

Undermining the Primacy of Evangelism

Introduction:

Attacks on the primacy of evangelism are multitudinous. They may cause the believer to question: (1) those who led him to Christ; (2) his home church; (3) the faith of his parents; or (4) his own perspective. False teachers prey on the untaught and un-established by bringing up doubts in their minds. These doubts rarely lead toward the primacy of New Testament evangelism, but away from it. They rarely confirm the faith of the Christian, but bring up countless doubts and unending confusion of mind.

These attacks on the primacy of evangelism come in many shapes and sizes. The following illustrates four primary areas within which doubts may be grouped: biblical authority, hermeneutics, theological systems, and missional emphases:

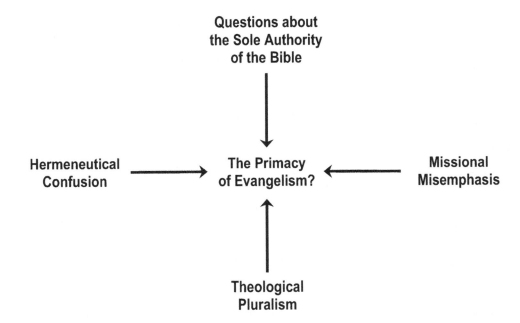

CHAPTER 6

Motivations and Urgency of Evangelism

Motivations for Evangelism

Introduction:

A. Evangelism for the Apostle Paul, who wrote, "be imitators of me, even I also am of Christ" (1 Cor 11:1), was not a matter of "if", it was a matter of "where", Acts 16:6ff.
1. While he had to be commanded to speak and not to be silent, Acts 18:9-10…
2. In Acts 16:6 he had to be forbidden to "speak the word in Asia"
3. Where did Paul get such motivation? From the OT!
    a. Notice how Ezek 3:18-19 impacted him (e.g. Acts 20:26-27; Rom 1:14; 1 Cor 9:19; 2 Cor 5:11)
4. Did he communicate this motivation in his writings? Yes!
    a. His sense of obligation, Rom 1:14
    b. His sense of compulsion, 1 Cor 9:16
    c. His sense of servitude, 1 Cor 9:19
    d. His view of grace to labor, 1 Cor 15:10

B. Seven Motivations from 2 Corinthians 4 and 5:
1. Focusing on the unseen, 2 Cor. 4:16-18
2. Having as our ambition to please God, 2 Cor. 5:9
3. The judgment seat of Christ, 2 Cor. 5:10
4. The fear of God, 2 Cor. 5:11
5. The love of Christ, 2 Cor. 5:14
6. Ministry given, 2 Cor. 5:18
7. Position as ambassador, 2 Cor. 5:20

C. Two major motivations and an expansion on some others…[284]

I. **"For This Purpose Also I Labor":**

Introduction: The Push of Purpose

A. A Look at Purpose:
1. Loving God: Deut 6:5; Matt 22:37
2. Loving neighbor: Lev 19:18; Matt 22:39;
3. Seeking the kingdom of God first: Matt 6:33;
4. Suffering: 1 Pet 2:21;
4. Sanctification: 1 Thess 4:7 (godliness, 1 Tim 4:7)
5. Great Commission: Luke 24:46-49
6. Reaping, John 4:38, "I sent you to reap"

B. Examples of Purpose:

1. Jesus:
    a. Revelatory, John 17:6
    b. Redemptive, Matt 20:28; Mark 10:45; John 1:29; 12:27
    c. Prophetic, Luke 24:44-45
    d. Evangelistic, Mark 1:38; Luke 4:42-43; Luke 19:10:
        1) Luke 4:43, "But He said to them, 'I must evangelize the kingdom of God to the other cities also [καὶ ταῖς ἑτέραις πόλεσιν εὐαγγελίσασθαί με δεῖ τὴν βασιλείαν τοῦ Θεοῦ], for I was sent <u>for this purpose</u> [ὅτι εἰς τοῦτο ἀπέσταλμαι].'"
    e. Exemplary, John 13:34-35

---

[284]Frank Shivers wrote of many convicting motivations for personal evangelism in his *Spurs to Soul Winning: 531 Motivations for Winning Souls* (La Vergne, TN: Lightning Source, 2012).

2. The Apostle Paul's sense of mission: 1 Cor 10:33; Phil 1:21; 3:14 (cf. imitation of Paul's purpose, 1 Cor 11:1; 2 Tim 3:10):

    As mentioned Solomon Stoddard: "Christ knew how to deal with Souls, and Paul followed His Example"[285]

    a. Acts 22:14-15, "And he said, 'The God of our fathers has appointed you to know His will, and to see the Righteous One, and to hear an utterance from His mouth. For **you will be a witness** for Him to all men of what you have seen and heard.'"

    b. Acts 26:16 (NKJ), "But rise and stand on your feet; for I have appeared to you for this purpose, **to make you** [from προχειρίζομαι] a minister and a witness both of the things which you have seen and of the things which I will yet reveal to you"

    c. Rom 1:1, "Paul, a bond-servant of Christ Jesus, called *as* an apostle, set apart for the gospel of God"

    d. Rom 1:15 (my translation), "Thus, for my part, I am eager to evangelize among you also who are in Rome"

    e. 1 Cor 9:19-23, "For though **I** am free from all *men*, **I** have made myself a slave to all, that **I** might win the more. And to the Jews **I** became as a Jew, that **I** might win Jews; to those who are under the Law, as under the Law, though not being myself under the Law, that **I** might win those who are under the Law; to those who are without law, as without law, though not being without the law of God but under the law of Christ, that **I** might win those who are without law. To the weak **I** became weak, that **I** might win the weak; **I** have become all things to all men, that **I** may by all means [effort] save some. And **I** do all things for the sake of the gospel, that **I** may become a fellow partaker of it."

    f. 1 Cor 10:33, "just as I also please all men in all things, not seeking my own profit, but the *profit* of the many, that they may be saved"

    g. Gal 1:16, "so that I might evangelize Him among the Gentiles [ἵνα εὐαγγελίζωμαι αὐτὸν ἐν τοῖς ἔθνεσιν]"

    h. Gal 2:7, "But on the contrary, seeing that I had been entrusted [from πιστεύω] with the gospel to the uncircumcised, just as Peter *had been* to the circumcised"

    i. Eph 3:7 (CSB), "I was made a servant of this *gospel* by the gift of God's grace that was given to me by the working of His power"

    j. Eph 6:20, "for which I am an ambassador in chains; that in *proclaiming* it I may speak boldly, as I ought to speak"

    k. Phil 1:12, "Now I want you to know, brethren, that my circumstances have turned out for the greater progress of the gospel"

    l. Phil 1:16, "the latter *do it* out of love, knowing that I am appointed for the defense of the gospel"

        Other possible translations of "defense of the Gospel" [being that it does not need to be defended, but rather proclaimed and guarded]—again, defense leads to a defensive posture, not exemplified in the Book of Acts

        Is there a word that more accurately portrays the positive-aggressive nature of Gospel proclamation, while still using the work of a lawyer in defending his client? How about:

        "Knowing that I am appointed unto **the plea** for the Gospel"

        Use of the word "plea" also corresponds with the teaching of 2 Cor 5:20; 6:1; 1 Pet 3:15

        Was this not the argumentation of Jesus with the Woman at the Well (John 4), bringing her to the point of faith in Him?

    m. Col. 1:29, "And for this purpose also I labor, striving according to His power, which mightily works within me"

    n. 1 Tim 2:6, "And for this I was appointed a preacher and an apostle (I am telling the truth, I am not lying) as a teacher of the Gentiles in faith and truth"

    o. 2 Tim 1:11, "for which I was appointed a preacher and an apostle and a teacher"

    p. 2 Tim 2:10, "For this reason I endure all things for the sake of those who are chosen, so that they also may obtain the salvation which is in Christ Jesus *and* with *it* eternal glory,"

---

[285]Richard L. Bushman, ed. *The Great Awakening: Documents on the Revival of Religion, 1740-1745* (Chapel Hill, NC: University Press, 1969), 13.

Comparison of Luke 4:43 and Gal 1:16

Passage	Luke 4:42-43	Gal 1:15-16
Person	Jesus	Paul
Preamble	And when day came, He departed and went to a lonely place; and the multitudes were searching for Him, and came to Him, and tried to keep Him from going away from them.	But when He who had set me apart, *even* from my mother's womb, and called me through His grace, was pleased [16] to reveal His Son in me,
Ministry	But He said to them, "I must preach [evangelize] the kingdom of God to the other cities also [καὶ ταῖς ἑτέραις πόλεσιν εὐαγγελίσασθαί με δεῖ τὴν βασιλείαν τοῦ Θεοῦ]	that I might preach [evangelize] Him among the Gentiles [ἵνα εὐαγγελίζωμαι αὐτὸν ἐν τοῖς ἔθνεσιν]
Purpose Statement	for I was sent for this purpose." [ὅτι εἰς τοῦτο ἀπέσταλμαι]	

3. The Christian's Purpose:
   a. "I have sent you to reap," John 4:38
   b. "Do not fear, from now on you will be taking men alive," Luke 5:10
   c. "Follow Me, and I will make you [become] fishers of men," Matt 4:19; Mark 1:17
   d. "You are witnesses of these things," Luke 24:48
   etc.

II. "The Love of Christ Compels Us":

The Love of Christ, 2 Cor 5:14 (cf. Phil 1:16)

> Love will, of course, find many creative and imaginative ways to come alongside those who are strangers to God. The love of Christ controlling a local church will drive its members out all the time in sustained evangelism.[286]

Variety in Translating of συνέχω in 2 Cor 5:14
Internal versus External Motivation

Greek (Byzan-tine)	Jerome's Vulgate (435)	Wycliffe's 2nd edition (1388)	Tyndale (1534); cf. Geneva, KJV, ASV	NKJ, NIV; cf. CSB	RSV, NAS, ESV, NET; cf. NLT	NRV (1989)	God's Word for the Nations (1995)	Douay-Rheims (1899)	New American Bible (1901)	New Jerusalem Bible (1985)	ABS' Cont. English Version (1991)
	Urget	Drives	Constrains	Compels	Controls	Urges	Guides	Presses	Impels	Over-whelms	Are ruled by
Ἡ γὰρ ἀγάπη τοῦ χριστοῦ συνέχει ἡμᾶς	caritas enim Christi urget nos	For the charite of Crist dryueth vs	For the love of Christ costrayn-eth vs	For the love of Christ compels us	For the love of Christ controls us	For the love of Christ urges us on	Clearly, Christ's love guides us	For the charity of Christ presseth us	For the love of Christ impels us	For the love of Christ over-whelms us	We are ruled by Christ's love for us.

Notice that the history of Catholic translations (Douay-Rheims, New American, New Jerusalem, Contemporary English Version) seem to internalize the evangelistic motivation in this verse by using words such as overwhelms, impels, and presses; the most passive being the Contemporary English Version, "are ruled by."

It would seem like the question that remains for Protestant or Evangelical translations is this: does this verse describe an outward motivation or action in evangelizing? If it does, this outward emphasis seems best translated by Wycliffe's "driveth" or the Holman Christian Standard's "compel".

---

[286]David Prior, *Bedrock: A Vision for the Local Church* (London; Houghton & Stoughton, 1980), 80, quote from Johanne Lukasse, *Churches with Roots* (Bromley, Kent, England; MARC, 1990), 117.

III. Other Motivations:

A. Desire to glorify God, John 15:8

B. The Fear of the Lord, 2 Cor 5:11 (cf. Luke 12:4-5, 1 Pet 2:17)

On the Translation of ὁ ἄνθρωπος in 2 Cor 5:11

Wycliffe	Tyndale (1534); Bishops (1595)	Geneva (1560); KJV; NKJ	Murdock (1852); ASV; RSV; NASB	Bible in Basic English (1949)	NIV (1984)	NAB✠ (1991)	NRSV (1989); ESV	New Living Translation (2001)	New Jerusalem Bible✠ (1985)	Holman Christian Standard (2005)	ABS' CEV✠ (1991)
Men							Others			People	Everyone
Men	Men	Men	Men	Men	Men	Others	Others	Others	People	People	Everyone
Dread	To be feared	Terrour	Fear	Fear	Fear	Fear	Fear	Fearful Responsibility	Fear	Fear	Respect
Therfor we witynge the drede of the Lord, councelen men, for to God we ben opyn; and Y hope, that we ben opyn also in youre consciencis.	Seynge then that we knowe how the lorde is to be feared we fare fayre with men. For we are knowen wel ynough vnto God. I trust also that we are knowen in youre con-sciences.	Knowing therefore that terror of the Lord, we persuade men, & we are made manifest vnto God, & I trust also that we are made manifest in your con-sciences.	Therefore because we know the fear of our Lord we persuade men; and we are made manifest unto God; and I hope also, we are made manifest to your minds.	Having in mind, then, the fear of the Lord, we put these things before men, but God sees our hearts; and it is my hope that we may seem right in your eyes.	Since, then, we know what it is to fear the Lord, we try to persuade men. What we are is plain to God, and I hope it is also plain to your conscience.	Therefore, since we know the fear of the Lord, we try to persuade others; but we are clearly apparent to God, and I hope we are also apparent to your conscious-ness.	Therefore, knowing the fear of the Lord, we try to persuade others; but we ourselves are well known to God, and I hope that we are also well known to your con-sciences.	Because we understand our fearful responsibilit y to the Lord, we work hard to persuade others. God knows we are sincere, and I hope you know this, too.	And so it is with the fear of the Lord always in mind that we try to win people over. But God sees us for what we are, and I hope your consciences do too.	Knowing, then, the fear of the Lord, we persuade people. We are completely open before God, and I hope we are completely open to your consciences as well.	We know what it means to respect the Lord, and we encourage everyone to turn to him. God himself knows what we are like, and I hope you also know what kind of people we are.

C. Compulsion of the Spirit, 1 Cor 9:16 (e.g. Acts 17:16)

D. Ministry given/committed, 1 Cor 9:16-17, 2 Cor 5:18-19

E. Giving grace to those who hear, Eph 4:29, Col 4:6

F. The Great Worth of a Soul, Psa 49:7-9 (cf. John 3:16)

G. The Great Cost of Our Salvation:
1. The reality of the great cost, Phil 2:7-8, 1 Pet 1:17-21, Heb 2:3, 12:28.
2. The great cost as a motivation, Rom 12:1, Phil 2:12-13.

H. The Need to Obey Our Savior:
1. The need to obey:
   a. Old Testament, Deut 4:1-2, 5-6, 14, 40, 5:1, 31-33, 6:1-3, 28:1-2, 15, Jos. 1:7-8, Psa 119:1-2
   b. New Testament, John 3:36, 14:21, 1 John 2:3-6
2. The urgency of obedience:
   a. The tragic removal of the lampstand, Rev 2:5
   b. The departure of the Spirit of the Lord, Ezek 10:4, 18; 11:22.
3. Obedience as a motivation, 1 Cor 9:16-17

I. God's Grace Must not Be Received in Vain!
1. The reality of grace being received in vain:
   a. Vain labor, 1 Cor 15:10

A Study of Translation Issues Based on the French Translations of 1 Corinthians 15:10

Greek Byzantine/ Latin Vulgate	French Lefèvre✠ (1530)	French Louvain✠ (1550)	French Geneva (1560-1616)	French Ostervald (1744)	French Louis Segond (1910)	French Jerusalem✠ (1973)	IBS French Le Semeur✠ (1992, 1999)*	French Bible Français Courant (1997)
καὶ ἡ χάρις αὐτοῦ ἡ εἰς ἐμὲ οὐ κενὴ ἐγενήθη, ἀλλὰ περισσότερον αὐτῶν πάντων ἐκοπίασα	and his grace was not [at all] idle in me, but I labored more abundantly than they all	and his grace was not [at all] idle in me. * But I labored more abundantly than they all	and his grace that [is] toward me, was not [at all] in vain: so I worked much more than they all	and his grace toward me was not [at all] in vain, but I worked much more than they all	and has grace toward me was not in vain; far from that, I worked more than they all	and his grace on my behalf was not sterile. Far from that, I worked more than they all	and this grace that was testified to me was not ineffective. Far from there, I have pained at the task more than all the other apostles	and the grace that he provided me has not been ineffective: on the contrary, I worked more than all the other apostles
et gratia eius in me vacua non fuit sed abundantius illis omnibus laboravi	& sa grace na point este oyseuse enmoy / may iay laboure plus abondamment q euly tous	& sa grace n'a point esté oyseuse en moy. * Mais i'ay labouré plus abondamment que eux tous	et sa grace qui [est] envers moi, n'a point esté vaine: ains j'ai travaillé beaucoup plus qu'eux tous	et sa grâce envers moi n'a point été vaine, mais j'ai travaillé beaucoup plus qu'eux tous	et sa grâce envers moi n'a pas été vaine; loin de là, j'ai travaillé plus qu'eux tous	et sa grâce à mon égard n'a pas été stérile. Loin de là, j'ai travaillé plus qu'eux tous	et cette grâce qu'il m'a témoignée n'a pas été inefficace. Loin de là, j'ai peiné à la tâche plus que tous les autres apôtres	et la grâce qu'il m'a accordée n'a pas été inefficace: au contraire, j'ai travaillé plus que tous les autres apôtres
Note the translation of Jerome was usually a word-for-word translation of the Greek	"ne … point" is an emphasized "ne … pas"	A strong break is added to the text, with both a period and a star	This shows the literal historic French Protestant translation: changed "idle" to "vain", "labor" to "work"; note the removal of the Louvain strong break	This version replaced the Geneva as the Protestant translation	Segond translated περισσότερον as "far from that"	This Catholic translation followed the punctuation of the French Louvain, changing "vain" to "sterile"	Marketed like the NIV for French Protestants by the UBS, it exceeds other Catholic translations in theologically Catholic renderings	[analyze this translation in light of the translation history]

*The 1995 Contemporary English Version is close to the 1992, 1999 French *Le Semeur*: "But God was kind! He made me what I am, and his wonderful kindness wasn't wasted. I worked much harder than any of the other apostles, although it was really God's kindness at work and not me" [notice the seeming aversion to the word "grace"].

      b. Vain preaching, 1 Cor 15:14

  2. The effective reception of God's grace:
      a. Through spiritual work, 1 Cor 15:58, Eph 2:10
      b. Through participation in the Gospel, Phil 1:5

IV. Thoughts for Consideration:

  A. What is your motivation in life? You must have one, what is it?

  B. Are your motivations "the worries of the world, and the deceitfulness of riches, and the desires for other things" which "enter in and choke the word, and it becomes unfruitful" (Mark 4:19)?

  C. Are you motivated to share the Gospel?

  D. Won't you make this your one motivation?

The Urgency of Evangelism

Introduction:

A. Jonathan Edwards in his sermon "Sinners in the Hand of an Angry God" touched on the urgency of getting right with God. This sermon was based on Deuteronomy 32:35 which clearly uses four terms to exemplify the urgency involved in God's judging of His people (recipients of the message). This same urgency is a part of the proclamation of the message, in our case, evangelism. The New Testament also testifies of the importance of the "now" (2 Cor 6:2) and of "today" (Heb 4:7). The following notes highlight the biblical foundation for an urgent evangelism.

B. Ezekiel 12:21-28 shows that the urgency for following Christ can be lost. God wants the urgency maintained for His glory.

C. This urgency should match the power of the gospel we preach (Rom 1:16):

> "In other words, my confession of Christ consists not only in the content of what I say but also in the style or manner in which I say it. If I display no personal urgency in claiming that my message should grasp and sway others, I am not likely to be believed. I am not myself infected, I cannot infect others. Spurgeon is one over whom hi Lord exercises power. Hence power (*exousia*) goes out of him too."[287]

D. Examples of an urgent witness for Christ:
  1. Acts 4:19-20 (cf. Acts 5:29), "Whether it is right in the sight of God to give heed to you rather than to God, you be the judge; for we cannot stop speaking what we have seen and heard."
  2. John Knox cried out, "Give me Scotland or I die!"
  3. William Booth, founder of the Salvation Army, displayed the same boldness and zeal when he wrote in King Edward VII's registry:

      > Your Majesty, Some men's ambition is art.
      > Some men's ambition is fame.
      > Some men's ambition is gold.
      > My ambition is the souls of men.

Preaching from a Gospel Wagon, 1890s, Saginaw, Michigan

  4. Spurgeon in his *The Soul Winner* spoke of the earnestness of the message that we preach:

      > "How earnest we ought to be when we remember that in our work we are dealing with souls that are immortal, with sin that is eternal in its effects, with pardon that is infinite, and with terrors and joys that are to last forever and ever."[288]

E. The Bible teaches, "Be strong in the Lord and in the strength of His might." (Eph 6:10) The Apostle Paul who was beaten, stoned, whipped, arrested, and threatened and cursed for the name of the Lord (cf. 2 Cor 11:23-28). He bore shame and rebuke for the Gospel (cf. 1 Cor 4:8-13, 2 Cor 6:4-10). Then he exhorts Christians to follow in his steps (cf. 1 Cor 11:1).

F. The same Holy Spirit resides in us as resided in the Apostles of old or in the great Reformers. Can we become too busy with the cares of the world? (Matt 13:22) Are we available to forsake all for our Lord? Do we allow sin to entangle us? (Heb 12:1) Are we free to do bold service for our King?

G. Isaiah pronounced a woe on those who were busy with merrymaking in life. (Isaiah 5:11-14; Jer 15:17-18) They had forgotten the Lord their God. In fact, the prophet explains that those whose words and lifestyle exemplify no concern for God become spiritually starved. Their lives have rendered them spiritually famished and incapable of having a positive spiritual ministry in the lives of others. They have become incapable of feeding others any worthwhile spiritual food.

---

[287]Helmut Thielicke, "Foreword," in Charles H. Spurgeon, *The Soul Winner* (Grand Rapids, MI: Eerdmans, 1964, 1995), 7.

[288]Charles H. Spurgeon, *The Soul Winner* (New Kensington, PA: Whitaker House, 1995), 63-64.

H. Philemon 6 (NIV) reads, "I pray that you may be active in sharing your faith, so that you will have a full understanding of every good thing we have in Christ." Spiritual anorexia results from a lack of activity in sharing the Good News of Jesus Christ. Whereas growth in understanding proceeds from active evangelism.

I. Why is evangelism so important? There are many reasons for evangelism to be the first priority in the Church. And among these reasons are the **Urgencies of Evangelism**. These **Urgencies** propel the Church forward in her mission to reach the lost:
    1. Jesus Christ is coming back quickly!
    2. The lost are really lost and headed for hell!
    3. The Christian is accountable for the lost whom he should reach!
    4. Time is short and the harvest is great!

1. Jesus Christ Is Coming Back Quickly!

Millard J. Erickson wrote:

> "In view of the certainty of the second coming and the finality of the judgment which will follow, it is imperative that we act in accordance with the will of God."[289]

A. B. Simpson called the church to hasten the return of Christ through world evangelism:

> "And furthermore let us never forget that this movement is intimately and immediately connected with the blessed hope of our Lord's return. Never let us forget our great missionary watchword, 'This Gospel of the kingdom must be preached in all the world for a witness to all nations, and then shall the end come.'"

> "On the great missionary movement hangs the appointed hour of the millennial dawn, of the marriage of the Lamb, of the glory of the resurrection, of the time of the restitution of all things. In yonder heavens He waits until we have fulfilled the last condition that precedes His advent, and then how gladly He will make haste to meet us with the recompense of our service and the grander opportunities of that kingdom of glory, whose crowns and sovereignties we shall share with Him."[290]

Sample Old Testament Scripture Regarding the Coming Day of Judgment

1. "Be silent before the Lord LORD! For the day of the LORD is near," Zeph 1:7.
2. "For the day of their calamity is near, And the impending things are hastening upon them," Deut 32:35
3. "Wail, for the day of the LORD is near! It will come as destruction from the Almighty," Isa 13:6
4. "Your doom has come to you, O inhabitant of the land. The time has come, the day is near," Ezek 7:7
5. "For the day is near, Even the day of the LORD is near; It will be a day of clouds, A time *of doom* for the nations," Ezek 30:3
6. "Alas for the day! For the day of the LORD is near, And it will come as destruction from the Almighty," Joel 1:15
7. "Blow a trumpet in Zion, And sound an alarm on My holy mountain! Let all the inhabitants of the land tremble, For the day of the LORD is coming; Surely it is near, A day of darkness and gloom, A day of clouds and thick darkness," Joel 2:1-2
8. "For the day of the LORD is near in the valley of decision," Joel 3:14
9. "For the day of the LORD draws near on all the nations," Obad 1:15
10. "Near is the great day of the LORD, Near and coming very quickly; Listen, the day of the LORD! In it the warrior cries out bitterly. A day of wrath is that day, A day of trouble and distress, A day of destruction and desolation, A day of darkness and gloom, A day of clouds and thick darkness," Zeph 1:14-15
11. "Then I will draw near to you for judgment; I will be a swift witness," Mal 3:5.
12. "Before the LORD for He is coming; For He is coming to judge the earth." Psa 96:13.
13. "The Lord laughs at him; For He sees his day is coming," Psa 37:13
14. "Behold, the day of the LORD is coming, Cruel, with fury and burning anger, To make the land a desolation; And He will exterminate its sinners from it," Isa 13:9
15. "Behold, the day! Behold, it is coming! *Your* doom has gone forth… their silver and their gold shall not be able to deliver them in the day of the wrath of the LORD," Ezek 7:10, 19
16. "'Behold, the days are coming,' declares the LORD, 'that I will punish all who are circumcised with the uncircumcised," Jer 9:25 (NKJ); Amos 8:11

    [By the way, Jeremiah makes a clear move from days of judgment to days of salvation!
    ["'Behold, *the* days are coming,' declares the LORD, 'When I shall raise up for David a righteous Branch; And He will reign as king and act wisely And do justice and righteousness in the land," Jer 23:5 (cf. Jer 23:7; 30:3; 31:27, 31, 38; 33:14)]

---

[289]Millard J. Erickson, *Christian Theology* (Grand Rapids: Baker, 1991), 1204.

[290]A. B. Simpson, *Annual Report of the Missionary Crusade* (1892), 62-63.

17. "'For behold, the day is coming, burning like a furnace; and all the arrogant and every evildoer will be chaff; and the day that is coming will set them ablaze,' says the LORD of hosts, 'so that it will leave them neither root nor branch,'" Mal 4:1
18. "For the LORD of Hosts will have a day…," Isa 2:12
19. "In that Day," Isa 2:17, 20, Amos 8:9, Mic 5:10-15, Zech 12:3-9.
20. "'Behold, it is coming and it shall be done,' declares the Lord God. 'That is the day of which I have spoken,'" Ezek 39:8
21. "But who can endure the day of His coming? And who can stand when He appears?" Mal 3:2

Sample New Testament Scripture Regarding the Second Coming

1. "(Behold,) I am coming quickly," Rev 3:11, 22:12, 20.
2. "For yet a little while, He who is coming will come, and will not delay," Heb 10:37 (cf. Hab 2:3).
3. "A little while, and you will no longer behold me; and again a little while, and you will see Me," John 16:16.
4. "For you yourselves know full well that the day of the Lord will come just like a thief in the night," 1 Thess 5:2
5. "But the day of the Lord will come like a thief," 2 Pet 3:10.
6. "Behold, I am coming like a thief," Rev 16:15.
7. "I will come like a thief," Rev 3:3
8. "In the day of judgment," Matt 10:15; 11:22, 24; 12:36
9. "You are storing up wrath for yourself in the day of wrath and revelation of the righteous judgment of God," Rom 2:5
10. "The Lord knows how to rescue the godly from temptation, and to keep the unrighteous under punishment for the day of judgment," 2 Pet 2:9
11. "That we may have confidence in the day of judgment," 1 Jn 4:17
12. "Kept for the day of judgment and destruction of ungodly men, 2 Pet 3:7
13. "In eternal bonds under darkness for the judgment of the great day," Jude 1:6
14. "Behold, the Judge is standing right at the door," Jms 5:9.
15. "Recognize that He is near, right at the door," Matt 24:33, Mark 13:29.
16. "For the time is near," Rev 1:3, 22:10.
17. "The Lord is near," Phil 4:5.
18. "The kingdom of God is near," Luke 21:31.
19. "But encouraging *one another*; and all the more, as you see the day drawing near," Heb 10:25
20. "Knowing the time ... for now salvation is nearer to us," Rom 13:11.
20. "It is the last hour," 1 John 2:18.
21. "The day is at hand," Rom 13:12.
22. "The kingdom of heaven is at hand," Matt 10:7.
23. "The coming of the Lord is at hand," James 5:8.
24. "The end of all things is at hand," 1 Pet 4:7.
25. "The things which must shortly take place," Rev 1:1, 22:6.
26. "For the Son of Man is coming at an hour when you do not think He will," Matt 24:44.
27. "For the Son of Man is coming at an hour when you do not expect," Luke 12:40.
28. "The master will come on a day when he does not expect him and at an hour which he does not know," Matt 24:50; Luke 12:46.
29. "But as to the day and hour no one knows," Matt 24:36, Mark 13:32.
30. "For you do not know which day the Lord is coming," Matt 24:42.
31. "Be on the alert," Matt 24:42, 25:13.
32. "Be ready," Matt 24:44, Luke 2:40.

Passages Affirming the Reality of/Need for a Future Expectation

1. "Even we ourselves groan within ourselves, waiting eagerly [ἀπεκδέχομαι] our adoption as sons, the redemption of our body," Rom 8:23
2. "But if we hope for what we do not see, with perseverance we wait eagerly [ἀπεκδέχομαι] for it," Rom 8:25
3. "Awaiting eagerly [ἀπεκδέχομαι] the revelation of our Lord Jesus," 1 Cor 1:7
4. "For we through the Spirit, by faith, are waiting [ἀπεκδέχομαι] for the hope of righteousness," Gal 5:5
5. "For our citizenship is in heaven, from which also we eagerly wait [ἀπεκδέχομαι] for a Savior, the Lord Jesus Christ," Phil 3:20
6. "And to wait [ἀναμένω] for His Son from heaven, whom He raised from the dead, that is Jesus, who rescues us from the wrath to come," 1 Thess 1:10
7. "Looking for [προσδέχομαι] the blessed hope and the appearing of the glory of our great God and Savior, Christ Jesus," Titus 2:13
8. "So Christ also, having been offered once to bear the sins of many, shall appear a second time for salvation without *reference to* sin, to [for] those who eagerly await [ἀπεκδέχομαι] Him," Heb 9:28
9. "Be patient, therefore, brethren, until the coming of the Lord," James 5:7

10. "Since all these things are to be destroyed in this way, what sort of people ought you to be in holy conduct and godliness, looking for [προσδοκάω] and hastening [σπεύδω] the coming of the day of God, on account of which the heavens will be destroyed by burning, and the elements will melt with intense heat!" 2 Pet 3:11-12
11. "But according to His promise we are looking for [προσδοκάω] new heavens and a new earth, in which righteousness dwells," 2 Pet 3:13
12. Therefore, beloved, since you look for [προσδοκάω] these things, be diligent to be found by Him in peace, spotless and blameless," 2 Pet 3:14
13. "Keep yourselves in the love of God, waiting anxiously [προσδέχομαι] for the mercy of our Lord Jesus Christ to eternal life," Jude 21

The Soon Advent of the Kingdom of God
Ought to Be Central to the Christian's Message

1. It was central in the message of John the Baptist:
   a. "Repent, for the kingdom of heaven is at hand," Matt 3:2
2. It was central in the preaching of Jesus:
   a. "From that time Jesus began to preach and say, 'Repent, for the kingdom of heaven is at hand,'" Matt 4:17
   b. "And after John had been taken into custody, Jesus came into Galilee, preaching the gospel of God, and saying, 'The time is fulfilled, and the kingdom of God is at hand; repent and believe in the gospel,'" Mark 1:14-15
3. It was central in the preaching of the apostles, "And as you go, preach, saying, 'The kingdom of heaven is at hand,'" Matt 10:7
4. Remembering, unfortunately, that false prophets will also have this emphasis, Luke 21:8, "And He said, 'See to it that you be not misled; for many will come in My name, saying, "I am *He*," and, "The time is at hand"; do not go after them.'"

The Return of Christ as Motivation

1. Motivation to faith, Luke 18:8
2. Motivation to persevere, Heb 10:36-37
3. Motivation for holiness of life, 2 Pet 3:11-12
4. Motivation to live for Christ, Matt 24:46-51, 25:13, 24-30.
5. Motivation to live zealous for good deeds, Titus 2:11-14
6. Motivation to preach, 2 Tim 4:1-2
7. Motivation to hasten the return of Jesus through evangelism, Matt 24:14, Mark 13:10 > 2 Pet 3:11-12

   Not surprisingly, there are nay-sayers on this point—they teach that only biblicists and literalists believe in the hastening the return of Christ through evangelism.[291] But it must be stated that this expectation is what the Bible teaches, and furthermore these verses sparked the urgency of evangelism during the Great Century of Protestant Missions.

8. Motivation to persevere in evangelism, Matt 10:23.

Commitment: "Lord, May I Always Live Remembering Your Soon Return."

---

[291]"Evangelism is not a mechanism to hasten the return of Christ, as some suggest" (David J. Bosch, *Transforming Mission: Paradigm Shifts in Theology of Mission* (Maryknoll, NY: Orbis, 1991), 420).

2. The Lost Are Really Lost!

To restate this in other words, individuals who are not born-again believers in Jesus Christ are spiritually dead (lifeless), heading for an eternal hell, and in desperate need of the Savior! … "But God, I know that they are not committed Christians, but they really seem like decent people!"

Consider in comparison the urgency to raise funds expressed by John Lorioth, early leader of cyclist Lance Armstrong's foundation Livestrong:

"'We've always said we have to pound on the door and maybe kick it in,' says Korioth. 'If people get their feelings hurt, tough crap. People are dying. We're not going to wait around.'"[292]

According to the article, nearly 600,000 people a year die from cancer in the U.S. Livestrong is committed to reduce that number. However, another statistic is even more alarming, the number of people in the U.S. who die without salvation by grace through faith in Jesus Christ. While only God knows the true numbers, is it illegitimate to say that between 5%-10% of Americans are truly born again and living for the Lord? With the U.S. Census Bureau reporting 2,424,000 deaths in the U.S. in 2007, and if 90% of these were lost people, the number is an alarming 2,181,600 people dying in the U.S. every year without Christ. Or approximately 3.6 times more people than die from cancer—and give urgency to Lance Armstrong's cancer foundation!

Consider the urgency of the founders of the "Whosoever Will Rescue Mission, San Francisco, California (early 1900s). Was that not an urgency fueled by a concern for the salvation of lost souls?[293]

Spurgeon wrote:

"When a Christian fears for others, his heart cries out, 'They will perish, they will perish; they will sink into hell; they will forever be banished from the presence of the Lord." When this fear oppresses his soul, weighs him down, and then drives him to go out and preach with tears, then he will plead with men so as to prevail."[294]

David Hesselgrave rightly summarized in his paper on the lostness of man:

"My conclusion is as short as it is simple. …Any Christian minister of missionary who would be faithful has a choice. The Bible is clear and lostness is of such gravity that we must teach and preach it with passion and purpose. More than that, the gravity of lostness can be communicated in the manner and style of Jonathan Edwards. It can also be communicated in the style and manner of Rev. Hashimoto. But it must be preached."[295]

---

[292]Chuck Salter, "Can Livestrong Survive Lance?" *Fast Company* (Nov 2010), 114.

[293]Photo available at http://biblebelievers.com/misc_periodical_articles/chr-workers_003.html; accessed: 25 Oct 2006; Internet.

[294]Spurgeon, *The Soul Winner* (New Kensington, PA: Whitaker House, 1995), 152.

[295]David J. Hesselgrave, Contextualizing Great Commission Fundamentals: "Lecture three: Contextualizing the Gravity of the Lostness: Preaching and Teaching the Wrath of God and the Judgment of Man." Lecture delivered at Midwestern Baptist Theological Seminary (25 Oct 2012), 8.

The Lostness of Man without Christ

1. Helpless/Hopeless, Rom 5:6, Eph 2:12
    Notice the progression in translating the phrase in Rom 5:6, "For while we were still helpless" [Ἔτι γὰρ χριστός, ὄντων ἡμῶν ἀσθενῶν]:

    French Geneva (1560-1616), "Car du temps que nous estions encore desnuez de toute force"
       Trans "For from the time that we were still denuded of all strength"
    English Geneva (1560), "For Christ, when we were yet of no strength"
    English KJV (1611/1769), "For when we were yet without strength"
    French Martin (1707), "Car lorsque nous étions encore privés de toute force"
       Trans "For when we were still deprived of all strength"
    French Ostervald (1744), "Car, lorsque nous étions encore sans force"
       Trans "For, when we were still without strength"
    English ASV (1901), "For while we were yet weak"
    English NASB (1977), "For while we were still helpless"

2. Sinners, Rom 5:8
3. Enemies of God, Rom 5:10
4. Under the empire of the flesh/sin, Rom 3:9, 7:5
    Consider the dually-doctrinally-powerful language in Deut 31:29:
    "for being corrupt you will act corruptly [כִּי־הַשְׁחֵת תַּשְׁחִתוּן]…"
5. Sons of disobedience, Eph 2:2
6. By nature children of wrath, Eph 2:3
7. Spiritually dead, Eph 2:1, 5, Col 2:13
8. Can do no good in the eyes of God, Rom 3:12
9. "For the gate is wide, and the way is broad that leads to destruction, and many are those who enter by it." Matt 7:13

God's Judgment of Sinners

Introduction:

"Just as in the past, the question of the future states of the wicked has created a considerable amount of controversy in our day. The doctrine of an everlasting punishment appears to some to be outmoded or sub-Christian view."[296]

For example, John Stott wrote:

"But the issue is too important to suppress, and I am grateful to you for challenging me to declare my mind. I do not dogmatise about the position to which I have come. I hold it tentatively. But I do plead for frank dialogue among Evangelicals on the basis of Scripture. I also believe that the ultimate annihilation of the wicked should at least be accepted as a legitimate, biblically founded alternative to eternal conscious torment."[297]

A. The Reality of Judgment:

1. A God who sees all sin, Job 34:21-22, Psa 69:5, Prov 24:12, Jer 16:17 (cf. Psa 119:168):
    a. God looks at the heart, I Sam. 16:7, 1 Chr 28:9
    b. God tests the sons of men, Psa 11:4-5
    c. "God will judge the secrets of men," Rom 2:16

2. God's reaction to sin:
    a. God is grieved because of sin, Gen 6:6, Psa 7:11, Eph 4:30 (e.g. Jer 6:7)
    b. God is angered because of sin, Rom 1:18, 32, 1 Cor 6:9-10, Gal 5:21, Eph 5:6, Col 3:6, Rev 21:8, 27 (cf. Psa 90:11, 137:9)

---

[296]Erickson, 1234-35; in his note on the last sentence, Erickson referenced Nels Ferré, *The Christian Understanding of God* (New York: Harper, 1951), 233-34.

[297]John R. W. Stott, in his response to David L. Edwards in *Evangelical Essentials: A Liberal-Evangelical Dialogue* (Downers Grove, IL: InterVarsity, 1988), 319-20; cited by David J. Hesselgrave, Contextualizing Great Commission Fundamentals: "Lecture three: Contextualizing the Gravity of the Lostness: Preaching and Teaching the Wrath of God and the Judgment of Man." Lecture delivered at Midwestern Baptist Theological Seminary (25 Oct 2012), 4.

3. God's judgment of sin:
   a. "God the judge of all." Heb 12:23
   b. God judges according to His Word, Psa 149:9, John 12:48, and Rev 19:13->15->21 (cf. Rom 2:12)
   c. God will judge wickedness, Psa 58:10-11, 76:8-9, 94:2, 23, 96:13; Ezek 18:4, 20, 22:31, "their ways I have brought upon their heads;" Hos 13:7-8; Rom 14:10-12; 2 Pet 3:7; Jude 14-15; Rev 20:11-15
   d. Some aspects of God's judgments:
      1) Temporal judgments of God, Psa 78:33, Prov 11:31, 13:6, e.g. Lev 10:1-2, 2 Kg 5:26-27
      2) Eternal judgment of God, Matt 13:40, 24:51, Rom 6:23, 14:10, Gal 5:21, Heb 9:27, Rev 21:8

4. Reasons for/Results of God's judgment:

   Introduction:
   > "Fill their faces with dishonor,
   > "That they may seek Thy name, O Lord.
   > "Let them be ashamed and dismayed forever;
   > "And let them be humiliated and perish,
   > "That they may know that Thou alone, whose name is the Lord,
   > "Art the most high over all the earth,"
   > Psa 83:17-18

   a. That people may know that the Lord is God, Psa 83:17-18:
      1) "Thus you will know that I am the Lord God." Ezek 23:49, 24:24, 25:5, 17
      2) "And they will know that I am the Lord." Ezek 25:11 (found 45 times in Ezekiel!)

   b. Other reasons:
      1) Judgment magnifies and sanctifies God's name, Ezek 38:16
      2) "For the Lord who judges her is strong," Rev 18:8
      3) "That the nations may know Me," Ezek 38:16 (cf. Ezek 38:23)
      4) To get man's attention, Job 36:15
      5) The fear of God, Psa 64:9
      6) Consideration of God's work, Psa 64:9
      7) That people may turn from sin, Ezek 16:41-43
      8) That people may come to salvation, Job 33:13-22, 29-30
      9) Declaring the works of God, Psa 64:9

   Conclusion:
   > "But God will shoot at them with an arrow;
   > "Suddenly they will be wounded.
   > "So they will make him stumble;
   > "Their own tongue is against them;
   > "All who see it will shake the head.
   > "Then all men will fear,
   > "And will declare the work of God,
   > "And will consider what He has done.
   > "The righteous will see it and be glad in the Lord, and will take refuge in Him;
   > "And all the upright in heart will glory" (Psa 64:7-10).

B. The Reality of Hell as the Everlasting Conscious Punishment of Unsaved Man:[298]

1611, from "A Declaration of Faith of English People Remaining at Amsterdam in Holland":

> "27. That after the resurrection all men shall appear before the judgment seat off CHRIST to be judged according to their workes, that the Godlie shall enjoy life Eternall, the wicked being condemned shallbee tormented everlastinglie in Hell. Mat. 25-26."[299]

1990:

> "The truth of hell is that eternal punishment is a vital doctrine. It cannot, it must not, be ignored or abandoned. We must have the courage to preach it from the pulpits, in Bible schools and seminaries, and to a lost world. Vernon Grounds is correct, 'It is impossible to exaggerate the seriousness and urgency that the doctrine of hell imparts to life here and now.'"[300]

1. Temporal Descriptions of Hell:
   a. "Second death," Rev 20:14; 21:8
   b. "Eternal destruction," 2 Thess 1:9
   c. "Eternal judgment," Heb 6:2
   d. "Eternal punishment," Matt 25:46
   e. "Eternal fire," Matt 18:8; 25:41; Jude 7
   f. "Unquenchable fire," Matt 3:11; Mark 9:43; Luke 3:17
   g. "For whom is reserved the blackness of darkness forever," 2 Pet 2:17 (NKJ)
   h. "Black darkness has been reserved forever," Jude 13
   i. "Tormented day and night forever and ever," Rev 20:10
   j. "And the smoke of their torment goes up forever and ever, and they have no rest day and night," Rev 14:11
   k. "Where the worm does not die and the fire is not quenched," Isa 66:24; Mark 9:48

2. Physical Descriptions of Hell:

   a. Regarding Fire (cf. Isa 30:30-33):
      1) "Upon the wicked He will rain snares [or: coals of fire]; fire and brimstone and burning wind will be the portion of their cup," Psa 11:6
      2) "A Place for burning," Matt 13:30
      3) "Burned up with fire," Rev 18:8 (cf. Rev 18:9)
      4) "Fire," Matt 3:10; 7:19; 13:40; Luke 3:9; John 15:6; Heb 10:27; 2 Pet 3:7
      5) "Fiery hell," Matt 5:22; 18:9
      6) "Furnace of fire," Matt 13:42, 50
      7) "Eternal fire," Matt 18:8; 25:41; Jude 7
      8) "Unquenchable fire," Matt 3:12; Mark 9:43; Luke 3:17
      9) "Where the fire is not quenched," Mark 9:44, 46, 48
      10) "Lake of fire," Rev 20:14, 14, 15
      11) "Lake of fire that burns with brimstone," Rev 19:20
      12) "Lake that burns with fire and brimstone," Rev 21:8
      13) "Lake of fire and brimstone," Rev 20:10
      14) "Tormented with fire and brimstone," Rev 14:10
      15) "And he cried out, 'I am in agony in this flame,'" Luke 16:24

---

[298]J.I. Packer in *Evangelical Affirmations* (Grand Rapids: Zondervan, 1990), 123-24, stated that many protestant theologians and cultists have adopted an 'annihilationism or conditionalism' view of God's Judgment. Cited are some prominent evangelical theologians, notably Philip E. Hugues and John R. W. Stott. In his favorable response to Packer, John Ankerberg (139-41) proposed seven excellent affirmations with regard to universalism and the denial of an eternal hell. These are: "(1) Jesus Christ is the principle figure responsible for the doctrine of eternal punishment. The denial of eternal punishment is tantamount to the denial of the deity of our Lord and Savior. (2) Rejection of hell is a denial of biblical authority which opens the door to additional revisionist and syncretistic tendencies in other areas. (3) The problem is not a scriptural issue but an emotional issue, contaminated by secularist and humanistic thinking. (4) To reject eternal punishment and accept other ways of salvation is to affirm that the cross of Christ was unnecessary. (5) To affirm universalism is the denial of the church's mission to preach the gospel and warn men to escape God's wrath and eternal punishment (2 Cor 5:11; Luke. 3:7, 9, 17, 18). (6) The doctrine of eternal punishment is the watershed between evangelical and non-evangelical thought. (7) Universalism logically repudiates the doctrine of justification by faith."

[299]"A Declaration of Faith of English People Remaining at Amsterdam in Holland" (Amsterdam, 1611); in William L. Lumpkin, *Baptist Confessions of Faith* (Valley Forge: Judson, 1959), 123.

[300]John Ankerberg and John Weldon, "Response to J.I. Packer" in *Evangelical Affirmations* (1990), 147.

     b. Other Descriptions:
        1) "Hell," Matt 5:29, 30, 10:28, 23:33; Mark 9:43, 45, 47; Luke 12:5; James 3:6; 2 Pet 2:4
        2) "Destruction," Matt 7:13; Rom 9:22; Phil 3:19; 1 Thess 5:3; Heb 10:39; 2 Pet 2:12, 3:7; Rev 17:8, 11
            [These verses are often used as proof texts for annihilationism]
        3) "Sheol," Isa 5:14
        4) "Weeping and gnashing of teeth," Matt 8:12; 13:42, 50; 22:13; 24:51; 25:30
        5) "Torment," Luke 16:23
        6) "Tribulation and distress," Rom 2:9
        7) "Abyss," Luke 8:31, Rev 20:1, 3
        8) "Pits of darkness," 2 Pet 2:4
        9) "Black darkness," 2 Pet 2:17; Jude 13
        10) "Outer darkness," Matt 8:12; 22:13; 25:30
        11) "Depths of the earth," Psa 63:9
        12) As mere relational separation from God?
            [These verses are used in the "reconciliation model" of the atonement; hell is mere "separation from God"—and *not* fire and brimstone; separation is also taught in the *Catechism of the Catholic Church*[301]]
            a) "And then I will declare to them, 'I never knew you; **depart from Me**, you who practice lawlessness,'" Matt 7:23 (cf. Luke 13:27)
            b) "And later the other virgins also came, saying, 'Lord, lord, **open up for us**.' But he answered and said, 'Truly I say to you, I do not know you.'" Matt 25:11-12
            c) "**Depart from Me**, accursed ones, into the eternal fire which has been prepared for the devil and his angels," Matt 25:41
            [Notice that relational separation is combined with eternal fire in this verse]

     c. There is no way to leave hell, Luke 16:26

C. The Reality of a Literal Hell for All Unsaved Persons:

    1. In many of the above occurrences of a designation for hell, the context refers directly to people (as opposed to a simile in a parable, e.g. Matt 13:30):

      a. The case of the rich man and Lazarus, wherein the rich man was conscious of the burning pain, Luke 16:23-24

      b. Various grammatical designations of people:
        1) "You", Matt 5:29, 30, 18:8, 9
        2) "Him", Matt 22:13, 24:51
        3) "These", Matt 25:46, Rev 19:20
        4) "Them", Matt 13:42
        5) "Anyone", Rev 20:15
        6) "Whoever," Matt 5:22
        7) "For whom," Jude 13
        8) "For every soul who does evil," Rom 2:9
        9) "Many are those who enter by it," Matt 7:13

      c. A designation of people condemned to hell according to the sin(s) which they commit:

        1) Those breaking the 1st and 2nd commandments:
            a) "Idolaters," 1 Cor 6:9; Rev 21:8, and those who practice "idolatry," Gal 5:20
            b) "Sorcerers," Rev 21:8, and those who practice "sorcery," Gal 5:20
            c) "Unbelievers," Luke 12:45
            d) Those who are, "cowardly, unbelieving," Rev 21:8

        2) Those breaking the 6th Commandment, "You shall not murder':
            a) "Murderers," Rev 21:8
            b) "Whoever shall say, 'You fool,'" Matt 5:22

---

[301]"To die in mortal sin without repenting and accepting God's merciful love means remaining separated from him for ever by our own free choice. This state of definitive self-exclusion from communion with God and the blessed is called 'hell.' … The chief punishment of hell is eternal separation from God, in whom alone man can possess the life and happiness for which he was created and for which he longs" (*Catechism of the Catholic Church* [Mahwah, NJ: Paulist, 1994], 269, 270 [§1033 and §1035]).

    3) Those breaking the 7th Commandment, "You shall not commit adultery":

> a) "Fornicators," 1 Cor 6:9, "immoral persons," Rev 21:8, and those who practice "immorality," Gal 5:19
> b) "Adulterers, effeminate, homosexuals," 1 Cor 6:9
> c) Those who practice "immorality, impurity, sensuality" Gal 5:19
> d) "Abominable," Rev 21:8—probably referring the all the abominations of the Canaanites prior to God spitting them out of the land (cf. Lev 18:1-30; 20:1-23)

    4) Those breaking the 8th Commandment, "You shall not steal":

> a) "Thieves," 1 Cor 6:10
> b) "Swindlers," 1 Cor 6:10

    5) Those breaking the 9th Commandment, "You shall not bear false witness":

> a) "All liars," Rev 21:8

    6) Those breaking the 10th Commandment, "You shall not covet":

> a) "Covetous," 1 Cor 6:10, and those who commit "envying," Gal 5:21

    7) Other sins:

> a) "All stumbling blocks, and those who commit lawlessness," Matt 13:41
> b) "Drunkards, revilers," 1 Cor 6:10; those who commit "drunkenness, carousing," Gal 5:20
> c) Those who commit, "enmities, strife, jealousy, outbursts of anger, disputes, dissensions, factions," Gal 5:20

  d. A designation according to a spiritual state or label:

> 1) "The sons of the kingdom," Matt 8:12
> 2) "The worthless slave," Matt 25:30
> 3) "Sons of disobedience," Eph 5:6
> 4) "Children of wrath," Eph 2:3

  e. Designation according to their name:

> 1) "And if anyone's name was not found written in the book of life, he was thrown into the lake of fire," Rev 20:15

2. The designation is so clearly associated to literal people that body parts are mentioned:

  a. "The eye," Matt 5:29, 30; 18:9
  b. "The hand and the foot," Matt 18:8
  c. "Whole body," Matt 5:29, 30
  d. "Cut him to pieces," Matt 24:51; Luke 12:46 (assumes a physical body)

3. People are alive in hell:

  a. "These were thrown alive into the lake of fire," Rev 19:10
  b. "Where the worm does not die," Mark 9:44, 46, 48

4. People remain conscious in hell:

  a. "Their torment goes up forever and ever," Rev 14:11
  b. "Tormented day and night forever and ever," Rev 20:10
  c. "They have no rest day and night," Rev 14:11
  d. "Weeping and gnashing of teeth," Matt 8:12; 13:42, 50; 22:13; 24:51; 25:30

5. In all these contexts the mentioning of hell by Jesus or John is used as a deterrent to evil behavior and an encouragement to good behavior. Were hell not a reality, to threaten with a fictional concept to change behavior, is completely inconsistent with the truth admonitions and claims of the Bible. For in the Bible the end never justifies the means when sin or deceit is the means. Satan is the father of lies (John 8:44), not God or Jesus. Thus, the Bible clearly teaches the everlasting conscious punishment of the unsaved in hell.

These Realities as Motivation

1. The reality of hell as motivation, Proverbs 24:11-12[302]

2. The lostness of man as motivation, 1 Cor 9:19, 22-23 (e.g. Acts 18:9-11; Rom 9:1-3; Jude 22-23):
   a. The lost have no hope if they do not hear, Rom 2:12, 10:14-15
   b. The lost need to call on God while He is near, Isa 55:6 (cf. Psa 32:6)

   "Even if we produce Christians who live as full brothers with men of other races, but do not burn with desire that those others may have eternal life, their 'quality' is certainly in doubt."[303]

3. God's judgment actually prepares people for the Gospel, Psa 58:11

Commitment: "Lord, May My Heart Burn with Desperation for Lost Souls."

---

[302]Mark D. Liederbach, Associate Professor of Christian Ethics at Southeastern Baptist Theological Seminary, in his "Ethical Evaluation of Modern Motivations for Evangelism" (Valley Forge, PA: Evangelical Theological Society, 2005, 2), wrote, "The idea that believers should practice evangelism because unbelievers will go to hell if they do not tell the good news … [is] utilitarianism. … Clearly, however, the motivational tool employed is concern for the consequences of failing to join the 'harvest team'" (ibid., 2-3).

After his section "Twisted Form of Motivation" Liederbach had a section, "Dangerous Results": "The subtle and most insidious nature of this utilitarian motivation is the implication that instead of a sinner being guilty of their own damnation, it is the lazy Christian's fault. … Each encounter with a lost person becomes one in which the eternal destiny of their soul depends upon the believer's actions. One wonders if the good news at this point is really good because it offers someone else an opportunity to know their Creator or because telling it assuages the potential guilt of failing to do so" (ibid., 3).

Liederbach ascribed to Dietrich Bonhoeffer his theological foundation for placing the worship of God, the who, before obedience, the how (ibid., 1). In his concluding point, Liederbach wrote, "Christians must understand that the purpose of the Great Commission is directly linked to the very nature and fabric of the universe and was the reason it was created in the first place—to spread the worship of God to the ends of the earth and magnify the glory of God in all places and times!" (ibid., 10). "The utilitarian assessment is exactly right—the lost will perish without Christ. But the energy to seek and to save them does not primarily rest in the fact that they are lost, but that their lostness robs God of the glory He alone is due. … We are commanded to evangelize because evangelism's primary function is to promote the glory of God and the worship of the King of the universe! … By commanding us, God is instructing us on how to have the fullest and best life now!" (ibid., 11).

[303]Donald A. McGavran, *Understanding Church Growth* (Grand Rapids: Eerdmans, 1970), 45.

3. The Christian is Accountable for the Lost Whom He Should Reach!

Accountability in the Old Testament

1. Cain's rhetorical question: "Am I my brother's keeper?" Gen 4:9

2. "Rebuke your brother frankly so you will not share in his guilt." Lev 19:17 (NIV)

3. Guilt for keeping silent: 2 Kings 7:9, "Then they said to one another, 'We are not doing right. This day is a day of good news, but we are keeping silent; if we wait until morning light, punishment will overtake us. Now therefore come, let us go and tell the king's household.'"

4. Ezekiel 3:16-21, 33:1-20:

   Introduction: Blackwood explained that the fourth commissioning of Ezekiel focused on the individual responsibility of the proclaimer and not on that of the hearer, as others do (Ezek 18). This distinction is important, particularly in light of the different commissions Jesus in the New Testament. It also emphasizes the mandate of speaking God's revelation to the point of moral decision:

   > "The fourth commission has burning relevance for the ministry today. … Many consider Exekiel's emphasis upon individual responsibility his chief contribution to our faith. … The fourth commission emphasizes the prophet's responsibility to speak to the point of moral decision, whether his hearers listen or not. …
   >
   > "The focus of the attention in the fourth commission is upon the watchman and his responsibility. In later developments of the thought, particularly in Chapter 18, the focus is upon the hearer rather than the one who gives warning."[304]

   a. Accountability towards the sinner: To tell him that God's Word says, *"You shall surely die!"* Ezek 3:18, 33:8

   b. Accountability towards the righteous: To warn him, Ezek 3:20-21

   c. Result of not declaring or warning—bloodguiltiness: "his blood I will require at your hand," Ezek 3:18, 20. 33:8 (cf. Prov 28:17)
      As far as antecedent Scripture, bloodguilt is first considered in Genesis 4, when Cain kills Able, and Abel's blood speaks from the ground unto God (Gen 4:10). This concept of bloodguilt is then addressed after the flood, basically stating blood for blood (Gen 9:5-7).
      A further understanding of the concept of bloodguilt is found in Deut 21:1-9. In this passage we find that bloodguilt is not necessarily tied to direct involvement in murder, but merely for finding a corpse in the vincinity of a town or city. Further, that murder brings guilt on the entire town or city. Further, atonement needs to be made for that bloodguilt of which the town or city is ignorant of who perpetrated the act.
      In Ezekiel, the concept is taken a step further: bloodguilt is tied not to physical death, but to spiritual death. And the guilt is associated with not warning people that they are living in sin, and need to repent. It appears that in God's economy of spiritual life, spiritual life must needs be communicated from man to man via warning, and that through that warning, God allows some to take heed (unto salvation and life), while others remain in their sin (to remain in spiritual death, and ultimately eternal judgment).
      As far as not being guilty of death, consider the young woman (Deut 22:25-26) who is raped in the field, she is not guilty of death, as she could not be heard crying out. Here we have an example of a different level of guilt or non-guilt.

   d. Is this applicable to every believer? Yes! Is God fair in this? Yes, Ezek 33:17-20

   Notice, for example, how Paul refers to this passage in his direct address in Acts, bringing the concept into New Testament revelation:
   Acts 18:6 (NKJ), "But when they opposed him and blasphemed, he shook *his* garments and said to them, 'Your blood *be* upon your *own* heads; I *am* clean. From now on I will go to the Gentiles.'"
   Acts 20:26-27 (NKJ), "Therefore I testify to you this day that I *am* innocent of the blood of all *men*. For I have not shunned to declare to you the whole counsel of God."

---

[304]Andrew W. Blackwood, Jr., *Ezekiel: Prophecy of Hope* (Grand Rapids: Baker, 1965), 52-53, 54.

Likewise, F. F. Bruce wrote of Acts 20:25-27:

> Like the trustworthy watchman in Ezek 33:1-6, he had sounded the trumpet aloud so that all the province of Asia had heard: if there were any who paid no heed, their blood would be upon their own heads; Paul was free of responsibility for their doom."[305]

Chart of Ezekiel 3:18-21

Conditional Element	To the Wicked [NT Evangelism]	To the Righteous [NT Discipleship]	Result to OT Prophet or NT Evangelist
If you do not warn...	**Ezek 3:18** When I say to the wicked, 'You shall surely die'; and you do not warn him or speak out to warn the wicked from his wicked way that he may live, that wicked man shall die in his iniquity, but his blood I will require at your hand.	**Ezek 3:20** Again, when a righteous man turns away from his righteousness and commits iniquity, and I place an obstacle before him, he shall die; since you have not warned him, he shall die in his sin, and his righteous deeds which he has done shall not be remembered; but his blood I will require at your hand.	**Bloodguilty**
Yet if you have warned...	**Ezek 3:19** Yet if you have warned the wicked, and he does not turn from his wickedness or from his wicked way, he shall die in his iniquity; but you have delivered yourself	**Ezek 3:21** However, if you have warned the righteous man that the righteous should not sin, and he does not sin, he shall surely live because he took warning; and you have delivered yourself	**Deliverance from bloodguiltiness**

Accountability in the New Testament

1. Accountability in the teaching of Jesus:
   a. Accountability to obedience, Matt 24:46-51, 25:21, 23, 26-30, 31-46
   b. Accountability to bear fruit, John 15:6
   c. Accountability for every word, Matt 12:36
   d. Accountability for a brother, Matt 18:15, Luke 17:3
   e. Accountability to following Christ in fishing for men, Matt 4:19; Mark 1:17
   f. Accountability to not be ashamed of Christ before wicked men, Mark 8:38
   g. Accountability to take men alive, Luke 5:10

2. Accountability as motivation in the writings of Paul:

   a. Accountability for evangelism before God:

      1) Acts 18:6 (NKJ), "But when they opposed him and blasphemed, he shook *his* garments and said to them, 'Your blood *be* upon your *own* heads; I *am* clean. **From now on I will go** to the Gentiles.'"

      2) Acts 20:26-27, Paul says to the Ephesian elders, "Therefore, I testify to you this day that I am innocent of the blood of all men. For **I did not shrink** from declaring to you the whole purpose of God."

      3) 1 Cor 9:16-17, "For if I preach the gospel [evangelize], I have nothing to boast of, for **I am under compulsion** [ἀνάγκη γάρ μοι ἐπίκειται]; for woe is me if I do not preach the gospel [evangelize]. For if I do this voluntarily, I have a reward; but if against my will, I have **a stewardship** entrusted to me." (cf. 1 Cor 10:31-33, 11:1).

      4) 2 Cor 5:9-11, "Therefore also we have as our ambition, whether at home or absent, to be pleasing to Him. For we must all appear before the judgment seat of Christ, that each one may be recompensed for his deeds in the body, according to what he has done, whether good or bad. Therefore **knowing the fear of the Lord, we persuade men**, but we are made manifest to God; and I hope that we are made manifest also in your consciences."

---

[305]F. F. Bruce, *Commentary on the Book of Acts* (Grand Rapids: Eerdmans, 1954), 415.

b. Accountability to the unsaved for their salvation:

1) Rom 1:14-16, "**I am under obligation** [ὁ ὀφειλέτης; lit "indebted"] both to the Greeks and to the barbarians, both to the wise and to the foolish. Thus for my part, I am eager to preach the gospel [to evangelize among] to you also who are in Rome. For I am not ashamed of the gospel for it is the power of God for salvation to every one who believes."

2) 1 Cor 9:19, "For though I am free from all men, **I have made myself a slave to all** [δουλόω; to be made a slave], so that I may win more"
Gk, Ἐλεύθερος γὰρ ὢν ἐκ πάντων, πᾶσιν ἐμαυτὸν ἐδούλωσα, ἵνα τοὺς πλείονας κερδήσω.
Lit trans, "For being free from all, unto all I myself am become enslaved, in order that more I may win."

3) 1 Cor 9:22-23, "To the weak I became weak, that I might win the weak; **I have become all things to all men**, so that I may by all [means] save some. I do all things for the sake of the gospel, so that I may become a fellow partaker of it."
Gk of v 9b, Τοῖς πᾶσιν γέγονα τὰ πάντα, ἵνα πάντως τινὰς σώσω.
Lit trans of v 9b, "Unto all I do everything in order that by everything (I do) I may save some."

4) 1 Cor 10:33-11:1, "Just as **I also please all men in all things**, not seeking my own profit but the profit of the many, so that they may be saved. Be imitators of me, just as I also am of Christ."
Gk of v 10:33, καθὼς κἀγὼ πάντα πᾶσιν ἀρέσκω, μὴ ζητῶν τὸ ἐμαυτοῦ συμφέρον, ἀλλὰ τὸ τῶν πολλῶν, ἵνα σωθῶσιν.
Lit trans of 10:33, "Just as I myself please all in all, not seeking my own benefit, but that of the many, in order that they might be saved."

3. Other areas of accountability:
   a. Accountability to God for the sake of a brother, Rom 14:10-13
   b. Accountability for a weaker brother, 1 Cor 8:10
   c. The special accountability of the leader, James 3:1

Summary of the Christian's accountability

The Christian is not accountable for the person's response to God's Word; rather he is responsible to faithfully declare God's Word.

A Response to This accountability

"And who is adequate for these things?" 2 Cor 2:16

"And such confidence we have through Christ toward God. Not that we are adequate in ourselves to consider anything as coming from ourselves, but our adequacy is from God, who also made us adequate as servants of a new covenant, not of the letter, but of the Spirit; for the letter kills, but the Spirit gives life," 2 Cor 3:4-6

Accountability as Motivation

1. Accountability as motivation to action, Prov 24:11-12, Ezek 3:16-21, 33:1-20, 1 Cor 9:16-17, 27, 2 Cor 5:9-11, Heb 12:28-29
2. Pleasing God as motivation, 1 Cor 9:27, 2 Cor 5:9
3. A charge given as motivation, 1 Cor 9:16-17, 2 Cor 5:18-20
4. Not receiving the grace of God in vain, 1 Cor 15:10, 2 Cor 6:1 (vs. *"fruitful labor", karpos ergou*, Phil 1:22)
5. Need as motivation, Rom 10:14.

Judgment as motivation

1. Mark 8:38, "For whoever is ashamed of Me and My words in this adulterous and sinful generation, the Son of Man will also be ashamed of him when He comes in the glory of His Father with the holy angels."
2. Rom 14:10, "For we shall all appear before the judgment seat of God."
3. Rom 14:12, "So then each one of us shall give an account of himself to God."
4. 1 Cor 3:13, "Each man's work will become evident; for the day will show it, because it is to be revealed with fire; and the fire itself will test the quality of each man's work."
5. 2 Cor 5:10, "For we must all appear before the judgment seat of Christ, that each one may be recompensed for his deeds in the body, according to what he has done, whether good or bad."
6. 2 Tim 4:1-2, "I solemnly charge you in the presence of God and of Jesus Christ, who is to judge the living and the dead ... preach the word; be ready in season and out of season."
7. 1 Pet 4:17, "For it is time for judgment to begin with the household of God; and if it begins with us first, what will be the outcome for those who do not obey the gospel of God?"

"Men! Women! You are bound to be wise in winning souls. Perhaps already souls have perished, because you have not put forth the wisdom which you might in saving them. The city is going to hell. Yes, the world is going to hell, and must go on, 'til the Church finds out what to do to win souls."[306]

Commitment: "Lord, May My Heart Stir Within Me to Reach Out to Lost Souls around Me."

---

[306]Charles G. Finney, in E. E. Shelhamer, ed. *Finney on Revival* (Minneapolis: Bethany House), 73-74.

4. Time Is Short and the Harvest Is Ripe!

The Fact of Limited Time

1. Psa 39:4, "Lord make me know my end, And what is the extent of my days, Let me know how transient I am." (cf. Psa 90:12)
2. John 4:35, "Do you not say, 'There are still four months and then comes the harvest'? Behold, I say to you, lift up your eyes and look at the fields, for they are already white for harvest!"
3. John 4:36, "Already, he who reaps is receiving wages, and is gathering fruit for life eternal"
4. John 9:4, "We must work the works of Him who sent Me, as long as it is day; night is coming, when no man can work."
5. Acts 22:16, "Now why do you delay? Get up and be baptized, and wash away your sins, calling on His name"
6. Rom 13:11-12, "And this do, knowing the time, that it is already the hour for you to awaken from sleep; for now salvation is nearer to us than when we believed. The night is almost gone, and the day is at hand. Let us therefore lay aside the deeds of darkness and put on the armor of light."
7. 1 Cor 7:29, "But this I say, brethren, the time has been shortened, so that from now on both those who have wives should be as though they had none."
8. 2 Cor 6:2, "Behold now is 'the acceptable time,' behold, now is the day of salvation."
9. Eph 5:15-16, "Therefore be careful how you walk, not as unwise men, but as wise, making the most of your time because the days are evil."

The Preparedness of People to Hear the Gospel

1. The harvest is plentiful, Matt 9:37-38, Luke 10:2
2. The harvest is ready, John 4:35
3. Sower and reaper rejoice together, John 4:36
4. The reaper overtakes the sower! Amos 9:13
5. Now is the acceptable time, 2 Cor 6:2
6. Some are waiting to hear, Isa 25:9; 42:4; 51:5
7. Some are anxious to hear, Acts 10:33

Limited Time as Motivation

1. **Need as motivation:**
   a. The ripeness of the harvest, Matt 9:37-38, John 4:35-36 (Prov 10:5)
   b. There are needs in the next town, Luke 4:43-44, 2 Cor 10:15-16
   c. The crying need for laborers, Matt 9:37-38

2. **Work as motivation:**
   a. "I (we) must work the work of Him who sent Me (us)," John 9:4
   b. Working today because God is at work today, John 5:17 (2 Pet 3:8-9)
   c. "He who gathers in summer is a son who acts wisely, But he who sleeps during harvest is a son who acts shamefully." Prov 10:5 (cf. Rom 13:11-12, Eph 5:15-16)

3. **Time as motivation:**

   a. Purchasing back the time (ἐξαγοράζω – 4 NT uses [referring to the atonement, Gal 3:13; 4:5], 1 OT LXX use):
      a. Making the best use of time, Eph 5:15-16
         Lit. "redeeming the time"; Gk. ἐξαγοραζόμενοι τὸν καιρόν.
      b. Making the most of every opportunity, Col 4:5-6
         Lit. "redeeming the time"; Gk. τὸν καιρὸν ἐξαγοραζόμενοι.
      c. These are likely quoted from Daniel 2:8 (LXX):
         "That you may gain [buy] time" [ὅτι καιρὸν ὑμεῖς ἐξαγοράζετε]

Translations of Eph 5:16
(Note the changes in the poignant word picture, "redeeming the time")

Byzan-tine	Latin Vulgate	KJV, NKJ, Revised Webster	Murdock (1852)	New American Bible‡ (1901, 1991)	Bible in Basic English (1949/ 1964)	RSV (1952)	NAS (1977)	NIV (1984)	CEV‡ (1995)	God's Word to the Nations (1995)	Complete Jewish Bible (1988)	The NET Bible (2003)	Holman Christian Standard (2003)
ἐξαγορα-ζόμενοι τὸν καιρόν, ὅτι αἱ ἡμέραι πονηραί εἰσιν.	Redimen-tes tempus quoniam dies mali sunt	Redeeming the time, because the days are evil	who purchase their oppor-tunity; because the days are evil	making the most of the oppor-tunity, because the days are evil	Making good use of the time, because the days are evil	making the most of the time, because the days are evil	making the most of your time, because the days are evil	making the most of every oppor-tunity, because the days are evil	These are evil times, so make every minute count.	Make the most of your oppor-tunities because these are evil days	Use your time well, for these are evil days	taking advantage of every oppor-tunity, because the days are evil	making the most of the time, because the days are evil

b. Realizing the shortness of life and the need to be doing God's will, Rom 13:11-12 (cf. Jos. 13:1)

4. Let's not be slack about God's will, Jos. 18:3

Conclusion: Perhaps the fact of limited time is one of the first urgencies that is removed in the quest for politically-correct evangelism.[307]

Commitment: "Lord, May My Heart Be Moved to Action in Evangelism Today."

Other Biblical Statements Paralleling these Urgencies

A. 2 Cor 3:12 (NKJ), "Therefore, since we have such hope, we use great boldness of speech."

B. 2 Cor 4:1 (NAS), "Therefore, since we have this ministry, as we received mercy, we do not lose heart [NEG, 'nous ne perdons pas courage']"

C. 2 Cor 4:6 (My reworking), "For God, who said, 'From darkness shall shine forth the Light,' has [also] shone forth in our hearts to radiate forth the knowledge of the glory of God in the face of Christ"
BYZ, Ὅτι ὁ θεὸς ὁ εἰπὼν ἐκ σκότους φῶς λάμψαι, ὃς ἔλαμψεν ἐν ταῖς καρδίαις ἡμῶν πρὸς φωτισμὸν τῆς γνώσεως τῆς δόξης τοῦ θεοῦ ἐν προσώπῳ Ἰησοῦ χριστοῦ.
NAS, "For God, who said, 'Light shall shine out of darkness,' is the One who has shone in our hearts to give the light of the knowledge of the glory of God in the face of Christ"

D. 2 Cor 4:13, "But having the same spirit of faith, according to what is written, 'I believed, therefore I spoke,' we also believe, therefore also we speak"

E. Eph 6:15 (French NEG, trans mine), "Place as shoes on your feet the zeal which comes from the Gospel of peace."

F. Eph 6:19-20, "and *pray* on my behalf, that utterance may be given to me in the opening of my mouth, to make known with boldness the mystery of the gospel, for which I am an ambassador in chains; that in *proclaiming* it I may speak boldly, as I ought to speak."
[Even from prison, Paul did not want to give up nor to give in—and to stop speaking about salvation in Christ (cf. Acts 18:9-10)!]

G. 2 Tim 4:2 (Eng Darby), "Proclaim the word; be urgent in season *and* out of season, convict, rebuke, encourage, with all longsuffering and doctrine."

Interaction with the Urgencies

A. Is God justified in causing His people to live with constant urgency?

1. Is it not God who makes the rules, and not His people?

Rom 9:21, "Or does not the potter have a right over the clay, to make from the same lump one vessel for honorable use, and another for common use?"

---

[307]Mittelberg explained why he encouraged a "process-oriented evangelism": "I've learned the hard way that pressing people to take steps for which they are not ready will backfire. In some cases it can even short-circuit the whole process" (Mark Mittelberg, *Building a Contagious Church* [Grand Rapids: Zondervan, 2000], 59.).

2. There must be [is] a loving purpose in the urgency of evangelism, although we may not always understand it, and it is directly related to our [and other people's] salvation:

Rom 9:23, "And *He did so* in order that He might make known the riches of His glory upon vessels of mercy, which He prepared beforehand for glory."

3. Whatever the case, God wants His people to live with urgency, and for that urgency to be directly related to evangelizing

B. How can these urgencies be used as motivational tools?
1. Jesus Christ is coming back quickly!
2. The lost are really lost and headed for hell!
3. The Christian is accountable for the lost whom he should reach!
4. Time is short and the harvest is great!

C. How do these urgencies coexist with the quietness of soul mentioned in Psa 131:1-2?
1. There seems to be a supernatural *non sequitur* released in the life of urgent evangelism:
   a. The peace and joy come, not from seeking them, but from telling of Christ and seeing Him at work in the hearts of others
   b. Evangelizing allows the evangelist to see God [and Satan] at work first hand, and that often brings great peace and assurance
2. Healthy quietness of soul comes from being fully available to the will of God, and having the release of pressure that comes from knowing that He is in control
   a. It follows, then, that true quietness of soul is not found by meditating in a grotto somewhere, virtually starved to death, as was the case of [St.] Benedict who in 529 A.D. gave Rome its Benedictine vows (poverty, chastity, and obedience)
   b. New Testament quietness of soul comes from being constantly aware of our spiritual condition ("Pray without ceasing" and "Be on the alert"), as well as the spiritual condition of others around us ("warning every man" Col 1:28 NKJ)

D. Urgency vs. Anxiety, Phil 4:6-7

Prayer of the Soul-Winner

"O Lord, open my lips, That my mouth may declare Your praise" (Psa 51:15, NAS).

[By the way, notice the disappointing KJV translation of this verse—
"O Lord, open thou my lips; and my mouth shall shew forth thy praise"]

Chapter 6 Appendixes

The Gospel of Christ or the Glory of God
As the Central Interpretive Motif?

Introduction:

The glory of God and the Gospel of Christ are two parallel concepts in the Bible, as such they are not mutually exclusive, but rather complementary. However, when it comes to the mission and purpose of the church, the Great Commission, and evangelism, each of the aforementioned concepts formulate different trajectories. If the Gospel of Christ is the Central Interpretive Motif (CIM), and correspondingly, if all of Holy Writ from beginning to end focuses on the Gospel, then the church and all of the Christian life focus on the Gospel, salvation, and the work of the Gospel—evangelism. However, if the glory of God is the CIM, and correspondingly if all of Holy Writ focuses on worship and the glory of God, then the church and the Christian life focus on the glory of God and His worship. In this latter option, salvation and evangelism seem secondary, whereas worship becomes preeminent, as does understanding the triune nature of God and perhaps even the hypostatic union; in the first option, salvation and evangelism are preeminent, and worship is a mere byproduct of redemption, as believers give praise and glory to God.

Again these two points are not mutually exclusive, but they lead the church down two completely different trajectories. It may be beneficial, therefore, to analyze these concepts in detail to see the major arguments of each to determine if the "Great Commission hermeneutic" is indeed valid, with its emphasis on the Gospel of Christ, or one the other hand, if the glory of God hermeneutic is in line with the Scripturally-based CIM.

Beginning Points:

1. Conservative Christians who affirm the inerrancy of Scripture and the Substitutionary Atonement are on both sides of this debate.

2. Christians who believe in and affirm the primacy of evangelism and practice it are on both sides of this debate.

3. While such a debate is in some ways unfortunate, as it provides ammunition to the enemies of the Gospel (where those who believe in the inerrancy of Scriptures differ), as they seek to discredit the Evangelicals:[308]
    a. Likewise, these issues will never be fully solved, and must be re-debated in each generation to further the work of the Gospel in as unhindered a way as possible.
    b. In a way, the issues revolve around hermeneutics and the plain reading of the text.

4. It does seem, however, that teaching the preimminent place of the "glory of God" or the foundational value of the "doctrines of grace" acts like a kind of "gnosis" (a special knowledge, if you will), whereby new believers or untrained Christians are apprenticed into the deeper things of the word of God:
    a. Are some adherents of the "Doctrines of Grace" not taught to move beyond a somewhat naïve focus on the Gospel of Christ, the cross of Christ, and the salvation of lost souls?
        i.   Whereas the simple and untrained stop mid-point (with the gospel), the properly trained move beyond (in the chronological progression of time) to what really matters from eternity past to eternity future;
        ii. In this system, the simple and untrained prove their lack of knowledge by focusing on the cross of Christ, evangelism, and the salvation of lost souls

---

[308]"If the Protestants knew at its depth how was formed their religion, with how many variations and inconsistencies their confessions of faith have been dressed; how they separated themselves first from us, then from each other; by how many subtleties, detours, and equivocations they have worked to repair their divisions, and to reassemble the distant members of their dis-unified Reformation, this Reform, in which they pride themselves, would not please them; and frankly to say what I think, it would inspire them to despise themselves" (Jacques-Benigne Bossuet, *Histoire des variations des églises protestantes* [Paris: Chez la veuve de Sebastien Mabre-Cramoisy, 1688; Paris: Librairie monarchique de N. Pichard, 1821], 5. Translation mine).

      iii. Fully trained adherents of the "Doctrines of Grace" for their part, focus on the glory of God, the sovereignty of God, and the worship of God;

      iv. The outcome can be quite different.

  b. Hence, say they, the fully trained Christian ought to move beyond to the chronological end-game of theology—the glory of God—the reason for it all—, where conversion and justification are a merely a means, or hiccup (if you will) to a further end

  c. That further end, say they, is the unabated worship of God and His glory from eternity past to eternity future!

5. By the way, there exist other Central Interpretive Motifs which may or may not relate to this discussion (for example):[309]

  a. God's election (often A parallel for the glory of God)

  b. God's sovereignty (another parallel of the glory of God)

  c. Justification by faith (often a parallel for the Gospel of Christ)

  d. The person of Christ as CIM, Col 1:27; 2:3, which can drift into philosophical consideration of the two natures of Christ, and their interrelationship to:

      v. The inspiration of Scripture (God's and man's involvement)[310]

      vi. Signs and symbols in salvation (sacraments and the spiritual work they "represent," versus faith alone and Scriptures alone)[311]

      vii. God and man in salvation (Calvinism versus Arminianism)

      viii. How the Christian or the Church relates to pagan culture:

        1) Syncretism with

        2) Accommodation to

        3) Separation from, or

        4) Isolation from (often due to persecution)

      ix. Or, "In light of Calvary the issue is no longer a *sin* issue. The issue is a *Son* issue."[312]

  e. The Holy Spirit and His gifts

  f. Reconciliation, peace, and social justice

  g. "It's all about the Virgin Mary," etc...

6. These notes provide introductory material to a very complex debate, and they should therefore be taken as introductory.

Reasoning for Gospel of Christ as CIM:

1. The Great Commission, particularly in Luke, affirms that ***the Gospel of Christ*** is the central message of the church which Christ directly commanded his disciples to preach (cf. Luke 24:46-47):

  a. "Thus it is written

  b. "That the Christ should suffer

---

[309]These issues are also discussed in the context of the Great Commission, at the end of Chapter 10.

[310]"Claiming to reduce the role of the exegete to that of a translator (or ignoring that translating the Bible is already doing the work of exegesis) and refusing to follow them [higher critical exegetes] farther in their studies, the fundamentalists do not take into account that, by a very praisable concern of complete faithfulness to the Word of God, they engage themselves in reality along paths that distance them from the exact meaning of the biblical texts as well as the full acceptance of the consequences of the Incarnation" (Commission biblique pontificale, *L'interprétation de la Bible dans l'Église* (Quebec: Éditions Fides, 1994; Paris: Les Éditions du Cerf, 1994), 97). "The foundational problem with this fundamental reading is that, refusing to keep in mind the historical character of divine revelation, she finds herself incapable of fully accepting the truth of the Incarnation itself. Fundamentalism flees the narrow relationship between the divine and the human as regards relations with God. He refuses to admit that the inspired Word of God was expressed in human language and that it was transmitted, under divine inspiration, by human authors with limited capacities and resources" (ibid., 49).

[311]"For as Augustine, the egregious Doctor, says in the book *on Christian Doctrine* [notation: Chapter 2, n. 2; here and in the next passage, but with many words omitted by Master (Peter) and not a few added or changed]: 'Every doctrine is of things, and/or signs. But even things are learned through signs. But here (those) are properly named things, which are not employed to signify anything; but signs, those whose use is in signifying'" (Master Peter Lombard, *The Four Books of Sentences*; available from http://www.franciscan-archive.org/lombardus/opera/ls1-01.html; accessed 16 May 2006; translated from Latin text, *Opera Omnia S. Bonaventurae*, Ad Claras Aquas, 1882, Vol. 1, pp. 26).

[312]Lewis Sperry Chafer quoted by Bob Wilkin, "Our Evangelism Should Be Exegetically Sound" (paper delivered at the Evangelical Theological Society, San Diego, CA, 15 Nov 2007), 3.

c.   "And rise again from the dead the third day

d.   "And that repentance for forgiveness of sins

e.   "Should be proclaimed in His name to all the nations, beginning from Jerusalem."

2.   Jesus, also in Luke 24:44-45, reiterated that He was the fulfillment of the prophecies of the Old Testament (OT), thereby affirming that His person and work was the CIM for the OT:

a.   "These are My words which I spoke to you while I was still with you,

b.   "That all things which are written about Me in the Law of Moses and the Prophets and the Psalms must be fulfilled.

c.   "Then He opened their minds to understand the Scriptures."

3.   The Gospel (τὸ εὐαγγέλιον) is the sole message in Mark's Great Commission: "And He said to them, 'Go into all the world and preach the gospel to all creation'" (Mark 16:15).

a.   This message of the Gospel is glorious, 1 Tim 1:11

Translations of "glory" in 1 Timothy 1:11
Is God glorious or is the Gospel glorious?

Byzantine	Vulgate*	Wycliffe (1388)	Tyndale (1534); cf. Bishop's	Young's (1862, 1898)	ASV (1901); cf. NJB*	ABS' CEV* (1991)	GNT* (1993)	God's Word to the Nations (1995)	Geneva (1560); cf. KJV; RSV; NAS; NIV; NKJ; NLT; CSB
	Gospel of the glory of God					Glorious God		"that contains"? How? The glory in the host?	Paul's Gospel is glorious
κατὰ τὸ εὐαγγέλιον τῆς δόξης τοῦ μακαρίου θεοῦ, ὃ ἐπιστεύθην ἐγώ.	quae est secundum evangelium gloriae beati Dei quod creditum est mihi	that is aftir the euangelie of the glorie of blessid God, which is bitakun to me.	accordinge to the gospell of the glory of the blessed God which gospell is committed vnto me.	according to the good news of the glory of the blessed God which I was entrusted.	according to the gospel of the glory of the blessed God, with which I was committed to my trust.	of the good news that the glorious and wonderful God has given me.	That teaching is found in the gospel that has been entrusted to me to announce, the Good News from the glorious and blessed God.	Moses' Teachings were intended to be used in agreement with the Good News that contains the glory of the blessed God. I was entrusted with that Good News.	Which is according to the glorious Gospel of the blessed God, which is committed vnto me.

4.   This Gospel was the message that Christ unfolded to the disciples throughout His ministry, even though they did not understand it (see the Book of Luke on Jesus' unfolding of the Gospel to His disciples throughout His ministry, as well as their lack of understanding in Luke 24)

5.   Paul emphasized the preaching of the cross, for which he was persecuted:

a.   In Galatians:

i.   **The cross** was a stumbling block, "But I, brethren, if I still preach circumcision, why am I still persecuted? Then the stumbling block of the cross has been abolished" (Gal 5:11)

ii.   False teachers avoided a unique focus on **the cross**, rather emphasizing some work or spiritual discipline; their motive—to avoid persecution: "Those who desire to make a good showing in the flesh try to compel you to be circumcised, simply that they may not be persecuted for the cross of Christ" (Gal 6:12)

iii.   **The cross** was the only boast of Paul, "But may it never be that I should boast, except in the cross of our Lord Jesus Christ, through which the world has been crucified to me, and I to the world" (Gal 6:14)

1) The French Geneva (Calvin's translation) translates the verb "to boast" as "to glorify oneself in", hence:

   a. "Mais pour moi, ja ne m'advienne que je me glorifie, sinon en la croix de nostre Seigneur Jesus Christ, par laquelle le monde m'est crucifié, et moi au monde" (Gal 6:14)[313]

2) This verse makes the cross the subject of glorification (not however, adoration of the crucifix), and not the illusive glorification of the mysteries of the Godhead (as in Peter the Lombard's *Sentences*, based on his reading of Augustine):

   a. The mystery of the Incarnation (God became flesh), or
   b. The mystery of the Godhead, three-in-one

3) Is not the glorification of the cross parallel to the glorification and running of the word through evangelism (cf. 2 Thess 3:1-2)?

   a. "Finally, brethren, pray for us that the word of the Lord may spread rapidly and be glorified, just as *it did* also with you; and that we may be delivered from perverse and evil men; for not all have faith" (2 Thess 3:1-2)

b. In Corinthians:

   i. **The cross** could be nullified by clever speech, "For Christ did not send me to baptize, but to preach the gospel, not in cleverness of speech, that the cross of Christ should not be made void" (1 Cor 1:17)
   ii. **The cross** was foolishness to those who are perishing, and the power of God to those who are being saved, "For the word of the cross is to those who are perishing foolishness, but to us who are being saved it is the power of God" (1 Cor 1:18)
   iii. **The cross** was a stumbling block to Jews, foolishness to Gentiles, "but we preach Christ crucified, to Jews a stumbling block, and to Gentiles foolishness" (1 Cor 1:23)
   iv. **The cross** was the wisdom of God and the power of God to who are called, "but to those who are the called, both Jews and Greeks, Christ the power of God and the wisdom of God" (1 Cor 1:24)
   v. **The cross** was the central message of the Apostle Paul to the church that was already in existence was Christ and His crucifixion: 1 Cor 2:2, "For I determined to know nothing among you except Jesus Christ, and Him crucified."

6. This Gospel was clearly stated by Paul, and was said to be the central message by which members of the church are saved and by which they persevere in their salvation (1 Cor 15:1-8):

   a. "Now I make known to you, brethren, the gospel
      i. "Which I preached to you
      ii. "Which also you received
      iii. "In which also you stand,
      iv. "By which also you are saved, if you hold fast the word which I preached to you, unless you believed in vain.

   b. "For I delivered to you as of first importance what I also received
      i. "That Christ died for our sins according to the Scriptures,
      ii. "And that He was buried
      iii. "And that He was raised on the third day according to the Scriptures
      iv. "And that He appeared to Cephas, then to the twelve.
      v. "After that He appeared to more than five hundred brethren at one time, most of whom remain until now, but some have fallen asleep;
      vi. "Then He appeared to James, then to all the apostles;
      vii. "And last of all, as it were to one untimely born, He appeared to me also.

7. In Romans:

   a. **The Gospel** is the central theme of Romans, Rom 1:16-17
      i. The apostle Paul was set apart for **the Gospel**, Rom 1:10; 15:15-16
      ii. Paul's ambition was to preach **the Gospel**, Rom 15:18-21
      iii. Paul's blessing is based on **the Gospel** and His preaching, Rom 16:25-27

---

[313]"Bible de Geneve"; available at: http://biblegeneve.com/bibles-php/index.php?version=nt1669-cm; accessed: 29 June 2006; Internet.

    b. **Justification by faith alone** being a corollary theme to the Gospel, Rom 1:16-17

        i. **No justification** through works, Rom 3:4, 20

        ii. **Justification** as a gift, Rom 3:24-4:5

        iii. However, **full and immediate justification by faith**, Rom 4:23-5:2, as is the evident purpose for Christ's death and resurrection (cf. Luke 24:46-47)

    c. Focusing on the glory of God was part of the Old Covenant:

        i. Making one's boast in God, Rom 2:17

        ii. To the Israelites belongs, "the glory," Rom 9:4

        iii. Through Christ, the Gentiles also glory in God, Rom 15:7-12

        iv. Paul provided the bridge between Christ and glory:

            1) Paul's glory is now Jesus Christ!
Rom 15:17, "Therefore I have reason to **glory in Christ Jesus** in the things *which pertain* to God."

            2) And it is via Jesus Christ that God receives glory:
Rom 16:17, "to God, alone wise, *be* **glory through Jesus Christ** forever. Amen."

        v. The New Covenant emphasis is for man to glory in Christ Jesus, when this is done through a focus on the gospel, then Christ Himself brings glory to God (John 17:1)!

            1) Could it not rightly be said that man is usurping the role of Jesus, if he seeks to glorify God directly, without going in and through Christ and His cross?

            2) Was this not the problem of Augustine and the Medieval scholastics, who sought to bring glory to God directly, with the primary focus on Jesus being His incarnation (as part of the Trinity), the mystery of His dual natures, and Rome's false doctrine of the Sacraments proceeding from contemplation of this dual nature?

8. In John:

    a. The Gospel of John is the Gospel of belief:

        i. The verb πιστεύω is found 100 times in 86 verses in the Gospel of John.

    b. Belief is related to the object of belief; in the book of John the object of belief is:

        i. Verbal confessions of faith:
            1) "I believe," John 9:38
            2) "Yes, Lord; I have believed that You are the Christ, the Son of God, *even* He who comes into the world," John 11:27

        ii. In an question:
            1) "Do you believe this?" John 11:26
            2) "Did I not say to you, if you believe, you will see the glory of God?" John 11:40
            3) "Do you now believe?" John 16:31

        iii. Dealing with Christ:
            1) In Him, John 1:7; 3:15, 16, 18; 4:39; 5:46; 6:35, 40, 47; 7:38, 39; 8:31; 9:36; 10:42; 11:25, 26, 48; 12:42, 46; 14:12; 17:20
            2) "In Me," John 12:44; 14:1
            3) In His name, John 1:12; 2:23
            4) The name of the only begotten Son of God, John 3:18
            5) You are the holy One of God, John 6:69
            6) Jesus is the Christ the Son of God, John 20:31
            7) That "I am," John 8:24; 13:19
            8) In the Son, John 3:36
            9) In the Son of man, John 9:35
            10) In Jesus, John 12:11
            11) That the Father is in Me and I in Him, John 10:38 (not found in NA27); 14:10, 11
            12) In the light, John 12:36
            13) The word of Christ, John 1:50; 2:22; 4:21, 41, 42, 50; 8:30; 12:47 (not found in NA27); 14:29
            14) Because of His signs, John 2:11, 23; 4:48, 53; 7:31; 10:37, 38; 11:45; 14:11
            15) Christ's ability to raise the dead, John 10:15

16) The empty tomb, John 20:8
17) Because of seeing the resurrected Christ, John 20:29
18) Believe though not seeing the resurrected Christ, John 20:29

    iv. Dealing with the Scriptures:
      1) Believing the Scriptures, John 2:22
      2) Believing Moses, John 5:46
      3) In the testimony of John, John 19:35

    v. Dealing with God:
      1) In God, John 14:1

    vi. Dealing with God sending Jesus:
      1) Believing in the One who sent Jesus, John 5:24; 6:29; 12:44
      2) Not believing the One God sent, John 5:38
      3) That God sent Jesus, John 10:42; 17:8, 21
      4) Christ came forth from God, John 16:27, 30

    vii. Dealing with unbelief
      1) Of Nicodemus' unbelief, John 3:12
      2) Of brothers' unbelief, John 7:5
      3) Of the rulers and Pharisees not believing, John 7:48
      4) Jews not believing in the healing of the blind man, John 9:18
      5) Due to receiving glory from man, John 5:44
      6) Disbelief in the Scriptures, John 5:47
      7) Disbelief in the words of Christ, John 5:47; 8:45, 46; 10:25
      8) Needing a sign to believe, John 6:30
      9) Even though they saw Christ, John 6:36
      10) Even though Jesus performed many signs, John 12:37
      11) Who do not believe, John 6:64; 10:26; 14:9
      12) Isaiah's prophecy, "LORD, who has believed our report?" John 12:38
      13) Inability to believe, John 12:39
      14) Of Thomas' need for proof, John 20:25

    viii. Of Jesus' lack of trust in man, John 2:23

c. Note the role of faith in relation to salvation:
    i. Faith being a gift from God
    ii. Yet man being the subject of believing

d. Note the centrality of Christ's sacrifice in the message of John, John 1:29, "Behold, the Lamb of God who takes away the sin of the world!"

9. In Revelation:

a. Considering an interesting shift between Rev 4 and Rev 5:
    i. Whereas the songs of Rev 4 focus on the glory of God
      1) A shift takes place after the entrance of the "Lamb as if slain"
    ii. The songs of Rev 4 address specifically:
      1) "Lord God Almighty," Rev 4:8
      2) "O Lord," Rev 4:11
      3) Trinitarian considerations aside, as well as the nuance of the link between the OT YHWH and the NT ὁ Κύριος for Jesus
    iii. Once Jesus is introduced in Rev 5:1-7, the songs change focus
      1) First to Jesus only:
        a. "You are worthy ... for You were slain, And have redeemed ...," Rev 5:9
        b. "Worthy is the Lamb that was slain," Rev 5:12
      2) Then to both God and the Lamb:
        a. "To Him who sits on the throne, And to the Lamb," Rev 3:13
    iv. Perhaps in this last song we have our balance: worshipping both God (and His glory) and Jesus (and His cross)!

b. Considering interpretive options between Rev 4 and Rev 5:
   i. Dispensational:
     1) Could not Rev 4, with its emphasis on the glory of God, be reminiscent of the OT dispensation?
     2) Could not also the revelation of the Lamb as worthy in Rev 5:1-7 be reminiscent of the ministry and passion of Jesus Christ?
     3) The hermeneutical question in this schema becomes why the next two songs focus on Jesus, and then the last song focus on both God and the Lamb?
   ii. Varieties of Trinitarian worship:
     1) Could it be that the different emphases in the focus of the worship of the songs in Rev 4 and 5 are merely coincidental, and not significant in a chronological way?
     2) Much as the church today sings songs both to worship God for who He is, and the Lamb for what He has done, similarly, perhaps, could not Revelation merely portray the breadth of the worship in heaven?
     3) Likewise, Rev 19 continues the emphasis found in Rev 4, wherein God is worshiped for his righteous judgment of the Harlot Babylon and affirming His eternal reign

c. Furthermore, Jesus will be worshiped as "the Lamb that was slain" (Rev 5:12) throughout all eternity, focusing on the priority of the atonement in His ministry:
   i. The word "Lamb" is used 26 times in the book of Revelation (all referring to Jesus, except Rev 13:11)
   ii. Uses of Lamb with a term for the atonement:
     1) Rev 5:6, "Lamb as it had been slain"
     2) Rev 5:12, "Lamb that was slain"
     3) Rev 7:14, "the blood of the Lamb"
     4) Rev 12:11, "the blood of the Lamb"
     5) Rev 13:8, "the Lamb slain from the foundation of the world"
   iii. Other references to the atonement:
     1) Rev 5:9, "Worthy art Thou to take the book, and to break its seals; for Thou wast slain, and didst purchase for God with Thy blood *men* from every tribe and tongue and people and nation"
     2) Rev 7:14, "they have washed their robes and made them white in the blood of the Lamb"
     3) Rev 12:11, "they overcame him because of the blood of the Lamb…"
     4) Rev 19:13, "And *He is* clothed with a robe dipped in blood"

d. The angel goes forth "to evangelize an eternal Gospel to all those who live on the earth" Rev 14:6

10. The Gospel is the primary message of the church in the pastoral epistles (see Appendix to Chapter 26):
a. "Remember Jesus Christ," 2 Tim 2:8

11. That the cross is not central in the Gospels is evident because:
a. The life of Jesus was lived under the Old Covenant
b. The teachings of Jesus often related to the Old Covenant, Matt 5, 22
c. Christ had not yet died

12. Christ as the Lamb of God was in the mind of God before He created the world, 1 Pet 1:20; Rev 13:8; and Christ as the Passover Lamb is one of the main elements of the Pentateuch's prophecy regarding the first coming of Jesus Christ

13. It is difficult to doubt that the Gospel (the cross, the blood, justification by faith, salvation in Christ, and believing in Christ) is the CIM of the NT church from a plain reading of the text:

a. While seeking to avoid endless debates over hermeneutics, I am advocating a plain reading of the text, rather than a theologically-forced reading

b. For example, some who advocate a forced reading are those who adhere to:
   i. "Oneness Theology"—baptism in the name of "Jesus only" (modalistic monarchianism)
   ii. Assured healing of the sick by the prayer of faith
   iii. Finding the Virgin Mary and/or the Eucharist on every page in Scripture.

Reasoning for the Glory of God as CIM:

1. It is interesting to note, by way of introduction, that Calvin likewise accused the Schoolmen (*Theologiens Sorboniques*) of misappropriately emphasizing God over Jesus Christ:[314]

    a. Calvin acknowledged that by the Holy Spirit man must seek Christ for salvation in order to find God[315]

    b. But then Calvin appears to have fallen prey to the same framing of the question, using:
        i. Medieval categories and logical progressions
        ii. Quoting Augustine, whose quotations fill the pages of Rome's quintessential Schoolmen, Peter the Lombard[316] and Thomas Aquinas

    c. While Calvin acknowledged the need for profession of truth from the mind, "by the submission of our mind"…[317]

    d. Like many other theologians before him and after him, the concept of and need for evangelizing was lost in:
        i. A state-church *a priori*—assuming that people will come to the approved state church to hear the Gospel, not usually a good assumption on two levels:
            1. That they will come to church (although infant Baptism is required and some other annual religious rites depending on the church and time)
            2. That the state church is actually preaching the Gospel of salvation

---

[314]"This evil, therefore, must, like innumerable others, be attributed to the Schoolmen [*theologiens Sorboniques*], who have in a manner drawn a veil over Christ, to whom, if our eye is not directly turned, we must always wander through many labyrinths" (John Calvin, *Institutes of the Christian Religion,* Henry Beveridge, trans. [available at: http://www.ccel.org/ccel/calvin/institutes.html (online); accessed: 16 Sept 2007; Internet], 470).

[315]"It is true, indeed, that faith has respect to God only; but to this we should add, that it acknowledges Jesus Christ whom he has sent. God would remain far off, concealed from us, were we not irradiated by the brightness of Christ. All that the Father had, he deposited with his only begotten Son, in order that he might manifest himself in him, and thus by the communication of blessings express the true image of his glory. Since, as has been said, we must be led by the Spirit, and thus stimulated to seek Christ, so must we also remember that the invisible Father is to be sought nowhere but in this image" (ibid., 470).

[316]Notice the Master of the Sentences, Peter the Lombard's use of Augustine from the very beginning of Book One, "On the Unity and Trinity of God"; Distinction One; Chapter One, "Every doctrine concerns things and/or signs": "While considering the contents of the Old and New Law again and again by diligent chase ['*indagine*'], the prevenient grace of God has hinted to us, that a treatise on the Sacred Page is ['*versari*'] chiefly about things and/or signs. For as Augustine, the egregious Doctor, says in the book *on Christian Doctrine* ['Chapter 2, n. 2; here and in the next passage, but with many words omitted by Master (Peter) and not a few added or changed']: « Every doctrine is of things, and/or signs. But even things are learned through signs. But here (those) are properly named things, which are not employed to signify anything; but signs, those whose use is in signifying ». But of these there are some, whose every use is in signifying, not in justifying, that is ['The Vatican text and edition 4, not so well, omit *that is*'], which we do not use except for the sake of signifying something, as (are) some Sacraments of the Law ['*legalia*']; others, which not only signify, but confer that which helps inwardly, as the evangelical Sacraments (do). 'From which it is openly understood, what are here named signs: those things namely, which are employed to signify something. Therefore every sign is also some thing. For because it is no thing, as Augustine said in the same (book), it is entirely nothing; but conversely ['The Vatican text and editions 4 and 6 have *diversely* in place of *conversely*'] not every thing is a sign', because it is not employed to signify anything. And since the studious and modest speculation of theologians is intent upon these, it turns toward the Sacred Page to hold the form prescribed in doctrine. Of these, therefore, there is to be an orderly discussion ['*disserendum est*'] by us who want, with God as (our) leader, to open an approach towards understanding to some extent the things divine; and first we would discuss in an orderly manner things, afterwards signs" (Master Peter Lombard, "Prologue," *Four Books of Sentences*; accessed 16 May 2006; from http://www.franciscan-archive.org/lombardus/opera/ ls1-01.html; Internet).

[317]"We do not obtain salvation either because we are prepared to embrace every dictate of the Church as true, or leave to the Church the province of inquiring and determining; but when we recognize God as a propitious Father through the reconciliation made by Christ, and Christ as given to us for righteousness, sanctification, and life. By this knowledge, I say, not by the submission of our understanding, we obtain an entrance into the kingdom of heaven. For when the Apostle says, "With the heart man believeth unto righteousness; and with the mouth confession is made unto salvation," (Rom. 10:10); he intimates, that it is not enough to believe implicitly without understanding, or even inquiring. The thing requisite is an explicit recognition of the divine goodness, in which our righteousness consists" (John Calvin, *Institutes of the Christian Religion*, 471-72). By the way, Calvin never quoted Rom 10:9 in his institutes, in interesting omission, in light of the fact that, in part, his institutes were meant to refocus the teaching of the Schoolmen back to the Word of God in the area of salvation.

      ii. Regeneration through infant Baptism, which he taught included partaking in "all his [Christ's] blessings." Note all the terminology that Calvin subsumed into infant Baptism, the promise of:[318]

        1. The washing of regeneration
        2. Renewing by the Holy Ghost
        3. Free pardon of sins
        4. Imputation of righteousness
        5. The grace of the Holy Spirit, to form us again into newness of life
        6. Being ingrafted into the death and life of Christ
        7. United to Christ himself
        8. Partakers of all his blessings.

2. Belief in the glory of God as the unique Central Interpretive Motif seems a bit more philosophically derived:

    a. The Gospel (in a limited view) seems to be only a temporary or preliminary message (leading to immediate salvation), whereas the glory of God is considered an eternal truth, which continues both in this life and throughout eternity

      i. Which is interesting in light of the songs of heaven (for all eternity) which refer to Jesus as "the Lamb that was slain."

    b. Similarly, the message of the Gospel is only necessary to initiate a lost soul to salvation, after his/her conversion, worship of God in all His glory (almost a worship of the transcendence of God) replaces an emphasis on the Gospel

    c. The glory of God is mentioned in several places in Scripture:

      i. In Ephesians 1, as the ultimate goal of salvation, thereby bringing to completion a temporary emphasis on the Gospel

      ii. In the OT Scriptures, such as in the Pentateuch and the Psalms

      iii. "Do all to the glory of God" (1 Cor 10:31) becomes the CIM (even though 1 Cor 2:2 and 15:1-8 are found in the same book of the Bible).

3. In fact, belief in the glory of God as the unique CIM has become for some a true the test of true faith:

    a. An emphasis on the glory of God has provided, for some, a tried and true test to avoid lapse into spiritual downgrade of human works and the Pelagian heresy (exemplified in Catholicism)

      i. Consider my remarks on the Second Council of Orange as an Appendix to Chapter 10, to show that the Pelagianism considered in that rebuttal seems to be nothing else than NT evangelism

    b. For some, it is only the message of "God and His glory" (as opposed to the Christ and His cross) that puts man in his place (e.g. total depravity and total inability), and therefore avoids the pitfalls of Arminianism with its emphasis on human ability (with the counter-measures of duty faith and duty repentance)

4. Sample Scriptural Proof for the glory of God as the CIM:

    a. Psa 96:3, "Tell of His glory among the nations, His wonderful deeds among all the peoples" (and similar; see Chapter 2 for many more examples)

      i. The only problem with this verse as proof, is that the salvation of God is also listed as that which ought to be shared to all the world

      ii. Notice Psa 96:2, "Sing to the LORD, bless His name; Proclaim good tidings of His salvation from day to day"

      iii. In fact, in these verses, salvation is listed as the message prior to the glory of God!

---

[318]"He elsewhere uses the same argument—viz. that we are circumcised, and put off the old man, after we are buried in Christ by baptism (Col. 2:12). And in this sense, in the passage which we formerly quoted, he calls it 'the washing of regeneration, and renewing of the Holy Ghost' (Tit. 3:5). We are promised, first, the free pardon of sins and imputation of righteousness; and, secondly, the grace of the Holy Spirit, to form us again to newness of life.

"6. The last advantage which our faith receives from baptism is its assuring us not only that we are ingrafted into the death and life of Christ, but so united to Christ himself as to be partakers of all his blessings" (ibid., 799).

b. 1 Cor 10:31, "Therefore, whether you eat or drink, or whatever you do, do all to the glory of God"
   i. What of 1 Cor 2:2, "For I determined not to know anything among you except Jesus Christ and Him crucified"? In the same book, and more clearly in a section where Paul was speaking about the message. In chapters 8-10 Paul was discussing meat sacrificed to idols.
   ii. Is the "glory of God" in 1 Cor 10:31 more important than the Gospel expounded in 1 Cor 15:1-8?
   iii. What of the twice mentioned concept of "doing"—man needing to do and being commanded to do something, even in this verse?

c. The glory of God in Ephesians 1:
   i. Once appears, "to the praise of the glory of His grace," Eph 1:6
   ii. Twice appears the phrase, "to the praise of His glory," Eph 1:12, 14
   iii. The prepositions "to" (εἰς) in these three references are taken with such causal weight and with such a hermeneutical *a priori*, as to overturn or negate all of the above emphases on the Gospel, Christ, the cross, or justification by faith as the CIM
   iv. Could we not, likewise, take the verses that mention the praise and glorification of the Word of God with the same causal weight (cf. Psa 56:10-11; 138:2; Acts 13:48; 2 Thess 3:1)?

d. In Revelation:
   i. The "Hallelujah Chorus" in Revelation emphasizes the glorious reign of God, Rev 19:6, "Hallelujah! For the Lord our God, the Almighty reigns."
   ii. Yes, note also the corollary song in Rev 19:1, "Hallelujah! Salvation and glory and power belong to our God…" Notice that we do not worship the power of God, but rather affirm that He has power; we do not worship the salvation of God, but rather affirm that He provides salvation; we do not worship the glory of God, but rather affirm that unto Him belong all glory.

e. Other examples:
   i. Herod was eaten up by worms because he took the glory due to God alone, Acts 12:20-23
   ii. Many other examples may also be noted and cited

Interaction:

1. There are good reasons for Christians to emphasize the glory of God:
   a. It is found in Scripture
   b. It is a safeguard to heresy and the ever-present overemphasis on human merits and human work to obtain salvation

2. It is not a matter of truth and falsehood:
   a. For example, consider the teaching of Apollos, Acts 18:24-28:
      i. Apollos "spoke accurately the things of the Lord, though he knew only the baptism of John" (Acts 18:25)
      ii. Yet Priscilla and Aquila took him aside to explain "the way of God more accurately" (Acts 18:26)
      iii. This resulted in Apollos following in the methodology of Paul, "he vigorously refuted the Jews publicly, showing from the Scriptures that Jesus is the Christ" (Acts 18:27; cf. Acts 9:20; 17:2-3; 28:23)
   b. Rather than being a matter of "right versus wrong," it is a matter of emphasis and misemphasis:
      i. Is the glory of God really the emphasis in the NT?
      ii. Is the Gospel of Christ the emphasis in the NT?
      iii. Is there a clear covenantal distinction between the message of the Old Covenant and the message of the New Covenant?
   c. Notice how this issue can spin us off into many directions of debate!

3. Thus, emphasizing the glory of God *over* the Gospel of Christ seems problematic for several reasons:
   a. It undermines the centrality of the Gospel in the Old Testament (Luke 24:44-45) and in the New Testament (as seen above in Luke, Romans, 1 Corinthians, Galatians, the Pastorals, and Revelation)
   b. It undermines the emphases taught in the Great Commission passages (Luke 24:46-47)

    c. It undermines the centrality of evangelism in the NT church

    d. It undermines the urgency of evangelism[319]

    e. It leads to a theological-philosophical approach in the interpretation of Scripture, rather than focusing on:

       i. The plenary interpretation of Scripture

      ii. The clear meaning of every text.

4. We cannot add to the glory of God by some type of worship of Him:

    a. He is already glorious!

       i. John 12:28, "'Father, glorify Thy name.' There came therefore a voice out of heaven: 'I have both glorified it, and will glorify it again'"

      ii. Even the greatest act of worship is not enough to express the true glory of God!

     iii. Isa 40:16-17, "Even Lebanon is not enough to burn, Nor its beasts enough for a burnt offering. All the nations are as nothing before Him, They are regarded by Him as less than nothing and meaningless"

    b. What God wants from a rebellious and stiff-necked people is humility and obedience:

       i. Example of worship without obedience:

         1) 1 Sam 15:22-23, "And Samuel said, 'Has the LORD as much delight in burnt offerings and sacrifices As in obeying the voice of the LORD? **Behold, to obey is better than sacrifice**, *And* to heed than the fat of rams. For rebellion is as the sin of divination, And insubordination is as iniquity and idolatry. Because you have rejected the word of the LORD, He has also rejected you from *being* king.'"

         2) The issue is not lack of worship or added worship, the issue is obedience versus disobedience (1 Pet 2:8)

         3) In fact, according to 1 Sam 15, obedience [e.g. to the Great Commission] is "better than" or prior or superior to worship [or sacrifice]

      ii. Example of worship without honor:

         1) Leviticus 10:1-3, "Now Nadab and Abihu, the sons of Aaron, took their respective firepans, and after putting fire in them, placed incense on it and offered strange fire before the LORD, which He had not commanded them. And fire came out from the presence of the LORD and consumed them, and they died before the LORD. Then Moses said to Aaron, 'It is what the LORD spoke, saying, "By those who come near Me I will be treated as holy, And before all the people I will be honored."' So Aaron, therefore, kept silent."

         2) A right relationship with God precedes appropriate worship, this is why the cross is prior to and above any worship that we can give God

     iii. The Pharisee and the Tax Gatherer, Luke 18:9-14:

         1) The Pharisee puts worship prior to having a right relationship with God, his prayers go unheard

         2) The tax gatherer knows that he is meaningless in the sight of God, he confesses his sin and his need for mercy; God hears his prayer

     iv. Luke 17:10, "So you too, when you do all the things which are commanded you, say, 'We are unworthy slaves; we have done *only* that which we ought to have done'":

         3) Even when we do all that God has commanded (and who does? Eccl 7:20), we have no right or position before God, we remain unworthy servants

         4) Our worship does not gain some kind of special worth because of who we are or what we have done—it is always and only because of the blood of Jesus shed for us!

    c. The central issue is our sin and God's plan of redemption, not some overarching goal of God to finally get humans to admit to His glory through worship:

       i. Yes, He desires those who worship Him to do so "in spirit and in truth," John 4:23-24

         1) John 4:23-24, "But an hour is coming, and now is, when the true worshipers shall worship the Father in spirit and truth; **for such people the Father seeks to be His worshipers**. God is spirit, and those who worship Him must worship in spirit and truth."

         2) Notice in this context, that God is first seeking worshipers, not the worship

---

[319]See Mark Liederbach quote above (Chapter 5, "The Urgencies of Evangelism"; 3. "The Lost Are Really Lost and Going to Hell").

    ii. It is Christ Who remains the stumbling block:
        1) Isa 28:16, "Therefore thus says the Lord God, "Behold, I am laying in Zion a stone, a tested stone, A costly cornerstone *for* the foundation, firmly placed. He who believes *in it* will not be disturbed"
        2) Rom 9:32-33, "Why? Because *they did* not *pursue it* by faith, but as though *it were* by works. They stumbled over the stumbling stone, just as it is written, "Behold, I lay in Zion a stone of stumbling and a rock of offense, And he who believes in Him will not be disappointed""
        3) 1 Pet 2:6-8, "For *this* is contained in Scripture: 'Behold I lay in Zion a choice stone, a precious corner *stone*, And he who believes in Him shall not be disappointed.' This precious value, then, is for you who believe. But for those who disbelieve, 'The stone which the builders rejected, This became the very corner *stone*,' and, 'A stone of stumbling and a rock of offense'; for they stumble because they are disobedient to the word, and to this *doom* they were also appointed"
        4) It is not an issue of atheism versus theism
        5) It is an issue of the Gospel of salvation in Jesus Christ

    iii. Because of its esoteric nature, an emphasis on worshipping the glory of God must needs morph into philosophical theology, as found from Augustine to Peter the Lombard, where the worship of the glory of God is reduced to worshipping speculations of:
        1) The mystery and magnificence of beauty[320]
        2) The mystery and magnificence of the Incarnation
        3) The mystery and magnificence of the Trinity

    iv. Meanwhile in Medieval philosophical theology (again founding itself on Augustine's writings), an emphasis on worshipping the glory of God above obedience to the Gospel of Christ morphed into worship of:
        1) The crucifix
        2) The signs by which the grace of God was deemed to be bestowed (holy water, holy oil, the Host in the Eucharist, etc.)

  d. As one evangelist recently told me, "Worship without obedience is absurd!"
    i. Soteriology must precede doxology (regardless of the practices of the Seeker Church movement and what Emergent writers are saying)
    ii. Without soteriology preceding doxology, there is a dangerous blurring of the bibical distinction between saved and the lost, the wicked and the righteous (cf. Lev 10:10; Mal 3:18)

  e. God is already glorious!
    i. He doesn't need our worship to affirm His glory or to enhance it in some minuscule way
    ii. What He desires is our obedience, not sacrifice (1 Sam 15:22), and as it relates to this discussion, our obedience to the Great Commission!

---

[320]"Again, while still a Manichæan Augustin had thought and written much about beauty. On this point also, the throwing off of Manichæism and the adoption of a Platonizing Christianity brought about a revolution in his conceptions. The exactness with which he has followed Plotinus in his ideas of the beauty of God and of his creatures is remarkable. This we could fully illustrate by the citation of parallel passages. But we must content ourselves with remarking that Augustin himself acknowledged his indebtedness, and that his idea of beauty was an important factor in his polemics against Manichæism. According to Augustin (and Plotinus) God is the most beautiful and splendid of all beings. He is the beauty of all beauties; all the beautiful things that are the objects of our vision and love He Himself made. If these are beautiful what is He? All beauty is from the highest beauty, which is God. Augustin follows Plato and Plotinus even in neglecting the distinction between the good and the beautiful. The idea of Divine beauty Augustin applies to Christ also. He speaks of Him as beautiful God, beautiful Word with God, beautiful on earth, beautiful in the womb, beautiful in the hands of his parents, beautiful in miracles, beautiful in being scourged, beautiful when inciting to life, beautiful when not caring for death, beautiful when laying down his life, beautiful when taking it up again, beautiful in the sepulchre, beautiful in Heaven. The beauty of the creation, which is simply a reflection of the beauty of God, is not even disturbed by evil or sin. Beauty is with Augustin (and the Platonists) a comprehensive term, and is almost equivalent to perfect harmony or symmetry of parts, perfect adaptation of beings to the ends for which they exist.

"It is patent that this view of the beauty of God and His creation is diametrically opposed to the crude conceptions of Mani, with reference to the disorder of the universe, a disorder not confined even to the Kingdom of Darkness, but invading the Realm of light itself" (Albert H. Newman, "An Introductory Essay on the Manichæan Heresy," in Philip Schaff, ed., *Nicene and Post-Nicene Fathers* [Edinburgh: T & T Clark; Grand Rapids: Eerdmans]; available at: http://www.ccel.org/ccel/schaff/npnf104.doc; accessed: 24 April 2007; Internet).

f.   Yet the balance of Rev 5:13 may help Bible-believing Christians bridge this gap: both Him who sits on His throne and the Lamb that was slain are both given the same honor, glory, and power, forever and ever. May it ever be so with us!

g.   Two amazing distinctions:

   i.   Present vs. future:

      1)   The glory of God is future: Rom 5:2, "we glory in the hope of the glory of God

      2)   The Gospel of Christ is for the present: Mark 15:16, "Go into all the world and preach the Gospel to all creation"

   ii.   Work vs. Motivation:

      1)   The glory of God motivates action: "Do all to the glory of God," 1 Cor 10:31; etc.

      2)   The Gospel demands work, cf. note the concept of "the work of the Gospel," Acts 13:2; 14:26; 1 Cor 15:58; 2 Cor 6:1; Phil 2:30; 1 Thess 3:2; 2 Tim 4:5

h.   For us, New Testament Christians, is it not really all about the glory of Christ Jesus and His cross?

   Rom 15:17, "Therefore I have reason to **glory in Christ Jesus** in the things *which pertain* to God"

   Gal 6:14 (ASV), "But far be it from me to glory, save in the cross of our Lord Jesus Christ, through which the world hath been crucified unto me, and I unto the world"

   Phil 3:3, "for we are the *true* circumcision, who worship in the Spirit of God and **glory in Christ Jesus** and put no confidence in the flesh"

   i.   Jesus was crowned with glory and honor:
   John 2:11, "This beginning of *His* signs Jesus did in Cana of Galilee, and manifested His glory, and His disciples believed in Him"
   John 7:39, "But this He spoke of the Spirit, whom those who believed in Him were to receive; for the Spirit was not yet *given*, because Jesus was not yet glorified"
   John 8:54, "Jesus answered, 'If I glorify Myself, My glory is nothing; it is My Father who glorifies Me, of whom you say, "He is our God"'"
   Acts 3:13, "The God of Abraham, Isaac, and Jacob, the God of our fathers, has glorified His servant Jesus, *the one* whom you delivered up, and disowned in the presence of Pilate, when he had decided to release Him"
   Titus 2:13, "looking for the blessed hope and the appearing of the glory of our great God and Savior, Christ Jesus"
   Heb 2:9, "But we do see Him who has been made for a little while lower than the angels, *namely*, Jesus, because of the suffering of death crowned with glory and honor, that by the grace of God He might taste death for everyone"
   James 2:1 (ESV), "My brothers, show no partiality as you hold the faith in our Lord Jesus Christ, the Lord of glory"
   2 Pet 3:18, "but grow in the grace and knowledge of our Lord and Savior Jesus Christ. To Him *be* the glory, both now and to the day of eternity. Amen"

   ii.   Jesus glorified the Father when He Himself was glorified:
   John 11:4, "But when Jesus heard it, He said, 'This sickness is not unto death, but for the glory of God, that the Son of God may be glorified by it.'"
   John 13:31, "When therefore he had gone out, Jesus said, 'Now is the Son of Man glorified, and God is glorified in Him'"
   John 17:1, "These things Jesus spoke; and lifting up His eyes to heaven, He said, 'Father, the hour has come; glorify Thy Son, that the Son may glorify Thee'"

   iii.   We glorify God by/through/in Jesus Christ:
   Implications of prepositions: "by" = instrumentality; "through" = causality; "in" = participation.
   Rom 16:27, "to the only wise God, through Jesus Christ, be the glory forever. Amen"
   Rom 5:11 (DRA), "And not only so; but also we glory in God, through our Lord Jesus Christ, by whom we have now received reconciliation"
   Eph 3:21 (NKJ), "to Him *be* glory in the church by Christ Jesus to all generations, forever and ever. Amen"
   Phil 1:11, "having been filled with the fruit of righteousness which *comes* through Jesus Christ, to the glory and praise of God"

1 Pet 4:11, "If anyone speaks, *let him speak* as the oracles of God. If anyone ministers, *let him do it* as with the ability which God supplies, that in all things God may be glorified through Jesus Christ, to whom belong the glory and the dominion forever and ever. Amen"

    iv.   Yes, we must glorify God and live to the glory of God:

Rom 15:6, "that with one accord you may with one voice glorify the God and Father of our Lord Jesus Christ"

1 Cor 10:31, "Whether, then, you eat or drink or whatever you do, do all to the glory of God"

    v.   In fact, one tangible way we glorify God is by confessing Jesus:[321]

Phil 2:11, "and that every tongue should confess that Jesus Christ is Lord, to the glory of God the Father"

Alternative translation by William Graham MacDonald,

Phil 2:11, "and every tongue would voice the acclamation: Kvrios Y-soûs Christòs ['Lord Jesus Christ!'], to the glory of Father God"

The verb "is" or the the preposition "as" are supplied by almost every other English translation: "Jesus Christ [is] Lord" or "Jesus Christ [as] Lord."[322]

For comments on varying views of confessing, see Chapter 7 under the verb "confessing."

    vi.   Yes, Christ and God cannot be separated in glory:

2 Cor 4:6, "For God, who said, 'Light shall shine out of darkness,' is the One who has shone in our hearts to give the light of the knowledge of the glory of God in the face of Christ"

    vii.   Our ultimate gift is gaining the reward of the glory of the Godhead:

2 Thess 2:14, "And it was for this He called you through our gospel, that you may gain the glory of our Lord Jesus Christ"

1 Pet 5:10, "And after you have suffered for a little while, the God of all grace, who called you to His eternal glory in Christ, will Himself perfect, confirm, strengthen *and* establish you"

    viii.   Therefore, it appears that seeking to glorify God directly, apart from going through Jesus Christ (and his cross and the gospel) appears to disregard the New Testament pattern:

        1) It is reverting back to an Old Testament approach, which does not take into account the revelation of Christ (Rom 2:17);

        2) It is following the historical pattern of what we know of the early church downgrade into philosophical and sacramental theology, with their focus away from the Great Commission and Christ crucified to discussion of the Trinity and the Hypostatic Union.

    ix.   It may be that to truly accomplish "Sola Deo Gloria," our cry should therefore be "Gloria ad Christum"!

  i.   The amazing examples of Stephen and Paul:

    i.   Other than the transfiguration of Jesus, the only two people in the New Testament actually saw the glory of God were Stephen and Paul. Their experience and its relationship to a discussion of the glory of God versus the gospel of Christ is quite fascinating

    ii.   Stephen:

        1) His face shone like an angel, Acts 6:15

        2) Had an actual epiphany of the glory of God, Acts 7:55-56

        3) All in the midst of evangelizing the Gospel of Christ to a very hostile crowd, Acts 7:54

    iii.   Paul:

        1) Went to the third heaven, 2 Cor 12:1-4

        2) Although unsure of the exact setting, most commentators conjecture that it took place when he was stoned and left for dead in Lystra, Acts 14:1-20

        3) Again, a vision of the glory of God was given when he was evangelizing the Gospel of Christ and receiving the hostilities of the Jews from Antioch and Iconium for doing so, Acts 14:19-20

---

[321]Another way we glorify God is by bearing fruit: John 15:8, "By this is My Father glorified, that you bear much fruit, and *so* prove to be My disciples."

[322]Chapter 21, "A. Commitment Is at the Heart," includes a chart on various translations of Rom 10:9.

iv. This link is also hinted at in the words of Jesus:
1) Mark 8:38, "For whoever is ashamed of Me and My words in this adulterous and sinful generation, the Son of Man will also be ashamed of him when He comes in the glory of His Father with the holy angels"
2) John 21:19, "Now this He said, signifying by what kind of death he [Peter] would glorify God. And when He had spoken this, He said to him, 'Follow Me!'"

v. So there is a strong link between seeing the glory of God and martyrdom experiences because of the gospel of Christ—an amazing thing!

j. Let's strive to love one another, put aside our differences, and be obedient unto death to the command to tell the whole world about the sacrifice of Jesus Christ on the cross for our sins!

i. Rev 12:11 (NKJ), "And they overcame him by the blood of the Lamb and by the word of their testimony, and they did not love their lives to the death"

Evangelism and Predestination

Predestination has been a very volatile subject among evangelists in the past. For example, consider this interchange between George Whitefield and John Wesley. Wesley preached and published the following sermon, title "Free Grace" in 1740:

> "The grace or love of God, whence cometh our salvation, is FREE IN ALL, and FREE FOR ALL.
> "I. It is free in all to whom it is given.
> "II. The doctrine of predestination is not a doctrine of God.
> "III. Predestination destroys the comfort of religion, the happiness of Christianity.
> "IV. This uncomfortable doctrine also destroys our zeal for good works.
> "V. Furthermore, the doctrine of predestination has a direct and manifest tendency to overthrow the whole Christian Revelation.
> "VI. And at the same time, makes that Revelation contradict itself.
> "VII. Predestination is a doctrine full of blasphemy."[323]

George Whitefield explained the timing of the sermon and its publication in a letter titled, "A Letter in Answer to Wesley's Sermon 'Free Grace'":

> "*'But when Peter was come to Antioch, I withstood him to the face, because he was to be blamed' (Gal. 2:11).*
> ### PREFACE
> "I am very well aware what different effects publishing this letter against the dear Mr. Wesley's Sermon will produce. Many of my friends who are strenuous advocates for *universal redemption* will immediately be offended. Many who are zealous on the other side will be much rejoiced. They who are lukewarm on both sides and are carried away with carnal reasoning will wish this matter had never been brought under debate.
>
> "The reasons I have given at the beginning of the letter, I think are sufficient to satisfy all of my conduct herein. I desire therefore that they who hold election would not triumph, or make a party on one hand (for I detest any such thing)—and that they who are prejudiced against that doctrine be not too much concerned or offended on the other.
>
> "Known unto God are all his ways from the beginning of the world. The great day will discover why the Lord permits dear Mr. Wesley and me to be of a different way of thinking. At present, I shall make no enquiry into that matter, beyond the account which he has given of it himself in the following letter, which I lately received from his own dear hands:
>
> *London, August 9, 1740*
>
> "*My dear Brother,*
> "*I thank you for yours, May the 24th. The case is quite plain. There are bigots both for predestination and against it. God is sending a message to those on either side. But neither will receive it, unless from one who is of their own opinion. Therefore, for a time you are suffered to be of one opinion, and I of another. But when his time is come, God will do what man cannot, namely, make us both of one mind. Then persecution will flame out, and it will be seen whether we count our lives dear unto ourselves, so that we may finish our course with joy. I am, my dearest brother,*
>
> "*Ever yours,*
>
> "*J. WESLEY*
>
> "Thus my honoured friend, I heartily pray God to hasten the time, for his being clearly enlightened into all the doctrines of divine revelation, that we may thus be closely united in principle and judgment as well as heart and affection. And then if the Lord should call us to it, I care not if I go with him to prison, or to death. For like Paul and Silas, I hope we shall sing praises to God, and count it our highest honour to suffer for Christ's sake, and to lay down our lives for the brethren.
>
> "[Follows Whitefield's Letter to Wesley]"[324]

With this example of disagreement between evangelists of the same time, language, and country, it would be wise to consider this topic very gently. With this in mind, here are some thoughts on evangelism and predestination.

1.   Man Cannot Predestine Anyone:

Infant Baptism: Man cannot predestine a baby unto salvation through infant baptism, although this appears to be the teaching of many Christian denominations[325]

---

[323] John Wesley, "Free Grace"; available at: http://gbgm-umc.org/UMhistory/Wesley/sermons/serm-128.stm (Online) accessed: 30 Oct 2006; Internet.

[324] George Whitefield, "A Letter from George Whitefield to the Rev. Mr. John Welsey"; available at: http://www.sounddoctrine.net/stanford/George%20Whitefield.pdf (Online); accessed: 1 July 2016; Internet.

Marriage: Mankind cannot predestine an unsaved person to be saved through the institution of marriage:

> 1 Cor 7:16, "For how do you know, O wife, whether you will save your husband? Or how do you know, O husband, whether you will save your wife?"

Any Other Rite or Ritual:

> Psa 49:7-9, "No man can by any means redeem *his* brother, Or give to God a ransom for him—For the redemption of his soul is costly, And he should cease *trying* forever—That he should live on eternally; That he should not undergo decay."

Even a Sinner's Prayer?

> Matt 15:8, "This people honors Me with their lips, But their heart is far away from Me"; cf. Mark 7:6.

God's Word does not give man the dispensation of granting eternal life to anyone:

> John 1:12-13, "But as many as received Him, to them He gave the right to become children of God, *even* to those who believe in His name, who were born not of blood, nor of the will of the flesh, nor of the will of man, but of God."

2. **Only God can Predestine**:

> Rom 9:10-13, "And not only this, but there was Rebekah also, when she had conceived *twins* by one man, our father Isaac; for though *the twins* were not yet born, and had not done anything good or bad, in order that God's purpose according to *His* choice might stand, not because of works, but because of Him who calls, it was said to her, 'The older will serve the younger.' Just as it is written, 'Jacob I loved, but Esau I hated.'"

3. **God's Predestination Is Veiled from Human Eyes**:

The case of the verb "believe" in John

4. **God Has Provided One "Means of Grace" for His Predestination to Be Conferred on Those to Who Are Predestined unto This End**:

The preaching of the Word of God

Combined with a "hearing of faith"

5. **God's Means of Grace Does not Result in a Robotic Obedience from Man**:

> 1 Cor 9:19-23, "For though I am free from all *men*, I have made myself a slave to all, that I might win the more. And to the Jews I became as a Jew, that I might win Jews; to those who are under the Law, as under the Law, though not being myself under the Law, that I might win those who are under the Law; to those who are without law, as without law, though not being without the law of God but under the law of Christ, that I might win those who are without law. To the weak I became weak, that I might win the weak; I have become all things to all men, that I may by all means save some. And I do all things for the sake of the gospel, that I may become a fellow partaker of it."

> 1 Cor 10:33, "just as I also please all men in all things, not seeking my own profit, but the *profit* of the many, that they may be saved."

6. **The Result of God's Means Is Not Readily nor Fully Apparent to the Human Mind**:

The 3 receptive soils in the Parable of the Soil

The case of Judas Iscariot

The case of stumbling blocks

The case of a baptized believer in Acts, e.g. Simon the Sorcerer

The case of Saul of Tarsus

And yet, we are to baptize those that we know to be true disciples, Matt 28:19

7. **To God Alone Be the Glory:**

Because God and only God saves, to Him belongs all the glory and praise and honor!

---

[325]See the Appendix, "Eight Views of Baptism" following the material in Chapter 24, "Evangelism and Baptism."

Thoughts on the Extent of the Atonement

Introduction: Another area which at times can divide conservative Christians one from another is the extent of the atonement. The issue can be summarized in this way:

1. Unlimited Atonement: Believing that Christ's death was efficacious for all mankind

   "Christ's redeeming work made it possible for everyone to be saved but did not actually secure the salvation of anyone. Although Christ died for every man, only those that believe in Him are saved. His death enable God to pardon sinners on the condition that they believe, but it did not actually put away anyone's sins. Christ's redemption becomes effective only if man chooses to accept it."[326]

2. Limited Atonement: Believing that Christ's death was efficacious only for the elect

   "Christ's redeeming work was intended to save the elect only and actually secured salvation for them. His death was a substitutionary endurance of the penalty of sin in the place of certain specified sinners. In addition to putting away the sins of his people, Christ's redemption secured everything necessary for their salvation, including faith which unites them to Him. The gift of faith is infallibly applied by the Spirit to all for whom Christ died, thereby guaranteeing their salvation."[327]

3. Possible combination: "Sufficient for all, efficient for the elect"

   "Sufficient we say, then, was the sacrifice of Christ for the redemption of the whole world, and for the expiation of all the sins of all and every man in the world. … and, therefore, it is denied that the blood of Christ was a sufficient price or ransom for all and every one, not because it was not sufficient, but because it was not a ransom [for all]."[328]

Some preliminary comments:
1. There are good Christians on both sides of this issue!
2. In some cases this discussion can lead to endless debate and produce bad blood among followers of Christ
3. There is a sense in which the doctrine of the limited atonement:
   a. Seems derived from philosophical theology, and a string of logical progressions, much like the teaching on faith healing and the oneness of God; and furthermore, it
   b. Seems to be a reactionary doctrine, reacting against universalism, which teaches that all men will ultimately be saved
4. The questions naturally follows from these two points: Has the doctrine of the limited atonement gone beyond Scripture in the area of the atonement?
5. This question necessitates a look at particular Scripture

Passages that seem to teach a universal atonement:
1. John 1:9, "There was the true light which, coming into the world, enlightens every man."
2. John 1:29, "The next day he saw Jesus coming to him, and said, "Behold, the Lamb of God who takes away the sin of the world!"
3. John 3:17, "For God did not send the Son into the world to judge the world, but that the world should be saved through Him."
4. John 4:42, "and they were saying to the woman, 'It is no longer because of what you said that we believe, for we have heard for ourselves and know that this One is indeed the Savior of the world.'"
5. John 6:33, "For the bread of God is that which comes down out of heaven, and gives life to the world."
6. John 12:32, "And I, if I be lifted up from the earth, will draw all men to Myself."
7. John 12:47, "And if anyone hears My sayings, and does not keep them, I do not judge him; for I did not come to judge the world, but to save the world.
8. Rom 5:18-19, "So then as through one transgression there resulted condemnation to all men, even so through one act of righteousness there resulted justification of life to all men. For as through the one man's disobedience the many were made sinners, even so through the obedience of the One the many will be made righteous."
9. Rom 11:12-15, "Now if their transgression be riches for the world and their failure be riches for the Gentiles, how much more will their fulfillment be! But I am speaking to you who are Gentiles. Inasmuch then as I am an

---

[326]David N. Steele and Curtis C. Thomas, *The Five Points of Calvinism: Defined, Defended, Documented* (Philipsburg, NJ: Presbyterian and Reformed, 1963), 17.

[327]Ibid.

[328]John Owen, *Death of Death in the Death of Christ* (Edinburgh: Banner of Truth, 1959), 183-84.

apostle of Gentiles, I magnify my ministry, if somehow I might move to jealousy my fellow countrymen and save some of them. For if their rejection be the reconciliation of the world, what will *their* acceptance be but life from the dead?"

10. 2 Cor 5:18-19, "Now all *these* things are from God, who reconciled us to Himself through Christ, and gave us the ministry of reconciliation, namely, that God was in Christ reconciling the world to Himself, not counting their trespasses against them, and He has committed to us the word of reconciliation."

11. 1 Tim 2:5-6, "For there is one God, *and* one mediator also between God and men, *the* man Christ Jesus, who gave Himself as a ransom for all, the testimony *borne* at the proper time."

12. Titus 2:11, "For the grace of God has appeared, bringing salvation to all men…"

13. 1 John 2:1-2, "My little children, I am writing these things to you that you may not sin. And if anyone sins, we have an Advocate with the Father, Jesus Christ the righteous; and He Himself is the propitiation for our sins; and not for ours only, but also for *those of* the whole world."

14. 1 John 4:14, "And we have beheld and bear witness that the Father has sent the Son *to be* the Savior of the world."

Passages that speak of the fallenness and condemnation of the world (see also my notes Jesus on Total Depravity following Chapter 8):

1. 1 Cor 11:32, "But when we are judged, we are disciplined by the Lord in order that we may not be condemned along with the world."

2. Rom 3:9-12, "What then? Are we better than they? Not at all; for we have already charged that both Jews and Greeks are all under sin; as it is written, 'There is none righteous, not even one; There is none who understands, There is none who seeks for God; All have turned aside, together they have become useless; There is none who does good, There is not even one.'"

3. Rom 3:19-20, "Now we know that whatever the Law says, it speaks to those who are under the Law, that every mouth may be closed, and all the world may become accountable to God; because by the works of the Law no flesh will be justified in His sight; for through the Law *comes* the knowledge of sin."

4. Eph 2:1-3, "And you were dead in your trespasses and sins, in which you formerly walked according to the course of this world, according to the prince of the power of the air, of the spirit that is now working in the sons of disobedience. Among them we too all formerly lived in the lusts of our flesh, indulging the desires of the flesh and of the mind, and were by nature children of wrath, even as the rest."

5. Phil 2:14-16, "Do all things without grumbling or disputing; that you may prove yourselves to be blameless and innocent, children of God above reproach in the midst of a crooked and perverse generation, among whom you appear as lights in the world, holding fast the word of life, so that in the day of Christ I may have cause to glory because I did not run in vain nor toil in vain."

6. 1 John 2:15-17, "Do not love the world, nor the things in the world. If anyone loves the world, the love of the Father is not in him. For all that is in the world, the lust of the flesh and the lust of the eyes and the boastful pride of life, is not from the Father, but is from the world. And the world is passing away, and *also* its lusts; but the one who does the will of God abides forever."

7. 1 John 3:1, "See how great a love the Father has bestowed upon us, that we should be called children of God; and *such* we are. For this reason the world does not know us, because it did not know Him."

8. 1 John 3:13, "Do not marvel, brethren, if the world hates you."

Passages that include both universal and limited considerations:

1. John 1:16, "For of His fulness we have all received, and grace upon grace."

2. John 3:16, "For God so loved the world, that He gave His only begotten Son, that whoever believes in Him should not perish, but have eternal life."

3. John 6:51, "I am the living bread that came down out of heaven; if anyone eats of this bread, he shall live forever; and the bread also which I shall give for the life of the world is My flesh."

4. John 8:12, "Again therefore Jesus spoke to them, saying, 'I am the light of the world; he who follows Me shall not walk in the darkness, but shall have the light of life.'"

5. John 14:17, "*that is* the Spirit of truth, whom the world cannot receive, because it does not behold Him or know Him, *but* you know Him because He abides with you, and will be in you."

6. John 15:18-19, "If the world hates you, you know that it has hated Me before *it hated* you. If you were of the world, the world would love its own; but because you are not of the world, but I chose you out of the world, therefore the world hates you."

7. John 17:14-18, "I have given them Thy word; and the world has hated them, because they are not of the world, even as I am not of the world. I do not ask Thee to take them out of the world, but to keep them from the evil *one*. They are not of the world, even as I am not of the world. Sanctify them in the truth; Thy word is truth. As Thou didst send Me into the world, I also have sent them into the world.

8. John 17:25, "O righteous Father, although the world has not known Thee, yet I have known Thee; and these have known that Thou didst send Me"

9. 1 Tim 4:10, "For it is for this we labor and strive, because we have fixed our hope on the living God, who is the Savior of all men, especially of believers"

10. 1 John 4:9, "By this the love of God was manifested in us, that God has sent His only begotten Son into the world so that we might live through Him."

Other interesting passages:
1. John 6:37, "All that the Father gives Me shall come to Me, and the one who comes to Me I will certainly not cast out."
2. John 6:39, "And this is the will of Him who sent Me, that of all that He has given Me I lose nothing, but raise it up on the last day."
3. John 6:45, "It is written in the prophets, 'And they shall all be taught of God.' Everyone who has heard and learned from the Father, comes to Me."
4. John 10:27-29, "My sheep hear My voice, and I know them, and they follow Me; and I give eternal life to them, and they shall never perish; and no one shall snatch them out of My hand. My Father, who has given *them* to Me, is greater than all; and no one is able to snatch *them* out of the Father's hand."
5. 1 Tim 1:15, "It is a trustworthy statement, deserving full acceptance, that Christ Jesus came into the world to save sinners, among whom I am foremost *of all*."

Passages that seem to teach a limited atonement:
1. Deut 32:43, "Rejoice, O nations, *with* His people; For He will avenge the blood of His servants, And will render vengeance on His adversaries, And will atone for His land *and* His people."
2. Matt 20:28, "Just as the Son of Man did not come to be served, but to serve, and to give His life a ransom for many."
3. Mark 10:45, "For even the Son of Man did not come to be served, but to serve, and to give His life a ransom for many."
4. Rev 5:9-10, "And they sang a new song, saying, 'Worthy art Thou to take the book, and to break its seals; for Thou wast slain, and didst purchase for God with Thy blood *men* from every tribe and tongue and people and nation. And Thou hast made them *to be* a kingdom and priests to our God; and they will reign upon the earth.'"

Some questions about particularity as a Central Interpretive Motif (CIM):
1. Could it be that a single minded focus on particularity as a CIM is an OT holdover of the particularity of the Jewish nation, that was changed to include Gentiles in the NT?
   a. This OT focus on particularity being the reason why adherents of the same often glean much from the pages of the OT as regards, a focus on particularity, a focus on the glory of God, etc.
   b. It must be remembered that Acts 10-11 and Gal 2 seeks to readdress association with Gentiles from a NT theology point-of-view
2. Is it possible to maintain a view of limited atonement as a CIM, and to simultaneously maintain an ardent heart wherein the Great Commission to preach the Gospel to all peoples and all nations is the CIM?

Concerning John's [and Paul's] supposed use of hyperbolic language:
1. Is it not dangerous as an interpretive principle to argue John's use of hyperbolic language on one hand (e.g. for limited atonement), while maintaining literal interpretation on the other hand (e.g. the depravity of the world and of all individuals therein, or the assurance that in Christ alone we are definitely and completely saved)?

Conclusions:
1. There are clearly passages on both sides of this issue
2. Both sides are not mutually exclusive, but rather dovetail together beautifully, if they are both held in a biblical tension:
   a. Those who cannot accept that they dovetail and are not incompatible seem to have placed their reasoning above Scripture (Isa 55:8-9), and need to take care lest they add or subtract from Scripture, and therefore come under its condemnation
3. The difficulty seems to lie in emphasizing one side so strongly, that the other is erased from the pages of Scripture
4. It would clearly seem, then, that:
   a. All men are sinners, and all are destined for an eternity in hell
   b. Christ died for all men, and for the sins of every and all men
   c. God gives a "hearing of faith" to some as they hear the Gospel (e.g. the narrow road):
      1) Those who receive a "hearing of faith" must necessarily repent and believe (at the appointed time, upon effectual hearing)
      2) However, remembering that some are made uncomfortable by the Gospel, who never come to salvation (e.g. Felix, Acts 24:25)
      3) And even among those who appear to believe, we have Jesus teach that:
         a) Some will fall away (scandalize), Matt 13:20-21 (and parallels)
         b) Some will bring no fruit to maturity, Matt 13:22 (and parallels)

    d.   Only those who repent and believe are saved (and/or converted), and are justified by the atonement of Christ:

        1)   "Sufficient for all, efficient for the elect"

        2)   Christ then becomes their ransom, in a particular sense

    e.   Only those who are thus saved (by repenting and believing) will go to heaven

    f.   Therefore it is expedient, necessary, and exceedingly urgent for all Christians to preach the Gospel to all nations and to all creation so that God may call out His own unto salvation.

Evangelism in the Pentateuch, or
Proclamational Aspects of the Pentateuch

Introduction: A Sunday School teacher asked Evangelist Keith Fordham what the Pentateuch had to say about evangelism, several introductory items need to be addressed:

1. It must be understood that the Sunday School teacher was pushing Evangelist Keith Fordham into a Catch 22:
   a. Framing the question of the Gospel and evangelism from the Pentateuch, that which it does not clearly or explicitly teach, being that the Gospel and the Great Commission is a New Testament emphasis, see Luke 24
   b. Thereby forcing Keith to argue what involves innumerable theological issues (hermeneutical relationship between Old and New Covenants, theology of the Pentateuch, etc.)

2. However, the most prominent aspects of "evangelism" addressed in the Pentateuch involved the message of salvation. Total depravity, or man's need for salvation, was addressed in a number of places. God's choosing His people was noted. The Passover celebration and Jesus as the Passover Lamb are a clear foreshadowing of the cross, which continued into the Book of Revelation where Jesus is called "the Lamb that was slain." Another allusion to God's deliverance of His people in the Pentateuch was the Exodus event.

3. However, the Pentateuch was the Law of Moses (John 1:17), and its commissioning was focused on individuals, such as a Great Commission was directed to Moses:

   Deut 4:14, "The LORD commanded me at that time to teach you statutes and judgments, that you might perform them in the land where you are going over to possess it."

   Deut 5:5, "I was standing between the LORD and you at that time, to declare to you the word of the LORD"

   In the NT, a similar commission is given to all the disciples of Christ, after His death and resurrection. Therefore, a universal Great Commission is a distinctly New Testament emphasis, although prophesied and exemplified in the Old Testament.

4. While not discussing material on the hermeneutical differences between the OT and NT (e.g. Heb 8:13), this study will focus on the several proclamational passages in the Pentateuch.

A. Sample proclamational texts in the Pentateuch (NAS translation):
   Exod 9:16, "But, indeed, for this cause I have allowed you to remain, in order to show you My power, and in order to **proclaim** [saphar] My name through all the earth"
   Exod 18:19-20, "Now listen to me: I shall give you counsel, and God be with you. You be the people's representative before God, and you bring the disputes to God, [20] then **teach** [zahar] them the statutes and the laws, and **make known** [yada'] to them the way in which they are to walk, and the work they are to do"
   Lev 10:9-11, "Do not drink wine or strong drink, neither you nor your sons with you, when you come into the tent of meeting, so that you may not die-- it is a perpetual statute throughout your generations-- [10] and so as to make a distinction between the holy and the profane, and between the unclean and the clean, [11] and so as to **teach** [yarah] the sons of Israel all the statutes which the LORD has spoken to them through Moses."
   Deut 4:5-8, "See, I **have taught** [lamad] you statutes and judgments just as the LORD my God commanded me, that you should do thus in the land where you are entering to possess it. [6] "So keep and do *them*, for that is your wisdom and your understanding in the sight of the peoples who **will hear** [shama] all these statutes and say, 'Surely this great nation is a wise and understanding people.' [7] "For what great nation is there that has a god so near to it as is the LORD our God whenever we call on Him? [8] "Or what great nation is there that has statutes and judgments as righteous as this whole law which I am setting before you today?"
   Deut 4:9, "Only give heed to yourself and keep your soul diligently, lest you **forget** [pen shakach] the things which your eyes have seen, and lest they **depart** [pen sur] from your heart all the days of your life; but **make them known** [yada'] to your sons and your grandsons"
   Deut 4:13, "So He **declared** [nagad] to you His covenant which He commanded you to perform, *that is*, the Ten Commandments; and He wrote them on two tablets of stone"
   Deut 4:14, "And the LORD commanded me at that time **to teach** [lamad] you statutes and judgments, that you might perform them in the land where you are going over to possess it"
   Deut 5:4-6, "The LORD **spoke** [dabar] to you face to face at the mountain from the midst of the fire, [5] *while* I was standing between the LORD and you at that time, to **declare** [nagad] to you the word of the LORD; for you were afraid because of the fire and did not go up the mountain. He said, [6] 'I am the LORD your God, who brought you out of the land of Egypt, out of the house of slavery...'"

Deut 6:6-7, "And these words, which I am commanding you today, shall be on your heart; [7] and you **shall teach** [shanan] them diligently to your sons and **shall talk** [dabar] of them when you sit in your house and when you walk by the way and when you lie down and when you rise up"

Deut 11:19, "And you shall **teach** [lamad] them to your sons, **talking** [dabar] of them when you sit in your house and when you walk along the road and when you lie down and when you rise up"

Deut 30:18, "I **declare** [nagad] to you today that you shall surely perish. You shall not prolong *your* days in the land where you are crossing the Jordan to enter and possess it"

Deut 32:1-6, "**Give ear** [azan], O heavens, and let me **speak** [dabar]; And let the earth **hear** [shama] the words of my mouth. [2] "Let my teaching drop as the rain, My speech distill as the dew, As the droplets on the fresh grass And as the showers on the herb. [3] "For I proclaim the name of the LORD; Ascribe greatness to our God! [4] "The Rock! His work is perfect, For all His ways are just; A God of faithfulness and without injustice, Righteous and upright is He. [5] "They have acted corruptly toward Him, *They are* not His children, because of their defect; *But are* a perverse and crooked generation. [6] "Do you thus repay the LORD, O foolish and unwise people? Is not He your Father who has bought you? He has made you and established you"

B. The messenger or intended messenger (by way of admonition or command):
1. God, Exod 9:16; Deut 4:13
2. The Lord, Deut 5:4-5
3. Moses, Exod 18:19-20; Deut 5:4-5, 14; 30:18; 32:1-6
    a. Notice the intermediary role of Moses in these verses (cf. 2 Cor 5:20)
    b. Also notice the commissioning of Moses in Deut 4:14
4. Sons of Aaron, Lev 10:9-11
5. Fathers and mothers, Deut 4:9; 6:6-7; 11:19
6. Reflexive verb, Deut 4:6

C. Methods of proclamation (verbs, see chart in Chapter 7, F, "Toward Translating Proclamational Words in the Old Testament"):
1. To declare [nagad], Deut 4:13; 5:5; 30:18
2. To proclaim [saphar], Exod 9:16
3. To teach [zahar], Exod 18:20
4. To teach [yarah], Lev 10:11
5. To teach [lamad], Deut 4:5, 14; 11:19
6. To teach [shanan], Deut 6:7
7. To speak [dabar], Deut 5:4; 6:7; 11:19; 32:1
8. To make known [yada'], Exod 18:20; Deut 4:9
9. To [cause to] hear [shama], Deut 4:6; 32:1
10. To give ear [azan], Deut 32:1
11. Not to forget, Deut 4:9
12. Not to depart, Deut 4:9

D. The message:
1. His covenant, the Ten Commandments, Deut 4:13
    a. Notice that this declaration was the condemning work of the OT Law, of which speaks Gal 3:23-25, which held faith in custody
2. The word of the LORD [the Ten Commandments], Deut 5:5
3. These words which I am commanding you, Deut 6:6
4. All the statutes, Lev 10:11
5. All these statutes, Deut 4:6
6. Statutes and laws, Exod 18:19-20
7. Statutes and judgments, Deut 4:5, 14
8. The name of God, Exod 9:16
9. The judgment of God, Deut 30:18 ("perish you shall perish")
10. What your eyes have seen, Deut 4:9
11. Aspects of the message in the Song of Moses:
    a. The words of my [Moses'] mouth, Deut 32:1
    b. The name of the LORD, Deut 32:3-4
    c. The depravity of the people of Israel, Deut 32:5-6
    d. God's election of His people, Deut 32:8-9
    e. God's saving of His people, Deut 32:10-12
    f. God's blessing of His people, Deut 32:13-14…
    g. The judgment of God, Deut 32:35

E. Recipient of the message:
   1. Heavens and earth, Deut 32:1
   2. Throughout all the earth, Exod 9:16
   3. The peoples, Deut 4:6
   4. People of Israel, Exod 18:19-20; Deut 4:5, 13-14; 5:4-6
   5. Sons of Israel, Lev 10:9-11
   6. Sons, Deut 6:7
   7. Sons and grandsons, Deut 4:9

Conclusions:
   1. it is indeed interesting that there are quite a few verses which specifically address the concept of proclamation in the Pentateuch, which is not surprising in light of Matt 23:15
   2. The link between the message spoken and the very words of God is very clear in the portions that delineate the message
   3. Perhaps the most comprehensive delineation of the Pentateuch's message is found in Deut 32:1-6ff.
   4. While parents are commissioned in Deut 6:7 and 11:19, the clearest commissioning in the Pentateuch (in style and language) is found in Deut 4:14, with the commissioning of Moses to teach the sons of Israel
   5. While Jesus clearly emphasized preaching to all nations, this concept was not foreign to the Pentateuch
   6. This study also shows that the proclamational emphases found in the Psalms and Isaiah are not foreign to the Pentateuch (See *Evangelizology*, Chapters 2 and 10)

CHAPTER 7
Defining Evangelizing

Introduction:

A. To what does the following list refer?
   1. Mass meetings
   2. Decisional speaking
   3. Door-to-door

B. No, it is not old-fashioned evangelism! Rather it was the 2012 (or 2016) presidential elections in the United States:[329]
   1. *Contra* the constant drone against New Testament evangelism (for cultural and/or psychological reasons): when the political parties are urgent to get out votes, they use urgent methods![330]
   2. However, these terms also describe methods used for urgent evangelism in the church
   3. When the urgency of salvation and conversion is lost among second generation Christians, then urgent evangelism becomes a thing of the past, to be replaced with non-urgent methods that are much more oriented to lifestyle or relationship.[331]

C. On a definition of evangelizing:

   1. Note the words of noted missiologist Gustav Warneck [1904, 1906] as to what he considered was a *lack of clarity* in defining of the word "evangelize":

> In view of the ambiguous definitions which have been and are still given of the watchword "evangelisation," [referring to John R. Mott's] it is difficult to say exactly what is to be understood by it. [John R.] Mott in his book, *The Evangelization of the World in this Generation* (London, 1900), written with a burning enthusiasm, explains that it means "that a sufficient opportunity shall be offered to all men to become acquainted with Jesus Christ as their Redeemer, and to become His disciples," but not "Christianisation in the sense of interpenetration of the world with Christian ideas," although educational, literary, and medical work are not excluded, and the proclamation of the Gospel is not to be of a superficial character. Dr. [A. T.] Pierson understands the word as only "preaching and testimony. These two words embrace all that is meant by evangelisation." What the definitions lack in clearness is supplied by the principles laid down as to methods of practical action. …
>
> This last task is the task of missions [the solid founding of the Christian church]; the limitation of this task to mere* evangelisation confounds means and goal. Mere* preaching does not suffice; it is to be the

---

[329]"'He needs you to keep making those calls, doing that hard work. Knocking on those doors. Treacherous work, right? Tiring work. He needs you to keep registering those voters. You know, the ones, you know, that aren't registered and you gotta get 'em and shake 'em. Find them, get them registered,' Michelle Obama said at the campaign event" ("Michel Obama: Find Unregistered Voters and Shake 'em" [10 July 2012]; available at: http://realclearpolitics.com/video/2012/07/10/michelle_obama_you_have_to_find_unregistered_voters_and_shake_em. html [online]; accessed 11 July 2012; Internet).

[330]"'Less than four years after Obama won Wisconsin, Democrats lost in an election of their own making. That's because the GOP excelled at our ground game, now giving us a significant advantage for the presidential race,' Priebus argues. 'Working with the Wisconsin GOP, the RNC ran joint voter contact Victory operations and opened 26 statewide offices. Since January, our volunteers made over 4 million voter contacts, more than the GOP did in the entire 2008 campaign and substantially more than Democrats and their union allies in this election. ... In the process, more than 3,400 Wisconsin volunteers have signed up to help the party. And the data collected by door-to-door volunteers for Governor Walker was all promptly added to the RNC's data center, thanks to the use of iPads, iPhones, and iPods'" (Alexander Burns, "Priebus memo claims Wis. boost"; available at: http://www.politico.com/blogs/burns-haberman/2012/06/priebus-memo-claims-wisconsin-boost-125399.html (online); accessed: 6 June 2012; Internet).

[331]"I reminded them that door-to-door is just about the least effective method out there, and encouraged them to take what they learned to share with people they already knew" (Alvin Reid, *Sharing Jesus {without Freaking Out}— Evangelism the Way You Were Born to Do It* [Nashville: B & H Academic, 2017], 98). Interestingly, Jesus did not evangelize according to Reid's advice in Mark 6—where his hometown people rejected Him:
"…And they were offended at Him. But Jesus said to them, 'A prophet is not without honor except in his own country, among his own relatives, and in his own house.' Now He could do no mighty work there, except that He laid His hands on a few sick people and healed *them*. And He marveled because of their unbelief. Then He went about the villages in a circuit, teaching" (Mark 6:3-6, NKJ).

means of laying the foundation of the Church. …mere* announcement of the Gospel is not sufficient for this.[332]

> *Warneck used a very emotive German term "bloß" three times, which root meaning is naked or bare; hence, "naked evangelism," "naked preaching," and "naked announcement."

2. The late David Bosch in 1991 telegraphed the same view of a lack of clarity in defining the concept of evangelize as his predecessor Warneck:

> It remains difficult, however, to determine precisely what authors mean by evangelism or evangelization. Barrett lists seventy-five definitions, to which many more could be added. Broadly speaking, controversy prevails in two areas: the differences (if any) between "evangelism" and "mission", and the scope or range of evangelism. These issues are, moreover, intimately interrelated. …
>
> [Arthur P.] Johnston, for instance, claims, "Historically the mission of the church is evangelism alone." The more "inclusive" understanding of the enterprise, Johnston says actually began with the Edinburgh Conference of 1910. …
>
> 1. *I perceive mission to be wider than evangelism.* "Evangelization is mission, but mission is not merely evangelization (Moltmann). …
>
> [additional definitional points 2-17] …
>
> 18. *Evangelism is not only verbal proclamation.* … There is no single way to witness to Christ, however.[333]

3. In sharp contradistinction to the definitional quandary and quagmire of Warneck and Bosch, note the 1944 words of Samuel Zwemer:

> "It is time that protest be made against the misuse of the word evangelism. It has only one etymological, New Testament, historical and theological connotation, namely, to tell the good news of One who came to earth to die on the cross for us: who rose again and who ever lives to intercede for those who repent and believe the Gospel. To evangelize is to win disciples, to become fishers of men, to carry the Gospel message directly to all nations."[334]

---

[332]Gustav Warneck, *Outline of the History of Protestant Missions,* 3rd English edition [translated from 8th German edition of 1904] (New York: Revell, 1906), 406-07. These words are the full exposition of what Warneck had said in the 1900 New York Ecumenical Missionary Conference:

"It is a hopeful sign of the increase in missionary interest that a growing enthusiasm for the work is spreading among young men and students. Very energetically are the watchwords promulgated nowadays, 'expansion,' 'diffusion,' 'evangelization of the world in this generation." I will not deny that in view of the present openings all the world over, such mottoes are entitled to consideration, and so far as this is the case, I certainly have no wish to weaken their force. But without due limitation and completion, I consider them dangerous. The mission command bids us 'go' into all the world, not 'fly.' *Festina lente* applies also to missionary undertakings The kingdom of heaven is like a field in which a crop is healthily growing at a normal rate, not like a hothouse" (Gustav Warneck, "Special Principles" in *Ecumenical Missionary Conference, New York, 1900* [New York: American Tract Society, 1900]: 1:289-90).

[333]David J. Bosch, *Transforming Mission: Paradigm Shifts in Theology of Mission* (Maryknoll: Orbis, 1991), 409, 410, 411-12, 420. All 18 of his points are as follows: "1. I perceive mission to be wider than evangelism. … 2. Evangelism should therefore not be equated with mission. …3. Evangelism may be viewed as an essential 'dimension of the total activity of the Church.' … 4. Evangelism involves witnessing to what God has done, is doing, and will do. … 5. Even so, evangelism does aim at a response. … 6. Evangelism is always invitation. … 7. The one who evangelizes is a witness not a judge. … 8. Even though we ought to be modest about the character and effectiveness of our witness, evangelism remains an indispensable ministry. … 9. Evangelism is only possible when the community that evangelizes-the church-is a radiant manifestation of the Christian faith and exhibits an attractive lifestyle. … 10. Evangelism offers people salvation as a present gift and with it assurance of eternal bliss. … 11. Evangelism is not proselytism. … 12. Evangelism is not the same as church extension. … 13. To distinguish between evangelism and membership recruitment is not to suggest, though, that they are disconnected. … 14. In evangelism, only people can be addressed and only people can respond. … 15. Authentic evangelism is always contextual. … 16. Because of this, evangelism cannot be divorced from the preaching and practicing of justice. … 17. Evangelism is not a mechanism to hasten the return of Christ, as some suggest. … 18. Evangelism is not only verbal proclamation" (ibid., 412-20).

[334]Samuel Zwemer, *Evangelism Today: Message not Method,* 4th ed. (New York: Revell, 1944), 17.

4. Repeating the uncertainty of his predecessors, Emergent Church guru, Brian McLaren, felt the need to provide a disclaimer for using the word "evangelism" in the title of his book:

> "However ironic as it may sound in a book with 'evangelism' in its title, I believe *evangelism* may be a less and less useful term in the future. I find myself replacing it with the term *disciple-making*."[335]

Therefore, it must be that McLaren used the word "evangelism" (1) to please his publisher, (2) to sell books, and/or (3) to influence those who do believe in evangelism to move in his direction.

D. Notice also some other contemporary changes in terminology:

1. Now we do not speak about the "lost souls", we speak about:
   a. The un-churched or pre-churched
   b. Seekers or "doubters welcome"
   c. Pre-Christian, and therefore "pre-evangelism"

2. Instead of speaking about the Gospel, we speak about:
   a. Christian worldview
   b. Sacraments
   c. God (e.g. "do you know God?" "Would you like to receive God?")

3. Instead of the power of the Word of God, we speak of:
   a. The power of drama
   b. The power of story

4. Instead of "Evangelize" or "preach the Gospel," its:
   a. Share the love of God
   b. Show the love of Jesus
   c. Engage lostness or engage culture
   d. Be relevant to people's needs

5. Instead of speaking about repentance and faith in Jesus Christ, we say:
   a. Try Jesus
   b. Believe in God
   c. Connect with God; "Come connect with God and others"
   d. Experience God; in some churches the Lord's Supper is seen as an opportunity for unbelievers to "experience God"!

Food for Thought:

a. Notice, by the way, that all of these changes impact how one views the Gospel, salvation, and evangelism

b. Does terminology matter? Is it no big deal?

c. Is not the subtle change in terminology possibly due to the desire to remove the reproach of the cross from terminology?
   Galatians 5:11, "But I, brethren, if I still preach circumcision [lifestyle], why am I still persecuted? Then the stumbling block of the cross has been abolished."

d. Or how about how the word "evangelism" is leverage to unsuspecting Christians?
   1) We need a new building: "Give to the building program, it's for 'evangelism'!"
   2) We want to start a weekly Saturday evening service: "Come to church on Saturday night, it's for 'evangelism'!"
   3) We need to start a segmented midweek outreach service: "Come to the church within a church: It's for 'evangelism'!"
   4) We need to preach more "relevant" messages: "It's for 'evangelism'!"
   5) We cannot preach expository sermons: "It's for 'evangelism'!"
   6) We need more aggressive music: "It's for 'evangelism'!"
   7) We need to improve the public relations of our church: "It's for 'evangelism'!"
   8) We need to do disaster relief: "It's for 'evangelism'!"
   9) We need to feed the hungry: "It's for 'evangelism'!"

---

[335]Brian McLaren, *More Ready than You Realize: Evangelism as Dance in the Postmodern Matrix* (Grand Rapids: Zondervan, 2002), 161.

e. While these ideas are not wrong in and of themselves, it is amazing how the word "evangelism" can be leveraged to get Christians to give to or to do a whole variety of things:

1) Are these points valid or not?
2) What actually is evangelism?
3) The answers to the legitimacy of these issues is often dependent on one's definition of evangelism, thus the reason that a definition of evangelism is often hotly debated!

E. As far as evangelizing, is it possible to develop **a normative definition of evangelizing**? Has God clouded this verb used 54/55/56 times in the New Testament,[336] or is knowledge of a "Regulative Principle" for evangelizing achievable?[337] It is my thesis that it is very possible to approach an authoritative definition:

1. Of the Protestant Reformers' use of the "Regulative Principle":

a. If one compares the Three or Five Solas of the Protestant Reformation, while one could easily add "the blood alone" (1 Pet 1:17-19) or "the cross of Christ alone" (1 Cor 2:2), it appears that three solas a conspicuously missing…

b. **Verbal Alone** [or perhaps *Solum Verbale*] as found in Acts 15:7, "that by my mouth":
1) Luther did acknowledge this as the need for the "Outward Word" or for preaching;
2) However, in the State-Church model where it was assumed that everyone goes to the state church, this "preaching" was limited to preaching within the local church;
3) Hence, the non-use of the verb "evangelizing" in German and English Bible translations lost the emphasis of proclamation in contexts that are non-receptive or positive;
4) Balthasar Hubmaier seemed to pick up on the need for preaching in contexts that are non-receptive with his emphasis on Mark 8:38 in his "Conclusions."

c. **Hearing Alone** [or perhaps *Per Solum Audire*], as found in Acts 15:7, "the Gentiles should hear the word of the gospel":
1) The need to "hear" to "believe" is found throughout the NT;
2) However, in a system wherein salvation is Sacramentally-wrought through Infant Baptism, hearing is subjugated beneath the Christological nature of the species of the water of baptism, whereby the recipient of salvation, the infant is uninvolved and ignorant of the salvation that it is presumably receiving, further this salvation is received without: (1) any repentance on its part; (2) any faith on its part; or (3) any verbal response or affirmation on its part.

d. **Believers Baptism Alone** [*Credobaptism* (versus *Pedobaptism*)], as found in Acts 18:8, "And many of the Corinthians, hearing, believed and were baptized":
1) Baptism is always listed after repentance, believing, and/or receiving the word, here as in Mark 16:16; Acts 2:38, 41; 8:12, 13, 36-38; 16:14-15; 31-33…
2) Only already "made disciples" are to be baptized according to Matt 28:19, following the use of the word "them" [αὐτός in the masculine plural accusative, αὐτοὺς] in that important text.

2. Further:

a. While the New Testament has far more to say about evangelizing than it does local church leadership, some conservative theologians will parse every passage on church leadership (in books on theology for example), while seemingly overlooking the more plentiful terminology and issues in evangelism

b. Similarly, sparks fly when divorce and remarriage are discussed. Verses on this issue are also quite sparse in the New Testament, while every verse on any issue is important and

---

[336]The use of three numbers is due to variant readings. Of the 55 uses in the Byzantine text tradition, the critical edition Greek removes the second use of εὐαγγελίζω from Rom 10:15. Hence, 54. Further, the Codex Bezae uses εὐαγγελίζω instead of καταγγέλλω in Acts 16:17, leading to 56 total possible uses of καταγγέλλω in the Greek NT.

[337]Chad Owen Brand and David E. Hankins explain the "Regulative Principle": "Some Baptists hold, somewhat strictly, that the New Testament lays out a very clear guideline for virtually everything related to church order, that this guideline is inflexible, and that we are duty bound to imitate it. Historically, this idea is known as the Regulative Principle of Church Order" (Chad Owen Brand and David E. Hankins, *One Sacred Effort: The Cooperative Program of Southern Baptists* [Nashville: Broadman, 2005], 54-55).

authoritative. Yet there seems to be more time spent exegeting verses on divorce and remarriage or gender roles, than to discuss what God says about evangelism…

    c.   Isn't it time to get back to the Bible in the area of evangelism?

MAIN IDEA: The main idea of this chapter is therefore to determine where and how to find a normative definition of evangelizing!

CHAPTER BREAKDOWN:

[For the benefit of teachers and students: begin with Point J., "Toward a Working Definition" followed by a brief overview of Point A., "Some Historical Definitions of Evangelism." Points D-E-F-G all follow in a sequence, seeking to show the benefits of using the word 'evangelize' in English language translations. The main 'meat' of this chapter is Point I., "Five Categories of New Testament Terms for Evangelism"]

A.   Select Historic Definitions of Evangelism

B.   A Long Historic Look at Terms for Evangelism

C.   Toward Translating Proclamational Words in the Old Testament

D.   A History of the Translation of εὐαγγελίζω in the English New Testament

E.   A Look at "Evangelize" in Several Translation Histories: Latin, English, French, and German

F.   On the Translation of Proclamational Terms in English Bibles

G.   Turning the Tide—Unleashing the Word Evangelize!

H.   Arguments for and against Translating εὐαγγελίζω as "Evangelize"

I.   Five Categories of New Testament Terms for Evangelizing

J.   Toward a Working Definition

K.   Concluding Considerations

A. Select Historic Definitions of Evangelism:[338]

1. Archbishop's Third Committee of Inquiry (1918):[339]

   "To evangelize is so to present Christ Jesus in the power of the Holy Spirit, that men shall come to put their trust in God through Him, to accept Him as Saviour, and serve Him as their King in the fellowship of His Church."[340]

2. D. T. Niles (1951):

   Evangelism is "one beggar telling another beggar where to get food."[341]

3. Michael Green (1970):

   "Evangelism in the strict sense is proclaiming the good news of salvation to men and women with a view of their conversion to Christ and incorporation in his church (1970:7)."

4. C. Peter Wagner (1971):

   "The mission of the church is to so incarnate itself in the world that the gospel of Christ is effectively communicated by word and deed toward the end that all men and women become faithful disciples of Christ, and responsible members of His church."

5. J. I. Packer (1966):

   "According to the New Testament, evangelism is just preaching the Gospel, the evangel. It is a work of communication in which Christians make themselves mouthpieces of God's message of mercy to sinners.... The way to tell whither in fact you are evangelizing is not to ask whether conversions are known to have resulted from your witness. It is to ask whether you are faithfully making known the Gospel message."

6. World Congress on Evangelism, Berlin, 1966:

   "Evangelism is the proclamation of the Gospel of the crucified and risen Christ, the only Redeemer of men, according to the Scriptures, with the purpose of persuading condemned and lost sinners to put their trust in God by receiving and accepting Christ as Savior through the power of the Holy Spirit, and to serve Christ as Lord in every calling of life and in the fellowship of his church, looking toward the day of his coming in glory (1967:I:6)."

7. Ronan Hoffman, from Catholic University of America (1972):

   "The Church is missionary by its very nature and must strive to carry out the work of evangelization, namely, of presenting Jesus Christ so that as many men as possible may come to know Him, and to accept Him as their Savior, and serve Him and their fellowmen in Him."[342]

8. The Lausanne Covenant—The Nature of Evangelism (1974):[343]

   "To evangelize is to spread the good news that Jesus Christ died for our sins and was raised from the dead according to the Scriptures, and that as the reigning Lord he now offers the forgiveness of sins and the

---

[338]Uncited quotes are from C. Peter Wagner, *Frontiers in Missionary Strategy* (Chicago: Moody, 1971).

[339]*The Evangelistic Work of the Church, Being the Report of the Archbishops' Third Committee of Inquiry* (London: Society for the Promoting Christian Knowledge for the National Mission, 1918), 18.

[340]This definition was used by Billy Graham (Billy Graham, "The Work of an Evangelist," in Frank Colquhoun, ed., *Introducing Billy Graham: The Work of an Evangelist. An Address Given in the Assembly Hall of the Church House, Westminster, on 20th March, 1952* [London: World Evangelical Alliance, 1953, 1961], 15). Templeton, the first full-time evangelist hired by the National Council of Churches, wrote, "The Archbishop's Committee of the Church of England framed a definition of evangelism which later became a part of the 'Report of the Archbishop's Commission' (popularly known as 'Towards the Conversion of England') and has, with some minor changes, been adopted as a definition of evangelism by the Madras Foreign Missions Council [1938], the National Council of the Churches of Christ in the U.S.A., the Commission on Evangelism of the Presbyterian Church, U.S.A., and other bodies" (Charles B. Templeton, *Evangelism for Tomorrow* [New York: Harper and Brothers, 1957], 41-42). Later Templeton authored his convictions in *Farewell to God: My Reasons for Rejecting the Christian Faith* (Toronto: McClelland and Stewart, 1996).

[341]Norman E. Thomas, *Classic Texts in Mission and World Christianity* (Maryknoll, NY: Orbis, 1995), 156.

[342]Ronan Hoffman, [in response to: 1967: Are Conversion Missions Outmoded?] "Yes! Conversion and the Mission of the Church," in Donald McGavran, ed., *Eye of the Storm: The Great Debate in Mission* (Waco, TX: Word, 1972), 83.

[343]From John R. W. Stott, *Making Christ Known: Historic Mission Documents from the Lausanne Movement* (Grand Rapids: Eerdmans, 1996), 20.

liberating gift of the Holy Spirit to all who repent and believe. Our Christian presence[344] in the world is indispensable to evangelism, and so is that kind of dialogue[345] whose purpose is to listen sensitively in order to understand. But evangelism itself is the proclamation of the historical, biblical Christ as Saviour and Lord, with a view to persuading people to come to him personally and so be reconciled to God. In issuing the Gospel invitation we have no liberty to conceal the cost of discipleship.[346] Jesus still calls all who would follow him to deny themselves, take up their cross, and identify themselves with his new community.[347] The results of evangelism include obedience to Christ, incorporation into his church and responsible service in the world."[348]

9. Paul VI's *Evangelii Nuntiandi*:

"Thus it has been possible to define evangelization in terms of proclaiming Christ to those who do not know Him, of preaching, of catechesis, of conferring Baptism and the other sacraments."[349]

"To live the sacraments in this way, bringing their celebration to a true fullness, is not, as some would claim, to impede or to accept a distortion of evangelization: it is rather to complete it."[350]

"In a certain sense it is a mistake to make a contrast between evangelization and sacramentalization, as is sometimes done."[351]

10. Baptist Faith and Message (2000):

"It is the duty and privilege of every follower of Christ and of every church of the Lord Jesus Christ to endeavor to make disciples of all nations. The new birth of man's spirit by God's Holy Spirit means the birth of love for others. Missionary effort on the part of all rests thus upon a spiritual necessity of the regenerate life, and is expressly and repeatedly commanded in the teachings of Christ. The Lord Jesus Christ has commanded the preaching of the gospel to all nations. It is the duty of every child of God to seek constantly to win the lost to Christ by *verbal* witness undergirded by a Christian lifestyle, and by other methods in harmony with the gospel of Christ. Genesis 12:1-3; Exodus 19:5-6; Isaiah 6:1-8; Matthew 9:37-38; 10:5-15; 13:18-30, 37-43; 16:19; 22:9-10; 24:14; 28:18-20; Luke 10:1-18; 24:46-53; John 14:11-12; 15:7-8,16; 17:15; 20:21; Acts 1:8; 2;

---

[344]Bassham located the origin of the concept of "Christian presence" to the "worker-priest movement" in France from 1944-1945. This then led to the "Christian Presence Series" of M. A. C. Warren, used by the World Student Christian Federation in the 1960s (Rodger C. Bassham, *Mission Theology: 1948-1975 Years of Worldwide Creative Tension Ecumenical, Evangelical, and Roman Catholic* [Pasadena: William Carey Library, 1979], 70). Bassham added, "Through its adoption of *The Church of Others*, the term [Christian presence] became practically a slogan for ecumenical mission strategy and was obvious in the preparatory documentation for the Fourth Assembly at Upsalla" (ibid., 71). "Presence" then appeared in Johannes Blauw's *The Missionary nature of the Church,* and "became a central component in later ecumenical mission theology" (ibid., 72).

[345]Bassham also traced the concept of dialogue to the report on evangelism by D. T. Niles at the Second Assembly of the WCC in Evanston, Illinois, in 1954. He recommended a "new approach in our evangelizing task" (ibid., 84). According to Bassham, dialogue was encouraged at the Third General Assembly of the WCC in New Delhi, 1961. "Dialogue" was then picked up by Paul VI in his 1964 encyclical *"Ecclesiam Suam,"* where he introduced the concentric circles, encouraging dialogue with those in "the circle of Christianity" ("But we must add that it is not in our power to compromise [in dialogue] with the integrity of the faith [Catholic doctrine] or the requirements of charity [the sacraments]" (Paul VI, *Ecclesiam Suam,* 6 August 1964, sec. 109). This encyclical came out four months prior to Vatican II's *Lumen Gentium,* 21 November 1964).

[346]Likewise, Reinhold Niebuhr decried the individualism of Billy Graham's message: "But whatever the church may do to spread the gospel, it must resist the temptation of simplifying it in either literalistic or individualistic terms, thus playing truant to positions hard-won in the course of history. We cannot afford to retrogress in regard to the truth for the sake of seeming to advance or in order to catch the public eye" (Reinhold Nieburh [editorial], "Literalism, Individualism, and Billy Graham," *Christian Century,* 23 May 1956, 642).

[347]Nieburh also decried the longevity of conversions at a Graham crusade: "The new life which should begin at conversion cannot endure very long in isolation; yet isolation is almost inevitable under the circumstances of a Graham crusade" (Reinhold Nieburh [editorial], "Mass Conversions" *Christian Century,* 29 May 1957, 678).

[348]"Both 'Presence' and 'Dialogue', which had a history of usage in ecumenical and Roman Catholic mission theology, were imported into the Lausanne 1974 definition of evangelism, as was also the 'cost of discipleship,' the 'new community,' and 'responsible service.' Each of these concepts served to blunt the cutting edge of the universal affirmative of the proclamation of the gospel as the only mission of the church" (Thomas P. Johnston, *Examining Billy Graham's Theology of Evangelism* [Eugene, OR: Wipf & Stock, 2003], 130).

[349]Paul VI, *Evangelii Nuntiandi: On Evangelization in the Modern World* (Rome, 8 Dec 1975), §17; available at: http://listserv.american.edu/catholic/church/papal/paul.vi/p6evang.txt (online); accessed: 8 Sept 2004; Internet.

[350]Ibid., sec. 28.

[351]Ibid., sec. 47.

8:26-40; 10:42-48; 13:2-3; Romans 10:13-15; Ephesians 3:1-11; 1 Thessalonians 1:8; 2 Timothy 4:5; Hebrews 2:1-3; 11:39-12:2; 1 Peter 2:4-10; Revelation 22:17."[352]

11. Seeker-Sensitive Example Definition of Evangelism (2003):

"a. To communicate the gospel in a relevant manner to seekers who live in our church field;

"b. To provide opportunities to seekers [outreach events] to respond to the gospel in a manner that both satisfies the demands of scripture and is culturally-relevant;

"c. Focus on family units whenever possible."[353]

12. From *Charta Oecumenica—Guidelines for Growing Cooperation among the Churches of Europe* (2006):

"2. Proclaiming the Gospel together:

"The most important task of the churches in Europe is the common proclamation of the Gospel, in both word and deed, for the salvation of all. The widespread lack of corporate and individual orientation and falling away from Christian values challenge Christians to testify to their faith, particularly in response to the quest for meaning which is being pursued in so many forms. This witness will require increased dedication to Christian education (e.g. catechism classes) and pastoral care in local congregations, with a sharing of experiences in these fields. It is equally important for the whole people of God together to communicate the Gospel in the public domain, which also means responsible commitments to social and political issues.

"We commit ourselves:

- "to discuss our plans for evangelisation with other churches, entering into agreements with them and thus avoiding harmful competition and the risk of fresh divisions;

- "to recognise that every person can freely choose his or her religious and church affiliation as a matter of conscience, which means not inducing anyone to convert through moral pressure or material incentive, but also not hindering anyone from entering into conversion of his or her own free will [the reader will note that this commitment corresponds to the 1994 Colson-Neuhaus Declaration quoted below]."[354]

13. T4G: "Together for the Gospel, "Affirmations and Denials, Article IX (2006):

"Article IX

"We affirm that the Gospel of Jesus Christ is God's means of bringing salvation to His people, that sinners are commanded to believe the Gospel, and that the Church is commissioned to preach and teach the Gospel to all nations.

"We deny that evangelism can be reduced to any program, technique, or marketing approach. We further deny that salvation can be separated from repentance toward God and faith in our Lord Jesus Christ."[355]

14. "Evangelistic Effectiveness" in "Vision for Ministry" from *Foundational Documents*; Gospel Coalition (2007, 2011):

"2. Evangelistic Effectiveness: Because the gospel (unlike religious moralism) produces people who do not disdain those who disagree with them, a truly gospel–centered church should be filled with members who winsomely address people's hopes and aspirations with Christ and his saving work. We have a vision for a church that sees conversions of rich and poor, highly educated and less educated, men and women, old and young, married and single, and all races. We hope to draw highly secular and postmodern people, as well as reaching religious and traditional people. Because of the attractiveness of its community and the humility of its people, a gospel–centered church should find people in its midst who are exploring and trying to understand Christianity. It must welcome them in hundreds of ways. It will do little to make them "comfortable" but will do much to make its message understandable. In addition to all this, gospel–centered churches will have a bias toward church plantingas one of the most effective means of evangelism there is."[356]

---

[352]"XI. Evangelism and Missions" in *The Baptist Faith and Message* [2000]; accessed 14 August 2002; available from: http://www.sbc.net/bfm/default.asp; Internet. The word "verbal" is italicized as it was added to the 1963 Baptist Faith and Message.

[353]From a WillowCreek Association local church handout. Notice the importance of the word "relevance" in this definition. By the way, if culture frames the question, then the Bible no longer does!

[354]From *Charta Oecumenica—Guidelines for Growing Cooperation among the Churches of Europe*; accessed 10 Aug 2006; available from http://www.cec-kek.org/English/ChartafinE.htm; Internet.

[355]"Affirmations and Denials, Article IX"; available at: http://t4g.org/about/affirmations-and-denials-2/ (online); accessed: 19 Mar 2014; Internet.

[356]"Foundational Documents"; available at: http://thegospelcoalition.org/about/foundation-documents/vision/ (online); accessed 19 Mar 2014; Internet.

Conclusion: These historic definitions are helpful, in that they provide a history of the understanding of the evangelism mandate. However, they may be less helpful in that the variety of views expressed leaves the Christian with uncertainty as to what is evangelism. Our goal is a normative definition of evangelism. Therefore, with a certain measure of uncertainty (although this author fully ascribes to the *Baptist Faith and Message 2000*) we delve into historical terms for evangelism.

B. A Long Historic Look at Terms for Evangelism:

   1. On the Demise of Evangelizing and Conversion Theology during the Patristic Era and Early Middle Ages:

   Introduction: It would seem that evangelism, evangelizing, and conversion suffer from a lack of sources. Ronan Hoffman formed an *a priori* argument based on this lack of source information.[357] It would seem more likely, however, that the lack of sources is primarily due to the lack of necessary transmission of the evangelistic or missional texts by the monks of the Church of Rome.

   a. Jerome (340-420) and absolution—Jerome interpreted Daniel 4 to record Daniel's promise of an indulgence to Nebuchadnezzar for absolution of his sin based on corresponding good works.

   > "'*It may be that God will forgive thy sins.*' In view of the fact that the blessed Daniel, foreknowing the future as he did, had doubts concerning God's decision, it is very rash on the part of those who boldly promise pardon to sinners. And yet it should be recognized that indulgence was promised to Nebuchadnezzar in return, as long as he wrought good works."[358]

   b. Augustine (354-430): His *Confessions*, Evangelism, and Philosophical Theology:

   Introduction: Augustine's *Confessions*, hugely important in the development of Western Church theology, provides fertile ground for the development of philosophical theology, particularly in the areas of evangelism and conversion. Today, it may be that some conservative Evangelicals have similarly adopted a type of Philosophical Calvinism which mirrors Augustine's surprising silence on proclamational evangelism. Augustine begins with an ode to predestination and election, and continues without anywhere mentioning even a breath about the human side of evangelism.

      1) Augustine's Two Part Conversion Experience:

         a) As explained by his translator: "We can observe two separate stages in Augustine's "conversion." The first was the dramatic striking off of the slavery of incontinence and pride which had so long held him from decisive commitment to the Christian faith. The second was the development of an adequate understanding of the Christian faith itself and his baptismal confession of Jesus Christ as Lord and Saviour."[359]

         b) Augustine explained his first mysterious conversion.[360]

---

[357]"For, in repudiating the deeply rooted notion that the Church is to seek the general conversion of the human race, it is important to understand that this is not a repudiation of any former teaching which might be found in the Scriptures, in Patristic sources, or in the teachings of theology or the general councils. There is no such teaching; it has been merely an assumption, though admittedly widespread. Consequently, it is necessary to note carefully the absence of teaching on this point" (Ronan Hoffman, [A Catholic response to: 1967: Are Conversion Missions Outmoded?] "Yes! Conversion and the Mission of the Church," in Donald McGavran, ed., *Eye of the Storm: The Great Debate in Mission* [Waco, TX: Word, 1972], 71).

[358]*Jerome's Commentary on Daniel,* trans. by Gleason L. Archer, Jr. (Grand Rapids: Baker, 1958), 52.

[359]Augustine, *Confessions* [Book 3, Part 6], ed. and trans. Albert C. Oulter; from http://www.ccel.org/a/augustine/confessions/ confessions_enchiridion.txt; accessed 11 September 2002; Internet; Preface.

[360]"I was saying these things and weeping in the most bitter contrition of my heart, when suddenly I heard the voice of a boy or a girl I know not which--coming from the neighboring house, chanting over and over again, "Pick it up, read it; pick it up, read it." [This is the famous *Tolle, lege; tolle, lege*] Immediately I ceased weeping and began most earnestly to think whether it was usual for children in some kind of game to sing such a song, but I could not remember ever having heard the like. So, damming the torrent of my tears, I got to my feet, for I could not but think that this was a divine command to open the Bible and read the first passage I should light upon. For I had heard [Doubtless from Ponticianus, in their earlier conversation] how Anthony, accidentally coming into church while the gospel was being read, received the admonition as if what was read had been addressed to him: "Go and sell what you have and give it to the poor, and you shall have treasure in heaven; and come and follow me" [Matt. 19:21]. By such an oracle he was forthwith converted to thee" (ibid., Book 8, Chap 12).

c) The passage that he read [Matt 19:21] was more befitting of accepting monastic vows (a Greek asceticism), rather than verbally repenting for the forgiveness of sins and verbally placing his faith in the atoning work of Christ alone:[361]

Matt 19:21 (NKJ), "Jesus said to him, 'If you want to be perfect, go, sell what you have and give to the poor, and you will have treasure in heaven; and come, follow Me.'"

d) For Augustine, the forgiveness of his sins was not yet bestowed until baptism.[362]

2) Elements related to evangelism:

a) The personification of "faith" as praying to God, "My faith prays to you, Lord, this faith which you gave me and with which you inspired me through the Incarnation of your Son and through the ministry of the Preacher."[363]

   (1) What of the cross? Is it the incarnation that saves? Is that a part of the 1 Corinthians 15 Gospel?

   (2) What of repentance for the forgiveness of sins?

b) Augustine described a God-shaped vacuum in man's heart (cf. Eccl 3:11),[364]

   (1) Is this God-shaped vacuum a part of the Gospel? Where or how is it a part of the order of salvation?

   (2) Is this not a witness of God through creation, which is either awakened or deadened through the ministry of evangelizing (cf. Acts 14:17, "yet He did not leave Himself without a witness")

c) Evangelism as an action of God in giving the soul a yearning for Him.[365]

d) An emphasis on another person's prayer [or goodness] in evangelism, "Yet, though he did not believe in Christ, he did not break the hold over me of my mother's goodness and did not stop me believing"[366]

e) A clue that the "Manicheans" did emphasize speaking the Gospel [evangelizing], "O Truth, Truth, how inwardly even then did the marrow of my soul sigh for thee when, frequently and in manifold ways, in numerous and vast books, [the Manicheans] sounded out thy name though it was only a sound!"[367]

   (1) Another clue as to the nature of "Augustine's Manichean Dilemna" is found in a book review for a book by the same title.[368]

---

[361]"So I quickly returned to the bench where Alypius was sitting, for there I had put down the apostle's book when I had left there. I snatched it up, opened it, and in silence read the paragraph on which my eyes first fell: "Not in rioting and drunkenness, not in chambering and wantonness, not in strife and envying, but put on the Lord Jesus Christ, and make no provision for the flesh to fulfill the lusts thereof' [Rom. 13:13]. I wanted to read no further, nor did I need to. For instantly, as the sentence ended, there was infused in my heart something like the light of full certainty and all the gloom of doubt vanished away [Note the parallels here to the conversion of Anthony and the *agentes in rebus*]" (ibid.).

[362]"But that faith allowed me no rest in respect of my past sins, which were not yet forgiven me through thy baptism" (ibid., Book 9, Chap 4)

[363]*The Confessions of St. Augustine,* trans. by Rex Warner (New York: Mentor, 1963), 17.

[364]"And man desires to praise thee, for he is a part of thy creation; he bears his mortality about with him and carries the evidence of his sin and the proof that thou dost resist the proud. Still he desires to praise thee, this man who is only a small part of thy creation. Thou hast prompted him, that he should delight to praise thee, for thou hast made us for thyself and restless is our heart until it comes to rest in thee" (*Confessions,* ed. and trans. Albert C. Oulter; Book 1, Chap 1).

[365]"But as for the souls that thirst after thee and who appear before thee—separated from 'the society of the [bitter] sea' by reason of their different ends--thou waterest them by a secret and sweet spring, so that 'the earth' may bring forth her fruit and--thou, O Lord, commanding it--our souls may bud forth in works of mercy after their kind [Gen 1:10f.]" (ibid., Book 13, Chap 17).

[366]*Confessions,* trans. by Rex Warner, 29.

[367]*Confessions,* ed. and trans. Albert C. Oulter; Book 3, Chap 6.

[368]"BeDuhn identifies the Manichean subtext to be found in nearly every work written by Augustine between 388 and 401, and demonstrates Augustine's concern with refuting his former beliefs without alienating the Manichaeans he wished to win over. To achieve these ends, Augustine modified and developed his received Nicene Christian faith, strengthening it where it was vulnerable to Manichean critique and taking it in new directions where he found room within the an orthodox frame of reference to accommodate Manichean perspectives and concerns. Against this

    f)   Not surprisingly, baptism became the main message of the Great Commission for Augustine.[369]

3)   Clues to philosophical Christianity:

    a)   An emphasis on sin a negation (a lack of love), "And not to love you, is this not itself misery enough?"[370] "Not weeping at his own death, caused by lack of love for you."[371]

    b)   An emphasis on truth rather than the Pauline Gospel.[372]

4)   Augustine's *Contra Manichean*:

    a)   Was not this document an example of the "Fallacy of Irrelevant Proof," "the "Fallacy of Negative Proof," the "Fallacy of False Analogy," or the "Fallacy of Proof by Analogy"?[373] In which case, as Augustine was developing his argumentation against the non-sacramental theology of the more evangelically-oriented Donatists, he found that they resembled in some [tangential] ways the teachings of Mani. Augustine, therefore, painted the Donatists as Manicheans, easily undermining the teachings of Mani, and further giving the Church of Rome an easy label and a weapon against Evangelicals after that time.

    b)   Likewise, 20th Century U.S. Evangelicals are considered Manichean by scholars such as George Marsden[374] and Mark Noll.[375]

---

background, Beduhn is able to shed new light on the complex circumstances and purposes of Augustine's most famous work, *The Confessions*, as well as his distinctive reading of Paul and his revolutionary concept of grace, *Augustine's Manichaean Dilemma, 2* demonstrates the close interplay between Augustine's efforts to work out his own "Catholic" persona and the theological positions associated with his name, between the sometimes dramatic twists and turns of his own personal life and his theoretical thinking" (From the publisher, Review of Jason D. BeDuhn, *Augustine's Manichaean Dilemma, 2: Making a "Catholic" Self, 388-401 C.E.*; University of Pennsylvania Press, Spring 2013 Catalog, 38).

[369]"For, by the ministry of thy holy ones, thy mysteries have made their way amid the buffeting billows of the world, to instruct the nations in thy name, in thy Baptism" (*Confessions,* ed. and trans. Albert C. Oulter, Book 13, Chap 20).

[370] *Confessions,* trans. by Rex Warner, 20.

[371]Ibid., 31.

[372]"O Truth, Truth, how inwardly even then did the marrow of my soul sigh for thee when, frequently and in manifold ways, in numerous and vast books, [the Manicheans] sounded out thy name though it was only a sound! And in these dishes—while I starved for thee—they served up to me, in thy stead, the sun and moon thy beauteous works—but still only thy works and not thyself; indeed, not even thy first work. For thy spiritual works came before these material creations, celestial and shining though they are. But I was hungering and thirsting, not even after those first works of thine, but after thyself the Truth, 'with whom is no variableness, neither shadow of turning' [James 1:17]" (*Confessions,* ed. and trans. Albert C. Oulter; Book 3, Chap 6).

[373]David H. Fischer, *Historians' Fallacies: Toward a Logic of Historical Thought* (New York: Harper Colophon, 1970).

[374]"Even though the political attitudes of most fundamentalists were much like those of their non-fundamentalist Republican neighbors, the development of hyper-American patriotic anti-communism is a puzzle and an irony in the history of fundamentalism. How could premillennialists, whose attention was supposed to be directed away from politics while waiting for the coming King, embrace this highly politicized view? It is difficult to account for a phenomenon on simply rational grounds. Perhaps the puzzle can be solved by understanding a type of mentality, or disposition of thought, sometimes associated with fundamentalism. Richard Hofstadter aptly described this mentality as 'essentially Manichean.' The world, in this view, is 'an arena of conflict between absolute good and evil....' This outlook lies behind a view of history that has often appeared on the American political scene. 'History *is* a conspiracy, set in motion by demonic forces of almost transcendent power....' This view, says Hofstadter, led to 'the paranoid style' often seen in American political thought [footnote: Richard Hofstadter, *Anti-Intellectualism in American Life* (New York, 1962), 135; *The Paranoid Style in American Politics, and Other Essays* (New York, 1963), 29].

"This syndrome has a near affinity to the view of history central to the fundamentalists' outlook. They held, as other Christians often had, that history involved a basic struggle between God and Satan. This premise in itself was not particularly conducive to conspiracy theories. The fundamentalists, however, were disposed to divide *all* reality into neat antitheses: the saved and the lost, the holy and the unsanctified, the true and the false. Moreover, their common sense philosophical assumptions added the assurance that they could clearly distinguish these contrasting factors when they appeared in everyday life. Add to these predispositions the fundamentalist experience in social displacement (which Hofstader makes much of) and the 'Manichean mentality' becomes comprehensible" (George Marsden, *Fundamentalism and American Culture: The Shaping of Twentieth-Century Evangelicalism, 1870-1925* [Oxford: University Press, 1980], 210-211).

c) Note some of the issues:

1) As noted in the footnote above, the categories "saved and lost" are essentially Manichean; just that statement right there includes everyone who believes in conversion as "essentially Manichean"!

2) Likewise, is not the belief in Total Depravity Manichean?

3) Is not the belief that there is no holiness in the bread of the altar of the Lord Manichean?

4) Is not the belief that there is no sacredness in a Crucifix, or in the statues of the Blessed Virgin, or the saints, essentially considered being Manichean?

5) Or holy water, or holy relics, or holy pilgrimage places…

6) Where not Genesis 6:5, Psalms 14 and 53, Jeremiah 17:9, Romans 3:9-20, or Ephesians 2:1-3 in the Bible of Augustine? Certainly they were!

d) It would seem his line of reasoning in *Contra Manichean* would and should give Evangelical scholars a more guarded view of Augustine than is often noted, not to mention his clear antagonism of Evangelicalism as noted in his *Contra Donatisten* (against the self-governing Donatist Puritan-type churches in North Africa).

5) Some comments on the use of Augustine:

a) Perhaps an important study of Augustine is the study of how Thomas Aquinas cited him in his *Summa Theologica*. Aquinas portrayed Augustine as a Medieval philosophical scholar.

b) However, it would seem that Calvin cited Augustine to counter the charge that his reading of Scripture (particularly in the area of Predestination) was novel and new (a typical charge brought by Rome against anyone who disagrees with them).

c) Note also the sharp words of Catholic Medieval historian Léon-E. Halkin as regards Augustine' contribution to Medieval theology, and especially Inquisition![376]

---

[375]"To make room for Christian thought, evangelicals must also abandon the false disjunctions that their distinctives have historically encouraged. The cultivation of the mind for Christian reasons does not deny the appropriateness of activism, for example, but it does require activism to make room for study. Similarly, it is conversionism along with a consideration of lifelong spiritual development and trust in the Bible along with a critical use of wisdom from other sources (especially from the world that God made) that will lead to a better day. Modifying the evangelical tendency to Manichaeism may cost some of the single-minded enthusiasm of activism, but it will be worth it in order to be able to worship God with the mind" (Mark Noll, *The Scandal of the Evangelical Mind* [Grand Rapids: Eerdmans, 1994], 245).

[376]"One must turn to Saint Augustine to understand how the New Testament could be exploited by an acrobatic exegesis during all the Middle Ages, and beyond, for Saint Augustine inspired successively Saint Thomas and Calvin.

"Saint Augustine shared the indulgence of the ancient Fathers when he composed his first writings. His evolution was only more noticeable. Exaggerate the excesses of the African dissidents and conquer by the political violence of Christian emperors, he concluded that the repression of error was a legitimate defense.

"Ceding to the temptation of efficiency, Saint Augustine accepted recourse from the secular arm, the use of violence against the heretics, but nonetheless not to the point of the death penalty. His conclusions, carefully founded upon psychology as upon history, could do nothing but gain ground with [the march of] time, with the progresses and reversals of evangelization.

"The time was ripe for Inquisition. For sure, heresy is illegal there where reigns a state religion; error, for a theologian, has no place, it is a serious sin. The simplicity of these principles will always lead to the most dire extremes among spirits of systematicians who are incapable of distinguishing, in daily realities rather than only in theory, between thesis and hypothesis. Contemporary and colleague of the first Inquisitors, Saint Thomas Aquinas interpreted the Parable of the [Wheat and the] Tares in an unpredictable sense. If one is to believe it, the Lord diminished his prohibition to cut out the tares by saying precisely, 'for fear that in pulling the tares, you may likewise pull out the wheat.' Where there is no fear of this result, concluded the Angelic Doctor, citing Augustine, the persecution of heretics is legitimate. [footnote: *Summa*, SS: Q10, A8; Q11, A3]

"The celebrated canonist Hostiensis made further efforts to justify punishment by [burning at] the stake by citing the example of the branch that is thrown into the fire: *si quis in me non manserit, mittetur foras sicut palmes, et arescet, et colligent eum et in ignem mittent, et ardet.* [footnote: John 15:6]

"Such misunderstanding of the eschatological emphasis of the parables cannot but astonish us. Already Saint Augustin had interpreted in his own way the parable of the banquet [Luke 19:23] to promote the harshness of his religious politicization" (Léon-E. Halkin, *Initiation à la critique historique* [Paris: Armand Colin, 1963], 203-04; translation mine).

Conclusion: It is important to remember that Augustine read the same Bible that we read today—in other words, he had the same access to all five Great Commission passages, the verbal elements of the Book of Acts, the Pauline Gospel in 1 Corinthians 15, other elements of evangelism as found in 2 Corinthians 3-6 and the Book of Philippians. Rather, it would seem that he chose to deemphasize evangelism in his *Confessions* and to lead or follow the Church of Rome into philosophical theology.

c. The "Evangelism" methodologies of Pope Gregory I (590-604):

Introduction: The impact of Gregory I was enormous. He centralized the hierarchy of the Roman Catholic church, beginning to gather the entire Latin-speaking church under his control. The first monk to become a pope, his "evangelism" methodologies, still used in the Roman church, displayed a growing non-biblical shift in the Roman church.

1. Syncretism with other religious systems[377]

2. Continued redefinition of sin:
    a. Providing the final number of "Cardinal Sins" as being seven[378]
    b. Thereby changing Rome's Gospel message to syncretize with Greek philosophy, and its Cardinal virtues—the Cardinal sins being their antithesis!
    c. Those who believed in total depravity were deemed Manichean, using Augustine as described above.

3. Gradual conversion (versus instantaneous conversion):[379]
    a. As sin became philosophical, so salvation became gradual self-improvement, whereby the Roman church provided Christianized tools through which this salvation was confirmed.

---

[377]"Therefore, when by God's help you reached our most reverend brother, Bishop Augustine, we wish you to inform him that we have been giving careful thought to the affairs of the English, and have come to the conclusion that the temples of the idols among that people should on no account be destroyed, but the temples themselves are to be aspersed with holy water, altars set up in them, and relics deposited there. For if these temples are well-built, they must be purified from the worship of demons and dedicated to the service of the true God. In this way, we hope that the people, seeing that their temples are not destroyed, may abandon their error and, flocking more readily to their accustomed resorts, may come to know and adore the true God. In this way, we hope that the people, seeing that their temples are not destroyed, may abandon their error and, flocking more readily to their accustomed resorts, may come to know and adore the true God. And since they have a custom of sacrificing many oxen to demons, let some other solemnity be substituted in its place, such as a day of Dedication or the festivals of the holy martyrs whose relics are enshrined there. On such occasions they might well construct shelters of boughs for themselves around the churches that were once temples, and celebrate the solemnity with devout feasting. They are no longer to sacrifice beasts to the Devil, but they may kill them for food to the praise of God, and give thanks to the Giver of all gifts for the plenty they enjoy. If the people are allowed some worldly pleasures in this way, they will more readily come to desire they joys of the spirit." (Gregory I, "Pope Gregory's Letter to the Abbot Mellitus," in Bede, *A History of the English Church and People*, trans. by L. Sherley-Price, rev. R. E. Latham [Harmondsworth, Middlesex, England: Penguin Books, 1979], 86-87).

[378]"According to St. Thomas (II-II:153:4) 'a capital vice is that which has an exceedingly desirable end so that in his desire for it a man goes on to the commission of many sins all of which are said to originate in that vice as their chief source.' It is not then the gravity of the vice in itself that makes it capital but rather the fact that it gives rise to many other sins. These are enumerated by St. Thomas (I-II:84:4) as vainglory (pride), avarice, gluttony, lust, sloth, envy, anger. St. Bonaventure (Brevil., III, ix) gives the same enumeration. Earlier writers had distinguished eight capital sins: so St. Cyprian (De mort., iv); Cassian (De instit. cænob., v, coll. 5, de octo principalibus vitiis); Columbanus ('Instr. de octo vitiis princip.' in 'Bibl. max. vet. patr.', XII, 23); Alcuin (De virtut. et vitiis, xxvii sqq.). The number seven, however, had been given by St. Gregory the Great (Lib. mor. in Job. XXXI, xvii), and it was retained by the foremost theologians of the Middle Ages" ("Sin," *Catholic Encyclopedia* (1911); available from http://www.newadvent.org/ cathen/14004b.htm#III; accessed 16 Jan 2003; Internet).

[379]"For it is certainly impossible to eradicate all errors from obstinate minds at one stroke, and whoever wishes to climb a mountain top climbs gradually step by step, and not in one leap. It was in this way that the Lord revealed Himself to the Israelite people in Egypt, permitting the sacrifices formerly offered to the Devil to be offered thenceforward to Himself instead. So He bade them sacrifice beasts to Him, so that, once they became enlightened, they might abandon one element of the sacrifice and retain another. For, while they were to offer the same beasts as before, they were to offer to God instead of to idols, so that they would no longer be offering the same sacrifices. Of your kindness, you are to inform our brother Augustine of this policy, so that he may conduct consider how he may best implement it on the spot" (Bede, *A History of the English Church and People*, 87).

      b. Gradual conversion was a necessity in the sacramental system Gregory further established; those who disagreed with Rome's sacramental system were persecuted as Manichean.

    4. Political manipulation for ecclesial control:

      a. Sending bishops to influence the king, the queen, or a prince[380]

      b. Leading to mass politically-motivated conversions[381]

    5. Formalism:

      a. Through the sending of bishops in order to absorb non-Catholic Christian churches[382]

      b. Which led to the squelching of Celtic Christianity, and their absorption into the Roman rite[383]

Result: Gregory I's theology of evangelism continued the process of displacing evangelists and those with an Evangelical theology away from mainstream Roman Catholicism, resulting in persecution and much bloodshed following the 11th Century.

e. Peter the Lombard (Archbishop of Paris, d. 1161/1164) on salvation:

    1. The Roman Pope and Peter the Venerable (of Cluny) had taken a strong stand against the evangelist Henry the Monk (aka. Henry of Lausanne; see below); In their time, Peter the Lombard's *Sentences* did not help the cause of New Testament evangelism!

    2. Salvation was not just a product of faith alone, but of outward signs, called sacraments[384]

    3. Again, he affirmed the Greek idea of virtues[385]

---

[380]In 579, it seems Visigoth King Leovigild's son, Hermenigild, married the daughter of the King of Austrasia, Ingunthis, who was devoutly orthodox. "Under the joint influence of his wife and of Leander [the orthodox (aka. Roman Catholic) bishop], Hermenigild himself was converted to orthodoxy and given the name John" (Sir Henry H. Howorth, *Gregory the Great* [London: John Murray, 1912], 131). This led to family infighting over the faith. Leovigild feared that his son might revolt and began to patronize the orthodox (or Roman Catholic), though he himself was Arian.

[381]In regards to the state imposing religion on its people, Clovis, when he converted to Christianity in 496 AD, "used no force to induce the Franks to conform to his behavior" (Kenneth S. Latourette, *A History of the Expansion of Christianity* [Grand Rapids: Zondervan, 1970], 1:207). By contrast, Reccared, King of the Visigoths, "summoned a synod at Toledo, in which he deliberately abjured Arianism, and induced many of the Bishops to follow his example" (Frederick H. Dudden, *Gregory the Great* [London: Longmans, Green, 1905; New York: Russell and Russell, 1967], 1:408. It must be stated that "It was probably a political motive that induced Reccared to accept the orthodox creed" [ibid., 1:407]). While no clear statements of Gregory I seem to encourage the imposing of a religion on its people, his theology did not discourage it. "Like Augustine, Gregory taught that the State must be in alliance with the Kingdom of God, and must use its power for the furtherance of Divine law and worship" (Dudden, 2:413). Latourette confirms the use of this approach, "Conversions were often en masse and engineered by the recognized rulers" (Latourette, 2:17)."

[382]"Of the eight kingdoms of the Anglo-Saxon Confederation, that of Kent alone was exclusively won and retained by the Roman monks whose first attempts among the East Saxons and Northumbrians ended in failure. In Wessex and East Anglia the Saxons of the West and the Angles of the East were converted by the combined action of continental missionaries and Celtic monks. As to the two Northumbrian kingdoms and those of Essex and Mercia, which comprehended in themselves more than two-thirds of the territory occupied by the German (Saxon) conquerors, those four countries owed their final conversion exclusively to the peaceful invasion of the Celtic monks, who not only rivaled the zeal of the Roman monks, the first obstacles surmounted, showed much more perseverance and gained much more success" (Count of Montalembert, *Monks of the West from St. Benedict to St. Bernard* [London: William Blackwood, 1867)], 3:369).

[383]"Wilfrid appeared: by a fifty years' struggle, and at the cost of his peace, safety, and even his personal freedom, he first neutralised, and finally annihilated, the Celtic spirit, without at any time being guilty of persecution, coercion, or violence towards the vanquished. He did more than check the Celtic movement; he sent it back into chaos; he extirpated all the ritual and liturgic differences which served as a veil and pretext for the prejudices of race and opinion; he extirpated them not only in his immense diocese, the vast region of Northumbria, but throughout all of England; and not in England only, but, by the contagion of his example and influence, in Ireland, in Scotland, and finally in the very sanctuary of Celtic Christianity, at Iona" (Montalembert, 4:116-117).

[384]"For as Augustine, the egregious Doctor, says in the book *on Christian Doctrine* [notation: 'Chapter 2, n. 2; here and in the next passage, but with many words omitted by Master (Peter) and not a few added or changed'], 'Every doctrine is of things, and/or signs. But even things are learned through signs. But here (those) are properly named things, which are not employed to signify anything; but signs, those whose use is in signifying'" (Peter the Lombard, *Sentences,* Book 1, Distinction 1, Chap 1, "Every doctrine concerns things and/or signs"; available from: http://www.franciscan-archive.org/lombardus/opera/ls1-01.html; accessed: 16 May 2006; Internet).

4. He moved the focus of the center of the Christian life from the Gospel and its proclamation to God and His glory:

    a) "The things, therefore, which one is to enjoy, are the Father and the Son and the Holy Spirit"[386]
    b) "It is therefore established, because[4] we ought to enjoy God, not use (Him)"[387]
    c) "Of which all, before we treat of signs, must be dealt with, and first of the things, which are to be enjoyed, namely, the Holy and Undivided Trinity"[388]
    d) For example, note the chapter titles of Peter the Lombard, *Sentences,* Book 1, Distinction 44, "Chapter I: Whether God can make something better, than He has made it, and/or in another and/or better manner, than He has. Chapter II: Whether God can always do everything which He could do"[389]

Summary: Peter the Lombard provided the Roman church "the most commented on book of the 13-16th Centuries", shifting doctrine toward a philosophical and non-Evangelical emphasis; his efforts were advanced by the Dominican Thomas Aquinas (1225-1274) and his *Summa theologica.*[390]

f. [Pope] Innocent III squelched Evangelicalism in Metz, Lorraine, France, as noted in his apostolic letter "Cum ex Iniuncto" (12 July 1199):

"Our venerable brother, the Bishop of Metz [Lorraine, France], We have come to know from his letter that in his diocese as well as in the town of Metz a rather important number of lay people and of women, drawn in some way by a desire for the Scriptures, made for themselves translations into the French language of the Gospels, the epistles of Paul, the Psalter, the Moralia of Job, and many other books; … (with the result being) that in the secret gatherings lay people and woman dare to belch forth to each other and to mutually preach, and they equally despise the company of those who are not mixed up in such things … Some of them also despise the simplicity of their priests, and when a word of salvation is proposed to these latter, they whisper in secret that they have better in their writings and that they are capable of express them more judiciously.

"Even if a desire to understand the divine Scriptures and the care to exhort in conformity with them is not to blame but quite the opposite commendable, these people deserve nevertheless to be reprimanded that they hold secret conventicles, and that they usurp the office of preaching, that they scoff at the simplicity of the priests and that they distain the company of those that do not attach themselves to such practices. God in fact … hates to this point the works of darkness that he commanded and said (to the apostles): "What I tell you in the dark, say it in the daylight; that which you hear in the deep of your ear proclaim it from the rooftops" (Matt 10:27); by this it is clearly manifest that the preaching of the Gospel ought to be proposed not in secret conventicles, as is done by the heretics, but publicly in the Church, in conformity with Catholic custom. …

"But the hidden mysteries of the faith ought not to be exhibited everywhere by all, because they cannot be understood by all, but only unto them that are seized by a believing intelligence; this is why the apostle said of the simple: "As unto little children in Christ, it is milk that I made you drink, not solid food" (1 Cor 3:2) …

"Such is the depth of the holy Scriptures that not only simple and uncultivated people, but even those who are wise and learned are not able to scrutinize the meaning. This is why the Scripture says: "For many of those who sought failed in their search"(Psa 64:7). Also was it correct that it was established in the divine Law that if an animal touches the Mountain (of Sinai) he should be stoned (cf. Heb 12:20; Ex 19:12ff), in order that in fact no simple or uncultivated man should have the presumption to touch upon the sublimities of the holy Scripture or to preach it to others. It is written in fact: "Do not seek that which is too high for you" (Sir 3:22). This is why the apostle said: "Do not seek more than what is necessary to seek, but seek with sobriety" (Rom 12:3).

"Similarly just as the body numbers many members, but not all the members have the same activity, likewise, the Church counts many levels, but not all have the same duty, for according to the Apostle "The

---

[385]"One is to use, therefore, the virtues and through them to enjoy the most high Good; thus we speak and from a good will" (ibid., Book 1, Distinction 1, Chap 3, "What is it 'to enjoy' and 'to use'?").

[386]Ibid., Book 1, Distinction 1, Chap 2, "On the things which one is to enjoy, and/or to use, and on those which enjoy and use". Noting Augustine, On Christian Doctrine, ch. 4.

[387]Ibid., Book 1, Distinction 1, Chap 3.

[388]Ibid., Book 1, Distinction 1, Chap 3.

[389]"Writings"; available at http://www.franciscan-archive.org/lombardus; accessed 25 Jan 2007.

[390]My paper, "The Holy Spirit's Work according to Peter the Lombard's *Four Books of Sentences*" (available at: http://www.evangelismunlimited.com/documents/The-Holy-Spirit's-Work-According-to-Peter-the-Lombard's-Four-Books-of-Sentences.pdf?v=29 [Online]; accessed 25 Nov 2018; Internet), documents Lombard's preparatory arguments for the seven Sacraments in Books 1-3, and his detail on those Sacraments in Book 4.

Lord has given some as apostles, others as prophets, but others as doctors, etc." (Eph 4:11). Therefore the doctor is in some ways the principal in the church and this is why no one ought to usurp without deference the office of preacher."[391]

2. Evangelizing during the 13th Century in Southern France:

Introduction:

With the repression of Manicheans, Donatists, and Paulicians in the early Dark Ages, we move to 12th Century Southern France, which was a center for the Gospel and evangelism. It was during this century that "evangelizing" became *the sign* of being a heretic for Roman Catholicism.

Medieval Evangelistic *Sitz im Leben*:

Jacques Dalarun, former director of Medieval Studies at the French School of Rome and director of the Institute for Research and History of Texts (I.R.H.T.), wrote:

"In the middle of the 12th Century, it was under the fire of the cross of Bernard of Clairvaux and Peter the Venerable that the South [of France] was assigned its heresy."[392]

Dominique Iogna-Prat, professor at the University of Bourgogne, France, translated the summary of the 1135-1140 treatise of Peter the Venerable (of the Cluny "Reform movement") as to the five heretical propositions of Henry of Lausanne, who had evangelized throughout Southern France:

"1. Refusal to baptize infants, under the pretext that it is faith that saves and that a young infant could not have sufficient conscience to believe.

"2. Rejection of holy places; the Church of God does not consist of an assemblage of stones but of a spiritual reality, the communion of the faithful.

"3. The cross is not an object of adoration; it is on the contrary a detestable object, as the instrument of the torture and suffering of Christ.

"4. Priests and bishops dispense a lying teaching as to the matter of the Eucharist. The body of Christ was consumed only one time and only by the disciples, during the communion that preceded the Passion. All other later consumption is only vain fiction.

"5. The funeral liturgy in its whole (offerings, prayers, Masses, and alms) is useless; the dead can hope in nothing more than what they received when they were alive."[393]

Similarly, Reinerius Sacho, inquisitor of the Waldensians stated that they believed "all the articles and symbols of the apostles" (e.g. Apostle's, Nicene, Chalcedonian, and Athanasian Creeds):

"Of all the sects that have been or that are still, there has never been one more pernicious for the church as that of the Waldenses, and this for three reasons. First she is the oldest of all, some find her to go back to the pope Sylvester [Note: "Sylvester, bishop of Rome, contemporary of Emperor Constantine (4th Century)], and others back to the time of the Apostles. Next, she is more extended than any other, for there is barely a place on earth that she has not penetrated. Finally, quite different from the other sects, who inspire at first horror among those who hear their pernicious doctrines, by the horrible blasphemes that they vomit, this one seduces the world *by the appearance of great piety*. The Waldenses lead *a righteous life* before men, and believe as regards God all that there is to believe. They accept *all the articles and symbols of the apostles*, only they blaspheme against the Roman Church and the clergy"[394]

---

[391]Innocent III, "Cum ex iniuncto: On the Necessity for the Magisterium of the Church for the [proper] Interpretation Scripture" [12 July 1199] (online); from *1996 Denzinger* online (DS 770-771); accessed: 8 Nov 2008; available at: http://www.catho.org/9.php?d=bwh; Internet; translation mine.

[392]Jacques Dalarun, "Conclusion," in *Évangile et évangélisme (XIIe-XIIIe siècle)*, Cahiers de Fanjeaux 34 (Toulouse, France: Éditions Privat, 1999), 336; translation mine.

[393]Dominique Iogna-Prat, "L'argumentation défensive: de la Polémique grégorienne au 'Contra Petrobrusianos' de Pierre le Vénérable," in *Inventer l'hérésie: Discours polémiques et pouvoirs avant l'inquisition*, Monique Zerner, ed., Collection du centre d'études médiévales de Nice, vol. 2 (Paris: C.I.D., 1998), 88; translation mine.

[394]Reinerius Sacho, "Témoignage rendu aux vaudois par un inquisiteur" [testimony given of the Waldenses by an inquisitor], in Franck Puaux, *Histoire de la Réformation Française* (Paris: Michel Lévy Frères, 1859), 1:424-25; taken from Bossuet, *Histoire des variations,* 11:55-54 [sic]; translation into English mine.

Even present days scholars believe that the Waldensians were not-at-all heretics, such as Jean-Louis Biget, professor emeritus, École Normale Supérieure, Fontenay/St. Cloud, France:

"He [Michel Rubellin] showed that at their origin they [the Waldenses] were not-at-all heretical [*nullement hérétiques*]. During the six years, between 1173 and 1179, Waldo and his own were utilized by the Archbishop, Guichard of Pontigny, a Cistercian, to wrestle against the Cathedral Chapter of Lyons. After John of Bellesmains ascended to the Episcopal seat, the Waldenses were defined as heretical because they refused to obey the rule that prohibited preaching by the laity."[395]

As far as the Albigenses, Jacques Dalarun explained that rulers would accuse one another of heresy for political reasons beginning in the 12th Century. Those that wanted to listen to these accusations listened.[396] He explained a political motive was the desire to gain territory, as was the case for the territory of the Albigenses. Dalarun continued:

"It had to be that the land tempting the appetite of the *Capétien* [King of France] become heretical in order to be conquered. 'Albigensian' became synonymous to heretical and a crusade followed, legitimizing the conquest. Today the preferred nomenclature for this country is "Country of the Cathars," which is nothing more than the latent but zealous echo of the propaganda for crusade. Thus the identity constructs itself by looking at the other."[397]

Similarly and interestingly, the Anglican Archbishop's Third Committee of Inquiry on Evangelization (1918) dismissed medieval revivalism as passé:

"In mediæval times there was deep in the consciousness of those revival preachers a terror of God the Avenger and the fear of hell. The overwhelming reaction when men were convinced that God had forgiven them and that they were redeemed was the most characteristic feature of many movements of revival. Safety was what men wanted: The Gospel that offered them that came as glorious news and was accepted with enthusiasm. To-day it is otherwise."[398]

---

[395]"Il [Michel Rubellin] a montré qu'à l'origine ils [les vaudois] ne sont nullement hérétiques. Durant six ans, entre 1173 et 1179, Valdo et les siens sont utilisés par l'archevêque, Guichard de Pontigny, un cistercien, pour lutter contre le chapitre cathédral de Lyon. Après que Jean de Bellesmains a succédé au siège épiscopal, les vaudois sont définis hérétiques parce qu'ils refusent d'obéir à la règle faisant aux laïcs interdiction de prêcher" (Jean-Louis Biget, Round Table Discussion, *Évangile et évangélisme*, 246). Ian Forrest admitted, "inquisitors often pursued people who were essentially orthodox but not easily accommodated within the structures of the church" (Ian Forrest, *The Detection of Heresy in Late Medieval England* [Oxford: Clarendon, 2005], 13).

[396]"Les prince locaux avaient commencé à jouer avec le feu dès le XIIe siècle, en s'accusant réciproquement d'hérésie comme on se passe le mistigri: le Trencavel l'eurent plus souvent en main que les autres" (Jacques Dalarun, "Conclusion," in *Évangile et évangélisme (XIIe-XIIIe siècle)*, 335).

[397]"Il fallait que ce pays tenant les appétits du Capétien soit hérétique pour être conquis. « Albigeois » devint synonyme d'hérétique et la Croisade s'ensuivit, légitimant la conquête. On préfère dire aujourd'hui ce pays « Pays cathares », ce qui n'est jamais que l'écho tardif mais zélé d'une propagande de croisade. Ainsi l'identité se construit-elle au regard de l'autre" (*ibid.*, 336).

[398]*The Evangelistic Work of the Church, Being the Report of the Archbishops' Third Committee of Inquiry* (London: Society for the Promoting Christian Knowledge for the National Mission, 1918), 13.

Unfortunately for the Christianity planted by Henry of Lausanne and for the Waldenses,[399] Roman Catholics called their evangelism "hereticking"!

From the 12th Century and following, the Roman Catholic Popes and clergy sought to control evangelism by prohibiting "lay preaching" or what is contemporaneously called "lay visitation", which often involved (1) house-to-house or door-to-door evangelism; they also prohibited (2) street, open-air, or outdoor evangelism. In subsequent centuries Rome prohibited the translation of the Bible into the vernacular language, as well as printing, selling, owning, or reading a vernacular Bible (and even some Latin Bibles), or even gathering in homes to read the Bible.[400]

According to the various Roman Catholic decrees of 1179, 1184, 1199, and 1215, New Testament itinerant evangelists were the pests of society. They were to be hated by all and shunned by all. No business was to be transacted with them, they were not to be given food or lodging, nor were they to be listened to at all. Thus was the lot of the "wandering preachers" (German *wanderprediger*). Yet the "poor men of Lyons" and the Albigenses continued to flourish, despite the harsh measures against them. It was then that Pope Innocent III called for even harsher treatment, by conspiring with the King of France to pronounce war against the region of Toulouse—it was called a "crusade" or holy war.

Once any hope of political asylum was shattered by the Fall of Toulouse, numerous inquisitors hunted the "poor men of Lyons" and the Albigenses throughout Southern France.

Gallagher explained the purpose of the harsh Inquisition legislation:

"Most of the legislation that has just been discussed was certainly intended to frighten the faithful against the danger of being led into heresy and also to compel the heretics to come to their senses and repent."[401]

The following is a list of the inquisition records transcribed by Jean Duvernoy, with some minor additions (in parentheses are the name of the inquisitors, the towns where they inquisited, and the document names if not identified with an inquisitor or town):[402]

a) Inquisition records with known dates:
    a)   1241-1242 (Pierre Cellan)
    b)   1243-1247 (Bernard de Caux; ms XXII, Bibliothèque Nationale, Paris)
    c)   1245-1246, 1253 (Ferrer and Pons de Parnac, Toulouse; manuscript 609, Bibliothèque Municipale, Toulouse)
    d)   1254, 1256 (Jean de Saint-Pierre and Réginald de Chartres)
    e)   1262-1309 (Pierre de Fenouillet and Hugue de Saissac)

---

[399]"3. Finally, the history of Waldo in Lyons appears exemplary as regards the invention of the heresy and the establishment of the 'Society of Persecution' that Robert Ian Moore described. Waldensianism as a heresy is not born in Lyon with Waldo, as the same, if my hypothesis is correct, collaborates with the Archbishop. It is outside of Lyon that it is born from the moment where this collaboration is rejected, and that Waldo and his followers have become not only useless but more so dangerous, and as a consequence they are condemned and chased out of Lyon" [3. Enfin, l'histoire lyonnaise de Valdès apparaît exemplaire quant à l'invention de l'hérésie et à la mise en place de la "société de persécution' que décrit Robert Ian Moore (*La persécution: Sa formation en Europe [Xe-XIIIe siècle]* [Paris, 1991]). Le valdéisme en tant qu'hérésie ne naît pas à Lyon avec Valdès, puisque celui-ci, si mon hypothèse est la bonne, collabore alors avec l'archevêque. Il naît hors de Lyon à partir du moment où cette collaboration est rejetée, et que Valdès et ses partisans sont devenus non seulement inutiles mais encore dangereux, et qu'en conséquence on les condamne et on les chasse de Lyon"] (Michel Rubellin, "Au temps où Valdès n'étais pas hérétique: hypothèses sur le rôle de Valdès à Lyon," in Monique Zerner, ed., *Inventer l'hérésie? Discours polémiques et pouvoirs avant l'inquisition*, Collection du centre d'études médiévales de Nice, vol. 2 [Paris: C.I.D., 1998], 217).

[400]Decrees, councils, and apostolic letters were promulgated against reading the Bible in the vernacular and against the other mentioned concerns in the years: 1179, 1184, 1199, 1211, 1215, 1229, 1234, 1246, 1408, 1414-1416, 1545-1565, 1559, 1564, 1590, 1664, 1836, 1864, 1897 (see *Histoire du Livre Saint en France*; available at http://perso.wanadoo.fr/hlybk/bible/ france.htm; accessed 2 February 2005; Internet; as well as Daniel Lortsch, *Histoire de la Bible en France*; available at: http://www.bibliquest.org/Lortsch/Lortsch-Histoire_Bible_France-1.htm; accessed 5 March 2005; Internet).

[401]Clarence Gallagher, *Canon Law and the Christian Community: The Role of Law in the Church according to the Summa Aurea of Cardinal Hostiensis* (Roma: Universita Gregoriana, 1978), 193.

[402]Manuscripts and dates reconstructed primarily from the writings and translations of Jean Duvernoy, as found on his website: http://jean.duvernoy.free.fr.

    f)   1266-1275 (ms 161, Bibliothèque Municipale, Carcassonne)

    g)   1273-1280 (Toulouse: Ranuphle de Plassac, Pons de Parnac, Pierre Arsieu, Hugues Amiel, and Hugues Bouniols; ms Fonds Doat t. XXV and XXVI, Bibliothèque Nationale, Paris)

    h)   1284-1289 (Jean Galand and Guillaume de Sainte-Seine; ms XXVI, Bibliothèque Nationale, Paris)

    i)   1308-1309 (Carcassonne, Geoffroy d'Albis; ms 4269, Bibliothèque Nationale, Paris)

    j)   1318-1325 (Jacques Fournier, who later became Pope Benedict XII; ms J 127, departmental archives, Ariège)

    k)   1319 (trial of Fr. Bernard Delicieux)

    l)   1319 (Carcassonne: Jean de Beaune; ms J 127, departmental archives, Ariège)

    m)   1323 (Lodève), 1324 (Pamiers), 1325-1327 (Carcassonne; registre DDD; ms Doat 28, Bibliothèque Nationale, Paris)

    n)   1328-1329 (Carcassonne, Prouille, Narbonne, Pamiers, Béziers, Carcassonne; registre GGG; ms Doat XXVII, Bibliothèque Nationale, Paris)

b)   Dates so far unknown to me of the records of other inquisitors:

    (1)   Arnaud de Gouzens et Arnaud de Brassac, inquisitors of the Bishop of Toulouse (mentioned as inquisitors in ms 609, Toulouse)

    (2)   Bernard Gui

    (3)   Bertrand de Tays (ms 4030, Vatican Library)

    (4)   Ferrier et Pons Gary (Fragment of ms 3 J 596, departmental archives of Aude)

    (5)   Guillaume Pelhisson

    (6)   Guillaume de Puylaurens

c)   Dates so far unknown to me of other sites inquisited:

    (1)   Monségur

    (2)   Carcassonne (ms 124 and 202, departmental archives, Haute-Garonne)

    (3)   "Registre du greffier épiscopal de Carcassonne" (Bibliothèque Municipale, Clermont-Ferrand)

d)   Books to assist with inquisitions:

    (1)   Bernard Gui, *Practica Inquisitionis*

    (2)   Raynier Sacconi, O.P., *Summula contra hereticos* (ms Doat XXXVI, Bibliothèque Nationale, Paris; ms 379, Bibliothèque Municipale, Toulouse)

e)   These documents represent a mere fraction of all the available records in various archives and municipal, departmental, and national libraries, as well as a mere fragment of the inquisitions that actually took place (predominantly) in Southern France, as many inquisition records were burned by Jesuits when Napoleon lost power in France. Likewise the Vatican library has not released the Inquisition records for study even after 350 years, so noted Léon-E. Halkin.[403]

f)   It is clear that from the founding of the inquisition as a policy under Pope Lucius III in 1184, in which he instituted organized searches to ferret out heretics, the Roman Catholic church developed a very complex structure for this "Holy Office". In 1184, bishops were assigned this task, that of busying themselves with the task of searching out heretics, arresting then, and turning them over to the secular arm for appropriate punishment [usually burning at the stake]. This specific role of the bishops was reaffirmed in the Fourth Lateran Council of 1215. The entire inquisition complex in every diocese across the Europe [and now the world] engendered a massive amount of records which are stored in Rome.

a.   *Sitz im Leben*—Canons of the Third Lateran Council (aka. 11th Ecumenical Council; 1179).

    "4. Since the apostle decided that he ought to support himself and those accompanying him by his own hands, *so that he might remove the opportunity of preaching from false apostles* and might not be

---

[403]"It is impossible for the historian to describe and to judge the activity employed by the inquisition as organized by Paul III [1534-1549], because not one document bears witness of it. The archives of the Holy Office in Rome must contain a certain number, but they are not entirely permitted to be visited. If the present congregation of the Holy Office persists in its system that is being almost everywhere abandoned of keeping its historical acts as an absolute secret, old as they are by three and a half centuries, not only is she doing a disservice to historical studies, but also to herself, as innumerable are the people who continue to hold as true the worst accusations held against the institution of the Roman inquisition" (Léon-E. Halkin, *Initiation à la critique historique* [Paris: Armand Colin, 1963], 212, n.1; quote of L. Pastor, *Histoire des Papes,* trans. from the German by A. Poizat [Paris, 1930], 12:916; translation mine).

burdensome to those to whom he was preaching, it is recognized that it is a very serious matter and calls for correction that some of our brethren and fellow bishops are so burdensome to their subjects in the procurations demanded that sometimes, for this reason, subjects are forced to sell church ornaments and a short hour consumes the food of many days."

"27. … For this reason, since in Gascony and the regions of Albi and Toulouse and in other places the loathsome heresy of those whom some call the Cathars, others the Patarenes, others the Publicani, and others by different names, has grown so strong that they no longer practise their wickedness in secret, as others do, but proclaim their error publicly and draw the simple and weak to join them, we declare that they and their defenders and those who receive them are under anathema, and we forbid under pain of anathema that anyone should keep or support them in their houses or lands or should trade with them. …we likewise decree that those who hire, keep or support them, in the districts where they rage around, should be denounced publicly on Sundays and other solemn days in the churches, that they should be subject in every way to the same sentence and penalty as the above-mentioned heretics and that they should not be received into the communion of the church, unless they abjure their pernicious society and heresy. As long as such people persist in their wickedness, let all who are bound to them by any pact know that they are free from all obligations of loyalty, homage or any obedience. On these {18, "princes"} and on all the faithful we enjoin, for the remission of sins, that they oppose this scourge with all their might and by arms protect the christian people against them. Their goods are to be confiscated and princes free to subject them to *slavery*" [404]

    1)   Please note the highlighted descriptions of evangelism (above and below).

b.   *Sitz im Leben*—Third Canon of the Fourth Lateran Council (aka. 12th Ecumenical Council; 1215):

"3. on Heretics. We excommunicate and anathematize every heresy raising itself up against this holy, orthodox and catholic faith which we have expounded above. *We condemn all heretics, whatever names they may go under.* They have different faces indeed but their tails are tied together inasmuch as they are alike in their pride. Let those condemned be handed over to the secular authorities present, or to their bailiffs, for due punishment. Clerics are first to be degraded from their orders. The goods of the condemned are to be confiscated, if they are lay persons, and if clerics they are to be applied to the churches from which they received their stipends. Those who are only found suspect of heresy are to be struck with the sword of anathema, unless they prove their innocence by an appropriate purgation, having regard to the reasons for suspicion and the character of the person. Let such persons be avoided by all until they have made adequate satisfaction. If they persist in the excommunication for a year, they are to be condemned as heretics. Let secular authorities, whatever offices they may be discharging, be advised and urged and if necessary be compelled by ecclesiastical censure, if they wish to be reputed and held to be faithful, to take publicly an oath for the defence of the faith to the effect that they will seek, in so far as they can, to expel from the lands subject to their jurisdiction all heretics designated by the church in good faith. Thus whenever anyone is promoted to spiritual or temporal authority, he shall be obliged to confirm this article with an oath. If however a temporal lord, required and instructed by the church, neglects *to cleanse his territory of this heretical filth*, he shall be bound with the bond of excommunication by the metropolitan and other bishops of the province. If he refuses to give satisfaction within a year, this shall be reported to the supreme pontiff so that he may then declare his vassals absolved from their fealty to him and make the land available for occupation by Catholics so that these may, after they have expelled the heretics, possess it unopposed and preserve it in the purity of the faith—saving the right of the suzerain provided that he makes no difficulty in the matter and puts no impediment in the way. The same law is to be observed no less as regards those who do not have a suzerain."

"Catholics who take the cross and gird themselves up for the expulsion of heretics shall enjoy the same indulgence, and be strengthened by the same holy privilege, as is granted to those who go to the aid of the holy Land. *Moreover, we determine to subject to excommunication believers who receive, defend or support heretics…*"

"'Let therefore all those who have been forbidden or not sent to preach, and yet dare publicly or privately to usurp the office of preaching without having received the authority of the apostolic see or the catholic bishop of the place', be bound with the bond of excommunication and, unless they repent very quickly, be punished by another suitable penalty." [405]

404"Third Lateran Council [A.D. 1179]," accessed 28 June 2003; from http://www.dailycatholic.org/history/ 11ecume1.htm; Internet.
    405"Fourth Lateran Council [A.D. 1215]," accessed 28 June 2003; from http://www.dailycatholic.org/ history/12ecume1.htm; Internet.

c. From 1243-1247 Inquisition records: *Cahiers de Bernard de Caux* [O.P.]:[406]

Evangelism was called "hereticking" from to heretic (from French *hérétiquer*; from Latin *hereticare*):[407]

Heretic (from French *hérétiquer*; from Latin *hereticari*): "Item I never saw them heretic anybody" (Lat *Item dixit quod nunquam vidit aliquem hereticari*) (op. cit., 43). For another use of this form see (op. cit., 75, 117, 133, 135, 146, 147).

Heretication (from French *hérétiquation*; from Latin *hereticationi*): "Item when my uncle Raymond de Grimoard went to Corbarieu to be hereticked there, me myself, William Faure of Peche-Hernier, Bertrand of Saint-Andrew, Hugo and John of Cavalsaut and Peter Beraut accompanied this Raymond up to Corbarieu in order that he might be hereticked there. But I did not attend the heretication. It was about twenty years ago" (op. cit., 59)

Hereticked (from French *hérétiquèrent*; from Latin *hereticaverunt*) (op. cit., 29). Other uses of this form see (op. cit., 59, 137, 146, 151)

Hereticking (from French *hérétiquant*; from Latin *hereticantes*): "I saw in the house of Stephen Sans, the "perfects" [Lat *hereticos*; Fr *parfaits*] Pons and Serny hereticking this Stephen Sans at Castelsarrasin" (first apparent use as a verb in *Cahiers de Bernard de Caux,* 21). For other uses see (op. cit., 77, 79, 118).

Was hereticked (from French *fut hérétiqué*; from Latin *fuit hereticatus*): "Item I heard it said to the heretics that Stephen Geraud, father of Bernard Geraud, cousin of the actual Stephen Geraud and of Pons, was hereticked at Moissac. Where he assisted the burning (?) of Vital Grimoard, father of Peter Grimoard ... twenty years ago" (op. cit., 23).[408] Other use of this form (op. cit., 35). For other forms see (op. cit., 97, 117, 126, 127, 131, 133, 134, 135, 145, 151, 155, 164).

Four heretics **who were hereticking** [him] (from French *quatres parfaits qui l'hérétiquaient*; from Latin *quatuor hereticos hereticantes*) (op. cit., 78-79).

Total of at least 31 uses of "hereticking" as a verb in this 1243-1247 document.

On Methodology: The major methodology used by the "Albigenses" was door-to-door evangelism two-by-two and street evangelism. This methodology was recorded throughout the inquisition interrogations, as well as in histories of the Dominicans as they described the methods of their "enemies," the Albigenses:

"Bishop Diego, borrowing from the enemy, recommended to the legates a new type of apostolate. They should give up their other business and devote themselves zealously to preaching. They should send away their followers, travel on foot without money and beg their bread from door to door, imitating the way of life and preaching of the apostles. This was a startling suggestion and the legates were unwilling to accept it. But if someone in authority, a bishop, would go before them, they would gladly follow. Diego was as good as his word. He dismissed his servants, sending them with his horses and baggage back to Osma. He kept at his side only Dominic, his subprior.

---

[406]"Cahiers de Bernard de Caux: Bas-Quercy, Toulousain" Jean Duvernoy, text and trans (Ms Doat XXII, bibliothèque nationale de Paris, 1243; 1988); accessed 8 Sept 2004; from http://jean.duvernoy.free.fr/sources/ sinquisit.htm; Internet; translated into English, Thomas P. Johnston.

[407]"I was a heretic by covering for three and a half years thirty years ago" (Bernard de Caux; Duvernoy, 9). ("Heretic by covering" from Fr *hérétique revêtue;* Lat *heretica induta*). "Item in the other house of Toulouse I saw Guilhabert de Castre, Bishop of the Heretics, and four others perfect [Lat *hereticos*] companions with him. I saw with them Pons Grimoard and John Pagan. It was about twelve years ago" (*ibid.,* 17). "I saw several times William Faure of Peche-Hermier give praise to the sect of the heretics" (*ibid.,* 69). (see also p 127).

[408]Notice the recording of William Faure's abjuration before the inquisitors: "He recognized that he had done wrongly, after having abjured heresy before his inquisitors at Castelsarrasin, to receive the heretics and to adore them [?] as was said. Item he recognized that he had done wrongly yesterday, having sworn by oath and having been requited, to hide skillfully the truth on that which precedes against his own oath. He swore, upon this fact, to hold to the orders of the Church and of the words of the inquisitors *to receive the punishment of perpetual prison or of exil*, all heresy abjured" (*Cahier de Bernard de Caux,* trans. by Duvernoy into French and by Johnston into English, 23).

"…Catholic itinerant missionaries, beginning with Robert of Arbissel at the opening of the twelfth century and ending with Fulk of Neuilly at its close, preached apostolic poverty. Diego's merit lies in seizing upon it now as a method in the Catholic campaign against the Albigenses."[409]

It must be noted, however, that the "Albigensian" evangelists in Southern France did *not* beg for food, as did the Dominicans and Franciscans.[410]

Vaudoisie—to Waldensize (also from *Cahiers de Bernard de Caux*):

Link between hereticking and the Waldenses:

"Also I never saw nor believed heretics, nor did I ever hear the preaching of the Waldenses (Interrogated as to the period of these Waldenses): It is not twenty years, but it may be fifteen to sixteen years ago" (op. cit., 47)
"I saw the Waldenses strolling [*déambulant*] in public on the streets of Montauban, but I never said anything to them. About twenty-years ago [speaking of about 1224]" (op. cit., 115).
"In the year of our Lord 1246, the fourth of the kalendes of July (28 June 1246) the horseman William-Raymond of Castlar, requisitioned to tell the truth on himself and on others dead or alive on the crime of heresy and Waldensizing [*vaudoisie*] testifying under oath said" (op. cit., 121).
Other use of Waldensize in this way (op. cit., 145).

d.   From 1245-1246, 1253, more inquisition depositions from Bernard de Caux:[411]

Waldensize became a part of the interrogation of the inquisitors: "Have you seen the heretics or heard Waldensize in public"
Lat *valdenses* (Bibliothèque Municipale de Toulouse, Manuscript 609A [1245-1246, 1253], Duvernoy [1994-1997], section 163, p 31; section 165, p 31; section 168, p 32; sec 199, p 46; sec 201, p 46; sec 212, p 46; Man 609B, sec 243, p 54; sec 243, p 244; sec 39-43, p 345; sec 98, p 349; sec 1, p 373)
Lat *valdensibus* (Man 609A sec 408, p 105; Man 609B, sec 66-68, p 211; sec 243, 244; sec 98, p 349; sec 5, p 443)
Lat *valdensem* (Man 609B, sec 75, p 424)

e.   From [St.] Thomas Aquinas, O.P., *Summa Theologica* (circa 1275):

Remembering that Aquinas was and is *THE* teacher of the Roman Church, being called the "Angelic Doctor" by at least five of the last ten popes.[412] By the way, notice that this title is found on both sides of Vatican II, showing that Vatican II did not change the status of Aquinas as the "Angelic Doctor," and confirming that Vatican II did not change the essence of the teaching of the Church of Rome.

1)   Evangelism as the sin of sowing discord against Charity (SS, Q[37], A[1]):

"I answer that, Discord is opposed to concord. Now, as stated above (Q[29], AA[1],3) concord results from charity, in as much as charity directs many hearts together to one thing, which is chiefly

---

[409]William A. Hinnebusch, O.P., *The History of the Dominican Order: Origins and Growth to 1500* (Staten Island, NY: Alba House, 1965), 1:23.

[410]The Albigenses believed in hard work, and were not allowed to beg individually, as Duvernoy has made clear (Jean Duvernoy, *Le Catharisme: la religion des Cathares* [Toulouse, France: Privat, 1976], 248-49).

[411]"Le Manuscript 609 [Lauragais]," Bibliothèque Municipale de Toulouse; transcribed by Duvernoy (1994-1997); (online) accessed 8 Sept 2004; from http://jean.duvernoy.free.fr/sources/sinquisit.htm; Internet; translated into English, Thomas P. Johnston.

[412]"Although he made much of the supernatural character of faith, the Angelic Doctor did not overlook the importance of its reasonableness; indeed he was able to plumb the depths and explain the meaning of this reasonableness" (John Paul II, *Fides et Ratio* [14 Sept 1998], 43; the title referring to Thomas Aquinas is found six times in this encyclical, 43, 43, 44, 57, 58, 61). Pius XII, *Mystici Corpis* (29 June 1943), 62; Pius XII, *Divino Afflante Spiritu* (30 Sept 1943), 3, 37; Pius XII, *Mediator Dei* (20 Nov 1947), 32; Pius XII, *Ad Caeli Reginam* (11 Oct 1954), 44; Pius XI, *Casti Connubii* (31 Sept 1930), 6, 94; Pius XI, *Ad Catholici Sacerdotii* (20 Dec 1935), 35, 73, 76; "And let it be clearly understood above all things that when We prescribe scholastic philosophy We understand chiefly that which the Angelic Doctor has bequeathed to us, and We, therefore, declare that all the ordinances of Our predecessor on this subject continue fully in force, and, as far as may be necessary, We do decree anew, and confirm, and order that they shall be strictly observed by all" (Pius X, *Pascendi Dominici Gregis* [8 Sept 1907], 54); Leo XIII, *Providentissimus Deus* (18 Nov 1893), 18.

the Divine good, secondarily, the good of our neighbor. Wherefore discord is a sin, in so far as it is opposed to this concord."[413]

2) The Evangelism of Schismatics (and Evangelicals) as scandalizing (SS, Q[43], A[1]):

"On the contrary, Jerome in expounding Mat. 15:12, 'Dost thou know that the Pharisees, when they heard this word,' etc. says: 'When we read "Whosoever shall scandalize," the sense is "Whosoever shall, by deed or word, occasion another's spiritual downfall."'

"I answer that, As Jerome observes the Greek {skandalon} may be rendered offense, downfall, or a stumbling against something. For when a body, while moving along a path, meets with an obstacle, it may happen to stumble against it, and be disposed to fall down: such an obstacle is a {skandalon}.

"In like manner, while going along the spiritual way, a man may be disposed to a spiritual downfall by another's word or deed, in so far, to wit, as one man by his injunction, inducement or example, moves another to sin; and this is scandal properly so called.

"Now nothing by its very nature disposes a man to spiritual downfall, except that which has some lack of rectitude, since what is perfectly right, secures man against a fall, instead of conducing to his downfall. Scandal is, therefore, fittingly defined as 'something less rightly done or said, that occasions another's spiritual downfall.'"[414]

3) SS, Q[10], A[7], "Whether one ought to dispute with unbelievers in public?"

"Objection 1: It would seem that one ought not to dispute with unbelievers in public. For the Apostle says (2 Tim. 2:14): 'Contend not in words, for it is to no profit, but to the subverting of the hearers.' But it is impossible to dispute with unbelievers publicly without contending in words. Therefore one ought not to dispute publicly with unbelievers [Whereas the Dominican Order, of which Thomas Aquinas was a member, did dispute heretics in public at certain times].

"…On the other hand, in the second case it is dangerous to dispute in public about the faith, in the presence of simple people, whose faith for this very reason is more firm, that they have never heard anything differing from what they believe. Hence it is not expedient for them to hear what unbelievers have to say against the faith."[415]

---

[413]Thomas Aquinas, *Summa Theologica*, SS, Q[37], A[1], "Whether discord is a sin?" This section later reads: "On the other hand, to arouse a discord whereby an evil concord (i.e. concord in an evil will) is destroyed, is praiseworthy. In this way Paul was to be commended for sowing discord among those who concorded together in evil, because Our Lord also said of Himself (Mat. 10:34): 'I came not to send peace, but the sword.'"

[414]Thomas Aquinas, *Summa Theologica*, SS, Q[43], A[1], "Whether scandal is fittingly defined as being something less rightly said or done that occasions spiritual downfall?"

[415]Thomas Aquinas, *Summa Theologica*, SS, Q[10], A[7], from: http://www.ccel.org/ccel/aquinas/summa.html; accessed: 19 June 2008; Internet. Because this entire section is devoted to evangelism from a Roman Catholic point-of-view, I will insert it into this footnote:
"Objection 1: It would seem that one ought not to dispute with unbelievers in public. For the Apostle says (2 Tim. 2:14): "Contend not in words, for it is to no profit, but to the subverting of the hearers." But it is impossible to dispute with unbelievers publicly without contending in words. Therefore one ought not to dispute publicly with unbelievers.
"Objection 2: Further, the law of Martianus Augustus confirmed by the canons [*De Sum. Trin. Cod. lib. i, leg. Nemo] expresses itself thus: "It is an insult to the judgment of the most religious synod, if anyone ventures to debate or dispute in public about matters which have once been judged and disposed of." Now all matters of faith have been decided by the holy councils. Therefore it is an insult to the councils, and consequently a grave sin to presume to dispute in public about matters of faith.
"Objection 3: Further, disputations are conducted by means of arguments. But an argument is a reason in settlement of a dubious matter: whereas things that are of faith, being most certain, ought not to be a matter of doubt. Therefore one ought not to dispute in public about matters of faith.
"On the contrary, It is written (Acts 9:22, 29) that 'Saul increased much more in strength, and confounded the Jews," and that "he spoke . . . to the gentiles and disputed with the Greeks.'
"I answer that, In disputing about the faith, two things must be observed: one on the part of the disputant; the other on the part of his hearers. On the part of the disputant, we must consider his intention. For if he were to dispute as though he had doubts about the faith, and did not hold the truth of faith for certain, and as though he intended to probe it with arguments, without doubt he would sin, as being doubtful of the faith and an unbeliever. On the other hand, it is praiseworthy to dispute about the faith in order to confute errors, or for practice.
"On the part of the hearers we must consider whether those who hear the disputation are instructed and firm in the faith, or simple and wavering. As to those who are well instructed and firm in the faith, there can be no danger in disputing about the faith in their presence. But as to simple-minded people, we must make a distinction; because either

4) SS, Q[10], A[8], "Whether unbelievers ought to be compelled to the faith?"

> "On the contrary, It is written (Lk. 14:23): 'Go out into the highways and hedges; and compel them to come in.' Now men enter into the house of God, i.e. into Holy Church, by faith. Therefore some ought to be compelled to the faith. …

> "On the other hand, there are unbelievers who at some time have accepted the faith, and professed it, such as heretics and all apostates: such should be submitted even to bodily compulsion, that they may fulfil what they have promised, and hold what they, at one time, received.

> "…Accordingly the meaning of Our Lord's words, 'Suffer both to grow until the harvest,' must be gathered from those which precede, 'lest perhaps gathering up the cockle, you root the wheat also together with it.' For, Augustine says (Contra Ep. Parmen. iii, 2) 'these words show that when this is not to be feared, that is to say, when a man's crime is so publicly known, and so hateful to all, that he has no defenders, or none such as might cause a schism, the severity of discipline should not slacken.'"[416]

[In this article Aquinas provided an explanation for the Dominican Order's use of force (i.e. torture) to persuade the Albigenses and Waldenses to recant of their heresy, prior to excommunicating them and turning them over to the secular sword for extirpation (publicly being burned alive, strangled, stretched on a wheel, drowned, or buried alive)].

5) SS, Q[10], A[9] Whether it is lawful to communicate with unbelievers?

> "Communication with a particular person is forbidden to the faithful, in two ways: first, as a punishment of the person with whom they are forbidden to communicate; secondly, for the safety of those who are forbidden to communicate with others."[417]

---

they are provoked and molested by unbelievers, for instance, Jews or heretics, or pagans who strive to corrupt the faith in them, or else they are not subject to provocation in this matter, as in those countries where there are not unbelievers. In the first case it is necessary to dispute in public about the faith, provided there be those who are equal and adapted to the task of confuting errors; since in this way simple people are strengthened in the faith, and unbelievers are deprived of the opportunity to deceive, while if those who ought to withstand the perverters of the truth of faith were silent, this would tend to strengthen error. Hence Gregory says (Pastor. ii, 4): 'Even as a thoughtless speech gives rise to error, so does an indiscreet silence leave those in error who might have been instructed.' On the other hand, in the second case it is dangerous to dispute in public about the faith, in the presence of simple people, whose faith for this very reason is more firm, that they have never heard anything differing from what they believe. Hence it is not expedient for them to hear what unbelievers have to say against the faith.

"Reply to Objection 1: The Apostle does not entirely forbid disputations, but such as are inordinate, and consist of contentious words rather than of sound speeches.

"Reply to Objection 2: That law forbade those public disputations about the faith, which arise from doubting the faith, but not those which are for the safeguarding thereof.

"Reply to Objection 3: One ought to dispute about matters of faith, not as though one doubted about them, but in order to make the truth known, and to confute errors. For, in order to confirm the faith, it is necessary sometimes to dispute with unbelievers, sometimes by defending the faith, according to 1 Pet. 3:15: 'Being ready always to satisfy everyone that asketh you a reason of that hope and faith which is in you [*Vulg.: "Of that hope which is in you" St. Thomas' reading is apparently taken from Bede].' Sometimes again, it is necessary, in order to convince those who are in error, according to Titus 1:9: 'That he may be able to exhort in sound doctrine and to convince the gainsayers.'"

[416]Thomas Aquinas, *Summa Theologica*, SS, Q[10], A[8], from: http://www.ccel.org/ccel/aquinas/summa.html; accessed: 19 June 2008; Internet.

[417]"I answer that, Communication with a particular person is forbidden to the faithful, in two ways: first, as a punishment of the person with whom they are forbidden to communicate; secondly, for the safety of those who are forbidden to communicate with others. Both motives can be gathered from the Apostle's words (1 Cor. 5:6). For after he had pronounced sentence of excommunication, he adds as his reason: 'Know you not that a little leaven corrupts the whole lump?' and afterwards he adds the reason on the part of the punishment inflicted by the sentence of the Church when he says (1 Cor. 5:12): 'Do not you judge them that are within?'

"Accordingly, in the first way the Church does not forbid the faithful to communicate with unbelievers, who have not in any way received the Christian faith, viz. with pagans and Jews, because she has not the right to exercise spiritual judgment over them, but only temporal judgment, in the case when, while dwelling among Christians they are guilty of some misdemeanor, and are condemned by the faithful to some temporal punishment. On the other hand, in this way, i.e. as a punishment, the Church forbids the faithful to communicate with those unbelievers who have forsaken the faith they once received, either by corrupting the faith, as heretics, or by entirely renouncing the faith, as apostates, because the Church pronounces sentence of excommunication on both.

"With regard to the second way, it seems that one ought to distinguish according to the various conditions of persons, circumstances and time. For some are firm in the faith; and so it is to be hoped that their communicating with unbelievers will lead to the conversion of the latter rather than to the aversion of the faithful from the faith. These are

6) SS, Q[10], A[10] Whether unbelievers may have authority or dominion over the faithful?[418]

7) SS, Q[10], A[11] Whether the rites of unbelievers ought to be tolerated?[419]

8) SS, Q[10], A[12] Whether the children of Jews and other unbelievers ought to be baptized against their parents' will?

9) SS, Q[11], A[3] Whether heretics ought to be tolerated?

> "For it is a much graver matter to corrupt the faith which quickens the soul, than to forge money, which supports temporal life. Wherefore if forgers of money and other evil-doers are forthwith condemned to death by the secular authority, much more reason is there for heretics, as soon as they are convicted of heresy, to be not only excommunicated but even put to death.
>
> "On the part of the Church, however, there is mercy which looks to the conversion of the wanderer, wherefore she condemns not at once, but 'after the first and second admonition,' as the Apostle directs: after that, if he is yet stubborn, the Church no longer hoping for his conversion, looks to the salvation of others, by excommunicating him and separating him from the Church, and furthermore delivers him to the secular tribunal to be exterminated thereby from the world by death. …"
>
> "According to Decret. (xxiv, qu. iii, can. Notandum), 'to be excommunicated is not to be uprooted.' A man is excommunicated, as the Apostle says (1 Cor. 5:5) that his 'spirit may be saved in the day of Our Lord.' Yet if heretics be altogether uprooted by death, this is not contrary to Our Lord's command, which is to be understood as referring to the case when the cockle cannot be plucked up without plucking up the wheat, as we explained above (Q[10], A[8], ad 1), when treating of unbelievers in general."[420]

---

not to be forbidden to communicate with unbelievers who have not received the faith, such as pagans or Jews, especially if there be some urgent necessity for so doing. But in the case of simple people and those who are weak in the faith, whose perversion is to be feared as a probable result, they should be forbidden to communicate with unbelievers, and especially to be on very familiar terms with them, or to communicate with them without necessity" (Thomas Aquinas, *Summa Theologica*, SS, Q[10], A[9], from: http://www.ccel.org/ccel/aquinas/summa.html; accessed: 19 June 2008; Internet).

[418]"And so the Church altogether forbids unbelievers to acquire dominion over believers, or to have authority over them in any capacity whatever. … Yet, if there be reason to fear that the faithful will be perverted by such communications and dealings [working the lands of unbelievers], they should be absolutely forbidden" (Thomas Aquinas, *Summa Theologica*, SS, Q[10], A[10], from: http://www.ccel.org/ccel/aquinas/summa.html; accessed: 19 June 2008; Internet).

[419]"On the contrary, Gregory [*Regist. xi, Ep. 15: cf. Decret., dist. xlv, can., Qui sincera] says, speaking of the Jews: 'They should be allowed to observe all their feasts, just as hitherto they and their fathers have for ages observed them.'

"I answer that, Human government is derived from the Divine government, and should imitate it. Now although God is all-powerful and supremely good, nevertheless He allows certain evils to take place in the universe, which He might prevent, lest, without them, greater goods might be forfeited, or greater evils ensue. Accordingly in human government also, those who are in authority, rightly tolerate certain evils, lest certain goods be lost, or certain greater evils be incurred: thus Augustine says (De Ordine ii, 4): 'If you do away with harlots, the world will be convulsed with lust.' Hence, though unbelievers sin in their rites, they may be tolerated, either on account of some good that ensues therefrom, or because of some evil avoided. Thus from the fact that the Jews observe their rites, which, of old, foreshadowed the truth of the faith which we hold, there follows this good—that our very enemies bear witness to our faith, and that our faith is represented in a figure, so to speak. For this reason they are tolerated in the observance of their rites. On the other hand, the rites of other unbelievers, which are neither truthful nor profitable are by no means to be tolerated, except perchance in order to avoid an evil, e.g. the scandal or disturbance that might ensue, or some hindrance to the salvation of those who if they were unmolested might gradually be converted to the faith. For this reason the Church, at times, has tolerated the rites even of heretics and pagans, when unbelievers were very numerous" (Thomas Aquinas, *Summa Theologica*, SS, Q[10], A[11], from: http://www.ccel.org/ccel/aquinas/summa.html; accessed: 19 June 2008; Internet).

[420]Thomas Aquinas, *Summa Theologica*, SS, Q[11], A[3], from: http://www.ccel.org/ccel/aquinas/ summa.html; accessed: 19 June 2008; Internet.

f.   From 1273-1280, "Registre de l'Inquisition de Toulouse: Registre de [Pons de] Parnac [O.P.]" Trans. into French by Jean Duvernoy:[421]

Asked about what they knew about heresy or Waldensizing (*vaudoisie*):

"In the year of our Lord 1273, day before the kalendes of July [30 June] Michael of Peche-Rodil from Burgundy who lives in Peche-Rodil in the diocese of Rodez testifies under oath and interrogated on the question of heresy and Waldensizing, if he has seen perfects [heretics], says he knows nothing at all" (p 8)

"...Jean Leroux says the same thing as the others except that when he was in his country of Burgundy he saw two Waldenses burned [at the stake]," p 8

"...interrogated on the fact of heresy and of Waldensizing, said nothing as before. He said however after having been silent and denied the truth: ... [long deposition]" (p 17)

"The year of our Lord 1273, Thursday before the chair of Saint Peter [16 Jan] Gardouche, cavalier from Mauremont testified under oath and required to tell the truth on the fact of heresy and of Waldensizing both on himself as on others dead or alive, said that after confessing to the inquisitor Bernard de Caux and to his colleague, he had neither seen nor worship [with] the perfects [heretics], had not eaten or drunk, had not sent any of his goods to the perfects, had had no contact with them, had not thought that they were good men and that they say the truth, nor that we could be saved by them, nor had received any *faidits* or fugitives for heresy. He said the same thing for the Waldenses. He deposed this before the Brothers Ranulphe de Plassac and Pons de Parnac, OP, inquisitors. Testified by Robin, sergeant guard of those condemned to the Wall, and me Bernard Bonnet, notary public of the inquisition who wrote it" (p 45) [footnote states that the man deposed had been jailed at the Wall approximately 30 years]

g.   From 1308-1309, "Registre de Geoffroy d'Ablis":[422]

Includes many uses of hereticking [verbal form of heretic]

Albigensian [Fr. *Albigeois*] used as a description of the sect (p 153)

h.   From the 1318-1325 Inquisition Record of Jacques Fournier, who became Pope Benedict XII (1334-1342), comes a summary of the house to house evangelism of a Cathar missionary from the preface of Emmanuel Le Roy Ladurie:

"Conversion to heresy, as well, was accomplished by successive blocks, house by house, and not necessarily by individual persons. Pierre Authié, the admirable Cathar missionary of Sabartès, believed that conversion to the faith was operated household by household, hearth to hearth, much more than individual conscience to conscience: "God wanted that I come to your home," said he to the gathered family of Raymond Peyre, "so that I can save the souls of the people who live in this home." For Pierre Authié homes are the packages of souls, that are rallied in block to such and such a faith."[423]

i.   Roman Catholics Persons and Methods Used for Mission (i.e. "Great Commission") in 12th and 13th Centuries:

1)   Persons in question:

a)   12th Century: Roman Catholic Bernard of Clairvaux (Cistercian) and Peter the Venerable (Cluniac), and during the time of the Evangelical Henry of Lausanne (see above)

b)   13th Century: Roman Catholic Francis of Assisi and Dominic, founder of the Dominicans

2)   Mission for the Roman Catholics:

a)   Reclaiming the Holy Land (crusades for the "Kingdom of God," i.e. the Church) for Bernard of Clairvaux (nor had he any appreciation for the Albigenses, by the way)

---

[421]"Registre de l'Inquisition de Toulouse: Registre de Parnac," Jean Duvernoy, trans.; (online) accessed 8 Sept 2004; from http://jean.duvernoy.free.fr/sources/ sinquisit.htm; Internet; translated into English, Thomas P. Johnston.

[422]"Registre de Geoffroy d'Ablis," Ms Latin 4269, Bibliotheque Nationale de Paris; et notes, Jean Duvernoy, ed and trans into French (1980); (online) accessed 8 Sept 2004; from http://jean.duvernoy.free.fr/sources/ sinquisit.htm; Internet; translated into English, Thomas P. Johnston.

[423]Emmanuel Le Roy Ladurie, "Preface," in *Le Registre d'Inquisition de Jacques Fournier,* translated by Jean Duvernoy (Paris: Bibliotheques des Introuvables, 2006), 1:viii-ix.

b)   "Extirpating heresy," from Southern France for the Dominicans[424]

3)   Used method of the "enemy", the heretic Albigenses:

a)   Door-to-door apostolic preaching[425]

b)   The Albigenses, however, believed in hard work, and were not allowed to beg individually as did the Dominicans[426]

4)   The Message of the Preaching Orders:

a)   Other than the title "preaching orders" given to the Franciscans and Dominicans, because of their itinerant open air "preaching" (not being attached to one diocese in particular), the exact message of these Friars is hard to ascertain, other than apostolic poverty and the importance of a proper allegiance to all the teachings of the Church of Rome for "true" salvation[427]

b)   Francois Giraud explained the primary message of Dominic:

"While he was seeking in fasting, penitence, and prayer the method to effectively oppose the Albigenses, he had an apparition of the Holy Mary that told him, 'Know that the principle weapon that was used by the Holy Trinity to reform the world was the Angelic Psalter [the Rosary] that is the foundation of the New Testament; this is why, if you want to win unto God these hardened hearts, preach the Psalter.' Beginning from this day, Saint Dominic never ceased to recite and preach the meditation of the Angelic Psalter. He obtained wonderful results, founded numerous brotherhoods for the recitation of this prayer, as well as the order of the Dominicans and, finally, the cathar heresy was extinguished in the 14th Century."[428]

c)   Notice how this coincides with the message of salvation (reserved only for Bishops) in the Council of Trent:

"But since the preaching of the Gospel is no less necessary to the Christian commonwealth than the reading thereof, and since this is the chief duty of the bishops … either personally or, if they are lawfully impeded, through others who are competent, feed the people committed to them with wholesome words in proportion to their own and their people's mental capacity, by teaching them those things that are necessary for all to know in order to be saved, and by impressing upon them with briefness and plainness of speech the vices that they must avoid and the virtues that they must cultivate, in order that they may escape eternal punishment and obtain the glory of heaven."[429]

---

[424]"By an official document, which is still extant, Bishop Foulques constituted Brother Dominic and his companions preachers in the diocese of Toulouse. They were to [1] extirpate heresy, [2] combat vice, [3] teach the faith, and [4] train men in good morals" (Pierre Mandonnet, O.P., *St. Dominic and His Work,* trans by Mary Benedicta Larkin, O.P. [St. Louis: B. Herder, 1948], 27). "Extirpate" is defined as "root out, extirpate; pull/pluck out/up by roots; eradicate root and branch" (*Whittaker's Words*; BibleWorks 9.0).

[425]William A. Hinnebusch, O.P., *The History of the Dominican Order*, 1:23.

[426]Jean Duvernoy, *Le Catharisme: La Religion des Cathares* (Toulouse, France: Privat, 1976), 248-49.

[427]Notice how [Pope] Clement XIII described proper preaching for leaders in the Church of Rome: "They should go to both testaments of the Bible, to the traditions of the Church, and to the writings of the holy fathers, as if they were going to springs from which pours forth a pure and undefiled teaching of faith and character. They should read often and reflect upon the Roman Catechism, the summation of Catholic teaching, which provides holy sermons to give to the faithful" (Clement XIII, *A Quo Die* [13 Sept 1758]; available at: http://www.ewtn.com/library/ENCYC/C13AQUOD.HTM; accessed: 22 April 2001; Internet).

[428]"En 1214, alors qu'il cherchait dans le jeûne, la pénitence et la prière une manière de s'opposer efficacement aux Albigeois, il eut une apparition de la Vierge Marie qui lui dit : 'Sache que la principale arme dont s'est servie la Sainte Trinité pour réformer le monde a été le Psautier Angélique qui est le fondement du Nouveau Testament ; c'est pourquoi, si tu veux gagner à Dieu ces cœurs endurcis, prêche mon Psautier'. A partir de ce jour, Saint Dominique ne cessa de réciter et de prêcher ma méditation du Psautier Angélique. Il obtint de merveilleux résultats, fonda de nombreuses confréries de récitation de cette prière en plus de l'ordre des Dominicains et, finalement, l'hérésie cathare s'éteignit au XIV siècle" (Francois Giraud, "Le Rosaire"; from http://francois.giraud1.free.fr/annexes/rosaire/rosaire.htm; accessed: 5 July 2003).

[429]"Council of Trent [1545-1563]: Concerning Reform [17 June 1546], Chapter 2"; from http://www.forerunner.com/chalcedon/X0020_15._Council_of_Trent.html; accessed 8 Jan 2005; Internet.

i. Sample articles against John Wycliffe from the Council of Constance:[430]

"7. If a person is duly contrite, all exterior confession is superfluous and useless for him."

"13. Those who stop preaching [cf. evangelizing] or hearing the word of God on account of an excommunication issued by men are themselves excommunicated and will be regarded as traitors of Christ on the day of judgment."

"42. It is ridiculous to believe in the indulgences of popes and bishops."

j. Sample articles against John Hus also from the Council of Constance:

"17. A priest of Christ who lives according to his law, knows scripture and has a desire to edify the people, ought to preach [cf. evangelize], notwithstanding a pretended excommunication. And further on: if the pope or any superior orders a priest so disposed not to preach, the subordinate ought not to obey."

"18. Whoever enters the priesthood receives a binding duty to preach [cf. evangelize]; and this mandate ought to be carried out, notwithstanding a pretended excommunication."[431]

k. Similar statements in the Council of Trent regarding preaching:

"But since the preaching of the Gospel is no less necessary to the Christian commonwealth than the reading thereof, and since this is the chief duty of the bishops…"

"…Regulars of whatever order, unless they have been examined by their superiors regarding life, morals and knowledge and approved by them, may not without their permission preach even in the churches of their order, and they must present themselves personally with this permission before the bishops and ask from these the blessing before they begin to preach."

"…Moreover, let bishops be on their guard not to permit anyone, whether of those who, being regulars in name, live outside their monasteries and the obedience of their religious institute, or secular priests, unless they are known to them and are of approved morals and doctrine, to preach in their city or diocese, even under pretext of any privilege whatsoever, till they have consulted the holy Apostolic See on the matter; from which See it is not likely that privileges of this kind are extorted by unworthy persons except by suppressing the truth or stating what is false."[432]

3. **Summary of Primary 13th and 14th Century Terminology for Evangelism:**

"Dogmatizing in public and openly preaching:"

1221   "The heretics lurk in this region [Bosnia] from their dens," wrote [Pope] Honorius III in 1221, "but, after the example of the vampire that breastfeeds its young with naked breast, they dogmatize in public and openly preach their depraved errors."[433]

"Secretly circulating … preaching the Gospel:"

1215   From Dutch Dominican inquisition guidelines: "Question him thus: … How often have you confessed to the teachers of the heretics, who secretly circulate that they have come into the world in the place of the apostles, to go from place to place, preaching the Gospel?"[434]

"Secretly… spreading divers strange errors:"

1215   From "the papistic writer Trithemius": "At this time, namely A. D. 1215, there were very many heretics secretly, men as well as women, who spread divers strange errors throughout all Germany, France, and Italy; of whom great numbers were apprehended and burned alive."[435]

---

[430]"Council of Constance [1414-1418]," accessed 23 Sept 2004; available from http://www.dailycatholic.org/history/16ecume1.htm; Internet.

[431]Ibid.

[432]"Council of Trent [1545-1563]: Concerning Reform, Chapter 2 [17 June 1546]"; from http://www.forerunner.com/chalcedon/X0020_15._Council_of_Trent.html; accessed 8 Jan 2005; Internet.

[433]Christine Thouzellier, *Un traité cathare inédit du debut du XIIIe siècle d'après le Liber Contra Manicheos de Durand de Huesca* (Louvain: Publications Universitaires, 1961), 38; citing Potthast 6725; T. Smičiklas, *Codex…*, III, p. 196 (171), 3 déc. 1221; - Potthast 6749; *Codex…*, p. 198 (174), 5 déc. 1221: *"in partibus Bosnie… heretici receptati… dogmatizando palam sue pravitatis errores"*; translation from the French mine.

[434]From the 1215 Dominican "Mode of Examination" of the suspected Waldenses; Thieleman J. van Braght, *The Bloody Theater or Martyrs Mirror of the Defenseless Christians Who Baptized Only Upon Profession of Faith…*, trans by Joseph F. Sohm (1660; 1748; 1837; 1853; Scottdale, PA: Herald Press, 2007), 312.

[435]From Trithemius, *Chron. Hirsaug.*, in van Braght, *The Bloody Theater,* 313.

"**Hereticking**" (Latin, *hereticari*)

"**Waldensizing**" (French, *vaudoisie*)

"**Lollardy**" (English, of followers of Wycliffe and their preaching)[436]

"**Preaching without [Papal] authorization**":

> 1215   Innocent III's Article in the Fourth Lateran Council, "preaching without having received the authority."[437]

> 1382   Archbishop of Canterbury, William Courtenay, in meeting at Chapter house of Blackfriars, London, "in the arrest of unauthorized preachers."[438]

4.   **Sample 15th-16th Century Terminology for Evangelism (both positive and negative uses):**

"**Announcer of the Word of God**" [15th Century]:

> "M. Iean Beverlan, announcer of the Word of God [1413]."[439]

---

[436]"This book is an attempt to step back from recent debates, and examine lollardy from a different, and really quite unfashionable, point of view: as a sin and a crime" (Ian Forrest, *The Detection of Heresy in Late Medieval England*, vii). "After [William] Courtenay became archbishop of Canterbury he attacked the problem of Lollardy, a movement of stemming from adherents of Wyclif. A council of made up of seven bishops and a large group of learned theologians met at the Chapter house of Blackfriars, London, on May 1382. After study of the twenty-four propositions, ten were condemned as heretical, four as erroneous. Parliament shortly afterwards enacted a statute providing that government would assist the hierarchy in the arrest of unauthorized preachers" (Dorothy B. Weske, "Book Review," of Joseph Dahmus, *William Courtenay, Archbishop of Canterbury, 1382-1396* (University Park, PA: Pennsylvania State University, 1966), in *Speculum*, 43:3 [July 1968], 502). "Also important to the initial spread of Wycliffe's ideas were the various clerics who favoured such beliefs. Preaching amongst the laity was an important way to spread dissent, especially after a purge of Oxford University in 1382. Preachers received protection from local knights and manual craftsmen, like William Smith in Leicester, were able to spread Lollard ideas to a wider audience" ("Lollardy," from: http://www.britannia.com/history/articles/lollardy.html; accessed 30 April 2007; Internet).

[437]"There are some who holding to the form of religion but denying its power (as the Apostle says), claim for themselves the authority to preach, whereas the same Apostle says, How shall they preach unless they are sent? Let therefore all those who have been forbidden or not sent to preach, and yet dare publicly or privately to usurp the office of preaching without having received the authority of the apostolic see or the catholic bishop of the place', be bound with the bond of excommunication and, unless they repent very quickly, be punished by another suitable penalty." ("Fourth Lateran Council [A.D. 1215]," accessed 28 June 2003; from http://www.dailycatholic.org/history/12ecume1.htm; Internet).

[438]Dorothy Weske, "Book Review," 502.

[439]Jean Crespin, *Histoire des vrays Tesmoins de la verite de l'evangile, qui de leur sang l'ont signée, depuis Jean Hus iusques autemps present* (Geneva, 1570; reproduction, Liège, 1964), 14b. Translation mine.

Council of Trent: "**Aggressive Spirits**" (of the door-to-door Bible salesmen):
> Defining the evangelism of evangelists as displaying "aggressive spirits" or in the French, "esprits agressifs" (Latin: *petulantia*)
> Compare with Noll's conceptual parallel below under "Activism" (1994)

From Lortsch (citing Migne, 1840)[440]	From Fordham.edu (unknown translation into English)[441]
§ 16. Pour arrêter et contenir les esprits agressifs (petulantia),	§ 2. Furthermore, to check[442] unbridled spirits,
le Concile ordonne que dans les choses de la foi ou de la conduite en tant que celle-ci concerne le maintien de la doctrine chrétienne, personne, se confiant en son propre jugement, n'ait l'audace de tirer l'Écriture sainte à son sens particulier, ni de lui donner des interprétations, ou contraires à celles que lui donne et lui a données la Sainte Mère l'Église	it decrees that no one relying on his own judgment shall, in matters of faith and morals pertaining to the edification of Christian doctrine, distorting the Holy Scriptures in accordance with his own conceptions,[5] presume[443] to interpret them contrary to that sense which holy mother Church,[444]
à qui il appartient de juger du véritable sens et de la véritable interprétation des Saintes Écritures,	to whom it belongs to judge of their true sense and interpretation,[6] has held and holds, [this last phrase is placed before Holy Mother Church in French]
ou opposées au sentiment unanime des Pères,	or even contrary to the unanimous teaching of the Fathers,
encore que ces interprétations ne dussent jamais être publiées (*1).	even though such interpretations should never at any time be published.
Les contrevenants seront déclarés par les ordinaires (*2), et soumis aux peines fixées par le droit.	Those who act contrary to this shall be made known by the ordinaries and punished in accordance with the penalties prescribed by the law.
(1) *Etiamsi nullo unquam tempore in lucem edendae forent.* Donc, ce que le Concile interdit, ce n'est pas seulement de *publier*, c'est aussi de *concevoir* des interprétations contraires à celle de l'Église [trans. "Therefore, what the Council prohibits, is not only the act of *publishing*, it is also the *conceiving* interpretations contrary to those of the Church"]. (2) *L'Ordinarius*, c'est le chef du diocèse	[5] Acts 5:41; Eph 2:14. [6] Ps 68:14.[445]

"**Brought poor ignorant ones to Jesus Christ**" (1562)[446]

Throughout Crespin one finds biblical language used to describe the ministry of the martyrs for the Gospel, which should come as no surprise, being the Bible was the source from which ministry was defined for the nascent Reformed church in France and Switzerland.

"**Confession of the Gospel**":

"Five men of Northfolk [England] were put to death for [their] confession of the Gospel [1507-1512]."[447]

"**Disturber of the peace of a Christian Republic**" [of French Bible colporteur Bartholomew Hector]:

"As obstinate and declared a **heretic, schismatic, reproved and separated from the church**, and returned to the secular judge to be burned according to the law. … The said court has condemned and condemns the said Bartholomew Hector to be burned alive in the plaza of the castle of the town on the day of the market, as heretic and schismatic declared by the sentence of the above mentioned Vicar and

---

[440]Samuel Lortsch, *Histoire de la Bible en France* (available at: http://www.bibliquest.org/Lortsch/Lortsch-Histoire_Bible_France-1.htm; accessed 5 March 2005; Internet).

[441]Council of Trent, Fourth Session (8 Apr 1546), "Decree Concerning the Edition and Use of the Sacred Books" (from: http://www.forerunner.com/chalcedon/X0020_15._Council_of_Trent.html; accessed: 8 Jan 2005; Internet).

[442]Notice the combination of two verbs into, "check." The verbs in French are "to stop and contain."

[443]Instead of "presume," a better translation, if the French is more accurate, is the verb "to have temerity." It appears that the English translation softens the emotionally-charged language considerably.

[444]Notice the lack of capital letters on "holy mother" as related to Church in English.

[445]Notice that the English translation, prepared for a mainly Protestant audience, includes Scritural citations in the footnotes.

[446]Crespin, 600v. Translation mine.

[447]Ibid., 56. Translation mine.

Inquisitor, and **as seducer and disturber of the peace of the Christian republic, and breaker of the King's edicts and ordinances.**[448]

"Dogmatizers"—1558 French edicts against the "**dogmatizers**" [Fr. les dogmatizants]:[449]

"The King having come there [to Paris], and having firstly taken advice from the guardian of the seal, interviewed them [the enemies of the Gospel], and added grievous edicts to counter those who call themselves Sacramentalists, for not wanting to receive transubstantiation, **to counter the dogmatizers**, of those who find themselves in assemblies [churches], or who are found caught with [heretical] books."[450]

"To dogmatize" was the charge against member of the Paris Parliament, Anne du Bourg, who was soon to be martyred:

"Asked then the names of those with whom he took Communion, prior to his arrest, he refused, as he had already done, at the time of his first questioning, saying that his profession was not that of a denouncer, and that anyways he could declare with a clear conscience that, other than four people whom he recognized, 'each kept themselves covered and disguised, fearing being known, as it is done in such assemblies and congregations.' The clerk, after having taken note of the answers, warned that he had an order from the Court to arrest him, if, when he left City Hall, 'he meddled **to dogmatize** or speak things contrary to the honor of God and o our Holy Mother the Church and the commandments of the same.'" Du Bourg responded that he had no desire **to dogmatize** nor to 'give any occasion for the people to be scandalized.'"[451]

"Dogmatizing" (used in French, from the interrogation of a colporteur before his death sentence):

"And to ensure that the errors of the heretics not pollute [further], the aforementioned Court [of Bordeaux, France] inhibits and forbids every kind of person, with the penalty of heresy [i.e. excommunication = the death penalty[452]], to gather and convene, nor to **dogmatize** and hold any propositions not consonant with the holy faith."[453]

"Evangelizing" (used in French):

"There were Bible colporteurs, similar to ours, for whom the primary work was **evangelization**."[454]

---

[448]Crespin, 440b. Translation mine. Similarly, Benoit Romyen was called [im]pertinent (Fr. pertinax), ibid., 472.

[449]Note that the French Geneva Bible of 1560 translated μαθητεύω in Matthew 28:19 as "dogmatize".

[450]Crespin, 491a-b. Translation mine.

[451]Matthieu LeLièvre, *Portraits et récits Huguenots,* première série (Toulouse: Société des Livres Religieux, 1903), 246-47; LeLièvre quoted *Mémoires de Condé*, 1:302. Translation mine.

[452]Thomas Aquinas, O.F.P., that "Great Angelic Doctor," wrote his *Summa Theologica* as an apologetic for Catholicism and the practices of his Order, the Dominicans, in their inquisition against and extirpation of the Evangelical Albigenses. For example, in the Section "Secunda Secundae", Question 11, Aquinas addressed "Heresy":
Article 1 defined heresy: "Therefore heresy is a species of unbelief, belonging to those who profess the Christian faith, but corrupt its dogmas."
Article 2 defined heretical faith by quoting Jerome: "If anything therein has been incorrectly or carelessly expressed, we beg that it may set aright by you who hold the faith and see of Peter. If however this, our profession, be approved by the judgment of your apostleship, whoever may blame me, will prove that he himself is ignorant, or malicious, or even not a catholic but a heretic."
Article 3, explained whether heretics should be tolerated: "I answer that, With regard to heretics two points must be observed: one, on their own side; the other, on the side of the Church. On their own side there is the sin, whereby they deserve not only to be separated from the Church by excommunication, but also to be severed from the world by death. ...much more reason is there for heretics, as soon as they are convicted of heresy, to be not only excommunicated but even put to death.
"On the part of the Church, however, there is mercy which looks to the conversion of the wanderer, wherefore she condemns not at once, but 'after the first and second admonition,' as the Apostle directs: after that, if he is yet stubborn, the Church no longer hoping for his conversion, looks to the salvation of others, by excommunicating him and separating him from the Church, and furthermore delivers him to the secular tribunal to be exterminated thereby from the world by death" (Thomas Aquinas, "Heresy" from Section "Secunda Secundae", Question 11, *Summa Theologica* [from http://www.newadvent.org/summa/3011.htm]; accessed 2 Oct 2007; Internet).

[453]Crespin, 436b. Translation mine.

[454]Lortsch, *Histoire de la Bible en France* [accessed: 5 March 2005; from: http://www.bibliquest.org/Lortsch/Lortsch-Histoire_Bible_France-1.htm; Internet], 1:26).

"Explaining":

"Students and gentilmen, said Calvin, were transformed into colporteurs, and, under the shadow of selling their merchandise, they offered all the faithful the weapons for the holy combat of the faith. They crossed the kingdom [of France], selling and **explaining** the Gospels."[455]

"Huguenoted":

"Many of those who followed [the Duke of Guise], Jacquais and pages, rejoiced to themselves of the plan [to destroy the Huguenots of Vaissy, France], saying, that the pillaging would be for them, vowed death and blood for **those that would have been Huguenoted**."[456]

"Imparting [heresy]"

"The final sentence reproaches him thus: That has come to pass concerning thee which the Apostle says (2 Tim. iii. 13), 'But evil men and seducers shall wax worse and worse, deceiving and being deceived;' for in Venice, and throughout many following years, proceeding from bad to worse, not only hast thou persisted in former heresies, but thou hast adopted others, imparting them to other persons similarly heretical and suspected, as well by reading many of the heresiarchs, Martin Luther's works, and those of other heretical and prohibited authors, as also by thy sustained intercourse with many and divers heretics."[457]

"Initiating ... to the Gospel":

"It was Olivétan who was, the first, **to initiate his cousin John Calvin to the Gospel**. He caused him 'to taste something of pure religion,' said Theodore Beza. He counseled him to read the Scriptures. 'Calvin, having followed this counsel, began to become distracted from papal superstitions.'"[458]

"To maintain the just quarrel of the Gospel":

"All know only too well that the said Portuguese and even the French who travelled to these regions [Brazil], never spoke one word of our Lord Jesus Christ to the poor folk of that country. Seeing that the three persons (the death of whom is contained hereafter) who exposed themselves to death as the first fruits **to maintain the just quarrel of the Gospel**. It would be an unthoughtful thing and of very terrible consequence, to leave their memory as buried and snuffed out among men. And it would come one day their blood will ask vengeance because of the forgotten memory of those who had the opportunity to make it heard in all the earth."[459]

"Ministry of the divine Word"; "Minister of the Word of God":

"In the year 1558, Brother Hans Smit, a minister of the Word of God, was sent forth by the church to seek and gather those that were eager for the truth. Acts 13:3. When he therefore, being divinely called, undertook to travel through the Netherlands, he, together with five brethren and six sisters, was apprehended in the city of Aix-la-Chapelle, on the ninth of January. While they were assembled there in a house, to speak the Word of God, and were engaged in prayer, many servants and children of Pilate came there in the night through treachery, with spears, halberds, and bare swords, and well provided with ropes and bonds, and surrounded the house, and bound and apprehended these children of God."[460]

"Thus did God help him [Hans Brael] to make his escape that night, which took place in the year 1559, and thus he returned in peace and with joy to the church of the Lord, his brethren. Subsequently he again went up into the country, several times, as the ministry of the divine Word had been committed to him."[461]

---

[455]Ibid., 1:25.

[456]Crespin, 591b. Translation mine.

[457]Leopold Witte, *A Glance at the Italian Inquisition: A Sketch of Pietro Carnesecchi: His Trial ... and His Martyrdom in 1566*; translated from the German by John T. Betts (London: The Religious Tract Society, 1885), 44.

[458]"C'est Olivétan qui, le premier, initia son cousin Jean Calvin à l'Évangile. Il lui fit 'goûter quelque chose de la pure religion,' dit Théodore de Bèze. Il lui conseilla de lire l'Écriture. 'Calvin, ayant suivi ce conseil, commença à se distraire des superstitions papales'" (Lortsch, *Histoire de la Bible en France*; accessed: 5 March 2005; from: http://www.bibliquest.org/Lortsch/ Lortsch-Histoire_Bible_France-2.htm; Internet], 2:4).

[459]Crespin, 442b. Translation mine.

[460]Van Braght, 588.

[461]Van Braght, 563.

"Missionary work": Samuel Lortsch, writing of the evangelistic work of Bible translator, Pierre Robert Olivétan:

> "He returned to the valleys [of the Alps] in July, in order to return to **his missionary work**."[462]

"Preach," "dogmatize," and "Exhort" (used in French, from the interrogation of a colporteur before his death sentence):

> "Interrogated if he had **preached** and **dogmatized** in the aforementioned valleys and elsewhere where he brought his books, if there were **preachers** there, if he had heard them, and who sent them, and if those of Geneva sent him to carry these books. He responded that he was not a minister with such and such a holy charge. Well had he **exhorted** those with whom he had something to do, to live according to the commandments of God, and not according to those of the Roman church, which were actually against God. … He had also remonstrated them to live as Christians. Not to be lazy, thieves, nor swear, neither drunkards, which he said, not as preaching, but rather as familiar advise without being sent, and that from any movement."[463]

After first being assured safe passage, the same, Bartholomew Hector, was judged by the Vicar and Inquisitor of Turin [Italy] (on the 19 June 1556)—see above under "disturber of the peace of a Christian republic."

"Seducer" [see above with "disturber of the peace of a Christian Republic"].

"Spread errors or scandals … preach heresies":

> "But if, which heaven avert, a preacher should **spread errors or scandals** among the people, let the bishop forbid him to preach, even though he preach in his own or in the monastery of another order. Should he **preach heresies**, let him proceed against him in accordance with the requirement of the law or the custom of the locality"[464]

"Persuade" in Queen Elizabeth I's 1593 "Act against the Puritans"[465]

"Preach, or teach, or to give audience" in Queen Elizabeth I's 1558 first proclamation to limit preaching.[466] Her 1559 "Act of Uniformity" expounded on the same theme, making the Book of Common prayer the measure of all preaching: "or shall preach, declare, or speak anything in the

---

[462] "Il retourna aux Vallées en juillet, afin d'y reprendre ses travaux missionnaires." (Ibid., 2:6).

[463] Crespin, 438. Translation mine.

[464] "Council of Trent [1545-1563]: "Concerning Reform," Chapter 2 [17 June 1546]"; from http://www.forerunner.com/chalcedon/X0020_15._Council_of_Trent.html; accessed 8 Jan 2005; Internet.

[465] "…If any person or persons above the age of sixteen years… by printing, writing, or express words or speeches, advisedly and **purposely practise or go about to move or persuade** any of her majesty's subjects, or any other within her highness's realms or dominions, to deny, withstand, and impugn her majesty's power and authority in causes ecclesiastical, united, and annexed to the imperial crown of this realm; or **to that end or purpose shall advisedly and maliciously move or persuade** any other person whatsoever to forbear or abstain from coming to church to hear divine service, or to receive the communion according to her majesty's laws and statutes aforesaid, **or to come to or be present at any unlawful assemblies, conventicles, or meetings**, under colour or pretence of any exercise of religion, contrary to her majesty's said laws and statutes… that then every such person so offending as aforesaid, and being thereof lawfully convicted, shall be committed to prison" ("The Acts against Puritans [1593]"; from http://history.hanover.edu/texts/engref/er86.html; accessed 20 Sept 2008).

[466] "The queen's majesty understanding that there be certain persons having in times past the office of ministry in the Church, which now do purpose to use their former office in preaching and ministry, and partly have attempted the same, assembling specially in the city of London, in sundry places, great number of people, whereupon riseth among the common sort not only unfruitful dispute in matters of religion, but also contention and occasion to break common quiet, hath therefore, according to the authority committed to her highness for the quiet governance of all manner her subjects, thought it necessary to charge and command, like as hereby her highness doth charge and command, all manner of her subjects, as well those that be called to ministry in the Church as all others, that they do **forbear to preach, or teach, or to give audience** to any manner of doctrine or preaching other than to the Gospels and Epistles, commonly called the Gospel and Epistle of the day, and to the Ten Commandments in the vulgar tongue, without exposition or addition of any manner, sense, or meaning to be applied and added; or to use any other manner of public prayer, rite, or ceremony in the Church, but that which is already used and by law received; or the common Litany used at this present in her majesty's own chapel, and the Lord's Prayer, and the Creed in English; until consultation may be had by Parliament, by her majesty and her three estates of this realm, for the better conciliation and accord of such causes, as at this present are moved in matters and ceremonies of religion" ("Queen Elizabeth's Proclamation to Forbid Preaching [1558]"; from: http://history.hanover.edu/texts/ENGref/er77.html; accessed 20 Sept 2008; Internet; taken from Henry Gee and William John Hardy, eds., *Documents Illustrative of English Church History* [New York: Macmillan, 1896], 416-17).

derogation or depraving of the said book, or anything therein contained, or of any part thereof…"[467] In the 1571 Canons, Elizabeth forbid preaching without permission from the Bishop of the area.[468]

"Publique preaching" in the "42 Articles of the Church of England" (Thomas Cranmer, 1552; this article is identical [other than changes in spelling] to Article 23 of the 39 Articles of Religion of the Church of England [Matthew Parker, 1563, 1571, 1572]):

"XXIV. *No man ne maie minister in the Congregation, except he be called.* **It is not lawful for any man to take vpon him the office of Publique preaching,** or ministring the sacramentes in the congregation, before he be lawfullie called, and sent to execute the same. And those we ought to iudge lawfullie called, and sent, whiche be chosen, and called to this woorke by menne, who haue publique auctoritie geuen vnto them in the congregation, to cal, and sende ministres into the Lordes vineyarde."[469]

"Publish … preaching … announcing the way of salvation":

"Even though Satan knew how to kindle and oppose the rage of his own against the truth of the Gospel, the Sons of God always showed their own virtue above that of all power, and that there was no obstacle that was able to hinder the work of those who were ordained **to publish it**. And how much in this time it seemed that all access to **the preaching** of the same, was closed in the country of France, if it would not have been for some who surmounted all difficulty, exposed their lives **to announce to the ignorant the way of salvation**."[470]

5.   Sample 16ᵗʰ Century Terminology for Methodology:

Bible Colporteurs prior to and following the Reformation of Geneva:

"Shortly before the arrival of the Bishop and the Duke, another power had arrived in Geneva; this power was the Gospel. At the end of the prior year, in October and November 1522, Lefèvre had published his French translation of the New Testament. At the same time, the friends of the Word of God chased from Paris, found refuge in various provinces. The negotiator Vaugris, nobleman from Du Blet, was in Lyons, and he sent from there Gospels and New Testaments to [the regions of] Bourgogne, in Dauphiné, to Grenoble and Vienna, such that in 1523 the Word of God, which would soon abolish the pagan superstitions, and that would now abolish the embryonic interests of Rome, had arrived on the shores of *Lac Léman* [aka. Lake Geneva]. … The names of the pious men, who first carried to the people of Geneva the Holy Scriptures, have not been any better preserved than those of the second century missionaries; it is quite ordinary that in the darkest night great fires are lit. Several Genevans 'gathered with them and purchased their books,' added the [Roman] manuscript. … What! They had hoped that the pompous entrance of Charles and Beatrice would assure their triumph, and come-to-find that an unknown book, mysteriously entered into the town, without pomp, without coverings, without golden draperies, humbly carried on the back of several poor colporteurs, seems destined to produce greater impact that the presence of the brother-in-law of [Holy Roman Emperor] Charles V and of the daughter of the King of Portugal."[471]

"There were Bible colporteurs, similar to ours, for whom the primary work was evangelization."[472]

---

[467]"Elizabeth's Act of Uniformity (1559)"; from http://history.hanover.edu/texts/engref/er80.html; accessed 20 Sept 2008.

[468]"No one without the bishop's permission shall publicly preach in his parish, nor shall he venture hereafter to preach (concionari) outside his cure and church, unless he has received permission so to preach" (from http://history.hanover.edu/texts/engref/er82.html; accessed 20 Sept 2008.).

[469]"42 and 39 Articles of Religion"; from: http://www.episcopalian.org/efac/1553-1572.htm; Accessed: 21 Oct 2004; Internet.

[470]Crespin, 450. Translation mine.

[471]J.-H. Merle D'Aubigné, *Histoire de la Réformation en Europe au Temps de Calvin* (Paris: Michel Lévy Frères, 1863), 1:327-30. Translation mine.

[472]Hereafter is the context in French: "Le colportage des Livres saints ne se faisait pas seulement sous forme indirecte. Il y eut des colporteurs bibliques, analogues aux nôtres, pour qui la grande affaire c'était l'évangélisation. Réfugiés à Genève, à Lausanne et à Neuchâtel, pour fuir la persécution qui faisait rage en France, ils étaient troublés en pensant que, de l'autre côté du Jura, les moissons blanchissantes réclamaient des ouvriers. Alors ils partaient, emportant avec eux un ballot de livres, qu'ils dissimulaient de leur mieux, souvent dans une barrique, que les passants supposaient contenir du vin ou du cidre. Ce fut de cette manière que *Denis Le Vair*, qui avait évangélisé les îles de la Manche, essaya de faire pénétrer en Normandie une charge de livres de l'Écriture. Comme il faisait marché avec un charretier pour le transport de son tonneau, deux officiers de police, flairant une marchandise suspecte, lui demandèrent si ce n'étaient point par hasard des 'livres d'hérésie' qu'il transportait ainsi. — 'Non,' répondit Le Vair, 'ce sont des livres de

"These colporteurs later carried forbidden Bibles from Geneva into France. They evangelized and some founded churches where they went. Many of them were caught and paid the ultimate sacrifice for their zeal for the Gospel and the Word of God. Lortsch named eleven such French Bible colporteur who died as martyrs, sometimes burned with their Bibles, sometimes preaching before they died, sometimes with their tongues cut out so that they could not preach when they were burning: Denis Le Vair, Philibert Hamelin, Jean Joëry and his servant, Étienne de La Forge [friend of Farel and Calvin], Macé Moreau, Nicolas Nail, Nicolas Ballon, Étienne Pouillot, Marin Marie, and Jacques de Loo."[473]

The **Bible colporteur** methodology continued to be used until the time of Dwight L. Moody and beyond [notice that a Bible colporteur does Bible colportage]:

"Early in 1896, he [Moody] established the Bible Institute Colportage Association, headed by his son-in-law, A. P. Fitt. This effort reached millions of people with Christian literature. In an era before Christian bookstores, 2000 individuals, or 'colporteurs,' sold the books, keeping a small commission from each sale."[474]

From a **Carrier of Images** to a **Carrier** [Fr. Porteur] **of the Books of the Holy Scriptures**:

"Macé Moreau touched by the fear of God, and of a desire to be instructed in the true knowledge of the Word, retired to Geneva: wherein being there for not a short time, by a sudden change of quality and of his first condition, from a **carrier of** [religious] **images**, he became a **carrier of the books of the Holy Scriptures**. It came to be that being loaded with a number of the aforementioned books, he made his way to France, to sell and distribute them there. [he was burned alive with his Bible in 1550 in Troyes, France]"[475]

Gospel Tracts used to convert Margaret of Valois (1523), sister of Francis I, King of France:

"But there was especially one soul, in the court of Francis I, who seemed prepared for the evangelical influence of the doctor from Étaples and the Bishop of Meaux. Margaret, uncertain and unsure, in the midst of the corrupt society that surrounded her, sought something firm, and she found it in the Gospel. She turned herself to this new wind that was reinvigorating the world, and she inhaled with delight the emanations from heaven. She learned from several of the ladies in her court what was being taught by the new doctors; **their writings were communicated to her, their small books, called in the language of the times 'tracts'**; they spoke to her of 'the primitive church, the pure Word of God, worship in spirit and in truth, Christian liberty that removes the yoke of the superstitions and traditions of men to attach itself uniquely to God.' Soon this princess met Lefèvre, Farel, and Roussel; their zeal, their piety, their beliefs, everything in them struck her; but it was especially the Bishop of Meaux [Briçonnet], long acquaintance of hers, who became her guide in the path of faith."[476]

Gospel Tracts then used by Margaret of Valois to convert princess Philabert of Savoie (d. 1524), Margaret's mother's sister:

"She became attached to Margaret, who by her talents and virtues exercised a great influence over all around her. Philabert's grief opened her heart to the voice of religion. Margaret imparted to her all she read; and the widow of the lieutenant-general of the Church began to taste the sweets of the doctrine of salvation."[477]

Tracts, which were often included articles for a disputation, sermons, or parts of sermons, were used extensively by the so-called Anabaptist Balthasar Hubmaier in the 1520s, as well as by the English Baptists in the 1630s and 40s. This pattern seemed to continue until well after the founding of the following printing societies (a mere sampling):

English Baptist Missionary Society was founded in 1792
London Tract Society was founded in 1799

---

la Sainte Écriture, contenant toute "vérité.'" Il ne cacha pas qu'ils lui appartenaient et l'usage qu'il voulait en faire. Traîné de prison en prison, il fut finalement condamné, par le parlement de Rouen, à être brûlé vif, et il souffrit le martyre avec une admirable constance" (Lortsch, *Histoire de la Bible en France*, 1:30-33).

[473]*Ibid.*

[474]George Sweeting, "Moody's Legacy: A Century after His Death His Ministries Continue to Touch Lives;" accessed 18 April 2006; from http://www.moodymagazine.com/articles.php?action=view_article&id=559; internet.

[475]Jean Crespin, 181v. Translation mine.

[476]J.-H. Merle d'Aubigné, *Histoire de la Réformation du Seizième Siècle* (Paris: Firmin Didot Frères, 1867), 3:508-09. Translation mine.

[477]J. H Merle d'Aubigné, *History of the Reformation of the Sixteenth Century,* trans by H. White and Heidelberg, revised by the author (Edinburgh: Oliver & Boyd, 1849), 450.

British and Foreign Bible Society was founded in 1804 (from a discussion in the board room of the London Tract Society)

New-York Tract Society was founded in 1812

Baptist Board of Foreign Missions was founded in 1814

American Bible Society was founded in 1816

Baptist General Tract Society was founded in 1824.[478]

In the case of the British and Foreign Bible Society they could report in their Sixteenth Report (1820): "The Auxiliaries of the Society itself amount to 265, and the Branch Societies to 364; forming together a total as of last year, of 629."[479]

Conclusion: We conclude this section with [Pope] Leo XIII's assessment of the Reformation Era, a time period which the shedding of much blood, both Anabaptist, Protestant, and many other non-Catholics, and allowed some freedom to evangelize:

> "The terrible storm which swept over the Church in the sixteenth century, deprived the vast majority of the Scottish people, as well as many other peoples of Europe, of that Catholic Faith which they had gloriously held for over one thousand years."[480]

6. **Evangelizing in American Colonial Period—primarily as "The Work of Conversion":**

a. Richard Baxter (1615-1691), in *The Reformed Pastor*: "**The work of conversion**, of repentance from dead works, and faith in Christ, must be taught first and in a frequent and thorough manner."[481]

b. Increase Mather, president of Harvard (1685-1701), stated in 1683:

> "There is already a great death upon religion, little more left than a name to live.... Consider we then how much it is dying representing the [very] being of it, by the general failure of **the work of conversion**, whereby only it is that religion is propagated, continued and upheld in being, among any people. As converting doth cease, so does religion die away; though more insensibly, yet most irrecoverably.... How much it is dying, respecting the visible profession and practice of it, partly by the formality of churches, but more by the hypocrisy and apostasy of formal hypocritical professors."[482]

c. Solomon Stoddard (1643-1729), grandfather of Jonathan Edwards, in a sermon titled "A Plea for Fervent Preaching," spoke of the general "want of good preaching" in his day in 1723:

His outline was as follows:

> "1. If any be taught that frequently men are ignorant of the **Time of their Conversion**, that is not good preaching;
>
> "2. If any be taught that Humiliation is not necessary before Faith, that is not good preaching;
>
> "3. When Men don't Preach much about the danger of Damnation, there is a want of good preaching;
>
> "4. If they give a wrong account of the nature of Justifying Faith, that is not good preaching;
>
> "5. If any do give false sign of Godliness, that is not good preaching;

---

[478]Thomas P. Johnston, "Organizing for Outreach—A Historical and Theological Look at Organizational Development Among Baptists With a Particular Emphasis on the Early Nineteenth Century," Seminar paper given at the Southern Baptist Theological Seminary, 1999.

[479]"British and Foreign Bible Society, Abstract of Sixteenth Report," *Christian Watchman & Baptist Register,* Vol 2, New Series No. 7 (January 27, 1821): 1.

[480]Leo XIII, *Caritatis Studium* (25 July 1898); available at: http://www.ewtn.com/library/ENCYC/ L13CARIT.HTM; accessed: 8 Sept 2004; Internet.

[481]Richard Baxter, *The Reformed Pastor* (Portland, OR: Multnomah, 1982; based on William Orme's edition of 1920, first edition, 1656), 15. "The work of conversion is the first and most vital part of our ministry. For there are those who are Christian only in name, who have need to be truly 'born again.' ... The next part of the ministry is the upbuilding of those that are truly converted'" (ibid., 73). Baxter even extolled the benefits of personal ministry [evangelism], "Personal ministry is a vital advantage for the conversion of many souls" (ibid., 106), and encouraged church members in personal witness, "(2) Urge them to step out and visit their poor, ignorant neighbors. (3) Urge them to go often to the impenitent and scandalous sinners around them, to deal with them in all possible skill and earnestness" (ibid., 136).

[482]Increase Mather quoted in Isaac Backus, *A History of New England With Particular Reference to the Denomination of Christians Called Baptists,* vols. 1-3, 2nd ed. with notes (1777, 1784, 1796; Newton, MA: Backus Historical Society, 1871; New York: Arno Press and The New York Times, 1969), 1: 458-59.

"The reading of sermons is a dull way of Preaching."[483]

He continued, "See the reason why there is little effect in preaching. There is much good preaching, and yet there is want of good preaching."
"1. For hence it is that there is **so little Conversion**;
"2. Hence many men that make a high profession, lead Unsanctified lives."[484]

Other concepts used by Stoddard in this sermon:
1) "No Saving Knowledge of Christ";
2) "No Experience of a Saving Change"
3) "No experience of a work of Humiliation";
4) "A sincere Convert";
5) "The way of Salvation is Preached";
6) "Paul knew the time of his conversion";
7) "Conversion is the greatest change that men undergo in this world, surely it falls under Observation";
8) "Accept the calls of the Gospel in Sincerity";
9) "Men must feel themselves dead in sin, in order to their Believing";
10) "If sinners dn't hear often of Judgment and Damnation, few will be Converted";
11) "Christ knew how to deal with Souls, and Paul followed His Example";
12) "Jutifying Faith is set forth in the Scriptures by many figurative expressions; Coming to Christ, Opening to Him, sitting under his Shadow, flying to Him for Refuge, building on Him as on a foundation, feeding on Him, etc.";
13) "Why is there seldom noise among the Dry Bones";
14) "Conversion-work will fail very much where there is not Sound Preaching."[485]

d.   Jonathan Edwards (1703-1758) also used "**work of conversion**" multiple times in his *A Narrative of Surprising Conversions*: "And the work of *conversion* was carried on in a most *astonishing* manner, and increased more and more; souls did as it were come by flocks to Jesus Christ."[486] Other terms used by Edwards were:

1) **Awakened, awakening**:

"The continual news kept alive the talk of religion, and did greatly quicken and rejoice the hearts of God's people, and much awakened those who looked on themselves as *left behind,* and made them the more earnest that they might also *share* in the great blessings that others had obtained."[487]

"This has appeared to be a very extraordinary dispensation, in that the Spirit of God has so much extended not only his *awakening,* but *regenerating* influences, both to *elderly* persons, and also to those who are *very young.*"[488]

2) **Harvests** (the term of his grandfather, Solomon Stoddard):

"And as he [The Rev. Mr. Stoddard] was eminent and *renowned* for his gifts and grace; so he was blessed, from the beginning, with *extraordinary success* in his ministry, in the conversion of many souls. He had five harvests, as he called them. The *first* was about 57 years ago; the *second* about 53; the *third* about 40; the *fourth* about 24; and the *fifth* and last about 18 years ago. . . .but in each of them, I have heard my grandfather say, the greater part of the *young* people in the town, seemed to be mainly concerned for their eternal salvation."[489]

3) **Concerned for their eternal salvation**: "the greater part of the young people in the town, seemed to be mainly concerned for their eternal salvation."[490]

---

[483]Richard L. Bushman, ed. *The Great Awakening: Documents on the Revival of Religion, 1740-1745* (Chapel Hill, NC: University Press, 1969), 11-15.

[484]Ibid., 15-16.

[485]Ibid., 11-16.

[486]*Jonathan Edwards on Revival* (Edinburgh: Banner of Truth, 1999), 13. Similarly, William Cooper used the term "Preaching of it [the gospel]" (ibid., 75-76, William Cooper, "Preface," in *The Distinguishing Marks of a Work of the Spirit of God* [1741]).

[487]Ibid., 16-17.

[488]Ibid., 20.

[489]Ibid., 8-9.

[490]Ibid.

4) **"Conversion of many souls"**:[491]

"Our *young people*, when they met, were to spend the time talking of the *excellency* and dying *love* of JESUS CHRIST, the glory of the way of *salvation*, the wonderful, free, and sovereign grace of God, his glorious work in the *conversion* of the soul, the *truth* and certainty of the great things of God's word, the sweetness of the views of his perfections, *&c.*"[492]

5) **"Converting influences"**[493]

6) **Convince others**:

"They are so greatly taken by their new discovery, and things appear so plain and so rational to them, that they are often at first ready **to think that they can convince other**s; and are apt to engage in talk with every one they meet with, *almost* to this end; and when they are disappointed , are ready to wonder that their reasonings seem to make no more impression."[494]

7) **House to house**:

"She felt a strong inclination immediately to go forth to warn sinners; and proposed it the next day to her brother to assist her in going house to house; but her brother restrained her by telling her the unsuitableness of such a method."[495]

8) **"Ingathering of souls"**[496]

9) **Justification by faith alone**: "There were some things said *publicly* on that occasion, concerning *justification by alone*."[497]

10) **Making converts**: Some accused Edwards of being "fond of making a great many converts and of magnifying the matter."[498]

11) Results of evangelism, according to Edwards a person "truly born again," and "the revival of religion."[499] Edwards described a woman who "longed to have the whole world saved."[500] He explained this woman's zeal, "[This same woman] expressed, on her deathbed, an exceeding longing, both for persons in a natural state, that they might be converted, and for the godly, that they might see and know more of God."[501]

e. Gibert Tennent, in "The Danger of Unconverted Ministry" (1740):

"What if some instances could be shown of unconverted ministers being instrumental in **convincing persons of their lost state**? The thing is very rare and extraordinary. And, for what I know, as many instances may be given of Satan's convincing persons by his temptations. Indeed, it's a kind of chance-medly, both in respect of the father and his children, when any such event happens. And isn't this the reason why **a work of conviction and conversion** has been so rarely heard of for a long time in the churches till of late, that the bulk of her spiritual guides were stone-blind and stone-dead?"[502]

---

[491]Ibid.

[492]Ibid., 14-15.

[493]Ibid., 42.

[494]Ibid., 43.

[495]Ibid., 57-58.

[496]Ibid., 9, 17, 17.

[497]Ibid., 11.

[498]Ibid., 21.

[499]Ibid, 20, 148.

[500]Ibid., 60.

[501]Ibid., 61.

[502]Gilbert Tennent, "The Danger of Unconverted Ministry"; accessed: 20 Oct 2008; from: http://www.sounddoctrine.net/Classic_Sermons/Gilbert%20Tennent/danger_of_ unconverted.htm; Internet.

7. **Sample Terminology in the 19ᵗʰ Century:**

a. Charles Grandison Finney, *Finney on Revival:* One of the chapters in *Finney on Revival* is titled "How to Approach Sinners." In this chapter Finney discussed practical pointers in evangelism:

1) **Conversing**: "Seize the *earliest opportunity* to **converse** with those around you who are careless. Do not put it off from day to day, thinking a better opportunity will come."[503]

2) **Interview**: "Appoint a time or place, and get an **interview** with your friend or neighbour, where you can speak to him freely."[504]

3) In conclusion: "Make it an object of constant study, and of daily reflection, and pray to learn **how to deal with sinners** so as to promote their conversion. It is the great business on earth of every Christian to **save souls**. ... *Now if you are thus neglecting the MAIN BUSINESS of life, what are you living for?*"[505]

b. Charles Grandison Finney, *Lectures on Revival*:

1) **"Witness," "spread the Gospel," and "preach the Gospel"**:

"God leaves the Christian in the world to be his witnesses, as our text affirms [Isa 43:10]. ... When the church at Jerusalem herded together instead of going out into all the world to spread the Gospel as Christ had commanded, God allowed persecution and dispersed them. Then they preached the Gospel everywhere as God's appointed witnesses."[506]

2) Finney's 1835 Compromise? Adding to proclamation "Mainly by their lives":

"Christians should speak for Christ on every proper occasion—by their lips, **but mainly by their lives**. Christians have no right to silence themselves. They should rebuke, exhort, and persuade with all patience, and with right doctrine. **But their main influence as witness is by example**. They witness in this way **because example teaches with force superior to words**. This is universally accepted: 'Actions speak louder than words.' But where both word and deed are applied, even stronger influence persuades the mind."[507]

By the way, there seems to be a definite change in tone between the Finney in *Finney on Revival* and the Finney in *Lectures on the Revival of Religion*. This is definitely worth further study (e.g. Was this change due to Finney or was it his editors? Was his methodological change chronological?)!

c. *Harper's Magazine* (1883):

Quaker Exhorter: In the July 1883 edition of *Harper's Magazine* was found the woodcut of a "**Quaker exhorter**" in a New England town square.[508]

From 1568-1570 the office of "**Exhorter**" was a part of the Church of Scotland, as recorded in their

---

[503]Charles G. Finney, *Finney on Revival,* arranged by E. E. Shelhamer (1834, 1839, 1850, 1868; Minneapolis: Bethany House, 1988), 75.

[504]Ibid., 75.

[505]Ibid., 78.

[506]Charles Grandison Finney, *Lectures on Revival,* Kevin Walter Johnson, ed., a modified edition of *Lectures on Revivals of Religion,* 1835 (Minneapolis: Bethany House, 1988), 94.

[507]*Ibid.,* 95-96.

[508]William W. Sweet, *The Story of Religion in America* (New York: Harper & Bros, 1930), ii.

Register of Ministers, Exhorters, and Readers (1830).[509]

The Church of God, Cleveland, Tennessee, used the level, "**Exhorter Rank**," in its 1993 Ministerial Guide.[510] Their *Minutes of the 2012 Church of God* explained the five "Qualifications of Exhorters" and seven "Rights and Authorities."[511]

According to *Encyclopedia of Protestantism*, the exhorter was an unordained lay preacher, appearing in the Moravian Church, but also among 19th Century Methodists.[512]

d. James Gall's *The Evangelistic Baptism* (1888):

1) **Evangelise**:

"The second great exhibition and experiment for which this world was selected as the theatre was intended to show the grandeur and power of Divine love as the only antidote for sin; and commenced upon the day of Pentecost, when the Holy Ghost was poured forth on the hundred and twenty disciples, and when they were definitely sent out to **evangelise** the world."[513]

"As it required an entire Christ to redeem and sanctify the Church, so it requires a whole Church to **evangelise** the world."[514]

2) **Propagative power**:

"But Old Testament Christianity was not **evangelistic**, and had no **propagative power**."[515]

3) **Evangelistic**:

"What, then, was to be the special and peculiar work which the Holy Ghost was to carry on, after the preliminary work had been completed, and when the Church was enabled to go forth, enriched and equipped with the Holy Scripture complete? It was purely and strictly **evangelistic**."[516]

4) **Witness-bearing**:

"**Witness-bearing** lay at the bottom of the whole system, and without **witness-bearing** there is no Paraclete. 'After the Holy Ghost is come upon you,' 'ye shall be witnesses unto me, both in

---

[509]Alexander McDonald, *Register of Ministers, Exhorters, and Readers*, No. 5 (Glasgow: Maitland Club, 1830). For example, page 44 of this book includes nine people with the office of Exhorter in various towns in Scotland from 1567-1572.

[510]Church of God [Cleveland, Tennessee], *Study Guide for Ministerial Licensure: Exhorter Rank* (Cleveland, TN: Church of God, Office of Ministerial Development, 1993).

[511]"I. Qualifications of Exhorters: 1. The church recognizes the exhorter as a regular rank of the ministry. It is, however, the primary rank, and all applicants for the ministry must serve as exhorter before being promoted in rank, except ordained ministers coming from other reputable organizations. 2. Must have the baptism in the Holy Ghost. 3. The candidate for exhorter must be actively engaged in this ministry either in evangelistic or pastoral work before being recommended for licensing. 4. Must be thoroughly acquainted with the Teachings and Doctrines of the Church of God a set forth by the International General Assembly. 5. Must successfully pass the examination given by a duly constituted board of examiners.

"II. Rights and Authorities: The exhorter shall have full right and authority to 1. Preach and defend the gospel of Jesus Christ. 2. Serve as evangelist. 3. Serve as pastor of a church. 4. In cases of emergency the exhorter may be authorized by the state overseer to baptize converts and receive believers into fellowship of church membership. 5. When an exhorter is serving as pastor, and where state laws recognize the credential of an exhorter as those of a duly authorized minister of the gospel, the exhorter may solemnize the rites of matrimony. 6. Exhorters who are serving as helpers and assistants may receive tithes when available. 7. The exhorter must be active in the ministry, and shall be required to pay tithes [into the local church where his or her membership is located] and make monthly reports to the state overseer and to the secretary general. The exhorter may be promoted to the rank of ordained minister when deemed qualified by the state overseer and others concerned" (Daniel L. Black, ed. *Minutes of the 2012 Church of God (Cleveland, TN)*, 154-55; available at: http://books.google.com/books?id=Zk4FrxyR-R4C&pg=PA154&dq=exhorter&hl=en&sa=X&ei=qVsEVN_MBs-dyATxhoKwAw&ved=0CFIQuwUwCA#v=onepage&q=exhorter&f=false (online); accessed: 1 Sept 2014; Internet.

[512]"Exhorter" in J. Gordon Melton, ed. *Encyclopedia of Protestantism* (Facts on File, 2005).

[513]James Gall, *The Evangelistic Baptism Indispensable to the Church for the Conversion of the World*, in "Science of Mission" series (Edinburgh: Gall and Inglis, 1888), 29.

[514]*Ibid.*, 45.

[515]*Ibid.*, 49.

[516]*Ibid.*, 101.

Jerusalem, in all Judea, and in Samaria, and unto the uttermost part of the earth.' It was to fit them for this **witness-bearing** that the Holy Ghost came upon them."[517]

e.   Personal evangelism as "**personal work**": D. A. Reed (1887) [quoted below], R. A. Torrey (1901),[518] John T. Faris (1916),[519] Charles Zahniser (1927):[520]

"In concluding, let me summarize: 'What can the ordinary church do to reach the masses?' ... (6) **Make much of personal work**, the efforts of individuals whose hearts are full of love for souls. Have a band of men and women trained in the Bible, who shall know how to use it and love to use it, ready to work in all meetings of an evangelistic character in the inquiry-room, ready to go and see individuals and converse with them about their spiritual needs, wise to win souls."[521]

f.   Door-to-door Canvassing:
Charles F. Thwing in *The Working Church* (New York: Baker and Taylor, 1888, 1889) devoted a chapter explaining the importance that every church, city and rural, by canvassing every home in their area to ascertain their spiritual needs. He called for the use of religious surveys.

8.   **Sample Terminology in the 20th Century:**

See also "Negative Views of Evangelism" and "Evangelism as Proselytism" below.

a.   **Prompter, Prompting**:

The ministry of a prompter was to urge people to go forward when an invitation was given.[522]

b.   "Evangelization" in Modern Roman Catholicism:

1965-1968, Note the unusual change in the use of "evangelization" in modern Roman Catholicism, remembering that neither Vatican II nor the 1994 *Catechism of the Catholic Church* changed Rome's understanding of salvation, the Eucharist, works, "faith alone," indulgences, or any of its other distinctive [or heretical] doctrines:[523]

"First, the Council began the recovery of the word *evangelization* for Catholics. In contrast to Vatican I, which used the term *gospel* only once, Vatican II mentions the *gospel* 157 times, *evangelization* 31 times, and *evangelize* 18 times."[524]

---

[517]*Ibid.*, 101-02.

[518]Reuben A. Torrey, *Personal Work* [part one of *How to Work for Christ*] (New York: Revell, 1901).

[519]John T. Faris, *The Book of Personal Work* (New York: Doran, 1916).

[520]Charles Reed Zahniser, *Case Work Evangelism: Studies in the Art of Christian Personal Work* (New York: Revell, 1927).

[521]Rev. Dr. D. A. Reed, "Proceedings of the Second Convention of Christian Workers in the United States and Canada, Sept 21-28, 1887," from Charles F. Thwing, *The Working Church* (New York: Baker and Taylor, 1888, 1889), 125.

[522]" A number of them said that they got many people to go to church; others said they had persuaded some to go forward when the invitation was given" (Dawson Trotman, *Born to Reproduce* [Colorado Springs: NavPress, 1984], 18-19).

[523]"The Second Vatican Council wished to be, above all, a council on the Church. Take in your hands the documents of the Council, especially "Lumen Gentium", study them with loving attention, with the spirit of prayer, to discover what the Spirit wished to say about the Church. In this way you will be able to realize that there is not—as some people claim—a 'new church', different or opposed to the 'old church', but that the Council wished to reveal more clearly the one Church of Jesus Christ, with new aspects, but still the same in its essence" (John Paul II, "Mexico Ever Faithful," *Osservatore Romano* [5 Feb 1979], 1). By the way, the "old" and "new" language has been regularly used by the Roman church to equivocate on the role of Vatican II in the life of the Roman Catholic Church (e.g. John Paul II, *Tertio Millennio Adviente,* 14 November 1994, section 18).

[524]Thomas P. Rausch, S.J., "Introduction," in *Evangelizing America,* ed. by Thomas P. Rausch (Mahwah, NJ: Paulist, 2004), 3. Rausch cited Avery Dulles, "John Paul II and the New Evangelization—What Does It Mean?" in *John Paul and the New Evangelization,* ed. by Ralph Martin and Peter Williamson (San Francisco: Ignatius, 1995), 25.

1975, Paul VI, *Evangelii Nuntiandi—On Evangelization in the Modern World* (Rome, 8 Dec 1975).

Analyzing as Avery Dulles above, the encyclical *Evangelii Nuntiandi*, building on the momentum from Vatican II, used the following words:

"Evangelization", 108 times;
"Evangelizing", 32 times;
"Evangelizers", 14;
"John the Evangelist", once;
"Evangelists", once; and
"Evangelism", none.

One must keep in mind that, according to Roman Catholic teaching, the encyclical *Evangelii Nuntiandi* provided the Church's infallible interpretation on "evangelization" being from the Vicar of Christ, the Pope.

The 20th Century Roman church, therefore, decided to use the terminology of heretics ("evangelize") in order to absorb the heretics, much like the 13th Century Roman church used the methodology of heretics ("apostolic preaching")in order to extirpate the heretics. In large part, the 20th Century strategy was successful (as was the 13th Century strategy). Mainline Protestant churches have authored and signed agreement after agreement with the Vatican since Vatican II. Quoting from one of my papers on the subject:

"In fact, according to Paul VI, *Evangelii Nuntiandi* (8 Dec 1975), without the Catholic Church Evangelicals are not obeying the Great Commission:

"'16. There is thus a profound link between Christ, the Church and evangelization. During the period of the Church that we are living in, it is she who has the task of evangelizing. This mandate is not accomplished without her, and still less against her.[525]

"Nor do those without the Roman hierarchy have complete evangelism without the sacraments:

"'47. Evangelization thus exercises its full capacity when it achieves the most intimate relationship, or better still, a permanent and unbroken intercommunication, between the Word and the sacraments. In a certain sense it is a mistake to make a contrast between evangelization and sacramentalization, as is sometimes done.[526]

"Also, without the proper Eucharist, Evangelicals and Baptists do not have the full Gospel message:

"'28. …For in its totality, evangelization—over and above the preaching of a message—consists in the implantation of the Church, which does not exist without the driving force which is the sacramental life culminating in the Eucharist.[527]

"And further, evangelism without the universal church has no power:

"'63.[§3] Evangelization loses much of its force and effectiveness if it does not take into consideration the actual people to whom it is addresses, if it does not use their language, their signs and symbols, if it does not answer the questions they ask, and if it does not have an impact on their concrete life. But on the other hand, evangelization risks losing its power and disappearing altogether if one empties or adulterates its content under the pretext of translating it; if, in other words, one sacrifices this reality and destroys the unity without which there is no universality, out of a wish to adapt a universal reality to a local situation.

---

[525]This portion continues as follows: "It is certainly fitting to recall this fact at a moment like the present one when it happens that not without sorrow we can hear people--whom we wish to believe are well-intentioned but who are certainly misguided in their attitude--continually claiming to love Christ but without the Church, to listen to Christ but not the Church, to belong to Christ but outside the Church. The absurdity of this dichotomy is clearly evident in this phrase of the Gospel: "Anyone who rejects you rejects me." And how can one wish to love Christ without loving the Church, if the finest witness to Christ is that of St. Paul: "Christ loved the Church and sacrificed himself for her"?" (Paul VI, *Evangelii Nuntiandi* [8 Dec 1975]).

[526]This portion also continues: "It is indeed true that a certain way of administering the sacraments, without the solid support of catechesis regarding these same sacraments and a global catechesis, could end up by depriving them of their effectiveness to a great extent. The role of evangelization is precisely to educate people in the faith in such a way as to lead each individual Christian to live the sacraments as true sacraments of faith--and not to receive them passively or reluctantly." (ibid).

[527]Ibid.

Now, only a Church which preserves the awareness of her universality and shows that she is in fact universal is capable of having a message which can be heard by all, regardless of regional frontiers.[528]

"So there we are, Baptists and Evangelicals, like little lost sheep out in the cold: no commission, no evangelism, no message, no power, and on top of that, no church!"[529]

It would seem that this sudden change in the use of the verb "evangelize," ever so nuanced as it was, became enough to convince leading Evangelicals like Billy Graham, that the Roman Catholic church had changed, and had become open to Great Awakening evangelism. They were sorely mistaken. The church had not changed.[530]

1994   *Catechism of the Catholic Church*:

The words "Evangelism" and "Evangelist" are not found in the index of the Catechism. Perhaps these words and what they signify was deemed an unnecessary inclusion as many Evangelicals were then ready to sign the regional Evangelicals and Catholics Together Statement by 1994.

9. Sample Negative Views of Evangelism:

Evangelists as an Epidemic:

1178   Henry of Clairveaux: "This epidemic had made such an advance, that these people not only have given themselves priests and pontiffs, but that they also had evangelists, who, corrupting and annulling the truth of the gospel, were shaping other gospels. They preach on the Gospels and the epistles and other Holy Scriptures that they corrupt in explaining them, as the teachers of error incapable of being disciples of the truth, since the preaching and explanation of the Scriptures are absolutely prohibited to lay people."[531]

Preaching without Papal authorization as heresy:

1215   "There are some who holding to the form of religion but denying its power (as the Apostle says), claim for themselves the authority to preach, whereas the same Apostle says, How shall they preach unless they are sent? Let therefore all those who have been forbidden or not sent to preach, and yet dare publicly or privately to usurp the office of preaching without having received the authority of the apostolic see or the catholic bishop of the place', be bound with the bond of excommunication and, unless they repent very quickly, be punished by another suitable penalty."[532]

1275   Thomas Aquinas (see quotes above)

---

[528]Ibid.

[529]Thomas P. Johnston, "The Shifting Ecumenical Posture of Roman Catholicism" (Kansas City, MO: Midwestern Baptist Theological Seminary, Oct 2005), 26-27.

[530]Note the words of John Paul II on the pretended change: "The Second Vatican Council wished to be, above all, a council on the Church. Take in your hands the documents of the Council, especially "Lumen Gentium", study them with loving attention, with the spirit of prayer, to discover what the Spirit wished to say about the Church. In this way you will be able to realize that there is not—as some people claim—a "new church", different or opposed to the "old church", but that the Council wished to reveal more clearly the one Church of Jesus Christ, with new aspects, but still the same in its essence" (John Paul II, "Mexico Ever Faithful," *Osservatore Romano* [5 Feb 1979], 1). Similarly nuanced language on the "old" and "new" has been used elsewhere by John Paul II to equivocate on the role of Vatican II (e.g. John Paul II, *Tertio Millennio Adviente,* 14 November 1994, section 18).

[531]"Ce fléau avait pris une telle extension, écrit vers 1178 l'abbé Henri de Clairveaux, que ces gens non seulement s'étaient donné des prêtres et des pontifes, mais qu'ils avaient aussi des évangélistes, lesquels, corrompant et annulant la vérité évangélique, leur façonnaient de nouveaux Évangiles. Ils prêchent sur les Évangiles et les épîtres et d'autres Saintes Écritures qu'ils corrompent en les expliquant, comme des docteurs d'erreur incapables d'être disciples de la vérité, puisque la prédication et l'explication des Écritures est absolument interdite aux laïques" (Henry of Clairvaux, "Actes de l'Inquisition" [1178], cités par Limborch dans son *Histoire de l'Inquisition*, chap. VIII; cited by Daniel Lortsch, *Histoire de la Bible en France* [available from: http://www.bibliquest.org/Lortsch/ Lortsch-Histoire_Bible_France-1.htm]; accessed: 4 March 2005).

[532]"Fourth Lateran Council [A.D. 1215]," accessed 28 June 2003; from http://www.dailycatholic.org/ history/12ecume1.htm; Internet.

Street evangelizing as fanaticism (*contra* Wycliffe and the Lollards):

1382   See quote on the "problem of Lollardy" above.

1551   Thomas More denounced a street evangelist who was "preaching in public … more zealously than wisely" because he "condemned all other rites as profane and loudly denounced their celebrants as wicked and impious men fit for hell fire."[533]

1553   Forty-Two Articles of the Church of England, Article 24 prohibited preaching without authorization;[534] this article was included identically as Article 23 of the 1563, 1571 Thirty-Nine Articles of Religion of the Church of England.

Personal interpretation of Scripture as fanaticism:

1688   Bossuet called Protestants "fanatics" because of their personalistic, individualistic, and "literalistic interpretation" of Scripture, and because of their lack of acceptance of Providence guiding the living [ever-changing] interpretations of the Roman church.[535]

Underground evangelism and church planting as fanaticism:

1698   In the list of offenses for which Desert Preacher/Evangelist Claude Brousson was put to death, was listed: "Diverse notebooks written by the hand of the said Brousson, by which it appeared, that he did all that was possible to revive Fanaticism [evangelism and planting of Reformed churches] in [the County of] *le Vivarez*."[536]

Conversionism as fanaticism, enthusiasm, or confusion:

1830s   Friedrich Schleiermacher, "The idea that every Christian must be able to point to the very time and place of his conversion is accordingly an arbitrary and presumptuous restriction of divine grace, and can only cause confusion."[537]

1910   *Archbishop's Third Committee of Inquiry*:

"In Mediæval times there was deep in the consciousness of those who listened to revival preachers a terror of God the Avenger and the fear of hell. The overwhelming reaction when men were convinced that God had forgiven them and that they were redeemed was the most characteristic feature of movements of revival. Safety is what men wanted: The Gospel that offered them that came as glorious news and was accepted with enthusiasm. To-day if is otherwise."[538]

1936   Emil Brunner:

"There are reasons for our dislike of the word Conversion; it has done and still does much mischief. We all know of particularly devout persons who pounce upon their amazed fellow men at work, on the street, in the street-car with the sudden question, Tell me, are you converted? This was not the manner and method of the New Testament."[539]

---

[533]Thomas More, *Utopia* (1516; Arlington Heights, IL: AHM, 1949), 71.

[534]"XXIV. *No man ne maie minister in the Congregation, except he be called.* It is not lawful for any man to take vpon him the office of Publique preaching, or ministring the sacramentes in the congregation, before he be lawfullie called, and sent to execute the same. And those we ought to iudge lawfullie called, and sent, whiche be chosen, and called to this woorke by menne, who haue publique auctoritie geuen vnto them in the congregation, to cal, and sende ministres into the Lordes vineyarde" ("42 and 39 Articles of Religion"; from: http://www.episcopalian.org/efac/1553-1572.htm; accessed: 21 Oct 2004; Internet).

[535]Jacques B. Bossuet, *Histoire des variations des églises Protestantes* (Paris, 1688, 1740, 1760, 1821). 3:205.

[536]"Divers Cahiers écrits de la main dudit Brousson, par lesquels il paroit, qu'il fait tout ce qu'il pû pour faire revivre le Fanatisme dans le Vivarez" (From copy of official paper, in Walter C. Utt and Brian E. Strayer, *The Bellicose Dove: Claude Brousson and Protestant Resistance to Louis XIV, 1647-1698* [Brighton, Great Britain: University of Sussex, 2002], 151).

[537]Friedrich Schleiermacher, *The Christian Faith*, 2nd ed. (Edinburgh: Clark, 1960), 487.

[538]*The Evangelistic Work of the Church, Being the Report of the Archbishops' Third Committee of Inquiry* (London: Society for the Promoting Christian Knowledge for the National Mission, 1918), 13.

[539]The quote continues, "Jesus went through the villages and towns of Galilee, and cried, 'Repent for the Kingdom of God is at hand.' That the Christian life must be a daily repentance or conversion, was the first of Luther's Ninety-five Theses, with which the Reformation began. … This then is conversion: that we seek first the Kingdom of God; that God's desire, namely, service to our neighbor, becomes our chief concern" (Emil Brunner, *Our Faith* [New York: Scribner's, 1936], 99, 102).

1951   H. Richard Niebuhr in *Christ and Culture* strongly denounced conversionist Christians as irrelevant to task of social reform. Note his unscrupulously antagonistic terminology.[540]

1956   Reinhold Niebuhr decried the invitation of Graham coming to New York for his 1957 crusade, "The Protestant leaders seem to have reached the decision which will bring Billy Graham, the evangelist, to New York City in about two years. We dread the prospect."[541]

1956   Reinhold Niebuhr accused Graham of irrelevancy, stating:

"Graham still thinks within the framework of pietistic moralism. He thinks that the problem of the atom bomb could be solved by converting the people to Christ, which means that he does not recognize the serious perplexities of guilt and responsibility, and of guilt association with responsibility, which Christians must face."[542]

1957   Martin E. Marty wrote of Graham's crusade:

"Behind the methods and message of Billy Graham, behind the revivalistic phenomenon which has just extended its lease on Madison Square Garden and emerged on national television, is a portentous development to which the nation's press and most of its churches are curiously blind. It is the attempted revival of fundamentalism as a major factor in Protestant life. The narrow and divisive creed which the churches rejected a generation ago is staging a comeback. … If the effort succeeds it will make mincemeat of the ecumenical movement, will divide congregations and denominations, will set back Protestant Christianity a half-century."[543]

Evangelizing as Activism:[544]

1975   A Bolivian Manifesto on Evangelism in Latin America Today:

"We are ashamed of having mistaken proselytism for evangelism, of **having satisfied ourselves with an intermittent and organized activism which we have named "evangelism,"** of having accepted to be a religious institution closed on itself, dominated by routine, conformity and apathy."[545]

1984   A Biblical Standard for Evangelists:

"**Evangelists are activists**. Traveling, meeting new people, organizing, and preaching keep us busy. But we must remember that it is not so much our *activity* for Christ as our *captivity* for Him that is most important."[546]

---

[540]"Half-baked and muddle-headed men abound in the anticultural movement as well as elsewhere; doubtless hypocrisy flourishes here too. Yet the single-heartedness and sincerity of the great representatives of this type are among their most attractive qualities. … Doubtless the individualistic ideal of soul-regeneration is not an adequate key to the attitude of radical Christians; but neither is the hope of social reform. …Secondly, the question about the nature and prevalence of sin is involved in the answer to the Christ-and-culture question. The logical answer of the radical seems to be that sin abounds in culture, but that Christians have passed out of darkness into the light, and that the fundamental reason for separation fro the world is preservation of the holy community from corruption. … Yet this solution of the problem of sin and holiness is found, by the exclusive Christians themselves, to be inadequate" (H. Richard Niebuhr, *Christ and Culture* [New York: Harper and Row, 1951], 65, 67, 78). One wonders why the "Emergent Church" movement is turning to Niebuhr as one of their prophets (cf. John G. Stackhouse quoted in Leonard Sweet, ed. *The Church in Emerging Culture: Five Perspectives* [El Cajon, CA: EmergentYS, 2003; Grand Rapids: Zondervan, 2003], 13).

[541]Reinhold Niebuhr, "Editorial Notes," *Christianity and Crisis*, 5 March 1956, 18.

[542]Reinhold Niebuhr, "Literalism, Individualism and Billy Graham," *Christian Century*, 23 May 1956, 641.

[543]"Editorial: Fundamentalist Revival," *The Christian Century,* 19 June 1957, 749.

[544]"There are the four qualities that have been the special marks of Evangelical religion: *conversionism*, the belief that lives need to be changed; *activism*, the expression of the gospel in effort; *Biblicism*, a particular regard for the Bible; and what may be called *crucicentrism*, a stress on the sacrifice of Christ n the cross. Together they form a quadrilaterial of priorities that is the basis of Evangelicalism" (David Bebbington, *Evangelicalism in Modern Britain: A History from the 1730s to the 1980s* [London: Unwin Hyman, 1989; Grand Rapids: Baker, 1992], 3).

[545]"A Bolivian Manifesto on Evangelism in Latin America Today," in Norman E. Thomas, ed., *Classic Texts in Mission and World Christianity* (Maryknoll, NY: Orbis, 1995), 165.

[546]Billy Graham, *A Biblical Standard for Evangelists* (Minneapolis: World Wide, 1984), 81.

1994   Mark Noll's critique in *The Scandal of the Evangelical Mind*:[547]

> "To make room for Christian thought, evangelicals must also abandon the false disjunctions that their distinctives have historically encouraged. The cultivation of the mind for Christian reasons does not deny the appropriateness of **activism**, for example, but it does require **activism** to make room for study. Similarly, it is conversionism along with a consideration of lifelong spiritual development and trust in the Bible along with a critical use of wisdom from other sources (especially from the world that God made) that will lead to a better day. **Modifying the evangelical tendency to Manichaeism may cost some of the single-minded enthusiasm of activism, but it will be worth it in order to be able to worship God with the mind.**"[548]

Evangelizing as Mental Manipulation?

2000   French Antisect Law (Called the "Loi About-Picard", the French Antisect Law passed unanimously [with one absention] by the Parliament of France, 30 May 2000):

> "The socialists deputies plan also to create a 'mental manipulation' offence, which should allow to launch more easily judicial suits against cults. It should apply to 'important and reiterated pressures' exerted against a person 'in order to create and exploit a physical or psychological dependence' state, by a 'group having as purpose or as effect to create or to exploit' these dependences."[549]

---

[547]With the following downplaying of evangelism as activism, this author is concerned with the place assigned to evangelism in Mark Noll's writings, as for example in his history of Protestant colleges in America: William Ringenberger and Mark Noll, *The Christian College: A History of Protestant Higher Education in America* (RenewedMinds, 2006).

[548]Mark Noll, *The Scandal of the Evangelical Mind* (Grand Rapids: Eerdmans, 1994), 245.

[549]"'The French Assemblée Nationale ready to start war against cults'; PARIS, 11 juin (AFP) - Paris, june 11, 2000: (AFP) The struggle against cults should be considerably reinforced by a specific judicial arsenal, according to a bill initiated by the socialist group, and shall be examined on june 22d by the national assembly.

"The parliament has 'hesitated for long' before planning specific anti-cult dispositions, but this time, it has decided to 'take the bull by horns', said the deputy PS Catherine PICARD, reporter of the text and president of the Task Force to study cults in the french assembly.

"Socialist congressmen have planned to the order of the day the discussion about the bill of the french senator UDF Nicolas ABOUT, which was adopted in the Senate in December. The text's purpose is to allow the political authorities to dissolve 'moral entities' having been condemned many times - either themselves or their executives, for some typically cultic offences, such as endangering people, illegal school studies, abuse of trust, etc.

"But they have prepared a series of motions to make this bill more efficient and to rewrite its bases.

"The socialist deputies want to attribute to justice, and not the political power, the possibility to dissolve cults having been sentenced at least twice by justice.

"This possibility to dissolve was asked, between else, by the french Mission to Combat Cults (MILS).

"'MENTAL MANIPULATION' MISDEMEANOR

"The socialists deputies plan also to create a 'mental manipulation' offence, which should allow to launch more easily judicial suits against cults. It should apply to 'important and reiterated pressures' exerted against a person 'in order to create and exploit a physical or psychological dependance' state, by a 'group having as purpose or as effect to create or to exploit' these dependances.

"The offence would be punished up to 200000 FF amend and two years jail, according to the text. The punishment could amount to 5 years and 500000 FF if it was committed against specially vulnerable persons.

"A Congress source added that the text could allow to engage proceedings without having to ask if the person having been victimized was agreeing or not.

"The struggle against cults should be the more easy by the fact that "for the first time, the legislator gives an embryo of definition of what is a cult", has said the same source.

"The propositions of the socialist group should find a large agreement into the congress, as they take most of the disposals from the RPR deputy Eric Doligé, author of a Bill on mental manipulation, or Jean Tiberi, Paris Mayor.

"Like M. Tiberi, socialists have proposed to forbid a cult having been already sentenced to install itself near a school, an hospital, a dispensary or other institutions dealing with vulnerable persons.

"They suggest as well, as did M. Tiberi, to forbid advertisement toward young people, from a cult already sentenced.

"Moreover, to facilitate the sentencing of cults by justice, the socialist deputies included also the senatorial bill to extend the penal responsability of moral entities to some other offences: offence to impede assistance or to omit to assist, provocation to suicide, family abandon complicity or complicity regarding cure deprival or food deprival to minor of less than 15" (From: http://fr.news.yahoo.com/000611/121/g5hb.html; accessed: 3 Nov 2000; Internet). For a paper describing a judicial process using this law, see http://www.cesnur.org/2006/sd_palmer.htm. For a French website decrying this abridgement of civil liberties, see www.la-liste-noire.nouvelle-religion.fr. On 28 June 2006 a commission

10. Evangelism as Proselytism:

A recent book, *Proselytism and Orthodoxy in Russia: The New War for Souls,* provided an overview of religious rights in Russia emphasizing primarily the 20th Century.[550] One of the major emphases in this book is the tension between anti-proselytism, religious repression, and a totalitarian religion (the Russian Orthodox) versus allowing evangelism, freedom of conscience, and the existence of many faiths. This same tension is noted in virtually every century of the church!

The consideration of evangelism as proselytism is not new, nor are the various approaches toward this topic…

1534   Before the "Placards Incident" in Paris, John Calvin draws attention to himself because of his proselytism:

> "Déjà avant cette action, Calvin attire l'attention en confessant publiquement sa foi évangélique et en faisant du prosélytisme."[551]

> "Already before this action, Calvin draws attention to himself by publicly confessing his evangelical faith and by doing proselytism." (translation mine).

1598   Non-Proselytism in the French "Edict of Nantes" (an edict by which Catholic politicians and police were encouraged to "tolerate" the Huguenots):

> "Not only was the Edict *not* a guarantee of religious tolerance (given the negative connotation of *tolerer* in Early Modern France), but its 148 articles also introduced many barriers – religious, social, and political – to divide the Catholic majority from the Protestant minority. Calvinists were quarantined in 'safe zones' (the places of refuge) like Jews isolated in urban ghettos; they could worship only in places where their faith had been established by 1597. **And they could not proselytize, publish, or promote their faith freely.**"[552]

1967   Jacques Blocher, French Evangelical Pastor:

> "In fact, today the Protestant theologians who want to be up to date, insist that evangelization should no longer seek to win new members to the church; this would be a type of **proselytizing**, something severely condemned in this century of ecumenism. According to these theologians, the Christian evangelizes through his activities in the world just by his presence and without trying to win anyone to his ideas. Though this theory of evangelism is not unanimously accepted—far from it—it nevertheless seems to us to be an important cause for the drop off in the number of Protestants, especially of those who do not practice their religion."[553]

1970   Catholic-World Council of Churches, "Common Witness and **Proselytism**":

> "Witness should avoid behavior such as: … c) Every exploitation of the need or weakness or of the lack of education of those to whom the witness is offered, in view of inducing adherence to a Church. d)

---

of inquiry on "the influence of sects on minors" was established by the Assemblee Nationale to investigate encroachments of the antisect law.

[550]John Witte, Jr. explained the changes in Russia, "A decade ago, Russia embraced religious liberty for all. President Mikhail Gorbachev's revolutionary ideals of *glasnost* and *perestroika* broke from the harsh establishment of Marxist-Leninist atheism, and awakened the sundry traditional faiths of Russia. … These favorable policies toward religion were soon translated into strong legal terms. On October 1, 1990, Gorbachev signed a comprehensive new law, "On the Freedom of Conscience and on Religious Organizations" for the USSR. … By far the greatest expressions of concern, however, came from the Moscow Patriarchate of the Russian Orthodox Church. Already in 1991…. By 1993, the Moscow Patriarchate's resentment was directed more generally at all 'well-organized and well-financed' mission groups, particularly from the West. Unwelcome 'foreign proselytizing faiths' now included various Roman Catholics, mainline Protestants, and Western Evangelicals, alongside religious mavericks and totalitarian cults" (John Witte Jr., "Introduction," in John Witte Jr. and Michael Boudreaux, eds., *Proselytism and Orthodoxy in Russia: The New War for Souls* [Maryknoll, NY; Orbis, 1999], 2, 6, 7).

[551]Georg Plasger, "Cours de base: l'histoire de la théologie réformées"; available at: http://www.reformiert-online.net/t/fra/bildung/grundkurs/gesch/lek3/lek3.pdf (online); accessed: 17 Jan 2017; Internet.

[552]Walter C. Utt and Brian E. Strayer, *The Bellicose Dove: Claude Brousson and Protestant Resistance to Louis XIV, 1647-1698* (Brighton, Great Britain: University of Sussex, 2002), 5-6; noting Brian E. Strayer, *Huguenots and Camisards as Aliens in France* (Lewiston: Mellin Press, 2001), 42-43, 69-80, 87-90.

[553]Jacques Blocher, "French-speaking Europe," in *One Race, One Gospel, One Task: World Congress on Evangelism, Berlin, 1966, Official Reference Volumes: Papers and Reports*, eds. Carl F. H. Henry and W. Stanley Mooneyham (Minneapolis: World Wide, 1967), 1:250.

Everything raising suspicion about the "good faith" of others –"bad faith" can never be presumed; it should always be proved."[554]

1973 Orthodox and Catholic Common Declaration:

"In the name of Christian charity, **we reject all forms of proselytism**, in the sense of acts by which persons seek to disturb each other's communities by recruiting members from each other through methods, or because of attitudes of mind, which are opposed to Christian love or to what should characterize the relationships between Churches. Let it cease where it may exist."[555]

1975 A Bolivian Manifesto on Evangelism in Latin America Today:

"**We are ashamed of having mistaken proselytism for evangelism**, of having satisfied ourselves with an intermittent and organized activism which we have named "evangelism," of having accepted to be a religious institution closed on itself, dominated by routine, conformity and apathy."[556]

1976 ICCPR—International Covenant on Civil and Political Rights:

This covenant is being used as precedent to describe and censor "**hate-speech**" on social media.

"Each State Party to the present Covenant undertakes to respect and to ensure to all individuals within its territory and subject to its jurisdiction the rights recognized in the present Covenant, without distinction of any kind, such as race, colour, sex, language, religion, political or other opinion, national or social origin, property, birth or other status."[557]

Three articles in this covenant are of special interest to evangelism:

Article 18
1. Everyone shall have the right to freedom of thought, conscience and religion. This right shall include freedom to have or to adopt a religion or belief of his choice, and freedom, either individually or in community with others and in public or private, to manifest his religion or belief in worship, observance, practice and teaching.
2. No one shall be subject to coercion which would impair his freedom to have or to adopt a religion or belief of his choice.
3. Freedom to manifest one's religion or beliefs may be subject only to such limitations as are prescribed by law and are necessary to protect public safety, order, health, or morals or the fundamental rights and freedoms of others.
4. The States Parties to the present Covenant undertake to have respect for the liberty of parents and, when applicable, legal guardians to ensure the religious and moral education of their children in conformity with their own convictions.

Article 19
1. Everyone shall have the right to hold opinions without interference.
2. Everyone shall have the right to freedom of expression; this right shall include freedom to seek, receive and impart information and ideas of all kinds, regardless of frontiers, either orally, in writing or in print, in the form of art, or through any other media of his choice.
3. The exercise of the rights provided for in paragraph 2 of this article carries with it special duties and responsibilities. It may therefore be subject to certain restrictions, but these shall only be such as are provided by law and are necessary:
(a) For respect of the rights or reputations of others;
(b) For the protection of national security or of public order (ordre public), or of public health or morals.

Article 20
1. Any propaganda for war shall be prohibited by law.

---

[554]"Common Witness and Proselytism—A Study Document," form the Joint Working Group between the Roman Catholic Church and the WCC, 1970; in Michael Kinnamon and Brian Cope, eds., *The Ecumenical Movement: An Anthology of Key Texts and Voices* (Geneva: World Council of Churches, 1997; Grand Rapids: Eerdmans, 1997), 352.

[555]"1973 Common Declaration," in Thomas B. Stransky and John B. Sheerin, eds., *Doing the Truth in Charity: Statements of Pope Paul VI, Popes John Paul I, John Paul II, and the Secretariat for the Promoting of Christian Unity,* Ecumenical Documents I (Maryknoll, NY Paulist, 1982), 248.

[556]"A Bolivian Manifesto on Evangelism in Latin America Today," in Norman E. Thomas, ed., *Classic Texts in Mission and World Christianity* (Maryknoll, NY: Orbis, 1995), 165.

[557]United Nations, Human Rights, Office of the High Commissioner, "International Covenant on Civil and Political Rights"; adopted and opened for signiature, ratification and accession by General Assembly resolution 2200A (XXI) of 16 December 1966; entry into force 23 March 1976, in accordance with Article 49; available at: http://www.ohchr.org/EN/ProfessionalInterest/Pages/CCPR.aspx (online); accessed: 5 July 2017; Internet.

2. Any advocacy of national, racial or religious hatred that constitutes incitement to discrimination, hostility or violence shall be prohibited by law.[558]

1980   the Lutheran-Catholic Conversation, "Ways to Community, 1980":

Part II, Article 2, 1. "Naturally *discrimination* must cease if ministers are to cooperate on all levels. Partners cannot cast aspersions on each other and **must renounce every form of proselytism** (though not mutual criticisms or requests for change)."[559]

1982   WCC Committee on World Mission and Evangelism:

"Surely, many ambiguities have accompanied this development and are present even today, not the least of which is **the sin of proselytism** among other Christian confessions."[560]

Note likewise how speaking about other gods to entice others to worship them was a capital crime in Israel.[561]

1986   *The Evangelical-Roman Catholic Dialogue on Mission 1977-1984: A Report*:

"We turn in our last chapter from theological exploration to practical action. ... [this chapter is titled "The Possibilities of Common Witness"]

"We feel the need to allude to the practice of seeking to evangelize people who are already church members, since this causes misunderstanding and even resentment, especially when Evangelicals are seeking to 'convert' Roman Catholics. ...

"There are forms of witness, however, which we would all describe as 'unworthy', and therefore as being 'proselytism' rather than 'evangelism'. We agree, in general, with the analysis of this given in the study document entitled *Common Witness and Proselytism* (1970), and in particular three aspects of it.

"First, **proselytism takes place** when our *motive* is unworthy...

"Second, **we are guilty of proselytism whenever** our *methods* are unworthy, especially when we resort to any kind of 'physical coercion, moral constraint or psychological pressure'...

"Thirdly, **we are guilty of proselytism whenever** our message includes 'unjust or uncharitable reference to the beliefs or practices of other religious communities in the hope of winning adherents." ...

"We who have participated in ERCDOM III are agreed that every possible opportunity for common witness should be taken, except where conscience forbids. ..."[562]

1991   David J. Bosch, South African missiologist:

"11. *Evangelism is not proselytism*. ... Only too often, then, evangelism has been used as a means of reconquering lost ecclesiastical influence, in Catholicism *and* Protestantism. ... Whether intended or not, this mentality suggests that it is not by grace, but by becoming adherents of our denomination, that people will be saved."[563]

1994   Evangelicals and Catholics Together:

"Today, in this country and elsewhere, Evangelicals and Catholics **attempt to win 'converts'** from one another's folds. In some ways, this is perfectly understandable and perhaps inevitable. In many instances, however, such efforts at recruitment undermine the Christian mission by which we are bound by God's Word and to which we have recommitted ourselves in this statement. ...At the same time, our

---

[558]Ibid.

[559]"Ways to Community, 1980," in Harding Meyer and Lukas Vischer, *Growth in Agreement: Reports and Agreed Statements of Ecumenical Conversations on a World Level,* Ecumenical Documents II (Maryknoll, NY: Paulist, 1984), 235.

[560]"Mission and Evangelism—An Ecumenical Affirmation," WCC Commission on World Mission and Evangelism, 1982; in Kinnamon and Cope, 373.

[561]"If your brother, your mother's son, or your son or daughter, or the wife you cherish, or your friend who is as your own soul, entice you secretly, saying, 'Let us go and serve other gods' (whom neither you nor your fathers have known, of the gods of the peoples who are around you, near you or far from you, from one end of the earth to the other end), you shall not yield to him or listen to him; and your eye shall not pity him, nor shall you spare or conceal him. But you shall surely kill him; your hand shall be first against him to put him to death, and afterwards the hand of all the people. So you shall stone him to death because he has sought to seduce you from the LORD your God who brought you out from the land of Egypt, out of the house of slavery. Then all Israel will hear and be afraid, and will never again do such a wicked thing among you" (Deut 13:6-11).

[562]Basil Meeking [Roman Catholic] and John Stott [Evangelical], *The Evangelical Roman Catholic Dialogue on Mission 1977-1984: A Report* (Exeter, Devon, Great Britain: Paternoster, 1986): being a "Report on the meetings held in Venice in 1977, Cambridge in 1982, and in Landévennec, France in 1984"

[563]David J. Bosch, *Transforming Mission*, 414, 415.

commitment to full religious freedom compels us to defend the legal freedom to **proselytize** even as we call upon Christians to refrain from such activity."[564]

1994 Colson-Neuhaus Declaration:

"There is a necessary distinction between evangelizing [non-Christians] and what is today commonly called **proselytizing or 'sheep stealing.'**" For "in view of the large number of non-Christians in the world and the enormous challenge of the common evangelistic task, it is neither theologically legitimate nor a prudent use of resources for one Christian community to **proselytize** among active adherents of another Christian community." Thus, "**We condemn the practice of recruiting people** from another community for the purposes of denominational or institutional aggrandizement."[565]

Please note also that Colson-Neuhaus borrowed and formalized the 1972 language of Catholic University of America's Ronan Hoffman:

"He [Christ] reproached them [the Pharisees] not for their missionary zeal but because this zeal was animated less by a desire of promoting God's glory and the good of men than by the desire of **self-aggrandizement and of boasting of the increase in the numbers of their sect**."[566]

[In his antagonism to an Evangelical view of conversion, Hoffman seems to have Southern Baptists in mind with this comment!]

Note also how the skillful dialectic of the Colson-Neuhaus Declaration curiously coincides with the teaching of Clement XIII, *In Dominico Agro* [In the field of the Lord]—On the Instruction in the Faith (1761), written not long after the First Great Awakening:

"2. It often happens that certain unworthy ideas come forth in the Church of God which, although they directly contradict each other, plot together to undermine the purity of the Catholic faith in some way. **It is very difficult to cautiously balance our speech between both enemies in such a way that We seem to turn Our backs on none of them, but to shun and condemn both enemies of Christ equally**. Meanwhile the matter is such that diabolical error, when it has artfully colored its lies, easily clothes itself in the likeness of truth while very brief additions or changes corrupt the meaning of expressions; and confession, which usually works salvation, sometimes, with a slight change, inches toward death."[567]

Please note also that Spurgeon addressed the topic of "sheep-stealing" in his *The Soul Winner*, first published in 1859:

"We do not regard it as soulwinning to steal members from other established churches and train them to say our particular creed. We aim to bring souls to Christ rather than to make converts to our churches. Sheep-stealers roam abroad, concerning whom I will say nothing except that they are not brothers, not acting in brotherly fashion."[568]

---

[564]"Evangelicals and Catholic Together: The Christian Mission in the Third Millennium," in Keith A. Fournier, with William D. Watkins, *A House United? Evangelicals and Catholics Together: A Winning Alliance for the 21st Century* (Colorado Springs: NavPress, 1994), 346.

[565]Geisler and MacKenzie, *Roman Catholics and Evangelicals: Agreements and Differences* (Grand Rapids: Baker, 1995), 493. Interestingly, the mention of "institutional aggrandisement" is reminiscent of the Council of Constance's "Sentence condemning the various articles of John Wyclif'," which stated, "We learn from the writings and deeds of the holy fathers that the catholic faith without which (as the Apostle says) it is impossible to please God, has often been attacked by false followers of the same faith, or rather by perverse assailants, and by those who, desirous of the world's glory, are led on by proud curiosity to know more than they should; and that it has been defended against such persons by the church's faithful spiritual knights armed with the shield of faith. Indeed these kinds of wars were prefigured in the physical wars of the Israelite people against idolatrous nations" ("Council of Constance, 1414-1418 A.D.," from: http://www.dailycatholic.org/history/16ecume1.htm; accessed 24 Sept 2004; Internet; italics mine).

[566]Ronan Hoffman, [in response to: 1967: Are Conversion Missions Outmoded?] "Yes! Conversion and the Mission of the Church," in Donald McGavran, ed., *Eye of the Storm: The Great Debate in Mission* (Waco, TX: Word, 1972), 71.

[567]Clement XIII, *In Dominico Agro*—On Instruction in the Faith (14 June 1761); available at: http://www.ewtn.com/library/ENCYC/C13INDOM.HTM; accessed: 8 Sept 2004; Internet.

[568]Charles H. Spurgeon, *The Soul Winner* (New Kensington, PA: Whitaker House, 1995), 7.

2006   Note some of the points from the report on the "Inter-religious Consultation on
'Conversion—Assessing the Reality," affirmed by the Vatican and the World Council of
Churches, on 12-16 May 2006, in Lariano/Velletri, Italy:

3.   We affirm that while everyone has a right to invite others to an understanding of their faith, it should
not be exercised by violating other's rights and religious sensibilities. At the same time, all should
heal themselves from the obsession of converting others.

4.   Freedom of religion enjoins upon all of us the equally non-negotiable responsibility to respect faiths
other than our own, and never to denigrate, vilify or misrepresent them for the purpose of affirming
superiority of our faith.

5.   We acknowledge that errors have been perpetrated and injustice committed by the adherents of every
faith. Therefore, it is incumbent on every community to conduct honest self-critical examination of its
historical conduct as well as its doctrinal/theological precepts. Such self-criticism and repentance
should lead to necessary reforms *inter alia* on the issue of conversion.

6.   A particular reform that we would commend to practitioners and establishments of all faiths is to
ensure that conversion by "unethical" means are discouraged and rejected by one and all. There
should be transparency in the practice of inviting others to one's faith.

10. We see the need for and usefulness of a continuing exercise to collectively evolve a "code of conduct"
on conversion, which all faiths should follow. We therefore feel that inter-religious dialogues on the
issue of conversion should continue at various levels.[569]

A headline for an article from this consultation read: "Vatican/WCC study on conversion affirms
freedom of religion, warns about 'obsession of converting others'"

"A study process jointly sponsored by the Vatican and the World Council of Churches (WCC)
kicked off this week by affirming the freedom of religion as a 'non-negotiable' human right valid for
everyone everywhere **while at the same time stressing that the 'obsession of converting others'
needs to be cured**. ...

"The report makes a bold recommendation: 'All should heal themselves from the obsession of
converting others'. Acknowledging that 'errors have been perpetrated and injustice committed by the
adherents of every faith,' it suggests that 'it is incumbent on every community to conduct honest self-
critical examination' of its historical record as well as its doctrines.

"As a result of such 'self-criticism and repentance,' some reforms should take place in order to
ensure a healthier approach to the issue of conversion. Some concrete suggestions include:
discouraging and rejecting 'unethical means', avoiding taking advantage of 'vulnerable' people like
children and disabled persons, and doing humanitarian work 'without any ulterior motives'.

"The report, issued by the 27 participants from Buddhist, Christian, Hindu, Muslim, Jewish and
Yoruba religious backgrounds, recognizes that 'many differences and disagreements' remained
among them, but nonetheless a 'convergent understanding of the several aspects of the issue of
religious conversion' developed."[570]

2007   World Evangelical Alliance's general secretary Rev. Dr Geoff Tunnicliffe gave full approval
of the WEA's involvement in the further development of the 2006 **"code of conduct to guide
activities seeking converts to Christianity"** [above] with the Vatican and the WCC to be
finalized by 2010.[571]

Since, it seems, that the WEA has approved this measure, severely limitations may be
enacted against the evangelism activities of WEA member churches, such as in France,
where an anti-sect law is now on the books (as of 31 May 2000). France chose to define
"sectarian" as being congregational, and not being a member of either the Roman Catholic
church, the French Protestant Federation, or the French Evangelical Alliance. The "face off"
is now for 2010, perhaps with implementation to follow!

---

[569]"Report from inter-religious consultation on 'Conversion – assessing the reality'"; available from
http://www.oikoumene.org/index.php?id=2252&L=0; accessed 2 Nov 2007; Internet.

[570]"Vatican/WCC study on conversion affirms freedom of religion, warns about 'obsession of converting
others'" available from: http://www.oikoumene.org/en/news/news-management/all-news-english/display-single-
english-news/browse/25/article/1634/vaticanwcc-study-on-conv.html; accessed 2 Nov 2007; Internet.

[571]"Christian code of conduct on religious conversion wins broader backing"; available from:
http://www.oikoumene.org/en/news/news-management/eng/a/article/1634/christian-code-of-conduct.html; accessed: 24
Sept 2009; Internet.

2016   The EU-Vatican appoints a world "Special Envoy for the Promotion of Freedom of Religion or Belief Outside the EU":

> The European Union (EU) has appointed a man tasked with imposing 'European values' on the entire globe, and solving time-old divisions over culture, and religious conflict.
>
> EU Commission President Jean-Claude Juncker named the new 'Special Envoy for the promotion of freedom of religion or belief outside the EU' at the Vatican on Friday.
>
> Mr. Ján Figeľ served as the European Commissioner for Education, Training, Culture and Youth before becoming the First Deputy-Prime Minister of the Slovak Republic in 2010.
>
> Speaking at the Vatican on the occasion of the award of the Charlemagne Prize for European integration to Pope Francis, President Juncker seemed optimistic about the new grandiose initiative and monumental task before Mr. Figel:
>
> "Freedom of religion or belief is a fundamental right which is part of the foundation of the European Union. The persistent persecution of religious and ethnic minorities makes protecting and promoting this freedom inside and outside the EU all the more essential", he said.
>
> Adding: "I trust that Ján Figeľ, our Special Envoy, will help us in this endeavour, sharpening our focus and ensuring that this important issue gets the attention it deserves."
>
> The initiative for a new special envoy was called for in a European Parliament resolution on the 4th February this year.[572]

2016   New Russian law making "missionary activity" outside prescribed places illegal:

> "The legislation, which was abruptly introduced into the package of antiterrorism bills on June 20, defines missionary activity as public worship and other religious rites and ceremonies; the distribution of religious literature, printed, audio, and video materials; public fundraising for religious purposes; conducting worship and religious meetings; and preaching."[573]

> "'An anti-terrorism package is almost certainly one that will pass,' SOVA Center for Information and Analysis Director Aleksandr Verkhovsky commented to Forum 18 from Moscow on 22 June. So adding the sharing belief restrictions to such a package was 'a clever move.'"[574]

Terminology in the Law: "missionary activity"?

In the Press:
  "Sharing belief"
  "Sharing the faith"
  "Evangelism"
  "Evangelizing"

Reason: "extremism" (Muslim), or Islamic "radicalization" (French).

2018, July 24-26 (Washington D.C.) First ever "Ministerial to Advance Religious Freedom"—watching for anti-proselytism rhetoric

> "On July 24-26, the State Department will bring together religious leaders, civil society groups, survivors of religious persecution, and delegations from foreign governments for the first-ever Ministerial to Advance Religious Freedom in Washington, D.C. Vice President Mike Pence and other senior Trump administration officials will also be participating. Our goal is simple: to promote the God-given human right to believe what you want to believe."[575]

---

[572]"European Union Appoints Man To Solve All Global Religious Conflict"; available at: http://www.breitbart.com/london/2016/05/09/european-union-appoints-man-solve-global-religious-conflict/ (Online); accessed: 9 May 2016; Internet.

[573]"Adventists Observe Day of Prayer as Russia Moves to Limit Missionary Activity: An Adventist leader also appeals to the Russian president to reject the legislation." http://www.adventistreview.org/church-news/story4134-adventists-pray-for-russia-not-to-restrict-missionary-activity; accessed 17 July 2016; Internet.

[574]"RUSSIA: Putin signs sharing beliefs, 'extremism', punishments" (July 8 2016); http://www.forum18.org/archive.php?article_id=2197; accessed 17 July 2016; Internet.

[575]"Religious Persecution in Iran, China Must End Now" by Michael R. Pompeo, Secretary of State; available at: https://www.state.gov/secretary/remarks/2018/07/284447.htm (Online); accessed: 25 July 2018; Internet. Following the above quote were listed the following purposes:
"We need partners to advance religious freedom
"To advance the cause of religious freedom, we need all these voices to work together.
"We need civil society groups, who are often the first to hear reports of violations, to continue their courageous work on the front lines.

May the Lord protect us in our New Testament evangelism as we fulfill His Great Commission!

Conclusions on Historical Terminology:

Evangelism has been discussed and fiercely debated throughout the history of the churches. Its seeming lack of attention in many "church history" classes is likely due to its omission in the history books, and due to the fact that most evangelists and evangelistic movements were extirpated by the Roman Catholic church. Later, among liberalizing Protestants, evangelism was shunned because it was viewed as "fanaticism," and among ecumenical Christians, evangelism was condemned as proselytizing. Simultaneously, bringing up past issues like the hundreds of thousands of Second Millennium martyrdoms in Western Europe at the hand of Rome (prior to the Enlightenment) in "church history" classes is deemed an unnecessary digging up of the "weaknesses of the past"[576] [ignoring or covering up the past is quite novel if one is to learn from the past], and one must remember that supposedly "both sides were to blame."[577]

"We need religious leaders of every faith to articulate to their adherents that violence is not a righteous way to propagate belief.

"We need governments to recognize religious discrimination and persecution, take a firm stand against it, and treat religious freedom as a foreign policy priority.

"And we need to hear the stories of those persecuted, tortured, falsely imprisoned, and killed for their faith. We can honor their sacrifices by preventing these atrocities from happening again.

"Promoting religious freedom for all not only advances the interests of individuals, but countries and faith groups around the world. Where fundamental freedoms of religion, speech, press, and peaceful assembly exist, ideas compete with one another and different views are discussed openly. Greater understanding comes from this free exchange. Countries that champion individual freedoms are often the most secure, economically vibrant, and prosperous in the world. Religious freedom is an indispensable building block of free societies.

"The Trump administration is passionate about promoting and defending international religious freedom. But the challenge is too big for any one nation. We need every country to protect and defend freedom of religion for everyone. I look forward to welcoming my counterparts to the U.S. State Department as we fight for the persecuted, speak out for the voiceless, and work together to pave the way for greater religious freedom around the world" (ibid.).

[576]See John Paul II, *Tertio Millennio Adviente* (14 Nov 1994), which speaks in very general terms of the weaknesses of the past: "She [the Church] cannot cross the threshold of the new millennium without encouraging her children to purify themselves, through repentance, of past errors and instances of infidelity, inconsistency and slowness to act. Acknowledging the weaknesses of the past is an act of honesty and courage which helps us to strengthen our faith, which alerts us to face today's temptations and challenges, and prepares us to meet them. 34. Among the sins which require a greater commitment to repentance and conversion should certainly be counted those which have been detrimental to the unity willed by God for his people. In the course of the 1,000 years now drawing to a close, even more than in the first millennium, ecclesial communion has been painfully wounded, a fact 'for which, at times, men of both sides were to blame.'" (*op. cit.,* par. 33-34).

[577]Some would say here, "After all, didn't Calvin have his Servetus?" [note the last sentence in the prior footnote from a Papal encyclical] Servetus was executed under the command of Geneva's town council for his denial of the Trinity, a capital crime all over Catholic Europe at the time. However, according to Crespin's martyrology (Geneva, 1570), there were 12 martyred Huguenots in France at the hand of Rome's clergy in 1553, that same year Servetus was executed (M. Dymonet martyred for heresy in Lyon; L. de Marsac, and his cousin, and E. Gravot burned at the stake for heresy in Lyon; S. Laloé martyred in Dijon, his executer, J. Sylvestre, was converted as a result; D. Peloquin burned at the stake in Ville-franche; N. Nail arrested with Bibles from Geneva burned over a fire in Paris; A. Magne burned alive in Paris; G. Neel burned at the stake in Evreux; E. le Roy and P. Denocheau executed in Chartres; P. Serre burned at the stake in Toulouse), the year before, 1552, there were eight martyred by Rome's clergy for the Gospel in France (The Lausanne five: M. Alba, P. Escrivain, B. Seguin, C. Favre and P. Navihère, arrested on their third day in Lyon, imprisoned, judged guilty of heresy, and strangled and burned at the stake; P. Bergier also strangled for the faith in Lyon; H. Gravier martyred in Bourg-en-Bresse; R. Poyet burned at the stake in Anjou), and the year after, 1555, there were nine martyred by Rome's clergy for their faith in Christ in France (P. Panier is decapitated in Dole of Bourgogne; J. Filleul and J. Leveillé hung and burned alive in Paris; F. Gamba burned at the stake at Bresse in Lombardie; D. Le Vayr colporter of Geneva Bibles, raised from the fire three times before being burned alive in Rouen; G. Dalençon, Bible colporter, betrayed after several trips, martyred along with a dyer of cloth in Montpelier; R. Lefevre arrested in Lyons, burned at the stake in Paris; P. de la Vau burned alive in Nimes). This does not count the 850 Waldensian-Lutheran's killed in the cities of Merindol and Cabrières, France, when they were destroyed in 1545, nor for the 100,000 Huguenots massacred in the St. Bartholomew massacre in Paris in 1572 (during a wedding celebration of a Huguenot prince with the daughter of the King of France), wherein Rome's Cardinal Richelieu killed the first man, the Huguenot Admiral of the French army, Coligny. In England the martyrdoms were only beginning (with the beheading of Lady Jane Gray) under Queen Mary who took the throne in 1553. In 1555 there were 12 martyrdoms throughout England (including in London J. Rogers, the first heretic burned alive under reign of Queen Mary; Bishop J. Hooper burned in Gloucester; H. Gudaker, primate of Ireland poisoned; Minister and Lawyer R. Taylor thrown in the fire at Aldham

From Edwards to Finney, Christians reacted for or against the First Great Awakening. After Finney, many conservatives Christians were for his evangelism[578] or against his theology and practice,[579] as he had piercingly negative words against the Westminster Confession,[580] as well as election and predestination, much like John Wesley 100 years before him.[581]

During Billy Graham's ministry in the 1950s, Christians were divided three ways over his ministry: (1) separation from; (2) agreement with; and (3) anti-conversionist.[582] And so the historical cycle regarding what constitutes proper evangelization continues.

One can be so weighed down by false views and responding to the multitudinous conferences and dialogues, that one can forget to "Do the work of an evangelist", and change the Great Commission to say, "Go into all the world and right all the wrong views of the Gospel and evangelism." This trap must be avoided, while not ignoring the hard lessons of false views.

Common; L. Saunders, minister in London, burned at the stake in Coventry; Pastor G. Marsh burned at the stake at Westchester; T. Thomkins burned on hand prior to being burned at the stake in London; T. Causton burned at Raleigh; W. Pygat at Braintree; T. Higby at Horndon; S. Knight at Malden; W. Hunter at Brentwood; J. Lawrence, R. White, and W, Dighel at Glouchester; J. Alcock died in prison; W. Flower burned at Westminster for a whistle during mass). In fact, under Queen Mary, 800 Protestants were killed in the first 2 years of her reign according to Crespin's 1570 Martyrology. It is unimaginable to compare "Calvin's Servetus" to the many martyrs and even massacres at the hands of the Catholic clergy during the same years!

[578]Two examples of those who were "for" Finney were R. A. Torrey, who emphasized the Spirit-filled life and personal soul-winning, are Bill Bright, whose "How to Have a Spirit-Filled Life" is like a page from Finney, and V. Raymond Edman, former president of Wheaton College who wrote, *Finney Lives On: The Secret of Revival in Our Time* (Wheaton, IL: Scripture Press, 1951).

[579]For example, see Ian Murray, *The Invitation System* (Edinburgh: Banner of Truth, 1967) and *Revival and Revivalism: The Making and Marring of American Evangelicalism, 1750-1858* (Edinburgh: Banner of Truth, 1994), or Erroll Hulse, *The Great Invitation* (Welwyn: Evangelical Press, 1986).

[580]"Every uninspired attempt to frame for the church an authoritative standard of opinion which shall be regarded as an unquestionable exposition of the word of God, is not only impious in itself, but it is also a tacit assumption of the fundamental dogma of Papacy. The Assembly of Divines did more than to assume the necessity of a Pope to give law to the opinions of men; they assumed to create an immortal one, or rather to embalm their own creed, and preserve it as the Pope of all generations; or it is more just to say, that those who have adopted that confession of faith and catechism as an authoritative standard of doctrine, have absurdly adopted the most obnoxious principle of Popery, and elevated their confession and catechism to the Papal throne and into the place of the Holy Ghost. That the instrument framed by that assembly should in the nineteenth century be recognized as a standard of the church, or of an intelligent branch of it, is not only amazing, but I must say that it is highly ridiculous. It is as absurd in theology as it would be in any other branch of science, and as injurious and stultifying as it is absurd and ridiculous. It is better to have a living that a dead Pope. If we must have an authoritative expounder of the word of God, let us have a living one, so as not to preclude the hope of improvement. 'A living dog is better than a dead lion;' so a living Pope is better than a dead and stereotypexd confession of faith, that holds all men bound to subscribe to its unalterable dogmas and unvarying terminology" (Charles G. Finney, "Preface," *Systematic Theology*, ed. by J. H. Fairchild [E. J. Goodrich, 1878; South Gate, CA: Porter Kemp, 1944], xii). By the way, the reader will note that Alexander Campbell, by several years an elder to Finney, was also very iconoclastic as regarded all denominations of his day.

[581]"VII. 1. This premised, let it be observed, that this doctrine represents our blessed Lord, 'Jesus Christ the righteous,' 'the only begotten Son of the Father, full of grace and truth,' as an hypocrite, a deceiver of the people, a man void of common sincerity. For it cannot be denied, that he everywhere speaks as if he was willing that all men should be saved. Therefore, to say he was not willing that all men should be saved, is to represent him as a mere hypocrite and dissembler. It cannot be denied that the gracious words which came out of his mouth are full of invitations to all sinners. To say, then, he did not intend to save all sinners, is to represent him as a gross deceiver of the people. You cannot deny that he says, 'Come unto me, all ye that are weary and heavy laden.' If, then, you say he calls those that cannot come; those whom he knows to be unable to come; those whom he can make able to come, but will not; how is it possible to describe greater insincerity? ... 3. This is the blasphemy clearly contained in the horrible decree of predestination! And here I fix my foot. On this I join issue with every assertor of it. ... 4. This is the blasphemy for which (however I love the persons who assert it) I abhor the doctrine of predestination, a doctrine, upon the supposition of which, if one could possibly suppose it for a moment, (call it election, reprobation, or what you please, for all comes to the same thing) one might say to our adversary, the devil, 'Thou fool, why dost thou roar about any longer? Thy lying in wait for souls is as needless and useless as our preaching. Hearest thou not, that God hath taken thy work out of thy hands; and that he doeth it much more effectually?'" (John Wesley, "Free Grace," Sermon 128 [1740 sermon from 1872 edition]; available at : http://gbgm-umc.org/UMhistory/Wesley/sermons/serm-128.stm; accessed 30 Oct 2006).

[582]See Thomas P. Johnston, *Examining the Evangelistic Theology of Billy Graham* (Eugene, OR: Wipf & Stock, 2003), Chapter 5, "Cooperation."

A study of historical terminology for evangelizing opens a "Pandora's Box" of theological and practical considerations. In the quest for a normative definition of evangelizing, we are brought to seek insight from the pages of the Bible. Now ... finally ... the truth of Scripture weighs in on this very emotive topic—a definition of evangelism!

C. Toward Translating Proclamational Words in the Old Testament:

Introduction:

The first two verbs in Psalm 19 happen to be proclamational verbs. While speaking of general revelation, they none the less exhibit a practice which was far too common in the translation practices of the King James Bible.

The following chart displays the wide range of verbs used to translate the verbs in Psalm 19:1, "The heavens are telling of the glory of God; And their expanse is declaring the work of His hands."

On the Translation of the verbs in Psalm 19:1

Hebrew	Greek	Latin	Wycliffe 2nd ed (1388)	Coverdale (1534)	KJV	Douais-Rheims (1899)	RSV (1952)	NAS (1977)	NIV (1984)	New Jerusalem (1985)	ABS' GNT (1993)	NET (2004, 2005)
Saphar	διηγέομαι	enarrant	tellen	declare	declare	shew forth	are telling	are telling	declare	declare	reveals	declare
Nagad	ἀναγγέλλω	adnuntiat*	tellith	sheweth	sheweth	declare	proclaims	is declaring	proclaim	proclaims	shows	displays

*The New Latin Vulgate changed this verb to "annuntiat"

The question that jumps out, especially from the second verb, is as follows: is the Hebrew *nagad* proclamational or is it visual?

Brown-Driver-Briggs encouraged the following translations: 1) tell, announce, report; 2) declare, make known, expound; 3) inform of; 4) publish, declare, proclaim; 5) avow, acknowledge, confess

The *Theological Wordbook of the OT* used two terms as translations of *nagad*: tell, make known

The *Holiday Lexicon* included the following verbs: put forward, report, announce, tell; speak out; denounce; explain, solve.

From these lexicons, the answer is that the verb *nagad* is always verbal. But just like the variance of translation of this verb, so there is a wide variance in the translation of many proclamational verbs in the OT, particularly those that are most closely related to evangelism!

English verbs used to translate Psalm 19:1-2:

As a test case for the translation of proclamational words;

A test case in understanding the value and role of general revelation:

The First Four Verbs in Psalm 19 [18]:1-2

Version	#1	#2	#3	#4
Hebrew (JPS)	ספר	נגד	נבע	חוה
Greek (GOT)	διηγέομαι	ἀναγγέλλω	ἐρεύγομαι	ἀναγγέλλω
Latin (Clem)	enarro	annuntio	eructo	indico
Wycliffe (1388)	tell	tell	tell	shew
Bishops (1568)	declare	shew	occasion talk	teach
Geneva (1560)	declare	shew	utter	teach
KJV (1611)	declare	shew	utter	shew
KJV (1769)	declare	shew	utter	shew
Webster's (1833)	declare	show	utter	show
Leeser (1853)	relate	tell	utter	show
Darby (1884/1890)	declare	shew	utter	shew
Young's (1862/1898)	recount	declare	utter	shew
ERV (1885)	declare	shew	utter	shew
ASV (1901)	declare	show	utter	show
JPS (1917)	declare	show	utter	reveal
Cambridge (1949)	sound	make clear	send	give
RSV (1952)	tell	proclaim	pour forth	declare
NAS (1977)	tell	declare	pour forth	reveal
NKJ (1982)	declare	show	utter	reveal
NIV (1984)	declare	proclaim	pour forth	display
NJB (1985)	declare	proclaim	discourse	hand on
NRSV (1989)	tell	proclaim	pour forth	declare
NAB (1991)	declare	proclaim	convey	impart
GNT (1993)	reveals	plainly show	announce	repeat
CEV (1991/1995)	keep telling	declare	inform	announce
NIRV (1998)	tell	show	speak	make [known]
TNIV (2001)	declare	proclaim	pour forth	display
NLT (2004)	proclaim	display	continue to speak	make [known]
HCSB (2005)	declare	proclaim	pour out	communicate
NET (2006)	declare	display	speak	reveal
NAB (2010)	declare	proclaim	pour forth	whispers
NIV (2011)	declare	proclaim	pour forth	reveal
ESV (2016)	declare	proclaim	pour out	reveal
CSB (2017)	declare	proclaim	pour out	communicate
Movement	Steady with the verb "declare"	From "show" to "proclaim"	From "utter" to "pour forth/out"	From "show" to mixed: from "whisper" [hidden], to "display" [visual], to "reveal" [cognitive], to "communicate" [verbal]
Emphasis	Maintained declarative emphasis	Movement from a visual display (show and tell) to declarative only	From an anthropomorphic rendering of verb to more literal	From declarative (likely meaning of *chavah*) to a broad mixture of ideas

Here is another striking example of this perplexing variety:

Deut 26:17-18, "You have today declared the LORD to be your God, and that you would walk in His ways and keep His statutes, His commandments and His ordinances, and listen to His voice. And the LORD has today declared you to be His people, a treasured possession, as He promised you, and that you should keep all His commandments;"

Translations of 'amar (to say, tell) in Deut 26:17-18

Hebrew	Geneva (1560)	KJV (1611/1769)	Young's (1862)	Darby (1885)	Douais-Rheims✲ (1899)	RSV (1952)	NAS (1977)	NIV (1984)	NJB✲ (1985)	NRSV	NAB✲ (1985)	Holman (2005)
'amar	hast set vp	hast avouched	hast caused to promise	hast this day accepted	hast chosen	have declared	have today declared	have declared	have obtained this declaration	have obtained the Lord's agreement	are making this agreement	have affirmed
'amar	hathe set thee vp	hath avouched thee	hath caused thee to promise	hath accepted thee	hath chosen thee	has declared this day concerning you	has today declared you	has declared this day that you	has obtained this declaration from you	has obtained your agreement	is making this agreement with you	has affirmed that you

The following chart is meant to whet the appetite as to what studies are possible when a particular word is studied in the original languages. This chart considers the translation of 9 uses of *nagad* in Deuteronomy in several English translations, with the addition of Deut 25:9, in which the NASB used "declare."

On the Translation of *nagad* in Deuteronomy (with the addition of Deut 25:9)

Reference	Hebrew	Greek	Latin	KJV	NAS	NIV	NJB✲
Deut 4:13	w + nagad	καί + ἀναγγέλλω	et + ostendit	And he declared	So he declared	He declared	He revealed
Deut 5:5	Nagad	ἀναγγέλλω	adnuntiarem	to shew	to declare	to declare	to let you know
Deut 17:4	w + nagad + lqa + shama	καὶ ἀναγγελῇ σοι καὶ ἐκζητήσεις	et hoc tibi fuerit nuntiatum	And it be told thee, and thou hast heard *of it*	and if it is told you and you have heard of it	and this has been brought to your attention	and this person is denounced to you
Deut 17:9	Nagad	ἀναγγέλλω	indicabunt	they shall shew	they shall declare	they shall give	And let you know
Deut 17:10	Nagad	ἀναγγέλλω	dixerint	shall shew	they declare	shall give	they give
Deut 17:11	Nagad	ἀναγγέλλω	-	they shall shew	they shall declare	they give	they have given
Deut 25:9	'anah + 'amar	ἀποκρίνομαι + λέγω	et dicet	and shall answer and say	and she shall declare	and say	and pronounce the following words
Deut 26:3	Nagad	ἀναγγέλλω	profiteor	I profess	I declare	I declare	I declare
Deut 30:18	Nagad	ἀναγγέλλω	praedico	I denounce	I declare	I declare	I tell
Deut 32:7	Nagad	ἀναγγέλλω	adnuntiabit	he will shew	he will inform	he will tell	let him explain

Using the Old Testament as an example, the chart below examines the translation of Hebrew words into Greek, Latin, and English. A lack of clarity in translation is sometimes apparent by use of the word "shew" in key verses of the KJV, most often found when in the context of 1st person renderings.

A Proclaimed or Spoken Witness in the Old Testament
(Often Focused toward the Nations, the Peoples, a People Yet to be Born, etc.)
A Select Translation Analysis Organized by (1) Hebrew Verbs and (2) Greek translation
[this study supplies examples only, and is not exhaustive—see the note following this chart]

#	Passage	Person/Form	Hebrew	Stem	LXX	Latin	KJV	NAS
1.	Psa 9:14	1st person, sg	Saphar	Piel	ἐξαγγέλλω	Adnuntiem	Shew forth	Tell
2.	Psa 71:15	My mouth	Saphar	Piel	ἐξαγγέλλω	Adnuntiabit	Shew forth	Tell
3.	Psa 73:28	1st person, sg	Saphar	Piel	ἐξαγγέλλω	Praedicationes	Declare	Tell
4.	Psa 79:13	1st person, pl	Saphar	Piel	ἐξαγγέλλω	Adnuntiabimus	Shew forth	Tell
5.	Psa 107:22	3rd person, pl	Saphar	Piel	ἐξαγγέλλω	Adnuntien	Declare	Tell
6.	Psa 119:13	1st person, sg	Saphar	Piel	ἐξαγγέλλω	Pronuntiavi	Declare	Tell
7.	Psa 22:30	P generation	Saphar	Piel	ἀναγγέλλω	Conspectu	Be accounted to	Tell
8.	Psa 96:3	Imperative, pl	Saphar	Piel	ἀναγγέλλω	Adnuntiate	Declare	Tell
9.	Psa 102:21	Infinitive	Saphar	Piel	ἀναγγέλλω	Narretur	Declare	Tell
10.	Psa 78:4	Participle, pl	Saphar	Piel	ἀπαγγέλλω	Narrantes	Shew	Tell
11.	Psa 78:6	Next generation	Saphar	Piel	ἀπαγγέλλω	Narrabunt	Declare	Tell
12.	Ezek 12:16	A few	Saphar	Piel	ἐκδιηγέομαι	Narrent	Declare	Tell
13.	Psa 118:17	1st person	Saphar	Piel	ἐκδιηγέομαι	Narrabo	Declare	Tell
14.	Psa 9:1	1st person	Saphar	Piel	διηγέομαι	Narrabo	Shew forth	Tell
15.	Psa 19:1 (1)	Heavens	Saphar	Piel	διηγέομαι	Enarrant	Declare	Tell
16.	Psa 26:7 (2)	1st person	Saphar	Piel	διηγέομαι	Enarrem	Tell	Declare
17.	Psa 48:13	2nd person	Saphar	Piel	διηγέομαι	Enarretis	Tell	Tell
18.	Psa 50:16	The wicked	Saphar	Piel	διηγέομαι	Enarras	Declare	Declare
19.	Psa 66:16	1st person	Saphar	Piel	διηγέομαι	Narrabo	Declare	Tell
20.	Psa 75:1	Works/men	Saphar	Piel	διηγέομαι	Narrabimus	Declare	Declare
21.	Psa 88:11	In the grave	Saphar	Pual	διηγέομαι	Narrabit	Declare	Declare
22.	Psa 145:6 (2)	3rd person	Saphar	Piel	διηγέομαι	Narrabunt	Declare	Tell
23.	Isa 43:21	People formed	Saphar	Piel	διηγέομαι	Narrabit	Shew forth	Declare
24.	Exod 9:16	God	Saphar	Piel	διαγγέλλω	Narretur	Declare	Proclaim
25.	Psa 2:7 (1)	1st person	Saphar	Piel	διαγγέλλω	Praedicans	Declare	Surely tell
26.	1 Chron 16:24	Imperative	Saphar	Piel	ἐξηγέομαι[583]	Narrate	Declare	Tell
27.	Psa 40:5 (1)	1st person	Nagad	Hiph	ἀπαγγέλλω	Adnuntiavi	Declare	Declare
28.	Psa 71:17	Psalmist	Nagad	Hiph	ἀπαγγέλλω	Pronuntiabo	Declare	Declare
29.	Psa 71:18	Psalmist	Nagad	Hiph	ἀπαγγέλλω	Adnuntiem	Shew	Declare
30.	Psa 145:4	One generat'n	Nagad	Hiph	ἀπαγγέλλω	Pronuntiabunt	Declare	Declare
31.	Psa 147:19	God	Nagad	Hiph	ἀπαγγέλλω	Adnuntiat	Shew	Declare
32.	Deut 4:13	God	Nagad	Hiph	ἀναγγέλλω	Ostendit	Declare	Declare
33.	Deut 5:5	Moses	Nagad	Hiph	ἀναγγέλλω	Adnuntiarem	Shew	Declare
34.	Deut 30:18	Moses	Nagad	Hiph	ἀναγγέλλω	Praedico	Denounce	Declare
35.	Deut 32:7	Your father	Nagad	Hiph	ἀναγγέλλω	Adnuntiabit	Shew	Inform
36.	1 Sam 3:13	God	Nagad	Hiph	ἀναγγέλλω	Praedixi	Have told	Have told
37.	2 Sam 1:20 (1)	Negative use	Nagad	Hiph	ἀναγγέλλω	Adnuntiare	Tell	Tell
38.	Job 33:23	An angel	Nagad	Hiph	ἀναγγέλλω	Adnuntiet	Shew	Remind
39.	Psa 9:11	Command	Nagad	Hiph	ἀναγγέλλω	Adnuntiate	Declare	Declare
40.	Psa 19:1 (2)	Firmament	Nagad	Hiph	ἀναγγέλλω	Adnuntiat	Shew forth	Declare
41.	Psa 22:31	N. generation	Nagad	Hiph	ἀναγγέλλω	Adnuntiabunt	Declare	Declare
42.	Psa 30:9	The dust	Nagad	Hiph	ἀναγγέλλω	Adnuntiabit	Declare	Declare
43.	Psa 50:6	Heavens	Nagad	Hiph	ἀναγγέλλω	Adnuntiabunt	Declare	Declare
44.	Psa 51:15	1st person	Nagad	Hiph	ἀναγγέλλω	Adnuntiabit	Shew forth	Declare
41.	Psa 64:9	Men	Nagad	Hiph	ἀναγγέλλω	Adnuntiaverunt	Declare	Declare
42.	Psa 92:2	Infinitive	Nagad	Hiph	ἀναγγέλλω	Adnuntiandum	Shew forth	Declare
43.	Psa 92:15	The righteous	Nagad	Hiph	ἀναγγέλλω	Adnuntient	Shew	Declare

---

[583] 1 Chron 16:24 is not found in Ralph's LXX Septuagint (BibleWorks 9.0), but is found in the Greek Orthodox Text.

#	Passage	Person	Hebrew	Stem	LXX	Latin	KJV	NAS
44.	Psa 97:6	Heavens	*Nagad*	Hiph	ἀναγγέλλω	*Pronuntiabo*	Declare	Declare
45.	Psa 111:6	God	*Nagad*	Hiph	ἀναγγέλλω	*Adnuntiabit*	Shew	Made known
46.	Isa 42:12	The inhabitants	*Nagad*	Hiph	ἀναγγέλλω	*Nuntiabunt*	Declare	Declare
47.	Isa 58:1 (4)	Imperative	*Nagad*	Hiph	ἀναγγέλλω	*Adnuntia*	Shew	Declare
48.	Isa 66:19	Those far off	*Nagad*	Hiph	ἀναγγέλλω	*Pronuntiabunt*	Declare	Declare
49.	Jer 4:5	Imperative	*Nagad*	Hiph	ἀναγγέλλω	*Adnuntiate*	Declare	Declare
50.	Jer 4:15	3rd person	*Nagad*	Hiph	ἀναγγέλλω	*Adnuntiatis*	Declare	Declare
51.	Jer 5:20	Imperative	*Nagad*	Hiph	ἀναγγέλλω	*Adnuntiate*	Declare	Declare
52.	Jer 31:10	Imperative	*Nagad*	Hiph	ἀναγγέλλω	*Adnuntiate*	Declare	Declare
53.	Psa 75:9	1st person	*Nagad*	Hiph	ἀγαλλιάω	*Adnuntiabo*	Declare	Declare
54.	1 Chron 17:10	The Lord	*Nagad*	Hiph	αὐξάνω	*Adnuntio*	Tell	Tell
55.	1 Sam 31:9	Philistines of the death of Saul	*Basar*	Piel	εὐαγγελίζω	*Adnuntiaretur*	Publish	Carry the good news
56.	2 Sam 1:20 (2)	Negative use	*Basar*	Piel	εὐαγγελίζω	*Adnuntietis*	Publish	Proclaim
57.	2 Sam 18:19	Of Ahimaaz	*Basar*	Piel	εὐαγγελίζω	*Nuntiabo*	Bear … tidings	Bring … news
58.	2 Sam 18:26	Of one running	*Basar*	Piel	εὐαγγελίζω	*bonus est nuntius*	Brings tidings	Bringing good news
59.	1 Kgs 1:42	Of a Jonathan	*Basar*	Piel	εὐαγγελίζω	*bona nuntians*	Bring good tidings	Bring good news
60.	Psa 40:9 (1)	1st person	*Basar*	Piel	εὐαγγελίζω	*Adnuntiavi*	Preach	Proclaim glad tidings
61.	Psa 68:11	Women	*Basar*	Piel	εὐαγγελίζω	*Evangelizantibus*	Publish	Proclaim
62.	Psa 96:2	Imperative	*Basar*	Piel	εὐαγγελίζω	*Adnuntiate*	Shew forth	Proclaim good tidings
63.	Isa 40:9 (1)	Participle	*Basar*	Piel	εὐαγγελίζω	*Quae evangelizas*	That bringeth good tidings	Bearer of good news
64.	Isa 40:9 (3)	Participle	*Basar*	Piel	εὐαγγελίζω	*Quae evangelizas*	That bringeth good tidings	Bearer of good news
65.	Isa 52:7 (1)	Him	*Basar*	Piel	εὐαγγελίζω	*Adnuntiantis*	Bring good tidings	Bring good news
66.	Isa 52:7 (3)	Him	*Basar*	Piel	εὐαγγελίζω	*Adnuntiantis*	bring good tidings	Bring good news
67.	Isa 60:6	3rd person plural	*Basar*	Piel	εὐαγγελίζω	*Adnuntiantes*	Shew forth	Bear good news
68.	Isa 61:1 (1)	Infinitive	*Basar*	Piel	εὐαγγελίζω	*Adnuntiandum*	Preach good tidings	Bring good news
69.	Joel 2:32 [3:5]	Middle [of God]	*Basar*	[unclear]	εὐαγγελίζω	*In residuis*	In the remnant	among the survivors
70.	Nah 1:15 [2:1] (1)	Him	*Basar*	Piel	εὐαγγελίζω	*Evangelizantis*	Bringeth good tidings	Brings good news
71.	1 Chron 16:23	Imperative m-pl	*Basar*	Piel	ἀναγγέλλω	*Adnuntiate*	Shew forth	Proclaim
72.	Isa 41:27	The Lord will give	*Basar*	Piel	παρακαλέω	*Evangelistam*	one that bringeth good tidings	a messenger of good news
73.	Jer 4:16	Imperative	*Shama*	Hiph	ἀναγγέλλω	*auditum est*	Publish	Proclaim
74.	Nah 1:15 [2:1] (2)	Him	*Shama*	Hiph	ἀπαγγέλλω	*Adnuntiantis*	Publish	Announce
75.	Deut 4:6	Imperfect	*Shama*	Qal	ἀκούω	*Audientes*	Shall hear	Will hear
76.	Deut 32:1 (3)	Imperfect	*Shama*	Qal	ἀκούω	*Oris*	Hear	Hear
77.	Psa 26:7 (1)	1st person	*Shama*	Hiph	ἀκούω	*Audiam*	Publish	Proclaim
78.	Jer 4:5	Imperative	*Shama*	Hiph	ἀκούω	*Auditum*	Publish	Proclaim
79.	Jer 4:15	Participle	*Shama*	Hiph	ἀκούω	*Notum facientis*	Publish	Proclaim
80.	Jer 5:20	Imperative	*Shama*	Hiph	ἀκούω	*Auditum facite*	Publish	Proclaim
81.	Psa 66:8	Imperative	*Shama*	Hiph	ἀκουτίζω	*Auditam facite*	Make … to be heard	Sound
82.	Psa 106:2 (2)	Rhetorical question	*Shama*	Hiph	ἀκουστός + ποιέω	*Auditas faciet*	Shew forth	Show forth—NIV declare
83.	Isa 52:7 (4)	Him	*Shama*	Hiph	ἀκουστός + ποιέω	*Praedicantis*	Publish	Announce
84.	Isa 62:11 (1)	The Lord	*Shama*	Hiph	ἀκουστός + ποιέω	*Auditum fecit*	Proclaim	Proclaim

#	Passage	Person	Hebrew	Stem	LXX	Latin	KJV	NAS
85.	Isa 52:7 (2)	Him	*Shama*	Hiph	ἡ ἀκοή (noun)	*Praedicantis*	Publish	Announce
86.	Neh 8:15 (1)	3rd person	*Shama*	Hiph	σημαίνω	*Praedicent*	Publish	Proclaim
87.	Prov 1:21 (1)	Wisdom	*Qara'*	Qal	κηρύσσω	*Clamitat*	Cry	Cry
88.	Isa 61:1 (2)	Infinitive	*Qara'*	Qal	κηρύσσω	*Praedicarem*	Proclaim	Proclaim
89.	Jon 1:2	God to Jonah	*Qara'*	Qal	κηρύσσω	*Praedica*	Cry	Cry
90.	Jon 3:2	God to Jonah	*Qara'*	Qal	κηρύσσω	*Praedica*	Preach	Proclaim
91.	Jon 3:4 (1)	Jonah	*Qara'*	Qal	κηρύσσω	*Clamavit*	Cry	Cry
92.	Deut 32:3 (1)	Moses in 1st pers	*Qara'*	Qal	καλέω	*Invocabo*	Publish	Proclaim
93.	Isa 61:2	Infinitive	*Qara'*	Qal	καλέω	*Praedicarem*	Proclaim	Proclaim
94.	Prov 9:3	Wisdom	*Qara'*	Qal	συγκαλέω	*Vocarent*	Cry	Call
95.	Isa 58:1 (1)	Imperative	*Qara'*	Qal	ἀναβοάω	*Clama*	Cry	Cry
96.	Deut 32:7	The elders	*'amar*	Qal	λέγω	*Dicent*	Tell	Tell
97.	1 Chron 16:31	3rd person	*'amar*	Qal	λέγω	*Dicant*	Say	Say
98.	Psa 2:7 (2)	The Lord	*'amar*	Qal	λέγω	*Dixit*	Say	Say
99.	Psa 40:10 (2)	1st person	*'amar*	Qal	λέγω	*Dixit*	Declare	Speak
100.	Psa 40:16	3rd person	*'amar*	Qal	λέγω	*Dicant*	Say	Say
101.	Psa 70:4	3rd person	*'amar*	Qal	λέγω	*Dicant*	Say	Say
102.	Psa 96:10	Imperative	*'amar*	Qal	λέγω	*Dicete*	Say	Say
103.	Psa 106:48	All the people	*'amar*	Qal	λέγω	*Dicet*	Say	Say
104.	Psa 107:2	The redeemed, imperative	*'amar*	Qal	λέγω	*Dicant*	Say	Say
105.	Psa 118:4	Imperfect	*'amar*	Qal	λέγω	*Dicant*	Say	Say
106.	Psa 145:6 (1)	3rd person	*'amar*	Qal	λέγω	*Dicent*	Speak	Speak
107.	Psa 145:11 (1)	3rd person	*'amar*	Qal	λέγω	*Dixit*	Shew	Speak
108.	Prov 1:21 (2)	Wisdom	*'amar*	Qal	λέγω	*Dicens*	Uttereth	Utters
109.	Isa 6:9	Imperative	*'amar*	Qal	λέγω	*Dixit*	Tell	Tell
110.	Isa 40:9 (6)	Evangelist (*bashar*, εὐαγγελίζω)	*'amar*	Qal	λέγω	*Dic*	Say	Say
111.	Isa 44:5	Imperfect	*'amar*	Qal	λέγω	*Dicet*	Say	Say
112.	Isa 45:24	Perfect	*'amar*	Qal	λέγω	*Dicet*	Say	Say
113.	Isa 52:7 (5)	Him	*'amar*	Qal	λέγω	*Praedicantis*	Say	Say
114.	Isa 62:11 (2)	Imperative	*'amar*	Qal	λέγω	*Dicite*	Say	Say
115.	Isa 65:1	Of the Lord	*'amar*	Qal	λέγω	*Dixi*	Say	Say
116.	Ezek 2:4	Prophet	*'amar*	Qal	λέγω	*Dices*	Say	Say
117.	Jon 1:9	Jonah	*'amar*	Qal	λέγω	*Dixit*	Say	Say
118.	Jon 3:4 (2)	Jonah	*'amar*	Qal	λέγω	*Dixit*	Say	Say
119.	Exod 4:12	Moses	*Dabar*	Piel	λαλέω	*Loquaris*	Say	Say
120.	Deut 5:4	God	*Dabar*	Piel	λαλέω	*Locutus*	Talked	Spoke
121.	Deut 6:7 (2)	2nd person	*Dabar*	Piel	λαλέω	*Meditaberis*	Talk	Talk
122.	Deut 11:19 (2)	Infinitive	*Dabar*	Piel	λαλέω	*Meditentur*	Speak	Talk
123.	Deut 32:1 (2)	Moses	*Dabar*	Piel	λαλέω	*Loquor*	Speak	Speak
124.	Psa 40:5 (2)	1st person	*Dabar*	Piel	λαλέω	*Locutus*	Speak	Speak
125.	Psa 116:10	1st person; 2 Cor 4	*Dabar*	Piel	λαλέω	*Locutus*	Spoken	Said
126.	Psa 119:46	1st person	*Dabar*	Piel	λαλέω	*Loquebar*	Speak	Speak
127.	Psa 145:11 (2)	3rd person	*Dabar*	Piel	λαλέω	*Loquentur*	Talk	Talk
128.	Psa 145:21	1st person	*Dabar*	Piel	λαλέω	*Loquentur*	Speak	Speak
129.	Isa 52:6	God	*Dabar*	Piel	λαλέω	*Loquebar*	Speak	Speak
130.	Ezek 3:18	2nd person	*Dabar*	Piel	λαλέω	*locutus [fueris]*	Speakest [to warn]	Speak out [to warn]
131.	Ezek 33:8	2nd person	*Dabar*	Piel	λαλέω	*Fueris locutus*	Speak [to warn]	Speak [to warn]
132.	Amos 5:10	Participle	*Dabar*	Qal	ὁ λόγος (noun)	*Loquentem*	Speak	Speak
133.	2 Sam 23:1 (1)	David	*Ne'um*	(noun)	πιστός (adj)	*Dixit*	Say	Declare
134.	2 Sam 23:1 (2)	David	*Ne'um*	(noun)	πιστός (adj)	*Dixit*	Say	Declare
135.	Psa 35:28	1st person	*Hagah*	Qal	μελετάω	*Meditabitur*	Speak	Declare

#	Passage	Person	Hebrew	Stem	LXX	Latin	KJV	NAS
136.	Psa 71:24	1st person	*Hagah*	Qal	μελετάω	*Meditabitur*	Talk	Utter
137.	Psa 78:2	1st person	*Naba'*	Hiphil	φθέγγομαι	*Eloquar*	Utter	Utter
138.	Psa 19:2 (1)	Heavens	*Naba' + dabar*	Hiphil	ἐρεύγομαι	*Eructat +verbum*	Uttereth + speech	Pours forth + speech
139.	Psa 119:171	1st person	*Naba'*	Hiphil	ἐξερεύγομαι	*Eructabunt*	Utter	Utter
140.	Psa 145:7	3rd person	*Naba'*	Hiphil	ἐξερεύγομαι	*Eructabunt*	Utter	Utter
141.	Psa 106:2 (1)	Rhet. question	*Malal*	Piel	λαλέω	*Loquetur*	Utter	Speak
142.	Isa 38:19	The father	*Yada'*	Hiphil	ἀναγγέλλω	*Notam*	Make known	Tell
143.	Isa 12:4 (3)	Imperative	*Yada'*	Hiphil	ἀναγγέλλω	*Notas*	Declare	Make remember
144.	Psa 89:1	1st person	*Yada'*	Hiphil	ἀπαγγέλλω	*Adnuntiabo*	Make known	Make known
145.	Psa 105:1	Imperative	*Yada'*	Hiphil	ἀπαγγέλλω	*Adnuntiate*	Make known	Make known
146.	2 Sam 22:50 (1)	1st person	*Yada'*	Hiphil	ἐξομολογέω	*confitebor*	Give thanks	Give thanks
147.	Psa 7:17	1st person	*Yada'*	Hiphil	ἐξομολογέω	*confitebor*	Praise	Give thanks
148.	Psa 119:7	1st person	*Yada'*	Hiphil	ἐξομολογέω	*confitebor*	Praise	Give thanks
149.	1 Sam 16:3	The Lord	*Yada'*	Hiphil	γνωρίζω	*Ostendam*	Will show	Will show
150.	1 Chron 16:8	Imperative	*Yada'*	Hiphil	γνωρίζω	*Notas*	Make known	Make known
151.	Ezra 7:25	2nd person	*Yada'*	Haphel	γνωρίζω	*Docete*	Teach	Teach
152.	Psa 78:5	Fathers	*Yada'*	Hiphil	γνωρίζω	*Facere*	Make known	Teach
153.	Psa 88:12	In the grave	*Yada'*	Niphal	γνωρίζω	*Cognoscentur*	Known	Make known
154.	Psa 145:12	Infinitive	*Yada'*	Hiphil	γνωρίζω	*Notam*	Make known	Make known
155.	2 Sam 22:50	1st person sing	*Yada'*	Hiphil	ἐξομολογέω	*Confitebor*	Give thanks	Give thanks
156.	Psa 18:49 (1)	1st person sing	*Yada'*	Hiphil	ἐξομολογέω	*Confitebor*	Give thanks	Give thanks
157.	Psa 57:9	1st person sing	*Yada'*	Hiphil	ἐξομολογέω	*Confitebor*	Praise	Give thanks
158.	Psa 92:1	Infinitive	*Yada'*	Hiphil	ἐξομολογέω	*Confiteri*	Give thanks	Give thanks
159.	Psa 108:3	1st person sing	*Yada'*	Hiphil	ἐξομολογέω	*Confitebor*	Praise	Give thanks
160.	Deut 4:9 (3)	2nd person	*Yada'*	Hiphil	συμβιβάζω	*Docebis*	Teach	Make known
161.	Exod 18:20 (2)	2nd person	*Yada'*	Hiphil	σημαίνω	*Colendi*	Shew	Make known
162.	Isa 64:2	Prayer to the Lord	*Yada*	Hiphil	φανερός + εἰμι	*Notum fiere*	Make known	Make known
163.	2 Sam 22:50 (2)	1st person sing	*Zamar*	Piel	ψάλλω	*Cantabo*	Sing praises	Sing praises
164.	Psa 18:49 (2)	1st person sing	*Zamar*	Piel	ψάλλω	*Psalmum dico*	Sing praises	Sing praises
165.	Psa 57:9	1st person sing	*Zamar*	Piel	ψάλλω	*Cantabo*	Sing	Sing praises
166.	Psa 92:1	Infinitive	*Zamar*	Piel	ψάλλω	*Psallere*	Sing praises	Sing praises
167.	Psa 108:3	1st person sing	*Zamar*	Piel	ψάλλω	*Cantabo*	Sing praises	Sing praises
168.	Psa 6:5	2nd person	*Zeker*	Verbal noun	μνημονεύω	*Memor*	Remembrance	Mention
169.	Psa 71:16	1st person	*Zakar*	Hiphil	μιμνήσκω μιμνήσκομαι	*Memorabore*	Make mention	Make mention
170.	Isa 12:4 (4)	Imperative	*Zakar*	Hiphil	μιμνήσκω μιμνήσκομαι	*Mementote*	Make mention	Make remember
171.	Jer 4:16	Imperative	*Zakar*	Hiphil	ἀναμιμνήσκω	*Concitate*	Make mention	Report
172.	Exod 18:20 (1)	2nd person	*Zahar*	Hiphil	διαμαρτύρομαι	*Ostendasque*	Teach	Teach
173.	2 Chron 19:10	Leaders	*Zahar*	Hiphil	διαστέλλομαι	*Ostendite*	Warn	Warn
174.	Ezek 3:18 (1)	2nd person	*Zahar*	Hiphil	διαστέλλομαι	*Adnuntiaveris*	Warn	Warn
175.	Ezek 3:18 (2)	Infinitive	*Dabar + Zahar*	Hiphil	λαλέω + διαστέλλομαι	*Locutus fueris ut avertatur*	Speakest to warn	Speak out to warn
176.	Ezek 3:19	2nd person	*Zahar*	Hiphil	διαστέλλομαι	*Adnuntiaveris*	Warn	Warn
177.	Ezek 3:20	2nd person	*Zahar*	Hiphil	διαστέλλομαι	*Adnuntiasti*	Give warning	Warn
178.	Ezek 3:21	2nd person	*Zahar*	Niphal	διαστέλλομαι	*Adnuntiasti*	Warn	Take warning
179.	Ezek 3:17	2nd person	*Zahar*	Hiphil	διαπειλέω	*Adnuntiabis*	Give warning	Warn
180.	Ezek 3:18 (2)	Infinitive	*Dabar + Zahar*	Hiphil	λαλέω + διαστέλλομαι	*Locutus fueris ut avertatur*	Speakest to warn	Speak out to warn
181.	Ezek 33:8	Infinitive	*Dabar + Zahar*	Hiphil	λαλέω + φυλάσσω	*Custodiat*	Speak to warn	Speak to warn
182.	Ezek 33:9	2nd person	*Zahar*	Hiphil	προαπαγγέλλω	*Adnuntiante*	Warn	Warn

#	Passage	Person	Hebrew	Stem	LXX	Latin	KJV	NAS
183.	Ezek 33:7	2nd person	*Zahar*	Hiphil	[n/a]	*Adnuntiabis*	Warn	Give warning
184.	Prov 24:25	Participle	*Yakach*	Hiphil	ἐλέγχω	*Arguunt*	Rebuke	Rebuke
185.	Amos 5:10	Participle	*Yakach*	Hiphil	ἐλέγχω	*corripientem*	Rebuketh	Reprove
186.	Isa 59:12	Our sins	*'Anah*	Qal	ἀνθίστημι	*Responderunt*	Testify	Testify
187.	1 Chron 16:9	Imperative	*Siyach*	Qal	διηγέομαι	*Narrate*	Talk	Speak
188.	Psa 105:2	Imperative	*Siyach*	Qal	διηγέομαι	*Narrate*	Talk ye	Speak
189.	Deut 4:14	Infinitive	*Lamad*	Piel	διδάσκω	*Docerem*	Teach	Teach
190.	Deut 5:31	2nd person	*Lamad*	Piel	διδάσκω	*Docebis*	Teach	Teach
191.	Deut 11:19 (1)	2nd person	*Lamad*	Piel	διδάσκω	*Docete*	Teach	Teach
192.	2 Chron 17:7	Infinitive	*Lamad*	Piel	διδάσκω	*Docerent*	Teach	Teach
193.	Ezra 7:10	Infinitive	*Lamad*	Piel	διδάσκω	*Doceret*	Teach	Teach
194.	Psa 51:13	1st person	*Lamad*	Piel	διδάσκω	*Docebo*	Teach	Teach
195.	Jer 31:34	3rd person	*Lamad*	Piel	διδάσκω	*Docebunt*	Teach	Teach
196.	Deut 4:5	1st person	*Lamad*	Piel	δείκνυμι	*Docuerim*	Taught	Taught
197.	Deut 33:10	3rd person plural	*Yarah*	Hiphil	δηλόω	*Iudicia*	Teach	Teach
198.	Lev 10:11	Infinitive	*Yarah*	Hiphil	συμβιβάζω	*Doceatisque*	Teach	Teach
199.	Deut 6:7 (1)	2nd person	*Shanan*	Piel	προβιβάζω	*Narrabis*	Teach diligently	Teach diligently
200.	Judges 5:11	3rd person imperf	*Tanah*	Piel	δίδωμι	*Narrentur*	Rehearse	Recount
201.	Isa 12:6 (1)	Imperative	*Tsahal*	Qal	ἀγαλλιάω	*Exulta*	Cry out	Cry aloud
202.	Psa 20:5 (1)	1st person plural	*Ranan*	Piel	ἀγαλλιάω	*Leatabimur*	Rejoice	Sing for joy
203.	Isa 12:6 (2)	Imperative	*Ranan*	Qal	εὐφραίνω	*Lauda*	Shout	Shout for joy
204.	Prov 1:20 (1)	Wisdom	*Ranan*	Qal	ὑμνέω	*Praedicat*	Cry	Shout
205.	Psa 20:5 (2)	1st person plural	*Dagal*	Qal	μεγαλύνω	*Magnificabimur*	Set up banners	Set up banners
206.	Isa 40:9 (2)	Evangelist (*basereth*, εὐαγγελιζόμενος)	*Rum*	Hiphil	ὑψόω	*Exalta*	Lift up [thy voice]	Lift up [your voice]
207.	Isa 40:9 (4)	Evangelist (*basereth*, εὐαγγελιζόμενος)	*Rum*	Hiphil	ὑψόω	*Exalta*	Lift *it* up	Lift *it* up
208.	Isa 58:1 (3)	Imperative	*Rum*	Hiphil	ὑψόω	*Exalta*	Lift up	Raise
209.	Prov 1:20 (2)	Wisdom	*Nathan*	Qal	ἡ παρρησία (noun)	*Vocem*	Uttereth	Lifts [her voice]
210.	Neh 8:15 (2)	2nd person	*'abar*	Hiphil	ἡ σάλπιγξ (noun)	*Divulgent vocem*	Proclaim	Circulated a proclamation
211.	Deut 32:3 (2)	Imperative plural	*Yahab*	Qal	δίδωμι + ἡ μεγαλωσύνη (noun)	*Date magnificentiam*	Ascribe greatness	Ascribe greatness
212.	1 Chron 16:28 (1)	Imperative plural	*Yahab*	Qal	δίδωμι	*Adfert*	Give	Ascribe
213.	1 Chron 16:28 (2)	Imperative plural	*Yahab*	Qal	δίδωμι ... ἡ δόξα + ἡ ἰσχύς (nouns)	*Adferte ... gloriam et imperium*	Give ... glory and strength	Ascribe ... glory and strength
214.	1 Chron 16:29	Imperative plural	*Yahab*	Qal	δίδωμι + ἡ δόξα (noun)	*Date ... gloriam*	Give ... the glory	Ascribe ... the glory
215.	Psa 29:1 (1)	Imperative plural	*Yahab*	Qal	φέρω	*Adferte*	Give	Ascribe
216.	Psa 29:1 (2[3])	Imperative plural	*Yahab*	Qal	φέρω + ἡ δόξα (noun)	*Adferte ... gloriam*	Give ... glory and strength	Ascribe ... glory and strength
217.	Psa 29:2	Imperative plural	*Yahab*	Qal	φέρω + ἡ δόξα (noun)	*Adferte ... gloriam*	Give ... the glory	Ascribe ... the glory
218.	Psa 96:7 (1)	Imperative plural	*Yahab*	Qal	φέρω	*Adferte*	Give	Ascribe
219.	Psa 96:7 (2)	Imperative plural	*Yahab*	Qal	φέρω + ἡ δόξα + ἡ τιμή (nouns)	*Adferte ... gloriam et honorem*	Give ... glory and strength	Ascribe ... glory and strength
220.	Psa 96:8	Imperative plural	*Yahab*	Qal	φέρω + ἡ δόξα (noun)	*Adferte ... gloriam*	Give ... the glory	Ascribe ... the glory
221.	Prov 15:7	3rd person	*Zarah*	Piel	δέω	*Disseminabunt*	Disperse	Spread
222.	Psa 19:2 (2)	Heavens	*Chavah + da'ath*	Piel	ἀναγγέλλω	*Indicat + scientiam*	Sheweth + knowledge	Reveals + knowledge

#	Passage	Person	Hebrew	Stem	LXX	Latin	KJV	NAS
223.	Prov 11:30	Participle	*Laqach*	Qal	ἀφαιρέω	*Suscipit*	Winneth [souls]	Wins [souls]
224.	Deut 32:1 (1)	Moses	*Azan*	Hiphil	προσέχω	*Audite*	Give ear	Give ear
225.	Isa 40:9 (5)	2nd person	*Lo yare'*	Qal	μή + φοβέω	*Noli timere*	Be not afraid	Do not fear
226.	Psa 40:9 (2)	1st person	*Lo kala'*	Qal	μή + κωλύω	*Non prohibebo*	Not refrain	Not restrain
227.	Psa 40:10 (1)	1st person	*Lo kasah*	Piel	οὐ + κρύπτω	*Non abscondi*	Not hid	Not hidden
228.	Psa 40:10 (3)	1st person	*Lo kachad*	Piel	οὐ + κρύπτω	*Non abscondi*	Not concealed	Not concealed
229.	Isa 62:6 (1)	Of the watchmen	*Lo chashah*	Qal	οὐ + σιωπάω	*Non tacebunt*	Never hold their peace	Never keep silent
230.	Isa 62:6 (2)	Of the watchmen	*Lo demiy*	[noun]	οὐ + διορθόω	*Ne taceatis*	Keep not silent	Take no rest
231.	Deut 4:9 (1)	2nd person	*Pen shakach*	Qal	μή + ἐπιλανθάνομαι	*Ne obliviscaris*	Lest ... forget	Lest ... forget
232.	Deut 4:9 (2)	2nd person	*Pen sur*	Qal	μή + ἀφίστημι	*Ne excedant*	Lest ... depart	Lest ... depart

Please note the many other instances of proclamational verbs in the Book of Psalms **NOT INCLUDED** in the above chart (using KJV references):

Using the verb *saphar*: Psa 22:18, 22; 40:5, 7; 44:1; 45:1; 56:8; 59:12; 64:5; 69:26, 28; 73:15; 78:3; 87:6; 119:26; 139:16, 18;

Using the verb *nagad*: Psa 52:1; 142:2;

Using the verb *basar*: 2 Sam 4:10; 18:20 (twice), 31; 1 Chron 10:9;

Using the verb *shama*: approx 80 uses in the Psalms, this chart cites only 14;

Using the verb *qara'*: approx 49 uses in the Psalms, this chart cites 9; consider also, for example, Deut 33:19;

Using the verb *'uwd*: Deut 8:19; etc.

Furthermore, the semantic ranges of some of the above verbs lead them to have a further proclamational emphasis depending on context:

For example, the Hebrew *zakar*, sometimes translated by the Greek μνημονεύω (to remember), can have a verbal element to it, e.g. to recall or bring to mind or remind, cf. 1 Chron 16:12, 15; Psa 6:5; 63:6

Preliminary Statistics (from above chart):

231 proclamational verb uses (+2 nouns) in the OT

40 Hebrew stems

multiple Greek verbs, 5 additional cognates, and 4 nouns

Observations (expanded from above chart):

Notice the 5 uses of κηρύσσω (26 OT uses; 61 NT uses) compared to the 8 uses of the Latin *praeco* and *praecento* (6 OT uses, 4 of which coincide with the LXX use of khru,ssw) and *praedico* (48 OT uses; 85 NT uses)

Notice also the 16 uses of εὐαγγελίζω above (20/21 total OT uses; 54/55/56 NT uses) compared to the use of the Latin *evangelizo* (3 total OT uses; 43 NT uses)

While the verb lema or stem *basar* is found 24 times as a verb, 21 of those are translated as εὐαγγελίζω according to the Tov-Polak 2004 *Hebrew-Greek Parallel Text*

Interestingly, five of these uses are found in a non-spiritual sense in 2 Sam 18:19-31;

Of the 10 uses in the early prophets, 8 in 1 & 2 Samuel and the one in 1 Chronicles refers to news of battle, and one in 1 Kings refers to political good news

The remaining 10 uses profer a spiritual meaning, and one a non-spiritual meaning (Jer 20:15):

The three in Psalms: 40:10; 68:12; 96:2

The six in Isaiah: 40:9 (twice); 52:7 (twice); 60:6; 61:1

And the two other prophetic uses: Jer 20:15; Nah 2:1

Notice the 7 uses of διδάσκω (79 OT uses; 98 NT uses) compared to the 9 uses of the Latin *doceo* (cf. Matt 28:19-20, in Matthew's Great Commission)

Further Observations:

It must be born in mind that the verses above were chosen because they had an "evangelistic feel." By that I mean that the audience was (for the most part) broader than the people of Israel. The recipients included: the heavens and earth, the earth, all the ends of the earth, the coastlands, the islands, the world and all that springs from it, inhabitants of the world, sons of men, many, men; the nations, all the families of the nations, families of the peoples, peoples, kingdoms, kings, young men and virgins, old men and children; this generation, the next generation, the coming generation, a generation to come, all generations, one generation to another, children; transgressors, sinners, those who hate the Lord, and the wicked (etc.). Therefore numerous verses like Psalm 22:22 were not included in the above chart (as listed above), although they use proclamational terms:

Psa 22:22, "I will tell [Heb. *saphar*, Gk. διηγέομαι, Lat. *narrabo*] of Thy name to my brethren; In the midst of the assembly I will praise Thee."

Comparing Hebrews 2:12 to Psalm [21:23] 22:22

Psa [21:23] 22:22			Heb 2:12	
NAS	**BHS**	**LXX**	**NA27**	**NAS**
I will tell of Thy name to my brethren; In the midst of the assembly I will praise Thee.	אֲסַפְּרָה שִׁמְךָ לְאֶחָי בְּתוֹךְ קָהָל אֲהַלְלֶךָּ׃	διηγήσομαι τὸ ὄνομά σου τοῖς ἀδελφοῖς μου, ἐν μέσῳ ἐκκλησίας ὑμνήσω σε.	λέγων· ἀπαγγελῶ τὸ ὄνομά σου τοῖς ἀδελφοῖς μου, ἐν μέσῳ ἐκκλησίας ὑμνήσω σε,	saying, "I will proclaim Thy name to My brethren, In the midst of the congregation I will sing Thy praise."

Note that the Heb. *saphar* is translated διηγέομαι by the LXX, whereas the author of Hebrews used the Greek verb ἀπαγγέλλω.

Notice how the author of Hebrews changed the proclamational verb found in the LXX. Perhaps he himself was translating from the Hebrew, as was also likely in Peter's use of Isaiah 43:21 in 1 Peter 2:9 (see Chapter 2)

Some thoughts about the use and translation of proclamational words in the Old Testament. First, note the number and breadth of the proclamational terms. I was once told by a prominent Old Testament scholar that there was not enough proclamational material in the Book of Psalms for a Th.M.! It was my Bible reading in the 1975 (1977, 1979) French Geneva Bible that led to this study. Second, the King James Bible seems abitrary in its translation of some of these terms, especially with its use of the word "shew," "shew forth," and "bring [glad tidings]." Third, the Septuagint, while seeming like quite a literal translation, did choose to translate proclamational terms quite differently depending on context.

It would be recommended that many Septuagint uses of εὐαγγελίζω (from the Hebrew *basar* 20 out of 22 times) be translated "evangelize" to show the Old Testament precedent behind the New Testament authors' intend in their usage of this word. This is especially the case for verses quoted or alluded to in New Testament contexts of mission, such as these from Isaiah (note my adaptations of the text of the NASB, with a one-to-one ratio in the use of proclamational verbs, while using the verb "evangelize"):

Some OT passages Especially Significant to Evangelism:

1. Psa 68:11 [67:12]:

    a. My translation: "The Lord gives the word; Those evangelizing are a great host."

    b. NASB: "The Lord gives the command; The women who proclaim the *good* tidings are a great host."

    c. LXX (GOT): Κύριος δώσει ῥῆμα τοῖς εὐαγγελιζομένοις δυνάμει πολλῇ,
        Ettheridge: "The Lord God will give a word to them that preach *it* in a great company"

2. **Isaiah 40:9:**

    a. **My translation: "On a high place, get up, you who evangelizes Zion, lift up your voice mightily, you who evangelizes Jerusalem, get up, do not fear. Speak unto the cities of Judah, 'Behold, your God!'"**

    Depection of John Buyan preaching

    b. NASB: "Get yourself up on a high mountain, O Zion, bearer of good news, Lift up your voice mightily, O Jerusalem, bearer of good news; Lift *it* up, do not fear. Say to the cities of Judah, "Here is your God!"

    c. Compare with Wycliffe's 1st ed. on this verse: "Thou that evangelisist Sion."[584]

---

[584]David Barrett, *Evangelize! A Historical Survey of the Concept* (Birmingham, AL: New Hope, 1987), 22.

d. NT quotes and allusions: Matt 3:1; 10:6-7; 11:1; Mark 3:14; 6:6, 7-13; Luke 3:3; 4:42-44; 8:1.

3. **Isaiah 52:7:**

a. **My translation: "How lovely on the mountains are the feet of him who evangelizes publishing peace, who evangelizes good [news], who publishes salvation, saying unto Zion, 'Your God reigns!'"**

b. NASB: "How lovely on the mountains Are the feet of him who brings good news, Who announces peace And brings good news of happiness, Who announces salvation, *And* says to Zion, 'Your God reigns!'"

c. New Living Translation: "How beautiful on the mountains are the feet of the messenger who brings good news, the good news of peace and salvation, the news that the God of Israel reigns!"

   1) Notice in this verse how the NLT has collapsed, subsumed, or reduced the five proclamational verbs in this verse into one verb, while duplicating the English predicate "good news," and then repeating with a third use of the noun "news."

   2) The two uses of "good news" are duplicated from one "evangelizing good" (*basar tob*) and another "publishing peace" (*shama shalom*); the word "news" seems to be repeated as if there was a series of three uses of the neuter "good" which needed nouns to be supplied.

   3) These changes completely smother the proclamational emphasis of this verse, emphasizing rather message rather than method (reminiscent of many contemporary English translations of Gal 1:8-9).

d. OT parallel, Nahum 1:15 [2:1], "Behold, on the mountains the feet of him who brings good news, Who announces peace!"

e. NT quotes and allusions: Matt 4:17; 10:6-7; Mark 3:14; Luke 4:42-44; Rom 10:15.

4. **Isaiah 61:1-2a:**

a. **My translation: "The Spirit of the Lord LORD is upon me, because the LORD has anointed me to evangelize the afflicted; He has sent me to bind up the brokenhearted, to proclaim liberty to captives And freedom to prisoners; To proclaim the favorable year of the LORD."**

b. NASB: "The Spirit of the Lord God is upon me, Because the LORD has anointed me To bring good news to the afflicted; He has sent me to bind up the brokenhearted, To proclaim liberty to captives, And freedom to prisoners; To proclaim the favorable year of the LORD"

c. NT quotes and allusions: Matt 11:4-6; Luke 4:18-19; 7:22.

D. A Survey of the Translation of εὐαγγελίζω in the English New Testament:

Introduction:

One conservative NT scholar recently admitted to me why he does not affirm translating εὐαγγελίζω as evangelize:

> "I just am concerned that some people seeing only 'evangelize' [rather than 'preach the gospel'] in a NT translation will read it with the assumption of modern practice."

His reasoning, therefore, was not linguistic but catechetic. *He was concerned for the potential impact to readers if they would see the word in their Bibles.* That is *exactly why* the word "evangelize" needs to be unleashed in our Bibles!

Luther had the privilege of reading the word "evangelize" in his Latin Vulgate (*evangelizare* rather than *praedico*). When he saw Johan Tetzel selling indulgences for the forgiveness of sins, the word "evangelize" found three times in Galatians 1:8-9 gave him the biblical affirmation to preach against this ongoing heretical practice,[585] and even to stand against the Roman Catholic Church. Luther saw that the Roman Catholic evangelism methodology (that of selling indulgences) was not in keeping with the evangelism in the book of Acts.[586] **In fact, it was Luther's theology of evangelism that brought us the Protestant Reformation!**

Yes, the word "evangelize" is a powerful term!

On the next page, please note the facsimile of a page from Jacques Lefèvre authorized French Bible of 1530. It contains chapter one and two of Galatians. The discriminating reader will see the use of the French "evangelise" 6 times in chapter one. The next page shows that the 1550 reauthorized French Louvain removed these six uses of evangelize, choosing the word "announce" instead. The Louvain removed the word "evangelize" in 28 of the other 32 times Lefèvre used that word. Had the French language changed that much in 20 years? This section will show the intense polemic involved in the translation of the word εὐαγγελίζω. As I was taught in a Hebrew class with Gleason Archer, "Make words your friends. Find out how they act in different contexts and around other words." In this next section of notes I have sought to make the word εὐαγγελίζω my friend.

Let's unleash the word "evangelize"!

---

[585]Consider this verse from the deuterocanonical book of Tobith, "For alms delivereth from death, and the same is that which purgeth away sins, and maketh to find mercy and life everlasting" "(Tobith 12:9, Douay-Rheims American Ed., 1899). Many other verses in Tobith and Sirach teach the same doctrine. The 1993 *Catechism of the Catholic Church* (edited by Joseph Cardinal Ratzinger, Benedict XVI) also taught the validity of indulgences for absolution from sin, even for dead persons: "Since the faithful departed now being purified are also members of the same communion of the saints, one way we can help them is to obtain indulgences for them, so that the temporal punishments due for their sins may be remitted" (par 1479).

[586]The sections in question are entitled, "The Argument from the Book containing the Acts of the Apostles" and "The Commendation of the Book containing the Acts of the Apostles," in Martin Luther, *A Commentary on St. Paul's Epistle to the Galatians: Based on Lectures Delivered by Martin Luther at the University of Wittenberg in the Year 1531 and First Published in 1535* (Westwood, NJ: Revell, n.d.), 201-07. See also Luther's pointed comments on nullifying the grace of God in his commentary on Galatians 2:21.

Page from the 1382 and 1388 Parallel Wycliffe Editions[587]

4 Jhesu Crist, thee which ʒaf him silf for oure synnes, that he schulde delyuere vs off this present weyward world, vp the wil 5 of God and oure fadir, to whom is 'honour and glorie in to worldis of worldis. Amen; 6 'so be it. I wondre, that thus so soone ʒe ben born ouer fro him that clepide ʒou into the grace of Crist, into an other 7 gospel; the which is not other, 'no but ther ben summe that disturblen ʒou, and wolen mysturne the euangelie of Crist. 8 But thouʒ we, or an aungel of heuene, euangelise to ʒou, bisydis that that we 9 han euangelisid to ʒou, cursid be he. As I bifore seide, and now eftsoone I seye, if ony 'schal euangelise out taken that that 10 ʒe han takun, cursid be he. 'I counceile now to men, or to God? or 'I seke for to plese to men? If I 'ʒit pleside to men, I were not the seruaunt of Crist. 11 Sotheli, britheren, I make the gospel knowun to ʒou, the which is euangelisid, 'or prechid, of me, for it is not vp man; 12 sothli nether I took it of man, nether lernyde, but by the reuelacioun of Jhesu 13 Crist. Forsothe ʒe herden my lyuynge sum tyme in the Juwerie, for ouer manere I pursuwide the chirche of God, and 14 fauʒte aʒens it. And I profitide in Jurye aboue many myn euene eeldis in my kyn, beynge more haboundantly louere, 'or folower, of my fadryn tradiciouns. 15 Forsoth whanne it pleside to him, that departide me fro the wombe of my modir, 16 and clepid by his grace, that he schulde schewe in me his sone, that I schulde preche hym in hethene men, anoon I acor- 17 dide not to fleisch and blood; nether I cam to Jerusalem to my bifore goeris apostlis, but I wente forth into Arabye,

Jhesu Crist, that ʒaf hym silf for oure 4 synnes, to delyuere vs fro the present wickid world, bi the wille of God and of oure fadir, to whom is worschip and 5 glorie in to worldis of worldis. Amen. I wondur, that so soone ʒe be thus 6 moued fro hym that clepid ʒou in to the grace of Crist, in to another euangelie; which is not anothir, but that ther ben 7 summe that troublen ʒou, and wolen mysturne the euangelie of Crist. But 8 thouʒ we, or an aungel of heuene, prech- ide to ʒou, bisidis that that we han prechid to ʒou, be he acursid. As Y 9 haue seid bifore, and now eftsoones Y seie, if ony preche to ʒou bisidis that that ʒe han vndurfongun, be he curside. For now whether counsele Y men, or 10 God? or whether Y seche to plese men? If Y pleside ʒit men, Y were not Cristis seruaunt. For, britheren, Y make knowun 11 to ʒou the euangelie, that was prechid of me, for it is not bi man; ne Y took 12 it of man, ne lernyde, but bi reuelacioun of Jhesu Crist. For ʒe han herd my 13 conuersacioun sumtyme in the Jurie, and that Y pursuede passyngli the chirche of God, and fauʒt aʒen it. And 14 Y profitide in the Jurie aboue many of myn eueneldis in my kynrede, and was more aboundauntli a folewere of my fadris tradiciouns. But whanne it ples- 15 ide hym, that departide me fro my mo- dir wombe, and clepide bi his grace, to 16 schewe his sone in me, that Y schulde preche hym among the hethene, anoon Y drowʒ me not to fleisch and blood; ne Y cam to Jerusalem to the apostlis, 17 that weren tofor me, but Y wente in to Arabie, and eftsoones Y turnede aʒen

e Om. v. f fro p. g Om. v. h after GMPQ. bi v. i Om. v. k Om. GMPQVX. l Om. NQ. m Om. v. n another v. o but if x. p disturben sx. distroublen vw. q eny man v pr. m. r euangelizith v. t we Q. u Now counseile I GMPQ. Forwhi counseile I now v. w seke I MPQ. speke v. x Om. MPQSX. y Om. x. z wolde ʒit pleese v. a Om. v. b prechid o. c Om. GMOPQX. or preching к. d after GMPQV. e for v. f take T. g lerede sx. h Om. G pr. m. op. i Om. G pr. m. MPQ. k wick- edly ouer o. l maner, or mesure Q. m the Jurie N. n men KV. o the louer G sec.m. a loueere v. p Om. x. q fadres GMOPQVY sec.m. r tradicioun N. s But v. t among v. u coorded G pr. m. w the flesche T. x to blood o. blood, that is, nether to vices of my fleische, nether to kynred of blode Q.

b Om. EIQRbceghkoaβ. c troublith b. d ony man M pr. m. h pr. m. e acursid CEIKMQRuabceghkoaβ. f to men K. g Om. EIQ pr. m. gaβ. h Om. k. i euene eldris IQegha. k Om. A pr. m. a. l modris CEI MQRacegka. m hethene men к sec.m. R. n ether acordide к marg. o ether biforgoers к marg. bifore a.

Please note that one important difference in the text between the so-called "First Edition" and "Second Edition" Wycliffe texts (remembering that these manuscripts originated prior to the use of the printing press) is in the translation of the Latin *evangelizare* into two different English words: in the First Edition of 1382, 36/43 Latin uses of *evangelizare* is translated "evangelize" in the Second Edition of 1388, only 3/43 uses of "evangelize" remain, as is noted on this page.

587 Josiah Forshall and Frederic Madden, *The Holy Bible, Containing the Old and New Testaments, with the Apocryphal Books, in the Earliest English Versions Made from the Latin Vulgate by John Wycliffe and His Followers* (Oxford: University Press, 1850), 4:397.

Page of Galatians 1 from the 1230-1330 Cathar New Testament[588]
[By Cathar is meant either Waldensian or Albigensian]

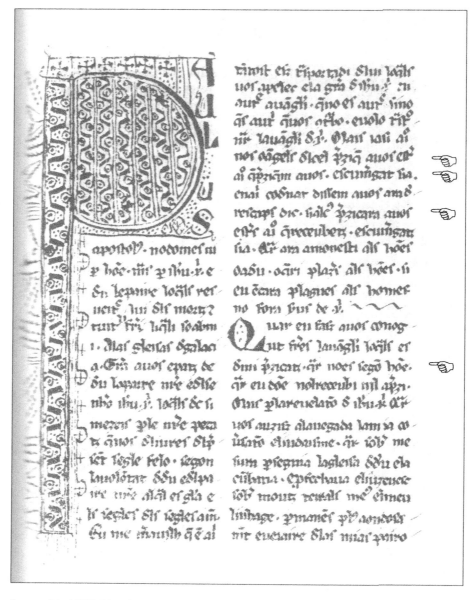

This amazing book was titled "Waldensian Bible" and included the New Testament in the Occitan language, a Medieval language in Southern France, along with a "Cathar Ritual." The Bible seems to be primarily a translation of the Latin Vulgate into Occitan, and the "Cathar Ritual" included several Gospel presentations and instructions for evangelism in difficult areas. The manuscript is located in the Library of Lyon (bibliothèque municipale de Lyon), France, and is numbered PA 36 (PA stands for "Palais des Arts")[589]

In this pre-versified Bible, the four uses of evangelize are translated "preach," as noted by the four hands in the margin (from Gal 1:8-9, 11). The first reads *pziq*, which, with the abbreviations above stands for *preziquam*, meaning "preach." The second reads *qpzqiqm*, which when stands for *que*, meaning "which," and *preziquam* for "preach." The third reads *pzicara*, or *prezicara*, another verbal form of *preziquam*. The fourth reads *prezicatz*. Thus this possible 13th Century translation did not follow the Latin Vulgate's use of the word *evangelizare*.

---

[588]L. Clédat, *Le Nouveau Testament: traduit au XIIIe siècle en langue provençale suivi d'un ritual cathar* (1887; Geneva: Slatkine Reprints, 1968), 395.

[589]Further information available at www.jean.duvernoy.free.fr. in a document titled "occitan NT_0intro.pdf."

Galatians 1-2 from the 1530 French Authorized Lefèvre Bible[590]

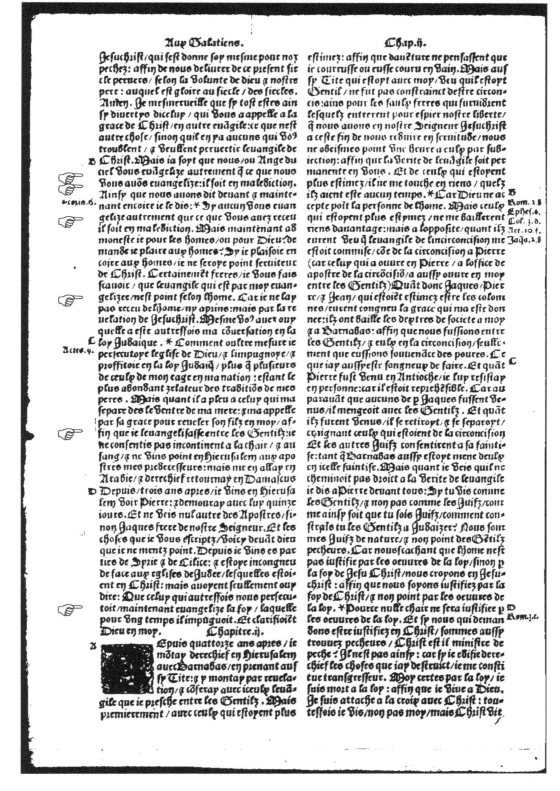

This New Testament which was originally translated in 1522 by Jacques Lefebvre d'Etaples was later deemed to be Lutheran, and was replaced by the Louvain version in 1550. Lefebvre translated 37 of the Vulgate's 43 uses of *evangelizare*.

---

[590]Lefevre and Louvain Bibles available at http://gallica.bnf.fr:/12148/bpt6k54287d; accessed via link at http://www.lexilogos.com/bible.htm; 16 Sep 2006.

Galatians 1 from the 1550 French Louvain Bible

II. Aux Corinthiens.   66

née. Et il adioufte generale exhortation, & falutations.

Chapitre .xiij.

Deu. 19 d
Mat. 18. b.
Ioh. 8. c.
heb. 10. c d

Voicy, c'eft la troifiefme fois que ie viens à vous. En la bouche de deux ou trois tefmoings, toute parolle fera arreftée. I'ay prediét, & predy côme prefent, & maintenât abfent, à ceux qui ont peché parauant, & à tous autres: que fi ie viens derechef, ie ne les efpargneray point. Demâdez vous l'experiéce de Chrift, qui parle en moy? Lequel n'eft poit foible enuers vous, mais eft puiffant en vous. Car iafoyt qu'il ayt efté crucifié par infirmité, neantmoins il vit par la puiffance de dieu. Car nous auffy fommes foibles en luy, mais nous viuerons auec luy de la puiffance de Dieu enuers vous. Experimentez vous vous mefmes, fi vo' eftes en la foy. Efprouuez vous vous mefmes. Ne vous cognoiffez poit vous mefmes, que Iefu Chrift eft en vous? fi d'auenture vous n'eftes reprouuez. Mais i'efpere, que vous cógnoiffez, que nous ne fommes point reprouuez. Et nous prions Dieu, que vous ne faciez rien de mal, non point à celle fin que nous apparoiffions approuuez, mais à fin que vous faciez ce qui eft bon, & que nous foyons comme reprouuez. Car nous ne pouuons rien contre verité, mais pour verité. Nous eliouyffons certes, q̃ nous fommes foibles, & que vous eftes puiffants. Ce auffy prions nous, c'eft, voftre perfectió. Pour tant i'efcry ces chofes abfent, à fin que prefent ne faice plus rigoreufement, felon la puiffance, que le Seigneur m'a donné à edification, & non point à deftruction. Du furplus freres, efiouyffez vo', foyez parfaiétz, foyez exhortez, foyez d'vn confentement. Ayez paix, & le Dieu de paix, & de deléction fera auec vous. Saluez l'vn l'autre en fainét baifer. Tous les fainétz vous faluent. La grace de noftre Seigneur Iefu Chrift, & la charité de Dieu, & la communication du fainét Efprit, foyt auec vous tous. Amen.

Fin de la feconde epiftre de Sainct Paul aux Corinthiens.

Epiftre de Sainct
Paul Apoftre aux Galatiens.

S. L'Apoftre reprend les Galates, qu'ilz fe font permis mettre hors de verité, laquelle ilz auoyent receu par luy. Laquelle il n'a point appris par homme, mais par la reuelation de Iefuchrift. Et aprés le reuôquée, adiouftant que Dieu l'auoyt feparé pour prefcher l'Euangile.

Chapitre premier.

PAVL Apoftre, non point de par les hommes, ne par homme, mais par Iefu Chrift, & par Dieu le pere, qui l'a refufcité des mortz, & tous les freres, q̃ font auec moy, aux eglifes de Galatie. Grace à vous, & paix, de par Dieu le pere, & noftre Seigneur Iefu Chrift, qui s'eft dôné foy mefme pour noz pechez à fin de nous deliurer de ce prefent fiecle peruers, felon la voluntéde Dieu, & noftre pere, auquel eft gloire au fiecle des fiecles Amé. Ie m'efmerueille q̃ fi toft eftes ainfy tranfportez de celuy, q̃ vous a appellé à la grace de Chrift, en autre Euangile, lequel n'eft autre, finon qu'il en y a aucuns qui vous troublent, & veulent peruertir l'Euangile de Chrift. Mais iafoyt que nous, ou ange du ciel, vous annôce l'Euangile autrement que ce que nous vous auons annoncé, il foyt en malediction. Ainfy que nous auons dit deuant, & maintenât encores ie le dy, Si aucun vous annonce l'Euangile autrement q̃ ce que vous auez receu, il foit en malediction. Car maintenant admonefte ie pour les homes, ou pour Dieu? demande ie plaire aux homes? fi ie plaifoye encores aux homes, ie ne feroye poit feruiteur de Chrift. ✠ Certainement freres, ie vous fay fçauoir, que l'Euangile qui eft p̃ moy annoncé, n'eft point felon l'home. Car ie ne l'ay pas receu d'home, n'y appris, mais par la reuelation de Iefu Chrift. Car vous auez ouy autrefois ma conuerfation en la loy Iudaique, comment oultre mefure ie perfecutoye l'eglife de Dieu, & la degaftoye, & profitoye en la loy Iudaique, plus que plufieurs de mon eage, en ma nation, eftant le plus abondant zelateur des traditions de mes peres. Mais quand il a pleu à celuy qui m'a feparé dez le ventre de ma mere, & m'a appellé fa grace, pour reueler fon filz en moy, à fin que ie l'annonçaffe entre les Gentilz, ie ne confenty pas incontinent à la chair, & au fang, & ne vins point en Ierufalem aux Apoftres mes predeceffeurs, mais m'en allay en Arabie, & derechef retournay en Damas. Depuis, trois ans aprés, ie vins en Ierufalé veoir Pierre, & demouray auprés de luy, quinze iours. Et ne vey aucun autre des apoftres, finon Iaques frere du Seigñr. Et les chofes que ie vous efcripz, voicy deuant Dieu, que ie ne mentz point. ✱ Depuis ie vins és parties de Syrie, & de Cilice: & eftoye incogneu de face aux eglifes de Iudée, lefquelles eftoyent en Chrift, mais auoy ent feulement ouy dire: Que celuy qui autrefois nous perfecutoit, maintenât annonce la foy, laquelle pour vn téps il impugnoit, & clarifioyent Dieu en moy.

S. Paul a toufiours enfeigné franchement la verité de l'Euangile entre les Gentilz. Les principaulx Apoftres approuoaãt iceluy Euangile, receurgt Paul en compaignon, lequel auffy publiquement reprint Pierre, demonftrant que perfone ne peult eftre iuftifié par les œuures de la loy, mais par la foy qui eft en Iefus Chrift.

Chapitre.ij.

Depuis quatorze ans aprés, ie montay derechef en Ierufalem auec Barnabé, en prenant auffy Tite, & y montay par reuelation, & communiquay auec iceux l'Euangile q̃ ie prefche entre les Gentilz, mais en particulier, auec

Please note that the 1550 Louvain revision of the Lefèvre Bible, changed all the uses of evangelize (in this passage) from "evangelize" to "announce." Likewise, the Louvain only retains 4 uses of "evangelize." Hence 4 of the Vulgate's 43 or 4 of Lefebvre's 37, thereby drastically reducing the evangelistic emphasis of the New Testament.

1535 printing of the 1534 Olivétan proto-French "Geneva Bible"

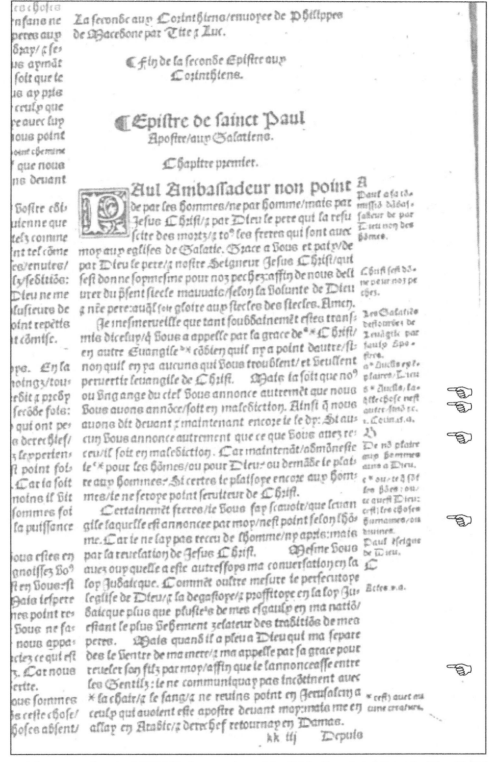

It must be noted, however, that the 1535 Olivétan version of the Bible (translated from the Greek) did not translate εὐαγγελίζω as "evangelize" in Galatians 1, but rather as the French word for "announce."

Olivétan's translation, however, was changed in the 1560 French Geneva version to include 4 of the 6 uses of the Greek εὐαγγελίζω in Galatians 1 in the French Geneva Bible (one of the "minor revisions") by either Jean Calvin, Theodore de Bèze, or Clément Marot (who focused on poetic portions).

1. One of the problems with translating evangelizing in English is presumably that of a lack of usage of the term evangelize:

   a. David Barrett wrote a review of the English use of the word *evangelize* in his *Evangelize! A Historical Survey of the Concept*. In this book Barrett ascribed the first English use of the word *evangelize* to John Wycliffe:

      "In 1382 in England, John Wycliffe completed the first translation of the whole Bible in the English language, using the Latin Vulgate. In the earlier of his two extant versions, Wycliffe translated almost all usages of the Latin *evangelizare* (and hence the Greek *euangelizein*) into the new English word 'euangelisen' (in some orthographies, 'evangelisen')."[591]

   b. Wycliffe first edition (circa 1382) used *evangelize* as a transliteration the Latin Vulgate's *evangelizare*. Wycliffe died in 1384. Then the second Wycliffe version, revised posthumously by John Purvey and other of Wycliffe's followers in 1388 removed almost all the uses of evangelize (see sample page above from the 1850 critical edition the 1382 and 1388 Wycliffe Bibles side-by-side):

      "[The 1388 John Purvey revised Wycliffe] replaced all of these English words commencing 'evangel-' by, in most cases, 'prechinge', and sometimes by synonyms like 'schewinge the Lord Jhesu'"[592]

   c. The change from "evangelize" to "preaching" continued through William Tyndale's translation and "has been perpetuated in all subsequent Bible translations up to the present day"[593] Two points here: Barrett missed both the 1884 English John Darby translation of Luke 7:22 which used the word "evangelize" and the 1899 Roman Catholic Douay-Rheims Bible Luke 8:1 which used the word "evangelize" (recently, the 1999 *Holman Christian Standard Bible* used the word "evangelize" 6 times; the 2009 CSB 7 times!). Listen to the concluding paragraphs of Barrett on this important word:

      "This deliberate removal of 'euangelisen' from the English Bible explains the almost total absence of the word 'evangelize' and derivatives from English church usage and English Christian vocabulary, language, and literature over the following 425 years. The words were not used at all by Chaucer or Shakespeare. When the Anglican Reformers drew up The Thirty-Nine Articles of Religion in 1562 and when they produced *The Book of Common Prayer* in 1552, no such words were included. 'Evangelize' is absent also from The Westminster Confession and all other English-language statements emanating from the Protestant Reformation of the 16th Century.

      "Rightly or wrongly, these words were construed by the Reformers as preserves of the Roman Church, as unreformed Latinized hybrids which therefore required to be reformed, replaced, and thoroughly translated into vernaculars. At the same time, however, this exclusion of 'evangelize' from the English vocabulary was also in part another consequence of the Reformer's general disinterest in human activity relating to the Great Commission and their resulting neglect of foreign missions."[594]

   d. In the French language, the 1530 Jacques Lefevre version (authorized by the King Francis I of France, and based on Jerome's Vulgate) used the word "evangelize" 38 times, as noted above and below.

   e. The 1535 Olivétan[595] Bible (a.k.a. French Geneva Bible) used by Calvin, which he slightly modified in 1560, used the word evangelize 13 times. By the way, the Olivétan was not merely a

---

[591]David B. Barrett, *Evangelize! A Historical Survey of the Concept* (Birmingham, AL: New Hope, 1987), 22.

[592]Ibid.

[593]Ibid.

[594]Ibid.

[595]It must be remembered that Pierre Robert [Louis] Olivétan shared the Gospel with his cousin Jean Calvin, was a schoolmaster in Neuchatel and in Geneva, was proficient in both Greek and Hebrew, was an evangelist involved in many mission trips to the Alps, and that he likely died at 29 years old from poisoning on a trip to Rome in 1538, three years after the first publication of his Bible 1535 (Samuel Lortsch, *Histoire de la Bible en France*; accessed: 4 March 2005; available at: http://www.bibliquest.org/Lortsch/Lortsch-Histoire_Bible_France-2.htm; Internet). As to Olivétan initiating Calvin in the Gospel, here is the exact text "C'est Olivétan qui, le premier, initia son cousin Jean Calvin à l'Évangile. Il lui fit 'goûter quelque chose de la pure religion', dit Théodore de Bèze. 'Il lui conseilla de lire l'Écriture. Calvin, ayant suivi ce conseil, commença à se distraire des superstitions papales.'" "'Quand Olivétan,' a dit M. Doumergue, 'n'aurait fait qu'initier Calvin à la Réforme, il mériterait un souvenir et une reconnaissance impérissables" [Doumergue, Calvin, I, 119]).

revision of the 1530 Lefèvre, as some purport. Lefèvre worked with the understanding that the Latin Vulgate was authoritative[596]—understandable as his colleague Briçonnet, Bishop of Meaux, was executed for the Lutheran heresy in 1529, and Louis de Berquin was strangled and burned at the stake as a Lutheran heretic that same year in Paris.[597] Olivétan, however, worked from an authoritative Greek, quite different from the Vulgate at key theological points. For example, in Romans 9:1-16 there are 54 translation variants between Lefèvre and Olivétan, some of which can only be understood in light of a different original manuscript.

    f.   Later, by 1669, the French Geneva Bible included 24 uses of the word "evangelize," meaning that someone had added 11 more uses than Olivétan (possibly Jean Calvin, Théodore de Bèze, or Clément Marot). The 1707 David Martin's French Geneva revision kept the 24 uses of the word "evangelize," with the exception of Romans 1:15, while adding a parenthetical use of "evangelize" in Gal 1:8.

    g.   A chart below shows all the NT uses of the word εὐαγγελίζω, shows when it was translated as "evangelize", and provides an overview of its translation since the Reformation.

2.   The following chart uses the Byzantine Textform (Majority Text) of the Greek for several reasons:

    a.   It was the foundational Greek to the pre-Tischendorf translations of the Bible (~1869). Therefore early translations noted below emanate from the Vulgate or the Greek, they are translated from the Byzantine Textform, rather than from the Tischendorf-Westcott-Hort-Nestle-Aland-Black-Metzger-Martini-Karavidopoulos tradition.

    b.   In fact, it seems to be more accurate to use the Byzantine Textform (cf. Majority Text, *Textus Receptus*, etc.), rather than the constantly changing Minority "Textpuzzle", which likely increases the input of the reasonings of men in determining the original text.[598]

---

[596]The title of the 1530 Lefevre Bible reads, "La Saincte Bible en Francois translatee selon la pure et entiere traduction de Saint Hierome conferer et entierement revisitee selon les plus anciens et plus correctz exemplaires" [The Holy Bible in French translated according to the pur and entire translation of Saint Jerome confered and entirely revised according to the most ancient and most correct examples] (beginning of the title on the cover page of the 1530 Lefevre Authorized Bible; available at http://gallica.bnf.fr/ark:/12148/bpt6k54287d/ f2.pagination; accessed 16 Sept 2006); translation mine. Also note that the Roman Catholic Council of Trent affirmed the absolute authority of the Jerome's Latin translation, probably, among other things, because of the 29 times it reads "do penance" instead of "repent." Hence reads the "19th Ecumenical Council," the Council of Trent: "Moreover, the same holy council considering that not a little advantage will accrue to the Church of God if it be made known which of all the Latin editions of the sacred books now in circulation is to be regarded as authentic, ordains and declares that the old Latin Vulgate Edition, which, in use for so many hundred years, has been approved by the Church, be in public lectures, disputations, sermons and expositions held as authentic, and that no one dare or presume under any pretext whatsoever to reject it" (from http://www.forerunner.com/chalcedon/X0020_ 15._Council_of_Trent.html; accessed 8 Jan 2005)

[597]Jean Crespin, *History of the True Martyrs of the True Gospel...* (Geneva, 1570), 70b-71b.

[598]Note the cautionary comment of Matthew Henry in this regard, considering that the freethinkers and manipulators of the text in his day are likely similar to those in our day: "And now I appeal to him who knows the thoughts and intents of the heart that in all this I think freely (if it be possible for a man to know that he does so), and not under the power of any bias. Whether we have reason to think that those who, without any colour of reason, not only usurp, but monopolize, the character of free-thinkers, do so, let those judge who easily observe that they do not speak sincerely, but industriously dissemble their notions; and one instance I cannot but notice of their unfair dealing with their readers—that when, for the diminishing of the authority of the New Testament, they urge the various readings of the original, and quote an acknowledgment of Mr. Gregory of Christ-church, in his preface to his Works, *That no profane author whatsoever, &c.,* and yet suppress what immediately follows, as the sense of that learned man upon it, *That this is an invincible reason for the scriptures' part, &c.*" (Matthew Henry, Preface to Volume V [1721, From Bibleworks]).

E. "Evangelize" in Select Translation Histories:

A Translation History of Translating of Evangelize as Evangelize[599]
(with some contextual words supplied for a sense of the translation)

#	Texts	Greek (Byzantine Textform)	Latin Vulgate	Waldensian Bible (circa. 1280)	Wycliffe 1st edition (1382)	Wycliffe 2nd edition (1388)	Jacques Lefèvre d'Étaples NT (1522)	Pierre Robert Olivétan (1535)	French Louvain (1550)	English Geneva (1560)	French Geneva (1605)	King James (1611)
1	Matt 11:5	καὶ πτωχοὶ εὐαγγελίζονται	pauperes evangelizantur	li paubres so prezicat	pore men ben 'taken to prechynge of the gospel	Poor men are taken to preaching the gospel	[page not available on website]	Les paoures receoivent bonnes nouuelles	aux pauvres l'Evangile est annôcé	the poore receiue the Gospel	l'Evangile est annoncé aux povres	the poore have the Gospel preached to them
2	Luke 1:19	καὶ εὐαγγελίσασθαί σοι ταῦτα	et haec tibi evangelizare	et aiso a tu prezicar	and to euangelize [telle, schewe] to the thes thingis	and to evangelise to thee these things	& pour te annoncer ces choses	& pour te annoncer ces choses	& pour t'annôcer ces choses	to shewe thee these good tidings	et t'annoncer ces bonnes nouvelles	to shew thee these glad tidings
3	Luke 2:10	γὰρ εὐαγγελίζομαι ὑμῖν χαρὰν μεγάλην	ecce enim evangelizo vobis gaudium magnum	quar vec vos que eu preziqui a os gran gaug	lo sothely I euangelize (or preche) to zou greet joye	I preach to you a great joy	car voicy ie vous euangelise	Car voicy ie vous annonce	car ie vous annôce	I bring you tidings	ie vous annonce	I bring you good tidings
4	Luke 3:18	εὐηγγελίζετο τὸν λαόν	evangelizabat populo	prezicavat al pople	euangelizide to the puple (or peple)	and preached to the people	& euangelisoit au people	& evangelizoit au peuple	annonçoit au peuple	he preached	il evangelizoit au peuple	preached he
5	Luke 4:18	εὐαγγελίσασθαι πτωχοῖς	evangelizare pauperibus	prezicar los paubres	to euangelize to pore men	to preach	po' euangelizer	pour evangelizer	pour annoncer l'Euangile	that I shulde preach the Gospel	pour evangelizer	to preach the Gospel
6	Luke 4:43	εὐαγγελίσασθαί με δεῖ	oportet me evangelizare	cove a mi prezicar	it bihoueth me for to euangelise	it behooves me to preach	Il me fault aussy euangelizer	Il me faut aussi annoncer	Il me faut aussi annoncer	Surely I must also preache	Il me faut aussi bien evangelizer	I must preach
7	Luke 7:22	πτωχοὶ εὐαγγελίζονται	pauperes evangelizantur	paubri so prezicat	pore men ben take to preche (or prechinge of) the gospel	Poor men are taken to preaching of the gospel	les poures sont euangelisez	Les paoures receoivent bonnes nouuelles	aux pauvres est l'euangile annoncée	the poore receiue the Gospel	l'Evangile est presché aux povres	to the poore the Gospel is preached
8	Luke 8:1	κηρύσσων καὶ εὐαγγελιζόμενος	et castella praedicans, et evangelizans regnum Dei	et per los castels prezicanz e 'vangelizantz	prechynge & euangelizynge	and castles, preaching and evangelising	preschant & euangelizant	preschant et annonceant	preschant & annônçans	preaching, and publishing	preschant & annonçant	preaching, and shewing the glad tidings
9	Luke 9:6	κατὰ τὰς κώμας, εὐαγγελιζόμενοι	per castella evangelizantes	los castels prezicantz	euangelyzynge	preaching	euangelizastes	evangelizans	annonçans l'euangile	preaching the Gospel	evangelizans	preaching the Gospel
10	Luke 16:16	εὐαγγελίζεται	evangelizatur	Prezicat	is euangelizide (is prechid)	is evangelised	est euangelize	est annonce	est annoncé	is preached	est evangelizé	is preached
11	Luke 20:1	εὐαγγελιζομένου	evangelizante	e prezicantz	& euangelizynge (prechinge the gospel)	and preached the gospel	& qu'il euangelizoit	& q'l evangelizoit	& qu'il annôçoit l'Euangile	and preached the Gospel	& evangelizoit	and preached the Gospel
12	Acts 5:42	εὐαγγελιζόμενοι	evangelizantes	essenhantz e prezicantz Ihesu Crist	techynge & euuangelisynge Jhu' c'st	to teach and to preach Jesus Christ	enseigner & euangelizer Jesu Christ	de enseigner et annoncer Jesus-Christ	d'enseigner & d'annoncer Jesus-Christ	to teache, and preache Iesus Christ	d'enseigner & annoncer Iesus Christ	to teach and preach Iesus Christ
13	Acts 8:4	εὐαγγελιζόμενοι τὸν λόγον	evangelizantes	prezicantz la paraula Deu enaviro las cuitatz e'ls castels	Passyden forth, euangelysinge the worde of god	passed forth, preaching the word of God	passoient de tous costez en euangelizant la parolle de Dieu	en annonceant la parolle [de Dieu]	passoient de tous costez, annôçans la parole	went to and fro preaching the worde	alloyent ça & là annonçans la parole de Dieu	went euery where preaching the word
14	Acts 8:12	εὐαγγελιζομένῳ	evangelizanti	Prezicant	euangelysinge of (or euangelist of)	that preached	qui euangelizoit	q' annonceoit les choses touchant	qui annonçoit	which preached the things that concerned	annonçant ce qui appartient au	preaching the things concerning

---

[599]Latin Vulgate (1880 Migne edition; BibleWorks 7.0); Occitan Bible aka. "Waldensian Bible" or "Cathar Bible" for Matt, Luke, Acts [except 13:32], Apoc (available at http:www.jeanduvernoy.free.fr; accessed 8 Sept 2004; Internet), remainder from L. Clédat, Le Nouveau Testament (1887; Geneva: Slatkine Reprints, 1968); 1382 Wycliffe, ed by Pickering (1848; http://books.google.com/books); The Wycliffe New Testament 1388, with modern spelling (1388; The British Library, 2002); French Jacques Lefevre and Louvain Bibles (link from lexilogos.com/bible.html); accessed 16-Sep-2006); French Olivétan (Berne, 1535); 1611 King James Version (1611; Thomas Nelson, 1982); French Geneva (La Rochelle, 1616) David Martin (from www.lirelabible.com; accessed 29-June-06); Holman Christian Standard (from www.biblegateway.com); all other versions from BibleWorks 7, 8, or 9. Use εὐαγγελίζω in Acts 16:17, found in Codex Bezae (cf. BW 9.0), is not included in this chart.

A Translation History of Translating of Evangelize as Evangelize (cont.)

#	Texts	French David Martin (1707)	Jean Frédéric Ostervald (1744)	J.W. Etheridge from Syriac (1849)	John Darby French NT (1859)	John Darby English NT (1884)	Douay-Rheims (1899)	Louis Segond (1910)	New American Standard (1977)	French La Colombe (1978)	Nouvelle Edition Genève (1979)	Holman Christian Standard (2009)	MacDonald Idiomatic (2006)	Total
1	Mt 11:5	l'Evangile est annoncé aux pauvres	l'évangile est annoncé aux pauvres	and the poor are evangelized	l'évangile est annoncé aux pauvres	poor have glad tidings preached to them	the poor have the gospel preached to them	la bonne nouvelle est annoncée aux pauvres	and the poor have the gospel preached to them	la bonne nouvelle est annoncée aux pauvres	la bonne nouvelle est annoncée aux pauvres	the poor are told the good news	Good news is being proclaimed to the poor	2
2	Lk 1:19	et pour t'annoncer ces bonnes nouvelles	et t'annoncer ces bonnes nouvelles	and to announce to thee these things	pour t'annoncer ces bonnes nouvelles	to bring these glad tidings to thee	to bring thee these good tidings	pour t'annoncer cette bonne nouvelle	to bring you this good news	et t'annoncer cette bonne nouvelle	pour t'annoncer cette bonne nouvelle	and tell you this good news	to announce this good news to you	3
3	Lk 2:10	je vous annonce	car je vous annonce	I announce to you	je vous annonce	I announce to you glad tidings	I bring you good tidings	Je vous annonce	I bring you good news	je vous annonce la bonne nouvelle	je vous annonce une bonne nouvelle	I proclaim to you good news	I have good news for you	3
4	Lk 3:18	il évangélisait	en lui annonçant l'Évangile	and preached to the people	il évangélisait	he announced *his* glad tidings	did he preach	Jean annonçait la bonne nouvelle	he preached the gospel	Jean annonçait la bonne nouvelle	Jean annonçait la bonne nouvelle	he proclaimed good news	preached good news to the people	7
5	Lk 4:18	pour évangéliser	pour annoncer l'Évangile	to evangelize	Pour annoncer de bonnes nouvelles	to preach glad tidings	to preach the gospel	pour annoncer de bonnes nouvelles	to preach the gospel	pour annoncer une bonne nouvelle	pour annoncer une bonne nouvelle	to preach good news	to announce good news	7
6	Lk 4:43	il faut que j'évangélise	Il faut que j'annonce	must I go to announce	Il faut que j'annonce	I must needs announce the glad tidings	I must preach the kingdom of God	Il faut aussi que j'annonce … la bonne nouvelle	I must preach	Il faut aussi que j'annonce … la bonne nouvelle	Il faut aussi que j'annonce … la bonne nouvelle	I must proclaim the good news	I must preach the good news	5
7	Lk 7:22	que l'Evangile est prêché aux pauvres	l'évangile est annoncé aux pauvres	and the poor are evangelized	l'évangile est annoncé	poor are evangelized	to the poor the gospel is preached	la bonne nouvelle est annoncée aux pauvres	*the* poor have the gospel preached to them	la bonne nouvelle est annoncée aux pauvres	la bonne nouvelle est annoncée aux pauvres	the poor are told the good news	The poor are getting good news	4
8	Lk 8:1	prêchant et annonçant	prêchant et annonçant la bonne nouvelle	and preached and announced	prêchant et annonçant	preaching and announ-cing the glad tidings of	preaching and evan-gelizing	prêchant et annonçant la bonne nouvelle	proclaiming and preaching	il prêchait et annonçait la bonne nouvelle	prêchant et annonçant la bonne nouvelle	Preaching and telling the good news	proclaiming the good news	6
9	Lk 9:6	Évangélisant	annonçant l'évangile	evangelized	évangéli-sant	announcing the glad tidings	preaching the gospel	annonçant la bonne nouvelle	preaching the gospel	ils annon-çaient la bonne nouvelle	annonçant la bonne nouvelle	proclaiming the good news	announcing good news	8
10	Lk 16:16	est évangélisé	est annoncé	is preached	est annoncé	the glad tidings of … are announced	is preached	est annoncé	the gospel … is preached	est annoncé comme une bonne nouvelle	est annoncé	the good news … has been proclaimed	is being announced as good news	6
11	Lk 20:1	et qu'il évangélisait	et qu'il annonçait l'Évangile	and evangelized	et évangélisait	and announcing the glad tidings	and preaching the gospel	et qu'il annonçait la bonne nouvelle	and preaching the gospel	et qu'il annonçait la bonne nouvelle	et qu'il annonçait la bonne nouvelle	and proclaiming the good news	and proclaiming good news	8
12	Ac 5:42	d'enseigner, et d'annoncer Jésus-Christ	d'enseigner et d'annoncer Jésus-Christ	to teach … and to preach	d'enseigner et d'annoncer Jésus *comme* le Christ	teaching and announcing the glad tidings that Jesus *was* the Christ	Teach and preach Christ Jesus	d'annoncer la bonne nouvelle de Jésus-Christ	they kept right on teaching and preaching Jesus *as the* Christ	d'enseigner et d'annoncer la bonne nouvelle du Christ-Jésus	d'enseigner, et d'annoncer la bonne nouvelle de Jésus-Christ	they continued teaching and proclaiming the good news …	they did not cease teaching and preaching Jesus *as the* Christ	3
13	Ac 8:4	allaient çà et là annonçant la parole de Dieu	annonçant la bonne nouvelle de la Parole	went about and preached the word of Aloha	allaient çà et là, annonçant la parole	went through *the countries* announcing the glad tidings of the word	went about preaching the word of God	allaient de lieu en lieu, annonçant la bonne nouvelle de la parole	went about preaching the word	allaient de lieu en lieu, en annonçant la bonne nouvelle de la parole	allaient de lieu en lieu, annonçant la bonne nouvelle de la parole	went on their way preaching the message of good news	went on their way preaching the message	3
14	Ac 8:12	Philippe leur annonçait touchant	qui leur annonçait la bonne nou-velle de ce qui concerne	who evangelized	qui leur annonçait les bonnes nouvelles touchant	announcing the glad tidings concerning	preaching of	qui leur annonçait la bonne nouvelle	preaching the good news	qui leur annonçait la bonne nouvelle	qui leur annonçait la bonne nouvelle	as he preached the good news about	Philip's preaching about	4

A Translation History of Translating of Evangelize as Evangelize (cont.)

#	Texts	Greek	Latin	Waldensian	Wycliffe 1st ed.	Wycliffe 2nd ed.	French Lefèvre	French Olivétan	French Louvain	English Geneva	French Geneva	King James
15	Ac 8:25	εὐηγγελί-σαντο	evangeli-zabant	e prezicavo	& euuangelize-den (or euangelisi-den)	and preached	& annonceoient 'Leuangile	& annonceoient leuangile	& annôçoient l'Euangile	and preached the Gospel	& annoncerent l'Evangile	and preached the Gospel
16	Ac 8:35	εὐηγγελίσατο	evangelizavit	preziquet e lui Ihesu	euuanglizide (or euangeliside) to hym' Jhu	preached to him Jesus	luy euangeliza Jesus	luy annoncea Jesus	lui annonça Iefus	preached vnto him Iesus	lui annonça Iesus	and preached vnto him Iesus
17	Ac 8:40	εὐηγγελίζετο	evangelizabat	e traspasantz predicava	and (he) passynge forth euuangelizide	he passed forth and preached	annonceoit 'Leuangile	annonceoit Leuangile	annonçoit l'Evangile	& he walked to and fro preaching	& en paasant annonça l'Evangile	and passing thorow he preached
18	Ac 10:36	εὐαγγελι-ζόμενος	adnuntians	Anunciantz	schewynge (or schewinge) pees	showing peace	Annonceant	Annonceant	annonçant	preaching	annonçant	preaching
19	Ac 11:20	εὐαγγελι-ζόμενοι	adnuntiantes	anunciant Ihesu Crist	schewyng	preached	Annonçans	Annonceans	annonçans	preached	annonçans	preaching
20	Ac 13:32	εὐαγγελι-ζόμεθα	adnuntiamus	Anonciama	And we schewen to zou	we show to you	nous vous annonceons	nous vous annonceons	Et nous vous annonçons	we declare	Et nous aussi vous annonçons	we declare vnto you glad tidings
21	Ac 14:[6]7	εὐαγγελι-ζόμενοι	evangeli-zantes	Et aqui eran prezicantz	and they weren prechynge there ye gospel	And they preached there the gospel	& la estoyent annonceantz leuangile	& la estoient annonceans Leuangile	& là eftoyent annonçants l'euangile	And there were preaching the Gospel	Et là estoyent annonçans l'Evangile	And there they preached the Gospell
22	Ac 14: [14] 15	εὐαγγελι-ζόμενοι	adnuntiantes	Anonciantz	schewinge to zou	show to you	vous annonceans	vous annonceans	vous annonçans	preache	vous annonçans	preach
23	Ac 14:[20] 21	Εὐαγγελι-σάμενοί τε τὴν πόλιν ἐκείνην	Cumque evangelizas-sent civitati illi	E co preziquesso en aicela ciutat	And whanne thei hadde[n] euangelysid[e] to the ilke cytee [or cite]	And when they had preached	annonce leuangile	Et apres q'lz eurent annonce Leuangile	Et aprés qu'ilz eurent annoncé l'euâgile	And after they had preached	Et apres qu'ils eurent annoncé l'Evangile	And when they had preached the Gospel
24	Ac 15:35	διδάσκοντες καὶ εὐαγγελι-ζόμενοι	evangeli-zantes	essenhatz e prezicanz	techinge and euangelysinge the word of the Lord	teaching and preaching	enseignans & euangelizans	enseignans et annonceans	enseignans & euangelizans	teaching and preaching	enseignans & annonçans	teaching and preaching
25	Ac 16:10	εὐαγγελί-σασθαι αὐτούς	evangelizare	prezicar ad els	to euangelize to [t]hem	to preach to them	po'leur euangeliser	pour leur euangelizer	pour leurs annoncer l'euangile	to preache the Gospel	pour leur evangelizer	to preach the Gospel
26	Ac 17:18	εὐηγγελίζετο [αὐτοῖς]	adnuntiabat	Anonciava	for he tolde them (or telde to hem) Jhesu	for he told them	pour ce quil leur annonceoit	pource quil leur annonceoit	pour ce quil leur annonçoit	because he preached vnto them	pource qu'il leur annonçoit	Because hee preached
27	Ro 1:15	ὑμῖν τοῖς ἐν Ῥώμῃ εὐαγγελί-σασθαι	evangelizare	Evangelizer	so that [that] is in me [is] reedy (or redy) for to euangelize & to zou	so that that is in me is ready to preach the gospel	ie suis prest deuagelizer	ie suis prest deuangelizer	ie suis prest d'euangelizer	to preache the Gospel	je suis prest d'evangelizer	I am ready to preach the Gospel
28	Ro 10:15 (1)	εὐαγγελιζο-μένων	evangelizan-tium pacem	evangelizantz la pantz	Men euuangeli-zynge (or euangelisinge) pees,	them that preach peace	des euangelisant la paix	De ceulx qui annoncent la paix	de ceuх qui annoncent la paix	which bring glad tydings of peace	de ceux qui annoncent paix	them that preach the Gospel of peace
29	Ro 10: 15 (2)	[εὐαγγελιζο-μένων]	evangelizan-tium bona	przicantz les bes	of prechynge (or preschinge) good thingis	them that preach good things	des euangelisant les biens	De ceulx qui annoncent les biens	de ceux qui annoncent les choses bónes	and bring glad tydings of good things	voire de ceux qui annoncent les choses bonnes	and bring glad tidings of good things

A Translation History of Translating of Evangelize as Evangelize (cont.)

#	Texts	French Martin	French Ostervald	Etheridge from Syriac	French Darby	English Darby	Douay-Rheims	French Segond	New American Standard	French La Colombe	New French Geneva	English Holman	MacDonald Idiomatic	Total
15	Ac 8:25	et annoncèrent l'Evangile	et prêchèrent l'Évangile	and evangelized	et ils évangélisaient	and announced the glad tidings	preached the gospel	en annonçant la bonne nouvelle	announced the glad tidings	en évangélisant	en annonçant la bonne nouvelle	evangelizing	En route they were evangelizing	7
16	Ac 8:35	lui annonça Jésus	lui annonça l'Évangile de Jésus	preaching to him concerning our Lord Jhesu	Lui annonça Jésus	announced the glad tidings of Jesus to him	preached unto him Jesus	lui annonça la bonne nouvelle de Jésus	he preached Jesus to him	lui annonça la bonne nouvelle de Jésus	lui annonça la bonne nouvelle de Jésus	proceeded to tell him the good news about Jesus	preached Jesus to him	3
17	Ac 8:40	Il annonça l'Evangile	il évangélisait	and from thence he itinerated and evangelized	Il évangélisa	passing through he announced the glad tidings	he preached the gospel	en évangélisant	he kept preaching the gospel	il évangélisa	en évangélisant	evangelizing	evangelizing	10
18	Ac 10:36	en annonçant	annonçant la bonne nouvelle	and hath announced to them	annonçant la bonne nouvelle	preaching	preaching	annonçant	Preaching	Annonçant la bonne nouvelle	annonçant	proclaiming the good news	by preaching the gospel of peace	0
19	Ac 11:20	annonçant	Annonçant	and evangelized	annonçant	announcing the glad tidings	preaching	et leur annoncèrent la bonne nouvelle	Preaching	et leur annoncèrent la bonne nouvelle	et leur annoncèrent la bonne nouvelle	proclaiming the good news about	the good news featuring the Lord Jesus	1
20	Ac 13:32	nous vous annonçons	Et nous aussi, nous vous annonçons la bonne nouvelle	we preach to you	Et nous, nous vous annonçons la bonne nouvelle	*we* declare	we declare unto you	Et nous, nous vous annonçons cette bonne nouvelle	we preach to you the good news	Et nous, nous vous annonçons cette bonne nouvelle	Et nous, nous vous annonçons cette bonne nouvelle	proclaim to you the good news	We preach good news to you	0
21	Ac 14:[6]7	Et ils y annoncèrent l'Evangile	Et ils y annoncèrent l'Évangile	and there evangelized	et ils y évangélisaient	and there they were announcing the glad tidings	and were there preaching the gospel	Et ils y annoncèrent la bonne nouvelle	and there they continued to preach the gospel	Ils y annoncèrent la bonne nouvelle	Et ils y annoncèrent la bonne nouvelle	And there they kept evangelizing	They kept on preaching the good news there	4
22	14:[14]	nous vous annonçons	Nous vous annonçons une bonne nouvelle	who preach to you	nous vous annonçons	preaching	preaching	vous apportant une bonne nouvelle	preach the gospel	et nous vous annonçons, comme une bonne nouvelle	vous apportant une bonne nouvelle	we are proclaiming good news	Preaching	0
23	14:[20]	Et après qu'ils eurent annoncé l'Evangile	Et après avoir annoncé l'Évangile	And when they had preached	Et ayant évangélisé	And having announced the glad tidings	And when they had preached the gospel	Quand ils eurent évangélisé	And after they had preached the gospel	après avoir évangélisé	Quand ils eurent évangélisé	After they had evangelized	After they had evangelized	8
24	Ac 15:35	enseignant et annonçant	enseignant et annonçant	and taught and preached	enseignant et annonçant	teaching and announcing the glad tidings	teaching and preaching	enseignant et annonçant ... la bonne nouvelle	teaching and preaching	enseignant et annonçant ... la bonne nouvelle	enseignant et annonçant ... la bonne nouvelle	teaching and proclaiming	teaching and preaching	4
25	Ac 16:10	Pour leur évangéliser	à y annoncer l'Évangile	to evangelize them	à les évangéliser	to announce to them the glad tidings	to preach the gospel to them	à y annoncer la bonne nouvelle	to preach the gospel to them	à y annoncer l'Évangile	à y annoncer la bonne nouvelle	to evangelize them	to evangelize them	10
26	Ac 17:18	Parce qu'il leur annonçait	car il leur annonçait la bonne nouvelle	he preached unto them	parce qu'il leur annonçait	because he announced the glad tidings of	because he preached to them	l'entendant annoncer	because he was preaching	parce qu'il annonçait la bonne nouvelle	l'entendant annoncer	because he was telling them the good news about	because he preached	0
27	Ro 1:15	je suis prêt d'annoncer	je suis prêt à vous annoncer aussi l'Évangile	and so am I urged to evangelize unto you	je suis tout prêt à vous annoncer l'évangile	to announce the glad tidings	I am ready to preach the gospel to you	j'ai un vif désir de vous annoncer aussi l'Évangile	I am eager to preach the gospel to you	de là mon vif désir de vous annoncer l'Évangile	j'ai un vif désir de vous annoncer aussi l'Évangile	So I am eager to preach the good news	I am all set to expound the gospel	8
28	Ro 10:15 (1)	de ceux qui annoncent la paix	de ceux qui annoncent la paix	who evangelize peace	ceux qui annoncent la paix	them that announce glad tidings of peace	them that preach the gospel of peace	ceux qui annoncent la paix	[omitted in NA27]	[omitted in NA27]	ceux qui annoncent la paix	[omitted in NA27]	[omitted in NA27]	5
29	Ro 10:15 (1)	de ceux qui annoncent de bonnes choses	de ceux qui annoncent de bonnes choses	who evangelize good things	ceux qui annoncent de bonnes choses	that announce glad tidings of good things	that bring glad tidings of good things	ceux qui annoncent de bonnes nouvelles	those who bring glad tidings of good things	ceux qui annoncent de bonnes nouvelles	ceux qui annoncent de bonnes nouvelles	those who announce the gospel of good things	announcing good news	3

A Translation History of Translating of Evangelize as Evangelize (cont.)

#	Texts	Greek	Latin	Waldensian	Wycliffe 1st ed.	Wycliffe 2nd ed.	French Lefevre	French Olivétan	French Louvain	English Geneva	French Geneva	King James
30	Ro 15:20	φιλοτιμού-μενον εὐαγγελί-ζεσθαι	praedicavi evangelium	prezianiangit evangli	Forsooth so I haue prechid[e] this gospel,	And so I have preached the gospel	Et ay ainsy presche ceste Euangile	Et ainsi ay prins courage de annonce de luy	Et i'ay ainsy presché cest Euangile	Yea, so I enforced my selfe to preache the Gospel	M'estudiant ainsi affectueuseme nt d'annoncer l'Evangile	So haue I striued to preach the Gospel
31	1 Co 1:17	ἀλλ' εὐαγγελί-ζεσθαι	evangelizare	Prezicam	but for to euuangelize (or preche thee gospel)	but to preach the gospel	mais pour euangeliser	mais pour Euangelizer	mais pour prescher l'Éuágile	but to preache the Gospel	mais pour evangelizer	but to preach the Gospel
[*]	1 Co 2:1	καταγγέλλων ὑμῖν	adnuntians	?	?	tellynge	vous annoncer	?	vous annonçant	shewing vnto you	en vous annonçant	declaring unto you
32	1 Co 9: 16 (1)	εὐαγγελί-ζωμαι	evangeliz-avero	prezica...	for whi zif I schal preche ye gospel	For if I preach the gospel	car ia foit ce que ie euangelise	Car ia foit q' ie euangelize	car ia foit ce que i'euangelize	for thogh I preache the Gospel	Car encore que j'evangelize	though I preach the Gospel
33	1 Co 9:16 (2)	εὐαγγελί-ζωμαι	evangeliz-avero	Prezicirsi	wo to me, zif I schal not euuangelise	if I preach not the gospel	sy ie ne euangelise	si ie ne euangelize	si ie n'euangelize	if I preache not the Gospel	si ie n'evangelize	if I preach not the Gospel
34	1 Co 9:18	ἵνα εὐαγγελι-ζόμενος ἀδάπανον θήσω	evangelium praedicans	prezivantz levanglei	yat I prechynge (or preche, or preching) ye gospel	preaching the gospel	Que en preschant leuangile ie mette leuangile riens prendre	Que en preschant Leuangile ie mette Leuangile de Christ sans rien prendre	Qu'en presçhant l'Euangile, ie mette l'Euangile sans despens	verely that when I preache the Gospel	c'est que en preschant l'Evangile, ie propose l'Evangile de Christ	When I preach the Gospel
35	1 Co 15:1	τὸ εὐαγγέλιον ὃ εὐηγγελι-σάμην ὑμῖν	praedicavi	Prezicant	[the] which[e] I haue prechid[e] to zou	which I have preached to you	laquelle ie vous ay presche	lesquelles ie vous ay annocees	leq'l ie vous ay presché	which I preached vnto you	que ie vous ai annoncé	which I preached vnto you
36	1 Co 15:2	τίνι λόγῳ εὐηγγελι-σάμην ὑμῖν	praedicaverim	Prezicat	by which[e] resoun[e] I haue prechid[e] to zou	By which reason I have preached to you	po' quelle raison le vous ay presche sy en souuenance	par quel maniere [les] vous ay annocees	le vous ay presché, sy en auez souuenance	after what maner I preached it vnto you	en quelle maniere ie le vous ai annoncé	What I preached vnto you
37	2 Co 10:16	εὐαγγελί-σασθαι	sunt evangelizare	enancelar ... prezicar	also [for] to preche into yo [tho] thingis	also to preach	Affin que nous euangelizons	affin que nous euangelizions	à fin aussy que nous annonçons l'Euangile	And to preache the Gospel	lusques à evangelizer	To preach the Gospel
38	2 Co 11:7	εὐαγγέλιον εὐηγγελι-σάμην ὑμῖν	evangelizavi	preziqui avor lavangeli	for fre[e]ly I euangelizide to zou the euangelie of god [God]	for freely I preached to you the gospel of God	vous ay euangelize leuangile de Dieu	Pourtant que de pur don vous ay annonce L'euangile de Dieu	ie vous ay annoncé l'Euangile de Dieu	I preached to you the Gospel of God	ie vous ai annoncé l'Evangile de Dieu	I haue preached to you the Gospel of God
39	Ga 1:8 (1)	εὐαγγελίζηται ὑμῖν	evangelizet	Preziquan	euuangelize [euangelise] to zou[,] bisidis [bysidis]	preached to you beside	vous euangelize	vous annonce autrement	vous annôce l'Euangile	preache vnto you otherwise	vous evangelizeroit	preach *anyother Gospel* vnto you
40	Ga 1:8 (2)	ὃ εὐηγγελι-σάμεθα ὑμῖν	evangeliz-avimus	Preziquam	that that we [t]han[e] euuangelizide (euangelisid) to zou	that that we have preached to you	ce que nous vous avons euangelize	que nous vous avons annonce	ce que nous vous auons annoncé	then that which we haue preached vnto you	ce que nous vous avons evangelizé	then that which wee haue preached vnto you,
41	Ga 1:9	εἴ τις ὑμᾶς εὐαγγελίζεται	evangeliz-averit	Prezicara	zif any [if ony] schal euuangelize [euangelise or euangelizith] out taken	preach to you beside	vous euangelize autrement	vous annonce autrement	vous annonce l'Euangile autrement	preache vnto you otherwise	vous evangelize outré	preach any other Gospel vnto you
42	Ga 1:11	τὸ εὐαγγέλιον τὸ εὐαγγελισ-θὲν ὑπ' ἐμοῦ	evangeliz-atum	Preziquanz	the whiche is euangelize [euangelisid (or prechid)] of me	the evangely that was preached of me	que leuangile qui est par moy euangelizee	que leuangile laquelle est annoncee par moy	que l'Euangile qui est p moy annoncé	the Gospel which was preached of me	que l'Evangile qui a esté annoncé par moi	the Gospel which was preached of me
43	Ga 1:16	ἵνα εὐαγγελί-ζωμαι αὐτὸν	evangeliz-arem	que preziquans sun e la gentz	that I shulde preche hym in hethen[e] men	that I should preach Him among the heathen	affin que ie leuangelis-asse	affin que ie lannonceasse entre les Gentilz	à fin que ie l'annoncasse	that I shulde preache him	afin que je l'Evangeliz-asse	that I might preach him

A Translation History of Translating of Evangelize as Evangelize (cont.)

#	Texts	French Martin	French Ostervald	Etheridge from Syriac	French Darby	English Darby	Douay-Rheims	French Segond	New American Standard	French La Colombe	New French Geneva	English Holman	MacDonald Idiomatic	Total
30	Ro 15:20	M'attachant ainsi avec affection à annoncer l'Evangile	Prenant ainsi à tâche d'annoncer l'Évangile	being anxious to preach	mais aussi m'attachant à évangéliser	and so aiming to announce the glad tidings	And I have so preached this gospel	Et je me suis fait honneur d'annoncer l'Évangile	thus I aspired to preach the gospel	Et je me suis fait un point d'honneur d'annoncer l'Évangile	Et je me suis fait honneur d'annoncer l'Évangile	My aim is to evangelize	to realize my ambition of evangelizing	3
31	1 Co 1:17	pour évangéliser	mais c'est pour annoncer l'Évangile	but to preach	mais évangéliser	but to preach glad tidings	but to preach the gospel	c'est pour annoncer l'Évangile	but to preach the gospel	mais pour annoncer l'Évangile	c'est pour annoncer l'Évangile	but to evangelize	but to preach the good news	8
[*]	1 Co 2:1	en vous annonçant	pour vous annoncer	did I evangelize to you	en vous annonçant	announcing to you	declaring unto you	que je suis allé vous annoncer	proclaiming to you	que je suis allé vous annoncer	que je suis allé vous annoncer	announcing ... to you	I continued to proclaim to you	1
32	1 Co 9:16 (1)	que j'évangélise	si je prêche l'Évangile	Yet also in preaching	si j'évangélise	if I announce the glad tidings	For if I preach the gospel	Si j'annonce l'Évangile	if I preach the gospel	Évangéliser	Si j'annonce l'Évangile	For if I preach the gospel	For if I preach the gospel	8
33	1 Cor 9:16 (2)	si je n'évangélise pas	si je ne prêche pas l'Évangile	unless I preach	si je n'évangélise pas	if I should not announce the glad tidings	if I preach not the gospel	si je n'annonce pas l'Évangile	if I do not preach the gospel	si je n'évangélise	si je n'annonce pas l'Évangile	if I do not preach the gospel	were I not to preach the gospel	9
34	1 Co 9:18	c'est qu'en prêchant l'Evangile, je prêche l'Evangile de Christ	qu'en prêchant l'Évangile, j'établirai l'Évangile de Christ	That while preaching ... I may perform the annunciation	C'est que, en évangélisant, je rends l'évangile	in announcing the glad tidings	That preaching the gospel, I may deliver the gospel	C'est d 'offrir gratuitement l'Évangile que j'annonce	when I preach the gospel	C'est en évangélisant, d'annoncer	C'est d 'offrir gratuitement l'Évangile que j'annonce	To preach the gospel	It is that I might preach	2
35	1 Cor 15:1	que je vous ai annoncé	que je vous ai annoncé	which I have announced to you	Que je vous ai annoncé	the glad tidings which I announced to you	which I preached to you	que je vous ai annoncé	which I preached to you	que je vous ai annoncé	que je vous ai annoncé	I proclaimed to you	I preached to you	0
36	1 Co 15:2	en quelle manière je vous l'ai annoncé	tel que je vous l'ai annoncé	the word I have preached to you	Que je vous ai annoncée	which I announced to you as the glad tidings	after what manner I preached unto you	tel que je vous l'ai annoncé	which I preached to you	dans les termes où je vous l'ai annoncé	dans les termes où je vous l'ai annoncé	I proclaimed to you	through this message of good news I preached to you	0
37	2 Cor 10:16	Jusques à évangéliser	Pour prêcher l'Évangile	to evangelize	pour évangéliser	to announce the glad tidings	to preach the gospel	et d'annoncer l'Évangile	so as to preach the gospel	en évangélisant	en évangélisant	so that we may proclaim the good news	We hope to preach the good news	9
38	2 Co 11:7	je vous ai annoncé l'Évangile de Dieu	en vous annonçant gratuitement l'Évangile de Dieu	because I have preached to you the gospel of God freely	parce que je vous ai annoncé gratuitement l'évangile	I gratuitously announced to you the glad tidings	Because I preached unto you the gospel of God freely	je vous ai annoncé gratuitement l'Évangile	because I preached the gospel of God to you without charge	je vous ai annoncé gratuitement l'Évangile	je vous ai annoncé gratuitement l'Évangile	because I preached the gospel of God to you	I preached to you the good news from God	3
39	Ga 1:8 (1)	[vous évangélis-erions]; vous évangélise-rait	vous annoncerait un évangile	should preach to you	vous évangélise-rait	announce as glad tidings to you	preach a gospel to you	annoncerait un autre Évangile	should preach to you a gospel	vous annonçait un évangile différent	annonçait un évangile s'écartant	should preach to you a gospel	preached a different gospel	6
40	Gal 1:8 (2)	ce que nous vous avons évangélisé	de celui que nous vous avons annoncé	what we have preached to you	ce que nous vous avons évangélisé	what we have announced as glad tidings to you	that which we have preached to you	que celui que nous vous avons prêché	to that which we have preached to you	que nous vous avons annoncé	de celui que nous vous avons prêché	what we have preached to you	that which we proclaimed to you	6
41	Ga 1:9	vous évangélise outre	vous annonce un évangile	preach to you	vous évangélise	announce to you as glad tidings	preach to you a gospel	vous annonce un autre Évangile que celui	if any man is preaching to you a gospel	vous annonce un évangile différent de celui	vous annonce un évangile s'écartant de celui	preaches to you a gospel	If anyone preaches to you a gospel	6
42	Ga 1:11	l'Evangile que j'ai annoncé	l'Évangile que j'ai annoncé	the gospel which is preached by me	qui a été annoncé	the glad tidings which were announced by me	the gospel which was preached by me	qui a été annoncé	the gospel which was preached by me	qui a été annoncé	qui a été annoncé	that the gospel preached by me	the gospel I preach	3
43	Ga 1:16	afin que je l'évangélis-asse	afin que je l'annonçasse	that I should preach	afin que je l'annonçasse	that I may announce him as glad tidings	that I might preach him	afin que je l'annonçasse	that I might preach Him	pour que je l'annonce	afin que je l'annonce	So that I could preach Him	that I might preach him	4

A Translation History of Translating of Evangelize as Evangelize (cont.)

#	Texts	Greek	Latin	Waldensian	Wycliffe 1st ed.	Wycliffe 2nd ed.	French Lefevre	French Olivétan	French Louvain	English Geneva	French Geneva	King James
44	Gal 1:[22] 23	νῦν εὐαγγελίζεται τὴν πίστιν	evangelizat	a prezica...	now euangelizith the feith	preached now the faith	maintenant euangelize la foy	maintenant annonce la foy	maintenât annonce la foy	now preacheth the faith	annonce maintenant la foi	Now preacheth the faith
[*]	Gal 3:8	προευηγγελίσατο τῷ Ἀβραὰμ	praenuntiavit	denant anoncier	tolde [toold] bifore	told tofore	Predist	a devant annonce	prediȼt	preached before ye Gospel	a devant evangelizé	preached before the Gospel
45	Gal 4:13	εὐηγγελισάμην ὑμῖν τὸ πρότερον	evangelizavi	Preziqui	I haue euangelizide [euangelisid] to zou now bifore	I have preached to you now before	ie vous ay pieça euangelize	ie vous ay paravant euangelizer	Aussi vous sçauez comment ie vous ay pieça annoncer l'Euangile	I preached the Gospel vnto you at the first	ci-devant ... ie vous ai evangelizé	I preached the Gospel vnto you at the first
46	Eph 2:17	καὶ ἐλθὼν εὐηγγελίσατο εἰρήνην ὑμῖν	evangelizavit	e venentz evangelizer patz a vos	and he comynge euangelizide pees to zow	preached peace	il euangeliza	il annoncea la paix	il annonça	and preached peace	il a evangelize la paix	preached peace
47	Eph 3:8	[ἐν] τοῖς ἔθνεσιν εὐαγγελίσασθαι	evangelizare	evangelizer	for to euangelie [euangelise] in hethen [men]	to preach among heathen men	po' euangelizer aux Gentilz	pour annoncer entre les Gentilz	pour annoncer entre les Gentilz	that I shulde preache among the Gentiles	pour annoncer entre les Gentils	that I should preach among the Gentiles
[*]	Phil 4:15	ὅτι ἐν ἀρχῇ τοῦ εὐαγγελίου	quod in principio Evangelii	quel comancement de lavangeli'	[?]	[?]	qu' au commencement de levangile	[?]	que au commencement de l'Evangile	in the beginning of the Gospel	qu'au commencement de la predicasion de l'Evangile	in the beginning of the gospel
48	1 Thess 3:6	καὶ εὐαγγελισαμένου ἡμῖν τὴν πίστιν	adnuntiante	et anonciant	and tellinge to vs	and tell to us	il nous a annonce	& nous ayant annonce vostre foy	& nous annoncé vostre foy	and broght vs good tidings	nous ayant apporté de joyeuses nouvelles	brought vs good tidings
49	Heb 4:2	καὶ γάρ ἐσμεν εὐηγγελισμένοι	nuntiatum	Anonciat	Forsoth it is told to vs,	it is told to us	il nous a este annonce	il nous a este annonce	il no' a esté annoncé	vnto vs was the Gospel preached	Car il nous a esté evangelisé	vnto vs was the Gospel preached
50	Heb 4:6	καὶ οἱ πρότερον εὐαγγελισθέντες	adnuntiatum	nocaia [?]	and thei to whiche the firste it is tolde	they to which it was told tofore	A ceul y ausquelz premierement a este annonce	& ceulx ausquelz premierement a este annonce	& ceux ausquelz premierement a esté annoncé	they to whome it was first preached	& que ceux ausquels premierement il a esté evangelizé	they to whom it was first preached
51	1 Pet 1:12	διὰ τῶν εὐαγγελισαμένων ὑμᾶς	evangelizaverunt	Anonciadar	bi [t]hem that euangelizeden to zou	by them that preached to you	par ceut'y qui vous ont evangelize	par ceulx qui vous ont annonce leuangile	par ceux qui vous ont annoncé l'Euangile	by them which haue preached vnto you the Gospel	par ceux qui vous ont [presc]hé l'Euangile	that haue preached the Gospel vnto you
52	1 Pet 1:25	τοῦτο δέ ἐστιν τὸ ῥῆμα τὸ εὐαγγελισθὲν εἰς ὑμᾶς	evangelizatum	Prezienda	sothely this is the worde[,] that is euangelizide to zou	And this is the word that is preached to you	Et icelle est la parolle laquelle vous est euangelizee	Or icelle est la parolle laquelle vous est annoncee	Et icelle est la parolle, laquelle vous est annoncée	and this is the worde which is preached among you	& ceste est la Parole qui vous a esté evangelizee	& this is the word which by the Gospel is preached vnto you
53	1 Pet 4:6	εὐηγγελίσθη	evangelizatum	Prezicat	it is euangelizid[e] (or ben made)	for this thing it is preached also	a este euangelize	Car pource aussi a este euangelize	A esté annoncé l'Euangile	was the Gospel preached	Car pource aussi a-il esté evangelizé	was the Gospel preached
54	Rev 10:7	ὡς εὐηγγέλισεν τοὺς δούλους αὐτοῦ τοὺς προφήτας	evangelizavit	co evangelizes per les seus servs prophetas	As he euangelizide bi his seruauntis prophetis	as He preached by His servants, prophets	côme il a euangelize par ses serviteurs prophetes	comme il a denonce a ses serviteurs prophetes	côme il a denôcé par ses serviteurs Prophetes	as he hathe declared to his seruants the Prophetes	comme il a declaré à ses serviteurs Prophetes	as hee hath declared to his seruants the Prophets
55	Rev 14:6	ἔχοντα εὐαγγέλιον αἰώνιον εὐαγγελίσαι	evangelium aeternum ut evangelizaret	avant evangeli durable que avangeliçes	hauynge the everlastynge gospel[,] that he schulde euangelize	having an everlasting gospel that he should preach	aiant leuangile eternelle: affin quil euangelisast	ayant lLeuangile eternel: affin quil euangelizast	ayant l'Euangile eternel: à fin qu'il annôçast	hauing an euerlasting Gospel, to preache	ayant l'Evangile eternel, afin qu'il evangelizast	Hauing the euerlasting Gospel, to preach
#	Texts	Greek	Latin	Waldensian	Wycliffe 1st ed.	Wycliffe 2nd ed.	French Lefèvre	Olivétan	French Louvain	English Geneva	French Geneva	King James
Totals		55 uses in Byzantine Text; 54 in Nestle-Aland	43/55 Latin uses (78% of Greek uses)	7/43 (17% of Lat) (13% of Gk)	36/55 (84% of Lat) (65% of Gk)	3/55 (7% of Lat) (5% of Gk)	37/54 [1 page miss] (70% of Gk)	13/55 (24% of Gk)	4/55 (7% of Gk)	0/55 (0% of Gk)	24/55 (44% of Gk)	0/55 (0% of Gk)

A Translation History of Translating of Evangelize as Evangelize (cont.)

#	Texts	French Martin	French Ostervald	Etheridge from Syriac	French Darby	English Darby	Douay-Rheims	French Segond	New American Standard	French La Colombe	New French Geneva	English Holman	MacDonald Idiomatic	Total
44	Gal 1:[22] 23	annonce maintenant la foi	annonce maintenant la foi	now preacheth	annonce	announces the glad tidings of	doth now preach	annonce	preaching	annonce	annonce	preaches	now preaches	3
[*]	Gal 3:8	a auparavant évangélisé	a évangélisé par avance	evangelized before	a d'avance annoncé la bonne nouvelle	announced beforehand the glad tidings	told unto Abraham before	a d'avance annoncé la bonne nouvelle	preached the gospel beforehand	a d'avance annoncé cette bonne nouvelle	a d'avance annoncé la bonne nouvelle	foretold the good news	proclaimed good news to Abraham back in that day	4
45	Gal 4:13	je vous ai ci-devant évangélisé	je vous ai annoncé ci-devant l'Évangile	I preached to you at the first	je vous ai évangélisé au commence-ment	I announced the glad tidings to you at the first	I preached the gospel to you heretofore	que je vous ai pour la première fois annoncé l'Évangile	that I preached the gospel to you the first time	que je vous ai pour la première fois annoncé l'Évangile	que je vous ai annoncé pour la première fois l'Évangile	previously I preached the gospel	in the beginning … when I evangelized you	8
46	Eph 2:17	Il a évangélisé	il est venu annoncer	he preached peace to you	et a annoncé la bonne nouvelle	he has preached the glad tidings	he preached peace to you	annoncer la paix à vous	preached peace to you	annoncer comme une bonne nouvelle …	annoncer la paix à vous	He proclaimed the good news	he proclaimed the good news	6
47	Eph 3:8	pour annoncer parmi les Gentils	d'annoncer, parmi les Gentils	that I should preach among the Gentiles	d'annoncer parmi les nations	to announce among the nations the glad tidings	to preach among the Gentiles	d'annoncer aux païens	to preach to the Gentiles	d'annoncer aux païens comme une bonne nouvelle	d'annoncer aux païens	to proclaim to the Gentiles	that I should announce good news	4
[*]	Phil 4:15	qu'au commence-ment [de la prédication] de l'Evangile	que, au commence-ment de la prédication de l'Évangile	that in the commence-ent of the gospel	qu'au commence-ment de l'évangile	that in the beginning of the gospel	that in the beginning of the gospel	au commence-ment de la prédication de l'Évangile	that at the first preaching of the gospel	au commence-ment (de la prédication) de l'Évangile	au commence-ment de la prédication de l'Évangile	in the early days of the gospel	when this area began to be evangelized	1
48	1 Thess 3:6	il nous a apporté d'agréables nouvelles	nous a apporté de bonnes nouvelles	and gave us intelligence of	ayant apporté les bonnes nouvelles	brought to us the glad tidings	and related to us	nous a donné de bonnes nouvelles	has brought us good news	il nous a donné de bonnes nouvelles	nous a donné de bonnes nouvelles	brought us good news about	He announced to us the good news	0
49	Heb 4:2	il nous a été évangélisé	l'heureuse promesse nous a été faite	For we have been evangelized	nous avons été évangélisés	indeed we have had glad tidings presented to us	For unto us also it hath been declared	cette bonne nouvelle nous a été annoncée aussi	we have had good news preached to us	Car la bonne nouvelle nous a été annoncée aussi	Car cette bonne nouvelle nous a été annoncée aussi	we also received the good news	we, too, have been recipients of good news	4
50	Heb 4:6	il a été évangélisé	que ceux à qui l'heureuse promesse a été première-ment faite	they who had it announced first	que ceux qui auparavant avaient été évangélisés	those who first received the glad tidings	to whom it was first preached	que ceux à qui d'abord la promesse a été faite	those who formerly had good news preached to them	que ceux qui avaient reçu les premiers cette bonne nouvelle	que ceux à qui d'abord la promesse a été faite	that those who formerly received the good news	the first hearers of the good news	3
51	1 Pet 1:12	qui vous ont prêché l'Evangile	qui vous ont prêché l'Évangile	who have preached to you	qui vous ont annoncé la bonne nouvelle	who have declared to you the glad tidings	which are now declared to you	qui vous ont prêché l'Évangile	who preached the gospel to you	par ceux qui vous ont prêché l'Évangile	ceux qui vous ont prêché l'Évangile	who preached the gospel to you	who preached the gospel to you	3
52	1 Pet 1:25	qui vous a été évangélisée	dont la bonne nouvelle vous a été annoncée	which is preached unto you	qui vous a été annoncée	which in the glad tidings is preached to you	which by the gospel hath been preached unto you	qui vous a été annoncée par l'Évangile	which was preached to you	qui vous a été annoncée par l'Évangile	qui vous a été annoncée par l'Évangile	that was preached as the gospel to you	preached as the evangel to you	5
53	1 Pet 4:6	qu'il a été évangélisée	l'Évangile a été aussi annoncé	also have been evangelized	qu'il a été évangélisé	were the glad tidings preached	was the gospel preached	l'Évangile a été aussi annoncé	For the gospel has … been preached	que les morts aussi ont été évangélisés	l'Évangile fut aussi annoncé	the gospel was also preached	the good news was preached	9
54	Rev 10:7	comme il l'a déclaré à ses serviteurs	comme il l'avait déclaré à ses serviteurs	as he hath declared to his servants	comme il en a annoncé la bonne nouvelle à ses esclaves	as he has made known the glad tidings to his own bondmen	as he hath declared by his servants	comme il l'a annoncé à ses serviteurs	as He preached to His servants	comme il en avait annoncé la bonne nouvelle à ses serviteurs	comme il l'a annoncé à ses serviteurs	as He announced to His servants	in accordance with his good news announced by his servants	4
55	Rev 14:6	ayant l'Evangile éternel, afin d'évangéliser	portant l'Évangile éternel, pour l'annoncer	had the ever-lasting gospel to preach to them who dwell on the earth	ayant l'évangile éternel pour l'annoncer	having the everlasting glad tidings to announce	having the eternal gospel, to preach unto them	ayant un Évangile éternel, pour l'annoncer	having an eternal gospel to preach	il avait un Évangile éternel, pour l'annoncer	il avait un Évangile éternel, pour l'annoncer	Having an eternal gospel to announce	His task was to announce the good news of the eternal gospel	7
#	Texts	French Martin	French Ostervald	Etheridge from Syriac	French Darby	English Darby	Douay-Rheims	French Segond	New American Standard	French La Colombe	New French Geneva	English Holman	MacDonald Idiomatic	#
	Totals	23/55 (42% of Gk)	2/55 (4% of Gk)	19/55 (35% of Gk)	21/55 (38% of Gk)	1/55 (2% of Gk)	1/55 (2% of Gk)	2/55 (4% of Gk)	0/54 [NA27] (0% of Gk)	7/54 [NA27] (13% of Gk)	3/55 (5% of Gk)	7/54 [NA27] (13% of Gk)	7/54 [NA27] (13% of Gk)	260/1206 22%

A Study of the Translation of Evangelize in the Other Modern Romance Languages

#*	Verse	Italian (La Buona Novella, 1991) La Nuova Diodati	Italian (Geneva Bible Society, 1994) La Sacra Bibbia Nuova Riveduta	Italian (San Paolo Editione, 1996) Nuovissima Versione della Bibbia	Portuguese (Bible Society of Brazil, 1969) João Ferreira de Almeida, Revista e Corrigida	Portuguese (Bible Society of Brazil, 1993) João Ferreira de Almeida, Revista e Atualizada, 2nd edition	Portuguese (1994) A Biblia Sagrada Traduzida em Portuguese por João Ferreira de Almeida	Portuguese (Trinitarian Bible Society of Brazil, 1995) João Ferreira de Almeida, Corrigida Fiel	Portuguese (Sociedade Bíblica de Portugal, 2005) Modern Language Translation	Spanish (Herder, 2003): Castilian La Biblia	Subtotal	Total-with prior chart
Language		Italian			Portuguese					Spanish		
OT	Isa 61:1			Evangelizzare							1	1
4	Luke 3:18	Evangelizzava	Evangelizzava								2	9
5	Luke 4:18	Evangelizzare	Evangelizzare		Evangelizar	Evangelizar	Evangelizar	Evangelizar			6	13
7	Luke 7:22								Evangelizados		1	5
9	Luke 9:6	Evangelizzando	Evangelizzando								2	10
11	Luke 20:1		Evangelizzava				Evangelizar				2	10
14	Acts 8:12					Evangelizava					1	5
15	Acts 8:25	Evangelizzato	Evangelizzando	Evangelizzando		Evangelizavam				Evangelizaban	5	12
17	Acts 8:40	Evangelizzò	Evangelizzò	Evangelizzando		Evangelizava				Evangelizando	5	15
18	Acts 10:36			Evangelizzando							1	1
21	Acts 14:7	Evangelizzare	Evangelizzare								2	6
23	Acts 14:21	Evangelizzato	Evangelizzato	Evangelizzato						Evangelizar	3	11
24	Acts 15:35									Evangelizando	1	5
**	Acts 15:38			Evangelizza-zione							1	1
25	Acts 16:10									Evangelizarlos	1	11
27	Rom 1:15	Evangelizzare									1	9
30	Rom 15:20	Evangelizzare									1	4
**	Rom 15:23	Evangelizzare									1	1
31	1 Cor 1:17	Evangelizzare	Evangelizzare		Evangelizar		Evangelizar	Evangelizar		Evangelizar	6	14
**	1 Cor 3:5							Evangelizar			1	1
32	1 Cor 9:16 (1)		Evangelizzo								1	9
33	1 Cor 9:16 (2)		Evangelizzo								1	10
34	1 Cor 9:18				Evangelizando	Evangelizando	Evangelizando	Evangelizando			4	6
37	2 Cor 10:16	Evangelizzare	Evangelizzare								2	11
**	Gal 2:7									Evangelización	1	1
45	Gal 4:13	Evangelizzai	Evangelizzai								2	10
46	Eph 2:17				Evangelizou	Evangelizou	Evangelizou	Evangelizou			4	10
47	Eph 3:8			Evangelizzare							1	5
51	1 Pet 1:12			Evangelizzato						Evangelización	2	5
52	1 Pet 1:25				Evangelizada	Evangelizada		Evangelizada			3	8
53	1 Pet 4:6			Evangelizzati							1	10
	Subtotal	13	13	9	5	8	4	5	2	8	66	209

*Column number keyed to Greek, Latin, English, French chart. Only versions with known uses of "evangelize" were included in this chart, and only the verses with the word "evangelize."

**Word εὐαγγελίζω not found in original Greek text of these verses.

A Study of German Translations of Evangelize (in key texts)*

Introduction: Barrett wrote, "There is no German transliteration of the verb *euangelizo* in Bible versions."[600]

Texts	Greek (GOT)	Luther Bibel (1545)	Unrevidierte Elberfelder (1905)	Luther Bibel (1912)	Schlachter Version (1951)	Münchener (1998)
Luke 4:43	ὁ δὲ εἶπε πρὸς αὐτοὺς ὅτι καὶ ταῖς ἑτέραις πόλεσιν εὐαγγελίσασ-θαί με δεῖ τὴν βασιλείαν τοῦ θεοῦ· ὅτι εἰς τοῦτο ἀπέσταλμαι.	Er aber sprach. zu ihnen: Ich muß auch andern Städten das Evangelium predigen vom Reich GOttes; denn dazu bin ich gesandt	Er aber sprach zu ihnen: Ich muß auch den anderen Städten das Evangelium vom Reiche Gottes verkündigen, denn dazu bin ich gesandt worden	Er sprach aber zu ihnen: Ich muß auch andern Städten das Evangelium verkündigen vom Reiche Gottes; denn dazu bin ich gesandt	Er aber sprach zu ihnen: Ich muß auch den andern Städten die frohe Botschaft vom Reiche Gottes verkündigen; denn dazu bin ich gesandt	Der aber sprach zu ihnen: Auch den anderen Städten muß ich verkünden das Königtum Gottes, weil ich dazu geschickt wurde
Luke 9:6	ἐξερχόμενοι δὲ διήρχοντο κατὰ τὰς κώμας εὐαγγελιζόμενοι καὶ θεραπεύοντες πανταχοῦ.	Und sie gingen hinaus und durchzogen die Märkte, predigten das Evangelium und machten gesund an allen Enden	Sie gingen aber aus und durchzogen die Dörfer nacheinander, indem sie das Evangelium verkündigten und überall heilten	Und sie gingen hinaus und durchzogen die Märkte, predigten das Evangelium und machten gesund an allen Enden	Und sie gingen aus und durchzogen die Dörfer, predigten das Evangelium und heilten allenthalben	Hinausgehend aber durchzogen sie die Dörfer, (das Evangelium) verkündend und heilend überall
Luke 20:1	Καὶ ἐγένετο ἐν μιᾷ τῶν ἡμερῶν ἐκείνων διδάσκοντος αὐτοῦ τὸν λαὸν ἐν τῷ ἱερῷ καὶ εὐαγγελιζομένου ἐπέστησαν οἱ ἱερεῖς καὶ οἱ γραμματεῖς σὺν τοῖς πρεσβυτέροις	Und es begab sich der Tage einen, da er das Volk lehrte im Tempel und predigte das Evangelium, da traten zu ihm die Hohenpriester und Schriftgelehrten mit den Ältesten	Und es geschah an einem der Tage, da er das Volk im Tempel lehrte und das Evangelium verkündigte, da traten die Hohenpriester und die Schriftgelehrten mit den Ältesten herzu	Und es begab sich an der Tage einem, da er das Volk lehrte im Tempel und predigte das Evangelium, da traten zu ihm die Hohenpriester und Schriftgelehrten mit den Ältesten	Es begab sich aber an einem der Tage, als er das Volk im Tempel lehrte und das Evangelium verkündigte, da traten die Hohenpriester und die Schriftgelehrten samt den Ältesten herzu	Und es geschah an einem der Tage, als er das Volk im Heiligtum und (das Evangelium) verkündete, hinzutraten die Hochpriester und die Schriftkundigen mit den Ältesten
Acts 8:40	Φίλιππος δὲ εὑρέθη εἰς Ἄζωτον, καὶ διερχόμενος εὐηγγελίζετο τὰς πόλεις πάσας ἕως τοῦ ἐλθεῖν αὐτὸν εἰς Καισάρειαν.	Philippus aber ward funden zu Asdod und wandelte umher und predigte allen Städten das Evangelium, bis daß er kam gen Cäseräa	Philippus aber wurde zu Asdod gefunden; und indem er hindurchzog, verkündigte er das Evangelium allen Städten, bis er nach Cäsarea kam	Philippus aber ward gefunden zu Asdod und wandelte umher und predigte allen Städten das Evangelium, bis daß er kam gen Cäsarea	Philippus aber wurde zu Azot gefunden, und er zog umher und verkündigte das Evangelium in allen Städten, bis er nach Cäsarea kam	Philippos aber wurde gefunden in Azotos; und umherziehend verkündete er (das Evangelium) allen Städten, bis er kam nach Kaisareia
Acts 16:10	ὡς δὲ τὸ ὅραμα εἶδεν, εὐθέως ἐζητήσαμεν ἐξελθεῖν εἰς τὴν Μακεδονίαν, συμβιβάζοντες ὅτι προσκέκληται ἡμᾶς ὁ Κύριος εὐαγγελίσασθαι αὐτούς.	Als er aber das Gesicht gesehen hatte, da trachteten wir alsobald zu reisen nach Mazedonien, gewiß, daß uns der HErr dahin berufen hätte, ihnen das Evangelium zu predigen	Als er aber das Gesicht gesehen hatte, suchten wir alsbald nach Macedonien abzureisen, indem wir schlossen, daß der Herr uns gerufen habe, ihnen das Evangelium zu verkündigen	Is er aber das Gesicht gesehen hatte, da trachteten wir alsbald, zu reisen nach Mazedonien, gewiß, daß uns der HERR dahin berufen hätte, ihnen das Evangelium zu predigen	Als er aber dieses Gesicht gesehen hatte, trachteten wir alsbald nach Mazedonien zu ziehen, indem wir daraus schlossen, daß uns der Herr berufen habe, ihnen das Evangelium zu predigen	Als er aber das Gesicht sah, suchten wir sogleich, wegzukommen nach Makedonia, folgernd, daß uns Gott herbeigerufen hat, zu verkünden ihnen (das Evangelium)
1 Cor 1:17	οὐ γὰρ ἀπέστειλέ με Χριστὸς βαπτίζειν, ἀλλ᾽ εὐαγγελίζεσθαι, οὐκ ἐν σοφίᾳ λόγου, ἵνα μὴ κενωθῇ ὁ σταυρὸς τοῦ Χριστοῦ.	Denn Christus hat mich nicht gesandt zu taufen, sondern das Evangelium zu predigen, nicht mit klugen Worten, auf daß nicht das Kreuz Christi zunichte werde	Denn Christus hat mich nicht ausgesandt zu taufen, sondern das Evangelium zu verkündigen; nicht in Redeweisheit, auf daß nicht das Kreuz Christi zunichte gemacht werde	Denn Christus hat mich nicht gesandt, zu taufen, sondern das Evangelium zu predigen, nicht mit klugen Worten, auf daß nicht das Kreuz Christi zunichte werde	enn Christus hat mich nicht gesandt zu taufen, sondern das Evangelium zu verkündigen, nicht in Redeweisheit, damit nicht das Kreuz Christi entkräftet werde	Denn nicht schickte mich Christos zu taufen, sondern (das Evangelium) zu verkünden, nicht in Weisheit (des) Wortes, damit nicht leer gemacht werde das Kreuz des Christos
1 Cor 9:16	ἐὰν γὰρ εὐαγγελίζωμαι, οὐκ ἔστι μοι καύχημα· ἀνάγκη γάρ μοι ἐπίκειται· οὐαὶ δὲ μοί ἐστιν ἐὰν μὴ εὐαγγελίζωμαι·	Denn daß ich das Evangelium predige, darf ich mich nicht rühmen; denn ich muß es tun. Und wehe mir, wenn ich das Evangelium nicht predige!	Denn wenn ich das Evangelium verkündige, so habe ich keinen Ruhm, denn eine Notwendigkeit liegt mir auf; denn wehe mir, wenn ich das Evangelium nicht verkündigte!	Denn daß ich das Evangelium predige, darf ich mich nicht rühmen; denn ich muß es tun. Und wehe mir, wenn ich das Evangelium nicht predigte!	Denn wenn ich das Evangelium predige, so ist das kein Ruhm für mich; denn ich bin dazu verpflichtet, und wehe mir, wenn ich das Evangelium nicht predige!	Denn wenn ich (das Evangelium) verkünde, nicht ist es mir Ruhm; denn Zwang liegt auf mir; denn ein Wehe ist mir, wenn ich nicht verkünde (das Evangelium).
Gal 1:8	ἀλλὰ καὶ ἐὰν ἡμεῖς ἢ ἄγγελος ἐξ οὐρανοῦ εὐαγγελίζηται ὑμῖν παρ᾽ ὃ εὐηγγελισάμεθα ὑμῖν, ἀνάθεμα ἔστω.	Aber so auch wir oder ein Engel vom Himmel euch würde Evangelium predigen anders, denn das wir euch gepredigt haben, der sei verflucht!	Aber so auch wir oder ein Engel aus dem Himmel euch etwas als Evangelium verkündigte außer dem, was wir euch als Evangelium verkündigt haben: er sei verflucht!	Aber so auch wir oder ein Engel vom Himmel euch würde Evangelium predigen anders, denn das wir euch gepredigt haben, der sei verflucht !	Aber wenn auch wir oder ein Engel vom Himmel euch etwas anderes als Evangelium predigen würde außer dem, was wir euch verkündigt haben, der sei verflucht!	Doch auch wenn wir oder ein Engel aus (dem) Himmel (das Evangelium) [euch] verkündete vorbei an (dem), das wir (als Evangelium) euch verkündeten, Fluch soll sein!
1 Peter 1:25	τὸ δὲ ῥῆμα Κυρίου μένει εἰς τὸν αἰῶνα τοῦτο δέ ἐστι τὸ ῥῆμα τὸ εὐαγγελισθὲν εἰς ὑμᾶς.	aber des HErrn Wort bleibet in Ewigkeit. Das ist das Wort, welches unter euch verkündiget ist	aber das Wort des Herrn bleibt in Ewigkeit." Dies aber ist das Wort, welches unter euch verkündigt worden ist	aber des HERRN Wort bleibt in Ewigkeit." Das ist aber das Wort, welches unter euch verkündigt ist	Das ist aber das Wort, welches euch als frohe Botschaft verkündigt worden ist	das Wort aber (des) Herrn bleibt in den Aion. ‹ Dies aber ist das Wort, das (als Evangelium) an euch verkündete

*All texts from BibleWorks 7, 8, 9, 10.

---

[600]David Barrett, *Evangelize!*, 30-31.

Comments:

While there is a strong history of translating εὐαγγελίζω as "evangelize" in French going back to Lefèvre's authorized translation into French (1530), neither the English nor German have followed this pattern.[601] However, the Italian and Portuguese Versions seem to have followed the French Geneva tradition of translating using "evangelize," as well as a new 2003 Spanish version. The reason for the French Geneva influence may very well be the evangelism and publishing efforts of the Geneva church in the 16th Century. Jean Crespin's Martyrology (1554, 1555, 1556, 1560, 1561, 1564, 1570) included quite a number of Protestant martyrs from Geneva who were evangelizing in Italy and Spain. Upon the promise of peace of Villegaignon, the Geneva Reformed church sent a colony to Brazil to begin colonizing that land in 1555-1556. Once established in Brazil, Villegaignon turned on the Reformed church pastors forcing them to adopt transubstantiation, resulting in 5 martyrs for the Gospel in 1557. So also, a Geneva mission to Sicily resulted in 6-12 martyrs in 1556.

Along with several French Bibles, the Geneva publisher, Jean Crespin, published (not including the Geneva Bible publishing of Robert Estienne):

☞ 1554, Italian version of the Psalter

☞ 1555, Italian New Testament

☞ 1556, Spanish New Testament (trans by Juan Pérez); as well as an English Bible, Psalms, and prayer book (trans by Th. Sternhold, J. Hopkins, and W. Whittingham); and an Italian commentary on Romans by Juan de Valdez

☞ 1557, 150 Psalms in Spanish (trans by Juan Pérez); a Spanish tract called "The Image of the Antichrist" (trans by Alonso de Peñafuerte); a Spanish tract on the reign of King Philip; and a commentary on First Corinthians by Juan de VV[aldez]

☞ 1559, An Italian tract on Freedom of Conscience (by Francesco Negri)

☞ 1560, two books in Spanish by Juan Pérez

☞ 1569, English Geneva Bible[602]

Crespin also published many other tracts in Italian and Spanish. While more research is necessary in early German versions, it seems that in the 1545 Luther Bible, as well as in major German 20th Century translations, εὐαγγελίζω was never translated as "evangelize."

Several additional comments: First, notice the importance of the precedent of the Latin Vulgate's translation to *adnuntio* (7 times) or *preadicatio* (4 times) or *nuntio* (1 time) in which texts later French or English translations translated εὐαγγελίζω as announce or preach (note the exceptions of Rom 10:15 (1) [removed from the Nestle-Aland Greek] and Gal 3:8 [not evangelize in Greek]). Second, notice that the early French Protestant translations did not translate the word evangelize in the Book of Acts (Lefèvre 6/10, Olivétan 1/10, Geneva (1/10), Martin, 1/10, Ostervald 0/10). But they rather chose to use "evangelize" in the epistles of Paul (Lefèvre 17/21, Olivétan 6/21, Geneva 12/21, Martin 10[11]/21, Ostervald 1/21). Darby reversed that trend, translating more in Acts (5/10) while still keeping some Pauline uses (10/21). It is not known who added 11 additional uses of "evangelize" to the French Geneva between the years 1535-1669. My guess is that Calvin and de Beze (or Beza) worked on this foundational translation and may have added these renderings. Third, notice that the English Geneva version did *not* follow Olivétan's French translation of the verb εὐαγγελίζω. Rather, the translators of the English Geneva Bible translated the word 55 uses of εὐαγγελίζω as follows:

•   Bring glad tidings, Luke 2:10; Rom 10:15 (twice)
•   Bring good tidings, 1 Thess 3:6
•   Declare, Acts 13:32; Rev 10:7
•   Gospel preached, Heb 4:2; 1 Pet 4:6

---

[601]Of the German language Bibles, Barrett wrote, "There is no German transliteration of the verb *euangelizo* in Bible versions" (David B. Barrett, *Evangelize! A Historical Survey of the Concept* [Birmingham, AL: New Hope, 1987], 31).

[602]Jean François Gilmont, *Bibliographie des éditions de Jean Crespin 1550-1572* (Veviers, Switzerland: P. M. Gason, 1981); Jean François Gilmont, *Jean Crespin: Un éditeur réformé du XVIe Siecle* (Geneva: Dros, 1981).

- Preach, Luke 3:18; 4:43; 16:16; Acts 5:42; 8:4, 12, 35, 40; 10:36; 11:20; 14:15; 15:35; 17:18; 1 Cor 15:1, 2; 2 Cor 11:7; Gal 1:8 (twice), 9, 11, 16, 22[23]; Eph 2:17; 3:8; Heb 4:6; 1 Pet 1:25; Rev 14:6
- Preach the glad tidings of the Gospel, Acts 14:21
- Preach the Gospel, Luke 4:18; 9:6; 20:1; Acts 8:25; 14:7; 16:10; Rom 15:20; 1 Cor 1:17; 9:16 (twice), 18; 2 Cor 10:16; 1 Pet 1:12
- Preach ye Gospel, Rom 1:15; Gal 4:13
- Publish, Luke 8:1
- Receive Gospel, Matt 11:5; Luke 7:22
- Shew, Luke 1:19

Similarly, although John Darby used "evangelize" 21 times in his French translation, in his English translation he used the word "evangelize" only once in Luke 7:22!

The 2000 Holman Christian Standard, however, has broken the English pattern of very rarely ever translating "evangelize" as "evangelize" by translating it this way six times, then a seventh time in 2009! May this pattern of using the English "evangelize" continue and increase in English translations, so that English Christians can experience the word "evangelize" in their Bibles just as French Protestants have for almost five centuries (albeit far less in the last two centuries)!

The variation in translating this word may show the following:
- The old French translations did not mimic one another as to translating the word "evangelize"
- The tendency in French Protestant translation history has been to slowly eliminate the use of the word "evangelize"
- There was varying opinion as to the translation of this term in French history, largely Catholic versus Protestant, as well as variation as to the use of "evangelize" in particular passages
- Catholic translation history, exemplified in the 1550 Louvain, although linguistically only 20 years apart from Lefèvre, reversed the pattern of Lefèvre's 37/55 Greek uses (or more accurately 37/43 Latin Vulgate uses) to 4/54 uses, likely accommodating to a historical-theological-methodological bias against proclamational evangelism dating from as early as Peter the Venerable's antagonism to Henry of Lausanne in 1130-1145 A.D. or going back as far as the 529 A.D Council of Orange; it wasn't until 200 years after the 1550 Louvain that the 1744 French Protestant Ostervald version followed the Catholic precedent of removing most uses of the word "evangelize" with 2/55. It could very well be that the translation of the word "evangelize" as "preach the Gospel" is one of the translations-interpretations with which the contemporary Roman Catholic church quietly agrees.[603]
- English translations have succeeded in "putting a cover" on the term "evangelize" in the Bible, as is especially exemplified in the 1560 English Geneva Bible which did not translate *any* of the 24 French Geneva Bible's "evangelize"; not surprisingly, the Lollard evangelistic movement begun or encouraged by Wycliffe died down as the word "evangelize" no longer appeared in English Bibles. There seems to be a direct correlation between viewing evangelism as fanaticism, and the lack of use of the term in the English Bible.

---

[603]"Some committees have considered the possibility of explaining different Roman Catholic and Protestant beliefs by noting that one interpretation is held by Roman Catholics and another by Protestants. Such a procedure does not seem wise, for it tends to accentuate the differences; nor is it necessary, for most diversities of interpretation can be covered more objectively by marginal notations on alternative readings, if the issue in question is important. Where the matter is not of great consequence, it is better simply to omit reference in the interest of joint undertakings" (Thomas F. Stransky, C.S.B. and John B. Sheerin, C.S.B., "Guiding Principles for Interconfessional Cooperation in Translating the Bible," *Doing the Truth in Charity*, Ecumenical Documents 1 [New York: Paulist, 1982], 162).

F. On the Translation of Proclamational Terms in English Bibles:

1. The King James Version's Generous Use of the English word "Shew":

While the French Protestant Bibles continued to use the word "evangelize", the **English King James Version** continued in the seemingly anti-proclamational translation of "evangelize" as "shew" in conjunction with using the same word to translate numerous other *visual, cognitive,* **and** *proclamational* terms. This has left those who read only the English with a clouded view of (1) proclamational aspects of a definition of evangelism, and of its corollary (2) the Great Commission:

The word "shew" or "shew forth" was a favorite NT translation for the KJV for numerous proclamational terms, in addition to its visual usage or its abstract cognitive usage. The next several pages provide an example of "back-translation", a method that has gone out of date since the rise of Eugene Nida's "dynamic equivalence." Perhaps this study will solidify its usefulness as a translation method, as well as note the theological and methodological dangers of not using back-translation.

First, let us note the terms which the KJV in the NT translated "shew" or "shew forth" in a visual sense, "to cause to see" (e.g. Isa 39:4); ἀναδείκνυμι (Acts 1:24); ἡ ἀνάδειξις (Luke 1:80); γίνομαι (Acts 4:22); δείκνυω (Matt 8:4; Mark 14:15; Luke 5:15; John 20:20); δίδωμι (Matt 24:24; Mark 13:22; Acts 2:19); ἐμφανής (Acts 10:40); ἐνεργέω (Matt 14:2; Mark 6:4); ἐπιδείκνυμι (Matt 16:1; Acts 9:39); ὁράω (Acts 7:26); παρέχω (Acts 28:2); παρίστημι (Acts 1:3); ποιέω (Luke 1:51; 10:37; John 6:30; Acts 7:36); ὑποδείκνυμι (Luke 6:47; Acts 9:16; 20:35); φανερόω (John 7:4; 21:1, 14).

For example, consider these examples of "cause to see" where "shew" is a translation of the verb δείκνυω, whose primary meaning is "to cause to see, show [visually]":

Matt 4:8 (KJV), "Again, the devil taketh him up into an exceeding high mountain, and **sheweth** him all the kingdoms of the world, and the glory of them."

John 14:9 (KJV), "Jesus saith unto him, Have I been so long time with you, and yet hast thou not known me, Philip? he that hath seen me hath seen the Father; and how sayest thou *then*, **Shew** us the Father?"

The KJV also used "shew" with its abstract cognitive meaning, "to cause to know" to translate other NT Greek words (cf. Isa 40:14): κατατίθημι (Acts 24:27); μεγαλύνω (Luke 1:58); μηνύω (Luke 20:37; John 11:57); ἡ πρόφασις (Luke 20:47; Acts 9:16; 10:28).

In the OT the KJV used "shew" as a translation for proclamational words: *basar* (bear tidings; cf. Psa 96:2; Isa 60:6), *saphar* (count, recount, relate; cf. Psa 9:1; 71:15; 79:13; Isa 43:21), for *nagad* (declare, tell; cf. Psa 19:1; 51:15; Isa 41:22; 58:1), and for *shama* ([cause] to hear; cf. Psa 106:2; Isa 43:12).

In the NT the KJV translated the following as "shew" or "shew forth": ἀναγγέλλω (John 13:14, 15, 16, 25; Acts 19:18; 20:20), ἀπαγγέλλω (Matt 11:4; 28:11; Luke 7:18; 14:21; Acts 11:13; 12:17; 26:20; 28:21; 1 Thess 1:9; 1 Jn 1:2), διηγέομαι (Luke 8:39), ἐμφανίζω (Acts 23:22), ἐπιδείκνυμι (Acts 18:28), εὐαγγελίζω (Luke 1:19; 8:1), ἐξαγγέλλω (1 Pet 2:9), καταγγέλλω (Acts 16:17; 26:23; 1 Cor 11:26), λέγω (1 Cor 15:51), προκαταγγέλλω (Acts 3:18; 7:52).

If the semantic range of "shew" as used by the KJV was placed on the chart, its range would be as follows:

KJV'S GENEROUS SEMANTIC RANGE FOR "SHEW" IN THE NEW TESTAMENT

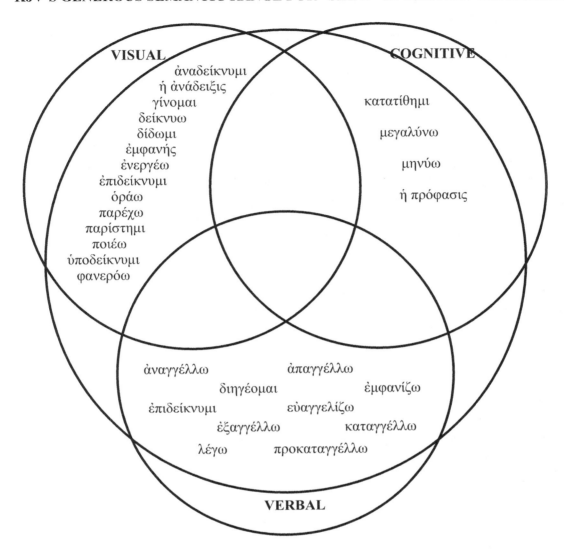

The reader will note that the translators of the KJV may have stretched the English word "shew" likely beyond its true semantic range by its generous usage of the term, especially as they translated a wide variety of visual, cognitive, and proclamational terms as "shew."

One word which Wycliffe's 1388 edition used to replace the translation of "evangelize" was "schewinge the Lord Jhesu."[604] Consider that the word "show" today is basically the same etymologically as what is found in an Old English online dictionary, for the word scéawung (showing):

"scéawung [] ƒ (-e/-a) **1**. a looking at, seeing, contemplation, consideration; **2**. respect, regard; **3**. reconnoitering, surveying, inspection, examination, scrutiny; **4**. a spectacle, show; **5**. a show, appearance, pretence; **6**. *as a technical term, the same as* ostensio; a showing, exhibiting, manifestation; **7**. toll on exposure of goods."[605]

The semantic range of this term in the Old English has not changed much from the current definition of show.[606] Consider that the word "shew," then, as now, is only related to proclamation in a very tertiary way.

---

[604]David B. Barrett, *Evangelize! A Historical Survey of the Concept* (Birmingham, AL: New Hope, 1987), 22.

[605]"Dictionaries: Old English-Modern English"; available at http://home.comcast.net/~modean52/ oeme_dictionaries.htm; accessed 3 Feb 2007; Internet.

[606]"Main Entry: **Show** (*verb*) [Etymology: Middle English *shewen, showen,* from Old English *sceawian* to look, look at, see; akin to Old High German *scouwon* to look, look at, and probably to Latin *cavere* to be on one's guard] *transitive verb*: **1** : to cause or permit to be seen : **exhibit** <*showed* pictures of the baby>; **2** : to offer for sale <stores were *showing* new spring suits>; **3** : to present as a public spectacle : **perform 4** : to reveal by one's condition, nature, or behavior <*showed* themselves to be cowards>; **5** : to give indication or record of <an anemometer *shows* wind

Notice, for example, notice several uses of the word "shew" in the KJV:

Gen 12:1, "Now the Lᴏʀᴅ had said unto Abram, Get thee out of thy country, and from thy kindred, and from thy father's house, unto a land that I will shew [Heb *ra'ah*: Gk δείκνυμι] thee"
The basic meaning of the Hebrew verb *ra'ah* is to see or be seen; in the Hiphil stem, as in this verse, *ra'ah* means "to show or exhibit"
The basic meaning of the Greek verb δείκνυμι is "to show" (as God showed Moses the promised land in Deut 34:1)

Deut 34:1, "And Moses went up from the plains of Moab unto the mountain of Nebo, to the top of Pisgah, that *is* over against Jericho. And the Lᴏʀᴅ shewed [Heb *ra'ah*: Gk δείκνυμι] him all the land of Gilead, unto Dan"
Same verbs used in Greek and Hebrew, same stem in Hebrew.

2. A Study of Sample Proclamational Terms in the New American Standard:

Intro: Comparing uses of εὐαγγελίζω **and** κηρύσσω in the Greek:

Possible Semantic Ranges of εὐαγγελίζω and κηρύσσω
[both of which are translated "preach"]

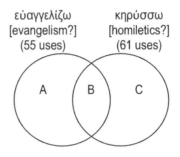

What if these words were in some way referring to evangelism or homiletics?

Comparing Evangelism and Homiletics

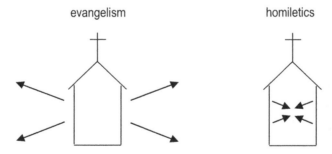

Rather than being fearful of unleashing the term "evangelize" in the Bible (as my friend mentioned above), if there were a clear translation of the biblical term "evangelize" in English (as in the *CSB,* except all or most of the 55 uses), it would allow for better theological and methodological examination, as evangelism is normally practiced by less educated mother-tongue-only [English-only] Bible-reading practitioners.

---

speed>; **6 a :** to point out : direct attention to <*showed* the view from the terrace>; **b : conduct, usher** <*showed* me to an aisle seat>; **7 : accord; bestow** <*shows* them no mercy>; **8 a :** to set forth : **declare b : allege; plead** -- used especially in law <*show* cause>; **9 a :** to demonstrate or establish by argument or reasoning <*show* a plan to be faulty>; **b : inform, instruct** <*showed* me how to solve the problem>; **10 :** to present (an animal) for judging in a show; *intransitive verb;* **1 a :** to be or come in view <3:15 *showed* on the clock>; **b :** to put in an appearance <failed to *show*>; **2 a :** to appear in a particular way <anger *showed* in their faces>; **b : seem, appear: 3 a :** to give a theatrical performance; **b :** to be staged or presented; **4 a :** to appear as a contestant; **b :** to present an animal in a show; **5 :** to finish third or at least third (as in a horse race); **6 :** to exhibit one's artistic work" (Merriam-Webster Dictionary online; available at http://www.m-w.com/dictionary/show; accessed 3 Feb 2007; Internet).

In order to properly understand what we do read in the English Bible, we will examine the use of various proclamational verbs, as exemplified in the New American Standard Bible, Updated Edition (1995)—NASB…

Semantic Study of the Verb "Preach" in the NT

Notice the variety of Greek verbs translated "preach" in the NASB. It would seem that the word "preach" has been overused by English translators to the detriment of other verbs available in English, such as "evangelize." The English verb "preach" is the primary term in the New Testament, found 104 times to translate the following Greek verbs (descending order of use):

  a. εὐαγγελίζω (50 uses), Matt 11:5; Luke 3:18; 4:18; 4:43; 7:22; 8:1; 9:6; 16:16; 20:1; Acts 5:42; 8:4, 12, 25, 35, 40; 10:36; 11:20; 13:32; 14:7, 15, 21; 15:35; 16:10; 17:18; Rom 1:15; 15:20; 1 Cor 1:17; 9:16 (twice), 18; 15:1, 2; 2 Cor 10:16; 11:7; Gal 1:8 (twice), 9, 11, 16, 23; 4:13; Eph 2:17; 3:8; Heb 4:2, 6; 1 Pet 1:12, 25; 4:6; Rev 10:7; 14:6;
  b. κηρύσσω (40 uses), Matt 3:1; 4:17; 10:7; 11:1; 24:14; 26:13; Mark 1:4, 7, 14, 38, 39; 3:14; 6:12; 13:10; 14:9; 16:15, 20; Luke 3:3; 4:44; Acts 10:42; 15:21; 19:13; 20:25; 28:31; Rom 2:21; 10:8, 14, 15; 1 Cor 1:23; 9:27; 15:11, 12; 2 Cor 1:19; 4:5; 11:4 (twice); Gal 2:2; 5:11; Phil 1:15; 2 Tim 4:2;
  c. τό κήρυγμα (6 uses), Matt 12:41; Luke 11:32; Rom 16:25; 1 Cor 1:21; 2:4; 15:14;
  d. [verb supplied] (3 uses), Rom 1:9; Phil 4:15; Col 1:25;
  e. διδάσκω (once), Acts 21:28;
  f. ὁ λόγος (once), 1 Tim 5:17;
  g. παρακαλέω (once) 1 Tim 6:2;
  h. πληρόω (once), Rom 15:19;
  i. προευαγγελίζομαι (once), Gal 3:8.

Semantic Range of the English Verb "Preach" in the NT

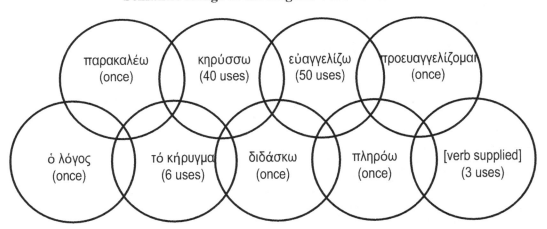

Conclusion: The verb "evangelize" is behind almost half (50/104) the English verbs "preach" in the NASB, and the verb "preach" (κηρύσσω) is behind 40/104.

The confusion to the English reader is obvious, as they understand "preaching" in the formal sense of homiletics (inside the church by ordained clergy to an audience quietly sitting in pews),[607] rather than the informal sense of "evangelism"[608] or "evangelize."[609]

---

[607]Note Webster's semantic range of the English verb, preach: "1) to deliver a sermon; 2) to urge acceptance or abandonment of an idea or course of action; 3) to deliver (as a sermon) publicly; 4) to bring, put, or affect by preaching" (*Webster's New Collegiate Dictionary,* 1977).

[608]"Evangelism: 1) the winning or revival of personal commitments to Christ; 2) militant or crusading zeal" (*ibid.*).

[609]"Evangelize: 1) to preach the gospel to; 2) to convert to Christianity" (*ibid.*).

Semantic Study of the Verb "Proclaim" in the NT

The secondary word for verbal proclamation in the NT is the word "proclaim" used 48 times. The verb is used for the following Greek verbs. The verbs are organized by frequency…

  a. κηρύσσω (20 uses), Matt 4:23; 9:35; 10:27; Mark 1:45; 5:20; 7:36; Luke 4:18, 19; 8:1, 39; 9:2; 12:3; 24:47; Acts 8:5; 9:20; 10:37; Col 1:23; 1 Thess 2:9; 1 Tim 3:16; Rev 5:2;
  b. καταγγέλλω (17 uses), Acts 4:2; 13:5, 38; 15:36; 16:17, 21; 17:3, 13, 23; 26:23; Rom 1:8; 1 Cor 2:1; 9:14; 11:26; Phil 1:17, 18; Col 1:28;
  c. ἀπαγγέλλω (4 times), Matt 12:18; Heb 2:12; 1 John 1:2, 3;
  d. [supplied] (twice), Luke 16:16; Eph 6:20;
  e. διαγγέλλω (twice), Luke 9:60; Rom 9:17;
  f. ἐξαγγέλλω (once), 1 Pet 2:9;
  g. λαλέω (once), Acts 17:19;
  h. προκηρύσσω (once), Acts 13:24.

Semantic Range of the English Verb "Proclaim" in the NT

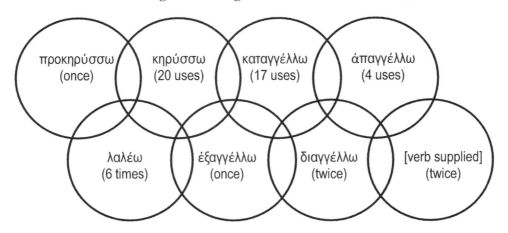

Semantic Study of the Verb "Declare" in the NT

The tertiary word for verbal proclamation in the NT is the word "declare" used 12 times (interestingly used 104 times in the OT—this dispensational differentiation does not appear warranted in the use of the verbs).[610] The verb is used for the following Greek verbs. The NT verbs for "declare" are organized by frequency…

  a. ἀναγγέλλω (3 times), John 4:25; Acts 20:20, 27;
  b. ἀπαγγέλλω (3 times), Luke 9:47; Acts 26:20; 1 Cor 14:25;
  c. ἀποφθέγγομαι (once), Acts 2:14;
  d. ἐπιβοάω/βοάω (once), Acts 25:24;
  e. ὁμολογέω (once), Matt 7:23;
  f. ὁρίζω (once), Rom 1:4;
  g. παραγγέλλω (once), Acts 17:30;
  h. [supplied] (once), Mark 7:19.

---

[610]A similar dispensational differentiation has occurred in use of the English word "rebel" and its derivatives, quite likely because of its relationship to the doctrine of man's sin and depravity. Out of 131 NASB uses of "rebel*" (including "rebel," "rebelled," "rebellion," "rebellious," "rebels"), 126 are in the Old Testament, while only 5 are found in the New Testament. A thorough study of Hebrew and Greek words is necessary to establish if this dichotomy is warranted linguistically, or if it derives from a softened approach to the theology of man's sin in NT translations. Whereas the 1599 English Geneva has 134 uses of "rebel*" (133 in the OT and 1 NT [Rom 7:23]), the KJV has 98 uses of "rebel*" (all OT), having removed 35 uses of this polemic term.

Semantic Range of the English Verb "Declare" in the NT

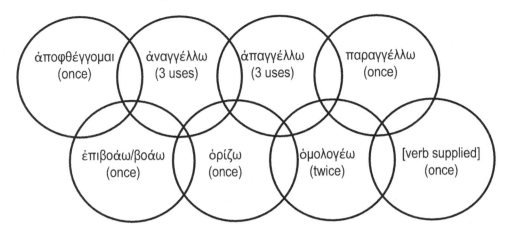

Semantic Study of the Verb "Announce" in the NT

An almost unused English word for verbal proclamation in the NT is the word "announce" used 7 times and 7 times in the OT (NASB). It is interesting that the Latin Vulgate used the verb *adnuntio* a total of 177 times and in the 1977 French Geneva the verb *annoncer* is used a total of 215 times. In the 1977 NAS, the verb "announce" is used for the following four Greek verbs:

a. ἀναγγέλλω (2 times), 1Pe 1:12; 1 John 1:5
b. ἀπαγγέλλω (2 times), John 20:28; Acts 12:14
c. προκαταγγέλλω (2 times), Act 3:18; 7:52
d. καταγγέλλω (1 time), Act 3:24.

Semantic Range of the English Verb "Announce" in the NT

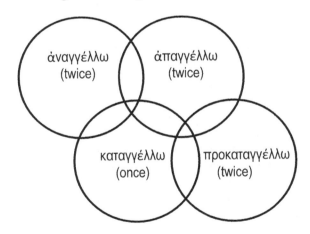

Concluding Comments:

   While some verbs are used very regularly by translators, often translating multiple cognate groups of
      verbs, for example:
      Verbs "say, saying, said, or says" are found 7,949 times in the Bible
      Verbs "speak, speaking, speaks, spoke" are found 1,253 times in the Bible
      Verbs "tell, tells, telling, told" are found 599 times in the Bible

   Note the dispensational or covenantal similarities or differentiations in the use of certain verbs:
      Almost uniquely OT—"Declare":
         Verbs "declare, declared, declares, declaring" are used 479 times (97.6%) in the OT, but only 12
            times (2.4%) in the NT (491 total uses).

Fairly neutral OT/NT—"Proclaim":
> Verbs "proclaim, proclaimed, proclaims, proclaiming" are used 81 times (62.3%) in the OT, and 48 times (37.2%) in the NT (129 total uses).

Almost uniquely NT—"Preach"—perfectly suited for NT church Christianity:
> Verbs "preach, preached, preaches, preaching" are used 1 time (0.94%) in the OT, and 105 times (99.06%) in the NT (106 total uses).

Conclusion: There seems to be a shift from "declare" as a primary term for proclamation in the OT to "preach" as a primary term in the NT; which shift appears to have more to do with the comfort or style of translation history than it does the actual translation of proclamational verbs.

Even considering the translation of proclamational verbs seems unstudied. For example, note the study, "Synomyms of the New Testament," that seems to have missed the nuance around the various Greek words for preaching, focusing mainly on the NT use of nouns:[611]

For example, never considered are the verbs: διαλέγομαι, διδάσκω, εὐαγγελίζω, καταγγέλλω, κηρύσσω, and μαρτυρέω (or διαμαρτύρομαι);

Paradoxically, both on the front and back covers of this book, is the logo of the school:

COLLEGIUM THEOLOGIAE LONDINENSE – VAE MIHI SI NON EVANGELIZAVERO

"London College of Theology – Woe to me if I preach not the gospel" [a quote of 1 Cor 9:16].

As a case study, therefore, the following provides a look at the English (NASB) renderings of certain communicatory verbs:
Verb "acclaim" once in NT in Mark 15:18 for the verb ἀσπάζομαι which is used 60 times in the NT, and 2 times in Rahlf's LXX;
Verb "address" is used 7 times, 6 in NT;
Verb "adjure" is used 9 times, 3 in NT;
Verb "admonish" is used 18 times, 8 in NT;
Verb "appeal" is found 18 times, 15 times in NT;
Verb "argue" is found 14 times, 8 times in NT;
Verbal phrase "empty chatter" is found twice in the NT;
Verb "circulate" [a proclamation] is used 3 times in OT;
> Adjective "circulation" [of a report] is used once in OT;
Verb "claim" is found 9 times, 4 in NT;
Verb "clamor" is found twice, once in NT;
Verb "command" is found about 483 times;
Verb "commission" is found 4 times in OT only;
Verb "communicate" is used once in the Bible, only in the NT (Rev 1:1);
Verb "confess" is found 41 times in the Bible, 24 times in the NT;
Verb "confront" is used 10 times in the Bible, only once in NT;
Verb "consult" is found 23 times, 2 in the NT;
Verb "contend" is found 41 times in the Bible, only once in the NT;
Verb "contest" is used once in the Bible (OT), and that not for communication;
Verb "converse" is used twice in the NT;
Verb "convince" is used 10 times in the Bible (all NT);
Verb "decry" is **not used** in the NASB;
Verb "demand" is found 12 times in the Bible (5 in NT; 3 times for 3 verbs, for one noun, and once supplied);
Verb "denigrate" is **not used** in NASB;
Verb "denounce" is found 6 times in the Bible, once in the NT;
Verb "dialogue" is **not used** in NASB;
Verb "discourse" is used 10 times in the, once in the NT and only as a noun;
Verb "discuss" is used 14 times in the Bible, 13 in the NT;
Verb "evangelize" is **not used** in NASB;
Verb "exchange" is used 15 times in the Bible, 7 times in NT (only once in relation to communication);
Verb "exclaim" is **not used** in the NASB;
Verb "expound" is used once in the Bible (OT);
Verbal phrase "give an account" is used 4 times, 3 times in NT;

---

[611]Richard C. Trench [Archbishop of Dublin], *Synonyms of the New Testament*, 10th ed. (London: Kegan Paul, Trench, & Co., 1886).

Verbal phrase "give an accounting" is used twice in NT;

Verb "interchange" is **not used** in NASB;

Verb "lecture" is **not used** in NASB;

Verb "plead" is found 19 times in the Bible, 4 in the NT;

Verb "portend" is **not used** in NASB;

Verb "profess" is used 3 times and only in the NT;

Verb "pronounce" is used 36 times in the Bible, 3 times in the NT for 3 different Greek verbs;

Verb "protest" is found 4 times in the Bible, 2 of 3 NT uses are merely supplied for context, 1 Cor 15:31 was changed to "affirm" in the 1995 NASB update;

Verb "reclaim" is not used in NASB;

Verb "recount" is found 3 times in the OT, although it is the primary literal meaning for the Hebrew *saphar* (which has 102 OT uses);

Verb "relate" is found 27 times in the Bible, 7 in the NT;

Verb "remand" is **not used** in NASB;

Verb "remonstrate" is **not used** in NASB;

Verb "renounce" is found once in the Bible (NT);

Verb "repeat" is found 12 times in the Bible, twice in the NT, and one of those is verbal;

Verb "reprimand" is found 3 times in Bible, once in NT;

Verb "reproach" is found 86 times, 18 times in NT;

Verb "retell" is **not used** in NASB;

Verb "share" is used 31 times in the NT, usually of sharing materially, but twice related to "sharing joy" [from συγχαίρω];

Verb "state" (e.g. "state your case") is found twice in the OT and not at all in the NT: "stated" is found twice in NT; "stating" is found 3 times in the NT;

Verb "verbalize" is **not used** in NASB.

Gerhard Friedrich (in Kittel's *Theological Dictionary*) also noted the same narrowing of vocabulary because of the overuse of the word "preach":

> "When we think of the proclaiming of God's Word by men, we almost necessarily think of preaching, and with few exceptions Luther always uses this word (*predigen*) in translation of κηρύσσειν. The NT is more dynamic and varied in its modes of expression than we are to-day. ... [follows a list of 31 synonyms] Naturally there are differences between these verbs. **But our almost exclusive use of "preach" for all of them is a sign, not merely of poverty of vocabulary, but of the loss of something which was a living reality in primitive Christianity."**[612]

Could it be that the coyly communicated antagonism of men like Sir Thomas More to street evangelism and street preaching (as well as Thomas Aquinas and many papal encyclicals) has made its way into lexicons and translations of the Bible? [613]

It may be that there may not be a proper translation of certain communicatory terms into English, because of a lack of use of the full breadth of the English language. This deficit may be especially evident if one attempts a back translation of the many communicatory synonyms which we will see below.

Therefore:

This difficulty may have been why John Wycliffe transliterated "evangelize" from the Latin to provide us another communicatory verb in English, which continues in common usage in the English

---

[612]Gerhard Freidrich, "κῆρυξ (ἱεροκῆρυξ), κηρύσσω, κήρυγμα, προκηρύσσω," in *Theological Dictionary of the New Testament*, ed. By Gerhard Kittel, trans. by Geoffrey Bromiley (Grand Rapids: Eerdmans, 1965), 3:703. Consider also that the Greek language is still being spoken in Greece—a language rooted with similar verbal constructs to Classical and Koine Greek. Thus, it seems logical that a similar range and breadth of vocabulary remains the inheritance of the Greeks to this day.

[613]"Those among them that have not yet accepted the Christian religion do not restrain others from it or abuse the converts to it. While I was there, only one man among the Christians was punished. This newly baptized convert, in spite of all our advice, was preaching in public on the Christian worship more zealously than wisely. He grew so heated that he not only put our worship before all others, but condemned all other rites as profane and loudly denounced their celebrants as wicked and impious men fit for hell fire. After he had been preaching these things for a long time, they seized him. They convicted him not on a charge of disparaging their religion, but of arousing public disorder among the people, and sentenced him to exile" (Thomas More, *Utopia* [1516; Arlington Heights, IL: AHM, 1949], 71).

language to this day. However, antagonism to this and other "borrowed terms" continues in various forms.[614]

The great semantic range of original language verbs translated in English "shew" in the KJV, or "preach," "proclaim," and "declare" in the NASB should be sufficient to *show* that greater clarity may be needed in translating certain proclamational words into English.

Therefore, in light of the (1) importance and volatility of these terms and (2) number of communicatory terms in the Hebrew and the Greek, it would seem that:
   (a) Greater consistency in the translation of communicatory verbs may be considered
   (b) Use could be made of some of the unused or minimally used terms in English, such as "contest," "exclaim," "evangelize," "profess," and "recount," and especially in the NT

Also, in light of the primacy of the Great Commission and the communication of the Gospel, it may be expedient for a thorough study of this subject to guide a linguistically and evangelistically-transparent translation of the Bible.

---

[614]Remembering the 1968 and 1987 "Guidelines for Interconfessional Cooperation in Translating the Bible" are against the use of "borrowed terms."

G. Turning the Tide—Unleashing the Word Evangelize!

A well-meaning acquaintance (with a Ph.D.) once told me, "The Gospels and the Book of Acts speak of evangelism, but it cannot be found in the epistles." This statement, by a man of letters, exemplifies why the word evangelize needs to be unleashed in the Pauline letters. Indeed, the word εὐαγγελίζω is found 21 times in the Pauline epistles. However, this learned man was unaware of that fact, as was I at the time. Notice above that 12 of the 24 translations of εὐαγγελίζω in the French Olivétan version (i.e. proto-French Geneva Bible) are in the Pauline letters, while it is found only once the Book of Acts. It was obvious that this acquaintance was not reading the French Geneva Bible in his devotions!

However, what if your Bible read like this? …

Several OT precedents (of the 22 total OT LXX uses) of the verb εὐαγγελίζω from the LXX (revising the NKJ):

Psa 40:9, "**I have evangelized** righteousness In the great assembly; Indeed, I do not restrain my lips, O LORD, You Yourself know"

Psa 68:11, "The Lord gave the word; Great *was* the company of **those evangelizing**"

Psa 96:2, "Sing to the LORD, bless His name; **Evangelize** His salvation from day to day"

Isa 40:9, "O Zion, **You who evangelizes**, Get up into the high mountain; O Jerusalem, **You who evangelizes**, Lift up your voice with strength, Lift *it* up, be not afraid; Say to the cities of Judah, 'Behold your God!'"

Isa 52:7, "How beautiful upon the mountains Are the feet of **him who evangelizes**, Who proclaims peace, **Who evangelizes** good, Who proclaims salvation, Who says to Zion, 'Your God reigns!'"

Isa 60:6, "The multitude of camels shall cover your *land*, The dromedaries of Midian and Ephah; All those from Sheba shall come; They shall bring gold and incense, And **they shall evangelize** the praises [LXX: 'the salvation'] of the LORD"

Isa 61:1, "The Spirit of the Lord GOD *is* upon Me, Because the LORD has anointed Me **To evangelize** the poor; He has sent Me to heal the brokenhearted, To proclaim liberty to the captives, And the opening of the prison to *those who are* bound"

Joel 2:32 (revising Brenton), "And it shall come to pass *that* whosoever shall call on the name of the Lord shall be saved: for in mount Sion and in Jerusalem shall the saved one be as the Lord has said, and **they that are evangelized**, whom the Lord has called"

Nahum 1:15, "Behold, on the mountains The feet of him **who evangelizes**, Who proclaims peace! O Judah, keep your appointed feasts, Perform your vows. For the wicked one shall no more pass through you; He is utterly cut off"

The following translates εὐαγγελίζω as evangelize in its 25/26 uses in Luke-Acts (10 in Luke and 15/16 in Acts), revising the NASB translation:

Luke 1:19, "And the angel answered and said to him, "I am Gabriel, who stands in the presence of God; and I have been sent to speak to you, and **to evangelize** this thing.""

Luke 2:10, "And the angel said to them, 'Do not be afraid; for behold, **I evangelize** you a great joy which shall be for all the people.'"

Luke 3:18, "So with many other exhortations also **he** [John the Baptist] **evangelized** the people."

Luke 4:18 (cf. Luke 7:22), "The Spirit of the Lord is upon Me, Because He anointed Me **to evangelize** the poor. He has sent Me to proclaim release to the captives, And recovery of sight to the blind, To set free those who are downtrodden."

Luke 4:43, "But He [Jesus] said to them, "I must **evangelize** the kingdom of God to other cities also, for I was sent for this purpose.""

Luke 7:22, "And He answered and said to them, 'Go and report to John what you have seen and heard: *the* blind receive sight, *the* lame walk, *the* lepers are cleansed, and *the* deaf hear, *the* dead are raised up, *the* poor **are evangelized**.'"

Luke 8:1, "And it came about soon afterwards, that He *began* going about from one city and village to another, proclaiming and **evangelizing** the kingdom of God; and the twelve were with Him."

Luke 9:6, "And departing, they *began* going about among the villages evangelizing and healing everywhere."

Luke 16:16, "The Law and the Prophets *were proclaimed* until John; since then the gospel of the kingdom of God **is evangelized**, and everyone is forcing his way into it."

Luke 20:1, "And it came about on one of the days while He was teaching the people in the temple and **evangelizing**, that the chief priests and the scribes with the elders confronted *Him*."

Acts 5:42, "And every day, in the temple and from house to house, they kept right on teaching and **evangelizing** Jesus *as* the Christ."

Acts 8:4, "Therefore, those who had been scattered went about **evangelizing** the word."

Acts 8:12, "But when they believed Philip **evangelizing** about the kingdom of God and the name of Jesus Christ, they were being baptized, men and women alike."

Acts 8:25, "And so, when they had solemnly testified and spoken the word of the Lord, they started back to Jerusalem, and **were evangelizing** the many villages of the Samaritans."

Acts 8:35, "And Philip opened his mouth, and beginning from this Scripture **he evangelized** him about Jesus."

Acts 8:40, "But Philip found himself at Azotus; and as he passed through **he kept evangelizing** all the cities, until he came to Caesarea."

Acts 10:36, "The word which He sent to the sons of Israel, **evangelizing** peace through Jesus Christ (He is Lord of all)."

Acts 11:20, "But there were some of them, men of Cyprus and Cyrene, who came to Antioch and *began* speaking to the Greeks also, **evangelizing** the Lord Jesus."

Acts 13:32, "And **we evangelize** you of the promise made to the fathers."

Acts 14:5-7, "And when an attempt was made by both the Gentiles and the Jews with their rulers, to mistreat and to stone them, they became aware of it and fled to the cities of Lycaonia, Lystra and Derbe, and the surrounding region; and there they continued **to evangelize**."

Acts 14:15, "And saying, 'Men, why are you doing these things? We are also men of the same nature as you, and **evangelize** you in order that you should turn from these vain things to a living God, who made the heaven and the earth and the sea, and all that is in them.'"

Acts 14:21, "And after **they had evangelized** that city and had ~~made~~ [won] many disciples, they returned to Lystra and to Iconium and to Antioch."

Acts 15:35, "But Paul and Barnabas stayed in Antioch, teaching and **evangelizing**, with many others also, the word of the Lord."

Acts 16:10, "And when he had seen the vision, immediately we sought to go into Macedonia, concluding that God had called us **to evangelize** them."

[Acts 16:17, "Following after Paul and us, she kept crying out, saying, 'These men are bond-servants of the Most High God, who are **evangelizing** to you the way of salvation.'" (from the variant found only in Codex Bezae)]

Acts 17:18, And also some of the Epicurean and Stoic philosophers were conversing with him. And some were saying, 'What would this idle babbler wish to say?' Others, 'He seems to be a proclaimer of strange deities,'— because **he was evangelizing** Jesus and the resurrection.'"

Or note these 22/23 Pauline uses:

Rom 1:15, "Thus, for my part, I am eager **to evangelize** you also who are in Rome."

Rom 10:15, "And how shall they preach unless they are sent? Just as it is written, 'How beautiful are the feet of those **who evangelize** [NKJ: peace, **who evangelize**] good things!'"

Rom 15:20, "And thus I aspired **to evangelize**, not where Christ was *already* named, that I might not build upon another man's foundation."

1 Cor 1:17, "For Christ did not send me to baptize, but **to evangelize**, not in cleverness of speech, that the cross of Christ should not be made void."

1 Cor 9:16, "For if **I evangelize**, I have nothing to boast of, for I am under compulsion; for woe is me if I do not **evangelize**."

1 Cor 9:18, "What then is my reward? That, when **I evangelize**, I may offer the gospel without charge, so as not to make full use of my right in the gospel."

1 Cor 15:1-2, "Now I make known to you, brethren, the gospel by which **I evangelized** you, which also you received, in which also you stand, by which also you are saved, if you hold fast the word by which **I evangelized** you, unless you believed in vain."

2 Cor 10:16, "So that **we may evangelize** regions beyond you, not boasting about what has already been done in someone else's area of ministry."

2 Cor 11:7, "Or did I commit a sin in humbling myself that you might be exalted, because **I evangelized** the gospel of God to you without charge?"

Gal 1:8-9, "But even though we, or an angel from heaven, should evangelize you contrary to how **we evangelized** you, let him be accursed. As we have said before, so I say again now, if any man **is evangelizing** contrary to that which you received, let him be accursed."[615]

Gal 1:11, "Now I want you to know, brothers, that the gospel which **I evangelize** is not based on a human point of view."

Gal 1:16, "to reveal His Son in me, that **I might evangelize** Him among the Gentiles, I did not immediately consult with flesh and blood"

Gal 1:23, "they simply kept hearing: 'He who formerly persecuted us now **evangelizes** the faith he once tried to destroy.'"

---

[615]Note the parallel translation of David Martin in his 1744 version in French, "Mais quand nous-mêmes [vous évangéliserions], ou quand un Ange du Ciel vous évangéliserait outre ce que nous vous avons évangélisé, qu'il soit anathème. Comme nous l'avons déjà dit, je le dis encore maintenant : si quelqu'un vous évangélise outre ce que vous avez reçu, qu'il soit anathème " (Gal 1:8-9; Epître de Saint Paul Apôtre aux Galates; accessed 29 June 2006; available from http://www.biblemartin.com/bible/bible_frm.htm; Internet).

Gal 4:13, "but you know that it was because of a bodily illness that **I evangelized** you the first time."

Eph 2:17, "And He came and **evangelized** peace to you who were far away, and peace to those who were near"

Eph 3:8, "This grace was given to me—the least of all the saints!—**to evangelize** to the Gentiles the incalculable riches of the Messiah."

1 Thess 3:6, "But now that Timothy has come to us from you, and **has evangelized** us of your faith and love, and that you always think kindly of us, longing to see us just as we also long to see you"

Heb 4:2, "For indeed **we were evangelized**, just as they also; but the word they heard did not profit them, because it was not united by faith in those who heard"

Heb 4:6, "Therefore, since it remains for some to enter it, and those who formerly **were evangelized** failed to enter because of disobedience"

Or in other portions:

Matt 11:5, "*The* blind receive sight and *the* lame walk, *the* lepers are cleansed and *the* deaf hear, and *the* dead are raised up, and *the* poor **are evangelized**."

1 Pet 1:12, "It was revealed to them that they were not serving themselves, but you, in these things which now have been announced to you through those **who evangelized** you by the Holy Spirit sent from heaven— things into which angels long to look"

1 Pet 1:25, "'but the word of the Lord endures forever.' And this is the word by which you were evangelized."

1 Pet 4:6, "For this purpose those who are dead **have been evangelized**, that though they are judged in the flesh as men, they may live in the spirit according to *the will of* God."

Rev 10:7, "but in the days of the voice of the seventh angel, when he is about to sound, then the mystery of God is finished, as **He evangelized** His servants the prophets"

Rev 14:6, "And I saw another angel flying in midheaven, having an eternal gospel **to evangelize** to those who live on the earth, and to every nation and tribe and tongue and people."

Conclusions about the usage of εὐαγγελίζω:

a. Lack of usage of "evangelize" in the English Bible makes the term more nebulous, the topic of endless debate among missiologists and practitioners.

b. Lack of usage of "evangelize" in the English Bible confuses evangelizing (lost people) with homiletics—formal preaching (in a church to primarily saved people)—and the many other Greek terms often translated "preach", like καταγγέλλω.

c. Many lexical definitions of this term may fall short in their definitions as they seem to rely on non-biblical usage and seem to have a ecclesiological agenda in their treatment of the term.

d. Had biblical authors wanted to use a verb (ἀγγέλλω, καταγγέλλω, κηρύσσω, etc.) + the noun (τό εὐαγγέλιον) they could have. In fact there are verses where the author uses both the verb (εὐαγγελίζω) and the noun (τό εὐαγγέλιον): 1 Cor 9:18; 2 Cor 11:7; Gal 1:11; Rev 14:6. Also, when needed, the authors could have use the verb (κηρύσσω) and the noun (τό εὐαγγέλιον), as in Mark 16:15 (cf. Gal 2:2).

As noted above, the 2009 *Holman Christian Standard Bible* (CSB) broke the "censorship" of the word "evangelize" and translated 7 of the 54 NA27 uses of εὐαγγελίζω as "evangelize" (13% of the NT uses)—the following lists all of the *CSB* uses of the verb "evangelize" with the verses in which they are found:

1) Acts 8:25, "Then, after they had testified and spoken the message of the Lord, they traveled back to Jerusalem, **evangelizing** the many villages of the Samaritans."

2) Acts 8:40, "Philip appeared in Azotus, and passing through, he was **evangelizing** all the towns until he came to Caesarea."

3) Acts 14:7, "And they kept **evangelizing**."

4) Acts 14:21, "After they had **evangelized** that town and made many disciples, they returned to Lystra, to Iconium, and to Antioch."

5) Acts 16:10, "After he had seen the vision, we immediately made efforts to set out for Macedonia, concluding that God had called us to **evangelize** them."

6) Rom 15:20, "So my aim is to **evangelize** where Christ has not been named, in order that I will not be building on someone else's foundation."

7) 1 Cor 1:17, "For Christ did not send me to baptize, but to **evangelize**—not with clever words, so that the cross of Christ will not be emptied of its effect."

This was a bold move for the *CSB* which has become the first English translation since A.D. 1382 to use the English "evangelize" for the Greek verb εὐαγγελίζω! Note: Two other English translations also used the term in the intervening 621 years: one use in Darby's 1884 translation of Luke 7:22, and one use of "evangelize" in the 1899 Douay-Rheims translation of Luke 8:1.

Likewise, the 2006 Idiomatic Translation of the New Testament by William Graham MacDonald also used the verb "evangelize" in 7 of the 55 NT uses of εὐαγγελίζω as "evangelize" (13% of the NT uses)—5 of which are the same verses as found in the CSB, one of which is added as implied in the text:

1) Acts 8:25, "Then after the apostles had given extensive testimony and had spoken the word of the Lord, they returned to Jerusalem. En route they were **evangelizing** many of the Samaritan towns."
2) Acts 8:40, "Philip, on the other hand, was found at Azotus. So he passed through all the (western) towns, **evangelizing** until he came to Caesarea."
3) Acts 14:21, "After they had **evangelized** in Derbe and had made many disciples, they returned to Lystra, Iconium, and (Pisidian) Antioch."
4) Acts 16:10, "After his vision, we at once were seeking to depart for Macedonia, inferring that God had called us to **evangelize** them."
5) Rom 15:20, "in such a way as to realize my ambition of **evangelizing** where Christ has not been named, so that I might not build on another man's foundation."
6) Gal 4:13, "You know that in the beginning of our relationship when I **evangelized** you, I did so while being physically debilitated."
7) Phil 4:15, "You Philippians also know that when this area began to be **evangelized**, when I set out from Macedonia, no church shared with me in the matter of giving and receiving—except you alone."

The bold move by the 1999 CSB seems to have been emulated in the 2006 MacDonald text, and then increased by one in the 2009 CSB. May this trend continue!

H. Arguments Against and For Translating εὐαγγελίζω as "Evangelize"

In light of all these considerations, biblical, historical, and linguistic, a perceptive student asked me why the word εὐαγγελίζω should be translated evangelize. The following seeks to explain the arguments on both sides of the fence, reasons against translating εὐαγγελίζω as "evangelize" and reasons for translating εὐαγγελίζω as "evangelize."

REASONS AGAINST
Some reasons why εὐαγγελίζω has not been and should not be translated as "evangelize" in English Bible Translations

1. Because it follows six centuries of historical precedent—going back to prior to the Protestant Reformation—especially with regards to English and German language Bible translation, which also includes the stated opinions in **all** English lexicons (many of which were translated from the German at some point), all commentaries, and all other grammatical helps.

   Rx: True, up until very recently (1987+), but not a valid argument in and of itself.

2. Because at times (1/55 in NT) the usage of εὐαγγελίζω relates merely to the telling of good news, seemingly unrelated to the proclamation of the Gospel (unless there was a methodological war in that church as in most churches), e.g. 1 Thess 3:6, "But now that Timothy has come to us from you, and has brought us good news of your faith and love, and that you always think kindly of us, longing to see us just as we also long to see you"

   Rx. One case should not decide the 54/55/56 other cases, especially when the context clearly warrants another translation. Additionally, the Thessalonian's view of Paul had a spiritual element to it. Therefore, included in Timothy's good news was the fact that they remained spiritually attentive, and were not "labor in vain" as may have been the case for other churches.

   By way of interest, at other times in similar contexts Paul used the verb δηλόω, perhaps indicating the unusual spiritual nature of the 1 Thess 3 usage of εὐαγγελίζω, as exemplified in 1 Thess 1:9-10:
   1 Cor 1:11, "For I have been informed concerning you, my brethren, by Chloe's *people*, that there are quarrels among you"
   Col 1:8, "and he also informed us of your love in the Spirit"

3. Because the transliteration of Greek or Latin terms, called "borrowing," is reproved by leading translation theorists.[616]

   Rx. The theological emphases of "loan words" are so weighty, that it appears that moderating translation theorists would prefer to dilute these terms, when expedient to their cause, in the name of proper translation theory; including words like: justification, justify, election, predestination, propitiation, expiation, and evangelize!

   A balanced look at loan words in English, for example, finds that there are so many loan words from Greek, Latin, and French in English that it is virtually impossible to know where to stop and draw a linguistic line.

   Further, loan words play the important role of adding a new worldview concept into a culture that may not have existed in a cultural language group up to that time.

---

[616]"Roman Catholics and Protestants have exhibited two rather distinct tendencies in borrowing. For the most part, Roman Catholics have borrowed largely from Latin while Protestants have borrowed from Greek, Hebrew, or modern European languages, with theological terms coming from Greek and Hebrew and cultural terms from European languages.

"For major languages borrowing should be kept at a strict minimum, for all such languages have a sufficiently large vocabulary or phrasal equivalence to make borrowing relatively unnecessary. For minor languages borrowing should be made from those major living languages from which the languages in question normally appropriate such terms as may be required by expanding technology, commerce, and social intercourse" ("Guiding Principles for Interconfessional Cooperation in Translating the Bible," in Thomas F. Stransky, C.S.P., and John B. Sheerin, C.S.B., eds. *Doing the Truth in Charity: Statements of Pope Paul VI, Popes John Paul I, John Paul II, and the Secretariat for Promoting Christian Unity 1964-1980* [New York: Paulist, 1982], 164-65).

4. Because on several occasions, Paul uses the word "evangelize" when speaking to Christians (e.g. Rom 1:15; 1 Cor 15:1-2; Gal 1:8-9), thereby proving that the word is not limited to an unsaved audience.

    Rx. The only unclear passage, other than 1 Thess 3:6 as above, is Rom 1:15; the other passages are speaking of the beginning of faith, which would be at the reception of the Gospel, which would be when evangelized and won as a disciple.

5. Because the contexts of "evangelize" in Luke are paralleled with the use of "preach" in the other Gospels, indicating that the words can and should be used interchangeably (or rather than interchangeably, "preach" should be used uniquely).

    Rx. Only true in one case; 7 of Luke's 10 uses of evangelize (1:19; 2:10; 3:18; 4:18; 7:22; 8:1; 16:16) are from contexts unique to Luke;[617] only three passages have synoptic parallels:
Luke 4:43 is parallel to Mark 1:38, in which case Luke uses εὐαγγελίζω and Mark uses κηρύσσω;
Luke 9:6 parallels Mark 6:12-13, in which case Luke uses εὐαγγελίζω and Mark uses a compound phrase, "preach that men should repent [Byz, ἐκήρυσσον ἵνα μετανοήσωσιν; NA27, ἐκήρυξαν ἵνα μετανοῶσιν]";
Luke 20:1 is parallel to both Matt 21:23 and Mark 11:27; whereas Luke uses the verb "teach" [διδάσκω] and "evangelize" [εὐαγγελίζω], Matt uses only teach [διδάσκω], and Mark does not contain a word for the type of ministry Jesus was having, only that he was walking through the Temple.

    The only conclusions from this data can be as follows:
Luke 4:43 and Mark 1:38: there is a semantic overlap between εὐαγγελίζω and κηρύσσω (which we know already from translation history);
Luke 9:6 and Mark 6:12-13: εὐαγγελίζω seems to include more than mere preaching or proclamation of a message (as κηρύσσω), but also preaching for repentance (or for a decision)

    From Luke 20:1, Matt 21:23, and Mark 11:27:
We may conclude that evangelizing includes a geographic movement (as in Mark 11:27), and as exemplified in Acts 8:25, 40;
We may also conclude that evangelizing is more than mere teaching (as in Matt 21:23), which Luke wanted to emphasize
We also notice that Luke picks up these same two verbs in his next use of εὐαγγελίζω in Acts 5:42, perhaps showing that the disciples were doing the same thing that Jesus had done in Luke 20:1, and were also persecuted just as He was!

6. Because it follows methodological precedent of limiting "preaching" to ordained clergy only, as noted above, the prohibition against lay preaching was very important to the persecution and slaughter of the so-called "Lollards," "Albigenses," and "Waldenses":

    This argument brings in ecclesiastical practice into Bible translation;
Its weight of authority is based on the "Sacrament of Holy Orders"—a means of imparting and giving grace;
Further, its weight was hardened into place by years of arrests, trials, and executions, of which Thomas Aquinas became defense attorney in Paris and a guide through his *Summa Theologica*.

    Rx. This is especially true in a state church model, wherein it is not every believers' mandate to verbally share the Gospel on the highways and byways. The "go ye" and "ye shall be" for all disciples in Christ's Great Commission must needs be restrcited to include only a particular group, i.e. clergy.

7. Because, closely following the prohibition against lay preaching was the prohibition against sharing the Gospel outside a church building.
This concept in today's French is called "Laïcité"—meaning secularism, ordinary, lay, civil,

---

[617]Albert Huck, *A Synopsis of the First Three Gospels,* 9th edition, revised by Hans Lietzmann (Tübingen: J. C. B. Mohr, 1936).

non-religious—a very powerful term in which French Catholics become militant to keep religion out of everyday life (which obviously includes evangelism).[618]

With this French understanding of the role of the laity, the term "lay preaching" is a *non sequitur* or an oxymoron.

Rx. This is true; from the Third Lateran Council and on, the Roman Catholic Church fiercely opposed anyone who had the audacity to preach without authorization from a Bishop who was rightly aligned to the Pope and the Church of Rome.

8. Because territorial and mainstream denominations do not endorse "proselytism," as noted above, seeing "evangelize" in the text would encourage aggressiveness in evangelism, which has been labeled "proselytism" and "sheep-stealing" for "institutional aggrandizement."

Rx. Territorial (Catholic, Lutheran, Anglican) and mainstream (United Methodist, Presbyterian Church U.S.A., etc.) are less comfortable with the seeming fanatical evangelism of the fundamentalist types.

9. Because the majority of New Testament scholars are not comfortable with aggressive evangelism (note their denominations of origin), they find it more appropriate to translate εὐαγγελίζω as "preach" (thereby focusing it within the local church by the ordained) because this translation fits more closely with their methodological presuppositions, as well as their denominational theological bias.

Rx. Translators who do not affirm the importance of every believer fulfilling the Great Commission, or to be approved by a publisher or by peers in the academy, may not be willing to translate εὐαγγελίζω as evangelize for methodological, pecuniary, or status reasons.

10. Because many professors of missions and evangelism[619] are more comfortable with discipleship (or mentoring), spiritual disciplines, church growth, leadership development, and community transformation, than with a single-minded focus on the verbal proclamation of the gospel; they sound no opposition to continuing with the status quo of translating εὐαγγελίζω as "preach the gospel".

Rx. It is strange that many who teach or write about evangelism no longer practice it themselves in an aggressive way; there seems to be a movement towards mediocrity in this area with the pressures to publish and to please academia and antagonistic students.

11. Because likely, especially to unlearned Christians, seeing "evangelize" in the English text would be the endorsement of religious fanaticism, evangelism; whereas those who currently read εὐαγγελίζω in the Greek or "evangelizare" Latin are limited to the learned and ordained.

Rx. Reaching the laity is the very reason that the word should be properly translated; it is very difficult to motivate the learned to this task, as a large part of learning moves the learned away from the fundamental truths of the Bible; hence Peter the Lombard's *Sentences* moved many a young monk into philosophical theology and scholasticism and away from evangelizing!

12. Because unsophisticated Christian lay people, seeing "evangelize" in the text, would likely confuse it with the modern practice of evangelism (see quote earlier in this section).

Rx. Seeing the word in the text given in the contexts given to us by God would have a revolutionary impact on lay people; they would and could allow Scripture to interpret Scripture, just as they are to do in other areas of theology and practice.

---

[618]"*La laïcité doit s'imposer partout*', a déclaré Manuel Valls, en préambule de l'annonce des mesures pour l'Education" ("DIRECT. Manuel Valls et Najat Vallaud-Belkacem détaillent les mesures pour l'Education et la laïcité"; from: http://www.francetvinfo.fr/faits-divers/attaque-au-siege-de-charlie-hebdo/direct-manuel-valls-detaille-les-mesures-pour-l-education_804047.html [online]; accessed: 23 Jan 2015; Internet).

"3/ 'Le seul enjeu qui importe, la laïcité, la laïcité, la laïcité. Parce que c'est le cœur de la République'" ("Terrorisme : les cinq phrases à retenir du discours d'hommage de Manuel Valls"; available at: http://www.lefigaro.fr/politique/le-scan/citations/2015/01/13/25002-20150113ARTFIG00336-terrorisme-les-cinq-phrases-a-retenir-du-discours-d-hommage-de-manuel-valls.php [online]; accessed: 23 Jan 2015; Internet).

[619]For example, see David J. Bosch, *Transforming Mission*, 420.

13. Because Christ could not expect all of His followers to be involved in such demeaning and socially unacceptable behavior as evangelizing.

   Rx. Fortunately, evangelizing is the joyful obligation and duty of every true believer in Christ; many have considered evangelizing the touchstone of true conversion, based on Matt 10:32-33; Mark 8:38; Luke 12:8-9

14. Because socially-unacceptable fanatical behavior already exists among some Christian groups, even with the word "evangelize" translated as "preach", and that fanaticism exists especially among certain sectarian groups (e.g. Southern Baptists), young people, and other "simplistic" readers; how much worse would that fanaticism be if these "literalistic" Christians actually saw all or most of the 54/55/56 NT uses of "evangelize," as in Luke-Acts (25 times) and the Pauline epistles (23 times)—it might radically transform their approach to evangelism!

   Rx. It is my prayer that God will transform the evangelizing of His people as they see this word rightly translated in their Bibles!

May the astute reader read the above comments in context, as they constitute the reasoning which may well have hindered the translation of the word εὐαγγελίζω as "evangelize" in the English text of the Bible for over 600 years. Let us now see reasons why it would be commendable for the New Testament (and some Old Testament, e.g. Isa 52:7; 61:1) uses of εὐαγγελίζω to be translated "evangelize."

REASONS FOR
Reasons why "evangelize" should be the preferential English translation
of the New Testament Greek εὐαγγελίζω

Introduction: Could it be that the reasons Delos Miles did not appreciate "Deductive" approaches to evangelism was because of translators confusing evangelizing with preaching? (See his chart at the end of Chapter 31). Delos rather posited "Inductive" approaches as a conversational alternative. Unfortunately, in seeking to remedy the confusion in translation, without differentiating between "preaching" in the text and "evangelizing," it can lead to lack of doctrinal clarity—both for preaching and for evangelizing!

1. **STYLE**: Translating εὐαγγελίζω as "preach" confuses it with formal preaching (cf. homiletics):
   - Monological—the preacher preaches while the audience listens,[620]
   - Within the four walls of a church, from a lectern or podium,
   - To a stable grouping of people or regular congregation, and
   - In prepared homiletical style (such as "three points and a poem").

   Most New Testament evangelism, however, is of a different nature:
   - Dialogical—the evangelists asks questions, hears the answers, and seeks to frame his message to the specific spiritual need of the individual[621]
   - On the highways and byways (outside of the church walls),
   - Individually (one-on-one), to groups, or to crowds; to "those who happen to be present" (Acts 17:17), and
   - In spontaneous style (unprepared, unrehearsed, and individually-guided).

2. **APPROACH**: Translating εὐαγγελίζω as "preach" has had the tendency for it to be confused with classical rhetoric, which includes:
   - A non-confrontational approach, and
   - Sophistication and cultured reasoning.

   Whereas New Testament evangelism includes:
   - Confrontation,
   - Persuasion, and
   - The unsophisticated communication by all Christians (e.g. Acts 8:4) of the death and resurrection of Jesus, and repentance for the forgiveness of sins.

3. **LOCATION**: Translating εὐαγγελίζω as "preach" limits the itinerant nature of the New Testament command and example, wherein "preaching," as understood today, generally occurs:
   - Within the four walls of a church, and
   - In one location for years (i.e. non-itinerating).

   New Testament evangelism most often took place:
   - In the streets (outside of the church walls),[622]
   - From city-to-city (emphasizing an itinerating ministry),
   - In homes or from house-to-house,
   - In the Temple and in synagogues,
   - In the judgment halls (cf. Phil 1:13; e.g. Acts 25:23-26:32)
   - Individually (one-on-one), to groups, or to crowds, and
   - In spontaneous style (unprepared, unrehearsed, and individually-guided).

---

[620]For example, the "herald" of the king (ὁ κῆρυξ) was not sent to dialogue with people, but rather to read the proclamation of the King to the people.

[621]Consider for example the 165 questions in the Book of Luke and the 75 questions in the Book of Acts (240 questions off the pen of Luke) and the 167 questions in the Gospel of John. In total, the gospels and Acts have 705 questions (Jimmie Hancock, *All the Questions in the Bible* [Lulu.com, 2011], using the KJV for determine number of questions). With its emphasis on evangelism training, the Book of Romans includes 88 questions.

[622]Midwestern student Matthew Parks wrote of the ministry of George Whitefield, "Rather than expecting the common folk to come to church, Whitefield took the gospel to the people by preaching in open fields the gospel in simple terms" (Matthew Parks, History of Christianity II, Source Material Assignment, Fall 2016).

In this context, note the change of emphasis (and power) in verses such as 1 Corinthians 9:16, which the Holy Spirit has given us in the first person:

- "For if I preach the gospel, I have nothing to boast of, for I am under compulsion; for woe is me if I do not preach the gospel"
  Note the formal feel of this verse, seeming to imply that Paul is under compulsion to stand behind a podium to preach to a gathered congregation (in which case this verse applies only to pastors), which betrays the context of Jesus' use of the term in Luke 4:43, and of Paul's example in the Book of Acts (e.g. Acts 16:10).
- "For if I evangelize, I have nothing to boast of, for I am under compulsion; for woe is me if I do not evangelize"
  Note the informal emphasis and universal applicability. If this verse were translated in this way, many a Christian and many a pastor would pronounce a curse upon themselves for their lack of evangelism!

4. **PERSON**: Who does New Testament evangelism involve…?
   - Uniquely ordained clergy or unordained and untrained laity?
     In many denominations, men are "ordained to preach the Gospel," thereby limiting or particularizing preaching only to the ordained.
     Likewise a pastor may say, "I am called to preach"; for he was set aside from among the lay people, in a particularistic sense, in order to "preach the Gospel."
     Hence, all the passages that use the word "preach" are naturally ignored or overlooked by lay people as not being applicable to them. No wonder it is so difficult to get lay people to evangelize, they do not see it in their Bibles, as their hermeneutical grid is that only certain people are called to "preach the Gospel." Lay people tune out most or all "preaching" portions in the Pauline epistles as: (1) for called "preachers" only, thus, (2) dealing with homiletics, and (3) related to what happens within the four walls of the church only.
     Preaching being limited to the ordained was the rule when the Roman Catholic began prohibiting evangelism or lay preaching beginning in the 12th and 13th Centuries. In the New Testament, however, evangelism is for all Christians, not just for the ordained clergy (cf. John Wesley, "All at it; always at it!")[623]
   - Women evangelizing (but not preaching)?
     In many denominations, preaching is limited to men, as only men can be ordained. The New Testament, however, does not limit evangelism only to men, women can and ought to evangelize.

5. **AUDIENCE**: Related to one's definition of evangelizing is the recipient of the message. According to 1 Cor 15:1-2, it appears that the verb "evangelize" was used by Paul in this context to refer to that hearing of the gospel which came to lost people leading them to faith in Jesus Christ. Therefore, a differentiation between the broadly used "preach" and the more narrowly used "evangelize" is the audience—that being unsaved people. This audience follows the teaching of Jesus in Mark 8:38 in which He warned against being ashamed of Him and His words in the midst of an adulterous and sinful generation.

6. **SEMANTIC 1**: The use of the the cognate verb related to an important noun in the NT is quite common to provide a unique semantic range for that verb. For example, the noun prophet and the verb prophesy. In this case, it is clear that the use of that proclamational verb is closely related to the meaning of the term prophet. The same appears true with the nouns gospel and evangelist, and the verb evangelize in the Greek.

7. **SEMANTIC 2**: The division or deflating[624] of the word "evangelize" into multiple words, such as "bring good news,"[625] "preach the gospel" or "publish glad tidings," divides the message

---

[623]For example in the Third Lateran Council (1179): "For this reason, since in Gascony and the regions of Albi and Toulouse and in other places the loathsome heresy of those whom some call the Cathars, others the Patarenes, others the Publicani, and others by different names, has grown so strong that they no longer practise their wickedness in secret, as others do, but proclaim their error publicly and draw the simple and weak to join them" (From: http://www.dailycatholic.org/history/11ecume1.htm; accessed: 28 June 2003; Internet).

[624]If conflation is defined as "to bring together or combine"—in the court of law it is used of seeking to insert a tangential argument or concept into a case, it would seem that the division of the word "ev" and "angelize" into two

(gospel) from the method (preach); this division actually *changes the emphasis* and therefore the meaning of Scripture, as in the case of Galatians 1:8-9:

- "But even if we, or an angel from heaven, should preach to you a gospel contrary to what we have preached to you, he is to be accursed! As we have said before, so I say again now, if any man is preaching to you a gospel contrary to that which you received, let him be accursed" (NAS)

  [Note that the emphasis is almost uniquely on the "what" of the message of the Gospel.]

- "But thogh that we, or an Angel from heauen preach vnto you otherwise, then that which we haue preached vnto you, let him be accursed. As we said before, so say I now againe, If anie man preache vnto you otherwise, then yt ye haue receiued, let him be accursed" (1560 English Geneva)

  [Notice how the emphasis shifts to the "how" of the methodology of evangelism.]

The very preaching of these false teachers was an accursed thing. It is quite likely that they disagreed with Paul not only in their content of preaching, but even as to their methodology of preaching. Paul seems to have pick up his very strong language of cursing from Deut 7:26:

- "Nor shall you bring an abomination into your house, lest you be doomed to destruction like it. You shall utterly detest it and utterly abhor it, for it *is* an accursed thing" (NKJ)

- "You shall not bring an abomination into your house, and become accursed [ἀνάθημα] like it, detesting you shall detest and abhorring you shall abhor, because it [is] accursed [ἀνάθημά]" (translation mine).

Had Paul wanted to use κηρύσσω ("preach") with a separate word delineating the message, he could done so, as he did in 2 Corinthians 11:4, which is a parallel passage to Galatians 1:

- "For if one comes and preaches another Jesus whom we have not preached, or you receive a different spirit which you have not received, or a different gospel which you have not accepted, you bear *this* beautifully"

- Εἰ μὲν γὰρ ὁ ἐρχόμενος ἄλλον Ἰησοῦν κηρύσσει ὃν οὐκ ἐκηρύξαμεν, ἢ πνεῦμα ἕτερον λαμβάνετε ὃ οὐκ ἐλάβετε, ἢ εὐαγγέλιον ἕτερον ὃ οὐκ ἐδέξασθε, καλῶς ἠνείχεσθε.

It was clearly in Paul's semantic range to use the word κηρύσσω when he wanted to emphasize differences in the message preached.

However, Paul's use in Galatians 1 contextually emphasized method, as well as message. In fact God used the very words "preach the Gospel" when He wanted a divided emphasis:

- Matt 4:23, "And *Jesus* was going about in all Galilee, teaching in their synagogues, and proclaiming the gospel [κηρύσσων τὸ εὐαγγέλιον] of the kingdom, and healing every kind of disease and every kind of sickness among the people"

- Matt 9:35, "And Jesus was going about all the cities and the villages, teaching in their synagogues, and proclaiming the gospel [κηρύσσων τὸ εὐαγγέλιον] of the kingdom, and healing every kind of disease and every kind of sickness"

- Matt 24:14, "And this gospel of the kingdom shall be preached [κηρυχθήσεται τοῦτο τὸ εὐαγγέλιον] in the whole world for a witness to all the nations, and then the end shall come"

- Matt 26:13, "Truly I say to you, wherever this gospel is preached [ὅπου ἐὰν κηρυχθῇ τὸ εὐαγγέλιον τοῦτο] in the whole world, what this woman has done shall also be spoken of in memory of her"

- Mark 1:14, "And after John had been taken into custody, Jesus came into Galilee, preaching the gospel [κηρύσσων τὸ εὐαγγέλιον] of God"

- Mark 13:10, "And the gospel must first be preached [κηρυχθῆναι τὸ εὐαγγέλιον] to all the nations"

- Mark 14:9, "And truly I say to you, wherever the gospel is preached [κηρυχθῇ τὸ εὐαγγέλιον (τοῦτο)] in the whole world, that also which this woman has done shall be spoken of in memory of her"

---

terms becomes a matter of deflation or disflation—dividing a common word into two disperate concepts, therefore diffusing its meaning centrifugally—losing the original power, thrust, and biblical context of the verb.

[625]Conflation also takes place in the translation of the verb ἀπαγγέλλω, where it is conflated from announce to "bring ... word" in the KJV of Matt 2:8, 28:8; it is also translated as the visually-focused verb "shew" in Matt 11:4; 12:18; 28:11; Luke 7:18; 14:21; Acts 11:13; 12:17; 26:20; 28:21; 1 Thess 1:9; 1 John 1:2.

- Mark 16:15, "And He said to them, 'Go into all the world and preach the gospel [κηρύξατε τὸ εὐαγγέλιον] to all creation'"
- Gal 2:2, "And it was because of a revelation that I went up; and I submitted to them the gospel which I preach [τὸ εὐαγγέλιον ὃ κηρύσσω] among the Gentiles, but *I did so* in private to those who were of reputation, for fear that I might be running, or had run, in vain"
- 1 Thess 2:9, "For you recall, brethren, our labor and hardship, *how* working night and day so as not to be a burden to any of you, we proclaimed to you the gospel [ἐκηρύξαμεν εἰς ὑμᾶς τὸ εὐαγγέλιον] of God."

Likewise, Paul could have used the word καταγγέλλω ("proclaim") with τό εὐαγγέλιον ("gospel"), as in 1 Cor 9:14:

- "So also the Lord directed those who proclaim the gospel to get their living from the gospel"
- οὕτως καὶ ὁ κύριος διέταξεν τοῖς τὸ εὐαγγέλιον καταγγέλλουσιν ἐκ τοῦ εὐαγγελίου ζῆν.

When Paul wanted to highlight the attitude in preaching, he did not feel it necessary to repeat the verb, as in Phil 1:15:

- "Some, to be sure, are preaching Christ even from envy and strife, but some also from good will"
- τινὲς μὲν καὶ διὰ φθόνον καὶ ἔριν, τινὲς δὲ καὶ δι᾽ εὐδοκίαν τὸν Χριστὸν κηρύσσουσιν·

8. **SEMANTIC 3**: Dividing the verb into a verb and predicate, using the term "glad tidings" or "good news," does not seem to take into account that the gospel is the smell of death to those who are dying, and not really a good thing at all:

- 2 Cor 2:15-16, "For we are a fragrance of Christ to God among those who are being saved and among those who are perishing; to the one an aroma from death to death, to the other an aroma from life to life. And who is adequate for these things?"

Is not the hearing of the gospel in the case of the dying a cause for future judgment and condemnation?

9. **SEMANTIC 4**: The old "divide the thought into two words" trick:

Notice the theological and practical presuppositions of Jerome when he translated "repent" into two words "do penitence," instead of using the wooden, strained, borrowed, or irrelevant word "repent." Thus Jerome (or someone in his time) chose to turn the "repent" into something you do, by dividing the thought into two words: the verb "to do" + the noun "penance." Hence the 1899 Douay-Rheims has 29 uses of the English phrase "do penance." It took over 1,000 years for a minority in the Western church to divest themselves of Jerome's doctrinally-misguided translation—and that only after an inordinate amount of bloodshed! Dividing a verb into a noun and a verb is not always appropriate, especially when it negatively impacts the proclamation and reception of the Gospel.[626]

The same is being done today in Romans with the verb "justify." For example, rather than using "being justified by grace" in Romans 5:1, some contemporaneous translations are substituting "since we have been declared righteous by faith" (NET, CSB). Their logic, "justified" and "declared righteous" mean the same thing. Unfortunately, **that is not the case**:

- The novel translation is unnecessary and leaves the English-only reader (for whom the translation is made) unable to compare uses of the verb "justify" in their text (as the translator would do in the original language without even thinking about it).
- Also, in this particular case, it plays into the hand of the Roman Catholic Church, in which priests declare righteous by pronouncing absolution after acceptable confession and penance are made. By the way, the God's Word to the Nations translation is even worse, as it translates justify as "we have God's approval."
- Again, if God would have wanted a verbal phrase in His Word, both the verb "declare" and the noun "righteous" are also available in the Greek language.

---

[626]Conversely, Jesus used the verb + noun (ποιέω + ὁ ἁμαρτία), "Whosoever works sin is a slave to sin" (John 8:34), which the NIV dutifully simplified into using one verb only, "Everyone who sins is a slave to sin."

Impact of Translating δικαιόω as "Justify" or "Declare Righteous"

Translations of δικαιόω	Justify	Declare Righteous
Two Contemporary Translations (by way of example)	[New King James] Rom 4:5 But to him who does not work but believes on Him who justifies the ungodly, his faith is accounted for righteousness,	[Holman Christian Standard] Rom 4:5 But to the one who does not work, but believes on Him who declares righteous the ungodly, his faith is credited for righteousness.
Theological weight	Imputed righteousness (in man's nature)	Declarative righteousness (apart from man's nature)
Temporality	Finished action, changing man's nature (Rom 5:1; 2 Cor 5:17, etc.)	Possibly temporary, not necessarily making a permanent change in man's nature
Finished or temporary	Unequivocal: completed action, "once and for all!" (2 Cor 5:21; Heb 9:26-28; 1 Pet 2:9-10, 24; 3:18)	Equivocal: may be understood as a declaration that needs repetition (as in Rome's confessionals), depending on how it is understood

Note also the difference in feel when καταλαλέω is translated into one verb or two in 1 Pet 2:12:

- Two words (NKJ), "having your conduct honorable among the Gentiles, that when they speak against you as evildoers, they may, by *your* good works which they observe, glorify God in the day of visitation."
- One word (NAS), "Keep your behavior excellent among the Gentiles, so that in the thing in which they slander you as evildoers, they may on account of your good deeds, as they observe *them*, glorify God in the day of visitation."

While these differences are subtle, they influence the feel, power, and accessibility of the text.

It is difficult to understand why anyone would want to dumb-down the Bible by removing even mildly technical terms that any Junior High school student can easily be taught and understand. It leaves us with a Bible without any theological teeth.[627] As regards some contemporary logic in translation, perhaps Tyndale and Olivétan did die in vain.

10. **SEMANTIC 5**: Paul's use of the verb εὐαγγελίζω with the noun τό εὐαγγέλιον for the message doubly intensifying the power of the noun "gospel" when used in combination with the verb of the same root (when God determined that the context specifically needed an emphasis on the verb and the noun), in 1 Cor 15:1, Gal 1:11, and Rev 14:6:

- "Now I make known to you, brethren, the gospel by which I evangelized you, which also you received, in which also you stand" [Γνωρίζω δὲ ὑμῖν, ἀδελφοί, τὸ εὐαγγέλιον ὃ εὐηγγελισάμην ὑμῖν, ὃ καὶ παρελάβετε, ἐν ᾧ καὶ ἑστήκατε]
  Perhaps a better translation of this vebal grouping would be either:
  "...the gospel by which I gospelized you"[628] or
  "...the evangel by which I evangelized you."
- Gal 1:11, "the gospel evangelized by me" [τὸ εὐαγγέλιον τὸ εὐαγγελισθὲν ὑπ' ἐμοῦ];
- Rev 14:6, "having an eternal gospel to preach" [ἔχοντα εὐαγγέλιον αἰώνιον εὐαγγελίσαι].

These examples suggests that if Paul was emphasizing the noun in Gal 1:8, first of all, he would certainly have included the noun τό εὐαγγέλιον ("gospel") in the sentence, and second of all, he would not have needed to repeat use of the verb εὐαγγελίζω as in Gal 1:8 and 2 Cor 11:4.

It was not uncommon for Paul to use a noun with its cognate verb together for increased emphasis. For example:

---

[627]"Imagine a chemistry book edited to exclude all chemistry terms! What chemistry teacher would want to use such a book?" For other translation fallacies, see my "32 Possible Fallacies in Bible Translation" found as an appensix of Chapter 8.

[628]"Imperfect middle indicative of εὐαγγελίζω to 'gospelize.'" (A.T. Robertson, *Word Pictures of the New Testament*, vol 3, "Acts of the Apostles" [Nashville: Broadman, 1930, 1966, 1991]: Acts 17:18.

- In 1 Cor 16:10, Paul used the noun τό ἔργον and it cognate verb ἐργάζομαι to describe the positive ministry of Timothy; this same pair is also used 5 other times in the NT: Matt 26:10; Mark 14:6; John 6:28; 9:4; and Acts 13:41.
- In Col 1:29, Paul used the noun ἡ ἐνέργεια (power) and its cognate verb ἐνεργέω (to work) as a type of amplification, after the style of Hebraic parallelism;
- In Rom 15:3, Paul uses the noun ὁ ὀνειδισμός (reproach) with the cognate verb ὀνειδίζω (to reproach), which provides an intensity to the concepts;
- So in 1 Cor 11:2, Paul again uses another root dual, this time to intensify that which is passed on or turned over—the verb παραδίδωμι and the noun ἡ παράδοσις.

11. **SEMANTIC 6**: Old Testament usage of the word "evangelize" (22 LXX uses of the verb εὐαγγελίζω) affirms the translation of evangelize as evangelize, especially as it relates to Isa 40:9; 52:7; and 61:1. Several non-spiritual OT uses of evangelize does not negate the fact that the NT in all cases but one assigned a clear spiritual use to the word, especially since Isaiah already had done so in his prophecies.

Similarly, the OT makes use of the word for "Gospel" merely for good news of military or political victory (τό εὐαγγέλιον, 2 Sam 4:10; ἡ εὐαγγελία, 2 Sam 18:20, 22, 25, 27; 2 Kings 7:9), but we do not slight Jesus for giving this word a new usage in the NT (e.g. Mark 1:15; 8:35; 10:29; 13:10; 14:9; 16:15).

12. **SEMANTIC 7**: The use of "evangelize" in several unusual contexts does not provide conclusive evidence that the word should *not* be translated as "evangelize":
- Luke 1:19 uses the word "evangelize" to explain the message of the angel Gabriel to Zacharias
- Luke 2:10, similarly, the angels announce the good news of the birth of Christ to the shepherds in the field
- Luke 3:18, the term is used to describe the preaching of John the Baptist
- 1 Thess 3:6 is a context in which Timothy shares the good report of the concern of the Thessalonian church for Paul

None of the above uses of evangelize provides conclusive evidence that other uses of "evangelize" cannot be properly understood if translated "evangelize' into English. There are many theological terms that have uses in both the spiritual and physical sense—quite likely to protect the proper translation of the term.

13. **ETYMOLOGICAL 1**: Translating εὐαγγελίζω in two parts: εὐ an abbreviation for τό εὐαγγέλιον; and ἀγγελίζω as a verbal derivation of the verbal root ἀγγέλλω (found only once in the NT, in John 20:18), merely divides the word into two units of thought.

While further research into other languages may be warranted, this division into two words seems not to have occured prior to Luther's 15[45] translation (e.g. Gal 1:8-9), with the first use of εὐαγγελίζω in verse 8 and its use in verse 9:

Gal 1:8-9, "Aber so auch wir oder ein Engel vom Himmel euch würde **Evangelium predigen** anders, denn das wir euch **geprediget** haben, der sei verflucht! Wie wir jetzt gesagt haben, so sagen wir auch abermal: So jemand euch **Evangelium predigt** anders, denn das ihr empfangen habt, der sei verflucht!" [Perhaps Luther wanted to emphasize the word "Gospel"]

In the Vulgate, the French Olivétan, the French Geneva, and the English Geneva, the alternative translation to "evangelize" was either "announce" or "preach," emphasizing the mode of communication, rather than the content or message of communication. Here is an example from the 1605 French Geneva (Berjon):

Gal 1:8-9, "Or quand bien nous-mesmes, ou vn Ange du ciel **vous euangelizeroit** outre ce que nous **vous auons euangelizé**, qu'il soit execration. Ainsi que nous auons desia dit, maintenant aussi [le] di-ie derechef, si quelcun **vous euangelize** outre ce que vous avez receu, qu'il soit execration."

Notice that the word "other" in this case [*outre*] as adverbs twice modifying the verb "evangelize" does not refer uniquely to the message, but also to combined method and message.

Following the pattern of Luther's German translation of 90 years before, the King James Bible inserted "any other Gospel" (in v. 9) which modified the interpretation of the English Geneva which read, "preach unto you otherwise," from the mode of communication to the message communicated.

Therefore the etymological division of the word εὐαγγελίζω into two words is historically quite late.

14. **ETYMOLOGICAL 2**: Could it be that dividing the verb εὐαγγελίζω into two words is falling prey to the "Root Fallacy" as described by Donald Carson?

> "One of the most enduring errors, the root fallacy presupposes that every word actually *has* a meaning bound up with its shape or its components. In this view, meaning is determined by etymology; that is by the root or roots of a word."[629]

Notice, for example, the Hebrew word *yatab* in Deut 8:16, meaning "to do be good or to do good to," wherein the emphasis is truly the concept "good." This word actually contains the root *tob* or "good." However, the Hebrew *basar*, which was verb translated εὐαγγελίζω 20 times in the 2nd Century B.C. LXX, does not contain the term "good" or "gospel" as later incorporated into the NT text through Jerome's Vulgate. *Basar* rather simply means "to bear tidings" (BDB), or "publish, bear (good) tidings, preach, show forth" (TWOT), or "1. Bring (good or bad) news; 2. Make known" (Holladay).[630]

It would seem therefore that the semantical division of the term εὐαγγελίζω comes down from the tradition established through Jerome's Vulgate. Notice for example Rom 15:20:

Analyzing the Text of Romans 15:20

Greek Orthodox Text*	NKJ	Douais-Rheims (1899)※	Latin Vulgate
οὔτω δὲ φιλοτιμούμενον εὐαγγελίζεσθαι οὐχ ὅπου ὠνομάσθη Χριστός	And so I have made it my aim to preach the gospel, not where Christ was named	And I have so preached this gospel, not where Christ was named	Sic autem praedicavi Evangelium hoc, non ubi nominatus est Christus

*The only difference between the GOT and the Nestle-Aland text is the οὕτως rather than the GOT's οὔτω.

The observant reader will notice two major changes in Jerome's Vulgate: (1) the removal of any translation for the verb φιλοτιμούμενον, "make it my ambition"; and (2) the dissecting of the verb εὐαγγελίζεσθαι into two parts, translating it rather as "preached" and "gospel." Needless to say, these translation adaptations correspond to the historic antagonism of the Church of Rome to NT evangelism.

Could it be that Jerome utilized the "Root Fallacy" to disperse the emotive power of the verb "evangelize" in this poignant passage? And could it be that his translation has influenced many English translations since that time? By the way, the above Latin translation is verified in the 1230 Occitan New Testament and Wycliffe's 1382 translation, both translated from the Latin.

15. **INSTRUCTIVE/CATECHETIC**: If students of the Bible had the opportunity to see the biblical word "evangelize" in its context, this could alleviate current definitional difficulties:

- Assist readers in developing a normative biblical definition of evangelizing, as opposed to the confusion and conflict that now exists
- Provide an understanding as to the role of evangelizing as it relates to the Great Commission
- Assist in understanding the commonality and differences in the biblical weight of evangelizing and discipling, cf. Acts 14:21

---

[629]Donald Carson, *Exegetical Fallacies*, 2nd ed. (Grand Rapids: Baker, 1996), 28.
[630]BibleWorks 8.0.

16. **DIFFERENTIATION** between the role of "clergy" and "laity"?

Could it be that the merging of the NT concept of "evangelizing" into "preaching" served the purpose of accentuating the differences between the clergy and laity?

Could it be that, if the contexts of "preaching" and "evangelizing" were studied separately, that the latter would be considered far more urgent, than is normally the case today, and the former would not be lifted on a pedestal to the degree that it is in some circles today?

Recommendation: a thorough study of both concepts side-by-side may enable the researcher to get "behind" hundreds of years of cultural conditioning from English translation history, as all the uses of "evangelize" have been translated using the restrictive word "preach."

17. **FAULTY EXPECTATIONS**: Due to confusing the New Testament uses of "preach" and "evangelize," may a pastor/preacher have a lack of clarity related to:

- His preaching within the church is the primary and preferred way for souls to be saved?
- His responsibility to "evangelize" among those who will never set foot in his church?
- Whether or not, in his interactions with people outside the church, he has the obligation to "evangelize" them to the point of decision?

Further, is it not possible that this same non-differentiating pastor/preacher, using a non-differentiating Bible translation, may deride the people within his church, whom he is to shepherd, because they are not constantly "making decisions" for Christ? Potentially then leading him to:

(a) Find fault with his faithful church members because they are so carnal as to not be "making decisions for Christ" every Sunday morning?

(b) Brow-beat his faithful church members, rather than treat them gently as a shepherd (cf. Isa 40:11)?

Hence, is a primary NT context for "Decisional Preaching" more "evangelizing" passages in the Book of Acts, outside the four walls of the church (e.g. Acts 16:14, 30-31)? Whereas Paul's preaching to the elders from the church in Ephesus (Acts 20), while being evangelistic in content, was not decisional to unsaved persons.

While this author is thoroughly convinced of the need for and importance of decisional preaching, I am also keenly aware of using methods of persuasion that are not consistent with the text of the Scripture being preached or with the *sensus plenior* of the Scriptures.

18. **IMPROPER USE OF TIME**: Because of a non-differentiation between the clergy-only "preaching"; as opposed to all believers "evangelizing":

- Pastors can spend all of their time studying within the church, in order to prepare a "rip-roaring" sermon for next Sunday to be preached within the four walls of the church, while people living in the shadow of the church, who need the gospel, will never set foot in the church to hear that sermon!
- Thereby, partly due to an improper translation of evangelize, and partly from ignoring, overlooking, or reinterpreting the many commands and examples to "go" in the NT (which have not been tainted), pastors/preachers may be misusing their tithe-paid time!

These reasons, and perhaps others known only to God (Who chose to use the Greek word εὐαγγελίζω), make it commendable to translate εὐαγγελίζω as "evangelize" in the New Testament, as well as possibly in some places in the Old Testament.

TOWARD UNDERSTANDING THE SPECIFIC CONTEXTS AND WORD USAGE OF EVANGELISTICALLY-RELATED TEXTS IN THE NEW TESTAMENT...

FIVE CATEGORIES OF NT TERMS FOR EVANGELISM
(This chart refers to the next sections of the notes)

1. Person
4. Spiritual Dynamic

2. Method[631]
3. Movement and Location

5. Result

---

[631]It appears that the concept of a biblical "method" of evangelism motivated George Whitefield to (a) outdoor evangelism and to (b) initiate the "Calvinist Methodist" conference—several years before the term Methodist was reconfigured by John Wesley.

I. Five Categories of New Testament Terms for Evangelizing:[632]

Introductory: The remainder of this chapter is devoted to a verbal and contextual study of New Testament evangelizing. It is organized in the following five categories, section two being the largest and having its own index below:

1. **PERSON**—terms highlighting the person involved in evangelism

2. **METHOD**—terms highlighting the method of evangelism

3. **MOVEMENT AND/OR LOCATION** of Evangelism Ministry

4. **SPIRITUAL DYNAMIC** of the Word of God

5. **RESULT** of Evangelism Ministry

1. **PERSON**—terms highlighting the person involved in evangelism:

Select Terms for the Evangelist

Positive Terms	Positive Terms	Negative Terms	Other Terms Not Used of Evangelists	Of God / Of Jews
General Terms: 　1) ὁ εὐαγγελιστής [1]; 　2) ὁ ἄγγελος [12]; 　3) ὁ κῆρυξ [3]; 　4) ὁ διδάσκαλος [2]; 　5) ὁ ἀπόστολος [3]; 　6) ὁ διάκονος [7]; 　7) ὁ θεράπων [0]; 　8) ὁ οἰκονόμος [4]; 　9) ὁ λειτουργός [1]; 　10) ὁ ὑπηρέτης [3]; 　11) ὁ μάρτυς [2]. Cooperative Terms: 　12) ὁ σύνδουλος [1]; 　13) ὁ συνεργός [13]; 　14) ὁ συστρατιώτης [2]; 　15) ὁ σύζυγος [1]; 　16) ὁ ἀδελφός [1].	Metaphorical Terms: 　17) ὁ ἁλιεύς [2]; 　18) ὁ θερίζων [3]; 　19) ὃ ἐποικοδόμησεν [1]; 　20) ὁ θυρωρός [0]; 　21) ὁ ἡγούμενος [0]. Soteriological Terms: 　22) ὁ ἀκούων [3]; Terms from the OT: 　23) οἱ τρέχοντες [0]; 　24) ὁ ἀροτριῶν [1]; 　25) ὁ ἀλοῶν [1]; 　26) ὁ ἀλοητὸς [1]; 　27) τὸν τρύγητον [1]; 　28) ὁ πρέσβυς [0].	World's View: 　29) τὸ θέατρον [2]; 　30) οἱ θεατριζόμενοι [1]; 　31) τὸ περίψημα [1]. Derogatory: 　32) ὁ πλάνος [2]; 　33) ὁ σπερμολόγος [1]; 　34) ὁ καταγγελεύς [1].	35) ὁ γόης [1]; 36) ὁ γραμματεύς [2]; 37) οἱ καπηλεύοντες [1]; 38) ὁ/ἡ κυνηγός [0]; 39) ἡ ματαιολογία [2]; 40) ὁ συζητητής [1]; 41) ὁ ψευδόμαρτυς [1].	Of God the Father: 　42) ὁ ἐπαγγειλάμενος [3]; 　43) ὁ καλῶν [1]; 　44) τὸν λαλοῦντα [3]. Of the Bible Itself: 　45) ἡ γραφή [8] 　(46) ὁ λόγος [16]. Paul Described the Jews: 　47) ὁ ὁδηγός [1]; 　48) τὸ φῶς [1]; 　49) ὁ παιδευτής [1]; 　50) ὁ διδάσκαλος [1].

a. **Positive Terms:**

1) ὁ εὐαγγελιστής: 2 Tim 4:5, "Do the work of an **evangelist**." (e.g. Acts 8):
    Acts 21:8, "And on the next day we departed and came to Caesarea; and entering the house of Philip the evangelist, who was one of the seven, we stayed with him."
    Eph 4:11, "And He gave some *as* apostles, and some *as* prophets, and some *as* evangelists, and some *as* pastors and teachers,"
    2 Tim 4:5, "But you, be sober in all things, endure hardship, do the work of an evangelist, fulfill your ministry."

    Psa 68:11 (NKJ), "The Lord gave the word; Great *was* the company of those who proclaimed *it*" [Heb. הַמְבַשְּׂרוֹת צָבָא רָב; Gk. τοῖς εὐαγγελιζομένοις δυνάμει πολλῇ]"

    Consider that an evangelist (ὁ εὐαγγελιστής) evangelizes (εὐαγγελίζω) the Evangel (τὸ εὐαγγέλιον), that is the "gospel"!

---

[632]The translation in this study is based on the New American Standard Bible. Chapter 17: What Is the Gospel?, "Biblical Terms," similarly notes biblical terms for the Gospel when used as nouns with these verbs. David C. Barrett in *Evangelize!* (Birmingham, AL: New Hope, 1987) has a helpful look at the biblical terms used for evangelism, as well as a brief historical look at translations of this term in various languages.

2) ὁ ἄγγελος (179 total NT uses), meaning messenger; normally translated "angel":

Of the messengers-angels (or "spies," in Joshua 2) who visited Rahab the harlot:

> James 2:25, "And in the same way was not Rahab the harlot also justified by works, when she received the messengers and sent them out by another way?" (those by whom she was proto-evangelized)
>
> In Joshua they were sent to "secretly scope out" the land (Gk. κατασκοπεύω, Jos 2:1; 6:23), using a verb; while they are not labelled spies in Joshua, they are called "spies" in Heb 11:31, using the cognate noun (Gk. ὁ κατάσκοπος).
>
> Interestingly, in Judges 1:24, different "spies" were called "guardians," again using a verb (Gk. οἱ φυλάσσοντες).

> To these "spies," Rahab cried out for deliverance, four times using the personal name of God, the LORD, and finally requesting:
>
> Joshua 2:13, "And spare ['capture alive'] my father and my mother and my brothers and my sisters, with all who belong to them, and deliver our lives [souls] from death."

In 2 Chron 36:16, the king of Israel sent out messengers (hence, angels):

> 2 Chron 36:16, "καὶ ἦσαν μυκτηρίζοντες τοὺς ἀγγέλους αὐτοῦ"
>
> 2 Chron 36:16 (LXE), "Nevertheless they sneered at his messengers"

In LXX reading of Deut 32:8 and 33:2: Imagine the difference if the criteria for God's separation is (1) The people of Israel, or (2) Those who are messengers on His behalf!

> "Angels of God" or "sons of Israel"?
>
> Deut 32:8 (LXE, representing LXX), "When the Most High divided the nations, when he separated the sons of Adam, he set the bounds of the nations according to the number of the **angels of God** [ἀγγέλων θεοῦ]."
>
> Deut 32:8 (NAS, representing MT), "When the Most High gave the nations their inheritance, When He separated the sons of man, He set the boundaries of the peoples According to the number of the **sons of Israel** [בְּנֵי יִשְׂרָאֵל]."

> "Angels," "flashing lightning," or "fiery law"?
>
> Deut 33:2 (LXE, representing LXX), "And he said, The Lord is come from Sina, and has appeared from Seir to us, and has hasted out of the mount of Pharan, with the ten thousands of Cades; on his right hand *were* **his angels** [αὐτοῦ ἄγγελοι] with him."
>
> Deut 33:2, (NAS, representing MT), "And he said, 'The LORD came from Sinai, And dawned on them from Seir; He shone forth from Mount Paran, And He came from the midst of ten thousand holy ones; At His right hand there was **flashing lightning** [אֵשׁ דָּת] for them.'"
>
> Deut 33:2 (NKJ, representing MT), "And he said: 'The LORD came from Sinai, And dawned on them from Seir; He shone forth from Mount Paran, And He came with ten thousands of saints; From His right hand *Came* **a fiery law** [אֵשׁ דָּת] for them.'"

> Consider, for example, this statement of Jesus:
>
> Mark 8:38, "For whoever is ashamed of Me and My words in this adulterous and sinful generation, the Son of Man will also be ashamed of him when He comes in the glory of His Father with the **holy angels** [μετὰ τῶν ἀγγέλων τῶν ἁγίων]."

Of John the Baptist:

> Matt 11:10, "This is the one about whom it is written, 'Behold, I send My **messenger** [τὸν ἄγγελόν μου] before Your face, Who will prepare Your way before You,'" (Jesus was quoting of Mal 3:1; cf. Mark 1:2; Luke 7:27)

Of the messengers of John the Baptist:

> Luke 7:24, "And when the **messengers** of John [δὲ τῶν ἀγγέλων Ἰωάννου] had left, He began to speak to the multitudes about John, 'What did you go out into the wilderness to look at? A reed shaken by the wind?'"

Of the messengers of Jesus:

> Luke 9:52, "and He sent **messengers** on ahead of Him [καὶ ἀπέστειλεν ἀγγέλους πρὸ προσώπου αὐτοῦ]. And they went, and entered a village of the Samaritans, to make arrangements for Him."

Of the shining on the face of Stephen, just prior to his bearing witness of the Gospel to the antagonistic audience:

> Acts 6:15, "And fixing their gaze on him, all who were sitting in the Council saw his face like the face of an **angel** [τὸ πρόσωπον αὐτοῦ ὡσεὶ πρόσωπον ἀγγέλου]."

Of the giving of the Law by angels/messengers:

> Act 7:53, "you who received the law as ordained by **angels** [εἰς διαταγὰς ἀγγέλων], and *yet* did not keep it" (cf. Gal 3:19 seems to favor the use of the word "angel" in Acts 7:53).

Of Paul:

> Gal 4:14, "and that which was a trial to you in my bodily condition you did not despise or loathe, but you received me as an **angel** of God [ἀλλ᾽ ὡς ἄγγελον θεοῦ ἐδέξασθέ με], as Christ Jesus *Himself*."

In the Gospel, commissioning, and proclamation of Paul:

> 1 Tim 3:16, "And by common confession great is the mystery of godliness: He who was revealed in the flesh, Was vindicated in the Spirit, Beheld by **angels** [ὤφθη ἀγγέλοις], Proclaimed among the nations, Believed on in the world, Taken up in glory"
>
> Thisauthor must confess that, from the standpoint of the Great Commission and the proclamation of the Gospel, as obeyed by messengers of the same, the translation "messengers" seems to be more appropriate in this context.

Of the angels/messengers/pastors of the Seven Churches in Revelation:

> Rev 2:1, "To the angel of the church in Ephesus [Τῷ ἀγγέλῳ τῆς ἐν Ἐφέσῳ ἐκκλησίας] write: The One who holds the seven stars in His right hand, the One who walks among the seven golden lampstands, says this"
> cf. Rev 2:8, 12, 18; 3:1, 7, 14

Yet, of a clear distinction between angels and the seed of Abraham:

> Heb 2:16, "For indeed He does not give aid to angels [Οὐ γὰρ δήπου ἀγγέλων ἐπιλαμβάνεται], but He does give aid to the seed of Abraham."

3) ὁ κῆρυξ (3 total NT uses):

> 1 Tim 2:7 (NIV), "And for this purpose I was appointed a **herald** [εἰς ὃ ἐτέθην ἐγὼ κῆρυξ] and an apostle."
> 2 Tim 1:11 (NAS), "the gospel, for which I was appointed a **preacher** [εἰς ὃ ἐτέθην ἐγὼ κῆρυξ] and an apostle and a teacher."
> 2 Pet 2:5, "but preserved Noah, a **preacher** [κήρυκα] of righteousness."

Select other biblical uses of "preacher":

> The noun "preacher" in Romans 10:14 is derived from the verb κηρύσσω (participle-present-active-genetive-masculine-singular), hence: κηρύσσοντος
> The noun "preacher" in Eccl 1:1, 2, 12; 7:27; 12:8, 9, 10 is a translation of the noun, ὁ ἐκκλησιαστής (derived from the Hebrew *dabar,* this noun means "a member of the assembly or church") from which the book is named Ecclesiastes.

4) ὁ διδάσκαλος (58 total NT uses):

> 1 Tim 2:7, "For this I was appointed a preacher and an apostle (I am telling the truth, I am not lying) as a **teacher** of the Gentiles in faith and truth"
> 2 Tim 1:11, "the gospel, for which I was appointed a preacher and an apostle and a **teacher**."

5) ὁ ἀπόστολος (81 total NT uses):

> Matt 10:1-2, "And having summoned His twelve **disciples**, He gave them authority over unclean spirits, to cast them out, and to heal every kind of disease and every kind of sickness. Now the names of the twelve **apostles** are these: …":
>
> (1) Only use of the word **apostle** [ὁ ἀπόστολος] in Matthew, in the context of the evangelism training of Matt 9:35-11:1 (whereas the word **disciple** [ὁ μαθητής] is found approx 75 times in Matthew);
> (2) The **disciples** became **apostles** when they actually went out into the harvest to evangelize;
> (3) The word **apostle** [ὁ ἀπόστολος] is derived from the verb "to send" [ἀποστέλλω], therefore **apostle** literally means "sent one";
> (4) There is a sense in which every Christian is a "sent one of Jesus Christ" (Titus 1:1), as the Great Commission is applicable to every believer.
>
> 1 Tim 2:7, "And for this purpose I was appointed a herald and an **apostle**"
> 2 Tim 1:11, "the gospel, for which I was appointed a preacher and an **apostle** and a teacher"
> (cf. Rom 1:1; Gal 2:7)

Restricted use of the word "apostle" may come for several reasons:

Due to the fact that the apostles seem to be listed as a closed group:
Their names are listed as "the twelve apostles" in Matt 10:2-4 (Mark 6:7), Luke providing distinctions in nomenclature:

Luke 6:13, "And when day came, He called His disciples to Him; and chose twelve of them, whom He also named as apostles."

These twelve apostles were in the upper room, Luke 22:14.
Their names (minus Judas Iscariot) are given as being on the twelve foundations of heaven, Rev 21:14, giving them a closed number;
Likewise in 2 Pet 3:2, they appear to have a closed number;
As in Acts 1:26; 15:2, 4, 6, 22, 23.

To counter false-apostles:
Due to false apostles considering that they speak with the authority of the Word of God, adding to Scripture, which is prohibited in Rev 22:18.
Paul also wrote against the "false apostles" plaguing the church in Corinth, 2 Cor 11:13, as well as "exceedingly super apostles," 2 Cor 12:11; as did John in Rev 2:2.

The importance of fixed-apostles (a fixed number of first century-only apostles):
The standards for a fixed-apostle were enumerated in Acts 1:21-22
The doctrine of the fixed-apostles became foundational for the teaching of the church, Acts 2:42.

Open use of the word "apostle" may come for several reasons:

We begin to read an interesting *non sequitur* in Acts 8:1—the "sent ones" (apostles) did not go out from Jerusalem—one wonders why not?

Acts 8:1, "and they were all scattered throughout the regions of Judea and Samaria, except the apostles."

The issue of Barnabas as an apostle:
Barnabas is distinct from the apostles, Acts 4:36; 9:27
Luke calls Barnabas an apostle, Acts 14:4
At least three important things happened before that event:
James, the apostle, was murdered, Acts 12:1;
Barnabas was sent out by the church and by the Holy Spirit, Acts 13:3-4
The name change of Paul and reversal of names:
From Barnabas and Saul, Acts 13:2
To Paul and Barnabas, Act 13:46

The raising of the title "elder" used repeatedly in conjunction with apostle, prior to its "apostle" no longer being used in Acts:
See Acts 15:2, 4, 6, 22, 23; 16:4;
Acts 16:4 being the last use of "apostle" in the Book of Acts.

The use of "apostles" as the recipients of the letter from the Jerusalem conclave:
Acts 15:33 (BYZ), ποιήσαντες δὲ χρόνον ἀπελύθησαν μετ᾽ εἰρήνης ἀπὸ τῶν ἀδελφῶν πρὸς τοὺς ἀποστόλους.
Acts 15:33 (NKJ), "And after they had stayed *there* for a time, they were sent back with greetings from the brethren to the apostles."

Consider also that this verse includes a key variant—to lock in "apostle" as a set category to be used only for the highest office in the Church:
Acts 15:33 (BGT), ποιήσαντες δὲ χρόνον ἀπελύθησαν μετ᾽ εἰρήνης ἀπὸ τῶν ἀδελφῶν πρὸς τοὺς ἀποστείλαντας αὐτούς.
Acts 15:33 (NAS), "And after they had spent time *there*, they were sent away from the brethren in peace to those who had sent them out."

Normally translated as "messengers" in English, the plural "apostles" in 2 Cor 8:23 (French Geneva) was translated "ambassadors" in 2 Cor 8:23:
"Quant à nos freres, ils sont ambassadeurs des Eglises."

6) ὁ διάκονος, servant (30 NT uses):

1 Cor 3:5 (NKJ), "Who then is Paul, and who *is* Apollos, but **ministers** through whom you believed, as the Lord gave to each one?"

Notice the instrumentality of the servant in bringing belief!

ἀλλ᾽ ἢ διάκονοι δι᾽ ὧν ἐπιστεύσατε

"But if [not] servants through whom [through which/by whom] you believed."

2 Cor 3:6, "who also made us adequate *as* **servants of a new covenant** [διακόνους καινῆς διαθήκης], not of the letter, but of the Spirit; for the letter kills, but the Spirit gives life."

2 Cor 6:4, "but in everything commending ourselves as **servants of God** [θεοῦ διάκονοι], in much endurance, in afflictions, in hardships, in distresses."

Col 1:6-7 (NKJ), "which has come to you, as *it has* also in all the world, and is bringing forth fruit, as *it is* also among you since the day you heard and knew the grace of God in truth; as you also learned from Epaphras, our dear fellow servant, who is **a faithful minister of Christ** on your behalf [ὅς ἐστιν πιστὸς ὑπὲρ ὑμῶν διάκονος τοῦ χριστοῦ]."

Col 1:23, "and not moved away from the hope of the gospel that you have heard, which was proclaimed in all creation under heaven, and of which I, Paul, was made a **minister**."

Col 1:25 (Eng. Gen), "Whereof I am a **minister**, according to the dispensation of God, which is giuen mee vnto you ward, to fulfill the word of God."

1 Thess 3:2 (NKJ), "and sent Timothy, our brother and **minister of God** [διάκονον τοῦ θεοῦ], and our fellow laborer in the gospel of Christ, to establish you and encourage you concerning your faith."

Note also that in 1 Thess 3:2 ὁ διάκονος was removed from the Greek NA27

NKJ	BYZ	NA27	NIVO
and sent Timothy, our brother and minister of God, and our fellow laborer in the gospel of Christ, to establish you and encourage you concerning your faith	καὶ ἐπέμψαμεν Τιμόθεον τὸν ἀδελφὸν ἡμῶν καὶ διάκονον τοῦ θεοῦ καὶ συνεργὸν ἡμῶν ἐν τῷ εὐαγγελίῳ τοῦ χριστοῦ, εἰς τὸ στηρίξαι ὑμᾶς καὶ παρακαλέσαι ὑμᾶς περὶ τῆς πίστεως ὑμῶν	καὶ ἐπέμψαμεν Τιμόθεον, τὸν ἀδελφὸν ἡμῶν καὶ συνεργὸν τοῦ θεοῦ ἐν τῷ εὐαγγελίῳ τοῦ Χριστοῦ, εἰς τὸ στηρίξαι ὑμᾶς καὶ παρακαλέσαι ὑπὲρ τῆς πίστεως ὑμῶν	We sent Timothy, who is our brother and God's fellow worker in spreading the gospel of Christ, to strengthen and encourage you in your faith

The Greek Orthodox text retained the helpful link between serving God and co-laboring in the work of the Gospel of Christ!

7) ὁ θεράπων, attendant, servant—of one who serves freely (1 NT use), only of Moses:

Heb 3:5, "Now Moses was faithful in all His house as a servant, for a testimony of those things which were to be spoken later"

Notice the progression at the end of the verse:

Servant [ὁ θεράπων] > bearing testimony [τὸ μαρτύριον] > to what would be said [λαλέω]

ὡς θεράπων, εἰς μαρτύριον τῶν λαληθησομένων

As a servant, unto testimony of that which must/would be spoken

8) ὁ οἰκονόμος (10 total NT uses), meaning steward, manager, administrator, treasurer:

1 Cor 4:1, "Let a man regard us in this manner, as servants of Christ, and stewards of the mysteries of God."

1 Cor 4:2, "In this case, moreover, it is required of stewards that one be found trustworthy."

Tit 1:7, "For the overseer must be above reproach as God's steward, not self-willed, not quick-tempered, not addicted to wine, not pugnacious, not fond of sordid gain,"

1 Pet 4:10, "As each one has received a *special* gift, employ it in serving one another, as good stewards of the manifold grace of God."

9) ὁ λειτουργός (10 OT LXX uses; 5 NT uses), meaning to "minister" as a priest:

Rom 15:16, "to be a minister [ὁ λειτουργός] of Christ Jesus to the Gentiles, ministering as a priest [ἱερουργέω] of the gospel of God, that *my* offering of the Gentiles might become acceptable, sanctified by the Holy Spirit."

Whereas the term "priest of the gospel" is fairly equivocal in Roman Catholic contexts, due to the renaming of leaders in the church as "priests," whose function is to offer the "sacrifice of the Mass," notice the different French translation history with this noun and its corresponding verb:

Comparative French Translations of the phrase ἱερουργοῦντα τὸ εὐαγγέλιον τοῦ θεοῦ in Rom 15:16

LeFebvres[‡] (1522)	Louvain[‡] (1550)	French Geneva (1605)	Ostervald (1724)	Martin (1744)	French Darby (1859)	Segond (1910)	French Jerusalem[‡] (1973)	TOB* (1988)	Le Semeur (1992, 1999)
En sainctement administrant leuangile de Dieu	Sanctifiant l'Evangile de Dieu	Vacquant au sacrifice de l'Evangile de Dieu	Et d'exercer les saintes fonctions de l'Évangile de Dieu	M'employant au sacrifice de l'Evangile de Dieu	Exerçant la sacrificature dans l'évangile de Dieu	M'acquittant du divin service de l'Évangile de Dieu	Ministre de l'Évangile de Dieu	Consacré au ministère de l'Évangile de Dieu	J'accomplis ainsi la tâche d'un prêtre en annonçant la Bonne Nouvelle de Dieu
By administering the gospel of God with holiness	Bringing holiness to the Gospel of God	Occupied with the sacrifice of the Gospel of God	And exercising the holy functions of the Gospel of God	Employing myself in the service of the Gospel of God	Exercising the priesthood in the gospel of God	Acquitting myself of the divine service of the Gospel of God	A minister of the Gospel of God	Consecrated to the ministry of the Gospel of God	I thus accomplish the task of a priest through announcing the Good News of God

*Traduction oecumenique de la Bible.

10) ὁ ὑπηρέτης (20 NT uses) – Minister [as an official position]; servant; assistant, helper:

Luke 1:2, "just as those who from the beginning were eyewitnesses and **servants** of the word have handed them down to us"

Acts 26:16, "to appoint you a **minister** and a witness"

1 Cor 4:1, "Let a man regard us in this manner, as **servants** of Christ, and stewards of the mysteries of God"

11) ὁ μάρτυς/οἱ μάρτυρες - witness/witnesses, perhaps a better translation is testifier/testifiers:

ὁ μάρτυς – witness (singular): Acts 1:22; 22:15; 26:16; 1 Pet 5:1; Rev 2:13:

Consider a precedent in the OT, Isa 43:12:

(GOT) ὑμεῖς ἐμοὶ μάρτυρες καὶ ἐγὼ κύριος ὁ θεός

(Hence, Brenton's), "ye are my witnesses, and I am the Lord God."

(Ralph's) ὑμεῖς ἐμοὶ μάρτυρες κἀγὼ μάρτυς λέγει κύριος ὁ θεός

(NETS), "You are my witnesses; I too am a witness, says the Lord God."

Notice the interesting use of ὁ μάρτυς in Heb 12:1:

Heb 12:1 (NAS), "Therefore, since we have so great a cloud of **witnesses** surrounding us, let us also lay aside every encumbrance, and the sin which so easily entangles us, and let us run with endurance the race that is set before us."

Now, notice how the change in one translation changes the feel, providing further interpretive power to the verse:

Heb 12:1 (Johnston), "Therefore, since we have so great a cloud of **testifiers** surrounding us, let us also lay aside every encumbrance, and the sin which so easily entangles us, and let us run with endurance the race that is set before us"

οἱ μάρτυρες – witnesses (plural): Acts 2:32; 3:15; 5:32; 10:39, 41; 13:31; Rev 17:6 (cf. Isa 43:10-13, 44:8)—amazed at the following differences on such key passages!

Luke 24:48 (GOT) ὑμεῖς δέ ἐστε μάρτυρες τούτων; "And you are **testifiers** of these things."
Luke 24:48 (NA28) ὑμεῖς μάρτυρες τούτων; "You are **testifiers** of these things."

Acts 1:8 (GOT) καὶ ἔσεσθέ μοι μάρτυρες – Acts 1:8, "and you shall be **testifiers** of me"
Acts 1:8 (NA28) καὶ ἔσεσθέ μου μάρτυρες – Acts 1:8, "and you shall be my **testifiers**."

Some OT insights from Deut 17:6:

The noun ὁ μάρτυς (witness) is used 3 times in Deut 17:6, simultaneously, so is the verb ἀποθνήσκω (to die, to put to death, to be put to death):

Linking with the NT idea of being "witnesses" of the death of Jesus:
Luke 24:48, "And you are witnesses of these things"

Acts 5:27-28, "And when they had brought them, they set *them* before the council. And the high priest asked them, saying, 'Did we not strictly command you not to teach in this name? And look, you have filled Jerusalem with your doctrine, and intend to bring this Man's blood on us!'"

As well as being witnesses to the resurrection of Jesus:

Acts 1:21-22, "Therefore, of these men who have accompanied us all the time that the Lord Jesus went in and out among us, beginning from the baptism of John to that day when He was taken up from us, one of these must become a witness with us of His resurrection."

The phrase "at the mouth" (in Hebrew) is found twice in the Hebrew of Deut 17:6, which word is not found in the Greek, but rather is subsumed into the word "witness," as is also done in most modern English translations:

Deut 17:6 (KJV), "**At the mouth** of two witnesses, or three witnesses, shall he that is worthy of death be put to death; *but* **at the mouth** of one witness he shall not be put to death"

This phrase, and especially the word "mouth," provides two NT links:

Witness by the "mouth" in the Book of Acts:
Acts 8:35, "Then Philip opened his mouth, and beginning at this Scripture, preached Jesus to him"
Acts 15:7, "And after there had been much debate, Peter stood up and said to them, 'Brethren, you know that in the early days God made a choice among you, that by my mouth the Gentiles should hear the word of the gospel and believe'"
Cf. Acts 3:18, 21; 4:25; 10:34

Links the command to be a witness, with the need for verbal testimony:
Acts 1:8, "and you shall be witnesses to Me"

The tongue has the power of life and death:

Prov 18:21, "Death and life *are* in the power of the tongue, And those who love it will eat its fruit"

Notice that in the OT, death is in the power of two or three witnesses, Deut 17:6

However, in the NT, eternal life is available through the mouth of only one witness, Acts 8:35; 10:34; 15:7

Likewise, the OT law is a minister of death unto death, but the Gospel of Christ is a minister of life unto life everlasting, 2 Cor 3:6

Food for thought:
A distinction is often made between evangelizing and "witnessing" (at least since 1835).[633] Rather than evangelism dealing with the verbal and witnessing the non-verbal elements of the Christian life, I suggest that they both speak of the verbally testifying of Jesus Christ (e.g. Acts 23:11). Many other passages deal with the Christian's lifestyle.

A witness in the courtroom always needs to testify verbally in some way, so that the court reporter can accurately record what is said. So with the Christian if he is to be a witness of Christ, he must speak of Christ. J.E. Conant clearly tied these two ideas together:

"'And preach the Gospel,' if it means anything, must certainly mean to witness, or to tell the Good News of salvation through Christ, and this defines the central activity of the Church.'"[634]

---

[633]Consider this new inclusion into his lectures from the "Later Finney" stage:
"But their main influence as witness is by example. They witness in this way because example teaches with force superior to words. This is universally accepted: 'Actions speak louder than words.' But where both word and deed are applied, even stronger influence persuades the mind" (Charles G. Finney, *Lectures on Revival,* Kevin Walter Johnson, ed., a modified edition of *Lectures on Revivals of Religion,* 1835 [Minneapolis: Bethany House, 1988], 95-96).
[634]J.E. Conant, *Every Member Evangelism* (New York: Harper, 1922), 6.

Four Views of Witnessing*

Initiating the witnessing conversation	Proactively bearing witness in conversation	Bearing witness when asked	Living as a witness
Proactive Evangelism	**Reactive Evangelism**	**Passive Evangelism**	**Silent Evangelism**[635]

*Notice how using the verb "testify" instead of "witness" clears up some of the misunderstanding.

b. Cooperative Terms:

12) ὁ σύνδουλος (10 NT uses), meaning fellow servant:
Col 1:7, "just as you learned *it* from Epaphras, our beloved **fellow bond-servant**, who is a faithful servant of Christ on our behalf"

13) ὁ συνεργός (13 NT uses, listed as an adjective), meaning fellow worker, helper:
Rom 16:3, "Greet Prisca and Aquila, my **fellow workers** in Christ Jesus"
Rom 16:9, "Greet Urbanus, our **fellow worker** in Christ, and Stachys my beloved"
Rom 16:21, "Timothy my **fellow worker** greets you, and *so do* Lucius and Jason and Sosipater, my kinsmen"
1 Cor 3:9, "For we are God's **fellow workers**; you are God's field, God's building."
2 Cor 1:24, "Not that we lord it over your faith, but are **workers with** you for your joy; for in your faith you are standing firm."
2 Cor 8:23, "As for Titus, *he is* my partner and **fellow worker** among you; as for our brethren, *they are* messengers [lit. apostles] of the churches, a glory to Christ."
Phil 2:25, "But I thought it necessary to send to you Epaphroditus, my brother and **fellow worker** and fellow soldier, who is also your messenger and minister to my need."
Phil 4:3, "Indeed, true comrade, I ask you also to help these women who have shared my struggle in *the cause of* the gospel, together with Clement also, and the rest of my **fellow workers**, whose names are in the book of life."
Col 4:11, "and *also* Jesus who is called Justus; these are the only **fellow workers** for the kingdom of God who are from the circumcision; and they have proved to be an encouragement to me."
1 Thess 3:2 (NKJ [GOT]), "and sent Timothy, our brother and minister of God, and our **fellow laborer** in the gospel of Christ, to establish you and encourage you concerning your faith"
(GOT) of underlined phrase: καὶ διάκονον τοῦ θεοῦ καὶ συνεργὸν ἡμῶν ἐν τῷ εὐαγγελίῳ τοῦ χριστοῦ
The NA28 removes "our fellow laborer" reading as such:
1 Thess 3:2 (NASB), "and we sent Timothy, our brother and God's fellow worker in the gospel of Christ, to strengthen and encourage you as to your faith."
(NA28) of underlined phrase: καὶ συνεργὸν τοῦ θεοῦ ἐν τῷ εὐαγγελίῳ τοῦ Χριστοῦ;
Notice that our key word for this section is omitted from the NA28 and hence the NASB.
Philm 1:1, "Paul, a prisoner of Christ Jesus, and Timothy our brother, to Philemon our beloved *brother* and **fellow worker**."
Philm 1:24, "*as do* Mark, Aristarchus, Demas, Luke, my **fellow workers**."

---

[635]"21. Above all the Gospel must be proclaimed by witness. Take a Christian or a handful of Christians who, in the midst of their own community, show their capacity for understanding and acceptance, their sharing of life and destiny with other people, their solidarity with the efforts of all for whatever is noble and good. Let us suppose that, in addition, they radiate in an altogether simple and unaffected way their faith in values that go beyond current values, and their hope in something that is not seen and that one would not dare to imagine. Through this wordless witness these Christians stir up irresistible questions in the hearts of those who see how they live: Why are they like this? Why do they live in this way? What or who is it that inspires them? Why are they in our midst? Such a witness is already a silent proclamation of the Good News and a very powerful and effective one. Here we have an initial act of evangelization. ...

"41. Without repeating everything that we have already mentioned, it is appropriate first of all to emphasize the following point: for the Church, the first means of evangelization is the witness of an authentically Christian life, given over to God in a communion that nothing should destroy and at the same time given to one's neighbor with limitless zeal. ...

"As such they have a special importance in the context of the witness which, as we have said, is of prime importance in evangelization. At the same time as being a challenge to the world and to the Church herself, this silent witness of poverty and abnegation, of purity and sincerity, of self-sacrifice in obedience, can become an eloquent witness capable of touching also non-Christians who have good will and are sensitive to certain values" (Paul VI, *Evangelii Nuntiandi* (8 December 1975), §21, 41, 69; available at: http://listserv.american.edu/catholic/church/papal/ paul.vi/p6evang.txt (online); accessed: 8 Sept 2004; Internet).

3 John 1:8, "Therefore we ought to support such men, that we may be **fellow workers** with the truth."

14) ὁ συστρατιώτης (2 NT uses), meaning fellow soldier:[636]

Phil 2:25, "But I thought it necessary to send to you Epaphroditus, my brother and fellow worker and **fellow soldier**, who is also your messenger and minister to my need"

Phm 1:2, "and to Apphia our sister, and to Archippus our **fellow soldier**, and to the church in your house"

15) ὁ σύζυγος (1 NT use), literally, "yoke fellow," carrying the meaning: companion, comrade:

Phil 4:3, "Indeed, **true comrade**, I ask you also to help these women who have shared my struggle in *the cause of* the gospel, together with Clement also, and the rest of my fellow workers, whose names are in the book of life"

16) Of a certain brother (ὁ ἀδελφός), 2 Cor 8:18:

The Meaning of "in the Gospel" in 2 Cor 8:18

Greek Byzantine	Latin Vulgate	Wycliffe 2nd ed (1388)	Tyndale (1534)	Geneva (1560); Bishops; KJV; Webster's; NKJ	Young's (1862)	Darby (1884)	English Revised (1885); ASV
οὗ ὁ ἔπαινος ἐν τῷ εὐαγγελίῳ διὰ πασῶν τῶν ἐκκλησιῶν	cuius laus est in evangelio per omnes ecclesias	whose preisyng is in the gospel bi alle chirchis	whose laude is in the gospell thorow out all the congregacions	whose praise *is* in the Gospel throughout all the Churches	whose praise in the good news *is* through all the assemblies	whose praise *is* in the glad tidings through all the assemblies	whose praise in the gospel *is spread* through all the churches

RSV (1952)	NAB* (1971)	NASB (1977)	ABS' GNT* (1993)	ESV (2001)	HCSB (2003)	NLT (2004)	NET (2004)
who is famous among all the churches for his preaching of the gospel	who is praised in all the churches for his preaching of the gospel	whose fame in *the things of* the gospel *has spread* through all the churches	Who is highly respected in all the churches for his work in preaching the gospel	who is famous among all the churches for his preaching of the gospel	who is praised throughout the churches for his gospel ministry	All the churches praise him as a preacher of the Good News	who is praised by all the churches for his work in spreading the gospel

---

[636]Notice the Louw-Nida's seeming attempt to remove the warfare imagery of Paul in this term: "34.19 συστρατιώτης, ου *m*: (a figurative extension of meaning of συστρατιώτης 'fellow soldier,' not occurring in the NT) one who serves in arduous tasks or undergoes severe experiences together with someone else – 'one who struggles along with, one who works arduously along with, fellow struggler.' Ἀπφίᾳ τῇ ἀδελφῇ καὶ Ἀρχίππῳ τῷ συστρατιώτῃ ἡμῶν 'to our sister Apphia and our fellow soldier Archippus' Phm 2 [sic]. A strictly literal translation of συστρατιώτης in Phm 2 might imply that Paul himself was a soldier and therefore, in a sense, a secret agent of some military force. Accordingly, it may be necessary to employ a simile, for example, 'who works like a fellow soldier' or 'one who experiences great hardships along with us'" (Louw-Nida Lexicon; from Bibleworks 8.0).

c. Metaphorical Terms:

Consider this unusual OT use of some of these terms, which may explain why the concept of evangelizing is socially odius—this passage speaks of the Babylonian invasion of Judah:

> Jer 16:16, "'Behold, I am going to send for many **fishermen** [ὁ ἁλιεύς],' declares the LORD, 'and **they will fish** [ἁλιεύω] **for them**; and afterwards I shall send for many **hunters** [ὁ θηρευτής], and **they will hunt** [θηρεύω] **them** from every mountain and every hill, and from the clefts of the rocks.'"

In considering contexts for metaphorical terms for evangelism, it is important to note oppositional uses, of which we can be sure that Jesus was aware when He called His disciples to function as fishermen (for example).

17) ὁ ἁλιεύς, fisherman:
   Matt 4:19, "I will make you **fishers** of men"
   Mark 1:17, "I will make you become **fishers** of men"

18) ὁ θερίζων, a harvester/a reaper:
   John 4:36 (NLT), "**The harvesters** are paid good wages, and the fruit they harvest is people brought to eternal life. What joy awaits both the planter and the **harvester** alike!"
   John 4:36 (HCSB), "**The reaper** is already receiving pay and gathering fruit for eternal life, so the sower and **reaper** can rejoice together."
   John 4:37 (HCSB), "For in this case the saying is true: 'One sows and another reaps.'"

19) ὃ ἐποικοδόμησεν (from ἐποικοδομέω, meaning to build), a builder:
   1 Cor 3:14, "If any man's work **which he has built** upon it remains, he shall receive a reward."
   GOT has a different verb form than NA28 and BYZ

20) ὁ θυρωρός (from ἡ θύρα, meaning door), a doorman:
   The "doorman" being someone who welcomes people, and even invites them into the House of the Lord, i.e., the evangelistic function of he who invites and greets people at the door!

   Building on the idea of Jesus being the door of the sheep:
   John 10:9, "I am the door; if anyone enters through Me, he shall be saved, and shall go in and out, and find pasture."

   Building on the idea of Jesus knocking at the door of men's hearts:
   Rev 3:20, "Behold, I stand at the door and knock; if anyone hears My voice and opens the door, I will come in to him, and will dine with him, and he with Me."

   Therefore, working with Jesus, the job of the doorkeeper is to open the door to the sheep:
   John 10:3, "To him the doorkeeper opens, and the sheep hear his voice, and he calls his own sheep by name, and leads them out."

   Including the idea of Psalmist's preference to be a doorman in the house of the Lord:
   Psa 84:10 (NKJ), "For a day in Your courts *is* better than a thousand. I would rather be a doorkeeper in the house of my God Than dwell in the tents of wickedness."

   The role of a doorman is to invite people to come in and to welcome them when they do come in to the house of the Lord.

21) ὁ ἡγούμενος (from ἡγέομαι, meaning lead or chief):
   a) ὁ ἡγούμενος τοῦ λόγου—Acts 14:12, "He was the chief **speaker**," literally "the chief of words"
   b) ἀπέστειλεν τοὺς ἡγουμένους αὐτοῦ καὶ τοὺς υἱοὺς τῶν δυνατῶν ... διδάσκειν ἐν πόλεσιν Ιουδα (**teaching teams** of officials):
      2 Chron 17:7, "Then in the third year of his reign he [Jehoshaphat] sent his officials, Ben-hail, Obadiah, Zechariah, Nethanel and Micaiah, to teach in the cities of Judah"

d. Soteriological Term:

22) ὁ ἀκούων – from the verb ἀκούω (436 total NT uses), meaning to hear, heed, listen, understand:
   "And let him who hears say, 'Come!'" Rev 22:17
   Speaking of someone with a hearing of faith, cf. Gal 3:2, 5

e. **Several OT precedents:**[637]

23) οἱ τρέχοντες (i.e. those who run, from the Greek verb τρέχω [62 OT LXX uses; 20 NT uses], maning "to run"), meaning courier, post, postman (KJV, "posts," from which we gain the term "postman"):

2 Chron 30:6, 10, "**couriers**":

"And the **couriers** went throughout all Israel and Judah with the letters from the hand of the king and his princes, even according to the command of the king, saying, 'O sons of Israel, return to the LORD God of Abraham, Isaac, and Israel, that He may return to those of you who escaped *and* are left from the hand of the kings of Assyria.'" 2 Chron 30:6

"So the **couriers** passed from city to city through the country of Ephraim and Manasseh, and as far as Zebulun, but they laughed them to scorn, and mocked them." 2 Chron 30:10.

a) Used in the natural sense of one who runs for a prize in 1 Cor 9:24;

b) Compare with the running Word, 2 Thess 3:1:

2 Thess 3:1, "Finally, brethren, pray for us that the word of the Lord may spread rapidly and be glorified, just as *it did* also with you."

c) Compare also with 2 Sam 18:26, which correlate the verb run [τρέχω] and evangelize [εὐαγγελίζω]:

2 Sam 18:26, "Then the watchman saw another man running [τρέχω]; and the watchman called to the gatekeeper and said, 'Behold, *another* man running [τρέχω] by himself.' And the king said, 'This one also is bringing good news [εὐαγγελίζω].'"

24) ὁ ἀροτριῶν; as a participle of the verb, ἀροτριάω, meaning to plow:
1 Cor 9:10, "Or is He speaking altogether for our sake? Yes, for our sake it was written, because **the plowman** ought to plow in hope, and the thresher *to thresh* in hope of sharing *the crops*."

25) ὁ ἀλοῶν (1 OT LXX and 1 NT use), meaning "thresher"; from the verb ἀλοάω, to thresh:
1 Cor 9:10, "Or is He speaking altogether for our sake? Yes, for our sake it was written, because the plowman ought to plow in hope, and **the thresher** *to thresh* in hope of sharing *the crops*.".

26) ὁ ἀλοητὸς (2 uses in OT LXX), meaning the plowman, Amos 9:13 (cf. Lev 26:5):
Amos 9:13, "'Behold, days are coming,' declares the LORD, 'When **the plowman** will overtake the reaper And the treader of grapes him who sows seed; When the mountains will drip sweet wine, And all the hills will be dissolved.'"

27) τὸν τρύγητον (3 OT LXX uses), meaning the reaper, Amos 9:13 (cf. Lev 26:5; 1 Sam 8:12).
Amos 9:13, "'Behold, days are coming,' declares the LORD, 'When the plowman will overtake **the reaper** And the treader of grapes him who sows seed; When the mountains will drip sweet wine, And all the hills will be dissolved.'"

28) ὁ πρέσβυς, messengers, (11 OT uses, as a translation of *malak*, 213 OT uses):
Deut 2:26, "So I sent messengers [πρέσβεις] from the wilderness of Kedemoth to Sihon king of Heshbon with words of peace, saying" (cf. Num 21:21)
  (1) It was a group of messengers
  (2) They were sent by Moses
  (3) With words [or a message] of peace, cf. Isa 52:7

The OT ὁ πρέσβυς is used for servants [ambassadors] of the king of Assyria (Isa 37:6) and the king of Babylon (Isa 39:1), as well as for messengers in general, Num 22:5; Isa 57:9; 63:9

The NT word "ambassador" is derived from the verb, πρεσβεύω, meaning to function as an ambassador (2 Cor 5:20; cf. Eph 6:20):

2 Cor 5:20 (Johnston), "Therefore, we ambassader for Christ, as though God were entreating through us; we beg you on behalf of Christ, be reconciled to God."

---

[637]For a good deal more examples, see Chapter 2, Section 2, "Metaphors Related to Evangelism," C. "Other Biblical Metaphors Relating the Christian and Evangelism," 1. "Old Testament Metaphors."

The NT adjective ὁ πρεσβύτερος, for elder (e.g. Titus 1:5), also implies a teaching function in the context of evangelism, because it deals with contradictors (Titus 1:9; cf. Acts 13:45; 28:22).

f. The World's View of the Evangelist:

29) τὸ θέατρον (Ø OT LXX uses; 3 NT uses) – meaning theater, amphitheater, spectacle:
> 1 Cor 4:9, "For I think that God has displayed us, the apostles, last, as men condemned to death; for we have been made **a spectacle** to the world, both to angels and to men"

Consider its metaphorical use as described in Thayer:
> "2. equivalent to θεά and θέαμα, *a public show* (Aeschines dial. socr. 3, 20; Achilles Tatius 1, 16, p. 55), and hence, metaphorically, *a man who is exhibited to be gazed at and made sport of*: 1 Cor. 4:9 (A. V. *a spectacle*)"[638]

Used in this case by Paul of his being put on display to the world, for example:
> Acts 25:23, "And so, on the next day when Agrippa had come together with Bernice, amid great pomp, and had entered the auditorium [ἀκροατήριον] accompanied by the commanders and the prominent men of the city, at the command of Festus, Paul was brought in"

Theater (τὸ θέατρον) was also used in the NT in a natural sense, as the large area o location where all the city was able to gather together, Acts 19:29, 31.

30) οἱ θεατριζόμενοι, from the verb θεατρίζω (Ø OT LXX uses; 1 NT use), verb used as noun (participle) meaning to be made a gazingstock, a public spectacle:
> Heb 10:33, "partly, by **being made a public spectacle** through reproaches and tribulations, and partly by becoming sharers with those who were so treated"

31) τὸ περίψημα (Ø OT LXX uses; 1 NT use) – meaning dirt, dregs, scum:
> 1 Cor 4:13 when we are slandered, we try to conciliate; we have become as **the scum** of the world, the dregs of all things, *even* until now"

g. Derogatory Terms:

32) ὁ πλάνος (4 NT uses), meaning to deceive:
> Matt 27:63, "and said, 'Sir, we remember that when He was still alive that **deceiver** said, "After three days I *am to* rise again."'"
> 2 Cor 6:8, "by glory and dishonor, by evil report and good report; *regarded* as **deceivers** and yet true;"

33) ὁ σπερμολόγος (Ø OT LXX uses; 1 NT use), see various posited meanings below:
> Acts 17:18 "What does this **idle babbler** want to say?"
>> Friberg: "picking up seeds, rag-picker, parasite; fig. babbler, chatterer, empty talker"[639]
>> Gingrich: "gossip, chatterer, ragpicker"
>> Louw-Nida: also added the concepts of "'ignorant show-off, charlatan"[640]
> Whatever the case, this NT and LXX *hapax legomena* was likely quite a derisive comment!

34) ὁ καταγγελεύς (Ø OT LXX uses; 1 NT use) – meaning proclaimer, preacher:
> Acts 17:18, "He seems to be a **proclaimer** of strange deities"

> Using "κατά" (meaning against with the gen) as a prefix, normally ascribes a negative or emphatic emphasis to the word (e.g. consider the verb καταργέω, to bring to naught, abolish); this

---

[638]BibleWorks 8.0.

[639]"24759 σπερμολόγος, on literally *picking up seeds*, of birds, such as rooks and crows; figuratively and substantivally in the NT, of one who lounges in the marketplace and subsists on scraps, what falls off loads, etc. *rag-picker, parasite*; figuratively, of a false teacher who picks up and passes on scraps of truth or information *babbler, chatterer, empty talker* (AC 17.18)" (Friberg, from BibleWorks 7.0).

[640]"27.19 σπερμολόγος, ου *m*: (a figurative extension of meaning of a term based on the practice of birds in picking up seeds) one who acquires bits and pieces of relatively extraneous information and proceeds to pass them on with pretense and show – 'ignorant show-off, charlatan.' τινες ἔλεγον, Τί ἂν θέλοι ὁ σπερμολόγος οὗτος λέγειν 'some said, What is this ignorant show-off trying to say?' Ac 17.18. The term σπερμολόγος is semantically complex in that it combines two quite distinct phases of activity: (1) the acquiring of information and (2) the passing on of such information. Because of the complex semantic structure of σπερμολόγος, it may be best in some languages to render it as 'one who learns lots of trivial things and wants to tell everyone about his knowledge,' but in most languages there is a perfectly appropriate idiom for 'a pseudo-intellectual who insists on spouting off.' For a different focus on the meaning of σπερμολόγος in Ac 17.18, see 33.381."

noun in particular is derived from the verb καταγγέλλω, meaning to "proclaim abroad." The verb, found 14 times in the NT, is used of proclaimers of the gospel from the mouth of antagonistic priests (Acts 4:2), a demon-possessed woman (Acts 16:17) and her owners (Acts 16:21), starting a riot. It is also used by Paul (Acts 13:38; 17:23; 26:23; 1 Cor 2:1; Col 1:28) and of Paul (Acts 17:3).

h.   Biblical Terms *not* Used for an Evangelist:

35) ὁ γόης, impostors, 2 Tim 3:13 (DRA, "seducers"; NAB, "charlatans")

36) ὁ γραμματεύς, scribe or town clerk (Acts 19:35; cf. 1 Cor 1:20)

37) οἱ καπηλεύοντες, plural participle from the verb καπηλεύω, meaning peddlers, hawkers, or hucksters:[641]
    2 Cor 2:17, "For we are not like many, peddling the word of God"
    [καπηλεύοντες τὸν λόγον τοῦ θεοῦ]

38) ὁ/ἡ κυνηγός, hunter, used in OT, e.g. Gen 10:9; 25:27; 1 Chron 1:10

39) ἡ ματαιολογία: empty-talker, (from μάταιος, meaning futile, worthless, useless; cf. 1 Cor 15:17; cognate ματαιολογία means empty talk), 1 Tim 1:6; Titus 1:10

40) ὁ συζητητής (hapax), disputant, debater, 1 Cor 1:20:
    Friberg: "as one who investigates";
    Louw-Nida, "likely to be involved in expressing strong differences of opinion"

41) ὁ ψευδόμαρτυς (3 total NT uses) a false witness:
    1 Cor 15:15, "Moreover we are even found *to be* **false witnesses** of God, because we witnessed against God that He raised Christ, whom He did not raise, if in fact the dead are not raised."

g.   Of God:

42) God as "the Promising One"—ὁ ἐπαγγειλάμενος:
    Heb 10:23, "Let us hold fast the confession of our hope without wavering, for **He who promised** is faithful"
    Rom 4:21, "and being fully assured that what **He had promised**, He was able also to perform"
    Consider aslso the Geneva and the ESV, which focus on God making the promise, rather than on what He promised:
        Rom 4:21, (GEN), "Being fully assured that he which had promised, was also able to doe it."
        Rom 4:21 (ESV), "fully convinced that God was able to do what he had promised."
    Heb 12:26, "And His voice shook the earth then, but now **He has promised**, saying, 'Yet once more I will shake not only the earth, but also the heaven'"

43) God as "the calling One"—ὁ καλῶν:
    1 Thess 5:24, "Faithful is **He who calls** you, and He also will bring it to pass"
    1 Thess 5:24, Πιστὸς ὁ καλῶν ὑμᾶς, ὃς καὶ ποιήσειΑ

    Reminiscent of numerous passages in Jeremiah (from NKJ):
        Jer 7:13-14, "'And now, because you have done all these works,' says the LORD, 'and I spoke to you, rising up early and speaking, but you did not hear, and I called you, but you did not answer, therefore I will do to the house which is called by My name, in which you trust, and to this place which I gave to you and your fathers, as I have done to Shiloh.
        Jer 7:25-26, "Since the day that your fathers came out of the land of Egypt until this day, I have even sent to you all My servants the prophets, daily rising up early and sending *them*. Yet they did not obey Me or incline their ear, but stiffened their neck. They did worse than their fathers"
        See also: Jer 11:7; 25:[3], 4; 26:5; 29:19; 32:33; 35:14-15; 44:4

44) God as "the speaking One"—τὸν λαλοῦντα:

    a)   God as "He who speaks":
        Heb 12:25, "See that you do not refuse he who speaks" [Βλέπετε μὴ παραιτήσησθε τὸν λαλοῦντα]

---

[641]Robertson wrote on this term: "Corrupting (*kapêleuontes*). Old word from *kapêlos*, a huckster or peddlar, common in all stages of Greek for huckstering or trading. It is curious how hucksters were suspected of corrupting by putting the best fruit on top of the basket. Note Paul's solemn view of his relation to God as a preacher (from God *ek theou*, in the sight of God *katenanti theou*, in Christ *en Christôi*)."

b) God who speaks through testifiers of His Gospel, especially in times of persecution:

Matt 10:19-20, "But when they deliver you up, do not worry about how or what you should speak. For it will be given to you in that hour what you should speak; for it is not you who speak, but the Spirit of your Father who speaks in you" [v. 20, οὐ γὰρ ὑμεῖς ἐστε οἱ λαλοῦντες, ἀλλὰ τὸ πνεῦμα τοῦ πατρὸς ὑμῶν τὸ λαλοῦν ἐν ὑμῖν]

We get the impression, that there is a point in which the Holy Spirit takes over, and it is no longer us who speak, but the Father who speaks!]

c) The author of Hebrews calls this New Covenant speech, God speaking from heaven:

Heb 12:25, "See to it that you do not refuse Him who is speaking. For if those did not escape when they refused him who warned *them* on earth, much less *shall* we *escape* who turn away from Him who *warns* from heaven"

d) Perhaps it is for this reason that Jesus made the startling statement:

Matt 10:40, "He who receives you receives Me, and he who receives Me receives Him who sent Me"

h. Of the Bible itself:

45) ἡ γραφὴ (51 NT uses), the Scriptures:

John 7:42, "Has not the Scripture said that the Christ comes from the offspring of David, and from Bethlehem, the village where David was?"

John 19:37, "And again another Scripture says, 'They shall look on Him whom they pierced.'"

Rom 4:3, "For what does the Scripture say? 'And Abraham believed God, and it was reckoned to him as righteousness.'"

Rom 9:17, "For the Scripture says to Pharaoh, 'For this very purpose I raised you up, to demonstrate My power in you, and that My name might be proclaimed throughout the whole earth.'"

Rom 10:11, "For the Scripture says, 'Whoever believes in Him will not be disappointed.'"

Gal 3:8, "And the Scripture, foreseeing that God would justify the Gentiles by faith, preached the gospel beforehand to Abraham, *saying*, 'All the nations shall be blessed in you.'"

Gal 3:22, "But the Scripture has shut up all men under sin, that the promise by faith in Jesus Christ might be given to those who believe."

2 Tim 3:16, "All Scripture is inspired by God and profitable for teaching, for reproof, for correction, for training in righteousness."

Other uses of Scripture as the subject of a verb (nominative), that are maybe not quite evangelistic, Rom 11:2; Gal 4:30; 1 Tim 5:18; James 4:5.

46) ὁ λόγος (51 NT uses), the Word [of God]:

John 1:14, "And the Word became flesh, and dwelt among us, and we beheld His glory, glory as of the only begotten from the Father, full of grace and truth."

John 12:48, "He who rejects Me, and does not receive My sayings, has one who judges him; the word I spoke is what will judge him at the last day."

John 17:17, "Sanctify them in the truth; Thy word is truth."
[Or: "the word which is thine is truth"].

Acts 6:7, "And the word of God kept on spreading; and the number of the disciples continued to increase greatly in Jerusalem, and a great many of the priests were becoming obedient to the faith."

Acts 12:24, "But the word of the Lord continued to grow and to be multiplied."

Acts 13:26, "Brethren, sons of Abraham's family, and those among you who fear God, to us the word of this salvation is sent out."

Acts 13:49, "And the word of the Lord was being spread through the whole region."

Acts 17:13, "But when the Jews of Thessalonica found out that the word of God had been proclaimed by Paul in Berea also, they came there likewise, agitating and stirring up the crowds."

Acts 19:20, "So the word of the Lord was growing mightily and prevailing."

1 Cor 1:18, "For the word of the cross is to those who are perishing foolishness, but to us who are being saved it is the power of God."

1 Thess 1:8, "For the word of the Lord has sounded forth from you, not only in Macedonia and Achaia, but also in every place your faith toward God has gone forth, so that we have no need to say anything."

2 Thess 3:1, "Finally, brethren, pray for us that the word of the Lord may spread rapidly and be glorified, just as *it did* also with you."

2 Tim 2:9, "for which I suffer hardship even to imprisonment as a criminal; but the word of God is not imprisoned."

Heb 4:2, "For indeed we have had good news preached to us, just as they also; but the word they heard did not profit them, because it was not united by faith in those who heard."

Heb 4:12, For the word of God is living and active and sharper than any two-edged sword, and piercing as far as the division of soul and spirit, of both joints and marrow, and able to judge the thoughts and intentions of the heart."

Heb 7:28, "For the Law appoints men as high priests who are weak, but the word of the oath, which came after the Law, *appoints* a Son, made perfect forever."

Other uses of Word as the subject of the verb, Col 3:16; Heb 2:2; 1 John 2:14; Rev 19:13.

h.   Of Jews who have revealed truth from the Law of Moses, Paul described their ministry to those who were not given this truth:

47) ὁ ὁδηγός (5 NT uses; 1 OT use; 4 Apocryphal uses), meaning leader, guide:
Rom 2:19, "and are confident that you yourself are **a guide** to the blind, a light to those who are in darkness"
Used three times in Matthew to describe the Pharisees as "blind guides" (Matt 15:14; 23:16, 24), and one to describe Judas who guided those who arrested Jesus (Acts 1:16).

48) τὸ φῶς (70 NT uses), meaning light:
Rom 2:19, "and are confident that you yourself are a guide to the blind, **a light** to those who are in darkness"
See my notes in Chapter Two on "Metaphors Related to Evangelism."

49) ὁ παιδευτής (2 NT uses), meaning instructor, corrector; one who chastens (cf. Heb 12:9):
Rom 2:20, "**a corrector** of the foolish, a teacher of the immature, having in the Law the embodiment of knowledge and of the truth"

50) Also, ὁ διδάσκαλος (as found above):
Rom 2:20, "a corrector of the foolish, **a teacher** of the immature, having in the Law the embodiment of knowledge and of the truth"

2. **METHOD**—terms highlighting the method of evangelism (not exhaustive, all terms as translated in the NASB)/**Context**:

Verbs Used For Evangelism...

Introduction: Through many years of study, this section of verbs has grown quite large to include 125 different Greek verbs. I have attempted to keep verb cognates organized by their root, which sometimes overlaps meaning with other verbal groups. However the following are the main categories by which the verbs may be more quickly identified and searched (the index at the rear of the text also lists every Greek verb and noun in this study alphabetically):

1—EVANGELIZE AND COGNATES
2—TO PROCLAIM
3—TO TESTIFY
4—TO SPEAK OR SAY
5—TO TEACH OR EXPLAIN
6—TO DEMONSTRATE OR PROVE
7—TO ADMONISH, WARN, PERSUADE, BEG
8—MISCELLANEOUS PROCLAMATIONAL VERBS
9—METAPHORICAL VERBS FOR EVANGELIZING

Further Studies:
10—CATEGORIES OF COMMUNICATORY VERBS NOT USED FOR EVANGELISM
   1.   COMMUNICATORY VERBS *NOT* USED FOR EVANGELIZING
   2.   VERBS DESCRIBING THE *OPPOSITE* OF EVANGELIZING
   3.   VERBS *DISAVOWED* IN EVANGELIZING
   4.   VERBS USED BOTH *FOR AND NOT FOR* EVANGELIZING.

Totals from the following study:

763 total NT uses of the 179 verbs (14 OT LXX verbs not included) and 107 verbal uses of the 22 nouns for a total of 870 NT verbal terms in evangelism contexts!

179 NT verbs used in the context of evangelism, as compared to 1,832 total individual verbs in the Byzantine Textform (NT), or 9.0% of the total verbs;[642]

763 total uses is a 2.7% of the 28,672 total verbs used in the NT;[643] (1,832 NT verbs are used 28,672 times; therefore, each verb is used an average of 15.7 times).

Of the 870 NT evangelistic uses:

81 verbs and 11 nouns are used only one time in NT evangelism contexts, for a total of 92 verbal forms;

28 verbs and 2 nouns are used twice in NT evangelism contexts, for a total of 30 verbal forms;

So 122 NT verbal forms are used once or twice only to describe the activity of evangelism.

It appears that God has provided a fairly extensive semantic range by which the concept of NT evangelizing may be ascertained!

It is also made evident from this study that the Great Commission is not only commanded, but it is also exemplified and clearly elaborated in the pages of the NT.

---

[642]According to the parsing search engine of BibleWorks 9.0, using the Byzantine Textform NT Greek.
[643]Ibid; e.g., there are 2,500 uses of the verb εἰμί and 2,315 uses of λέγω in the Byzantine Textform NT.

Chart of Verbs and Verbal Nouns in Evangelism Contexts by Category

Numbers after each verb represent evangelistic contexts in the following notes (0 for LXX only use).

Disclaimer: Categories are general in nature, as cognate verbs and nouns are kept together and due to varieties of contexts; thus there may be some overlap or duplication in categories. Verbs, nouns, or verbal combinations are listed only once.

Literal Terms	Literal Terms	Metaphorical Terms	Metaphorical Terms
Evangelize and Cognates (1) ἀναγγέλλω [9]; (2) ἀπαγγέλλω [10]; (3) διαγγέλλω [2]; (4) ἐξαγγέλλω [2]; (5) ἐπαγγέλλομαι [5]; (n1) τὸ εὐαγγέλιον [34]; (6) εὐαγγελίζω [54/55/56]. **Proclaim** (7) καταγγέλλω [18]; (8) παραγγέλλω [1]; (9) προκαταγγέλλω [0]; (10) προεπαγγέλλω [1]; (11) προκαταγγέλλω [2]; (12) προευαγγελίζομαι [1]; (13) κηρύσσω [31]; (14) προκηρύσσω [1]; (15) διηγέομαι [2]; (16) ἐκδιηγέομαι [0]; (17) ἐξηγέομαι (2); (18) προφητεύω [2]. **Testify** (19) μαρτυρέω [41]; (20) μαρτύρομαι [1]; (n2) ἡ μαρτυρία [3]; (n3) τὸ μαρτύριον [1]; (21) διαμαρτύρομαι [5]; (22) συμμαρτυρέω [2]. **Speak or Say** (23) λαλέω [51]; (24) προσλαλέω [1]; (25) λέγω [14]; (26) ἀπολογέομαι [6]; (n4) ἡ ἀπολογία [5]; (27) διαλέγομαι [6]; (28) ὁμολογέω [7]; (29) ἐξομολογέω [4]; (n5) ἡ ὁμολογία [1]; (n6) ὁ λόγος [1]; (30) ἀκούω [160]; (n7) ἡ ἀκοή [16]; (31) εἰσακούω [1]; (32) προακούω [1]; (33) ἀκουτίζω [0]; (34) φθέγγομαι [1]; (35) ἀποφθέγγομαι [3]; (36) φημί [4]; (37) ἀναφωνέω [1] (38) προσφωνέω [3]; (39) παρρησιάζομαι [9]; (n8) ἡ παρρησία [10]; (40) τολμάω [1]; (41) ὀνομάζω + Χριστός [1]; (n9) ἡ κοινωνία [4]; (n10) ὁ συγκοινωνός [2]; (42) ἐρεύγομαι [1]; (43) ὁρίζω [1].	**Asking and Answering a Question** (44) ἐρωτάω [2] (45) ἀποκρίνομαι [11] **Teach or Explain** (46) διδάσκω [18]; (47) γνωρίζω [15]; (48) διαγνωρίζω [1]; (49) γινώσκω [7] (50) ἐκτίθημι [2]; (51) παρατίθημι [1]; (52) ἀνοίγω [13]; (53) διανοίγω [1]; (54) διασαφέω [1] (55) φράζω [1] (56) ὀρθοτομέω [1]; (57) μηνύω [1]; (58) διερμηνεύω [1]; (59) συνετίζω [0]. **Demonstrate or Prove** (60) δείκνυω [2]; (61) ἐπιδείκνυμι [1]; (62) ἐνδείκνυμι [1]; (63) ὑποδείκνυμι [3]; (64) συμβιβάζω [1]. **Admonish, Warn, Persuade, Beg*** (65) νουθετέω [2]; (66) διαπειλέω [0]; (67) διαστέλλω [0]; (68) φυλάσσω [0]; (69) ὀνειδίζω [1]; (70) ἐλέγχω [8]; (71) διακατελέγχομαι [1]; (72) ἐπιτιμάω [1]; (73) πείθω [7]; (74) δέομαι [3]; (75) χρηματίζω [1]; (76) καλέω [1]; (77) συγκαλέω [3] (n11) ἡ κλῆσις [11] (78) ἐκκαλέω [0]; (79) παρακαλέω [3]; (80) παραινέω [2]; (81) φάσκω [1]. **Miscellaneous**** (82) ἐπαίρω [1]; (83) ἀγαλλιάω [0]; (84) βεβαιόω [1]; (n12) ἡ βεβαίωσις [1]; (85) φανερόω [9]; (n13) ἡ φανέρωσις [1]; (86) ἀναστρέφω [4]; (n14) ἡ ἀναστροφή [2]; (87) πολιτεύομαι [1]. **Function and Habit** (88) πρεσβεύω [2]; (89) εἴωθα / ἔθω [2].	**Fruitfulness** (90) ποιέω + ὁ καρπός [3]; (91) φέρω + ὁ καρπός [4]; (92) ἔχω + ὁ καρπός [1]; (93) καρποφορέω [6]. **Throw/Sow/Reap/Thresh/Plant** (94) βάλλω [3]; (95) σπείρω [15]; (96) θερίζω [5]; (97) ἀροτριάω [2]; (98) ἀλοάω [3]; (99) περκάζω [0]; (100) φυτεύω [3]. **Fishing** (101) ποιέω + ὁ ἁλιεύς [1] (102) ποιέω + γίν. + ὁ ἁλιεύς [1] (103) βάλλω + τὸ δίκτυον [1] (104) χαλάω + τὸ δίκτυον [2] **Carrying or Taking Up** (105) μεταδίδωμι [1]; (106) παραδίδωμι [2]; (107) ἐπέχω [1]; (108) περιφέρω [1]; (109) εἰσφέρω [1] (110) ἐκφέρω [0]; (111) βαστάζω [2]; (112) λαμβάνω [1]; (113) ἐπιλαμβάνομαι [2]; (114) αἴρω [3]; (115) ὑψόω [4]; **Holding Forth/Establishing** (116) κρατέω [1]; (117) τίθημι [1]. **Capturing People** (118) ζωγρέω [1]; (119) αἰχμαλωτεύω [1]; (120) αἰχμαλωτίζω [1]; (121) καθαιρέω [1]; (n15) ἡ καθαίρεσις [1]. **Seeking/Guiding/Compelling** (122) ζητέω [1]; (123) ἐκζητέω [3]; (124) ἐπιζητέω [2]; (125) ὁδηγέω [1] (126) κατευθύνω [1] (127) ἄγω [1]; (128) εἰσάγω [1]; (129) ἀναγκάζω [1]; (130) ἁρπάζω [1]. **Gathering** (131) συνάγω [2]; (n16) ὁ καταρτισμός [1]; (132) κατανατάω [1]; (133) συναρμολογέω [1]; (134) ἐκκλησιάζω [0]; (135) συντυγχάνω [1]. **Working [for the] Lord** (136) ἐργάζομαι + ὁ κύριος [1]; (137) κοπιάω [2] + ὁ κύριος [1].	**Death Working** (138) ὁ θάνατος + ἐνεργέω [1]; **Laboring [in things] Holy** (139) ἐργάζομαι + τὸ ἱερόν [1]; (140) προσεδρεύω + τὸ θυσιαστ.[1]. **Outward Expansion** (141) ἀποστέλλω [3]; (142) ἐξαποστέλλω [3]; (143) ἐξηχέομαι [1]; (144) ἐξέρχομαι [2]; (145) πάρειμι [1]. **Spread of Gospel** (146) διαφημίζω [2]; (147) πληρόω [3]; (148) ἀνταναπληρόω [1]; (149) πληροφορέω [2]; (n17) τὸ πλήρωμα [1]; (150) πίμπλημι [0]; (151) ἐμπίμπλημι [1]; (152) αὐξάνω [4]; (153) πληθύνω [4]; (154) πλεονάζω [1]; (155) περισσεύω [3]; (156) ὑπερπερισσεύω [1]; (n18) ἡ προκοπή [1]; (157) ἐξερεύγομαι [0]. **Shining Forth**** (158) λάμπω [1]; (159) φαίνω [4]; (160) ἐπιφαίνω [3]; (161) φωτίζω [2]; (n19) ὁ φωστήρ [1]; (n20) ὁ φωτισμός [1] **Sounding Forth** (162) σαλπίζω [1] **Displaying** (163) θριαμβεύω [1] (164) ἀποδείκνυμι [3] **Spiritual Dynamic** (165) διαφέρω [1]; (166) ἰσχύω [1]; (167) τρέχω [2]. **Struggling/Pressing on** (168) πυκτεύω [1] (169) ἀγωνίζομαι [2] (170) ἀνταγωνίζομαι [1]; (171) ἐπαγωνίζομαι [1]; (172) ἀντικαθίστημι [1]; (173) φιλοτιμέομαι + εὔαγγελ. [1]. **Other** (174) συνίστημι/συνιστάω [3]; (175) δουλεύω [2]; (176) διακονέω [1]; (n21) ἡ διακονία [8] (177) ἱερουργέω [1]; (178) οἰκοδομέω [2]; (n22) ἡ οἰκονομία [1]; (179) ἐπισκέπτομαι [2].

*And βλέπω (take heed) Acts 13:40. **Additional verbs describe testifying in the OT, e.g. sing aloud in Psa 51:13-15 (see above); consider sing, psalmify, and bless in Psa 96:2-3; 105:1-2; e.g. Acts 16:25; especially in light of Deut 6:13; 10:20. ***Consider also being an "aroma" in 2 Cor 2:14-16; cf. Ezek 20:41.

1—EVANGELIZE AND COGNATES

a. ἀγγέλλω (1 NT use; Eng. "angel") and cognates:[644]

1) ἀναγγέλλω (211 OT LXX uses; 14 total NT uses)—to declare, tell, announce, disclose, unveil:

Of OT uses:

>   In Deut 8:3, where it is translated for the Heb *yadah*, to make known or teach

>   In Deut 17:4, it is used for the Heb *nagad*, in reference to speaking forth to report a false teacher

>   In Deut 30:18, it is also used for the Heb *nagad*, and due to its context elicited a variety of translations…

Translations of *nagad* (ἀναγγέλλω) in Deut 30:18

English Geneva (1560)	KJV (1611, 1769); Darby; ERV; ASV	Isaac Leeser (1853); NKJ	Young's (1862, 1887, 1898)	Joseph (1868-1902); JPS; RSV; NAS; NIV; ESV	Cambridge BBE (1949, 1964)	NJB* (1985); NAB*; GWN; HCSB	DRA* (1899)
I pronounce vnto you this day	I denounce unto you this day	I announce unto you this day	I have declared to you this day	I declare unto you, today	I give witness against you this day	I tell you today	I foretell thee this day

a) Psa 51:15, "O Lord, open my lips, That my mouth may **declare** [Heb. *nagad*, hiph; Gk. ἀναγγέλλω] Thy praise."

b) Isa 42:12, "Let them give glory to the LORD, And **declare** [Heb. *nagad*, hiph, "**declare, tell**"; Gk. ἀναγγέλλω] His praise in the coastlands"

c) Isa 52:15, "For what had not been **told** [Heb. *saphar*, pual, "count, recount, relate"; Gk. ἀναγγέλλω] them they will see, And what they had not heard they will understand" (cf. Rom 15:21)

d) John 4:25, "He will **declare** all things to us"

e) Acts 19:18, "confessing and **disclosing** their practices"

f) Acts 20:20, "**declaring** to you anything that was profitable..."

g) Acts 20:27, "**declaring** to you the whole purpose of God"

h) Rom 15:21, "but as it is written, 'They who **had no news** of Him shall see, And they who have not heard shall understand'":

Paul apparently quoted Isa 52:15 here:

>   "Thus He will sprinkle many nations,
>   "Kings will shut their mouths on account of Him;
>   "For what **had not been told** them they will see,
>   "And what they had not heard they will understand."

In the case of the first negation of Isaiah, he used the Hebrew verb *saphar* (to be recounted, related rehearsed); further the verb is used in parallel with the Hebrew *shama'* (to hear).

i) 1 Pet 1:12, "these things now having been **announced** to you..."

j) 1 John 1:5, "**announce** to you"

Another OT use:

>   Of taking heed to the teaching of the Levites regarding leprosy, Deut 24:8

---

[644]A word about cognates. Cognates are words with the same root that have a variety of prefixes or suffixes attached to them. The prefixes or suffixes add nuance to the meaning of the word. Luke was particularly adept at using a wide range of terms, utilizing the entire range of cognates for emphasis. For example note Acts 16:6-10, in which he uses multiple aorist cognates of the word ἔρχομαι: v. 6 διελθόντες; v. 7 ἐλθόντες; v. 8 παρελθόντες; v. 10 ἐξελθεῖν. The preposition or lack thereof as a prefix gives a slightly different meaning to the word. At times the meanings change considerably. There are numerous cognate words in the book of Acts for the proclamation of the Gospel. However, unfortunately, many of the nuances of these cognates are lost in translation.

NT uses:

This same verb is used to describe the ministry of the Holy Spirit: John 16:13, 14, 15;
Used for sharing/explaining/disclosing one's testimony of turning from sin, Acts 19:18;
Also use of Timothy recounting the love of the Corinthian church for Paul, 2 Cor 7:7.

2) ἀπαγγέλλω (200 OT LXX uses; 45 total NT uses):
   a) Matt 11:4, "Go and **report** to John the things you hear and see"
   b) Matt 12:18, "Behold, My Servant whom I have chosen; My Beloved in whom My soul is well-pleased; I will put My Spirit upon Him, And He **shall proclaim** justice to the Gentiles" (quoting Isa 42:1)
   c) Mark 5:19, "Go home to your people and **report** to them what great things the Lord has done for you."
   d) Luke 7:22, "Go and **report** to John what you have seen and heard."
   e) Luke 18:37, "And they **told** him that Jesus of Nazareth was passing by."
   f) Acts 17:30, "God is now **declaring** to men that all everywhere should repent."
   g) Acts 26(19)-20, "Consequently, King Agrippa, I did not prove disobedient to the heavenly vision, but *kept* **declaring** both to those of Damascus first, and *also* at Jerusalem and *then* throughout all the region of Judea, and *even* to the Gentiles, that they should repent and turn to God, performing deeds appropriate to repentance"
   h) Heb 2:12, "saying, 'I will **proclaim** Thy name to My brethren, In the midst of the congregation I will sing Thy praise'" (quoting Psa 22:22[23]; Heb. *Saphar*; LXX διηγέομαι)
   i) 1 John 1:2, "**proclaim** to you the eternal life"
   j) 1 John 1:3, "we **proclaim** to you"

3) διαγγέλλω – to proclaim; publish abroad (6 OT LXX uses; 3 total NT uses):
   NT: Luke 9:60, "**proclaim** everywhere the kingdom of God"

   NT citation of OT proto-evangelization:
   Rom 9:17, "that my name **might be proclaimed** throughout the whole earth."
   Paul here quoted Exod 9:16, in which text the LXX contains διαγγέλλω as a translation of the Hebrew verb *saphar* in the piel stem

   OT use in Psa 2:7 with a clear Christological focus to proclamation (cf. 1 Cor 2:2):
   Psa 2:7 is another example of διαγγέλλω being the translation of the Hebrew verb *saphar* in the piel stem[645]
   Psa 2:7, "**I will surely tell** of the decree of the LORD: He said to Me, 'Thou art My Son, Today I have begotten Thee'"
   Psa 2:7 (NKJ), "**I will declare** the decree: The LORD has said to Me, 'You *are* My Son, Today I have begotten You.'"

   OT interesting double use of the verb διαγγέλλω, the Day of Atonement is to be proclaimed (or sounded abroad) by use of a trumpet throughout the land:
   Lev 25:9, "You shall then **sound** a ram's horn **abroad** on the tenth day of the seventh month; on the day of atonement you shall **sound** a horn all through your land"

4) ἐξαγγέλλω – to announce, to declare (9 OT LXX uses; 1[2] NT uses), also meaning to exclaim, profess, publish, herald:
   Friberg Lexicon: ἐξαγγέλλω 1aor. ἐξήγγειλα; *report widely, proclaim throughout, tell everywhere*
   Liddell-Scott Lexicon: ἐξαγγέλλω - ἐξ-αγγέλλω, f. ελῶ, *to send out* tidings, *report,* of traitors and the like, Il., Att.:-Med. *to cause to be proclaimed,* Hdt., Soph.; c. inf. *to promise to* do, Eur.:-Pass. *to be reported,* Hdt.; impers., ἐξαγγέλλεται *it is reported,* Id.
   a) Mark 16:S, άντα δὲ τὰ παρηγγελμένα τοῖς περὶ τὸν Πέτρον συντόμως ἐξήγγειλαν (NLT), "Then they briefly reported all this to Peter and his companions."
   b) I Peter 2:9, ὅπως τὰς ἀρετὰς ἐξαγγείλητε, "that you may proclaim [exclaim, profess] the excellencies"

5) ἐπαγγέλομαι - to proclaim, to promise (2 OT LXX uses; 15 NT uses), often in NT with God as Evangelist:
   a) 1 Tim 6:21, "which some have **professed** [concerning false teaching]"
   b) Heb 10:23, "for He who **promised** is faithful."
   c) James 1:12, "crown of life, which the Lord has **promised** to those who love Him."
   d) James 2:5, "heirs of the kingdom which He **promised** to those who loved Him."

---

[645]See the chart, "A Proclaimed or Spoken Witness in the Old Testament," earlier in this chapter for 26 other examples of translations of the Hebrew *saphar* (only 2 of which are translated as διαγγέλλω in the LXX).

e)   1 John 2:25, "And this is the promise which He Himself **made** to us: eternal life."

n1) τὸ εὐαγγέλιον – noun (1 OT LXX use; 77 NT uses), meaning Gospel, in some cases translators have considered an elliptical use appropriate to the context, and have added a proclamational verb, in others the use of the noun implies proclamation:

a)   Definite use with διὰ and the genitive or accusative:
(1) 1 Cor 4:15 (NKJ), "For though you might have ten thousand instructors in Christ, yet *you do* not *have* many fathers; for in Christ Jesus I have begotten you through the [**preaching of the**] gospel"
(2) 1 Cor 9:23 (NKJ), "Now this I do for the [**preaching of the**] gospel's sake, that I may be partaker of it with *you*."
e.g. 1 Cor 9:23 (NLT), "I do everything to spread the Good News and share in its blessings"
(3) Eph 3:6 (NKJ), "that the Gentiles should be fellow heirs, of the same body, and partakers of His promise in Christ through the [**preaching of the**] gospel"
(4) 2 Thess 2:14 (NRSV), "For this purpose he called you through our proclamation of the good news, so that you may obtain the glory of our Lord Jesus Christ"
e.g. 2 Thess 2:14 (NLT), "He called you to salvation **when we told you** the Good News; now you can share in the glory of our Lord Jesus Christ"
(5) 2 Tim 1:10 (NAS), "but now has been revealed by the appearing of our Savior Christ Jesus, who abolished death, and brought life and immortality to light through the [**preaching of the**] gospel"

b)   Definite use with ἐκ and the genitive:
(1) 1 Cor 9:14 (NKJ), "Even so the Lord has commanded that those who preach the gospel should live from the [**preaching of the**] gospel"

c)   Definite use with ἐν and the dative:
(1) Rom 1:9 (NAS), "For God, whom I serve in my spirit in the *preaching of the* gospel of His Son, is my witness *as to* how unceasingly I make mention of you"
(2) 1 Cor 9:18 (NKJ), "What is my reward then? That when I preach the gospel, I may present the gospel of Christ without charge, that I may not abuse my authority in the [**preaching of the**] gospel"
(3) 2 Cor 8:18 (RSV), "With him we are sending the brother who is famous among all the churches for **his preaching of** the gospel"
(4) 2 Cor 10:14 (ESV), "For we are not overextending ourselves, as though we did not reach you. For we were the first to come all the way to you with the gospel of Christ"

d)   Definite and indefinite uses with εἰς and the accusative:
(1) Rom 1:1 (NEG), "Paul, serviteur de Jésus-Christ, appelé à être apôtre, mis à part pour **annoncer** l'Évangile de Dieu"
(2) 2 Cor 2:12 (ESV), "When I came to Troas to **preach** the gospel of Christ, even though a door was opened for me in the Lord"
(3) Phil 1:5 (NLT), "for you have been my partners in **spreading** the Good News about Christ from the time you first heard it until now"
(4) Phil 2:22 (NLT), "But you know how Timothy has proved himself. Like a son with his father, he has served with me in **preaching** the Good News"
See also 2 Cor 9:13

e)   Definite use with κατὰ and the accusative:
(1) Rom 2:16 (NKJ), "in the day when God will judge the secrets of men by Jesus Christ, according to my [**preaching of the**] gospel"
e.g. Rom 2:16 (GWN), "This happens as they face the day when God, through Christ Jesus, will judge people's secret thoughts. He will use the Good News that I am spreading to make that judgment"
(2) Rom [14:24] 16:25 (CSB), "Now to Him who has power to strengthen you according to [**the preaching of**] my gospel and the proclamation of Jesus Christ, according to the revelation of the sacred secret kept silent for long ages"
(3) 1 Tim 1:11 (NKJ), "according to the [**proclamation of the**] glorious gospel of the blessed God which was committed to my trust"
(4) 2 Tim 2:8 (NAS), "Remember Jesus Christ, risen from the dead, descendant of David, according to my gospel [**proclamation**]"

f)   With a definite article and no preposition:
(1) Rom 1:16 (NAS), "For I am not ashamed of the [**preaching of the**] gospel, for it is the power of God for salvation to everyone who believes, to the Jew first and also to the Greek"

(2) Rom 10:16 (NKJ), "But they have not all obeyed the [**preaching of the**] gospel. For Isaiah says, 'Lord, who has believed our report?'"

(3) Rom 11:28 (NKJ), "Concerning the [**preaching of the**] gospel *they are* enemies for your sake, but concerning the election *they are* beloved for the sake of the fathers"

(4) Rom 15:19 (NKJ), "in mighty signs and wonders, by the power of the Spirit of God, so that from Jerusalem and round about to Illyricum I have fully **preached** the gospel of Christ"

(5) Rom 15:29 (NKJ), "But I know that when I come to you, I shall come in the fullness of the blessing of the [**preaching of the**] gospel of Christ"

(6) 2 Cor 4:3 (NKJ), "But even if our gospel [*preached*] is veiled, it is veiled to those who are perishing"

(7) Gal 1:7 (NKJ), "which is not another; but there are some who trouble you and want to pervert the [**preaching of the**] gospel of Christ"

(8) Gal 2:7 (NKJ), "But on the contrary, when they saw that the [**preaching of the**] gospel for the uncircumcised had been committed to me, as the *[**preaching of the**] gospel* for the circumcised *was* to Peter"

(9) Eph 6:15 (CSB), "and your feet sandaled with readiness for the [**preaching of the**] gospel of peace"

(10) Phil 1:12 (ESV), "I want you to know, brothers, that what has happened to me has really served to advance the [**preaching of the**] gospel"

(11) Phil 1:27 (CSB), "Just one thing: live your life in a manner worthy of the [**preaching of the**] gospel of Christ. Then, whether I come and see you or am absent, I will hear about you that you are standing firm in one spirit, with one mind, working side by side for the faith of the [**preaching of the**] gospel"

e.g. Phil 1:27 (MacDonald), "Your exclusive concern should be to live as citizens worthy of the gospel of Christ. Do this in order that whether I come and see you or remain away, I will hear concerning you: *that you stand unanimously in one spirit, like one person, contending for the [**preaching of the**] gospel faith*"

(12) Phil 4:15 (MacDonald), "You Philippians also know that when this area began **to be evangelized**, when I set out from Macedonia, no church shared with me in the matter of giving and receiving—except you alone"

e.g. Phil 4:15 (NAS), "And you yourselves also know, Philippians, that at the first **preaching of the** gospel, after I departed from Macedonia, no church shared with me in the matter of giving and receiving but you alone"

Translations of ἐν ἀρχῇ τοῦ εὐαγγελίου in Phil 4:15
Verse presumes that the Gospel has a beginning point in the lives of people, or does it?

Proclamational							Cognitive			Historical
MacDonald (2008)	NAS (1977)	Stern (1988)	NLT (2003)	Cambridge (1949)	NIRV (1998)	Wycliffe (1388); Tyndale, Geneva, Bishops, KJV, ERV, ASV, RSV, NKJ, ESV	NIV (1984)	NAB (2010)	NJB (1985); CSB	NET (2006)
when this area began to be evangelized	at the first preaching of the gospel	in the early days of my work spreading the Good News	when I first brought you the Good News	when the good news first came to you	That was in the early days when you first heard the good news	in the bigynnyng of the gospel	in the early days of your acquaintance with the gospel	at the beginning of the gospel	in the early days of the gospel	at the beginning of my gospel ministry

(13) 1 Thess 1:5 (Noyes), "because the gospel **preached by us** came not to you in word only, but also in power, and in the Holy Spirit, and in much assurance; as ye well know what sort of persons we became among you for your sake"

(14) 1 Thess 2:4 (NRSV), "but just as we have been approved by God to be entrusted with **the message of** the gospel, even so we speak, not to please mortals, but to please God who tests our hearts"

(15) 2 Tim 1:8 (NKJ), "Therefore do not be ashamed of the testimony of our Lord, nor of me His prisoner, but share with me in the sufferings for the [**preaching of the**] gospel according to the power of God"

(16) Philm 13 (NKJ), "whom I wished to keep with me, that on your behalf he might minister to me in my chains for the [**preaching of the**] gospel"

g) With singular or plural personal pronoun—seeming to imply the impact of the gospel in the midst of a sharing situation:

(1) Singular:
  (a) Rom 2:16, "in the day when God will judge the secrets of men by Jesus Christ, according to **my gospel**."
  (b) Rom 16:25, "Now to Him who is able to establish you according to **my gospel** and the preaching of Jesus Christ, according to the revelation of the mystery kept secret since the world began."
  (c) 2 Tim 2:8-9, "Remember that Jesus Christ, of the seed of David, was raised from the dead according to **my gospel**, for which I suffer trouble as an evildoer, *even* to the point of chains; but the word of God is not chained."

(2) Plural:
  (a) 2 Cor 4:3, "And even if **our gospel** is veiled, it is veiled to those who are perishing."
  (b) 1 Thess 1:5, "for **our gospel** did not come to you in word only, but also in power and in the Holy Spirit and with full conviction; just as you know what kind of men we proved to be among you for your sake."
  (c) 2 Thess 2:14, "And it was for this He called you through **our gospel**, that you may gain the glory of our Lord Jesus Christ."

6) εὐαγγελίζω – to evangelize, to announce glad tidings (22 OT LXX uses; 54 NT uses in Nestle-Aland; 55 in Byzantine Textform [+1 variant in Codex Bezae = 56])[646]
[Lat *evangelizare* translated into Eng "evangelize" in Wycliffe's 1ˢᵗ edition of 1382]

The interesting correlation between the nouns Gospel (εὐαγγέλιον) and evangelist (εὐαγγελιστές), and the verb evangelize (εὐαγγελίζω) necessitates further study, perhaps from an evangelistically-oriented scholar.

Consider also, by contradistinction, that καταγγελέω means, "to bring evil tidings" [Liddell-Scott].

The practical and theological issues involved are comparable to other root words, such as:
(1) Glory (δόξα) and glorify (δοξάζω) in John 8:54; 11:4; 17:5; 2 Cor 3:10; 1 Pet 4:11, 14:

  1 Pet 4:14 (NKJ), "If you are reproached for the name of Christ, blessed *are you*, for the Spirit of glory and of God rests upon you. On their part He is blasphemed, but on your part **He is glorified**"

(2) Grace (χάρις) and engratiated (χαριτόω) in Eph 1:6[-7]; for example note Wycliffe's literal translation of this verse:

  Eph 1:6-7 (WYC), "in to the heriyng of the glorie of his grace; in which he hath glorified vs in his dereworthe sone"

(3) Righteous (δίκαιος), righteousness (δικαιοσύνη), justify (δικαιόω), a form of the verb "those who justify" (οἱ δικαιοῦντες, Luke 16:15), [righteous] requirement (δικαίωμα, Rom 2:26; 5:16, 18; 8:4...), and righteous judgment (δικαιοκρισία, Rom 2:5):

  Rom 3:26 (NKJ), "to demonstrate at the present time His righteousness, that He might be just and the justifier of the one who has faith in Jesus"

a) Consider the variations in the English translations of εὐαγγελίζω (verb without predicate) into English:

(1) **No use of a verb**:
  (a) "news," Isa 52:7 (2) (NLT)

(2) **Verb only**:
  (a) "Are evangelized," Luke 7:22 (Eng Darby)
  (b) "Evangelizing," Luke 8:1 (Douay-Rheims)

---

[646]For an canonical listing in English of all the 54/55/56 uses of εὐαγγελίζω, please see in this chapter, Section G., "Turning the Tide—Unleashing the Word Evangelize!"

(c) "Preached," Luke 3:18 (Eng Gen); Acts 5:42 (KJV); "Preaching," Acts 8:40 (Eng Gen)

    [1] "Preach" is the second most common translation today, especially when the text supplies a word for the message

(d) "Publishing," Luke 8:1 (Eng Gen)

(3) Non-proclamational verb with noun:

(a) "Bring glad tidings," Rom 10:15 (NAS)

(b) "Bring good news," Luke 1:19 (NAS), 2:10 (NAS); "Brought good news," 1 Thess 3:6 (NAS)

(c) "Giving the good news," Luke 8:1 (Bible in Basic Eng)

(d) "Receiue the Gospel" (Eng Gen), Matt 11:5; Luke 7:22

(e) "Showing the glad tidings," Luke 8:1 (Webster's)

(f) "Spread the good news," Acts 8:12 (God's Word to the Nations)

(4) Proclamational verb with noun:

(a) "Announcing the glad tidings," Luke 8:1; 9:6; 20:1 (Eng Darby)

(b) "Preach the gospel" (NAS), Luke 4:18, Acts 14:7, 15, 16:10, Rom 1:15, 15:20, 1 Cor 1:17, 9:16, 16, 18, 2 Cor 10:16; "Preached the gospel" (NAS), Luke 3:18, Acts 14:21, 2 Cor 11:7 , Gal 3:8, 4:13, 1 Pet 1:12

    [1] "Preach the Gospel" is by far the most common translation of εὐαγγελίζω today, especially when no noun is provided for the message.

(c) "Proclaim good news," Luke 4:18 (ESV); Luke 4:43 (CSB)

(d) "Telling the good news," Luke 20:1 (NRSV)

b) A look at the NASB translations of the 54 uses εὐαγγελίζω, as found in the NA27 (sometimes with associated nouns):

(1) Non-proclamational verb with noun:

(a) "Bring glad tidings of good things," Rom 10:15

    [MT adds a second verb here, omitted in the Nestle-Aland tradition]

(b) "Bring good news," Luke 1:19, 2:10

(c) "Brought us good news," 1 Thess 3:6 [not directly an evangelistic context]

(2) Proclamational with no noun supplied by translators:

(a) "As he preached," Rev 10:7

(b) "That which we have preached," Gal 1:8 (2)

(3) Proclamational (only) with noun in context:

(a) Noun in context is "gospel":

    [1] "Having an eternal gospel to preach," Rev 14:6

    [2] "Preached the gospel," 2 Cor 11:7

    [3] "The gospel which I preached," 1 Cor 15:1

    [4] "The gospel which was preached by me," Gal 1:11

(b) Noun in context is Christ or Jesus:

    [1] "Preach Him," Gal 1:16

    [2] "Preach … the unfathomable riches of Christ," Eph 3:8

    [3] "Preached Jesus," Acts 8:35

    [4] "Preaching Jesus and the resurrection," Acts 17:18

    [5] "Preaching Jesus as the Christ," Acts 5:42

    [6] "Preaching the Lord Jesus," Acts 11:20

(c) Noun in context is "the word":

    [1] "The word which was preached to you," 1 Pet 1:25

    [2] "The word which I preached," 1 Cor 15:2

    [3] "Preaching the word," Acts 8:4

    [4] "Preaching … the word of the Lord," Acts 15:35

(d) Noun in context is the kingdom of God:

    [1] "Preach the kingdom of God," Luke 4:43

    [2] "Preaching the kingdom of God," Luke 8:1

(e) Noun in context is something else:

    [1] "Preached peace," Eph 2:17

    [2] "Preaching peace through Jesus Christ," Acts 10:36

    [3] "Preaching the faith," Gal 1:23

(4) Proclamational verb with noun supplied by translators:

(a) "Good news preached," Heb 4:2, 6

(b) "Gospel preached," Gal 1:11, 1 Pet 4:6

(c) "Had preached the gospel," Acts 14:21

(d) "Had the good news preached to them," Heb 4:6

(e) "Have had the good news preached to us," Heb 4:2

(f) "Have the Gospel preached," Matt 11:5; Luke 7:22

(g) "Is preaching to you a gospel," Gal 1:9

(h) "Preach good news," Acts 13:32

(i) "Preach the gospel," Luke 4:18, Acts 14:15, 16:10, Rom 1:15, 15:20, 1 Cor 1:17, 9:16, 16, 18, 2 Cor 10:16; Gal 1:8, 9

(j) "Preached the gospel," Luke 3:18, Acts 8:25; 2 Cor 11:7; Gal [3:8]; 4:13; 1 Pet 1:12

(k) "Preaching the gospel," Luke 9:6, 20:1, Acts 8:40

(l) "Should preach to you a gospel," Gal 1:8 (1)

(5) Proclamational verb with noun supplied by translators + noun in context:

(a) "The gospel of the kingdom of God is preached," Luke 16:16

(b) "Preach to you the good news of the promise," Acts 13:32

(c) "Preaching the good news about the kingdom of God," Acts 8:12

(6) Proclamational verb + verb in the original with noun supplied:

(a) "They continued to preach the gospel," Acts 14:7

c) A study of the Bible's grammatical uses of εὐαγγελίζω:

Consider the words of David B. Barrett as he explained Wycliffe's 1382 use of the verb :

> "He [Wycliffe] employed the verb 'euangelisen' in the intransitive (without an object) and the transitive, and so the exact modern equivalent of 'euangelisen', as we can see from his Acts 5:42 and 8:4 above, is 'evangelize concerning' *A* to *B*, where *A* equals the subject matter (Jesus Christ, the word of God), and *B* equals the recipient (Sion, the city, the Jews, etc.)."[647]

(1) Intransitive uses of εὐαγγελίζω:

(a) In the passive voice:

[1] Verbal subject, Heb 4:2, 4;

[2] Subject, the poor, Matt 11:5; Luke 7:22

[3] Subject, the kingdom of God, Luke 16:16

[4] Subject, the dead, 1 Pet 4:6

(b) Middle voice, Luke 8:1; 20:1; 8:25; 14:7; 15:35; 1 Cor 1:17; 9:16 (twice); 2 Cor 10:16; Gal 1:8 (twice); 1:9

(2) Transitive uses of εὐαγγελίζω with an object for the message:

(a) The kingdom of God, Luke 4:43; 8:1

(b) Jesus the Christ, Acts 5:42

(c) The word, Acts 8:4

(d) [Things] concerning the kingdom of God and the name of Jesus Christ, Acts 8:12

(e) Peace through Jesus Christ, Acts 10:36

(f) The Lord Jesus, Acts 11:20

(g) Jesus and the resurrection, Acts 17:18

(h) Peace, Rom 10:15

(i) Good [things], Rome 10:15

(j) The Gospel of Christ without charge, 1 Cor 9:18

(k) The faith, Gal 1:23

(l) Unsearchable riches in Christ, Eph 3:8

(3) Transitive uses of εὐαγγελίζω with an object for the recipient of the message:

(a) The people, Luke 3:18

(b) The poor, Luke 4:18

(c) The many villages, Acts 8:40

(d) Also that city, Acts 14:21

(e) Them (the Macedonians), Acts 16:10

(f) Unto you (pl) in Rome, Rom 1:15

[this is actually the theme statement for the book of Romans, of which vv. 16-17 are a series of prepositional clauses]

(g) Not where Christ was [already] named, Rom 15:20

(h) Unto you (pl), Gal 4:13; 1 Pet 1:12

---

[647]David B. Barrett, *Evangelize! A Historical Survey of the Concept* (Birmingham, AL: New Hope, 1987), 22.

(i)   Unto them dwelling on the earth, Rev 14:6

(4) Transitive uses of εὐαγγελίζω with an object for the proclaimer:
(a) Through His servants the prophets, Rev 10:7

(5) Transitive uses of εὐαγγελίζω with an objects for both recipient and message:
(a) You (sg), these things, Luke 1:19
(b) You (pl), great joy, Luke 2:10
(c) To him, Jesus, Acts 8:35
(d) Unto you (pl) … that which unto our fathers was promised, Acts 13:32
(e) Unto you (pl) from these vanities to turn, turning unto the God, the living One, Acts 14:15
(f) The Gospel … you (pl), 1 Cor 15:1
(g) The word [λόγος] … you (pl), 1 Cor 15:2
(h) The word [ῥῆμα] … unto you (pl), 1 Pet 1:25
(i) The Gospel of God … to you (pl), 2 Cor 11:7
(j) Him unto the heathen, Gal 1:16
(k) Peace to you, Eph 2:17

(6) Transitive uses of εὐαγγελίζω with an object for both message and proclaimer:
(a) The Gospel … by me, 1 Cor 1:11

(7) Transitive uses of εὐαγγελίζω with an object for both sender and recipient:
(a) From you to us, 1 Thes 3:6

d) A look at the subjects used as those doing the evangelizing:

(1) Jesus evangelized, Matt 11:5; Luke 4:18; 43; 7:22; 8:1; 20:1
(a) In the letters of Paul, Eph 2:17

(2) Angels evangelized:
(a) Gabriel, Luke 1:19
(b) A host of angels, Luke 2:10
(c) A seventh angel, Rev 10:7
(d) Another angel, Rev 14:6

(3) John the Baptist evangelized, Luke 3:18

(4) The disciples evangelized:
(a) The 12 disciples evangelized, Luke 9:6
(b) The disciples of the apostolic church evangelized, Acts 5:42
(c) Those scattered from Jerusalem evangelized, Acts 8:4; 11:20 (disciples from Cyprus and Cyrene)
(d) Philip evangelized, Acts 8:12; 35; 40
(e) Peter and John evangelized, Acts 8:25

(5) God evangelizes, Acts 10:36

(6) Paul evangelized:
(a) Paul and Barnabas, Acts 13:32; 14:7, 15, 21; 15:35
(b) Paul, Silas, Timothy, and Luke, Acts 16:10
(c) Paul, Acts 17:18
(d) In his letters, Rom 1:15; 15:20; 1 Cor 1:17; 9:16, 18; 15:1, 2; 2 Cor 10:16; 11:7; Gal 1:8 (twice), 9, 11, 16, 23; 4:13; Eph 3:8

(7) Sent ones evangelize, Rom 10:15

(8) Timothy evangelized, 1 Thess 3:6 (bringing good news of the spiritual health of the Thessalonians)

(9) General, 1 Pet 1:12

(10) Unclear, 1 Pet 4:6

(11) Passive uses of the verb (no subject), Luke 16:16; Heb 4:2, 6; 1 Pet 1:25

e) Some other NT verbs beginning with the prefix εὐ (for the sake of comparison and consideration, based on a study of the Byzantine Textform):
(1) εὐαρεστέω (3 NT uses), meaning to "be pleased, please," Heb 11:5, 6; 13:16
(2) εὐδοκέω (21 NT uses), meaning to "think well," e.g. Matt 3:17

(3) εὐοδόω (4 NT uses), meaning to "prosper," cf. Rom 1:10

(4) εὐεργετέω (1 NT use), meaning to "do good works," Acts 10:38

(5) εὐκαιρέω (3 NT uses), meaning to "have the opportunity, time," cf. Mark 6:31

(6) εὐλαβέομαι (2 NT uses), meaning to "reverence or respect," Acts 23:10; Heb 11:7

(7) εὐλογέω (40 NT uses), meaning to "bless" or "speak well of," cf. Matt 5:44

(8) εὐθυδρομέω (2 NT uses), meaning to "set a straight course for," Acts 16:11; 21:1

(9) εὐθυμέω (3 NT uses), meaning to "be cheerful, cheer up," Acts 27:22, 25; James 5:13

(10) εὐθύνω (2 NT uses), meaning to "make straight," John 1:23; James

(11) εὐνοέω (1 NT use), meaning to "be in agreement with," Matt 5:25

(12) εὐνουχίζω (2 NT uses), meaning to "make a eunuch of," Matt 19:12 (twice)

(13) εὐσεβέω (2 NT uses), meaning to "show piety or profound respect for," Acts 17:23; 1 Tim 5:4

(14) εὐφορέω (1 NT use), meaning to "bear good crops, be fruitful," Luke 12:16

(15) εὐφραίνω (14 NT uses), meaning to "rejoice," Luke 12:19

(16) εὐχαριστέω (40 NT uses), meaning to "give thanks," cf. Matt 15:36

(17) εὔχομαι (7 NT uses), meaning to "pray," e.g. Acts 26:29

(18) εὐψυχέω (1 NT use), meaning to "be glad, have courage," Phil 2:19

f) Conclusions:

(1) As to the variety of translations in Section (a): it seems that almost any translation of εὐαγγελίζω into English is deemed fine to one degree or another, just **not** the use of the word "evangelize"!

(2) As to the NAS translations in (b): Because of avoiding the translation of the verb εὐαγγελίζω as "evangelize," the term has a wide variety of translations based on the context. It is clear that the translators made a choice: (1) when the verb should or should not be proclamational, and (2) whether a noun needed to be supplied or not. For example, the emphatic εὐαγγελίζω + εὐαγγέλιον is lost in the translation (1 Cor 15:1; 2 Cor 11:7; Gal 1:11; Rev 14:6), and problems of misemphasis and possible misapplication (as in Gal 1:8-9) occur as discussed above.

(3) As to the variety of uses of εὐαγγελίζω in the New Testament (c): The wide range of uses of the word in many contexts shows that it has a definite purpose and meaning in the New Testament, and need not be blended or merged with the translations of other proclamational words, such as κηρύσσω or καταγγέλλω.

2—TO PROCLAIM

7) καταγγέλλω (Ø OT LXX uses; 18 NT uses) – to proclaim (perhaps to denounce, decry, declare, confront, contest, protest, challenge, promulgate, propagate, disseminate, countermand):

Could this word have been translated "protesting" in an early French translation of 1 Cor 11:26, leading to the following phrase on the poster for the 1534 "placard incident"?

> "The fruit of the holy scene of Jesus Christ [the Lord's Supper] is to publicly make a protest of one's faith and insure confidence of one's salvation have memory of the death and passion of Jesus Christ, through which we are redeemed from damnation and perdition."[648]

No, the 1522 LeFevre translated that verb καταγγέλλω as "announce" in 1 Cor 11:26, as did also the 1669 French Geneva.

Friberg: 14694 καταγγέλλω impf. κατήγγελλον; 1aor. κατήγγειλα; 2aor. pass. κατηγγέλην; used of solemn religious messages; (1) *proclaim (solemnly), announce* something (AC 4.2); (2) *proclaim, tell about* someone (PH 1.17).

Liddell-Scott Lexicon: καταγγέλλω κατ-αγγέλλω, f. ελῶ, *to denounce, betray,* Xen. 2. *to declare,* πόλεμον Lys. Hence κατάγγελτος.

---

[648]"True articles on the horrible, great and unbearable abuses of the Papal Mass..." [online]; accessed 12 Oct 2005; available from http://www.bethel-fr.com/afficher_texte.php?id=891.6; Internet; translation mine. [P.S. I could not access this website when I tried in September 2006]. I have placed my translation of the text of this poster on my website at: http://www.evangelismunlimited.org/08b_placard_contre_la_messe_1534-English.doc.

Notice for example another of many verbs with the prefix "κατά" whose meaning is amplified in a negative or emphatic sense:

κατακρίνω (17 NT uses), with "κατά" (against with gen) + "κρίνω" (to judge), combined meaning: to condemn;

καταφιλέω (6 NT uses), with "κατά" (against with gen) + "φιλέω" (to love), combined meaning: to kiss fervently or affectionately;

καταφρονέω (9 NT uses), with "κατά" (against with gen) + "φρονέω" (to think), combined meaning: to despise.

So is mentioned of "κατά" in Liddell-Scott:

"III. *against,* in hostile sense, as καταγιγνώσκω, κατακρίνω.
"IV. often only to strengthen the notion of the simple word, as κατακόπτω, καταφαγεῖν."

a) "All the prophets who have spoken, from Samuel and *his* successors onward, also **announced** these days," Acts 3:24

b) "**Proclaiming** in Jesus the resurrection from the dead," Acts 4:2

c) "They began **to proclaim** the word of God," Acts 13:5

d) "Forgiveness of sins **is proclaimed** to you," Acts 13:38

e) "**We proclaimed** the word of the Lord," Acts 15:36

f) "These men are bond-servants of the Most High God, who **are proclaiming** to you the way of salvation," Acts 16:17

g) "And **are proclaiming** customs which it is not lawful for us to accept or to observe, being Romans," Acts 16:21

h) "This Jesus who **I am proclaiming** to you is the Christ." Acts 17:3

i) "The Word of God **had been proclaimed** by Paul in Berea also," Acts 17:13

j) "Therefore what you worship in ignorance, this **I proclaim** to you," Acts 17:23

k) "He should be first to **proclaim** light," Acts 26:23 (of Jesus proclaiming)

l) "because your faith **is being proclaimed** throughout the whole world, Rom 1:8

m) "**Proclaiming** to you the testimony of God," 1 Cor 2:1

n) "Those who **proclaim** the Gospel," 1 Cor 9:14

o) "**Proclaim** the Lord's death," 1 Cor 11:26

p) "The former **proclaim** Christ out of selfish ambition," Phil 1:17

q) "Only that in every way, whether in pretense or in truth, Christ **is proclaimed**; and in this I rejoice, yes, and I will rejoice," Phil 1:18

r) "And **we proclaim** Him [Jesus]," Col 1:28

Comparing Translations of καταγγέλλω (order based on variations of Rom 1:8)

Texts	Nestle-Aland 27th Ed Greek	Latin Vulgate (4th-5th Century)	French Geneva (1616)	New Jerusalem Bible (1956)	King James Version (1611)	New International Version (1984)	American Standard Bible (1901)	Geneva Bible (1560)	New American Bible (1899)
Rom 1:8	καταγγέλ-λεται	adnuntiatur	est renommée [is made famous]	is talked of	is spoken of	being reported	is proclaimed	is published	is heralded
Acts 4:2	καταγγέλ-λειν	adnuntiarent	annonçaient	proclaiming	Preached	proclaiming	proclaimed	preached	proclaiming
Acts 16:17	καταγγέλ-λουσιν	adnuntiant	annoncent	to tell	Shew	Telling	proclaim	shewe	proclaim
Acts 16:21	καταγγέλ-λουσιν	adnuntiant	annoncent	advocating	Teach	advocating	set forth	preache	advocating

8) παραγγέλλω (13 OT LXX uses; 30 NT total uses) commanding, order; declaring:

Acts 17:30, "Therefore having overlooked the times of ignorance, God is now **declaring** to men that all *people* everywhere should repent"

Acts 17:30 (NKJ), "Truly, these times of ignorance God overlooked, but now **commands** all men everywhere to repent"

Consider the more common use of παραγγέλλω as to give an order or instruction:

Acts 10:42, "And He **ordered** us to preach to the people, and solemnly to testify that this is the One who has been appointed by God as Judge of the living and the dead"

Acts 23:30, "And when I was informed that there would be a plot against the man, I sent him to you at once, also **instructing** his accusers to bring charges against him before you."

9) προαπαγγέλλω (1 OT LXX only): Ezek 33:9, "But if you on your part **warn** [Heb. *zahar*] a wicked man to turn from his way and he does not turn from his way, he will die in his iniquity, but you have delivered your life."

10) προεπαγγέλλω (Ø OT LXX uses; 2 NT uses): Rom 1:2, "which He **promised beforehand** through His prophets in the holy Scriptures."

11) προκαταγγέλλω (Ø OT LXX uses; 2 NT uses): announced beforehand:
   a) "But the things which God **announced beforehand** by the mouth of all the prophets, that His Christ should suffer, He has thus fulfilled," Acts 3:18
   b) "Which one of the prophets did your fathers not persecute? They killed those **who had previously announced** the coming of the Righteous One, whose betrayers and murderers you have now become," Acts 7:52

12) προευαγγελίζομαι (Ø OT LXX uses; 1 NT use): Gal 3:8, "The Scriptures **preached the Gospel beforehand** to Abraham"
   a. Compare with the combination in Heb 4:6, οἱ πρότερον εὐαγγελισθέντες, "those previously evangelized"
   b. Compare also the nuance of the prefix "pro-" added to the word judge, when used in the noun πρόκριμα (in 1Ti 5:21), to judge beforehand, prejudice, discrimination, or bias

Considering ἀγγέλλω and its Cognates

[word] (# total NT uses, # uses deemed in evangelistic contexts)

[No LXX or NT use of the verb ἀνταγγέλλω]

Some OT examples (of the 22 OT LXX uses of εὐαγγελίζω):

"The Lord gives the command; The women **who evangelize** are a great host," Psa 68:11 [translation mine]:

κύριος δώσει ῥῆμα τοῖς εὐαγγελιζομένοις δυνάμει πολλῇ

"**Evangelize** from day to day of his salvation," Psa 96:2 [translation mine]:
ὐαγγελίζεσθε ἡμέραν ἐξ ἡμέρας τὸ σωτήριον αὐτοῦ

"Behold, on the mountains the feet of him **who evangelizes, Who evangelizes** peace!" Nah 1:15 [2:1] (parallel to Isa 52:7) [translation mine]:
ἰδοὺ ἐπὶ τὰ ὄρη οἱ πόδες εὐαγγελιζομένου καὶ ἀπαγγέλλοντος εἰρήνην

"And it shall come to pass *that* whosoever shall call on the name of the Lord shall be saved: for in mount Sion and in Jerusalem shall the saved one be as the Lord has said, and they that are evangelized, whom the Lord has called," Joel 2:32 [3:5] [Translation adapted from Brenton]:
καὶ ἔσται πᾶς ὃς ἂν ἐπικαλέσηται τὸ ὄνομα κυρίου σωθήσεται ὅτι ἐν τῷ ὄρει Σιων καὶ ἐν Ιερουσαλημ ἔσται ἀνασῳζόμενος καθότι εἶπεν κύριος καὶ εὐαγγελιζόμενοι οὓς κύριος προσκέκληται

Also, as noted above, Isaiah 40:9 (twice); 52:7 (twice); and 61:1

Interesting verb + noun groupings:
εὐαγγελίζω + ἀγαθά , Isa 52:7
εὐαγγελίζω + Ἰησοῦν, Acts 8:35
εὐαγγελίζω + κύριον Ἰησοῦν, Acts 5:42; 11:20
εὐαγγελίζω + εἰρήνην διὰ Ἰησοῦ Χριστοῦ, Acts 10:36
εὐαγγελίζω + τὸν λόγον, Acts 8:4
εὐαγγελίζω + τὴν πίστιν, Gal 1:23
εὐαγγελίζω + περὶ τῆς βασιλείας τοῦ θεοῦ καὶ τοῦ ὀνόματος Ἰησοῦ Χριστοῦ, Acts 8:12

Notice (as considered above) the use of εὐαγγέλιον with no proclamational verb, while the verb is assumed by the context (e.g. considered an ellipsis):
2 Cor 2:12:
BYZ: Ἐλθὼν δὲ εἰς τὴν Τρῳάδα εἰς τὸ εὐαγγέλιον τοῦ χριστοῦ, καὶ θύρας μοι ἀνεῳγμένης ἐν κυρίῳ
NAS: "Now when I came to Troas for the gospel of Christ and when a door was opened for me in the Lord,"
NKJ: "Furthermore, when I came to Troas to *preach* Christ's gospel, and a door was opened to me by the Lord,"

b.   κηρύσσω and cognate:

13) κηρύσσω - preach, proclaim (found a total of 61 times in NT):

a)   Translations of κηρύσσω in evangelism situations (including John the Baptist):
(1)   Having preached, 1 Cor 9:27
(2)   I may preach, Mark 1:38
(3)   I preach, Gal 2:2; 5:11
(4)   Is preached, Matt 26:13; Mark 14:9; 1 Cor 15:12
(5)   Preach (imperative), Matt 10:7
(6)   Preach, Phil 1:15
(7)   Preach Jesus Christ as Lord, 2 Cor 4:5
(8)   κηρύξατε τὸ εὐαγγέλιον - Preach the Gospel, Mark 16:15
(9)   Preach the word, 2 Tim 4:2
(10) Preached, Mark 6:12; 16:20
(11) Preached that men should repent, Mark 6:12
(12) Preaches, Acts 19:13; 2 Cor 11:4
(13) Preacher, Rom 10:14
(14) Preaching, Matt 4:23; 9:35; Mark 1:4, 7, 14, 39; Luke 3:3; 4:40, 44; 8:1, 39; Acts 8:5; 9:20; 20:25; 28:31; Rom 10:8:

Notice Some Translations of this Verb in Mark 1:7

Byzantine	KJV	NASB	Bible in Basic English	NIV	New Jerusalem Bible*	New American Bible*	NLT	CSB	NET
Καὶ ἐκήρυσσεν, λέγων	And preached, saying	And he was preaching, and saying	And he said to them all	And this was his message	In the course of his preaching he said	And this is what he proclaimed	John announced	He was preaching	He proclaimed

(15) Preaching Christ, Phil 1:15

(16) Preaching the kingdom of God, Acts 28:31

(17) Proclaim (κηρύξατε), Matt 10:27

(18) Proclaim, Mark 7:36

(19) Proclaim Jesus, Acts 9:20

(20) Proclaimed, Luke 8:39; Acts 10:37; 1 Tim 3:16

(21) Proclaimed to you the Gospel of God, 1 Thess 2:9

(22) Καὶ κηρυχθῆναι ἐπὶ τῷ ὀνόματι αὐτοῦ μετάνοιαν εἰς ἄφεσιν ἁμαρτιῶν - Luke 24:47, "And that repentance for the forgiveness of sins should be proclaimed in His name"

(23) ἐκήρυσσέ αὐτοῖς τὸν χιστόν - "Proclaiming Christ to them," Acts 8:5

(24) Shall be preached, Matt 24:14; Mark 13:10; Luke 24:47

(25) They preach, Rom 10:15

(26) To preach, Matt 4:17; 11:1; Mark 1:45; 3:14; 5:20; Luke 9:2

(27) To proclaim, Luke 4:18, 19; Acts 10:42

(28) Was preached, 2 Cor 1:19

(29) Was proclaimed, Col 1:23

(30) We have [not] preached, 2 Cor 11:4; 1 Thess 2:9

(31) We preach, Rom 10:8; 1 Cor 1:23; 15:11; 2 Cor 4:5

b) Interesting combinations of verbs with κηρύσσω:

(1) ἀκούω and κηρύσσω (hear and preach), Matt 10:27; Rom 10:14; Col 1:23

(2) διδάσκω and κηρύσσω (teach and preach), Matt 11:1

(3) διδάσκω, κηρύσσω, and θεραπεύω (teaching, preaching, and healing), Matt 4:23; 9:35

(4) κηρύσσω and ἐκβάλλω (preaching and casting out), Mark 1:39

(5) κηρύσσω and λέγω:

(a) Preach, saying (κηρύσσετε λέγοντες), Matt 10:7

(b) Preaching, saying (ἐκήρυσσεν λέγων), Mark 1:7

(c) To preach and to say (κηρύσσειν καὶ λέγειν), Matt 4:17

c) κηρύσσω with nouns:[649]

(1) Preaching the gospel, Mark 16:15

(2) Preaching "the word of faith" (rather than the word of works), Rom 10:8

d) Some thoughts comparing the NT usage of κηρύσσω with εὐαγγελίζω:

(1) κηρύσσω obviously always necessitates a predicate as the message, whereas in contemporary translation, the predicate "gospel," "good news," or "glad tidings" is supplied when none is provided as the object of εὐαγγελίζω

(2) κηρύσσω seems to be used much more frequently in summary statements of the ministries of John the Baptist, Jesus, or Paul; likewise, εὐαγγελίζω seems to be used in particular cases describing particular instances of evangelizing

(3) Both terms are usually used to describe the first hearing of the gospel, or that hearing of the gospel that led to the conversion of the recipient (as opposed to weekly preaching in a church, as is used today); if this is so, neither κηρύσσω nor εὐαγγελίζω in the NT actually refer to what is generally called homiletics, but rather to evangelistic preaching (by the way, please note my study of NT verbs used for follow-up ministry in Chapter 26)

14) προκηρύσσω – Acts 13:24, "after John had **proclaimed before** His coming a baptism of repentance to all the people of Israel"

c. ἡγέομαι and cognate:

15) διηγέομαι – "declare:"

a) "The people whom I formed for Myself, Will declare (Heb. *saphar*, piel, "recount, rehearse, declare") My praise," Isa 43:21

b) "Return to your house and describe what great things God has done for you," Luke 8:39

16) ἐκδιηγέομαι – "tell, relate" (2 NT uses; in LXX from Hebrew *saphar*, "count, recount, relate"), Psa 118:17; Ezek 12:6:

a) "Behold, you scoffers, and marvel, and perish; For I am accomplishing a work in your days, A work which you will never believe, though someone should describe it to you," Acts 13:41; citing Hab 1:5 (Heb. *saphar*, pual, to be recounted)

---

[649]Chapter 17 includes a study of nouns associated with these many verbs.

Consider also the cognate adjective, "indescribable" ἀνεκδιήγητος as found in 2 Cor 9:15, the negation of our verb:

2 Cor 9:15, "Thanks be to God for His indescribable gift!"

17) ἐξηγέομαι – "explain, report, describe; reveal, make fully known" (6 NT uses; 6 in LXX from Hebrew saphar, "count, recount, relate"), Job 28:27:

    a)   "And they *began* to relate their experiences on the road and how He was recognized by them in the breaking of the bread," Luke 24:35

    b)   "No man has seen God at any time; the only begotten God, who is in the bosom of the Father, He has explained *Him*," John 1:18

18) προφητεύω – "speaking what God wants to make known: preach, expound; foretell" (28 NT uses; 110 in OT LXX), Job 28:27

    a)   "But one who prophesies speaks to men for edification and exhortation and consolation," 1 Cor 14:3

    b)   "As to this salvation, the prophets who prophesied of the grace that *would come* to you made careful search and inquiry," 1 Pet 1:10

Comparing Select Grammatical Forms of Proclamational Verbs in Evangelistic Contexts

Form	κηρύσσω	εὐαγγελίζω	καταγγέλλω
Imperative-present-active-2nd plural	κηρύσσετε (preach), Matt 10:7		
Imperative-aorist-active-2nd singular	κήρυξον (preach), 2 Tim 4:2		
Imperative-aorist-active-2nd plural	κηρύξατε (preach), Matt 10:27; Mark 16:15		
Indicative-present-active-1st singular	κηρύσσω (I preach), Gal 2:2; 5:11		καταγγέλλω (I proclaim), Acts 17:3, 23
Indicative-present-active-3rd singular	κηρύσσει (preaches), Acts 19:13; 2 Cor 11:4		
Indicative-present-active-1st plural	κηρύσσομεν (we preach), Rom 10:8; 1 Cor 1:23; 15:11; 2 Cor 4:5		καταγγέλλομεν (we proclaim), Col 1:28
Indicative-present-active-2nd plural			καταγγέλλετε (you proclaim), 1 Cor 11:26
Indicative-present-active-3rd plural	κηρύσσουσιν (preach), Phil 1:15		καταγγέλλουσιν (proclaim), Acts 16:17, 21; 1 Cor 9:14; Phil 1:16
Indicative-present-middle-1st singular		εὐαγγελίζομαι (I evangelize), Luke 2:10	
Indicative-present-middle-1st plural		εὐαγγελιζόμεθα (we evangelize), Acts 13:32	
Indicative-present-passive-3rd singular	κηρύσσεται (is preached), 1 Cor 15:12	εὐαγγελίζεται (is evangelized), Luke 16:16; Gal 1:9, 23	καταγγέλλεται (is proclaimed), Acts 13:38; Rom 1:8; Phil 1:18
Indicative-present-passive-3rd plural		εὐαγγελίζονται (are evangelized), Matt 11:5; Luke 7:22	
Indicative-aorist-active-3rd singular	ἐκήρυξεν (proclaimed), Acts 10:37	εὐηγγέλισεν (evangelized), Rev 10:7	
Indicative-aorist-active-1st plural	ἐκηρύξαμεν (we have [not] preached), 2 Cor 11:4; 1 Thess 2:9		κατηγγείλαμεν (we proclaimed), Acts 15:36
Indicative-aorist-active-3rd plural	ἐκήρυξαν (preached), Mark 6:12; 16:20		κατήγγειλαν (announced), Acts 3:42
Indicative-aorist-middle-1st singular		εὐηγγελισάμην (I evangelized), 1 Cor 15:1, 2; 2 Cor 11:7; Gal 4:13	
Indicative-aorist-middle-3rd singular		εὐηγγελίσατο (he evangelized), Acts 8:35	
Indicative-aorist-middle-1st plural		εὐηγγελισάμεθα (we evangelized), Gal 1:8 (2)	
Indicative-aorist-middle-3rd plural		εὐηγγελίσαντο (they were evangelizing), Acts 8:25	
Indicative-aorist-passive-3rd singular	ἐκηρύχθη (proclaimed), 1 Tim 3:16	εὐηγγελίσθη (were evangelized), 1 Pet 4:6	
Indicative-future-passive-3rd singular	κηρύσσειν (shall be preached), Matt 24:14		
Indicative-imperfect-active-3rd singular	ἐκήρυσσεν (preaching), Mark 1:7; Acts 8:5; 9:20		
Indicative-imperfect-active-3rd plural	ἐκήρυσσον (proclaim), Mark 7:36		κατήγγελλον (they preached), Acts 13:5
Indicative-imperfect-middle-3rd singular		εὐηγγελίζετο (he evangelized), Luke 3:18; Acts 8:40; 17:18	
Subjunctive-present-middle-1st singular		εὐαγγελίζωμαι (I evangelize), 1 Cor 9:16 (twice); Gal 1:16	
Subjunctive-present-middle-3rd singular		εὐαγγελίζηται (he should preach), Gal 1:8 (1)	
Subjunctive-aorist-active-1st singular	κηρύξω (I may preach), Mark 1:38		
Subjunctive-aorist-passive-3rd singular	κηρυχθῇ (is preached), Matt 26:13; Mark 14:9		
Subjunctive-aorist-active-3rd plural	κηρύξωσιν (they preach), Rom 10:15		
Infinitive-present-active	κηρύσσειν (to preach), Matt 4:17; 11:1; Mark 1:45; 3:14; 5:20; Luke 9:2		καταγγέλλειν (preached), Acts 4:2; 26:23
Infinitive-present-middle		εὐαγγελίζεσθαι (to evangelize), Rom 15:20; 1 Cor 1:17	

Form	κηρύσσω	εὐαγγελίζω	καταγγέλλω
Infinitive-aorist-active	κηρύξαι (to proclaim), Luke 4:18, 19; Acts 10:42	εὐαγγελίσαι (to evangelize), Rev 14:6	
Infinitive-aorist-middle		εὐαγγελίσασθαί (to evangelize), Luke 1:19; 4:18, 43; Acts 16:10; Rom 1:15; 2 Cor 10:16; Eph 3:8	
Infinitive-aorist-passive	κηρυχθῆναι (be preached), Mark 13:10; Luke 24:47		
Participle-present-active-nominative-masculine-singular	κηρύσσων (preaching), Matt 4:23; 9:35; Mark 1:4, 14, 39; Luke 3:3; 4:44; 8:1, 39; Acts 20:25; 28:31		καταγγέλλων (declaring), 1 Cor 2:1
Participle-present-active-genitive-masculine-singular	κηρύσσοντος (preacher), Rom 10:14		
Participle-present-middle-nominative-masculine-singular		εὐαγγελιζόμενος (evangelizing), Luke 8:1; Acts 10:36; 1 Cor 9:18	
Participle-present-middle-nominative-masculine-plural		εὐαγγελιζόμενοι (evangelizing), Luke 9:6; Acts 5:42; 8:4; 11:20; 14:7, 15; 15:35	
Participle-present-middle-dative-masculine-singular		ὑαγγελιζομένῳ (evangelizing), Acts 8:12	
Participle-present-middle-genetive-masculine-singular		εὐαγγελιζομένου (evangelizing), Luke 20:1	
Participle-present-middle-genetive-masculine-plural		εὐαγγελιζομένων (evangelizing), Rom 10:15 (twice)	
Participle-aorist-active-nominative-masculine-singular	κηρύξας (having preached), 1 Cor 9:27		
Participle-aorist-middle-nominative-masculine-plural		εὐαγγελισάμενοί (they had evangelized), Acts 14:21	
Participle-aorist-middle-genetive-masculine-singular		εὐαγγελισαμένου (evangelizing), 1 Thess 3:6	
Participle-aorist-middle-genetive-masculine-plural		εὐαγγελισαμένων (have evangelized), 1 Pet 1:12	
Participle-aorist-passive-nominative-neuter-singular		εὐαγγελισθὲν (was evangelized), Gal 1:11; 1 Pet 1:25	
Participle-aorist-passive-nominative-masculine-plural		εὐαγγελισθέντες (were evangelized), Heb 4:6	
Participle-aorist-passive-genetive-neuter-singular	κηρυχθέντος (was proclaimed), Col 1:23		
Participle-aorist-passive-nominative-masculine-singular	κηρυχθείς (was preached), 2 Cor 1:19		
Participle-perfect-passive-nominative-masculine-plural		εὐηγγελισμένοι (we were evangelized), Heb 4:2	
Some Totals for Comparison	4 Imperatives (3 forms) 10 Indicative-present (5 forms) 6 Indicative-aorist (4 forms) 1 Indicative-future (1 form) 4 Indicative-imperfect (2 forms) 4 Subjunctive-aorist (3 forms) 6 Infinitive-present (1 form) 5 Infinitive-aorist (2 forms) 12 Participle-present (2 forms) 3 Participle-aorist (3 forms) **61 Total uses**	7 Indicative-present (4 forms) 9 Indicative-aorist (6 forms) 3 Indicative-imperfect (1 form) 4 Subjunctive-present (2 forms) 2 Infinitive-present (1 form) 8 Infinitive-aorist (2 forms) 14 Participle-present (5 forms) 6 Participle-aorist (5 forms) 1 Participle-perfect (1 form) **55 Total uses**	11 Indicative-present (5 forms) 2 Indicative-aorist (2 forms) 1 Indicative-imperfect (1 form) 2 Infinitive-present (1 form) 1 Participle-present (1 form) **18 Total uses**
Preliminary Thoughts	κηρύσσω is uniquely used for imperatives (4 uses at 7%), including 15 participles (25%)	εὐαγγελίζω is used predominantly in narratives relating to evangelizing, including 21 participles (39%)	καταγγέλλω is used especially when speaking of evangelizing (positively or negatively), most uses being in the indicative form (78%)
Contextual Emphases	κηρύσσω appears to be an umbrella term for proclaiming, which receives the imperative emphases	εὐαγγελίζω seems to speak to that proclamation of the Gospel which leads to a hearing of faith followed by a response of faith in the Gospel (cf. 1 Cor 15:1-2)	καταγγέλλω seems to be used in contexts where there is an emotionally-negative response by the hearer or a more emotionally-charged context of proclamation

3—TO TESTIFY

d. μαρτυρέω (Eng. martyr) and cognates:

Introduction: The 1669 French Geneva Bible's three use of the word "protest," came from translating μαρτυρέω twice and διαμαρτύρομαι once, all in edification contexts.[650]

19) μαρτυρέω (76 NT uses; 46 Johanine; 11 in Acts) – bearing witness, testifying:
Evangelistic Uses:
   John 1:7, 8, 15, 32, 34; 3:11, 3:26, 32; 4:39; 5:31, 32 [2], 33, 36, 37, 39; 8:13, 14, 18 [2]; 10:25; 12:17; 15:26, 27; 18:37; 19:35; 21:24; Acts 10:43; 14:3; 23:11; Rom 3:21; 1 Cor 15:15; 1 Tim 6:13; Heb 7:17; 10:15; 1 John 1:2, 4:14; 5:9, 10; Rev 1:2; 22:20
   Translated as "Protest" in 1560 English Geneva Bible, Rev 22:18
Food for thought: a less equivocal translation of μαρτυρέω: **to testify** (e.g. NAS translation of 1 Tim 6:13)

a) Several evangelistic examples:
   (1) "He **will bear witness** of Me, and you *will* **bear witness** also," John 15:26-27
   (2) "**Bearing witness** [testifying] to the word of His grace," Acts 14:3
   (3) "So **you must witness** [testify] in Rome also," Acts 23:11
   (4) "But now apart from the Law *the* righteousness of God has been manifested, **being witnessed** by the Law and the Prophets," Rom 3:21
   (5) "I charge you in the presence of God, who gives life to all things, and of Christ Jesus, who **testified** the good confession before Pontius Pilate," 1 Tim 6:13
   (6) "And the life was manifested, and we have seen and **bear witness** and proclaim to you the eternal life, which was with the Father and was manifested to us," 1 John 1:2

b) Varieties of translation of John 3:26, "And they came to John and said to him, 'Rabbi, He who was with you beyond the Jordan, to whom **you have borne witness**, behold, He is baptizing, and all are coming to Him.'"

Various Translations of μαρτυρέω in John 3:26

Testified	Have testified	Said	Gavest testimony	Have born witness	Barest witness
New International	**New King James**	**New Living Translation**	**Douay-Rheims**	**New American Standard**	**King James**

c) Translations of 1 Tim 2:6, "who gave Himself as a ransom for all, the testimony *borne* at the proper time"

Various Translations of μαρτυρέω in 1 Timothy 2:6

Greek Byzantine	Future Tense Etheridge (from Syriac)	Future Tense KJV	Present Tense NAS (1977)	Past Action NAU (1995)	Past Tense NIV	Past Tense Murdock (from Syriac)
ὁ δοὺς ἑαυτὸν ἀντίλυτρον ὑπὲρ πάντων, τὸ μαρτύριον καιροῖς ἰδίοις	who gave himself a ransom for every man; a testimony which cometh in its time.	Who gave himself a ransom for all, to be testified in due time	who gave Himself as a ransom for all, the testimony *borne* at the proper time	who gave Himself as a ransom for all, the testimony *given* at the proper time	who gave himself as a ransom for all men--the testimony given in its proper time.	who gave himself a ransom for every man; a testimony that arrived in due time.

Some evangelistic implications of the translation of μαρτυρέω in 1 Timothy 2:6:
   Is Paul referring to past completed action: hence the sending of Christ by God to earth as a testimony?
   Is Paul referring to continued action: hence, the testimony of Jesus as he heralds (see 1 Tim 2:7) it in one city and another?

---

[650]See examples in Chapter 26.

Can "testimony" in 1 Timothy 2:6 also apply to the testimony of Christians today, as they bear witness of Christ in due season to persons who have not yet heard? In which case, when they hear, it becomes their kairos moment?

d) The Holy Spirit also bearing witness of the work of Christ:

Heb 10:15, 17, "And the Holy Spirit also **bears witness** to us; for after saying, ...And their sins and their iniquities will I remember no more"

1 John 5:6-7, "This is the one who came by water and blood, Jesus Christ; not with the water only, but with the water and with the blood. And it is the Spirit who **bears witness**, because the Spirit is the truth"

e) God also bore witness by giving the Holy Spirit:

Acts 15:8, "And God, who knows the heart, **bore witness** to them, giving them the Holy Spirit, just as He also did to us"

f) Example of NT use in a non-evangelistic context:

Acts 26:5 , "Since they have known about me for a long time previously, if they are willing **to testify**, that I lived *as* a Pharisee according to the strictest sect of our religion"

g) **A look at the translation of μαρτυρέω in Heb 11:2:**

Having more to do with being and/or giving testimony or witness

Byzantine Textform	Tyndale; Geneva	Bishops; KJV	Young's	Darby; DRA✠; NKJ	ERV; ASV	NAS	CSB	RSV
ἐμαρτυρήθησαν	were well reported of	obtained a good report	were ... testified of	have obtained testimony	had witness borne to them	gained approval	were approved	received divine approval
ἐν ταύτῃ γὰρ ἐμαρτυρήθησαν οἱ πρεσβύτεροι.	By it the elders were well reported of	For by it, the elders obtained a good report	for in this were the elders testified of	For in *the power of* this the elders have obtained testimony	For therein the elders had witness borne to them	For by it the men of old gained approval	For by it our ancestors were approved	For by it the men of old received divine approval

Having less to do with being and/or giving testimony or witness

GNT✠	NIV	ESV	NET	NJB✠	NAB✠	NLT	CEV✠	Message
won God's approval	were commended for	received their commendation	received God's commendation	are acknowledged	were well attested	earned a good reputation	made ... pleasing to God	distinguished ... set them above
It was by their faith that people of ancient times won God's approval	This is what the ancients were commended for	For by it the people of old received their commendation	For by it the people of old received God's commendation	It is for their faith that our ancestors are acknowledged	Because of it the ancients were well attested	Through their faith, the people in days of old earned a good reputation	It was their faith that made our ancestors pleasing to God.	The act of faith is what distinguished our ancestors, set them above the crowd.

(1) Possible proclamatory translations:

Mine: "For by it the elders received testimony [μαρτυρέω@viap3p]"

Mine: "For by it the elders were testifying"

Mine: "For by it the elders were bearing witness"

Mine: "For by it the elders bore witness"

Mine: "For by it testified the men of old"

And wherein they still speak, cf. Heb 11:4

Much like the heavens declare the glory of God, Psa 19:1

(2) Can the passive voice...

Include an emphatic element at times?

Include the element that they themselves were the testimony of which they were bearing witness?

(3) For example:

"By faith Adoniram Judson went to Burma to evangelize the Burmese"

"Adoniram Judson bore witness of his faith"

(4) Other passive uses of (following Gingrich's delineation for passive use):

    (a) "Be witnessed, have witness born":

      Rom 3:21, "But now the righteousness of God apart from the law is revealed, being witnessed [μαρτυρέω@vpppnfs] by the Law and the Prophets,"

      Heb 7:8, "Here mortal men receive tithes, but there he *receives them*, of whom it is witnessed [μαρτυρέω@vpppnms] that he lives."

      Heb 7:17 (NKJ), "For He testifies [μαρτυρέω@vipa3s]: 'You *are* a priest forever According to the order of Melchizedek.'"

      Heb 7:17 (NAS), "For it is witnessed [μαρτυρέω@vipp3s] *of Him*, 'Thou art a priest forever According to the order of Melchizedek.'"

    (b) "Be well spoken of, be approved":

      Acts 6:3, "Therefore, brethren, seek out from among you seven men of *good* reputation [μαρτυρέω@vpppamp], full of the Holy Spirit and wisdom, whom we may appoint over this business;"

      Acts 10:22, "And they said, 'Cornelius *the* centurion, a just man, one who fears God and has a good reputation [μαρτυρέω@vpppnms] among all the nation of the Jews, was divinely instructed by a holy angel to summon you to his house, and to hear words from you.'"

      Acts 16:2, "He was well spoken of [μαρτυρέω@viip3s] by the brethren who were at Lystra and Iconium."

      Acts 22:12, "Then a certain Ananias, a devout man according to the law, having a good testimony [μαρτυρέω@vpppnms] with all the Jews who dwelt *there*,"

      Heb 11:2, "For by it the elders obtained a *good* testimony [μαρτυρέω@viap3p]."

      Heb 11:4, "By faith Abel offered to God a more excellent sacrifice than Cain, through which he obtained witness [μαρτυρέω@viap3s] that he was righteous, God testifying of his gifts; and through it he being dead still speaks."

      Heb 11:5, "By faith Enoch was taken away so that he did not see death, 'and was not found, because God had taken him'; for before he was taken he had this testimony [μαρτυρέω@vixp3s], that he pleased God."

      Heb 11:39, "And all these, having obtained a good testimony [μαρτυρέω@vpapnmp] through faith, did not receive the promise,"

Concerning συμμαρτυρέω (3 NT uses)—to bear witness with or within by the conscience:[651]

    Rom 2:15, "in that they show the work of the Law written in their hearts, their conscience bearing witness, and their thoughts alternately accusing or else defending them"

    Rom 8:16, "The Spirit Himself bears witness with our spirit that we are children of God"

    Rom 9:1, "I am telling the truth in Christ, I am not lying, my conscience bearing me witness in the Holy Spirit"

20) μαρτυρομαι (5 NT uses) – testifying:

    a) Evangelistic context – Acts 26:22, "And so, having obtained help from God, I stand to this day **testifying** both to small and great, stating nothing but what the Prophets and Moses said was going to take place"

n2) ἡ μαρτυρία (37 NT uses), testimony, evidence + ἔχω (710 NT uses) to hold, maintain, have:

    Introduction: Interesting for this word, is that Psalm 119 uses it 23 times in the plural (based on the LXX) to refer to God's special revelation. As if God's testimony is not solely locked in a book, but in the New Testament, Christians are commanded to verbalized those words through bearing witness of the Gospel.

      The issue of "lifestyle evangelism" versus "verbal evangelism" flows from this word: is it the lifestyle of the believer that is a witness (e.g. outward obedience to monastic vows, etc.) or is it the words of the believer that bear witness? In fact, 2 Cor 3:2-3 seems to link the two ideas together, as Paul is referring to the work of the Holy Spirit in the lives of those that he led to Christ. A work that produces not only visible fruit through the changed life of the believer, but also the fruit of verbal witness, 2 Cor 5:11, 14, 19-20.

    a) "And because of the testimony which they had maintained," Rev 6:9

    b) "And have the testimony of Jesus Christ," Rev 12:17 (NKJ)

---

[651]Notice the emphatic emphasis of the Louw-Nida Lexicon: "33.266 συμμαρτυρέω: to provide confirming evidence by means of a testimony – 'to support by testimony, to provide supporting evidence, to testify in support.' συμμαρτυρούσης αὐτῶν τῆς συνειδήσεως 'their consciences testify in support of this' Ro 2.15. It may be necessary in some languages to translate this phrase in Ro 2.15 as 'their consciences say to them that this is true.'"

Translations of the μαρτυρία + ἔχω Word Pair in Rev 12:17
[Notice the proclamational or non-proclamational emphases based on a preposition or verb]

Byzan-tine Greek	Latin Vulgate	Tyndale; Geneva; Bishops; KJV; NKJ	Young's (1862)	ERV (1885); ASV	NASB; NIV	RSV	NAB✠	NJB✠	TNIV	CSB	NLT	NET
καὶ ἐχόντων τὴν μαρτυρίαν Ἰησοῦ	et habent testimo-nium Jesu Christi	and have the testimony of Iesus Christe	and having the testimony of Jesus Christ	and hold the testimony of Jesus	and hold to the testimony of Jesus	and bear testimony to Jesus	and bear witness to Jesus	and have in them-selves the witness of Jesus	and hold fast their testimony about Jesus	and have the testimony about Jesus	and maintain their testimony for Jesus	and hold to the testimony about Jesus

    c)   "Your brethren who hold the testimony of Jesus," Rev 19:10

    For similar usages, see:
        (1)   "What further need do we have of testimony?" Luke 22:71
        (2)   "But the witness which I have is greater than *that of* John," John 5:36
        (3)   "Moreover he must have a good testimony among those who are outside, "1 Tim 3:7 (NKJ)

n3) τὸ μαρτύριον (19/20 NT uses) – **giving witness** to the resurrection of the Lord Jesus, Acts 4:33

21) διαμαρτύρομαι (15 NT uses) – affirm solemnly, testify emphatically, warn [cf. Lk 16:28], "protest" [1560 English Geneva Bible, 2 Tim 2:14] (also used of follow-up):
    a)   That he may **warn** them, Luke 16:28
    b)   Solemnly testifying to the Jews, Acts 18:5, 20:21 (and Greeks), 28:23
    c)   Solemnly to testify, Acts 10:42 (prior to their salvation)
    d)   Solemnly witnessed, Acts 23:11
    e)   Testify solemnly, Acts 20:24

    Consider the importance of the usage of this verb in Mose's warning to heed his Song:
        Deut 32:46, "he said to them, 'Take to your heart all the words with which **I am warning** you today, which you shall command your sons to observe carefully, *even* all the words of this law.'"

22) συμμαρτυρέω (3 total NT uses; 2 evangelistic) – to bear witness, confirm:
    Rom 2:15, "in that they show the work of the Law written in their hearts, their conscience **bearing witness**, and their thoughts alternately accusing or else defending them."
    Rom 8:16, "The Spirit Himself **bears witness** with our spirit that we are children of God."

    Also one non-evangelistic use:
    Rom 9:1, "I am telling the truth in Christ, I am not lying, my conscience **bearing** me **witness** in the Holy Spirit, that I have great sorrow and unceasing grief in my heart."

*) An interesting verse of interest in the μαρτυρέω word group:
    a)   Acts 23:11 includes in parallel form both διαμαρτύρομαι and μαρτυρέω:
        "But on the night *immediately* following, the Lord stood at his side and said, 'Take courage; for as **you have solemnly witnessed** to My cause at Jerusalem, so **you must witness** at Rome also,'" Acts 23:11

4—TO SPEAK OR SAY

e. λαλέω and cognate:

23) λαλέω (296 NT uses), to talk, speak (cf. Matt 13:3):
    a)   For it is not you who **speak** , but *it is* the Spirit of your Father who **speaks** in you, Matt 10:20; cf. Mark 13:11; Luke 12:11-12
    b)   What I tell you in the darkness, **speak** in the light, Matt 10:27
    c)   All these things Jesus spoke to the crowds in parables, and He did not **speak** to them without a parable (most uses of Jesus "speaking" are not included in this list), Matt 13:34; cf. Matt 13:10-17; Mark 4:10-13, 33-34; Luke 8:9-10; John 10:6; 16:25
    d)   And many were gathered together, so that there was no longer room, not even near the door; and He was **speaking** the word to them, Mark 2:2

e)   and continued to **speak** of Him to all those who were looking for the redemption of Jerusalem, Luke 2:38

f)   The two disciples heard him **speak**, and they followed Jesus, John 1:36

g)   The officers answered, "Never has a man spoken the way this man **speaks**," John 1:46

h)   For I did not **speak** on My own initiative, but the Father Himself who sent Me has given Me a commandment *as to* what to say and what to **speak.** I know that His commandment is eternal life; therefore the things I **speak**, I **speak** just as the Father has told Me, John 12:49-50

i)   Jesus answered him, "I **have spoken** openly to the world; I always taught in synagogues, and in the temple, where all the Jews come together; and I **spoke** nothing in secret, Joh 18:20

j)   And as they were **speaking** to the people, Acts 4:1

k)   Let us warn them to **speak** no more to any man in this name, Acts 4:17

l)   For we cannot stop **speaking** what we have seen and heard, Acts 4:20

m) Grant that Thy bond-servants may **speak** Thy word with all confidence, Acts 4:29

n)   **Speak** the Word of God, Acts 4:31, Phil 1:14

o)   Stand and **speak** to the people in the temple the whole message of this Life, Acts 5:20

p)   They flogged them and ordered them to **speak** no more in the name of Jesus, Acts 5:40

q)   they were unable to cope with the wisdom and the Spirit with which he was **speaking**, Acts 6:10

r)   We have heard him **speak** … This man incessantly **speaks**, Acts 6:11, 13

s)   **Had ... spoken** the word of the Lord, Acts 8:25

t)   While Peter was still **speaking** these words, Acts 10:44, cf. Acts 11:15

u)   He shall **speak** words to you by which you will be saved, Acts 11:14

v)   **Speaking** the word to no one except to Jews alone, Acts 11:19

w) **Speaking** to the Greeks also, preaching the Lord Jesus, Acts 11:20

x)   That these things may be **spoken** to them the next Sabbath, Acts 13:42

y)   Contradicting the things **spoken** by Paul, Acts 13:45

z)   The same heard Paul **speaking**, Acts 14:9

aa) **Had spoken** the word, Acts 14:25

ab) **Speak** the word, Acts 16:6

ac) The Lord opened her heart to respond to the things **spoken** by Paul, Acts 16:14

ad) And they **spoke** the word of the Lord to him, Acts 16:32

ae) Go on **speaking** (vs. fearful silence), Acts 18:9

af) he was **speaking** and teaching accurately the things concerning Jesus, Acts 18:25

ag) Allow me to **speak** to the people, Acts 21:39

ah) And I **speak** to him with confidence, Acts 26:26

ai) Some were being persuaded by the things **spoken**, but others would not believe, Acts 28:24

aj) We **speak** in Christ in the sight of God, 2 Cor 2:17

ak) I believed, therefore I **spoke**, 2 Cor 4:13

al) We believe therefore we **speak**, 2 Cor 4:13

am) That in *proclaiming* it I may speak boldly, as I ought to **speak**, Eph 6:20

an) Have far more courage to **speak** the word of God without fear, Phil 1:14

Unpacking this powerful verse:

NKJ: "and most of the brethren in the Lord, having become confident by my chains, are much more bold to speak the word without fear," Phil 1:14

Greek (Byzantine): καὶ τοὺς πλείονας τῶν ἀδελφῶν ἐν κυρίῳ, πεποιθότας τοῖς δεσμοῖς μου, περισσοτέρως τολμᾶν ἀφόβως τὸν λόγον λαλεῖν

πείθω (verb) – "persuaded by my chains" (54 NT uses)

περισσοτέρως (adverb) – "[have] abundantly" (13 NT uses)

τολμάω (verb) – to dare, be brave, have courage:

15 NT uses:

Of the scribes and pharisees no longer daring to ask Jesus questions, Matt 22:46; Mark 12:34; Luke 20:40

Of Joseph of Arimathaea daring to ask for the body of Christ, Mark 15:43):

Of the disciples not daring to ask if it was Jesus, John 21:12

Of no one daring to join the disciples (due to the signs and wonders of the apostles), Acts 5:13

Of Moses not daring to look at the burning bush, Acts 7:32

Of one perhaps daring to die for a good man, Rom 5:7

Of Paul not daring to take credit for any other man's work, Rom 15:18

Of a Christian daring to take another to court, 1 Cor 6:1

Of the accusation of the Corinthian church of Paul's boldness when absent, 2 Cor 10:2, or in his letters, 2 Cor 10:12

Of Paul matching boldness for boldness, 2 Cor 11:21

> Of Michael the archangel not daring to pronounce an accusation against the devil, Jude 9
> Hence "are abundantly daring" or "have abundant courage"
> ἀφόβως (adverb) – fearlessly (4 NT uses, Luke 1:74; 1 Cor 16:10; Jude 12)
> τὸν λόγον λαλεῖν - to speak the word

Other translations of Phil 1:14:

> 1560 English Geneva: "In so muche that manie of the brethren in the Lord are boldened through my bandes, and dare more frankely speake the worde"
> King James: "And many of the brethren in the Lord, waxing confident by my bonds, are much more bold to speak the word without fear"
> English Darby: "and that the most of the brethren, trusting in *the* Lord through my bonds, dare more abundantly to speak the word of God fearlessly"
> My amalgamation: "And that many of the brethren in the Lord, persuaded by my chains, dare more abundantly to speak the word of God fearlessly"

ao) So that we may **speak** forth the mystery of Christ … in he way I ought to **speak**, Col 4:3-4

ap) To s**peak** to you the Gospel of God, 1 Thess 2:2
(note the "Bible in Basic English" [1949, 1964] translation: "we gave you the good news")

aq) But just as we have been approved by God to be entrusted with the gospel, so **we speak**, 1 Thess 2:4

ar) Hindering us from **speaking** to the Gentiles that they might be saved, 1 Thess 2:16

24) προσλαλέω (2 NT uses) – to speak to:
   a) I requested to see you and **to speak with you**, Acts 28:20

f.   λέγω and cognates:

25) λέγω (2353/2356 total NT uses) - speak:
   a) Or what you **are to say**, Luke 12:11
   b) Giving attention to what was **said** by Philip, Acts 8:6
   c) "**Say it**," Acts 13:15
   d) And Paul and Barnabas spoke out boldly and **said**, Acts 13:46
   e) And **saying**," Acts 14:15
   f) **Saying** these things, Acts 14:18
   g) What would this babbler **say**? Acts 17:18
   h) He spoke to them in the Hebrew dialect, **saying**, Acts 21:40
   i) And when the governor had nodded for him **to speak**, Paul responded, Acts 24:10
   j) "You are permitted **to speak** for yourself," Acts 26:1
   k) **Saying** nothing but, Acts 26:22
   l) Some were being persuaded by the things **spoken**, Acts 28:24
   m) **Saying**, "Know the LORD," Heb 8:11
   n) And let him who hears **say**, "Come!" Rev 22:17

26) ἀπολογέομαι (10 total NT uses) – say in defense:
   a) Do not worry about how or what you are to speak in your defense, Luke 12:11
   b) Not to prepare beforehand to defend yourselves, Luke 21:14
   c) I cheerfully make my defense, Acts 24:10
   d) Paul stretched forth his hand, and answered for himself, Acts 26:1
   e) I consider myself fortunate, King Agrippa, that I am about to make my defense before you today, Acts 26:2
   f) And while *Paul* was saying this in his defense, Acts 26:24

For further consideration—does this verb lean toward?

> Trying to develop rational proofs of or for the Gospel—as in seeking to defend it, because the Gospel needs to be defended, as does the defense attorney in the court of law?

> Or: Explaining it to those who do not understand it, as the Gospel needs no defense:
> For the Gospel is powerful in and of itself
> For God makes it self-evident to those whom He wants to reach ("Let him who has ears hear")?

> Does Paul, in his "defense" or in "defense" of the Gospel, ever provide rational proofs, either in the Book of Acts, which has ample judicial material from the hand of Luke,

or in his epistles, which also have opportunity for such topics, be it Romans 1, 1 Corinthians 1-2, or the book of Galatians?

How are the English noun "explanation" and verb "explain" generally used in the NT?

The English word "explanation" is found three times in the NAS: Eccl 7:25, 27; Dan 5:12:

In Eccl 7:25 it translates as a noun the Hebrew *cheshbon* (reasoning), the Greek ψῆφος (smooth stone), and the Latin *rationem*

In Eccl 7:27 it translates as a noun the Hebrew *cheshbon* (reasoning), the Greek λογισμός (reasoning), and the Latin *rationem*

In Dan 5:12 it translates as a verb the Aramaic *'achavah* (declaration) and the Greek ἀναγγέλλω (report, make known)

The English verb "explain" is used 12 times for the NAS as translations of:

φράζω (Matt 13:36 [BYZ]; 15:15; 2 total uses in NT)
or from: διασαφέω (Matt 13:36 [NA27]; 18:31; 2 total uses in NT)
ἐπιλύω (Mark 4:34; 2 total NT uses), the other use is Acts 19:29 in which it is translated "determined"
διερμηνεύω (Luke 24:27; 6 total NT uses)
διανοίγω (Luke 24:32; Acts 17:3; 8 total NT uses)
ἐξηγέομαι (John 1:18; Acts 10:8; 6 total NT uses)
ἐκτίθημι (Acts 11:4; 18:26; 28:23; 4 total NT uses)
δυσερμήνευτος λέγειν (Heb 5:11; this is the single NT use of the adjective δυσερμήνευτος)

Conclusions:

The English noun "explanation" is never used in the NT of the NAS

Whereas the English verb "explain" is used to translate 6 verbs and one verbal group, none of which are for the verb ἀπολογέομαι

Could there be a predisposed translation of the the word ἀπολογέομαι and ἀπολογία (below) using the English root "defense" due to the predetermined historical-theological uses of these verses to provide prooftexts for the field of apologetics and many other philosophical-theological areas of inquiry within Christianity?

n4) ἡ ἀπολογία (8 total NT uses; Eng. apologetics) – noun: a speech in defense (almost exclusively in a judicial sense):

a) Hear my defense which I now *offer* to you, Acts 22:1
What if ἀπολογία were translated "explanation"?
b) In the defense [of the Gospel], Phil 1:7
c) Knowing that I am appointed for the defense of the gospel, Phil 1:16
d) At my first defense no one supported me, 2 Tim 4:16
e) Always being ready to make a defense, 1 Pet 3:15

Various Translations of πρὸς ἀπολογία in 1 Peter 3:15

Johnston Modified (2007)	New American Standard (1978)	King James (1611/1769)	New Living Translation (2004)	New American Bible (1991)	Douay-Rheims (1899)
tell the reason	to make a defense	to *give* an answer	to explain it	to give an explanation	to satisfy
always eager to tell the reason to everyone who requests a word about the hope that is in you	always *being* ready to make a defense to everyone who asks you to give an account for the hope that is in you	and *be* ready always to *give* an answer to every man that asketh you a reason of the hope that is in you	And if you are asked about your Christian hope, always be ready to explain it	Always be ready to give an explanation to anyone who asks you for a reason for your hope	being ready always to satisfy every one that asketh you a reason of that hope which is in you

27) διαλέγομαι (13 NT uses; Eng. dialogue) - "**reason**" (1560 English Geneva Bible, "dispute"):

Introduction: This word is used 10 times in Acts, and primarily for evangelism; but it is also used for follow-up discipleship (Acts 19:9), and to explain that Paul did not seem to evangelize during his last visit to Jerusalem (Acts 24:12). It is also used from the mouth of the Lord in Isa 63:1:

Isa 63:1, "Who is this who comes from Edom, With garments of glowing colors from Bozrah, This One who is majestic in His apparel, Marching in the greatness of His strength? '**It is I who speak in righteousness, mighty to save.**'"
'ἐγὼ διαλέγομαι δικαιοσύνην καὶ κρίσιν σωτηρίου.'

cf. Acts 24:15, "And as he was discussing righteousness, self-control and the judgment to come, Felix became frightened and said, 'Go away for the present, and when I find time, I will summon you.'"
Διαλεγομένου δὲ αὐτοῦ περὶ δικαιοσύνης

Jerome's Latin Vulgate translated this Greek term by three Latin verbs:
disputo [11 times] meaning to weigh, examine, investigate, treat, discuss, explain;[652]
dissero [1 time, Acts 17:2!] meaning to examine, argue, discuss, speak, harangue, discourse, treat;[653]
dico [1 time, Heb 12:5] meaning to say, speak, utter, tell, mention, relate, affirm, declare, state, assert[654]
The student of church history recognizes the use of this word by way of the numerous "disputations" that have taken place between people of differing points of view, the most famous of these may be the Ninety-Five Theses of Martin Luther as he called for a "disputation" on the concepts enumerated in 1517.[655]

Today the term could be confused with the modern missiological concept of "dialogue", as used by the World Council of Churches,[656] a term which has taken on the meaning of the

---

[652]"**dis-putō** āvī, ātus, āre, to weigh, examine, investigate, treat, discuss, explain: *de singulis sententiis breviter: ad id: multa de sideribus,* Cs.: *de omni re in contrarias partes: esse in utramque partem disputatum,* Cs. — To argue, maintain, insist: *palam: copiose: non ita disputo,* such is not my argument: *qui contra disputant,* opponents: *pro omnibus et contra omnia: isti* in eo disputant, Contaminari non decere fabulas, T.: *nihil contra: contra te: quod disputari contra nullo pacto potest,* cannot be disputed: *quid desiderem, non quid viderim,* the question is, etc." (Charlton T. Lewis, *An Elementary Latin Dictionary* [1890]).

[653]"**dis-serō** ruī, rtus, ere, to examine, argue, discuss, speak, harangue, discourse, treat: *mecum: pluribus verbis sit disserendum: philosophiae pars, quae est disserendi: de omnibus rebus in contrarias partīs: pro legibus,* L.: *contra ista: permulta de eloquentiā cum Antonio: haec subtilins: alquae in contione huiuscemodi verbis,* S.: *libertatis bona,* Ta.: *nihil esse in auspiciis*" (ibid.).

[654]Ibid.

[655]"In the desire and with the purpose of elucidating the truth, a disputation will be held on the underwritten propositions at Wittemberg, under the presidency of the Reverend Father Martin Luther, Monk of the Order of St. Augustine, Master of Arts and of Sacred Theology, and ordinary Reader of the same in that place. He therefore asks those who cannot be present and discuss the subject with us orally, to do so by letter in their absence. In the name of our Lord Jesus Christ. Amen" (Martin Luther, "Preamble: Ninety Five Theses"; available at: http://www.ccel.org/ccel/luther/first_prin.iv.i.ii.html [online]; accessed: 9 Oct 2006; Internet).

[656]"It was not until the 1950s that the relationship of Christianity to other faiths again became a vital concern. A theologian from Asia, D. T. Niles, again raised the issue at the Evanston Assembly [of the World Council of Churches] in 1954. The Report on Evangelism spoke of the renascent non-Christian religions which 'necessitate a new approach in our evangelizing task.' This led to a long-term study on 'The Word of God and the Living Faiths of Men,' endorsed by both the Central Committee of the WCC in 1956 and the Ghana Assembly of the IMC [International Missionary Council] in 1958. A meeting in Nagpur, India in 1961 evaluated the work done in a number of consultations, and indicated points of agreement and those requiring further discussion. These included the realization that religions are living faiths; an awareness of human solidarity in common humanity; the need for a re-evaluation of the relationship of the gospel to other religions; and the need for a fresh approach to the task of Christian witness. The New Delhi Assembly of the WCC in 1961 voted to continue the study, 'The Word of God and the Living Faiths of Men,' through work at local study centers. It also encouraged dialogue in order to witness effectively. ...

"The Mexico City statement [1963] affirmed that dialogue is a serious endeavor. Through dialogue Christians seek to be open to hearing the other partner, yet without denying the finality of the Christian revelation since both partners are open to the dialogue of God with humanity" (Rodger C. Bassham, *Mission Theology: 1948-1975 Years of Worldwide Creative Tension Ecumenical, Evangelical, and Roman Catholic* (Pasadena: William Carey Library, 1979), 84-85).

Greek συμβάλλω (Acts 17:18, meaning to converse, confer; consider, ponder) or perhaps the Greek word διαλογίζομαι [see below under "Words NOT Used for Evangelizing"]; "dialogue" was then used in a missiological sense in 1964 by Rome[657] and then in 1974 by Evangelicals in the Lausanne Covenant.[658]

a) "And according to Paul's custom, he went to them, and for three Sabbaths **reasoned** with them from the Scriptures," Acts 17:2
b) "So he was **reasoning** in the synagogue with the Jews and the God-fearing *Gentiles*, and in the market place every day with those who happened to be present," Acts 17:17
c) "And he was **reasoning** in the synagogue every Sabbath and trying to persuade Jews and Greeks," Acts 18:4
d) "And they came to Ephesus, and he left them there. Now he himself entered the synagogue and **reasoned** with the Jews," Acts 18:19
e) "**Reasoning** and persuading *them* about the kingdom of God, Acts 19:8
f) "He was **discussing** righteousness, self-control and the judgment to come," Acts 24:25

Consider also, for example, the context and use of διαλέγομαι in other NT contexts, which is quite different than the concept of "dialogue" as used in the Lausanne:
Mark 9:34 (NIV), "But they kept quiet because on the way **they had argued** about who was the greatest"
Heb 12:5, "and you have forgotten the exhortation which **is addressed** to you as sons, 'My son, do not regard lightly the discipline of the Lord, Nor faint when you are reproved by Him'"
Jude 1:9, "But Michael the archangel, when he disputed with the devil and **argued** about the body of Moses, did not dare pronounce against him a railing judgment, but said, 'The Lord rebuke you.'"

For a consideration of the NT weight of διαλέγομαι, there are two other terms available to Luke in writing:
(1) συμβάλλω, "converse," from Luke 14:31; Acts 4:15; 17:18; 18:27; 20:14
(2) ὁμιλέω [from which derives the English "homiletics"], "converse," from Luke 24:14, 15; Acts 20:11, 24:26

In consideration of Paul's ill consideration of the thoughts of man in 1 Corinthians 1-3:
Psa 94:11, "The LORD knows the thoughts of man, That they are a *mere* breath ["vain" or "futile"]."
Isa 55:8-9, "For My thoughts are not your thoughts, Neither are your ways My ways," declares the LORD. "For *as* the heavens are higher than the earth, So are My ways higher than your ways, And My thoughts than your thoughts."

---

[657]Part III, the final portion of the 1964 encyclical *Ecclesiam Suam* of Paul VI is titled, "The Dialogue," comprising of sections 58-118. In this portion Paul VI explained: "we think it [mission] can be described as consisting of a series of concentric circles around the central point in which God has placed us" (Paul VI, *Ecclesiam Suam: On the Ways in Which the Church Must Carry Out Its Mission in the Contemporary World* [6 August 1964], §96; available at: http://www.ewtn.com/library/ENCYC/P6ECCLES.HTM; accessed 15 June 2001; Internet). Paul VI then explained three circles for their mission of dialogue: (1) "All things human" (ibid., §97); (2) Monotheists, e.g. Jews and Muslims (ibid., §107-08); (3) "...the circle of Christianity. In this field the dialogue, which has come to be called ecumenical, has already begun, and in some areas is making real headway. There is much to be said on this complex and delicate subject, but our discourse does not end here. ... But we must add that it is not in our power to compromise with the integrity of the faith [distinctive Catholic doctrine] or the requirements of charity [including use of the sacraments and antagonism to schism]" (Ibid., §109). This encyclical was published just four months prior to what is often considered Vatican II's most important decree, *Lumen Gentium* (21 November 1964), in which the order of these concentric circles is reversed, similarly to the 1994 *Catechism of the Catholic Church*, under the portion, "Who Belongs to the Church" (§836-845).

[658]From the 1974 Lausanne Covenant: "Our Christian presence in the world is indispensable to evangelism, and so is that kind of dialogue whose purpose is to listen sensitively in order to understand. But evangelism itself is the proclamation of the historical, biblical Christ as Saviour and Lord, with a view to persuading people to come to him personally and so be reconciled to God" (John R. W. Stott, *Making Christ Known: Historic Mission Documents from the Lausanne Movement* [Grand Rapids: Eerdmans, 1996], 20).

28) ὁμολογέω, confess; admit, declare, say plainly; promise (24 NT uses):

Introduction: The word, ὁμολογέω, has been made into a complex term, with quite a number of historico-theologico-ecclesial variations of interpretation, for example:

(1) Is it reactive, as in [sheepishly] confessing in response to the question of another person, e.g. acknowledging Christ as Savior when asked?

(2) Is it sacramental, such as going to a confessional booth to make a confession before a priest, thereby "acknowledging" some particular sin to receive penance and absolution?

(3) Is it liturgical, such as reciting a certain confession about some philosophical aspects of Trinitarian theology or Christology:

    E.g. "Let us [all] now confess our faith"—Then, everyone in the given church building recites or reads the Apostles Creed, Nicene Creed, Creed of Chalcedon, or Creed of Athanasius?

(4) Is it conversionistic, such as verbally and publicly declaring a one's faith in Christ's atoning death in order to be saved (a one times experience)?

    Consider, for example:
        If one is to hold to a particular redemption, and yet practice a generalized Infant Baptizing method of salvation (everyone who is born in a given country is Infant Baptized into the State-Church of that country);
        Is not one means of affirming true election the outward profession of Christ (Matt 10:32-33) which then becomes the seal on those who were genuinely saved at their Baptism—as understood within their system?

(5) Is it baptistic, such as confessing Christ by being water baptized following one's conversion, following the order of the verbs in Matt 28:19 and Mark 16:16?

(6) Is it proactive (declarative), such as in taking the initiative to evangelize Christ before men as often as possible?

(7) Is it a combination of some of the above?

Interestingly, God has allowed that the NT provides ample examples to assist in its proper translation and application. For example, please note that the *Louw-Nida Lexicon* includes three entries for the verb ὁμολογέω:
    33.221, to make an emphatic declaration,[659]
    33.274, to express open allegiance,[660] and
    33.275, to acknowledge a fact publicly.[661]

---

[659]"33.221 ὁμολογέω: to make an emphatic declaration, often public, and at times in response to pressure or an accusation - 'to declare, to assert.' τότε ὁμολογήσω αὐτοῖς ὅτι Οὐδέποτε ἔγνων ὑμᾶς 'then I will declare to them, I never knew you' Mt 7.23; τῆς ἐπαγγελίας ἧς ὡμολόγησεν ὁ θεὸς τῷ 'Αβραάμ 'the promise which God had declared to Abraham' Ac 7.17" (ibid.).

[660]"33.274 ὁμολογέω; ὁμολογία, ας f; ἐξομολογέομαι: to express openly one's allegiance to a proposition or person - 'to profess, to confess, confession.' ὁμολογέω: ὅστις ὁμολογήσει ἐν ἐμοὶ ἔμπροσθεν τῶν ἀνθρώπων, ὁμολογήσω κἀγὼ ἐν αὐτῷ ἔμπροσθεν τοῦ πατρός μου 'whoever confesses me before people, I will confess him before my Father' Mt 10.32. ὁμολογία: κατέχωμεν τὴν ὁμολογίαν τῆς ἐλπίδος 'let us hold on to the hope we profess' He 10.23. ἐξομολογέομαι: διὰ τοῦτο ἐξομολογήσομαί σοι ἐν ἔθνεσιν 'therefore I will confess you before the Gentiles' Ro 15.9. For another interpretation of ἐξομολογέομαι in Ro 15.9, see 33.359.

"It is often extremely difficult, if not impossible, to translate ὁμολογέω, ὁμολογία, and ἐξομολογέομαι by the usual expression for 'confess,' since this would usually imply that one has done something wrong. It is normally necessary, therefore, to employ quite a different type of relationship, usually involving a public utterance and an expression of confidence or allegiance. For example, in Mt 10.32 it may be necessary to translate 'whoever tells people publicly that he is loyal to me, I will tell my Father that I am loyal to that person.' Similarly, in He 10.23 one may translate 'let us hold on to the hope in which we have told people we have such confidence.' Likewise, in Ro 15.9 one may translate 'therefore I will tell the Gentiles how I have put my confidence in you'" (*Louw-Nida Lexicon*, BibleWorks 7.0)

[661]"33.275 ὁμολογέω; ἐξομολογέομαι: to acknowledge a fact publicly, often in reference to previous bad behavior - 'to admit, to confess.' ὁμολογέω: ἐὰν ὁμολογῶμεν τὰς ἁμαρτίας ἡμῶν 'if we confess our sins' 1 Jn 1.9. ἐξομολογέομαι: ἐξομολογούμενοι τὰς ἁμαρτίας αὐτῶν 'they confessed their sins' Mt 3.6. In translating Mt 3.6 in some

Interestingly, two of these three definitions coincide with the Hebrew *shaba'*, to swear, to swear an oath, to swear allegiance to:

Deut 6:13, "You shall fear *only* the LORD your God; and you shall worship Him, and swear by [or: 'swear allegiance to'] His name"

Deut 10:10, "You shall fear the LORD your God; you shall serve Him and cling to Him, and you shall swear by [or: 'swear allegiance to'] His name"

Likewise interesting, is that ὁμολογέω relates directly, in some contexts, to evangelizing (as is noted below). Nuances in the ecclesiastical-theological-liturgical grid of a translator (as noted above), however, can be and are often injected into the translation of this important word.

It would seem that Jerome's translation of ὁμολογέω using the verb "confiteor"[662] (by the way the sacramental application of this term makes for interesting study)[663] has been transliterated into the English as "confess," which in English is used primarily in the sense of "admitting" or making a "profession" within a church. In this sense, note Webster's English definition for "confess "is somewhat tangential to NT usage of this term.[664]

New Testament use of the verb ὁμολογέω, however, seems to be much more public and initiative than is currently communicated by the English verb "confess," which has a passive feel to it:

See for example (by way of introduction):

Matt 7:23, "And then I [Jesus] will declare [ὁμολογέω] to them, "I never knew you; depart from Me, you who practice lawlessness'"

Matt 14:7, "Thereupon he [Herod] promised [ὁμολογέω] with an oath to give her [the daughter of Herodias] whatever she asked"

John 1:20, "And he [John the Baptist] confessed [ὁμολογέω], and did not deny, and he confessed [ὁμολογέω], 'I am not the Christ.'"

John 9:22, "His parents said this because they were afraid of the Jews; for the Jews had already agreed, that if anyone should confess [ὁμολογέω] Him to be Christ, he should be put out of the synagogue."

John 12:42-43, "Nevertheless many even of the rulers believed in Him, but because of the Pharisees they were not confessing [ὁμολογέω] *Him*, lest they should be put out of the synagogue; for they loved the approval of men rather than the approval of God"

---

languages, it may be useful to restructure the expression somewhat, for example, 'they admitted to people that they had sinned' or 'they admitted publicly to God ...'

"In Php 2.11 the statement πᾶσα γλῶσσα ἐξομολογήσηται ὅτι κύριος Ἰησοῦς Χριστός ('that everyone may confess that Jesus Christ is Lord') means simply to acknowledge a fact publicly, and in this instance there is no implication of previous bad behavior" (ibid.).

[662]"**Cōnfiteor** fessus, ērī, dep. com- + fateor, to acknowledge, confess, own, avow, concede, allow, grant: *confitere*, T.: *confitentem audire alqm: non infitiando confiteri videbantur: Confessas manūs tendens*, in surrender, O.: *scelus: amorem nutrici*, O.: *se victos*, Cs.: *se*, reveal, O.: *deam*, V.: *se hostem: hoc de statuis: hoc confiteor iure Mi obtigisse*, T.: *sese plurimum ei debere*, Cs.: *largitionem factam esse: O cui debere salutem confiteor*, O. — Fig., to reveal, manifest, show: *confessa voltibus iram*, O" (Charlton T. Lewis, *An Elementary Latin Dictionary* [1890]).

[663]The following may show how Jerome translated the Greek verb ὁμολογέω into Latin, assuming that the Greek text that he translated from was similar to the text that is available to us today (Byzantine or Nestle-Aland):

(1) As a verbal phrase with the adjective *confessus* (1a) "make [a] confession" (*confessus fuerit*), Luke 12:8; Rom 10:10; 1 John 4:15 (1b) "do confession" (*confessus est*), John 1:20 (twice); (1c) "confessed a good confession" (*confessus bonam confessionem*), 1 Tim 6:12;

(2) As the verb "confess" (*confiteor*), Matt 7:23; 10:32 (twice); John 9:22; 12:42; Acts 23:8; 24:14; Rom 10:9; Tit 1:16; Heb 11:13; 13:15; 1 John 1:9; 4:2; 2 John 7; Rev 3:5;

(3) As the verb *solvo* meaning, "loosen, unbind, unfasten, unfetter, untie, release," 1 John 4:3 (the "New" Vulgate [by order of Paul VI, and authorized by John Paul II] solved the problem with this translation by using the standard *confiteor*).

[664]"Confess: (1) to tell or make known (as something wrong or damaging to oneself): ADMIT; (2a) to acknowledge (sin) to God or to a priest; (2b) to receive the confession of (a penitent); (3) to declare faith in or adherence to: PROFESS; (4) to give evidence of ~ (1): (4a) to disclose one's faults; specifically: to unburden one's sins or the state of one's conscience to God or to a priest; (4b) to hear a confession; (2) ADMIT" (*Webster's New Collegiate Dictionary* [Springfield, MA: Merriam, 1977]).

Acts 23:8, "For the Sadducees say that there is no resurrection, nor an angel, nor a spirit; but the Pharisees acknowledge [ὁμολογέω] them all"

Acts 24:14 (Paul to Felix), "But this I admit [ὁμολογέω] to you, that according to the Way which they call a sect I do serve the God of our fathers, believing everything that is in accordance with the Law, and that is written in the Prophets"

Rom 10:9, "that if you confess [ὁμολογέω] with your mouth Jesus *as* Lord, and believe in your heart that God raised Him from the dead, you shall be saved;

[Note how one little change in this verse changes, adding "*as*" emphasizes the element of making a creedal "confessional," rather than an evangelistic profession, e.g. note the KJV on this verse "That if thou shalt confess with thy mouth the Lord Jesus"][665]

Rom 10:10, "for with the heart man believes, resulting in righteousness, and with the mouth he confesses [ὁμολογέω], resulting in salvation."

1 Tim 6:12, "Fight the good fight of faith; take hold of the eternal life to which you were called, and you made the good confession [καὶ ὡμολόγησας τὴν καλὴν ὁμολογίαν] in the presence of many witnesses."

[Here Paul congratulates and encourages Timothy who "confessed a good confession"; note the KJV on this phrase, "and hast professed a good profession before many witnesses"]

Titus 1:16, "They profess [ὁμολογέω] to know God, but by *their* deeds they deny *Him*, being detestable and disobedient, and worthless for any good deed"

Heb 11:13, "All these died in faith, without receiving the promises, …, and having confessed [ὁμολογέω] that they were strangers and exiles on the earth"

Heb 13:15 (CSB), "Therefore, through Him let us continually offer up to God a sacrifice of praise, that is, the fruit of our lips that confess His name"

1 John 1:9, "If we confess [ὁμολογέω] our sins, He is faithful and righteous to forgive us our sins and to cleanse us from all unrighteousness"

[Did not the Samaritan woman openly confess her sin to the townspeople, this being her witness to Christ which led to a revival in the town of Sychar, John 4:39-42?]

1 John 4:2, "By this you know the Spirit of God: every spirit that confesses [ὁμολογέω] that Jesus Christ has come in the flesh is from God"

1 John 4:3, "and every spirit that does not confess [ὁμολογέω] Jesus is not from God…"

1 John 4:15, "Whoever confesses [ὁμολογέω] that Jesus is the Son of God, God abides in him, and he in God"

2 John 7, "For many deceivers have gone out into the world, those who do not acknowledge Jesus Christ *as* coming in the flesh. This is the deceiver and the antichrist"

[Isn't it interesting that Mormons and Jehovah's Witnesses do not confess their sins or their sinfulness in their witness (1 John 1:8-10)? Neither do they confess Christ and the need for the blood atonement]

Rev 3:5, "…and I will confess his name before My Father, and before His angels"

[a parallel to the words of Jesus in Mark 8:38]

It would seem, therefore, that the word "confess" in English is about the least intentional and active translation of the word ὁμολογέω, as compared with "declare," "profess," and even "acknowledge."

a) "Everyone therefore who **shall confess** Me before men," Matt 10:32

Notice that it is before others, and before others plural ("men"), in the context of persecution because of the name of Jesus:

Matt 10:22-23, "And you will be hated by all on account of My name, but it is the one who has endured to the end who will be saved. But whenever they persecute you in this city, flee to the next…"

Notice also that our confession of God, listed first, mirrors Christ's confession of us in Matt 10 and Luke 12, as well as inversely in Mark 8

How about translating with the word "profess" just like the translation of this word (ὁμολογέω) in Titus 1:16? "Therefore everyone who professes Me before men, I will also profess him before My Father who is in heaven."

---

[665]Chapter 21, "A. Commitment Is at the Heart," includes a chart on various translations of Rom 10:9.

Notice also the gloss of the evangelistic Anabaptist Martyr, Balthasar Hubmaier, which explains his interpretation of this verse: "If anyone confessed Christ before men, not fearing them, though they rage as lions, Christ will confess him, in the presence of the Father, (Matt. 10 Mark 8)"[666]

Note, in reference to Hubmaier's Mark 8, Jesus in the instance of Mark 8 only mentions the negative, using the verb "being ashamed" rather than deny: Mark 8:38, "For whoever is ashamed of Me and My words in this adulterous and sinful generation, the Son of Man will also be ashamed of him when He comes in the glory of His Father with the holy angels" (cf. Luke 9:26)

b) "Everyone who **confesses** Me before men," Luke 12:8
c) "If any man should **confess** Him to be Christ," John 9:22
d) "Nevertheless many even of the rulers believed in Him, but because of the Pharisees they were **not confessing** *Him*, lest they should be put out of the synagogue," John 12:42
e) "But this I admit [confess] to you," Acts 24:14
f) "Whoever confesses that Jesus is the Son of God, God abides in him, and he in God," 1 John 4:15

Translations of ὁμολογέω in 1 John 4:15

NIV (1984); NJB*; NAB*	Young's (1885)	English Geneva (1560); Bishop's; RSV; NAS; NKJ; NET; ESV	KJV (1611); ERV; ASV;	Norton (1881) [from Syriac]	BBE (Cambridge, 1949/1964); CEV*	GWN (1995); GNT*	Nouvelle édition Genève (1975)*
Acknowledges	May Confess	Confesseth	Shall Confess	Profess	Says openly	Who declare	Will publicly declare
"If anyone acknowledges that Jesus is the Son of God, God lives in him and he in God"	"whoever may confess that Jesus is the Son of God, God in him doth remain, and he in God"	"Whosoeuer confesseth that Iesus is the Sonne of God, in him dwelleth God, and he in God"	"Whosoeuer shall confesse that Iesus is the Sonne of God, God dwelleth in him, and he in God"	"Whoever professes that Jesus is the Son of God, God is continuing in him, and he is continuing in God"	"Everyone who says openly that Jesus is the Son of God, has God in him and is in God"	"God lives in those who declare that Jesus is the Son of God, and they live in God"	"He who will publicly declare that Jesus is the Son of God, God dwells in him, and he in God"

*My translation of "Celui qui déclarera publiquement que Jésus est le Fils de Dieu, Dieu demeure en lui, et lui en Dieu"

[666]Balthasar Hubmaier, "Conclusions of Balthasar Friedberg, Pastor at Waldshut and a Spiritual Brother of Ulrich Zwingli. They are Addressed to John Eck at Ingolstadt, But He Forbade Them to Be Examined," from "The Writings of Balthasar Hubmaier," collected and photographed by W. O. Lewis, translated by G. D. Davidson (Liberty, MO: Archives, William Jewell College Library), 1:38.

g)   "The fruit of lips **confessing** of His name," Heb 13:15 (trans. mine)

Translations of ὁμολογέω in Hebrews 13:15

Greek Byzantine	Latin Vulgate*	Wycliffe 2nd (1388)	ABS' CEV* (1991)	KJV (1611/ 1769); cf. NASB; NKJ	ABS' GNT* (1993)	ASV (1901)	Bible in Basic English (1949/ 1964)	RSV (1952); cf. ESV; NET	NET	NLT (2004)	Eng. Geneva (1560); cf. NIV	CSB (2003)
ὁμολο-γέω	confiteor*	[ac]know-ledge	**	give thanks	Confess	make confes-sion	give witness	acknow-ledge	acknow-ledging	proclaim allegiance to	confesse	that confess
τοῦτ' ἔστιν, καρπὸν χειλέων ὁμολογ-ούντων τῷ ὀνόματι αὐτοῦ.	id est fructum labiorum confiten-tium nomini eius	that is to seye, the fruyt of lippis knoulech-inge to his name	in the name of Jesus	that is, the fruit of *our* lips giving thanks to his name	which is the offering presented by lips that confess him as Lord	that is, the fruit of lips which make confes-sion to his name	that is to say, the fruit of lips giving witness to his name	that is, the fruit of lips that acknow-ledge his name	the fruit of our lips, acknow-ledging his name	Proclaim-ing our allegiance to his name	that is, the frute of the lippes, which confesse his Name	the fruit of our lips that confess His name
			Least evangel-istic (verb ὁμολογέω removed)		Change as liturgy: "His name" to "as Lord"	Perhaps passive evangel-istic						Most evangel-istic

*[from Charlton T. Lewis, *An Elementary Latin Dictionary* (1890)] cōnfiteor: fessus, ērī, dep. com- + fateor, to acknowledge, confess, own, avow, concede, allow, grant.

**This entire verse in the CEV is abbreviated to, "Our sacrifice is to keep offering praise to God in the name of Jesus."

29) ἐξομολογέω (146 total uses; 10 in NT), meaning confess, profess; give praise, to thank (Matt 11:25; Luke 10:21—herein God is the audience!):

Acts 19:18, "Many also of those who had believed kept coming, **confessing** [openly] and disclosing their practices"

Rom 14:11, "For it is written: '*As* I live, says the LORD, Every knee shall bow to Me, And every tongue **shall confess** to God.'"

Or: "every tongue **shall openly confess** God"

Rom 15:9, "and for the Gentiles to glorify God for His mercy; as it is written, 'Therefore **I will give praise** to Thee among the Gentiles, And I will sing to Thy name.'"

Or: "Therefore I will **openly confess** you among the Gentiles"

Phil 2:11, "and that every tongue **should confess** that Jesus Christ is Lord, to the glory of God the Father."

Or: "that every tongue **should openly confess** the Lord Jesus Christ"

Open confession often accompanies genuine revival, Acts 19:18 (cf. John 4:39)!

Mark 1:5, "And all the country of Judea was going out to him, and all the people of Jerusalem; and they were being baptized by him in the Jordan River, **confessing** their sins."

Consider also confession within the context of genuine discipleship in the context of Christian fellowship:

Jam 5:16, "Therefore, **confess** [ἐξομολογεῖσθε] your sins to one another, and pray for one another, so that you may be healed. The effective prayer of a righteous man can accomplish much."

Of Judas:

Luke 22:6, "And he **consented**, and *began* seeking a good opportunity to betray Him to them apart from the multitude."

Compare with the use of ἐξομολογέω in Psa 6:5 and 30:12 (among the 136 OT LXX uses):

NAS: Psa 6:5, "For there is no mention of Thee in death; In Sheol who will **give** Thee **thanks**?"

BYZ: Psa 6:6, ὅτι οὐκ ἔστιν ἐν τῷ θανάτῳ ὁ μνημονεύων σου· ἐν δὲ τῷ ᾅδῃ τίς ἐξομολογήσεταί σοι;

NAS: Psa 30:12, "That *my* soul may sing praise to Thee, and not be silent. O LORD my God, I will give thanks to Thee forever.

BYZ: Psa 29:13, ὅπως ἂν ψάλῃ σοι ἡ δόξα μου καὶ οὐ μὴ κατανυγῶ. κύριε ὁ θεός μου, εἰς τὸν αἰῶνα ἐξομολογήσομαί σοι.

n5) ὁ ὁμολογία, "let us hold fast [κατέχω] the **confession** of our hope," Heb 10:23

n6) ὁ λόγος (as plural a noun) – 2 Tim 4:15, "Be on guard against him yourself, for he vigorously opposed **our teaching** [τοῖς ἡμετέροις λόγοις]"

g. ἀκούω and cognates:

30) ἀκούω (1495 OT LXX uses; 435 total NT uses; likely 160 are evangelistic) – hear, listen to; give a hearing; listen, pay attention to; call to listen; cause to hear:

Some OT examples: Isa 6:10; 42:18; 55:2; 66:19

NT examples:
John 10:27, "My sheep **hear** My voice, and I know them, and they follow Me"
"He who hears, hear": Matt 11:15 (2x); 13:9 (2x), 43 (2x); Mark 4:9 (2x), 23 (2x); 7:16 (2x); Luke 8:8 (2x); 14:35 (2x)
"He who has an ear, hear": Rev 2:7, 11, 17, 29; 3:6, 13, 22; 13:9
Luke 10:16 (2x), "The one who **listens** to you **listens** to Me, and the one who rejects you rejects Me; and he who rejects Me rejects the One who sent Me."
Acts 16:14, "And a certain woman named Lydia, from the city of Thyatira, a seller of purple fabrics, a worshiper of God, **was listening**; and the Lord opened her heart to respond to the things spoken by Paul."
Rom 10:14, "How then shall they call upon Him in whom they have not believed? And how shall they believe in Him whom **they have** not **heard**? And how **shall they hear** without a preacher?"
Rom 15:21, "but as it is written, 'They who had no news of Him shall see, And they who have not heard shall understand.'" Citing Isa 52:15.
2 Tim 2:2, "And the things which you have heard from me in the presence of many witnesses, these entrust to faithful men, who will be able to teach others also."
Heb 4:2, "For indeed we have had good news preached to us, just as they also; but the word **they heard** did not profit them, because it was not united by faith in those who heard.".

List of NT evangelistic uses:
Matt 7:24, 26; 10:14; 11:5; 13:13-23 (14x); 15:10
Mark 4:12-20 (6x); 33
Luke 4:10-18 (6x), 28; 5:1; 6:47, 49; 7:22 (2x); 15:1; 16:29, 31
John 1:37, 40; 4:42; 5:24, 25 (2x), 28; 6:45, 60; 8:9, 47 (2x); 10:3, 8, 16, 20, 27; 12:47; 18:37
Acts 2:11, 22, 37; 3:22, 23; 4:4; 5:33; 7:54; 8:6; 10:22, 33, 44; 13:7, 16, 44, 48; 14:9; 15:7; 16:14; 17:32 (2x); 18:8; 19:5, 10; 22:1, 2, 7, 14, 15, 22; 24:24; 25:22; 26:3, 14, 29; 28:22, 26, 27 (2x), 28:28
Rom 10:14 (2x); 11:8; 15:21
Eph 1:13; 4:21, 29
Col 1:6, 23
1 Tim 4:16; 2 Tim 1:13; 2:2; 4:17
Heb 2:1, 3; 3:7, 15, 16; 4:2, 7
1 John 1:1, 3, 5; 2:7, 24 (2x); 3:11; 4:6; 2 John 6
Rev 1:3; 3:3, 20; 22:17, 18

n7) ἡ ἀκοή (24 total NT uses; 16 uses) – hearing, report, news:
Matt 4:24, "And the **news** about Him went out into all Syria."
Matt 13:14, "And in their case the prophecy of Isaiah is being fulfilled, which says, 'You will keep on hearing [**hearing** you will hear] but will not understand; And you will keep on seeing, but will not perceive,'"
Matt 14:1, "At that time Herod the tetrarch heard the **news** about Jesus."
Mark 1:28, "And immediately the **news** about Him went out everywhere into all the surrounding district of Galilee."
Luke 7:1, "When He had completed all His discourse in the **hearing** of the people, He went to Capernaum."
John 12:38, "that the word of Isaiah the prophet might be fulfilled, which he spoke, 'LORD, who has believed our **report**? And to whom has the arm of the Lord been revealed?'"
Acts 17:20, "For you are bringing some strange things to our **ears**; we want to know therefore what these things mean."

Acts 28:26, "saying, 'Go to this people and say, "You will keep on hearing [**hearing** you will hear], but will not understand; And you will keep on seeing, but will not perceive.""'"

Rom 10:16, "However, they did not all heed the glad tidings; for Isaiah says, 'LORD, who has believed our **report**?'"

Rom 10:17, "So faith *comes* from **hearing**, and **hearing** by the word of Christ."

Gal 3:2, "This is the only thing I want to find out from you: did you receive the Spirit by the works of the Law, or by **hearing** with faith?"

Gal 3:5, "Does He then, who provides you with the Spirit and works miracles among you, do it by the works of the Law, or by **hearing** with faith?"

1 Thess 2:13, "And for this reason we also constantly thank God that when you received from us the word of God's **message**, you accepted *it* not *as* the word of men, but *for* what it really is, the word of God, which also performs its work in you who believe."

Heb 4:2, "For indeed we have had good news preached to us, just as they also; but the word they **heard** did not profit them, because it was not united by faith in those who heard."

Heb 5:11, "Concerning him we have much to say, and *it is* hard to explain, since you have become dull of **hearing**."

31) εἰσακούω (5 total NT uses) – to listen, to hear:
　　1 Cor 14:21, "In the Law it is written, 'By men of strange tongues and by the lips of strangers I will speak to this people, and even so they will not **listen** to Me,' says the Lord."

32) προακούω (1 NT use) – to hear beforehand:
　　Col 1:5, "because of the hope laid up for you in heaven, of which you **previously heard** in the word of truth, the gospel,"

33) ἀκουτίζω (8 uses in LXX; None in NT) – to cause to hear:
　　Psa 66:8, "Bless our God, O peoples, And **sound** His praise **abroad**"
　　Psalm 76:8, "Thou didst **cause** judgment **to be heard** from heaven; The earth feared, and was still"

　　See also:
　　　　SSol 2:14, "O my dove, in the clefts of the rock, In the secret place of the steep pathway, Let me see your form, **Let me hear** your voice; For your voice is sweet, And your form is lovely."
　　　　SSol 8:13, "O you who sit in the gardens, *My* companions are listening for your voice—**Let me hear** it!"

h.　φθέγγομαι and cognates:

34) φθέγγομαι – speak (with the lips)—3 total NT uses:
　　a)　Acts 4:18, "They commanded them not to **speak** or teach at all in the name of Jesus"
　　b)　Psa 78:2, "I will **utter** dark sayings of old"
　　c)　Compare with use of μελετάω in Psa 35:28 ("speak"); 71:24 ("talk"):
　　　　Friberg: **17690 17690 μελετάω** 1aor. ἐμελέτησα; *give careful thought to, meditate on, think about* (1T 4.15); in a negative sense *plot, conspire, premeditate* (AC 4.25)

35) ἀποφθέγγομαι – speak out, declare—3 total NT uses:
　　a)　Acts 2:4, "And they were all filled with the Holy Spirit and began to speak with other tongues, as the Spirit was **giving** them **utterance**."
　　b)　Acts 2:14, "But Peter, taking his stand with the eleven, raised his voice and **declared** to them…"
　　c)　Acts 26:25, "But Paul said, 'I am not out of my mind, most excellent Festus, but **I utter** words of sober truth.'"

　　d)　Consider also that the cognate noun of this verb has a significant usage in the LXX's version of the Song of Moses:
　　　　Deut 32:2, "Let my teaching [τὸ ἀπόφθεγμά μου] drop as the rain, My speech distill as the dew, As the droplets on the fresh grass And as the showers on the herb."

i.　(36) φημί – say, mean, imply (introducing direct discourse; introducing quotations; introducing interpretations):
1)　And he [Stephen] said (ἔφη) [before the Council]," Acts 7:2
2)　And he said to them (ἔφη), Acts 10:28
3)　And Paul stood in the midst of the Areopagus and said (ἔφη), Acts 17:22
4)　they became even more quiet; and he said (φησίν), Acts 22:2

j.　Cognates of φωνέω:

37) ἀναφωνέω – cry out loudly, exclaim:
　　Luke 1:42, "And she cried out with a loud voice, and said, "Blessed among women *are* you, and blessed *is* the fruit of your womb!"

38) προσφωνέω (7 NT uses) – speak unto:

Luke 13:12, "And when Jesus saw her, He **called** her over and said to her, 'Woman, you are freed from your sickness.'"

Acts 21:40, "And when he had given him permission, Paul, standing on the stairs, motioned to the people with his hand; and when there was a great hush, **he spoke** to them in the Hebrew dialect, saying."

[textual variant on this verb in Acts 21:40: NA27 has it in the aorist, BYZ has it in the imperfect]

Acts 22:2, "And when they heard that **he was addressing** them in the Hebrew dialect, they became even more quiet; and he said."

k. Cognates of παρρησιάζομαι:

39) παρρησιάζομαι to speak boldly (9 NT uses):

a) Without an additional verb:
(1) How at Damascus he had **spoken out boldly** in the name of Jesus, Acts 9:27
(2) **Speaking out boldly** in the name of the Lord, Acts 9:28

On the translation of παρρησιαζόω in Acts 9:27

Byzantine Textform (2004)	Vulgate, rev.⁑ (1969, 1975, 1983)	Wycliffe's 2nd Ed (1388)	Tyndale (1534)	Geneva (1560)	King James (1611, 1769)	James Murdock (1852)	Young's Literal (1862)	Douay-Rheims⁑ (1899)	Bible in Basic English (1949, 1964)	NIV (1984)
ἐπαρρη-σιάσατο	fiducialiter egerit	he dide tristili	he had done boldely	he had spoken boldely	he had preached boldly	he had discoursed openly	he was speaking boldly	he had dealt confidently	he had spoken out boldly	he had preached fearlessly
καὶ πῶς ἐν Δαμασκῷ ἐπαρρη-σιάσατο ἐν τῷ ὀνόματι τοῦ Ἰησοῦ.	et quomodo in Damasco fiducialiter egerit in nomine Iesu	and hou in Damask he dide tristili in the name of Jhesu.	and how he had done boldely at damas-co in the name of Iesu.	and how he had spoken boldely at Damascus in ye Name of Iesus.	and how he had preached boldly at Damascus in the name of Jesus.	and how, in Damascus, he had discoursed openly in the name of Jesus.	and how in Damascus he was speaking boldly in the name of Jesus.	and how in Damascus he had dealt confidently in the name of Jesus.	and how in Damascus he had spoken out boldly in the name of Jesus.	and how in Damascus he had preached fearlessly in the name of Jesus.

b) With the verb λαλέω:
(1) I speak to him also **with confidence**, Acts 26:26
(2) That in *proclaiming* it I may **speak boldly**, as I ought to speak [ἵνα ἐν αὐτῷ παρρησιάσωμαι ὡς δεῖ με λαλῆσαι], Eph 6:20

(3) But after we had already suffered and been mistreated in Philippi, as you know, **we had the boldness** in our God to speak to you the gospel of God amid much opposition [ἐπαρρησιασάμεθα ἐν τῷ θεῷ ἡμῶν λαλῆσαι], 1 Thess 2:2

On the translation of παρρησιαζόω in 1 Thess 2:2

Byzantine Textform (2004)	Vulgate, rev. (1969, 1975, 1983)	Wycliffe's 2nd Ed (1388)	Tyndale (1534)	Geneva (1560)	King James (1611, 1769)	James Murdock (1852)	English Revised (1885)	Douay-Rheims (1899)	New American Bible (1901, 1991)	American Standard Version (1901)
ἐπαρρησια-σάμεθα ἐν τῷ θεῷ ἡμῶν	fiduciam habuimus in Deo nostro	hadden trust in oure Lord	were we bolde in oure God	we were bolde in our God	we were bold in our God	with confidence in our God	we waxed bold in our God	we had confidence in our God	we drew courage through our God	we waxed bold in our God

Bible in Basic English (1949, 1964)	Revised Standard Version (1952)	New American Standard (1977)	New King James (1982)	New International Version (1984)	New Jerusalem (1985)	Good News for the World (1995)	New Living Translation (2004)	NET Bible (2004, 2005)	Holman Christian Standard (2004)	Johnston's Modified (2009)
by the help of God … without fear	we had courage in our God	we had the boldness in our God	we were bold in our God	but with the help of our God we dared	God gave us the courage	But our God gave us the courage	Yet our God gave us the courage	we had the courage in our God	we had the courage in our God	being embold-dened in our God

c) With the verb λέγω:
  (1) And Paul and Barnabas spoke out boldly and said [Παρρησασάμενοι δὲ ὁ Παῦλος καὶ ὁ Βαρνάβας εἶπον], "It was necessary that the word of God should be spoken to you first; since you repudiate it, and judge yourselves unworthy of eternal life, behold, we are turning to the Gentiles," Acts 13:46

d) With the verb διατρίβω:
  (1) Therefore they spent a long time *there* **speaking boldly** *with reliance* upon the Lord, Acts 14:3

e) With the verb ἄρχω:
  (1) And he began to **speak out boldly** in the synagogue, Acts 18:26

f) With the verb διαλέγομαι and πείθω:
  (1) And he entered the synagogue and continued **speaking out boldly** for three months, reasoning and persuading *them* about the kingdom of God, Acts 19:8

n8) ἡ παρρησία + with other verbs "speak openly [bold speech]":
  a) ἡ παρρησία + λαλέω (cf. Mark 8:32; John 16:25, 29):
    (1) Positive:
      (a) "He is **speaking publicly**," John 7:26
      (b) "I **have spoken openly** to the world," John 18:20
      (c) "Grant that Thy bond-servants may **speak** Thy word **with all confidence**," Acts 4:29
      (d) "And *began* **to speak** the word of God **with boldness**," Acts 4:31
    (2) Negative:
      (a) "Yet no one **was speaking openly** of Him for fear of the Jews," John 7:13
  b) ἡ παρρησία + ἀναγγέλλω: "but will **tell you plainly** of the Father," John 16:25
  c) ἡ παρρησία + γνωρίζω: "**To make known with boldness** the mystery of the Gospel," Eph 6:19
  d) ἡ παρρησία + κηρύσσω + διδάσκω: "preaching the kingdom of God, and teaching concerning the Lord Jesus Christ **with all openness**, unhindered," Acts 28:31
  e) ἡ παρρησία + χράω/χράομαι: "Having therefore such a hope, **we use great boldness in our** speech" (πολλῇ παρρησίᾳ χρώμεθα), 2 Cor 3:12
    Lit. "Having therefore such a hope, we freely use great boldness of speech."
  f) ἡ παρρησία + εἰμί: "when he himself seeks to be *known* publicly," John 7:4

40. τολμάω verb (16 total NT uses), meaning to dare, have courage, be brave; presume; be courageous; 1 use in an evangelistic context:

> Phil 1:14, "and that most of the brethren, trusting in the Lord because of my imprisonment, have far more **courage** to speak the word of God without fear."
> Phil 1:14 (NA27), καὶ τοὺς πλείονας τῶν ἀδελφῶν ἐν κυρίῳ πεποιθότας τοῖς δεσμοῖς μου περισσοτέρως τολμᾶν ἀφόβως τὸν λόγον λαλεῖν

Other uses are:

> The word is used of the scribes and Pharisees not "daring" to ask Jesus another question (Matt 22:46; Mark 12:34; Luke 20:40);
> Of unsaved persons not daring to join the early apostolic church, Acts 5:13;
> Of false teachers daring to revile things that they do not understand, 2 Pet 2:10;
> Of Michael the Archangel not reviling Satan, Jude 9;
> Of any man's lack of courage to die for someone righteous (Rom 5:7);
> It is also used of Joseph of Arimathea daring to request for the body of Jesus (Mark 15:43), of the disciples not daring to ask if it was Jesus after the resurrection (John 21:12), of Moses not daring to look at God (Acts 7:32);
> It is used by the Apostle Paul:
>> Of the audacity of taking a fellow believer to secular court (1 Cor 6:1);
>> Of Paul's courage to confront sinful attitudes in person (2 Cor 10:2);
>> Of his boldness in writing to the church members who were in Rome (Rom 15:15);
>> Of the audacity of boasting in someone else's work in the Lord (Rom 15:18);
>> Of the audacity of fellow Christian workers comparing themselves to others (2 Cor 10:12);
>> Of Paul when he was made to boast of his persecutions for the work of Christ (2 Cor 11:21).

Non-evangelistic cognate noun τολμητής used once:

> 2 Pet 2:10, "and especially those who indulge the flesh in *its* corrupt desires and despise authority. **Daring**, self-willed, they do not tremble when they revile angelic majesties."

Parallel cognate comparative adjective/adverb τολμηρός used once:

> Rom 15:15, "But I have written **very boldly** to you on some points, so as to remind you again, because of the grace that was given me from God."

41. ὀνομάζω (10 NT uses) + Χριστός (563 uses) [1]

Evangelistic use:

> Rom 15:20, "And thus I aspired to preach the gospel, not where Christ **was** *already* **named**, that I might not build upon another man's foundation."

Use as sign of commitment:

> 2 Tim 2:19, "'Nevertheless, the firm foundation of God stands, having this seal, "The Lord knows those who are His,' and, 'Let everyone **who names** the name of the Lord abstain from wickedness.'"

Figurative use:

> Eph 1:21, "far above all rule and authority and power and dominion, and every name **that is named**, not only in this age, but also in the one to come."
> Compare with Deut 6:13 10:20-21

Non-evangelistic uses:

> Acts 19:13, "But also some of the Jewish exorcists, who went from place to place, attempted **to name** over those who had the evil spirits the name of the Lord Jesus, saying, 'I adjure you by Jesus whom Paul preaches.'"

1. ἡ κοινωνία (Eng. koinonia) and cognate word groups:

(n9) ἡ κοινωνία:

> Philm 6 (NIV, 1984), ἡ κοινωνία τῆς πίστεώς σου, "sharing your faith":
>> (1) NIV (1984), "I pray that you may be active in sharing your faith, so that you will have a full understanding of every good thing we have in Christ."
>> (2) NIV (2011), "I pray that your partnership with us in the faith may be effective in deepening your understanding of every good thing we share for the sake of Christ."

Five Translations of ἡ κοινωνία τῆς πίστεώς σου ἐνεργὴς γένηται in Philemon 6

You may be active in sharing your faith	The sharing of your faith may become effective	The communication of thy faith may become effectual	Your participation in the faith may become effective	The fellowship of your faith may become effective
New International Version (1984)	**English Standard Version**	**King James Version**	**Holman Christian Standard**	**New American Standard Updated**

Phil 1:5, τῇ κοινωνίᾳ ὑμῶν εἰς τὸ εὐαγγέλιον; "in view of your participation in the gospel"

Heb 13:16, Τῆς δὲ εὐποιΐας καὶ κοινωνίας μὴ ἐπιλανθάνεσθε; (KJV) "But to do good and to communicate forget not"

Three Translations of ἡ κοινωνία Backtranslated from the Syriac in Heb 13:16

Byzantine Textform	James W. Etheridge (1849)	James Murdock (1851)	William Norton (1881)
Κοινωνίας	**Communicate**	**Communication**	**Giving of gifts to the poor**
Τῆς δὲ Εὐποιΐας καὶ Κοινωνίας μὴ Ἐπιλανθάνεσθε· τοιαύταις γὰρ θυσίαις εὐαρεστεῖται ὁ θεός.	And forget not compassion and communication to the poor: for with these sacrifices a man pleaseth Aloha	And forget not commiseration and communication with the poor; for with such sacrifices a man pleaseth God.	And forget not kindness and the giving of gifts to the poor; for by these slain offerings man pleases God
Text of translation	"a translation of the NT Peshitta that was very literal"	"from the Syriac Peshito Version"; said to be a revision and improvement of Etheridge	"A Translation of the Peshito-Syriac Text"
Denomination of Translators	Wesleyan-Methodist preacher (from 1824)	Ordained as a Congregational minister (1801)	unknown

Translating ἡ κοινωνία in Heb 13:16

Byzantine Textform	French Geneva (1669)*	KJV (1769); ERV; ASV	Young's (1862)	Darby (1884)	Douais-Rheims (1899)⸸	Tyndale (1534); English Geneva, Bishops	NAS (1977); NKJ; CSB	French Martin (1707)**	RSV (1952); NJB⸸; NET; ESV; NAB⸸	NIV (1984)	Bible in Basic English (1949)	NLT (2007)
	Communication					**or**						**Sharing?**
Κοινω-νίας	Communi-cation	Communi-cate	Fellowship	Communi-cating *of your substance*	Impart	Distribute	Share	Sharing of your goods	Share what you have	Share with others	Giving to others	Share with those in need
Τῆς δὲ Εὐποιΐας καὶ Κοινωνία ς μὴ Ἐπιλανθά νεσθε· τοιαύταις γὰρ θυσίαις εὐαρεστεῖ ται ὁ θεός.	Do not bring to forgetful-ness welldoing and communi-cation: for God finds pleasure in such sacrifices	But to do good and to communi-cate forget not: for with such sacrifices God is well pleased	and of doing good, and of fellowship, be not forgetful, for with such sacrifices God is well-pleased	But of doing good and communi-cating *of your substance* be not forgetful, for with such sacrifices God is well pleased	And do not forget to do good, and to impart; for by such sacrifices God's favour is obtained	To do good and to distribute forget not for with suche sacrifises god is pleased	And do not neglect doing good and sharing; for with such sacrifices God is pleased	Do not forget welldoing and the sharing of your goods; for God finds pleasure in such sacrifices	Do not neglect to do good and to share what you have, for such sacrifices are pleasing to God	And do not forget to do good and to share with others, for with such sacrifices God is pleased	But go on doing good and giving to others, because God is well-pleased with such offerings	And don't forget to do good and to share with those in need. These are the sacrifices that please God

*"Or ne mettez point en oubli la beneficence et la communication: car Dieu prend plaisir à de tels sacrifices."

**"Or n'oubliez pas la béneficence et de faire part de vos biens ; car Dieu prend plaisir à de tels sacrifices."

1 John 1:3, "What we have seen and heard we proclaim to you also, that you also may have **fellowship** with us; and indeed our fellowship is with the Father, and with His Son Jesus Christ."

(n10) ὁ συγκοινωνός:

> 1 Cor 9:23, πάντα δὲ ποιῶ διὰ τὸ εὐαγγέλιον ἵνα συγκοινωνὸς αὐτοῦ γένωμαι, "And I do all things for the sake of the gospel, that I may become a fellow partaker of it"
>
> Phil 1:7, συγκοινωνούς μου τῆς χάριτος; "participants with me of grace"

m. (42) ἐρεύγομαι – utter, proclaim: Matt 13:35, "so that what was spoken through the prophet might be fulfilled, saying, 'I will open My mouth in parables; I will **utter** things hidden since the foundation of the world'" (citing Psa 78:2; Hebrew *naba*; LXX uses φθέγξομαι)

n. (43) ὁρίζω (8 NT uses; 21 OT LXX), meaning III: declare, appoint, determine (hence to declare with a sense of formality):

> Rom 1:4, "who was **declared** the son of God with power"

See also:

> Heb 4:7 (NKJ), "again He **designates** a certain day, saying in David, 'Today,' after such a long time, as it has been said: 'Today, if you will hear His voice, Do not harden your hearts'"

5—TO ASK OR ANSWER A QUESTION

o. (44) ἐρωτάω – "to ask, request, entreat" [basically to ask a question]:[667]

> Matt 15:23, "But He did not answer [ἐρωτάω] her a word. And His disciples came to *Him* and kept asking Him, saying, 'Send her away, for she is shouting out after us.'"
>
> Matt 16:13, "Now when Jesus came into the district of Caesarea Philippi, He *began* asking [ἐρωτάω] His disciples, saying, 'Who do people say that the Son of Man is?'"

p. (45) ἀποκρίνομαι – "to answer" (248 NT uses):

> "Let your speech always be with grace, seasoned, *as it were*, with salt, so that you may know **how you should respond** [ἀποκρίνομαι] to each person" Col 4:6
>
> Ὁ λόγος ὑμῶν πάντοτε ἐν χάριτι, ἅλατι ἠρτυμένος, εἰδέναι πῶς δεῖ ὑμᾶς ἑνὶ ἑκάστῳ ἀποκρίνεσθαι [infinitive present middle or passive deponent]

1) There is an interesting use of this verb in the OT LXX in relationship to a confession to God:

> Deut 21:7-8, "and they shall answer [ἀποκρίνομαι] and say, 'Our hands did not shed this blood, nor did our eyes see *it*. Forgive Your people Israel whom You have redeemed, O Lord, and do not place the guilt of innocent blood in the midst of Your people Israel.' And the bloodguiltiness shall be forgiven them'"

2) This verb is often used in conversations, in response to a statement or a question:

> Matt 11:4, "And Jesus answered [ἀποκρίνομαι] and said to them, 'Go and report to John what you hear and see...'"
>
> Matt 12:38-39, "Then some of the scribes and Pharisees answered [ἀποκρίνομαι] Him, saying, 'Teacher, we want to see a sign from You.' But He answered [ἀποκρίνομαι] and said to them, 'An evil and adulterous generation craves for a sign; and *yet* no sign shall be given to it but the sign of Jonah the prophet...'"
>
> Matt 15:1-3, "Then some Pharisees and scribes came to Jesus from Jerusalem, saying, 'Why do Your disciples transgress the tradition of the elders? For they do not wash their hands when they eat bread.' And He answered [ἀποκρίνομαι] and said to them, 'And why do you yourselves transgress the commandment of God for the sake of your tradition?'"
>
> Matt 15:21-28, "And Jesus went away from there, and withdrew into the district of Tyre and Sidon. And behold, a Canaanite woman came out from that region, and *began* to cry out, saying, 'Have mercy on me, O Lord, Son of David; my daughter is cruelly demon-possessed.' But He did not answer [ἀποκρίνομαι] her a word. And His disciples came to *Him* and kept asking Him, saying, 'Send her away, for she is shouting out after us.' But He answered [ἀποκρίνομαι] and said, 'I was sent only to the lost sheep of the house of Israel.' But she came and *began* to bow down before Him, saying, 'Lord, help me!' And He answered [ἀποκρίνομαι] and said, 'It is not good to take the children's bread and throw it to the dogs. But she said, 'Yes, Lord; but even the dogs feed on the crumbs which fall from their masters' table.' Then Jesus answered and said to her, 'O woman, your faith is great; be it done for you as you wish.' And her daughter was healed at once."
>
> Matt 16:16, "And Simon Peter answered [ἀποκρίνομαι] and said, 'Thou art the Christ, the Son of the living God.' And Jesus answered [ἀποκρίνομαι] and said to him, 'Blessed are you, Simon

---

[667]Cf. Randy Newman, *Questioning Evangelism: Engaging People's Hearts the Way Jesus Did* (Grand Rapids: Kregel, 2004).

Barjona, because flesh and blood did not reveal *this* to you, but My Father who is in heaven…"
[see also parallels]

Acts 3:12, "But when Peter saw *this*, he replied [ἀποκρίνομαι] to the people, 'Men of Israel, why do you marvel at this, or why do you gaze at us, as if by our own power or piety we had made him walk? …'"

Acts 24:10, "And when the governor had nodded for him to speak, Paul responded [ἀποκρίνομαι]: 'Knowing that for many years you have been a judge to this nation, I cheerfully make my defense'"

6—TO TEACH OR EXPLAIN

o. (46) διδάσκω – "teach" (97 total uses in NT [Byzantine Textform]; cf. Matt 5:2):
1) And He was passing through from one city and village to another, **teaching**, and proceeding on His way to Jerusalem, Luke 13:22
2) And it came about on one of the days while He was **teaching** the people in the temple and preaching the gospel [evangelizing], Luke 20:1
3) They kept on insisting, saying, "He stirs up the people, **teaching** all over Judea…" Luke 23:5
4) Jesus went up into the temple, and *began to* **teach**, John 7:14
5) Jesus therefore cried out in the temple, **teaching** and saying, John 7:28
6) Jesus answered him, "I have spoken openly to the world; I always **taught** in synagogues, and in the temple, where all the Jews come together; and I spoke nothing in secret, Joh 18:20
7) **Teaching** the people and proclaiming [καταγγέλλω] the resurrection from the dead, Acts 4:2
8) They commanded them not to speak [φθέγγομαι] or **teach** at all in the name of Jesus, Acts 4:18
9) They entered into the temple about daybreak, and *began* to **teach**, Acts 5:21
10) "Behold, the men whom you put in prison are standing [ἵστημι] in the temple and **teaching** the people!" Acts 5:22
11) We gave you strict orders not to continue **teaching** in this name, and behold, you have filled Jerusalem with your **teaching**, Acts 5:28
12) And every day, in the temple and from house to house, they kept right on **teaching** and preaching [evangelizing] Jesus *as* the Christ, Acts 5:42
13) But Paul and Barnabas stayed in Antioch, **teaching** and preaching [evangelizing], with many others also, the word of the Lord, Acts 15:35
14) He was speaking [λαλέω] and **teaching** accurately the things concerning Jesus, Acts 18:25
15) Crying out, "Men of Israel, come to our aid! This is the man who **preaches** [διδάσκω] to all men everywhere against our people and the Law and this place, …" Acts 21:28
16) Preaching [κηρύσσω] the kingdom of God, and **teaching** concerning the Lord Jesus Christ, Acts 28:31
17) **Teaching** every man, Col 1:28
18) Notice this unusual negative use of teach [Gk. διδάσκω; Heb. *lamad*]:
"And **they shall not teach** everyone his fellow citizen, And everyone his brother, saying, 'Know the LORD,' For all shall know Me, From the least to the greatest of them," Heb 8:11 (quote of Jer 31:34)

Several interesting OT usages of διδάσκω:
2 Chron 17:7, "Then in the third year of his reign he sent his officials, Ben-hail, Obadiah, Zechariah, Nethanel, and Micaiah, to teach in the cities of Judah."
Itinerant teachers were the instrument God used in to bring revival under Jehoshaphat, King of Judah, 2 Chron 17:1ff.
Psa 51:13, "*Then* I will teach transgressors Thy ways, And sinners will be converted to Thee."
Evangelism is a natural outflow of receiving forgiveness, cf. Luke 7:47

Consider also the cognate noun διδαχή, discussed earlier in this chapter related to defining evangelism, and more fully in Chapter 17, "What Is the Gospel?"

p. γνωρίζω and cognate:

47) γνωρίζω:

a) "Know the Lord," Heb 8:11 (from quote of Jer 31:34)

Translations of "Know the Lord" in Heb 8:11

Byzantine Textform (2005)	Wycliffe (1388)	Tyndale (1534); Young's	Geneva (1560); Bishops; KJV; Darby; ERV; RSV; NAS; NKJ; NIV; NET; ESV	Bible in Basic English (Cambridge, 1949)	New Jerusalem Bible* (1985)	New living Translation (2004)
Γνῶθι τὸν κύριον	"Knowe thou the Lord"	"Knowe thou the Lorde"	"Knowe ye Lord"	"This is the knowledge of the Lord"	"Learn to know the Lord!"	"You should know the LORD"

b) Made known, Luke 2:15, 17; John 15:15, 17:26; Rom 16:26; Eph 1:9, 3:5, 10; 2 Pet 1:16 (Acts 2:28)

c) Make known, John 17:26; Rom 9:23; 1 Cor 15:1; Eph 6:19; Col 1:27

(1) ἐν παρρησίᾳ γνωρίσαι τὸ μυστήριον τοῦ εὐαγγελίου - Eph 6:19, "make known the mystery of the Gospel."

Who Makes Known [γνωρίζω] the Gospel?

God?	Jesus?	?	Man?	The Church?
"He made known [γνωρίσας] to us the mystery of His will, according to His kind intention which He purposed in Him" (Eph 1:9; cf. Rom 9:22, 23; Eph 3:3 [5]; Col 1:27)	"and I have made Thy name known [ἐγνώρισα] to them, and will make it known; that the love wherewith Thou didst love Me may be in them, and I in them" (John 17:26)	"but now is manifested, and by the Scriptures of the prophets, according to the commandment of the eternal God, has been made known [γνωρισθέντος] to all the nations, *leading* to obedience of faith" (Rom 16:26)	"Now I make known [γνωρίζω] to you, brethren, the gospel which I preached to you, which also you received, in which also you stand" (1 Cor 15:1; cf. 1 Cor 12:3; 2 Cor 8:2; Gal 1:11; Eph 6:19, 21; 2 Pet 1:16)	in order that the manifold wisdom of God might now be made known [γνωρισθῇ] through the church to the rulers and the authorities in the heavenly *places* (Eph 3:10)

48) διαγνωρίζω (1 NT use in Byzantine Text; No LXX uses; No Critical Edition NT uses; NA27 uses only γνωρίζω):

Meaning: "give an exact report": Luke 2:17, "And when they had seen this, they made known the statement which had been told them about this Child"

Friberg: "**6199 διαγνωρίζω** 1aor. **διεγνώρισα**; *give an exact report, tell accurately* (LU 2.17)"

Gingrich: "**1528 διαγνωρίζω** *give an exact report* Lk 2:17 v.l.* [pg 45]"

Thayer: "**1297 διαγνωρίζω** 1 aorist διεγνωρισα; *to publish abroad, make known thoroughly*: περί τίνος, Luke 2:17 R G. Besides, only in (Philo, quod det. pot. sec. 26, i. 210, 16, Mang. edition and) in Schol. in Bekker Anecd., p. 787, 15 to discriminate.*"

Verb related to the noun ἡ διάγνωσις (from which we get diagnosis), another *hapax*, found in Acts 25:21, a legal decision

Friberg: "**6201 διάγνωσις**, εως, ἡ strictly *act of discernment, determination*; as a legal technical term *judicial hearing, decision, judgment* (AC 25.21)"

Louw-Nida: 56.21 διαγινώσκω ; διάγνωσις, εως f: to make a judgment on legal matters, with the implication of thorough examination - 'to decide a case, to arrive at a verdict after examination.' διαγινώσκω: εἶπας, Ὅταν Λυσίας ὁ χιλίαρχος καταβῇ διαγνώσομαι τὰ καθ' ὑμᾶς 'I will decide your case, he told them, when the commander Lysias arrives' Ac 24.22. διάγνωσις: τοῦ δὲ Παύλου ἐπικαλεσαμένου τηρηθῆναι αὐτὸν εἰς τὴν τοῦ Σεβαστοῦ διάγνωσιν 'when Paul made his appeal to be held over for the Emperor to decide his case' Ac 25.21.

This verbal group is also related to ἡ πρόγνωσις (from which we get prognosis), used twice in NT (Acts 2:23; 1 Pet 1:2), meaning predetermination or foreknowledge.

49) γινώσκω (582 OT LXX uses, 222 NT uses):

    a)   Some uses in the Psalms—often in passive, in prayer, often God as evangelist:
        Psa 9:20, "Put them in fear, O LORD; **Let** the nations **know** that they are but men. Selah."
        Psa 46:10, "Cease *striving* and **know** that I am God; I will be exalted among the nations, I will be exalted in the earth."
        Psa 59:13, "Consume *them* in wrath, consume *them*, That they *may* not *be*; And **let them know** that God rules in Jacob To the ends of the earth. Selah."
        Psa 67:2, "That Your way **may be known** on earth, Your salvation among all nations."
        Psa 78:3, "Which we have heard and **known**, And our fathers have told us."
        Psa 78:6, "That the generation to come **might know**, *even* the children *yet* to be born, *That* they may arise and tell *them* to their children."
        Psa 83:18, "That **they may know** that Thou alone, whose name is the LORD, Art the Most High over all the earth."
        Psa 100:3, "**Know** that the LORD Himself is God; It is He who has made us, and not we ourselves; *We are* His people and the sheep of His pasture."
        Psa 109:27, "And **let them know** that this is Thy hand; Thou, LORD, hast done it."

    b)   Some uses in the Isaiah:
        Isa 43:10, "'You are My witnesses,' declares the LORD, 'And My servant whom I have chosen, In order that **you may know** and believe Me, And understand that I am He. Before Me there was no God formed, And there will be none after Me.'"
        Isa 45:6, "That men **may know** from the rising to the setting of the sun That there is no one besides Me. I am the LORD, and there is no other."
        Isa 48:6, "You have heard; look at all this. And you, will you not declare it? I proclaim to you new things from this time, Even hidden things which you have not known."
        Isa 52:6, "Therefore My people shall know My name; therefore in that day I am the one who is speaking, 'Here I am.'"—as a set up for the important passage on evangelizing, Isa 52:7.

    c)   Of Jesus' use of parables to "evangelize" the masses:
        Matt 13:11, "And He answered and said to them, 'To you it has been granted **to know** [ὅτι Ὑμῖν δέδοται γνῶναι] the mysteries of the kingdom of heaven, but to them it has not been granted.'"
        Mark 4:11, "And He was saying to them, 'To you has been given [**to know**] the mystery of the kingdom of God; but those who are outside get everything in parables.'"
        Luk 8:10, "And He said, 'To you it has been granted **to know** the mysteries of the kingdom of God, but to the rest *it is* in parables, in order that seeing they may not see, and hearing they may not understand.'"

    d)   Other NT uses—often in direct address:
        Luke 10:11, "'Even the dust of your city which clings to our feet, we wipe off *in protest* against you; yet **be sure** of this, that the kingdom of God has come near.'"
        Acts 2:36, "Therefore **let** all the house of Israel **know** for certain that God has made Him both Lord and Christ-- this Jesus whom you crucified."
        Acts 22:14, "And he said, 'The God of our fathers has appointed you **to know** His will, and to see the Righteous One, and to hear an utterance from His mouth.'"
        2 Cor 3:2, "You are our letter, written in our hearts, known and read by all men."

    e)   Not considered an evangelistic use: of God giving knowledge in a particular way (see also John 3, etc.):
        1 Cor 2:14, "But a natural man does not accept the things of the Spirit of God; for they are foolishness to him, and he cannot understand them, because they are spiritually appraised."

    The usual context of the use of the verb γινώσκω ("to know") refers to the completed knowledge of Christ, or to the finality of salvation and eternal life. Thus the verb is used numerous times in 1 John, "By this we know…"

q.   Cognates of τίθημι:

50) ἐκτίθεμι (4 NT uses) – explaining:
    Acts 18:26, "They took him aside and **explained** to him the way of God more accurately"
    Acts 28:23, "He **was explaining** to them by solemnly testifying about the kingdom of God"

51) παρατίθημι (19 NT uses) – meaning to place or put before, hence "giving"; translated **"giving evidence"**:

> Acts 17:3, "Explaining and **giving evidence** that the Christ had to suffer and rise again from the dead…"
>
> Note also this verb used in a type of prayer: Acts 20:32, "And now I **commend** you to God and to the word of His grace, which is able…"

*) Note also the cognate ἀνατίθημι (2 NT uses), used verbally, but not used evangelistically in Acts 25:14; Gal 2:2, meaning "laid out, laid before, communicated, declared"

r.   ἀνοίγω and cognate:

52) ἀνοίγω – meaning to open:

    a) Physical use:

        (1) Of opening doors, Matt 25:11; Luke 13:25; John 10:3; Acts 5:19, 23; 12:10, 14, 16; 16:26, 27

        (2) Of opening eyes, Matt 20:33; John 9:10, 14, 17, 21, 26, 30, 32; 10:21, 37; Acts 9:40

        (3) Of opening tombs, Matt 27:52; cf. Rom 3:13

        (4) Of opening the mouth of a fish, Matt 17:27

        (5) Of the tongue being loosed [opened], Luke 1:64

        (6) Of the heavens opening, Acts 7:56

    b) Figurative sense:

        (1) Of God opening doors, Matt 7:7-8; Luke 11:9-10; cf. Rev 3:7, 8

        (2) Of the sky opening in a vision, Acts 10:11

        (3) Of that which comes out of the mouth, Rom 3:13

    c) Of evangelizing:

    Some antecedent Scripture:

> Psalm 51:15, "O Lord, **open my lips**, That **my mouth** may declare Thy praise."
>
> Ezek 3:27, "But when I speak to you, **I will open your mouth**, and you will say to them, 'Thus says the Lord God.' He who hears, let him hear; and he who refuses, let him refuse; for they are a rebellious house" (cf. Ezek 29:21)

        (1) Used in combination with the word "mouth" (ἀνοίξας τὸ στόμα αὐτοῦ):

            (a) Of Jesus:

                [1] Prophecy of Jesus opening his mouth in parables, Matt 13:35 (Psa 78:2)

                [2] Speaking to the crowds, Matt 5:2

            (b) Of Philip opening up his mouth to evangelize, Acts 8:35

            (c) Of Peter opening his mouth to preach the Gospel, Acts 10:34; cf. Acts 15:7

            (d) Of Paul opening his mouth, Acts 18:14 (almost); Eph 6:19 (to evangelize)

        (2) Of God opening doors:

            (a) Of God opening a door of faith among the Gentiles, Acts 14:27

            (b) Of God opening a door for the Gospel, 1 Cor 16:9; 2 Cor 2:12

            (c) Of God opening a door for the Word, Col 4:3

        (3) Of God opening the eyes of the Gentiles unto salvation, Acts 26:18

        (4) Of ministry [including evangelism] with/from an open heart, 2 Cor 6:11

        (5) Of the need for an open heart in receiving [a] the Gospel and [b] the continued ministry of the Gospel, 2 Cor 6:13

        (6) Of a person [singular], opening themselves to the voice of Christ, Rev 3:20

53) διανοίγω – literally "to open," hence **"explaining"**:

    a) Physical use:

        (1) Of ears being opened, Mark 7:34-35

        (2) Of the womb being opened, Luke 2:23

    b) Of opening in a figurative or spiritual sense:

        (1) Of the opening of the eyes [of understanding], Luke 24:31

        (2) Of the opening of the mind, Luke 24:45

      c)   Christ opening the Scriptures, Luke 24:32 [NAS, "explained"]

      d)   Paul "opened" the Gospel, Acts 17:3
            "**Explaining** and giving evidence that the Christ had to suffer and rise again from the dead, and…"
            διανοίγων καὶ παρατιθέμενος ὅτι τὸν χριστὸν ἔδει παθεῖν καὶ ἀναστῆναι ἐκ νεκρῶν καὶ…

      e)   God "opened" the heart (ὁ κύριος διήνοιξεν τὴν καρδίαν), Acts 16:14

s.   (54) διασαφέω (2 NT uses; 10 LXX uses, including 8 apocryphal uses)– to report, explain:
      Evangelistic/explanatory:
          Mat 13:36, "Then He left the multitudes, and went into the house. And His disciples came to Him, saying, '**Explain** to us the parable of the tares of the field.'"

      Non-evangelistic: Mat 18:31, "So when his fellow slaves saw what had happened, they were deeply grieved and came and **reported** to their lord all that had happened."

      One OT use: Deut 1:5, "Across the Jordan in the land of Moab, Moses undertook **to expound** this law, saying,"

t.   (55) φράζω (1 NT use; 4 LXX uses)– to explain, interpret:
      Evangelistic/explanatory:
          Matt 15:15, "And Peter answered and said to Him, '**Explain** the parable to us.'"

u.   (56) ὀρθοτομέω (1 NT use; 2 LXX uses)– "Rightly teaching/dispensing/imparting/dividing/ handling," in 2 Tim 2:15:
    1)   Meaning:
          Friberg: literally, as cutting a straight road through difficult terrain *make a straight path*; figuratively in the NT, with reference to correctly following and teaching God's message *hold to a straight course, teach accurately* (2T 2:15)
          Gingrich: to guide along a straight path
          Louw-Nida: to give accurate instruction – 'to teach correctly, to expound rightly.' σπούδασον σεαυτὸν … ὀρθοτομοῦντα τὸν λόγον τῆς ἀληθείας 'do your best ... to teach the word of truth correctly' 2 Tim 2:15
          Thayer: 3830 ὀρθοτομέω ὀρθοτομέω, ὀρθοτόμω; (ὀρθοτομος cutting straight, and this from ὀρθός and τέμνω); **1.** *to cut straight*: τάς ὁδούς, to cut straight ways, i. e. to proceed by straight paths, hold a straight course, equivalent to to do right (for רשׁי), Prov. 3:6; 11:5 (viam secare, Vergil Aen. 6, 899). **2.** dropping the idea of cutting, *to make straight and smooth*; Vulgate *recte tracto, to handle aright*: τόν λόγον τῆς ἀληθείας, i. e. to teach the truth correctly and directly, 2 Tim. 2:15; τόν ἀληθῆ λόγον, Eustathius, opuscc., p. 115, 41. (Not found elsewhere (except in ecclesiastical writings (Winer's Grammar, 26); e. g. constt. apost. 7, 31 ἐν τῷ τοῦ κυρίου δόγμασιν; cf. Suicer ii. 508f). Cf. καινοτομέω, *to cut new veins* in mining; dropping the notion of cutting, *to make something new, introduce new things, make innovations or changes,* etc.)*
    2)   Two LXX uses:
          Prov 3:6 ("he will rightly direct" thy paths)
          Prov 11:5 (the righteousness of the upright "shall rightly direct" his paths)
    3)   Notice also in the discussion of the verb πειθώ [persuade] below, that πειθώ is used to translate the Hebrew verb עסשׁ (shaw-saw), meaning to divide or be divided e.g. "having a divided hoof" 5 times; and of David persuading his men in 1 Sam 24:7, "And David **persuaded** his men with *these* words and did not allow them to rise up against Saul"

Conclusions: It is highly likely, from these examples, that rightly dividing has an implication of verbally persuading to follow a right or proper action

How Proclamational is ὀρθοτομέω in 2 Timothy 2:15?

More Verbal/ Proclamational											Less Verbal/ Proclamational								
James Murdock (1852)	Holman Christian Standard (2004)	NET Bible (2005)	French Martin (1669)	French Geneva Revised (1977)	Ostervald (1744)	NRSV (1989)	New Living Trans (2004)	New American Bible (1971)	French Geneva (1669)	Le Semeur (1992, 1999)	Tyndale (1534)	Geneva (1560)	Bishops (1595); KJV; Webster's; Young's; NKJV	Darby (1884)	NASB (1977)	English Revised (1885); ASV	ESV (2005)	NIV (1982)	Wycliffe (1388); RSV
Correctly announcing	Correctly teaching	Teaching ... accurately	Teaching purely	Dispensing rightly	Dispensing with accuracy	Rightly explaining	Correctly explains	Imparting ... without deviation	Detailing rightly	Correctly transmitting	Dividing ... justly	Dividing ... aright	Rightly dividing	Cutting in as straight line	Handling accurately	Handling aright	Rightly handling	Correctly handles	Rightly treating
(Murdock) And study to present thyself before God, perfectly, a laborer who is not ashamed, one who correctly announceth the word of truth.		(NET) Make every effort to present yourself before God as a proven worker who does not need to be ashamed, teaching the message of truth accurately.		(Fr. Gen) Make effort to present yourself before God as a man approved, a worker who need not to blush, dispensing rightly the word fo truth.		(NRSV) Do your best to present yourself to God as one approved by him, a worker who has no need to be ashamed, rightly explaining the word of truth		(NAB) Be eager to present yourself as acceptable to God, a workman who causes no disgrace, imparting the word of truth without deviation		(Fr LS) Make every effort to present yourself before God as a man who has proven himself a worker who need not blush correctly transmitting the word of truth	(Eng Gen) Studie to shewe thy selfe approued vnto God, a workeman that nedeth not to be ashamed, diuiding the worde of trueth aright		(Darby) Strive diligently to present thyself approved to God, a workman that has not to be ashamed, cutting in a straight line the word of truth		(English Rev) Give diligence to present thyself approved unto God, a workman that needeth not to be ashamed, handling aright the word of truth		(NIV) Do your best to present yourself to God as one approved, a workman who does not need to be ashamed and who correctly handles the word of truth	

*English texts and translations that are not shown are: Holman, "Be diligent to present yourself approved to God, a worker who doesn't need to be ashamed, correctly teaching the word of truth."; French Martin, "Study you to render yourself approved to God, a workman without reproach, teaching purely the word of truth"; French Ostervald, "Make effort to show yourself approved before God, as a worker above reproach, dispensing with accuracy the word of truth"; NLT, "Work hard so you can present yourself to God and receive his approval. Be a good worker, one who does not need to be ashamed and who correctly explains the word of truth"; French Geneva, "Study to render yourself approved to God, a worker without blame, detailing rightly the word of truth"; Tyndale, "Study to shewe thy silfe laudable vnto god a workman that nedeth not to be a shamed dividynge the worde of trueth iustly"; Bishop's, ""Studie to shewe thy selfe approued vnto God, a workman not to be ashamed, rightlie deuidyng the worde of trueth; NASB, "Be diligent to present yourself approved to God as a workman who does not need to be ashamed, handling accurately the word of truth"; ESV, "Do your best to present yourself to God as one approved, a worker who has no need to be ashamed, rightly handling the word of truth"; Wycliffe, "Bisili kepe to yyue thi silf a preued preisable werkman to God, with oute schame, riytli tretinge the word of treuthe."

**The French originals are as follows: French Martin, "Etudie-toi de te rendre approuvé à Dieu, ouvrier sans reproche, enseignant purement la parole de la vérité."; French Geneva Revised, "Efforce-toi de te présenter devant Dieu comme un homme éprouvé, un ouvrier qui n'a point à rougir, qui dispense droitement la parole de la vérité"; French Ostervald, "Efforce-toi de te montrer éprouvé devant Dieu, comme un ouvrier irréprochable, dispensant avec droiture la parole de la vérité."; French Geneva, "Estudie-toi de te rendre approuvé à Dieu, ouvrier sans reproche, détaillant droitement la parole de vérité"; and the French Le Semeur, "Efforce-toi de te présenter devant Dieu en homme qui a fait ses preuves, en ouvrier qui n'a pas à rougir de son ouvrage, parce qu'il transmet correctement la Parole de vérité."

    v. (57) μηνύω (4 NT uses) – make known, reveal, "But that the dead are raised, even Moses **showed**, in the *passage about the burning* bush, where he calls the Lord the God of Abraham, and the God of Isaac, and the God of Jacob," Luke 20:37

    w. (58) διερμηνεύω (6 total NT uses) – "He **explained** to them the things concerning Himself in all the Scriptures," Luke 24:27

x. (59) συνετίζω (No NT uses; 13 uses in Ralf's LXX) – to instruct, cause to understand; (pass) give insight:

1) Of God instructing:
    Psa 16:7, "I will bless the LORD who **has counseled** me; Indeed, my mind instructs me in the night"
    Psa 32:8, "I **will instruct** you and teach you in the way which you should go; I will counsel you with My eye upon you"
    Neh 9:20, "And Thou didst give Thy good Spirit **to instruct** them, Thy manna Thou didst not withhold from their mouth, And Thou didst give them water for their thirst"

2) Of requesting God to teach: Psa 119:27, "**Make me understand** the way of Thy precepts, So I will meditate on Thy wonders" (cf. Psa 119:34, 73, 125, 144, 169)

3) Of God's Word: Psa 119:130, "The unfolding of Thy words gives light; It **gives understanding** to the simple"

4) Of an angel: Dan 8:16, "And I heard the voice of a man between *the banks of* Ulai, and he called out and said, 'Gabriel, **give** this *man* **an understanding** of the vision'"

5) Of the revival under Ezra and Nehemiah:
    Neh 8:7, "Also Jeshua, Bani, Sherebiah, Jamin, Akkub, Shabbethai, Hodiah, Maaseiah, Kelita, Azariah, Jozabad, Hanan, Pelaiah, and the Levites, **explained** the law to the people while the people *remained* in their place"
    Neh 8:9, "Then Nehemiah, who was the governor, and Ezra the priest *and* scribe, and the Levites who **taught** the people said to all the people, 'This day is holy to the LORD your God; do not mourn or weep.' For all the people were weeping when they heard the words of the law"

7—TO DEMONSTRATE OR PROVE

y. δείκνυω and cognates:

60) δείκνυω (31 NT uses in BYZ; none in Ralph's; 34 uses of δείκνυμι in NA27 and 126 in Ralph's LXX), meaning, (1) to shew, point out; (2) to bring to light, to portray, represent, mid. To display, set before one; (3) to point out, make known, esp. by words, to tell, explain, teach, to shew, prove, abs. perfect, it is clear; (4) of accusers, to inform against; (in an idiomatic construct) as a pledge (Scott):
    Matt 8:4, "And Jesus said to him, 'See that you tell no one; but go, show yourself to the priest, and present the offering that Moses commanded, for a testimony to them'"
    Mark 1:44, "and He said to him, 'See that you say nothing to anyone; but go, **show** yourself to the priest and offer for your cleansing what Moses commanded, for a testimony to them'"
    For a better understanding, as used related to abstract ideas, see Matt 16:21; Acts 10:28; 1 Tim 6:15; Heb 8:5; James 2:18.

61) ἐπιδείκνυμι – "**demonstrating** [KJV, shewing] by the Scriptures." Acts 18:28
    Friberg Lexicon: ἐπιδείκνυμι 1aor. ἐπέδειξα; literally, as causing to be seen *show, exhibit, demonstrate* (MT 16.1); figuratively, as proving to be true *show beyond doubt, prove, demonstrate convincingly* (AC 18.28).

62) ἐνδείκνυμι (8 OT LXX uses; 11 NT uses):
    Rom 9:17, "For the Scripture says to Pharaoh, 'For this very purpose I raised you up, **to demonstrate** My power in you, and that My name might be proclaimed throughout the whole earth'" (quote of Exod 9:16)
    Rom 9:22, "What if God, although willing **to demonstrate** His wrath and to make His power known, endured with much patience vessels of wrath prepared for destruction?"
    Appears to be especially an action which demonstrates a value: cf. Eph 2:17; 1 Tim 1:16; 2 Tim 4:14; Tit 2:10; 3:10; Heb 6:10-11

63) ὑποδείκνυμι (6 NT uses), meaning show, demonstrate, reveal; hence warn: Acts 20:35
    Matt 3:7, "You brood of vipers, who **warned** you to flee from the wrath to come?"
    Luke 3:7, "You brood of vipers, who **warned** you to flee from the wrath to come?"
    Luke 12:5, "But I **will warn** you whom to fear: fear the One who after He has killed has authority to cast into hell; yes, I tell you, fear Him!"

    Friberg Lexicon: ὑποδείκνυμι or ὑποδεικνύω fut. ὑποδείξω; 1aor. ὑπέδειξα; (1) strictly *show secretly, give a glimpse of*; hence *intimate, suggest*; (2) figuratively, with the dative of person *show, make known, point out* (LU 6.47; AC 9.16); in a negative sense *warn* (MT 3.7)

z. (64) συμβιβάζω – to hold together, instruct, confirm, or teach (9 OT LXX uses; 7 NT uses):

Of Paul:

Acts 9:22, "**proving** that this Jesus is the Christ"

Col 2:2, "that their hearts may be encouraged, having been **knit together** in love, and *attaining* to all the wealth that comes from the full assurance of understanding, *resulting* in a true knowledge of God's mystery, *that is*, Christ *Himself*,"

Of the Lord instructing:

Acts 16:10, "And when he had seen the vision, immediately we sought to go into Macedonia, **concluding** that God had called us to preach the gospel to them"

Of man instructing God:

1 Cor 2:16, "For who has known the mind of the Lord, that he **should instruct** Him? But we have the mind of Christ"

Of the church being fit with instruction in Christ:

Eph 4:16, "from whom the whole body, being fitted and **held together** by that which every joint supplies, according to the proper working of each individual part, causes the growth of the body for the building up of itself in love"

Col 2:19, "and not holding fast to the head, from whom the entire body, being supplied and **held together** by the joints and ligaments, grows with a growth which is from God"

In the OT LXX:

a) συμβιβάζω is the word used in Lev 10:11 after a discussion of the need to distinguish, "and **so as to teach** [συμβιβάσεις] the sons of Israel all the statutes which the LORD has spoken to them through Moses."

b) συμβιβάζω has some other interesting uses in the Pentateuch, Exod 4:12, 15; Deut 4:9; cf. Judges 13:8

Of the cognate προβιβάζω:

a) Notice the use of προβιβάζω in Deut 6:7, translated "teach diligently" (NAS); "inculcate" (cf. French NEG), versus the use of συμβιβάζω in Deut 4:9

b) προβιβάζω is also used in the Byzantine of Acts 19:33 where the Nestle-Aland chose instead συμβιβάζω.

8—TO ADMONISH, WARN, PERSUADE, BEG

aa. (65) νουθετέω (8 NT uses, all Pauline [one in Acts 20:31]), meaning "to admonish, exhort," (cf. Col 3:16):

"I myself am also persuaded about you, my brothers, that you yourselves are full of goodness, filled with all knowledge, able also **to admonish others**" (Rom 15:14 RPTE)"

"And we proclaim Him, **admonishing every man** and teaching every man with all wisdom, that we may present every man complete in Christ" Col 1:28.

ab. (66) διαπειλέω – "to threaten violently" [Liddell-Scott Greek Lexicon, Abridged]:

1) One OT LXX use: "I have made thee a watchman to the house of Israel; and thou shalt hear a word of my mouth, and **shalt threaten** them from me" Ezek 3:17 (Brenton).

"Son of man, I have appointed you a watchman to the house of Israel; whenever you hear a word from My mouth, **warn** them from Me" (Ezek 3:17).

2) διαπειλέω is also used twice in 3 Maccabees:

"or when he heard the shouting and saw them all fallen headlong to destruction, he wept and angrily **threatened** his friends, saying," (3 Macc 6:23)

"But we very severely **threatened** [σκληρότερον διαπειλησάμενοι] them for these acts, and in accordance with the clemency which we have toward all men we barely spared their lives. Since we have come to realize that the God of heaven surely defends the Jews, always taking their part as a father does for his children" (3 Macc 7:6)

ac. (67) διαστέλλω – "warn" and combination:

1) διαστέλλω:

"When I say to the wicked, 'You shall surely die,' and you **do not warn** him [οὐ διεστείλω] ..." Ezek 3:18

"Yet if you have warned [διαστείλῃ] the wicked, and he does not turn from his wickedness or from his wicked way, he shall die in his iniquity; but you have delivered yourself," Ezek 3:19

2) λαλέω + διαστέλλω:
> "When I say to the wicked, 'You shall surely die,' and you do not warn him or **speak out to warn** (οὐδὲ ἐλάλησας τοῦ διαστείλασθαι) the wicked from his wicked way that he may live," Ezek 3:18

ad. (68) φυλάσσω – "guard against": "When I say to the wicked, 'O wicked man, you shall surely die,' and you do not speak to warn (μὴ λαλήσῃς τοῦ φυλάξασθαι) the wicked from his way," Ezek 33:8

Also, it is worth considering the impact of this verb as it relates to other verses:
> "Guard" is in parallel with "contend" in Jude 3, "Beloved, while I was making every effort to write you about our common salvation, I felt the necessity to write to you appealing that you contend earnestly for the faith which was once for all delivered to the saints."
> Guard here may point to an alternative translation of 2 Tim 4:7, "I have fought the good fight, I have finished the course, I have guarded the faith"
> > Consider the impact of changing the translation of τηρέω from a passive "kept" to the active "guarded."

ae. (69) ὀνειδίζω - reproach, revile, heap insults (cf. Matt 5:11); reproach [justifiably], upbraid:
> Matt 11:20, "Then He began to **reproach** the cities in which most of His miracles were done, because they did not repent."

af. ἐλέγχω and cognate:

70) ἐλέγχω (18 NT uses) – to expose, convict, reprove:

Evangelistic Uses:
> Luke 3:19, "But when Herod the tetrarch **was reproved** by him on account of Herodias, his brother's wife, and on account of all the wicked things which Herod had done"
> John 16:8, "And He, when He comes, **will convict** the world concerning sin, and righteousness, and judgment"
> 1 Cor 14:24, "But if all prophesy, and an unbeliever or an ungifted man enters, he **is convicted** by all, he is called to account by all"
> Eph 5:11, "And do not participate in the unfruitful deeds of darkness, but instead even **expose** them"
> 2 Tim 4:2, "Preach the word; be ready in season and out of season; **reprove**, rebuke, exhort, with great patience and instruction"
> > [It is highly likely here that Paul is already exhorting Timothy to do the work of an evangelist in this verse, cf. Mark 16:15, "Preach the Gospel"]
> Titus 1:9, "Holding fast the faithful word which is in accordance with the teaching, that he may be able both to exhort in sound doctrine and **to refute** those who contradict"
> > [Anti-lego (to "contradict"), is also found in an evangelistic context in Luke 20:27; Acts 13:45 (twice); 28:19, 22]
> Titus 1:12-13, "One of themselves, a prophet of their own, said, 'Cretans are always liars, evil beasts, lazy gluttons.' This testimony is true. For this cause **reprove** them severely that they may be sound in the faith"
> > [Perhaps an example of the need for resolve of steel, as found in Ezek 3:8]
> Jude 15, "To execute judgment upon all, and **to convict** all the ungodly of all their ungodly deeds which they have done in an ungodly way"

Verb [and phrase] omitted from the "Critical Edition" Greek text in John 8:9:
> (1) "And when they heard it, they *began* to go out one by one, beginning with the older ones, and He was left alone, and the woman, where she was, in the midst," John 8:9 (NAS)
> (2) "Then those who heard *it*, **being convicted** by *their* conscience [καὶ ὑπὸ τῆς συνειδήσεως ἐλεγχόμενοι], went out one by one, beginning with the oldest *even* to the last. And Jesus was left alone, and the woman standing in the midst," John 8:9 (NKJ)
> Analysis of this omission:
> > Notice that the conviction comes from hearing the words of Jesus, and the conviction is in their conscience
> > It appears that the Evangelical belief in the necessity of the conviction of the Holy Spirit (John 16:8) with a "hearing of faith" (Gal 3:2, 5) for salvation is removed from this text

Notice also how this verb is closely linked with the exposing attribute of light:

(1) "For everyone who does evil hates the light, and does not come to the light, lest his deeds **should be exposed**," John 3:20

(2) "But all things become visible when they **are exposed** by the light, for everything that becomes visible is light," Eph 5:13 (cf. v. 11 above)

Note also how this root word is used in Proverbs:

Prov 6:23, "For the commandment is a lamp, and the teaching is light; And reproofs [ἔλεγχος] for discipline are the way of life"

Prov 24:25, "But to those who rebuke [ἐλέγχω] the *wicked* will be delight, And a good blessing will come upon them."

71) διακατελέγχομαι – "**refuted** the Jews," Acts 18:28 (note the adverb with this verb, εὐτόνως, meaning "with vehemence", cf. Luke 23:10)

ag. (72) ἐπιτιμάω – to mete out due measure, hence to censure: "Preach the word; be ready in season and out of season; reprove, **rebuke**, exhort, with great patience and instruction." 2 Tim 4:2

ah. (73) πείθω (54 NT uses [17 in Acts]; in addition see Acts 14:19; 23:21; 26:26)—below I note the passive use of this verb, as a response to the Gospel:

Notice the interesting OT usage of this verb (only a few examples):

a) From the Heb. *chacah*:

2 Sam 22:3, "My God, my rock, in whom **I take refuge** [μου πεποιθὼς ἔσομαι]; My shield and the horn of my salvation, my stronghold and my refuge; My savior, Thou dost save me from violence."

2 Sam 22:31, "As for God, His way is blameless; The word of the LORD is tested; He is a shield to all **who take refuge** in Him [ὑπερασπιστής ἐστιν πᾶσιν τοῖς πεποιθόσιν ἐπ᾽ αὐτῷ]."

Psa 2:12, "Do homage to the Son, lest He become angry, and you perish *in* the way, For His wrath may soon be kindled. How blessed are all **who take refuge** in Him [μακάριοι πάντες οἱ πεποιθότες ἐπ᾽ αὐτῷ]!"

Psa 11:1, "In the LORD **I take refuge** [ἐπὶ τῷ κυρίῳ πέποιθα]; How can you say to my soul, 'Flee *as* a bird to your mountain.'"

Cf. Psa 57:1; 117:8.

b) From the Heb. *batach*:

Psa 25:2, "O my God, in Thee **I trust** [ἐπὶ σοὶ πέποιθα], Do not let me be ashamed; Do not let my enemies exult over me."

Psa 49:6, "Even those **who trust** in their wealth [οἱ πεποιθότες ἐπὶ τῇ δυνάμει αὐτῶν], And boast in the abundance of their riches?"

Cf. Psa 115:8; 125:1; 135:18; 146:3.

1) "Paul and Barnabas, who, speaking to them, were **urging** them to continue in the grace of God," Acts 13:43

2) Trying **to persuade**, Acts 18:4, 28:23

3) "This man **persuades** men to worship God contrary to the law," Acts 18:13

4) "Reasoning and **persuading** *them* about the kingdom of God," Acts 19:8

a) The French Segond (1910) Geneva (1979) translate this verbal pair (διαλέγομαι and πειθώ) as "forcefully persuading" ("s'efforçant de persuader ceux qui l'écoutaient")

5) "This Paul has **persuaded** and turned away a considerable number of people," Acts 19:26

6) "Agrippa *replied* to Paul, 'In a short time you will **persuade** me to become a Christian,'" Acts 26:28

7) "and he was explaining to them by solemnly testifying about the kingdom of God, and trying to persuade them concerning Jesus, from both the Law of Moses and from the Prophets, from morning until evening," Act 28:23

a) Of special interest is the use of the same verb πειθώ in v. 24 for the response to the gospel proclamation, along with its antithesis, "And some **were being persuaded** by the things spoken, but others would not believe," Act 28:24

8) "Therefore knowing the fear of the Lord, we **persuade** men," 2 Cor 5:11

9) In Deut 28:52, the people "trusted" (or were persuaded) in the strength of their city walls to protect them from the enemy:

a) The translation of this verb comes from the Hebrew בָּטַח (baw-takh)

b) This Hebrew verb is normally translated "trust," such as in Psa 37:3, "Trust in the LORD"

c) Herein the translaters of the LXX show that there is a semantic overlap between "trust" and "being persuaded"; which is interesting in the NT case of Acts 28 as noted above.

10) Another interesting OT LXX use of πείθω 1 Sam 24:7, "And David **persuaded** his men with *these* words and did not allow them to rise up against Saul. And Saul arose, left the cave, and went on *his* way":

    a) The translation of this verb comes from the Hebrew שסע (shaw-saw)

    b) The 9 uses of the verb שסע in the Hebrew, it is used 5 times of an animal with "divided" hooves, Lev 11:3, 7, 26; Deut 14:6, 7; once of tearing a bird, Lev 1:17; twice of Samson tearing the jaw of the lion, Judges 14:6; and figuratively, once of David **dividing** the word of the Lord to his men, 1 Sam 24:7

    c) Could this use of "dividing" in 1 Sam 24:7 relate to 2 Tim 2:15 (KJV), "rightly dividing the word," and Heb 4:12, "For the word of God *is* quick, and powerful, and sharper than any two-edged sword, piercing even to the dividing asunder of soul and spirit"?

    d) There are three elements to David's dividing this concept to his men:

        (1) David had to study the "anointing oil" in the Pentateuch to come to this conclusion;

        (2) David had to come to a decision upon what it meant, enough to be convinced of it, and to submit to the teaching of the Word of God;

        (3) David communicated what he learned to his men to keep them from disobeying the Word of the Lord.

ai. (74) δέομαι – "beg," beseech:

    1) "But Paul said, 'I am a Jew of Tarsus in Cilicia, a citizen of no insignificant city; and I **beg** you, allow me to speak to the people,'" Acts 21:39

    2) "Therefore I **beg** you to listen to me patiently," Acts 26:3

    3) "We **beg** you on behalf of Christ, be reconciled to God," 2 Cor 5:20.

aj. (75) χρηματίζω (10 OT LXX uses; 9 NT uses) – warn; impart a revelation, injunction, or warning; bear a name, be called, named:

Heb 12:25, "See to it that you do not refuse Him who is speaking. For if those did not escape when they refused him who **warned** *them* on earth, much less *shall* we *escape* who turn away from Him who *warns* from heaven"

On the Translation of the Proclamational Verbs in Hebrews 12:25

Greek	Latin	Tyndale; Eng Geneva	Bishops; KJV; Web-ster's	Young's	Darby	ERV; ASV	Bible in Basic English	NAS	French Geneva Revised*	NKJ	NIV	NJB*
λαλέω	Loquen-tem	that speaketh	that speaketh	who is speaking	that speaks	that speaketh	which comes	who is speaking	who speaks	who speaks	who speaks	when he speaks
χρημα-τίζω	Loque-batur	spake	Spake	was divinely speaking	who uttered the oracles	that warned	the voice	who warned	published oracles	who spoke	who warned	to a warning
	Loquen-tem	*speaketh*	[speak-eth]	*speaketh*	*who does so*	that *warneth*	whose voice	who *warns*	who speaks	who *speaks*	who warns	a voice that warns

*(French Geneva Revised, 1977), "Gardez -vous de refuser d'entendre celui qui parle; car si ceux qui refusèrent d'entendre celui qui publiait des oracles sur la terre n'ont pas échappé combien moins échapperons-nous, si nous nous détournons de celui qui parle du haut des cieux"

Similarly, God used the verb "warn" as the primary verb in Ezek 3:18-21 to describe the responsibility of the watchman toward the wicked one who sins and the righteous one who sins.

The verb χρηματίζω is used in the mocking answer of Elijah to the Prophets of Baal in 1 Kings 18:27:

1 Kings 18:27 (LXE), "And it was noon, and Eliu the Thesbite mocked them, and said, Call with a loud voice, for he is a god; for he is meditating, or else perhaps he is engaged in **business** [teaching], or perhaps he is asleep, and is to be awaked."

This verb χρηματίζω is used 8 times in the Book of Jeremiah:

    a) Of false prophets speaking falsely in the name of God (Jer 29:23):

Jer 29:23, "because they have acted foolishly in Israel, and have committed adultery with their neighbors' wives, and **have spoken** words in My name falsely, which I did not command them; and I am He who knows, and am a witness," declares the LORD."

b) Of God revealing Himself (Jer 25:30):

Jer 25:30, "Therefore you shall prophesy against them all these words, and you shall say to them, 'The LORD **will roar** from on high, And utter His voice from His holy habitation; He **will roar** mightily against His fold. He will shout like those who tread *the grapes*, Against all the inhabitants of the earth.'"

c) In a command of God to teach the people of Israel coming into the Temple in Jerusalem (Jer 26:2):

Jer 26:2, "Thus says the LORD, Stand in the court of the LORD's house, and **speak** to all the cities of Judah, who have come to worship *in* the LORD's house, all the words that I have commanded you to **speak** to them. Do not omit a word!"

d) It was used of God's instruction to Jeremiah, in relation to the admonition for Jeremiah to write the words in a book (Jer 30:2; 36:2, 4):

Jer 30:2, "Thus says the LORD, the God of Israel, 'Write all the words which I **have spoken** to you in a book."

ak. καλέω and cognate:

76) καλέω (146 NT uses; 513 OT LXX uses) – to call: "invite," Matt 22:9:

Matt 4:21, "And going on from there He saw two other brothers, James the *son* of Zebedee, and John his brother, in the boat with Zebedee their father, mending their nets; and He **called** them."

Matt 9:13, "But go and learn what *this* means, 'I desire compassion, and not sacrifice,' for I did not come **to call** the righteous, but sinners."

Matt 22:3, "And he sent out his slaves **to call** those who had been invited to the wedding feast, and they were unwilling to come."

Matt 22:4, "Again he sent out other slaves saying, 'Tell those who have been **invited**, "Behold, I have prepared my dinner; my oxen and my fattened livestock are *all* butchered and everything is ready; come to the wedding feast.""'"

Matt 22:8, "Then he said to his slaves, 'The wedding is ready, but those **who were invited** were not worthy."

Matt 22:9, "Go therefore to the main highways, and as many as you find *there*, **invite** to the wedding feast."

Mark 1:20, "And immediately He **called** them; and they left their father Zebedee in the boat with the hired servants, and went away to follow Him."

Mark 2:17, "And hearing this, Jesus said to them, '*it is* not those who are healthy who need a physician, but those who are sick; I did not come **to call** the righteous, but sinners.'"

Luke 5:32, "I have not come **to call** the righteous but sinners to repentance."

Luke 14:13, "But when you give a reception, **invite** the poor, *the* crippled, *the* lame, *the* blind,"

Luke 14:16-17, "But He said to him, 'A certain man was giving a big dinner, and he **invited** many; and at the dinner hour he sent his slave to say to those **who had been invited**, 'Come; for everything is ready now.'"

Luke 14:24, "For I tell you, none of those men who were invited shall taste of my dinner."

John 10:3, "To him the doorkeeper opens, and the sheep hear his voice, and **he calls** his own sheep by name, and leads them out."

Rom 8:30, "and whom He predestined, these He also **called**; and whom **He called**, these He also justified; and whom He justified, these He also glorified."

Rom 9:11, "for though *the twins* were not yet born, and had not done anything good or bad, in order that God's purpose according to *His* choice might stand, not because of works, but because of Him **who calls**."

Rom 9:24-25, "*even* us, whom **He** also **called**, not from among Jews only, but also from among Gentiles. As He says also in Hosea, '**I will call** those who were not My people, "My people," And her who was not beloved, "beloved.""'"

1 Cor 1:9, "God is faithful, through whom you **were called** into fellowship with His Son, Jesus Christ our Lord."

1 Cor 7:17-18, 20-22, 24, "Only, as the Lord has assigned to each one, as God **has called** each, in this manner let him walk. And thus I direct in all the churches. Was any man **called** *already* circumcised? Let him not become uncircumcised. Has anyone been **called** in uncircumcision? Let him not be circumcised. … Let each man remain in that condition in which **he was called**. Were you **called** while a slave? Do not worry about it; but if you are able also to become free, rather do that. For he who **was called** in the Lord while a slave, is the Lord's freedman; likewise he who **was called** while free, is Christ's slave. … Brethren, let each man remain with God in that *condition* in which he **was called**."

Gal 1:6, "I am amazed that you are so quickly deserting Him **who called** you by the grace of Christ, for a different gospel."

Gal 1:15, "But when He who had set me apart, *even* from my mother's womb, and called me through His grace, was pleased."

Gal 5:8, "This persuasion *did* not *come* from Him **who calls** you."

Eph 4:1, "I, therefore, the prisoner of the Lord, entreat you to walk in a manner worthy of the calling with which you **have been called**."

Eph 4:4, "*There is* one body and one Spirit, just as also you **were called** in one hope of your calling."

Col 3:15, "And let the peace of Christ rule in your hearts, to which indeed you **were called** in one body; and be thankful."

1 Thess 2:12 (NKJ), "that you would walk worthy of God **who calls** you into His own kingdom and glory."

1 Thess 4:7, "For God has not **called** us for the purpose of impurity, but in sanctification."

1 Thess 5:24, Faithful is He who **calls** you, and He also will bring it to pass."

2 Thess 2:14, "And it was for this He **called** you through our gospel, that you may gain the glory of our Lord Jesus Christ."

1 Tim 6:12, "Fight the good fight of faith; take hold of the eternal life to which you **were called**, and you made the good confession in the presence of many witnesses."

2 Tim 1:9, "who has saved us, and **called** us with a holy calling, not according to our works, but according to His own purpose and grace which was granted us in Christ Jesus from all eternity"

Heb 9:15, "And for this reason He is the mediator of a new covenant, in order that since a death has taken place for the redemption of the transgressions that were *committed* under the first covenant, those who **have been called** may receive the promise of the eternal inheritance."

1 Pet 1:15, "but like the Holy One **who called** you, be holy yourselves also in all *your* behavior."

1 Pet 2:9, "But you are a chosen race, a royal priesthood, a holy nation, a people for *God's* own possession, that you may proclaim the excellencies of Him **who has called** you out of darkness into His marvelous light."

1 Pet 2:21, "For you **have been called** for this purpose, since Christ also suffered for you, leaving you an example for you to follow in His steps."

1 Pet 3:9, "not returning evil for evil, or insult for insult, but giving a blessing instead; for **you were called** for the very purpose that you might inherit a blessing."

1 Pet 5:10, "And after you have suffered for a little while, the God of all grace, **who called** you to His eternal glory in Christ, will Himself perfect, confirm, strengthen *and* establish you."

2 Pet 1:3, "seeing that His divine power has granted to us everything pertaining to life and godliness, through the true knowledge of Him **who called** us by His own glory and excellence."

Rev 19:9, "And he said to me, 'Write, "Blessed are those **who are invited** to the marriage supper of the Lamb."' And he said to me, 'These are true words of God.'"

Consider from the OT:

Jer 7:13, "'And now, because you have done all these things,' declares the LORD, 'and I spoke to you, rising up early and speaking, but you did not hear, and **I called** you but you did not answer.'"

Or consider also:

Rom 4:17, "(as it is written, 'A father of many nations have I made you') in the sight of Him whom he believed, *even* God, who gives life to the dead and **calls** into being that which does not exist."[668]

Rom 9:7, "neither are they all children because they are Abraham's descendants, but: 'through Isaac your descendants **will be named**.'"

---

[668]"The gospel itself is the power of God unto salvation to everyone that believeth. Now, there are different ways of preaching the gospel. There is the plan of preaching the gospel and looking forward to the gradual enlightenment of the people, to their being saved as it were by a process of gradual instruction and preaching. And there is another method of preaching the gospel; believing it to be the power of God unto salvation; preaching it in the *expectation* that He who first brought light out of darkness can and will at once and instantaneously take the darkest heathen heart and *create light within*. That is the method that is successful. It has been my privilege to know many Christians – I am speaking within bounds when I say a hundred – who have accepted Jesus Christ as their Saviour the first time they ever heard of Him. The gospel itself is the power of God unto salvation" (J. Hudson Taylor, "The Source of Power," *Ecumenical Missionary Conference, New York, 1900* [New York, American Tract Society, 1900]: 1:91; italics mine).

Examples of Various Soteriological Uses of καλέω [to Call] and ἐπικαλέω [to Call, Invoke]

καλέω			ἐπικαλέω		
God Calls	Jesus Calls	Man Calls Man	Man Calls Man	Man Is Assured Salvation	Calling as a Descriptor
Rom 8:30, "and whom He predestined, these **He** also **called**;	Luke 5:32, "I have not come **to call** the righteous but sinners to repentance."	Matt 22:3, "And he sent out his slaves **to call** those who had been invited to the wedding feast	Acts 22:16, "And now why do you delay? Arise, and be baptized, and wash away your sins, **calling** on His name."	Rom 10:13, "for 'Whoever **will call** upon the name of the LORD will be saved.'"	1 Cor 1:2, "to the church of God which is at Corinth, to those who have been sanctified in Christ Jesus, saints by calling, with all **who** in every place **call** upon the name of our Lord Jesus Christ, their *Lord* and ours."

77) συγκαλέω (8 total NT uses)

Luke 15:6, "And when he comes home, he **calls together** his friends and his neighbors, saying to them, 'Rejoice with me, for I have found my sheep which was lost!'"

Luke 15:9, "And when she has found it, she **calls together** her friends and neighbors, saying, 'Rejoice with me, for I have found the coin which I had lost!'"

Acts 10:24, "And on the following day he entered Caesarea. Now Cornelius was waiting for them, and had **called together** his relatives and close friends."

Act 28:17, "And it happened that after three days he **called together** those who were the leading men of the Jews, and when they had come together, he *began* saying to them, 'Brethren, though I had done nothing against our people, or the customs of our fathers, yet I was delivered prisoner from Jerusalem into the hands of the Romans.'"

n11) ἡ κλῆσις (3 OT LXX uses; 11 NT uses) – meaning calling:

Rom 11:29, "for the gifts and **the calling** of God are irrevocable."

1 Cor 1:26, "For consider your **calling**, brethren, that there were not many wise according to the flesh, not many mighty, not many noble."

1 Cor 7:20, "Let each man remain in that **condition** in which he was called."

Eph 1:18, "*I pray that* the eyes of your heart may be enlightened, so that you may know what is the hope of His **calling**, what are the riches of the glory of His inheritance in the saints."

Eph 4:1, "I, therefore, the prisoner of the Lord, entreat you to walk in a manner worthy of **the calling** with which you have been called."

Eph 4:4, "*There is* one body and one Spirit, just as also you were called in one hope of your **calling**."

Phil 3:14, "I press on toward the goal for the prize of the upward **call** of God in Christ Jesus."

2 Thess 1:11, "To this end also we pray for you always that our God may count you worthy of your **calling**, and fulfill every desire for goodness and the work of faith with power."

2 Tim 1:9, "who has saved us, and called us with a holy **calling**, not according to our works, but according to His own purpose and grace which was granted us in Christ Jesus from all eternity."

Heb 3:1, "Therefore, holy brethren, partakers of a heavenly **calling**, consider Jesus, the Apostle and High Priest of our confession."

2 Pet 1:10, "Therefore, brethren, be all the more diligent to make certain about His **calling** and choosing you; for as long as you practice these things, you will never stumble."

78) ἐκκαλέω (0 NT uses; 2 OT LXX uses) – to call out, call forth, summon forth; hence "offer":

First OT LXX use: the wicked men of Sodom solicit and demand sexual interaction from the angels who visited Lot in their city:

Gen 19:5, " and they called to Lot and said to him, 'Where are the men who came to you tonight? **Bring** them **out** to us that we may have relations with them.'"

Other OT LXX use is linked with making an offer of "peace"!

Deut 20:10, "When you approach a city to fight against it, **you shall offer** it terms of peace"

Parallel ideas:

1) The prophecied message of the evangelists was peace, Isa 52:7
2) The disciples were to go from city to city offering peace, Matt 10:11-13; Luke 10:1, 5

      3)   Peace was evangelized by the disciples in Acts:
           Acts 10:36, "The word which *God* sent to the children of Israel, preaching [εὐαγγελίζω] peace through Jesus Christ—He is Lord of all"
      4)   Christ Jesus came evangelizing peace:
           Eph 2:17, "And He came and preached [εὐαγγελίζω] peace to you who were afar off and to those who were near"

*) ἐπικαλέω (187 uses in the OT LXX; 32 uses in the NT) – meaning to invoke or call is included in the responses to the gospel below.

79) παρακαλέω – entreat, exhort (cf. 1 Tim 6:2):

    In the New Testament:
        Luke 3:18, "So with many other exhortations also he preached the gospel to the people" [Πολλὰ μὲν οὖν καὶ ἕτερα παρακαλῶν εὐηγγελίζετο τὸν λαόν]
        2 Cor 5:20, "As though God where **entreating** through us [ὡς τοῦ θεοῦ παρακαλοῦντος δι' ἡμῶν]"
        2 Tim 4:2, "Preach the word; be ready in season and out of season; reprove, rebuke, **exhort**, with great patience and instruction"

    Also in the Old Testament LXX:
        Deut 13:6 (NRS), "If anyone secretly **entices** you-- even if it is your brother, your father's son or your mother's son, or your own son or daughter, or the wife you embrace, or your most intimate friend-- saying, 'Let us go worship other gods,' whom neither you nor your ancestors have known"

    The word παρακαλέω is especially essential for proper spiritual growth, as noted in Chapter 26. Yet, the word παρακαλέω is also an important word in the invitation to commitment,[669] as well as one of the predominant words used for follow-up in the Acts (cf. Acts 25:2), see *Evangelizology,* Chapter 26.

al. (80) παραινέω – urge, advise, recommend (in the case of specific action):
    Acts 27:9-10, "And when considerable time had passed and the voyage was now dangerous, since even the fast was already over, Paul *began* **to admonish** them, and said to them, 'Men, I perceive that the voyage will certainly be *attended* with damage and great loss, not only of the cargo and the ship, but also of our lives'"
    Acts 27:22, "And *yet* now **I urge** you to keep up your courage, for there shall be no loss of life among you, but *only* of the ship"

am. (81) φάσκω: speaking with certainty, assert, claim, declare—used by a third party to describe Paul's evangelism:
    Acts 25:19, "but they *simply* had some points of disagreement with him about their own religion and about a certain dead man, Jesus, whom Paul **asserted** to be alive"

    Also found:
        Gen 26:20, "the herdsmen of Gerar quarreled with the herdsmen of Isaac, saying, 'The water is ours!" So he named the well Esek, because they **contended** with him'"
        Acts 24:9, "And the Jews also joined in the attack, **asserting** that these things were so"
        Rom 1:22, "**Professing** to be wise, they became fools."

9—MISCELLANEOUS PROCLAMATIONAL VERBS

an. (82) ἐπαίρω – "raise [his voice]" - Acts 2:14, "But Peter, taking his stand with the eleven, raised his voice and declared to them…" (ἐπῆρεν τὴν φωνὴν αὐτου)

ao. (83) ἀγαλλιάω – speaking with extreme joy, Psa 75:9 (unusual LXX translation of Heb *nagad* [declare])

ap. βεβαιόω and verbal adjective – confirmation:

    84) βεβαιόω (7 NT uses) – "**confirmed** to us by those who heard [of salvation]," Heb 2:3

---

[669]Consider the discussion of παρακαλέω as "beside-call" in Keith Fordham and Tom Johnston, *The Worth and Work of the Evangelist for Christ's Great Commission Church* (Liberty, MO Evangelism Unlimited, 2013), 142.

n12) ἡ βεβαιώσις (noun) – "**confirmation** of the Gospel," Phil 1:7

Interestingly, the verb βεβαιόω is often an action of God establishing, e.g. 1 Cor 1:8, but it is also part of a command for the believer to grow in Christ, Col 2:6-7. The semantic struggle occurs with the addition of the concept of "Confirmation" as a life-cycle rite of passage in some ritualistic churches.

aq. φανερόω and cognate:

85) φανερόω - to reveal, make known, show:
John 17:6, "I **manifested** Thy name to the men whom Thou gavest Me out of the world"

Translations of φανερόω in John 17:6a
[Notice the semantic struggle over the verbal and initiative elements in the translation of this verb]

King James (1611); RSV (1952); ASV (1901); NAS (1977)	NIV (1984); CSB (2003); NET (2005)	Bible in Basic English (1949)	French Louis Segond and 1977 Geneva	Tyndale (1534); English Geneva (1560); Bishops (1595)
Manifested	Revealed	Given knowledge	Made known	Declared
I **have manifested** thy name unto the men which thou gavest me out of the world	I **have revealed** Your name to the men You gave Me from the world	I have **given knowledge** of your name to the men whom you gave me out of the world	J'ai fait connaître [i.e. '**made known**'] ton nom aux hommes que tu m'as donnés du milieu du monde	I **have declared** thy Name vnto the men which thou gauest me out of the worlde

Rom 3:21 (NKJ), "But now the righteousness of God apart from the law is **revealed**, being witnessed by the Law and the Prophets," cf. Rom 16:26
2 Cor 2:14 (NKJ), "Now thanks *be* to God who always leads us in triumph in Christ, and through us **diffuses** the fragrance of His knowledge in every place [τὴν ὀσμὴν τῆς γνώσεως αὐτοῦ φανεροῦντι]"

Translations of φανερόω in 2 Cor 2:14
[Notice the same semantic struggle over the verbal and initiative elements as was noted in John 17:6a]

Young's (1862)	Tyndale (1534); Bishop's (1595)	NKJ (1982)	NAS (1977)	English Geneva (1560); KJV; Webster's; Darby; ERV; ASV	RSV (1952); NIV; CSB; ESV	Bible in Basic English (1949)	NET (2005)
He is manifesting	Openeth	Diffuses	Manifests	Maketh manifest	Spreads	Makes clear	Makes known
and the fragrance of His knowledge He is manifesting through us in every place	and openeth the saver of his knowledge by vs in every place	and through us diffuses the fragrance of His knowledge in every place	and manifests through us the sweet aroma of the knowledge of Him in every place	and maketh manifest the sauour of his knowledge by vs in euerie place	and through us spreads the fragrance of the knowledge of him everywhere	and makes clear through us in every place the value of the knowledge of him	who makes known through us the fragrance that consists of the knowledge of him in every place

Notice that if God reveals [φανερόω] Himself through us (evangelizing Christians), as appears to be taught in this verse, that the evangelist is placed in the order of salvation as a subsection of God's revelation of Himself to lost persons!

Consider also that in 2 Cor 2:14 the verb φανερόω + the noun ἡ ὀσμή is placed in parallelism with the verb θριαμβεύω, to "trimphalize" or "march in triumphal procession" (see below).

2 Cor 4:10, "Always carrying about in the body the dying of Jesus, that the life of Jesus also **may be manifested** in our body"
2 Cor 4:11, "For we who live are constantly being delivered over to death for Jesus' sake, that the life of Jesus also **may be manifested** in our mortal flesh."
2 Cor 5:11 (NKJ), "Knowing, therefore, the terror of the Lord, we persuade men; but we are **well known** to God, and I also trust are **well known** in your consciences"
Phil 1:13 (1560 English Geneva), "So that my bandes in Christ **are famous** throughout all the iudgement hall, and in all other *places*"
Col 4:4 (Geneva), "In order that I **may make it clear** in the way I ought to speak," Col 4:4 (NAS) "That I **may vtter it**, as it becometh me to speake"
["Et le faire connaître (i.e. '**made it known**') comme je dois en parler," Col 4:4 (NEG)]

Rev 15:4 (NKJ), "Who shall not fear You, O Lord, and glorify Your name? For *You* alone *are* holy. For all nations shall come and worship before You, For Your judgments **have been manifested**."

This same verb is used as an affirmation of a positive response to the ministry of evangelism (cf. 2 Cor 3:3), as we may consider in Chapter 26.

n13) ἡ φανέρωσις (2 NT uses) – to disclose, announce: φανερώσει τῆς ἀληθείας – "disclosing the truth," 2 Cor 4:2:

    [Other NT use is 1 Cor 12:7, "But to each one is given the **manifestation** of the Spirit for the common good"]

Translations of ἡ φανέρωσις in 2 Cor 4:2b
[Notice the proclamational spectrum, though arranged chronologically]

Byzantine	Latin Vulgate	Wycliffe (2nd) 1388	Tyndale (1534)	Geneva (1560)	Bishop's (1595)	KJV (1611, 1769); cf. ERV; ASV; NAS; NKJ	New American Bible* (1901)	RSV (1952); cf. ESV	NIV (1984)	New Jerusalem Bible* (1985)	Cont English Version* (1995)	NET (2005)
Φανέρωσις	manifesta-tione	Schewynge	Walke	declaration	openyng	manifes-tation	open declaration	open statement	setting forth ... plainly	...showing ... openly	speak	open proclama-tion
συνίστημι	commen-dantes	comen-dynge	Reporte	approue	report	commen-ding	commend	commend	commend	Commend	will be sure	commend
ἀλλὰ Τῇ φανε-ρώσει τῆς ἀληθείας συνιο-τῶντες ἑαυτοὺς πρὸς πᾶσαν συνεί-δησιν ἀνθρώ-πων ἐνώπιον τοῦ θεοῦ	sed in manifesta-tione veritatis commen-dantes nosmet ipsos ad omnem con-scientiam hominum coram Deo	but in schewynge of the treuthe comen-dynge vs silf to ech conscience of men bifor God	but walke in open trueth and reporte oure selves to every mannes conscience in the sight of God	but in declaration of the trueth we approue our selues to euerie mans conscience in the sight of God	but in openyng of the trueth, and report our selues to euery mans conscience in the syght of God	But by manifes-tation of the truth commen-ding ourselves to every man's conscience in the sight of God	but by the open declaration of the truth we commend ourselves to everyone's conscience in the sight of God	but by the open statement of the truth we would commend ourselves to every man's conscience in the sight of God	On the contrary, by setting forth the truth plainly we commend ourselves to every man's conscience in the sight of God	instead, in God's sight we commend ourselves to every human being with a conscience by showing the truth openly	God is our witness that we speak only the truth, so others will be sure that we can be trusted	but by open proclama-tion of the truth we commend ourselves to everyone's conscience before God

Some French translations, by way of example:
  French Louis Segond [1910] and Nouvelle édition Genève [1979], "But, in publishing the truth" ["Mais, en publiant la vérité"]
  French *Le Semeur* [IBS, 1992,1999], "On the contrary, in making known the truth" ["Au contraire, en faisant connaître la vérité"]

    ar. ἀναστρέφω and cognate:
        Perhaps this verb and noun provide an important and necessary link between evangelistic fervor and behavior; one not excluding the other, but both being important simultaneously!

      86) ἀναστρέφω (11 NT uses), in passive voice: live, behave, conversation:[670]
        2 Cor 1:12, "For our proud confidence is this, the testimony of our conscience, that in holiness and godly sincerity, not in fleshly wisdom but in the grace of God, **we have conducted ourselves** in the world, and especially toward you"
        Heb 10:33 (Tyndale), "partly whill all men wondred and gased at you for the shame and trioulacion that was done vnto you and partly whill ye became companyons of the which so **passed their tyme**"—of fellowshipping with those in prison for the gospel"
        Heb 13:18, "Pray for us, for we are sure that we have a good conscience, desiring **to conduct ourselves** honorably in all things"
        1 Pet 1:17, "And if you address as Father the One who impartially judges according to each man's work, **conduct yourselves** [ἀναστράφητε] in fear during the time of your stay"

---

[670]Gingrich described the passive reflexive figurative use of ἀναστρέφω: "b. fig., of human conduct, *act, behave, conduct oneself,* or *live* in the sense of the practice of certain principles; always with the kind of behavior more exactly described: α. by an adverb, Hb 13:18; β. by prep. phrases, Eph 2:3; 2 Pt 2:18; 1 Ti 3:15; 1 Pet 1:17 [(ASV), "And if ye call on him as Father, who without respect of persons judgeth according to each man's work, pass the time of your **sojourning** in fear"]; γ. with adv. and prep. phrase; δ. with more than one ἐν in var. mngs., 2 Cor 1:12; Heb 10:33" (William Arndt and F. Wilbur Gingrich, *A Greek-English Lexicon of the New Testament and Other Early Christian Literature*, 4th ed. [Chicago: University of Chicago Press, 1957]).

(n14) ἡ ἀναστροφή (13 NT uses), translated: living (Wycliffe 1st ed); conversation (Wycliffe
2nd ed and KJV); behavior (NAS); etc.:

Gal 1:13 (Wycliffe 1st ed), "Forsothe ye herden of my **lyuynge** [or: living] sum tyme in the Juwerie,
for ouer manere I pursuwide the chirche of God, and faugte agaens it"

Gal 1:13 (Wycliffe 2nd ed), "For ye han herd my **conversacioun** sumtyme in the Jurie, and that
Y pursued passyngli the chirche of God, and faugt agen it"

1 Pet 2:12, "Keep your **behavior** excellent among the Gentiles, so that in the thing in which they
slander you as evildoers, they may on account of your good deeds, as they observe *them*,
glorify God in the day of visitation"

Translations of the noun ἡ ἀναστροφή in 1 Pet 2:12

Tyndale (1534); Geneva (1560); Bishops (1595); KJV (1611); Darby (1884)	Young's (1862); ERV (1885); ASV (1901); NAS (1977)	RSV (1952); CSB (2003); NET (2005)	Webster's (1833)	NIV (1984); GWN (1995); NLT (2002)	New Jerusalem (1985)
Verbal Element	**Lifestyle Emphasis**				
Conversation	Behavior	Conduct	Manner of life	Life/live	Behave
and se that ye have honest conversacion amonge the getyls that they which backbyte you as evyll doars maye se youre good workes and prayse god in the daye of visitacion.	having your behaviour among the nations right, that in that which they speak against you as evil-doers, of the good works having beheld, they may glorify God in a day of inspection.	Maintain good conduct among the Gentiles, so that in case they speak against you as wrongdoers, they may see your good deeds and glorify God on the day of visitation.	Having your manner of life honest among the Gentiles: that, whereas they speak against you as evil-doers, they may by {your} good works, which they shall behold, glorify God in the day of visitation	Live such good lives among the pagans that, though they accuse you of doing wrong, they may see your good deeds and glorify God on the day he visits us	Always behave honourably among gentiles so that they can see for themselves what moral lives you lead, and when the day of reckoning comes, give thanks to God for the things which now make them denounce you as criminals

as. (87) πολιτεύομαι (2 NT uses), translated "conversation" (KJV); conduct (NAS):[671]

Phil 1:27 (KJV), "Only let your conversation be as it becometh the gospel of Christ: that whether I come
and see you, or else be absent, I may hear of your affairs, that ye stand fast in one spirit, with one
mind striving together for the faith of the gospel"

This verb may be considered to speak of lifestyle rather than only of verbal communication, for
example, the other use of the verb is Acts 23:1:

Acts 23:1 (KJV), "And Paul, earnestly beholding the council, said, Men *and* brethren, I have lived in
all good conscience before God until this day"

And yet, as with Paul, there exists a close link almost impregnable link between one's words
(that which comes out of the heart) and one's manner of life!

---

[671]The Middle English "conversacion," from the French, is said to mean "conversation, manner of life"
(Stratmann and Bradley, *Middle English Dictionary* [1891]). The 1875 Liddell-Scott Greek Lexicon emphasized the
lifestyle aspect: 1. To be a citizen or free-man of a free state [as opposed to under a monarchy]; 2. To have a certain
form of government, hence to be governed.

10—METAPHORICAL VERBS FOR EVANGELIZING

at. Verbs dealing with one's function and habit or custom:

88) πρεσβεύω (2 NT uses) – to function as an ambassador, 2 Cor 5:20; Eph 6:20, hence to represent; note the cognage noun πρεσβύτερος [presbuteros] translated "priest" before the Protestant Reformation, and now often translated "elder":

> Because this verb, used twice in the NT and never as a verb in the LXX, links the person evangelizing with the message of the Gospel, as can be expected, its translation has an interesting provenance…

> 2 Cor 5:20, "Therefore, we are ambassadors for Christ ['Υπὲρ χριστοῦ οὖν πρεσβεύομεν], as though God were entreating through us; we beg you on behalf of Christ, be reconciled to God"

Translations of πρεσβεύω 2 Cor 5:20

(Pre-1900)

Greek	Latin	Wycliffe	Tyndale; Bishops	Geneva; KJV; Noyes	Etheridge	Murdock	Young's; Rotherham	Darby	ERV; ASV	DRA
'Υπὲρ χριστοῦ οὖν πρεσβεύομεν,	pro Christo ergo legationem fungimur	Therfor we vsen message for Crist,	Now then are we messengers in the roume of Christ:	Now then are we ambassadours for Christ:	We are ambassadors then for the Meshiha,	We are therefore ambassadors for the Messiah,	in behalf of Christ, then, we are ambassadors,	We are ambassadors therefore for Christ,	We are ambassadors therefore on behalf of Christ,	For Christ therefore we are ambassadors,

(Post-1900)

RSV; NJB; NAB (1991, 2010)	NAS; NET; ESV; CSB	NKJ; RWB	NIV (1984, 2011); TNIV	NLT	MacDonald	BBE	GWN	CEB	NIRV
So we are ambassadors for Christ,	Therefore, we are ambassadors for Christ,	Now then, we are ambassadors for Christ,	We are therefore Christ's ambassadors,	So we are Christ's ambassadors	Therefore, in behalf of Christ we serve as God's ambassadors,	So we are the representatives of Christ,	Therefore, we are Christ's representatives,	So we are ambassadors who represent Christ.	So we are Christ's official messengers.

Is this verb speaking more of the message or the messenger?
> Is the emphasis on the Christian as an ambassador-messenger of the gospel of Christ, or the Christian as a ambassador-person representing Christ?
> Hence "We are representing Christ, …"[672]
> The context appears to be more the message and less the messenger

Particularizing the role of the messenger in this verse can result in some negative connotations:
> If "representative" refers only to the Pope, then the plural use of Paul could be a problem—for the Catholic apologist only the Pope speaks for Christ on earth;
> However, if "Christ" refers to the pope: ambassadors for Christ may be understood as "conquistadores for the Vicar of Christ"
> If "we" refers to apostolic authority: *pro Christo ergo legationem fungimur* may be understood as "Therefore we function as legislators for Christ"—people actually writing ecclesiastical legislation, called canonical law
> If "we" refers to ordained clergy only: then this verse only refers to "Christ's official messengers," not to all followers of Christ
> However, the implication of this verse seems to be more general: "I, Paul, those with me, and you all in Corinth" are currently representating [present active] Christ!

In most of the above versions, the English reader:
> Would almost never understand that the concept of "ambassador" results from the translation of a Greek verb. Most would assume that it results from the translation of a very specialized noun.

---

[672]Please see study of English translations using derivatives of the word represent at the end of this chapter.

Would never know that it is a participle, "messengering"—in the present tense (continuous), "We therefore are messengering of Christ" or even, "We therefore are representing Christ, …"

Interestingly, the other Greek word often translated "messenger" in the Bible is angel (ἄγγελος), from which derives the verb evangelize (εὐαγγελίζω).

Eph 6:20, "for which I am an ambassador in chains; that in *proclaiming* it I may speak boldly, as I ought to speak"

Translations of πρεσβεύω Eph 6:20

Greek	Latin	Wycliffe	Tyndale; Bishops	Murdock; NJB	Geneva	KJV	Etheridge; ERV; ASV; RSV; NAS; NKJ; NIV; NRS; NAB; Stern; TNIV; NET; ESV	Noyes	Young's; DRA	Darby
ὑπὲρ οὗ πρεσβεύω ἐν ἁλύσει,	pro quo legatione fungor in catena	for which Y am set in message in a chayne;	whereof I am a messenger in bondes	of which I am a messenger in chains;	Whereof I am the ambassadour in bonds,	For which I am an ambassador in bonds:	for which I am an ambassador in chains,	in behalf of which I am an ambassador in chains;	for which I am an ambassador in a chain,	for which I am an ambassador *bound* with a chain,

Rotherham	BBE	CEV	GNT	GWN	NIRV	NLT	Magiera	MacDonald	CSB	CEB
In behalf of which I am conducting an embassy in chains,	For which I am a representative in chains,	I was sent to do this work, and that's the reason that I am in jail.	For the sake of this gospel I am an ambassador, though now I am in prison	Because I have already been doing this as Christ's representative, I am in prison.	Because of the good news, I am being held by chains as the Lord's messenger.	I am in chains now, still preaching this message as God's ambassador.	for which I am its ambassador in chains,	on whose behalf I am an ambassador, as evidenced by my "chain,"	For this I am an ambassador in chains.	I'm an ambassador in chains for the sake of the gospel.

Compare also with the OT LXX noun πρέσβυς (used 11 times) considered above under the "Section A, The Person"

89) εἴωθα/ἔθω (4 total NT uses), meaning to have a custom of, be accustomed to:

Luke 4:16, "So He came to Nazareth, where He had been brought up. And as His **custom was**, He went into the synagogue on the Sabbath day, and stood up to read."

Acts 17:2, "Then Paul, as his **custom was**, went in to them, and for three Sabbaths reasoned with them from the Scriptures."

au. Verbs dealing with fruitfulness:

Some thoughts concerning fruit:

The interrelationship between an action and its fruit is exemplified in Rom 6:21:

Rom 6:21 (NKJ), "What fruit did you have then in the things of which you are now ashamed? For the end of those things *is* death"

Here is the question: How does fruit relate to the action in question?

Sin	Whose fruit is?	Shame	Whose end is?	Death	For whom?	(1) To those who practice it; (2) To the unrepentant
Evangelism	Whose fruit is?	Souls (and joy)	Whose end is?	Eternal life	For whom?	(1) To those who testify; (2) To those who have a hearing of faith

What is "fruit for eternal life" (John 4:36)? Is it not souls?

When a seed is planted in the ground, does it not reproduce a plant which multiplies that original seed 30, 60, and 100 times?

Some OT precedents:
From the Hebrew *asah* (do, make) + *peri* (fruit):
2 Kgs 19:30, "And the surviving remnant of the house of Judah shall again take root downward and bear fruit upward"
Isa 37:31, "And the surviving remnant of the house of Judah shall again take root downward and bear fruit upward"
Jer 12:2 (NKJ), "You have planted them, yes, they have taken root; They grow, yes, they bear fruit. You *are* near in their mouth But far from their mind"
Ezek 17:23, "On the high mountain of Israel I shall plant it, that it may bring forth boughs and bear fruit, and become a stately cedar"
Hos 9:16, "Ephraim is stricken, their root is dried up, They will bear no fruit. Even though they bear children, I will slay the precious ones of their womb"
From the Hebrew *asah* (do, make) + *enab* (grape):
Isa 5:2, "And He dug it all around, removed its stones, And planted it with the choicest vine. And He built a tower in the middle of it, And hewed out a wine vat in it; Then He expected *it* to produce *good* grapes, But it produced *only* worthless ones"
Isa 5:4, "What more was there to do for My vineyard that I have not done in it? Why, when I expected *it* to produce *good* grapes did it produce worthless ones?"
From the Hebrew *nasa or nasah* (carry) + *peri* (fruit)
Ezek 17:8, "It was planted in good soil beside abundant waters, that it might yield branches and bear fruit, *and* become a splendid vine"
From the Hebrew *nub* (bear fruit):
Psa 92:14, "They will still yield fruit in old age; They shall be full of sap and very green"

90) ποιέω (do, make) + ὁ καρπός (fruit):
Matt 3:10, "And the axe is already laid at the root of the trees; every tree therefore that does not bear good fruit is cut down and thrown into the fire" (cf. Luke 3:9)
Matt 7:18, "A good tree cannot produce bad fruit, nor can a bad tree produce good fruit"
(cf. Luke 6:43)
Matt 7:19, "Every tree that does not bear good fruit is cut down and thrown into the fire"

91) φέρω (to bear) + ὁ καρπός (fruit):
John 15:2, "Every branch in Me that does not bear fruit, He takes away; and every *branch* that bears fruit, He prunes it, that it may bear more fruit"
John 15:4, "Abide in Me, and I in you. As the branch cannot bear fruit of itself, unless it abides in the vine, so neither *can* you, unless you abide in Me"
John 15:8, "By this is My Father glorified, that you bear much fruit, and *so* prove to be My disciples"
John 15:16, "You did not choose Me, but I chose you, and appointed you, that you should go and bear fruit, and *that* your fruit should remain…"

92) ἔχω (have) + ὁ καρπός (fruit):
Rom 1:13, "And I do not want you to be unaware, brethren, that often I have planned to come to you (and have been prevented thus far) in order that I might **obtain** some **fruit** among you also, even as among the rest of the Gentiles"
Cf. Rom 6:21-22.

93) καρποφορέω (8 NT uses; 1 OT LXX use)—meaning to bear fruit or crops, yield (a crop):

An OT precedent:
Hab 3:17-18, "Though the fig tree should not **blossom**, And there be no fruit on the vines, *Though* the yield of the olive should fail, And the fields produce no food, Though the flock should be cut off from the fold, And there be no cattle in the stalls, Yet I will exult in the LORD, I will rejoice in the God of my salvation"

Matt 13:23, "And the one on whom seed was sown on the good soil, this is the man who hears the word and understands it; who indeed **bears fruit**, and brings forth, some a hundredfold, some sixty, and some thirty"
Mark 4:20, "And those are the ones on whom seed was sown on the good soil; and they hear the word and accept it, and **bear fruit**, thirty, sixty, and a hundredfold"
Luke 8:15, "And the *seed* in the good soil, these are the ones who have heard the word in an honest and good heart, and hold it fast, and **bear fruit** with perseverance"

Rom 7:4, "Therefore, my brethren, you also were made to die to the Law through the body of Christ, that you might be joined to another, to Him who was raised from the dead, that we might **bear fruit** for God" (cf. Rom 7:5)

Col 1:5-6, "…the gospel, which has come to you, just as in all the world also it is constantly **bearing fruit** and increasing…"

Col 1:10, "so that you may walk in a manner worthy of the Lord, to please *Him* in all respects, **bearing fruit** in every good work and increasing in the knowledge of God"

Two non-evangelistic contexts
Of the agricultural process of a seed sprouting, Mark 4:27;
Of sin's fruit being death, Rom 7:5.

av. Verbs dealing with agricultural motifs:

94) βάλλω (125 NT uses; 56 OT LXX uses), literal meaning: to throw, cast; by analogy: to bring, lay, pour:

Matt 7:6, "Do not give what is holy to dogs, and do not **throw** your pearls before swine, lest they trample them under their feet, and turn and tear you to pieces."

Matt 13:47, Again, the kingdom [rule] of heaven is like a dragnet **cast** into the sea, and gathering *fish* of every kind."

Mark 4:26, "And He was saying, 'The kingdom of God is like a man who **casts** seed upon the soil.'"

An OT LXX variant:
Psa 126:6 (Brenton), "They went on and wept as **they cast** their seeds; but they shall surely come with exultation, bringing their sheaves *with them*."

Psa 125[126]:6 (GOT), πορευόμενοι ἐπορεύοντο καὶ ἔκλαιον **βάλλοντες** τὰ σπέρματα αὐτῶν· ἐρχόμενοι δὲ ἥξουσιν ἐν ἀγαλλιάσει αἴροντες τὰ δράγματα αὐτῶν.

*Ralph's LXX reads αἴροντες in the place of the GOT βάλλοντες, whereas the latter seems to be the verb behind Brenton's translation use of "they cast" in this verse.

95) σπείρω (53 NT uses; 56 OT LXX uses), meaning to sow [seed]; other synonyms: spreading seed, casting seed, bearing seed:

Some OT precedents:
Psa 126:5, "Those who **sow** in tears Shall reap in joy"
[Heb. *zara'*; Gk. σπείρω]

Psa 126:6 (NKJ), "He who continually goes forth weeping, **Bearing seed** for **sowing**, Shall doubtless come again with rejoicing, Bringing his sheaves *with him*"
[Heb. *meshech* + *zara'*; Gk. αἴρω + σπέρμα]

Prov 11:18, "The wicked earns deceptive wages, But he who **sows** righteousness *gets* a true reward"
[Heb. *zara'* + tsedaqah; Gk. σπέρμα + δίκαιος]

Prov 15:7, "The lips of the wise **spread** knowledge, But the hearts of fools are not so"
[Heb. *zara'* is translated in the LXX by δέω, meaning "to bind"]

Matt 13:3 And He spoke many things to them in parables, saying, 'Behold, the **sower** went out to **sow** [ὁ σπείρων τοῦ σπείρειν]'" (cf. Mark 4; Luke 8)

Matt 13:4, "and as he **sowed** [Καὶ ἐν τῷ σπείρειν αὐτόν]…"

Matt 13:18, "Hear then the parable of the **sower**"

Matt 13:19, "When anyone hears the word of the kingdom, and does not understand it, the evil *one* comes and snatches away what **has been sown** in his heart. This is the one on whom seed **was sown** beside the road"

Matt 13:20, "And the one on whom seed **was sown** on the rocky places…"

Matt 13:22, "And the one on whom seed **was sown** among the thorns…"

Matt 13:23, "And the one on whom seed **was sown** on the good soil, this is the man who hears the word and understands it; who indeed bears fruit, and brings forth, some a hundredfold, some sixty, and some thirty"

Matt 13:24, "He presented another parable to them, saying, 'The kingdom of heaven may be compared to a man who sowed good seed in his field'" (Matt 13:27)

Matt 13:31, "He presented another parable to them, saying, 'The kingdom of heaven is like a mustard seed, which a man took and **sowed** in his field'" (cf. Mark 4:31-32)

Matt 13:37, "And He answered and said, 'The one who **sows** the good seed is the Son of Man'"

Matt 25:24, "And the one also who had received the one talent came up and said, 'Master, I knew you to be a hard man, reaping where you did not **sow**, and gathering where you scattered no *seed*'" (cf. Matt 25:26; Luke 19:21-22)

John 4:36 (NKJ), "And he who reaps receives wages, and gathers fruit for eternal life, that both he who **sows** and he who reaps may rejoice together"

John 4:37, "For in this *case* the saying is true, 'One **sows**, and another reaps'"

1 Cor 9:11, "If we **sowed** spiritual things in you, is it too much if we should reap material things from you?"

2 Cor 9:6, "Now this *I say*, he who **sows** sparingly shall also reap sparingly; and he who **sows** bountifully shall also reap bountifully"

Also used of false teachers or of the Devil himself:

Matt 13:25, "But while men were sleeping, his enemy came and sowed tares also among the wheat, and went away" (cf. Matt 13:39)

96) θερίζω (21 NT uses; 24 OT LXX uses), meaning to reap, harvest:

Psa 126:5, "Those who sow in tears **Shall reap** in joy"

John 4:36 (NKJ), "And **he who reaps** receives wages, and gathers fruit for eternal life, that both he who sows and he who **reaps** may rejoice together"

John 4:37, "For in this *case* the saying is true, 'One sows, and another **reaps**.'"

John 4:38, "I sent you **to reap** that for which you have not labored; others have labored, and you have entered into their labor"

1 Cor 9:11, "If we sowed spiritual things in you, is it too much if we should reap material things from you?"

2 Cor 9:6, "Now this *I say*, he who sows sparingly shall also **reap** sparingly; and he who sows bountifully shall also **reap** bountifully"

Regarding fruitlessness:

As a curse:

Psa 129:7, "With which **the reaper** does not fill his hand, Nor he who binds sheaves, his arms"

Resulting from overthinking—"Need more cultural and sociological analysis to really understand these people":

Eccl 11:4, "He who observes the wind will not sow, And he who regards the clouds will not reap"

Complaining because of God's method of sowing (cf. Luke 19:20-21):

Matt 25:24, "And the one also who had received the one talent came up and said, 'Master, I knew you to be a hard man, reaping where you did not sow, and gathering where you scattered no *seed*'"

Matt 25:26, "But his master answered and said to him, 'You wicked, lazy slave, you knew that I reap where I did not sow, and gather where I scattered no *seed*'"

97) ἀροτριάω (13 OT LXX uses and 3 NT uses), meaning to plow:

1 Cor 9:10, "Or is He speaking altogether for our sake? Yes, for our sake it was written, because **the plowing** [man] ought **to plow** in hope, and the thresher *to thresh* in hope of sharing *the crops*."

Consider these verses on plowing:

Isa 28:24-26 (NKJ), "Does the plowman keep plowing all day to sow? Does he keep turning his soil and breaking the clods? When he has leveled its surface, Does he not sow the black cummin And scatter the cummin, Plant the wheat in rows, The barley in the appointed place, And the spelt in its place? For He instructs him in right judgment, His God teaches him."

98) ἀλοάω (8 OT LXX uses; 3 NT uses), meaning to thresh [tread out]:

1 Cor 9:9-10, "For it is written in the law of Moses, 'You shall not muzzle an ox while it **treads out** the grain.' Is it oxen God is concerned about? Or does He say *it* altogether for our sakes? For our sakes, no doubt, *this* is written, that he who plows should plow in hope, and he who **threshes** in hope should be partaker of his hope."

1 Tim 5:8, "For the Scripture says, 'You shall not muzzle an ox while it treads out the grain,' and, 'The laborer *is* worthy of his wages.'"

Consider these verses on threshing:

Isa 28:27-29 (NKJ), "For the black cummin is not threshed with a threshing sledge, Nor is a cartwheel rolled over the cummin; But the black cummin is beaten out with a stick, And the cummin with a rod. Bread *flour* must be ground; Therefore he does not thresh it forever, Break *it with* his cartwheel, Or crush *it with* his horsemen. This also comes from the LORD of hosts, *Who* is wonderful in counsel *and* excellent in guidance."

99) περκάζω (1 OT LXX use), meaning to turn dark [from treading the grapes]:
   Amos 9:13, "'Behold, days are coming,' declares the LORD, 'When the plowman will overtake the reaper And the treader of grapes him who sows seed; When the mountains will drip sweet wine, And all the hills will be dissolved.'"

100) φυτεύω (42 OT LXX uses; 11 NT use)
   1 Cor 3:6-8, "I planted [φυτεύω], Apollos watered, but God was causing the growth. So then neither the one who plants [φυτεύω] nor the one who waters is anything, but God who causes the growth. Now he who plants [φυτεύω] and he who waters are one; but each will receive his own reward according to his own labor."

   Consider these OT precedents:
      Psa 1:3, "And he will be like a tree *firmly* **planted** [φυτεύω] by streams of water, Which yields its fruit in its season, And its leaf does not wither; And in whatever he does, he prospers."
      Psa 92:13, "**Planted** [φυτεύω] in the house of the LORD, They will flourish in the courts of our God"
      Eccl 3:2, "A time to give birth, and a time to die; A time to plant [φυτεύω], and a time to uproot what is planted"
      Isa 5:1-2, "Let me sing now for my well-beloved A song of my beloved concerning His vineyard. My well-beloved had a vineyard on a fertile hill. And He dug it all around, removed its stones, And **planted** [φυτεύω] it with the choicest vine. And He built a tower in the middle of it, And hewed out a wine vat in it; Then He expected *it* to produce *good* grapes, But it produced *only* worthless ones."
      Jer 12:2, "Thou hast **planted** [φυτεύω] them, they have also taken root; They grow, they have even produced fruit. Thou art near to their lips But far from their mind."

aw. Verbal phrases dealing with fishing:

Consider this very unusual Old Testament LXX use of nouns and verbs related to the concept of fishermen and hunters used to describe the Babylonian invaders of Judea:

   Jer 16:16, "'Behold, I am going to send for many **fishermen** [ὁ ἁλιεύς],' declares the LORD, 'and **they will fish** [ἁλιεύω] **for them**; and afterwards I shall send for many **hunters** [ὁ θηρευτής], and **they will hunt** [θηρεύω] **them** from every mountain and every hill, and from the clefts of the rocks.'"

It behooves us to bear in mind the odius nature of "fishing for men" in sociological circles.

1) Verbal phrases with ὁ ἁλιεύς—"fisherman":

   (101) ποιέω + ὁ ἁλιεύς + ὁ ἄνθρωπος (5 NT uses of ὁ ἁλιεύς) – meaning "make" + "fishermen" + "of men":
      Matt 4:19, "And He said to them, 'Follow Me, and I will make you fishers of men.'"

   (102) ποιέω + γίνομαι + ὁ ἁλιεύς + ὁ ἄνθρωπος (5 NT uses of ἁλιεύς) – meaning "make" + "become" + "fishermen" + "of men":
      Mark 1:17, "And Jesus said to them, 'Follow Me, and I will make you become fishers of men.'"

2) Verbs with δίκτυον—"net":

   (103) βάλλω + τὸ δίκτυον (1 NT use of this pair) – meaning "throw, put cast" + "net":
      John 21:6, "And He said to them, '**Cast the net** on the right-hand side of the boat, and you will find *a catch*.' They **cast** therefore, and then they were not able to haul it in because of the great number of fish."

   (104) χαλάω + τὸ δίκτυον (2 NT uses of this pair) – meaning "let down" + "net":
      Luke 5:4, "And when He had finished speaking, He said to Simon, 'Put out into the deep water and **let down** your **nets** for a catch.'"
      Luke 5:5, "And Simon answered and said, 'Master, we worked hard all night and caught nothing, but at Your bidding I will **let down** the **nets**.'"

ax. Verbs dealing with carrying or taking up:

1) Two cognates of δίδωμι:

   (105) μεταδίδωμι (5 NT uses) – impart, share, give:
      1 Thess 2:8, "Having thus a fond affection for you, we were well-pleased to **impart** to you not only the gospel of God but also our own lives, because you had become very dear to us"

(106) παραδίδωμι (121 NT uses) – hand over, deliver, betray; give (over); pass down:
> 1 Cor 15:3, "For I **delivered** to you as of first importance what I also received, that Christ died for our sins according to the Scriptures"

Various Translations of παρέδωκα in 1 Corinthians 15:3

I have taught you	For I have communicated to you	I told you	For I passed on to you	I brought you [as a package]	For I deliuered vnto you	I transmitted to you	I handed on to you	The tradition I handed on to you
Je vous ai enseigné	Car je vous ai communiqué			ie vous ay baille; ie vous ay baillé; je vous ai baillé*		Je vous ai [donc] transmis		
Fr. New Geneva (1976)	Fr. Darby (1859)	Contemporary English Version (1995)✠	Holman Christian Standard (cf. NIV; NLT; NET)	Fr. Lefevre (1530), Louvain✠ (1550), Geneva (1669)	English Geneva (1560); KJV; ASV; RSV; NAS; NKJ; ESV	French Jerusalem Bible (1973)✠; French Le Semeur (1992, 1999)✠	New American Bible (1901)✠	English New Jerusalem Bible (1985)✠

*The semantic range of this interesting French verb is fairly broad: "Donner, remettre, livrer, présenter" [give, return, deliver, present]. The 16th Century Bible colporteurs were called in French "portebaille" [carriers of packages]; which is consistent with certain French translations of 2 Chron 30:6, 10, the "posts" or "couriers" of King Hezekiah who delivered the plea of invitation to Passover from the king. This French verb "bailler" is also used as a translation of "to give" in Deut 31:9 (FGN), when Moses "gave" the scroll of "this Law" to the priests for safe-keeping.

> 1 Cor 11:2, "Now I praise you because you remember me in everything, and hold firmly to the traditions, just as **I delivered** them to you" (cf. 1 Cor 11:23)

Consider, please, several OT parallel uses and thoughts:

> The first OT LXX use of παραδίδωμι is in Gen 14:20 (for the Heb *magan*) wherein Melchizedek blessed the Lord for delivering (placing) the enemies of Abraham into his hands;
> Of special interest was the act of "placing something in the hands" of someone else, which is what the Apostle Paul was accomplishing in writing a letter, that being what we now call 1 Corinthians:
>> Gen 14:20, "'And blessed be God Most High, Who has delivered your enemies into your hand.' And he gave him a tenth of all."

> Another verse of interest is Deut 24:1, 3, in which a written certificate of divorce is "given into the hands of" the disfavored wife, using the Heb verb for "give" (*nathan*):
>> Deut 24:3, "and if the latter husband turns against her and writes her a certificate of divorce and puts *it* in her hand and sends her out of his house…"

> In like way, a Gospel tract, New Testament, or Bible is placed into the hand of a contact for the Gospel, with the hope that the individual will read it, and that the Gospel will take hold of their heart, and that they will be saved!

107) ἐπέχω (5 NT uses), often translated "holding forth" (KJV) or "holding fast" (Tyndale) in Phil 2:[15]-16, also translated hold toward, aim at; fix one's attention; take pains; notice; stop, stay:

> Phil 2:15-16 (KJV), "among whom ye shine as lights in the world; Holding forth the word of life"
>> The punctuation between the verses also seems to have been changed from a comma (Geneva, Bishops) to a semi-colon to a period
>> Likewise, the verse break changed between the French Geneva and English Geneva, as the French Geneva has verse 16 begin after the word "life"
>> It seems like there has been a desire by some to divide these two phrases, likewise rendering the word in as non-evangelistic a way as possible
> One cannot help but notice in the translations of this word in Phil 2:16, especially following precedent of the *Nova Vulgata* (shrewdly revised after Vatican II), that this phrase is viewed less and less in an evangelistic manner (see chart below):

Translations of λόγον ζωῆς ἐπέχοντες Phil 2:16

Migne's Clemen-tine Vulgate (1598, 1880)	DRA⚕ (1899)*	Nova Vulgata (1979)⚕	NJB⚕ (1985)**	Ethe-ridge Syriac (1849)	Mur-dock Syriac (1851)	Tyndale (1534); Bishops; RSV; NAS; NKJ; ESV	Geneva (1560); KJV; ERV; ASV	Bible in Basic English (1949)	ABS' GNT⚕ (1993)	NIV (1984)	NAB⚕ (1991)** *	ABS' CEV⚕ (1991)** *	TNIV (1995)** *	CSB (2005)
verbum vitae conti-nentes	Holding forth the word of life	verbum vitae firmiter tenentes	Proffer-ing to it the Word of life	to be unto them for a place of salvatio n	so that ye may be to them in place of life	holdinge fast the worde of lyfe	Holding forthe the worde of life	Offering the word of life	as you offer them the messag e of life	as you hold out the word of life	as you hold on to the word of life	as you hold firmly to the messag e that gives life	as you hold firmly to the word of life	Hold firmly the messag e of life

*The Douais-Rheims seems to be a very literal translation of the earlier Vulgate

**The New Jerusalem Bible is a translation conforming to the 1973 French Bible de Jerusalem, which seems to follow the updated Vulgate in its translation.

***The Church of Rome "New American Bible" translates this phrase even more closely with the *Nova Vulgata*, with the TNIV being a more exact translation of the *Nova Vulgata*.

3) Two cognates of φέρω:

(108) περιφέρω (3 NT uses) – "to carry about," also in Mark 6:55 and Eph 4:14:
2 Cor 4:10, "always **carrying about** in the body the dying of Jesus, that the life of Jesus also may be manifested in our body"
This verb is used in parallel form with "manifested" [φανερόω].

(109) εἰσφέρω [1]:
Act 17:20, "For you **are bringing** some strange things to our ears; we want to know therefore what these things mean."

(110) ἐκφέρω (77 OT LXX uses [for Heb *yatsa*]; 8 NT uses) – "bear forth":
Psa 37:6, "And He **will bring forth** your righteousness as the light, And your judgment as the noonday"
Isa 42:3, "A bruised reed He will not break, And a dimly burning wick He will not extinguish; He will faithfully **bring forth** justice [lit. judgment]"

Note also this negative use:
Prov 10:18, "He who conceals hatred *has* lying lips, And he who **spreads** slander is a fool"

Likewise, in NT it is used of bearing bad fruit:
Heb 6:8, "but if it **yields** thorns and thistles, it is worthless and close to being cursed, and it ends up being burned."

In this light, consider the power and the metaphorical implications of Deut 28:38 as a curse related to evangelism:
Deut 28:38, "You shall **bring out** much seed to the field but you shall gather in little, for the locust shall consume it."

Concerning the literal use of ἐκφέρω as "bring out" in Deut 22:15:
On a side note, it may not be accurate to use "bring" (as in "bring out") when translating εὐαγγελίζω , e.g. as "**bring** good news" as is often done, since numerous other words, such as ἐκφέρω, are and could easily have been used if that was the intended meaning of the original Hebrew or Greek.

For example, consider how these two primary passages may quite likely be a mistranslation of εὐαγγελίζω:
Isa 52:7 (KJV), "How beautiful upon the mountains are the feet of him that **bringeth** good tidings, that publisheth peace; that **bringeth** good tidings of good, that publisheth salvation; that saith unto Zion, Thy God reigneth!"

Rom 10:15 (KJV), "And how shall they preach, except they be sent? as it is written, How beautiful are the feet of them that preach the gospel of peace, and **bring** glad tidings of good things!"

Note, however, that while Psa 126:5 does use the verb αἴρω, "to take up, carry," in a metaphorical way to describe evangelizing, this use of a figurative verb is no warrant to mistranslate the proclamational term, as in the KJV's translation of both uses of εὐαγγελίζω in Isa 52:7.

111) βαστάζω (27 NT uses) – "pick up; carry, bear; carry away, remove":
Acts 9:15, "But the Lord said to him, 'Go, for he is a chosen instrument of Mine, to **bear** My name before the Gentiles and kings and the sons of Israel'"
Greek Byzantine: Εἶπεν δὲ πρὸς αὐτὸν ὁ κύριος, Πορεύου, ὅτι σκεῦος ἐκλογῆς μοι ἐστιν οὗτος, τοῦ **βαστάσαι** τὸ ὄνομά μου ἐνώπιον ἐθνῶν καὶ βασιλέων, υἱῶν τε Ἰσραήλ·
Rev 2:3, "I know you are enduring patiently and **bearing up** for my name's sake, and you have not grown weary"
Greek Byzantine: καὶ ὑπομονὴν ἔχεις καὶ **ἐβάστασας** διὰ τὸ ὄνομά μου καὶ οὐκ ἐκοπίασας.

Other interesting uses of this verb include:
Matt 10:12, "**Carry** no purse, no bag, no shoes; and greet no one on the way"
Luke 14:27 "Whoever does not **carry** his own cross and come after Me cannot be My disciple"
John 19:17 They took Jesus therefore, and He went out, **bearing** His own cross, to the place called the Place of a Skull, which is called in Hebrew, Golgotha"
Acts 15:10, "Now therefore why do you put God to the test by placing upon the neck of the disciples a yoke which neither our fathers nor we have been able **to bear**?"
Gal 6:5, "For each one **shall bear** his own load"
Gal 6:17, "From now on let no one cause trouble for me, for I **bear** on my body the brand-marks of Jesus"

5)   λαμβάνω and cognate:

(112) λαμβάνω (263 NT uses) – "take up" (take up, take hold of, catch, draw):
Matt 10:38, "And he who does not **take** his cross and follow after Me is not worthy of Me"

(113) ἐπιλαμβάνομαι (19 NT uses) – lay hold, take hold:
1 Tim 6:12, "take hold of the eternal life to which you were called"
[The prior phrase and the following phrase correspond to the evangelistic call of Timothy, making it highly likely that this command has an evangelistic emphasis]
1 Tim 6:19 (NKJ), "storing up for themselves a good foundation for the time to come, that they may lay hold on eternal life"
[The critical edition Greek in this verse changes "eternal life" for "that which is life"]

114) αἴρω (102 NT uses) – "take up" (raise, lift, take up, pick up; take, carry away, remove):
Psa 126:6, "He who goes to and fro weeping, **carrying** *his* bag of seed, Shall indeed come again with a shout of joy, bringing his sheaves *with him*."
Matt 16:24, "Then Jesus said to His disciples, 'If anyone wishes to come after Me, let him deny himself, and **take up** [imperative] his cross, and follow Me.'"
Mark 8:34, "And He summoned the multitude with His disciples, and said to them, 'If anyone wishes to come after Me, let him deny himself, and **take up** [imperative] his cross, and follow Me.'"
Luke 9:23, "And He was saying to *them* all, 'If anyone wishes to come after Me, let him deny himself, and **take up** [imperative] his cross daily, and follow Me.'"

115) ὑψόω (20 NT uses) – "raised up":
John 3:14, "And as Moses **lifted up** the serpent in the wilderness, even so must the Son of Man **be lifted up**."
John 8:28, "Jesus therefore said, 'When you **lift up** the Son of Man, then you will know that I am *He*, and I do nothing on My own initiative, but I speak these things as the Father taught Me.'"
John 12:32, "And I, if **I be lifted** up from the earth, will draw all [men] to Myself."
John 12:34, "The multitude therefore answered Him, 'We have heard out of the Law that the Christ is to remain forever; and how can You say, "The Son of Man **must be lifted up**"? Who is this Son of Man?'"

ay. Verbs relating to holding forth/establishing:

116) κρατέω (47 NT uses) – 1. take into one's possession or custody: a. arrest, apprehend; b. take hold of, grasp, seize; attain; 2. Hold, hold back, restrain; be prevented; hold fast, keep, retain:

Heb 4:14, "Since then we have a great high priest who has passed through the heavens, Jesus the Son of God, **let us hold fast** our confession"

[Get the idea of someone seizing the horns of the altar, grasping tightly to a verbal confession, in the context of a very powerful Word (Heb 4:12-13), a powerful Savior (Heb 4:14), and a compassionate Savior (Heb 4:15)]

[Not merely holding to the content of the confession of Christ, in a passive sense, but holding forth a confession of Him before all creatures, knowing that there is no creature hidden "from His sight" (Heb 4:13), as well as holding forth the need for verbal confession of Christ (Matt 10:32; Luke 12:18)]

[Christ sympathizing with our weaknesses, in the next verse, seems to acknowledge the great difficulty of regularly holding fast to this confession before men, cf. Mark 8:38]

For a similar emphasis, See also:
#68, φυλάσσω, cf. Ezek 33:8;
#170, ἀνταγωνίζομαι, cf. Heb 12:4;
#171, ἐπαγωνίζομαι, cf. Jude 1:3
#172, ἀντικαθίστημι, cf. Heb 12:4.

117) τίθημι (493 OT LXX uses; 100 NT uses), meaning to set, place, establish:
1 Cor 3:10, "According to the grace of God which was given to me, as a wise master builder **I laid** [τίθημι] a foundation, and another is building upon it. But let each man be careful how he builds upon it."

az. Verbs relating to capturing people:

118) ζωγρέω (2 NT uses; 8 OT uses) – "**capturing men alive**":
The Greek meaning of ζωγρέω is to "capture" alive, based on the OT LXX translation;
7 of the 8 OT use of ζωγρέω comes from a translation of the hiphil (5) or piel (2) of the Hebrew *chayah* (287 total uses) to preserve alive, to revive; the 8th use is in 2 Chron 25:12, and come from two Hebrew words *shabah* (to capture) and *chay* (alive)

Luke 5:10, "Do not fear, from now on you will be **catching** men [or: taking men alive]"

Translations of ζωγρῶν in Luke 5:10

Greek Byzantine	Latin Vulgate	Wycliffe 2nd ed	Geneva	NAS	Louis Segond (my trans)	Louis Segond
Μὴ φοβοῦ· ἀπὸ τοῦ νῦν ἀνθρώπους ἔσῃ ζωγρῶν	noli timere ex hoc iam homines eris capiens	Nyle thou drede; now fro this tyme thou schalt take men.	Feare not: from hence forthe thou shalt catch men	Do not fear, from now on you will be catching men	Do not fear, from now on you will be a fisher of men	Ne crains point; désormais tu seras pêcheur d'hommes

a) The verb ζωγρέω is used 8 times in the OT LXX:

Num 31:15, "Have you **spared** all the women?
[τί ἐζωγρήσατε πᾶν θῆλυ]"

Num 31:18, "But all the girls who have not known man intimately, **spare** for yourselves"

Deut 20:16, "you shall not leave alive anything that breathes
[οὐ ζωγρήσετε ἀπ' αὐτῶν πᾶν ἐμπνέον]"

Translations of ζωγρῶν in Deut 20:16 (especially last phrase)

Greek Byzantine	Brenton (1851)	Latin Vulgate	Wycliffe 2nd ed	Geneva	KJV, RSV, ASV, ESV	NAS, NIV	NKJ	NIRV	NLT	CSB	CEB*
οὐ ζωγρήσετε ἀπ' αὐτῶν πᾶν ἐμπνέον	ye shall **not take** any thing **alive**	tibi nullum omnino permittes vivere	thou schalt **not suffre** eny **to lyue**	thou shalt **save no person alive**	thou shalt **save alive nothing** that breatheth	you shall **not leave alive** anything that breathes	you shall **let nothing** that breathes **remain alive**	**Kill** everything in those cities that breathes	**destroy** every living thing	you must **not let** any living thing **survive**	you must **not spare** any living thing
δοὺ δὲ ἀπὸ τῶν πόλεων τῶν ἐθνῶν τούτων ὧν κύριος ὁ θεός σου δίδωσίν σοι κληρονομεῖν τὴν γῆν αὐτῶν οὐ ζωγρήσετε ἀπ' αὐτῶν πᾶν ἐμπνέον	[...] *Of these* ye shall not take any thing alive.	de his autem civitatibus quae dabuntur tibi nullum omnino permittes vivere	Sotheli of these citees that schulen be youun to thee, thou schalt not suffre eny to lyue,	But ye cities of this people, which the Lord thy God shal giue thee to inherit, thou shalt save no person alive	But of the cities of these people, which the LORD thy God doth give thee *for* an inheritance, thou shalt save alive nothing that breatheth	Only in the cities of these peoples that the LORD your God is giving you as an inheritance, you shall not leave alive anything that breathes	But of the cities of these peoples which the LORD your God gives you *as* an inheritance, you shall let nothing that breathes remain alive	But what about the cities the LORD your God is giving you as your own? Kill everything in those cities that breathes	In those towns that the LORD your God is giving you as a special possession, destroy every living thing	However, you must not let any living thing survive among the cities of these people the LORD your God is giving you as an inheritance	But in the case of any of the cities of these peoples—the ones the LORD your God is giving you as an inheritance--you must not spare any living thing

*Common English Bible.

Jos 2:13, "and **spare** my father and my mother and my brothers and my sisters, with all who belong to them, *and deliver our lives from death*"
French Geneva (1605), "Que vous sauverez la vie à mon pere, & à ma mere, à mes frères & à mes soeurs, & à tous ceux qui leur *appartiennent*, & deliurez nos personnes de la mort."
My translation: "That you save the life of my father… and deliver our persons from death."

Jos 6:25, "However, Rahab the harlot and her father's household and all she had, Joshua **spared**"

Jos 9:20, "This we will do to them, even **let them live**, lest wrath be upon us for the oath which we swore to them"

2 Sam 8:2, "And he defeated Moab, and measured them with the line, making them lie down on the ground; and he measured two lines to put to death and one full line **to keep alive**. And the Moabites became servants to David, bringing tribute"

2 Chron 25:12, "The sons of Judah also **captured** 10,000 **alive** and brought them to the top of the cliff, and threw them down from the top of the cliff so that they were all dashed to pieces"

b) Compare the OT use of ζωγρέω (above) with the OT use of the verb ζωοποιέω:

Judges 21:14, "And Benjamin returned at that time, and they gave them the women whom they **had kept alive** from the women of Jabesh-gilead; yet they were not enough for them."

2 Kings 5:7, "And it came about when the king of Israel read the letter, that he tore his clothes and said, 'Am I God, to kill and **to make alive**, that this man is sending *word* to me to cure a man of his leprosy? But consider now, and see how he is seeking a quarrel against me.'"

Neh 9:6, "Thou alone art the LORD. Thou hast made the heavens, The heaven of heavens with all their host, The earth and all that is on it, The seas and all that is in them. Thou **dost give life** to all of them And the heavenly host bows down before Thee."
Consider, this is almost a play on the name LORD [YHWH], the Ever-Existing One, YHWH, who gives life, [CHYH] *chayah*.

Psa 71:20, "Thou, who hast shown me many troubles and distresses, Wilt revive me again, And wilt bring me up again from the depths of the earth."

Eccl 7:12, "For wisdom is protection *just as* money is protection. But the advantage of knowledge is that wisdom preserves the lives of its possessors."

Job 36:6, "He does not keep the wicked alive, But gives justice to the afflicted."

c) Other than Luke 5:10, the only other NT use of ζωγρέω in NT is in 2 Tim 2:26:

> 2 Tim 2:26 (NAS), "The Lord's bond-servant must not be quarrelsome, but be kind to all, able to teach, patient when wronged, with gentleness correcting those who are in opposition, if perhaps God may grant them repentance leading to the knowledge of the truth, and they may come to their senses *and escape* from the snare of the devil, **having been held captive** by him [ἐζωγρημένοι ὑπ αὐτοῦ] to do his will"

d) Notice several verbs on capturing that Jesus **did not use** in this context:
   (1) ζωογονέω (2 Byz or 3 UBS NT uses) to give life to, make alive (1 Tim 6:13 in UBS text; Byz uses ζωοποιέω); preserve alive, keep alive (Luke 17:33; Acts 7:19)
   (2) ζωοποιέω (12 Byz or 11 UBS NT uses) to make alive, give life to, bring to life (e.g. Rom 4:17; 1 Cor 15:36)
   (3) Clearly, God alone generates life within [ζωογονέω] or makes alive [ζωοποιέω] those whom He saves; man for his part is to capture men alive [ζωγρέω].

119) αἰχμαλωτεύω (2 NT uses) – meaning to take captive, Eph 4:8; 2 Tim 3:6:

Used positively, Eph 4:8 (of Jesus taking captive)—two main readings of this text, regarding who Jesus took captive, a multitude (of people) into captivity:

   (1) "A host of captives":
      > Eph 4:8 (NAS), "Therefore it says, 'When He ascended on high, He **led captive** a host of captives, And He gave gifts to men'"

   (2) The reading that states "He led captivity captive" is a reading from Jerome's Latin Vulgate (Migne):
      > Eph 4:8 (Douais-Rheims), "Wherefore he saith: Ascending on high, he **led** captivity **captive**; he gave gifts to men"

Used negatively, 2 Tim 3:6 (of evil men capturing weak women):
   > 2 Tim 3:6 (NAS), "For among them are those who enter into households and **captivate** weak women weighed down with sins, led on by various impulses"

120) αἰχμαλωτίζω (3 NT uses, Luke 21:24 [of war in end times]; Rom 7:23 [of sin capturing]; 2 Cor 10:5 [of Christian activity]), meaning to capture at war, take captive, subdue; mislead:

> 2 Cor 10:4-5 (1560 Eng Geneva), "⁴ (For the weapons of our warrefare are not carnal, but mightie through God, to cast downe holdes) ⁵ Casting downe the imaginations, and euerie high thing that is exalted against the knowledge of God, and **bringing into captiuitie** euerie thoght to the obedience of Christ"

Herein Paul seems to explain his emphasis in evangelizing, so clearly highlighted elsewhere (Acts 20; 1 Cor 9; 2 Cor 5), highlighting its apologetic nature:
Paul clearly mentioning that the Word of God was the Sword of the Spirit in Eph 6:17 in another warfare passage
Every "thought" of man in 2 Cor 10:5 apparently being a figure of speech (synecdoche) for the totality of a man

Therefore a reading of this passage may be (revising the NAS):

> 2 Cor 10:4-5, "for the weapons of our warfare are not of the flesh, but divinely powerful for the destruction of fortresses, destroying speculations and every lofty thing raised up against the knowledge of God, and **taking captive** every thought [of man] unto the obedience of Christ

In fact, the verb destroying, reminiscent of Jeremiah's call (Jer 1:10), is used in parallel to our αἰχμαλωτίζω, in which God used six verbs:
Heb. nathash; Gk. ἐκριζόω; to root up
Heb. nathats; Gk. κατασκάπτω; to tear down
Heb. abad; Gk. ἀπόλλυμι; to destroy
Heb. haras; Gk. [not translated]; to pluck up
Heb. banah; Gk. ἀνοικοδομέω; to build
Heb. nata; Gk. καταφυτεύω; to plant

However, rather than using κατασκάπτω for tearing down or ἀπόλλυμι for destroy, as found in Rahlf's LXX, Paul used the word καθαιρέω for tear down/destroy…

3)   καθαιρέω and cognate:

(121) καθαιρέω (9 NT uses: 2 in Mark, 6 in Luke-Acts, 1 in Paul), meaning tear down, bring down; tear down, overpower, destroy:
   2 Cor 10:5 (NAS), "*We are* **destroying** speculations and every lofty thing raised up against the knowledge of God, and *we are* taking every thought captive to the obedience of Christ."

(n15) ἡ καθαίρεσις (3 NT uses, all in 2 Cor: 10:4; 10:8; 13:10):
   2 Cor 10:4 (NAS), "for the weapons of our warfare are not of the flesh, but divinely powerful for the **destruction** of fortresses."

ba. Verbs related to compelling people:

1)   ζητέω and cognate:

(122) ζητέω (118 NT uses) – to seek:
   Luke 19:10, "For the Son of Man has come **to seek** and to save that which was lost."

   Other interesting uses of ζητέω related to the gospel submission or gospel ministry:
      Matt 6:33, "But **seek** first His kingdom [or: rule] and His righteousness; and all these things shall be added to you."
      Matt 7:7-8, "Ask, and it shall be given to you; **seek**, and you shall find; knock, and it shall be opened to you. For everyone who asks receives, and he who **seeks** finds, and to him who knocks it shall be opened."
      Matt 13:45-46, "Again, the kingdom of heaven is like a merchant **seeking** fine pearls, and upon finding one pearl of great value, he went and sold all that he had, and bought it."
      Luke 5:18, "And behold, *some* men *were* carrying on a bed a man who was paralyzed; and **they were trying** to bring him in, and to set him down in front of Him."
      Luke 12:31, "But **seek** for His kingdom [or: rule], and these things shall be added to you."
      Luke 11:9-10, "And I say to you, ask, and it shall be given to you; **seek**, and you shall find; knock, and it shall be opened to you. For everyone who asks, receives; and he who **seeks**, finds; and to him who knocks, it shall be opened."
      Luke 12:29-31, "And **do not seek** what you shall eat, and what you shall drink, and do not keep worrying. For all these things the nations of the world eagerly seek [ἐπιζητέω]; but your Father knows that you need these things. But **seek** for His kingdom, and these things shall be added to you."
      Luke 13:24, "Strive to enter by the narrow door; for many, I tell you, will **seek** to enter and will not be able."
      Luke 17:33, "Whoever **seeks** to keep his life shall lose it, and whoever loses *his life* shall preserve it."
      Luke 19:3, "And **he was trying** to see who Jesus was, and he was unable because of the crowd, for he was small in stature."
      John 1:38, "And Jesus turned, and beheld them following, and said to them, 'What **do you seek**?' And they said to Him, 'Rabbi (which translated means Teacher), where are You staying?'"
      John 4:23, "But an hour is coming, and now is, when the true worshipers shall worship the Father in spirit and truth; for such people the Father **seeks** to be His worshipers."
      John 6:26, "Jesus answered them and said, 'Truly, truly, I say to you, **you seek** Me, not because you saw signs, but because you ate of the loaves, and were filled.'"
      Acts 17:26-27, "and He made from one, every nation of mankind to live on all the face of the earth, having determined *their* appointed times, and the boundaries of their habitation, that **they should seek** God, if perhaps they might grope for Him and find Him, though He is not far from each one of us."
      1 Cor 1:22, "For Jews request a sign, and Greeks **seek** after wisdom."
      1 Cor 10:33, "just as I also please all men in all things, **not seeking** my own profit, but the *profit* of the many, that they may be saved."

(123) ἐκζητέω (7 NT uses) – to seek out, inquire:
      Acts 15:17, "In order that the rest of mankind **may seek** the Lord, And all the Gentiles who are called by My name."
      Rom 3:11, "There is none who understands, There is none who **seeks** for God."

Heb 11:6, "And without faith it is impossible to please *Him*, for he who comes to God must believe that He is, and *that* He is a rewarder of those who **seek** Him."

Interesting OT use:

Ezek 34:8, "'As I live,' declares the Lord God, 'surely because My flock has become a prey, My flock has even become food for all the beasts of the field for lack of a shepherd, and My shepherds **did not search** for My flock, but *rather* the shepherds fed themselves and did not feed My flock.'"

(124) ἐπιζητέω (15 NT uses) – to eagerly seek:

Acts 13:7, "who was with the proconsul, Sergius Paulus, a man of intelligence. This man summoned Barnabas and Saul and **sought** to hear the word of God."

Rom 11:7 (NKJ), "What then? Israel has not obtained what it **seeks**; but the elect have obtained it, and the rest were blinded.

Other interesting uses:

Heb 11:14, "For those who say such things make it clear that **they are seeking** a country of their own."

Heb 13:14, "For here we do not have a lasting city, but **we are seeking** *the city* which is to come."

125) ὁδηγέω (1 evangelistic use; 5 total NT uses; 44 OT LXX uses), to lead, guide, teach:

Evangelistic use:

To Philip the Evangelist: Acts 8:31, "And he said, 'Well, how could I, unless someone **guides** me?' And he invited Philip to come up and sit with him."

Positive uses:

Of Holy Spirit: John 16:13, "But when He, the Spirit of truth, comes, **He will guide** you into all the truth; for He will not speak on His own initiative, but whatever He hears, He will speak; and He will disclose to you what is to come."

Of Jesus: Rev 7:17, "for the Lamb in the center of the throne shall be their shepherd, and **shall guide** them to springs of the water of life; and God shall wipe every tear from their eyes."

Negative uses:

Matt 15:14, "Let them alone; they are blind **guides** of the blind. And if a blind man **guides** a blind man, both will fall into a pit."

Luke 6:39, "And He also spoke a parable to them: 'A blind man cannot **guide** a blind man, can he? Will they not both fall into a pit?'"

126) κατευθύνω (1 evangelistic use; 3 total NT uses), meaning to lead, direct, guide (used of God guiding):

Luke 1:79, "To shine upon those who sit in darkness and the shadow of death, To guide our feet into the way of peace."

4) ἄγω and cognate:

(127) ἄγω (76 NT uses) – "to bring":

John 10:16, "And I have other sheep, which are not of this fold; **I must bring** them also, and they shall hear My voice; and they shall become one flock *with* one shepherd."

(128) εἰσάγω (10 NT uses) – "to bring in":

Luke 14:21, "Go out at once into the streets and lanes of the city and **bring in** here the poor and crippled and blind and lame."

129) αναγκάζω + εἰσέρχομαι – "compel" + "to come in":

Luke 14:23, "Go out into the highways and along the hedges, and **compel** *them* to come in, that my house may be filled" (cf. 2 Chron 34:32-33, which twice uses the word ποιέω).

130) ἁρπάζω – "to take by force":

Jude 23, "save others, **snatching** them out of the fire; and on some have mercy with fear, hating even the garment polluted by the flesh."

bb. Verb related to gathering people:

1) Another cognate of ἄγω (above):

(131) συνάγω (61 NT uses) – to gather:

Matt 12:30, "He who is not with Me is against Me; and he who does not **gather** with Me scatters"

Luke 11:23, "He who is not with Me is against Me, and he who does not **gather** with Me scatters"

As it was in the OT prophetic books about false teachers: Jer 23:1-4; Ezek 34:1-10 (cf. John 10:12)

Interestingly, this word is use in the LXX of God's ingathering of redeemed peoples from lands in the East and West, North and South—a wonderful parallel to the Great Commission (Rev 5:9):

Psa 107:3, "And gathered [συνήγαγεν] from the lands, From the east and from the west, From the north and from the south"

See also Isa 40:11; 43:5; 49:5; Micah 2:12; 4:6; 5:6

n16) ὁ καταρτισμός (1 NT use), meaning assembling; training, equipping:

Eph 4:12, "for the equipping [assembling?] of the saints for the work of service, to the building up of the body of Christ"

Translations of ὁ καταρτισμός in Eph 4:12

Greek Byzantine	Jerom's Vulgate (435)	Wycliffe 2nd ed (1388)	Tyndale (1534)	Cover-dale (1535)	English Geneva (1560)	French Geneva (1669)	English Geneva (1599)	KJV (1769); Darby; ERV; ASV	BBE (1949)	RSV (1952)	NAS (1977); NKJ	NIV (1984)
πρὸς τὸν καταρτισμὸν τῶν ἁγίων	Ad consummationem sanctorum	To the ful endying of the seyntes	That all the sainctes might have all things necessary	Wherby the sayntes mighte be coupled together	For the gathering together of the Saintes	For the assembling of the saints*	For the repairing of the Saintes	For the perfecting of the saints	For the training of the saints	To equip the saints	For the equipping of the saints	To prepare God's people
			Notice the evangelistic emphasis of these translations that seems to imply the need for an ingathering!									

*The 1979 Nova Vulgata changed the old Vulgate verb *consumationem* (perfecting), to the revised verb *instructionem* (instruction)

**The French text reads: "Pour l'assemblage des saints."

Is there a gathering element expressed in the term καταρτισμός, as hinted to in Coverdale's "coupled together," the 1560 English Geneva's "gathering together, and the 1696 French Geneva's "assembling"?

Hence, in Scott's lexicon, καταρτισμός is defined as "setting a bone"; whereas καταρτῖσις is defined as "restoring, preparing, training." It is interesting that my BW9 includes no lising for the "abridged" Liddell-Scott Lexicon of this word.[673]

---

[673]The following three lexical entries are taken from the 1875 Liddell-Scott (Henry George Liddell and Robert Scott, *A Greek-English Lexicon, base on the work of Francis Passow* [New York: Harper, 1875). Items omitted by BW9's Liddell-Scott Lexicon are underlined; items unique to BW9's Liddell-Scott Greek Lexicon in [] brackets:

[23234] καταρτίζω

[κατ-αρτίζω], f. ίσω, (κατά, ἀρτίζω) *to adjust* or *put in order again, restore,* ἐς τωὐτό, Hdt. 5, 106: *to settle by acting as mediator, reform,* Id. 5, 28, cf. καταρτιστήρ : *to repair, refit,* ναῦς, Polyb. : *to set* a broken bone, Medic [; κ. δίκτυα *to put* nets *to rights, mend* them, N.T.:-metaph. *to restore to a right mind,* Ib.]
II. in genl. *To prepare, train,* or [*to*] *furnish thoroughly* [*completely*: pf. pass. part. κατηρτισμένος, absol., *well-furnished, complete,* Hdt.,] N.T. Cf. καρτάω [Hence κατάρτισις].

[23235] κατάρτισις

κατάρτῖσις, εως, ἡ, (καταρτίζω) *as adjusting, restoring* [*restoration*], *a preparing* [N.T.

Before a wall of stones can be fit together, they need to be gathered (hence, the "evangelist" in Eph 4:11)

Once the stones are gathered or assembled, they can be fitted together (hence, some factories use an "assembly line")
  Hence the definition in Friberg: "as a process of adjustment that results in a complete preparedness *equipping, perfecting, making adequate.*"

While the 1599 English Geneva, "repairing," gives the impression that the wall was good at one time, and only needs to be repaired, the 1560 English Geneva, however, uses the words "gathering together"
  Could it be that this word includes both meanings, assembling and fitting together for effective ministry?

Being that ὁ καταρτισμός is a hapax legomena in both the NT and LXX, there is no other biblical passage available for the purpose of comparison.

132) καταντάω (13 NT uses), meaning to come, arrive (coupled with the gathering meaning of ὁ καταρτισμός above):

As a result of being gathered together:
  Eph 4:13 (Eng. Geneva), " Till we all **meete together** (in the vnitie of faith and that acknowledging of the Sonne of God) vnto a perfite man, and vnto the measure of the age of the fulnesse of Christ
  Eph 4:13 (NKJ), "till we all **come** to the unity of the faith and of the knowledge of the Son of God, to a perfect man, to the measure of the stature of the fullness of Christ

"Meet together" seems to be more active than "come together," which appears passive; furthermore, the text implies a progression, which we will see in the συναρμολογέω (below):
  v. 12, gather together
  v. 13, meet together
  v. 16, fitted together

If "gather together" is the proper translation of καταρτισμός, as noted above, then it provides purpose for the exhortation of Heb 10:25, "not forsaking the assembling of ourselves together, as is the habit of some."

Likewise, it exemplifies the importance of the "evangelist" in edification as found in Eph 4:11

133) συναρμολογέω (2 NT uses), meaning fitted or joined together:
  Following up on Eph 4:12, 13, συναρμολογέω is the final way in which Christ and man colabor in gathering together the elect in local church bodies for fellowship
  Eph 4:16, "from whom the whole body, **being fitted** and held together by that which every joint supplies, according to the proper working of each individual part, causes the growth of the body for the building up of itself in love."

See also Eph 2:21-22, where the verbs συναρμολογέω and συνοικοδομέω are used in another pattern, with an emphasis on salvation in Christ and His sovereign rule over His church.

II. *a] training, [education, discipline,]* Plut. [; and καρτιστήρ]
καταρτισμός
  καταρτισμός, οῦ, ὁ,= καταρτισις esp. *the setting* of a bone, Galen.

The differences, especially in the verb, are quite a few. The observant reader will notice that the meaning has been shifted from the initial "setting of a bone" or "fitting" (καταρτισμός) to a prolonged [monastic] "training, education, discipline" (καταρτισις). Does καταρτισμός in Eph 4:12 refer to the beginning of the process (setting), or to the continuation of the process (as if referring to the healing or to the physical therapy after the bone was healed)? The ideas of "acting as a mediator" or "being a medic" appear irrelevant to καταρτισμός.
  While the strength of Louw-Nida Lexicon (LNLEX) prioritizing "Semantic Domains" is extremely beneficial in finding and comparing words with the given sets of synonyms, it may also: (1) frame translations by placing words in semantic groupings and (2) remove words from the cognate root meanings, as is noted in removing καταρτισμός as a word in the public domain Liddell-Scott Lexicon.

134) ἐκκλησιάζω (6 uses in LXX [for Heb *qahal*]; 0 in NT), meaning "to gather [for a meeting; i.e. to get a group message]":
Lev 8:3, "and **assemble** all the congregation at the doorway of the tent of meeting"
Num 20:8, "Take the rod; and you and your brother Aaron **assemble** the congregation and speak to the rock before their eyes, that it may yield its water. …"
Deut 4:10, "…when the LORD said to me, '**Assemble** the people to Me, that I may let them hear My words…'"
Deut 31:12, "Assemble the people, the men and the women and children and the alien who is in your town, in order that they may hear and learn and fear the LORD your God, and be careful to observe all the words of this law"
Deut 31:28, "Assemble to me all the elders of your tribes and your officers, that I may speak these words in their hearing and call the heavens and the earth to witness against them"
Est 4:16, "Go, assemble all the Jews who are found in Susa, and fast for me…"

The idea of gathering is the logical opposite of scattering, which is used to describe the ministry of the false prophets both in Jer 23 and Ezek 34:
In Jer 23:3 the Hebrew gather is *qabats*, "to gather"; translated as the Greek εἰσδέχομαι;
In Ezek 34:8 the Hebrew word *darash*, "to search"; translated as the Greek ἐκζητέω.

135) συντυγχάνω (1 NT use), meaning to meet with, join—hence, the result of assembling:
Luke 8:19 (NKJ), "Then His mother and brothers came to Him, and **could** not **approach** Him because of the crowd."

bc. Verbs dealing with working for the Lord:

136) ἐργάζομαι (38 NT uses) + ὁ κύριος (747 NT uses) [1 NT example], meaning working for the Lord:
1 Cor 16:10, "Now if Timothy comes, see that he is with you without cause to be afraid; for **he is doing the Lord's work**, as I also am."
Lit. "for he is working the Lord's work; τὸ γὰρ ἔργον κυρίου ἐργάζεται

137) κοπιάω (23 NT uses) + ὁ κύριος (747 NT uses) [2 NT examples], meaning toiling for the Lord:
Rom 16:12, "Greet Tryphaena and Tryphosa, **workers in the Lord**. Greet Persis the beloved, **who has worked hard in the Lord**."
Lit, "who are toilers in the Lord. … who toils much in the Lord."

Other uses of κοπιάω:
Col 1:28-29, "Him we preach, warning every man and teaching every man in all wisdom, that we may present every man perfect in Christ Jesus. To this *end* I also **labor** [κοπιάω], striving according to His working which works in me mightily."
1 Thess 5:12, "But we request of you, brethren, that you appreciate **those who diligently labor** [κοπιάω] among you, and have charge over you in the Lord and give you instruction."

bd. Death Working:

(138) ὁ θάνατος + ἐνεργέω [1]: the noun, death + the verb, working in:
2Co 4:12, "So death works in us, but life in you."

be. Verbs dealing with laboring in things holy:

139) ἐργάζομαι (39 NT uses) + τὸ ἱερόν (2 NT uses) [1 NT example], meaning to work in holy [things]:
1 Cor 9:13, "Do you not know that those who **perform sacred** services eat the *food* of the temple, *and* those who attend regularly to the altar have their share with the altar?"

140) προσεδρεύω* (1 NT use) + τὸ θυσιαστήριον (23 NT uses) [1 NT example], meaning to attend to the altar:
1 Cor 9:13, "Do you not know that those who perform sacred services eat the *food* of the temple, *and* those who attend regularly to the altar have their share with the altar?"
*In the NA27 substitutes the verb παρεδρεύω instead, meaning to serve, wait upon, attend to.

bf. Terms expressing outward expression and expansion of evangelism:

141) αποστέλλω (132 NT uses; 521 LXX uses), to send:
Acts 10:36, "The word **which He sent** to the sons of Israel, preaching peace through Jesus Christ (He is Lord of all)—"

Acts 13:26 (NKJ), "Men *and* brethren, sons of the family of Abraham, and those among you who fear God, to you the word of this salvation **has been sent**."

Byzantine Textform here reads ἀποστέλλω, whereas the NA Critical Edition Greek text uses ἐξαποστέλλω

Acts 13:26 (NAS), "Brethren, sons of Abraham's family, and those among you who fear God, to us the word of this salvation **is sent out**."

Acts 28:28, "Let it be known to you therefore, that this salvation of God **has been sent** to the Gentiles; they will also listen."

142) ἐξαποστέλλω (13 NT uses; 232 LXX uses), to send forth:

OT LXX use:

Psa 43:3 (Young's), "**Send forth** Thy light and Thy truth, They—they lead me, they bring me in, Unto Thy holy hill, and unto Thy tabernacles"[674]

Mark 16:8b (NLT), "Afterward Jesus himself **sent them out** from east to west with the sacred and unfailing message of salvation that gives eternal life. Amen."

Acts 22:21, "And He said to me, 'Go! For I will **send you far away** to the Gentiles'"; literal word order, "Go, for I unto the Gentiles far away **send** you [out]."

Gal 4:4, "But when the fulness of the time came, God **sent forth** His Son, born of a woman, born under the Law"

Gal 4:6, "And because you are sons, God has **sent forth** the Spirit of His Son into our hearts, crying, 'Abba! Father!'"

143) ἐξηχέομαι (1 NT use), meaning to ring out, sound forth:

1 Thess 1:8, "For the word of the Lord has **sounded forth** from you."

144) ἐξέρχομαι (577 OT LXX uses; 222 NT uses), go out, come out; go forth:

1 Thess 1:8, "in every place your faith toward God has **gone forth**"

1 Cor 14:36, "What? was it from you that the word of God **went forth**? or came it unto you alone?"

Consider also in the OT:

Psa 19:4, "Their line has **gone out** through all the earth, And their utterances to the end of the world. In them He has placed a tent for the sun."

Isa 51:5, "My righteousness is near, My salvation **has gone forth**, And My arms will judge the peoples; The coastlands will wait for Me, And for My arm they will wait expectantly."

Isa 55:11, "So shall My word be which **goes forth** from My mouth; It shall not return to Me empty, Without accomplishing what I desire, And without succeeding *in the matter* for which I sent it."

Isa 55:12, "For you **will go out** with joy, And be led forth with peace; The mountains and the hills will break forth into shouts of joy before you, And all the trees of the field will clap *their* hands."

Isa 62:1 (KJV), "For Zion's sake will I not hold my peace, and for Jerusalem's sake I will not rest, until the righteousness thereof **go forth** as brightness, and the salvation thereof as a lamp *that* burneth."

145) πάρειμι (24 NT uses), [come unto]; be present; at one's disposal:

Col 1:5-6 "…of which you previously heard in the word of truth, the gospel, which **has come** to you, just as in all the world also it is constantly bearing fruit and increasing…"

bg. Terms dealing with the spread of the Gospel:

146) διαφημίζω (3 NT uses), meaning spread the news, spread widely, disseminate (cf. Matt 28:15):

Matt 9:31, "But they went out, and **spread the news** about Him in all that land"

Mark 1:45, "But he went out and began to proclaim it freely and **to spread the news** about, to such an extent that Jesus could no longer publicly enter a city, but stayed out in unpopulated areas; and they were coming to Him from everywhere."

---

[674]George Verwer, founder of Operation Mobilization in 1957, simultaneously founded "Send the Light" (now Send the Light Distribution: available at: http://www.stl-distribution.com/about/; accessed 19 Oct 2013) for the printing and providing of evangelistic literature for distribution. The mission of Send the Light Distribution is: "To advance the Christian faith and carry out the Great Commission through the effective distribution of Scripture-based and wholesome media."

3) πληρόω and cognate:

(147) πληρόω (88 NT uses), meaning to fill; fill up; finish; fulfill; complete:

Acts 5:28, "saying, 'We gave you strict orders not to continue teaching in this name, and behold, **you have filled** Jerusalem with your teaching, and intend to bring this man's blood upon us.'"

Acts 12:25, "And Barnabas and Saul returned from Jerusalem when **they had fulfilled** their mission [τὴν διακονίαν, cf. 2 Tim 4:5], taking along with *them* John, who was also called Mark"

Rom 15:18-19, "For I will not presume to speak of anything except what Christ has accomplished through me, resulting in the obedience of the Gentiles by word and deed, in the power of signs and wonders, in the power of the Spirit; so that from Jerusalem and round about as far as Illyricum I have **fully preached** the gospel of Christ"

Consider another perfect active use of πληρόω in Rom 13:8, "for he who loves his neighbor has **fulfilled** *the* law" [BYZ: ὁ γὰρ ἀγαπῶν τὸν ἕτερον, νόμον πεπλήρωκεν] [Meaning that Paul placed a geographic element on his obedience to the Great Commission, just as Christ gave it, "Go into all the world..." Mark 16:15]

Various Translations of πεπληρωκέναι in Romans 15:19

Byzantine Text	French Louis Segond*	French Geneva (1616)**	English Geneva (1560)	KJV, ASV, NAS	New Living Translation	Cont English Version✢	New American Bible✢	English Jerusalem✢°	French Jerusalem✢°	Douay-Rheims✢	IBS' *Le Semeur*✢ °°
πεπληρω-κέναι τὸ εὐαγγέλιον τοῦ χριστοῦ	I abundantly spread forth the gospel of Christ	I made to abound the Gospel of Christ	I haue caused to abunde the Gospel of Christ	I have fully preached the gospel of Christ.	I have fully presented the Good News of Christ	I have preached the good news about him all the way from ...	I have finished preaching the gospel of Christ.	I have fully carried out the preaching of the gospel of Christ	I procured the accomplish-ment of the gospel of the Christ	I have replenished the gospel of Christ	By shining in all directions, I made everywhere resound the message of the Christ
[infinitive perfect active of πληρόω]	Past completed but unfulfilled action (i.e. more work remains to do)			Past completed action, use of the English "fully" hints at the fulfillment of the work		Past completed geographic action, "all the way from"	Past completed and fulfilled action, especially the use of "finished" (i.e. no need for that kind of evangelism any more)			Unclear meaning	

*My translations of (respectively) "J'ai abondamment répandu l'Évangile de Christ"; **"J'ai fait abonder l'Évangile de Christ"; °"J'ai procuré l'accomplissement de l'Évangile du Christ"; °°"En rayonnant en tous sens, j'ai fait partout retentir le message du Christ."

(148) ἀνταναπληρόω (1 NT use), meaning to fill up, complete:

Col 1:24, "Now I rejoice in my sufferings for your sake, and in my flesh I do my share on behalf of His body (which is the church) in **filling up** that which is lacking in Christ's afflictions"

Of its evangelistic meaning:

Being presupposed from other verses that Christ has done it all, as far as our salvation ("it is finished," John 19:30);

Therefore that which was/is "lacking" in the cross was/is the "boots on the ground" of messengers of the Gospel sharing its excellencies; indeed that which we know Paul himself was doing [with significant intensity of zeal] from the Book of Acts!

Interestingly this verb (with "anta") is used with the noun ὑστέρημα (9 NT uses), meaning that which is lacking

However, the verb ἀναπληρόω (with "ana", 6 NT uses) with ὑστέρημα is found used twice: 1 Cor 16:17; Phil 2:30; both of which cases seems to imply the fulfilling of a physical or emotional need, rather than a strictly a spiritual need

Thus, Paul's use of "anta" (ἀνταναπληρόω) as the prefix seems to intensify or even change its meaning, whereas it seems to be currently translated much like ἀναπληρόω; the question arises, in what way is it mean to be intensified, especially with the stark words "in my flesh" which seems to directly relate to this verb?

The Church of Rome reads into this concept their entire sacramental theology of penance and absolution positing a "Bank of Merits" in heaven (wherein according to their Sacrament of Penance, priests, dispensing from this "bank" at Rome's unique disposal, declare absolution of the individual sins of those who confess in their confessionals), adding to the blood of Christ the merits of Mary and of all the Saints—a clearly unfortunate misreading of Paul's intention, which was rather evangelistic and not soteriological nor even part of personal spiritual perfectionism, but rather an outflow of his being a living sacrifice

Therefore, the translation of this intensified use of the verb is very tricky!

(149) πληροφορέω (5 NT uses), meaning to fill, fulfill, accomplish:

2 Tim 4:17, "But the Lord stood with me, and strengthened me, in order that through me the proclamation [τὸ κήρυγμα] **might be fully accomplished**, and that all the Gentiles might hear; and I was delivered out of the lion's mouth."

2 Tim 4:5, "But you, be sober in all things, endure hardship, do the work of an evangelist, **fulfill** your ministry [τὴν διακονίαν σου]."

(n17) τὸ πλήρωμα (17 NT uses), meaning that which fills, fullness:

Rom 15:29 (NKJ), "But I know that when I come to you, I shall come in the fullness of the blessing of the gospel of Christ."

Notice here that "the gospel of Christ":

Is a singular source of blessing

Is a sufficient source of blessing

Provides for the fullness of God's blessing.

Consider also, that there seems to appear a textual issue here:

Wherein the above sufficiency may be a threat to those who give and sell blessings from other sources (Holy Water, tappers (candles), the Sacraments, etc.)

3) πίμπλημι and cognate:

(150) πίμπλημι (104 OT LXX uses; 24 NT uses), meaning to fill; to fulfill; to be completed:

Dan 12:4, "But as for you, Daniel, conceal these words and seal up the book until the end of time; many will go back and forth, and knowledge **will increase**"

Hab 2:14, "For the earth will **be filled** With the knowledge of the glory of the LORD, As the waters cover the sea."

As a result of evangelism:

Matt 22:10, "And those slaves went out into the streets, and gathered together all they found, both evil and good; and the wedding hall **was filled** with dinner guests"

Of being filled with the Holy Spirit: Luke 1:15, 41, 67; Acts 2:4; 4:8, 31; 9:17; 13;9

Consider also:

Exod 40:34, 35, "the glory of the LORD **filled** the tabernacle."

1 Kings 8:10, "the cloud **filled** the house of the LORD"

1 Kings 8:11, "for the glory of the LORD **filled** the house of the LORD"

2 Chron 7:1, "and the glory of the LORD **filled** the house"

2 Chron 7:2, "because the glory of the LORD **filled** the LORD's house"

Note also the antithetic:

Gen 6:11, 13, "the earth was filled with violence";

2 Kings 21:16, "Moreover, Manasseh shed very much innocent blood until he **had filled** Jerusalem from one end to another" (cf. 2 Kings 24:4)

Ezra 9:11, "the peoples of the lands, with their abominations which **have filled** it from end to end *and* with their impurity"

Ezek 8:17, "that they **have filled** the land with violence and provoked Me repeatedly?"

Consider the use of this verb as prophetic of its fulfillment prior to the second coming of Christ:

Hab 2:14, "For the earth will be filled [πίμπλημι] With the knowledge of the glory of the LORD, As the waters cover the sea."

E.g. Matt 24:14, "And this gospel of the kingdom shall be preached in the whole world for a witness to all the nations, and then the end shall come."

(151) ἐμπίπλημι (116 OT LXX uses; 5 NT uses), meaning to fill, fill full, or to be filled with:

Isa 11:9, "They will not hurt or destroy in all My holy mountain, For the earth will be full of the knowledge of the LORD As the waters cover the sea."

Isa 58:10, "*If* you extend your soul to the hungry And satisfy the afflicted soul, Then your light shall dawn in the darkness, And your darkness shall *be* as the noonday"

Jer 31:25, "For I satisfy the weary ones and refresh everyone who languishes."

Luke 1:53, "He has filled the hungry with good things; And sent away the rich empty-handed."

Cf. Num 14:21; Deut 34:9; 2 Chron 5:13-14; Psa 22:27; 107:9; [Job 33:24]; Isa 27:6

152) αὐξάνω (23 NT uses), meaning to grow, cause to grow; increase:
Acts 6:7; 12:24; 19:20; Col 1:6

153) πληθύνω (12 NT uses), meaning to increase, multiply; grow, increase:

Introduction: This verb seems to emphasize the promise of or completed supernatural action, whether from God or from sin. Notice how πληθύνω is used in the OT:

As part of the blessing to man, Gen 1:28:
Gen 1:28 (Rahlf's), καὶ ηὐλόγησεν αὐτοὺς ὁ θεὸς λέγων αὐξάνεσθε καὶ πληθύνεσθε [πληθύνω] καὶ πληρώσατε τὴν γῆν
Gen 1:28 (Brenton), "And God blessed them, saying, Increase and **multiply**, and fill the earth"

To mean that man's sin was multiplied upon the earth, Gen 6:5:
Gen 6:5 (Rahlf's), ἰδὼν δὲ κύριος ὁ θεὸς ὅτι ἐπληθύνθησαν [πληθύνω] αἱ κακίαι τῶν ἀνθρώπων ἐπὶ τῆς γῆς
Gen 6:5 (Brenton), "And the Lord God, having seen that the wicked actions of men **were multiplied** upon the earth"
Similarly at the end of time: Matt 24:12 (CSB), "Because lawlessness will multiply, the love of many will grow cold"

To refer to God's blessing on Abraham [Hebrew dual]:
Gen 22:17 (Rahlf's), ἦ μὴν εὐλογῶν εὐλογήσω σε καὶ πληθύνων [πληθύνω] πληθυνῶ [πληθύνω] τὸ σπέρμα σου [cited in Heb 6:14]
Gen 22:17 (Brenton), "Surely blessing I will bless thee, and **multiplying** I **will multiply** thy seed"

In the fourfold use warning to kings not to multiply for themselves:
Deut 17:16-17 (Rahlf's), διότι οὐ πληθυνεῖ [πληθύνω] ἑαυτῷ ἵππον οὐδὲ μὴ ἀποστρέψῃ τὸν λαὸν εἰς Αἴγυπτον, ὅπως πληθύνῃ [πληθύνω] ἑαυτῷ ἵππον ὁ δὲ κύριος εἶπεν· οὐ προσθήσετε ἀποστρέψαι τῇ ὁδῷ ταύτῃ ἔτι. καὶ οὐ πληθυνεῖ ἑαυτῷ γυναῖκας, οὐδὲ μεταστήσεται αὐτοῦ ἡ καρδία·[675] καὶ ἀργύριον καὶ χρυσίον οὐ πληθυνεῖ ἑαυτῷ σφόδρα.
Deut 17:16-17 (Brenton),[676] "For he shall not multiply to himself horses, and he shall by no means turn the people back to Egypt, lest he should multiply to himself horses; for the Lord said, Ye shall not any more turn back by that way. And he shall not multiply to himself wives, lest his heart turn away; and he shall not greatly multiply to himself silver and gold."

To refer to God's blessing on the people (in a warning):
Deut 8:13 (Rahlf's), καὶ τῶν βοῶν σου καὶ τῶν προβάτων σου πληθυνθέντων [πληθύνω] σοι ἀργυρίου καὶ χρυσίου πληθυνθέντος [πληθύνω] σοι καὶ πάντων ὅσων σοι ἔσται πληθυνθέντων [πληθύνω] σοι
Gen 22:17 (Brenton), "and thy oxen and thy sheep **are multiplied** to thee, and thy silver and thy gold **are multiplied** to thee, and all thy possessions **are multiplied** to thee"

And the verb πληθύνω was also used of the spreading of the Gospel!

Acts 6:1 (NKJ), "Now in those days, when *the number of* the disciples **was multiplying**"
Acts 6:7 (NKJ), "Then the word of God spread, and the number of the disciples **multiplied** greatly in Jerusalem, and a great many of the priests were obedient to the faith"
Acts 9:31 (NKJ), "Then the churches throughout all Judea, Galilee, and Samaria had peace and were edified. And walking in the fear of the Lord and in the comfort of the Holy Spirit, they **were multiplied**"
Acts 12:24, "But the word of God grew and **multiplied**"

Concerning πολυπλασιάζομαι for multiply:

Consider, however, that for "multiply" Paul did not use the verb πολυπλασιάζομαι as found in Deut 8:1—even though in Deuteronomy it is three times paired with the important, "that you may live" [ζάω]; The exact form, "that you may live and

---

[675]The phrase, οὐδὲ μεταστήσεται αὐτοῦ ἡ καρδία, is found differently in the Greek Orthodox Text, ἵνα μὴ μεταστῇ αὐτοῦ ἡ καρδία.

[676]Brenton Translation available at: http://ebible.org/eng-Brenton/DEU17.htm (Online); accessed 1 Dec 2017; Internet.

multiply," [ἵνα ζῆτε καὶ πολυπλασιασθῆτε] is found 3 times in the LXX of Deuteronomy (Deut 4:1; 8:1; 11:8), the only uses of this verb in the LXX:

Deut 8:1, "All the commandments that I am commanding you today you shall be careful to do, that you may live and multiply, and go in and possess the land which the LORD swore *to give* to your forefathers."

Liddell-Scott: "πολυπλασιάζομαι = πολλαπλασιάζω"; "πολλαπλασιάζω, (πολλαπλάσιος) to multiply, magnify, Polyb. 30, 4, 13. Hence, ἡ πολλαπλασίασις, multiplication and ὁ πολλαπλασιασμός, Plut. 2, 388 , etc.

Paul, a Deuteronomic scholar, did not choose this word to describe the growth of the church in his epistles;

Nor did Luke use it in Luke-Acts, even though he did use the adjective πολλαπλασίων in Luke 18:30, where Jesus seems to pick up on the two Deuteronomic concepts, multiplication and life:

Luk 18:30, "who shall not receive many times [πολλαπλασίων] as much at this time and in the age to come, eternal life [ἡ ζωὴν]."

154) πλεονάζω – that the grace **which is spreading** to more and more people (ἵνα ἡ χάρις πλεονάσασα διὰ τῶν πλειόνων), 2 Cor 4:15 (cf. Rom 6:1, ἵνα ἡ χάρις πλεονάσῃ)
(NKJ) "that grace, having spread through the many"
(ESV) "so that as grace extends to more and more people"
Notice that the same verb is used of:
(1) The growth of sin (Rom 5:20 (twice); 6:1), in a construction with ὑπερπερισσεύω, refering over-abounding of grace
(2) The abounding of grace (2 Cor 4:5), in a construction with περισσεύω, refering to the increase of thanksgiving to thee glory of God
(3) The abundance of fruit (Phil 4:17)
(4) The abounding of love (1 Thess 3:12), used in parallel with περισσεύω (see below)
(5) The growth of love (2 Thess 1:3), in a construction with ὑπεραυξάνω

6) περισσεύω and cognate:

(155) περισσεύω (39 NT uses) – be abundant, overflow, excel; cause to abound:
Acts 16:5, "So the churches were being strengthened in the faith, and **were increasing** in number daily"
Rom 5:15, "much more did the grace of God and the gift by the grace of the one Man, Jesus Christ, **abound** to the many"
1 Cor 15:58, "always **abounding** in the work of the Lord"

(156) ὑπερπερισσεύω (2 NT uses) – grace abounded all the more (ὑπερεπερίσσευσεν ἡ χάρις), Rom 5:20 (cf. 2 Cor 7:4)

n18) ἡ προκοπή (3 NT uses), meaning: progress, advancement:
Phil 1:12, "Now I want you to know, brethren, that my circumstances have turned out for the greater **progress** of the gospel"
Greek of the last phrase: ὅτι τὰ κατ' ἐμὲ μᾶλλον εἰς προκοπὴν τοῦ εὐαγγελίου ἐλήλυθεν·
Possible translation: "that the [things] against me rather came unto the **advancement** of the Gospel."

Translations of ἡ προκοπή in Phil 1:12

Etheridge (1849)	Tyndale (1534); Geneva	Bishops (1595); KJV; Webster's; Murdock; Darby; Douais-Rheims✠; NKJ	Young's (1862); CSB	RSV (1952); NIV; ESV	NET (2005)	NAS (1977)	ERV (1885); ASV	God's Word to the Nations (1995); NLT	BBE (1949)	NJB✠
Most Active										**Most Passive**
Forward-ing	Further-ynge	Further-aunce	Advance-ment	served to advance	turned out to advance	Greater progress	Progress	helped to spread	cause … has been helped	helping rather than hindering the advance
tendeth the more to the forwarding of the gospel	is happened vnto the greater furtherynge of the gospel	hath come rather vnto the further-aunce of the Gospell	rather to an advance-ment of the good news have come	that what has happened to me has really served to advance the gospel	has actually turned out to advance the gospel	that my circum-stances have turned out for the greater progress of the gospel	have fallen out rather unto the progress of the gospel	that what happened to me has helped to spread the Good News	that the cause of the good news has been helped by my experiences	that the circum-stances of my present life are helping rather than hindering the advance of the gospel

157) ἐξερεύγομαι (in LXX), to "empty" from the Hebrew naba', meaning to pour forth, bubble forth, fig. utter:

> Liddell-Scott: ἐξ-ερεύγομαι, Pass., of rivers, *to empty themselves,* Hdt.
> Psa 119:171, "Let my lips utter praise"
> Psa 145:7, "Thine abundant goodness will I pour forth" (NAS, "eagerly utter")

bh. Of Shining Forth:

158) λάμπω (7 NT uses), meaning to shine:

> Matt 5:16, "Let your light **shine** before men in such a way that they may see your good works, and glorify your Father who is in heaven"

Concerning the results of evangelizing:

> 2 Cor 4:6, "For God, who said, 'Light **shall shine** out of darkness,' is the One who **has shone** in our hearts to give the light of the knowledge of the glory of God in the face of Christ."

ἀναλάμπω, a cognate verb is used prophetically of Jesus in Isa 42:4 (LXX):

> Isa 42:4 [LXE], "He shall shine out, and shall not be discouraged, until he have set judgement on the earth: and in his name shall the Gentiles trust."

159) φαίνω (31 NT uses), to shine, give light:

> John 1:5, "And the light shines in the darkness, and the darkness did not comprehend it"
> John 5:35, "He was the lamp that was burning and was shining and you were willing to rejoice for a while in his light."
> Phil 2:15, "that you may prove yourselves to be blameless and innocent, children of God above reproach in the midst of a crooked and perverse generation, among whom you appear as lights in the world"
> 2 Pet 1:19, "And *so* we have the prophetic word *made* more sure, to which you do well to pay attention as to a lamp shining in a dark place, until the day dawns and the morning star arises in your hearts"

160) ἐπιφαίνω (4 total NT uses), to shine, give light; to appear:

Luke 1:79, "To shine upon those who sit in darkness and the shadow of death, To guide our feet into the way of peace."

Acts 27:20, "And since neither sun nor stars appeared for many days, and no small storm was assailing *us*, from then on all hope of our being saved was gradually abandoned."

Titus 2:11, "For the grace of God has appeared, bringing salvation to all men"

Titus 3:4, "But when the kindness of God our Savior and *His* love for mankind appeared"

161) φωτίζω (11 NT uses), meaning to shine; give light, light up; enlighten, shed light upon; enlighten, reveal:

Eph 3:9 (Darby), "And **to enlighten** all *with the knowledge of* what is the administration of the mystery hidden throughout the ages in God, who has created all things"

2 Tim 1:10, "But now has been revealed by the appearing of our Savior Christ Jesus, who abolished death, and brought life and immortality **to light** through the gospel."

See also (some of these deal with the result of evangelism, enlightenment as to salvation):

John 1:9, "There was the true light which, coming into the world, **enlightens** every man."

Heb 6:4, "For in the case of those who have once **been enlightened** and have tasted of the heavenly gift and have been made partakers of the Holy Spirit"

Heb 10:32, "But remember the former days, when, after **being enlightened**, you endured a great conflict of sufferings"

n19) ὁ φωστήρ (noun, meaning a star; 2 NT uses):

Phil 2:15, "Among whom you appear as stars in the world" [ἐν οἷς φαίνεσθε ὡς φωστῆρες ἐν κόσμῳ]

n20) ὁ φωτισμός (noun, meaning to radiate forth, 2 NT uses: 2 Cor 4:4, 6):

2 Cor 4:6, "to give the light of the knowledge of the glory of God in the face of Christ" [πρὸς φωτισμὸν τῆς γνώσεως τῆς δόξης τοῦ θεοῦ ἐν προσώπῳ Ἰησοῦ χριστοῦ]

Evangelism as **radiating forth** the knowledge of God in the face of Jesus Christ, 2 Cor 4:6 (cf. Isa 60:1; Acts 13:47), being the very thing against which Satan seeks to blind the world (2 Cor 4:4)

bi. Sounding Forth:

162) σαλπίζω (12 total NT uses; 69 total LXX uses):

Joel 2:1, "**Blow** a trumpet in Zion, And sound an alarm on My holy mountain! Let all the inhabitants of the land tremble, For the day of the LORD is coming; Surely it is near."

Joel 2:15, "**Blow** a trumpet in Zion, Consecrate a fast, proclaim a solemn assembly."

Isa 27:13, "It will come about also in that day that a great trumpet **will be blown**; and those who were perishing in the land of Assyria and who were scattered in the land of Egypt will come and worship the LORD in the holy mountain at Jerusalem."

Isa 44:23, "Shout for joy, O heavens, for the LORD has done *it*! **Shout joyfully**, you lower parts of the earth; Break forth into a shout of joy, you mountains, O forest, and every tree in it; For the LORD has redeemed Jacob And in Israel He shows forth His glory."

Ezek 33:3, "and he sees the sword coming upon the land, and he **blows** on the trumpet and warns the people."

Rev 11:15, "And the seventh angel **sounded**; and there arose loud voices in heaven, saying, 'The kingdom of the world has become *the kingdom* of our Lord, and of His Christ; and He will reign forever and ever.'"

bj. Displaying:

163) θριαμβεύω (2 NT uses; Ø LXX uses), to celebrate a triumph: hence to march in triumphal procession, to lead a triumphal procession; to cause to triumph, to be victorious; or [hypothetically] "to triumphalize" (2 Cor 2:14; Col 2:15):

2 Cor 2:14 [mine], "But thanks be to God, who always **triumphalizes** us in Christ, and reveals by us in every place the sweet aroma of the knowledge of Him."

The question comes: What kind of parallelism is being made by Paul between the θριαμβεύω and the φανερόω ἡ ὀσμή? Is it synonymous, synthetic, or antithetical?

A similar concept seems to be ἀποδείκνυμι in 1 Cor 4:9, "For, I think, God has exhibited us apostles last of all, as men condemned to death."

Consider how this use of "triumphalizing" fits with the promise of Christ in His evangelism training sermon:

Matt 10:18, "and you shall even be brought before governors and kings for My sake, as a testimony [τὸ μαρτύριον] to them and to the Gentiles."

Mark 13:9, "But be on your guard; for they will deliver you to *the* courts, and you will be flogged in *the* synagogues, and you will stand before governors and kings for My sake, as a testimony [τὸ μαρτύριον] to them."

Luke 21:12, "But before all these things, they will lay their hands on you and will persecute you, delivering you to the synagogues and prisons, bringing you before kings and governors for My name's sake."

164) ἀποδείκνυμι (4 NT uses; 7 Apocryphal and 5 OT LXX uses), to exhibit, display; prove; proclaim; recommend, attest:

Acts 2:22, "Men of Israel, listen to these words: Jesus the Nazarene, a man **attested** to you by God with miracles and wonders and signs which God performed through Him in your midst, just as you yourselves know—"

1 Cor 4:9, "For, I think, God **has exhibited** us apostles last of all, as men condemned to death; because we have become a spectacle to the world, both to angels and to men."

2 Thess 2:4, "who opposes and exalts himself above every so-called god or object of worship, so that he takes his seat in the temple of God, **displaying** himself as being God."

bk. Spiritual Dynamic:

*) See also below in Section 4, "Spiritual Dynamic of the Word of God," regarding the use of the following metaphorical terms:

1) Verbs already addressed above:

#152, αὐξάνω, to grow, spread, increase, and become important, Acts 6:7; 12:24; 19:20; Col 1:6;

#93, καρποφορέω, meaning to bear fruit, Col 1:6;

#153, πληθύνω, intrans. grow, increase, hence "be multiplied," Acts 12:24 (cf. 2 Cor 9:10).

2) Verbs not addressed above:

(165) διαφέρω, meaning carry through, spread:

Acts 13:49, "And the word of the Lord **was being spread** through the whole region."

(166) ἰσχύω, to able, can, have resources, win over, defeat, be strong, grow strong:

Acts 19:20, "So the word of the Lord was growing mightily and **prevailing**."

(167) τρέχω, to run, exert oneself, make an effort:

1 Cor 9:26, "Therefore I run in such a way, as not without aim; I box in such a way, as not beating the air"

2 Thess 3:1, "Finally, brethren, pray for us that the word of the Lord **may spread rapidly** [lit. 'run'] and be glorified, just as *it did* also with you."

Note, however, the interesting balance of Scripture related to the verb τρέχω:

Rom 9:16, "So then it *does* not *depend* on the man who wills or the man **who runs**, but on God who has mercy."

bl. Pressing on in evangelism to the point of resisting or struggling against:

"For consider Him who has endured such hostility by sinners against Himself, so that you may not grow weary and lose heart. You have not yet resisted to the point of shedding blood in your striving against sin" (Hebrews 12:3-4)

168) πυκτεύω (*hapax* in NT; intransitive use: to box), evangelism requires effort, training, and concentration, just as does boxing, as well as clear direction:

1 Cor 9:26, "Therefore I run in such a way, as not without aim; I box in such a way, as not beating the air."

2)   ἀγωνίζομαι and Cognates:

(169) ἀγωνίζομαι (8 NT uses), meaning to compete, contend, strive, fight:

General commands:

Luke 13:24, "Strive [ἀγωνίζομαι] to enter by the narrow door; for many, I tell you, will seek to enter and will not be able"

1 Cor 9:25, "And everyone who competes [ἀγωνίζομαι] in the games exercises self-control in all things. They then *do it* to receive a perishable wreath, but we an imperishable."

1 Tim 6:12, "Fight [ἀγωνίζομαι] the good fight of faith; take hold of the eternal life to which you were called, and you made the good confession in the presence of many witnesses."

2 Tim 4:7, "I have fought [ἀγωνίζομαι] the good fight, I have finished the course, I have kept the faith."

Verses related directly to evangelism (also showing parallel uses of labor and strive, κοπιάω and ἀγωνίζομαι):

Col 1:28-29, "Him we preach, warning every man and teaching every man in all wisdom, that we may present every man perfect in Christ Jesus. To this *end* I also labor, striving [ἀγωνίζομαι] according to His working which works in me mightily."

1 Tim 4:10, "For it is for this we labor and strive, because we have fixed our hope on the living God, who is the Savior of all men, especially of believers."

(170) ἀνταγωνίζομαι (*hapax* in NT, meaning "struggle"; from ἀγωνίζομαι [7 NT uses], meaning to fight, struggle, strive, wrestle; cf. English, "agonize") – evangelism as wrestling with sin (Heb 12:4); again the context of enduring hostility by sinners to the point of shedding one's blood (martyrdom):

Heb 12:4, "You have not yet resisted to the point of shedding blood in your striving [ἀνταγωνίζομαι] against sin."

(171) ἐπαγωνίζομαι (*hapax* in NT, meaning Jude 1:3 BYM)

Jude 3, "Beloved, while I was making every effort to write you about our common salvation, I felt the necessity to write to you appealing that you contend earnestly [ἐπαγωνίζομαι] for the faith which was once for all delivered to the saints."

172)   ἀντικαθίστημι (*hapax* in NT; intransitive use: to oppose, resist) –
Idea being: evangelism as resisting sin unto death (Heb 12:4), in the context of the sufferings of Jesus, who endured harsh treatment from the hand of sinners (Heb 12:3), as an outworking of a life of faith in God's promise (Heb 11, for example, Heb 11:26):
Heb 12:4, "You have not yet resisted [ἀντικαθίστημι] to the point of shedding blood in your striving against sin."

173)   φιλοτιμέομαι (3 NT uses) + εὐαγγελίζω (54/55/56 NT uses): herein Paul expresses his inner drive and desire to evangelize, not where Christ has already been named:
Rom 15:20, "And thus I aspired to preach the gospel, not where Christ was *already* named, that I might not build upon another man's foundation."

On the translation of οὕτως δὲ φιλοτιμούμενον εὐαγγελίζεσθαι in Rom 15:20

An amazing variety of translations for this term!

Over-powering effort	Actual effort	Heartfelt desire—present tense	Heartfelt desire—past tense	Desired goal—present tense		Desired goal—past over-statement	Desired direction				Goal	Rule
Tyndale (1534); Geneva (1560); Bishops (1599)	KJV (1611); Webster's	Noyes (1868)	NAS (1977)	Rother-ham (1868)	RSV (1952); ESV	NIV (1984); NLT	Darby (1884)	ERV (1885); ASV; NKJ	HCSB (1999)	NET (2006)	CEB (2011)	NJB* (1985)
I have enforced myself	I strive to preach the gospel	Always earnestly desirous to preach it in this manner	I aspired to preach the gospel	As ambitious to be announcing the glad tidings	Making it my ambition	It has always been my ambition	Aiming to announce the glad tidings	Making it my aim so to preach the gospel	My aim is to evangelize	in this way I desire to preach	I have a goal to preach the gospel	It has been my rule to preach the gospel only
"So have I enforsed my selfe to preache the gospell not where Christ was named lest I shuld have bylt on another mannes foundacion"	"Yea, so have I strived to preach the gospel, not where Christ was named, lest I should build upon another man's foundation"	"but always earnestly desirous to preach it in this manner,—not where Christ had been named, that I might not build on another's foundation"	"And thus I aspired to preach the gospel, not where Christ was *already* named, that I might not build upon another man's foundation"	"Although, thus,—as ambitious to be announcing the glad-message—not where Christ had been named, lest, upon another's foundation, I should be building"	"thus making it my ambition to preach the gospel, not where Christ has already been named, lest I build on another man's foundation"	"It has always been my ambition to preach the gospel where Christ was not known, so that I would not be building on someone else's foundation"	"and so aiming to announce the glad tidings, not where Christ has been named, that I might not build upon another's foundation"	"yea, making it my aim so to preach the gospel, not where Christ was *already* named, that I might not build upon another man's foundation"	"So my aim is to evangelize where Christ has not been named, in order that I will not be building on someone else's foundation"	"And in this way I desire to preach where Christ has not been named, so as not to build on another person's foundation"	In this way, I have a goal to preach the gospel where they haven't heard of Christ yet, so that I won't be building on someone else's foundation"	and what is more, it has been my rule to preach the gospel only where the name of Christ has not already been heard, for I do not build on another's foundations"

Considering French Translations of οὕτως δὲ φιλοτιμούμενον εὐαγγελίζεσθαι in Rom 15:20

Olivétan (1535)*	Calvin (1551)	Calvin (1564)	Genève (1605)	Genève (1687)
I took courage to announce the gospel	I employed myself to announce the gospel	Striving in this way to announce the gospel	Affectionately applying** myself to announce the gospel	Attaching myself with affection to announce the gospel
Et ainsi ay prins courage de annoncer Levangile / non point ou Christ avoit este annonce: affin que ie ne ediffiasse sur le fondement daustruy /	Et me suis employé a annoncer l'Evangile, non point ou il avait esté faict mention de Christ, à fin que je n'edifiasse point sur le fondement d'autruy,	M'efforçant ainsi d'annoncer l'Evangile, non point où il avoit esté faict mention de Christ: à fin que ie n'edifiasse sur le fondement d'autrui:)	M'estudiant ainsi affectueusement d'annoncer l'Evangile, non point où il avoit esté fait mention de Christ, (afin que ie n'edifiasse sur la fondation d'autrui)	M'attachant ainsi avec affection à annoncer l'Evangile, là où Christ n'avoit pas encore été prêché, (afin que je n'édifiasse sur un fondement qu'un autre auroit posé).

*Before verse delineations were made.
**Literally "studying."

bm. Further terms dealing metaphorically with evangelism:

174) συνιστάω or συνίστημι (16 NT uses), meaning to commend, stand beside:
Of Paul's ministry:
2 Cor 4:2, "but we have renounced the things hidden because of shame, not walking in craftiness or adulterating the word of God, but by the manifestation of truth **commending ourselves** to every man's conscience in the sight of God"
2 Cor 6:4, "but in everything **commending ourselves** as servants of God, in much endurance, in afflictions, in hardships, in distresses"

Of God:

>Rom 5:8, "But God **demonstrates** His own love toward us, in that while we were yet sinners, Christ died for us"

Used negatively, of people "commending themselves," 2 Cor 10:12, 18

Interesting use, Gal 2:18, "I commend myself a transgressor."

175) δουλεύω (25 NT uses) – meaning, be a slave, be subject; serve [someone] as a slave, serve:

>Acts 20:19, "Serving the Lord with all humility and with tears and with trials which came upon me through the plots of the Jews."

>Phil 2:22 (NKJ), "But you know his proven character, that as a son with *his* father he **served** with me in the gospel":

>>Greek Byzantine: σὺν ἐμοὶ ἐδούλευσεν εἰς τὸ εὐαγγέλιον;

>>Hence following the Greek word order: "with me served in the Gospel."

>Note also the context of this negative use:

>>Rom 16:18 (NKJ), "For those who are such do not serve our Lord Jesus Christ, but their own belly, and by smooth words and flattering speech deceive the hearts of the simple";

>>By the way, could not "positive thinking" be considered "flattering speech"?

176) διακονέω (37 NT uses), meaning to wait upon, serve:

>2 Cor 3:3, "being manifested that you are a letter of Christ, **cared for** by us, written not with ink, but with the Spirit of the living God, not on tablets of stone, but on tablets of human hearts"

Translations of διακονηθεῖσα ὑφ᾽ ἡμῶν in 2 Cor 3:3

Perhaps the progression can be characterized as emphasizing the punctiliar beginning of ministry (aorist tense) to emphasizing the end result of an extended ministry. The emphasis seems to be the hypostatic union of the evangelist as a minister of the gospel for Christ. This symbiotic interrelationship could also be conveyed as a participle in English.

"Serving through us"	"Produced by us"	"Delivered by us"	"Prepared by us"	"Minister-ed by us"	"Adminis-tered by us"	"Cared for by us"	"Entrusted to our care"	"The fruit of our work"	"The result of our ministry"	"You are the result of our work for God"
Johnston's Conjecture	CSBO (2009)	RSV (1952); NET; CEB; ESV	NRSV (1989)	Tyndale (1534); Geneva; Bishops; KJV; Darby; Young's; ERV; ASV; NKJ	NAB☩ (1991, 2010)	NASB (1977)	NJB☩ (1985)	Bible in Basic English (1949)	NIV (1984, 2011); TNIV	NIRV (1998)

n21) ἡ διακονία (34 total NT uses) – meaning minister or (in this case) ministry (not exhaustive, but merely some examples):

>Acts 6:4, "But we will devote ourselves to prayer, and to the **ministry of the word**."

>Acts 12:25, "And Barnabas and Saul returned from Jerusalem when they had fulfilled **their mission**, taking along with *them* John, who was also called Mark."

>Acts 20:24, "But I do not consider my life of any account as dear to myself, in order that I may finish my course, and **the ministry** which I received from the Lord Jesus, to testify solemnly of the gospel of the grace of God."

>Acts 21:19, "And after he had greeted them, he *began* to relate one by one the things which God had done among the Gentiles through **his ministry**."

>Rom 11:13, "But I am speaking to you who are Gentiles. Inasmuch then as I am an apostle of Gentiles, I magnify **my ministry**."

>2 Cor 3:8, "how shall the **ministry of the Spirit** fail to be even more with glory?"

>2 Cor 3:9, "For if the ministry of condemnation has glory, much more does the **ministry of righteousness** abound in glory."

>2 Cor 4:1, "Therefore, since we have **this ministry**, as we received mercy, we do not lose heart."

177) ἱερουργέω (1 NT use) – meaning, to minister, perform holy service, act as a priest:

>Rom 15:16, "to be a minister of Christ Jesus to the Gentiles, ministering as a **priest the gospel of God** [ἱερουργοῦντα τὸ εὐαγγέλιον τοῦ θεου], that *my* offering of the Gentiles might become acceptable, sanctified by the Holy Spirit"

Consider also the 1560/1605/1616 French Geneva, which places the emphasis on the sacrifice of the gospel of God, rather than the OT functions of the priesthood:

> Rom 15:16 (FGN), "Afin que ie soye ministre de Iesus Christ envers les Gentils, vacquant au sacrifice de l'evangile de Dieu: a ce que l'oblation des Gentils soit agreeable, estant sanctifiee par le Saint Esprit."

> Rom 15:16 (my translation), "In order that I may be a minister of Jesus Christ towards the Gentiles, occupied with the sacrifice of the gospel of God: so that the oblation of the Gentiles may be agreeable, being sanctified by the Holy Spirit."

178) οἰκοδομέω (39 NT uses):

Evangelism as building a gospel foundation or spiritual foundation:

> Rom 15:20, "And thus I aspired to evangelize, not where Christ was *already* named, that I might not **build** [οἰκοδομῶ] upon another man's foundation"

Evangelism as gathering and arranging stones in a building:

> Matt 16:18, "And I also say to you that you are Peter, and upon this rock **I will build** [οἰκοδομήσω] My church; and the gates of Hades shall not overpower it"

n22) ἡ οἰκονομία (9 NT uses), meaning management, administration, plan [of salvation], training [in the way of salvation]:

> Eph 3:9 (1669 French Geneva), "Et pour mettre en evidence devant tous quelle est **la communication** du mystere, qui estoit caché de tous temps en Dieu, qui a creé toutes choses par Jesus Christ."[677]

> Eph 3:9 (my translation of the 1669 French Geneva), "And to put in evidence before all what is **the communication** of the mystery, which was hidden from all time in God, who created all things by Jesus Christ."

> Eph 3:9 (1560 English Geneva), "And to make clear vnto all men what the fellowship of the mysterie is, which from the beginning of the worlde hathe bene hid in god, who hathe created all things by Iesus Christ,"

> Eph 3:9 (NAS), "and to bring to light what is **the administration** of the mystery which for ages has been hidden in God, who created all things"

Compare with Jer 1:10:

> "See, I have appointed you this day over the nations and over the kingdoms, To pluck up and to break down, To destroy and to overthrow, **To build** [Heb. banah; Gk. ἀνοικοδομέω; to build] and to plant."

179) ἐπισκέπτομαι (140 OT LXX uses; 11 NT uses), meaning to visit, have care for:

> Luke 1:68, "Blessed *be* the Lord God of Israel, For He has visited [ἐπισκέπτομαι] us and accomplished redemption for His people."

> Acts 15:14, "Simeon has related how God first concerned [ἐπισκέπτομαι] Himself about taking from among the Gentiles a people for His name."

Some interesting verbal groupings:

Combinations and/or parallel use of verbs for proclamation:

ἀναγγέλλω, διδάσκω, and διαμαρτύρομαι, Acts 20:20-21
διαλέγομαι, διανοίγω, παρατίθημι, and καταγγέλλω Acts 17:2-3
    Dialoguing (reasoning), opening (explaining), setting forth (giving evidence), and protesting/challenging (proclaiming)
διακατελέγχομαι and ἐπιδείκνὺμι, Acts 18:28
διαμαρτύρομαι, λαλέω, and εὐαγγελίζω, Acts 8:25
διαμαρτύρομαι and μαρτυρέω, Acts 23:11
διδάσκω and εὐαγγελίζω, Luke 20:1; Acts 5:42; 15:35
διδάσκω and καταγγέλλω, Acts 4:2
διδάσκω and κηρύσσω, Matt 11:1
διδάσκω, κηρύσσω, and θεραπεύω, Matt 9:35

---

[677]Interestingly the French Protestant Martin (1707) used the same translation, but added "that was given to us" after it: "Et pour mettre en évidence devant tous quelle est **la communication** qui nous a été accordée du mystère qui était caché de tout temps en Dieu, lequel a créé toutes choses par Jésus-Christ" (from: From: http://lirelabible.com/bibles-php/index.php?version=martin-NT; accessed: 29 June 2006; Internet). The French Protestant Ostervald (1844) used "administration," likewise the French John Darby (1859); then French Protestant Louis Segond (1910) used the word "dispensation." In English, however, as with the translation of other terms, it appears that no major translation gave it the proclamational bent that is found in the French Geneva (which quite likely comes off the pen of John Calvin).

ἐνδείκνυμι and διαγγέλλω, Rom 9:17 (Exod 9:16)
ἐξομολογέω and ἀναγγέλλω, Acts 19:18
εὐαγγελίζω and κηρύσσω, Luke 4:18; Acts 8:4-5
εὐαγγελίζω and θεραπεύω, Luke 9:6
κηρύσσω and διδάσκω, Acts 28:31
κηρύσσω and διαμαρτύρομαι, Acts 10:42
κηρύσσω and εὐαγγελίζω, Luke 8:1; Rom 10:15
κηρύσσω and καταγγέλλω, Phil 1:15-16
κηρύσσω and λέγω, Matt 10:7
λαλέω, διδάσκω, and παρρησιαζόω, Acts 18:25-26
λαλέω and εὐαγγελίζω, Luke 1:19; 11:20
λαλέω, φανερόω, and λαλέω, Col 4:3-4
λαλέω and καταγγέλλω, Acts 3:24
μαθητεύω, βαπτίζω, and διδάσκω, Matt 28:19-20
μαρτύρομαι and λέγω, Acts 26:22
παρρησιαζόω and λαλέω, Acts 26:26
παρρησιαζόω, διαλέγομαι, and πειθώ, Acts 19:8
    Speaking out boldly, reasoning, and persuading
πειθώ and λέγω, Acts 28:24
πληροφορέω + τὸ κήρυγμα and ἀκούω, 2 Tim 4:17
    Fulfill + the proclamation and [cause to] hear
πληρόω, εὐαγγελίζω, and οἰκοδομέω, Rom 15:19-20
    Fully spread, evangelized, and established

Interesting combination of verbs in one verse—2 Cor 5:20:

Byzantine Textform: Ὑπὲρ χριστοῦ οὖν πρεσβεύομεν, ὡς τοῦ θεοῦ παρακαλοῦντος δι᾽ ἡμῶν· δεόμεθα ὑπὲρ χριστοῦ, καταλλάγητε τῷ θεῷ. (2Co 5:20 BYZ)

NAS: "Therefore, we are ambassadors for Christ, as though God were entreating through us; we beg you on behalf of Christ, be reconciled to God"

πρεσβεύω, meaning to be an ambassador, [function as] an ambassador, [work as] an ambassador
παρακαλέω, meaning beseech, urge, exhort, comfort, implore, entreat
δέομαι, meaning ask, pray beg

Combinations of 3+ Verbs Used for Evangelizing in Acts

	Acts 17:2-3	Acts 18:25-26	Acts 19:8	Acts 20:20-21	Acts 28:23	Total Uses
Speaking		λαλέω				1
Proclaiming				ἀναγγέλλω		1
Reasoning	διαλέγομαι		(2) διαλέγομαι			2
Opening (explaining)	διανοίγω					1
Explaining					ἐκτίθημι	1
Teaching		διδάσκω		διδάσκω		2
Setting forth (giving evidence)	παρατίθημι					1
Solemnly testifying				διαμαρτύρομαι	διαμαρτύρομαι	3
protesting/challenging/ declaring (proclaiming)	καταγγέλλω					1
Speaking boldly		παρρησιαζόω	(1) παρρησιαζόω			2
Persuading			(3) πειθώ		πείθω	2

The Intersection of 3 Key Passages

	Matthew 28:18-20; Luke 24:46-47	Acts 17:2-3	Acts 19:9-11
Paul's Method	"Go [and preach the Gospel]	Paul's custom: Went in Reasoned from the Scriptures Opening (explaining) Establishing (demonstrating)	Went into Spoke boldly Reasoning Persuading
Paul's Message	"All authority has been given to Me in heaven and on earth" "Thus it is written, and thus it was necessary for the Christ to suffer and to rise from the dead the third day, and that repentance and remission of sins should be preached in His name to all nations"	That the Christ had to suffer and rise again from the dead, and *saying* "This Jesus whom I preach to you is the Christ!"	"The things concerning the kingdom of God"
Negative Response		[But the Jews who were not persuaded, becoming envious...]	Became hardened Did not believe Spoke evil of the way
Positive Response	"Win disciples	And some of them were persuaded; and a great multitude ... joined Paul and Silas	Withdrew the disciples
Baptism	"Baptizing them...		
Teaching	"Teaching them to observe all things that I have commanded to you"	[Paul and Silas had to leave immediately by night, v. 10]	Reasoning daily in the school of Tyrannus

Preliminary Comments:

The "methodology" terms above include 179 verbs and 22 nouns used in some way to refer to action or method of evangelizing, that being the verbal proclamation of the Gospel, not including some verbs dealing with movement or motion (as shall be seen below), nor verbs dealing with the "work of the Lord," nor verbs denoting a response to the Gospel.[678]

Note also that a different cross-section or semantic range of (1) verbal words not used for evangelism—see below and (2) verbs is used for edification in the Bible (cf. Matt 28:20) (see below in the Chapter 26, "Follow-up is Important!").

There also exists a chart of both sets of terms, verbs for evangelism and follow-up, including terms that are found in both lists available at: www.evangelismunlimited.org.

---

[678]David Barrett, from whom I am indebted to four verbs in my list, explained how he found his 42 NT verbs for evangelizing: "To illustrate our point, we can arrange those synonyms closest to *euangelizein* in Table 1, page 16, in alphabetical order (by English transliteration), with the total number of occurrences [note: 'References and totals are from C. H. Bruder, *Concordantiae NT*, Liepzig, 1867]. ... After listing most of the 41 close synonyms, Kittel's *Theological Dictionary of the New Testament* (1935 and 1964) commented.... In Table 2 we have arranged alphabetically the English terms for all 42 Greek words as given in Liddell & Scott" (David B. Barrett, *Evangelize! A Historical Survey of the Concept* (Birmingham, AL: New Hope, 1987), 15, 16, 18, 80).

10—CATEGORIES OF COMMUNICATORY VERBS NOT USED FOR EVANGELISM

Introduction:

The sins of the tongue are enumerated in several places in the New Testament. These verbals sins are wrong and are not encouraged as part of New Testament evangelizing. The following chart provides a comparative of some of these lists:

Sample Lists of Nouns, Adjectives, and Phrases Describing Sins of the Tongue

Things coming out in speech	Rom 1:29-30	Rom 13:13	1 Cor 3:3	Gal 5:20	Phil 1:15	1 Tim 6:4	Titus 3:3
Envy	φθόνου				φθόνον	φθόνος	φθόνῳ
Strife, rivalry	ἔριδος	ἔριδι	ἔρις	ἔρεις, ἐριθεῖαι	ἔριν	ἔρις	
Guile, fraud	δόλου						
Backbiters	καταλάλους						
Arrogant	ὑβριστάς						
Proud	ὑπερηφάνους						
Boastful	ἀλαζόνας						
Jealousy		ζήλῳ	ζῆλος	ζῆλοι			
Ωρατη				θυμοί			
Disssension			διχοστασίαι	διχοστασίαι			
Divisions				αἱρέσεις			
Disputes						ζητήσεις	
Disputes about words						λογομαχίας	
Blasphemy						βλασφημίαι	
Malice, evil							κακία
Suspicion of evil						ὑπόνοιαι πονηραί	
Hateful							στυγητοί
Hating one another							μισοῦντες ἀλλήλους

Because some communicatory words relate to sins of the tongue, it was deemed important to look at these prior to embarking on the adventure of locating communicatory words not used for evangelizing in the Bible.

The verbs listed in the following section are organized without duplication into these categories:
1. Communicatory verbs [in NT] *NOT USED* for evangelizing
2A. Verbs describing the *OPPOSITE OF* evangelizing
2B. Verbs describing the *OPPOSITE OF* evangelizing—linked to an affirmation for the need to evangelize
3. Methods of Evangelizing Apparently *DISAVOWED*
4. Verbs used both *FOR AND NOT FOR* evangelizing

Communicatory-Related Verbs Not Used for Evangelizing*

Verbs Not Used	Opposite of Evangelizing	Disavowed or Mixed
Debating, Arguing, Discussing, Plotting:	**Cursing, reviling, speaking evil of:**	**Of Jesus:**
1) συζητέω [10], argue, debate, discuss, question;	32) ἀναθεματίζω [4], curse;	*) κράζω [60], cry out;
n1) ἡ ζήτησις [7], investigation, [controversial] discussion, debate;	33) καταναθεματίζω [1], place under a curse;	63) ἀνίστημι [4], send up; let go; let loose; etc.;
3) διαλογίζομαι [15/16], discuss, argue; consider, reason; wonder, question;**	34) καταράομαι [6] to curse;	64) ἀκούω [436], cause to be heard.
4) συμβάλλω [6], meet, encounter, discuss, confer; debate: "converse";	35) ὀμνύω [27], to swear;	**Of Paul:**
5) συμβουλεύω [4], advise; consult, plot;	36) ἐξουθενέω [11], to despise;	65) ἁμαρτάνω [43], to sin;
6) διαλαλέω [2], discuss, plot;	37) ἐξουδενόω/ἐξουδενέω [1], to despise;	66) καπηλεύω [1], peddle;
7) δημηγορέω [1], make a speech, deliver a speech, make an oration, harangue;	38) ἐμπαίζω [13], to mock;	a3) κρυπτός [19], hidden;
8) ὁμιλέω [4], converse, speak; cf. "homelics"	39) ἐκμυκτηρίζω [2], to ridicule, sneer;	n12) ἡ πανουργία [4], crafty;
aXX) φιλόνεικος, quarrelsome.	40) λοιδορέω [4] revile;	67) δολόω [1], adulterate;
Speaking with Anger, Malice, Confront, Curse:	n7) ἡ λοιδορία [3], speak reproachfully;	n13) ἡ πλάνη [10], deception;
9) ἐμβριμάομαι [5], be moved to anger, admonish sternly;	41) ἀντιλοιδορέω [1], revile in return;	n14) ἡ ἀκαθαρσία [10], impurity;
10) ἐπιπλήσσω [1], reprove, rebuke; strike at;	42) ψεύδομαι [12] lie, mislead, deceive;	n15) ὁ δόλος [11], treachery;
11) ἐφίστημι [21], confront, come upon;	43) ψευδομαρτυρέω [5] bear false witness;	n16) ἡ κολακεία [1] flattery;
12) κακολογέω [4], speak evil of, curse; e.g. to "bad mouth" [someone];	n8) ὁ ψευδολόγος [1] speaking falsely.	n17) ἡ πλεονεξία [10] covetousness;
13) κατηγορέω [22], accuse;	**Speaking against:**	68) ἀρέσκω [17], please;
14) ὀνειδίζω [9/10]: reproach, insult;	44) ἀπειλέω [6], to threaten;	69) ζητέω + ἡ δόξα, seek glory;
15) συνεπιτίθημι [1], to join in an attack [verbal], join in the charge, lit. make a joint attack [stand];	n9) ἡ ἀπειλή [4], a threat;	70) διαλέγομαι [13], carry on a discussion;
16) συντίθεμαι [4], agree together, collude.	45) ἀνθίστημι [14], stand against, oppose;	n18) ἡ ἐπισύστασις [2], insurrection
Commanding or Ordering:	46) ἀντιτάσσω [5], to resist;	n19) ὁ ὄχλος [174], crowd;
17) ἐκλαλέω [1], tell (emphatic);	47) βλασφημέω [35], to blaspheme	n20) ὁ θόρυβος [7], uproar;
18) ἐρέω [95], to say, declare (often referring to revelation);	48) κατανίστημι [0], to rise up against;	71) ὀχλαγωγέω [0], stir up a crowd.
19) προβιβάζω [1], cause to come forward, prompt;	49) ἀντιλέγω [9], speak against, gainsay, contradict; declare in opposition;	**Methods repeatedly used by Opponents of the Gospel:**
20) φάσκω [3], speak with certainty, assert, claim, declare.	n10) ἡ ἀντιλογία [4], contradiction, controversy, disputation;	72) ἐπεγείρω [2], arouse;
Revealing or Making Known:	XX) λογομαχέω [1], dispute about words;	73) κακόω [2], mistreat;
21) δηλόω [7], declare, testify, make known, reveal;	nXX) ἡ λογομαχία [1], verbal-swordplay;	74) πείθω [6], persuade;
22) σημαίνω [6], indicate, signify, reveal;	50) προφασίζομαι [0], set up as pretext;	75) ὀχλοποιέω [1], mob forming;
23) ἐμφανίζω [10], inform, make known, report [bring charges], declare plainly;	a5) προφασιστικοὺς λόγους [0], reproachful words;	76) θορυβέω [1], make a tumult;
24) κατηχέω [7], to sound in one's ears, to teach by word of mouth, to instruct; hence, "catechism";	51) κατενέγκη … ὄνομα πονηρὸν [0], to bring against … an evil name;	n*) ὁ θόρυβος [2]: an uproar.
XX) ἐξαγορεύω, to declare plainly, confess.	52) λαλέω + διαστρέφω [1], to speak perverse things;	**Other:**
Begging, Praying:	53) μάχομαι [4], fight, quarrel; fig. be quarrelsome, dispute;	77) φείδομαι/ψεύσομαι [2] from Heb. *Kachad*, conceal;
25) παραβιάζομαι [2], strongly urge, prevail upon.	54) οὐ + προσαγορεύω [1], not + to call, designate + object.	78) κρύπτω [16], hide;
Idle Speech, Vanity, Murmuring:	**Empty Conversation:**	79) ἀναφωνέω [1], cry aloud.
26) βατταλογέω [1], to babble;	55) ὁμιλέω [4], converse, discuss, speak;	**Words Used For and Not For Evangelizing:**
27) γογγύζω [7], murmur;	**Deceiving, Leading Astray, Taking Captive:**	80) λέγω [2,315], say;
a1) ἀνωφελής [2], unprofitable, useless;	56) ἐξαπατάω [5], to deceive, cheat	81) φημί [59], say;
n2) ὁ λῆρος [1]: idle talk, nonsense;	57) πλανάω [40], to lead astray, cause to wander; fig. mislead, deceive; to go astray, be led astray, wander about;	82) ἐρωτάω [57], pray, plead, ask, beg (of prayer).
a2) μάταιος [6], vain [things];	58) συλαγωγέω [1], take captive, carry off as captive;	83) βοάω [11], cry out;
a3) ματαιολόγος [1], empty talk, idly talking, empty talker;	n11) ἡ κληδών [0], to soothsay.	84) κράζω [60], cry out;
n3) ἡ ματαιολογία [1], empty, idle, fruitless talk;	**Opposite Linked with Commands:**	85) σκορπίζω [5], fig. scatter, disperse;
a4) μωρός [12], foolish;	59) ἀρνέομαι [31], to deny, disown, renounce, refuse;	86) ἀρέσκω [17], strive to please, accommodate;
n4) ἡ μωρολογία [1], silly talk;	60) ἐπαισχύνομαι [11], be ashamed of;	87) παραγγέλλω [30], command, order; declare;
n5) ἡ αἰσχρότης [1], filthiness, obscenity;	61) ὑποστέλλω [4], hold back, shrink back, keep silent about;	88) ζωγρέω [2], take men alive.
n6) ἡ εὐτραπελία [1] coarse jesting.	62) σιωπάω [10/11] be silent.	
Big Talk:		
28) καυχάομαι [37], to boast [in Lord, not ourselves];		
29) μεγαλορρημονέω [0], to magnify [themselves];		
30) βροντάω [0], thunder		
31) ἀνακράζω [5], cry out [scream].		

*Numbers after verbs = NT uses; these not an exhaustive. **NT uses of διαλογίζομαι and its counterpart λογίζομαι, including textual-historical-soteriological-missional critical concerns, would make for an interesting study. XX = unstudied words (of which there are plenty).

Off due to unnecessary complexity.

Addendum 1: Communicatory verbs [in NT] *NOT USED* **for evangelizing:**

Regarding Debating, Arguing, Discussing

a. συζητέω and cognate:

(1) συζητέω (10 NT uses); meaning: argue, debate, discuss, question:

Acts 6:9, "But some men from what was called the Synagogue of the Freedmen, *including* both Cyrenians and Alexandrians, and some from Cilicia and Asia, rose up and **argued** with Stephen"

(n2) ἡ ζήτησις (7 NT uses); meaning: investigation, controversial question, discussion, debate:

Paul also used the stem of συζητέω in its noun form as something to be avoided, with the adjectives "endless" (1 Tim 1:5), "foolish" (Tit 3:9), "foolish and unlearned" (2 Tim 2:23), or the verb "sick" (1 Tim 6:4):

Although Paul himself did have a great debate over the Gospel, Acts 15:2, as did John's disciples over keeping pure, John 3:25

Paul called the end result of these dissensions "worthless and useless," Tit 3:9

3) διαλογίζομαι (16 in NT), to discuss, argue; consider, reason; wonder, question:

Mark 8:17, "And Jesus, aware of this, said to them, 'Why do you **discuss** *the fact* that you have no bread?'"

Often today, it seems that what is called "dialogue" is not διαλέγομαι as noted in the prior section (reasoning with the purpose of persuading, e.g. Acts 17:2-3), but διαλογίζομαι as here (discussing with uncertainty).

For example, the 1974 Lausanne Covenant included "dialogue" as indispensible in its definition of evangelism.[679]

Consider, for example, this LXX use of διαλογίζομαι:

Psa 10:2 [9:23], ἐν τῷ ὑπερηφανεύεσθαι τὸν ἀσεβῆ ἐμπυρίζεται ὁ πτωχός, συλλαμβάνονται ἐν διαβουλίοις, οἷς διαλογίζονται.

Psa 9:23 (LXE), "While the ungodly one acts proudly, the poor is hotly pursued: *the wicked* are taken in the crafty counsels which they imagine"

4) συμβάλλω (6 NT uses): meet, encounter, discuss, confer; debate: "**conversing**," Acts 17:18, notice here that the subject of the verb is not Paul but the Stoic and Epicurean philosophers, thus technically it is not a term for evangelizing. Paul was reasoning, and they were batting back and forth ideas:

Friberg Lexicon: συμβάλλω impf. συνέβαλλον; 2aor. συνέβαλον; strictly *throw together*; (1) active; (a) transitively; (i) with λόγους (*words*) understood *confer, consult* (AC 4.15); (ii) *consider, ponder, think about seriously* (LU 2.19); (iii) *quarrel, dispute* (AC 17.18); (b) intransitively *meet, fall in with* (AC 20.14); in a hostile sense *meet in battle, wage war with, fight* (LU 14.31); (2) middle *help, give assistance to, contribute to* (AC 18.27)

5) συμβουλεύω (4 in NT), to plot, advise, counsel:

Matt 26:4, "and **they plotted** together to seize Jesus by stealth, and kill *Him*."

John 18:4, "Now Caiaphas was the one **who had advised** the Jews that it was expedient for one man to die on behalf of the people."

Acts 9:23, "And when many days had elapsed, the Jews **plotted** together to do away with him."

Rev 3:18, "**I advise** you to buy from Me gold refined by fire, that you may become rich, and white garments, that you may clothe yourself, and *that* the shame of your nakedness may not be revealed; and eye salve to anoint your eyes, that you may see."

---

[679]"To evangelize is to spread the good news that Jesus Christ died for our sins and was raised from the dead according to the Scriptures, and that as the reigning Lord he now offers the forgiveness of sins and the liberating gift of the Holy Spirit to all who repent and believe. Our Christian presence in the world is indispensable to evangelism, and so is that kind of dialogue whose purpose is to listen sensitively in order to understand. But evangelism itself is the proclamation of the historical, biblical Christ as Saviour and Lord, with a view to persuading people to come to him personally and so be reconciled to God. In issuing the Gospel invitation we have no liberty to conceal the cost of discipleship. Jesus still calls all who would follow him to deny themselves, take up their cross, and identify themselves with his new community. The results of evangelism include obedience to Christ, incorporation into his church and responsible service in the world" (John R. W. Stott, *Making Christ Known: Historic Mission Documents from the Lausanne Movement* [Grand Rapids: Eerdmans, 1996], 20).

6) διαλαλέω (2 in NT), to plot, advise, counsel:

Luke 1:65, "And fear came on all those living around them; and all these matters **were being talked** about in all the hill country of Judea."

Luke 6:11, "But they themselves were filled with rage, and **discussed** together what they might do to Jesus."

7) δημηγορέω (1 NT use): to make a speech, deliver a speech, make an oration, harangue (a long prepared speech), Acts 12:21

[hence English demagoguery]

Lidell-Scott: δημηγορέω, f. ήσω, (δημηγόρος) *to speak in the assembly,* Lat. concionari, Ar., etc.: Pass., τὰ δεδημηγορημένα *public speeches,* Dem.

II. *to make popular speeches, to speak rhetorically, use clap-trap,* Plat., etc.

May not demagoguery (classical rhetoric) sometimes be taught in some homiletics classes rather than preaching? *Contra* 1 Cor 1:17, 21-25.

8) ὁμιλέω (4 NT uses; word from which we get "homiletics"): to converse, Acts 24:26, "At the same time too, he was hoping that money would be given him by Paul; therefore he also used to send for him quite often and **converse** with him"

[four NT uses, Luke 24:14, 15; Acts 20:11; 24:26]

Regarding Speaking with Anger or Malice, to Curse

9) ἐμβριμάομαι (5 NT uses): "be moved to anger, admonish sternly":

1) Used of Jesus sternly warning people not to tell of his miracles, Matt 9:30; Mark 1:43;

2) Used of the disciples (esp Judas Iscariot, John 12:4-6) admonishing the woman who annointed Jesus with oil, Mark 14:5

3) Used of Jesus groaning in his spirit because of the response to the death of Lazarus, John 11:33, 38

10) ἐπιπλήσσω (1 NT use): to reprove, rebuke; strike at:

1 Tim 5:1, "Do not sharply rebuke an older man, but *rather* appeal to *him* as a father, *to* the younger men as brothers"

11) ἐφίστημι (21 in NT): confront, come upon:

Luke 20:1, "the chief priests and the scribes with the elders **confronted** [came upon] Him"

12) κακολογέω (4 NT uses): speaking evil of, curse [e.g. "to bad mouth (someone)," denegrate], Acts 19:9 (cf. Matt 15:4; Mark 7:10; 9:39)

The verb which combines "bad-speech" in Latin means to curse: *maledico;* which transliterates into French as the noun "malediction" (a curse) or the verb "maudire" (to curse).

Notice that when they received cursing for sharing the Gospel, it was the sign for them that they needed to "shake the dust off there feet" as it were, withdraw from the synagogue, and go elsewhere (cf. Acts 13:51; 18:6).

13) κατηγορέω (22 in NT): accuse:

Matt 12:10, "Mat 12:10 And behold, *there was* a man with a withered hand. And they questioned Him, saying, 'Is it lawful to heal on the Sabbath?'—in order that they might **accuse** Him."

14) ὀνειδίζω (9/10 NT uses): reproach, insult, Matt 5:11; 11:20; 27:44; Mark 15:32; 16:14; Luke 6:22; Rom 15:3; 1 Tim 3:7; 4:10; Heb 10:33; 11:26; 13:13; James 1:5; 1 Pet 4:14

Also 1 Tim 4:10 (NKJ), "For to this *end* we both labor and **suffer reproach**, because we trust in the living God, who is *the* Savior of all men, especially of those who believe."

See also noun ὀνειδισμός: Rom 15:3; 1 Tim 3:7; Heb 10:33; 11:26; 13:13

15) συνεπιτίθεμαι (1 NT use), to join in an attack [verbal], join in the charge, lit make a joint attack (stand);

Acts 24:9, "The Jews also **joined in the attack**, asserting that these things were so";

*) See also συνεπέστη (from συνεφίστημι), to join together in an attack:

Acts 16:22, "And the crowd **rose up together against them**" (1977 NAS)

16) συντίθεμαι (4 in NT BYM), to agree in covenant [for something bad], conspire, collude; Considered middle voice of συντίθημι (3 in NT BGM), meaning to agree together:

Luke 22:5, "And they were glad, and **agreed** to give him money."

John 9:22, "His parents said this because they were afraid of the Jews; for the Jews had already **agreed**, that if anyone should confess Him to be Christ, he should be put out of the synagogue."

Acts 23:20, "And he said, "The Jews **have agreed** to ask you to bring Paul down tomorrow to the Council, as though they were going to inquire somewhat more thoroughly about him."

Acts 24:9, "And the Jews also **joined in the attack**, asserting that these things were so."

Regarding Commanding, Ordering

17) ἐκλαλέω (1 NT use): tell (emphatic), Acts 23:22, "Therefore the commander let the young man go, instructing him, '**Tell** no one that you have notified me of these things.'"

18) ἐρέω (95 NT uses):

This verb has some difference of opinion in its parsing: the Bibleworks parsing of the Nestle-Aland assigns it as a derivative of the verb λέγω; the Byzantine Textform keeps it as a separate root form. Liddell-Scott assign this root as an Ionic and Epic verb meaning to say.

For example, of 30 uses in Matthew, and 12 of those times it relates to the fulfillment of prophecies, 7 times relates to quotations of the OT law, and 7 times it relates to the words of Christ directly or in parables, and 4 times it relates to the sayings of men in one way or another.

One interesting use is Matt 26:75:

Matt 26:75 (my adaptation), "And Peter remembered the **declaration** which Jesus had **declared**, 'Before a cock crows, you will deny Me three times.' And he went out and wept bitterly."

Matt 26:75 (BYZ), "Καὶ ἐμνήσθη ὁ Πέτρος τοῦ **ῥήματος** [ῥῆμα] τοῦ Ἰησοῦ **εἰρηκότος** [ἐρέω] αὐτῷ ὅτι Πρὶν ἀλέκτορα φωνῆσαι, τρὶς ἀπαρνήσῃ με. Καὶ ἐξελθὼν ἔξω ἔκλαυσεν πικρῶς.."

Further the Greek word ῥῆμα is clearly relate to divine revelation:

Deut 8:3 (my adaptation), "And He humbled you and let you be hungry, and fed you with manna which you did not know, nor did your fathers know, that He might make you understand that man does not live by bread alone, but man lives by everything [ῥῆμα] that proceeds out of the mouth of the LORD."

1 Pet 1:24-25 (my adaptation), "For, 'All flesh is like grass, And all its glory like the flower of grass. The grass withers, And the flower falls off, But the word of the Lord [τὸ δὲ ῥῆμα κυρίου] abides forever.' And this is the word [ῥῆμα] by which you were evangelized."

The evangelist tells about what has been declared by God. His power is in what God has declared, not what the evangelist personally declares or thinks.

19) προβιβάζω (NT *hapax* in NA27): used of Herodias' careful instruction to her daughter regarding the beheading of John the Baptist, Matt 14:8 ;
Used in BYZ in Acts 19:33.

20) φάσκω (3 NT uses): speaking with certainty, assert, claim, declare: Acts 25:19—used by third party to describe Paul's evangelism:

Acts 25:19 but they *simply* had some points of disagreement with him about their own religion and about a certain dead man, Jesus, whom Paul **asserted** to be alive

Also found:

Acts 24:9, "**asserting** that these things were so"

Rom 1:22, "**professing** to be wise"

Regarding Revealing, Making Known

21) δηλόω (7 NT uses), meaning to declare, testify, make known, reveal:

Heb 9:8, "The Holy Spirit *is* **signifying** this, that the way into the holy place has not yet been disclosed, while the outer tabernacle is still standing"

2 Pet 1:14, "knowing that the laying aside of my *earthly* dwelling is imminent, as also our Lord Jesus Christ **has made clear** to me."

Other NT uses: 1 Cor 1:11; 3:13; Col 1:8; Heb 12:27; 1 Pet 1:11.

Appears to be used in contexts where man reveals information about someone or something, 1 Cor 1:11; Col 1:8; where persons of the Trinity reveal something to someone, Heb 9:8; 1 Pet 1:11; 2 Pet 1:14; of revelation in interpreting Scripture, Heb 12:27; and of the future revelation of our works, 1 Cor 3:13.

22) σημαίνω (6 NT uses; 26 OT LXX uses): indicate, signify, reveal:

Acts 11:28, "And one of them named Agabus stood up and *began* **to indicate** by the Spirit that there would certainly be a great famine all over the world. And this took place in the *reign* of Claudius"

23) ἐμφανίζω (10 NT uses): inform, make known, report [bring charges], declare plainly (KJV); reveal, appear, John 14:21, 22; Acts 23:15, 22; 24:1; 25:2, 15 (cf. Matt 27:53):

John 14:22, "Judas (not Iscariot) said to Him, 'Lord, what then has happened that You are going to **disclose** Yourself to us and not to the world?'"

Acts 23:22, "So the commander let the young man go, instructing him, "Tell no one that you have **notified** me of these things.'"

24) κατηχέω (7 NT uses): "to sound a thing in one's ears, to teach by word of mouth, to instruct; Pass. to be informed" (Liddell-Scott):

Rom 2:18, "and know *His* will, and approve the things that are essential, **being instructed** out of the Law"

Regarding Begging, Praying

25) παραβιάζομαι (2 NT use), strongly urge, prevail upon:

Luke 24:29, "And **they urged** Him, saying, 'Stay with us, for it is *getting* toward evening, and the day is now nearly over.' And He went in to stay with them."

Regarding Idle Speech, Vanity, Murmuring

26) βατταλογέω (No LXX uses; 1 NT use), babble:

Matt 6:7, "And when you are praying, **do** not **use meaningless repetition**, as the Gentiles do, for they suppose that they will be heard for their many words."

27) γογγύζω (13 OT LXX uses; 7 NT uses), murmur, grumble:

Matt 20:11, "And when they received it, **they grumbled** at the landowner."

Luke 5:30, "And the Pharisees and their scribes *began* **grumbling** at His disciples, saying, 'Why do you eat and drink with the tax-gatherers and sinners?'"

John 6:41, "The Jews therefore **were grumbling** about Him, because He said, 'I am the bread that came down out of heaven.'"

John 6:43, "Jesus answered and said to them, '**Do** not **grumble** among yourselves.'"

John 6:61, "But Jesus, conscious that His disciples **grumbled** at this, said to them, 'Does this cause you to stumble?'"

John 7:32, "The Pharisees heard the multitude **muttering** these things about Him; and the chief priests and the Pharisees sent officers to seize Him."

1 Cor 10:10, "Nor **grumble**, as some of them did, and were destroyed by the destroyer."

a1) ἀνωφελής (1 NT use): idle talk, nonsense:

Titus 3:9, "But shun foolish controversies and genealogies and strife and disputes about the Law; for they are unprofitable and worthless."

n2) ὁ λῆρος (1 NT use): idle talk, nonsense:

Luke 24:11, "And these words appeared to them as **nonsense**, and they would not believe them"

5) μάταιος and cognate forms:

(a2) μάταιος (6 NT uses), vain [things]:

Acts 14:15, "and saying, 'Men, why are you doing these things? We are also men of the same nature as you, and preach the gospel to you in order that you should turn from these **vain things** to a living God, who made the heaven and the earth and the sea, and all that is in them.'"

1 Cor 3:20, "and again, 'The Lord knows the reasonings of the wise, that they are useless.'"

1 Cor 15:17, "and if Christ has not been raised, your faith is worthless; you are still in your sins."

Titus 3:9, "But shun foolish controversies and genealogies and strife and disputes about the Law; for they are unprofitable and **worthless**."

James 1:26, "If anyone thinks himself to be religious, and yet does not bridle his tongue but deceives his *own* heart, this man's religion is **worthless**."

1 Pet 1:18, "knowing that you were not redeemed with perishable things like silver or gold from your **futile** way of life inherited from your forefathers."

(a3) ματαιολόγος (1 NT use), empty talk, idly talking, empty talker:

Tit 1:10, "For there are many rebellious men, **empty talkers** and deceivers, especially those of the circumcision."

(n3) ἡ ματαιολογία (1 NT use), empty, idle, fruitless talk:

1 Tim 1:6, "For some men, straying from these things, have turned aside to **fruitless discussion**."

6) μωρός and cognate:

(a4) μωρός (7 OT LXX; 12 NT uses), foolish, fool:

2 Tim 2:23, "But refuse foolish and ignorant speculations, knowing that they produce quarrels."

(n4) ἡ μωρολογία (noun; *hapax*): idle talk, nonsense:

> Eph 5:4, "and *there must be no* filthiness and **silly talk**, or coarse jesting, which are not fitting, but rather giving of thanks."

n5) ἡ αἰσχρότης (1 NT use), filthiness, obscenity:

> Eph 5:4, "and *there must be no* **filthiness** and silly talk, or coarse jesting, which are not fitting, but rather giving of thanks."

n6) ἡ εὐτραπελία (1 NT use), coarse jesting:

> Eph 5:4, "and *there must be no* filthiness and silly talk, or **coarse jesting**, which are not fitting, but rather giving of thanks."

Big Talk

28) καυχάομαι (37 NT uses), to boast:

> 1 Cor 1:31, "that, just as it is written, 'Let **him who boasts**, boast in the Lord.'" (cf. 2 Cor 10:17)
>
> 1 Cor 3:21, "So then let no one **boast** in men."
>
> 1 Cor 4:7, "For who regards you as superior? And what do you have that you did not receive? But if you did receive it, why **do you boast** as if you had not received it?"
>
> 2 Cor 10:16, "so as to preach the gospel even to the regions beyond you, *and* not **to boast** in what has been accomplished in the sphere of another."
>
> 2 Cor 11:30, "If I have **to boast**, **I will boast** of what pertains to my weakness."
>
> Gal 6:14, "But may it never be that **I should boast**, except in the cross of our Lord Jesus Christ, through which the world has been crucified to me, and I to the world."
>
> James 4:16, "But as it is, **you boast** in your arrogance; all such boasting is evil."

29) μεγαλορρημονέω (4 OT LXX uses only), to magnify:

> Psalm 35:26, "Let those be ashamed and humiliated altogether who rejoice at my distress; Let those be clothed with shame and dishonor **who magnify** themselves over me."
>
> Psalm 38:16, "For I said, 'May they not rejoice over me, *Who*, when my foot slips, **would magnify** themselves against me.'"
>
> Psalm 55:12, "For it is not an enemy who reproaches me, Then I could bear *it*; Nor is it one who hates me **who has exalted** himself against me, Then I could hide myself from him."
>
> Ezek 35:13, "And you have spoken arrogantly against Me and **have multiplied** your words against Me; I have heard."

30) βροντάω (6/7 OT LXX uses only), to thunder:

> 1 Sam 7:10, "Now Samuel was offering up the burnt offering, and the Philistines drew near to battle against Israel. But the LORD **thundered** with a great thunder on that day against the Philistines and confused them, so that they were routed before Israel."
>
> 2 Sam 22:14, "The LORD **thundered** from heaven, And the Most High uttered His voice."

There are some forms of communication that are left only for God to accomplish!

31) ἀνακράζω (5 NT uses), to cry out [scream]:

> #84 is κράζω.
>
> Mark 1:23, "And just then there was in their synagogue a man with an unclean spirit; and he **cried out**."
>
> Mark 6:49, "But when they saw Him walking on the sea, they supposed that it was a ghost, and **cried out**."
>
> Luke 4:33, "And there was a man in the synagogue possessed by the spirit of an unclean demon, and he **cried out** with a loud voice."
>
> Luke 8:28, "And seeing Jesus, he **cried out** and fell before Him, and said in a loud voice, 'What do I have to do with You, Jesus, Son of the Most High God? I beg You, do not torment me.'"
>
> Luke 23:18, "But they **cried out** all together, saying, 'Away with this man, and release for us Barabbas!'"

Addendum 2A: Verbs describing the *OPPOSITE OF* evangelizing:

Cursing, Reviling, Speaking Evil of

1) ἀναθεματίζω and cognates:

    32) ἀναθεματίζω (4 in NT): to curse, Mark 14:71:
        Mark 14:71, "But he began to **curse** and swear, 'I do not know this man you are talking about!'"

    33) καταναθεματίζω (1 NT use): to place under a curse, Matt 26:74:
        Matt 26:74, "Then he began to **curse** and swear, 'I do not know the man!' And immediately a cock crowed."

    Consider also the nouns:
        a) τὸ ἀνάθεμα (6 NT uses): accused; used in a third person construction, but never in direct address to a lost soul;
        b) τὸ κατάθεμα (1 NT use): meaning "the curse," Rev 22:3.

34) καταράομαι (6 in NT) to curse:
    Matt 5:44 (NKJ), "But I say to you, love your enemies, bless those **who curse** you, do good to those who hate you, and pray for those who spitefully use you and persecute you."
    Matt 25:41, "Then He will also say to those on His left, 'Depart from Me, **accursed** ones, into the eternal fire which has been prepared for the devil and his angels.'"
    Luke 6:28, "bless those **who curse** you, pray for those who mistreat you."
    Rom 12:14, "Bless those who persecute you; bless and **curse** not."
    James 3:9-10 (NKJ), "With it we bless our God and Father, and with it we **curse** men, who have been made in the similitude of God. Out of the same mouth proceed blessing and cursing [cognate noun: κατάρα]. My brethren, these things ought not to be so"

35) ὀμνύω (27 in NT), to swear, take an oath:
    Matt 5:34, "But I say to you, **make no oath** at all, either by heaven, for it is the throne of God."
    Matt 5:36, "Nor shall you **make an oath** by your head, for you cannot make one hair white or black."
    Matt 23:16-22, "Woe to you, blind guides, who say, 'Whoever **swears** by the temple, that is nothing; but whoever **swears** by the gold of the temple, he is obligated.' You fools and blind men; which is more important, the gold, or the temple that sanctified the gold? And, 'Whoever **swears** by the altar, *that* is nothing, but whoever **swears** by the offering upon it, he is obligated.' You blind men, which is more important, the offering or the altar that sanctifies the offering? Therefore he who **swears** by the altar, **swears** *both* by the altar and by everything on it. And he who **swears** by the temple, **swears** *both* by the temple and by Him who dwells within it. And he who **swears** by heaven, **swears** *both* by the throne of God and by Him who sits upon it."
    Matt 26:74, "Then he began to curse and **swear**, 'I do not know the man!' And immediately a cock crowed."
    Mark 6:23, "And he **swore** to her, 'Whatever you ask of me, I will give it to you; up to half of my kingdom.'"
    Mark 14:71, "But he began to curse and **swear**, 'I do not know this man you are talking about!'"
    James 5:12, "But above all, my brethren, do not **swear**, either by heaven or by earth or with any other oath; but let your yes be yes, and your no, no; so that you may not fall under judgment."

36) ἐξουθενέω (11 in NT), to despise; to view with contempt:
    Luke 18:9, "And He also told this parable to certain ones who trusted in themselves that they were righteous, and **viewed** others **with contempt**."
    Luke 18:9 (NKJ), "Also He spoke this parable to some who trusted in themselves that they were righteous, and **despised** others."
    Rom 14:3, "Let not him who eats **despise** him who does not eat, and let not him who does not eat judge him who eats; for God has received him."

37) ἐξουδενόω/ἐξουδενέω (1 in NT), to despise, treat with contempt:
    Mark 9:12, "And He said to them, 'Elijah does first come and restore all things. And *yet* how is it written of the Son of Man that He should suffer many things and **be treated with contempt**?'"

38) ἐμπαίζω (13 in NT), to mock:
    Matt 20:19, "and will deliver Him to the Gentiles **to mock** and scourge and crucify *Him*, and on the third day He will be raised up."
    Luke 14:29, "Otherwise, when he has laid a foundation, and is not able to finish, all who observe it begin **to ridicule** him."

39) ἐκμυκτηρίζω (2 in NT), to ridicule, sneer:
    Matt 5:34, "But I say to you, **make no oath** at all, either by heaven, for it is the throne of God."

8. λοιδορέω and cognates:

   40) λοιδορέω (4 NT uses): revile, John 9:28; Acts 23:4; 1 Cor 4:12; 2 Pet 2:23, "and while **being reviled**, He did not revile in return"

   n7) ἡ λοιδορία (3 in NT), speak reproachfully, 1 Tim 5:14; 1 Pet 3:9

   41) ἀντιλοιδορέω (1 NT use): revile in return, 2 Pet 2:23, "and while being reviled, He **did not revile in return**"

9. ψεύδομαι and and other words with that same prefix:

   42) ψεύδομαι (12 NT uses) lie:
   Matt 5:11, "Blessed are you when *men* cast insults at you, and persecute you, and say all kinds of evil against you **falsely**, on account of Me"
   Acts 5:3, "But Peter said, 'Ananias, why has Satan filled your heart **to lie** to the Holy Spirit, and to keep back *some* of the price of the land?'"
   Col 3:9, "**Do not lie** to one another, since you laid aside the old self with its *evil* practices"
   Paul wrote, "I am not lying" three times: 2 Cor 11:31; Gal 1:20; 1 Tim 2:7
   Also note, "it is impossible for God to lie" (Heb 6:18).

   43) ψευδομαρτυρέω (5 NT uses) bear false witness: Matt 19:18; Mark 10:19; 14:56, 57; Luke 18:20.
   Three of the uses are when Jesus is quoting the Ten Commandments, and the two other uses are when the false witnesses are providing false testimony against Jesus, Mark 14:56-57.

   n8) ὁ ψευδολόγος (1 NT use) speaking falsely:
   1 Tim 4:2, "by means of the hypocrisy of **liars** seared in their own conscience as with a branding iron."

Speak Against

10. ἀπειλή and cognate verb:

   44) ἀπειλέω (2 NT uses; 9 OT LXX uses): to threaten, Acts 4:17; 2 Pet 2:23, "while suffering, He uttered no threats":

   n9) ἡ ἀπειλή (4 NT uses): a threat, Acts 4:17, 29; 9:1; Eph 6:9.

45) ἀνθίστημι (14 NT uses): to stand against, oppose, Acts 13:8

46) ἀντιτάσσω/ἀντιτάσσομαι (same 5 NT uses, parsing from two approaches)
   Acts 18:6, "And when **they resisted** and blasphemed, he shook out his garments and said to them, 'Your blood *be* upon your own heads! I am clean. From now on I shall go to the Gentiles.'"

47) βλασφημέω (35 NT uses), to blaspheme:
   Acts 18:6, "And when **they resisted** and blasphemed, he shook out his garments and said to them, 'Your blood *be* upon your own heads! I am clean. From now on I shall go to the Gentiles.'"

48) κατανίστημι (1 OT LXX use), to rise up against:
   Num 16:3, "And they assembled together against Moses and Aaron, and said to them, 'You have gone far enough, for all the congregation are holy, every one of them, and the LORD is in their midst; so why do you **exalt yourselves** above the assembly of the LORD?'"

15. ἀντιλέγω and cognate of ἀντιλογέω (not found in NT):

   49) ἀντιλέγω (9 NT uses): speak against, gainsay, contradict; declare in opposition:
   Acts 13:45, "But when the Jews saw the crowds, they were filled with jealousy, and *began* **contradicting** the things spoken by Paul, and were blaspheming"
   Luke 2:34 (NKJ), "Then Simeon blessed them, and said to Mary His mother, 'Behold, this *Child* is destined for the fall and rising of many in Israel, and for a sign which will be **spoken against**'"
   Titus 1:9, "holding fast the faithful word which is in accordance with the teaching, that he may be able both to exhort in sound doctrine and to refute those **who contradict**.'"

   n10) ἡ ἀντιλογία (4 NT uses; 3 in Heb, one in Jude); contradiction, controversy, disputation; in pl. opposing arguments, answering speeches:
   a) Used to describe the treatment that Jesus received from sinners, Heb 12:3, "For consider Him who has endured such **hostility** by sinners against Himself, so that you may not grow weary and lose heart"

b) Used to describe the rebellion of Korah, Jude 11, "Woe to them! For they have gone the way of Cain, and for pay they have rushed headlong into the error of Balaam, and perished in the rebellion of Korah"

c) Similarly, was not Elymas the Magician contradicting Saul, who became Paul in this encounter (Acts 13:6-12)?

OT precedent of ἡ ἀντιλογία also refers to a disagreement between persons requiring or resulting in judicial process (Deut 25:1), especially of the people of Israel contending with God's leadership through Moses (Deut 33:8):

> Exod 17:7 (NAS), "And he named the place **Massah** and **Meribah** because of the quarrel of the sons of Israel, and because they tested the LORD, saying, 'Is the LORD among us, or not?'"
> Exod 17:7 (LXX), καὶ ἐπωνόμασεν τὸ ὄνομα τοῦ τόπου ἐκείνου **πειρασμὸς** καὶ **λοιδόρησις** διὰ τὴν λοιδορίαν τῶν υἱῶν Ισραηλ καὶ διὰ τὸ πειράζειν κύριον λέγοντας εἰ ἔστιν κύριος ἐν ἡμῖν ἢ οὔ

> Deut 33:8, "And of Levi he said, '*Let* Thy Thummim and Thy Urim *belong* to Thy godly man, Whom Thou didst prove at **Massah**, With whom Thou didst contend at the waters of **Meribah**'"
> Deut 33:8, καὶ τῷ Λευι εἶπεν δότε Λευι δήλους αὐτοῦ καὶ ἀλήθειαν αὐτοῦ τῷ ἀνδρὶ τῷ ὁσίῳ ὃν ἐπείρασαν αὐτὸν ἐν **πείρᾳ** ἐλοιδόρησαν αὐτὸν ἐπὶ ὕδατος **ἀντιλογίας**

12) προφασίζομαι and cognate:

(50) προφασίζομαι (3 in OT LXX; 0 in NT), set up as pretext;
> 2 Kgs 5:7, "And it came about when the king of Israel read the letter, that he tore his clothes and said, 'Am I God, to kill and to make alive, that this man is sending *word* to me to cure a man of his leprosy? But consider now, and see how he is **seeking a quarrel** against me.'"
> Psa 141:4, "Do not incline my heart to any evil thing, **To practice deeds of wickedness** With men who do iniquity; And do not let me eat of their delicacies."
> This verse contains a Hebrew dual translated into Greek: τοῦ προφασίζεσθαι προφάσεις
> Pro 22:13, "The sluggard **says**, 'There is a lion outside; I shall be slain in the streets!'"

(a5) ἐπιθῇ … προφασιστικοὺς λόγους, place upon … reproachful words, Deut 22:14:
> Deut 22:14 (LXE), "and **attach to her reproachful words**, and bring against her an evil name, and say, I took this woman, and when I came to her I found not her tokens of virginity"
> This adjective is found only twice in the OT LXX, both times in this context, Deut 22:14, 17.

51) καταφέρω: κατενέγκῃ … ὄνομα πονηρόν, to bring against …an evil name, Deut 22:14
> Deut 22:14 (LXE), "and attach to her reproachful words, and **bring against her an evil name**, and say, I took this woman, and when I came to her I found not her tokens of virginity"

Consider the context of the NT parallels!
> Luke 6:22, "Blessed are you when men hate you, and ostracize you, and cast insults at you, and **spurn your name as evil**, for the sake of the Son of Man"
> Greek (BYZ): ἐκβάλωσιν τὸ ὄνομα ὑμῶν ὡς πονηρόν
> Or, Matt 5:11 (NKJ), "Blessed are you when they revile and persecute you, and **say all kinds of evil against you** falsely for My sake"
> Greek (BYZ): εἴπωσιν πᾶν πονηρὸν ῥῆμα καθ' ὑμῶν

52) λαλέω + διαστρέφω (1 NT use of this combination): speaking perverse things, Acts 20:30

53) μάχομαι (20 OT and 4 NT uses): lit. to fight (Acts 7:26); fig. to be quarrelsome (2 Tim 2:24), dispute (John 6:52; James 4:2):
> 2 Tim 2:24, "And the Lord's bond-servant must not be **quarrelsome**, but be kind to all, able to teach, patient when wronged"

54) οὐ προσαγορεύω, not + to call, designate + object:
> Deut 23:6[7] LXE, "Thou **shalt not speak** peaceably or profitably to them all thy days for ever."

Interestingly, notice the one NT use:
> Heb 5:10, "being designated by God as a high priest according to the order of Melchizedek"

Note also that this command has been used against the Jews by both the Muslims and the Roman Catholic Church through exacting higher taxes from Jews or placing on them restrictions that others did not have.

Empty Conversation

55) ὁμιλέω (4 NT uses) discuss, converse, speak;

Acts 24:26 describes the fruitless and ill-motivated discussions initiated by Felix with Paul:

Acts 24:26, "At the same time too, he was hoping that money would be given him by Paul; therefore he also used to send for him quite often and **converse** with him."

Also found in a positive sense in Luke 24:14 and Acts 20:11:

Luke 24:14, "And they were conversing with each other about all these things which had taken place."

Acts 20:11, "And when he had gone *back* up, and had broken the bread and eaten, he talked with them a long while, until daybreak, and so departed."

Deceive, Lead Astray, Take Captive

56) ἐξαπατάω (5 in NT), to deceive, cheat:

Rom 7:11, "for sin, taking opportunity through the commandment, **deceived** me, and through it killed me"

Rom 16:18, "For such men are slaves, not of our Lord Christ but of their own appetites; and by their smooth and flattering speech **they deceive** the hearts of the unsuspecting."

1 Cor 3:18, "Let no man **deceive** himself. If any man among you thinks that he is wise in this age, let him become foolish that he may become wise."

2 Cor 11:3, "But I am afraid, lest as the serpent **deceived** Eve by his craftiness, your minds should be led astray from the simplicity and purity *of devotion* to Christ."

2 Thess 2:3, "Let no one in any way **deceive** you, for *it will not come* unless the apostasy comes first, and the man of lawlessness is revealed, the son of destruction."

57) πλανάω (92 OT LXX uses; 40 NT uses): meaning (1) to lead astray, cause to wander; fig. mislead, deceive; (2) to go astray, be led astray, wander about; these below are but a sampling of this powerful word:

Deut 13:5, "But that prophet or that dreamer of dreams shall be put to death, because he has **counseled rebellion** against the LORD your God…"

Jer 23:13, "Moreover, among the prophets of Samaria I saw an offensive thing: They prophesied by Baal and **led** My people Israel **astray**"

Jer 23:32, "Behold, I am against those who have prophesied false dreams," declares the LORD, "and related them, and **led** My people **astray** by their falsehoods and reckless boasting; yet I did not send them or command them, nor do they furnish this people the slightest benefit," declares the LORD"

Matt 24:4-5, "And Jesus answered and said to them, 'See to it that no one **misleads** you. For many will come in My name, saying, "I am the Christ," and **will mislead** many'"

Matt 24:11, "And many false prophets will arise, and **will mislead** many"

Matt 24:24, "For false Christs and false prophets will arise and will show great signs and wonders, so as **to mislead**, if possible, even the elect"

2 Tim 3:13, "But evil men and impostors will proceed *from bad* to worse, **deceiving** and **being deceived**"

James 5:19, "My brethren, if any among you **strays** from the truth, and one turns him back"

1 John 2:26, "These things I have written to you concerning those who are trying **to deceive** you"

Rev 12:9, "And the great dragon was thrown down, the serpent of old who is called the devil and Satan, **who deceives** the whole world; he was thrown down to the earth, and his angels were thrown down with him"

58) συλαγωγέω (1 OT LXX use): take captive, carry off as captive:

Col 2:8, "See to it that no one **takes you captive** through philosophy and empty deception, according to the tradition of men, according to the elementary principles of the world, rather than according to Christ."

  1) συλαγωγέω is a *hapax legomena* in the NT and OT LXX

  2) This verb may be somewhat synonymous to ζωγρέω as in Luke 5:10 and 2 Tim 2:26

n11) ἡ κληδών (1 OT LXX use): to soothsay:

Deut 18:14 (NKJ), "For these nations which you will dispossess listened to **soothsayers** and diviners; but as for you, the LORD your God has not appointed such for you."

Thoughts:

What is amazing to me is that anathematizing became the chief method of the Church of Rome to deal with their theological foes. Apparently this was to be an expected byproduct of a part of the church becoming associated with the state, whereby its must needs determine and author binding regulations to administer the religious affairs of the realm. Clearly this level of dominance was not what Christ had in mind for the organization of His church, cf. Mark 10:42-45;

Framing as heretic was evident early in the 2nd Century. Further, these writings have been preserved for posterity! Anathematizing was in clear evidence at the Council of Trent (1545-1564), but even much earlier than that, the fires for the burning of heretics had been in stong use, beginning perhaps as late as 1002 or 1022 A.D.;

Taking up of arms against adversaries began with Constantine, but was especially in evidence with Charlemagne, and the many "Holy Roman Emperors" that followed after him;

So the three most prominent methods of Rome were: anathematizing their enemies, burning them at the stake (when politically possible), and subduing peoples by war or colonization for political domination—amazing how far they drifted from the example of Christ!

Addendum 2B: Verbs describing the *OPPOSITE OF* evangelizing—linked to an affirmation for the need to evangelize:

Opposite Linked with Commands

59) ἀρνέομαι: to deny, disown, renounce, refuse, Matt 10:33; 27:70, 72; Mark 14:68, 70; Luke 12:9; 22:53; John 18:25, 27

e.g., John 1:20, "And he confessed, and did not deny, and he confessed, 'I am not the Christ.'"

60) ἐπαισχύνομαι (11 total NT uses) to be ashamed of, Mark 8:38; Luke 9:26; Rom 1:16; 2 Tim 1:8, 12, 16:

1) Not only shame of Christ, but also shame of His words, Mark 8:38; Luke 9:26:

Mark 8:38, "For whoever is ashamed of Me and My words in this adulterous and sinful generation, the Son of Man will also be ashamed of him when He comes in the glory of His Father with the holy angels"

Luke 9:26, "For whoever is ashamed of Me and My words, of him will the Son of Man be ashamed when He comes in His glory, and *the glory* of the Father and of the holy angels"

2) Ashamed of the Gospel of Christ, Rom 1:16

3) Ashamed of the testimony of the Lord and of Paul, His prisoner, 2 Tim 1:8

4) This inward shame seems to lead to the verb before this, denial; or likewise, the shame is noticeable because of the lack of confessing!

61) ὑποστέλλω (4 NT uses): hold back, shrink back, keep silent about, Acts 20:20

1) Notice the uses of the cognate διαστέλλομαι (to warn) in Ezek 3:18, 19, 20, 21 to describe the communication required by God; Ezek 33:7 uses the Hebrew *zahar* (hiphil: to instruct, teach, warn); Ezek 33:8 uses the Hebrew word *dabar* (to speak) + *zahar* (to warn), or the Greek λαλέω (to speak) + φυλάσσω (to guard); Ezek 33:9 uses προαπαγγέλλω (to warn).

62) σιωπάω (10/11 NT uses): be silent, Acts 18:9; cf. Luke 19:40:

1) Note the parallel use of the verb ἡσυχάζω – to cease, to be silent, to rest, cf. Acts 11:18; 21:14

Addendum 3: Methods of Evangelizing Apparently *DISAVOWED*:

Of Jesus

Introductory: the three verbs in the prophecy regarding Jesus:

> Isa 42:2, "He will not **cry out** or **raise** *His voice*, Nor **make** His voice **heard** in the street"

> *) κράζω (60 NT uses), used first in Isaiah 42:2, means to cry out:
> #84 is κράζω, to cry out; #31 is ἀνακράζω, to cry out.

63) ἀνίημι, also in Isaiah 42:2, mean (from Scott): 1. to send up; 2. send back; 3. i. let go; ii. let loose; iii. set free; iv. allow; v. baring [her breast]; vi. let go free, leave untilled; vii. slacken, relax, let down, unstring; viii. Slacken, abate:
   a) In the context of Isa 42:2, it appears that the meaning follows 3.ii., to "let loose," which approximates the Hebrew concept of "raise up"
   b) The allusion here is that the Messiah, or Jesus, would *not* raise up [his voice], in parallel with "cry out"
   c) Jesus did, however, preach on the street, in the plain, from the shore, and from a mountain
   d) Therefore, the meaning must not be the level of the voice, but the strongly emotive connotation of "cry out"; implying that Jesus did not yell at people.
   e) Chrysosthom (Hom. xxiv) took this to imply that Jesus did not rebuke people, "But Jesus said nothing like this to him, nor did He rebuke him," as in the case of Nicodemus; but perhaps this is going too far, especially from other contexts where Jesus did rebuke (Matt 11:20; Mark 8:33; cf. 2 Tim 4:2).

64) ἀκούω, the third verb in the Isaiah 42:2 LXX verbal parallelism, in the passive voice means "cause to be heard" (also considered below under "Results of evangelizing")
   a) More problematic than the two verbs above, which can easily be explained that Jesus did not scream or yell as He preached; but what does it mean that He did not make His voice heard in the streets?
   b) Matthew Henry took this that the arrival of Jesus would not be pompous and boisterous, announced with loud trumpets, as is done among men at the arrival of a king, but rather quiet, gentle, and unassuming[680]
   c) Henry's explanation seems to coincide with the fulfillment of the prophecy, giving an explanation from synonymous parallelism with the first three verbs
   d) Therefore this verb cannot mean that:
      (1) Jesus did not do "street evangelism," which is proven false by the record in the Gospels
      (2) Jesus was merely a silent witness, or a witness by His lifestyle

Disavowals of Paul

65) ἁμαρτάνω (43 NT uses), to sin, do wrong, transgress:
   Acts 25:8, "while Paul said in his own defense, 'I have committed no offense either against the Law of the Jews or against the temple or against Caesar'" (cf. 1 Cor 10:32)
   Acts 25:8 ἀπολογουμένου αὐτοῦ ὅτι Οὔτε εἰς τὸν νόμον τῶν Ἰουδαίων, οὔτε εἰς τὸ ἱερόν, οὔτε εἰς Καίσαρά τι ἥμαρτον.

66) καπηλεύω (1 NT use), to be a vendor, trade in; to peddle, hawk, be a huckster:
   2 Cor 2:17, "For we are not like many, **peddling** the word of God, but as from sincerity, but as from God, we speak in Christ in the sight of God."

---

[680]"It shall not be proclaimed, *Lo, here, is Christ* or *Lo, he is there;* as when great princes ride in progress or make a public entry. He shall have no trumpet sounded before him, nor any noisy retinue to follow him. The opposition he meets with he shall not strive against, but patiently *endure the contradiction of sinners against himself.* His kingdom is spiritual, and therefore its weapons are not carnal, nor is its appearance pompous; it comes not with observation" (Matthew Henry, Isaiah 42; Bibleworks 9.0).

4) Three disavowals of Paul in 2 Cor 4:2:

2 Cor 4:2, "but we have renounced the (1) things hidden because of shame, not walking in (2) craftiness or (3) **adulterating** the word of God, but by the manifestation of truth commending ourselves to every man's conscience in the sight of God."

a3) κρυπτός (19 NT uses), hidden;
n12) ἡ πανουργία (4 NT uses), clever, crafty;
67) δολόω (1 NT use), falsify, adulterate.

5) Five Disavowals of Paul in 1 Thess 2:3-6:

1 Thess 2:3-6, "For our exhortation does not *come* from (1) error or (2) impurity or by way of (3) deceit; but just as we have been approved by God to be entrusted with the gospel, so we speak, not as pleasing men but God, who examines our hearts. For we never came with (4) flattering speech, as you know, nor with a pretext for (5) greed—God is witness—nor did we seek glory from men, either from you or from others, even though as apostles of Christ we might have asserted our authority."

n13) ἡ πλάνη (10 NT uses), error, deception; wandering [from the truth];
n14) ἡ ἀκαθαρσία (10 NT uses), uncleanness, impurity;
n15) ὁ δόλος (11 NT uses), deceit, treachery, fraud;
n16) ἡ κολακεία (1 NT use) flattery, exaggerated praise;
n17) ἡ πλεονεξία (10 NT uses) greed, covetousness.

6) Two Contrasts of Paul in 1 Thess 2:3-6:

1 Thess 2:3-6, "For our exhortation does not *come* from error or impurity or by way of deceit; but just as we have been approved by God to be entrusted with the gospel, so we speak, (1) not as pleasing men but God, who examines our hearts. For we never came with flattering speech, as you know, nor with a pretext for greed—God is witness—(2) nor did we seek glory from men, either from you or from others, even though as apostles of Christ we might have asserted our authority."

68) ἀρέσκω (17 NT uses), please, strive to please, accommodate; win favor; cf. Gal 1:10
69) ζητέω (118 NT uses), seeking + ἡ δόξα (168 hits), glory.

7) Two disavowals of Paul in Acts 24:12:

70) διαλέγομαι (13 total NT uses; 10 in Acts), to reason, dispute, argue, debate:
Acts 24:12, "And neither in the temple, nor in the synagogues, nor in the city *itself* did they find me **carrying on a discussion** [διαλεγόμενον] with anyone or causing a riot."
Act 24:12, καὶ οὔτε ἐν τῷ ἱερῷ εὗρόν με πρός τινα **διαλεγόμενον** ἢ ἐπισύστασιν ποιοῦντα ὄχλου, οὔτε ἐν ταῖς συναγωγαῖς, οὔτε κατὰ τὴν πόλιν.

1) Interestingly, this same verb is found to summarize Paul's customary ministry (as in Thessalonica), Acts 17:2-3, of his ministry in Ephesus, Acts 19:8-9, of his speech in Troas, Acts 20:9, and of his personal evangelism with Felix, Acts 24:25

2) In this context, therefore, his denial of διαλέγομαι (reasoning) in Jerusalem must mean either:

a) that it refers to the fact that Paul did not badger people with the Gospel in Jerusalem, thus in this context the word carries with it a negative connotation which is not implied in the other contexts; or

b) that Paul was not involved in aggressive personal evangelism while he was in Jerusalem, which corresponds to the lack of mention of Paul's evangelism in Acts 21:26-27

3) Remembering that in Jerusalem:

a) Paul did not follow his usual custom of evangelizing (Acts 17:2-3)

b) He rather seemed to change his custom to accommodate to the desire of those of James:
"For prior to the coming of certain men from James, he used to eat with the Gentiles; but when they came, he *began* to withdraw and hold himself aloof, fearing the party of the circumcision" (Gal 2:12)

c) Note also his rebuke of the First Century city of Jerusalem,
"Now this Hagar is Mount Sinai in Arabia, and corresponds to the present Jerusalem, for she is in slavery with her children" Gal 4:25

d) An analysis of Acts 21:20:
"And when they heard *it*, they glorified the Lord, and said unto him, Thou seest, brother, how many thousands of Jews there are which believe; and they are all zealous of the law" (KJV)

(1) Rejoiced in the right thing—the things which God had done among the Gentiles

(2) "The believers" apparently still kept the name "Jew" (the NAS translated the dative in the phrase ἐν τοῖς Ἰουδαίοις as "among the Jews")

(3) These Jewish believers were many ten thousands strong (seems like a strong percentage of Jerusalem

(4) These Jewish believers seemed zealous for the wrong thing, the Law, rather than for the Gospel, the Great Commission, Christ, or lost souls:

(5) Where were these ten thousands of Jewish believers when Paul was being beaten in the Temple (Acts 21:30-32)?

n20) ἡ ἐπισύστασις [BYM] (2 NT uses), uprising, disturbance, insurrection;
Or ἡ ἐπίστασις [NA27] (same 2 NT uses), disturbance, rioting; burden. Pressure + ποιέω (to do, make) + ὁ ὄχλος (crowd):

Acts 24:12, "And neither in the temple, nor in the synagogues, nor in the city *itself* did they find me carrying on a discussion with anyone or **causing a riot**."
Act 24:12, καὶ οὔτε ἐν τῷ ἱερῷ εὗρόν με πρός τινα διαλεγόμενον ἢ **ἐπισύστασιν ποιοῦντα ὄχλου**, οὔτε ἐν ταῖς συναγωγαῖς, οὔτε κατὰ τὴν πόλιν.

11) Two more disavowals of Paul in Acts 24:18:

Acts 24:18, "in which they found me *occupied* in the temple, having been purified, without *any* crowd or uproar. But *there were* certain Jews from Asia—"
Acts 24:18, ἐν οἷς εὗρόν με ἡγνισμένον ἐν τῷ ἱερῷ, οὐ μετὰ ὄχλου οὐδὲ μετὰ θορύβου, τινὲς ἀπὸ τῆς Ἀσίας Ἰουδαῖοι·

n21) ὁ ὄχλος (174 NT uses), crowd
(Paul was quietly minding his own business, i.e. not stirring up a crowd);

n22) ὁ θόρυβος (7 NT uses), uproar.

12) The OT prophet Amos was accused of the same thing:

71) ὀχλαγωγέω (1 use in OT LXX), meaning to draw a crowd, to stir up [a crowd]:
Amos 7:16, "And now hear the word of the LORD: you are saying, 'You shall not prophesy against Israel nor shall you **speak against** the house of Isaac.'"

These Same Methods Were Repeatedly Used by Opponents of the Gospel

13) Which methods, however, were repeatedly used of the Jews:

72) ἐπεγείρω: arousing, stirring up:

(a) ἐπεγείρω + ὁ διωγμός: arousing a persecution:
Acts 13:50, "But the Jews aroused the devout women of prominence and the leading men of the city, and **instigated a persecution** against Paul and Barnabas, and drove them out of their district."

(b) ἐπεγείρω + ἡ ψυχή: "stirring up … the souls," Acts 14:2:
Acts 14:2, "But the Jews who disbelieved **stirred up the minds** of the Gentiles, and embittered them against the brethren."

73) κακόω: mistreat, harm; corrupt [the minds]:

(a) κακόω: Acts 12:1, "Now about that time Herod the king laid hands on some who belonged to the church, in order **to mistreat** them."

(b) κακόω + ἡ ψυχη: corrupt the minds: Acts 14:2, "But the Jews who disbelieved stirred up **the minds** of the Gentiles, and **embittere**d them against the brethren."

74) πείθω: persuade, follow, obey:
Acts 5:36, "and all who **followed** him were dispersed and came to nothing"
Acts 5:37, "and all those who **followed** him were scattered"
Acts 14:19, "**having won over** the multitudes"

> Acts 19:26, "this Paul **has persuaded** and turned away many people, saying that they are not gods which are made with hands."
>
> Acts 26:28, "And Agrippa *replied* to Paul, 'In a short time you **will persuade** me to become a Christian'"
>
> Acts 27:11, "But the centurion **was** more **persuaded** by the pilot and the captain of the ship, than by what was being said by Paul."

75) ὀχλοποιέω (hapax): mob forming; Acts 17:5, "formed a mob" (cf. Acts 24:12):
From ὁ ὄχλος (crowd) + ποιέω (to do, make).

76) θορυβέω: make a commotion; Acts 17:5, "set all the city in an uproar"

n*) (see n20) ὁ θόρυβος: an uproar, tumult; Acts 20:1; 21:34.

Conclusion:

(a) The Jews accused Paul of using methods that they themselves used!

(b) Whereas, Paul, for his part, called on God's people to:
(1) Seek "to lead a quiet and peaceable" life, 1 Tim 2:2
(2) Remain subject to human [political] authority, Rom 13:1-7; cf. 1 Pet 2:13-17.

Other Verbal Forms

77) φείδομαι/ψεύσομαι (to falsify); from Heb. *Kachad*, for conceal [the holy words] Job 6:10; 27:11:
Job 6:10 (KJV), "Then should I yet have comfort; yea, I would harden myself in sorrow: let him not spare; for **I have not concealed** the words of the Holy One"
Job 6:10 (NAS), "But it is still my consolation, And I rejoice in unsparing pain, That **I have not denied** the words of the Holy One"
Job 27:11, "I will instruct you in the power of God; What is with the Almighty **I will not conceal**."

78) κρύπτω (16 NT uses), meaning to hide:
John 19:38, And after these things Joseph of Arimathea, being a disciple of Jesus, but a **secret** *one*, for fear of the Jews, asked Pilate that he might take away the body of Jesus; and Pilate granted permission. He came therefore, and took away His body."

79) ἀναφωνέω (1 NT uses), meaning to cry aloud:
Luke 1:42, "And she **cried out** with a loud voice, and said, "Blessed among women *are* you, and blessed *is* the fruit of your womb!"

Addendum 4: Verbs used both *FOR AND NOT FOR* **evangelizing:**

Words Used For and Not For Evangelizing*
[*this is a preliminary study to consider the issues involved here]

80) λέγω: to say [denying that he was with Jesus or one of His disciples], Luke 22:60; John 18:17, 25

81) φημί [NA27]: to say, "I am not [a follower of Christ]," Luke 22:58 [BYZ has the verb λέγω here]

82) ἐρωτάω (57 NT uses): pray, plead, ask, beg (often of prayer) [verb perhaps related to oratory]:
   Acts 16:39, "and they came and appealed to them, and when they had brought them out, they **kept begging** them to leave the city."
   Acts 18:20, "When they **asked** him to stay for a longer time"

83) βοάω: to "cry out," is used of antagonists of the Gospel in the Book of Acts:

   In Acts it is used:
   (1) To describe the cries of the demon-possessed, Acts 8:7
   (2) To describe the response of antagonists to the Gospel, Acts 17:6, 25:24

   However, elsewhere it is used as follows:
   (1) To describe the preaching of John the Baptist, Isa 40:3; Matt 3:3; Mark 1:3; Luke 3:4; John 1:23;
   (2) To describe the pleading prayers of God's people, Luke 18:7

   Cognate form: ἐπιβοάω (Byz Text), to cry out loudly, Acts 25:24.

84) κράζω: (3611): cry out, Acts 7:57:
   Mark 9:24, "Immediately the boy's father **cried out** and said, 'I do believe; help my unbelief.'"
   Luke 19:40, "But Jesus answered, 'I tell you, if these become silent, the stones will **cry out**!'"

   Some OT precedents:
   Prov 1:20-21, "Wisdom **shouts** in the street, She lifts her voice in the square; At the head of the noisy *streets* she **cries out**; At the entrance of the gates in the city, she utters her sayings"
   The Hebrew verb behind "shouts" in v 20 is *ranan*, meaning "to cry aloud" in the qal stem
   The Hebrew verb behind "cries out" in v 21 is *qara'*, having one meaning of "to call, proclaim" in the qal stem; this verb is translated κηρύσσω (to preach) in the Greek
   Isa 42:2, "He will not **cry out** or raise *His voice*, Nor make His voice heard in the street"

85) σκορπίζω (figurative), to scatter, disperse [broadcast?]:

   God scatters (his gifts):
   2 Cor 9:9, "as it is written, 'He scattered abroad, he gave to the poor, His righteousness abides forever.'"

   Those not gathering are scattering:
   Matt 12:30, "He who is not with Me is against Me; and he who does not gather with Me scatters."

86) ἀρέσκω (17 NT uses): strive to please, accommodate:

   Pleasing men:
   1 Cor 10:33, "just as I also please all men in all things, not seeking my own profit, but the *profit* of the many, that they may be saved"

   Not pleasing men, but God:
   1 Thess 2:4, "but just as we have been approved by God to be entrusted with the gospel, so we speak, not as pleasing men but God, who examines our hearts"

   Not pleasing men:
   Gal 1:10, "Am I striving to please men?"
   Gal 1:10, "If I were still trying to please men, I would not be a bond-servant of Christ"

87) παραγγέλλω (30 NT uses); used 11 times in Acts, once to describe Jesus' commissioning of His disciples (Acts 10:42), in an evangelistic context it is only used of God's declaring to men; rather than command, we beseech [δέομαι] men on behalf of Christ (2 Cor 5:20, 6:1):
   Acts 17:30, "Therefore having overlooked the times of ignorance, God is now declaring to men that all everywhere should repent" (cf. 1 Tim 4:11).

88) Many more verbs could be added to this list, such as ζωγρέω used:in Luke 5:10 and 2 Tim 2:26

Used prophetically of Jesus to Peter and the disciples:

Luke 5:10, "and so also James and John, sons of Zebedee, who were partners with Simon. And Jesus said to Simon, "Do not fear, from now on **you will be catching men**."

Used of the Devil's methodology:

2 Tim 2:24-26, "And the Lord's bond-servant must not be quarrelsome, but be kind to all, able to teach, patient when wronged, with gentleness correcting those who are in opposition, if perhaps God may grant them repentance leading to the knowledge of the truth, and they may come to their senses *and escape* from the snare of the devil, **having been held captive** by him to do his will."

3. MOVEMENT AND/OR LOCATION of Evangelism Ministry (which impacts the conception, description, and definition of methodology):
[i.e. not only within the church building; also assumes intentionality and precise missionary activity]

Introduction: Consider the travel language in the OT:

1) Walking to and fro – e.g. Psa 126:6, using a Hebrew dual of the verb *yalak*
(הָלוֹךְ יֵלֵךְ ; *halok yelek*):
Psa 126:6 (NKJ), "He who continually goes forth weeping, Bearing seed for sowing, Shall doubtless come again with rejoicing, Bringing his sheaves *with him*"

2) Emphasizing the feet – e.g. Isa 52:7:
Isa 52:7, "How lovely on the mountains Are the feet of him who brings good news, Who announces peace And brings good news of happiness, Who announces salvation, *And* says to Zion, "Your God reigns!""

3) Going out; going forth; being led out – e.g. Isa 55:12:
Isa 55:12, "For you will go out with joy, And be led forth with peace; The mountains and the hills will break forth into shouts of joy before you, And all the trees of the field will clap *their* hands."

a. Movement verbs for the messenger, rather than the message (sometimes used by itself to describe evangelism ministry):

1) εὑρίσκω (177 NT uses), find, discover, come upon:
Matt 22:9-10, "'Go therefore to the main highways, and as many as you **find** *there*, invite to the wedding feast.' And those slaves went out into the streets, and gathered together all they **found**, both evil and good; and the wedding hall was filled with dinner guests."
Luke 15:4-7, "What man among you, if he has a hundred sheep and has lost one of them, does not leave the ninety-nine in the open pasture, and go after the one which is lost, until he **finds** it? And when he has **found** it, he lays it on his shoulders, rejoicing. And when he comes home, he calls together his friends and his neighbors, saying to them, 'Rejoice with me, for I **have found** my sheep which was lost!' I tell you that in the same way, there will be *more* joy in heaven over one sinner who repents, than over ninety-nine righteous persons who need no repentance."
Luke 15:8-10, "Or what woman, if she has ten silver coins and loses one coin, does not light a lamp and sweep the house and search carefully until she **finds** it? And when she has **found** it, she calls together her friends and neighbors, saying, 'Rejoice with me, for I have **found** the coin which I had lost!' In the same way, I tell you, there is joy in the presence of the angels of God over one sinner who repents."
Luke 15:22-24, "But the father said to his slaves, 'Quickly bring out the best robe and put it on him, and put a ring on his hand and sandals on his feet; and bring the fattened calf, kill it, and let us eat and be merry; for this son of mine was dead, and has come to life again; he was lost, and has been **found**.' And they began to be merry" (cf. Luke 15:32)
John 1:41, "He **found** first his own brother Simon, and said to him, 'We have **found** the Messiah (which translated means Christ).'"
John 1:43, "The next day He purposed to go forth into Galilee, and He **found** Philip. And Jesus said to him, 'Follow Me.'"
John 1:45, "Philip **found** Nathanael and said to him, 'We have **found** Him of whom Moses in the Law and *also* the Prophets wrote, Jesus of Nazareth, the son of Joseph.'"
John 5:12, "Afterward Jesus **found** him in the temple, and said to him, 'Behold, you have become well; do not sin anymore, so that nothing worse may befall you.'"
John 9:35, "Jesus heard that they had put him out; and **finding** him, He said, 'Do you believe in the Son of Man?'"

2) ἐγγίζω (43 NT uses), come near, approach; draw near, come close:
Luke 10:11, "Even the dust of your city which clings to our feet, we wipe off *in protest* against you; yet be sure of this, that the kingdom of God **has come near**."

b. Movement verbs for travel:

1) ἐξέρχομαι (222 NT uses), go out, come out; go forth:
Luke 9:6, "And **departing**, they *began* going about among the villages, preaching the gospel, and healing everywhere"
1 John 4:1, "Beloved, do not believe every spirit, but test the spirits to see whether they are from God; because many false prophets **have gone out** into the world."

2) περιῆλθον or περιέρχομαι (4 NT uses; 13 OT LXX uses)†, go about; go from place to place (hence, itinerate); wander about:

    13 OT LXX uses: 8 in Joshua; 2 in Job; 1 in 2 Sam, Jer, Ezek:
        Jos 6:7, 11, 15: of the people of Israel marching around Jericho
        Jos 15:10; 16:6, 18:14; 19:13, 14: used to describe the turning of the perimeter of assigned
            territories
        2 Sam 14:20 (LXE), "In order that this form of speech **might come about**"
        Job 1:7, of Satan: "From **roaming about** on the earth and walking around on it"
        Jer 31:22 (LXE), "men shall **go about** in safety"
        Ezek 3:15 (LXE), "and [Ezekiel] **went round** *to* them that dwelt by the river of Chobar"

    Acts 19:13, "But also some of the Jewish exorcists, who **went from place to place** [τῶν περιερχομένων], attempted to name over those who had the evil spirits the name of the Lord Jesus, saying, 'I adjure you by Jesus whom Paul preaches'"
    Acts 28:13 (ASV), "And from thence we **made a circuit**, and arrived at Rhegium: and after one day a south wind sprang up, and on the second day we came to Puteoli"
    1 Tim 5:13, "And at the same time they also learn *to be* idle, as they **go around** from house to house [περιερχόμεναι τὰς οἰκίας]; and not merely idle, but also gossips and busybodies, talking about things not proper *to mention*"
    Heb 11:37, "They were stoned, they were sawn in two, they were tempted, they were put to death with the sword; they **went about** in sheepskins [περιῆλθον ἐν μηλωταῖς], in goatskins, being destitute, afflicted, ill-treated"

Sample Translations of περιέρχομαι as Applied to People*

		Aimless							Purposeful
Passage	Person	KJV; cf. Tyndale, Geneva, Bishops	Young's	ESV; cf. ASV	Darby; cf. DRA⁑	NIV	NAS; cf. BBE	RSV; cf. NKJ, NJB⁑, CSB, ESV	NLT
		Vagabond	Wandering	Strolling	Who went about	Went around	Who went from place to place	Itinerant	was traveling from town to town
Acts 19:13	Jewish exorcists	"Then certain of the vagabond Jews, exorcists"	"And certain of the wandering exorcist Jews"	"But certain also of the strolling Jews, exorcists"	"And certain of the Jewish exorcists also, who went about"	"Some Jews who went around driving out evil spirits"	"But also some of the Jewish exorcists, who went from place to place"	"Then some of the itinerant Jewish exorcists"	"A group of Jews was traveling from town to town casting out evil spirits"
1 Tim 5:13	Idle widows	"Wandering about from house to house"	"going about the houses"	"going about from house to house"	"to go about from house to house"	"going about from house to house"	"they go around from house to house"	" gadding about from house to house"	"will spend their time gossiping from house to house"
Heb 11:37	Men of faith	"they wandered about in sheepskins"	"they went about in sheepskins"	"They went about in skins of sheep"	"they went about in sheepskins"	"They went about in sheepskins"	"they went about in sheepskins"	"they went about in skins of sheep"	"Some went about wearing skins of sheep"

*Order based on the translation in Acts 19:13

3) περιάγω (6 NT uses; 5 OT LXX uses)† – to lead around, go about:
    Introduction: 4 of the 5 OT LXX uses speak of God's leading: Amos 2:10, God's leading the people out of Egypt; Ezek 37:2, God leading Ezekiel around the dry bones; Ezek 46:21; 47:2, of God leading Ezekiel around the Temple; the 5th use is figurative in Isa 28:27
    Matt 4:23, "And *Jesus* **was going about** in all Galilee, teaching in their synagogues, and proclaiming the gospel of the kingdom, and healing every kind of disease and every kind of sickness among the people"

Matt 9:35, "And Jesus **was going about** all the cities and the villages, teaching in their synagogues, and proclaiming the gospel of the kingdom, and healing every kind of disease and every kind of sickness"

Matt 23:15, "Woe to you, scribes and Pharisees, hypocrites, because you **travel about** on sea and land to make one proselyte; and when he becomes one, you make him twice as much a son of hell as yourselves"

Mark 6:6, "And He wondered at their unbelief. And He was **going around** the villages teaching"

Acts 13:11, "'And now, behold, the hand of the Lord is upon you, and you will be blind and not see the sun for a time.' And immediately a mist and a darkness fell upon him, and he **went about** seeking those who would lead him by the hand"

1 Cor 9:5, "Do we not have a right to **take along** a believing wife, even as the rest of the apostles, and the brothers of the Lord, and Cephas?"

Some Translations of περιάγω

Passage	Tyndale	KJV	Etheridge (from Syriac)	Young's	NLT	MacDonald's Idiomatic	ESV
Matt 4:23	Went about	Went about	Perambulated	Was going about	Traveled throughout	Circulated throughout	Went throughout
Matt 9:35	Went about	Went about	Itinerated in	Was going up and down	Traveled through	Made a circuit to	Went throughout
Matt 23:15	Compasse	Compass	Go over	Go round	Cross	Travel over	Travel across
Mark 6:6	Went about	Went round	Itinerated	Goiung round … in a circle	Went from	Made the rounds	Went about

4) μεταβαίνω (12 NT uses) – to depart:

Matt 11:1, "And it came about that when Jesus had finished giving instructions to His twelve disciples, He **departed** from there to teach and preach in their cities"

Luke 10:7, "And stay in that house, eating and drinking what they give you; for the laborer is worthy of his wages. **Do** not **keep moving** from house to house"

John 7:3 His brothers therefore said to Him, '**Depart** from here, and go into Judea, that Your disciples also may behold Your works which You are doing'"

Acts 18:7, "And he **departed** from there and went to the house of a certain man named Titius Justus, a worshiper of God, whose house was next to the synagogue"

c. Movement verbs coupled with verbs for proclamation:

1) Entering a location to teach or preach:

εἰσῆλθον (from εἰσέρχομαι, go in) + ἐδίδασκον(from διδάσκω, teach), Acts 5:21

εἰσῆλθεν (from εἰσέρχομαι, go in) + four verbs explaining proclamation, Acts 17:2-3

εἰσελθὼν (from εἰσέρχομαι, go in) + three verbs explaining proclamation, Acts 19:8

2) Going forth from a location to teach or preach:

ἀποστέλλω (sent out) πορεύομαι (go) + κηρύσσω (preach), λέγω (say), Matt 10:5, 7

ἐξέρχομαι (go out) + κηρύσσω (preach), μετανοέω (repent), ἐκβάλλω (casting out), and θεραπεύω (healing), Mark 6:12-13

ἐξέρχομαι (go out), διέρχομαι (pass through) + εὐαγγελίζω (evangelize), θεραπεύω (heal), Luke 9:6

πορεύομαι (go) + ἀπαγγέλλω (report), Matt 11:4; Luke 7:22

πορεύομαι (go) + μαθητεύω (win disciples), βαπτίζω (baptize), and διδάσκω (teach) Matt 28:19-20

πορεύομαι (go) + κηρύσσω (preach), Mark 16:15

μεταβαίνω (depart) + διδάσκω (teach), κηρύσσω (preach), Matt 11:1

3) Standing up in a location to teach or preach:

Intro: This combination is very common, and may even be overlooked; cf. Isa 40:9; 52:7[681]

ἵστημι (standing up [implying take a stand, cf. Isa 40:9; Eph 6:11, 13]) + ἐπῆρεν τὴν φωνὴν αὐτοῦ (raised his voice) and ἀποφθέγγομαι (declared), Acts 2:14

ἵστημι (stood) + ἀπαγγέλλω, Acts 5:25

ἵστημι (stood up) + φημί (said) Acts 17:22

ἀναστὰς (stood up) + κατασείσας τῇ χειρὶ (motioned with his hand) + εἶπεν (said), Acts 13:16 (cf. Acts 21:40)

---

[681]Johnston, *Charts for a Theology of Evangelism*, Chart 4, "Verbs for Great Commission Methodology," 16-17.

ἀνέστησαν (rose up) + συζητοῦντες (argued), Acts 6:9 (of antagonists)

d. Calling persons together:

a) συγκαλέω (9 OT LXX uses; 8 NT uses, 7 in Luke-Acts) – meaning to call together, used in contexts in preparation to evangelize:

Luke 9:1-2, "And He **called** the twelve **together**, and gave them power and authority over all the demons, and to heal diseases. And He sent them out to proclaim the kingdom of God, and to perform healing."

Acts 10:24, "And on the following day he entered Caesarea. Now Cornelius was waiting for them, and had **called together** his relatives and close friends."

Acts 28:17, "And it happened that after three days he **called together** those who were the leading men of the Jews, and when they had come together, he *began* saying to them, "Brethren, though I had done nothing against our people, or the customs of our fathers, yet I was delivered prisoner from Jerusalem into the hands of the Romans.""

e. Location: general terms for locations of evangelizing activity:

1) δημόσιος – publicly, Acts 20:20

2) House to house:
   a) κατ' οἴκους – house to house, Acts 5:42; 20:20
   b) εἰσερχόμενοι δὲ εἰς τὴν οἰκίαν – enter the house, Matt 10:12
   c) ἐξερχόμενοι ἔξω τῆς οἰκίας – depart from that house, Matt 10:14
   d) μὴ μεταβαίνετε ἐξ οἰκίας εἰς οἰκίαν – Do not keep moving from house to house, Luke 10:7
      (1) Seems to imply that prior to being received in to a home, they were going house to house
      (2) Also probably implies the need to follow-up on an open heart (i.e. a person unto whom God has granted peace and openness to listen)
   e) Notice that Jesus reveals Himself as One who knocks on doors, Rev 3:20
   f) Consider the ministry of Jesus that was done from individual receptive houses, and that reached the larger community (preaching, healing of the paralytic, etc.)
   g) Notice also false teachers who creep into homes (οἱ ἐνδύνοντες εἰς τὰς οἰκίας), 2 Tim 3:6-7

3) Cities (there is more about cities in the Gospels and the Acts than is recorded here):
   a) ἢ τῆς πόλεως ἐκείνης – or that city, Matt 10:14
   b) καὶ διερχόμενος εὐηγγελίζετο τὰς πόλεις πάσας – and passing through he was evangelizing all the cities, Acts 8:40
   c) Note the woes on particular cities, Luke 10:13-15

4) City and village:
   a) Καὶ περιῆγεν ὁ Ἰησοῦς τὰς πόλεις πάσας καὶ τὰς κώμας – And Jesus went about every city and village, Matt 9:35
   b) Εἰς ἣν δ' ἂν πόλιν ἢ κώμην εἰσέλθητε (BYZ) – And whatever city or village you enter, Matt 10:11
   c) καὶ αὐτὸς διώδευεν κατὰ πόλιν καὶ κώμην – and he [himself] went throughout every city and village, Luke 8:1
   d) Καὶ διεπορεύετο κατὰ πόλεις καὶ κώμας – And he was passing through from one village and city to another, Luke 13:22

5) City and place:
   a) καὶ ἀπέστειλεν αὐτοὺς ἀνὰ δύο πρὸ προσώπου αὐτοῦ εἰς πᾶσαν πόλιν καὶ τόπον οὗ ἔμελλεν αὐτὸς ἔρχεσθαι – and sent them two and two ahead of Him to every city and place where He Himself was going to come, Luke 10:2

6) Village, city, or countryside:
   a) Καὶ ὅπου ἂν εἰσεπορεύετο εἰς κώμας ἢ πόλεις ἢ ἀγρούς – and whenever he entered villages, or cities, or the countryside, Mark 6:56

f. Location: particular interior locations:
1) τῇ στοᾷ τῇ καλουμένῃ Σολομῶντος – Portico of Solomon, Acts 3:11; τῇ στοᾷ Σολομῶντος - Solomon's portico, Acts 5:12
2) Sanhedrin [gathered together in Jerusalem], Acts 4:5, 7; τῷ συνεδρίῳ – the Council, Acts 5:27; 6:12, 15
3) τῷ ἱερῷ - the Temple, Acts 5:42
4) οἰκίᾳ Ἰούδα - house of Judas, Acts 9:11
5) ταῖς συναγωγαῖς – the synagogues [of Damascus], Acts 9:20; ταῖς συναγωγαῖς τῶν Ἰουδαίων – synagogues of the Jews, Acts 13:5;

τὴν συναγωγὴν – the synagogue, Acts 13:14 (v 43);
τὴν συναγωγὴν τῶν Ἰουδαίων – synagogue of the Jews, Acts 14:1;
ἡ συναγωγὴ τῶν Ἰουδαίων – synagogue of the Jews, Acts 17:1

6) Home of Cornelius, Acts 10:25
7) Before Roman Commander, Acts 22:30
8) In private gatherings with Felix and Drussila, Acts 24:24-26
9) In the Tribunal of Festus, Acts 25:6
10) Auditorium before King Agrippa and Festus, Acts 25:23
11) Home of Publius on Malta, Acts 28:7
12) Paul's rented home in Rome, Acts 28:30
13) τὸ πραιτώριον – the judgment hall, Phil 1:13 (English Geneva); e.g. Acts 25:23-26:32

Translations of τὸ πραιτώριον in Philippians 1:13

Byzantine Textform	English Geneva	King James	New American Standard	New King James	New International Version
ἐν ὅλῳ τῷ πραιτωρίῳ καὶ τοῖς λοιποῖς πάσιν,	throughout all the iudgement hall, and in all other *places*,	in all the palace, and in all other *places*;	throughout the whole praetorian guard and to everyone else,	to the whole palace guard, and to all the rest,	throughout the whole palace guard and to everyone else

g. Location: particular exterior locations:
  Notice the interesting OT precedent in terms of location:
    a) Wisdom is described as a street preacher in Prov 1:20-21
    b) Jeremiah was specifically told "to stand" and speak:
       (1) At the gate of the Temple, Jer 7:2
       (2) At the gate of the city, Jer 17:19
       (3) In the court of the Lord's house, Jer 26:2
  1) τὴν θύραν τοῦ ἱεροῦ τὴν λεγομένην Ὡραίαν - Gate of the Temple called beautiful, Acts 3:2
  2) Οἱ μὲν οὖν διασπαρέντες διῆλθον - those who had been scattered went about, Acts 8:4
  3) πόλιν τῆς Σαμαρείας - city of Samaria, Acts 8:5
  4) πολλάς τε κώμας τῶν Σαμαριτῶν - many villages of the Samaritans, Acts 8:25
  5) τὴν ὁδὸν τὴν καταβαίνουσαν ἀπὸ Ἰερουσαλὴμ εἰς Γάζαν αὕτη ἐστὶν ἔρημος - the road that descends from Jerusalem to Gaza (which is called the desert *road*), Acts 8:26
  6) τὰς πόλεις πάσας ἕως τοῦ ἐλθεῖν αὐτὸν εἰς Καισάρειαν - all the cities until he came to Caesarea, Acts 8:40
  7) Φοινίκης καὶ Κύπρου καὶ Ἀντιοχείας - Phoenicia, Cyprus, and Antioch, Acts 11:19
  8) ἃς πόλεις τῆς Λυκαονίας Λύστραν καὶ Δέρβην καὶ τὴν περίχωρον – the cities of Lycaonia, Lystra and Derbe, and the surrounding region, Acts 4:6
  9) Unclear (interior or exterior, street or Temple), Acts 2:6; 6:8; 14:8-9

h. Location: interior locations for the gathering of the disciples/Christians/leaders:
  1) Home of Lydia, Acts 16:40
  2) Home of Jason, Acts 17:5-7
  3) School of Tyrannus, Acts 19:9
  4) Upper room in Troas, Acts 20:8
  5) Home of Philip the Evangelist, Acts 21:8-9
  6) Home of James, Acts 21:18

i. Location does influence methodology, a fact that was not lost to L.R. Scarborough:

  "Christ's churches were not meant to be indoor institutions only, but outdoor agencies as well. His kingdom was inaugurated in its earthly expression on the hills of Judea and the banks of the Jordan, John the Baptist, the first gospel evangelist, never preached in a church house. Most of Christ's preaching and teaching was done out in the open. Pentecost was a big street meeting. Paul's evangelism was carried on, in the main, on the streets and in the open places. The idea in most churches today seems to be 'if you will come to our meeting house, we will offer you the gospel.' In New Testament times, Christians worked on the theory of carrying the gospel to the people."[682]

---

[682]L. R. Scarborough, *With Christ After the Lost* (Nashville: Tennessee Sunday School Board, 1919; New York: George H. Doran, 1919; Nashville: Broadman, 1919, 1952, 1953; Fort Worth: Southwestern Library of Centennial Classics, 2008), 141.

4. SPIRITUAL DYNAMIC of the Word of God:

a. The Word of God as a Living Agent at Work:

1) "And the Word of God kept on spreading," Acts 6:7
   Message: "The word of God," Καὶ ὁ λόγος τοῦ θεοῦ
       Just like the parable of the sower, cf. Luke 8:11, "Now the parable is this: The seed is the word of God"
   ηὔξανεν καὶ ἐπληθύνετο (same construction as 12:24)
       "Kept on spreading," ηὔξανεν, from αὐξάνω, to grow, spread, increase, become important
       [the number of disciples] multiplied (πληθύνω) in Jerusalem greatly (σφόδρα)
       "multiplied," καὶ ἐπληθύνετο, from πληθύνω, intrans. grow, increase
       Notice that this same Greek verb was used related to the blessing of Abraham:
           Gen 22:17, ἦ μὴν εὐλογῶν εὐλογήσω σε καὶ πληθύνων πληθυνῶ τὸ σπέρμα σου ("assuredly blessing I will bless you and multiplying I will multiply your seed")
           Heb 6:14, ἦ μὴν εὐλογῶν εὐλογήσω σε καὶ πληθύνων πληθυνῶ σε ("assuredly blessing I will bless you and multiplying I will multiply you")
       So, in a way, the growth of the church in Acts was a direct fulfillment of God's promise to Abraham, as is the growth of the true church of God today, through souls being saved!
       Notice how Luke is drawing a parallel with the growth of the Hebrew nation in Egypt, as the same two verbs are also used in Acts 7:17 of their numerical growth

2) "But the word of the Lord continued to grow and to be multiplied," Acts 12:24
   Message:
       [Byzantine] "The word of God," Ὁ δὲ λόγος τοῦ θεοῦ
       [Wescott-Hort] "The word of the Lord," Ὁ δὲ λόγος τοῦ κυρίου
   ηὔξανεν καὶ ἐπληθύνετο
       "Continued to grow," ηὔξανεν, from αὐξάνω (see above)
       "And to be multiplied," καὶ ἐπληθύνετο, from πληθύνω, intrans. grow, increase

3) "And the word of the Lord was being spread through the whole region," Acts 13:49
   διεφέρετο δὲ ὁ λόγος τοῦ κυρίου δι' ὅλης τῆς χώρας
   Spread," διεφέρετο, from διαφέρω, meaning carry through, spread

4) "So the word of the Lord was growing mightily and prevailing," Acts 19:20
   Οὕτως κατὰ κράτος τοῦ Κυρίου ὁ λόγος ηὔξανεν καὶ ἴσχυεν
   ηὔξανεν, "growing mightily," from αὐξάνω (see above) same word used in 6:7 for "kept on spreading," and in 12:24 for "continued to grow"
   Here it is paralleled with prevailing, ἴσχυεν, from ἰσχύω, to able, can, have resources, win over, defeat, be strong, grow strong

5) "The gospel, which has come to you, just as in all the world it is constantly bearing fruit and increasing," Col 1:5-6
   ἐστὶν καρποφορούμενον, καὶ αὐξανόμενον
   καρποφορούμενον, from καρποφορέω, meaning to bear fruit
   αὐξανόμενον, from αὐξάνω (see above)

6) "For the word of the Lord has sounded forth from you, not only in Macedonia and Achaia, but also in every place your faith toward God has gone forth," 1 Thess 1:8
   Ἀφ' ὑμῶν γὰρ ἐξήχηται ὁ λόγος τοῦ κυρίου
   ἐξήχηται from ἐξηχέομαι, meaning to sound forth

7) "Pray for us that the word of the Lord may spread rapidly and be glorified," 2 Thess 3:1
   ἵνα ὁ λόγος τοῦ κυρίου τρέχῃ καὶ δοξάζηται
   "Spread rapidly," τρέχῃ, from τρέχω, to run, exert oneself, make an effort
   "be glorified," δοξάζηται, from δοξάζω, to praise, honor, glorify, exalt

8) This use of the Word of God as a supernatural active agent when proclaimed fits with other verses also:
   a. The kingdom of God "coming near" even to cities that reject the Gospel proclamation, Luk 10:11;
   b. The wind blowing here or there being related to one being born again, John 3:8;
   c. Verses on the power and activity of the Word of God, e.g. Heb 4:12; 1 Thess 2:13.

9) Likewise, note the superlative use of the word when Paul described the hyper-spreading of the faith of the Thessalonians:

> 2 Thess 1:3, "We are bound to thank God always for you, brethren, as it is fitting, because your faith **grows exceedingly** [ὑπεραυξάνω], and the love of every one of you all abounds toward each other"

In this case, the word ὑπεραυξάνω is used only once in the NT; its parallel use with growth in love for the brethren gives the impression that it relates more to evangelizing the lost than it does to spiritual growth, cf. 1 Thess 1:3, 8

b. Evangelism as the "THE MINISTRY OF THE WORD":

1) "But we will devote ourselves to prayer, and to **the ministry** of the word," Acts 6:4

2) The next time we find Peter and John ministering the word as follows:
   a. Confirming the ministry of Philip, Acts 8:14-15
   b. Ministering through edification in the word and traveling evangelism: "And so, when they had solemnly testified and spoken the word of the Lord, they started back to Jerusalem, and were preaching the gospel to [evangelizing] many villages of the Samaritans," Acts 8:25

3) In fact, ministering the Word was a reality for all Christ's followers:
   a. "And when they had prayed, the place where they had gathered together was shaken, and they were all filled with the Holy Spirit, and *began* to speak the word of God with boldness," Acts 4:31
   b. "Therefore, those who had been scattered went about preaching the word," Acts 8:4
   c. "So then those who were scattered because of the persecution that arose in connection with Stephen made their way to Phoenicia and Cyprus and Antioch, speaking the word to no one except to Jews alone," Acts 11:19

4) Ministering the Word was also Paul's calling and practice:
   a. "But I do not consider my life of any account as dear to myself, in order that I may finish my course, and **the ministry** which I received from the Lord Jesus, to testify solemnly of the gospel of the grace of God," Acts 20:24
   b. "And when they reached Salamis, they *began* to proclaim the word of God in the synagogues of the Jews; and they also had John as their helper," Acts 13:5
   c. "And the next Sabbath nearly the whole city assembled to hear the word of God. But when the Jews saw the crowds, they were filled with jealousy, and *began* contradicting the things spoken by Paul, and were blaspheming. And Paul and Barnabas spoke out boldly and said, "It was necessary that the word of God should be spoken to you first; since you repudiate it, and judge yourselves unworthy of eternal life, behold, we are turning to the Gentiles," Acts 13:44-46
   d. Et cetera…

c. Evangelism as "THE WORK OF GOD":

Introduction:

Moses asked God, "Let Your work appear to Your servants" (Psa 90:16). The NIV translates it this way: "May your deeds be shown to your servants." This request for God to make His work evident was repeated in the New Testament.

Some followers asked Jesus, "What shall we do, so that we may work the works of God?" (John 6:28). Jesus answered with an invitation to believe: "Jesus answered and said to them, 'This is the work of God, that you believe in Him whom He has sent'" (John 6:29)

How different was Jesus' call to faith from the Chuch of Rome's call to arms as the "work of God" in the Middle Ages (i.e. a misplaced ecclesiological and territorial emphasis):

> "Let nobles and the powerful in the army, and all who abound in riches, be led by the holy words of prelates so that, with their eyes fixed on the crucified one for whom they have taken up the badge of the cross, they may refrain from useless and unnecessary expenditure, especially in feasting and banquets, and let they give a share of their wealth to the support of those persons through whom **the work of God** may prosper; and on this account, according to the dispensation of the prelates themselves, they may be granted remission of their sins."[683]

---

[683]The full context is as follows, under Section 5 of the 13th Ecumenical Council, the First Council of Lyons (France), "Deeply sorrowful at the grievous dangers of the holy Land, but especially at those which have recently happened to the faithful settled there, we seek with all our heart to free it from the hands of the wicked. Thus with the

This misapplication of the "work of God" led to a skewed view of what was the "preaching the Cross":

> "No papal proclamation [concerning the crusades] after the first was itself enough to move Europe. General letters had to be followed up by personal visits and constant publicity, a process known as the **preaching of the Cross**. It was obviously important that the popes should have control over this and therefore over recruitment."[684]

This misplaced view of the work of God also led Pope Alexander III in 1487 to call the work of inquisition and annihilation of the Waldenses, "the Cause of God and the Faith."[685]

Yes, a variety of views as to the "work of God" have presented themselves in the history of the church.[686] However, the work of God is spiritual (John 18:36). The work of God involves faith. In fact, the work of God is evangelism!

---

approval of the sacred council, in order that the crusaders may prepare themselves, we lay it down that at an opportune time, to be made known to all the faithful by preachers and our special envoys, all who are ready to cross the sea should gather at suitable places for this purpose, so that they may proceed from there with the blessing of God and the apostolic see to the assistance of the holy Land. Priests and other clerics who will be in the christian army, both those under authority and prelates, shall diligently devote themselves to prayer and exhortation, teaching the crusaders by word and example to have the fear and love of God always before their eyes, so that they say or do nothing that might offend the majesty of the eternal king. If they ever fall into sin, let them quickly rise up again through true penitence. Let them he humble in heart and in body, keeping to moderation both in food and in dress, avoiding altogether dissensions and rivalries, and putting aside entirely any bitterness or envy, so that thus armed with spiritual and material weapons they may the more fearlessly fight against the enemies of the faith, relying not on their own power but rather trusting in the strength of God. Let nobles and the powerful in the army, and all who abound in riches, be led by the holy words of prelates so that, with their eyes fixed on the crucified one for whom they have taken up the badge of the cross, they may refrain from useless and unnecessary expenditure, especially in feasting and banquets, and let they give a share of their wealth to the support of those persons through whom the **work of God** may prosper; and on this account, according to the dispensation of the prelates themselves, they may be granted remission of their sins" (First Council of Lyons [A.D. 1245], accessed 1 Sept 2005; from: http://www.geocities.com/Heartland/Valley/8920/churchcouncils/ Ecum13.htm#On%20excommunication%201; Internet; emphasis mine).

[684]Jonathan Riley-Smith, *What Were the Crusades?* 3rd ed (San Francisco: Ignatius, 1977, 1992, 2002), 37.

[685]"We therefore having determined to use all our endeavors, and to imploy all our care, as we are bound by the duty of our Pastoral charge, to root up and extirpate such a detestable Sect, and the foresaid execrable Errors, that they may not spread further, and that the hearts of believers may not be damnably perverted from the *Catholick* Church; and to repress such rash undertakings; & having special confidence in the Lord concerning your Learning, your ripeness in counsel, your zeal in the faith, and your experience in the management of affairs; and in like manner hoping that you will truly and faithfully execute the things which we shall think good to commit unto you for extirpating such errours; we have thought good to constitute you at this time, **for the Cause of God and the Faith**, the Nuntio Commissioner of us, and of the Apostolic See, within the Dominions of our beloved Son *Charls* Duke of *Savoy*, and the *Delphinat*, and the Cities and Diocess of *Vienna*, and *Sedun*, and the adjacent Provinces, Cities, Lands and places whatsoever, to the end that you should cause the same Inquisitor to be received and admitted to the free exercise of his Office, and that you should induce the followers of the most wicked Sect of the *Waldenses*, and all others polluted with any other Heretical pravity whatsoever, to abjure their Errours, and to obey the Commandments of the same Inquisitor, and give way to your seasonable remedies: And that you may do this so much the more easily, by how much the greater Power and Authority is given you by us, to wit, a Power, that by your self, or by some other person or persons, you may admonish and require most instantly all Archbishops, and Bishops seated in … and command them by vertue of Holy obedience, that together with our Venerable Brethren …, to execute the Office which is injoyned you with the forenamed Inquisitor, a man no doubt endued with Learning and fervent Zeal for the salvation of souls, they do assist you in the premises; and together with you be able and willing to *proceed to the execution thereof against the forenamed Waldenses, and all other Hereticks whatsoever, to rise up in Arms against them, and by joint communication of processes, to tread them under foot, as venemous Adders*, and to procure diligently that the people committed to their charge do persist in the confession of the true Faith, and be confirmed therein… And to injoyn that all the moveable and immoveable goods of the Hereticks may be lawfully seized and given away by any body whatsoever; and to make a booty of all goods which the Hereticks bring, or cause to be brought unto the territories of Catholicks, or carry, or cause to be carried out of the same … and that they abstain from all commerce with the aforesaid Hereticks: And to declare, that neither they nor any others, who by any contract or otherwise are in any sort bound unto them to perform or pay any thing, are henceforth at all obliged, or by the same authority can be compelled thereunto" (Samuel Morland, *History of the Evangelical Churches of the Valleys of Piedmont* [London, 1658; Gallatin, TN: Church History Research and Archives, 1982], 199-200, 201, 203).

[686]For example, Chuck Colson wrote, "Salvation does not consist simply of freedom from sin; salvation also means being restored to the task we were given in the beginning—**the job of creating culture**" (Charles Colson and Nancy Pearcey, *How Now Shall We Live?* 295; emphasis mine).

Acts 13:41, "For I work a work in your days, A work which ye shall in no wise believe, if one declare it unto you"

Acts 14:26-27, "From there they sailed to Antioch, from which they had been commended to the grace of God for the work that they had accomplished [εἰς τὸ ἔργον ὃ ἐπλήρωσαν]. When they had arrived and gathered the church together, they *began* to report all things that God had done [ἐποίησεν ὁ θεὸς] with them and how He had opened a door of faith to the Gentiles"

Acts 21:19, "After he had greeted them, he *began* to relate one by one the things which God had done [ἐποίησεν ὁ θεὸς] among the Gentiles through his ministry"

Rom 14:20, "Do not tear down the work of God for the sake of food"

1 Cor 9:1-2, "Am I not free? Am I not an apostle? Have I not seen Jesus our Lord? Are you not my work in the Lord? If to others I am not an apostle, at least I am to you; for you are the seal of my apostleship in the Lord"

1 Cor 15:58, "Therefore, my beloved brethren, be steadfast, immovable, always abounding in the work of the Lord, knowing that your toil is not *in* vain in the Lord"

1 Cor 16:10, "Now if Timothy comes, see that he is with you without cause to be afraid; for he is doing the Lord's work, as I also am."

2 Cor 6:1, "And working together [Συνεργοῦντες] *with Him*, we also urge you not to receive the grace of God in vain"

Phil 2:30, "because he came close to death for the work of Christ"

Conclusion: Many other verses draw on evangelism as the work of God:

Col 4:3, "meanwhile praying also for us, that God would open to us a door for the word, to speak the mystery of Christ, for which I am also in chains"

1 Thess 2:13, "For this reason we also constantly thank God that when you received the word of God which you heard from us, you accepted *it* not *as* the word of men, but *for* what it really is, the word of God, which also performs its work in you who believe"

d. Evangelism as THE WORK OF MAN (i.e. man is not idle in the work!):[687]

Examples:

1 Cor 3:9, "For we are God's fellow workers" [θεοῦ γάρ ἐσμεν συνεργοί]

2 Cor 6:1, "And working together [Συνεργοῦντες] *with Him*"
The very next verb used for man working together with God is παρακαλέω, meaning beseech, urge, exhort
Closely followed by λέγει γάρ, "For He says"

1 Thess 3:2 [citing both BYZ-NKJ and NA27-NAS]:
BYZ: "...διάκονον τοῦ θεοῦ καὶ συνεργὸν ἡμῶν ἐν τῷ εὐαγγελίῳ τοῦ χριστοῦ..."
NKJ: "minister of God, and our fellow laborer in the gospel of Christ"
NA27: "...συνεργὸν τοῦ θεοῦ ἐν τῷ εὐαγγελίῳ τοῦ Χριστοῦ..."
NAS: "God's fellow worker in the gospel of Christ"

John the Baptist fulfilled his work, Acts 13:25

1) Other verses emphasizing evangelism as the work of man:

Acts 12:25, "And Barnabas and Saul returned from Jerusalem when they had fulfilled their mission [the service], taking along with *them* John, who was also called Mark"

Acts 13:2, "Set apart for Me Barnabas and Saul for the work to which I have called them"

Acts 14:26-27, "From there they sailed to Antioch, from which they had been commended to the grace of God for the work that they had accomplished [εἰς τὸ ἔργον ὃ ἐπλήρωσαν]. When they had arrived and gathered the church together, they *began* to report all things that God had done [ἐποίησεν ὁ θεὸς] with them and how He had opened a door of faith to the Gentiles"

Acts 19:21, "Now after these things were finished [fulfilled, accomplished], Paul purposed in the spirit to go to Jerusalem after he had passed through Macedonia and Achaia, saying, 'After I have been there, I must also see Rome.'"

1 Cor 3:5-8, "What then is Apollos? And what is Paul? Servants through whom you believed, even as the Lord gave *opportunity* to each one. I planted, Apollos watered, but God was causing the growth. So then neither the one who plants nor the one who waters is anything, but God who causes the growth. Now he who plants and he who waters are one; but each will receive his own reward according to his own labor [κατὰ τὸν ἴδιον κόπον]"

---

[687]Also see Chapter 11, "God and Man in Evangelism" which further considers this mystery, wherein the temporal touches the eternal.

1 Cor 3:9-15, "For we are God's fellow workers [θεοῦ γάρ ἐσμεν συνεργοί]; you are God's field, God's building. According to the grace of God which was given to me, as a wise master builder [ὡς σοφὸς ἀρχιτέκτων] I laid a foundation, and another is building upon it. But let each man be careful how he builds upon it. For no man can lay a foundation other than the one which is laid, which is Jesus Christ. Now if any man builds upon the foundation with gold, silver, precious stones, wood, hay, straw, each man's work [ἑκάστου τὸ ἔργον] will become evident; for the day will show it, because it is *to be* revealed with fire; and the fire itself will test the quality of each man's work [ἑκάστου τὸ ἔργον]. If any man's work [τινος τὸ ἔργον] which he has built upon it remains, he shall receive a reward. If any man's work [τινος τὸ ἔργον] is burned up, he shall suffer loss; but he himself shall be saved, yet so as through fire"

1 Cor 9:1, "Are you not my work [τὸ ἔργον μου] in the Lord?"

Phil 2:16, "holding fast the word of life, so that in the day of Christ I may have cause to glory because I did not run in vain nor toil in vain"

2 Tim 4:5, "do the work of an evangelist [ἔργον ποίησον εὐαγγελιστοῦ]"

2) Verb describing the spiritual battle or agonizing difficulty of this work:

a) συναθλέω (2 NT uses) – meaning to fight or contend beside:
Phil 1:27, "Only conduct yourselves in a manner worthy of the gospel of Christ; so that whether I come and see you or remain absent, I may hear of you that you are standing firm in one spirit, with one mind **striving together** for the faith of the gospel"
Phil 4:3, "Indeed, true comrade, I ask you also to help these women who have **shared my struggle in** *the cause of* the gospel, together with Clement also, and the rest of my fellow workers, whose names are in the book of life"

3) So strongly did Paul see his role in the salvation of others that he wrote:

Rom 1:5-6, "through whom we have received grace and apostleship to bring about *the* obedience of faith among all the Gentiles, for His name's sake, among whom you also are the called of Jesus Christ"
The phrase, "to bring about *the* obedience of the faith" comes from the Greek: εἰς ὑπακοὴν πίστεως
Therefore the NAS (quoted above) supplied the verb "bring about"
The verse might also read: "through whom we have received grace and apostleship unto obedience of faith…"
The issue involved seems to be this: is the obedience described in Rom 1:5 the obedience of the recipients of the Gospel ("all the Gentiles") or the obedience of those receiving grace to make known this Gospel unto "all the Gentiles"?
Perhaps this chart will help:

On the Translation of εἰς ὑπακοὴν πίστεως in Romans 1:5 in English Bible Translation History

Wycliffe 2nd ed (1388)	Tyndale (1534)	Cover-dale (1535)	Geneva (1560); cf. Bishops	KJV (1611, 1769)	Murdock (1851)*	ASV (1901)	Bible in Basic English (1949)**	RSV (1952)	NAS (1977)	NIV (1984)	NJB⌗ (1985)	God's Word for the Nations (1995)	NLT (2004)
	To bring .. that is	To set up the ... under	Might be given unto		To the end that	[name]'s sake	To make disciple	To bring about ... for the sake of	To bring about ... [name]'s sake	To call people from ... that comes from	Of winning the ... for the honour of	Who bring people ... that is asso-ciated with .... This is the honor of	To tell ... every-where what God has done for them, so that they will ... bring glory
to obeie to the feith in alle folkis for his name	to bringe all maner hethe people vnto obedience of the fayth that is in his name	amonge all Heythen, to set vp the obedience of faith vnder his name	(that obedience might be giuen vnto the faith) in his Name among al the Gentiles	for obedience to the faith among all nations, for his name	among all the Gentiles, to the end that they may obey the faith in his name	unto obedience of faith among all the nations, for his name's sake	to make disciples to the faith among all nations, for his name	to bring about the obedience of faith for the sake of his name among all the nations	to bring about the obedience of faith among all the Gentiles, for His name's sake	for his name's sake, ... to call people from among all the Gentiles to the obedience that comes from faith	of winning the obedience of faith among all the nations for the honour of his name	who bring people from every nation to the obedience that is associated with faith. This is for the honor of his name	to tell Gentiles every-where what God has done for them, so that they will believe and obey him, bringing glory to his name

*The Murdock translation of the Syriac translated "apostleship" as "mission", which creates an interesting read by removing the theologically loaded term "apostle": "by whom we have received grace, and a mission among all the Gentiles, to the end that they may obey the faith in his name"

**The Cambridge "Bible in Basic English" (NT, 1949) substituted "to make disciples" for "unto obedience." The whole verse reads: "Through whom grace has been given to us, sending us out to make disciples to the faith among all nations, for his name"

Rom 11:14, "if somehow I might move to jealousy my fellow countrymen and [I might] save some of them."
> Paul used the Greek verb σῴζω in the first person singular aorist subjunctive, σώσω, meaning "I might save";
> With the addition of the "and" and "some of them" the Greek reads: καὶ σώσω τινὰς ἐξ αὐτῶν

1 Cor 9:22, "To the weak I became weak, that I might win the weak; I have become all things to all men, that I may by all means save some"
> If the adverb does not split the last verbal phrase, it would read, "that by all means **I may save** [σώσω] some";
> Same form as Rom 11:14, the order of the "some" is reversed: ἵνα πάντως τινὰς σώσω
> Paul was quite secure that he had a role in other persons being saved!

By the way, the exact same form of the Greek verb σῴζω is used from the mouth of Jesus in John 12:47:
> John 12:47 "And if anyone hears My sayings, and does not keep them, I do not judge him; for I did not come to judge the world, but to save the world"

Col 1:24, "Now I rejoice in my sufferings for your sake, and in my flesh I do my share on behalf of His body (which is the church) in **filling up that which is lacking** in Christ's afflictions"

The issue was not that Paul was crucified for anyone (1 Cor 1:13), but rather that his role as evangelist was necessary, as part of God's work and plan, for the salvation of others!

e. Evangelism as the work of God and Man:

Acts 14:26-27, "From there they sailed to Antioch, from which they had been commended to the grace of God for the work that they had accomplished [εἰς τὸ ἔργον ὃ ἐπλήρωσαν]. When they had arrived and gathered the church together, they *began* to report all things that God had done [ἐποίησεν ὁ θεὸς] with them and how He had opened a door of faith to the Gentiles"

1 Cor 3:9, "For we are God's fellow workers [θεοῦ γάρ ἐσμεν συνεργοί]; you are God's field, God's building"

1 Cor 9:23, "And I do all things for the sake of the gospel, that I may become a fellow partaker of it"

1 Cor 15:10, "But by the grace of God I am what I am, and His grace toward me did not prove vain; but I labored even more than all of them, yet not I, but the grace of God with me"

2 Cor 3:2-4, "You are our letter, written in our hearts, known and read by all men; being manifested that you are a letter of Christ, cared for by us, written not with ink, but with the Spirit of the living God, not on tablets of stone, but on tablets of human hearts. And such confidence we have through Christ toward God."

Consider the uses of all three persons of the Trinity, "Christ," "Spirit," and "God," signifying the interrelationship of human work with the godhead—how many more verses would this section have if we considered "working with Christ" or "colaboring with the Spirit"?

2 Cor 6:1, "And working together *with Him*, we also urge you not to receive the grace of God in vain"

Three IBS/ABS Translations of 2 Corinthians 6:1

Byzantine Textform	New American Standard (1977)	ABS' Contemporary English Version (1991)	IBS' French *Le Semeur* (1992, 1999)*	ABS' Good News Translation (1993)
Συνεργοῦντες δὲ καὶ παρακαλοῦμεν μὴ εἰς κενὸν τὴν χάριν τοῦ θεοῦ δέξασθαι ὑμᾶς	And working together *with Him*, we also urge you not to receive the grace of God in vain	We work together with God, and we beg you to make good use of God's kindness to you.	Also, we who work together in this task, we invite you to not allow the grace that you received from God to be without effect.	In our work together with God, then, we beg you who have received God's grace not to let it be wasted.
		Notice this translation's typical removal of the concept of "in vain", changing it into the positive "make good use of"	Note the removal of the link between God and man in the word "working together" (from 5:21), adapting it to mean that men work together. Note also that grace must be "received" [as in the sacraments]	Again, the reception of grace is made passive, something to be received

*My translation of "Aussi, nous qui travaillons ensemble à cette tâche, nous vous invitons à ne pas laisser sans effet la grâce que vous avez reçue de Dieu."

Conclusion:

While evangelism is the work of God, while its power is the Word of God, it is a work to which God calls men, and which then also becomes the work of men!

For a further discussion of this issue, see Chapter 11, "God, Prayer, and Fasting in Evangelism," and the Section "God and Man in Evangelism"

5.   RESULT of Evangelism Ministry:

Chart of Verbs Used for the Result of Evangelism Ministry

Salvation Heard and Understood/ Salvation Urged	Salvation Urged/ Salvation Occurs	Metaph./ Result/ OT Precedents/ Profitable & Unprofitable Ministry	Profitable & Unprofitable Ministry, 1 Cor 14/ Results	Results of Evangelism
ἀκούω and cognates 1) ἀκούω, "hear" (13): ἀκούω + πληροφορέω, "hear + fulfill" (1); ἀκούω + πιστεύω, "hear + believe" (9); ἀκούω + λαμβάνω, "hear + receive" (3); ἀκούω + ποιέω, "hear + do" (5); n1) ἡ ἀκοή, "hearing" (5): ἡ ἀκοή + ἀκούω, "hearing + hear" (2); ἡ ἀκοή + πιστεύω, "hearing + believe" (2); ἡ ἀκοή + ἡ πίστις, "hearing + faith" (2); ἡ ἀκοή + ἀκούω + ἡ πίστις, "hearing + hear + faith" (1); ἡ ἀκοή + εἰσακούω + ἡ φωνή, "hearing + harkening + voice (1) 2) εἰσακούω, "harken" (0); 3) προακούω, "hear beforehand" (1); 4) ὑπακούω, "obey" (1); n2) τὸ νόημα, understanding (2); 5) ἐπακροάομαι (1). **Salvation Urged** **Exemplified:** 6) μετανοέω, "repent" (2); 7) πιστεύω, "believe" (6); 8) πείθω [active], "persuade" (5); 9) ἐπιστρέφω, "turn" (4); 10) σῴζω, "save" (3); 11) κερδαίνω, "win" (5). **Forceful Terms:** 12) ἀναγκάζω, "compel" (1); 13) ἀρπάζω, "take by force" (1); 14) ἵστημι, "made" (0).	**Salvation Occurs** **Outward Acceptance** 15) ἐπικαλέω/ ἐπικαλέομαι, "call upon" (2 + 24 OT!). **Inward Acceptance:** 16) πιστεύω, "believe" (28): πιστεύω + ἐπιστρέφω, "believe + turn" (1); 17) παραλαμβάνω, "received" (3); 18) δέχομαι, "receive" (10): δέχομαι + μετ᾽ εἰρήνης "received ... with peace" (1); 19) πείθω (passive), "were persuaded" (4); 20) ἐπιστρέφω, "turned" (2); 21) ἔρχομαι + ἡ ἐπίγνωσις + ἡ ἀλήθεια, "come unto knowledge of the truth" (2); 22) ὑπακούω + ἡ πίστις, "obey + faith" (1); n3) ἡ ὑπακοή + ἡ πίστις, "obedience + faith" (2). **Spiritual Transformation:** 23) γεννάω, "to beget" (2); 24) μαθητεύω, "disciple won/made" (4). **Divine Process:** 25) οὐ + δίδωμι, "not give" 26) ὁ κύριος + λέγω + μή + φοβέω + λαλέω + μή + σιωπάω, The Lord said... (1) 27) ἀκούω + μανθάνω + ἔρχομαι, "hear + learn + come" (1) 28) ἐνάρχομαι + τὸ ἔργον + ἀγαθός, "to begin + work + good" (1).	**Metaphorical:** 29) διανοίγω, "open" (1); n4) ὁ καρπός, "fruit" (4); n5) ἡ ἀπαρχή, "firstfruit" (2). **Result:** n6a) εἰς Χριστόν, "in Christ" (4); n6b) ἐν Χριστῷ, "in Christ" (97 total); n6c) Χριστὸς ἐν ὑμῖν, Christ in you (4); n7) ἐπιστολή + Χριστός, (1). **Further OT Precedents:** 30) συνθέλω, "consent" (0); p1) καὶ ἀπὸ τῶν δικαίων τῶν πολλῶν, "they that [turn] many to righteousness" (0) **Profitable & Unprofitable Ministry, 1 Cor 14** 31) οὐδεὶς γὰρ ἀκούει [ἀκούω], "no one can hear"; n8) ἡ οἰκοδομή, "edification" (3) n9) ἡ παράκλησις, "exhortation"; n10) ἡ παραμυθία, "consolation." 32) οἰκοδομέω, "to edify" (2). 33) ὠφελέω, "profit"; n11) ἡ ἀποκάλυψις, "revelation"; n12) ἡ γνῶσις, "knowledge"; n13) ἡ προφητεία, "prophecy"; n14) ἡ διδαχή, "teaching." a1) ἄδηλος + ἡ φωνη, "unclear + sound"; 34) παρασκευάζω, "prepare himself." a2) εὔσημος, "clear"; 35) γινώσκω + λαλέω, "know + say."	**Profitable & Unprofitable Ministry, 1 Cor 14 (cont)** 36) μὴ + εἰδῶ, "not + know." n15) ἡ γλῶσσα + ἄκαρπος, "a tongue + unfruitful." 37) λόγους διὰ τοῦ νοός μου λαλῆσαι, "speak words with my mind"; 38) κατηχέω, "teach." 39) ἐλέγχω, "convict"; 40) ἀνακρίνω, "to examine"; 41) γίνομαι + φανερός, "be + disclosed"; 42) πίπτω + τὸ πρόσωπον, "fall + face"; 43) προσκυνέω, "worship." **Salvation Rejected** 44) σκληρύνω:,[pass] "to become stubborn"; 45) ἀπειθέω, "to be disobedient"; 46) ἀπιστέω, "not believing"; 47) ζηλόω, "being moved to jealousy"; 48) πίμπλημι + ὁ ζῆλος, "filled with jealousy"; 49) ἀντιτάσσομαι, "resist, oppose"; 50) βλασφημέω, "blaspheme." **Results of false prophecying** 51) διαστρέφω, "turn away" [from the faith]; 52) ἀνατρέπω, "overturn" [whole households]. **Metaphorical Results** **General Results:** 53) λάμπω + τὸ φῶς, "shine + the light" (1); n16) ἡ ὀσμή, "an aroma" (2); n17) ἡ εὐωδία, "a fragrance" (1); 54) ἐγγίζω + ἡ βασιλεία, "Kingdom + comes near" (2).	**Particular Results:** 55) ζωγρέω ," taking men alive" (2) 56) ἁρπάζω, "snatching" (1); 57) ἕλκω/ἑλκύω, "draw, drag" (20; 58) Heb. laqach, "to snatch" (0) n18) τὸ τέκνον + μᾶλλον, "more + children" (0) 59) οἰκοδομέω, "built up" (1); 60) οὐ κενὴ γέγονεν, "was not in vain" (1). **Results to the Evangelist:** 61) Confession [ὁμολογέω] before men yields confession of Christ (2). **Deliverance from guilt:** 62) ῥύομαι, deliverance (0); 63) σῴζω, save (1); 64) καλύπτω, cover (1). **Edification occurs:** n19) ἡ κοινωνία, participation (1); n20) ὁ συγκοινωνός, fellow-partaker (1). **Extreme rejoicing:** 65) περισσεύω, abounds (1). **God is glorified:** 66) μεγαλύνω, exalting (1). **Lasting spiritual fruit:** n21) Crown of glory (1); n22) Glory and joy (1). **Purpose for living:** 67) ζάω, We live (1). **Divine result:** 68) κλητός, calling (1).

a.   Salvation heard—received or rejected:

1)   ἀκούω and cognates:

1)   ἀκούω (verb, 437 NT uses) to hear; heed, listen to; understand; [cause to] hear or learn of; learn; [give a] hearing:

(1)   Used in triplicate form:

Matt 13:17, "For truly I say to you, that many prophets and righteous men desired to see what you see, and did not see *it*; and **to hear** what **you hear**, and **did not hear** *it*"

Byz: καὶ ἀκοῦσαι ἃ ἀκούετε, καὶ οὐκ ἤκουσαν

Notice that the parallel "seeing" used two verbs: ὁράω, βλέπω, and ὁράω

(2)   Used in duplicate form:

Matt 13:9

Matt 13:9 (NAS), "He who has ears, let him hear."

N/A27: ὁ ἔχων ὦτα ἀκουέτω

Matt 13:9 (NKJ), "He who has ears to hear, let him hear!"

Byz: Ὁ ἔχων ὦτα ἀκούειν ἀκουέτω.

Similarly Matt 11:15; 13:43

Matt 13:13 "Therefore I speak to them in parables; because while seeing they do not see, and while **hearing they do not hear**, nor do they understand [συνίημι]"

(3)   Used in parallel with συνίημι (to understand):

Matt 15:10, "And after He called the multitude to Him, He said to them, "Hear, and understand"

(4)   Other uses:

Matt 18:15 "And if your brother sins, go and reprove him in private; if **he listens** to you, you have won your brother"

Matt 18:16, "But if **he does not listen** *to you*, take one or two more with you, so that by the mouth of two or three witnesses every fact may be confirmed"

Matt 19:22, "But when the young man **heard** this statement, he went away grieved; for he was one who owned much property"

Matt 19:25, "And when the disciples **heard** *this*, they were very astonished and said, 'Then who can be saved?'"

Matt 20:30, "And behold, two blind men sitting by the road, **hearing** that Jesus was passing by, cried out, saying, "Lord, have mercy on us, Son of David!"

Matt 22:22, And **hearing** *this*, they marveled, and leaving Him, they went away"

Matt 22:33, "And when the multitudes **heard** *this*, they were astonished at His teaching"

(5)   OT uses (see "A Proclaimed or Spoken Witness in the OT"):

Deut 4:6, "In the sight of the peoples **who will hear** all these statutes"

Deut 18:19, "And it shall come about that whoever will not **listen** to My words which he shall speak in My name, I Myself will require *it* of him"

Deut 32:1, "Give ear, O heavens, and let me speak; And let the earth **hear** the words of my mouth"

b)   Combinations with the verb ἀκούω:

(1)   ἀκούω + πληροφορέω (to fill, fulfill, accomplish) the κήρυγμα (preaching):

2 Tim 4:17, "But the Lord stood with me, and strengthened me, in order that through me **the proclamation might be fully accomplished**, and that all the Gentiles **might hear**; and I was delivered out of the lion's mouth."

(2)   ἀκούω + πιστεύω (to believe):

Luke 8:12, "And those beside the road are **those who have heard**; then the devil comes and takes away the word from their heart, so that **they may not believe** and be saved"

John 5:24, "Truly, truly, I say to you, **he who hears** My word, and **believes** Him who sent Me, has eternal life, and does not come into judgment, but has passed out of death into life"

John 12:47 (NKJ), "And if anyone **hears** My words and **does not believe** [NA27, φυλάσσω], I do not judge him; for I did not come to judge the world but to save the world"

Acts 4:4 (NKJ), "However, many of those who **heard** the word **believed**; and the number of the men came to be about five thousand"

Acts 13:48, "And when the Gentiles **heard** this, they *began* rejoicing and glorifying the word of the Lord; and as many as had been appointed to eternal life **believed**"

Acts 15:7, "And after there had been much debate, Peter stood up and said to them, "Brethren, you know that in the early days God made a choice among you, that by my mouth the Gentiles **should hear** the word of the gospel and **believe**"

Acts 18:8 (NKJ), "Then Crispus, the ruler of the synagogue, **believed** on the Lord with all his household. And many of the Corinthians, **hearing**, **believed** and were baptized"

Rom 10:14, "How then shall they call upon Him in whom **they have not believed**? And how **shall they believe** in Him whom **they have not heard**? And how **shall they hear** without a preacher?"

Eph 1:13, "In Him, you also, after **listening** to the message of truth, the gospel of your salvation—**having also believed**, you were sealed in Him with the Holy Spirit of promise"

[Because the verb ἀκούω translated as "listening" (in the NAS) is in the aorist tense, the NKJ use of "you heard," while not translating it as a participial (ἀκούσαντες), seems to place more emphasis on the punctiliar element of aorist use of hearing]

(3) ἀκούω + λαμβάνω (to receive):

Matt 13:20, "And the one on whom seed was sown on the rocky places, this is the man who hears the word, and immediately receives it with joy" (cf. Mark 4:16; Luke 8:13 uses δέχομαι)

John 3:32, "What He has seen and heard, of that He bears witness; and no man receives His witness"

Rev 3:3, "Remember therefore what you have received and heard; and keep *it*, and repent"

(4) ἀκούω + ποιέω (to do):

Matt 7:24, "Therefore everyone who hears these words of Mine, and acts upon them, may be compared to a wise man, who built his house upon the rock" (cf. Luke 6:47)

Matt 7:26, "And everyone who hears these words of Mine, and does not act upon them, will be like a foolish man, who built his house upon the sand" (cf. Luke 6:49)

Luke 8:21, "But He answered and said to them, 'My mother and My brothers are these who hear the word of God and do it.'"

John 9:31, "We know that God does not hear sinners; but if anyone is God-fearing, and does His will, He hears him"

Acts 2:37, "Now when they heard *this*, they were pierced to the heart, and said to Peter and the rest of the apostles, 'Brethren, what shall we do?'"

n1) ἡ ἀκοή (noun, 24 NT uses), [that which is] **heard** (faculty of hearing; organ of hearing; hearing; report; fame; message; preaching):

(1) Used in triplicate:

Romans 10:16-17 (NKJ), "But they have not all obeyed the gospel. For Isaiah says, 'Lord, who has believed our **report**?' So then faith *comes* by **hearing**, and **hearing** by the word of God"

(2) Other uses:

Acts 17:20, "For you are bringing some strange things to our **ears**; we want to know therefore what these things mean."

1 Thess 2:13 (NKJ), "For this reason we also thank God without ceasing, because when you received the word of God which **you heard** from us, you welcomed *it* not *as* the word of men, but as it is in truth, the word of God, which also effectively works in you who believe"

Tim 4:4 (NKJ), "and they will turn *their* **ears** away from the truth, and be turned aside to fables"

Heb 5:11, "Concerning him we have much to say, and *it is* hard to explain, since you have become dull of **hearing**"

(3) Verbal combinations with the noun ἡ ἀκοή:

(a) ἡ ἀκοή + ἀκούω (to hear):

Matthew 13:14, "And in their case the prophecy of Isaiah is being fulfilled, which says, 'You will keep on **hearing**, but **will not understand**; And you will keep on seeing, but will not perceive…'"

Acts 28:26, "saying, 'Go to this people and say, "You will keep on **hearing**, but **will not understand**; And you will keep on seeing, but will not perceive"'"

Cf. Exod 15:26; 19:5; 23:22; Deut 11:22; 28:2; 2 Sam 22:45; 1 Kings 10:7; 2 Chron 9:6; Psa 17:45; Job 37:2; 42:5; Obad 1:1; Jer 6:24; 17:24; 31:18; 49:14, 23; similarly Deut 11:13; 15:5; 28:1; Hab 3:2; Isa 6:9

(b) ἡ ἀκοή + πιστεύω (to believe):

John 12:38, "that the word of Isaiah the prophet might be fulfilled, which he spoke, 'LORD, who **has believed** our **report**? And to whom has the arm of the Lord been revealed?'"

Rom 10:16, "However, they did not all heed the glad tidings; for Isaiah says, 'LORD, who **has believed** our r**eport**?'"

(c) ἡ ἀκοή + ἡ πίστις (faith):
Gal 3:2, "This is the only thing I want to find out from you: did you receive the Spirit by the works of the Law, or **by hearing with faith**?"
ἐξ ἀκοῆς πίστεως
Gal 3:5, "Does He then, who provides you with the Spirit and works miracles among you, do it by the works of the Law, or **by hearing with faith**?"
ἐξ ἀκοῆς πίστεως

(d) ἡ ἀκοή + εἰσακούω (to [really] hear) + ἡ φωνή (voice) + ἀκούω (to hear):
Deut 28:1-2, "Now it shall be, if you will diligently obey [ἡ ἀκοή + εἰσακούω + ἡ φωνή] the LORD your God, being careful to do all His commandments which I command you today, the LORD your God will set you high above all the nations of the earth. And all these blessings shall come upon you and overtake you, if you will obey [ἡ ἀκοή + ἀκούω + ἡ φωνή] the LORD your God."

And negation: μὴ (not) + εἰσακούω (to [really] hear; thus, obey) + ἡ φωνή (voice):
Deut 28:15, "But it shall come about, if you will not obey the LORD your God, to observe to do all His commandments and His statutes with which I charge you today, that all these curses shall come upon you and overtake you."

(f) εὐαγγελίζω + ἡ ἀκοή + ἡ πίστις (faith) + ἀκούω (to hear):
Heb 4:2, "For indeed we have had good news preached [εὐαγγελίζω]to us, just as they also; but the word **they heard** [ἀκοή] did not profit them, because it was not united by faith [πίστις] in those who heard [ἀκούω]"

2) εἰσακούω (verb; 214 LXX uses; 5 NT uses), to listen or to hear; esp. to give ear or heed:

In NT:

Of man thinking himself heard in prayer, Matt 6:7

Of God hearing prayer, Luke 1:13; Acts 10:31; Heb 5:7

Of God speaking to His people through a people of strange tongue:
1 Cor 14:21, "In the Law it is written, 'By men of strange tongues and by the lips of strangers I will speak to this people, and even so they will not listen to Me,' says the Lord."

In the OT:

Of giving heed to the voice of the Lord:
Deut 4:30, "When you are in distress and all these things have come upon you, in the latter days, you will return to the LORD your God and **listen** to His voice"; Deut 11:13; 15:5; 27:10

Of giving heed to the false teaching of a family member:
Deut 13:8, "you shall not yield to him or **listen** to him; and your eye shall not pity him, nor shall you spare or conceal him"

μὴ +εἰσακούω + ποιέω:
Deut 28:15, "But it shall come about, if you **will not obey** [μὴ +εἰσακούω] the LORD your God, to observe **to do** [ποιέω] all His commandments and His statutes with which I charge you today, that all these curses shall come upon you and overtake you."
Deut 28:58, "If you are **not careful to observe** [μὴ +εἰσακούω + ποιέω] all the words of this law which are written in this book, to fear this honored and awesome name, the LORD your God."

3) προακούω (verb, hapax) to hear beforehand:
Col 1:5, "…because of the hope laid up for you in heaven, of which **you previously heard** in the word of truth, the gospel…"
[Byz] ἣν προηκούσατε ἐν τῷ λόγῳ τῆς ἀληθείας τοῦ εὐαγγελίου

4) ὑπακούω (verb, 21 NT uses) to listen (hence, to obey):
Rom 10:16 (KJV), "But they have not all **obeyed** the gospel. For Esaias saith, Lord, who hath believed our report?'"
[Byz] Ἀλλ' οὐ πάντες ὑπήκουσαν τῷ εὐαγγελίῳ.

n2) τὸ νόημα (6 total NT uses), understanding, that is the result of "hearing" (Fr. *entendement*):

2 Cor 3:14 (Noyes), "But their **understandings** were blinded; for until this day, when the old covenant is read, the same veil remaineth, since it is not unveiled to them that it is done away in Christ."

2 Cor 4:4 (Noyes), "in whom the God of this world blinded the **understandings** of the unbelieving, so that they cannot behold the light of the gospel of the glory of Christ, who is the image of God."

5) ἐπακροάομαι (1 NT use), meaning to listen to—in the sense of overhearing:

Acts 16:25, "But about midnight Paul and Silas were praying and singing hymns of praise to God, and the prisoners **were listening** to them."

b. Salvation urged:

6) μετανοέω, "**repent**" [as verb, describing the commitment to Christ], Mark 6:12; Acts 2:38; 3:19; 8:22; 17:30:

a) Acts 26:20, "I preached that they should **repent** [μετανοεῖν] and turn to God and prove their repentance [τῆς μετανοίας] by their deeds."

b) Acts 11:18, "God has granted to the Gentiles also the **repentance** [as a noun] *that leads* to life"

7) πιστεύω – "**believe**" [as needful or an imperative], Matt 9:28; Mark 9:23-24; Luke 8:12-13, 50; 24:25; John 1:7, 12; 3:12, 18; 5:47; 8:24, 45-46; 10:37-38; 11:25-26; 12:36; 13:19; 14:1, 10-11, 29; 19:35; 20-30-31; Acts 19:4; Rom 10:9:

a) Mark 1:15, "and saying, 'The time is fulfilled, and the kingdom of God is at hand; repent and **believe** in the gospel'"

b) Mark 5:36, "But Jesus, overhearing what was being spoken, said to the synagogue official, 'Do not be afraid *any longer*, only **believe**'"

c) John 6:39, "Jesus answered and said to them, 'This is the work of God, that you **believe** in Him whom He has sent'"

d) Acts 15:7, "After there had been much debate, Peter stood up and said to them, "Brethren, you know that in the early days God made a choice among you, that by my mouth the Gentiles would hear the word of the gospel and **believe**"

e) Acts 16:31, "They said, '**Believe** in the Lord Jesus, and you will be saved, you and your household'"

f) Acts 26:27, "King Agrippa, do you **believe** the Prophets? I know that you do."

8) πείθω (passive voice) – "**persuaded**" (cf. Acts 21:14):

a) "But he said to him, 'If they do not listen to Moses and the Prophets, they will not be **persuaded** even if someone rises from the dead," Luke 16:31

b) "And some of them were **persuaded** [ἐπείσθησαν] and joined [προσεκληρώθησαν] Paul and Silas," Acts 17:4

c) "This Paul has **persuaded** and turned away a considerable number of people," Acts 19:26

d) "When they had set a day for Paul, they came to him at his lodging in large numbers; and he was explaining to them by solemnly testifying about the kingdom of God and trying to **persuade** them concerning Jesus, from both the Law of Moses and from the Prophets, from morning until evening. Some were being **persuaded** by the things spoken, but others would not believe," Acts 28:23-24

e) In the LXX, the verb persuaded is used to refer to "trusting" in Deut 28:52, wherein the people "trusted" in their strong and high walls; in this case the translators of the LXX used πείθω in the active voice to translated the Hebrew בָּטַח (baw-takh; meaning to trust; e.g. Psa 37:3).

9) ἐπιστρέφω, turn (489 uses in LXX and NT; 37 uses in NT):

a) Some OT uses:

(1) Psa 51:13, "*Then* I will teach transgressors Thy ways, And sinners **will be converted** [Heb *shuwb*] to Thee"

(2) Psa 116[114]:7, "**Return** to your rest, O my soul, For the LORD has dealt bountifully with you"

(a) Hebrew: shuwb (meaning "turn");

(b) Latin: convertere (meaning "be ye converted")

(3) Isa 6:10 (KJV), "Make the heart of this people fat, and make their ears heavy, and shut their eyes; lest they see with their eyes, and hear with their ears, and understand with their heart, and **convert**, and be healed"

(4) There are many more OT examples of the use of this verb for a spiritual turning, e.g. Jer 3:10; 5:3; 8:5; Ezek 14:6; 18:30

b) Acts 3:19-20, "Repent therefore and **return**, that your sins may be wiped away, in order that times of refreshing may come from the presence of the Lord; and that He may send Jesus, the Christ appointed for you"

Some Translations of ἐπιστρέφω in Acts 3:19

NA27	VUL	WYC	GEN	KJV	Douay-Rheims	NAS	NKJ	NIV / GNT	CSB / NET	CEV*
μετανοή-σατε οὖν καὶ ἐπιστρέ-ψατε	paenitemini igitur et **conver-timini**	Therfor be ye repentaunt, and **be ye conuertid**	Amend your liues therefore, and **turne**	Repent ye therefore, and **be converted**	Be penitent, therefore, and **be converted**	Repent therefore and **return**	Repent therefore and **be converted**	Repent, then, and **turn to God**	Therefore repent and **turn back**	So **turn** to God! Give up your sins

*Apparently, the ABS' Contemporary English Version, having received the imprimatur of a Bishop of the Church of Rome, subsumes both the verbs "repent" and "be converted" as one verb, "turn". The next verse is less of a result clause and even more tentative, after being separated by a period from the prior clause, "Then that time will come when the Lord will give you fresh strength"

c) Acts 14:15, "and saying, 'Men, why are you doing these things? We are also men of the same nature as you, and preach the gospel to you in order that **you should turn** from these vain things to a living God, who made the heaven and the earth and the sea, and all that is in them.'"

d) Acts 26:20, "that they should repent and **turn** to God, doing works worthy of repentance"

e) 1 Thess 1:9, "For they themselves report about us what kind of a reception we had with you, and how **you turned** to God from idols to serve a living and true God"

10) σῴζω – "**save**," John 3:17; 1 Cor 9:22, 10:33; 1 Tim 2:4; Jude 23:

a) "I have become all things to all men, so that **I may** by all means **save** some (ἵνα πάντως τινὰς σώσω)," 1 Cor 9:22;

b) "just as I also please all men in all things, not seeking my own profit but the *profit* of the many, so that **they may be saved** (ἵνα σωθῶσιν)" 1 Cor 10:33;

c) "but others **save** with fear (οὓς δὲ ἐν φόβῳ σῴζετε), pulling *them* out of the fire, hating even the garment defiled by the flesh," Jude 23.

11) κερδαίνω – "**win**," 1 Cor 9:19-22 (cf. Prov 11:30):

a) "For though I am free from all *men*, I have made myself a slave to all, so that **I may win** more," 1 Cor 9:19;

b) "To the Jews I became as a Jew, so that **I might win** Jews," 1 Cor 9:20;

c) "To those who are under the Law, as under the Law though not being myself under the Law, so that **I might win** those who are under the Law," 1 Cor 9:20;

d) "To those who are without law, as without law, though not being without the law of God but under the law of Christ, so that **I might win** those who are without law," 1 Cor 9:21;

e) "To the weak I became weak, that **I might win** the weak," 1 Cor 9:22.

Six Approaches to "That I Might Win" (ἵνα … κερδήσω) in 1 Corinthians 9:19-22

Intentional	Passive 1	Passive 2	Passive 3	Selective	Patronizing	Mysterious
God uses the Christian to intentionally win others to Christ (e.g. "Follow Me and I will make you fishers of men")	God uses the Christian to passively win others to Christ (responding only when others initiate it, or speaking only within the church)	God uses the Christian to passively win others to Christ (without any knowledge of how to biblically share their faith)	Winning others to Christ is a result of their seeing the lifestyle of the Christian, and God leading them to seek out salvation on their own	Wining others to Christ is only for those with the gift of the evangelist or evangelism	Talking about "winning" sounds competitive, patronizing, and out-of-fashion	God wins others to Christ on His own in some mysterious way

A parallel to this discussion would be: "Who saves the soul?"—see references under the word "save" above.

Comparing Translations: 1 Cor 9:22-23

Byzantine Textform	New American Standard (1977)	ABS' Contemporary English Version (1995)	IBS's French *Le Semeur* (1992, 1999)*
Ἐγενόμην τοῖς ἀσθενέσιν ὡς ἀσθενής, ἵνα τοὺς ἀσθενεῖς κερδήσω. Τοῖς πᾶσιν γέγονα τὰ πάντα, ἵνα πάντως τινὰς σώσω.	To the weak I became weak, that I might win the weak; I have become all things to all men, that I may by all means save some.	When I am with people whose faith is weak, I live as they do to win them. I do everything I can to win everyone I possibly can.	In my relations with Christians who are poorly established in the faith, I live like one of them, in order to win them. It is in this way that I make myself all to all, in order to direct at least several unto salvation by all means.
Τοῦτο [NA27, πάντα] δὲ ποιῶ διὰ τὸ εὐαγγέλιον, ἵνα συγκοινωνὸς αὐτοῦ γένωμαι.	And I do all things for the sake of the gospel, that I may become a fellow partaker of it.	I do all this for the good news, because I want to share in its blessings.	Thus, all this, I do it for the cause of the Good News to have a part, with them, in the blessings that are brought by the Good News.

*My translation of "Dans mes relations avec les chrétiens mal affermis dans la foi, je vis comme l'un d'entre eux, afin de les gagner. C'est ainsi que je me fais tout à tous, afin d'en conduire au moins quelques-uns au salut par tous les moyens. Or, tout cela, je le fais pour la cause de la Bonne Nouvelle pour avoir part, avec eux, aux bénédictions qu'apporte la Bonne Nouvelle."

7) **Forceful terms for calling to commitment**:

(12) ἀναγκάζω – "compel," Luke 14:23:
  Luke 14:23, "And the master said to the slave, 'Go out into the highways and along the hedges, and **compel** *them* to come in, that my house may be filled.'"

(13) ἁρπάζω – "to take by force," Jude 23:
  Jude 23, "save others, **snatching** them out of the fire; and on some have mercy with fear, hating even the garment polluted by the flesh."

(14) ἵστημι – "made" 2 Chron 34:32:
  2 Chron 32:34, "Moreover, **he made** all who were present in Jerusalem and Benjamin to stand *with him*. So the inhabitants of Jerusalem did according to the covenant of God, the God of their fathers."

b. **Salvation Acceptance**:

Introduction:

Remembering that "Man looks at the outward appearance [εἰς πρόσωπον], God looks at the heart [εἰς καρδίαν]":
1 Sam 16:7, "But the LORD said to Samuel, 'Do not look at his appearance or at the height of his stature, because I have rejected him; for God *sees* not as man sees, for man looks at the outward appearance, but the LORD looks at the heart.'"
Basically: "Man sees the face, God sees the heart."

Consider also the interesting order of the phrases in Zech 13:9:
Zech 13:9, "And I will bring the third part through the fire, Refine them as silver is refined, And test them as gold is tested. They will call on My name, And I will answer them; I will say, 'They are My people,' And they will say, 'The LORD is my God.'"

Symbiotic Action: Man—God—Man:
1) They will call on My name,
2) And I will answer them; I will say, 'They are My people,'
3) And they will say, 'The LORD is my God.'"

15) ἐπικαλέω/ἐπικαλέομαι –to call upon for salvation:
Acts 2:21, "And it shall be, that everyone who calls on the name of the Lord shall be saved."
Rom 10:13, "for 'Whoever will call upon the name of the LORD will be saved.'"

Did not Philip lead the Ethiopian Eunuch to "call on the name of the Lord" to verbally affirm his salvation before baptizing him?
Acts 8:37 (NKJ), "Then Philip said, 'If you believe with all your heart, you may.' And he answered and said, 'I believe that Jesus Christ is the Son of God.'"

Did not Paul exhort the Philippian Jailer to "call on the name of the Lord" to be saved?
Acts 16:29-31, "And he called for lights and rushed in and, trembling with fear, he fell down before Paul and Silas, and after he brought them out, he said, 'Sirs, what must I do to be

saved?' And they said, 'Believe in the Lord Jesus, and you shall be saved, you and your household.'"

ἐπικαλέω–to call upon the Lord at other times in the Christian life:

Acts 7:59, "And they went on stoning Stephen as he called upon *the Lord* and said, 'Lord Jesus, receive my spirit!'"

2 Tim 2:22, "Now flee from youthful lusts, and pursue righteousness, faith, love *and* peace, with those who call on the Lord from a pure heart."

OT precedents:

In Romans 10:13, Paul cited one line from Joel 2:32, just as did Peter on the day of Pentecost in Acts 2:21:

Joel 2:32, "And it will come about that whoever calls on the name of the LORD Will be delivered; For on Mount Zion and in Jerusalem There will be those who escape, As the LORD has said, Even among the survivors whom the LORD calls."

Other OT contexts of calling upon the Lord:

Gen 4:26, "And to Seth, to him also a son was born; and he called his name Enosh. Then *men* began to call upon the name of the LORD."

Gen 12:8, "Then he [Abram] proceeded from there to the mountain on the east of Bethel, and pitched his tent, with Bethel on the west and Ai on the east; and there he built an altar to the LORD and called upon the name of the LORD."

Gen 13:3-4, "And he went on his journeys from the Negev as far as Bethel, to the place where his tent had been at the beginning, between Bethel and Ai, to the place of the altar, which he had made there formerly; and there Abram called on the name of the LORD."

Gen 21:33, "And *Abraham* planted a tamarisk tree at Beersheba, and there he called on the name of the LORD, the Everlasting God."

Deut 4:7, "For what great nation is there that has a god so near to it as is the LORD our God whenever we call on Him?"

2 Sam 22:3, "I call upon the LORD, who is worthy to be praised; And I am saved from my enemies."

2 Sam 22:7, "In my distress I called upon the LORD, Yes, I cried to my God; And from His temple He heard my voice, And my cry for help *came* into His ears."

1 Kgs 17:21, "Then he stretched himself upon the child three times, and called to the LORD, and said, 'O LORD my God, I pray Thee, let this child's life return to him.'"

1 Kgs 18:24, "'Then you call on the name of your god, and I will call on the name of the LORD, and the God who answers by fire, He is God.' And all the people answered and said, 'That is a good idea.'"

1 Chron 16:8, "Oh give thanks to the LORD, call upon His name; Make known His deeds among the peoples." (cf. Psa 105:1)

Psa 18:3, "I call upon the LORD, who is worthy to be praised, And I am saved from my enemies."

Psa 18:6, "In my distress I called upon the LORD, And cried to my God for help; He heard my voice out of His temple, And my cry for help before Him came into His ears."

Psa 31:17, "Let me not be put to shame, O LORD, for I call upon Thee; Let the wicked be put to shame, let them be silent in Sheol."

Psa 86:5, "For Thou, Lord [Adonai], art good, and ready to forgive, And abundant in lovingkindness to all who call upon Thee."

Psa 99:6, "Moses and Aaron were among His priests, And Samuel was among those who called on His name; They called upon the LORD, and He answered them."

Psa 105:1 [Psa 104:1 in LXX], "Oh give thanks to the LORD, call upon His name; Make known His deeds among the peoples." (cf. 1 Chron 16:8)

Psa 116:4, "Then I called upon the name of the LORD: 'O LORD, I beseech Thee, save my life!'"

Psa 116:13, "I shall lift up the cup of salvation, And call upon the name of the LORD."

Psa 118:5, "From *my* distress I called upon the LORD; The LORD answered me *and set me* in a large place."

Psa 145:18, "The LORD is near to all who call upon Him, To all who call upon Him in truth."

Lam 3:55, "I called on Thy name, O LORD, Out of the lowest pit."

Zeph 3:9, "For then I will give to the peoples purified lips, That all of them may call on the name of the LORD, To serve Him shoulder to shoulder."

Zeph 13:9, "And I will bring the third part through the fire, Refine them as silver is refined, And test them as gold is tested. They will call on My name, And I will answer them; I will say, 'They are My people,' And they will say, 'The LORD is my God.'"

Consider also the antithetical use of ἐπικαλέω in Psa 14:4:
> Psa 14:4, "Do all the workers of wickedness not know, Who eat up my people *as* they eat bread, *And* **do not call upon** the LORD?"
> The NAS did not capitalize "Lord" in this verse, whereas the KJV, ESV, and HCSB did.

c. **Inward Acceptance**:

16) πιστεύω–believed, John 1:50; 4:42; 8:30; 17:20-21; Acts 2:42; 4:4, 32; 8:12, 13; 9:42; 11:21; 13:12, 48; 14:1, 23; 15:5; 16:34; 17:12, 34; 18:8, 27; 19:18; Rom 3:22; 4:11, 24; 1 Cor 1:21; 3:5; for example:

Acts 9:42, "It became known all over Joppa, and many **believed** in the Lord"

Acts 14:1, "In Iconium they entered the synagogue of the Jews together, and spoke in such a manner that a large number of people believed, both of Jews and of Greeks"

Acts 17:12, "Many of them therefore believed"

Acts 18:8, "Crispus, the leader of the synagogue, believed in the Lord with all his household, and many of the Corinthians when they heard were believing and being baptized"

Acts 19:18, "Many also of those who had believed kept coming, confessing and disclosing their practices"

1 Cor 3:5, "What then is Apollos? And what is Paul? Servants **through whom you believed**, even as the Lord gave *opportunity* to each one"

πιστεύω (believed) + ἐπιστρέφω (turn):
> Acts 11:21, "And the hand of the Lord was with them, and a large number who **believed turned** to the Lord"

Other interesting uses of "believed": John 2:23-25; 8:31f.; 12:42; 20:28-29; Acts 8:13; 15:5; cf. Acts 21:20

2) Received:

(17) παραλαμβάνω (49 NT uses) "**received**" [or learned; took]:
> John 1:11-12, "He came to His own, and those who were His own **did not receive** Him. But as many as **received** Him, to them He gave the right to become children of God, *even* to those who believe in His name"
>
> 1 Cor 15:1-2, "Now I make known to you, brethren, the gospel which I preached to you, **which also you received**, in which also you stand, by which also you are saved, if you hold fast the word which I preached to you, unless you believed in vain"
>
> 1 Thess 2:13, "And for this reason we also constantly thank God that when **you received** from us the word of God's message, you accepted *it* not *as* the word of men, but *for* what it really is, the word of God, which also performs its work in you who believe"

(18) δέχομαι (58 NT uses), meaning "take, receive; welcome; accept, approve; put up with":
> Matt 10:40, "He who **receives** you **receives** Me, and he who **receives** Me **receives** Him who sent Me" (cf. Mark 9:37)
>
> Luke 10:8, "And whatever city you enter, and they **receive** you, eat what is set before you" (see also the negative response, Matt 10:15; Luke 10:10)
>
> Acts 8:14, "Now when the apostles in Jerusalem heard that Samaria **had received** the word of God, they sent them Peter and John"
>
> Acts 11:1, "Now the apostles and the brethren who were throughout Judea heard that the Gentiles also **had received** the word of God"
>
> Acts 17:11, "Now these were more noble-minded than those in Thessalonica, for they **received** the word with great eagerness, examining the Scriptures daily, *to see* whether these things were so"
>
> Eph 6:17, "And **take** the helmet of salvation, and the sword of the Spirit, which is the word of God"
>
> 1 Thess 1:6, "You also became imitators of us and of the Lord, **having received** the word in much tribulation with the joy of the Holy Spirit"
>
> 1 Thess 2:13, "And for this reason we also constantly thank God that when you received from us the word of God's message, you **accepted** *it* not *as* the word of men, but *for* what it really is, the word of God, which also performs its work in you who believe"
>
> James 1:21, "Therefore putting aside all filthiness and *all* that remains of wickedness, in humility **receive** the word implanted, which is able to save your souls"

δέχομαι + ἡ εἰρήνη – "**received** … **with peace**":
> Heb 11:31 (NKJ): "By faith the harlot Rahab did not perish with those who did not believe, when she **had received** the spies **with peace**"

19) πείθω (passive voice) - "**persuaded**"—use of persuade in the active voice above:

Luke 16:31, "But he said to him, 'If they do not listen to Moses and the Prophets, they will not be **persuaded** even if someone rises from the dead'"

Acts 17:4, "And some of them were **persuaded** [ἐπείσθησαν] and joined [προσεκληρώθησαν] Paul and Silas"

Acts 19:26, "This Paul has **persuaded** and turned away a considerable number of people"

Acts 28:23-24, "When they had set a day for Paul, they came to him at his lodging in large numbers; and he was explaining to them by solemnly testifying about the kingdom of God and trying to **persuade** them concerning Jesus, from both the Law of Moses and from the Prophets, from morning until evening. some were being **persuaded** by the things spoken, but others would not believe"

Seven Approaches to "Persuading" Others (ἐπείθοντο τοῖς λεγομένοις) in Acts 28:24[688]

→	→	→	✓	←	←	←
Evangelist persuades	Evangelist persuades	Evangelist persuades	God uses the Evangelist to persuade	God persuades	God persuades	God persuades
Evangelist does and says nothing	Using his own lifestyle; he says nothing	Using his own words or stories	Using His own words, as found in the Bible	Through evangelist's words or stories	Using evangelist's lifestyle; he says nothing	Evangelist does and says nothing

*Remembering 1 Cor 2:4, "And my message and my preaching were not in **persuasive** words of wisdom, but in demonstration of the Spirit and of power."

Persuasion as a result of God persuading:

Rom 8:38-39, "For **I am convinced** that neither death, nor life, nor angels, nor principalities, nor things present, nor things to come, nor powers, nor height, nor depth, nor any other created thing, shall be able to separate us from the love of God, which is in Christ Jesus our Lord."

On the Translation of πείθω in Rom 8:38

I Am Persuaded That	I Am Convinced That	I Am Absolutely Sure* That	I Am Sure* That	I Am Certain*
Geneva (1560), KJV, Webster's, Etheridge, Murdock, Darby, Noyes, Rotherham, Young's, ERV, ASV, NKJ, and CSB.	NAS (1979), NIV (1984, 2011), NRS, NAB (1991, 2010)⚭, GWN, TNIV, NLT, and NET.	NIRV (1998)	Tyndale (1534), Bishops, Douai-Rheims⚭, RSV, and ESV.	BBE (1949/1964) and NJB⚭.

*These translations seem to follow the Latin Vulgate which uses the adjective *certus* (meaning: fixed, settled, firm; certain; sure; resolved, reliable) here.

20) ἐπιστρέφω, turn:

Acts 11:21, "And the hand of the Lord was with them, and a large number who believed **turned** to the Lord"

1 Thess 1:9, "how you **turned** to God from idols to serve a living and true God"

OT Precedent:

Psa 51:13, "*Then* I will teach transgressors Thy ways, And sinners **will be converted** to Thee."

21) ἔρχομαι + ἡ ἐπίγνωσις + ἡ ἀλήθεια, come + knowledge + truth:

1 Tim 2:4, "who desires all men to be saved and to come to the knowledge of the truth."

2 Tim 3:7, "always learning and never able to come to the knowledge of the truth."

22) ὑπακούω + ἡ πίστις, obey + faith:

a)   "A great many of the priests were becoming obedient to the faith," Acts 6:7

---

[688]Chafer may have been theologically-motivated as he wrote: "The examples of soul-winning in the New Testament present a conspicuous contrast to some examples of present-day evangelism. So far as the divine record shows there seemed to be little urging or coaxing, nor was any person dealt with individually who had not first given evidence of a divinely wrought sense of need" (Lewis Sperry Chafer, *True Evangelism: Winning Souls by Prayer* [1911, 1919, Grand Rapids: Kregel, 1993], 58).

n3) ἡ ὑπακοή + ἡ πίστις, obedience [hearing unto obedience] + faith:

    a) "Through whom we have received grace and apostleship to bring about *the* **obedience of faith** among all the Gentiles, for His name's sake," Rom 1:5;

    b) "But now is manifested, and by the Scriptures of the prophets, according to the commandment of the eternal God, has been made known to all the nations, *leading* **to obedience of faith**," Rom 16:26;

εἰς ὑπακοὴν πίστεως – lit "unto an obedience of faith,"* identical phrase in both Rom 1:5 and 16:26 (NKJ), "for obedience to the faith"

*The issue surrounding the word "faith" is striking. Is "faith" a heartfelt trust in God, hence describing "from faith to faith," is it a body of truth to which one professes assent, or both? Perhaps Romans 8 and 10 provide the answer to this question.

d. Spiritual Transformation:

23) γεννάω–to beget; e.g. begotten, 1 Cor 4:15:

1 Cor 4:15, "For if you were to have countless tutors in Christ, yet *you would* not *have* many fathers; for in Christ Jesus I **became your father** through the gospel."

Philemon 10, "I appeal to you for my son Onesimus, whom **I have begotten** *while* in my chains."

Translations of the Verb γεννάω in 1 Cor 4:15

Tyndale (1534), Bishops, Geneva, KJV, Darby, DRA✳, NKJ	Young's (1862)	Rotherham (1868), ERV, ASV	Noyes	BBE (1949)	RSV (1952), NAS, NIV, NAB, NIRV, TNIV, NET, NLT, HCSB, ESV	NJB✳ (1985), CSBO
I have begotten you	I did beget you	I begat you	I begot you	I have given birth to you	I became your father	It was I who fathered you
For though ye have ten thousande instructours in Christ: yet have ye not many fathers. In Christ Iesu I have begotten you thorowe the gospell.	for if a myriad of child-conductors ye may have in Christ, yet not many fathers; for in Christ Jesus, through the good news, I—I did beget you.	For, though myriads of tutors ye should have in Christ, yet not many fathers; for, in Christ Jesus, through means of the joyful message, I, begat you.	For though ye have ten thousand teachers in Christ, yet have ye not many fathers; for in Christ Jesus I begot you through the gospel.	For even if you had ten thousand teachers in Christ, you have not more than one father: for in Christ Jesus I have given birth to you through the good news.	For though you have countless guides in Christ, you do not have many fathers. For I became your father in Christ Jesus through the gospel.	for even though you might have ten thousand slaves to look after you in Christ, you still have no more than one father, and it was I who fathered you in Christ Jesus, by the gospel.

From at OT perspective, Moses spoke of God begetting Israel:

Deut 32:18, "Of the Rock *who* **begot** you, you are unmindful, And have forgotten the God **who fathered** you."

In the NT the verb γεννάω is juxtaposed with the concept of being begotten of God (using NKJ translation):

John 1:12-13, "But as many as received Him, to them He gave the right to become children of God, to those who believe in His name: **who were born**, not of blood, nor of the will of the flesh, nor of the will of man, but of God."

1 John 2:29, "If you know that He is righteous, you know that everyone who practices righteousness is born of Him."

1 John 3:9, "Whoever **has been born of** God does not sin, for His seed remains in him; and he cannot sin, because he **has been born of** God."

1 John 4:7, "Beloved, let us love one another, for love is of God; and everyone who loves **is born of** God and knows God."

1 John 5:1, "Whoever believes that Jesus is the Christ **is born of** God, and everyone who loves Him **who begot** also loves him **who is begotten of** Him"

1 John 5:4:, "For whatever **is born of** God overcomes the world. And this is the victory that has overcome the world—our faith."

1 John 5:18, "We know that whoever **is born of** God does not sin; but he **who has been born of** God keeps himself, and the wicked one does not touch him"

This verb is also used in the command form, of a person needing to be "born again":

John 3:3, "Jesus answered and said to him, 'Most assuredly, I say to you, unless one **is born** again, he cannot see the kingdom of God.'"

John 3:5, "Jesus answered, 'Most assuredly, I say to you, unless one **is born** of water and the Spirit, he cannot enter the kingdom of God.'"

John 3:6, "That which is born of the flesh is flesh, and that which **is born** of the Spirit is spirit."

John 3:7, "Do not marvel that I said to you, 'You must **be born** again.'"

John 3:8, "The wind blows where it wishes, and you hear the sound of it, but cannot tell where it comes from and where it goes. So is everyone who **is born** of the Spirit."

24) μαθητεύω (4 total NT uses) – to teach, make disciples, win disciples, or proselytize—Hence, disciples are won to Christ (cf. "fishers of men"):

a) "To become a disciple" (NAS; aorist passive of μαθητεύω):

Indicating past completed action, which was at the beginning of becoming a disciple!

Matt 13:52, "And Jesus said to them, 'Therefore every scribe **who has become a disciple** of [into] the kingdom of heaven [Διὰ τοῦτο πᾶς γραμματεὺς μαθητευθεὶς εἰς τὴν βασιλείαν τῶν οὐρανῶν] is like a head of a household, who brings out of his treasure things new and old.'"

Matt 27:57, "And when it was evening, there came a rich man from Arimathea, named Joseph, who himself **had also become a disciple** of Jesus [ὃς καὶ αὐτὸς ἐμαθήτευσεν τῷ Ἰησοῦ]"

b) To win a disciples (NIV, aorist active of μαθητεύω):

Acts 14:21 (NIV), "They preached the good news in that city and **won** a large number of **disciples**"

Compare with Acts 6:7, "and the number of disciples continued to increased greatly in Jerusalem"

Matt 28:19 (mine), "Go therefore and **win disciples** of all the nations, baptizing them in the name of the Father and the Son and the Holy Spirit"

Views of Discipleship (impacted by or impacting the translation of μαθητεύσατε in Matthew 28:19)[689]

Impacting Others (the outer life)							Personalistic/Individualistic (the inner life)				
Win disciples		Multiply disciples			Mentor leaders		Follow Christ			Follow the Apostles	
Win souls, Acts 14: 21 [NIV]	Teach others to win disciples	Teach others to win disciples and live the Christian life	Teach others to live the Christian life and win disciples	Teach others to live the Christian life	Teach others to teach and lead others	Teach others to lead others	Identifica-tion with Christ	Imitate Christ	Live as a sequel to the life of Christ	Live as the apostles	Imitate the apostles
Vita evangelica (Wanderprediger?)		*regula evangelica (vir evangelicus?)*					*Identificatio Christi*	*Imitatio Christ*	*Sequela Christi*	*Vita apostolica*	*Imitatio apostolorum*

c) Consider the reoriented emphases in translating using "proselytize" for μαθητεύω (translations mine):

Matt 13:52, "And Jesus said to them, 'Therefore every scribe **proselytized** into the kingdom of heaven is like a head of a household, who brings out of his treasure things new and old.'"

Matt 27:57, "And when it was evening, there came a rich man from Arimathea, named Joseph, who himself **was proselytized** unto Jesus."

Acts 14:21, "They evangelized that city and **proselytized** many."

Matt 28:19, "Go **proselytize** in all nations, baptizing them in the name of the Father and the Son and the Holy Spirit"

e. **Divine Process:**

25) οὐ + δίδωμι (2,545 uses in LXX and NT), meaning to give:

Deut 29:4, "Yet to this day the LORD **has not given** [οὐ + δίδωμι] you a heart to know, nor eyes to see, nor ears to hear."

Yet consider Deut 30:6! "Moreover the LORD your God will circumcise your heart and the heart of your descendants, to love the LORD your God with all your heart and with all your soul, in order that you may live."

---

[689]Note the various translations of this term over the history of English (and French) Bible translation in Chapter 26, "Follow-up Is Important."

26) God has many people, even prior to their hearing and believing:

ὁ κύριος + λέγω + μή + φοβέω + λαλέω + μή + σιωπάω:

"And the Lord said to Paul in the night by a vision, 'Do not be afraid *any longer*, but go on speaking and do not be silent; For I am with you, and no man will attack you in order to harm you, for I have many people in this city [διότι λαός ἐστίν μοι πολὺς ἐν τῇ πόλει ταύτῃ]'" Acts 18:9-10.

a)   λέγω: God speaks;

b)   μή + φοβέω: Fear not;

c)   λαλέω: Speak;

d)   μή + σιωπάω: Be not silent;

e)   διότι ἐγώ εἰμι μετὰ σοῦ: For I am with you;

f)   καὶ οὐδεὶς ἐπιθήσεταί σοι τοῦ κακῶσαί σε: and no man will attack you in order to harm you;

g)   διότι λαός ἐστίν μοι πολὺς ἐν τῇ πόλει ταύτῃ:

NIV, "because I have many people in this city";

ESV, "for I have many in this city who are my people."

27) ἀκούω + μανθάνω + ἔρχομαι - "hear, learn, and come to the Father [unto salvation]":

John 6:45, "It is written in the prophets, 'And they shall all be taught of God.' Everyone who has **heard** and **learned** from the Father, **come**s to Me:

ἀκούω, hear [from the Father];

μανθάνω, learn [from the Father];

ἔρχομαι, come [to Jesus].

28) ἐνάρχομαι + τὸ ἔργον + ἀγαθός – begin + work + good:

"*For I am* confident of this very thing, that He who **began a good work** in you [ὅτι ὁ ἐναρξάμενος ἐν ὑμῖν ἔργον ἀγαθὸν] He who began a good work in you will perfect it until the day of Christ Jesus," Phil 1:6.

i.e. the work of God has a beginning!

f.   Metaphorical:

29) διανοίγω - "**open**":

a)   ἧς ὁ Κύριος διήνοιξε τὴν καρδίαν προσέχειν– "whose heart the Lord opened to respond," Acts 16:14:

New Testament Uses of "Open" – διανοίγω

Christ opens the mouth of a mute man	God opens a heart unto salvation	Christ reveals who He is	Christ explains the Scriptures	Christ opens the disciples' minds to understand the Scriptures	Paul opens the Scriptures in the synagogue*
Mark 7:34	Acts 16:14	Luke 24:31	Luke 24:32	Luke 24:45	Acts 17:3

*Psa 51:15, "O Lord, open my lips, That my mouth may declare Thy praise."

n4) ὁ καρπός – "**fruit**," John 4:36, "fruit for life eternal," 15:8, 16; Rom 1:13:*

John 4:36, "Already he who reaps is receiving wages, and is gathering fruit for life eternal; that he who sows and he who reaps may rejoice together."

John 15:8, "By this is My Father glorified, that you bear much fruit, and *so* prove to be My disciple."

John 15:16, "You did not choose Me, but I chose you, and appointed you, that you should go and bear fruit, and *that* your fruit should remain, that whatever you ask of the Father in My name, He may give to you."

Rom 1:13, "And I do not want you to be unaware, brethren, that often I have planned to come to you (and have been prevented thus far) in order that I might obtain some fruit among you also, even as among the rest of the Gentiles."

*These are examples of many more metaphors like this.

n5) ἡ ἀπαρχή (8 total NT uses) - "firstfruit":

Rom 16:5, "also *greet* the church that is in their house. Greet Epaenetus, my beloved, who is the **first convert** to Christ from Asia." [Asia being Ephesus and surroundings]

Rom 16:5 (NKJ), "Likewise *greet* the church that is in their house. Greet my beloved Epaenetus, who is the **firstfruits** of Achaia to Christ." [Achaia being Corinth and surroundings]

1 Cor 16:15, "Now I urge you, brethren (you know the household of Stephanas, that they were the **first fruits** of Achaia, and that they have devoted themselves for ministry to the saints)"

g. Result:

n6a) εἰς Χριστὸν –in Christ (13 verses total):

"Or do you not know that all of us who have been baptized into Christ Jesus have been baptized into His death?" Rom 6:3;

"Greet my beloved Epaenetus, who is the firstfruits of Achaia to Christ [Ἀσπάσασθε Ἐπαίνετον τὸν ἀγαπητόν μου, ὅς ἐστιν ἀπαρχὴ τῆς Ἀχαΐας εἰς χριστόν," Rom 16:5;

"Therefore the Law has become our tutor *to lead us* to Christ, that we may be justified by faith," Gal 3:24;

"For all of you who were baptized into Christ have clothed yourselves with Christ," Gal 3:27.

n6b) ἐν Χριστῷ –in Christ (97 verses total):*

"For the wages of sin is death, but the free gift of God is eternal life in Christ Jesus our Lord," Rom 6:23;

"There is therefore now no condemnation for those who are in Christ Jesus," Rom 8:1;

"So we, who are many, are one body in Christ, and individually members one of another," Rom 12:5;

"Greet Andronicus and Junias, my kinsmen, and my fellow prisoners, who are outstanding among the apostles, who also were in Christ before me," Rom 16:7;

"To the church of God which is at Corinth, to those who have been sanctified in Christ Jesus, saints by calling, with all who in every place call upon the name of our Lord Jesus Christ, their *Lord* and ours," 1 Cor 1:2;

"I thank my God always concerning you, for the grace of God which was given you in Christ Jesus," 1 Cor 1:4…

*Samples only.

n6c) Χριστὸς ἐν ὑμῖν, Christ in you:

"And if Christ is in you, though the body is dead because of sin, yet the spirit is alive because of righteousness," Rom 8:10;

"Test yourselves *to see* if you are in the faith; examine yourselves! Or do you not recognize this about yourselves, that Jesus Christ is in you-- unless indeed you fail the test?" 2 Cor 13:5;

"My children, with whom I am again in labor until Christ is formed in you—" Gal 4:19;

"To whom God willed to make known what is the riches of the glory of this mystery among the Gentiles, which is Christ in you, the hope of glory," Col 1:27.

n7) ἐπιστολή + Χριστός, "An epistle of Christ":

"And if Christ is in you, though the body is dead because of sin, yet the spirit is alive because of righteousness," Rom 8:10;

h. Further OT precedents:

30) συνθέλω (hapax) - "to consent with, have the same wish as":

Deut 13:8 (of the false teacher), "you shall not **yield** to him or listen to him; and your eye shall not pity him, nor shall you spare or conceal him"

p1) καὶ ἀπὸ τῶν δικαίων τῶν πολλῶν [Heb: וּמַצְדִּיקֵי הָרַבִּים] – "they that [turn] many to righteousness":

Dan 12:3, "And those who have insight will shine brightly like the brightness of the expanse of heaven, **and those who lead the many to righteousness**, like the stars forever and ever."

i. Profitable and Unprofitable Communication, 1 Cor 14:

1) Unprofitable Ministry #1, 1 Cor 14:2:

1 Cor 14:2, "For one who speaks in a tongue does not speak to men, but to God; **for no one understands**, but in *his* spirit he speaks mysteries."

(31) οὐδεὶς γὰρ ἀκούει [ἀκούω], "no one can hear."

2) Profitable Ministry #1, 1 Cor 14:3:

1 Cor 14:3, "But one who prophesies speaks to men for edification and exhortation and consolation."

(n8) ἡ οἰκοδομή, "edification" (once);

(n9) ἡ παράκλησις, "exhortation";

(n10) ἡ παραμυθία, "consolation."

3) Profitable Ministry #2, 1 Cor 14:4-5:

1 Cor 14:4-5, "One who speaks in a tongue **edifies** himself; but one who prophesies **edifies** the church. Now I wish that you all spoke in tongues, but *even* more that you would prophesy; and greater is one who prophesies than one who speaks in tongues, unless he interprets, so that the church may receive **edifying**."

(32) οἰκοδομέω, "to edify" (twice);

(n8) ἡ οἰκοδομή, "edification" (twice).

4) Profitable Ministry #3, 1 Cor: 14:6:

1 Cor 14:6, "But now, brethren, if I come to you speaking in tongues, what **shall I profit** you, unless I speak to you either by way of **revelation** or of **knowledge** or of **prophecy** or of **teaching**?"

(33) ὠφελέω, "profit";

(n11) ἡ ἀποκάλυψις, "revelation";

(n12) ἡ γνῶσις, "knowledge";

(n13) ἡ προφητεία, "prophecy";

(n14) ἡ διδαχή, "teaching."

5) Unprofitable Ministry #2, 1 Cor: 14:8:

1 Cor 14:8, "For if the bugle produces an indistinct sound, who will prepare himself for battle?"

(a1) ἄδηλος + ἡ φωνη, "unclear + sound [voice]";

(34) παρασκευάζω, "prepare himself."

6) Profitable Ministry #4, 1 Cor: 14:9:

1 Cor 14:9, "So also you, unless you utter by the tongue speech that is **clear**, how will it be **known** what **is spoken**? For you will be speaking into the air."

(a2) εὔσημος, "clear"—hence clarity of speech;

(35) γινώσκω + λαλέω, "know + say [passive]."

7) Unprofitable Ministry #3, 1 Cor: 14:11:

1 Cor 14:11, "If then I do not know the meaning of the language, I shall be to the one who speaks a barbarian, and the one who speaks will be a barbarian to me."

(36) μὴ + εἰδῶ, "not + know."

8) Profitable Ministry #5, 1 Cor 14:12:

1 Cor 14:12, "So also you, since you are zealous of spiritual *gifts*, seek to abound for the edification of the church."

(n8) ἡ οἰκοδομή, "edification" (thrice).

9) Unprofitable Ministry #4, 1 Cor: 14:14:

1 Cor 14:14 (NKJ), "For if I pray in a tongue, my spirit prays, but my understanding is unfruitful."

(n15) ἡ γλῶσσα + ἄκαρπος, "a tongue + unfruitful."

10) Profitable Ministry #6, 1 Cor: 14:19:

1 Cor 14:19, "however, in the church I desire to speak five words with my mind, that I may instruct others also, rather than ten thousand words in a tongue."

(37) λόγους διὰ τοῦ νοός μου λαλῆσαι, "speak words with my mind";

(38) κατηχέω, "teach."

11) Profitable Ministry #7, 1 Cor: 14:24-25:

> 1 Cor 14:24-25, "But if all prophesy, and an unbeliever or an ungifted man enters, **he is convicted** by all, he is **called to account** by all; the secrets of his heart **are disclosed**; and so **he will fall on his face** and **worship** God, declaring that God is certainly among you."

(39) ἐλέγχω, "convict";

(40) ἀνακρίνω, "to examine";

(41) γίνομαι + φανερός, "be + disclosed";

(42) πίπτω + τὸ πρόσωπον, "fall + face";

(43) προσκυνέω, "worship."

j. Interesting Combinations:

1) ἔλαβον ... τοῖς πιστεύουσιν, John 1:12 (receive and [those] believe[ing])
2) ἀκούω, hearing [from the Father], μανθάνω, learning [from the Father], ἔρχομαι, coming [to Jesus], John 6:45
2) πιστεύσας ἐπέστρεψεν, Acts 11:21 (believed and turned)
3) ἐπείσθησαν and προσεκληρώθησαν, Acts 17:4 (persuaded and joined)
4) ἐδέξαντο ... ἀνακρίνοντες, Acts 17:11 (received and examining)
5) ἀκούοντες ἐπίστευον καὶ ἐβαπτίζοντο, Acts 18:8 (hearing, believing, and being baptized)
6) πεπιστευκότων ἤρχοντο ἐξομολογούμενοι καὶ ἀναγγέλλοντες, Acts 19:18 (believing, coming, confessing, disclosing)
7) μετανοεῖν καὶ ἐπιστρέφειν, Acts 26:20 (repent and turned)
8) ἐπείθοντο or ἠπίστουν, Acts 28:24 (persuaded or not believing)
9) εὐηγγελισάμην, παρελάβετε, ἑστήκατε, σῴζεσθε, εὐηγγελισάμην, κατέχετε, ἐπιστεύσατε, 1 Cor 15:1-2 (preached, received, stand, saved, preached, hold fast, and believed)

k. Salvation rejected:

44) σκληρύνω: to make hard, rough, or harsh; passive, to be stubborn, "But when some were becoming **hardened** and disobedient," Acts 19:9
Like the hardening of Pharoah's heart, Exo 7:22ff.
Like the people of Israel, Psa 95:8 (cf. Heb 3:8ff)

45) ἀπειθέω: disobedience (and disbelieving):
   a) "But the Jews which believed not" (KJV), Acts 17:5 (Byzantine Textform [BYZ])
   b) "But when some were becoming hardened and **disobedient**," Acts 19:9

46) ἀπιστέω: not believing:
   a) "but others would not believe," Acts 28:24

b)   As used in 2 Tim 2:13…

Approaches to Translating 2 Timothy 2:13

Greek	Latin Vulgate (Migne, 1880)	Wycliffe (1388)	Tyndale (1534); Coverdale; Geneva; KJV	Douais-Rheims (1899)	Bishops' (1568); Darby	NAB (1970, etc.); NLT; NET	ERV (1885); ASV	RSV (1952); NAS; NKJ; NIV; CSB; ESV	NJB (1985)	Bible in Basic English (1949)	Young's (1862, etc.)
εἰ ἀπιστοῦμεν	si non credimus	if we bileuen not	Yf we beleve not	If we believe not	If we be vnfaythful	If we are unfaithful	if we are faithless	if we are faithless	If we are faithless	If we are without faith	if we are not stedfast
English translation and its implication	"Believe not": point-in-time implication, implying a lack of faith in a critical circumstance			"Unfaithful": implies a general quality of lacking faith in a linear sense		"Faithless": seems to imply never having faith, completely devoid of faith			Much like faithless		To lack faith in a particular circumstance?
ἐκεῖνος πιστὸς μένει	ille fidelis permanet	he dwellith feithful	yet abideth he faithfull	he continueth faithful	he abideth faithfull	he remains faithful	he abideth faithful	he remains faithful	he is faithful still	still he keeps faith	he remaineth stedfast

From Syriac Peshitta:
  Etheridge (1849): "And if we believe him not, He in his faithfulness abideth"
  Murdock (1851), "And if we shall have not believed in him, he abideth in his fidelity"

Perhaps the best implication of 2 Tim 2:13 is this "if we lack faith, he remains faithful"
  1 John 1:9, "He is faithful and just to forgive us our sins…"

47) ζηλόω: being moved to jealousy, Acts 17:5 (BYZ reads quite differently here);

48) πίμπλημι + ὁ ζῆλος: filled with jealousy, Acts 5:17; 13:45;

49) ἀντιτάσσομαι: resist, oppose, Acts 18:6;

50) βλασφημέω: blaspheme, Acts 18:6.

l.   Results of false prophecying:

51) διαστρέφω: turn away [from the faith], Acts 13:8; cf. Luke 23:2; Acts 13:10
    Compare with Ezek 13:18-23, which speaks of the false prophetesses, using the Hebrew *tsuwd* (צוּד), meaning "to hunt" (5 times in this passage); and the Greek, διαστρέφω, meaning to pervert, distort, mislead, lead astray, cf. Ezek 13:18-23;

52) ἀνατρέπω: overturn or subvert [whole households], Tit 1:11.

m.   Metaphorical terms for the result of evangelism:

1)   General Metaphorical Results:

(53) λάμπω + τὸ φῶς, "**Shine** + the **light** [of the gospel]":
    Matt 5:16, "Let your light shine before men in such a way that they may see your good works, and glorify your Father who is in heaven."

b)   The **aroma** of the gospel goes forth:

(n16) ἡ ὀσμή: meaning an aroma:
    2 Cor 2:14, "But thanks be to God, who always leads us in His triumph in Christ, and manifests through us the sweet aroma of the knowledge of Him in every place."
    2 Cor 2:16, "to the one an aroma from death to death, to the other an aroma from life to life. And who is adequate for these things?"

(n17) ἡ εὐωδία: meaning a fragrance:

> 2 Cor 2:15, "For we are a fragrance of Christ to God among those who are being saved and among those who are perishing."

54) ἐγγίζω + ἡ βασιλεία, "The **kingdom** [rule] of God **comes near**":

Following up on preaching that "the kingdom of heaven is at hand" Matt 3:2; 4:17; 10:7; and Mark 1:15, comes the post-evangelism affirmation that "the kingdom [or rule] of God has come near to you"—even when it is rejected!

(1) Where received, "And whatever city you enter, and they receive you, eat what is set before you; and heal those in it who are sick, and say to them, 'The kingdom of God has come near to you.'" (Luke 10:8-9)

(2) Where not received, "But whatever city you enter and they do not receive you, go out into its streets and say, 'Even the dust of your city which clings to our feet, we wipe off *in protest* against you; yet be sure of this, that the kingdom of God has come near.'" (Luke 10:10-11)

2) **Particular Metaphorical Results**:

55) ζωγρέω – "from now on you will be **catching** men [taking men alive]," Luke 5:10

(1) Only other NT use is of the Devil catching men in 2 Tim 2:26, "and they may come to their senses *and escape* from the snare of the devil, **having been held captive** [taken alive] by him to do his will"

(2) Compare with its LXX use in Joshua 2:13, "and **spare** [capture alive] my father and my mother and my brothers and my sisters, with all who belong to them"

(3) Add to this, Joshua 2:13, "and deliver our lives from death" [καὶ ἐξελεῖσθε (from ἐξαιρέω) τὴν ψυχήν μου ἐκ θανάτου]

56) ἁρπάζω [to take by force; take away, carry off; catch up (into heaven)] - "**snatching** them out of the fire," Jude 23

57) ἕλκω/ ἑλκύω [draw, pull, haul, drag]:

(1) This verb is used of Peter drawing his sword (John 18:10), drawing up a net (John 21:6, 11), as well as Paul being dragged before the authorities (Acts 16:19; 21:30) and Christians being dragged to court (James 2:6)

(2) It is used of the need for God to draw someone to Christ, John 6:44:
> John 6:44, "No one can come to Me, unless the Father who sent Me draws him; and I will raise him up on the last day."

(3) It is also used of Jesus "drawing" all [men] unto himself, if He is lifted up, John 12:32 (cf. Eph 1:21-22; Phil 2:9-10):
> John 12:32, "And I, if I be lifted up from the earth, will draw all men to Myself."

> It is highly doubtful, however, that John 12:32 is a universalist statement, meaning that all will be saved because Jesus was lifted up on a cross, as that would contradict the particularism taught in other passages, such as John 1:11-13.

58) Heb. *laqach* - "he who **snatches** souls is wise," Prov 11:30

Translations of *laqach* in Prov 11:30

Greek LXX (200 B.C.)	Brenton LXX (1844/1851)	Cambridge (1949)	RSV (1952)	NRSV (1989); NAB✣; GNT	CSB (2003)	Vulgate (375)	NJB✣ (1985)	Jewish Tanakh (1985)	ESV	Wycliffe 2nd ed (1388)	Youngs Lit (1898)	Coverdale (1535)	Bishops (1595); KJV; NKJ; NIV; NET	Darby (1885); ASV; NASB	NLT (2004)	DRA✣ (1899)
ἀφαιρέω	Negative subject of verb					Suscipio	Captivate		Capture	Take			Win			Gain
ἀφαιροῦνται δὲ ἄωροι ψυχαὶ παρανόμων	but the souls of transgressors are cut off before their time	but violent behaviour takes away souls	but lawlessness takes away lives	but violence takes lives away	but violence takes lives	et qui suscipit animas sapiens est	the sage captiveates souls	A wise man captiveates people	and whoever captures souls is wise	and he that takith soulis, is a wijs man	And whoso is taking souls *is* wise	a wyse man also wynneth mens soules	and he that winneth mens soules is wise	and the wise winneth souls	a wise person wins friends	and he that gaineth souls, is wise

n18) τὸ τέκνον + μᾶλλον, "For more are the children of the desolate Than of the one who has a husband [πολλὰ τὰ τέκνα τῆς ἐρήμου μᾶλλον ἢ τῆς ἐχούσης τὸν ἄνδρα]", Gal 4:27:

(1) The believer may have spiritual children [through evangelism] 30, 60, or 100 times, Mark 4:20

    (a) Likewise, Gal 4:28 calls these spiritual children "children of promise"

(2) Whereas, it is impossible for a woman to bear so many children naturally!

59) οἰκοδομέω, Of the church being "built up" and "multiplying" in a time of peace:

Acts 9:31, "So the church throughout all Judea and Galilee and Samaria enjoyed peace, being built up [οἰκοδομούμεναι]; and, going on in the fear of the Lord and in the comfort of the Holy Spirit, it continued to increase"

60) οὐ κενὴ γέγονεν – work "was not in vain," 1 Thess 2:1.

n.   Results to the Evangelist:

61) Confession [ὁμολογέω] before men yields Christ's confession before God:

a)   Matt 10:32, "Everyone therefore who shall confess Me before men, I will also confess him before My Father who is in heaven"

b)   Luke 12:8, "And I say to you, everyone who confesses Me before men, the Son of Man shall confess him also before the angels of God"

Note also the opposite response:

a)   Mark 8:38, "For whoever is ashamed of Me and My words in this adulterous and sinful generation, the Son of Man will also be ashamed of him when He comes in the glory of His Father with the holy angels"

2)   Deliverance from guilt:

62) ῥύομαι – Ezek 3:19, "Yet if you have warned the wicked, and he does not turn from his wickedness or from his wicked way, he shall die in his iniquity; but you have delivered yourself"

b)   Two phrases in James 5:19-20, My brethren, if any among you strays from the truth, and one turns him back, let him know that he who turns a sinner from the error of his way will save his soul from death, and will cover a multitude of sins:

(63) σῴζω – Will save his soul from death [σώσει ψυχὴν ἐκ θανάτου]

(64) καλύπτω – Will cover a multitude of sins [καλύψει πλῆθος ἁμαρτιῶν]

3)   Edification occurs:

n19) ἡ κοινωνία – Phil 1:5, "your **participation** in the Gospel" (cf. Phm 6)

n20) ὁ συγκοινωνός – 1 Cor 9:23, "that I may become a **fellow-partaker** of it [Gospel]."

    4) Extreme rejoicing:
       65) περισσεύω – "may cause the giving of thanks **to abound** to the glory of God" (τὴν εὐχαριστίαν περισσεύσῃ εἰς τὴν δόξαν τοῦ θεοῦ), 2 Cor 4:15

    5) God is glorified:
       66) μεγαλύνω (exalting) – "For they were hearing them speaking with tongues and exalting God," Acts 10:46

    6) Lasting spiritual fruit:
       n21) Those saved as a crown of glory – Τίς γὰρ ἡμῶν ἐλπὶς ἢ χαρὰ ἢ στέφανος καυχήσεως; Ἢ οὐχὶ καὶ ὑμεῖς (1 Thess 2:19):
         [NKJ] –"For what *is* our hope, or joy, or crown of rejoicing? *Is it* not even you"
         [NAS] – "For who is our hope or joy or crown of exultation? Is it not even you"
       n22) Those saved as glory and joy – "For you are our glory and our joy Ὑμεῖς γάρ ἐστε ἡ δόξα ἡμῶν καὶ ἡ χαρά]," 1 Thess 2:20

    7) Purpose for living:
       67) ζάω – to live; 1 Thess 3:8, "For now we live, if you stand fast in the Lord"

o. Divine result of evangelism:

    68) κλητός—[verbally] called, invited, Rom 1:6, "called of Jesus Christ" (cf. Matt 22:14)
       Rom 1:5-6, "through whom we have received grace and apostleship to bring about *the* obedience of faith among all the Gentiles, for His name's sake, among whom you also are the called of Jesus Christ"

    2) The church grows (note these verbs mentioned in the section above, "Spiritual Dynamic")
       a) αὐξάνω, to grow, spread, increase, and become important, Acts 6:7; 12:24; 19:20; Col 1:6
       b) διαφέρω, meaning carry through, spread, Acts 13:49
       c) ἰσχύω, to able, can, have resources, win over, defeat, be strong, grow strong, Acts 19:20
       d) πληθύνω, intrans. grow, increase, hence "be multiplied," Acts 12:24 (cf. 2 Cor 9:10)

p. Word *NOT USED* for calling for commitment in the NT:

    1) ποιέω – make, cause (KJV), compel (Geneva [1560])
       2 Chron 34:32, "Moreover, he **made** ["caused," KJV] all who were present in Jerusalem and Benjamin to stand *with him*."
       2 Chron 34:33, "Josiah removed all the abominations from all the lands belonging to the sons of Israel, and **made** ["compelled," Geneva Bible] all who were present in Israel to serve the LORD their God."

6. The Enumeration of New Testament Terms:

    1. **PERSON**—terms highlighting the person involved in evangelism:

       Approximately 50 NT nouns used positively, negatively, or not for evangelism;

    2. **METHOD**—terms highlighting the method of evangelism:

       Approximately 174 NT verbs and 22 nouns used in evangelizing contexts;

       Approximately 88 communicatory verbs not used for evangelism, as well as 23 nouns;

    3. **MOVEMENT AND/OR LOCATION** of Evangelism Ministry;

    4. **SPIRITUAL DYNAMIC** of the Word of God;

    5. **RESULT** of Evangelism Ministry:

       Approximately 68 verbs, 22 nouns, 2 adjectives, and one preposition related to actual evangelizing.

7. **An Evaluation of Biblical Terms:**

   a. These terms show the **character** of the evangelism that the Bible speaks of.

   b. The **breadth** and **depth** of the evangelism commanded by God's Word is also clarified.

   c. These terms show the **style** and **types** of evangelism intended in these biblical passages.

      1) "Showing" is not one of the terms used [except KJV's equivocal "shewing" as a translation of εὐαγγελίζω] (e.g. "Showing the Love of Christ"), with the exception of an equivocal translation of φανερόω (see above).

      2) Nor does the concept of μαρτυρέω express a non-verbal "witness".

      3) Nor is a non-verbal "lifestyle" a replacement for verbal evangelism, as is often ascribed to λάμπω in Matt 5:16 and in the noun ἀναστροφὴν (KJV, conversation; NAS, behavior) in 1 Pet 2:12 (see above)

J. Toward a Working Definition:

Introduction: Two portions explain the essence of the proclamation in the book of Acts:

Acts 17:2-3:
According to Paul's custom (κατὰ δὲ τὸ εἰωθὸς τῷ Παύλῳ)
He went to the synagogue
Paul reasoned (διελέξατο, aorist, 3rd person sg of διαλέγομαι)
This reasoning included opening (διανοίγων, participle)
And setting forth (παρατιθέμενος, participle)
Paul's proclamation was summarized as [bold] proclamation (καταγγέλλω, imp, mid, ind 1st p sg)
Length: three Sabbaths
Message: suffering, resurrection of the Christ

Acts 19:8:
Going to the synagogue
Paul spake boldly (ἐπαρρησιάζετο, indicative imperfect 3rd sg of παρρησιάζομαι)
This bold speech included reasoning (διαλεγόμενος, participle)
And persuading (πείθων, participle)
Length: three months
Message: kingdom of God

For methodology in Luke, note both the itinerant ministry (cf. 1 Cor 4:11) and the stationary ministry:
Traveling itinerant ministry of Jesus, Luke 4:42-43 (I must evangelize other cities also)
Traveling itinerant ministry of Jesus, Luke 8:1 (preaching and evangelizing)
Traveling itinerant ministry of His twelve disciples, Luke 9:6 (evangelizing and healing)
Traveling itinerant ministry of the seventy others, Luke 10:1, 3, 5
(appointed and sent; go and say)
Stationary ministry of Jesus in Temple, Luke 20:1 (teaching and evangelizing)

Signs and Wonders in Paul's First Missionary Journey
As a brief investigation into the necessity for the miraculous for effective evangelism[690]

City	Ministry term	Response	Miraculous	Response	Church founded?
Salamis	Proclaimed (καταγγέλλω) the word of God	None listed	None listed	None listed	Likely (cf. Acts 15:34)
Paphos	None listed	Sought to hear the word of God	Elymas blinded for a time	Proconsul believes, "being amazed at the teaching (didache) of the Lord"	Likely (cf. Acts 15:34)
Pisidian Antioch	Sermon of Paul, titled a "word of exhortation"	"Many of the Jews and of the God-fearing proselytes followed Paul and Barnabas"	None listed	None listed	Yes
Iconium	Speaking in such a manner that many believed … bold speech	Many believed	None listed	None listed	Yes
Lystra	Evangelizing	Lame man was listening	Heals lame man	Offer sacrifices to Paul and Barnabas; end up stoning Paul	Yes
Derbe	Evangelized	Won many disciples	None listed	None listed	Yes (cf. Acts 14:20-21; 16:1; 20:4)
Perga	Spoke the word	None listed	None listed	None listed	Likely (cf. Acts 14:25)

---

[690]See John Wimber, *Power Evangelism* (San Francisco: Harper and Row, 1986; North Pomfret, VT: Trafalgar Square, 2000).

Some thoughts:
1. Signs and wonders are not noted in every city in Paul's journey; and therefore do not appear as a necessary or preferred preparation for the Gospel
2. Signs and wonders are misunderstood in Lystra, the focus turning to the "healer" [Paul], rather than to God; therefore showing that a miraculous healing must be interpreted and received by the listeners in order to have a positive effect for the Gospel
3. The Bible teaches that the role of miracles is that of confirmation of the message already given (Deut 18:20-22), although at times God allows the miracle as a test to the hearers (Deut 13:1-5); so in the NT, miracles confirmed the message (Mark 16:20; Heb 2:3-4), though John the Baptist did no sign and his message was true (John 10:41).
4. Note the order of the verbs that include healing in the Gospels, healing is almost always listed after the teaching and preaching, for example:
    Matt 9:35, "And Jesus was going about all the cities and the villages, teaching in their synagogues, and proclaiming the gospel of the kingdom, and healing every kind of disease and every kind of sickness"

Contextual definition:
    Evangelizing is that verbal proclamation of the Gospel of Jesus Christ to the unsaved with the intent of leading them to salvation, in other words, beginning their walk with Jesus Christ (Gal 3:2; Phil 1:6; Heb 6:1):
        Evangelizing is exemplified in two of the first three commands of Christ, repent, believe the Gospel, and come follow Me and I will make you become fishers of men (Mark 1:14-17);
        Evangelizing is prerequisite for a person to become a disciple of Jesus Christ, who upon verbal confession ought to be baptized and taught to obey all that Christ has commanded (Matt 28:19-20);
        Evangelizing is distinct from and yet overlaps with the proclamation that is meant to strengthen and exhort believers (Acts 14:22), whereas Christ crucified for sins must remain the center of all true Christian proclamation (Luke 24:46-47; 1 Cor 2:2; 15:1-5; Col 1:28-29).

Practical definition:
    Evangelizing is the verbal proclamation of the Gospel of Jesus Christ to the unsaved in the power of the Holy Spirit, to the end of persuading them to repent of their sin, to believe in the work of Jesus Christ on their behalf, and to accept Him as their Savior and Lord, with the intent of baptizing those who repent and teaching them to observe all that Christ has commanded, as committed members of a local NT church.

1. The **bold proclamation**,[691] Mark 16:15, Luke 24:47, Rom 10:14-17, Eph 6:19-20
    a. Of the **Gospel of Jesus Christ**, Acts 8:35, 1 Cor 15:1-4
    b. To the **unsaved**, Matt 9:36-38
    c. In the **power of the Holy Spirit**, Luke 24:49 (cf. Acts 4:31, John 16:8, 1 Thess 1:5, 1 Pet 1:12)

2. To the end of **persuading** them, 2 Cor 5:11
    a. **To repent** of their sin, Luke 24:46-47, Acts 2:38
    b. **To believe** (in Jesus), Acts 16:31:
        1) In the **work of Jesus Christ**, Luke 24:46, 2 Cor 5:15
        2) **On their behalf**, John 1:29, 2 Cor 5:15
    c. **To accept** Him, Jean 1:12, Rev 3:20:
        1) As their **Savior**, Acts 16:30-31
        2) And **Lord**, Matt 10:38-39, 12:30

    [Herein is often argued a dividing line between evangelism and follow-up/discipleship]
    [See my notes in Chapter 26 for a brief discussion of the issues]

3. With the intent **to baptize them** and **teach them to oberve all that Christ has commanded**, Matt 28:19-20 (John 15:16, 1 Thess 5:11)

---

[691]Irving Hexham wrote in the Canadian Encyclopedia, "Evangelism is an English word derived from the combination of the 2 Greek words *euangelion* and *euangelizomai*, meaning 'good news,' or 'gospel' and 'to announce, proclaim, or bring good news.' Historically all Christians have been committed to proclaiming the gospel to make converts, and thus to evangelism. Today the term evangelical is used to describe theologically Conservative churches and interdenominational para-church organizations" (available from: http://www.thecanadianencyclopedia.com/index.cfm?PgNm=TCE&Params=A1ARTA0002671; accessed 13 Nov 2006).

4. That they might **become committed members** of a local NT church:
   a. Col 3:12-17, Heb 10:25, 1 John 1:3
   b. 1 Cor 12:7, 1 Pet 4:10

K. Concluding Considerations:

A. Some questions on the term "apologetic evangelism":[692]

In light of the use of the verb ἀπολογέομαι in Acts 25:8, without any emphasis on the proclamation of the Gospel, can the NT ἀπολογέομαι therefore be the basis for apologetic evangelism?
Acts 25:8, "while Paul said in his own defense, 'I have committed no offense either against the Law of the Jews or against the temple or against Caesar.'"

Again in light of Acts 25:8, as well as in light of 1 Corinthians 1-2, how are we to understand Paul's use of the phrase "knowing that I am appointed for the defense of the gospel [εἰδότες ὅτι εἰς ἀπολογίαν τοῦ εὐαγγελίου κεῖμαι]" in Phil 1:16 (note the punctuation of Phil 1:7 in the English Geneva Bible)?
Phil 1:7, "As it becommeth me so to iudge of you all, because I haue you in remembrance that both in my bands, and in my defence, and confirmation of the Gospell you all were partakers of my grace"

Does this one phrase in Phil 1:16 overturn the weight of what Paul said in 1 Cor 1-2; 9:16-23; 10:31-11:1; including the context of Paul's use of ἀπολογέομαι in Acts 26:1, 2, and 24; as well as Luke's summary of Paul's ministry in Acts 17:2-3?

B. Is evangelism an end in itself?

Must evangelism be wed to discipleship or church planting in order to be valid, or is [mere] evangelism or [mere] proclamation a legitimate end in itself?
See notes after Chapter 10, "Evangelism as a Means to an End or an End in Itself?"

Or again, do the Mark or Luke Great Commission passages stand alone complete by themselves, or must they always be interpreted in light of the Matthean Great Commission (as translated in the past 150 years)? See Chapter 10, "The Great Commission"

What difference does it make if Matthew's Great Commission is translated "win disciples" as I argue in Chapter 10?

Is proclaiming the wonderful salvation available in Jesus Christ a worthy task and a duty in and of itself, and is not God glorified in so doing?

Or similarly, does 1 Peter 2:9 with its "proclaim the excellencies" stand alone?

These questions are also addressed in chapter 10 as regards the Great Commission, and yet again in Chapter 26 in relationship to follow-up and discipleship.

---

[692]For further information on "Apologetic Evangelism: see Chapter 8, "The Doctrine of the Bible in Evangelism," F. "Concerning Other Sources of Truth."

Some Issues in a Definition of Evangelism:

ISSUES IN VERBALIZING THE GOSPEL

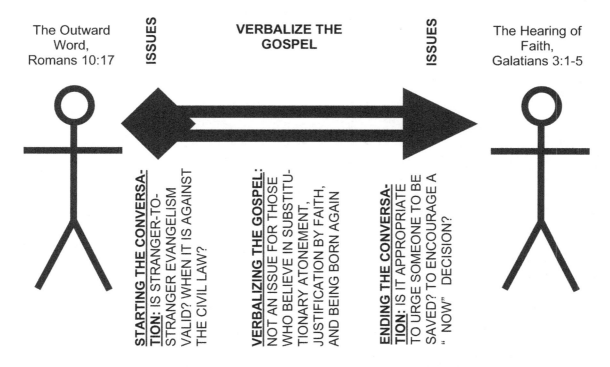

The Outward Word, Romans 10:17 — **ISSUES** — **VERBALIZE THE GOSPEL** — **ISSUES** — The Hearing of Faith, Galatians 3:1-5

STARTING THE CONVERSATION: IS STRANGER-TO-STRANGER EVANGELISM VALID? WHEN IT IS AGAINST THE CIVIL LAW?

VERBALIZING THE GOSPEL: NOT AN ISSUE FOR THOSE WHO BELIEVE IN SUBSTITUTIONARY ATONEMENT, JUSTIFICATION BY FAITH, AND BEING BORN AGAIN

ENDING THE CONVERSATION: IS IT APPROPRIATE TO URGE SOMEONE TO BE SAVED? TO ENCOURAGE A "NOW" DECISION?

LOWEST COMMON DENOMINATOR FOR THE MESSAGE?
"Christ is proclaimed; in this I rejoice. Yes, and I will rejoice." Phil 1:18; or similarly:
"and He said to them, 'Thus it is written, that the Christ should suffer and rise again from the dead the third day; and that repentance for forgiveness of sins should be proclaimed in His name to all the nations, beginning from Jerusalem.'" Luke 24:46-47

LOWEST COMMON DENOMINATOR FOR THE METHOD?
Initiating and closing a conversation are part of methodology.
Does the Bible give a lowest common denominator for methodology? How about Luke 24:47?

1. How can or must the conversation be started?
   a. Must there be friendship or service first?
   b. Must there be lifestyle (or "Presence") first?

2. What of the Gospel needs to be shared?
   a. Must there be reasoned arguments or an extended period of dialogue prior to sharing the Gospel (i.e. apologetics or Christian worldview)?
   b. Must there be a prolongued period of contrition prior to properly hearing and/or properly making a decision for Christ?
   c. Is there a lowest common denominator for the message?

3. Is the evangelist permitted to press for a decision?
   a. Can there be faith without repentance?
   b. Does the need for repentance imply urging for a decision?

Logical Implications of Defining Evangelism as Verbal Proclamation:[693]

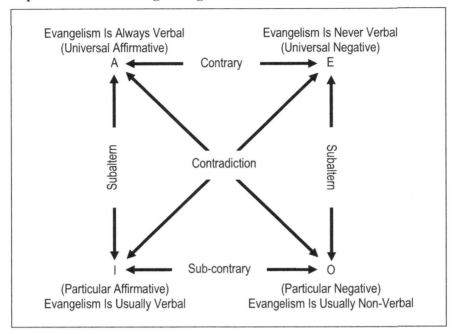

1. Have these notes addressed this square of opposition?

2. Where is the weight of biblical material as regards the definition of evangelism?

3. Is there enough biblical material on evangelism to develop a "Regulative Principle" by way of defining evangelizing?

4. Do theological predeterminations because of ecclesial background or predeterminations about conversion and salvation influence views of evangelism (and the Great Commission)?
   a. Chapter 8 considers views of conversion and the biblical material on conversion
   b. As will be noted there is a massive amount of historical-theological baggage that predetermines views of salvation, conversion, evangelism, and the Great Commission
   c. All of these concepts are inseparably wed in a coherent theological system, often colored by one's Central Interpretive Motif
   d. My Central Interpretive Motif, as hopefully exemplified in these notes, corresponds with the literal application of the Great Commission verses, as well as those on evangelizing.

---

[693]Seven similar charts are found in Johnston, *Charts for a Theology of Evangelism*, Chart 18, "Placing Views of Evangelism on the Square of Opposition," 38-41.

Chapter 7 Appendixes

Considering the Meaning of "Taking Oaths in the Name of the LORD" in Deut 6 and 10

The two passages in question:

> Deut 6:13 (NKJ) "You shall fear the LORD your God and serve Him, and **shall take oaths in His name**"
> Deut 10:20-21 (NKJ) "You shall fear the LORD your God; you shall serve Him, and to Him you shall hold fast, and **take oaths in His name**. He *is* your praise, and He *is* your God, who has done for you these great and awesome things which your eyes have seen"

Clearly, "taking oaths in His name" is the only verbal element in Deut 6, and in Deut 10, the command moves into boasting about or praising the Lord God.

Does "taking oaths in the name of the Lord" contradict or complement the Third Commandment?

> Exod 20:7 (NKJ), "You shall not take the name of the LORD your God in vain, for the LORD will not hold *him* guiltless who takes His name in vain"
> Deut 5:11 (NKJ) "You shall not take the name of the LORD your God in vain, for the LORD will not hold *him* guiltless who takes His name in vain"

In common English language, swearing is considered vulgarity; it is obvious that the follower of the LORD is not commanded to use the name of the LORD in vulgarity or frivolity

Furthermore, Jesus as He interpreted the Law denied that one ought to swear by heaven or earth:
Nor even to "swear by heaven, nor by earth" (Matt 5:34)

> Matt 5:34-37 (NKJ) "But I say to you, do not swear [ὄμνυμι] at all: neither by heaven, for it is God's throne; nor by the earth, for it is His footstool; nor by Jerusalem, for it is the city of the great King. Nor shall you swear by your head, because you cannot make one hair white or black. But let your 'Yes' be 'Yes,' and your 'No,' 'No.' For whatever is more than these is from the evil one"

Therefore, it is highly unlikely that Deut 6:13 and 10:20-21 are calls to use the name of the LORD to affirm or confirm truthfulness or finality in a contractual arrangement.

So what could "taking an oath in His name" mean?

Two Hebrew verbs at issue:

Shaba' (186 OT uses)—meaning "to swear" or to take an oath (as in the NKJ), Deut 6:13; 10:20:
> The power is in the preposition "in"

Does this mean taking all oaths "in" His name? Possibly prohibited in Matt 5:33-37
> In other words, "Do you swear to do such and such?" "Yes, I swear by the name of the LORD!" "OK then, as long as you swear in that name, I will accept your word!"

Or does it mean taking an oath unto His name? i.e. making a unique commitment to follow Him and Him only?
> In other words, "LORD God, I swear to love you, honor you, and serve you alone!"
> Does not this application seems to be the case in Psalm 119:106?

> > Psa 119:106, "I have sworn and confirmed That I will keep Your righteous judgments"

The second appears to be the emphasis of the LXX translation of Deut 6:13:

> Deut 6:13, κύριον τὸν θεόν σου φοβηθήσῃ καὶ αὐτῷ λατρεύσεις καὶ πρὸς αὐτὸν κολληθήσῃ καὶ τῷ ὀνόματι αὐτοῦ ὀμῇ

> My translation: "You shall fear the Lord your (sg.) God and serve/worship him and unto him shall you <u>cleave</u> [κολλάω] and unto his name alone"
> In other verses, the translators of the LXX translated this verb by the Greek ὄμνυμι or ὀμνύω—to swear (e.g. Deut 6:10, 18, 23).

By the way, does not the reading "swear by" of "cling to" coincide with a proper reading and application of the "Shamah" in Deut 6:5 (the direct context of the command):

Which is far more than a mere ontological reality (affirming philosophical monotheism)

But is a relational and soteriological reality (affirming the Lord's unique role in the choosing of and salvation of Israel as a nation of individuals [hence "your God" is often in the singular in Deut, except "your God" in 6:5], and by transference, our salvation)

Even "your God" in 6:13 is singular!

Consider also that "taking an oath" (as in Deut 6:13) is <u>verbal</u> (if that is actually the proper translation)—a prototype to a sinner's oath to God in prayer!

Otherwise, if "cling" or "cleave" is a better translation (as in the LXX), it is an affirmation of complete dependence!

Dabaq—meaning "to cling to", Deut 10:20

Which verb is used in parallel to *shaba'* (implying similarity and/or continuity of thought)

Interestingly, the LXX translated 10:20 identically to 6:13:

Deut 10:20 κύριον τὸν θεόν σου φοβηθήσῃ καὶ αὐτῷ λατρεύσεις καὶ πρὸς αὐτὸν κολληθήσῃ καὶ τῷ ὀνόματι αὐτοῦ ὀμῇ

Whereas, the Hebrew (Leningradensis) adds a fourth verb to the string in the third position (וּבוֹ תִדְבָּק; wa-bo tidbaq)

Therefore the Hebrew of Deut 10:20 includes both the verbs *dabaq* (cling to) and *shaba'* (swear by/unto)

Also interestingly, the Hebrew verb *dabaq* is used in Psa 119:25, and is translated with the Greek κολλάω ("cling to") as above in Deut 6:13!

Could it be that the translators of the LXX considered the concepts the same? In other words, spiritually clinging to the Lord = verbally bearing witness to His name?

Tehillah—meaning to praise (in Greek, translated καύχημα, "boast"), Deut 10:21

It seems that Deut 10:21 builds upon the emphasis of the verbal element in the prior verse, with a crescendo of praise, boasting in the Lord and His marvelous works

Deut 10:21 seems then to be a precursor of Psa 34:2, "My soul shall make its boast in the LORD; The humble shall hear *of it* and be glad"

As well as to Gal 6:14, "But God forbid that I should boast except in the cross of our Lord Jesus Christ, by whom the world has been crucified to me, and I to the world"

Also at issue, the application of this text by Jesus in His temptation—the "dynamic equivalent translation" of Jesus (if anyone has the right to dynamic equivalent translation, it is Jesus, who truly understands the mind of God!)

Jesus used two verbs when he responded to the temptation of Satan (purportedly quoting Deut 6:13):

Matt 4:10 (Byz) Τότε λέγει αὐτῷ ὁ Ἰησοῦς, Ὕπαγε ὀπίσω μου, Σατανᾶ· γέγραπται γάρ, Κύριον τὸν θεόν σου προσκυνήσεις, καὶ αὐτῷ μόνῳ λατρεύσεις.
"You shall kneel" (προσκυνέω), literally "genuflect"
"You shall worship" (λατρεύω), to worship or serve

Luke 4:8 (Byz) Καὶ ἀποκριθεὶς αὐτῷ εἶπεν ὁ Ἰησοῦς, Ὕπαγε ὀπίσω μου, Σατανᾶ· γέγραπται, Προσκυνήσεις κύριον τὸν θεόν σου, καὶ αὐτῷ μόνῳ λατρεύσεις.
[In the Greek Orthodox Text, the Byzantine textform, and the Nestle-Aland critical edition text-history, Luke uses the same two verbs as Matthew]

Notice that Jesus did not quote from the more obvious prohibition against bowing from the Second Commandment:

Exod 20:4-5 (NKJ) "You shall not make for yourself a carved image … you shall not bow down to them nor serve them"

Jesus seemed to ignore the first part of the temptation, "to fall down" before Satan, and rather emphasize the second part of the temptation "to worship" Satan;

Instead of using the prohibition against bowing and serving, to which it seems Satan was alluding, used the positive command of worship and consecration to the Lord:

Note also that the Second Command contextually relates to inanimate objects, graven images, which Satan was not.

So, for purposes of defeating the temptation, Jesus cited the more non-verbally related verbs of Deut 6:13 or 10:20: kneel and serve:

He did not use the third and/or fourth verb in the strings, which have a verbal emphasis, "to swear unto/by"

Further, notice the use of *shaba'* in the prophecy of Isaiah in 45:23, which is then picked up by Paul in Phil 2:11:

Isa 45:23 (NKJ), "I have sworn by Myself; The word has gone out of My mouth *in* righteousness, And shall not return, That to Me every knee shall bow, Every tongue shall take an oath [*shaba'*]"

Isa 45:23, κατ᾽ ἐμαυτοῦ ὀμνύω ἦ μὴν ἐξελεύσεται ἐκ τοῦ στόματός μου δικαιοσύνη οἱ λόγοι μου οὐκ ἀποστραφήσονται ὅτι ἐμοὶ κάμψει πᾶν γόνυ καὶ ἐξομολογήσεται πᾶσα γλῶσσα τῷ θεῷ

Isa 45:23 (ESV), "By myself I have sworn; from my mouth has gone out in righteousness a word that shall not return: 'To me every knee shall bow, every tongue shall swear allegiance [*shaba'*]"

Note several things, the LXX translated *shaba'* in this verse as ἐξομολογέω, meaning "to confess, profess" [in the NT also translated "promise, pray, praise"]

Two New Testament passages appear to allude to this great Isaiah text:
Psalm 18:49, cited by Paul in Rom 15:9 as related to the gospel going forth to the Gentiles
Acts 15:7, Peter stated that by his mouth the Gentiles heard the word of the gospel and believed

The outwardly verbal element of ἐξομολογέω is expressed by the people confessing their sins prior to John the Baptist baptizing them in Matt 3:6 and Mark 1:5

Consider also Jeremiah's use of *shaba'* in Jer 4:2:

Jer 4:2 (NAS), "And you will swear, 'As the LORD lives,' In truth, in justice, and in righteousness; Then the nations will bless themselves in Him, And in Him they will glory."

Jer 4:2 (GOT), καὶ ὀμόσῃ· ζῇ Κύριος μετὰ ἀληθείας ἐν κρίσει καὶ ἐν δικαιοσύνῃ, καὶ εὐλογήσουσιν ἐν αὐτῷ ἔθνη καὶ ἐν αὐτῷ αἰνέσουσι τῷ θεῷ ἐν Ἰερουσαλημ·

Here, again, the verb appears to speak of more than just swearing or taking an oath. Rather *shaba'* here leans more toward pledging allegiance to the Lord as a form of witness—a possible precursor to New Testament evangelizing, including the promsed blessing which follows the verbal witness (cf. Psa 96:1-3).

In Conclusion:

It would seem that translating *shaba'* as "swear allegiance" is more akin to the *sensus plenior* of the Bible:

What does it mean for the Muslim to swear allegiance to Allah and to Muhammad as his prophet?
What does it mean for a groom to swear allegiance to his bride?
What does it mean for the NT Christian to swear allegiance to Jesus Christ?

Could it not be something like this—expanding from the U.S. "Pledge of Allegiance" to the flag?

"I swear allegiance, unto Jesus Christ, my Lord, my Savior, and my God, who died on the cross for my sins, who rose again on the third day, and who is coming back quickly to judge all men. I swear to give Him my heart, my mind, my life, my all. So help me, Lord. Amen."

On one hand, then, is this not a prayer of commitment and surrender? Is this not calling on the name of the Lord to be saved (Joel 2:32; cf. Rom 10:13)?

Furthermore, is this not simultaneously confessing Christ before men?

Matt 10:32-33 (NKJ) "Therefore whoever confesses Me before men, him I will also confess before My Father who is in heaven. But whoever denies Me before men, him I will also deny before My Father who is in heaven" (cf. Luke 12:8-9)
Mark 8:38 (NKJ) "For whoever is ashamed of Me and My words in this adulterous and sinful generation, of him the Son of Man also will be ashamed when He comes in the glory of His Father with the holy angels" (cf. Luke 9:26; Heb 11:16)

Notice how verbal acknowledgement of Christ for salvation is linked to verbal acknowledgement of Him before men
How do some churches get around this verbal acknowledgement?
By couching it in the "Sacrament" of Baptism, before a child can speak, with the verbal acknowledgement of the parents before a priest or pastor within the four walls of a church building?

Considering the Meaning of
"Lifting Up the Name of the LORD in Vain"
in Exod 20 and Deut 5

The two passages in question:

Exod 20:7, "You shall not take* the name of the LORD your God in vain**, for the LORD will not hold *him* guiltless who takes His name in vain."

Deut 5:11, "You shall not take* the name of the LORD your God in vain**, for the LORD will not leave him unpunished who takes His name in vain."

*The Hebrew *nasa'* means "to lift, carry"—consider the translation of the dual "evangelize" in Isa 52:7, "to bring good news"
**The Hebrew *shav'* means "emptiness, vanity"—consider that false teachers are wells without water (2 Pet 2:17)

Link with some OT portions, especially wherein false prophets speak in the name of the Lord:

1 Kings 22:24, "Now Zedekiah the son of Chenaanah went near and struck Micaiah on the cheek, and said, 'Which way did the spirit from the LORD go from me to speak to you?'"

Jer 23:16-17, "Thus says the LORD of hosts: "Do not listen to the words of the prophets who prophesy to you. They make you worthless; They speak a vision of their own heart, Not from the mouth of the LORD. They continually say to those who despise Me, 'The LORD has said, "You shall have peace"'; And *to* everyone who walks according to the dictates of his own heart, they say, 'No evil shall come upon you.'"

Link with some NT concepts:

John 12:32, "And I, if I am lifted up from the earth, will draw all *peoples* to Myself."

Acts 13:6, "Now when they had gone through the island to Paphos, they found a certain sorcerer, a false prophet, a Jew whose name *was* Bar-Jesus, who was with the proconsul, Sergius Paulus, an intelligent man. This man called for Barnabas and Saul and sought to hear the word of God."

Acts 19:13-15, "Then some of the itinerant Jewish exorcists took it upon themselves to call the name of the Lord Jesus over those who had evil spirits, saying, 'We exorcise you by the Jesus whom Paul preaches.' Also there were seven sons of Sceva, a Jewish chief priest, who did so. And the evil spirit answered and said, 'Jesus I know, and Paul I know; but who are you?'"

Could taking the name of the Lord in vain not be related to speaking of the Lord or Jesus in a wrong way, much like these false teachers and false prophets above?

If so, the 3rd Commandment can be related to a polluted form of evangelism:

Prov 25:26, "A righteous *man* who falters before the wicked *Is like* a murky spring and a polluted well."

Matt 23:15, "Woe to you, scribes and Pharisees, hypocrites! For you travel land and sea to win one proselyte, and when he is won, you make him twice as much a son of hell as yourselves."

Semantic Studies:
Words Lightly Used in English Bible Translations?

Introduction:

There appears to be several reasons why particular words would not be found in most or all English translations of the Bible:

1) God never meant them to be used:
   a) Either the term or concept is never discussed, or
   b) God chose other terminology for the discussion of that concept; or

2) Editors thought the concept was somewhat vulgar, and not acceptable for Holy Writ:
   a) Perhaps a term in this category is the word "foreskin" (for ἀκροβυστία—17 total NT uses: Acts 11:3; Rom 2:26; Gal 2:7; 5:6; 6:15; etc., rather than ἀπερίτμητος (Act 7:51), wherein "uncirmcumcised" or "uncircumcision" is used for both in the New Testament...

3) As the English language has evolved, some terms are now used to express topics and issues, whereas translators continue to translate the ideas based on the precedent of old lexicons and common usage; or

4) Although particular concepts are truly found and addressed in the text of Scripture, using terms that could be translated differently, specific terms are not used because of some theological bias, whether it be historical, theological, exegetical, lexical, etymological, or practical:
   a) Consider the reason that a NT professor told me that it would not be wise to translate εὐαγγελίζω as "evangelize":

   > "I just am concerned that some people seeing only 'evangelize' [rather than 'preach the gospel'] in a NT translation will read it with the assumption of modern practice."

   Therefore, for him, he felt justified in not using the word "evangelize" because of his subjective judgment of "modern practice"—How does he define "modern practice," whose practice is meant by it, and in what part of the world?

The following examines some words that, though seemingly interrelated with biblical themes and ideas, for some reason are not or rarely used in the English Bible translations...

"Accountability", "accountable," "give ... account," "gave ... account":

Word study of uses of "account, accountability, accountable"
[Approximate chronological arrangement]

	TYN*	GNV*	BSP*	KJV	WEB	YLT	NOY	ROT	DBY	ERV	DRA	ASV	BBE	RSV	NAS	NKJ	NIVO	NJB	NRS	NABO	NAU	GWN	CJB	NIrV	NLT	TNIV	NET	CSBO	MGI	ESV	MIT	NIV	NAB	CEB	CSB	Total
Account	0	4	0	17	25	44	213	112	145	30	32	30	206	62	104	28	75	91	63	72	86	29	51	2	33	73	62	45	40	56	40	73	77	88	44	2152
Accountability	0	0	0	0	0	0	0	0	0	0	0	0	0	0	0	0	0	0	0	0	0	0	0	0	0	0	0	1	0	0	0	0	0	0	1	2
Accountable	0	0	0	0	0	0	0	0	1	0	0	0	0	1	2	0	8	1	5	2	2	2	0	64	6	8	19	8	0	2	0	8	5	11	8	163
Total	0	4	0	17	25	44	213	112	146	30	32	30	206	63	106	28	83	92	68	74	88	31	51	66	39	81	81	54	40	58	40	81	82	99	53	2317

*Spelling of words may be an issue in older Bibles.

"Allegiance":

Not found in KJV, NKJ

In NAS (6 uses, 3 in italics); HCSB (6 uses, some very interesting); ESV (4 uses)

"Brain":

Can the Greek word νοῦς ever mean "brain" (e.g 1 Cor 14:15)? Is there a word in Greek or Hebrew for the brain? If there is, it is interesting that it is never used in translations.

"Clarified," "clarify," "clarifying":

Another interesting word that is used in hermeneutical or exegetical or homiletical settings, but does not appear to be found in modern English translations, that seem to prefer words like "revelation" and "disclosure" for ἀποκάλυψις, following Friberg. While the NKJ, NAS, and ESV do not use this word root, the HCSB uses "clarify" once as the translation for "make known" (γνωρίζω) in 1 Cor 15:1.

"Conversation":

Consider for example, the 20 uses of the word "conversation" in the KJV and the 1 use in the NAS. Intriguing!

"Conversion," "convert," and "converting":

As an aside, but since it is first in the alphabet, it is interesting to note that an English word group which took on theological meaning has often been replaced by other words (see Chapter 6; for antagonists to conversion, see Chapter 8). This study seeks to understand the history of the usage and/or non-usage of the term related to the root "convert," as it relates to the moment of or experience of true salvation.

The trend-setter translations below are the NIV-family of translations, which the American Bible Society and United Bible Society mainstreamed into U.S. Evangelicalism in the mid-1980s: NIVO, NIVR, TNIV, and NIV. The uses of any terms with the root "convert" are respectively: NIVO (5), NIVR (0), TNIV (6), and NIV (2).

Word study of uses of "conversion," "convert," and "converting" in the NT
[Approximate chronological arrangement]

	TYN	KJV	WEB	ETH	MRD	YLT	NOY	ROT	DBY	ERV	DRA	ASV	BBE	RSV	NAS	NKJ	NIVO	NJB	NRS	NABO	NAU	GWN	CJB	NIVR	NLT	TNIV	NET	CSBO	MGI	ESV	MIT	NIV	NAB	CSB	CEB	Total
Conversion°	0	1	1	5	3	1	1	1	1	1	1	1	0	1	1	1	0	2	1	1	1	0	0	0	1	0	1	1	1	1	1	0	1	1	1	34
Convert*	1	1	1	5	2	1	2	2	0	1	3	1	0	2	2	0	4	3	4	3	2	2	1	0	2	5	4	2	2	2	1	1	3	2	3	70
Converted°°	5	7	7	8	7	0	0	0	6	0	16	0	0	0	2	2	1	5	0	5	2	3	0	0	2	1	0	3	2	0	0	1	5	3	1	94
Converting**	0	0	0	0	0	0	0	0	0	0	0	0	0	0	0	0	0	0	0	0	0	0	0	0	0	0	0	0	0	0	0	1	0	0	0	1
Total	6	9	9	18	12	2	3	3	7	2	20	2	0	3	5	3	5	10	5	9	5	5	1	0	5	6	5	6	5	3	3	2	9	6	5	199

° 27 versions use the word "conversion" in Acts 15:3, "...describing in detail the conversion of the Gentiles..."; The Greek word behind this word is ἐπιστροφή (1 NT use; 5 OT LXX uses); note that none of the 4 NIV translations use the word "conversion." The 5 uses in Etheridge are: Acts 15:3; Rom 11:15; 2 Tim 2:25; Heb 6:6; and 1 Pet 3:20; the 3 uses in Murdock are: Acts 15:3; Rom 11:15; and 2 Cor 7:10; the 2 uses in the New Jerusalem Bible are: Acts 13:8 and 16:34.

* "[New] convert" was used by Young's in 1 Tim 3:6 (for the Greek neophyte: νεόφυτος), and was followed by 18 other translations; "convert" was also used by Tyndale in James 5:19 (for the Greek ἐπιστρέψῃ); followed by a total of 9 other translations, including the KJV; "convert" was used by Rotherham in Matt 23:15 (for the Greek proselyte: προσήλυτος); this was followed by 10 translations, three of which use the word twice in that text; Etheridge's five uses of "convert" are: Luke 1:16; Acts 17:31; James 5:19; and Rev 2:5 and 21; Murdock also uses "convert" in Luke 1:16 and James 5:19; the Douai-Rheims adds Acts 3:26 to the list of verses with this word; the RSV adds Rom 16:5; the old NIV also used the word in Acts 6:5; the New Jerusalem translated "persuaded" (πείθω) as "trying to convert" in Acts 18:4

°°The KJV's 7 uses of "converted" are: Matt 13:15; 18:4; Mark 4:12; Luke 22:32; John 12:40; and Acts 3:19 and 28:27.

** Rom 2:29 (for οὐ γράμματι; NOY), "but he is a Jew who is one inwardly; and circumcision is of the heart, spiritual, not literal, whose praise is not of men, but of God"

"Cooperate," "cooperated," "cooperating," and "cooperation":

Never used in any English Bibles that I considered (of 34 English Bibles in my version of Bibleworks)...

1) Clearly an important subject in Christian fellowship (συνυπουργέω [2 Cor 1:11]; κοινωνία [Phil 1:5]; συγκοινωνός [1 Cor 9:23]; συγκοινωνέω [Phil 4:14]; συνεργέω [1 Cor 3:9; 2 Cor 6:1]; as well as even in Soteriology (the doctrine of salvation, and the steps thereof)

2) Clearly, mutual submission is an unimportant subject:
    a) In the hierarchical form of church leadership, where mutual submission is not the issue, but rather something akin to the "Vow of Obedience"

    b)   In the doctrine of salvation, a very solid philosophical wedge has been placed between God's role and man's role in salvation, therefore, terms that tend to nullify that distinction have been replaced with other words

    c)   In the preaching of the gospel, man's role is intimately involved; another wall of linguistic separation has been erected to avoid any hint of man's cooperation in salvation by obeying the Great Commission and preaching the Gospel

3)   However, "cooperation" is very much akin to a congregational form of church government, and is less a part of the mindset of an authoritarian bishop-rule state-church model, which model has ruled much of Christian history!

"Delight," "delighting," and "delight":

In NKJ, used 89 times in OT and only 2 times in NT. Apparently replaced by the English "well-pleased" in NT Greek lexicography.

"Deprave," "depraved," and "depraving":

Used 5 times in the New American Standard, and more thereafter in English language translation. The implications are obvious, as there are numerous words in Hebrew and Greek which describe the corrupt nature of human depravity. This word may be minimized from the view of English readers to reduce belief in "total depravity."

	WYC	TYN*	BSP	KJV	WEB	YLT	NOY	ROT	DBY	ERV	DRA	ASV	BBE	RSV	NAS	NKJ	NIVO	NJB	NRS	NABO	NAU	GWN	CJB	NIVR	NLT	TNIV	NET	CSBO	MGI	ESV	MIT*	NIV	NAB	CEB	Total
Depravation	0	0	0	0	0	0	0	0	0	0	0	0	0	0	0	0	0	0	0	0	0	0	0	0	0	0	0	0	0	0	0	0	0	1	**1**
Deprave	0	0	0	0	0	0	0	0	0	0	0	0	0	0	0	0	0	0	0	0	0	0	0	0	0	0	0	0	0	0	0	0	0	0	**0**
Depraved	0	0	0	0	0	0	0	0	2	0	1	0	0	2	3	0	5	4	2	11	3	0	2	0	3	6	2	5	0	1	4	6	10	0	**72**
Depraving	0	0	0	0	0	0	0	0	0	0	0	0	0	0	0	0	0	0	0	0	0	0	0	0	0	0	0	0	0	0	0	0	0	0	**0**
Depravities	0	0	0	0	0	0	0	0	0	0	0	0	0	0	0	0	0	0	0	0	1	0	0	0	0	0	0	0	0	0	0	0	0	0	**1**
Depravity	0	0	0	0	0	0	0	0	0	0	0	0	0	0	2	0	2	1	4	0	2	0	2	0	0	3	1	2	0	4	2	2	10	3	**40**
Total	**0**	**0**	**0**	**0**	**0**	**0**	**0**	**0**	**2**	**0**	**1**	**0**	**0**	**2**	**5**	**0**	**7**	**5**	**6**	**11**	**5**	**0**	**5**	**0**	**3**	**9**	**3**	**7**	**0**	**5**	**6**	**8**	**20**	**4**	**114**

*New Testament only.

"Discriminate" et al.:

This is an interesting English word, especially with the current discussion of racism in U.S. culture. In this regard, one thinks of the translation of διακρίνω in 1 Cor 4:7.

	WYC	TYN*	BSP	KJV	WEB	YLT	NOY	ROT	DBY	ERV	DRA	ASV	BBE	RSV	NAS	NKJ	NIVO	NJB	NRS	NABO	NAU	GWN	CJB	NIVR	NLT	TNIV	NET	CSB	MGI	ESV	MIT*	NIV	NAB	CEB	Total
Discriminate	0	0	0	0	0	0	0	0	0	0	0	0	0	0	0	0	0	1	0	0	0	1	0	0	0	1	1	0	2	0	2	1	0	0	**9**
Discriminated	0	0	0	0	0	0	0	0	0	0	0	0	0	0	0	0	1	0	0	0	0	0	0	0	1	1	0	1	0	0	0	1	0	0	**5**
Discriminates	0	0	0	0	0	0	0	0	0	0	0	0	0	0	0	0	0	1	0	0	0	0	0	0	0	0	0	0	0	0	0	0	0	0	**1**
Discriminating	0	0	0	0	0	0	0	1	0	0	0	0	0	0	0	0	0	0	0	1	0	1	1	0	0	0	0	0	1	0	1	0	1	0	**7**
Discrimination	0	0	0	0	0	0	0	0	0	0	0	0	0	0	0	0	0	0	0	0	0	0	0	0	1	0	0	0	0	1	0	0	0	1	**3**
Discriminations	0	0	0	0	0	0	0	1	0	0	0	0	0	0	0	0	0	0	0	0	0	0	0	0	0	0	0	0	0	0	0	0	0	0	**1**
Total	**0**	**0**	**0**	**0**	**0**	**0**	**0**	**2**	**0**	**0**	**0**	**0**	**0**	**0**	**0**	**0**	**1**	**2**	**0**	**1**	**0**	**2**	**1**	**0**	**2**	**2**	**1**	**1**	**3**	**0**	**4**	**2**	**1**	**1**	**26**

*New Testament only.

"Distinction"—i.e. "making a distinction," or distinguishing between

In NKJ one NT use of "distinguish": 1 Cor 4:10, "You are distinguished" [for ἔνδοξος].

In the OT the concept of "distinguishing between" is communicated in Lev 10:10; 11:47; 20:25..

"Elected," "election":

The word "elected" are not found in the CSB, ESV, NAS, and NIV; the word "election" is not found in the NAS, although found several times in the CSB, ESV, and NIV. Although the Greek verb χειροτονέω (from ἡ χείρ + τείνω; meaning to extent the hand, as in "to cast a vote") is found twice in the NT (Acts 14:23; 2 Cor 8:19), it is not usually translated in a such way as to affirm or promote congregational raising of hands for a vote. Perhaps this Greek word has been muffled because of ecclesiastical debates as to the propriety of congregational rule?

"Equivocal":

Not used in KJV, NAS, NKJ, HCSB, ESV.

Eternity:

Now here is an unexpected word to include in this list. "Eternity" is found only 3 times in the entire NKJ (Eccl 3:11; Isa 57:15; and Acts 15:18). And yet the noun translated "eternity" in Acts 15:18 (ὁ αἰών) is found 126 times in the Byzantine Greek NT and 583 times in the combined LXX-GNT. It must be remembered that this does not count use of the adjective for "eternal (αἰώνιος), used 71 times in the Byzantine Greek NT and 186 times in the LXX-GNT.

"Exhale," "exhaled," "exhaling":

Never used in any major English translation in any form.

1) The closest is "breathed out" in Heb 4:12 (ESV), "All Scripture is breathed out by God and profitable for teaching, for reproof, for correction, and for training in righteousness"

2) The divine inspiration and unique authority of the words of Scripture have been under attack almost from their being penned; thus, this word which links God's Word with His very breath understandably draws significant polemic attention

"Grasp," "grasped," "grasping," "grasps":

16 uses in English in NKJ, all OT—10 of which are in Eccl.

None in NT, which means that of the 58 uses of δέχομαι in the NT, none of them are translated with the English "grasp" in the NKJ—a very fascinating history of translation.

In the NAS, there are only two uses of "grasp" in the NT, John 10:39, "he eluded their hand"; and Phil 2:6, equality with God as "a thing to be grasped"—for the Greek noun ὁ ἁρπαγμός (booty, plunder).

"Inhale," "inhaled," "inhaling":

"Inhale": one use in NJB (Lev 26:31)

"Inhaled": one use in NABO and NAB (Wisdom 7:3)

"Inhaling": not used.

"Liberate," "liberated," "liberation":

Word study of uses of "liberate, liberated, liberateth, liberating, liberation, liberator, liberators"
[Approximate chronological arrangement]

	WYC	TYN	BSP	KJV	WEB	YLT	NOY	ROT	DBY	ERV	DRA	ASV	BBE	RSV	NAS	NKJ	NIVO	NJB	NRS	NABO	NAU	GWN	CJB	NIVR	NLT	TNIV	NET	CSBO	MGI	ESV	MIT	NIV	NAB	CEB	Total
Liberate	0	0	0	0	2	0	0	0	1	0	0	0	0	0	0	0	0	2	0	0	0	0	2	0	0	0	0	0	0	0	0	0	0	5	**12**
Liberated	0	0	0	0	1	0	0	0	0	0	0	0	0	0	0	0	1	2	2	1	0	0	2	0	0	1	1	3	0	0	0	1	1	3	**18**
Liberateth	0	0	0	0	0	0	0	1	0	0	0	0	0	0	0	0	0	0	0	0	0	0	0	0	0	0	0	0	0	0	0	0	0	0	**1**
Liberating	0	0	0	0	0	0	0	0	0	0	0	0	0	0	0	0	0	0	0	0	0	0	0	0	0	0	0	0	0	0	0	0	0	0	**0**
Liberation	0	0	0	0	0	0	0	1	0	0	0	0	0	0	0	0	0	3	0	0	0	0	0	0	1	1	0	1	0	0	0	0	0	0	**7**
Liberator	0	0	0	0	0	0	0	0	0	0	0	0	0	0	0	0	0	0	1	0	0	0	0	0	0	0	0	1	0	0	0	0	0	0	**2**
Liberators	0	0	0	0	0	0	0	0	0	0	0	0	0	0	0	0	0	0	0	0	0	0	0	0	0	0	0	0	0	0	0	0	0	1	**1**
Total	**0**	**0**	**0**	**0**	**3**	**0**	**0**	**2**	**1**	**0**	**0**	**0**	**0**	**0**	**0**	**0**	**1**	**7**	**3**	**1**	**0**	**0**	**4**	**0**	**1**	**1**	**1**	**5**	**0**	**0**	**0**	**1**	**1**	**9**	**41**

Webster's: Jer 34:9, 10, 11; Rotherham: Psa 146:7; Ezek 46:17; Darby: 2 Chron 23:8; NIVO: Rom 8:21; NJB: Lev 25:10; 2 Macc 2:22; Sir 51:3; Ezek 46:17; Luke 21:28; Acts 7:25; Gal 1:4; NRS: Acts 7:35; 2 Macc 2:22; 4 Esth 14:29; NABO: 2 Macc 2:22; CJB: Luke 1:68; 2:38; 21:28; 24:21;

NLT: Neh 9:27; TNIV: Rom 8:21; NET: Esth 4:14; CSBO: Esth 4:14; Rom 6:18, 22; 11:26; Gal 5:1; NIV (2011): Rom 8:21; NAB: 2 Macc 2:22; CEB: Isa 61:1; Matt 20:28; Mark 10:45; Luke 4:18; 1 Pet 1:18, 19; 4 Esth 12:34; 13:36; 14:29.

I was thinking of the use of "liberate" (from the power of sin) for "set free" in Rom 6:22 (NKJ), "But now having been set free from sin, and having become slaves of God, you have your fruit to holiness, and the end, everlasting life"—the Greek word being ἐλευθερόω, meaning to set free or exempt (from a liability).

However, on the other hand, it appears that the 2010 CEB, "Common English Bible," fans the flames of "liberation theology" by inserting the word "liberation" into the Isaiah 61 passage, "liberate" into the purpose statements of Jesus in the NT—in the place of "ransom" in Matt 20 and Mark 10; and in the place of "release" or "set free" in Luke 4), and to replace "redeemed" with "liberated" in 1 Pet 1:18-19 (supplying it as a verb in v. 19). Notice that the CEB does not use the word "liberate" in relation to sin, but rather in relation to the mission and purpose of Jesus!

Yes, words are important and they do carry with them significant meaning and power (cf. Acts 7:22).

"Literal" and "literally":

Word study of uses of "literally" [Fr. "à la lettre"]
[Approximate chronological arrangement]

	WYC	TYN	BSP	KJV	WEB	YLT	NOY	ROT	DBY	ERV	DRA	ASV	BBE	RSV	NAS	NKJ	NIVO	NJB	NRS	NABO	NAU	GWN	CJB	NIVR	NLT	TNIV	NET	CSBO	MGI	ESV	MIT	NIV	NAB	CEB	Total
Literal	0	0	0	0	0	0	1**	0	0	0	0	0	0	1**	1*	0	0	0	1**	0	1*	0	1**	0	0	0	0	0	0	0	0	0	0	0	6
Literally	0	0	0	0	0	0	0	0	0	0	0	0	0	0	0	0	0	0	0	0	0	0	1*	0	0	0	1°	0	1**	0	1°°	0	0	1**	5
Total	0	0	0	0	0	0	1	0	0	0	0	0	0	1	1	0	0	0	1	0	1	0	2	0	0	0	1	0	1	0	1	0	0	1	11

°Psa 19:3 (NET), "There is no actual speech or word, nor is its voice literally heard

°°Matt 1:23 (MIT), "Notice: The virgin will conceive and bear a son. His identity will be Immanuel. That designator means literally: with us [is] God"

*John 11:13 (supplied for clarification; NAS), "Now Jesus had spoken of his death, but they thought that He was speaking of literal sleep"

**Rom 2:29 (for οὐ γράμματι; NOY), "but he is a Jew who is one inwardly; and circumcision is of the heart, spiritual, not literal, whose praise is not of men, but of God."

Total # of English versions in this study of "literal" and "literally": 34
  # of versions with no use of either term: 24 (71%)
  # of versions with no use of the word "literal": 28 (83%)
  # of versions with no use of the word "literally": 29 (86%)

# of times either of "literal" or "literally" were used by philosophers in the Bibleworks database: 76, especially the phrase "literal meaning" (26 times).

"Mission," "missionaries", "missionary," "missions":

Mission: Multiple uses in many Bibles, from 19 in CEB (incl. Acts 20:24), 14 in the NJB (incl. Rom 1:5), 12 in NLT, 10 in HCSB (1 in NT: Acts 12:25), 9 in NIV, 7 in RSV (incl. Gal 2:8), 4 in ESV (1 NT: 2 Cor 11:12), 3 in NAS (incl. Acts 12:25), to 2 in NKJ (both in 1 Sam 15).

Missionaries: found once in GWN (Eph 4:11, used to replace the word "evangelist"); found 4 times in MIT (Acts 14:14; 16:22; 2 Cor 11:5; 12:11, used to replace the word "apostle").

Missionary found twice in GWN (Acts 21:8; 2 Tim 4:5, both times replacing the word "evangelist")

Missions: found once in the NIVO, TNIV, NIVO (1 Sam 21:5) and NJB (1 Kgs 8:44); found twice in the CEB (1 Sam 21:5 and 1 Macc 2:47).

Mode; "[Manner]; Style":
There are a significant number of uses of "manner".

	TYN	BSP	KJV	WEB	YLT	NOY	ROT	DBY	ERV	DRA	ASV	BBE	RSV	NAS	NKJ	NIVO	NJB	NRS	NABO	NAU	GWN	CJB	NIVR	NLT	TNIV	NET	CSBO	CSB17	MGI	ESV	MIT	NIV	NAB	CEB	Total
Mode	0	0	0	0	0	0	0	1	0	0	0	0	0	1	0	0	0	1	0	1	0	0	0	0	0	0	0	0	0	0	0	0	0	0	4
Style	0	0	0	0	0	0	0	3	0	0	0	0	2	0	1	0	2	3	0	0	0	3	0	0	0	18	1	1	1	2	4	0	0	0	41
Total	0	0	0	0	0	0	0	4	0	0	0	0	2	1	1	0	2	4	0	1	0	3	0	0	0	18	1	1	1	2	4	0	0	0	45

"Mix," "Mixed," "Mixing," "Mixt", "Mixture" [also consider "Admixture," "Unmixed"]:

Consider, for example, the noun ἡ ἁπλότης (with unmixed motivation, single-minded; hence simplicity) find 8 times in the NT (Rom 12:8; 2 Cor 1:12; 8:2; 9:11, 13; 11:3; Eph 6:5; Col 3:22).

"Mix": used 6 times in NJB (Acts 10:28 only NT use); used 5 times in ESV and 4 times in NAS and HCSB (only NT use in all three: Rev 18:6); 8 uses in NLT (only NT: Rev 8:3); NIVR uses "mix" 33 times (including 9 times in Num 28-29; Rev 18:6 only NT use).

"Mixed": many uses in many Bibles; e.g. Heb 4:2, a hearing "mixed with faith."

"Mixt": 8 times in Bishops Bible, 6 in English Geneva, and once in KJV and DRA (all of them OT only).

"Mixture": Most use "mixture" in John 19:39 (only NT use for Young's, ERV, ASV, RSV, NASB, NKJ, CEB, HCSB, ESV, NIV, NAB); of 3 uses in KJV (also NT: Rev 14:10); Young's has the most at 9 uses (8 in OT).

Reciprocal, Reciprocate, Reciprocated, Reciprocating, Reciprocity:

7 uses in MacDonald Idiomatic (2006): Luke 6:38; 12:8; 14:12, 14; Rom 11:35; 2 Cor 6:13; Rev 2:23;

2 Uses of "reciprocity" in David H. Stern's "Complete Jewish Bible" (1998): 2 Cor 8:13, 14:

Definitions of the Greek noun ἡ ἰσότης in these verses appear to be used to exchange the contextual divine reciprocity for a para-contextual Christianized socialism.

"Represent," "Representation," "Represented," "Representing" [also consider in this regard, Vicar]

[NT only]

Word study of uses of "represent, representation, represented, representing"
[Approximate chronological arrangement]

	WYC	TYN	BSP	KJV	WEB	YLT	NOY	ROT	DBY	ERV	DRA	ASV	BBE	RSV	NAS	NKJ	NIVO	NJB	NRS	NABO	NAU	GWN	CJB	NIVR	NLT	TNIV	NET	CSBO	MGI	ESV	MIT	NIV	NAB	CEB	Total
2 Cor 5:20	0	0	0	0	0	0	0	0	0	0	0	0	1	0	0	0	0	0	0	0	0	0	0	0	1	0	0	0	0	0	0	0	2	0	4
Heb 1:3	0	0	0	0	0	0	0	1	0	0	0	0	0	0	1	0	1	0	0	1	0	0	0	0	1	1	0	0	0	0	0	1	0	0	7
Heb 5:1	0	0	0	0	0	0	0	0	0	0	0	0	0	0	0	0	1	0	0	1	0	1	0	0	1	1	1	0	0	0	0	2	1	0	9
Other	0	0	0	0	0	0	1	0	0	0	5	0	0	1	0	0	3	3	1	9	1	7	0	0	26	2	6	0	1	0	43	2	8	6	125
Total	0	0	0	0	0	0	1	1	0	0	5	0	1	1	1	0	5	3	1	11	1	8	0	0	29	4	7	0	1	0	43	5	11	6	145

NJB: Psa 109:20; 2 Macc 15:33; NABO: Deut 15:18; Judges 18:4; 1 Kgs 5:20; Mic 3:11; Tob 2:12; 5:3; NAB: Deut 15:18; Tob 2:12; CEB: Deut 24:15; Ezra 4:14; John 6:7; Rom 4:4; 2 Cor 11:8.

"Reputation":

From 50 uses in NET Bible (incl. 4 NT: John 7:4; Gal 2:9; 1 Tim 5:10; Rev 3:1); to 5 uses in KJV (4 NT: Acts 5:34; Gal 2:2; Phil 2:7, 29).

"Salary":

Word study of uses of "salaried, salaries, salary"
[Approximate chronological arrangement]

	WYC	TYN	BSP	KJV	WEB	YLT	NOY	ROT	DBY	ERV	DRA	ASV	BBE	RSV	NAS	NKJ	NIVO	NJB	NRS	NABO	NAU	GWN	CJB	NIVR	NLT	TNIV	NET	CSBO	MGI	ESV	MIT	NIV	NAB	CEB	Total
Salaried	0	0	0	0	0	0	0	0	0	0	0	0	0	0	0	0	0	0	0	0	0	0	0	0	0	0	0	0	0	0	0	0	0	0	0
Salaries	0	0	0	0	0	0	0	0	0	0	0	0	0	0	0	0	0	0	0	0	0	0	0	0	0	0	0	0	0	0	0	0	0	1	1
Salary	0	0	0	0	0	0	0	0	0	0	0	0	0	0	0	0	0	2	0	6	0	0	0	0	0	0	0	0	0	0	0	0	2	4	14
Total	0	0	0	0	0	0	0	0	0	0	0	0	0	0	0	0	0	2	0	6	0	0	0	0	0	0	0	0	0	0	0	0	2	5	15

NJB: Psa 109:20; 2 Macc 15:33; NABO: Deut 15:18; Judges 18:4; 1 Kgs 5:20; Mic 3:11; Tob 2:12; 5:3; NAB: Deut 15:18; Tob 2:12; CEB: Deut 24:15; Ezra 4:14; John 6:7; Rom 4:4; 2 Cor 11:8.

It is interesting to note that all of these Bibles using the term "salary" and cognates, with the exception of the CEB, are Roman Catholic.

"Side-stepping" the law:

Consider οὐδὲ παράβασις **Rom 4:16**

BYZ Romans 4:15 ὁ γὰρ νόμος ὀργὴν κατεργάζεται· οὗ γὰρ οὐκ ἔστιν νόμος, οὐδὲ παράβασις.
NAS Romans 4:15 for the Law brings about wrath, but where there is no law, neither is there violation.

Byzantine	Latin	KJV; NKJ	CSB; ESV	ASV	NASB	German Luther
οὐδὲ παράβασις	nec praevaricatio	no transgression	there is no transgression	neither is there transgression	neither is there violation	keine Übertretung

Could this term be better translated, "where there is no law, there is no side-stepping"?

The idea might even be "hedging"?

Rather than the result of the violation: transgression; perhaps it is how the violation takes place: seeking to side-step the law?

Similarly, consider also the act of removing oneself:

There is an interesting translation of the preposition παρ' in Gal 1:9 in the French Revised Geneva (1979), which states:

Gal 1:9 (my translation of NEG), "As I have preceded to say, I know repeat at this time: if someone announces unto you a Gospel **separated from** [or: removed from] that which you have received, may he be anathema!"

Gal 1:9 (NEG), "Nous l'avons dit précédemment, et je le répète à cette heure: si quelqu'un vous annonce un évangile **s'écartant** de celui que vous avez reçu, qu'il soit anathème !"

"Stratagem", "Strategies", and "Strategy":

Word study of uses of "stratagem, strategies, strategy"
[Approximate chronological arrangement]

	WYC	TYN	BSP	KJV	WEB	YLT	NOY	ROT	DBY	ERV	DRA	ASV	BBE	RSV	NAS	NKJ	NIVO	NJB	NRS	NABO	NAU	GWN	CJB	NIVR	NLT	TNIV	NET	CSBO	MGI	ESV	MIT	NIV	NAB	CSB	CEB	Total
Stratagem	0	0	0	0	0	0	0	0	0	0	0	0	0	0	0	0	0	0	0	0	0	0	0	0	0	0	0	0	0	0	0	0	0	0	**0**
Strategies	0	0	0	0	0	0	0	1	0	0	0	0	0	0	0	0	0	0	0	0	0	2	0	0	2	0	0	2	0	0	0	0	2	0	**9**
Strategy	0	0	0	0	0	0	0	0	0	0	0	0	0	2	1	0	3	3	2	2	1	1	0	0	1	8	2	0	2	2	1	6	3	2	**42**
Total	0	0	0	0	0	0	0	1	0	0	0	0	0	2	1	0	3	3	2	2	1	3	0	0	2	1	8	4	0	2	2	1	6	5	2	**51**

The words stratagem, strategies, and strategy are found several times in the apocryphal books, which were not included in this study.

Wicked, Wickedness:

Noting that the LXX has translated the Heb *rashayim* as the Greek ungodly (ἀσεβής, cf. Psa 9-10), out of 448 uses of "wicked*" in the NAS, only 21 are NT. Thus there may be either (1) a covenantal shift in anthrolopogy between OT and NT, wherein man prior to Christ was more depraved than after Christ; or (2) the authors of the NT (a) did not see the need to repeat the clear OT theme of depravity, (b) followed the philosophical bent of the LXX in discussing wickedness, (c) followed the Greek worldview of this concept, (d) followed unrecorded teachings of Jesus on this issue, or (d) used terms to communicate the idea of wickedness which are not being properly translated as such; and/or (3) lexographers and translators have made the doctrinal choice to disemphasize the concept "wicked" and "wickedness" in NT translation activity.

Concluding Thoughts:

Ought anything be done about these apparent discrepancies?

Ought further study be initiated in the area of the history of translation tendencies?

Piggybacking on translation tendencies, ought any further study be initiated in the area of the history of textual variants, and their "source criticial" (communal, ecclesial, or church-based) provenance?

It must be understood that, these translation tendencies find their root in early church polemics; therefore, it is important to note that no lexical analysis from the past 1500 years is free from ecclesial-doctrinal bias.

While this issue may appear to be an insurmountable obstacle:

God appears to have guarded not only the text of His Word, but also the translation of His Word by cross-references of certain terms that are used in a physical sense, as well as in a figurative or doctrinal sense;

Further, God, who invented every language and all their intermiggling dialects, and understands, yea, allowed, and even guided every shift in meaning of every word in every dialect, has limited (or in actuality "magnified") His revelation to the use of terms in the original languages that He deemed fitting to be used for the entire history of the world since their authorship off the pen of His human instrumentality. God rendered holy what appears to be mere human words, but in actuality are His words constructed under His providential care!

Once proper studies are done, and the historical-doctrinal tendencies are understood, then translation can be done seeking to avoid, as much as possible, predisposed historical-doctrinal biases calculated to shift the meaning, interpretation, and application of Scripture.

Postscript 1: Concerning the different semantic ranges in the OT and NT

In previous study in this Chapter, I have noted that some proclamational terms appear reserved for an OT context in the minds of translators (and their readers). Hence the verb "declare" is used almost exclusively to signify some types of prophetic speech in the OT. Whereas, the same English verb is rarely found in the NT. Because the same Greek words are found in both Testaments, the reason for this dispensational distinction appears both:
(1) Lexical: reflecting translation usages recommended in Greek-English lexicons; and
(2) Practical: perhaps to discourage aggressive preaching in the practice of the church.

Theologically, on the other hand, the concept of "eternal life" as a reward for faith and/or obedience is very sparce in the OT, whereas it is very common in the NT. A focus on the resurrection is rather part of the New Covenant preaching of Jesus and the Apostles!

For other interesting cross-testamental studies of words in English translations, also consider:

Conceal (seems to be used in the OT only, at least in NKJ);

Conciliate, conciliation, conciliatory
    Found a total of once in a variety of verses in 7 versions
    Found 3 times in the NJB, one in Gen 32:20[21] and two in 1 Macc.

Conscientious, conscientiously, conscientiousness;

Consecrate (OT vs. NT);

Corrupt, corrupted, corrupting;

Declare, declared, declaring;

Decree, decreed, decreeing;

Deprive, deprivation;

Deviant;

Deviate, deviated, deviating;

Impossible;

Introduce, introduced, introducing;
    See the noun in Heb 7:19

Knowledgeable;

Minister (its broad semantic range in Greek words, esp Acts 13:2; Rom 13:6);

"Persevere" as a verb, even though the verb ὑπομένω is found 17 times; often translated "to endure":
    "endure" is passive; "persevere" is active.

Persist in John 8:31, as the translation of μένω, "If you persist in My word, you are My disciples indeed." (cf. 1605 French Geneva).

Perverse, pervert, perverted, perverting.

Plural in any form (.plural*) is found only once in all the English Bibles available to me in BibleWorks 9.0, Gal 3:16 (NJB);

Pride;

Proponent;

Putrid;

Reality;

Rebel, rebelled, rebellion, rebellious: in NKJ there are a total of 126 hits on rebel*, whereas only 9 of those (7%) are in the NT; of the 9 in the NT 7 are the noun "rebellion" and one is the noun "rebel." Hence there is only one use of the verb "rebel" in the NT in the NKJ (in Heb 3:16 for the Greek παραπικραίνω; which verb is found 43 times in the OT LXX—12 times in the Psalms and 20 times in Ezekiel [15 of those in chaps 2, 3, and 12]—and only once in the NT):

Jesus chose the word "adulterous" in the pairs "evil and adulterous" (Matt 12:39) and "wicked and adulterous" (Matt 16:4): the same Greek for both words. Mark 8:38 reads, "adulterous and sinful."

Rot, rotten, rottenness, rotting;

Stink, stinking (See French Geneva, Psa 14:3);

[In] Vain (especially in contemporary translations);

Zeal, zealous.

Made in the USA
Monee, IL
09 January 2022